The Oxford Companion
—TO—
Emotion and the Affective Sciences

The Oxford Companion

—— TO ——

Emotion and the Affective Sciences

EDITED BY

DAVID SANDER AND KLAUS R. SCHERER

OXFORD

UNIVERSITY PRESS

OXFORD
UNIVERSITY PRESS

Great Clarendon Street, Oxford OX2 6DP

Oxford University Press is a department of the University of Oxford.
It furthers the University's objective of excellence in research, scholarship,
and education by publishing worldwide in

Oxford New York

Auckland Cape Town Dar es Salaam Hong Kong Karachi
Kuala Lumpur Madrid Melbourne Mexico City Nairobi
New Delhi Shanghai Taipei Toronto

With offices in

Argentina Austria Brazil Chile Czech Republic France Greece
Guatemala Hungary Italy Japan Poland Portugal Singapore
South Korea Switzerland Thailand Turkey Ukraine Vietnam

Oxford is a registered trade mark of Oxford University Press
in the UK and in certain other countries

Published in the United States
by Oxford University Press Inc., New York

© Oxford University Press 2009

The moral rights of the author have been asserted
Database right Oxford University Press (maker)

First published 2009

British Library Cataloguing in Publication Data

Data available

Library of Congress Cataloging in Publication Data

Data available

Typeset by SPI Publisher Services, Pondicherry, India
Printed in Great Britain
on acid-free paper by
CPI Antony Rowe, Chippenham, Wiltshire

ISBN 978–0–19–856963–3

1 3 5 7 9 10 8 6 4 2

Contents

Contributors

Editors

David Sander, Swiss Centre for Affective Sciences and Department of Psychology, University of Geneva, Geneva, Switzerland.

Klaus R. Scherer, Swiss Centre for Affective Sciences, University of Geneva, Geneva, Switzerland.

Associate editors

John T. Cacioppo, Center for Cognitive and Social Neuroscience, University of Chicago, Chicago, IL, USA.

Tim Dalgleish, MRC Cognition and Brain Sciences Unit, Cambridge, UK.

Robert Dantzer, Integrative Immunology and Behavior Program, University of Illinois at Urbana-Champaign, Urbana, IL, USA.

Richard J. Davidson, Department of Psychology, University of Wisconsin-Madison, Madison, WI, USA.

Phoebe C. Ellsworth, Department of Psychology, University of Michigan, Ann Arbor, MI, USA.

Nico H. Frijda, Faculty of Social and Behavioural Sciences, University of Amsterdam, Amsterdam, The Netherlands.

George Loewenstein, Department of Social and Decision Sciences, Carnegie Mellon University, Pittsburgh, PA, USA.

Paula M. Niedenthal, Department of Psychology, University of Wisconsin-Madison, Madison, WI, USA.

Peter Salovey, Department of Psychology, Yale University, New Haven, CT, USA.

R. de Sousa, Department of Philosophy, University of Toronto, Toronto, ON, Canada.

Richard A. Shweder, Department of Psychology, University of Chicago, Chicago, IL, USA.

Contributors

Ralph Adolphs, Division of Humanities and Social Sciences, California Institute of Technology, Pasadena, CA, USA.

John J. B. Allen, Department of Psychology, University of Arizona, Tucson, AZ, USA.

Adam K. Anderson, Department of Psychology, University of Toronto, Toronto, ON, Canada.

Leonard Angel, Department of Philosophy and Humanities, Douglas College, New Westminster, BC, Canada.

Jens B. Asendorpf, Institute for Psychology, Humboldt University Berlin, Berlin, Germany.

James R. Averill, Department of Psychology, University of Massachusetts, Amherst, MA, USA.

Ozlem Ayduk, Department of Psychology, University of California Berkeley, Berkeley, CA, USA.

Jo-Anne Bachorowski, Department of Psychology, Vanderbilt University, Nashville, TN, USA.

Ishani Banerji, Wake Forest University, Winston-Salem, NC, USA.

Tanja Bänziger, University of Gävle, Gävle, Sweden.

Jack Barbalet, School of Social Sciences, Bankstown Campus, University of Western Sydney, NSW, Australia.

Simon Baron-Cohen, Autism Research Centre, Department of Psychiatry, University of Cambridge, Cambridge, UK.

Lisa Feldman Barrett, Department of Psychology, Boston College, Chestnut Hill, MA, USA.

Lawrence W. Barsalou, Department of Psychology, Emory University, Atlanta, GA, USA.

C. Daniel Batson, Department of Psychology, University of Kansas, Lawrence, KS, USA.

Roy F. Baumeister, Department of Psychology, Florida State University, Tallahassee, FL, USA.

Max H. Bazerman, Negotiations, Organizations, and Markets Department, Harvard Business School, Boston, MA, USA.

Antoine Bechara, Psychology Department, University of Southern California, Los Angeles, CA, USA.

Lane Beckes, Department of Psychology, University of Minnesota, Twin Cities Campus, Minneapolis, MN, USA.

Richard P. Bentall, School of Psychology, University of Bangor, Bangor, UK.

Aaron Ben-Ze'ev, Department of Philosophy, University of Haifa, Haifa, Israel.

Leonard Berkowitz, 5818 Anchorage Ave., Madison, WI, USA.

Gary G. Berntson, Ohio State University, Columbus, OH, USA.

Kent C. Berridge, Department of Psychology, University of Michigan, Ann Arbor, MI, USA.

Jarett D. Berry, Feinberg School of Medicine, Department of Preventive Medicine, Northwestern University, Chicago, IL, USA.

Joël Billieux, Cognitive Psychopathology and Neuropsychology Unit, Department of Psychology, University of Geneva, Geneva, Switzerland.

R. J. R. Blair, Mood and Anxiety Program, National Institute of Mental Health, Bethesda, MD, USA.

D. Caroline Blanchard, Department of Psychology, University of Hawaii, Honolulu, HI, USA.

Robert J. Blanchard, Department of Psychology, University of Hawaii, Honolulu, HI, USA.

Terry D. Blumenthal, Department of Psychology, Wake Forest University, Winston-Salem, NC, USA.

Iris Bohnet, Kennedy School of Government, Harvard University, Cambridge, MA, USA.

Derek Bolton, Institute of Psychiatry, King's College London, London, UK.

R. Thomas Boone, Department of Psychology, University of Massachusetts Dartmouth, North Dartmouth, MA, USA.

Philippe Borgeaud, History of Ancient Religions, Faculty of Arts, University of Geneva, Switzerland.

Stephanie Both, Department of Psychosomatic Gynaecology and Sexology, Leiden University Medical Centre, Leiden, The Netherlands.

Leaf Van Boven, Department of Psychology and Neuroscience, University of Colorado at Boulder, Boulder.

Anton van Boxtel, Department of Psychology, Tilburg University, Tilburg, The Netherlands.

Marc Brackett, Department of Psychology, Yale University, New Haven, CT, USA.

Margaret M. Bradley, University of Florida, Gainesville, FL, USA.

Seger M. Breugelmans, Department of Social Psychology, Tilburg University, Tilburg, The Netherlands.

Chris R. Brewin, Clinical, Educational & Health Psychology, University College London, Gower Street, London, UK.

Kerstin Brinkmann, Department of Psychology, University of Geneva, Geneva, Switzerland.

Leslie R. Brody, Department of Psychology, Boston University, Boston, MA, USA.

Tobias Brosch, Swiss Centre for Affective Sciences, University of Geneva, Geneva, Switzerland.

Ross Buck, Departments of Communication Sciences and Psychology, University of Connecticut, Storrs, CT, USA.

Brad J. Bushman, Institute for Social Research, University of Michigan, Ann Arbor, MI, USA and Vrije Universiteit, Amsterdam, The Netherlands.

Abraham P. Buunk, Social and Organizational Psychology, Royal Netherlands Academy of Arts and Sciences and University of Groningen, Groningen, The Netherlands.

Bernard Calvino, Laboratoire de Neurobiologie, CNRS UMR, ESPCI, Paris, France.

Joseph J. Campos, Department of Psychology, University of California Berkeley, Berkeley, CA, USA.

Lola Cañamero, Adaptive Systems Research Group, School of Computer Science, University of Hertfordshire, Hatfield, UK.

Turhan Canli, Department of Psychology, Stony Brook University, Stony Brook, NY, USA.

Lucile Capuron, Laboratory of Psychoneuroimmunology, Nutrition and Genetics, INRA UMR, University of Bordeaux II, CNRS, Bordeaux, France.

Sam Cartwright-Hatton, School of Psychological Sciences, University of Manchester, Manchester, UK.

Charles S. Carver, Department of Psychology, University of Miami, Coral Gables, FL, USA.

Justin V. Cavallo, Department of Psychology, University of Waterloo, Waterloo, Ontario, Canada.

James F. Cavanagh, Department of Psychology, University of Arizona, Tucson, AZ, USA.

Louis C. Charland, Departments of Philosophy and Psychiatry and Faculty of Health Sciences, University of Western Ontario, London, ON, Canada.

Robert B. Cialdini, Department of Psychology, Arizona State University, Tempe, AZ, USA.

Jason K. Clark, Department of Psychology, University of Alabama, Tuscaloosa, AL, USA.

Margaret Clark, Department of Psychology, Yale University, New Haven, CT, USA.

Gerald L. Clore, University of Virginia, Charlottesville, VA, USA.

Jeffrey F. Cohn, University of Pittsburgh, Pittsburgh, PA, USA.

Martin A. Conway, Institute of Psychological Sciences, Leeds Memory Group, University of Leeds, Leeds, UK.

Randolph R. Cornelius, Department of Psychology, Vassar College, Poughkeepsie, NY, USA.

Stephen L. Crites Jr, Department of Psychology, University of Texas at El Paso, El Paso, TX, USA.

Cynthia Cryder, Department of Social and Decision Sciences. Carnegie Mellon University, Pittsburgh, PA, USA.

Nele Dael, Swiss Centre for Affective Sciences, University of Geneva, Geneva, Switzerland.

Justin D'Arms, Department of Philosophy, The Ohio State University, Columbus, OH, USA.

Michael E. Dawson, Department of Psychology, University of Southern California, Los Angeles, CA, USA.

Ian J. Deary, Department of Psychology, University of Edinburgh, Edinburgh, UK.

Jean Decety, Department of Psychology and the College, University of Chicago, Chicago, IL, USA.

Jan De Houwer, Ghent University, Ghent, Belgium.

Sylvain Delplanque, Swiss Centre for Affective Sciences, University of Geneva, Geneva, Switzerland.

Susanne A. Denham, Applied Developmental Psychology, George Mason University, Fairfax, VA, USA.

Joseph de Rivera, Department of Psychology, Clark University, Worcester, MA, USA.

Julien A. Deonna, Swiss Centre for Affective Sciences, University of Geneva, Geneva, Switzerland.

Andreas Dick-Niederhauser, Department of Psychology, University of Redlands, Redlands, USA.

Wilco W. van Dijk, Department of Social Psychology, VU University Amsterdam, Amsterdam, The Netherlands.

John F. Dovidio, Department of Psychology, Yale University, New Haven, CT, USA.

Steve Duck, Department of Communication Studies, The University of Iowa, Iowa City, IA, USA.

Barnaby D. Dunn, MRC Cognition and Brain Sciences Unit, Cambridge, UK.

Barry R. Dworkin, Department of Neural and Behavioral Sciences, Pennsylvania State University, College of Medicine, Hershey PA, USA.

Nancy Eisenberg, Department of Psychology, Arizona State University, Tempe, AZ, USA.

Paul Ekman, Department of Psychiatry, University of California, San Francisco, CA, USA.

Phoebe C. Ellsworth, Department of Psychology, University of Michigan, Ann Arbor, MI, USA.

Robert A. Emmons, Department of Psychology, University of California, Davis, CA, USA.

Walter Everaerd, Department of Psychology, University of Amsterdam, Amsterdam, The Netherlands.

Michael W. Eysenck, Department of Psychology, Royal Holloway University of London, Egham, Surrey, UK.

Leandre R. Fabrigar, Department of Psychology, Queen's University at Kingston, Kingston, ON, Canada.

Contributors

Ernst Fehr, Institute for Empirical Research in Economics. University of Zurich, Zurich, Switzerland.

Daniel M. T. Fessler, UCLA Center for Behavior, Evolution, and Culture and Department of Anthropology, University of California, Los Angeles, CA, USA.

Andy P. Field, School of Psychology, School of Life Sciences, University of Sussex, Brighton, UK.

Susan T. Fiske, Department of Psychology, Princeton University, Princeton, NJ, USA.

Edna B. Foa, Department of Psychiatry, University of Pennsylvania School of Medicine, Philadelphia, PA, USA.

Susan Folkman, Osher Center for Integrative Medicine, University of California, San Francisco, CA, USA.

Johnny R. J. Fontaine, Faculty of Psychology and Educational Sciences, Ghent University, Ghent, Belgium.

Don C. Fowles, Department of Psychology, University of Iowa, Iowa City, IA, USA.

Martin E. Franklin, Center for the Treatment and Study of Anxiety, University of Pennsylvania School of Medicine, Philadelphia, PA, USA.

Shane Frederick, Sloan School of Management, Massachusetts Institute of Technology, Cambridge, MA, USA.

Barbara L. Fredrickson, Department of Psychology, University of North Carolina at Chapel Hill, Chapel Hill, NC, USA.

Andrew L. Geers, Department of Psychology, University of Toledo, Toledo, OH, USA.

Guido H. E. Gendolla, Department of Psychology, University of Geneva, Geneva, Switzerland.

Asif A. Ghazanfar, Neurosciences Institute, Department of Psychology, Princeton University, Princeton, NJ, USA.

John Gibson, Department of Philosophy, University of Louisville, Louisville, KY, USA.

Gerd Gigerenzer, Max Planck Institute for Human Development, Berlin, Germany.

Daniel T. Gilbert, Department of Psychology, Harvard University, Cambridge, MA, USA.

Thomas Gilovich, Department of Psychology, Cornell University, Ithaca, NY, USA.

Nicole R. Giuliani, Department of Psychology, Stanford University, Stanford, CA, USA.

Peter Goldie, Philosophy, University of Manchester, UK.

Celia M. Gonzalez, Department of Psychology, New York University, New York, NY, USA.

Guy M. Goodwin, University Department of Psychiatry, Warneford Hospital, Oxford, UK.

Stephanie H. M. van Goozen, School of Psychology, Cardiff University, Cardiff, UK.

Robert M. Gordon, University of Missouri St Louis, St Louis, MO, USA.

Ian H. Gotlib, Department of Psychology, Stanford University, Stanford, CA, USA.

Martijn Goudbeek, Department of Psychology, Tilburg University, Tilburg, The Netherlands.

Didier Grandjean, Swiss Centre for Affective Sciences and Department of Psychology, University of Geneva, Geneva, Switzerland.

James J. Gross, Department of Psychology, Stanford University, Stanford, CA, USA.

Jonathan Haidt, Department of Psychology, University of Virginia, Charlottesville, VA, USA.

Judith A. Hall, Department of Psychology, Northeastern University, Boston, MA, USA.

Seunghee Han, Department of Social and Decision Sciences, Carnegie Mellon University, Pittsburgh, PA, USA.

Valerie Gray Hardcastle, Departments of Philosophy and Science and Technology in Society, Virginia Tech, Blacksburg, VA, USA.

Shlomo Hareli, Graduate School of Management, University of Haifa, Haifa, Israel.

Paul L. Harris, Graduate School of Education, Harvard University, Cambridge, MA, USA.

Allison G. Harvey, Department of Psychology, University of California, Berkeley, CA, USA.

J. H. Harvey, Department of Psychology, University of Iowa, Iowa City, IA, USA.

Elaine Hatfield, Department of Psychology, University of Hawaii, Honolulu, HI, USA.

Dale Hay, School of Psychology, Cardiff University, Cardiff, UK.

Todd F. Heatherton, Department of Psychological and Brain Sciences, Dartmouth College, Hanover, NH, USA.

Paula T. Hertel, Department of Psychology, Trinity University, San Antonio, TX, USA.

Ursula Hess, Department of Psychology, University of Quebec at Montreal, Montreal, QC, Canada.

E. Tory Higgins, Department of Psychology, Columbia University, New York, NY, USA.

Julianne Holt-Lunstad, Department of Psychology, Brigham Young University, Provo, UT, USA.

Christopher K. Hsee, Graduate School of Business, University of Chicago, Chicago, IL, USA.

Marco Iacoboni, Ahmanson-Lovelace Brain Mapping Center, David Geffen School of Medicine at UCLA, Los Angeles, CA, USA.

Rick E. Ingram, Department of Psychology, University of Kansas, Lawrence, KS, USA.

Brad Inwood, Departments of Classics and Philosophy, University of Toronto, Toronto, ON, Canada.

Carroll E. Izard, Department of Psychology, University of Delaware, Newark, DE, USA.

W. Jake Jacobs, Department of Psychology, University of Arizona, Tucson, AZ, USA.

Daniel Jacobson, Department of Philosophy, Bowling Green State University, Bowling Green, OH, USA.

Steven Jones, Spectrum Centre for Mental Health Research, University of Lancaster, UK.

Jutta Joormann, Department of Psychology, University of Miami, Coral Gables, FL, USA.

Patrik N. Juslin, Department of Psychology, Uppsala University, Uppsala, Sweden.

Jerome Kagan, Department of Psychology, Harvard University, Cambridge, MA, USA.

Daniel Kahneman, Woodrow Wilson School of Public and International Affairs, Princeton University, Princeton, NJ, USA.

Keith W. Kelley, Laboratories of Integrative Immuno-physiology, Integrative Immunology and Behavior Program, University of Illinois, Urbana, IL, USA.

Kristen A. King, Department of Psychology, University of Delaware, Newark, DE, USA.

Leslie D. Kirby, Department of Psychology, Vanderbilt University, Nashville, TN, USA.

Shinobu Kitayama, Institute for Social Research, University of Michigan, Ann Arbor, MI, USA.

David Konstan, Department of Classics, Brown University, Providence RI, USA.

Sebastian Korb, Swiss Centre for Affective Sciences, University of Geneva, Geneva, Switzerland.

Nienke Korsten, Department of Mathematics, King's College London, London, UK.

Laura D. Kubzansky, Department of Society, Human Development, and Health, Harvard School of Public Health, Boston, MA, USA.

Peter Kuppens, Department of Psychology, University of Leuven, Leuven, Belgium.

Jaime L. Kurtz, University of Virginia, Charlottesville, VA, USA.

Ellen T.M. Laan, Department of Sexology and Psychosomatic Obstetrics and Gynaecology Academic Medical Center, University of Amsterdam, The Netherlands.

Kevin S. LaBar, Center for Cognitive Neuroscience, Duke University, Durham, NC, USA.

Gisela Labouvie-Vief, Department of Psychology, University of Geneva, Geneva, Switzerland.

Richard D. Lane, Department of Psychiatry, 1501 N. Campbell Ave., Tucson, AZ, USA.

Peter J. Lang, Department of Clinical and Health Psychology, University of Florida, Gainesville, FL, USA.

Jeff T. Larsen, Department of Psychology, Texas Tech University, Lubbock, TX, USA.

Andrew D. Lawrence, School of Psychology, Cardiff University, Cardiff, UK.

Mark R. Leary, Department of Psychology and Neuroscience, Duke University, Durham, NC, USA.

Joseph LeDoux, Center for Neural Science, New York University, New York, NY, USA.

Lawrence A. Lengbeyer, Department of Leadership, Ethics and Law, and Character, United States Naval Academy, Annapolis, MD, USA.

Jennifer S. Lerner, Department of Social and Decision Sciences, Carnegie Mellon University, Pittsburgh, PA, USA.

Howard Leventhal, Institute for Health and Department of Psychology, Rutgers, The State University of New Jersey, New Brunswick, NJ, USA.

Matthew D. Lieberman, University of California Los Angeles, Los Angeles, CA, USA.

Paul M. Litvak, Department of Social and Decision Sciences, Carnegie Mellon University, Pittsburgh, PA, USA.

Donald M. Lloyd-Jones, Northwestern University, Chicago, IL, USA.

Tyler Lorig, Department of Psychology, Washington and Lee, University, Lexington, VA, USA.

William Lyons, Department of Philosophy, School of Mental and Moral Science, Trinity College, Dublin, Ireland.

Sonja Lyubomirsky, Department of Psychology, University of California Riverside, Riverside, CA, USA.

Clark McCauley, Psychology Department, Bryn Mawr College, Bryn Mawr, PA, USA.

Samuel M. McClure, Department of Psychology, Stanford University, Stanford, CA, USA.

Diane M. Mackie, Department of Psychology, University of California, Santa Barbara, CA, USA.

Richard J. McNally, Department of Psychology, Harvard University, Cambridge, MA, USA.

Kateri McRae, Department of Psychology, Stanford University, Stanford, CA, USA.

G. Alan Marlatt, Addictive Behaviors Research Center, Department of Psychology, University of Washington, Seattle, WA, USA.

David Matsumoto, Department of Psychology, San Francisco State University, San Francisco, CA, USA.

Stephan Meier, Center for Behavioral Economics and Decision Making, Federal Reserve Bank of Boston, Boston, MA, USA.

Batja Mesquita, Department of Psychology, University of Leuven, Leuven, Belgium.

Janet Metcalfe, Department of Psychology, Columbia University, New York, NY, USA.

Wulf-Uwe Meyer, Department of Psychology, University of Bielefeld, Bielefeld, Germany.

William Ian Miller, Law School, University of Michigan, Ann Arbor, MI, USA.

Walter Mischel, Department of Psychology, Columbia University, New York, NY, USA.

Yuri Miyamoto, Department of Psychology, University of Wisconsin-Madison, Madison, WI, USA.

Richard G. Moore, Cambridgeshire and Peterborough NHS Foundation Trust, Addenbrookes Hospital, Cambridge, UK.

Agnes Moors, Department of Psychology, Ghent University, Ghent, Belgium.

Nicola Morant, Department of Social and Developmental Psychology, University of Cambridge, UK.

Marcello Mortillaro, Swiss Centre for Affective Sciences, University of Geneva, Geneva, Switzerland.

Judith Tedlie Moskowitz, Osher Center for Integrative Medicine, University of California, San Francisco, CA, USA.

Cristina M. Moya, UCLA Center for Behavior, Evolution, and Culture and Department of Anthropology, University of California, Los Angeles, CA, USA.

Kevin Mulligan, Department of Philosophy, Université de Genève, Genève, Switzerland.

Robin L. Nabi, Department of Communication, University of California, Santa Barbara, CA, USA.

Randolph M. Nesse, Department of Psychiatry and Psychology, and the Institute for Social Research, University of Michigan, Ann Arbor, MI, USA.

Jerome Neu, Cowell College, University of California, Santa Cruz, CA, USA.

Keith Oatley, Department of Human Development and Applied Psychology, University of Toronto, Toronto, ON, Canada.

Anna Ogarkova, Swiss Centre for Affective Sciences, University of Geneva, Geneva, Switzerland.

Arne Öhman, Psychology Section, Department of Clinical Neuroscience, Karolinska Institutet, Karolinska University Hospital, Stockholm, Sweden.

Andrew Ortony, School of Education and Social Policy, Northwestern University, Evanston, IL, USA.

Michael J. Owren, Department of Psychology and Center for Behavioral Neuroscience, Georgia State University, Atlanta, GA, USA.

Contributors

Brian Parkinson, Department of Experimental Psychology, University of Oxford, Oxford, UK.

W. Gerrod Parrott, Department of Psychology, Georgetown University, Washington, DC, USA.

Catherine Pelachaud, Laboratoire Traitement et Communication de l'Information (LTCI), UMR, CNRS/TELECOM ParisTech, Paris, France.

Louis A. Penner, Karmanos Cancer Center, Wayne State University and Research Center for Group Dynamics, University of Michigan.

Meinrad Perrez, Department of Psychology, University of Fribourg, Fribourg, Switzerland.

Christopher Peterson, Department of Psychology, University of Michigan, Ann Arbor, MI, USA.

Paolo Petta, Institute of Medical Cybernetics and Artificial Intelligence, Centre for Brain Research, Medical University of Vienna, Vienna, Austria.

Richard E. Petty, Department of Psychology, Ohio State University, Columbus, OH, USA.

Elizabeth A. Phelps, Department of Psychology, New York University, New York, NY, USA.

Rosalind W. Picard, MIT Media Laboratory, Cambridge, MA, USA.

Diego A. Pizzagalli, Department of Psychology, Harvard University, Cambridge, MA, USA.

Susan Polanco, Synovate Healthcare, Mahwah, NJ, USA.

Ryan Powell, Wake Forest University, Winston-Salem, NC, USA.

Michael J. Power, School of Health in Social Science, The University of Edinburgh Medical School, Edinburgh, UK.

Joëlle Proust, Institut Jean-Nicod, CNRS-EHESS-ENS, Paris, France.

Anat Rafaeli, Faculty of Industrial Engineering and Management, Technion – Israel Institute of Technology, Haifa, Israel.

David N. Rapp, Department of Psychology, Northwestern University, Evanston, IL, USA.

Richard L. Rapson, Department of History, University of Hawaii, Honolulu, HI, USA.

Judy S. Reilly, Department of Psychology, San Diego State University, San Diego, CA, USA.

Rainer Reisenzein, Institute of Psychology, University of Greifswald, Greifswald, Germany.

William Revelle, Department of Psychology, Northwestern University, Evanston, IL, USA.

Michael Richter, Geneva Motivation Lab, University of Geneva, Geneva, Switzerland.

Scott Rick, Department of Marketing, University of Michigan, Ann Arbor, MI, USA.

Jason Riis, Harvard Business School, Soldier Field, Boston MA, USA.

Bernard Rimé, Faculty of Psychology, University of Louvain, Louvain-la-Neuve, Belgium.

Jenefer Robinson, Department of Philosophy, University of Cincinnati, Cincinnati, OH, USA.

Michael D. Robinson, Psychology Department, North Dakota State University, Fargo, ND USA.

Lucien Rochat, Cognitive Psychopathology and Neuropsychology Unit, Department of Psychology, University of Geneva, Geneva, Switzerland.

Todd Rogers, Analyst Institute, Washington, DC, USA.

Edmund T. Rolls, Department of Experimental Psychology, University of Oxford, South Parks Road, Oxford, UK.

Ira J. Roseman, Department of Psychology, Rutgers University, Camden, NJ, USA.

Paul Rozin, Department of Psychology, University of Pennsylvania, Philadelphia, PA, USA.

Willibald Ruch, Department of Psychology, University of Zurich, Zurich, Switzerland.

John M. Ruiz, Department of Psychology, University of North Texas, Denton, TX, USA.

James A. Russell, Department of Psychology, Boston College, MA, USA.

Benoist Schaal, European Centre for the Science of Taste, CNRS, Dijon, France.

Anne M. Schell, Department of Psychology, Occidental College, Los Angeles CA, USA.

Daniela Schiller, Center for Neural Science and Psychology Department, New York University, New York, NY, USA.

Marc Schröder, German Research Centre for Artificial Intelligence, (DFKI) Saarbrücken, Germany.

Timothy Schroeder, Department of Philosophy, Ohio State University, Columbus, OH, USA.

Norbert Schwarz, Institute for Social Research, University of Michigan, Ann Arbor, MI, USA.

Patrick Seder, Department of Psychology, University of Virginia, Charlottesville, VA, USA.

Zindel V. Segal, Centre for Addiction and Mental Health – Clarke, Toronto, ON, Canada.

Norbert Semmer, Department of Psychology, University of Bern, Bern, Switzerland.

David R. Shanks, Division of Psychology and Language Sciences, University College London, London, UK.

Phillip R. Shaver, Department of Psychology, University of California Davis, Davis, CA, USA.

Baba Shiv, Graduate School of Business/Marketing, Stanford University, Stanford, CA, USA.

Peter Shizgal, Centre for Studies in Behavioural Neurobiology, Department of Psychology, Concordia University, Montreal, QC, Canada.

Jennifer S. Silk, Western Psychiatric Institute and Clinic, University of Pittsburgh, Pittsburgh, PA, USA.

Roxane Cohen Silver, Department of Psychology and Social Behavior, University of California Irvine, Irvine, CA, USA.

Wendy K. Silverman, Child Anxiety and Phobia Program, Department of Psychology, Florida International University, University Park, Miami, FL, USA.

Paul J. Silvia, Department of Psychology, University of North Carolina at Greensboro, Greensboro, NC, USA.

Jeffry A. Simpson, Department of Psychology, University of Minnesota, Twin Cities Campus, Minneapolis, MN, USA.

Craig A. Smith, Department of Psychology and Human Development, Vanderbilt University, Nashville, TN, USA.

Eliot R. Smith, Department of Psychological and Brain Sciences, Indiana University, Bloomington, IN, USA.

Alan Soble, Arts and Humanities, Abington College of Pennsylvania State University, Abington, PA, USA.

Ana Solodkin, Department of Neurology, The University of Chicago, Chicago, IL, USA.

Cristina Soriano, Swiss Centre for Affective Sciences, University of Geneva, Geneva, Switzerland.

Robert Soussignan, European Centre for the Sciences of Taste, CNRS, University of Burgundy, Dijon, France.

Laurence D. Steinberg, Department of Psychology, Temple University, Philadelphia, PA, USA.

Margaret S. Stroebe, Department of Clinical and Health Psychology, Utrecht University, Utrecht, The Netherlands.

Wolfgang Stroebe, Department of Social and Organizational Psychology, Utrecht University, Utrecht, The Netherlands.

Louise Sundararajan, Rochester Regional Forensic Unit, Rochester Psychiatric Center, Rochester, NY, USA.

Johan Sundberg, Department of Speech Music Hearing, School of Computer Science and Communication, KTH (Royal Institute of Technology), Stockholm Sweden.

Ed S. Tan, Department of Communication, University of Amsterdam, Amsterdam, The Netherlands.

Christine Tappolet, Department of Philosophy, Université de Montréal, Montréal, QC, Canada.

John G. Taylor, King's College London, Strand, London, UK.

Robert E. Thayer, Department of Psychology, California State University Long Beach, Long Beach, CA, USA.

Barry-John Theobald, School of Computing Sciences, University of East Anglia, Norwich, Norfolk, UK.

Sander Thomaes, Department of Developmental Psychology, Vrije Universiteit, Amsterdam, The Netherlands.

Franziska Tschan, Institute for the Psychology of Work and Organizational Psychology, University of Neuchâtel, Neuchâtel, Switzerland.

Hjalmar K. Turesson, Neuroscience Institute, Department of Psychology, Princeton University, Princeton, NJ, USA.

Graham Turpin, Clinical Psychology Unit, Department of Psychology, University of Sheffield, Sheffield, UK.

Tom R. Tyler, Department of Psychology, New York University, New York, NY, USA.

Bert N. Uchino, Department of Psychology, University of Utah, Salt Lake City, UT, USA.

Martial Van der Linden, Cognitive Psychopathology and Neuropsychology Unit, Department of Psychology, University of Geneva, Geneva, Switzerland.

Patrik Vuilleumier, Laboratory for Neurology and Imaging of Cognition, Department of Neurosciences and Clinic of Neurology, University Medical Center, Geneva, Switzerland.

Frans B. M. de Waal, Living Links, Yerkes Primate Center, Emory University, Atlanta, GA, USA.

Heather K. Warren, Applied Developmental Psychology, George Mason University, Fairfax VA, USA.

Edward Watkins, Mood Disorders Centre, School of Psychology, University of Exeter, Exeter, UK.

Duane T. Wegener, Department of Psychological Sciences, Purdue University, West Lafayette, IN, USA.

Bernard Weiner, Department of Psychology, University of California Los Angeles, Los Angeles, CA, USA.

Justin A. Wellman, Department of Psychology, University of Toledo, Toledo, OH, USA.

Paul J. Whalen, Department of Psychological and Brain Sciences, Dartmouth College, Hanover, NH, USA.

Timothy D. Wilson, Department of Psychology, University of Virginia, Charlottesville, VA, USA.

Piotr Winkielman, Department of Psychology, University of California, San Diego, La Jolla, CA, USA.

Katie Witkiewitz, Alcohol and Drug Abuse Institute, University of Washington, Seattle, WA, USA.

Joanne V. Wood, Department of Psychology, University of Waterloo, Waterloo, ON, Canada.

Camille B. Wortman, Department of Psychology, Stony Brook University, Stony Brook, NY, USA.

Rex A. Wright, Department of Psychology, University of Alabama at Birmingham, Birmingham, AL, USA.

Yang Yang, Tepper School of Business, Carnegie Mellon University, Pittsburgh, PA, USA.

Brendan Young, 105 Becker Communication Studies Building, The University of Iowa, Iowa City, IA, USA.

Vanda L. Zammuner, Department of Development and Socialization Psychology, University of Padova, Padova, Italy.

Leslie A. Zebrowitz, Department of Psychology, Brandeis University, Waltham, MA, USA.

Marcel Zeelenberg, Department of Economic and Social Psychology, Tilburg University, Tilburg, The Netherlands.

Christian Zehnder, Faculty of Business and Economics (HEC), University of Lausanne, Lausanne, Switzerland.

Note to the Reader

Entries are arranged in strict alphabetical order of their headword. Cross-references between entries are indicated either by an asterisk (*) in front of the word to be looked up, or by 'See' or 'See also' followed by the entry title in SMALL CAPITALS.

A

achievement motivation Achievement motivation refers broadly to striving toward standards of excellence that appears not to be prompted by a tangible reward (e.g. a monetary incentive) or intrinsic pleasure associated with the activity at hand (e.g. that associated with sexual behaviour) (see MOTIVATION). As an area of scientific study, it has roots in early research on aspiration levels (Lewin *et al.* 1944) and, especially, the need to achieve (Murray 1938, McClelland *et al.* 1953). Classic analyses posited that achievement motivation results from the interplay between the need to achieve and the need to avoid failure, assuming that these needs could be assessed via projective tests. A well-known research finding was that people high in the need to achieve and low in the fear of failure showed a preference for moderately difficult performance challenges. They did so, presumably, because these challenges provided a good opportunity to achieve and, at the same time, a limited chance to fail. In contrast, people low in the need to achieve and high in the fear of failure showed a preference for especially difficult challenges, presumably because failure could be excused. More modern analyses of achievement motivation assume that achievement behaviour is driven by multiple motives, with three receiving special attention: (1) that to appear capable, (2) that to avoid appearing incapable, and (3) that to achieve mastery within a performance realm. All of these motives involve an underlying concern with competence. In view of this, some investigators have recommended that the 'achievement' literature be reidentified as the 'competence' literature and that 'achievement motivation' be reidentified as 'competence motivation' (Elliot and Dweck 2005). An implication is that achievement behaviour should not be thought of as striving for no reward but rather as striving for a certain class of rewards.

REX A. WRIGHT

Elliot, A.J. and Dweck, C.S. (eds) (2005). *Handbook of competence and motivation.* New York: Guilford Press.

Heckhausen, H. (1991). *Motivation and action.* Berlin: Springer-Verlag.

action readiness The notion of action readiness designates the motivational aspect of emotions (see MOTIVATION). Most emotions contain readiness to change or maintain a relationship with the world, oneself, or some object of thought. They involve a position taken towards that object (e.g. rejection), and readiness to implement that position in action (e.g. by moving away). This relational aspect pertains even to nonaction, as in depressed apathy: it implements loss of motivation to entertain any relationship whatever.

A motivational perspective on emotions seeks to account for feelings of urge, but also for the flexibility of emotional behaviour. Most emotional behaviour varies with available actions (e.g. running or jumping in fear) and with context (e.g. object location and nature). The variations all share the same relational end (e.g. diminishing exposure); they embody some aim. Different states of action readiness are defined by different relational aims. Exuberance, as in joy, defines diffuse openness to contacts; hostility, as in anger, defines stopping or hurting the antagonist; aimless excitement defines absence of relational direction.

States of action readiness possess a second defining property. They possess 'control precedence': they take control of action, attention, and thought when circumstances and efforts at restraint permit. They thus embody priority settings for dealing with what elicits them. Control precedence is inferred from persistence in the face of interruption and obstacles, single-mindedness, being distracted by emotions, their interrupting ongoing action, and neglect of incompatible information. These features led to the earlier designation of emotions as 'passions': states by which one is overcome and that carry one away.

States of action readiness are of two different kinds: activation and deactivation states (e.g. diffuse excitement), and *action tendencies.

NICO H. FRIJDA

Frijda, N.H. (2007). *The laws of emotion.* Mahwah, NJ: Lawrence Erlbaum Associates.

action tendencies The term 'action tendency' was coined by Arnold (1960) to account for several major aspects of emotional *feelings: felt urge, felt direction of that urge (e.g. towards or away from), and aboutness of that urge. Felt emotional tendency is about a thing or situation. The notion has been expanded to refer to the internal motive states that are hypothesized to underlie such feelings, as well as overt behavioural phenomena with similar content.

Such inner states are conceived as those states of *action readiness that prepare and guide actions for achieving a particular relation with the object that the emotion is about (relations such as proximity, being remote from, or opposing). Action tendencies, both as felt and as transpiring from behaviour, are among the main features for assigning major emotion category labels to one's own emotions and those of other people or animals.

Action tendencies are distinguished by the kind of relational change at which they aim. The aims are inferred from self-reports, in which subjects may mention the content of their desire or urge ('I wanted to get away', 'I wanted to get back to him!'). They are also inferred from co-occurrence, in subject–event encounters, of behaviours that appear to share the function of modifying a relationship (e.g. self-protection, gaining proximity, rejection, expanding one's range of relationships), and that have led to inferring 'behaviour systems'. For example, intimidation, threat, attack, and insults all share in hurting an opponent and blocking offensive action; thinking of novel exploits, establishing new interpersonal contacts, and smiling at unknown people, all exemplify broadening-and-building.

Modes of action readiness and major emotion categories tend to correspond in unsurprising fashion. For instance, approach is often mentioned and observed in connection with desire, proximity-seeking with affection or love, moving away with fear, moving against with anger, rejecting with disgust (see APPROACH/WITHDRAWAL). A number of less obvious action tendencies are also meaningfully distinguished. For instance: dominance, or 'moving above', as the motive state that drives erect posture and vocal intensity in pride; 'moving below' or submission in humility, shame, and deference, as manifest in bent posture and downward glance; 'playful exuberance' that establishes brief and gratuitous contacts, as what drives joy; 'receptive openness', the unfocused attentional stance in many emotions of enjoyment; and inclination to fuse with some object, as in love and in mystical or 'oceanic' feelings.

States of action tendency can be felt without noticeable behavioural manifestations. One's 'heart swells up in pride'; one feels humbled by reading about Gandhi or Nelson Mandela; one strongly desires to be with someone one daydreams about. Action tendency, therefore, appears to exist regardless of motor action that implements it. As it should, of course, if it is the motive state that drives actions. States of action tendency thus appear to exist as fully central phenomena, without peripheral feedback. Two major sets of findings give support to that supposition. One comes from the analysis of mental representations underlying word meanings, notably by Barsalou (1999). These appear to be largely modal, that is, representations of visual, motor, and tactual impressions. The other consists of the activity of so-called mirror neurons in ventral prefrontal and inferior parietal cortex (Rizzolatti *et al.* 1996). These neurons are activated when performing actions, but also when viewing those actions in other individuals, and when viewing objects that are usually the objects of such actions. Certain of those neurons respond not to the movements of given actions, but to setting their aim; they appear to embody action readiness as such.

Representation of aims forms a theoretical problem, because action tendencies are not premeditated; they are not preceded by deliberate goal setting (see GOALS). However, actions that are both impulsive or emotional *and* purposive are common; eye fixation is an example. The purposiveness can be understood by the so-called efferent copy theory. Aims can be understood as setting 'efferent copies', that is, setting inner representations to which the outcomes of successful actions will match.

Outcome expectancies are produced by appraisal (see APPRAISAL THEORIES) of the event that elicits the emotion; they thus result from appraisal processes.

NICO H. FRIJDA

action unit Action units (AUs) refer to the functionally independent muscles identified and coded in the *facial action coding system (FACS) (Ekman and Friesen 1978). Each AU refers to the most elemental, independent movement of the facial mimetic musculature (see FACIAL EXPRESSION (OF EMOTION)). Most single muscles can move in only one way, producing one change of appearance on the face; each of these is identified by its own FACS AU code. Several muscles, however, can move in more than one way, producing multiple changes in appearance. The frontalis muscle across the forehead, for example, can move in the middle, raising the inner corners of the eyebrows, and on the outside, raising the outer corners of the eyebrows. Both of these actions are identified as distinct AUs in FACS, even though they refer to movements of the same single muscle. Orbicularis oris, the muscle in the lips, can be tightened and tensed, producing one change in appearance, or pressed together, producing a different change in appearance. These actions are also identified as distinct AUs in FACS, even though they refer to movements of the same muscle. In contrast, the *corrugator muscle group, which lowers the brows and brings them together, comprises three muscles, and one when is innervated they are all innervated, lowering the brows down and together and producing a single type of change in appearance. This action is identified as a single AU in FACS, even though it refers to movements of multiple muscles. For these reasons, AUs are based in functional, not structural, anatomy.

Any facial behaviour can be described in terms of the AUs that singly or in combination produce it. A smile of enjoyment, for instance, known as a Duchenne smile, involves AU 6 (orbicularis oculi) and AU 12 (*zygomatic major). Non-Duchenne smiles typically involve only AU 12. Expressions of sadness typically involve the raising of the inner corners of the eyebrows (AU 1), sometimes with corrugator (AU 4), and often with lowering of the corners of the lips (AU 15) and pushing up of the lower lip (AU 17). The eyebrow flash, which is used as a greeting in many cultures, involves the raising of both the inner and outer corners of the eyebrows (AUs 1 and 2).

DAVID MATSUMOTO

adaptation Adaptation refers to any action process or mechanism that reduces the effects of a constant or repeated stimulus. Adaptive processes range from behaviours that reduce exposure to that stimulus to molecular changes at the cellular level. For example, when we step from a dark building into sunshine, we adapt to the sun's brightness by turning away, by squinting, by the contraction of our pupils, and by photochemical changes occurring within our retinas.

Helson (1948, 1964) introduced the notion of an 'adaptation level'—the level of a stimulus that elicits no response or which is affectively neutral. He proposed that an individual's reaction to a stimulus is a function of the difference between the current stimulus level and the current 'adaptation level'. Helson's model captures the observations that the affective intensity of a stimulus depends on past levels of stimuli and diminishes over time for a constant stimulus. Thus, entering a room at 20°C feels more pleasurable when the temperature outside is really cold, but ceases to confer pleasure after we have been inside for a while.

Adaptive processes both reduce the harmful impacts of a stimulus (e.g. sweating is an adaptation to heat) and preserve perceptual sensitivity to small changes in the stimulus level. For example, when we first walk indoors from the afternoon sun everything looks dark, but after continued exposure we not only can see again but have regained sensitivity to small differences in luminance levels, permitting us to detect when a single light bulb burns out in a large auditorium (Frederick and Loewenstein 1999).

The power of adaptive processes is supported by studies showing that happiness is barely correlated with objective circumstances (see LIFE SATISFACTION). For example, lottery winners and recently paralysed people express levels of happiness that are comparable with those of people who have experienced neither

(Brickman et al. 1978). Similarly, as nations get wealthier, the reported well-being of its citizens does not increase (Easterlin 1995).

Such data have given rise to the concept of a 'hedonic treadmill' (Brickman and Campbell 1971), which suggests that happiness remains stationary despite efforts or interventions to advance it. The suitability of this metaphor remains in question, however. The research cited to support it relies on subjective self-reports whose interpretation is unclear. When asked 'How happy are you on a scale from 0 to 100?', respondents must judge for themselves what the endpoints of the scale represent. Someone who has lived a tough life might interpret '0' as unrelenting torture and '100' as pleasant comfort, whereas someone who has lived an easy life might interpret '0' as the absence of joy and '100' as heavenly bliss. If both people declared their happiness level to be a '60' (out of 100), it would obviously be wrong to conclude that they really are equally happy, since one has adopted a higher standard for the internal feeling that warrants that rating (Frederick and Loewenstein 1999, Kahneman 2000).

SHANE FREDERICK

addiction The exact definition and aetiology of addiction is disputed among health professionals and addiction researchers. The World Health Organization defines the term 'addiction' as: 'Repeated use of a psychoactive substance or substances, to the extent that the user (referred to as an addict) is periodically or chronically intoxicated, shows a compulsion to take the preferred substance (or substances), has great difficulty in voluntarily ceasing or modifying substance use, and exhibits determination to obtain psychoactive substances by almost any means. Typically, tolerance is prominent and a withdrawal syndrome frequently occurs when substance use is interrupted.'

The Diagnostic and Statistical Manual for Psychiatric Disorders, Fourth Edition (Text Revision) distinguishes between substance dependence and substance abuse. 'Substance dependence' is marked by symptoms of physiological tolerance, withdrawal, persistent desire and unsuccessful efforts to stop substance use, interruptions to work and social activities because of substance use, a large amount of time spent securing and using the substance or recovering from its effects, and continued substance use despite negative physical and psychological consequences of use. 'Substance abuse' is defined as recurrent failure to fulfil work, school, or home obligations because of substance use, substance use in physically hazardous situations, substance use resulting in legal problems, and continued use despite negative social and relationship consequences related to use. For many people, addiction results in compulsive craving, drug seeking, and drug use, which persists even in the face of severe adverse consequences.

Several models of addiction have been put forward, each attempting to explain and predict addictive behaviour. Benjamin Rush (1745–1813) was among the first to introduce the disease model of addiction, which defined addiction as a result of human weakness representing a defect of moral character. Individuals who endorse the moral model do not believe there is any biological or genetic basis for addiction and thus have little sympathy for people with severe addictions (Harding 1986; Peele 1987). The disease model, which is held by the American Medical Association and many addiction specialists around the world, views addiction as an illness that results from the impairment of neurochemical and/or biobehavioural processes (Jellinek 1960, Room 1983). Behavioural models, including classical and operant conditioning models, are based on the premise that addiction is a consequence of learning, such that problematic habits and maladaptive behaviour patterns are initiated and maintained by past and present *rewards (reinforcement), environmental access, family history, peer influences, and individual beliefs and expectations. The disease and behavioural models of addiction agree that a large component of addiction can be explained by neurochemistry and neuroadaptation following repeated exposure to drugs and/or alcohol (Robinson and Berridge 1993). All known drugs of abuse have the common effect of elevating the level of dopamine in the nucleus accumbens. Dopamine is a neurotransmitter that is part of the reward system, and continued use of drugs and alcohol will eventually result in the reward system reducing the amount of endogenous dopamine by causing a decrease in the number of dopamine receptors (Kalivas and Volkow 2005). Craving and withdrawal, two indicators of addiction, are directly related to reduction in dopamine receptors in the brain (Lowman et al. 2000).

Regardless of how addiction is defined or the aetiology of addiction explained, the fact that addictive behaviour often results in large costs to the individual and society is indisputable. For individuals the costs can be financial (medical and legal costs), physical (health and disease), and emotional (including the toll of addiction on family and friends). For society, costs are often attributed to medical and social welfare costs, the cost of drug-related law enforcement activity, and lost productivity due to drug use. For example, in the United States it is estimated that the annual costs of drug abuse and dependence (including costs to society and treatment costs) amount to more than $500 billion. Unfortunately only a small percentage of this amount is spent on treatment, even though with every dollar spent on addiction treatment there is a $4–7 reduction in the cost due to drug-related crimes (National Institute of Drug Abuse 2006).

To understand the treatment of addiction it is important to recognize addiction as a chronic, persistent condition that is complex but treatable (McLellan et al. 2000). Within many treatment settings the ultimate goal of addiction treatment is to enable an individual to achieve abstinence from drugs and/or alcohol. More immediate goals of treatment are to reduce the addictive behaviour, improve functioning, and minimize the physical and social consequences of addiction (harm reduction). Individuals who receive treatment for an addition may experience relapses even after long periods of abstinence (Moos and Moos 2006). In fact, relapse to drug abuse occurs at rates similar to that for other chronic medical illnesses such as diabetes, hypertension, and asthma. As such, addiction may require repeated treatments tailored to individual needs and relapse risk factors (Witkiewitz and Marlatt 2004).

G. ALAN MARLATT AND KATIE WITKIEWITZ

admiration/awe Admiration and awe are on few lists of *basic emotions, yet there can be little doubt that people sometimes feel a strong emotional response to extraordinarily talented, powerful, or famous people. An essay on Noam Chomsky (1928–) described the 'nearly theological reverence' that his students had for him: ' "It verged on worship", Robin Lakoff, a member of this group, later wrote. "To be in Chomsky's good graces meant that you were worthy of him, you partook in some small way in the godhead" ' (L. MacFarquhar in The New Yorker, 31 March 2003).

In their cognitive theory of emotions, Ortony et al. (1988) grouped admiration and awe together with esteem and respect and called them 'appreciation emotions'— triggered by positive appraisals (see APPRAISAL THEORIES) of the actions of an agent. Many social animals have emotions related to fear and submission, but none seem to have positive emotional responses to excellence. Why would humans have evolved such feelings? There is almost no empirical research on admiration or awe, so we are forced to confine ourselves to theoretical speculations.

Admiration

The word admiration comes from the Latin admirare, to wonder at, and the Oxford English Dictionary (OED) defines it as 'agreeable surprise; wonder mingled with reverence, esteem, approbation'. Perhaps the best way to understand the origins and functions of admiration is to view it as an emotion that facilitates learning (Henrich and Gil-White 2001). As humans were becoming cultural creatures who did most of their learning by copying others, it became adaptive to find the best role models to copy. Individuals who excel in any culturally valued skill therefore draw attention and followers. The followers, in turn, are motivated to build a relationship with the prestigious person to maximize their ability to learn further, and to share in his or her prestige. Admiration speeds cultural learning, and celebrity is what happens when a person is admired by many people. Admiration sometimes leads to inspiration, a highly positive state experienced as a transcending of one's old self and old limitations coupled with a motivation to emulate the admired person or otherwise to express what has been learned or discovered (Thrash and Elliot 2004).

Awe

The word awe comes from Old Norse *agi*, which referred to fear, dread, and terror, particularly with respect to God (see RELIGION AND EMOTION (PSYCHOLOGICAL PERSPECTIVES)). The OED shows how awe became a more positive emotion over time: 'From its use in reference to the Divine Being this passes gradually into: Dread mingled with veneration, reverential or respectful fear; the attitude of a mind subdued to profound reverence in the presence of supreme authority, moral greatness or sublimity, or mysterious sacredness'. In its modern usage the word awe has lost most of its connection to fear, and is often used to mean little more than admiration (for people) or appreciation (for natural or human-made beauty). Keltner and Haidt (2003) reviewed the literature in anthropology, sociology, and psychology to propose that awe should be understood as a family of emotional states that result when two appraisals are made: vastness, and the need for accommodation. Awe happens when we encounter something vast (usually physically vast, but sometimes small things reveal vast power, genius, or complexity) that cannot be comprehended using existing mental structures. There are at least five additional appraisals that create the variety of awe experiences and give them their particular flavour: perceptions of threat (as when in the presence of a dominant or powerful person), beauty (as in awe at nature), extraordinary ability (as with admiration), virtue (as with moral elevation), and the supernatural (as in older meanings of awe towards a divine being). Awe stops us dead in our tracks, and sometimes, when intense enough, acts like a reset button on the self. People sometimes emerge from awe experiences with new selves, values, and allegiances. For this reason awe is among the emotions most often implicated in spiritual transformations and religious conversion experiences.

JONATHAN HAIDT AND PATRICK SEDER

James, W. (1961/1902). *The varieties of religious experience*. New York: Macmillan.
Maslow, A.H. (1964). *Religions, values, and peak-experiences*. Columbus OH, Ohio State University Press.

adolescence (emotional development) Adolescence is a time of change in the social and biological systems that underlie and support emotional processes. The transition through adolescence is accompanied by physical, psychological, and social transformations (see CHILDHOOD (EMOTIONAL DEVELOPMENT)) that elicit novel experiences of emotional arousal. Although psychologists no longer view adolescence as a time of 'storm and stress', transitions in multiple life domains do tax emotional resources and challenge *coping abilities.

Social and pubertal changes at adolescence

Within the social realm, adolescents must renegotiate relationships with family (see FAMILY (ROLE OF EMOTION IN)), friends, and members of the opposite sex (see SOCIAL RELATIONSHIPS). As children enter the teenage years, they begin to spend less time with their families. The peer context becomes increasingly important, and experiences within this context have strong emotional content such as jealousy, competition, commitment, excitement, loneliness, loyalty, or betrayal (Larson and Asmussen 1991). Adolescents begin to turn more to their peers to discuss their emotions, although parental support remains critical in helping adolescents manage their emotions (see REGULATION OF EMOTION) and solve problems. The popular media also appear to play a role in adolescent emotionality, with the choices of music, television, and internet fare influencing (and influenced by) adolescents' emotions.

The onset of puberty in early adolescence also introduces the adolescent to new and intense emotional experiences. Although hormonal changes have rarely been directly linked to adolescent emotionality, hormone-induced physical maturation leads to changes in appearance that, in turn, lead to changes in treatment by others such as parents and opposite-sex peers. Socially mediated effects of hormonal changes and associated changes in physical appearance place the adolescent in new situations and social contexts. Experiences in new, quasi-adult roles (e.g. employee, romantic partner) are potentially both emotionally exhilarating as well as overwhelming, posing new challenges for the adolescent's capabilities of emotion regulation.

Adolescent brain maturation

These changes lead to a period of heightened emotional intensity coupled with increased need for self-competence in regulatory demands due to decreased adult supervision. Unfortunately, the 'adolescent brain' is not fully prepared to handle these challenges. Regions of the prefrontal cortex that play a critical role in emotion regulation mature slowly, continuing to show functional changes into late adolescence and early adulthood (Spear 2000). Furthermore, pubertal maturation has been occurring at much earlier ages in industrialized societies, particularly among girls. Thus, the adolescent may find himself or herself in affectively challenging social and interpersonal situations as much as a decade before having developed the full capacity to manage or regulate the associated affect.

Dahl (2004) describes this dilemma as 'starting the engines with an unskilled driver'. This may explain, in part, the fact that adolescents often make poor decisions (i.e. high rates of participation in dangerous activities, automobile accidents, drug use (see ADDICTION), and unprotected sex) despite understanding (cognitively) the risks involved (see RISK-TAKING) (Steinberg 2004). Some evidence suggests an imbalance in cognitive and emotional influences on decision-making and behaviour during adolescence, with the scale temporarily tipping toward affective influences until skills in cognitive control gradually 'catch-up'. For example, Ernst *et al.* (2006) have proposed that adolescence is characterized by a strengthening of neural systems involved in reward processing (e.g. the ventral striatum) combined with relatively weak harm avoidance (e.g. amygdala) and regulatory systems (e.g. ventromedial prefrontal cortex).

Clinical implications

Adolescence is also a period of heightened vulnerability for emotion-related disorders (see DISORDER (AFFECTIVE, EMOTIONAL)) such as mood disorders, anxiety disorders, substance abuse problems, and delinquency. Many of the health problems that emerge during adolescence are related to difficulties with the control of emotions, involving either dysregulation of emotion (e.g. depression, bipolar disorder, anxiety disorder) or poor decision-making in the face of emotional influence (e.g. unsafe sex, peer pressure to engage in substance abuse, or delinquency). Research is only beginning to delineate the specific role of emotional reactivity and regulation in adolescent mental health (e.g. Silk *et al.* 2003), but this appears to be an important area for future research. Adolescence is an important stage in which to investigate the influence of emotional reactivity and regulation on health outcomes because it represents not only a period of increased vulnerability for affect-related disorders but also a period ripe with opportunity for intervention (Dahl 2004). Given new evidence of considerable brain plasticity throughout adolescence, parents, peers, teachers, and mental health workers have the opportunity to have an impact on adolescent emotional development and the development and refinement of skills for regulating emotion during adolescence.

JENNIFER S. SILK AND LAURENCE D. STEINBERG

Dahl, R.E. (2004). Adolescent brain development: a period of vulnerabilities and opportunities. In: R.E. Dahl and L.P. Spear (eds), *Adolescent brain development, vulnerabilities and opportunities*, pp. 1–22. New York: New York Academy of Sciences.

Galambos, N.L. and Costigan, C.L. (2003). Emotional and personality development in adolescence. In: R.M. Lerner, M.A. Easterbrooks, and J. Mistry (eds) *Handbook of psychology, developmental psychology*, Vol. 6, pp. 351–72. Hoboken, NJ: John Wiley and Sons.

aesthetic emotions (philosophical perspectives)

If the term 'aesthetic emotion' is understood broadly to refer to the various roles that emotions can play in the arts, then there are at least three ways in which it can be understood: artworks sometimes *represent* emotions, as when Racine's (1639–99) *Phèdre* represents a woman in the throes of an uncontrollable passion; they sometimes *express* emotions, as when Goethe seems to express his nostalgia for *das Land wo die Zitronen blühen*; and they sometimes *arouse* emotions in audiences and spectators, as when we are horrified by a horror film or saddened by a sad piece of *music. But the term 'aesthetic emotion' has also been used more narrowly to refer to a special emotion thought (by some) to be induced when spectators or audiences engage with artworks, or a special way in which emotions are thought to be experienced when people are having *aesthetic experiences*, whether with artworks or with objects or scenes in nature.

A special aesthetic emotion?

Although theorizing about the arts goes back to the ancient Greeks, it was not until the 18th century that the term 'aesthetics' was coined and aesthetics became its own field of theoretical inquiry. In his *Critique of the Power of Judgment*, Kant (1790; 2000) describes *pleasure in the beautiful as a special kind of *disinterested* pleasure, which all rational persons can be necessarily expected to share. In enjoying a beautiful sunset, we feel a subjective pleasure that is more than just sensuous pleasure and that has no practical aspect: we do not enjoy the sunset because it is useful to us in some way. Schopenhauer (1818; 1966) developed this idea, arguing that aesthetic contemplation is one way in which we can remove ourselves from and hence endure the evils of ordinary life (which is governed by blind energy or will). These philosophers are the main source of the widely accepted idea that when our emotional responses to works of art are aesthetic, they are 'distanced' from real life (Bullough 1977). This thought finds its most extreme expression in the work of the Formalist art critic and theorist, Clive Bell (1914), who used the phrase 'aesthetic emotion' to describe a special kind of emotion that he thought was evoked by works of art (not nature) and that he explicitly distinguished from the emotions of life. Bell claimed that the 'aesthetic emotion' is aroused by works of art that have 'significant form', such as the work of the Post-Impressionist painter Cézanne (1839–1906). John Dewey (1959) and others disputed the idea that art evokes some special type of emotion unrelated to 'life emotions,' and indeed Bell can be construed as referring to ordinary 'life' emotions such as *admiration and awe that are directed towards paintings that exhibit a powerful or interesting or beautiful composition.

The arousal of emotion by artworks

There is also a strong tradition in writing about the arts, going back to the Greeks, that links them to the arousal of such basic 'life' emotions as sorrow, anger, and fear. Plato (1993) thought that the arts were morally unsound and dangerous, partly because they represent deceitful appearances rather than reality and partly because they appeal to the emotions rather than the reason, a 'higher' part of the soul. Aristotle (1987) agreed with Plato that the arts arouse emotions, but unlike Plato he thought this was a good thing because we *learn* through having our emotions aroused. His definition of a good tragedy included the requirement that it evoke a *catharsis* of pity and fear in its audience. Scholars debate about what exactly this means, but part of its meaning seems to be that a good tragedy, such as *Oedipus*, clarifies the emotions it arouses and helps us to understand the message of the play: it is partly by pitying Oedipus and fearing that we ourselves are just as vulnerable to the whims of fate that we grasp the terrible significance of his story.

Recently, there has been much discussion about *how* exactly literary works of fiction such as plays and novels arouse emotions. Do we need to *simulate* the emotions of characters such as Oedipus, and if so, does that mean that we somehow actually feel as the characters do, or do we only have to sympathize without actually putting ourselves in the character's shoes (Gerrig 1993, Feagin 1996, Harris 2000, Goldman 2006)? In watching *Oedipus* on stage or screen, it may be that our motor reactions (influenced by mirror neurons) mirror those of the actor playing Oedipus and thus help us to feel as Oedipus does. But to what degree this is possible is a matter of dispute.

One general problem that has received a lot of attention is how works of fiction can arouse emotions at all. Why should we pity Oedipus when he probably didn't even exist? This 'paradox of fiction' (see FICTION (AND EMOTION)) only arises, however, if one holds a particular version of the so-called 'judgement' or 'cognitive appraisal' theory of emotion (see APPRAISAL THEORY). If pitying Oedipus entails both believing that Oedipus exists and that he is having a terrible time, then one simply can't genuinely pity Oedipus. Appraisal theorists try to explain away the problem: one is only *imagining* of oneself that one pities Oedipus or one is experiencing a 'quasi-emotion', in the sense that one suffers some of the symptoms of the emotion but in the absence of its essential cognitive core (Walton 1990). If, however, one

gives up the idea that the core of an emotion is a belief, then the problem would seem to dissipate. It seems that we just do respond emotionally not only to actual events but to memories, imaginings, and thought which may or may not be about actual people or events (Robinson 2005). There is good evidence that imagining fearsome events evokes physiological responses characteristic of fear (e.g. Vrana *et al.* 1989).

Tragedy raises another paradox: why is it that people seem to enjoy hearing tales of terror and woe? Again, some people try to explain away the problem: we enjoy the interesting way in which the terrible tale is told, or we engage in a special process of 'distancing' our emotions, so that although the tale is still terrible we manage to cope with the terror. Both solutions assume that we have to somehow distract ourselves from the tale itself. A better solution is to acknowledge that pleasure is not the only reason why people engage with great *literature; the main reason is that people feel compelled to engage with works that deal with the most important issues facing humankind and that they learn something from such works (Lamarque 1995, Ridley 2003).

Finally, music—or at least 'pure' music without accompanying words—presents special problems for the cognitive appraisal theory of emotion. If a cognitive appraisal of loss is necessary for sadness, and of potential threat is necessary for anxiety, then how can music all by itself arouse these emotions? Yet there is lots of empirical evidence that 'pure' music can arouse at least sadness, happiness, anxiety, and tranquillity in listeners (Scherer and Zentner 2001, Sloboda and Juslin 2001). One possibility is that music arouses only *moods and that it does this by inducing physiological and motor changes of various sorts (cf. Hatfield *et al.* 1994). Possibly these mood states are labelled more precisely by listeners in light of other aspects of the music or the context of listening. Suppose a piece makes me *sad* because of its plodding rhythm and slow minor key melody. If it also continually delays harmonic resolution and induces in me a strong desire for resolution I may describe it as making me not just 'sad' but 'yearning' (Robinson 2005).

The expression of emotion in art

So far we have discussed only the emotions of audiences in their interactions with artworks. But artworks, such as novels and portraits, are also agreed to *represent* the emotions of the characters they contain and to *express* the emotions of their creators. One way in which representational works of art—plays, novels, films, (representational) paintings, sculptures, dance, etc.—express emotions is by representing characters who are themselves expressing their emotions. The *Weeping Madonna* by Bouts may express sorrow just because its subject matter is so obviously sorrowful. The 17th-century painter Charles Le Brun (1619–90), following Leon Battista Alberti (1404–72), systematized the representation of facial expressions that express the various passions (SEE EXPRESSION, PRINCIPLES OF EMOTIONAL). In the 17th century music, too, was often described as 'representing' the passions; indeed in Baroque suites and concerti the emotion represented by a movement was often a principal means of unifying it. However, the word 'represent' was used very generally, and usually no strict distinction was made between representing the passions and evoking them.

The idea that the arts could or should express emotion came into its own in the Romantic period. Romantic poets, painters, and composers talked of themselves as expressing their own deepest emotions in their work, so that when Shelley cried, 'I fall upon the thorns of life! I bleed!' his readers could take him to be expressing his very own emotions in his verse. At about the same period Hegel (1975) was arguing that art is a special mode of understanding, distinct from philosophy on the one hand and religion on the other. These two ideas come together in the aesthetic philosophy of Benedetto Croce (1992) and his English follower, R. G. Collingwood (1963). Collingwood defended the idea that art should be defined as the expression of emotion, but he used the term 'expression' in a quasi-technical sense. To 'express' an emotion for Collingwood is to get clear about it and bring it to consciousness. When an artist begins to create, he or she may have little idea how things will turn out; in the process of creating the poem or the symphony or whatever, the artist gradually comes to understand what emotion he or she is struggling to express, and the finished artwork will reveal that emotion. So in writing the *Ode to a Nightingale*, Keats expresses his longing for a timeless world of art and beauty far away from 'the weariness, the fever, and the fret' of our quotidian existence, and the finished poem articulates and elucidates this emotion.

Artworks, according to Collingwood, do not express emotions in the way that facial expressions or physiological symptoms do. To weep and frown is merely to *betray* emotion, whereas artistic expression is a mode of understanding. Similarly, to assert 'I am sad' is merely to categorize an emotion as belonging to a general type (sadness), whereas artistic expression elucidates an emotion in all its peculiarity and uniqueness. Artistic expression is a kind of cognitive monitoring of emotion, or, as Wordsworth put it, the recollection of emotion in tranquillity. The artistic expression of emotion is also distinct from the mere arousal of emotion; a poet who is genuinely expressing his or her own emotions is engaged in trying to clarify those emotions, not in manipulating the emotions of other people. On the other

hand, if a poet genuinely expresses his or her emotions in a work, then other people, on reading the work, will be able to recreate these emotions for themselves and to experience what the artist was expressing.

Not all art fits Collingwood's definition, of course. His account is probably more interesting as an account of artistic expression than as an account of art *per se*. One problem with the view is that it entails that all expressive art expresses the artist's very own feelings. But even if Keats the man had been indifferent to art and beauty, the dramatic speaker of his nightingale ode still expresses 'his' longing for those things. Instead of attributing the emotions expressed by a work to the actual author it is wiser to postulate an implied author as owner of the emotional states expressed (cf. Booth 1961). Once we introduce the idea of an implied author, we can see clearly the difference between what emotions a work represents a character as expressing and what the work itself expresses. Mr Collins in *Pride and Prejudice* expresses his gratitude to all and sundry; the implied author expresses not gratitude but amused contempt.

According to some analytic philosophers, artistic expression is just a matter of an artwork's possessing expressive qualities and need have no implications about the emotions of either the author or implied author of the work. In discussions of expressiveness in music, Peter Kivy (1989) and Stephen Davies (1994) have defended the view that music is expressive of sadness, say, in the same way as the face of a Saint Bernard or basset hound is expressive of sadness. The configuration of the dog's face makes it look sad, but we can draw no inferences from this expression about the way the dog is actually feeling. Similarly, sad music need not emanate from a sad composer or implied composer: to write a sad piece you simply have to mimic the falling tones of the sad human voice or the plodding movements of the sad human gait (Gabrielsson and Juslin 2003), or you employ conventions like a 'sad' minor key.

It is surely right to say that music can be called 'sad' because it mimics the movements or intonations of a person expressing their sadness, but some works, especially Romantic works, do more than this. Many Romantic lieder express the emotions of a protagonist in a truly Collingwoodian way, articulating not only the nature of particular unique emotional states but also the way that particular emotions can blend, conflict, and mutate. Some theorists have argued that some instrumental music can be heard in the same way, as the articulation of emotions in an imagined persona in the music (Levinson 1996). The ABA form of a Brahms Intermezzo, for example, can sometimes be interpreted as a conflict between two related emotional tendencies. Music is in many ways the quintessential art of emotional expression because it not only expresses emotions but also arouses them in listeners in a direct physiological way (Robinson 2005).

JENEFER ROBINSON

Hjort, M. and Laver, S. (eds) (1997). *Emotion and the arts*. New York: Oxford University Press.

Juslin, P.N. and Sloboda, J.A. (eds) (2001). *Music and emotion: theory and research*. Oxford: Oxford University Press.

Nussbaum, M.C. (2001). *Upheavals of thought: the intelligence of emotions*. Cambridge: Cambridge University Press.

Oatley, K. (1992). *Best laid schemes: the psychology of emotions, studies in emotion and social interaction*. Cambridge: Cambridge University Press.

Oatley, K. (2003). Creative expression and communication of emotions in the visual and narrative arts. In: R.J. Davidson, K.R. Scherer, and H.H. Goldsmith (eds), *Handbook of affective sciences*, pp. 481–502. New York: Oxford University Press.

aesthetic emotions (psychological perspectives)

The study of aesthetic emotions is an interdisciplinary region of affective science, involving scholars from psychology, philosophy, history of art, anthropology, and design theory. Psychological theories of aesthetics assume that mainstream theories of motivation and emotion can explain the central problems of aesthetic experience. This assumption is controversial to some aesthetic theories rooted in history of art and philosophy, but it enables scientists to apply successful theories of emotion to the study of aesthetics. Psychology's scientific interest in aesthetic emotions dates to Gustav Fechner (1876), who pioneered the use of experimental methods to examine aesthetic preference. Fechner's 'experimental aesthetics' was particularly interested in how proportions such as the golden ratio influenced preferences. The study of aesthetics was dormant until the late 1960s, when Daniel Berlyne (1971) applied his theory of motivation to understanding why people find art pleasing, interesting, and aversive. To emphasize its kinship with Fechner, Berlyne labelled his approach 'the new experimental aesthetics'. Berlyne's experimental, laboratory-based approach to aesthetics remains the dominant methodological perspective.

Modern research on aesthetic emotions focuses into two areas of interest. One area of research examines low-level features and processes that affect aesthetic experience. In visual art, for example, colour, proportion, symmetry, balance, angularity, complexity, and familiarity influence preference. A second area of research examines higher-order processes that affect aesthetic experience, such as knowledge relevant to the work, broad dimensions of personality, cultural norms, and expertise in art and design (Locher *et al.* 2006).

On the whole, the study of aesthetic emotions has focused more on simple, low-intensity preferences than on fully fledged emotions. Most research has measured self-reported pleasingness, liking, and preference for works of art. This emphasis fits the philosophical tradition of aesthetic experience as the experience of beauty; as refined, sublime feelings; or as feelings of disinterested pleasure. But equating aesthetic emotions with mild positive states underestimates the emotional power of the arts. People use aesthetic objects, particularly *music, movies, novels (see LITERATURE AND EMOTION), and rituals, to regulate their emotions. When research has examined discrete aesthetic emotions, it has emphasized positive emotions (particularly *enjoyment and *interest) over negative emotions. Cultural conflicts over the arts hinge on negative emotions—such as disgust, anger, and contempt in response to a controversial film—and artists often try to evoke negative emotions in their audience, so negative aesthetic emotions deserve more attention.

*Appraisal theories of emotion have recently appeared in both psychological and philosophical work on aesthetics (Robinson 2005, Silvia 2006a). These approaches connect aesthetic emotions to the patterns of appraisals that cause and constitute them. Although still in development, appraisal approaches to aesthetics have two primary virtues. First, appraisal theories root aesthetic emotions within mainstream models of emotion. Explaining aesthetic emotions with emotion theories may seem obvious to modern researchers, but historically the study of aesthetics has been rooted in cognitive and behavioural theories (Berlyne 1971). Second, appraisal theories can explain many of the major problems in aesthetic emotions—such as why people have different emotions in response to the same work and how expertise and knowledge influence aesthetic experience—and they make clear predictions for a wide range of positive and negative emotions.

PAUL J. SILVIA

Robinson, J. (2005). *Deeper than reason: emotion and its role in literature, music, and art*. New York: Oxford University Press.

Silvia, P.J. (2005). Emotional responses to art: from collation and arousal to cognition and emotion. *Review of General Psychology*, **9**, 342–57.

affect (philosophical perspectives)

When the term 'affect' is employed in the expression '*affective science' it is usually meant to demarcate a distinct scientific domain of inquiry (e.g. Panksepp 1998). An important feature of domain names of this sort is that their precise theoretical meaning depends on research in the very fields they are supposed to delimit. In the case of 'affect' this has led to an intriguing situation where both the term and the domain have been called into question. Indeed, scientific disputes about the meaning of 'affect' may have escalated to the point where a radical rethinking of the aims and boundaries of 'affective science' is required. One major issue is whether there can be unconscious affective states (see UNCONSCIOUS EMOTIONS), which many argue is as self-contradictory as the claim that there can be unfelt *feelings.

The Latin etymology of 'affect' suggests the receptive property of being influenced or acted on by something (*ad* + *facere*, to do; *afficere*, to cause change, to influence). This passivity is reflected in another conceptual assumption made by early pioneers of affective science like James, Wundt, and Titchener, which is that affect is a property of conscious experience. In the work of Wundt and Titchener, these two assumptions occur with the added proviso that felt experience in affect is characterized by a positive or negative hedonic tone. This is the idea of *valence, now a fundamental construct in affective science, but also a matter of great conceptual complexity and controversy (Colombetti 2005). Valence has been argued to be the fundamental building block of emotion (Barrett 2006a). It is also probably the most widely discussed component of affect, where it is the central ingredient in the extensive literature on 'bipolarity' (Russell 1999). Along with valence, the concepts of activation, *arousal, intensity, and duration have at various times been proposed as additional dimensions of affect and emotion (see DIMENSIONAL MODELS).

Nowadays, it is widely believed that 'feeling is synonymous with conscious affect' (Berkowitz 2000, p. 2). It is common for 'affect' to be defined as 'genuine subjective feelings and *moods (Russell 1999, p. 3). In some theories, affect in this conscious sense is said to be based on a primitive neurophysiological affective state called the '*core affect' which may, but need not, be conscious (Russell 2003). Nevertheless, most current research on 'affect' is exclusively devoted to 'affect' in its conscious sense (Barrett and Russell 1999). Recently, in an effort to scientifically extricate themselves from this conceptual straightjacket, some researchers have argued that the possibility of unconscious affect is an empirical matter for which there exists favourable evidence (Winkielman et al. 2005a). Comparable arguments have been made in defence of the existence of unfelt emotions (Prinz 2005). There is a tendency in some sectors of affective science to identify affect with the felt subjective experience of emotion. However, many resist this restriction and maintain that moods and feeling states other than those associated with emotion deserve to be included under the rubric of 'affect'. This does not negate the fact that affect, and in particular the valence dimension of affect, is probably the most important defining feature of emotion (Charland 2005b).

Despite the controversies over the definition of 'affect' there exists an indomitable optimism that the secrets of affect will eventually reveal themselves to science. When engaged in such a quest, it is easy to forget that science is not incompatible with mystery. In the scientific study of affect, we appear to have encountered such a mystery. In a situation reminiscent of the indeterminacies of quantum mechanics, it appears that apart from our efforts to measure and report affect, there is no objective fact of the matter about what it is we ultimately feel, and what it is our feelings ultimately mean (Charland 2005a). Modern clinical psychiatry may appear to bypass this problem when it limits 'affect' to 'a pattern of observable behaviors that is the expression of a subjectively experienced emotion state' (American Psychiatric Association 1994, p. 763). But limiting 'affect' to what is observable in this away also eliminates most of what counts as 'affect' in affective science today. In comparison, even if it does have its mysteries, the scientific quest to understand 'affect' in all its conscious—and possibly unconscious—glory and complexity seems a preferable route to take.

LOUIS C. CHARLAND

affect (psychological perspectives) The terms *affect* and the corresponding adjective *affective* are generally used in an overarching generic sense for a mental state that is characterized by emotional feeling as compared with rational thinking. The etymology of the term, from the Latin *affectus* (the past participle of *afficere*, meaning 'to act on, have influence on') has acquired the connotation of 'being touched or moved by an event to a greater extent than what a normal perception or thought would entail', sometimes implying a strong intensity in the reaction. Philosophers and psychologists generally see an evaluative feeling (sometimes considered a *judgement*) of an object, person, or event in terms of positive–pleasant versus negative–unpleasant *valence (at the extremes, pleasure and pain) as the defining characteristic of affect. Most psychologists also require a certain degree of arousal to differentiate the term from purely cognitive judgements, suggesting at least some degree of corresponding bodily *reaction (but not necessarily action; which is in line with the passive connotation of 'being touched'; see contributions in Clark and Fiske, 1982). The term is often used in a general sense to refer to a class or category of mental states that includes *emotions, *moods, *attitudes, *interpersonal stances, and affect dispositions (see PERSONALITY), with each of these class members differing in terms of origin, function, intensity, duration, bodily reaction, behavioural effects, and rapidity of change (Scherer 2005).

NICO H. FRIJDA AND KLAUS R. SCHERER

affect-as-information model Judgements, decisions, and emotions arise from unconscious processes. People therefore learn their likes, dislikes, preferences, and decisions from the thoughts and feelings they experience. Traditional theories emphasize that people make judgements and decisions using available information. It turns out that the critical information sometimes comes from *feelings rather than facts. Often judgements and decisions are based on actual and anticipated affect. Thus, according to the affect-as-information approach (Schwarz and Clore 1983), people make evaluative judgements essentially by asking, 'How do I feel about this?'. When affect is experienced as spontaneous, it can be very persuasive. The absence of affect can also be informative. Whether they are choosing a spouse or buying a house, people's confidence in their decisions would suffer if they discovered they had no feelings one way or the other.

Affect provides information about value and importance, but what is valuable and important depends on the person's attention at the time. Thus, positive affect may be experienced as liking during the evaluation of an object, but as feelings of efficacy during a task. Feelings of efficacy generate confidence in one's cognitions and inclinations, whereas negative affect can undermine such confidence, resulting in a focus on perception rather than cognition and in item-specific rather than categorical processing. Indeed, research shows that many textbook phenomena of cognitive psychology are especially reliable when individuals are in a happy mood but not when they are in a sad mood (Clore and Storbeck 2006). In both judgement and performance situations, the influence of affect can often be reversed when the affect is made to appear irrelevant to the object of judgement or performance on the task. Such effects show that it is the information from affect, rather than the affect itself, that is responsible for many affective influences on both judgement and performance.

GERALD L. CLORE

affect bursts While much of the facial and vocal *expression of emotion occurs during speech, there are also completely nonverbal emotion expressions that occur outside of or that intersperse speaking activity. The notion of *affect burst* has been proposed (Scherer 1994a) to refer to such sudden, full-blown displays of emotion in response to highly affectively charged, and often unexpected, events. These eruptive outbursts of emotion are considered as concomitants of automatically produced emotional response patterns (see PUSH/ PULL EFFECTS) that consist of brief, synchronized changes in facial, vocal, and possibly gestural and postural, expression. Consequently, raw affect bursts are reflexive displays produced by physiological reactions and adaptive behaviour tendencies (e.g. regurgitating in disgust) that are universal, but may show strong interindividual differences across situations due to differences in appraisal of events or in response tendencies.

While affect bursts are often produced in a spontaneous and unintentional fashion, sometimes defying efforts of expression control or emotion regulation, they can be produced intentionally and strategically, often with the aim of bestowing greater authenticity or naturalness to one's emotional display. The consequence of this strategic use has been the development of conventionalized (emblematic) forms of such emotional outbursts, which have been termed *affect emblems* (Scherer 1994a). The vocal component of such affect emblems have been 'domesticated' by language (e.g. 'yuk', 'ouch') and are often found as entries in dictionaries (with strong differences in the sound transcription between languages). Emoticons reflect the conventionalization of the facial component.

The production of affect emblems is governed by strongly culture-dependent templates, 'pulling' the expression into line with the model, and thus shows comparatively few and small individual differences. Raw affect bursts and conventionalized affect emblems are seen as extreme points on a continuum, and many different forms of intermediate productions can be found, determined by spontaneity or intentionality of production and the availability of conventionalized symbols. While the vocal part of such affect bursts (often referred to as 'interjections') has received some attention from speech scientists (e.g. Schröder, 2003), the complete phenomenon of an integrated vocal/facial/ bodily expression is curiously underresearched.

KLAUS R. SCHERER

affective computing Affective computing is computing that relates to, arises from, or deliberately influences emotion and other affective phenomena (Picard 1997). Its use is illustrated by the following encounter with a robot entering your kitchen one morning before guests arrive:

Before deciding whether to speak or interrupt, the robot tries to infer your affective state, and sees, probably through observing your face, gestures, and verbal language, that you appear to be quite probably upset. It reasons that people who are upset usually do not like energetic and cheery 'Good morning!' greetings and subsequently adjusts its internal state to 'subdued', which has the effect of lowering its vocal pitch and amplitude settings and toning down behavioural displays. While the robot is in this state, it avoids initiating unnecessary conversation. Suppose you exclaim, 'I burned the #@$!sauce and burned my hand and have to start all over!' While the robot's speech recognition may err, its assessment of your affect indicates that it should not look happy right now. If it understands being burned, it might also turn its head into a look of concern and search its empathetic response phrases, selecting,

'Ouch. Are you OK?' and perhaps 'I fried a transistor once', as opposed to choosing the semantically connected, 'Shall I list sauce recipes for you?'. It watches for signs of your affective state changing. When you indicate you are OK and appear calmer, it returns to a more neutral state, now again initiating conversation such as, 'How about if I scrub that pan?'. If it recognizes that you now appear to be pleased and approving, then it increments the positive level of its internal state and updates its learning system to indicate that the currently used strategy was successful.

Research in affective computing can be organized into four areas, although these are not mutually exclusive: (1) technology for sensing, recognizing, modelling, and predicting emotional and affective states, e.g. he looks and sounds angry now and if I say this it might make him angrier (see RECOGNITION OF EMOTION (NEURAL SYSTEMS FOR)); (2) methods for computers to respond intelligently and respectfully to handle perceived affective information, e.g. the strategy of acting subdued around a person who is upset; (3) technology for displaying emotional information or mediating the expression or communication of emotion, e.g. modulate pitch, word choice, and physical movements to indicate joy (see EXPRESSION, PRINCIPLES OF EMOTIONAL); and (4) computational mechanisms that simulate internal emotions or implement their regulatory and biasing functions, e.g. change the memory search strategy based on current affective state (see COMPUTATIONAL MODELS).

While it is easiest to see how to apply affective computing to robots or software agents that are modelled after people or other animals (Marsella et al. 2004, Breazeal and Picard 2006), the applications also extend to other areas. For example, affective computing can be used to improve product design by helping to identify experiences that cause stress, frustration, or other undesirable states, e.g. designing new automobile interfaces that improve driver safety (Healey and Picard 2005). There are also opportunities to use affective technology to assist people with special needs, such as people diagnosed with autistic spectrum conditions who usually have difficulty recognizing, predicting, and knowing how to respond to emotional information: technology that recognizes and anticipates social–emotional displays could assess another person's interest or boredom, displeasure or pleasure, ultimately helping a person with social–emotional challenges to choose ways to respond that are likely to lead to a better conversational experience (el Kaliouby et al. 2006). Affective computing is also used in commercial applications; for example, more than $US 400 million was spent in 2006 on call centre software that automatically detects if customers sound upset so that those calls can receive special attention (UPI 2006).

Research in affective computing combines engineering and computer science with psychology, cognitive science, neuroscience, sociology, linguistics, education, medicine, psychophysiology, value-centred design, ethics, and more, enabling advances in basic understanding of affect and its role in a broad range of human experience. For example, the dominant psychological theories in the affective sciences do not have a state labelled 'subdued'; however, a study comparing subdued and enthused speech showed that choosing subdued speech led to significantly better driver performance and safety when drivers were previously exposed to upsetting stimuli (Nass et al. 2004). In fact there are several affective states that arise commonly in human–technology interaction which are widely ignored by affect theories, e.g. frustration and boredom (D'Mello et al. 2006). Through the construction of interactive systems that can record and process affective aspects of interaction through use of technology, researchers in affective computing can monitor states that happen naturally, including their duration and frequency, psychophysiological, behavioural, and social–communicative characteristics. This information contributes to the synthesis and evaluation of improved affect theories that more fully explain and predict measurable human experience. Revised theories can then be implemented in technology and tested under natural usage, and this process iterated until the theory achieves descriptive and predictive accuracy.

Affective Computing researchers often situate their studies in contexts where emotion is coupled with other factors. For example, if the computer is a tutoring agent interacting with a learner, and she is making lots of mistakes and starts smiling at the tutor, then those smiles probably do not express feelings of happiness, even if her orbicularis oculi and *zygomaticus muscles are contracted, as seen in the case where children smiled more after failure than after success (Schneider and Josephs 1991). The smart computer tutor looks jointly at affective expressions such as facial cues together with nonaffective information such as performance, personality, and past history, in order to decide what the student is likely to be feeling and what pedagogical move to make next. Today's systems also recognize complex cognitive-affective states by analysing joint head and facial movements, and tracking how they change over time (el Kaliouby and Robinson 2005), such as when a look of interest morphs into one of concentration, then into one of confusion, then back into interest, then into confusion again, and perhaps from there into frustration or anger mixed with other feelings. One of the challenges in affective computing research is how to deal robustly with affective information even when it is not in a pure or static form.

Technology for sensing, recognizing, modelling, and predicting affective state

Emotion researchers have traditionally used question-naires, human observation, and physiological sensing to gather data for assessing emotional state. Affective computing enables new kinds of real-time, automatic, and sometimes less obtrusive measurements, giving technology the ability to read affective cues from tone of voice, language, facial expressions, posture, gestures, autonomic nervous system measures, and whatever combinations of modalities that people are comfortable with having sensed. Tools of pattern analysis and machine learning are typically used to discover possibly nonlinear combinations of the sensor data that enable recognition of emotions (Picard *et al.* 2001, Pantic and Rothkrantz 2003). These techniques can also construct statistical models to aid not only in recognizing the current state, but also in predicting the next state or states, much like speech models can be used to predict likelihoods of certain words following others.

This area of research raises many questions concerning an individual's privacy and the use of digital affective information. Great care must be taken to respect people's wishes about what is and is not sensed, clearly communicating whether collected information can be associated with their identity and what benefits and harms they may receive from sharing this information. These concerns are especially important because in some cases sensors can obtain affective information without people being aware that sensors are even being used, for example when thermal imaging is used for detection of deceit (Tsiamyrtzis *et al.* 2006).

Methods for computers to respond intelligently and respectfully to handle perceived emotions

When a person reveals affective information to a recipient, the latter can choose ways to respond that may be helpful or harmful. For example, if the recipient is a computer and a person reveals to it that its action is very frustrating, then the computer could be equipped to recognize that and take steps to alleviate the person's frustration. Fixing the problems that frustrate people can improve human experience with technology.

A different strategy for responding to human emotion is to provide *empathetic or caring responses. While it may sound absurd for a computer to express feelings when it does not have them, it is possible for a computer to empathize and appear caring without pretending to feel anything a person feels (see Fig. A1). Studies suggest that computer-provided empathy can reduce frustration and stress (Klein *et al.* 2002, Prendinger *et al.* 2005) and can impact upon perceptions of caring,

which could help in health-care technologies, among others (de Rosis *et al.* 2006).

The idea of having a computer show empathy grew out of findings that people interact with computers in a similar way to how they interact with other people (Reeves and Nass 1996); consequently, the theory of human–human interaction can be applied to make predictions about what will work in human–computer interaction. For example, if we know that Bob doesn't like it when Sally sings triumphant songs after Bob experiences misfortune, then we can predict that Bob won't like it when a computer plays triumphant songs after Bob experiences misfortune. While we do not expect people to treat computers exactly the same as people, many general principles about human–human interaction carry over to the case of human–computer interaction.

Technology for displaying emotional information or mediating the expression or communication of emotion

Technology can easily give the appearance of having emotion without having the components that traditionally accompany emotion (see Fig. A2). Apple computers display a smile when booting successfully, even though the computer has no accompanying feelings of happiness. Artists can masterfully craft robotic dogs, animated characters, and other technologies to look like they have emotions; however, the hardest challenge in real-time emotion display is figuring out *when* to display *which* affect. Without understanding social *display rules and other important cues about the interaction context, technology is quite likely to irritate people with its emotional displays. For example, the Microsoft Windows operating system plays a triumphant tune when it boots up, and this is suitable when all is well. However, if a person has to reboot because of a system crash and the first response they hear from the computer is triumphant music, then this is annoying. In contrast, people often smile after they make a mistake (e.g. Schneider and Josephs 1991), so the Apple's smile, while it may be perceived differently during a reboot, is socially acceptable.

The difficulty of accurately communicating emotion through text-based online interaction has led to the development of emoticons and other means for people to add affective intent. Increasingly, artists and interaction designers augment chat, instant messaging, and other technologies with new means of communicating emotion. Their aim is to take the sender's affective bits and redisplay them in ways that enable the receiver to experience something of the state that was encoded at the input.

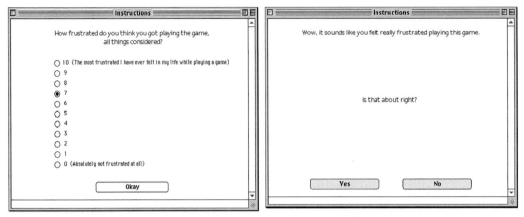

Fig. A1. Computers, even without using anthropomorphic faces and voices, can adapt responses to human emotion that subsequently influence the affective state of those whom they interact with. The empathetic example shown here (from Klein *et al.* 2002) did not pretend to have real feelings, but still conveyed the impression of active listening, empathy, and sympathy to help many frustrated computer users feel better.

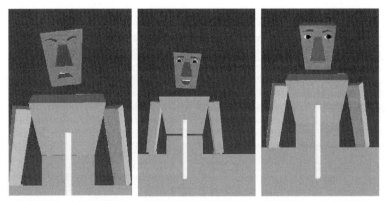

Fig. A2. It is easy to give machines the appearance of having emotion. It is much harder to give them the ability to know what emotion to express and when. The software agent shown here, created by Ken Perlin and John Lippincott, has a variety of continuously changing expressive parameters which have been hooked to sensors of human nonverbal communication (Burleson *et al.* 2004).

Computational mechanisms that simulate internal emotions or implement their regulatory and biasing functions

The most controversial area of affective computing arises when researchers start talking about giving machines emotions, because the topic quickly moves to whether machines can be conscious and have feelings in any sense resembling the human experience. To date, there is no evidence that they can, and no proof that they cannot, while there is ample evidence that computer scientists can implement computational *functions* that imitate biological emotion.

Emotion-like mechanisms can perform functions that may or may not appear emotional to an outside observer. When the emotion model within the Hasbro/iRobot toy doll My Real Baby evaluates inputs and then causes the doll's facial expressions and vocalizations to change, the doll can look quite emotional. Another example is where a cognitive appraisal (see APPRAISAL THEORIES) model within a software agent is used to trigger an emotional verbalization. In other cases, affective computing researchers implement less visible functions of emotion, such as ways in which affective states can improve machine *decision-making, attention regulation, learning (Gadanho 2003), and more (Trappl *et al.* 2003).

Trying to construct technologies with a variety of functions of emotion requires moving the light beam to focus on emotion at different angles and depths, asking not just 'What is this?' but also 'What exact function is it performing here, and when it interacts with this, and with that?'. These new perspectives contribute to an overall deeper understanding of affective phenomena while enabling affect to also play new roles in the development of technology for improving human experience.

ROSALIND W. PICARD

There are many special issues of journals that feature affective computing research, including:

Carberry, S. and de Rosis, F. (eds) (2008). *User Modeling and User-Adapted Interaction*, **18**(1–2) (special issue on affective modelling and adaptation).

Douglas-Cowie, E., Cowie, R., and Campbell, N. (eds) (2003). *Speech Communication*, **40**(1–2) (special issue on speech and emotion).

Isbister, K. and Höök, K. (eds) (2007). *International Journal of Human-Computer Studies*, **65**(4) (special issue on evaluating affective interactions).

The Humaine Portal <http://emotion-research.net/> contains an outstanding bibliography of research on emotion and human–machine interaction funded by the European Union.

affective forecasting From the life-altering to the mundane, the decisions we make depend largely on predictions of future happiness or heartbreak. Working over-time to be able to afford a new luxury car, choosing to marry one person over another, or even planning what to do on a Saturday night are all motivated by an *affective forecast* of how we think the decision will make us feel in the future (see DECISION-MAKING). Because these affective forecasts play a major role in the choices people make, accuracy in forecasting is essential.

The first step in successful affective forecasting is forming an accurate construal of the event in question. If we imagine a forthcoming picnic as a small gathering of close friends rather than what it turns out to be—a boisterous crowd of inebriated co-workers demanding that we take part in sack races—we will probably wrongly predict our enjoyment of it. But even when people construe an event accurately and have some idea of whether it will be good or bad, they are often poor at estimating just *how* good, or *how* bad. In other words, people make systematic errors, the most common of which is the *impact bias*: the tendency to overestimate the intensity and duration of emotional reactions to future events. Despite their predictions, people often recover from romantic break-ups more quickly than they think they will and underestimate how quickly a new plasma TV will become just another fixture in the living room.

The impact bias occurs for several reasons. First, when making an affective forecast, people typically think of a future event as existing in a vacuum, rather than as one filled with many other experiences that will dominate their thoughts and influence their feelings. This tendency, known as *focalism*, can be reduced by asking people to think about the things that are likely to occur at the same time as the future emotional event (Wilson *et al.* 2000).

A second reason for the impact bias is that people adapt to both positive and negative life events much more quickly than they anticipate (see ADAPTATION). When faced with a novel emotional experience, people typically make sense of it quickly by automatically assimilating it to a pre-existing schema or altering schemas to accommodate the event (Piaget 1952). Because of this sense-making process, events that were originally laden with emotion come to seem ordinary and elicit little if any emotional response. But because sense-making often operates outside of conscious awareness, people fail to anticipate how quickly it will occur and neutralize emotional events (Wilson and Gilbert 2008). One implication of this view is that people will have long-lasting negative reactions to painful events that are difficult to make sense of. People will also have long-lasting reactions to positive events that cannot be fully explained or understood, which Wilson *et al.* (2005) termed the *pleasures of uncertainty*.

A third reason for the impact bias is that people fail to anticipate how quickly they will mobilize psychological defences to deal with the pain of negative outcomes (Brickman *et al.* 1978). One reason that these defences are successful is that they occur unconsciously. People who are rejected by a romantic partner typically do not say, 'From now on I will decide that my partner was an unattractive bore, in order to make myself feel better'. Rationalization works better when it occurs unconsciously, such that spurned lovers come to believe that their ex-partners really were unsuitable, without recognizing that this change in view is a self-serving rationalization. But, because defensive processes occur unconsciously, people fail to take them into account when predicting their future emotional reactions (Wilson and Gilbert 2003). People's failure to recognize the ease with which they will defend against negative outcomes has a number of interesting consequences, such as the fact that a minor setback sometimes has a longer-lasting emotional impact than a major setback, because people are more motivated to defend against and repair the psychological damage done by the latter than the former (Gilbert *et al.* 2004).

In sum, the affective forecasting literature suggests that, despite the elation or heartbreak that an event may initially bring, the duration of these emotional reactions is often surprisingly short-lived. Research on affective forecasting has implications for many major life decisions. For example, the failure to recognize the ability to 'bounce back' from negative events may create excessive risk aversion. Overpredicting the elation that a future experience will bring can lead to disappointment. Ongoing research is examining how these limitations of self-knowledge influence people's attempts at happiness.

JAIME L. KURTZ, TIMOTHY D. WILSON, AND
DANIEL T. GILBERT

Wilson, T.D., Centerbar, D.B., Kermer, D.A., and Gilbert, D.T. (2005). The pleasures of uncertainty: prolonging positive moods in ways people do not anticipate. *Journal of Personality and Social Psychology*, **88**, 5–21.
Wilson, T.D. and Gilbert, D.T. (2003). Affective forecasting. In: M.P. Zanna (ed.), *Advances in experimental social psychology*, pp. 345–411. San Diego, CA: Academic Press.

affective neuroscience The term affective neuroscience is a relatively recent addition to the scientific lexicon. It was first introduced by Panksepp (1992) and Davidson and Sutton (1995) in the titles of review articles. Since that time there have been hundreds of scientific articles that have used this term, journals that now include 'affective neuroscience' within their title, laboratories that include this term in their name, and advertisements for academic positions naming this field. Thus, in a decade and a half, affective neuroscience has become a vibrant subdiscipline and is thriving in academia. Affective neuroscience is a term that broadly refers to

the study of the neural bases and correlates of emotion and related affective phenomena (see NEURAL ARCHITECTURE OF EMOTION). When Panksepp (1992) first used this term he was referring to the corpus of literature at the animal level that was directed at the study of the neural bases of emotion mostly from lesion studies in rodents. The Davidson and Sutton (1995) article was the first to advance the proposal of an affective neuroscience in humans. Notably, this latter paper appeared just at the time that functional magnetic resonance imaging (fMRI) was being developed. It was in 1996 that our laboratory was the first to publish a scientific article using fMRI to investigate the activation of the human amygdala in response to emotional stimuli (Irwin *et al.* 1996).

The field of affective neuroscience now has several major emphases that can be gleaned from a perusal of the current scientific literature. One major emphasis is the study of the neural basis of *regulation of emotion (e.g. Davidson 2004a, Ochsner and Gross 2005). A second major emphasis is on the neural bases of affect–cognition interaction. A particular focus here is on the relation between *attention and emotion (e.g. Pessoa 2008). A third major focus is on brain mechanisms underlying *disorders of emotion, e.g. anxiety and mood disorders (see, e.g. Johnstone *et al.*, 2007, for a recent exemplar study from our laboratory). The field of neuroeconomics (see ECONOMICS (ROLE OF EMOTION IN)) is now a central part of affective neuroscience, since the impact of emotion on decision-making is a key question (e.g. Fehr and Camerer 2007). Finally, another important modern trend is focused on developmental affective neuroscience where the concepts and methods from adult affective neuroscience are applied in a developmental context (e.g. Goldsmith *et al.* 2008).

Affective neuroscience in human research is methodologically diverse and includes all of the available methods to make inferences about brain–behaviour relations including the lesion method, neuroimaging, transcranial magnetic stimulation, and behavioural methods.

RICHARD J. DAVIDSON

Leknes, S. and Tracey, I. (2008). A common neurobiology for pain and pleasure. *Nature Reviews Neuroscience*, **9**, 314–20.
Seymour, B. and Dolan, R. (2008). Emotion, decision making, and the amygdala. *Neuron*, **58**, 662–71.

affective sciences The term affective sciences is increasingly used to refer to a rapidly growing interdisciplinary field of study devoted to all aspects of *affect and emotion. There are several reasons for this new development. Recent changes in social values and lifestyles mean that emotional experiences are seen as assets for well-being and self-fulfilment. Emotions have become fashionable and are very popular in the media and advertising. In research on the human mind and behaviour, two major changes have affected the social, behavioural, and life sciences over the last 20 years, leading to what can be considered an *affective revolution*: (1) The realization by leading scholars in many sciences (particularly in economics, psychology, and philosophy) that the fiction of humans as perfectly rational decision-makers, guided by a cognitive machinery that closely resembles computer architecture, could no longer be maintained, given the very nature of cognitive processes and *decision-making. The award of several Nobel prizes in economics to scholars who experimentally demonstrated the important role of affect in economic behaviour has confirmed this massive paradigm shift (see ECONOMICS (ROLE OF EMOTION IN)). (2) The ever-growing empirical evidence on the pervasive role of different affective determinants—motives, attitudes, moods, and emotions—in all of human functioning, including cognition and decision-making. These massive changes in human science are at the root of this new interdisciplinary area. Research over the last two decades has demonstrated that many phenomena, ranging from individual cognitive processing to social and collective behaviour, cannot be understood without taking into account affective determinants such as motives, attitudes, moods, and emotions.

Both research on cognition and affect are currently undergoing another major paradigm shift in the direction of a thoroughly neuroscientific approach (see AFFECTIVE NEUROSCIENCE). The enormous success in developing leading-edge technologies to measure the activation of neural centres and circuits in different regions in the brain has fundamentally changed the way in which questions about human behaviour are posed. The impact of recent neuroscience findings on our understanding of emotion is staggering, and judging from the explosion of research activity in this domain it is bound to grow exponentially. It is not surprising that the affective and social neurosciences, including neuroeconomy and neurofinance, are among the most rapidly growing areas.

Just as the 'cognitive revolution' of the 1960s has spawned the highly successful *cognitive sciences*, which link the disciplines studying cognitive functioning from different vantage points, the emerging field of the affective sciences promises to bring together the disciplines which study the biological, psychological, and sociocultural dimensions of emotion and other types of affect, in particular researchers from psychology, philosophy, economics, political science, law, psychiatry, neuroscience, education, sociology, ethology, literature, linguistics, history, and anthropology. The major challenge for this new interdisciplinary domain is to integrate research focusing on emotions, moods, attitudes, and affective personality dispositions that emerges from different perspectives, theoretical backgrounds, and levels of analysis.

KLAUS R. SCHERER

Davidson, R., Scherer, K.R, and Goldsmith, H. (eds) (2003). *Handbook of affective sciences*. New York: Oxford University Press.

affective style Affective style is a term that is used to refer to a broad range of variation in emotional responding and emotion regulation (see Davidson, 2000, for review). It has been proposed that individual differences in affective style are related to *temperament and *personality, *vulnerability to psychopathology and *resilience. An important feature of affective style as it has been explicated by Davidson (2000, 2004a) is the chronometry of emotional response. Variation in the onset, peak, and rise time to peak in response to an emotional stimulus, and recovery following an emotional stimulus, all constitute separable features of affective style. For example, it has been shown that phobic subjects exhibit earlier (i.e. faster) activation of the amygdala in response to a phobic stimulus compared with healthy controls (e.g. Larson *et al.* 2006). Variations in emotional response during an anticipatory period prior to the onset of an emotional stimulus also play an important role in governing features of affective style (e.g. Nitschke *et al.* 2006). Other data suggest important variation in the time course of recovery following a negative stimulus (e.g. Jackson *et al.* 2003). Individual differences in affective style can be objectively measured using a variety of behavioural, physiological, and neuroimaging methods.

Individual differences in affective style are also related to peripheral biology and, through bidirectional influences between the brain and body, may play a role in modulating physical health and illness. We have demonstrated, for example, that individuals with a profile of brain function that predisposes them to show increased positive affect and approach behaviour also have a more robust antibody titre response to influenza vaccine (Rosenkranz *et al.* 2003). In other research we have found that the same neural measures that reflect dispositional positive and negative affect are associated with cortisol in both human infants (Buss *et al.* 2003) and in rhesus monkeys (Kalin *et al.* 1998). In more recent studies we have found that individual differences in activation in specific components of the neural circuitry underlying emotion regulation predict lung function and inflammatory mediators in the lungs of asthmatics (Rosenkranz *et al.* 2005).

RICHARD J. DAVIDSON

Davidson, R.J. (2004). Well-being and affective style: neural substrates and biobehavioral correlates. *Philosophical Transactions of the Royal Society B: Biological Sciences*, **359**, 1395–411.

affect programs Tomkins (1962, p. 244) suggested that the affect system consists of a limited number of basic or fundamental emotions that are directly linked to the motivational system (see BASIC EMOTIONS). Following Darwin, Tomkins argued that basic emotions are subserved by phylogenetically evolved, genetically encoded, and universal affect programs. Although Tomkins did not describe the nature of these programs in detail, the assumption was that specific eliciting conditions (which Tomkins sought in different gradients of neural firing) would automatically trigger a pattern of reactions ranging from peripheral physiological responses to muscular innervations, particularly in the face and the voice (see VOCAL EXPRESSION OF EMOTION). The concept of discrete, basic emotions has been popularized by Ekman and Izard who extended the theory and attempted to obtain pertinent empirical evidence, particularly with respect to the early ontogenetic onset of the discrete emotion patterns and the *universality of these patterns. This theoretical tradition, which Griffiths (1997) has labelled the 'affect program conception of emotion', has dominated much of emotion research to date and is still one of the most influential models. The general assumption made by the protagonists of this tradition is that there are a limited number of evolutionary continuous basic emotions that are triggered by specific eliciting conditions and that are differentiated by tightly knit emotion-specific response programs that are universal and prepared at birth. Recently, both Ekman and Izard attempted to account for the large variety of emotional states in everyday life, renouncing the notion of a small repertoire of rigid neuromotor affect programs. However, they continue to predict emotion-specific response patterns, especially prototypical facial expressions, for basic emotions, and assume that affect programs run automatically and are resistant to change, although they assume multiple interactions between the different systems and allow for the existences of 'partial programs' (see Scherer and Ellgring 2007a, pp. 113–14).

KLAUS R. SCHERER

affiliation Affiliation refers to the state of one entity being associated in some way with another entity. In psychology, affiliation is a term used primarily by social psychologists to refer to people being or becoming associated with one another.

Most theorists believe that humans are inherently social creatures who need one another to survive and flourish in the world and therefore have a natural inclination to seek out and to affiliate with other individuals. The term affiliation generally implies a voluntary coming together of two or more people that serves a positive function for the individuals in question. Affiliation can refer to a short-term coming together for minutes or hours or longer-term bonding. Affiliation can involve low levels of interdependence between people, meaning that whereas each member does have an impact on the other the impact may take place in a single domain or only once, or high levels of interdependence.

The functions that the affiliation can serve for individuals are varied, and the nature of the affiliation between two or more people often is determined by the particular function or functions that affiliation is serving for people. Some functions of affiliation (e.g. affiliation that is sought to be able to socially compare one's values, emotions, or abilities with others, satisfying sexual needs) need not involve high levels of interdependence or long-term affiliation, although they might. Other functions (for instance establishing a mutual communal relationship in which each member cares for the other, knows a great deal about the other, and trusts the other) do require long-term, highly interdependent types of affiliation.

The term itself does not imply that the association in question is serving any particular function.

MARGARET CLARK

ageing (and emotional development) Research and theory on emotional development in adulthood and later life reveals a pattern of both gains and losses (Labouvie-Vief 2005). On the one hand a line of research has demonstrated that older individuals' understanding (see COMPETENCE, EMOTIONAL) and *regulation of emotion improves well into late middle age, until about the age of 60. However, another research tradition has pointed to regulation problems that result from later-life declines of certain resources that are implicated in emotion regulation. In particular, the prefrontal cortex, the neurobiological structure involved in processes of inhibiting and coordinating emotions, shows quite dramatic losses of volume throughout adulthood (Raz 2000). How is this pattern of apparently contradictory trends to be reconciled?

One strand of work begins with the observation that processes of positive development, including emotional development, continue beyond youth and into adulthood and later life. From childhood into midlife, an individual's awareness of emotions shows positive trends. For example, individuals develop a rich and highly complex vocabulary identifying and differentiating emotions. They are better able to experience emotions of opposite *valence simultaneously, without conflict, and as a result, can deal with affective complexity in self and others. They also develop a more astute understanding of emotional mechanisms, ranging from an awareness of the dependence of emotions on *norms and ideologies, to the contribution of one's own desires and unconscious processes. All of these findings suggest that mature and ageing adults may be superior at integrating the demands for objective judgement and control in emotions with those of flexible and rich emotional expressivity (Labouvie-Vief 2005). Some of these gains may continue into later life, as suggested by the observation that the balance of positive over negative affect increases into the 70s despite the increasing threats of ill-health, psychological decline, and looming death (Charles and Carstensen 2007).

A second strand of research points to the widely established findings that some cognitive processes, as well as the neurobiological structures that mediate them, are negatively affected by the ageing process (Raz 2000). A large body of research indicates that these losses can be related to impaired affect regulation. For example, the ability to represent mixed positive and negative emotions has been found to be impaired in ageing samples, particularly in situations of high demand on available resources, such as ill-health, intellectual decline, or extreme emotional activation. This impaired ability may lead to polarized evaluations as either positive or negative, and to stereotyped attribution of character flaws and/or ill-intent to a protagonist who has experienced negative outcomes of an interaction (Blanchard-Fields 1999). More generally, the elderly are more strongly affected by automatic processes. This can lead to poor cognitive and memory performance, especially in tasks that do not rely on accumulated experience and emotional knowledge. For example, the autonomic system of older adults is highly reactive to stress-inducing situations. In addition, they are more negatively affected by the activation of strong emotions in tasks that require complex cognitive performance. Findings such as these suggest that the ageing organism is more vulnerable to the effects of unanticipated emotional activation. In contrast, increased automaticity may even enhance performance in situations in which the ageing individual can readily integrate task demands with pre-existing knowledge structures (Labouvie-Vief 2005).

These various declines do not necessarily imply that the older individual is debilitated when it comes to the regulation of emotions. In general, the degree of debilitation depends not only on their physical health and the availability of cognitive resources, but also on aspects of life-long psychological health variables that are related to the efficacy of emotion regulation. Nevertheless, a majority of the elderly appear to adjust to these changes in adaptive ways. For example, they appear to be successful at gating out difficult to manage affect, or to reduce the complexity of their environments or social networks in an effort to minimize negative affect and conflict (Carstensen and Mikels 2005). These strategies are not merely compensatory, but may even reflect a degree of wisdom by which many ageing individuals develop a stronger focus on meaning, relationship, and spirituality—a form of wisdom that is thought to be the ideal of late life.

GISELA LABOUVIE-VIEF

Labouvie-Vief, G. and Márquez González, M. (2004). Dynamic integration: affect optimization and differentiation in development. In: D.Y. Dai and R.J. Sternberg (eds), *Motivation, emotion, and cognition: integrative perspectives on intellectual functioning and development*, pp. 237–72. Mahwah, NJ: Lawrence Erlbaum Associates.

Magai, C. (2001). Emotions over the life course. In: J.E. Birren and K.W. Schaie (eds), *Handbook of the psychology of aging*, 5th edn, pp. 399–426. San Diego, CA: Academic Press.

agency (philosophical perspectives) Agency refers to the capacity to act intentionally, i.e. to represent a *goal and try to achieve it through one's own bodily or mental effort, with or without the mediation of external agents or objects. A major philosophical issue is whether or not *attitudes play a causal role in intentional behaviour. Opponents of causal theories observe that causality holds between independent events, whereas there is no independence between the reasons that are supposed to cause the action and the action itself. In this anticausalist view, the reasons one has to act have nothing to do with the way the action is developing as a causal process. As for an intention or volition, it seems to give rise to a regress: either it is itself caused by a further intention or volition, or it merely happens to the agent. Action can rather be captured by a practical syllogism in which the relations of premises (desiring X, believing that you need to A to have X) to conclusion (deciding to A) can be drawn purely a priori. It is argued further that causes need to be tested experimentally, whereas an agent does not need to put to test the reason he or she has to act. Anticausalists of mental states may, however, maintain that the cause of an act is the agent who performs it (Taylor 1966).

Causal theorists of action, on the other hand, claim that an event can only be an action if it is caused by a mental state with a certain kind of content. Popular candidates for the relevant mental state include the reason to act—a specific combination of pro-attitude and beliefs (Davidson 1980)—and 'specialized' representations such as intentions (Searle 1983) or volitions (Ginet 1990). It is further claimed by causal theorists that a mental state supervenes on a physical event, and derives from the latter its causal capacity. What is the content of the relevant mental state? It must specify the conditions of success of the action, i.e. the description under which the action is intentional. For example, I flick the switch to turn on the light, not to frighten a burglar. Some causal theorists (Searle 1983) include causation as a constituent of the content represented in the intention or in the volition. According to this self-referential analysis of intention, to intentionally perform A, the agent must have a representation whose content includes that this very representation is causing a specific movement, and is thereby allowing the desired result to be reached. Other causal theorists, however, observe that it is doubtful that very young children or non-human animals can refer to their own intentions when acting. It can be argued, in response, that the corresponding intention–reflexive information is accessible to the agent in a non-conceptual format, representing the fact that the agent is active in a given ideational or motor process. Research on the psychopathology of agency indeed suggests that the sense of agency can be dissociated from the sense of moving in a goal-directed way (Stephens and Graham 2000).

A problem that causalist theories of action have to face is the existence of deviant causal chains between the mental antecedents and the resulting bodily movement. For example, A tries to kill B by shooting at him; he misses but stampedes a herd of wild pigs that trample B to death (Davidson 1980). In this case, one cannot maintain that A killed B intentionally. Several authors from the causalist camp try to rescue the causal definition of action by introducing nonconceptual contents meant to guide action in specifiable ways.

JOËLLE PROUST

Mele, A.R. (1992). *The springs of action*. New York: Oxford University Press.

Stephens, G.L. and Graham, G. (2000). When self-consciousness breaks, Cambridge, MA.: MIT Press.

Taylor, C. (1966). *Action and purpose*. Englewood Cliffs, NJ: Prentice-Hall.

agency (psychological perspectives)

agency (psychological perspectives) In modern emotions research, *agency* refers to an *appraisal of who or what caused something to happen (see, e.g., Ellsworth and Scherer 2003).

Conceptualization

Different theories identify different varieties of agency appraisals, e.g. internal versus external locus (Weiner 1986), or self versus other agent versus natural causation (Scherer 2001a). Currently, agency is perhaps most often conceptualized as having three main values: attributing causation to the self, or to some other person(s), or to impersonal circumstances (Roseman 2001). Other types of agency have also been proposed. For example, it has been suggested that a category of supernatural agency may be needed, for example to account for emotion-eliciting appraisals reported by African research participants (see Scherer 1997, Mesquita 2003). It appears that different agency appraisals are not mutually exclusive—the same event can be attributed (to equal or differing degrees) to multiple causes.

Related conceptualizations are appraisals of self- and other-person accountability, responsibility, and blame. Indeed, Smith and Lazarus (1990) contended that when agency appraisals conflict with appraisals of accountability, the latter are more closely related to emotional response (e.g. when another person is seen as causing but not responsible for a negative outcome, anger will not be felt). On the other hand, appraisals of accountability may be too complex to account for emotions such as anger and pride in young children (see Roseman et al. 1996).

Agency–emotion relationships

Appraisal theorists have proposed that different agency appraisals are characteristic of different emotions, and research has provided some support for several specific hypotheses (see, e.g., Roseman et al. 1996, Scherer 2001a). Perceived self-agency appears to be characteristic of pride, guilt, shame, and regret. Perceived causation by other persons has been linked to gratitude, affection (love), anger, contempt, and interpersonal dislike. Impersonal causation has been predicted for a variety of emotions, but empirical support has been weak. Roseman et al. (1996) suggested that emotions such as surprise, joy, sadness, fear, and frustration may be felt (1) when events are appraised as being caused by impersonal circumstances, (2) when no causal *attribution is made, or (3) when an event is seen as caused by self or other persons, but attention is focused on the event itself rather than its causal agent.

Theorists disagree about whether agency appraisals (in combination with motivations and other appraisals) are causes of emotions or components and/or consequences of emotions (e.g. Is attributing a negative event to another person a cause of anger? Is attributing a positive event to oneself a cause of pride?); and if causes, whether they are sufficient, necessary, or contributory causes. Research to date suggests appraisals of self- and other-person agency may be contributory causes, though much of the evidence is correlational and/or employs linguistic measures of emotion, which can be challenged if appraisal information is implicit in the meaning of emotion words (for a balanced discussion and excellent analysis of these issues see Frijda, 2007a).

Functions

It has been proposed that appraisals function to elicit those emotions whose characteristic *action tendencies are most likely to cope adaptively with the particular events faced by the appraising organism. For example, appraisals of other-person agency elicit emotions whose action tendencies (e.g. seeking interpersonal closeness in love, threatening or hurting someone in anger, socially excluding someone in contempt) may be especially suited for influencing other people who are causing positive or negative events; whereas self-agency appraisals elicit emotions whose responses (e.g. self-assertion in pride; self-reproach and reparation in guilt; social withdrawal in shame) are especially suited for coping adaptively with self-caused positive or negative events (Roseman 2001).

Variability

There are important developmental, cultural, and individual differences in agency appraisals and related emotions. For example, appraisals of self-agency and the emotions of pride, shame, and guilt are not present at birth, but emerge in childhood (e.g. Mascolo *et al.* 2003). Self-attributions are more common in Western cultures, attributions to fate in East Asia, and attributions to witchcraft in some African cultures (e.g. Scherer 1997, Mesquita 2003). Self-attributions for negative events are prominent in depression (at least in Western cultures); and excessive attribution of negative events to others in paranoid disorders.

Current issues

At present, additional research is needed to (1) resolve lingering disputes over whether agency appraisals play a causal role in eliciting emotions such as love, pride, anger, contempt, guilt, and shame (e.g. research manipulating appraisals and measuring emotional behaviours); (2) flesh out how agency appraisals are actually generated, often rapidly and unconsciously (e.g. from events, context, and stored information); and (3) understand more about developmental, cultural, and individual differences in agency appraisals and related emotions.

IRA J. ROSEMAN

Frijda, N.H. (2007a). Appraisal. In: *The laws of emotion*, pp. 93–121. Mahwah, NJ: Lawrence Erlbaum Associates.

Mascolo, M.F., Fischer, K.W., and Li, J. (2003). Dynamic development of component systems of emotions: pride, shame, and guilt in China and the United States. In: R.J. Davidson, K.R. Scherer, and H.H. Goldsmith (eds), *Handbook of affective sciences*, pp. 375–408. New York: Oxford University Press.

aggression (biological perspectives)

Aggression is the evolved response to challenge over sequesterable resources from another—generally, but not always, conspecific—animal (Wilson 1975). In most species territory and dominance position are major resources for dispute. Access to a reproductive partner is a prime cause for aggression in virtually all vertebrates.

Aggression is a dangerous behaviour. The still-popular belief that fights among conspecifics in nonhuman animals do not injure or kill has no scientific basis. Most mammalian species do have evolved mechanisms that tend to reduce injury in conspecific fights, including structures such as the manes of lions, that serve to protect the sites that are most often attacked in conspecific fights, as well as behavioural defences that are effective because they are exquisitely sensitive to features of both the attack and of the situation in which it occurs. Along with flight, freezing, etc., these evolved defences include defensive threat and defensive attack components that can injure the attacker. This 'defensive aggression' is motivated by *fear rather than resource challenge, which is associated with 'offensive aggression'. However, most serious fights involve both of these motivations and relatively little attention has been paid to separating them in research on the biology of aggression (Blanchard and Blanchard 2005). They are included without differentiation in the term 'impulsive aggression'.

Many of these same causal and behavioural mechanisms related to aggression are also found in people. Because aggression is dangerous to society and to individuals, every culture has made some attempt to delineate the circumstances in which aggression is allowed, and to institute sanctions for violations. Nonetheless, aggression is a persistent human social problem (see VIOLENCE). On an individual level, successful aggression produces an immediate gain of resources, obedience, prestige, or even relief from attack; rewards that may be sufficient to strengthen aggression as instrumental response and broaden the range of situations in which it occurs. When aggression is emitted without pronounced emotional accompaniment, and with clear reward possibilities, it tends to be called 'instrumental'; a term that says relatively little about aggression except that it is very sensitive to its rewarding or punishing outcomes.

Most current models of aggression involve some type of resource dispute, with territory or dominance most commonly featured. The 'resident-intruder' model places a strange conspecific in the home cage of the subject, who then attacks. Exposure to a strange male in conjunction with the subject's own female can elicit arousal in a number of limbic and diencephalic structures, including amygdala, hypothalamus, and cortex; structures that may be active in both the initiation and the inhibition of aggression. A selective vasopressin 1A receptor antagonist normalizes these activation patterns (Ferris *et al.* 2008). Vasopressin appears to interact with testosterone to enhance aggression, particularly in rodent models in which males dispute over territory, dominance status, or females.

Drugs and genetic manipulations of particular 5-hydroxytryptamine (serotonin, 5-HT) receptors have been found to strikingly alter aggression in animal models (Olivier *et al.* 1995) as do genetic manipulations that reduce the expression of monoamine oxidase A (MAOA) (Chen *et al.* 2007). In line with a view that animal models of aggression provide results that are relevant to human aggression as well, reduced 5-HT metabolism has been implicated in a pattern of impulsivity that may involve violence (Virkkunen and Linnoila 1997). Similarly, imaging of the brains of volunteers with genes linked to low expression of the MAOA enzyme (and increased risk for violent behaviour) has shown a hyper-responsive amygdala during emotional arousal and reduced reactivity of prefrontal regions that normally inhibit amygdala activation (Meyer-Lindenberg *et al.* 2006). Raine has also presented consistent findings of enhanced *impulsivity, including aggression, in individuals with reduced inhibitory functioning of the frontal cortex (Raine 2002a).

These and other studies of aggression suggest that aggressive behaviours have similar functions across mammalian species, even though the specific resources disputed and the overall magnitude of aggression, in terms of frequency and damage to individuals, may vary considerably. They suggest substantial similarities between human and nonhuman animals in the control of aggression by reward/punishment, as well as in biological (eliciting and inhibiting brain systems) factors in aggression.

ROBERT J. BLANCHARD AND D. CAROLINE BLANCHARD

aggression (psychological perspectives) In sports and in business, the term 'aggressive' is frequently used when the terms 'assertive', 'enthusiastic', or 'confident' would be more accurate. For example, an aggressive salesperson is one who tries really hard to sell you something. In psychology, the term 'aggressive' means something different. Most aggression researchers define human aggression as any behaviour that is intended to harm another person who wants to avoid the harm (Baron and Richardson 1994). This definition includes three important features. First, aggression is a behaviour. You can see it (e.g. you can see a person shoot, stab, hit, or curse someone). Aggression is not an emotion or a thought that occurs inside a person. Second, aggression is intentional. Aggression is not accidental, such as when a drunk driver accidentally runs over a child on a tricycle. Behaviours that are intended to harm others are still acts of aggression even if they don't actually harm them. For example, if a person shoots a gun at you but misses, it is still an act of aggression. Third, the victim wants to avoid the harm. For example, suicide and sadomasochistic sex play are not included because the victim is not motivated to avoid the pain or harm (and is in fact actively seeking it).

*Violence is aggression that has extreme physical harm as its goal, such as injury or death (Bushman and Anderson 2001). For example, one child intentionally pushing another off a tricycle is an act of aggression

but is not an act of violence. One person intentionally hitting, kicking, shooting, or stabbing another person is an act of violence. Thus, all violent acts are aggressive, but not all aggressive acts are violent—only the extreme physical ones are.

For decades psychologists have debated whether aggression is innate or learned. Given the universality of aggression and some of its features (e.g. young men are always most violent), and recent findings from heritability studies, there appears to be an innate basis for aggression. However, there is also clearly a role for learning. Many experts on aggression favour a middle ground in this debate. The available research evidence indicates that people do not need to learn how to behave aggressively—it comes naturally. What people need to learn is how to control their aggressive impulses (Tremblay and Nagin 2005).

Numerous factors can increase aggression, such as unpleasant situations (e.g. hot temperatures, loud noises, frustration, provocation, crowding, pollution, poverty). Unpleasant situations make people irritable and put them in a bad or angry mood (Berkowitz 1983). Aggressive cues, such as weapons and violent media (e.g. TV, film, video games) can increase aggression. Chemicals can also influence aggression. For example, high levels of testosterone (the male sex hormone), high levels of alcohol, low levels of serotonin (called the 'feel good' neurotransmitter), and low levels of cortisol (the stress hormone), have all been linked to aggression. Finally, culture can facilitate or inhibit aggression (Baumeister 2005). For example, people from honour cultures, in which threats to one's honour are met with a violent response, tend to be more aggressive than other cultures.

There are also individual differences in aggressiveness. Males use more direct aggression (e.g. hitting, stabbing, shooting), whereas females use more indirect aggression (e.g. spreading rumours). Narcissists, who have a grandiose view of themselves, are more aggressive than others, especially when they receive a blow to their ego. People who lack self-control also tend to be more aggressive. Age matters. Research shows that the most aggressive individuals are toddlers aged 1–3 years. They push and shove each other to get what they want because they lack the means to communicate in more constructive ways. Fortunately, they cannot do much damage at that age. *Serious* aggressive and violent behaviour peaks just past the age of puberty. After age 19, aggressive behaviours begin to decline for most people.

The fact that there is no single cause for aggression makes it hard to treat. A treatment that works for one individual may not work for someone else. There are two important general points to be made about treatments. First, successful treatments target as many causes of aggression as possible, and attempt to tackle them collectively. Most often, these interventions are aimed at reducing factors that promote aggression in the direct social environment (family, friends), general living conditions (housing and neighbourhood, health, financial resources), and occupation (school, work, spare time). Interventions that are narrowly focused at removing a single cause of aggression are bound to fail. Second, aggressive behaviour problems are best treated in early development, when they are still malleable. The better we are able to identify and treat early signs of aggression, the safer our communities will be.

BRAD J. BUSHMAN AND SANDER THOMAES

Anderson, C.A. and Bushman, B.J. (2002). Human aggression. *Annual Review of Psychology*, **53**, 27–51.

Loeber, R. and Hay, D. (1997). Key issues in the development of aggression and violence from childhood to early adulthood. *Annual Review of Psychology*, **48**, 371–410.

alexithymia The term alexithymia refers to difficulties in the experience, regulation, and expression of emotions. It was first coined by Sifneos (see Sifneos 1973) and comes from the Greek *alexis* (no words) and *thymos* (emotion). Alexithymia has five principal characteristics: (1) a reduction or absence of emotion experience; (2) a reduction or inability to verbalize one's emotions; (3) a reduction or incapacity to fantasize; (4) a reduced tendency to think about one's emotions; and (5) problems with emotion identification. Two main forms of alexithymia have been distinguished (see Larsen, J.K. *et al.* 2003): Type I alexithymia involves deficits in both experiential and cognitive aspects of emotion whereas Type II comprises deficits in emotion-related cognition, with sparing of emotion experience (even if the individual is unable to label it as such). This overall five-fold conceptualization of alexithymia is supported by numerous studies examining emotion processing, using combinations of self-report, experimental, and psychophysiological outcome measures. Alexithymia is thought to affect around 10% of the population and research suggests that it is a generally stable trait, though with some capacity for state-like variation.

Measurement

The gold standard measure of alexithymia is a self-report questionnaire—the Toronto Alexithymia Scale (TAS). Revisions of the original TAS have led to the development of a twenty-item measure (the TAS-20) with three factors: difficulty identifying feelings; difficulty describing feelings; and a tendency to think in externally orientated ways (Bagby *et al.* 1994). The TAS-20 has good psychometric properties. Criticisms of the TAS-20 are that it does not cover all of the five salient features of alexithymia outlined above, and that

it overly focuses on cognitive aspects of the construct. More recently, another measure—the Bermond–Vorst Alexithymia Questionnaire (BVAQ; Vorst and Bermond, 2001)—has been developed that addresses these concerns by also assessing emotionalizing and fantasizing. Beyond the domain of self-report, observer rated and interview measures (e.g. the Toronto Structured Interview for Alexithymia) have been developed.

Aetiology

It is currently unclear what might cause people to be alexithymic. Most theorists favour a biological conceptualization with at least three distinct neurobiological models dominating the literature (see Larsen, J.K. *et al.*, 2003, and Tabibnia and Zaidel, 2005, for reviews). The first focuses on dysfunction of the corpus callosum to provide an account of situations where individuals still experience basic emotional feelings but with an absence of conscious cognition concerning these feelings (Type II alexithymia). The second model focuses on dysfunction of the right hemisphere, and the third focuses on putative anterior cingulate dysfunction. These various views have garnered support from neuroimaging, neuropsychological, and brain lesion studies. More recent prospective-longitudinal research studies have also provided some support for a social-developmental model of alexithymia (e.g. Joukamaa *et al.* 2003).

Comorbidity

Alexithymia shows a small to moderate relationship with somatization and it has been suggested that, as a result, somatic sensations are more likely to be misinterpreted as physical illness. In this vein, alexithymia is correlated with a number of physical illnesses such as hypertension, irritable bowel syndrome, and functional dyspepsia. Alexithymia scores are also elevated in a range of psychiatric conditions such as panic disorder, major depression, eating disorders, somatoform disorders, posttraumatic stress disorder, and personality disorders, as well as other physical complaints such as chronic pain.

Treatment

Few treatments have been developed specifically to tackle alexithymia, partly as a result of its perception as a stable trait. Group interventions have the greatest promise. Most therapeutic literature regarding alexithymia has focused on the potential barrier it offers to successful outcome and/or its treatment in the context of interventions for other physical or psychiatric conditions.

TIM DALGLEISH

Sifneos, P.E. (1996). Alexithymia: past and present. *American Journal of Psychiatry*, **153**, 137–42.

Taylor, G.J. (2004). Alexithymia: 25 years of theory and research. In: I. Nyklicek, L. Temoshok, and A. Vingerhoets (eds),

Emotional expression and health, pp. 137–53. Andover: Brunner-Routledge.

altruism (economics perspectives) Human societies are based on a detailed division of labour and cooperation between genetically unrelated individuals in large groups. In many cases cooperation is only possible if people are willing to take costly actions that benefit other people. In this sense altruism is a vital pillar of cooperation in social and economic life (Andreoni 1990, Fehr and Fischbacher 2002).

The definition of altruism

Altruism is a concept which cuts across many disciplines. Unfortunately the definitions of altruism vary considerably across the different fields of research. It is uncontested that altruism refers to behaviour that confers economic benefits on other individuals, at a cost to the acting individual itself. However, while biologists regard all behaviours that exhibit these characteristics as altruistic, psychologists would only consider such actions as altruistic if the altruistic act is caused by an underlying intention to help other individuals. The problem with the psychological approach to altruism is its empirical operationalization. As a reliable direct measurement of intentions is not feasible, it is always possible to attribute an unobservable selfish motive to an action. Biological altruism, in contrast, is easier to identify because economic costs and benefits are often observable and measurable. In the following we therefore always refer to altruism in the biological sense.

It is obvious that the biological definition of altruism subsumes behaviours that stem from very different motivations. In the animal world the vast majority of altruistic actions are kin-directed (Hamilton 1964, Stevens and Hauser 2004, Boyd and Richerson 2005) and cooperation is therefore most often limited to small groups. Exceptions are social insects such as ants and bees, but their altruistic cooperation is also based on a substantial amount of genetic relatedness. In humans, however, three additional forms of altruism are of great importance. The first form is reciprocal altruism (Trivers 1971, Axelrod and Hamilton 1981). The basic idea of reciprocal altruism is straightforward: in many situations people do not only interact once but are involved in repeated encounters with the same persons. In such a situation it may benefit an individual to behave altruistically towards another if the favour is returned in the future. Thus, reciprocal altruists only act altruistically if the cost of the action is offset by future benefits. The second form of altruism is called reputation-based altruism (Alexander 1987, Nowak and Sigmund 1998). Reputation formation is relevant in situations where future interaction partners can observe the behaviour of an individual with his or her current and past partners. Similar to reciprocal altruism, the concept of reputation-based altruism also stipulates that individuals only act altruistically if the current costs are compensated by the future benefits of a good reputation. The third form of altruism is strong reciprocity (Gintis 2000, Fehr *et al.* 2002). Strong reciprocity is a combination of altruistic rewarding, which is a predisposition to reward others for cooperative, norm-abiding behaviours, and altruistic punishment, which is a propensity to impose sanctions on others for norm violations. In contrast to reciprocal and reputation-driven altruists strong reciprocators bear the cost of rewarding or punishing even if they gain no individual economic benefit whatsoever from their acts. Strong reciprocity thus constitutes a powerful incentive for cooperation even in nonrepeated interactions and when reputation gains are absent, because strong reciprocators will reward those who cooperate and punish those who defect.

Measuring altruism

Measuring the different forms of altruism using field data is very difficult. The problem is that altruistic behaviour in real-life circumstances can almost always be attributed to different motives. As a consequence, strong reciprocity, reciprocal altruism, and reputation-based altruism are very hard to separate. In laboratory experiments, in contrast, the specific motives behind altruistic acts can easily be isolated. Therefore, reliable knowledge about the relative importance of the different subcategories of altruism stems predominantly from controlled experiments.

Evidence of the relevance of altruism in human behaviour

In the following, we first discuss experimental evidence for the relevance of strong reciprocity. In these experiments interactions among kin, repeated encounters, and reputation formation have been ruled out. In a second step, we document how the possibility of future encounters and individual reputation formation changes subjects' behaviour. In all experiments discussed below, real money was at stake. Subjects never knew the personal identities of those with whom they interacted and they had full knowledge about the structure of the experiment, i.e. the available sequence of actions and the prevailing information conditions.

Evidence for strong reciprocity

Striking evidence for people's willingness to engage in altruistic punishment comes from experiments on the ultimatum game (Güth *et al.* 1982). In this game, two subjects have to agree on the division of a fixed sum of money. Person A, the proposer, can make exactly one proposal of how to divide the money. Then person B, the responder, can accept or reject the proposed division. In the case of rejection, both receive nothing, whereas in the case of acceptance, the proposal is implemented. A robust result in this experiment is that proposals giving the responder shares below 25% of the available money are rejected with a very high probability. Rejections in the ultimatum game can be viewed as altruistic acts because most people view the equal split as the fair outcome. Thus, a rejection of a low offer is costly for the responder and it punishes the proposer for the violation of a social norm. As a consequence, the proposer is likely to obey the norm in the future by making less greedy offers.

In the ultimatum game, the proposer's action directly affects the responder. However, with respect to norm enforcement, altruistic punishment is much more effective if even those who are not economically affected punish a violation of a norm. That such behaviour is indeed observed is shown in experiments on the third-party punishment game (Fehr and Fischbacher 2004). This game involves three subjects—an allocator, a recipient, and a third party. The allocator is endowed with 100 monetary units (MUs), the recipient has no endowment, and the third party is endowed with 50 MUs. The allocator is free to give whatever he wants to the 'poor' recipient. After the third party has been informed about the allocator's transfer to the recipient, he can spend money to punish the allocator. Every MU spent on punishment reduces the allocator's income by 3 MUs. Because it is costly to punish, no selfish third party will ever punish. But if a fairness norm applies to the situation, altruistic punishers are expected to punish unfair transfers. In fact, the evidence shows that more than half of the third parties punish the allocator for transfers below 50, and the lower the transfer, the higher the punishment.

The presence of altruistic rewarding can best be shown in sequentially played social dilemmas. The most prominent experimental designs in this respect are gift exchange games (Fehr et al. 1993), trust games (Berg et al. 1995), and sequentially played prisoners' dilemmas (Hayashi et al. 1999). While there are differences in the details of these games, the basic structure is always the same and can be captured by the following illustrative example: there is a trustor and a trustee, both of whom are endowed with 10 MUs. First, the trustor decides how many, if any, MUs to transfer to the trustee. Then the trustee decides how much of his or her endowment to send to the trustor. The experimenter doubles any amount sent to the other subject so that, collectively, the two subjects are best off if both transfer their whole endowment: if both keep what they have, each one earns 10 MUs; if both transfer their whole endowment, each earns 20 MUs. The problem

is that the trustee has always a material incentive to transfer nothing regardless of how much he received. Thus, for the trustor transferring is only attractive if he believes that the trustee resists this incentive and reciprocates. The evidence indeed shows that despite the incentive to cheat more than half of the trustees transfer money and their transfers are the higher the more the trustor transferred initially.

In everyday life cooperation is often not restricted to bilateral interactions. Thus, it is important to know to what extent the results from two-person games can be extended to situations involving larger groups. Public good experiments are the ideal set-up to investigate these questions (Marwell and Ames 1979, Ledyard 1995). By definition, a public good can be consumed by every group member regardless of the member's contribution to the good. Therefore, each member has an incentive to free-ride on the contributions of others. Altruistic rewarding in this situation implies that an individual's contributions increase if the expected contributions from the other group members increase. Individuals reward others if the latter are expected to raise their cooperation. In public goods experiments that are played only once, subjects typically contribute between 40% and 60% of their endowment, although selfish individuals are predicted to contribute nothing. There is also strong evidence that higher expectations about others' contributions induce individual subjects to contribute more. Cooperation is, however, rarely stable and deteriorates to rather low levels if the game is played repeatedly. The most plausible interpretation of the decay of cooperation is based on the fact that a large percentage of the subjects are strong reciprocators but that there are also many total free-riders who never contribute anything. The presence of the selfish players disappoints the initially high expectations of conditional cooperators and leads to a decrease of contributions over time. This breakdown of cooperation provides an important lesson. Despite the fact that there are a large number of strong reciprocators, they cannot prevent the decay of cooperation under these circumstances. This implies that it is not possible to infer the absence of altruistic individuals from a situation in which we observe little cooperation.

To maintain cooperation in n-person interactions, the upholding of the belief that all or most members of the group will cooperate is thus decisive. One possibility to achieve this is again altruistic punishment. If cooperators have the opportunity to target their punishment directly towards those who defect they impose strong sanctions on the defectors. Thus, in the presence of targeted punishment opportunities, strong reciprocators are capable of enforcing widespread cooperation by deterring potential noncooperators.

Evidence for the impact of repeated interactions and reputation formation on altruistic behaviour

Experimental evidence indicates that humans are very attentive to the possibility of repeated interactions with the same individual (reciprocal altruism). In repeated social dilemma experiments many individuals strictly condition their degree of cooperation on the past behaviour of their trading partner (Gächter and Falk 2002). Thus, altruistic behaviour in early periods of the experiment pays off as it triggers ongoing cooperation of the trading partner in later periods. As a consequence, relative to one-shot interactions average cooperation rates are much higher if subjects know that there is a possibility of meeting the same partners again in future periods.

Another powerful mechanism for the enforcement of cooperation is the possibility of building up a general reputation for behaving altruistically. This is nicely illustrated by the evidence for helping behaviour in indirect reciprocity experiments (Wedekind and Milinski 2000, Milinski et al. 2001). In the helping game, subjects are matched in pairs and one subject is randomly placed in the role of a donor and the other in the role of a recipient. The donor can help the recipient, and the donor's costs of helping are lower than the benefits for the recipient. The recipient's reputation is established by his past helping decisions. A crucial element in these experiments is that direct reciprocity is ruled out because no recipient will ever be put in a position where he can give to one of his previous donors. The helping rates in these experiments are between 50% and 90%. Furthermore, recipients with a history of generous helping decisions are significantly more likely to receive help themselves. This suggests that the donors' behaviour is driven by the desire to acquire a good reputation.

Limits of altruism

Strongly reciprocal individuals reward and punish in anonymous one-shot interactions. Yet they increase their rewards and punishment in repeated interactions or when their reputation is at stake. This suggests that a combination of altruistic and selfish concerns motivates them. Their altruistic motives induce them to cooperate and punish in one-shot interactions and their selfish motives induce them to increase rewards and punishment in repeated interactions or when reputation-building is possible. If this argument is correct, we should also observe that altruistic acts become less frequent as their costs increase. At a higher cost, individuals have to give up more of their own pay-off to help others, so that the individuals will exhibit less altruistic behaviour for a given combination of selfish and altruistic motives. The evidence from dictator games and public good games confirms this prediction (Andreoni and Miller 2002,

Anderson and Putterman 2006, Carpenter 2007). If the own pay-off that needs to be invested to produce one unit of the public good increases, subjects invest less into the public good. Likewise, if the cost of transferring 1 MU to the recipient in the dictator game increases, the dictators give less money to the recipients.

ERNST FEHR AND CHRISTIAN ZEHNDER

altruism (psychological perspectives) Altruism refers to a specific form of *motivation for benefiting another. Some biologists, economists, and psychologists speak of altruism as a type of helping behaviour (e.g. costly helping or helping with no external reward). However, such use fails to consider the motivation for the behaviour, which has historically been crucial for altruism. Comte (1875) coined the term altruism in juxtaposition to egoism, and soon thereafter it became prominent in philosophy. To the degree that one's ultimate goal in benefiting another (i.e. the state one is seeking) is to increase the other's welfare, the motivation is altruistic. To the degree that the ultimate goal is to increase one's own welfare, with increasing the other's welfare being an instrumental means to reach this goal, the motivation is egoistic. Accordingly, altruism may be defined as a motivational state with the ultimate goal of increasing another's welfare.

Dictionary definitions of altruism reflect this motivational focus. They typically define altruism as 'unselfish concern for the welfare of others' (e.g. Webster's Desk Dictionary of the English Language 1990). However, for scientific use it seems best to avoid the term 'unselfish' for two reasons. First, unselfish has clear evaluative connotations because of its juxtaposition to selfish. Second, to speak of 'unselfish concern' can lead to the assumption that self-sacrifice or net cost to self is a necessary component of altruism. This is not the case. Increasing the other's welfare, not decreasing one's own, is the focus of altruism.

The egoism–altruism debate

Clearly, humans devote much time and energy to helping others. Is this evidence of altruism? Proponents of altruism say not necessarily. Proponents of universal egoism say necessarily not; they claim that everything we do, no matter how noble and beneficial to others, is directed toward the ultimate goal of self-benefit (see EGO). They point out that even when helping involves material or physical cost we benefit by getting social and self-rewards (praise, esteem) and avoiding social and self-punishment (censure, guilt). Proponents of altruism do not deny that the motivation for helping is often egoistic. However, they claim more. They claim that at least some of us, to some degree, under some circumstances, help with an ultimate goal of benefiting the person in need. They point out that even though we get self-benefits for helping, these benefits may not be the reason why we helped. Rather than an ultimate goal, the self-benefits may be unintended consequences.

Over the past 50 years, the term altruism has been widely used in biology, where it has at times been suggested that altruism is contrary to natural selection and therefore cannot exist. Making a useful distinction, Sober and Wilson (1998) point out that these biologists are referring to *evolutionary altruism*—behaviour by one organism that reduces its individual, immediate reproductive fitness. Evolutionary altruism is quite different from what is normally meant by altruism (see above), which Sober and Wilson call *psychological altruism*. The existence of psychological altruism does not depend on the existence of evolutionary altruism.

Does altruism exist? The empathy–altruism hypothesis

In both earlier philosophical writings and in more recent psychological work, the most frequently mentioned possible source of psychological altruism is an other-oriented emotional reaction to seeing another person in need (see EMPATHY (NEUROSCIENCE PERSPECTIVES); EMPATHY (PHILOSOPHICAL PERSPECTIVES)). This emotional reaction has variously been called compassion, empathy, pity, sympathy, and tenderness. It is other-oriented in the sense that it involves feeling *for* the other—feeling sorry for, distressed for, concerned for the other. We can also feel direct, self-oriented sorrow, distress, or concern when we are faced with a distressing situation, including seeing someone in need. The direct distress experienced at witnessing another person in distress—sometimes called 'personal distress'—is distinct from other-oriented distress for that person (Batson 1991). To use the same terms for both other-oriented and self-oriented emotional reactions to seeing another in distress invites confusion. The relevant psychological distinction must be based not on whether terms like 'sad' or 'distressed' are used, but on whose welfare is the focus of the emotional response—the other person's welfare or one's own.

The proposal that other-oriented emotion felt for someone in need produces altruistic motivation to relieve that need has been called the *empathy–altruism hypothesis* (Batson 1991). In the past several decades, more than 30 experiments have tested this hypothesis against various egoistic alternatives. Although still controversial, results have been remarkably supportive of the empathy–altruism hypothesis, suggesting that psychological altruism does exist.

C. DANIEL BATSON

Batson, C.D. (1991). *The altruism question: toward a social-psychological answer*. Hillsdale, NJ: Lawrence Erlbaum Associates.

Sober, E. and Wilson, D.S. (1998). *Unto others: the evolution and psychology of unselfish behavior*. Cambridge, MA: Harvard University Press.

ambivalent emotions Many emotion types come in opposed pairs. Experience teaches us that we can feel both emotions of such a pair with respect to the same thing. Someone can both fear and be attracted by something, be sad and happy about the same event, love and hate the same person. In some cases, what happens is that the person undergoing ambivalent emotions switches back and forth from one emotion to the other. In other cases, it appears that both opposed emotions are present at the same time. Ambivalent emotions have been taken to show that emotions differ from judgements (Greenspan 1980). It can be rational to be both happy and unhappy that a friend got a promotion. But it would be irrational to judge that the event is good while also judging that it is bad. Happiness has thus to be distinguished from the judgement that something is good. One can reply that the concepts that are involved are more fine-grained. What the person who has ambivalent emotions could judge, if judgements are involved, is that the promotion is good in a way, while also bad in a way.

CHRISTINE TAPPOLET

amusement Amusement is the state of experiencing funny and often entertaining events or situations. Referring to the three dimensions of emotions of Wundt, amusement may be described as a pleasurable, relaxed excitation. While elicitors of amusement have the potential to induce unpleasurable states (for example, humour can be found aversive), amusement is a state we enjoy experiencing. The excitation component of the feeling state relates to the perception of intensity of the behaviour activated and its physiological concomitants. Among the facets of positive emotions, amusement is the one most frequently associated with *laughter. The peripheral physiological changes during laughter usually exceed the ones for the other emotions studied. However, amusement is also characterized by relaxation (see SERENITY). During laughter there is a relaxed posture and a typically lowered muscle tone, associated with a reduced readiness to respond attentively or with planned behaviour to changes in the surroundings. The laughing person has been described as abandoning himself or herself to the body response and as being in an unprotected state (Ruch and Ekman 2001). It was noted that one never sees purposeful acts and laughter together and that laughter and *goal-oriented behaviour are incompatible. In contrast to negative emotions such as anger or anxiety, the excitation during laughter occurs at a relaxed basis. The physiological changes occurring during laughter do not prepare the individual for 'fight or flight'; in this respect, they are more or less purposeless in terms of short-term consequences.

Whereas there are low levels of strain during the emotional response, a build-up of strain or *tension and its abrupt relief may precede amusement. For example, in humour, attention is paid to the eliciting event, and it is processed seriously until it is discovered that it is 'just fun.' The sudden annulment of seriousness and disengagement from prior problem-solving-like activity may be related to the feeling of 'lightness' ascribed to amusement (Ruch 1993). Incongruity is the essential ingredient in humour (Martin 2007). However, incongruity needs to be resolved, even if there is only an 'as if' (or pseudo-) resolution; i.e. the appearance of making sense out of incongruities without actually doing so. In humour the recipient's ability to make sense or to solve problems is exploited; after detecting the incongruity he or she is misled to resolve it, only to later discover that what made sense for a moment is not really making sense.

People are habitually differently inclined to respond to a funny stimulus with amusement. Such differences are typically ascribed to traits like cheerfulness, playfulness, or a sense of humour (Martin 1998). Likewise, the disposition for amusement varies across situations. Actual states, like a cheerful *mood or a playful frame of mind account for the fact that for most people, at some time, situations which would normally elicit amusement may not always have the same effect (Ruch 1997).

Amusement is not the only term used in this context and it is not used consistently. When researchers study laughter or the emotional response to humour, some speak of amusement, others of mirth or *enjoyment, and still others use hilarity or the German term *Erheiterung* (referring to a temporary increase in cheerful state, as expressed by the dated use of the English term 'exhilaration').

WILLIBALD RUCH

amygdala Named by the anatomist Karl Friedrich Burdach (1776–1847) in 1819, because of its almond-like shape, the amygdala is currently recognized by affective scientists as a key piece in the puzzle of the emotional brain (see NEURAL ARCHITECTURE OF EMOTION). Located in the temporal lobe, this structure is thought to play a critical role not only in emotion elicitation, emotional responses, and emotion regulation, but also in allowing prioritized or enhanced neural processing in various systems involved in perception, learning, memory, attention, vigilance, judgement, and decision-making. It is, therefore, critical to understand the nature of the computations performed by the amygdala, and how it interacts with other neural networks. However, the

anatomical unity of the amygdala and the issue of whether it functions as a system remain matters of debate (e.g. Davis and Whalen 2001), with some scholars even arguing that the amygdala does not exist as a unitary structure (Swanson and Petrovich 1998) while others reject this claim (e.g. Barton *et al.* 2003), sometimes suggesting that the unity of the amygdala also includes a so-called 'extended amygdala' containing, for instance, neurons located within the *substantia innominata* region of the ventral basal forebrain (see Aggleton 2000, Davis and Whalen 2001). The debate concerning the unity of the amygdala originates mainly from the variety of amygdala nuclei and nuclear divisions that make up the amygdala (see Fig. A3; see also Aggleton 2000), the variety of neuron subtypes in each nucleus, and also the confusion concerning the function of the amygdala. Current debates concerning the computational profile of the amygdala concern both the *domain* and the *level* of processing of the amygdala.

The amygdala's domain of processing

Historically, since the 1930s and until the end of the 20th century, the emotional role of the amygdala was typically associated with one emotion: *fear. This association was mainly based on clear evidence from animal research, brain imaging, and patient studies that the amygdala is important for fear learning, and, more generally, for the processing of threat-related information (see LEARNING, EMOTIONAL (NEUROSCIENCE PERSPECTIVES); RECOGNITION OF EMOTION (NEURAL SYSTEMS FOR)) (see Phelps and LeDoux 2005). These results ultimately led to the view that the amygdala is central to a 'defence system', 'fear system', or even a so-called 'fear module' (Öhman and Mineka 2001), the latter term implying that the domain of specificity of the amygdala is dedicated to fear-related computations. However, as argued by LeDoux (2008a), a critical issue is to understand whether the importance of the amygdala in fear reflects the importance of fear to the amygdala or whether fear is just the function that has been studied most.

In fact, although the role of the amygdala in fear is unchallenged, it is now clear that the processing domain of the amygdala is not restricted to fear-related information. A large body of evidence—which is too broad to be reviewed here—indicates that the amygdala is involved in processing not only information related to negative emotions other than fear, but also of positive information, such as humour-related stimuli, happy faces, pleasant pictures, movies, odours and tastes (see Fig. A4 and Sergerie *et al.*, 2008, for review), and reward learning (see Baxter and Murray 2002). How can the amygdala be considered central to both a 'fear module' (Öhman and Mineka 2001) and a 'reward system' (Baxter and Murray 2002)? As activity of the amygdala increases with the intensity of both negative

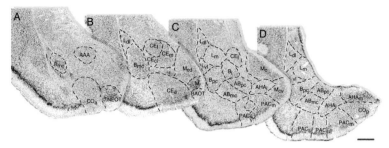

Fig. A3. Organization of amygdaloid nuclei and nuclear divisions adapted from Pitkänen *et al.* (1997) (scale bar 0.5 mm). Abbreviations. **Deep nuclei:** lateral nucleus (L) (dorsolateral division (L_{dl}), ventrolateral division (L_{vl}), medial division (L_m)); basal nucleus (B) (magnocellular division (B_{mc}), intermediate division (B_i), parvicellular division (B_{pc})); accessory basal nucleus (AB) (magnocellular division (AB_{mc}), parvicellular division (AB_{pc})). **Superficial nuclei:** nucleus of the lateral olfactory tract (NLOT); bed nucleus of the accessory olfactory tract (BAOT); anterior cortical nucleus (CO_a); medial nucleus (M) (rostral division (M_r), central division /dorsal part (M_{cd})/ventral part (M_{cv})); caudal division (M_c)); periamygdaloid cortex (periamygdaloid cortex (PAC), periamygdaloid cortex, medial division (PAC_m), periamygdaloid cortex, sulcal division (PAC_s)); posterior cortical nucleus (CO_p). **Other areas of the amygdala:** anterior amygdaloid area (AAA); central nucleus (CE) (capsular division (CE_c), lateral division (CE_l), intermediate division (CE_i), medial division (CE_m)); amygdalo-hippocampal area (AHA) (medial division (AHA_m), lateral division (AHA_l)); intercalated nuclei (I).

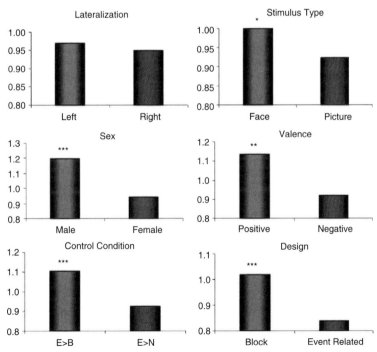

Fig. A4. Mean effect sizes associated with the human amygdala activation in functional neuroimaging studies for various conditions of interest (*$P < 0.05$, **$P < 0.01$, ***$P < 0.001$). E: Emotional stimuli, B: Baseline (low-level control), N: Neutral stimuli. From Sergerie *et al.* (2008).

and positive events, it was suggested that this structure is sensitive to the intensity or arousal of the emotion-eliciting stimulus, independently of its *valence (see Hamann 2003). However, it has been shown that the amygdala is involved in the processing of stimuli that are low on arousal, such as sadness-related information (see Fine and Blair 2000), that equally intense stimuli differentially activate the amygdala (e.g. Whalen et al. 2001), that arousal ratings in a patient with an amygdala lesion are impaired for negative but not positive emotions (e.g. Adolphs et al. 1999), and that neither valence nor intensity per se is coded in the amygdala (Winston et al. 2005). Taken together, these results contradict the view that the amygdala codes stimulus intensity or elicited arousal irrespective of valence.

As an alternative, and arguing for a unitary function of the human amygdala, Sander et al. (2003) proposed that the basic function of the amygdala is to detect events that are subjectively appraised as relevant given the individual's current goals, needs, values, and concerns. This proposal accounts for both inter- and intra-individual differences in amygdala sensitivity and emotional mechanisms. For instance, Phan et al. (2003) reported amygdala responses only when subjective ratings were incorporated in the analysis of brain activation as regressors. Another line of research highlighting the importance of taking into account inter-individual differences in amygdala sensitivity concerns the fact that response of the amygdala varies as a function of *personality or affective

traits. For instance, one can argue that the reason why happy faces particularly activate the amygdala in participants who are high on extraversion (Canli et al. 2002) is because such stimuli are particularly relevant for them. It is also important to consider intra-individual differences in terms of needs and goals. For instance, LaBar et al. (2001) showed that the amygdala was more activated by the visual presentation of food-related stimuli when participants were hungry than when they were satiated. Another dimension that may contribute to appraise a stimulus as relevant concerns its novelty or ambiguity, which is consistent with Whalen's proposal that the amygdala—in particular its more dorsal part—may be especially involved in increasing vigilance based on perceived stimulus ambiguity (see Davis and Whalen 2001). The fact that the amygdala is also sensitive to task-related goals and task performance (e.g. Schaefer et al. 2006, Wright and Liu 2006) also speaks in favour of a role for the amygdala in the processing of goal/need relevance. Importantly, this proposal is consistent with a preferential processing and learning for fear-related stimuli in many contexts, as such stimuli are usually more relevant than stimuli used in the other experimental conditions.

Anatomically, the amygdala seems to be particularly well located to serve this function, as it receives information from the thalamus and all sensory cortices, and as amygdalofugal projections to the cortex are massive (see Fig. A5; see also Aggleton 2000).

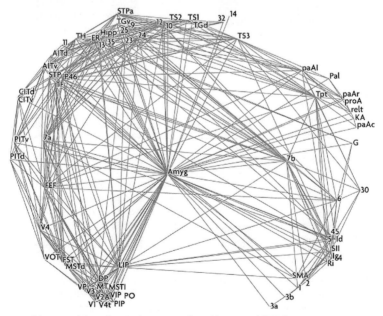

Fig. A5. Connectivity of the amygdala and cortical structures. From Young et al. (1994).

To conclude this section, it appears that the amygdala's domain of processing includes, but is not limited to, fear-related information as well as other negative arousing stimuli. Responses of the amygdala to positive as well as low-arousal stimuli that have a particular impact on the individual rather suggest that, as a structure, the amygdala's domain of processing consists of events that are subjectively appraised as relevant given the individual's current goals, needs, values, and concerns.

The amygdala's levels of processing

The levels of processing of the amygdala can be investigated from at least two approaches: (1) What are the primary features that are processed by the amygdala? (2) Does the amygdala compute information in an automatic way?

Concerning the issue of the primary features that are processed by the amygdala, several results indicate that simple perceptual cues have the power to elicit an amygdala response. This is particularly clear in fear conditioning paradigms in humans or other animals, during which a simple auditory tone or visual cue can elicit a response in the amygdala if it has been previously paired with an emotional stimulus (see LEARNING, EMOTIONAL (NEUROSCIENCE PERSPECTIVES)) (see Phelps and LeDoux 2005). Importantly, there is evidence that the amygdala is also sensitive to unconditioned low-level perceptual information such as low spatial frequencies in fearful faces (Vuilleumier et al. 2003), the sclera of fearful eyes (Whalen et al. 2004), or increasing sound intensity (Bach et al. 2008). Such results speak in favour of the fact that a rapid processing of coarse emotion-eliciting information takes place in the human amygdala. This is consistent with anatomical and functional evidence suggesting the existence of a dual-route architecture to the amygdala. Indeed, experiments on auditory fear conditioning in rats have shown the existence of a direct subcortical pathway from the auditory thalamus to the amygdala in addition to the more indirect cortical pathway (see Phelps and LeDoux 2005). Although uncontroversial anatomical evidence is lacking in humans, functional evidence suggests that a colliculo-pulvinar-amygdala subcortical pathway is involved in coarse and fast processing of visual stimuli in humans (e.g. Vuilleumier et al. 2003: see Vuilleumier 2005). A recent model has raised the question of whether such a pathway might be better conceptualized in the context of a two-stage architecture—rather than a dual route—according to which coarse and fast processing first occur in magnocellular pathways, then being complemented by slower parvocellular visual pathways (Vuilleumier 2005) (see ATTENTION AND EMOTION).

The existence of a low road in humans—or of a first processing stage—is also consistent with the view that the amygdala processes emotion-eliciting information at an automatic level. Indeed, strong evidence from experiments in blind-sight and neglect patients, as well as from studies using incidental, masking, or nonendogenous attention paradigms in normal individuals, suggest that the amygdala is able to process emotion-eliciting information implicitly, unconsciously, and independently of voluntary attention (see Vuilleumier 2005). Notably, the amygdala also seems able to process positive—therefore not only negative—stimuli in an unconscious way (e.g. Childress et al. 2008). The extent to which such automatic processes take place in a systematic context-independent way is still a question for further research, as there is evidence that amygdala responses may vary as a function of the attentional constraints of the task at hand (see Vuilleumier 2005, Pessoa 2008). The fact that task-set and top-down context-dependent processing can also modulate processing in the amygdala (see Vuilleumier 2005, Pessoa 2008) makes it flexible, which is consistent with its suggested role of appraising relevant stimuli.

To conclude this section, an analogy with the attention-constraints-based hypothesis proposed by Smith et al. (2001) to account for semantic activation seems useful to us in order to characterize the amygdala's levels of processing. According to these authors, semantic activation can be considered the *default setting* of the visual word recognition system. By analogy, it can be suggested here that evaluating emotion-eliciting stimuli reflects the *default setting* of the human amygdala, rather than an automatic process *per se* (in the strong sense of automaticity, implying total independence from capacity demands). With this suggestion, we mean that under *typical* cognitive conditions, processing in the amygdala may be unconscious, uncontrolled, independent of voluntary attention, efficient, and fast (see Moors and De Houwer 2006) (see AUTOMATIC APPRAISAL), but that automaticity is not a *necessary* condition in the sense that nontypical conditions (e.g. a highly demanding concurrent task) might not allow the *default setting* of the amygdala to be expressed (see also Vuilleumier, 2009).

Conclusion and perspectives

In order to accommodate the apparently multifaceted aspects of amygdala function, at least two kinds of explanation are possible. One explanation might be that the amygdala can implement as many processes as those directly suggested by the variety of experimental results. According to this view, some subregions within the amygdala might still be considered to implement a specific fear module, whereas other parts might subserve distinct processes such as intensity coding. Alternatively, another explanation argues that an extensive analysis of the different types of stimuli and tasks associated with amygdala involvement may point to a anger

common computational profile. Along this last line, a conceptual analysis of the domain and level of process- ing of the amygdala suggests that the function of the amygdala is best characterized as *default detection of stimuli appraised as relevant* given the individual's current goals, needs, values, and concerns.

Unfortunately, it is still not possible to draw straight- forward conclusions about the functional specialization of the amygdala's subnuclei, either from lesion studies or from brain imaging in humans. Therefore, methodo- logical advances in spatial and temporal imaging of the human amygdala will certainly be very important in order to provide an integrative framework capable of incorporating the current variety of experimental results on the sensitivity of the amygdala to relevant stimuli, including those concerning the precise neuronal cir- cuitry involved in fear learning (see Phelps and LeDoux 2005) and reward processing (see Baxter and Murray 2002). Identifying the neural pathways and temporal dynamics that modulate the human amygdala (e.g. dual-route or two-stage architecture), the internuclear connections within the amygdala, and how it interacts with other neural networks of specific cognitive systems remains a conceptual and methodological challenge to our understanding of how the amygdala is able to play such a central and integrative role in emotional processing.

DAVID SANDER

Aggleton, J. (ed.) (2000). *The amygdala: a functional analysis.* Oxford: Oxford University Press.

Davis, M. and Whalen, P.J. (2001). The amygdala: vigilance and emotion. *Molecular Psychiatry*, **6**, 13–34.

Phelps, E.A. and LeDoux, J.E. (2005). Contributions of the amygdala to emotion processing: from animal models to human behavior. *Neuron*, **48**, 175–87.

Vuilleumier, P. (2009). The role of the amygdala in perception and attention. In: P.J. Whalen and E.A. Phelps (eds), *The human amygdala*. New York: Guilford Press.

anger Anger is a negatively *valenced emotion charac- terized by high arousal and is considered to be one of the *basic emotions. Related states are *irritation, annoy- ance, fury, rage, etc.

Causes of anger

From a functional perspective, anger is assumed to be elicited by unwanted or harmful circumstances and to serve the purpose of mobilizing energy to remove or attack the cause of such circumstances. Psychological theories differ in how broadly the eliciting conditions should be conceived. The neo-associationistic theory of Berkowitz (Berkowitz and Harmon-Jones 2004) holds that anger can be elicited by any aversive condition, ranging from aversive sensory stimulation such as loud noise or heat to complex interpersonal events such as threat or

rejection. *Appraisal theories of emotions (Scherer et al. 2001a) propose more specific elicitors, holding that anger is elicited by the appraisal of an event as relevant (see RELE- VANCE DETECTION) and important for the self, incongruent with the individual's motives or well-being (see MOTIVE CONSISTENCY), and caused by someone else (and, according to some versions of appraisal theory, *power or *coping potential and illegitimacy (see LEGITIMACY) of the caused wrongdoing are also determining appraisals for anger). In this view, the combination of these appraisals elicits anger. Between these two positions, it has been argued that not all the appraisals are always necessary for anger to be experienced, but that some minimal anger-relevant ap- praisal is nevertheless necessary (Kuppens et al. 2003). For instance, anger can occur when the blame for a situation appraised as goal-incongruent is assigned to oneself instead of someone else.

The experience of anger is characterized by disposi- tional individual differences (referred to as trait-anger). These dispositional differences affect the tendency to appraise circumstances in anger-eliciting ways (see AP- PRAISAL STYLE), and are related to the personality dimen- sion of low agreeableness.

The experience of anger

The experience of anger is characterized by feelings of unpleasantness and high arousal, in the form of antag- onistic *feelings and *action tendencies. Antagonism refers to the urge to strike against or remove the obs- tacle of frustration. The experience of anger is further characterized by ruminative cognitions about the causes or blame and the consequences of the anger-eliciting event. The physiological and biological changes that accompany the experience of anger are characteristic of the generalized stress response to threat: elevated heart rate and blood pressure (see CARDIOVASCULAR SYS- TEM), elevated temperature, hormonal changes (most notably adrenaline and corticoid hormones), and the release of neurotransmitters (most notably acetylchol- ine, noradrenaline, and serotonin).

Consequences

The antagonistic behavioural tendency associated with the experience of anger, when not inhibited, motivates aggressive behaviour such as angry facial expression and verbal and physical *aggression. This type of anger behaviour is often referred to as anger-out behaviour. Due to learned societal norms and display rules, how- ever, aggressive behaviour is often inhibited or sup- pressed (referred to as anger-in) and is replaced by more socially acceptable behaviours. As a result, anger can be followed by a variety of behaviours including both aggressive and nonaggressive behaviours, such as avoidance, sulking, distracting activities, and social shar- ing (Van Coillie and Van Mechelen 2006).

The experience of anger can influence subsequent information-processing. Its experience can activate appraisal styles so that subsequent events are more easily appraised in anger-congruent ways. For instance, angry individuals display a heightened tendency to blame others (which can result in instances of displaced anger). There is further evidence that the experience of anger leads to a heightened tendency for risky *appetitive choice behaviour (Lerner and Keltner 2001), resulting from the feelings of control and coping potential assumed to be associated with its experience.

Several facets of anger experience have been associated with health risks such as increased blood pressure and risk for cardiovascular diseases (see HEALTH AND EMOTION). Chronic hostile cognitions such as distrust and the blameworthiness of others, referred to as the hostile component of Type A behaviour, have been especially related to such outcomes.

Control
Despite widely held beliefs in catharsis, the outward expression of the antagonistic, aggressive tendencies accompanying anger has not been proven to lower or control the intensity of felt anger (Bushman 2002). Interventions that are more effective in reducing anger are relaxation and cognitive restructuring or reappraisal.

PETER KUPPENS

Averill, J.R. (1982). *Anger and aggression: an essay on emotion.* New York: Springer.
Berkowitz, L. and Harmon-Jones, E. (2004). Toward an understanding of the determinants of anger. *Emotion,* 4, 107–30.

anhedonia First introduced in 1896 by the French psychologist Théodule-Armand Ribot (1839–1916), the term 'anhedonia' (from the Greek *an-*, 'without', and *hedone,* 'pleasure') refers to a decreased ability to experience *pleasure or react to pleasurable stimuli.

Anhedonia can be a state-like symptom of various psychiatric disorders as well as a trait indicating stable individual differences in the ability to experience pleasure. Anhedonia has been found to confer increased vulnerability to disorders such as depression, schizophrenia, and substance abuse. For example, anhedonic symptoms have been found to: (1) precede the onset of the disease; (2) show trait-like features (particularly in schizophrenia); (3) predict poor long-term outcome; (4) correlate with deficits in social functioning and illness severity; and (5) be present in unaffected biological relatives of individuals with schizophrenia or depression (Pizzagalli et al. 2005, Horan et al. 2006). Interestingly, recent animal and human research indicates that anhedonia is linked to dysfunction within the brain reward system (the dopaminergic mesocorticolimbic system). Overall, these findings indicate that the inability to

experience pleasure might represent a biological, probably genetically determined, *risk factor for various forms of psychopathology.

Over the decades, three basic methods have been utilized for assessing anhedonia: interview-based instruments, self-report measures, and laboratory-based assessments (Horan et al. 2006). Although the first two methods have been most widely used, it is important to consider that, in specific situations, their validity and reliability may be affected by individual's ability to recall and relate past pleasurable activities. Consequently, laboratory-based approaches have recently attracted considerable interest (Pizzagalli et al. 2005). Such objective assessments are expected to play an increasingly important role in improving our understanding of anhedonia, especially in light of recent advances in affective science indicating that pleasure is not a unitary construct but can be decomposed into distinct components (e.g. appetitive versus consummatory phases of reward processing).

DIEGO A. PIZZAGALLI

animal emotions Animal emotions used to be uncontroversial, as reflected in Darwin's (1872/1998) seminal work *The Expression of the Emotions in Man and Animals.* After a long interim during which American behaviourism imposed its taboos, new research has again opened the door to this topic. In a time in which animals are extensively used to explore the neural circuitry of fear, aggression, or affiliation, students of animal behaviour would do well to reconsider their traditional reluctance to consider animal emotions.

We may never be able to experience animal emotions, but the involvement of emotions in the organization of behaviour is open to objective investigation. Studies of the neural substrate of positively versus negatively *valenced affective states have thus far found no qualitative difference between humans and other animals (Berridge 2003a, Panksepp 2005) apart from a difference in emphasis on cortical versus subcortical regions that may be either an artefact of technique and conceptualization (Berridge 2003a) or due to differences in neural complexity between rodents and primates (Davidson 2003a).

When chimpanzees watch images with aversive content, their peripheral skin temperature drops, which in humans indicates negative arousal (Parr 2001). Moreover, their brain temperature shows human-like lateralized changes (Parr and Hopkins 2001). Psychopharmacological research shows that heightened emotional arousal in primates is associated with self-scratching (Schino et al. 2004), a behaviour which also increases during poor performance on cognitive tasks (Leavens et al. 2004). Self-scratching is also typical of victims of intragroup aggression, who are probably socially stressed. Remarkably, their rate of self-scratching returns to baseline following reconciliation with the opponent (Aureli and van Schaik 1991).

Since a rise in core body temperature, similar to the one associated with anxiety in humans, is measurable in response to mild stressors in mammals, reptiles, and birds, but not amphibians, it has been speculated that the first elements of emotional experience emerged in vertebrates after the amphibians (Cabanac 1999).

Facial expressions

Almost all communication among nonhuman primates seems emotionally mediated. We are familiar with the prominent role of emotions in human *facial expressions, but the facial musculature of humans and apes differs only marginally, and nonhuman primates have a similar array of expressions. If humans self-report certain emotions during a particular expressive display, such as laughing, it is logical to assume similar emotions in apes during a homologous display, known as the play face. From an evolutionary perspective, to assume emotional continuity between humans and apes is more parsimonious than to assume discontinuity (see EVOLUTION OF EMOTION).

Facial expressions are a powerful example of what early ethologists called an *Erbkoordination*, which in English became a fixed action pattern or FAP. In the same way that each species is characterized by structural features (e.g. wings, ears, digestive system), it is also endowed with stereotypical motor patterns. Since FAPs occur in recognizable form in all species members, they must have been subject to natural selection like any other trait. This permits us to apply the concept of 'homology' to similar FAPs in closely related species, i.e. their origin probably traces to a common ancestor (Preuschoft and van Hooff 1995). It also implies that we can look at FAPs as adaptations, i.e. we can assume natural selection for visual communication (Schmidt and Cohn 2001) (see FUNCTIONALIST THEORIES OF EMOTION).

Van Hooff (1967) was the first to provide detailed descriptions of facial expressions in a wider range of primates. He speculated about their causal underpinnings based on concomitant behaviour. A central concept is 'ritualization', i.e. the evolutionary transformation of instrumental behaviour to become more stereotypical and conspicuous so that it can serve a signal function. An example is van Hooff's (1967) suggestion that lip-smacking, common in many monkeys, derives from the consumption of particles picked up during foraging or grooming. Lips-macking has a friendly meaning, and often leads to grooming. This speculation is supported by the recent finding of a shared neural substrate between ingestion and orofacial communication (Ferrari *et al.* 2003).

Laugh and smile

Speculating its origin, grinning in primates (sometimes called the 'grimace'), has been proposed to derive from

a reflex in which the teeth are bared in response to sudden unpleasant or noxious stimuli. This response was rtiualized by exaggerating the muscle pull at the mouth corners and using it from a distance towards potentially harmful fellow group members. Reflexive teeth-baring thus evolved into a fearful or submissive expression (de Waal and Luttrell 1985; see Fig. A6).

In humans, however, the homologous expression, known as the smile, has different connotations. Not that fear is absent (e.g. someone who smiles too much is considered nervous), yet there is also an affectionate, even happy quality to the display. Smiling seems to have evolved as an indicator of cooperativity and altruism. In a phylogenetic analysis, van Hooff (1972) compared the way in which various primates employ the 'silent bared-teeth display' and concluded that the appeasing qualities of the human smile are not unique: there is a clear connection with the bared-teeth display of a great variety of primates, and in terms of its friendly use, the human display resembles one of the chimpanzee's bared-teeth expressions. Van Hooff further proposed the 'relaxed open-mouth display' of the chimpanzee and other primates as a homologue of human laughing. This expression, commonly known as the 'play face', occurs typically during tickling matches among apes, and is often accompanied by sounds reminiscent of guttural, breathy laughter.

Animal empathy

Qualitative accounts support the view that anthropoid apes show strong emotional reactions to others in pain or need (see EMPATHY (NEUROSCIENCE PERSPECTIVES)). Yerkes (1925, p. 246) reported how his bonobo, Prince Chim, was so extraordinarily concerned and protective towards his sickly chimpanzee companion, Panzee, that the scientific establishment might not accept his claims: 'If I were to tell of his altruistic and obviously sympathetic behaviour towards Panzee I should be suspected of idealizing an ape'. Ladygina-Kohts (1935, p. 121) noticed similar empathic tendencies in her young chimpanzee, Joni, whom she raised at the beginning of the 20th century, in Moscow. Kohts, who analysed Joni's behaviour in the minutest detail, discovered that the only way to get him off the roof of her house after an escape (much better than any reward or threat of punishment) was by appealing to his sympathy: 'If I pretend to be crying, close my eyes and weep, Joni immediately stops his plays or any other activities, quickly runs over to me, all excited and shagged, from the most remote places in the house, such as the roof or the ceiling of his cage, from where I could not drive him down despite my persistent calls and entreaties. He hastily runs around me, as if looking for the offender; looking at my face, he

(a)

(b)

Fig. A6. Ritualization turns reflexes into communication signals by making them more stereotypical and conspicuous. A cactus-eating female baboon (a) shows extreme lip retraction in reaction to noxious stimuli, a reflex which evolution has turned into the bared-teeth display shown by a rhesus monkey (b) as a signal of submission to an approaching dominant male. This display is thought to be homologous with the human smile. Photographs by Frans de Waal.

tenderly takes my chin in his palm, lightly touches my face with his finger, as though trying to understand what is happening, and turns around, clenching his toes into firm fists.'

Similar reports are discussed by de Waal (1996), who suggests that apart from emotional connectedness apes have an appreciation of the other's situation and a degree of perspective-taking. They show 'targeted help-ing', i.e. altruistic behaviour tailored to the specific needs of the other, such as the highly publicized case of Binti-Jua, a female gorilla who, in 1996, rescued a 3-year-old boy at the Brookfield Zoo, in Chicago.

A major difference between monkey and ape em-pathy is evident in so-called 'consolation' behaviour, i.e. friendly, reassuring contact by an uninvolved by-stander towards a distressed party, such as the loser of a fight (de Waal and van Roosmalen 1979; see Fig. A7). The hypothesis that consolation serves to alleviate the distress is supported by this behaviour being directed more at recipients of aggression than aggressors, and more at recipients of intense than mild aggression (de Waal and Aureli 1996).

Consolation has thus far been demonstrated only in the great apes. When de Waal and Aureli (1996) set out to apply exactly the same observation protocols as used on chimpanzees to detect consolation in monkeys, they failed to find any. This came as a surprise, because

Fig. A7. Consolation is common among chimpanzees. A juvenile puts an arm around a screaming adult male who has just been defeated in a fight with his rival. Consolation is known in humans and apes but not monkeys. Photograph by Frans de Waal.

'reconciliation' (i.e. a friendly reunion between former opponents) occurs in species after species (de Waal 2000). The consolation gap between monkeys and the Hominoidea (i.e. humans and apes) extends even to the one situation where one would most expect consolation to occur: macaque mothers fail to reassure offspring that have been attacked.

Why are humans and apes different? Possibly, one cannot take another's perspective without a well-developed self-representation. In other words, in order to understand that the source of a vicarious affective state is not oneself but the other, and to understand the specific cause of the other's distress, one needs a distinction between self and other. Following this line of reasoning, Gallup (1982) was the first to speculate about a possible connection between cognitive empathy and mirror self-recognition (MSR). This view is supported both ontogenetically by the co-emergence in children of advanced helping tendencies and phylogenetically by the same co-emergence in the Hominoidea. The only nonprimates for which we have similar accounts of targeted helping and consolation (albeit largely of an anecdotal nature) are dolphins and elephants, which are also the only animals apart from the Hominoidea to show MSR.

This doesn't mean that species that lack MSR possess no empathy at all. In fact, Preston and de Waal (2002) have proposed that empathy rests on a simple perception-action mechanism that provides an observer (the subject) with access to the subjective state of another (the object) through the subject's own neural and bodily representations. When the subject attends to the object's state, the subject's neural representations of similar states are automatically and unconsciously activated (see MIMICRY, SENSORIMOTOR ASPECTS). The more similar and socially close two individuals are, the easier the subject's identification with the object. Simple forms of empathy that do not require perspective-taking (often called 'emotional *contagion') may be widespread in mammals, as confirmed by pain-contagion in mice (Langford et al. 2006).

FRANS B. M. DE WAAL

Berridge, K.C. (2003). Comparing the emotional brain of humans and other animals. In: R.J. Davidson, K.R. Scherer, and H.H. Goldsmith (eds), *Handbook of affective sciences*, pp. 25–51. Oxford: Oxford University Press.

Darwin, C. (1872/1998). *The expression of the emotions in man and animals*, 3rd edn, ed. P. Ekman. New York: Oxford University Press.

van Hooff, J.A.R.A.M. (1967). The facial displays of the catarrhine monkeys and apes. In: D. Morris (ed.), *Primate ethology*, pp. 7–68. Chicago: Aldine.

Preston, S.D. and de Waal, F.B.M. (2002). Empathy: its ultimate and proximate bases. *Behavioral and Brain Sciences*, 25, 1–72.

de Waal, F.B.M. (1996). *Good natured: the origins of right and wrong in humans and other animals*. Cambridge, MA: Harvard University Press.

animal vocalizations Ever since Darwin (1809–82), and probably before him, animal vocalizations have been thought by many to be mindless and reflexive utterances conveying nothing but the emotional state of the vocalizer (see ANIMAL EMOTIONS). While it is certainly true that the vocalizations of animals convey emotions, we now know that they are, like human speech, very rich in their signalling properties and communicate emotional states in parallel with other types of information. Indeed, there are interactions between emotional states and the body condition of the vocalizer, habitat acoustics, and the role of the listener—all of which determine the roles vocalization plays in a social group.

There are three factors that shape the form–function relationship in animal vocalizations (see VOICE PRODUCTION AND ACOUSTICS). First, the vocalization reflects physical characteristics of the vocalizer, also known as 'indexical cues'. The acoustic structure of a vocalization can reveal an animal's size, reproductive status, gender, and age. For example, the length and shape of the vocal tract (the oral and nasal cavities above the vocal cords) determine which frequency bands get emphasized or suppressed (the resonance frequencies or *formants*). The larger animals within a species have longer vocal tracts and their formants are closely spaced, giving them deep sounding vocalizations, whereas the opposite is true for smaller animals. There is considerable variation in the shape of the vocal tract as well, and this can lead to signature spectral features in the formants of a given individual. Thus, with many vocalizations with formant structure (and probably other acoustic features), a listener can extract both the size (Ghazanfar et al., 2007) and possibly the identity (Owren and Rendall, 1997) of the individual caller. Such 'honest' signals—signals that can't be faked because they are constrained by the physical anatomy—may be useful in competitive situations (e.g. male–male competition) and when individuals are part of large, stable social hierarchies.

The second factor that can shape the acoustic structure of vocalizations is habitat acoustics, particularly for long-distance vocalizations that are used to induce group movements, defend territory, and/or attract mates. Different habitats (e.g. rain forest, riverine forest versus savannah) have different effects on the transmission of vocal signals to receivers. The 'noise' in these habitats can come from a variety of biotic and abiotic sources. One solution to habitat noise is to use very low-frequency vocalizations whose long wavelengths allow them essentially to go around many obstacles. Elephants use such vocalizations to communicate across distances sometimes exceeding 10 km. Female elephants are known to increase their rate of low-frequency call production during oestrous to attract males who may be some distance away from them (Payne *et al.* 2003). Another solution is to find clear channels within the habitat noise. The blue monkey (*Cercopithecus mitis*) is an arboreal species that lives in the rain forests of Uganda and Kenya. In these environments, background noise is at a minimum in the 100–1000 Hz frequency range. The blue monkey has exploited this channel by producing a long-distance 'boom' call whose frequency lies within the 125–200 Hz range. Naturally, the auditory system of this species reflects this specialization by its exquisite sensitivity to sounds within this range (Brown and Waser 1984).

Calls elicited by the emotional state of the signaller can be seen as serving the purpose of producing a desired effect in a listener. Where human speech often is produced to inform the listener, and hence tailored after her/him, animal vocalizations differ fundamentally in that they are produced with respect to the sender's own condition rather than the listener's (Owren and Rendall 2001). This kind of discrepancy between the interests of the sender and receiver leads us to the third factor in the form–function relationship. Specializations of the auditory system can be exploited by the sender to produce unconditioned emotional responses in listeners solely by virtue of the call's acoustics. High-amplitude calls with noxious spectral qualities and/or chaotic structure (such as screams and shrieks) are likely to elicit aversive responses in listeners. It has been proposed that in agonistic interactions, subordinates may use such noxious sounding calls to get a dominant individual to move away (Owren and Rendall 1997). Screams and shrieks can also elicit the well-known acoustic-startle reflex which evokes changes in the autonomic nervous system, shifts in attention, and interruption of ongoing activity. Similarly, tonally rich vocalizations can have up-sweeps which capture attention and increase arousal, or down-sweeps which have a soothing effect.

The three form–function factors described above demonstrate that vocalizations are certainly indicators of emotions (Jurgens 1979), and may in some cases modify the behaviours of distant listeners, but there is another level at which vocalizations can modify the behaviour of listeners. Vocalizations can be linked arbitrarily to events external to the caller. The classic example of such a signalling property (alternatively called 'functional reference' or 'semantics') is alarm calling, whereby vocalizations are associated with particular types of predators. Meerkats (*Suricata suricatta*), for in-

stance, produce several acoustically distinct calls to different classes of predators (Manser *et al.* 2001). Distinct calls are useful because listeners may have to respond in different ways depending on the predator. For example, their raptor alarm call is produced upon sighting an eagle, to which they respond by freezing and crouching on the spot, and scanning the sky. In contrast, the snake alarm call induces other group members to approach the caller and collectively mob the snake. Nevertheless, the link to affect is ever present, as alarm calls are modified in acoustic structure depending on the distance of the predator. Low-urgency calls tended to be clear and more harmonic while high-urgency calls are harsher and noisier.

HJALMAR K. TURESSON AND
ASIF A. GHAZANFAR

Seyfarth, R.M. and Cheney, D.L. (2003). Signalers and receivers in animal communication. *Annual Review of Psychology*, **54**, 145–73.

antecedents (of emotion) The antecedents of emotions are generally events that an organism perceives as important for its physical, social, or personal well being (see APPRAISAL THEORIES; RELEVANCE DETECTION). The event may be something that is actually happening in the present environment, or a thought or memory. The 'organism' is a person or some other higher mammal. It is somewhat unclear (or arbitrary) where in phylogenetic development animals can be said to experience emotions (see ANIMAL EMOTIONS). In most species (e.g. all insects) behaviour is motivated by specific triggering stimuli: the antecedents can be sufficiently described by the event itself and the response is automatic. The antecedents of emotions, however, are not the actual events but the events-as-perceived. Whether and how a person perceives an event as relevant to his or her well-being depends upon that person's *beliefs and *values, present circumstances and goals, and current biological state. What is offensive to a person from one culture, for example, may be innocuous to someone from another. A person's background *mood—hostile, anxious, or depressed—can affect the threshold for perceived relevance. A person who is phobic sees life-threatening danger where others see nothing; a person high on heroin may be oblivious to dangers perceived by others.

Most behavioural scientists believe that all antecedents of emotion involve *valence—the feeling that the event will have consequences that are good or bad, even if the perceiver is not yet sure which (e.g. when the telephone rings). Other commonly (although not universally) accepted criteria for emotional antecedents include *novelty, certainty, perceived *agency, coping ability (see COPING POTENTIAL), presence or absence of goal obstacles (see MOTIVE CONSISTENCY), engaging in a satisfying activity, and compatibility with personal or social norms.

A few antecedents seem to be universal (see INTRINSIC PLEASANTNESS). Sweet or bitter tastes, smiling or angry faces produce positive or negative feelings. A large rapidly approaching object or the threat of physical pain evokes fear; the death or illness of a loved one evokes sorrow; a severely disfigured person evokes disgust. Snakes and darkness are feared more often than not. Among emotional antecedents, a very few are universal; many, like snakes and insults and the sight of happy babies, are widely general and many others are culturally or individually idiosyncratic. Very abstract descriptions of antecedents (novelty, hazard, attack, success, loss, opportunity) are likely to be more general, but cultures and individuals differ in what they perceive as novel, dangerous, offensive, and so on, so that the particular events that result in these emotionally relevant perceptions are highly variable.

The perception that what is happening is relevant to the organism's *goals or *needs is a fundamental antecedent of emotion. Events seen as furthering the attainment of a goal lead to emotions such as joy, hope, and interest; events seen as obstacles to goal attainment lead to emotions such as frustration, anxiety, anger, or a sense of determination. Events that signal that a goal has been gained or lost are also important emotional antecedents. The perception that an event involves basic goals and needs, like physical welfare or group membership, or goals that are high in priority at the moment, displaces perceptions of events related to subordinate goals. The perception of one's ability to cope with threats to a goal also contributes to the emotional experience. Some theorists believe that goal-relevant perceptions are necessary antecedents to emotion; others believe that valence can be independent of the motivational state of the organism.

Different theorists have defined the sequence of events in the unfolding of an emotion in different ways (see EMOTION THEORIES AND CONCEPTS (PSYCHOLOGICAL PERSPECTIVES)), some beginning the sequence with the physiological response to the eliciting event (e.g. the James–Lange theory, some with the expressive behaviour, some with the appraisal of the event, some with the motivation to action, and some with the subjective feeling. Whether these various elements are *antecedents* of emotion or *components* of emotion is currently a matter of theoretical debate, and depends upon one's definition of emotion itself.

PHOEBE C. ELLSWORTH

Ekman, P. and Davidson, R.J. (1994). How is evidence of universals in antecedents of emotions explained? In: *The nature of emotion: fundamental questions*, pp. 144–77. New York: Oxford University Press.

Ellsworth, P.C. and Scherer, K.R. (2003). Appraisal processes in emotion. In: R.J. Davidson, K.R. Scherer, and H.H. Goldsmith (eds), *Handbook of affective sciences*, pp. 572–95. Oxford: Oxford University Press.

Frijda, N.H. (2007). *The laws of emotion*. Mahwah, NJ: Lawrence Erlbaum Associates.

anterior cingulate cortex The anterior cingulate cortex (ACC) is a complex structure on the medial surface of the frontal lobe adjacent to the corpus callosum. It is considered cortex that is somewhat more primitive than neocortex in part because it has fewer cell layers. The ACC has several subdivisions, including the ventral, rostral, and dorsal (see Fig. A8). Each of these subdivisions has unique functions by virtue of unique connectivity to other brain structures and cellular architecture, but all are highly interconnected with other medial prefrontal structures. There is a progressive increase in the degree of conscious and controlled information processing as one ascends from ventral to dorsal and a corresponding progression in the regulation of motor responses from more automatic and involuntary to more intentional and unrehearsed. There is also evidence of reciprocal activation of the dorsal and ventral subsectors of the ACC such that as one is activated the other is inhibited.

Attempts to describe the function of the ACC in a unified way are controversial. One view is that the ACC integrates the personal salience and environmental context of stimuli, as well as anticipated actions and their outcomes, to guide the behavioural response to any given environmental situation. The integration of internal and external information in the service of

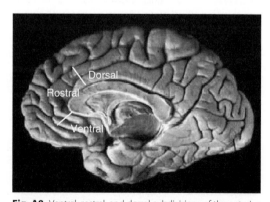

Fig. A8. Ventral, rostral, and dorsal subdivisions of the anterior cingulate cortex (ACC). The labels are superimposed on the ACC. The dividing line between subdivisions is approximate.

selecting behavioural responses constitutes a kind of 'motivated gear shift' function of the ACC.

The ventral (subgenual) ACC (vACC) includes Brodmann area (BA) 25, which is the principal site of autonomic regulation in the frontal lobe, as well as BA24 and BA32. The vACC has important bidirectional connections with the *amygdala, periaqueductal grey, nucleus accumbens, hypothalamus, anterior insula, and orbitofrontal cortex, all of which are structures involved in different aspects of the generation and processing of emotional responses. Due to this connectivity it has been labelled the 'affective division' of the ACC (Bush et al. 2000). The vACC is part of the ventromedial prefrontal cortex, the area at the base of the frontal lobe that mediates the 'somatic marker' function of integrating one's own emotional responses into decision-making (see SOMATIC MARKER HYPOTHESIS). The vACC participates in the evaluation of the emotional significance of stimuli including information about behavioural outcomes, a type of processing that probably occurs outside of conscious awareness (Williams et al. 2006). Due to its important role in regulating vegetative functions, and evidence of its hyperactivity in depression, BA25 has recently been the site of successful inhibitory deep brain stimulation in the treatment of refractory depression (Mayberg et al. 2005).

The rostral (pregenual) ACC (rACC) including Brodmann areas 24, 32, and 33 is just superior to and is closely related to the vACC as it has strong bidirectional connections with the amygdala. It is activated in a variety of emotional states and seems to participate both in conscious processing of emotional *feeling states as well as performing related cognitive operations, such as thinking about feeling and reflecting upon feeling. Neighbouring regions of medial prefrontal cortex participate in representing the mental states of self and other as well as self-relevant information more generally (Amodio and Frith 2006). Consistent with these functions, recent evidence indicates that the rACC plays a key role in emotional conflict resolution (Etkin et al. 2006). In posttraumatic stress disorder the rACC is underactive, contributing to hyperactivity of the amygdala and dysregulated fear responses.

The dorsal ACC (dACC), including Brodmann areas 24 and 32, is predominantly connected to the lateral prefrontal cortex, parietal cortex and pre- and supplementary motor areas, contributing to its label as the 'cognitive division' of the ACC (Bush et al. 2000). The dACC is highly sensitive to the organism's state of *arousal as it has the highest density of dopaminergic inputs from the ventral tegmental area in the brainstem (Paus 2001). The dACC plays a major role in the executive control of attention in that its activity increases with any mental effort, particularly when automatic prepo-

tent responses must be suppressed in favour of unrehearsed responses, and plays a major role in the resolution of conflict (choosing between alternative behavioural response options). The dACC participates in registering emotional signals, such as pain and the commission of errors, that inform behavioural responses and the choice of one action over another. Lesions in this area produce inattention and a clinical state called 'akinetic mutism', in which movement is not initiated. The range of motor behaviour influenced by the dACC is diverse, including autonomic regulation, emotional vocalizations, and behavioural responses to cognitive tasks (Bush et al. 2000, Paus 2001, Vogt 2009). The dACC (among other structures) has been shown to be overactive in obsessive–compulsive disorder, consistent with its role in action monitoring.

Emotion can be thought of as a mechanism for evaluating the extent to which an individual's goals are or are not being met in interaction with the environment, associated with an orchestrated physiological, behavioural, experiential, and cognitive resetting of the organism to deal with the outcome of that evaluation. Given the functions of the ACC described above, the ACC is a key player in the network of brain structures mediating the generation and implementation of emotional responses.

RICHARD D. LANE

Paus, T. (2001). Primate anterior cingulate cortex: where motor control, drive and cognition interface. Nature Reviews Neuroscience, **2**, 417–24.

Vogt, B.A. (ed.) (2009). Cingulate neurobiology and disease. Oxford: Oxford University Press.

antisocial behaviour Antisocial behaviour is an issue of significant social and clinical concern. Every year more than 1.6 million people are killed as a result of *violence (see AGGRESSION), and many more suffer from a range of physical or mental health problems (World Health Organization 2002). A recent survey showed that citizens of European nations see themselves as having 'significant' difficulties with antisocial behaviour, and that the problem was above all associated with people aged under 25 years (BBC News 2006). These responses predominantly concern rowdy, nuisance, and intimidating behaviour, as well as more extreme incidents committed by youngsters. 'Antisocial behaviour' involves not only aggression but also activities such as theft, vandalism, fire-setting, lying, truancy, running away from home, and oppositional behaviours.

Children who show antisocial behaviour from an early age onwards are at risk for a host of negative outcomes in adolescence and adulthood, including dropping out of school, criminality, social isolation, unemployment, dependence on welfare, depression, and substance abuse (Hill and Maughan 2001, Tremblay *et al.* 2005). Moreover, early violence breeds more violence. Aggressive children provoke aggressive responses from parents, who may themselves be violent, since antisocial behaviour runs in families from one generation to the next (Rutter and Silberg 2002). The contagious nature of aggressive behaviour means that victims of bullying may become aggressors, and group-based intervention programmes may actually lead to increased rates of aggression (Dishion *et al.* 2002)

Most individuals show antisocial behaviour from time to time. In normal development children occasionally disobey adults, tell lies, fight, and intimidate other children. However, when antisocial behaviour goes beyond occasional occurrences and has adverse effects on a child's functioning psychiatrists make a diagnosis of conduct disorder (CD) or oppositional defiant disorder (ODD; American Psychiatric Association 1994). These disorders are relatively common in school-age children, with estimated prevalences ranging from 5–10% (Hill and Maughan 2001). It is not clear whether such disorders grow out of normal levels of aggression and selfishness. There are two prominent schools of thought on the development of antisocial behaviour: the social learning hypothesis that aggression is learnt through reinforcement and observational learning processes, and the contrasting view, which holds that aggression is a fundamental human tendency that does not need to be taught (Tremblay *et al.* 2005). The latter perspective implies that virtually all children show aggression during the toddler years, but then learn to interact with other people in more socially acceptable ways. At present there is only limited evidence with which to evaluate these proposals, because relatively few studies of young children's aggression have been conducted, and different investigators use different definitions, units of analysis, sampling strategies, and experimental procedures. Observational studies and large surveys both show that 1-year-olds use force against family members and peers but do not reveal whether such young children deliberately intend to cause harm, i.e. whether the early use of force is truly aggressive. Individual differences in aggression emerge in late infancy (Tremblay *et al.* 2005); these findings suggest that many children are never aggressive but a minority of children show high levels of aggression. The sex differences that begin to emerge between 2 and 4 years of age derive partly from the escalation of aggression in a minority of boys (Hay 2007).

The origin of antisocial behaviour

There is a growing consensus that both individual (i.e. genetic, temperamental, cognitive) and social factors (e.g. early social adversity, family relations, peers) contribute to the development and maintenance of anti-social behaviour, although most research has focused on identifying the specific contextual or social factors that impinge on the developing child. For example, negative life events, family stress, parental psychopathology, and parental relationship problems have all been associated with antisocial behaviour problems in children. However, there is increasing evidence that factors organic to individual children explain or accentuate (mediate and/or moderate) risk to children who live with early social adversity: not all children exposed to social adversity develop antisocial behaviour, and some children become antisocial despite a favourable social background. Research suggests that a number of different biological, cognitive, and social factors may be involved in the development and maintenance of antisocial behaviour over time. To illustrate this, we focus on three factors that promote aggression: the biological stress system, early social experiences, and social cognitive deficits.

The biological stress system

When we consider young children it is most likely that the origin of antisocial behaviour lies in a combination of a child with a difficult *temperament and a nonoptimal environment in which ineffective socialization plays a key role: A difficult child elicits harsh, inconsistent, and negative socialization behaviours as a result of which a difficult temperament ultimately develops into aggressive or disruptive behaviour (Lykken 1995). Although there are factors that contribute to antisocial behaviour in childhood becoming chronic, not all antisocial children become antisocial adolescents, and not all antisocial adolescents become antisocial adults. A study of biological factors could help explain why these behavioural patterns change over time.

The systems that are involved in the regulation of *stress are the neuroendocrine hypothalamic–pituitary–adrenal (HPA) axis and the psychophysiological autonomic nervous system (ANS). Normal variations in stress system (re-)activity seem to play a clear role in temperamental differences between children, with higher activity being linked with a shy, inhibited, and fearful temperament and low activity with a more impulsive and aggressive temperament. It has also been proposed that a reduced activity of the stress systems is part of the biological predisposition to antisocial behaviour (Raine 2002b). Low activity or arousal has been linked to fearlessness, sensation-seeking, and/or risk-taking behaviour. A relative lack of fear would lead to antisocial behaviour because one is insensitive to the negative consequences of one's own or other people's behaviour in general and the experience of receiving punishment in particular. If this is the case, the implications for the treatment of these problem behaviours are clear: antisocial individuals will have problems in learning the association between behaviour and punishment and pointing out the negative consequences of behaviour, or punishing unacceptable behaviour, is likely to have a reduced effect relative to other children.

A different theory focuses on sensation-seeking (Zuckerman 1979). Here it is argued that a certain level of stress is needed in order to feel pleasant and that too little or too much stress is experienced as aversive. Aggressive individuals are considered to have an elevated threshold for stress: they are easily bored and not deterred by situations that the average person finds too arousing/exciting, stressful, or dangerous.

Antisocial individuals have lower resting levels of cortisol, skin conductance (SC), and heart rate (HR). There is also evidence of inverse relationships between these physiological variables and the severity of behavioural problems, and stress variables can predict antisocial behaviour over time. Raine et al. (1997) found that low resting HR measured at the age of 3 years predicted aggressive behaviour at age 11 years. Brennan et al. (1997) found that sons of criminal fathers who themselves did not become criminal had higher HR and SC than sons who did become criminal. Thus the former group seemed to be biologically protected by their heightened autonomic reactivity. Van Goozen et al. (2000) found that CD children had lower HR, SC, and cortisol reactivity when exposed to psychosocial stress than normal controls. However, although CD children appeared not to be affected by stress at a *biological* level, they reacted more angrily and aggressively to the frustration and provocation involved, and reported feeling quite upset. Thus, their appraisal of the situation did not lead to activation of autonomic or endocrine stress response systems. Children who, as a result of their risky or impulsive behaviour, place themselves in threatening or dangerous situations might gradually become further desensitized to stress, due to habituation. This leads to a vicious circle in which the child becomes increasingly resistant to stress and therefore places him- or herself in increasingly threatening situations (van Goozen et al. 2007).

Early social experience
Physical and biological problems during important phases in development (e.g. birth complications, chronic stress during pregnancy), together with early adversity (e.g. malnutrition, neglect, and abuse), make an important contribution to the development of personality and psychopathology. Antisocial children are more likely to come from adverse rearing environments involving atypical caregiver–child interactions (Rutter and Silberg 2002). It is also known that these children are more likely to experience compromised pre- or perinatal development due to maternal smoking, poor nutrition, or exposure to alcohol and/or drugs and maternal mental illness. It is possible that these factors have affected early brain development and resulted in a child with a difficult temperament. Given what we know about children who show severe antisocial behaviour, it is possible that a downregulation of the stress response system in the face of chronic stress has occurred (van Goozen et al. 2007). A genetic predisposition towards antisocial behaviour may be expressed in adverse rearing environments in which the child receives harsh or inconsistent discipline, or is exposed to high levels of interparental conflict or marital breakdown (Moffitt 2005). Conversely, the effects of such a predisposition may be minimized if the child is raised in an environment in which the parents express warmth or adopt a consistent, authoritative parenting style.

Cognitive deficits and peer rejection
One source of stress and frustration for young children is the demands made upon them by their parents and other people. Initially they may react with anger and aggression, but they gradually learn to deal with others and control their own behaviour in socially acceptable ways. Executive function deficits, associated with impairment in the frontal lobe, impede the development of self-regulation (Raine 2002b). By 4 years of age, typically developing children acquire 'theories of mind' (TOM), allowing them to make accurate inferences about the intentions and beliefs of other people (see THEORY OF MIND AND EMOTION). Some antisocial children have deficits in TOM, but some bullies have good TOM (Sutton et al. 1999). Development of TOM allows children to deceive other people, which may promote covert antisocial behaviour. Some aggressive children do have specific cognitive biases, where they interpret other people's behaviour as intentionally aggressive, and react accordingly; other children tend to respond in kind, which promotes aggression and leads to the rejection of aggressive children by their non-aggressive peers (Dodge et al. 2003). Peer rejection promotes loneliness (Pedersen et al. 2007), and encourages aggressive youth to spend time with other delinquent youngsters, which may further promote antisocial behaviour (Dishion et al. 2002).

Conclusion
Antisocial behaviour in youngsters is of significant concern: it can be persistent, difficult to treat, and develop into a range of other types of problems (Hill and Maughan 2001). Research on serious antisocial behaviour has shown that biological factors are involved in this behaviour. At present, we do not know what causes the pattern of neurobiological impairments observed in antisocial children, although it is clear that genetic factors are involved (Rutter and Silberg 2002, Moffitt 2005).

An important line of research suggests that psychosocial adversity affects the development of the brain in early life. Knowing that many antisocial children have problematic backgrounds, it seems possible that adverse experiences have had an effect on their biological and psychosocial development. There is a need for longitudinal research in high-risk children to shed more light on this issue.

A final point is that the understandable tendency to focus on the persistence of antisocial behaviour runs the risk of overlooking the fact that a substantial proportion of antisocial children do *not* grow up to be antisocial adults. Studying the neurobiological and social factors involved in early antisocial behaviour could account for this. Expanding on this research base is essential if we are to more adequately understand the causes, course, and consequences of antisocial behaviour and, most importantly, what can be done to reduce escalating societal impacts.

STEPHANIE H. M VAN GOOZEN AND DALE HAY

van Goozen, S.H.M., Fairchild, G., Snoek, H., and Harold, G.T. (2007). The evidence for a neurobiological model of childhood antisocial behavior. *Psychological Bulletin*, **133**, 149–82.

Hill, J. and Maughan, B. (2001). *Conduct disorders in childhood and adolescence*. Cambridge: Cambridge University Press.

Moffitt, T.E. (2005). The new look of behavioral genetics in developmental psychopathology: gene–environment interplay in antisocial behaviors. *Psychological Bulletin*, **131**, 533–54.

Tremblay, R.E., Hartup, W.W., and Archer, J. (2005). *Developmental origins of aggression*. New York: Guilford Press.

anxiety Anxiety is an aversive emotional state provoked by the prospect of future threat. Beyond this minimalist definition, there is considerable diversity of opinion on how to conceptualize and measure anxiety. Some view anxiety as a *basic emotion (Oatley and Johnson-Laird 1987), whereas others view it as a mixture of the fundamental emotion of *fear plus two or more other emotions (e.g. guilt, distress, anger; Izard 1977, p. 93).

Anxiety is distinguishable from fear. Anxiety is triggered by distal threat, whereas fear is triggered by immediate threat. The physiological activation (see AROUSAL) accompanying fear can mobilize the person for either fight or flight. Fear often has an abrupt onset and offset, whereas anxiety often does not. Prolonged anxiety may best be characterized as a *mood rather than an emotion.

Anxiety is sometimes described as free-floating as if dread can emerge without any object or focus of apprehension. The belief that anxious feelings can be entirely divorced from any cognitive content is probably a misconstrual arising from failure to ask the proper questions of the anxious person. Indeed, the cognitive aspect of anxiety—worry about possible future threats—is a central feature of the emotion (Borkovec and Inz 1990).

If the prominence of worry about future threat renders the notion of unconscious anxiety oxymoronic, what do we make of someone who exhibits apparent signs of anxiety in a threatening context yet denies feeling anxious? There are three possibilities. First, the person's denial may arise from differences in linguistic labelling. The person may acknowledge being aroused, but not anxious. Second, the person might be unwilling to acknowledge feeling anxious to others. Third, the signs of anxiety are fallible indicators of the inner state (see FEELINGS (PSYCHOLOGICAL PERSPECTIVES)), and they do not invariably covary. For example, people who deny feeling anxious despite contrary behavioural and physiologic evidence are called repressors. Research on individuals characterized by this repressive *coping style suggests a distinctive cognitive profile marked by hypervigilance for threat followed by avoidance of threat (Eysenck 2004).

Discrete state versus dimensions

Some scholars conceptualize emotions in terms of dimensions (see DIMENSIONAL MODELS) rather than as qualitatively discrete states (Russell and Mehrabian 1977). They believe that emotions differ in degree, not in kind, and that each seemingly discrete emotion can be represented by points on three orthogonal dimensions: *valence (pleasant versus unpleasant), arousal (high versus low), and dominance (in control versus being controlled). Anxiety, then, is characterized by unpleasant valence, high arousal, and low dominance. Lang (1985) likened the dimensional versus discrete state views of emotion to the wave and particle theories of light. Both enjoy independent empirical support.

State and trait anxiety

Psychologists distinguish between state anxiety and trait anxiety (Spielberger 1985). State anxiety is an occurrent concept, whereas trait anxiety is a dispositional concept (Fridhandler 1986). As an occurrence, episodes of state anxiety unfold in time, and are evinced by their empirical indicators. In contrast, as a disposition, trait anxiety does not unfold in time. Rather, it denotes individual differences in the proneness to experience episodes of state anxiety. Trait anxiety, however, must not be confused with a prolonged episode of state anxiety. Trait anxiety is never directly observed; it is inferred from the frequency of observable episodes of state anxiety.

The frequency of anxiety episodes provides the basis for inferring elevated trait anxiety, but it is not equivalent to trait anxiety. Indeed, a high-trait anxious person may infrequently experience elevations of anxiety if he or she happens to live a relatively stressor-free life. Analogously, a glass vase remains characterized by the disposition of fragility even if it is never shattered by a force. The disposition of fragility is instantiated in the microstructure of glass, and the disposition of trait anxiety is ultimately instantiated in the brain even though it is inferred only from observable episodes of state anxiety. It is the task of science to elucidate the causal powers that produce variations in observable anxiety.

How is anxiety measured?

Much relevant work does not distinguish between measures of fear and anxiety. For example, in his influential three-systems approach, Lang (1985) proposed that fear (or anxiety) consists of three loosely coupled response systems: one involving language, one involving motor behaviour, and the other involving visceral physiology. The systems usually covary under conditions of high (or low) threat. A person under serious, imminent threat is likely to exhibit activation in all three systems, expressing fear in language, in motor behaviour (e.g. flight), and in physiology (e.g. sweating palms, pounding heart). According to Lang, fear and anxiety are fundamentally about defensive action in response to danger.

Ordinary language recognizes the decoupling of these systems and their empirical indicators. A person who reports fear and exhibits heightened physiological responsivity, yet approaches the threat, is courageous rather than fearless.

Cognitive aspects of anxiety

There are two distinct cognitive approaches to understanding anxiety (McNally 2001). One approach considers anxiety as the product of threat-related beliefs and appraisals (see APPRAISAL THEORIES) ascertainable through introspective self-report and disclosed through language on questionnaires and during interviews (Beck et al. 1985). This approach awards casual significance to beliefs. What a person believes about future threat is key to understanding the person's emotional state of anxiety.

The other approach holds that anxiety results from information-processing biases (see COGNITIVE BIAS) whose casual influence is inferred from behavioural indicators (e.g. reaction time) on cognitive psychology tasks (Williams et al. 1997). This approach relies on applying the laboratory methods of experimental psychology to elucidate cognitive biases that often operate outside of awareness or occur too quickly to be captured by introspection (e.g. MacLeod et al. 1986).

Psychologists have documented that people with elevated trait anxiety or who suffer from anxiety disorders are characterized by a bias for selectively attending to threatening information (see ATTENTION AND EMOTION) (Bar-Haim et al. 2007). Although everyone will attend to highly threatening information, very anxious individuals will attend selectively to relatively mildly threatening information. Anxiety is also associated with either an interpretive bias favouring threatening construals of ambiguous events or the absence of a positivity bias that characterizes people not suffering from anxiety problems (Hirsch and Mathews 2000).

Psychologists have recently demonstrated that attentional and interpretive biases favouring threat are not merely epiphenomenal correlates of elevated anxiety (Mathews and MacLeod 2002). Indeed, inducing such biases renders people susceptible to experiencing heightened anxiety in response to subsequent stressors (Wilson et al. 2006). Among the most exciting recent developments are attempts to apply cognitive training methods to correct information-processing biases, thereby alleviating emotional suffering (MacLeod et al. 2004, Yiend and Mackintosh 2004).

Evolutionary aspects

Most psychologists regard the capacity to experience anxiety as an evolutionary adaptation (see EVOLUTION OF EMOTION). That is, the capacity to anticipate threat and to experience an aversive emotional state that motivates one to neutralize the threat must surely have fostered fitness in our ancestors. The evolutionary roots of anxiety encourage attempts to study it in nonhuman animals. Although there are certainly aspects of anxiety shared by human beings and other animals, Kagan (2006) has rightly warned about the tendency to overlook crucial differences in our attempts to detect the similarities. As he wrote: 'Because rats and mice, and perhaps apes as well, do not interpret their bodily changes, scientists should not equate the emotions of animals and humans. Although some scientists attribute 'fear' to both rats and humans, the psychological states in the two species are far from identical. Some scientists say that mice that freeze in a place where they had been shocked a day earlier or do not enter a brightly lit alley are 'anxious'. But readers should understand that the brain state of the mice is quite different from that of adults who refuse to fly because of anxiety over a possible crash.' (Kagan 2006, p. 208).

Indeed, human beings possess language and a self-representational capacity enabling them to become anxious about social threats (i.e. mice cannot be 'shy' in the same sense as people) and to experience guilt. They also can project themselves into the future and into the past, rendering them vulnerable to developing syndromes such as generalized anxiety disorder (GAD) and *posttraumatic stress disorder, both based on the capacity to escape the temporal prison of the present. In fact, although it is plausible that animals may experience a state akin to human fear in the presence of immediate threat, it is questionable whether they can experience anxiety about imagined threats lying in the future.

*Generalized anxiety disorder (GAD) is characterized by excessive and seemingly uncontrollable worry about a range of topics (e.g. school performance, work). The person with this disorder experiences intense worry more days than not, and the problem must have persisted for at least 6 months for the diagnosis to be warranted. Moreover, the person must also report at least three of the following symptoms: feeling keyed up, on edge, or restless; easily fatigued; difficulty concentrating; irritability; muscle tension; and difficulty sleeping. Many people with GAD say that they have been troubled by it most of their lives. GAD has a chronic, but fluctuating, course. Approximately 5% of the population suffers from GAD at some point in their lives. In community studies, about two-thirds of the cases are women.

RICHARD J. MCNALLY

Barlow, D.H. (2002). *Anxiety and its disorders: the nature and treatment of anxiety and panic*, 2nd edn. New York: Guilford Press.

McNally, R.J. and Reese, H.E. (2009). Information-processing approaches to understanding anxiety disorders. In: M.M. Antony and M.B. Stein (eds), *Oxford handbook of anxiety and anxiety disorders*, pp. 136–52. Oxford: Oxford University Press.

apathy Apathy derives from the Greek *apatheia* 'freedom from suffering' and *apathes* 'without feeling' (*a-* 'without' + *pathos* 'emotion, feeling, suffering'). Originally a positive quality (*apatheia*) (Sorabji 2000), the sense of 'an absence or lack of emotion or motivation' and 'an indifference to what should excite' dates from around the 18th century.

In the modern clinical literature, debate focuses on a putative 'apathy syndrome', defined by Marin (1996) as a primary loss of *motivation, manifest in a loss of interest, a loss of effortful behaviour, and a loss of emotional responsivity. According to Marin, diagnosing an apathy syndrome requires showing that lack of motivation is the primary explanation for lack of goal-directed activity, i.e. lack of motivation is not attributable to dysphoria or a diminished level of consciousness, for example. Thus defined, an apathy syndrome can be distinguished from other syndromes, such as major depressive disorder (see DEPRESSION), in which apathy can be a symptom. Marin's definition has been operationalized in the Apathy Evaluation Scale (AES), studies of which have indeed suggested that apathy as a syndrome can be discriminated from depression. Further, the AES predicts the extent of an individual's engagement in exciting activities, and is related to neural indices of attention to novel events. A putative apathy syndrome has been documented in several clinical conditions including Alzheimer's disease, Parkinson's disease, stroke, traumatic brain injury, drug addiction, and schizophrenia. Apathy is frequently associated with impaired effortful cognitive control. Evidence suggests that apathy is related to dysfunction of the basal ganglia–prefrontal systems of the brain, and that dopaminergic drugs may be useful in its treatment. In contrast to Marin, other authors (e.g. van Reekum *et al.* 2005) have argued that there are multiple kinds of apathy.

Affective science reveals motivation to be a complex, multifaceted process, encompassing dissociable goal-directing and energizing effects (Niv *et al.* 2006), but the study of apathy has yet to make substantial contact with the experimental investigation of motivation.

ANDREW D. LAWRENCE

appetitive motivational system The idea that complex behaviour can be reduced to combinations of two distinct classes of *action tendencies—*approach and avoidance—acquired new prominence in the 1990s, in a family of theories with roots in neuropsychology, psychopathology, and animal conditioning (Davidson 1998, Depue and Collins 1999, Gray 1994). The theories hold that appetitive *motivation and the approach behaviours that follow from it are managed by what various theorists termed a *behavioural activation system, behavioural approach system, or behavioural facilitation system. This is a regulatory system that organizes the approach of diverse incentives, thus being general-purpose rather then specialized (though some views also argue for partially independent special-purpose social appetitive systems). Positive affects associated with approach—excitement, eagerness, etc.—are generally attributed to the appetitive system. Some believe the appetitive system also is the root of certain negative affects, such as anger and sadness, which arise when appetitive motives are thwarted (see, e.g., Carver 2004). The appetitive system is assumed to vary in sensitivity among persons, with such variations manifested in ways such as differences in the desire for new incentives, energetic pursuit of incentive stimuli, and positive responses to the attainment of incentives.

CHARLES S. CARVER

applications (of emotion and affective science research) see AESTHETIC EMOTIONS (PSYCHOLOGICAL PERSPECTIVES); AGGRESSION (BIOLOGICAL PERSPECTIVES); AGGRESSION (PSYCHOLOGICAL PERSPECTIVES); CLIMATE, EMOTIONAL; COMPETENCE, EMOTIONAL; COMPUTATIONAL ANALYSIS OF EMOTION; DECISION-MAKING; ECONOMICS (ROLE OF EMOTION IN); EMBODIED CONVERSATIONAL AGENTS; INTELLIGENCE, EMOTIONAL; LAW (AND EMOTION); LIFE SATISFACTION; MARKETING (ROLE OF EMOTION IN); MEDIA COMMUNICATION; NEGOTIATION; STRESS; WORK SETTING (ROLE OF EMOTION IN).

appraisal style According to *appraisal theories the evaluation of emotion-eliciting events is highly subjective and depends on the perceiver's goals, values, and coping potential (Ellsworth and Scherer 2003). Thus one of the major strengths of appraisal theories is that they can explain why the same event can trigger highly disparate emotions in different people. Appraisal theories can also account for stable individual differences in the tendency to experience particular emotions more or less frequently (emotional dispositions) (Scherer *et al.* 2004) and for affective disorders, postulating that these trait-like characteristics could be due to systematic individual differences in appraisal tendencies or biases.

The literature on individual differences in cognitive processing suggests that a number of traits and cognitive styles may consistently affect appraisal processes (see van Reekum and Scherer 1997). There may be individual differences in how thoroughly events are appraised. Whereas one person may rapidly accept an initial appraisal, another may engage in repeated reappraisals before settling on an interpretation. One of the underlying variables might be the amount of cognitive effort that is characteristically expended. Furthermore, the cognitive style of the individual may influence the complexity of the appraisal, i.e. gross versus fine-grained appraisal, particularly with respect to the width of the categories used in inference and classification. For example, generally optimistic people might process emotional information more superficially than pessimists do (Schwarz 2001). Finally, people may differ in their sensitivity to spatial 'looming' and temporal urgency (Riskind *et al.* 2000).

Appraisal tendencies or biases may also involve systematic sensitization or distortion of particular appraisals. A well-known example is internal versus external control as the outcome of the agency appraisal, i.e. the attribution of responsibility to oneself rather than other people or circumstances. Such biases may exist for all the major appraisals: *novelty, *valence, certainty, control, goal conduciveness, and morality (see van Reekum and Scherer 1997). Optimists and pessimists may have different biases in the appraisal of valence; people who are shy or bold may differ in characteristic appraisals of certainty and control. A number of empirical studies have examined the effects of differences in performance goals and motivational styles (Smith and Kirby 2001) or in causal attribution and control beliefs (Wranik and Scherer 2008) on appraisals and the associated emotions.

While idiosyncratic appraisals and their accompanying emotions seem valid and realistic to the perceiver, other people in the social environment may evaluate them as more or less appropriate to the situation and the individual's actual *coping potential. If an appraisal deviates too far from such reality constraints, the resulting emotion will be seen as abnormal. Using this approach one can attempt to correlate appraisal malfunctions with clinically relevant affect disorders, and to conceptualize different types of emotional disorders in terms of appraisal biases or malfunctions (see Kaiser and Scherer 1998, Roseman and Kaiser 2001). Clinicians may object that these suggestions are merely reformulations of syndrome definitions; however, the effort to link theories of normal emotion to an understanding of the aetiology of affect disturbance may help to encourage more general studies of cognitive functioning and appraisal styles in patients suffering from affective illness in order to better understand the underlying mechanisms. In a similar vein, Watts (1992) provides an overview of potential applications of current cognitive theories of emotion to the conceptualization of emotional disorders. Once the role of appraisal biases in the aetiology and maintenance of affective illness is better understood, it may become possible to develop appropriate remedial or therapeutic approaches to eliminate pathogenic appraisal biases (something that is consistently practised, under somewhat different theoretical auspices, in *cognitive behaviour therapy).

KLAUS R. SCHERER AND PHOEBE C. ELLSWORTH

Ellsworth, P.C. and Scherer, K.R. (2003). Appraisal processes in emotion. In: R.J. Davidson, K.R. Scherer, H. Goldsmith (eds), *Handbook of affective sciences*, pp. 572–95. New York: Oxford University Press.

van Reekum, C.M. and Scherer, K.R. (1997). Levels of processing for emotion-antecedent appraisal. In: G. Matthews (ed.), *Cognitive science perspectives on personality and emotion*, pp. 259–300. Amsterdam: Elsevier Science.

appraisal theories The basic premise of appraisal theories is that emotions are elicited and differentiated by the subjective interpretation of the personal significance of events. This assumption has been made, at least implicitly, by many philosophers (e.g. Aristotle, Spinoza, Descartes, Hume) and psychologists (James, Stumpf, Schachter). While most current scholars in affective science research agree that some kind of appraisal plays a role in most emotional experience, the contribution of *appraisal theories* consists in (1) applying this conceptual framework to all instances of emotion, including automatic unconscious processing (see AUTOMATIC APPRAISAL), (2) explaining emotional response patterns as a direct consequence of appraisals, and (3) providing a theoretical framework specifying which configurations of appraisals are most important in differentiating among emotions.

The nature of appraisal

Following pioneering contributions by Arnold and Lazarus, a number of authors independently suggested that the nature of an emotional reaction can best be predicted by the individual's subjective evaluation or interpretation of an event, generating the theories that have come to be subsumed under the label 'appraisal theory' (see chapters by Roseman and Smith, and Schorr in Scherer *et al.* 2001a). Scherer (1999a) distinguished four major theoretical approaches to appraisal based on the nature of the appraisal dimensions postulated: criteria, attributions, themes, and meanings.

Criteria

Based on the early work of Arnold and Lazarus, appraisal theories propose a fixed set of (relatively molecular) criteria used in evaluating the significance of the events that happen to individuals. These criteria include: the *novelty or familiarity of objects or events; their *intrinsic pleasantness or unpleasantness; their significance for the individual's *needs or *goals (see MOTIVE CONSISTENCY); their perceived causes (self, another person, or circumstances); the individual's ability or power to influence or cope with the consequences of the event (see COPING POTENTIAL (APPRAISAL OF)), including the level of uncertainty; and the compatibility of the event with social or personal standards, *norms, or *values. Table 1 (adapted from Scherer, 1999a) shows a comparative listing of the major criteria. Theorists in this trad-

ition postulate that specific combinations of appraisal outcomes for these criteria determine the nature of the emotion (see Ellsworth and Scherer, 2003, and chapters by Frijda, Lazarus, Roseman, Scherer, and Smith and Kirby in Scherer *et al.*, 2001a).

Attributions

Social psychologists have been particularly interested in the nature of the causal attributions that are involved in emotion-antecedent appraisal. Thus, Weiner (1982) proposed that major emotions such as *anger, *pride, and *shame can be distinguished solely on the basis of internal versus external attribution of responsibility and the degree of perceived control (see ATTRIBUTION THEORY). Others (Roseman 1984, Scherer 1984a, Smith and Ellsworth 1985) have proposed *agency as an appraisal dimension, distinguishing among the self, other human agents, and impersonal circumstances as causes.

Themes

Lazarus (1991) proposed the notion of emotion-specific 'core-relational themes' focusing primarily on the implications of events for the individual's goals (e.g. 'loss of a valued person or object' for sadness). Smith and Lazarus

Table A1. Comparative overview of major appraisal dimensions as postulated by different theorists

Frijda	Roseman	Scherer	Smith/Ellsworth
Change Familiarity		Novelty suddenness familiarity predictability	Attentional activity
Valence		Intrinsic pleasantness	Pleasantness
Focality Certainty Presence Open/closed Urgency	Appetitive/aversive motives Certainty Motive consistency	Goal significance concern relevance outcome probability expectation conduciveness urgency	Importance Certainty Perceived obstacle Anticipated effort
Intent/self–other Modifiability Controllability	Agency Control potential	Coping potential cause: agent cause: motive control power adjustment	Human agency Situational control
Value relevance		Compatibility standards external internal	Legitimacy

Table A2. Examples of theoretically postulated appraisal profiles for different emotions

Stimulus evaluation checks	Joy/happiness	Anger/rage	Fear/panic	Sadness
Novelty	High	High	High	Low
Intrinsic pleasantness	High	Open	Low	Open
Goal significance				
Outcome probability/certainty	High	Very high	High	Very high
Conduciveness/consistency	Conducive	Obstructive	Obstructive	Obstructive
Urgency	Low	High	Very high	Low
Coping potential				
Agency/responsibility	Self/other	Other	Other/nature	Open
Control	High	High	Open	Very low
Power	High	High	Very low	Very low
Adjustment	High	High	Low	Medium
Compatibility with standards/value relevance/legitimacy	High	Low	Open	Open

(1993) have suggested a two-step model, combining both molecular (appraisal criteria) and molar (relational themes) elements. Starting from different premises, Oatley and Johnson-Laird (1987) and Stein and Trabasso (1992) also emphasize emotion-specific goal contingencies.

Meanings

Philosophers and cognitive scientists interested in evaluation (see EVALUATIVE PROCESSING) and judgements as a basis for emotion (Solomon 1976, Ortony et al. 1988) have focused on the analysis of the propositional nature of the semantic fields that underlie the use of specific emotion terms, illustrating the logical operations that determine the labelling of a feeling state with a specific emotion word. Thus Ortony et al. (1988) propose a structure of emotions as *valenced reactions to appraisals of events, objects, and agents.

The mechanism of appraisal

While there is a high degree of convergence on fundamental assumptions among these approaches, only the first, criteria-oriented, group of theorists have developed detailed models with respect to the nature of the appraisal process and the predicted emotional response patterning. The following overview focuses on these appraisal theories.

Appraisal theorists generally assume that appraisal is a central component of the emotion process (see Ellsworth and Scherer 2003, pp. 574–6) generating emotional response patterns in other components (physiological responses, expression, subjective experience, *action tendencies) in a dynamic, cumulative fashion (see COMPONENTIAL THEORIES). Specific configurations or profiles of appraisal outcomes correspond to specific *modal

emotions or emotion families, both with respect to prototypical response patterns and subjective feeling states, as labelled by standard emotion words. Table 2 (adapted from Scherer, 1999a) shows examples of such theoretically postulated profiles for several emotions (see Roseman, 1984, and his chapter in Scherer et al., 2001, for a somewhat different approach). Appraisal theories can also account for emotional experiences not captured by verbal labels, such as intermediate emotional states or 'incomplete' emotions.

A variety of different paradigms have been used to study the relationship between particular configurations of appraisals and the nature of the emotional reaction. The most frequently used method consists of asking subjects to recall specific emotional experiences and questioning them about the antecedent evaluation processes. Another method is to study naturally occurring events such as school examinations or to induce emotions experimentally and obtain verbal reports of the appraisal processes. A technique that is more closely related to the 'meanings approach' described above consists of having people judge the appraisal implications of emotion words. Finally, one can use vignettes or scenarios that systematically manipulate dimensions of appraisal, asking subjects to indicate the emotional reactions that they—or a fictitious other—might experience in this situation. On the whole, these studies provide substantial support for many of the theoretical predictions made by appraisal theorists. For example, a limited set of five to seven predictor dimensions generally allows correct classification of about 40–50% of the emotional states studied in this research.

The reliability of *self-reports of appraisals has been questioned, as the recall of the underlying appraisal processes (some of which may occur outside awareness) requires a fairly high level of conceptual processing. Instead of actually remembering their appraisals, participants may construct a rationale for their emotional response after the fact or rely on sociocultural representations of emotional meanings. However, much of this research taps recognition memory rather than recall memory, since there are specific probes for the postulated appraisal dimensions. Therefore many inferential processes that are potentially available to consciousness can be expected to be reported fairly accurately. Obviously, complex appraisal processes occurring below the level of consciousness cannot easily be studied by self-report (or by any other currently known technique).

Levels of appraisal

Critics of this approach often erroneously assume that appraisal processes are deliberate, conscious, and thus too slow and 'cognitivistic', questioning the likelihood that elaborate cognitive evaluations can be performed during the few milliseconds that seem sufficient to bring about many emotion episodes. In many cases emotions are produced by unconscious, nondeliberate, nonvoluntary factors. While some types of affective phenomena are outside the scope of appraisal theories (for example, free-floating moods, preferences, reflexive pain reactions, and emotional memories), most cases of automatic, unconscious emotion elicitation are included. Specifically, Leventhal and Scherer (1987) have suggested a '*levels of processing' approach to specify the mechanisms underlying appraisal. They suggested that all of the standard appraisal criteria can be processed on a sensorimotor, a schematic, or a conceptual level, in more or less rudimentary form and with different effects on the ensuing emotion. Viewing appraisal as a multi-level process corresponds to a number of similar approaches in other traditions (Van Reekum and Scherer, 1997; see Smith and Kirby chapter in Scherer *et al.*, 2001a). It should be noted that appraisal theorists, in contrast to dual-system notions, use the words appraisal or evaluation to cover a continuum of information processing from conscious, deliberative processes all the way down to unconscious, automatic processes.

The process of appraisal

Emotion episodes are characterized by continuous changes in the underlying appraisals and reactions (Scherer 1984a, 2001a, 2004, Frijda 1986). Thus, to specify a pattern of appraisals that is supposed to explain a static emotion as indexed by a label is at best a first entry point into the complexity of the underlying process. The dynamic nature of appraisal processes and their cumulative effects on the other components of emotion (such as subjective feeling, physiological responses, motor expression, and action tendencies) need to be examined

in terms of their temporal unfolding (see SEQUENCE OF APPRAISAL PROCESSES). Appraisal theorists differ in their assumptions about the sequentiality of appraisal. While some believe that the evaluation criteria are processed in a parallel fashion or in a sequence determined by context, others assume a partially (Ellsworth 1991) or a completely fixed sequence in a recursive process (Scherer, 1984, 2001a) (see COMPONENT PROCESS MODEL).

Links between appraisal and other components of emotion

Several appraisal theories have linked appraisals directly to other components of the emotion process. Generally, these theorists argue that, from a functional point of view, the appraisal process brings about appropriate adaptive reactions involving all the other emotion modalities. Scherer (1984, 2001a, 2004) postulates that every appraisal change directly affects the other subsystems (e.g. the somatic and autonomic nervous systems), and presents detailed prediction tables for the presumed effects of appraisal outcomes on facial and vocal expression, physiological responses, and behaviour tendencies. Similar attempts to link appraisal outcomes to specific response patterns have been suggested by Smith and Ellsworth (1985) for *facial expression and Frijda *et al.* (1989) for action tendencies. It is also likely that other components of emotion, such as physiological responses, can elicit related appraisals, once habitual patterns of emotional responses have developed.

To test these hypotheses, a variety of appraisal dimensions must be systematically manipulated and their effects on other emotion components measured. Some researchers have used cognitive tasks to manipulate appraisals in quasi-experiments (see chapter by Pecchinenda in Scherer *et al.* 2001a). In other work, various aspects of computer games (of the Pac-Man or space invader type) were manipulated so as to influence intrinsic pleasantness, goal conduciveness, control, and/or power (van Reekum *et al.* 2004; Lanctôt and Hess 2007). More recently, picture viewing paradigms have been used to manipulate novelty, intrinsic pleasantness, and goal conduciveness and to measure a variety of central and peripheral nervous system processes (Aue *et al.* 2007). On the whole, this work has provided strong support for the notion that appraisal outcomes drive changes in other emotion components.

Social and cultural context of appraisal

Social psychologists have strongly emphasized the role of social factors in appraisal (see Part IV in Scherer *et al.* 2001a). The explanatory principles that account for these effects can be grouped into two categories. First, social effects on the current motivational state, such as interacting with a specific kind of person (a macho friend or a very feminist woman) or with members of a particular group (a reference group or an outgroup) can change one's goal hierarchy by making certain needs or goals more or less important or desirable and can render certain values or norms more salient. Given the transactional nature of appraisal, this will change the resulting emotion. Second, social context may affect the appraisal process itself. An interactive or group setting may serve to define an ambiguous situation or event or it may produce greater certainty of appraisal results due to the perceived convergence in appraisal by group members. This effect may occur through verbal communication of appraisals or observation of others' emotional reactions, which suggest their underlying appraisals.

There is also empirical evidence for differences across cultures (1) in the actual frequency of particular events (e.g. crime), (2) in the relative importance of particular aspects of social life such as the family, (3) in the definition of self-identity, or (4) in the cultural value systems (see Mesquita *et al.* 1997) (see CULTURAL SPECIFICITY). Yet, the nature of the appraisal process and the set of evaluative criteria used (defined abstractly, e.g. novelty, goal-conduciveness, morally acceptable) might be universal. While specific goals are likely to be strongly determined by cultural values (e.g. raising fat pigs, honouring one's ancestors, or achieving maximal self-realization), the general appraisal of the goal conduciveness or controllability of an event might not be (Ellsworth 1994a).

Overall, intercultural research has shown that the appraisal mechanism itself seems to be quite general across cultures—the appraisal profiles for the major emotions are very similar across the large number of rather diverse countries studied. While the cultural differences in the use of appraisal dimensions found in intercultural studies are generally smaller than the emotional differences, they are nevertheless, at least for some emotions and for some appraisal dimensions, rather sizable, showing that members of different cultures seem to appraise emotion-antecedent events somewhat differently on at least some of the major dimensions. Specifically, 'complex' appraisal dimensions, requiring the use of cultural schemata, are more affected by intercultural differences than relatively basic dimensions related to stimulus characteristics or individual well-being.

An issue that also deserves research is the potential existence of subcultural differences in appraisal patterns, e.g. between rural and urban populations, differences between generations, or between specific subgroups. Of particular interest are strong individual differences in appraisal which may constitute potential risk factors for emotion dispositions and even affective disorders (see APPRAISAL STYLE).

Outlook

Appraisal theories represent a convergence of independently developed theoretical models, and have generated a sizable number of empirical studies supporting the basic tenets of the theories. The criticism of 'excessive cognitivism' is no longer tenable given the empirical demonstration that appraisal can occur at all levels of the central nervous system. Future research needs to be directed at the dynamic nature of these processes, particularly with respect to interlevel interaction (i.e. top-down priming, bottom-up elaboration) and the automatization of appraisals, such as schematization. Six major lines of theoretical and empirical development can be envisaged: (1) further refinement of concrete, falsifiable predictions, (2) systematic experimental induction of specific appraisals, (3) use of more sophisticated procedures to elicit verbal report of conscious experiences, (4) search for nonverbal indicators of appraisals, such as physiological reactions, expression patterns, or action tendencies, (5) increased attention to the social and cultural context of appraisal and integration of strategic behaviour and regulation attempts (see also chapters by Mesquita and Ellsworth and Parkinson in Scherer *et al.* 2001a), and (6) developmental research on the emergence of appraisals and emotions in children. Concern with clinical and applied issues may also foster the development of research paradigms that will search for ecological validity of the situation studied, such as earlier studies on emotions generated by university examinations (Folkman and Lazarus 1985, Smith and Ellsworth 1987) or the study of emotions following the discovery that one's luggage has been lost (Scherer and Ceschi 1997). Finally, theory development may also benefit from efforts to develop appraisal-based computational models of emotion.

KLAUS R. SCHERER AND PHOEBE C. ELLSWORTH

Ellsworth, P.C. and Scherer, K.R. (2003). Appraisal processes in emotion. In: R.J. Davidson, K.R. Scherer, and H.H. Goldsmith (eds), *Handbook of affective sciences*, pp. 572–95. Oxford: Oxford University Press.

Mesquita, B., Frijda, N.H., and Scherer, K.R. (1997). Culture and emotion. In: J.E. Berry, P.B. Dasen, and T.S. Saraswathi (eds), *Handbook of cross-cultural psychology: Vol. 2. Basic processes and developmental psychology*, pp. 255–97. Boston, MA: Allyn and Bacon.

Scherer, K.R. (1999). Appraisal theories. In: T. Dalgleish and M. Power (eds), *Handbook of cognition and emotion*, pp. 637–63. Chichester: Wiley.

Scherer, K.R. (2004). Feelings integrate the central representation of appraisal-driven response organization in emotion. In: A.S.R. Manstead, N.H. Frijda, and A.H. Fischer (eds), *Feelings and emotions: the Amsterdam Symposium*, pp. 136–57. Cambridge: Cambridge University Press.

Scherer, K.R., Schorr, A., and Johnstone, T. (eds) (2001). *Appraisal processes in emotion: theory, Methods, Research*. New York: Oxford University Press.

approach/withdrawal The terms approach and withdrawal behaviour have a long and distinguished history in the behavioural and biological sciences. Attention was drawn to this concept by Schneirla (1959) in his classic paper. In that article, the comparative psychologist highlighted the important role of approach and withdrawal behaviour at all levels of phylogeny and showed that, wherever behaviour was observed, approach- and withdrawal-related processes were evident. In a fundamental sense, approach and withdrawal represent the basic psychological decision an organism makes with respect to its environment.

In recent years, connections have been made between approach and withdrawal systems and emotion. Approach and withdrawal behaviour usually occur in an affective context and these behaviours can be observed in organisms which cannot provide verbal reports about their emotions—both infrahuman species as well as preverbal infants. Since this dimension of behaviour appears at all levels of phylogeny where behaviour itself is observed, some commentators have suggested that it is a more fundamental dimension of emotion than a simple positive–negative *valence dimension (e.g. Vrana et al. 1988). More recently, Davidson and his colleagues have suggested that prefrontal brain asymmetry may be associated with this fundamental dimension of approach and withdrawal (see FRONTAL BRAIN ASYMMETRY) (see, e.g., Davidson 2003b). Very recently Maxwell and Davidson (2007) explicitly manipulated approach and withdrawal motor behaviour to examine its potential impact on biasing behavioural measures of asymmetric hemispheric activation. They found evidence consistent with an embodiment hypothesis, namely that approach behaviour facilitated left-hemispheric processes while withdrawal behaviour facilitated right-hemispheric processes.

A promising extension of the approach/withdrawal framework has been to the study of psychopathology, particularly *depression. Some investigators have suggested that at least one subtype of depression might be characterized by a deficit in an approach system (see, e.g., Davidson et al. 2002). On this view, one would expect that measures of approach behaviour (e.g. reward sensitivity) should be deficient in this subtype. In a recent examination of this issue, Shankman et al. (2007) reported that patients with early onset depression showed decreased neural responsivity to reward, suggesting that this specific depression subgroup was associated with an abnormality in approach behaviour.

RICHARD J. DAVIDSON

Maxwell, J.S. and Davidson, R.J. (2007). Emotion as motion: asymmetries in approach and avoidant actions. *Psychological Science*, **18**, 1113–19.

arousal Phasic arousal refers to a short-term (phasic) increase in some process that can be viewed as involving excitatory processes—usually an increase in behaviour or physiological activity (see PERIPHERAL PSYCHOPHYSIOLOGY). Historically, 'arousal' has been applied to such processes as the massive increase in sympathetic nervous system (see AUTONOMIC NERVOUS SYSTEM) activity preparing for fight or flight in response to an imminent threat (identified by Cannon, 1927a) or to a phobic stimulus, increases in generalized drive due to hunger or thirst in animal learning experiments, activation of the ascending reticular activating system in response to sensory input and subsequent desynchronization of the electrical activity of the cerebral cortex as observed in the electroencephalogram, activation of the pituitary–adrenal axis to stressful stimuli (see STRESS), behavioural activation in response to cues promising response-contingent reward, nonspecific 'energizing' of behaviour due to punishment or threats of punishment (e.g. the *Yerkes–Dodson law), and the negative affect associated with anxiety in anticipation of potential threats. In recent years, technological advances have made it possible to record increases in activity or arousal in numerous parts of the brain. Most often 'phasic' arousal is applied to increases in arousal over a period of a few seconds to a few minutes, usually in response to an explicit or presumed stimulus. Increases over periods of an hour or more (e.g. the pituitary–adrenal axis response, hunger/thirst) might be viewed as phasic if viewed in a temporally broad theoretical context, but often the term would not be applied in such cases. Thus, the brevity associated with the concept of phasic is, to some degree, a matter of contrast with more prolonged time periods.

DON C. FOWLES

art (and emotion) see AESTHETIC EMOTIONS (PHILOSOPHICAL PERSPECTIVES); AESTHETIC EMOTIONS (PSYCHOLOGICAL PERSPECTIVES); FICTION AND EMOTION; LITERATURE AND EMOTION; MUSIC (EMOTIONAL EFFECTS).

associative processing Emotional reactions to situations or events are often grounded on associations. An otherwise harmless stimulus that reliably predicts a fear-inducing experience will itself become feared. At the opposite pole, a liked stimulus can support the transfer of positive affect to a previously neutral stimulus that predicts it. What is the nature of the associative processes that underlie these forms of learning? And can knowledge of associative mechanisms help us to understand affective processes and formulate therapeutic techniques?

The strength of an associative bond formed between a cue (in Pavlovian terminology the conditioned stimulus) and an outcome (or unconditioned stimulus) depends on a variety of properties such as the frequency and reliability with which they are paired, their precise temporal arrangement, and properties of the events themselves. For example, learning tends to be faster with more salient events, and can be influenced by the extent to which they 'belong' together: a taste will be easily associated with gastric illness and a flashing light with a shock, but it is much harder to learn to associate a taste with shock or a flashing light with illness (Garcia and Koelling 1966).

Formal theories of association formation have paid most attention to the frequency and reliability of the predictive relationship. In the influential theory of Rescorla and Wagner (1972), which relates strongly to learning processes in *connectionist models, the increment in the associative strength between a cue and an outcome (ΔV_i) on an occasion i in which they co-occur is a multiplicative function of the salience of the cue and the outcome (α and β, respectively, which take values between 0 and 1) and the difference between the maximum associative strength the outcome can support (λ, the asymptotic learning level) and the current associative strength of all the cues present on that occasion (ΣV_i): $\Delta V_i = \alpha\beta(\lambda - \Sigma V_i)$. The increment in associative strength is therefore a function of the degree to which the outcome is unpredicted by the cues present on that trial: the term in brackets is an *error* term. The asymptote λ is 1 for an outcome but 0 for a null event (that is, an occasion on which no outcome occurs, as in extinction). In a situation in which the outcome reliably follows the cue across several learning trials, the model predicts a gradual acquisition of associative strength to the cue, negatively accelerating towards a maximal value. With the assumption that associative strength maps in some monotonic fashion onto response strength, learning curves consistent with this formulation have been repeatedly observed.

One of the main achievements of this model is to present a mechanistic explanation for situations in which more than one predictor is present. Consider the classic example of *blocking*, in which cue A initially predicts the outcome O across several trials (A→O), and then A and another cue B together predict O across a second stage of trials (AB→O). The remarkable finding from such procedures (Kamin 1968) is that cue B will gain little control over behaviour, and hence little associative strength, despite that fact that it is paired on several occasions with the outcome. This is explained, in the Rescorla–Wagner theory, by the fact that cue A gains a near-asymptotic amount of associative strength during the first stage. In the second stage, the associative strength (ΣV_i) of all the cues present (A and B) is near 1, and hence learning is driven by a very small error term. Once it is recognized that all learning situations involve a multitude of cues (e.g. there is always a context cue in addition to the nominal cue), the importance of being able to account for cue interactions becomes central to models of associative processing. The Rescorla–Wagner theory stands as the precursor of many successful current models of cue interaction.

Another implication of this approach is that learning will be very dependent on the contingency or correlation between the cue and outcome. As might be hoped for an evolutionarily adaptive system, the associative strength of the cue will be increased the more frequently it is accompanied by the outcome, and decreased the more often it occurs without the outcome or vice versa. Studies across a range of species and learning preparations have confirmed that learning is often highly sensitive to cue–outcome correlation (Rescorla 1968, Shanks 2004).

How can a learned emotional response such as fear be extinguished? After pairings of a cue and a feared outcome, the simple presentation of the now fear-inducing cue in the absence of the outcome will lead to a loss of associative strength. According to the equation above this comes about since the absence of the outcome is surprising: ΣV_i is large, and because λ for a null outcome is 0, the critical term, $\lambda - \Sigma V_i$, is large and negative, leading to a reduction in the associative strength of the cue. Rescorla has recently explored an elegant technique—motivated directly by the theory—for accelerating the rate of extinction. If a feared cue is extinguished in the presence of another feared cue, extinction will be twice as fast. Suppose that A→O and B→O trials lead A and B each to have asymptotic strength for an emotion-inducing outcome O. Subsequent AB→no O trials will cause A to lose associative strength much faster than typical A→no O extinction trials because the presence of B will lead to a supernormal error term. Specifically, ΣV_i is 2λ for the AB→no O treatment against λ for the A→no O treatment, hence the change in associative strength on each trial, ΔV_i, is doubled. Rescorla (2000) tested and confirmed this important prediction which has considerable implications for behaviour therapy (see COGNITIVE BEHAVIOUR THERAPY; PHOBIAS)

Although the Rescorla–Wagner theory explains many of the conditions that promote or impede extinction, its theoretical interpretation of extinction is probably incorrect. In the theory, extinction is simply the opposite of acquisition, in other words, the weakening of an associative connection. Yet extinction does not return a cue to its original neutral state. Instead, extinction often appears to be better described as new learning. The associations created during cue–outcome pairings are rarely unlearned. A change in context or even the mere passage of time is often sufficient to reawaken what earlier appeared to be an extinguished response. If extinction is carried out in a context (Y) different from the original training context (X), the response is likely to recur when the cue is again tested in context (X), even if it was completely extinguished in context (Y) (renewal). Alternatively, presentation of a small number of outcome events (e.g. electric shocks) after extinction of the cue is usually sufficient to re-establish responding to the cue (reinstatement).

Association formation can drive changes in affect. Under certain conditions, the pairing of an affectively neutral cue with an affectively *valenced (liked or disliked) outcome can engender transfer of affect from the outcome to the cue. Such transfer appears generally to follow the same rules as transfer of response tendencies in traditional conditioning procedures, suggesting that affective responses for these purposes function just like bodily responses such as approach and blinking (De Houwer et al. 2001, Field 2005). Indeed this form of learning is often termed 'evaluative conditioning'. Thus in a differential fear conditioning procedure in which one cue predicts shock and another does not, two types of learning take place: learning of the signalling values of the cues (measured by conventional means such as skin conductance), and learning to like or dislike them (measured by valence judgements).

Do these two forms of learning obey similar rules? The answer to this is still under debate, but in the main it seems they do. Both, for instance, are sensitive to the cue–outcome contingency. Early findings did suggest one important difference, namely that affective responses were exceptionally resistant to extinction. However, more recent studies have suggested that this is a property of the measurement method rather than a fundamental attribute of evaluative learning (Lipp et al. 2003).

Much debate has focused on the relationship between associative processing on the one hand and cognitive or information processing on the other (see UNCONSCIOUS EMOTIONS). To what extent is the formation and expression of associative knowledge automatic or unconscious? How does it relate to attention and working memory? Numerous studies, pioneered by Thorndike (1931), have asked whether associations can be formed in conditions in which the individual is unaware of the cue–outcome contingency. Other studies have asked whether associations—once learned—may be expressed automatically and without requiring attentional resources. In neither case, however, is the picture clear. Conditioning in the absence of awareness has frequently been reported, yet methodological issues have clouded interpretation. For instance, tests of awareness for the contingency between a cue and outcome are usually administered via a posttask questionnaire, raising problems of sensitivity and task demands. Lovibond and Shanks (2002) concluded that when better assessment methods are used, awareness

appears to be a necessary (but not sufficient) condition for learning.

The automatic expression of learned associations has been studied by, for example, measuring responses to cues presented in the unattended channel in a dichotic listening task. Dawson and Schell (1982) reported that learned responses to such unattended stimuli were sometimes evoked, but this effect was greater when there was evidence of a slippage of attention to the supposedly unattended channel. It seems quite possible that undetected slippage explains the remaining responses and that in the complete absence of attention to the cue, no evocation of learned responses is possible (Lachter et al. 2004). Similarly, conditioning has been shown to make demands on central attentional resources (Carter et al. 2003).

Another reason to suppose that the associations formed in typical learning conditions are represented in cognitive structures is that they can be strongly influenced by verbal mediation. After an individual has learned in the laboratory that a cue predicts shock, conditioned responses are dramatically reduced (i.e. extinguished) if verbal instructions are presented which explain that the cue–outcome relationship no longer holds. Indeed a learned discrimination can be reversed by instructions (McNally 1981). Of course, clinically such effects are usually partial and incomplete: phobias can rarely be eliminated simply by verbal instruction.

DAVID R SHANKS

De Houwer, J., Thomas, S., and Baeyens, F. (2001). Associative learning of likes and dislikes: a review of 25 years of research on human evaluative conditioning. *Psychological Bulletin*, **127**, 853–69.

Hermans, D., Craske, M.G., Mineka, S., and Lovibond, P.F. (2006). Extinction in human fear conditioning. *Biological Psychiatry*, **60**, 361–8.

Lovibond, P.F. and Shanks, D.R. (2002). The role of awareness in Pavlovian conditioning: empirical evidence and theoretical implications. *Journal of Experimental Psychology: Animal Behavior Processes*, **28**, 3–26.

Pearce, J.M. and Bouton, M.E. (2001). Theories of associative learning in animals. *Annual Review of Psychology*, **52**, 111–39.

Rescorla, R.A. (2000). Extinction can be enhanced by a concurrent excitor. *Journal of Experimental Psychology. Animal Behavior Processes*, **26**, 251–60.

attachment At its core, attachment theory attempts to account for social and personality development in people 'from the cradle to the grave' (Bowlby 1979, p. 129) (see INFANCY (EMOTIONAL DEVELOPMENT IN); CHILDHOOD EMOTIONAL DEVELOPMENT; AGEING (AND EMOTIONAL DEVELOPMENT)). However, it is also a theory that was developed to explain the experience, expression, and regulation of emotion (i.e. affect) at both normative (i.e. species-typical) and individual difference (i.e. person-specific) levels of analysis. This is not surprising given how important emotions and processes of affect regulation are to interpersonal functioning in all types of close relationships (see Mikulincer and Shaver 2005).

Bowlby (1969, 1973, 1980) believed that the attachment system serves two principal functions: (1) to protect vulnerable individuals from potential threats or harm, and (2) to regulate negative affect following threatening or harmful events (see REGULATION OF EMOTION). The normative component of attachment theory specifies the stimuli and contexts that typically should elicit and terminate different kinds of emotions plus the sequence of emotions that are routinely experienced in response to certain relational events (see below). The individual difference component articulates how an individual's personal history of receiving care and support from attachment figures shapes the goals, working models (e.g. interpersonal attitudes, if/then expectancies, and schemas), and coping strategies that s/he utilizes when emotion-eliciting events occur in relationships.

Normative features of emotions and emotion regulation

Bowlby's fascination with the emotional ties that bind humans to one another began with an astute observation from ethology. In all human cultures and most primate species, young and vulnerable infants display a specific sequence of reactions following separation from their stronger, older, and wiser caregivers. Immediately following separation, infants protest vehemently, typically crying, screaming, or throwing temper tantrums as they search for their caregivers (Bowlby 1969). Bowlby believed that vigorous protest during the early phases of caregiver absence is a good initial 'strategy' to promote survival, especially in species born in a developmentally immature and highly dependent state. Intense protests usually draw the attention of caregivers to their infants, who, during evolutionary history, would have been vulnerable to injury or predation if left unattended.

If, however, loud and persistent protests fail to retrieve the caregiver, infants enter a second stage, despair, during which their motor activity declines and they fall silent. From an evolutionary standpoint, Bowlby argued that despondency is a good 'second' strategy to promote survival. Excessive movement could result in accident or injury, and loud protests combined with movement might draw predators. Accordingly, if protests fail to retrieve the caregiver in due time, the next best survival strategy would be to avoid actions that would increase the risks of self-inflicted harm or predation.

Bowlby also observed that, after a period of despair, infants who are not reunited with their caregivers enter a third and final stage—detachment. During this phase, the infant begins to resume normal activity without the caregiver, learning to behave in an independent and self-reliant manner. Bowlby (1982) conjectured that the function of emotional detachment is to permit the formation of emotional bonds with new caregivers. He reasoned that emotional ties with previous caregivers have to be relinquished before new bonds can be fully formed. From the standpoint of evolution, detachment allows infants to cast off old ties and begin forming new ones with caregivers who may be able and willing to provide the resources necessary for survival. Bowlby surmised that these normative stages and processes also characterize reactions to prolonged or irrevocable separations in adult attachment-based relationships, which might also have evolutionary adaptive value with regard to maintaining, casting aside, or creating new romantic pair-bonds.

Individual difference features of emotions and emotion regulation

Scholars following in the footsteps of Bowlby have proposed that different attachment patterns (in children) and attachment styles/orientations (in adults) reflect different ways of regulating affect, particularly controlling and dampening negative affect elicited in stressful, threatening, or challenging situations (Kobak and Sceery 1988, Simpson 1990, Mikulincer et al. 1993). Systematic individual differences in patterns of attachment in 12–18-month-old children were first documented by Mary Ainsworth and her colleagues (Ainsworth et al. 1978) using the Strange Situation. The Strange Situation involves a sequence of separations and reunions between caregivers (usually mothers) and their children. It assesses how children regulate negative emotions vis-à-vis their primary caregivers when they are upset. Although most children are visibly distressed when left alone at this age, securely attached children effectively use their caregivers as a 'secure base' to reduce negative affect and resume other activities fairly soon after reuniting with them. Anxious-resistant children, on the other hand, remain distressed and typically show signs of anger or resentment toward their caregivers during reunion episodes. And anxious-avoidant children, who show fewer overt signs of distress but tend to have elevated heart rates, remain distant and emotionally detached from their caregivers during reunions, opting to calm themselves in a self-reliant manner.

During later stages of development, therefore, one of the key differences between secure and different types of insecure individuals is how negative affect is regulated and controlled given the specific beliefs and expectancies that individuals have about the availability of comfort and support from their current attachment figures. According to Kobak and Sceery (1988), for example, highly secure individuals have learned through their own caregiving experiences to follow 'rules' that permit distress to be acknowledged and encourage them to rely on attachment figures as sources of comfort and support. Highly avoidant adults, on the other hand, have learned from their past caregiving experiences to follow rules that limit the acknowledgement of distress and encourage the use of self-reliant tactics to control and mitigate negative affect when it arises. And highly anxious people have learned to use rules that direct their attention toward their distress and to the possibility that their attachment figures may not meet their strong needs for comfort.

Expanding upon these ideas, Mikulincer and Shaver (2003) have developed a process model that explains the sequence of events that underlies the emotional coping and regulation strategies of people who have different attachment histories. For example, when stress or potential threats are perceived, highly secure individuals remain confident that their attachment figures will be attentive, responsive, and available to meet their needs and help them lower their distress/anxiety. These beliefs, in turn, increase their level of felt security, deactivating their attachment systems, and allowing more secure individuals to use constructive, problem-focused coping strategies that, over time, are more likely to solve or resolve chronic problems.

Highly insecure individuals, on the other hand, follow different emotional pathways. When highly anxious individuals encounter attachment-relevant stress or threats, they are uncertain that their attachment figures will be sufficiently attentive, available, and responsive to their needs. Such worries sustain their distress and keep their attachment systems 'on-line', resulting in the deployment of emotion-focused coping strategies (e.g. hypervigilance to signs of possible relationship loss, rumination about worst-case scenarios). When highly avoidant individuals feel stressed or threatened, they experience—but may not consciously acknowledge—anxiety at a physiological level. To keep their attachment systems deactivated, however, highly avoidant persons try to inhibit and control their emotional reactions by deploying avoidant coping strategies.

These three emotion regulation/coping strategies—problem-focused, emotion-focused, and avoidance-focused—are believed to drive many of the interesting cognitive and behavioural outcomes found in people who have different attachment styles/orientations (see Mikulincer and Shaver, 2003, for a review). More securely attached individuals, for example, experience more intense and mild positive emotions in their romantic relationships as well as fewer intense and mild negative emotions, whereas the reverse is true of more insecurely attached persons (Simpson 1990). Recent longitudinal research has also documented connections between early attachment patterns with mothers (i.e. being classified as secure versus insecure in the Strange Situation at age 1) and emotions experienced and expressed with romantic partners 20 years later in life. Specifically, individuals classified as insecure in the Strange Situation at age 1 tend to be rated by their teachers as being less socially competent during early primary/elementary school (years/grades 1–3). Lower social competence, in turn, predicts greater likelihood of being rated as insecurely attached to same-sex friends at age 16, which in turn predicts the experience and expression of greater negative affect in relationships with romantic partners when individuals are in their early 20s (Simpson *et al.* 2007). Thus, indirect but theoretically meaningful links exist between early attachment experiences and later attachment-based relationships in early adulthood, as Bowlby anticipated.

Conclusion
In conclusion, the experience, expression, and regulation of emotion—particularly negative emotion in response to events capable of triggering the attachment system—are central to attachment theory. The theory offers a unique account of both the normative and individual-specific processes that govern the regulation of emotions in close relationships.

JEFFRY A. SIMPSON AND LANE BECKES

attention and emotion Emotional processing involves both registration of the affective significance of events or stimuli in the environment, and adaptation of the current bodily and cognitive states in order to respond appropriately to these events. Changes in attention and awareness are among the most essential effects of emotions on cognitive operations, and recent research in human neuroscience has begun to reveal specific neural pathways that are responsible for many reciprocal interactions between emotion and attention.

Because perceptual systems have a limited capacity and cannot represent all stimuli that are bombarding our senses at any given moment, our brain has evolved complex mechanisms of attention allowing us to select salient or goal-relevant information. However, different mechanisms of selection may operate in parallel, and some of these may be driven by emotional processes in a relatively direct and unconscious manner. Behaviourally, a large number of attentional paradigms show that perception is facilitated for emotionally significant stimuli as compared with neutral ones. These include: visual search tasks where the detection of a target among distractors is quicker when the target is emotional rather than neutral (Öhman *et al.* 2001); attentional blink tasks or rapid serial visual presentations with masking where emotional items are missed less often than neutral items (Anderson and Phelps 2001); dot probe tasks where a target is reported faster or discriminated better when it is preceded by a cue with some emotional compared with neutral value at the same location (so-called valid cues) or compared with a cue with emotional value at another location (so-called invalid cues) (Phelps *et al.* 2006). Greater efficiency of search for emotional targets does not imply that emotional stimuli 'pop out' like targets defined by elementary features (e.g. colour), as sometimes interpreted in early studies, but rather that detection time slopes are shallower for emotional than neutral targets with increasing number of distractors, and therefore suggest that selective attention is preferentially 'guided' towards emotional items during search. Emotional processing may also enhance perception for stimuli presented under conditions of binocular rivalry or binocular suppression, and expand the breadth of attentional focus. Conversely, emotional stimuli may increase the cost of distractors during flanker tasks, visual search, or saccadic eye movements, and Stroop-like interference is observed in classification tasks when words are emotional rather than neutral, indicating that the emotional meaning of the stimuli may be extracted and influence selective attention even without conscious intention.

Emotional influences on attentional performance have been found not only with a variety of stimuli (e.g. faces, scenes, words, voices) but also with a range of different emotional dimensions. A majority of studies have reported stronger effects with negative or threat-related stimuli such as angry faces, snakes, or spiders (Öhman *et al.* 2001), but similar effects may also arise with positive or appetitive stimuli including baby faces (Brosch *et al.* 2007). This has been taken to suggest that arousal or self-relevance might be the critical factors responsible for emotional effects on attention, rather than threat *per se* (see RELEVANCE DETECTION). Nevertheless, threat cues might often be more effective because their emotional significance or relevance may be less dependent on context and task characteristics.

Many of these behavioural effects may vary between individuals and be partly modulated by some personality traits. This has been demonstrated in studies using visual search, cueing, blink, as well as Stroop tasks. Thus, enhanced detection of emotional targets or interference by emotional distractors tend to be amplified in people with higher anxiety, greater harm avoidance, or specific phobias. For instance, attention is directed faster to pictures of snakes than spiders in snake phobics, but vice versa in spider phobics (Öhman *et al.* 2001). This individual sensitivity may result from differences at various stages of both emotional and attentional processing (Bishop 2007). Moreover, because emotional influences on attention may affect either orienting towards, or disengagement away

from, emotional information, these different attentional components might be differentially modulated by anxiety factors (see ANXIETY; PHOBIAS).

At the brain level, neurophysiological and neuroimaging results also converge to indicate enhanced neural processing for emotionally arousing stimuli relative to neutral information, across different sensory modalities and different emotion categories. In the visual domain, 'boosting' of the neural responses to emotional stimuli may arise at several stages along the visual pathways, including primary visual cortex in occipital lobe and higher-level areas associated with object and face recognition. Such emotional modulation is typically found in cortical regions selective to the stimulus category, suggesting enhanced representation within neuronal populations coding for a specific stimulus type. For instance, scenes with emotional content produce greater activation in the lateral occipital cortex as compared with neutral scenes (Sabatinelli *et al.* 2005), whereas faces with emotional expressions (such as fear) produce selective increases in the fusiform face area (FFA; Vuilleumier *et al.* 2004) and emotional body expressions activate both the fusiform and extrastriate body areas (FBA and EBA). Likewise, in the auditory domain, vocal and nonvocal sounds with emotional significance (such as prosody, animal cries, or gunshots) may evoke significantly higher neural responses in auditory cortical areas as compared with similar but more mundane sounds (Grandjean *et al.* 2005). This emotional boosting may arise for a variety of different emotions but is often greater for negative or threat-related stimuli. It is also observed selectively for stimuli from the feared animal category in people with phobias, but not for similar stimuli in people without phobias (Sabatinelli *et al.* 2005). Similar increases have also been observed in visual cortex of monkeys in response to monkey faces with threatening expressions, which are defined by different features from human expressions.

These enhanced cortical activations are similar to the effects of selective attention on perceptual processing, and might thus mediate the enhanced attentional performance for emotional stimuli as observed in behavioural tasks. Selective attention is thought to involve a modulation of sensory pathways by top-down signals from higher regions in parietal and frontal cortex (Maunsell 2004), which can be generated by endogenous factors related to current *goals and internal needs, or exogenous factors such as abrupt changes and sensory saliency. Thus, frontal and parietal cortical regions are responsible for the ability to direct attention towards a particular location or object in a scene, and to enhance its representation by boosting neural activity in the corresponding sensory pathways, in preference to the representation of concurrent distractors. However, although attentional systems in frontal and parietal cortex might be influenced by emotional inputs (Maunsell 2004), there is abundant evidence that emotional influences on neural responses may involve distinct top-down signals that can act directly on sensory cortices, and thus operate partly independently or additively to the fronto-parietal attention system.

The *amygdala is thought to provide a major source for such direct emotional influences on sensory processing. Not only does it receive abundant inputs from all sensory modalities but it also sends dense projections back to many cortical regions, which could serve to amplify neural responses to emotionally salient stimuli, and perhaps promote learning or tuning to these stimuli (Freese and Amaral 2005). In vision, while sensory inputs converge primarily in the lateral nucleus of the amygdala, feedback connections project mainly from the basal nucleus towards all areas from the primary visual cortex (VI) to higher areas in the ventral temporal cortex (TE), with a precise topographic organization from posterior to anterior regions; area TE receives additional projections from the lateral and accessory basal nuclei (see Fig. A9). Interestingly, in monkeys, the densest projections target the superior temporal sulcus (STS), corresponding to regions that contain neurons with selective responses to faces (Freese and Amaral 2005). A similar pattern has been observed in the auditory system. These feedback loops might be ideally suited to provide a modulatory signal to cortical areas in response to emotional stimuli activating the amygdala, and potentially amenable to regulation through inputs from the *orbitofrontal cortex to the basal nucleus of the amygdala. In humans, the functional importance of

these projections has been demonstrated by both behavioural and neuroimaging studies of patients with damage to the amygdala. These patients do not show the normal advantage of emotional relative to neutral stimuli in attentional tasks (Anderson and Phelps 2001). Furthermore, amygdaloidal lesions may abolish the normal enhancement of cortical responses to emotional faces in visual areas within the ipsilesional hemisphere, while leaving intact the normal modulation by voluntary attention that is presumably driven by top-down signals from fronto-parietal areas (Vuilleumier et al. 2004). By contrast, patients with right parietal damage who are unable to direct attention towards the left side of space (hemispatial neglect syndrome) may still show enhanced activation of the visual cortex and enhanced detection for emotional relative to neutral stimuli in their impaired left hemispace.

Further evidence for parallel modulation by emotional and attentional processes has also been provided in healthy subjects by imaging studies that manipulated these two factors separately (see Fig. A10). For instance, an early functional magnetic resonance imaging (fMRI) experiment compared brain responses to fearful and neutral faces when faces appeared either at task-relevant or irrelevant locations (i.e. inside or outside the focus of attention) and found that even though activity of face-sensitive regions in fusiform cortex was reduced when attention was directed away from faces, rather than focused on faces, fusiform activity was always greater for fearful than neutral faces irrespective of whether faces were task-relevant or not (Vuilleumier et al. 2004). In other words, fear expression produced a significant boost to fusiform activity, in addition to the effect of spatial attention on this region. Moreover, the amygdala also responded to fearful expression regardless of spatial attention, suggesting that it could provide the source of this emotional modulation. A similar pattern was found in temporal cortex for voices with either emotional (angry) or neutral prosody that were presented to either task-relevant or irrelevant ears during a dichotic task (Grandjean et al. 2005), and in occipito-temporal cortex for emotional visual scenes that were presented in one visual hemifield, on either the same or different side to the current direction of voluntary attention (Keil et al. 2005). Taken together, these findings suggest that additive influences from emotion (operating largely without voluntary control) and attention (under voluntary control) may act simultaneously on similar cortical pathways to enhance perception, with emotional signals serving to enhance detection of potentially significant events arising outside the focus of attention. However, some studies suggested that emotional responses in both the amygdala and cortex might be suppressed when emotional signals are too weak or

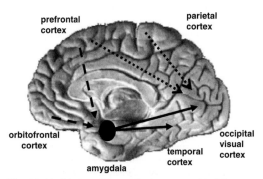

Fig. A9. Medial view of human brain anatomy. Modulatory influences on sensory processing in visual cortex involve top-down signals from parietal and frontal cortex for voluntary attention (dotted lines), as well as feedback signals from amygdala for emotional regulation (full lines). Feedback loops from amygdala might in turn be modulated by inputs from prefrontal and orbitofrontal areas (dashed lines).

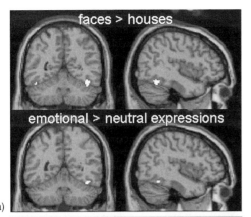

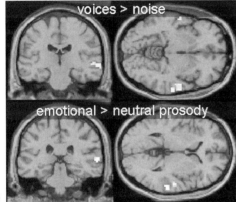

(a)

(b)

Fig. A10. Enhancement of cortical responses by emotional relative to neutral stimuli. (a) Faces with a fearful relative to neutral expression produce increased fMRI activation in fusiform cortex, overlapping with the fusiform area selectively activated by faces (FFA) as compared with houses. (b) Similarly, voices with angry prosody produce increased fMRI activation in temporal cortex, overlapping with an area in the superior temporal gyrus selectively activated by human voices as compared with noises with similar acoustic energy.

emotional responses have been recorded over frontal regions (or directly in orbitofrontal cortex) around 120 ms, prior to latencies of components usually associated with face and object categorization or associated with visual awareness (around 170–200 ms). This would be consistent with the idea that some emotional appraisal may arise prior to selective attention and influence ongoing perceptual processes within cortical areas. Accordingly, recordings of face-responsive neurons in temporal cortex of monkeys show that the initial phase of their responses discriminates faces from other object categories, while subsequent phases are modulated by emotional expression or familiarity, possibly through feedback signals received from the amygdala or other limbic regions.

Although these data converge to suggest that the amygdala may receive rapid sensory information prior to full cortical analysis, the exact pathways conveying this information remain undetermined (Rudrauf *et al.* 2008). A direct 'quick and dirty' subcortical route has been suggested based on animal studies showing that fear conditioning in the amygdala may still arise after the removal of sensory cortices, and human studies showing that amygdaloid responses may still be obtained for emotional faces presented in the blind visual field of patients with occipital damage (Morris *et al.* 2001), or presented in subliminal conditions (e.g. masked) in healthy subjects (Pessoa 2005). Alternatively, quick responses of the amygdala might arise through an initial feedforward sweep of processing along the visual pathways, consistent with some models of vision proposing that early activation in prefrontal or temporal areas based on coarse stimulus information might then serve to guide further cortical processing for conscious recognition and awareness (Bar 2004). Both a two-pathways and a two-stages mechanism would be consistent with recent neuroimaging findings that responses of the amygdala to fearful faces may be driven by coarse visual information (such as low spatial frequency or wide-open eyes) that does not optimally activate cortical areas (see Fig. A11) (Vuilleumier *et al.* 2003, Whalen *et al.* 2004). Coarse but fast processing of low spatial frequency information is known to occur in magnocellular pathways, phylogenetically derived from the primitive tectal (brainstem) visual system that exists in lower nonmammal species and is already functioning at birth in humans (unlike the more sophisticated cortical visual pathways). By contrast, cortical processing may rely more strongly or additionally on high spatial frequency information that is conveyed by slower parvocellular visual pathways. Moreover, low spatial frequency processing through magnocellular pathways is also responsible for motion perception, and provides the main source of retinal inputs from the peripheral visual field, two functional properties that might also be

reduced by high perceptual competition (Pessoa *et al.* 2002), but cortical responses were abolished even for neutral stimuli in the latter case.

Studies using event-related potentials (ERPs) reveal that emotional information may influence cortical responses at several processing stages (Olofsson *et al.* 2008). These differential effects may affect early perceptual components (100–200 ms postonset) related to initial sensory processing and attention (e.g. P1 or N1), as well as those related to stimulus recognition (e.g. N170 or posterior negative waveforms) (Schupp *et al.* 2006). Remarkably, very early

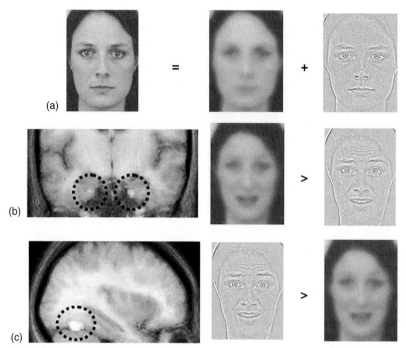

Fig. A11. Responses to faces in human fusiform cortex and amygdala. (a) Any visual stimulus contains both crude configural information (at low spatial frequencies of the image) and more detailed information (at high spatial frequencies of the image). (b) Activation of the amygdala is driven by coarse inputs at low spatial frequencies. (c) By contrast, activation of the fusiform cortex is driven by information at higher spatial frequencies.

important for efficient monitoring of significant events occurring outside the focus of attention.

Nevertheless, it remains unresolved to what extent emotional processing may arise without attention or prior to awareness, and in which processing pathways (Pessoa 2005). Pre-attentive or unconscious responses to emotional stimuli (as well as neutral stimuli for that matter) have been well established by many behavioural and neuroimaging studies (see UNCONSCIOUS EMOTIONS), but may potentially vary as a function of several factors such as concurrent task load, anticipation, habituation, or individual personality differences. Imaging and ERP studies comparing brain responses to emotional stimuli presented in attended or ignored conditions have reported partly discrepant results concerning respon-siveness of the amygdala, including an absence of sig-nificant different modulation (Vuilleumier *et al.* 2004), suppression of responses (Pessoa *et al.* 2002), unequal enhancements for either emotional or neutral stimuli, as well as modulations that vary with task demands. Fur-thermore, the effectiveness of emotional processing and

its attenuation by attentional control or goal settings might depend on anxiety levels (Bishop 2007) or other internal states, possibly implicating projections to the amygdala from orbitofrontal and cingulate cortex, as well as their reciprocal connections with other pre-frontal areas. These connections might provide the neural pathways through which emotional limbic cir-cuits might impact on ongoing cognitive processes me-diated by dorsal and lateral prefrontal areas, or vice versa.

Finally, although past research has concentrated on the amygdala and threat processing, other regions of the brain might be implicated in regulating attention based on affective or motivational cues. In particular, much remains to be explored concerning interactions between attention and reward (Maunsell 2004).

PATRIK VUILLEUMIER

Compton, R.J. (2003). The interface between emotion and attention: a review of evidence from psychology and neuroscience. *Behavioral and Cognitive Neuroscience Reviews*, **2**, 115–29.

Vuilleumier, P. (2005). How brains beware: neural mechanisms of emotional attention. *Trends in Cognitive Science*, **9**, 585–94.

attitudes (structure and change)

Attitudes refer to people's global evaluations of any object such as oneself, other people, issues, and so forth (see EVALUATIVE PROCESSING). Persuasion is said to occur when a person's attitude toward some object changes. Since Aristotle's (384–322 BC) *Rhetoric*, emotions have been assumed to play an important role in the structure of people's attitudes and in the processes by which they are modified. We consider each topic in turn.

Attitude structure

Emotion has traditionally been assumed to be a part of the underlying structure of attitudes. That is, attitudes are often conceptualized as consisting of three components: affective (emotional), cognitive, and behavioural (Katz and Stotland 1959). The overall attitude is assumed to be stored separately from the affective, cognitive, and behavioural information on which it is based. Although the three bases of attitudes are positively correlated with each other, they are separable constructs, and the attitude toward any given object can be based on affective, cognitive, or behavioural information (Cacioppo *et al.* 1989). There are also individual differences in the extent to which people's attitudes are based on affect versus cognition (Huskinson and Haddock 2004).

Importantly, there are meaningful consequences of the bases of an attitude. For example, Millar and Tesser (1986) showed that instrumental behaviours (those performed to accomplish a *goal independent of the behaviour itself) are driven primarily by cognitively based attitudes, whereas consummatory behaviours (those performed because the behaviour is intrinsically rewarding) are driven more by *affect. Chaiken *et al.* (1995) showed that when attitudes toward an object were inconsistent with the underlying affect or cognition associated with that object, the attitude was unstable. Furthermore, as discussed next, a growing body of research indicates that attitudes based largely on affect versus cognition are changed differently.

Attitude change

Messages using emotion: Just as attitudes can be sorted into those that are based primarily on emotion versus cognition (Crites *et al.* 1994), so too can persuasive appeals. The dominant finding in the literature is for a matching effect. That is, attitudes based primarily on affect are more easily changed with messages relying on emotion, and attitudes based primarily on cognition are more easily changed with informational appeals (Fabrigar and Petty 1999). This matching effect also holds for people who tend to base their attitudes on affect versus cognition (Huskinson and Haddock 2004).

The type of emotional message that has been the most studied is the fear appeal, perhaps because of its great potential relevance to health communications (see HEALTH AND EMOTION). The dominant theoretical perspective on fear appeals is *protection motivation theory* (Rogers 1983). Consistent with expectancy-value theories, this model holds that fear appeals will be effective to the extent that the message convinces the recipient that the consequences of not following the recommendation are very undesirable and very likely to occur. This theory also holds that effective fear messages should convey that the negative consequences are highly likely to be avoided if the recommended action is followed and that the recipient has the requisite skills to take the recommended action. These conditions reduce the likelihood that defence motives will lead people to dismiss or ignore the message.

Incidental emotions: In addition to studying emotion that is part of a persuasive message, researchers have examined how emotion that is incidental to the communication influences attitudes. For example, if emotions were produced by a television programme that preceded a political advertisement and not by the advertisement itself, what effect would this have on attitudes? Contemporary theories of persuasion such as the elaboration likelihood model (ELM; Petty and Cacioppo 1986) and heuristic-systematic model (HSM; Chaiken *et al.* 1989) provide a framework from which to understand these effects. The ELM in particular indicates that emotions play different roles depending on the level of cognitive effort individuals allocate to a persuasive message.

Low-thinking conditions: According to the ELM, when thinking is low (when people are unwilling or unable to scrutinize attitude-relevant information because, for example, it is low in personal relevance or many distractions are present), variables such as a person's emotional state have an impact on attitudes by the operation of relatively simple, low-effort processes such as forming a direct association between the feeling state and the attitude object. Or, emotion could serve as part of an affect or 'How do I feel about it' heuristic (e.g., I feel good, so I must like it or choose it; Schwarz and Clore 1988, Slovic *et al.* 2002) (see AFFECT-AS-INFORMATION MODEL). Under low-thinking conditions, an emotion generally impacts on attitudes in a manner consistent with its *valence. Thus, incidental positive affect produces more positive attitudes toward an object, but incidental negative affect elicits more negative attitudes. Early demonstrations of this phenomenon can be found in the extensive research on mere exposure and evaluative conditioning (Zajonc and Markus 1982). Repeatedly presenting an object or pairing it with stimuli that bring about positive feelings can lead to more positive attitudes compared with presenting the object a few times or pairing it with stimuli that produce negative reactions.

High-thinking conditions: Incidental affect can also influence attitudes under high-thinking conditions, but the processes are different. Under high-thinking conditions, when people are carefully scrutinizing persuasive messages for merit, emotional states themselves can also be scrutinized for their information value. Thus, for example, sadness (an emotion with negative value as a simple cue under low-thinking conditions) could be a positive attribute of a movie drama when processed as an argument (Martin *et al.* 1997). If the emotion is not scrutinized as evidence or is dismissed in this regard, it can still affect judgements by biasing one's evaluation of the evidence—especially if that evidence is ambiguous. Forgas (1995) refers to this as an *affect infusion* effect. Indeed, research suggests that *moods and emotions can affect the thoughts that come to mind when processing a message (Petty *et al.* 1993) as well as perceptions of the likelihood of various outcomes described in the message. For example, in one study (DeSteno *et al* 2004) participants who were made to feel sad rather than angry prior to receiving a message showed an increased estimate of the likelihood of sad versus angering consequences, and thus were more influenced by a message advocating that sad rather than angering consequences would follow the failure to adopt a recommendation. Participants made to feel angry were more persuaded by the message pointing to angering consequences.

Emotion can also affect confidence in people's thoughts in response to a persuasive message. Under high-thinking conditions, not only are people influenced by the number and valence of thoughts that they generate, but also by the confidence they have in those thoughts. The more confidence people have in their thoughts, the more they will use them to form attitudes (Petty *et al.* 2002). *Appraisal theories of emotion suggest that some emotions are related to certainty whereas others are linked to doubt (Smith and Ellsworth 1985). For example, happiness and anger are associated with more confidence than sadness and surprise. Thus, in high-thought conditions, experiencing the emotions associated with confidence after thought generation should be more *self-validating* and should therefore lead to greater use of the thoughts than experiencing the emotions associated with doubt. Consistent with this idea, Briñol *et al.* (2007) manipulated whether message recipients experienced happiness or sadness after a persuasive message. When the message was strong (and thoughts were thus mostly favourable), people who were happy following message processing were more persuaded than those who were sad. How-

ever, when participants received a weak message on the same topic (and thoughts were mostly unfavourable), the effects of the emotion induction were reversed. Furthermore, the self-validation effects for emotion were confined to high-thinking conditions. In contrast, under low-thinking conditions, emotions had a direct effect on attitudes, consistent with a simple cue effect.

Unconstrained thinking conditions: Emotions can also affect attitudes by influencing the extent of information processing when it is not already constrained by other variables to be high or low. In one early experiment, Bless *et al.* (1990) found that sad mood induced prior to a message created greater processing (a larger influence of argument quality on thoughts and attitudes; Petty and Cacioppo 1986) than happy mood.

Several theories have been proposed to explain why happiness tends to lead to less information processing than sadness. One view—*the affect-as-information* framework (Schwarz and Clore 1988)—holds that individuals' emotions serve as informational cues regarding the status of their environment. Negative affective states inform individuals that their current environment is problematic, and therefore engender a relatively high level of effortful processing to deal with this situation. In contrast, positive states signal that the current situation is safe and, therefore, do not require a high level of cognitive effort. Another possibility is suggested by the *hedonic contingency model* (Wegener *et al.* 1995). This framework suggests that individuals in a happy state will process less if the message is expected to undermine one's positive state. However, if the message is expected to induce positive feelings, then happiness will not undermine processing and may even increase it beyond neutral or sad states. A third explanation relies on the association between emotions and certainty. Specifically, emotions such as happiness and anger, which are associated with certainty, should decrease information processing relative to emotions such as sadness and surprise, which are associated with uncertainty (Tiedens and Linton 2001). Which of these mechanisms is responsible for the impact of emotional states on information processing probably depends on what goals are salient to the person at the time and what information the emotion conveys in that context.

Corrections for perceived effects of emotion

In closing, we note that the effects of incidental emotions that we have addressed tend to occur primarily when the underlying cause of the emotion is not clear. However, if people are aware of the source of the emotion, they might not want it to exert any biasing impact on their judgement. When incidental affect becomes salient and people do not want their judgements to become biased by it, they may attempt to correct for its assumed biasing impact if they have the ability to do so. According to the flexible correction model (FCM; Wegener and Petty 1997), in such situations people will attempt to correct their judgements based on their naïve theory regarding the expected effect of the emotion on judgement.

Because corrective efforts work to avoid or remove perceived biases, the FCM holds that corrections proceed in a direction opposite to the perceived bias and in a magnitude commensurate with the expected size of the bias. Because emotions are believed by most people to create emotion-congruent judgements, attempts to correct for bias often reduce emotion-congruent biases and can result in emotion-incongruent outcomes. For example, in one study in which emotion was made salient (DeSteno et al. 2000), individuals under high-thinking conditions made judgements of *lower* likelihood for sad events when feeling sad rather than angry, and for angering events when feeling angry rather than sad—the opposite of the normal biasing pattern, suggesting an overcorrection for a presumed bias.

Summary

There are many ways that emotions contribute to attitudes and persuasion. First, affect has long been recognized as one of the fundamental bases of attitudes. In addition, when the affect associated with an object is consistent with the overall attitude, the attitude is generally more consequential than when the attitude is inconsistent with object-relevant affect. With respect to persuasion, appeals based on emotion are most effective in changing attitudes based on emotion. However, the effectiveness of emotional messages, especially fear appeals, depends on a number of other variables. Emotions can also influence attitude change even if they stem from sources extraneous to the persuasive communication. The impact of such emotions is the result of different processes depending on whether thinking is high, low, or unconstrained. Finally, if the source of an incidental emotion is salient, people will sometimes correct their judgements for the presumed effect of the emotion, sometimes creating the opposite bias in judgements due to overcorrection.

RICHARD E. PETTY, DUANE T. WEGENER,
AND LEANDRE R. FABRIGAR

Clore, G.L. and Schnall, S. (2005). The influence of affect on attitude. In: D. Albarracin, B. Johnson, and M. Zanna (eds), *The handbook of attitudes*, pp. 437–89. Mahwah, NJ: Lawrence Erlbaum Associates.

Petty, R.E. and Wegener, D.T. (1998). Attitude change: multiple roles for persuasion variables. In: D. Gilbert, S. Fiske, and G. Lindzey (eds), *The handbook of social psychology*, (4th edn), pp. 323–90. New York: McGraw-Hill.

Petty, R.E., Fabrigar, L.R., and Wegener, D.T. (2003). Emotional factors in attitudes and persuasion. In: R.J. Davidson, K.R. Scherer, and H.H. Goldsmith (eds), *Handbook of affective sciences*, pp. 752–72. Oxford: Oxford University Press.

Zanna, M.P. and Rempel, J.K. (1988). Attitudes: a new look at an old concept. In: D. Bar-Tal and A.W. Kruglanski (eds), *The social psychology of knowledge*, pp. 315–34. Cambridge: Cambridge University Press.

attractiveness Attractiveness is a physical quality of face, voice, or body that elicits positive responses, or 'attraction'. There is no 'gold standard' of attractiveness, but rather a variety of interchangeable currencies. Facial attractiveness is augmented by averageness, symmetry, certain sexually dimorphic qualities, a positive expression or behaviour, youthfulness, or familiarity (Rhodes and Zebrowitz 2002). The components of vocal attractiveness include a less nasal, less monotonous, and more resonant voice as well as a small range of vocal pitch, a more mature sounding voice in college students, and lower-pitched voices in men. There is a curvilinear relationship between body attractiveness and weight, with lower attractiveness associated with the extreme high and low ends of the distribution. Body attractiveness is also related to sexually dimorphic cues, higher for women with a more 'feminine' waist-to-hip ratio and higher for men with a more 'masculine' ratio. Although cultural factors have an influence on the qualities deemed attractive, particularly the body qualities, some universal process is implicated by cross-cultural agreement in judgements of facial attractiveness coupled with the finding that even young infants prefer attractive faces. The nature of that universal process remains an active area of investigation that tests hypotheses derived from evolutionary, social, developmental, and cognitive psychology. These hypotheses have focused primarily on sexual attraction, but they can also concern attraction to infants, peers, and leaders. In addition to elucidating the components of attractiveness, research has identified myriad social consequences. People attribute more positive psychological traits to individuals with more attractive faces, voices, and bodies—the attractiveness halo. This effect appears early in development, and it is culturally widespread, although the particular positive traits may depend upon cultural values. Moreover, more attractive individuals receive more positive social outcomes across the lifespan in several domains, including close relationships, encounters with strangers, school, employment, and criminal justice settings.

LESLIE A. ZEBROWITZ

attributional style Attributional style, or explanatory style, is a cognitive personality variable that reflects how people characteristically explain the causes of bad events (Peterson and Seligman 1984) (see ATTRIBUTION THEORY; APPRAISAL STYLE) The construct emerged from the reformulation of the learned helplessness model of *depression, where it was proposed to influence the extent of deficits following experience with uncontrollability (Abramson *et al.* 1978). Individuals who explain bad events in pessimistic terms, with causes that are relatively internal ('it's me'), stable ('it's going to last forever'), and global ('it's going to undermine everything I do'), are thought to experience greater disruption following uncontrollable bad events than their more optimistic counterparts.

Attributional style is measured with a self-report questionnaire that asks respondents to imagine good or bad events happening to them, to offer in their own words a causal explanation for the events, and to rate the attributed cause along the dimensions of internality, stability, and globality. Attributional style can also be measured by content analysis of written or spoken material in which good or bad events are described and explained. However assessed, an optimistic explanatory style has been linked to positive mood and good morale, to perseverance and effective problem solving, to achievement in a variety of domains, to popularity, to good health, and even to long life and freedom from trauma. In contrast to these benefits of an optimistic attributional style is the finding that individuals who offer optimistic explanations for bad events may underestimate their future likelihood.

Attributional style becomes more optimistic during the process of cognitive therapy for depression, and this change occurs in tandem with the alleviation of depressive symptoms. Intervention programmes that teach individuals to offer more optimistic explanations for bad events effectively prevent future episodes of depression.

CHRISTOPHER PETERSON

attribution theory Attribution theory refers to a set of ideas concerning phenomenal causality, or the perceived causes of events (see Heider 1958, Jones *et al.* 1972). Causal *beliefs play a central role in determining emotions, both of the actor as well as involved observers. For example, if personal success is inferred by the actor as caused by high ability, then pride is often experienced, while observers sharing this causal belief may feel envy. On the other hand, when failure is ascribed by the actor to lack of ability, then shame or humiliation is a dominant experience. Observers, on the other hand, tend to react with sympathy, although scorn and contempt are also potential and less frequent emotional reactions. Attributional analyses of emotion thus fall under the general rubric of *appraisal theory, with feelings determined by thoughts. It is presumed that attributional beliefs are sufficient causes of some emotions, although only a subset of emotions has attributional *antecedents. For example, happiness and unhappiness are outcome-

dependent, attribution-independent feelings, determined by perceived success and failure, regardless of why these outcomes came about.

It also has been contended that emotions goad action and bridge the gap between attributional thinking and doing (Weiner 1995). In the above examples of ability-produced failure, the actor is anticipated to withdraw following shame and humiliation, whereas the sympathetic observer will offer help or some other pro-social action. Thus, the attribution–affect–action sequences can be portrayed as:

Failure ascribed personally to low ability—shame and humiliation—withdrawal

Failure of other ascribed to low ability—sympathy—pro-social action such as help

Inasmuch as there are an indefinite number of perceived causes of positive and negative outcomes, attribution theorists have attempted to identify their common properties and arrange causes within a taxonomic scheme. These causal characteristics are central in determining emotional experience. Three properties or dimensions of causes have been isolated, labelled locus, stability, and controllability. For example, ability and effort are of internal locus to the actor. Although they are distinct causal beliefs, both give rise to pride when causing success because they share the property of internality. Stability refers to the duration of a cause. Aptitude, for example, in addition to being internal to the actor, endures over time. Hence, failures due to lack of aptitude as well as other stable causes give rise to feelings of hopelessness. Finally, causal *controllability concerns the extent to which the cause is subject to volitional change and therefore the outcome 'could have been otherwise'. Controllability is a key determinant of perceived responsibility and a variety of social emotions, including guilt and anger. For example, personal failure due to lack of effort, which is under personal control, tends to give rise to guilt, whereas failure caused by the intentional acts of another produces anger. These affective experiences stimulate disparate actions so that the attribution–affect–action sequences can be depicted as:

Personal failure—ascribed to lack of effort—guilt—increased studying

Personal failure—ascribed to bad intentions of another—anger—retaliation

Causes elicit numerous emotions and overdetermined behaviours inasmuch as they have multiple properties. Failure to due lack of aptitude, for example, reduces personal esteem, promotes feelings of hopelessness, and elicits shame, three emotions that contribute to withdrawal from the setting.

In addition to the many feelings already mentioned (anger, contempt, envy, guilt, hopelessness, pride, self-esteem, shame, and sympathy), other affects elicited by causal beliefs include admiration (success of other due to internal causes), gratitude (personal success ascribed to volitional help from others, or external controllable causality), regret (internal controllable causality), and schadenfreude (failure of another following undeserved success) (see Hareli and Weiner 2002). Each of these emotions also has motivational significance. For example, admiration gives rise to positive interpersonal actions, while gratitude promotes reciprocation that 'evens the scales of justice'. In sum, causal attributions provide important insights into an extensive array of emotional experiences and motivated behaviour.

BERNARD WEINER

Schutz, P.A. and Pekrun, R. (eds) (2007). *Emotion in education.* Amsterdam: Elsevier/Academic Press.

Weiner, B. (2006). *Social motivation, justice, and the moral emotions.* Mahwah, NJ: Lawrence Erlbaum Associates.

autism Autism is a *spectrum* condition, in that it is manifested in varying degrees of severity. At one extreme a person may have no social skills, no language, and major learning difficulties. At the other end of this spectrum, a person may have normal or even above average IQ, precocious vocabulary development (though a lack of interest in small-talk or chatting), and social skills that are only odd by virtue of being one-sided or extremely self-centred. The former case would receive a diagnosis of classic autism. The latter case would receive a diagnosis of Asperger syndrome (AS). Both represent subgroups on the autistic spectrum. Both also share a strong preference for routines and repetition, and where the intellectual style is narrow and deep an 'obsessional' interest in highly specific topics. Up to 1% of the population are somewhere on the autistic spectrum.

Psychological aspects

The empathizing–systemizing (E-S) theory holds that there are empathizing deficits in autism, whilst systemizing is either intact or superior. *Empathy involves two major elements: (1) the ability to put oneself into someone else's shoes, to imagine their thoughts and feelings, and (2) having an emotional reaction that is appropriate to the other person's mental state (such as sympathy). Some children and adults with AS only show their empathizing deficits on age-appropriate adult tests. This deficit in empathizing underlies the difficulties such children have in social and communicative development and in the imagination of others' minds. Systemizing is the drive to analyse systems, in order to understand and predict the behaviour of inanimate events. Systems include technical, natural, and abstract systems. We make sense of systems in terms of under-

lying rules. People with autistic spectrum conditions show a precocious understanding of systems relative to their mental age. Moreover, the unusually strong repetitive behaviour, a strong desire for routines, and a 'need for sameness' can be interpreted in terms of the person's strong drive to systemize—striving to identify rules and regularities. Systemizing also requires excellent attention to detail, to understand what controls a system. This has been demonstrated on visual search tasks. The strong systemizing underlies the strengths that people with autism and AS have, whilst the empathizing deficits underlie the difficulties that they have (see Figs A12 and A13).

Neurobiological aspects

Anatomical abnormalities have been identified in many brain areas in autism. These include the cerebellum, the brainstem, frontal lobes, parietal lobes, hippocampus, and the *amygdala. Epilepsy also occurs in classic autism. In terms of neuropathology, the number of Purkinje cells in the cerebellar cortex is abnormally low. Abnormalities in the density of packing of neurons in the hippocampus, amygdala, and other parts of the limbic system have also been reported. Functional neuroimaging suggests

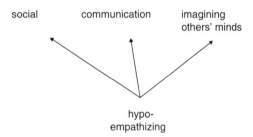

Fig. A12. Triad of difficulties.

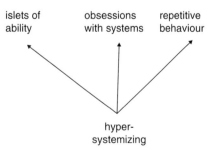

Fig. A13. Triad of strengths.

increased activity in sensory areas of the brain normally associated with stimulus-driven processing, and decreased activity in areas normally associated with higher-cognitive processing. Magnetic resonance imaging (MRI) morphometry shows volume deficits in the cerebellum, the brainstem, and posterior corpus callosum. Regarding the cerebellar abnormalities, a subgroup shows increased cerebellar volume. Using either MRI volumetric analysis or measures of head circumference, the autistic brain appears to involve transient postnatal macroencephaly. Using functional MRI (fMRI), abnormalities in autism have also been found in the amygdala and the orbito- and the medial frontal cortex, and these are associated with the empathizing deficits.

Genetic and hormonal aspects
The sibling risk-rate for autism is approximately 4.5%, or a four-fold increase over general population rates. Regarding twin studies, when a narrow phenotype is considered, 60% of monozygotic (MZ) pairs are concordant for autism versus no dizygotic (DZ) pairs. When a broader phenotype is considered, 92% of MZ pairs are concordant versus 10% of DZ pairs. Molecular genetic studies are under way. The marked sex ratio in autism may reflect genes and/or hormonal factors. Currently there are clues that foetal testosterone (FT) may play a role: within normal development, FT is inversely correlated with frequency of eye contact, rate of vocabulary development, empathy and social skills; and within normal development, FT is positively correlated with narrow interests and systemizing.

Early diagnosis and intervention
The earliest age at which classic autism has been reliably diagnosed is at 18 months, following a screening using an instrument called the CHAT (Checklist for Autism in Toddlers) which tests for the absence of 'joint attention' behaviours such as pointing and gaze following, and the absence of pretend play, all behaviours that are normally present by this age. Asperger syndrome has been reliably diagnosed by age 5 years, following a screening using an instrument called the CAST (Childhood Asperger Screening Test). The most effective interventions are special education, such as social skills teaching and speech therapy, the key ingredients being that the methods are highly structured, intensive, one-to-one, and begin early.

SIMON BARON-COHEN

Baron-Cohen, S. and Belmonte, M.K. (2005). Autism: a window onto the development of the social and the analytic brain. *Annual Review of Neuroscience*, **28**, 109–26.

Baron-Cohen, S., Knickmeyer, R.C., and Belmonte, M.K. (2005). Sex differences in the brain: implications for explaining autism. *Science*, **310**, 819–23.

Frith, U. (2006). *Autism: explaining the enigma*. Oxford: Blackwell.

<http://www.nas.org.uk/> The National Autistic Society is the main charity in the UK for families with a child on the autistic spectrum.

<http://www.autismresearchcentre.com/> The Autism Research Centre, Cambridge University, contains a searchable database of publications.

automatic appraisal The notion of automatic appraisal accommodates important observations regarding the elicitation of emotions. A first observation is that there are few if any one-to-one relations between stimuli and emotions. The same emotion (e.g. *anger) can be produced by different stimuli (e.g. an insult, a computer crash), and the same stimulus (e.g. an insult) can lead to different emotions (e.g. anger, *fear) on different occasions or in different individuals. Appraisal is invoked to explain this variable relation. It is the process that determines whether an emotion follows, and which one (see APPRAISAL THEORIES). Appraisal theorists have listed a number of appraisal variables or criteria, each of which deals with a specific aspect of the encounter, such as *novelty, *goal relevance, *motive consistency, *intrinsic pleasantness, *agency/intentionality, and *coping potential. The values of these variables combine into patterns of appraisal, which determine the nature of the ensuing emotion.

A second observation is that emotions are often elicited unexpectedly and unbidden. Thus, it is assumed that appraisal is often automatic. Most appraisal theorists assume that appraisal comes in (at least) two flavours: one is automatic, the other is nonautomatic. The assumption that appraisal can and often does occur in an automatic way is not an accessory assumption. Within the prevailing scientific climate, a process is accepted as a valid cause of emotions only when it is able to operate in an automatic sense. The notion of automatic appraisal also dovetails with the idea that emotions are adaptive in that they are able to mobilize the organism in a fast, automatic sense (e.g. in response to a life-threatening event).

The concept of automaticity is an umbrella term for a number of independent features such as unconscious, uncontrolled in the counteracting sense, unintentional (i.e. uncontrolled in the promoting sense), efficient (i.e. requiring only minimal attentional capacity), and fast. According to a decompositional view of automaticity (Moors and De Houwer 2006), each feature should be investigated separately. The presence of one feature cannot be inferred from the presence of another. For instance, evidence that a process is unconscious is not evidence that it is also unintentional. Features of (non) automaticity can be taken to provide information about operating conditions (Bargh 1992). Automatic processes are those that operate under suboptimal conditions (such as a lack of intention, consciousness, attentional capacity, and/or time); nonautomatic processes are those that require optimal conditions.

To demonstrate that an appraisal variable can be processed in an automatic way, one has to demonstrate (1) that the appraisal variable under study was processed (and not some other variable), and (2) that it was processed automatically (i.e. under suboptimal conditions). Support for the automaticity of individual appraisal variables has been obtained with various research methods (both behavioural and neuroscientific). Support for the automatic detection of goal relevance and novelty comes from studies using attentional bias tasks (e.g. the modified Stroop task, the dot probe task, the spatial cueing task, and the visual search task) demonstrating selective attention to goal-relevant compared with neutral stimuli (Gati and Ben-Shakar 1990). Support for automatic appraisal of novelty also comes from neuroscientific studies (e.g. Berns *et al.* 1997). The automatic appraisal of intrinsic pleasantness is amply documented in affective priming studies (Draine and Greenwald 1998) as well as in studies using the event-related potential method (Grandjean and Scherer 2008). Support for the automatic appraisal of motive consistency has been obtained with variants of the affective priming task, in which goals were manipulated and intrinsic pleasantness was kept neutral (Moors *et al.* 2005). There is also evidence that the appraisal component of agency/intentionality can be automatic. With regard to intentionality, recent studies have shown that people automatically attribute intentionality when seeing or reading about other people's actions (e.g. Hassin *et al.* 2005). Finally, data on the automatic assessment of control (Aarts 2007) and relative power or status (Moors and De Houwer 2005) suggest the possibility of automatic appraisal of coping potential.

Future efforts in both behavioural and neuroscientific studies should be more concerned with (1) clearly identifying and delineating the appraisal variables at stake, (2) extending the range of automaticity features examined, and (3) investigating whether the values on several appraisal variables can also be integrated in an automatic manner.

AGNES MOORS

autonomic nervous system The autonomic nervous system (ANS) is the set of peripheral nerves and ganglia, together with their central brain components, which innervate visceral and other internal organs of the body. This system has variously been termed the sympathetic nervous system, the vegetative nervous system, the visceral nervous system, or the ganglionic nervous system, but is now generally referred to as the autonomic nervous system after Langley (1916; see also Ack-

Table A3. Functional effects of sympathetic and parasympathetic activation

Organ system	Sympathetic	Parasympathetic
Heart	↑ Heart rate	↓ Heart rate
	↑ Contractility	Inhibits sympathetic
Cardiovascular	↑ Blood pressure	↓ Blood pressure
Pupils	Dilates pupil	Constricts pupil
Metabolism	↑ Metabolism	↓ Metabolism
	↓ Insulin release	↑ Insulin release
Gut	Slows digestion	Promotes digestion

erknecht, 1974, for early history). Descending (efferent) influences of the ANS serve to regulate the viscera and internal functions of the body, while ascending (afferent) components carry information on visceral states to reflex systems as well as higher levels of the brain. The ANS comprises the sympathetic division, the parasympathetic division, and the enteric (gut) division, although the latter is often considered its own distinct system but is innervated by the other autonomic divisions.

Many visceral organs are dually innervated by both the sympathetic and parasympathetic systems, which generally exert opposing actions. Walter Cannon (1871–1945) was an important early experimentalist and theorist, who proposed that the sympathetic system is particularly important in emergency states and adaptive threats, and serves to mobilize the organism for fight or flight. This division, he thought, was especially important in maintaining internal conditions in a steady state that is necessary for life, a process he termed homeostasis (Cannon 1932). In contrast, the parasympathetic system serves more as a conservation system, which promotes calm, decreases energy output, increases digestion, and otherwise opposes the activational effects of the sympathetic division. Table A3 lists some functional consequences of sympathetic and parasympathetic activation.

Visceral organs are often dually innervated, sympathetic and parasympathetic systems tend to have opposing actions, and it is often the case that the two divisions show reciprocal patterns of activation. Increased activity of one branch is often accompanied by decreased activity of the other, which can synergistically effect a common outcome. For example, activation of the sympathetic system, which speeds the beat of the heart (see CARDIOVASCULAR SYSTEM), may be accompanied by inhibition of the parasympathetic system, which normally serves to slow the heart beat. This reciprocal pattern of autonomic control affords a broad, synergistic control over the end organ, and is rather characteristic of homeostatic reflexes. Many such reflexes are organ- ized at the level of the brainstem. One example is the baroreceptor–heart rate reflex, whereby a decrease in blood pressure (e.g. from standing up and pooling of blood in the legs) results in a reflexive increase in sympathetic control of the heart and a reflexive decrease in parasympathetic control of the heart. Both of these changes increase heart rate, and thus cardiac output, and tend to oppose or compensate for the perturbation of blood pressure.

Modern conceptions

Control of the two autonomic branches is not always reciprocal, however, and may not always be homeo- static (Berntson *et al.* 1991, Berntson and Cacioppo 2007). Early studies tended to focus on relatively low-level brainstem homeostatic reflexes, where this reciprocal pattern of control is common. Walter Hess (1881–1973), however, was a pioneer in focusing attention on higher brain controls over the ANS, for which he shared the Nobel prize in 1949. Hess and his students demonstrated that higher levels of the brain, which are involved in behavioural and affective states, exert powerful controls over autonomic outflows (Hess 1957). Importantly,

these higher brain systems are not as rigid and immut- able as many brainstem reflexes, but can flexibly sculpt autonomic outflows or adaptively adjust to changing demands. In contrast to the rigid reciprocal coupling of lower autonomic reflexes, higher neural systems are able to generate patterns of autonomic outflows extend- ing from reciprocal to independent or even co-activation of the two autonomic branches (Berntson *et al.* 1991). In fact, a single regulated homeostatic level may not al- ways be optimal, as adaptive challenges may demand deviations from the steady state, and higher-level brain systems have been shown to be capable of bypassing or inhibiting homeostatic reflexes (Berntson and Cacioppo 2007; McEwen and Wingfield 2003).

These considerations have required a revision in the traditional conceptualization of autonomic control lying along a single bipolar continuum from sympathetic dominance at one end to parasympathetic dominance at the other. Rather, as illustrated in Fig. A14, a bivariate autonomic plane, with independent sympathetic and parasympathetic axes, is necessary to encompass the range of reciprocal, independent, and co-active modes of autonomic control (Berntson *et al.* 1991, Berntson and Cacioppo 2007).

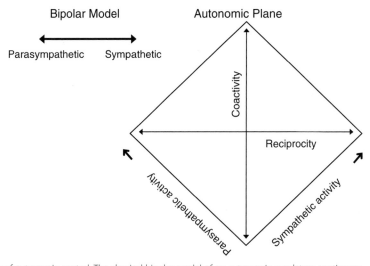

Fig. A14. Models of autonomic control. The classical bipolar model of an autonomic regulatory continuum extending from maximal parasympathetic to maximal sympathetic control is illustrated on the left. This is a reciprocal model in which increased activity in one autonomic branch is coupled to a decreased activity in the other. The right side illustrates the more comprehensive model of an autonomic plane, in which activities of the two autonomic branches can vary either independently or together (reciprocally or coactively). This model subsumes the more limited bipolar model as the reciprocal diagonal, but also captures other modes of autonomic control such as independent sympathetic activation, independent parasympathetic activation, and coactivation.

Ascending influences

Historically, psychophysiologists have often focused on the efferent autonomic control of organ systems (see PERIPHERAL PSYCHOPHYSIOLOGY), although the ANS also carries important visceral sensory information to the brain via afferent projections. About 70% of the axons in the vagus nerve (tenth cranial nerve—a major parasympathetic nerve) are afferent and convey visceral sensory information to the nucleus of the tractus solitarius (NTS), which is the major visceral relay nucleus in the medulla. This afferent information plays an important role in autonomic reflexes (e.g. baroreceptor reflexes), but is also relayed to higher brain levels, including the *amygdala, basal forebrain, and insula cortex. These latter projections may impact higher-level behavioural processes.

In 1884 William James (1842–1910) proposed that rather than emotion (e.g. fear in the presence of a bear) driving bodily changes (e.g. autonomic *arousal and fleeing), it is the perception of these bodily changes that is the emotion (see JAMES–LANGE THEORY). Although this conception no longer appears viable in its strongest form, visceral feedback may play a modulatory role in emotion and behaviour (Cacioppo *et al.* 1992, Damasio 1999). Ascending visceral feedback, for example, has been shown not only to influence emotion but also to enhance memory and to foster attention and cortical processing (for reviews see Berntson *et al.* 2003a, McGaugh and Cahill 2003). As illustrated in Fig. A15, these ascending influences may be related to visceral afferent inputs to the amygdala and the basal forebrain, where they can be relayed to higher cortical areas including the insula cortex and the medial prefrontal cortex (Berntson *et al.* 2003a).

Novel perspectives

Although the ANS has a well-established contribution to its traditional homeostatic role, recent research and theory suggest a much broader role in behavioural processes, health (see HEALTH AND EMOTION) and disease. In addition to the perspectives outlined above, the ANS has been shown to interact extensively with the immune system, and to both modulate and be regulated by immune processes. These findings have led to the development of the burgeoning field of *psychoneuroimmunology (e.g. see Ader *et al.* 2001). Additional recent findings that vagal stimulation may be medically effective in treating pain, depression, and intractable epilepsy (Groves and Brown 2005) suggest that the coming decade may see unprecedented advances in our understanding of the ANS.

GARY G. BERNTSON AND JOHN T. CACIOPPO

Berntson, G.G. and Cacioppo, J.T. (2007). Integrative physiology: homeostasis, allostasis and the orchestration of systemic physiology. In: J.T. Cacioppo, L.G. Tassinary, and G.G. Berntson (eds), *Handbook of psychophysiology*, 3rd edn, pp. 433–52. Cambridge: Cambridge University Press.

Berntson, G.G., Cacioppo, J.T., and Sarter, M. (2003). Bottom-up: implications for neurobehavioral models of anxiety and autonomic regulation. In: R.J. Davidson, K.R. Scherer, and H.H. Goldsmith (eds), *Handbook of affective sciences*, pp. 1105–16. New York: Oxford University Press.

Groves, D.A. and Brown, V.J. (2005). Vagal nerve stimulation: a review of its applications and potential mechanisms that mediate its clinical effects. *Neuroscience and Biobehavioral Reviews*, **29**, 493–500.

Korte, S.M., Koolhaas, J.M., Wingfield, J.C., and McEwen, B.S. (2005). The Darwinian concept of stress: benefits of allostasis and costs of allostatic load and the trade-offs in health and disease (review). *Neuroscience and Biobehavioral Reviews*, **29**, 3–38.

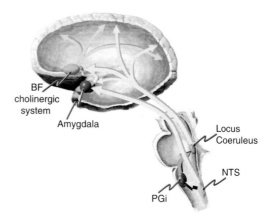

Fig. A15. Ascending pathways implicated in behavioural and cognitive effects of visceral priming. Vagal afferents convey visceral information to the nucleus tractus solitarius (NTS), the major visceral relay nucleus of the brainstem. The NTS issues a direct noradrenergic projection to forebrain areas such as the amygdala, and via an excitatory input to the nucleus paragigantocellularis (PGi) can also activate the ascending noradrenergic system arising in the locus coeruleus (LC). The LC, in turn, projects to the basal forebrain corticopetal cholinergic system (BF cholinergic system) as well as to the amygdala and the cortex. There are thus several routes (noradrenergic and cholinergic) by which ascending visceral information can affect cortical/cognitive processing. Reciprocal interactions between the amygdala and basal forebrain, together with their overlapping targets in the medial prefrontal cortex, constitute important processing substrates for emotion and cognition. From Berntson *et al.* (2003a).

autonomous agents In artificial intelligence and related disciplines, autonomous agents are artificial entities that interact with their environment with a relatively high level of independence to make and execute their own decisions, which are based on their relation to and perception of the environment as well as of their own state. Artificial autonomous agents can be classified in terms of their different types of embodiments, the environments they inhabit, and the tasks they perform. For example, at the First International Conference on Autonomous Agents (Müller 1997) they were divided into four broad categories: expert assistants—software agents that help humans in knowledge-processing tasks such as *decision-making; autonomous robots—physical agents that have to perform and interact in our physical and social world; softbots—programs that interact with software environments, such as operating systems, the internet, or the world-wide web; and synthetic agents—entertainment characters aiming to portray believable personalities and that operate in simulated environments, such as virtual worlds or video games. The conceptual traditions, models, techniques, and challenges underlying these different types of autonomous agents are very diverse, and it is not infrequent to see one of those subcommunities use the term 'autonomous agent' to denote the particular type of system that constitutes their object of study to the exclusion of the rest.

In addition, although autonomous agents research and applications are very widespread, the terms 'autonomous' and 'agent' are far from being used univocally. In the broadest sense of the term, an agent is a system that can exert some influence on its environment through its actions. However, other capabilities are usually required for a system to properly be called an 'agent' and distinguished from purely mechanical devices: an ability to maintain itself (to remain 'alive' or operational); an ability to control its own actions; awareness of executing an action; goal-directedness; purposive behaviour, etc. Present-day autonomous agents can only achieve some of those capabilities and in a limited way.

Autonomy refers to independence of external control or ability to self-regulate, and this is, again, a matter of degree. In the case of autonomous robots or more generally 'complete creatures' (to use the term coined by Rodney Brooks) that have to work towards their survival, for example, it usually ranges from (limited) energy independence (robots with on-board batteries) and independence of computer or human control (on-board computation), which can be present even in the most reactive robots that merely respond to external stimuli in a reflex-like manner, to relative independence of the external environment provided by simple internal

value systems and motivational states that drive decision-making (motivation-based robot control architectures), to independence of the demands of the motivational system achieved by 'second-order' control mechanisms akin to some of the roles that emotions considered as 'interrupts' of ongoing cognitive and behavioural activity play in biological systems, giving rise to emotion-based control architectures (see, e.g., Hudlicka and Cañamero, 2004, for some examples). Affective phenomena are thus key elements for autonomous agents (Trappl et al. 2003, Fellous and Arbib 2005) as they provide them with mechanisms that make them 'want' (see MOTIVATION) and 'like' to do things (see AISB '05 2005) and interact with other agents. In the case of robots that have to interact with other agents, particularly with humans, the development of attachment bonds is being used by some researchers (e.g. Cañamero et al. 2006) as a mechanism to initiate and maintain affective interactions and relations. Generally, emotions and other affective phenomena are being increasingly explored by researchers of autonomous agents as mechanisms for *adaptation to the physical and social environment, as well as tools to help understand emotions in biological systems (Cañamero 2005), as indeed adaptation (considered as adequacy of the behaviour of the agent to the environment in which it is embedded) is a key feature that (biologically inspired) autonomous agents must possess (see AFFECTIVE COMPUTING). The roles of emotions as mechanisms for adaptation have been investigated in robotics, artificial intelligence, and artificial life at different timescales, namely adaptation to short-term environmental changes in action selection, adaptation to changes along an individual's lifetime, from developmental and learning perspectives, and adaptation to very slow changes at the level of species.

However, some authors such as Tim Smithers or Luc Steels consider the above traits correct for automata but insufficient to describe truly autonomous systems, which must be not only self-regulating but also self-governing, developing and adapting the laws that govern their behaviour. Other characteristics of emotions, such as emotional control, would again be essential to achieve self-governing agents, providing not only the values to ground those laws, but also mechanisms to monitor their effects on the agent's survival and/or well-being, and to orient the change and adaptation of such laws accordingly. This would involve modelling emotions as adaptive mechanisms themselves.

LOLA CAÑAMERO

B

basic emotions One of the problems that plagues theory and research on emotion is the lack of consensus on definitions of emotion. One reason for this is that humans experience a wide range of affective phenomena, such as being tired, bored, sleepy, excited, hungry, angry, afraid, sad, ashamed, proud, embarrassed, happy, or jealous, and much of it is called 'emotion' by researchers and laypersons alike. Also, emotion is an aspect of psychology that all humans have a lifetime of access to, and a lifetime of contemplating the proper words to describe nuances of an inner physiological state or sensation. Thus it is difficult to arrive at a consensual definition of emotion that encompasses all the possible types of emotion. At the same time, it is important for researchers to make explicit their working definition of emotion so that they, and others, can understand what part of the affective world they are calling emotion. We do so here.

We consider the universe of affective phenomena to include emotion, moods, affect-related personality traits, some psychopathologies, and well-being; emotion, therefore, is one class of affective phenomena. We define emotion as *transient, bio-psychosocial reactions designed to aid individuals in adapting to and coping with events that have implications for survival and well-being.* They are biological because they involve physiological responses from the central and autonomic nervous systems. They are psychological because they involve specific mental processes required for elicitation and regulation of response. And they are social because they are often elicited by social interactions, and have meaning to those interactions. (We use the word 'social' here in the broadest sense in relation to our evolutionary history, which includes interactions not only with other humans, but also other living beings, such as snakes, bears, wild pigs, etc.)

Within the domain of emotion, humans experience different types of emotions, including self-conscious emotions, positive emotions, pro-social emotions, and moral emotions (see EMOTION CLASSIFICATION). Basic emotions are a class of emotions that share a unique set of characteristics that distinguish them from other emotions, including unique physiological signatures, distinctive changes in mental activities and attention, subjective experience, and reliable nonverbal signals

(Ekman 1999) (see more below). Moreover, these characteristics are universal to all people of all cultures (see UNIVERSALITY OF EMOTION). For now, the basic emotions include *anger, *disgust, *fear, *enjoyment, *sadness, and *surprise; future research may demonstrate that other emotions share the same characteristics as basic emotions.

In the basic emotions framework, each emotion label is a place-holder denoting a family of related emotions (Ekman 1999, 2003). For example, the anger family contains emotions denoted by the terms annoyed, irritated, frustrated, pissed off, angry, mad, hostile, exasperated, furious, and enraged. The fear family includes anxious, nervous, tense, worried, apprehensive, frightened, terrified, horrified, and mortified. Specific emotion labels often denote variations in intensity and/or the eliciting circumstances (Shaver *et al.* 1987). Thus the basic emotions framework is not about 'just' a small set of emotions, but about quite a large and varied emotional world.

The basic emotion system

Levenson (1999) proposed the existence of a basal processing system called the 'core emotion system', which describes a mechanism for emotion elicitation. He suggested that the core system developed to deal with species-constant problems related to survival in a time-tested, predictable, and automatic fashion. These problems could occur in interactions with nature or with other humans. The core emotion system is hard-wired, fairly impermeable to modification by experience, and relatively unchanged throughout the lifespan.

We extend this conceptualization by elaborating on several components and relabelling it the basic emotion system (see Fig. B1). The first stage of this system is perception, in which the sensory information obtained as individuals scan their environment is converted to schemas—mental representations of the situations or events being perceived. These schemas may consist of two components—one referring to the physical characteristics of the sensory information associated with the perceived event trigger and the other referring to psychological meanings or themes associated with the event trigger. In other words, perceived schemas may describe what the events are, and/or what they mean. There is no reason to prefer

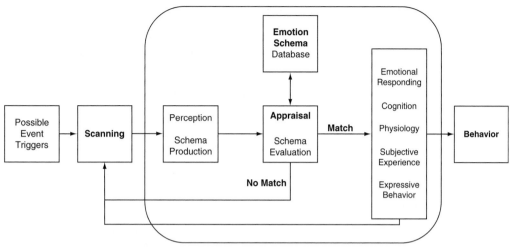

Fig. B1. The basic emotion system.

one version over the other at this point, and future research will need to address this issue.

Then, the created schemas are evaluated in an appraisal process (see APPRAISAL THEORIES) (Lazarus 1991), which is immediate, unbidden, opaque, unconscious, and automatic (Ekman 2003). In that process, perceived schemas must be compared with a known set of emotionally relevant schemas, that is, schemas that when matched should initiate an emotional response. We posit the existence of an *emotion schema database* that stores such schema information. (Ekman, 2003, referred to this as an 'emotion alert database'). For example, the perception of a coiled, cylindrical object that is hissing may match the schema of a snake in the emotion schema database, triggering the emotion of fear. The perception of the smell of faeces may match the schema of contamination in the emotion schema database, triggering the emotion of disgust.

If the perceived schemas do not match those in the emotion schema database, no emotion is elicited and the individual continues to scan the environment. A match, however, initiates a group of responses, including expressive behaviour, physiology, cognitions, and subjective experience. The group of responses is coordinated, integrated, and organized, and constitutes what is known as an emotion. Emotional responses, in turn, affect the scanning component of the system. In our view, the term 'emotion' is a metaphor that refers to this group of coordinated responses (see COMPONENTIAL THEORIES).

The emotion response system

Basic emotions evolved to help us cope with events and situations that have consequences for our *immediate* welfare. If humans didn't have emotions, they wouldn't know when to attack, defend, flee, care for others, reject food, or approach something useful, all of which were helpful in our evolutionary histories (as they are today as well) (see EVOLUTION OF EMOTION; FUNCTIONALIST THEORIES OF EMOTION). Thus basic emotions helped humans adapt to immediate needs in their environments, and were instrumental in our survival as a species. Other emotions also help humans adapt, but the events and situations that elicit nonbasic emotions are more long term, not immediate.

Basic emotions aid in adaptation because they recruit programmes that coordinate and orchestrate other evolved systems, such as perception, attention, inference, learning, memory, goal choice, motivational priorities, physiological reactions, motor behaviours, and behavioural *decision-making (Cosmides and Tooby 2000). Below we categorize these responses into four categories—cognitions, physiology, expressive behaviour, and subjective experience. Their engagement allows for the simultaneous activation of certain evolved systems and deactivation of others in order to prevent the chaos of multiple, competing systems being activated at the same time, and thus allowing for coordinated, orchestrated responses to environmental stimuli. Thus, anger prepares the body to fight, and fear prepares for flight. To be sure, not everyone who is angry actually does fight, nor does everyone who is afraid actually flee. In these cases, anger and fear *prepare* the individual to do so; engaging in such motor behaviours, however, depends on a host of other factors, both cultural and individual (Matsumoto and Wilson 2008).

Physiological reactions

Basic emotions are associated with distinct physiological signatures in both the autonomic and central nervous systems (Davidson *et al.* 2003b, Levenson 2003). These physiological changes help prepare individuals to respond to the eliciting stimulus immediately and effectively by initiating and maintaining whole-body activity (see ACTION READINESS). Anger, for instance, produces vasodilation, pupil constriction, foaming, and piloerection, each of which prepares the individual to fight; fear, however, produces vasoconstriction, pupil dilation, and bulging eyes, preparing the individual to flee (Levenson 2003). The same physiological signatures have been found in people of very different cultures (e.g. Levenson *et al.* 1992), and thus are strongly suggestive of a biologically innate, universal programme for emotional responding that is unique for each emotion.

Cognitions

When emotions are aroused, they recruit a host of cognitive processes that support the action preparedness of the individual. Two types of basic-level cognitive processes are associated with this arousal (Levenson 1999). One is the perceptual/attentional system, the function of which is to maximize attention to the elicitor and minimize attention to distractors. The other is the gating of higher mental processes, which limits the novelty of the response and aids in accessing memories and other knowledge stores helpful in determining the appropriate subsequent behavioural response.

Subjective experience

When emotions are aroused they elicit subjective experiences, which can signal to the individual that an emotion is occurring or has occurred (or that an event that requires a response has occurred), and thus inform oneself about goals, motivational priorities, inferences, and decision-making. Thus, subjective experience plays an important function by being the window to our internal experiences, and to the relationship between us and the environment (see FEELINGS (PSYCHOLOGICAL PERSPECTIVES)). Each of the basic emotions has a unique subjective feeling state and physiological sensations (Scherer and Wallbott 1994); thus, anger feels hot and pressurized, while fear feels cold and constricted.

Expressive behaviour

Darwin (1872/1998) suggested that expressive behaviours associated with emotion are the residual actions of more complete behavioural responses. Facial (and vocal) expressions are part of those actions, and occur in combination with other bodily responses—postural, gestural, skeletal muscle movements, and physiological responses. Thus, we express anger by furrowing the brow and tightening the lips with teeth displayed because these actions are part of an attack response; we express disgust with an open mouth, nose wrinkle, and tongue protrusion as part of a vomiting response. Facial expressions, then, are part of the coordinated response involving multiple systems (see EXPRESSION, PRINCIPLES OF EMOTIONAL).

Several lines of research provide strong evidence for the universality of expressive behaviour. One such line of evidence comes from judgement studies, in which observers in different cultures are shown various facial expressions and are asked to judge which emotion is being portrayed. Research has provided strong evidence for the universal recognition of facial expressions portraying the basic emotions across different stimulus sets, investigators, expressor ethnicities and sex, and response formats (Matsumoto 2001).

Even stronger evidence, however, comes from production studies, in which emotions are elicited and the resulting facial behaviours are measured. The most well-known of these is Ekman's (1972) classic study of Americans and Japanese college students. But since then there have been at least 74 other studies that measured facial behaviours occurring in reaction to emotionally evocative situations, reporting that the facial configurations originally posited by Darwin (1872/1998), and verified and somewhat modified by Ekman (Ekman and Friesen 1975) actually occur (Matsumoto *et al.* 2008). These studies have involved a variety of methodologies for the elicitation of emotion, and participants from many different countries and cultures, demonstrating the universality of facial expressions of emotion. Examples of the universal facial expressions of emotion are depicted in Fig. B2.

Moreover, the available evidence strongly suggests a biological basis of universality: (1) The universal facial expressions among humans have been observed in non-human primates (de Waal 2003) (see ANIMAL EMOTIONS). (2) Congenitally blind individuals spontaneously produce the same facial expressions as sighted individuals when emotion is aroused (Matsumoto and Willingham 2009) and (3) their expressions are more concordant with their kin than with strangers (Peleg *et al.* 2006). (4) Some facial expressions to emotionally provocative stimuli are more concordant among monozygotic twin pairs than dizygotic twins (Kendler *et al.* 2008).

Coherence among response system components

Because emotions evolved in order to aid humans by preparing us to engage in some action, the responses

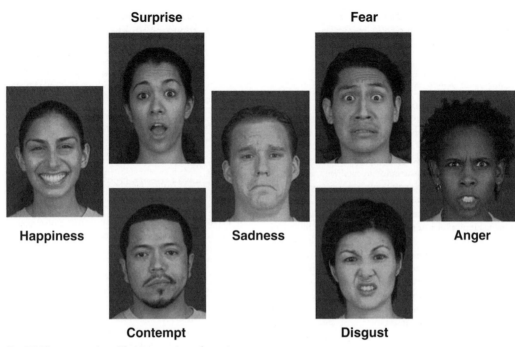

Surprise   **Fear**

Happiness   **Sadness**   **Anger**

Contempt   **Disgust**

Fig. B2. The seven universal facial expressions of emotion.

associated with emotion—physiology, expressive behaviour, cognitions, and subjective experience—need to be organized and coordinated. This notion is referred to as *response system coherence* (Levenson 1999), and has garnered empirical support over the last decade, especially in studies that use facial expressions as markers to signal when an emotion is occurring (e.g. Davidson *et al.* 1990a, Ekman *et al.* 1990, Rosenberg and Ekman 1994). These linkages also exist across cultures (Levenson *et al.* 1992).

Summary
The existence of basic emotions does not argue against other types of emotions; nonbasic emotions are important for a rich and varied emotional life. Basic emotions do, however, remind us how we are all linked together and with our phylogenetic relatives. Basic emotions and the universality of their expression are the closest thing we may have to a common human language.

DAVID MATSUMOTO AND PAUL EKMAN

Ekman, P. (2003). *Emotions revealed.* New York, Times Books.
Ekman, P. and Rosenberg, E.L. (eds) (2005). *What the face reveals: basic and applied studies of spontaneous expression using the Facial Action Coding System (FACS).* New York, Oxford University Press.
Matsumoto, D. and Willingham, B. (2009). Spontaneous facial expressions of emotion of blind individuals. *Journal of Personality and Social Psychology*, 96(1), 1–10.

behavioural activation system The behavioural activation system (BAS) acts as an approach-related (see APPROACH/WITHDRAWAL) incentive *motivational system that initiates behaviour towards conditioned or unconditioned appetitive or hedonic stimuli. The BAS also mediates the active avoidance of conditioned punishing stimuli (Gray and McNaughton 2000) (see PUNISHMENT). The ensuing motivational states may be simply described as 'reward seeking' and 'safety or relief', respectively (Fowles 1988).

Neurophysiology and neuroanatomy
Mesolimbic dopamine (DA) function in the ventral tegmental area (VTA; area A10) and nucleus accumbens (NAcc) has been theorized to underlie aspects of the incentive motivational drive of the BAS. DA activity in the nigrostriatal (substantia nigra–caudate–putamen) pathway may also be involved in the selection of motor actions which facilitate approach-oriented behaviour. Striatal DA receptor affinity has been hypothesized to moderate individual differences in BAS function. Low D_2 receptor affinity may lead to reduced dopaminergic inhibition of striatal output and greater BAS activity (Pickering and Gray 1999), and greater D_1 receptor affinity may facilitate long-term potentiation during reinforcement learning (Pickering and Gray 2001). A recent study has demonstrated that

genetic polymorphisms (*COMT* and *DRD2*) that interact to produce states of high tonic DA predict high scores on Carver and White's (1994) BAS scale (Reuter *et al.* 2006).

Personality

The specific ways in which the BAS relates to personality remain complex and not completely understood. BAS activity has been theorized to engender the trait of *impulsivity, which is analogous to a 30-degree rotation between Eysenck's *neuroticism and *extraversion dimensions. This behavioural facet has been further clarified over time as impulsive sensation seeking (Pickering and Gray 1999) or impulsive antisocial sensation seeking (Pickering and Gray 2001). Including aspects of antisocial impulsivity in a theory of BAS may account for shared variance between BAS and Eysenck's psychoticism dimension of personality (Pickering and Gray 2001). Evidence from multiple investigations has linked dopaminergic activities to the trait of extraversion, yet debate still ensues as to whether extraversion or impulsivity are phenomenological derivatives of the other characteristic's relation to dopaminergic activities (Pickering and Gray 2001). In Carver and White's (1994) behavioural inhibition system (BIS)/BAS scales, BAS emerges from the combination of three related subscales: fun seeking, drive, and reward seeking, with no specific account of impulsivity. Moreover, sympathetic activation under conditions of pure reward, arguably a clean indicator of BAS activity, was unrelated to self-reported BAS total or subscale scores (Brenner *et al.* 2005), raising concerns about the extent to which the BAS scales are sensitive to underlying individual differences in the neural systems of the BAS.

Psychopathology

A number of clinical states have been theoretically linked to individual differences in BAS function. Although schizophrenia is not specifically related to BAS function, both of these phenomena share a common hypothesized substrate of high mesolimbic DA activity, lending support to an aspect of psychotic personality traits in BAS-related function. Depression (low BAS) and mania (high BAS) may be broadly associated with alterations in reward responsive behaviour (Fowles 1988) as well as associated dopaminergic functions. Externalizing disorders (conduct disorder, attention-deficit hyperactivity disorder) have been hypothesized to result from the interaction between an underactive BAS and BIS, which thus drives self-stimulation behaviours without adequate regard for negative consequences (Brenner *et al.* 2005).

JAMES F. CAVANAGH AND JOHN J. B. ALLEN

Pickering, A.D. and Gray, J.A. (2001). Dopamine, appetitive reinforcement, and the neuropsychology of human learning: an individual differences approach. In: A. Eliasz and A. Angleitner (eds), *Advances in research on temperament*, pp. 113–49. Lengerich, Germany: PABST Science Publishers.

Reuter, M., Schmitz, A., Corr, P., and Hennig, J. (2006). Molecular genetics support Gray's personality theory: the interaction of COMT and DRD2 polymorphisms predicts the behavioral approach system. *International Journal of Neuropsychopharmacology*, **9**, 155–66.

behavioural inhibition system The behavioural inhibition system (BIS) was originally conceived as an aversive *motivational system that inhibits appetitive behavioural reactions to conditioned stimuli requiring passive avoidance of punishment or those engendering extinction (Gray 1982). The ensuing emotional states may be simply described as 'anxiety' and 'frustration', respectively (Fowles 1988). The theoretical concept of the BIS has evolved, however, such that the BIS inhibits prepotent approach or avoidant behaviours (see APPROACH/WITHDRAWAL) to resolve goal conflict between competing motivations (Gray and McNaughton 2000), including approach–approach, avoidance–avoidance, or approach–avoidance conflicts. The system currently hypothesized to mediate avoidance motivational reactions to aversive stimuli is the fight–flight–freeze system (FFFS), where the behavioural activation system (BAS) mediates motivational reactions to appetitive stimuli. Conflict between competing goals within a system (e.g. approach–approach) or between systems (approach–avoidance) is resolved by the BIS through risk assessment and cautious arousal processes ('defensive approach'), with a bias towards activation of the FFFS (Gray and McNaughton 2000).

Neuropsychology of anxiety

Gray's (1982) model highlighted the role of the septo-hippocampal system (SHS) in mediating aspects of the mammalian response to conditioned signals of punishment and nonreward, as well as to novel and innate fear stimuli. The SHS acts in concert with the Papez circuit (mammillary bodies of the hypothalamus, anterior thalamus, and cingulate cortex) and prefrontal cortex to compare actual with expected behavioural outcomes (Gray 1982). If there is a 'mismatch' in prediction (expected does not equal actual), or if the predicted consequence is aversive, the BIS acts to inhibit ongoing motor actions and heightened attention is paid to the next similar motor occurrence with a bias towards greater restraint. Thus, it is theorized that activity in the BIS (but not necessarily the SHS itself) constitutes the psychological and behavioural components of *anxiety. This deduction is bolstered by the fact that anxiolytic drugs (barbiturates, tranquillizers, and alcohol) act to reduce inhibition and arousal due to conditioned signals of punishment/nonreward and also to novel stimuli (Gray 1982). Anxiolytic drugs may directly diminish BIS activity by facilitating GABAergic inhibition as well as reducing monoaminergic activities within the SHS (Gray 1982).

Defensive distance

The processes of fear and anxiety are separable on multiple dimensions (functional, behavioural, and pharmacological), where fear is mediated via the FFFS and anxiety via the BIS (McNaughton and Corr 2004). Fear and anxiety are further separable on the dimension of defensive distance: where fear involves movement away from danger (via FFFS activity), anxiety may involve both FFFS activity and BAS-mediated movement towards danger (McNaughton and Corr 2004). These distinct responses are hypothesized to be elicited depending on the organism's response to the perceived physical distance between itself and the threatening stimuli. Unconditional threat requiring behavioural avoidance may only require FFFS activity. However, when approach may be necessary (such as in the case of defensive aggression or uncertainty of outcome), activity of the BAS is required and thus the BIS must mediate the interaction between these two systems (Gray and McNaughton 2000).

Personality

Individual differences in BIS activity have been theorized to underlie trait anxiety, with BIS activity giving rise to the subjective experiences of anxiety, frustration, worry, and rumination. The BIS was originally considered as a 30-degree rotation (labelled punishment sensitivity) between Eysenck's *neuroticism and *introversion dimensions (Gray 1982). Gray's reinforcement sensitivity theory (RST) has evolved from the original hypothesis of independent function of the BIS and BAS to a theory of interdependent processes between concurrent sensitivities to reward (BAS) and punishment (BIS or FFFS) (Corr 2004).

BIS/BAS, a system of personality derived from the study of neural systems, contrasts with other approaches to personality that comprise emergent trait constructs based on self-report or observation. Self-report scales have been developed, however, to capture individual differences in BIS/BAS activity. Carver and White's (1994) BIS/BAS scales are concise and evidence good reliability, but have been criticized as being more closely related to self-reported affect than to the underlying neural substrates of the BIS or BAS (Brenner et al. 2005). The BIS scale in particular might be more representative of the current conception of FFFS activity (Brenner et al. 2005) or of punishment sensitivity more generally (Carver and White 1994, Corr 2004).

Psychopathology

A recent revision of the RST defines most disorders of the anxiety spectrum along defensive avoidance (fear) and defensive approach (anxiety) dimensions (Gray and McNaughton 2000, McNaughton and Corr 2004). In this model, the defensive avoidance spectrum accounts for obsessive–compulsive, phobic or panic disorders as perceived defensive distance is lessened (danger is closer, less abstract, and behaviour depends on phylogenetically older brain regions). The defensive approach spectrum accounts for complex and social anxieties towards more generalized anxiety activity as defensive distance is diminished.

JAMES F. CAVANAGH AND JOHN J. B. ALLEN

Corr, P.J. (2004). Reinforcement sensitivity theory and personality. *Neuroscience and Biobehavioral Reviews*, **28**, 317–32.

McNaughton, N. and Corr, P.J. (2004). A two-dimensional neuropsychology of defense: fear/anxiety and defensive distance. *Neuroscience and Biobehavioral Reviews*, **28**, 285–305.

being moved You have just witnessed your daughter passing her swimming test. She waves at you from a distance, and you suppress a sob. Being moved is the feeling of being conquered. It takes one unawares, causing *embarrassment because of an urge to *cry. The emotion is ill-understood. Here an attempt is made to grasp it.

*Action readiness consists of a general weakening of control and autonomy, in response to a feeling of being overwhelmed. The appraisal is complex. Something very dear to you makes its appearance; there is a definite point in time when it strikes you (the supreme or rare moment); there is some difficulty linked to the dear object; at the supreme moment a profound change takes place, easing the difficulty. The dear object may be a person, as in a reunion, or a quality of a person or event: truth, virtue, innocence, vulnerability, heroism, purity, justice, beauty (e.g. Frijda 2007), the sacred, etc. The difficulty may be separation, rejection, struggle, impossibility, a misunderstanding, etc. The change may be a reversal of fortune or a definitive outcome (e.g. Efran and Spangler 1979). Victories in a difficult sports contest or witnessing true love finally triumph are examples. Being moved is hard to combine with *agency; it happens more often to the one witnessing events. Media events (real or fictional) are ideal triggers (Tan and Frijda 1999).

The adaptive function of being moved may originate in submission upon being overpowered: we yield to something bigger than ourselves. Crying emphasizes surrender to something greater than us (Plessner 1941). A favourable turn of events can render one helpless, perhaps because coping and negative expectations have abruptly become idle or have given way to what we unconsciously cherished all the time. Being moved probably has a great power in bonding.

Being moved offers a paradigm of the potential of emotions to signal to persons what is significant to them.

ED S. TAN

belief (philosophical perspectives) Many modern
accounts insist that emotions are not mere *feelings but
necessarily include cognitive components that at least in
part determine what specific kinds of emotions they are
and toward what objects they are directed or responsive.
A leading candidate for the crucial cognitive component
is belief (perhaps combined with evaluation). For example, if I did not believe that this gun is loaded, that
it might discharge, and that a discharge could cause
injury, I would experience no *fear* in handling it. Given
this plausible link between emotion and belief, understanding the former would seem to presuppose a clear
understanding of the latter.

Beliefs are typically conceived to be those informa-
tion-carrying mental entities that are created and modified by perception, reasoning, and reflection, and that,
combined with other, motivational entities like *desires
and plans, issue in behaviour. They are most straight-
forwardly (though not uncontroversially) depicted as
concrete, discrete representations in a person's head,
representations that take the form of sentences. And it
is generally agreed that beliefs are 'truth-directed',
meaning that they cannot be formed or maintained
where the person deems their contents not to be true
(Wedgwood 2002).

But the domain of such entities contains much internal diversity. For one thing, 'belief' sometimes refers
to an entity that is affirmed, possessed, or used by a
mind at a given moment in time (an 'occurrent' belief),
whether merely transiently and temporarily or as the
manifestation of a lasting constituent of the thinker's
cognitive endowment. In other common usages, by
contrast, 'belief' refers only to these enduring cognitive
constituents, sometimes called 'dispositional beliefs',
that stably persist to be called forth from memory for
thinking activity until they are altered, repudiated, or
permanently forgotten (Price 1969). A subset of dispositional beliefs comprises the 'global' beliefs that can be
attributed to a person as her 'real' view of things,
however much inconsistency exists between her dispositional beliefs and her occurrent beliefs, or even within
her corpus of dispositional beliefs itself.

If emotions are conceived, as is common, as occurrent
events or states of mind that persist only as long as whatever feelings are essential to them, then it would seem that
it is *occurrent* beliefs that are of primary importance to
emotion. To understand the arousal and control of emotion, then, we need to study also the processes by which
occurrent beliefs are formed, activated, manipulated,
altered, and extinguished.

Such study promises to make sense of two puzzling
phenomena that pose prima facie challenges to cognitivist models of emotion: (1) How is it that emotions can
be so volatile (e.g. flashing from love to hatred within

minutes), despite the relative stability of beliefs designed
to present a true picture of the world? (2) How is it that
emotions can sometimes exist without the supposedly
essential underlying beliefs (e.g. I might feel fear in
handling that gun even when confident that it's not
loaded)? Answers to these puzzles can be found in
distinguishing the 'micro' level of occurrent belief
from the 'macro' level of global belief. Occurrent
thought is, arguably, quite volatile—perhaps because
our minds are structured so as not to draw upon our
entire cognitive endowments (perspectives) at each moment of mental activity but only limited subsets ('per-
spects') whose activation is keyed not to topic but to
perceived mental task or situation. Such a cognitive
architecture would produce occurrent thinking that
sometimes shows considerable fluctuation among out-
looks that are all accepted unquestioningly when
deployed but that might take mutually divergent and
even inconsistent positions.

If cognition is fragmented in this fashion, and if emotions
are triggered in response to cognitive judgements (i.e. to
belief formation or activation), we would expect to see
somewhat disjointed emotional patterns—smoothed over
in part by inertia in the physiological responses that accompany many emotions, and by our general inattentiveness to
fine-grained cognitive and emotional shifts. We would also
expect to encounter emotional states that seem to clash
with beliefs. In this way, an important role for belief in
emotion—and for management of emotion via management of cognition, a project shared by ancient Stoicism and
present-day cognitive therapy—can be preserved in the face
of some of the major objections that have been levelled at it
(Nussbaum 1994).

A complete explanation here must also recognize the
substantial part played by nonsentential representations
in the cognitive contribution to emotion. The occurrent
thoughts that trigger emotions can be images, not just
beliefs. Thus, if my self-reassurances that the gun is not
loaded are repeatedly shoved aside by images of
weapons discharging or the gruesome aftermaths of
shootings, I will experience fear despite my firm conviction about the gun's harmlessness. Taking account of
imagistic cognitions in some fashion will also address
the concern that cognitivist accounts of emotion are not
sufficiently general to account for emotion in prelinguistic infants and nonlinguistic animals.

LAWRENCE A. LENGBEYER

Lengbeyer, L. (2007). Situated cognition: the perspect model. In:
D. Spurrett, D. Ross, H. Kincaid, and L. Stephens (eds),
*Distributed cognition and the will: individual volition and social
context* pp. 227–54. Cambridge, MA: MIT Press.
Schwitzgebel, E. (2006). Belief. In: E.N. Zalta (ed.), *Stanford
encyclopedia of philosophy*, Fall 2006 edn <http://plato.stan-
ford.edu/archives/fall2006/entries/belief/>.

belief (psychological perspectives) Beliefs link an object to a property or feature with some degree of likelihood. The object of the belief could be anything, including people, physical objects, actions, events, or even concepts. The properties or features could include physical characteristics (such as colour or height), nonphysical characteristics (such as desirability or prevalence), or states of being (such as existence or occurrence). Many statements of belief are unqualified, suggesting that no uncertainty exists regarding whether the object possesses the quality of interest, but beliefs can vary in the perceived likelihood of the object possessing that quality. Thus, one could hold beliefs as diverse as 'Albert Pujols is my favourite baseball player', 'the Eiffel Tower is probably made of iron', 'alien life is unlikely to exist', and 'nuclear holocaust would be horrific'. Beliefs can be generated when needed or stored in memory.

Beliefs can be distinguished from the related constructs of *attitudes and associations. Attitudes can be thought of as evaluative beliefs in which the quality of goodness or badness is viewed as a property of the object. Many beliefs do address properties of objects that are generally positive or negative. However, beliefs are broader in scope, because many belief statements are neutral (neither good nor bad) or only take on evaluative properties in context. For example, believing that a person is 7 feet tall is good if looking for a basketball centre but bad if looking for a racehorse jockey. Beliefs do 'associate' an object and quality, but the term belief generally implies that the quality is perceived 'as a property of the object', rather than the quality simply coming to mind at the same time as the object (simply being associated with the object). In this sense, beliefs are more like inferences than mere associations (see Carlston and Skowronski 2005).

The concept of belief is related to affect in a variety of ways.

Affect as a property of the object
In many settings, *affect forms the property or feature of the object in question. A person might believe that a friend is a happy person or that a certain group is emotional. A person might also believe that a certain object or event makes him/her feel certain emotions ('I'm afraid of snakes', or 'I get angry when my team loses'). These beliefs about affect can form the basis for attitudes toward the object. It is important to note that beliefs about affect need not be accurate. Indeed, the research on *affective forecasting suggests that people are often mistaken about how certain events will make them feel or how long that affect will last (Wilson and Gilbert 2005).

Beliefs influence affect
Beliefs themselves can also create or influence affect. Some beliefs reflect the cognitive appraisals (see APPRAISAL THE-

ORIES) that create emotions. For example, when one believes that an outgroup is threatening and one's own group is weak, these appraisals can combine to create fear (Mackie and Smith 2002). Other configurations of beliefs can produce different emotions. In a general sense, beliefs that are inconsistent with one another can produce cognitive dissonance, which is experienced in part as negative affect (Elliot and Devine 1994). Depending on the specific beliefs involved, other emotional states may be produced. For example, a person might believe that his/her actual characteristics or achievements fall short of his/her desired (ideal) standing. If so, the person experiences disappointment or sadness. However, the emotional consequences are different when the person believes that s/he falls short of what s/he believes important others expect. These actual–ought discrepancies produce anxiety or fear (Higgins 1987). Affect is not only produced by perceptions of one's static standing. Beliefs about progress toward *goals (which can be tempered by perceptions of one's self-efficacy) can also produce affect—positive if one is making sufficient progress, and negative if one is not making sufficient progress (Carver et al. 1996). Finally, people also hold beliefs about when and how their affective states can be managed. Therefore, once a person is experiencing the affective state, beliefs can guide one's actions to shorten or prolong the affect (Clark and Isen 1982).

Affect influences beliefs
Consistent with the idea that emotions activate the cognitive appraisals associated with them, experience of sadness makes sad events seem more likely to occur in the future, but the experience of anger makes angering events seem more likely (DeSteno et al. 2000). Moods can also influence perceptions of the desirability of an object or event (Schwarz and Clore 2007). However, these effects are most likely if the influences of emotion are not made salient to the social perceiver. If attention is drawn to potential influences of the emotions, cognitive corrections (guided by the perceiver's beliefs about how the emotions are influencing their perceptions) can diminish or even reverse these effects (DeSteno et al. 2000).

DUANE T. WEGENER AND JASON K. CLARK

Martin, L.L. and Clore, G.L. (eds) (2001). *Theories of mood and cognition: a user's guidebook.* Mahwah, NJ: Lawrence Erlbaum Associates.

Wyer, R.S. Jr and Albarracín, D. (2005). Belief formation, organization, and change: cognitive and motivational influences. In: D. Albarracín, B.T. Johnson, and M.P. Zanna (eds), *The handbook of attitudes*, pp. 273–322. Mahwah, NJ: Lawrence Erlbaum Associates.

bereavement Bereavement refers to the loss of a loved one through death (see LOSS; LOVE). The reaction to that loss is called *grief. The most prevalent symptom of grief is strong feelings of yearning or longing for the deceased. There is extraordinary variability in the nature and course of grief. Some people are devastated and never regain their psychological equilibrium, while others emerge relatively unscathed, perhaps even strengthened. Clarifying the antecedents and consequences of these patterns is an important focus of research.

For the past century, the predominant theoretical perspective has emphasized the importance of confronting and 'working through' one's feelings about the loss. Research has demonstrated, however, that thinking, talking, or writing about one's grief is not always beneficial. Researchers are attempting to clarify the conditions under which grief processing is most helpful, as well as the kinds of processing most likely to facilitate adaptation to the loss.

Past research has focused on the negative emotions associated with grief, such as depression, anxiety, and anger. In recent years, investigators have begun to examine positive emotions. Surprisingly, positive emotions have been found to be as prevalent, if not more prevalent, than negative emotions among the bereaved. This is the case even shortly after the loss. It will be important to learn more about how people cultivate and maintain positive emotions in the face of loss.

Risk factors predicting poor outcome following loss include a history of prior loss or trauma, the presence of concomitant stressors like chronic illness, and the absence of social support. Losses that are sudden, untimely, violent or mutilating, or that have occurred through others' negligence are associated with more intense and prolonged grief, as is the death of a child. Among those who lose a spouse, men are more at risk than women for adverse outcomes.

CAMILLE B. WORTMAN

Archer, J. (1999). *The nature of grief: the evolution and psychology of reactions to loss*. London: Routledge.

Stroebe, M.S., Hansson, R.O., Stroebe, W., and Schut, H. (eds) (2001). *Handbook of bereavement research*. Washington, DC: American Psychology Association.

bipolar disorder The story of bipolar disorder, or manic depression, starts with the ancient descriptions by Greek clinicians of the euphoria and psychosis associated with manic states (see MANIA), and the despair and suicidal inclinations associated with melancholia or *depression. The distinction between 'manic depressive insanity' and other forms of psychosis—especially schizophrenia—was made by Emil Kraepelin (1856–1926), in the late 19th century. He saw the worst cases of mental disorder, but contrasted the outcome in schizophrenia, which is usually poor, with that in manic depression, which is often compatible in the short term with complete recovery. Unfor-

tunately, it still results in long-term disability because of recurrent mood episodes, chronic symptoms, and impairment of attention and memory.

The emphasis on bipolarity arose in the 1960s when a clear distinction was drawn between patients experiencing mania and depression (thus bipolar disorder) and just depression (unipolar disorder). Bipolar I disorder is characterized by an elevation of mood that interferes seriously with everyday tasks and relationships, and may have psychotic features. Less severe mood elevation—hypomania—also occurs in association with depressive episodes, when the illness is then called bipolar II (see HYPOMANIA). Comorbidity with anxiety disorders and/or substance misuse is common.

The cause of bipolar disorder is largely attributed to genetic rather than environmental factors. The onset can be at any age, but is typically between 15 and 25 years. When the first manifestation is mania, it should be straightforward to recognize. If initial symptoms are anxiety or minor depression, an accurate diagnosis is often delayed by as much as 10 years. The course of illness is individually variable, from episodic with infrequent severe episodes punctuating a normally stable mood, to continuously cycling between mood elevation and depression. Effective treatment can be assisted by a range of psychotropic medications, often required in combination. Patient self-management contributes critically to mood stability.

GUY M GOODWIN

Goodwin, G.M. and Sachs, G. (2004). *Bipolar disorder*. Oxford: Healthpress.

blame The term blame refers to the assignment of responsibility for a particular act or event. In normal usage, blame is usually assigned for events that are unpleasant or unwanted by the person who assigns the blame (in contrast to the more neutral term 'attribution' (see ATTRIBUTION THEORY)). The assignment of blame is considered to be an important (appraisal) determinant for the elicitation and differentiation of the experience of different emotions. In particular, two important distinctions in the nature of blame are assumed to qualify the emotional response. First, blame can be assigned to another person, to circumstances (fate, luck, or some higher power), or to oneself. The assignment of blame to an external agent (other-blame, e.g. blaming someone else, an object, or circumstances) is considered to be an important determinant or component of *anger and *pity. In the case of an impersonal external agent, blame has also been related to feelings of depression or sadness. In contrast, when blame is assigned to oneself (self-blame), it is considered to be an important determinant or component of *shame and *guilt. A second important distinction concerns *controllability or *intentionality. Both other- and self-blame are assumed to correspond to different emotions, depending on whether the blamed behaviour is perceived as intentional/controllable or not. In the attributional theory of Weiner (1986), controllable other-blame is associated with anger, whereas uncontrollable other-blame is associated with pity, and controllable self-blame is associated with guilt, whereas uncontrollable self-blame is associated with shame.

PETER KUPPENS

bodily expression of emotion Emotions have a direct impact on the body of the person who is experiencing them. This effect is reflected in both internal physiological changes and external physical expressions, with these two elements being closely linked in serving the *action tendency triggered by the emotion (Frijda 1986).

Changes in physical appearance produced by emotional motor expressivity have been mainly investigated in terms of facial muscle actions (see FACIAL EXPRESSION OF EMOTION; FACIAL ACTION CODING SYSTEM) while body movements and postures have received much less attention (despite early efforts by linguists and ethologists to create a field of *kinetics* research; Harrigan 2005). This is surprising given Darwin's (1872/1998) early listing of emotion-specific body movements and postural configurations, along with facial expression patterns. For example, he suggested that in anger, among other behaviours, the whole body trembles, the head is erect, the chest is well expanded, feet are firmly on the ground, elbows are squared or the arms are rigidly suspended by the sides, and shoulders are squared (Darwin 1872/1998, Wallbott 1998, p. 880)

The description of body movements is extremely complex because each of the several parts of the body has several degrees of freedom with respect to the available movement dimensions. The elements that have been more extensively considered are head movements and position, arms, body lean, and legs (Harrigan 2005; see GESTURAL EXPRESSION OF EMOTION). While several attempts have been made to develop a comprehensive coding scheme for body movements, none of these is currently widely used.

If body movements and postures are generally recognized as being influenced by the emotional state, their capacity to convey specific emotions is highly debated. It is possible to identify two main perspectives in the field: (1) An *arousal perspective* (see AROUSAL) that assigns an ancillary role to body movements and postures in emotional expression, assuming that body movements and postures have a quantitative function (covarying with arousal, activity level, or intensity of the emotional state), often limiting the qualitative function (i.e. cues indicative of specific emotions) to facial expressions.

The respective authors argue that body movements are mainly used by observers to infer the level of arousal and intensity of the emotional experience. However, some authors recognize the possibility that some body and facial cues can, in some cases, separately communicate both the quantity and quality aspects of emotional experience (Ekman and Friesen 1967). (2) A *specificity perspective*—currently gaining more support—holding that body movements and postures constitute an autonomous channel of expression able to convey discrete emotions (see BASIC EMOTIONS) with or without the support of other modalities. In this perspective it is assumed that emotions are encoded through emotion-specific bodily movements and postures. Wallbott (1998) analysed portrayals of emotions by actors and identified some distinctive bodily characteristics, or patterns of them, that were used in a reliable fashion to encode various discrete emotional states. For example, hot anger was encoded by shoulders moving upwards, arms stretched frontally, or lateralized, the execution of various hand movements, as well as high movement activity, dynamism, and expansiveness.

Interestingly, these two perspectives originate from slightly different research foci. Authors claiming emotion-specificity of body movement adopted mainly production (or encoding) paradigms, whereas the arousal perspective is mostly based on recognition studies (see ENCODING/DECODING OF EXPRESSION). However, recent evidence shows that judges are able to infer specific emotions in recognition studies from body movements alone (De Meijer 1989). This suggests that there are both body movements and postures which mostly reflect the 'activity' level of the underlying emotion, as well as others that are associated in a distinctive way with specific emotions (Wallbott 1998). Much of the debate about emotion-specificity of body movement is being superseded by increasing attention given to links between body movements and postures with other expressive channels—face and voice—in synchronized emotional expressions (Scherer and Ellgring 2007b; see MULTIMODAL EXPRESSION OF EMOTION).

A further aspect of the bodily expression of emotions concerns touch, the *tactile* channel of communication. Some studies have highlighted the importance of touch in infant–caregiver communication, with the possibility of transmitting to or producing in the infant different emotionally valenced states (Hertenstein 2002). While this interpersonal communicative function of touch is generally accepted, the existence of specific characteristics of touch able to express discrete emotions has not yet received extensive empirical study. Clynes (1973) argued in favour of the existence of specific time curves of finger movements to express each discrete basic emotion through specific pressure curves. However,

Clynes' methodology has been widely criticized. Furthermore, it is not clear if and how these supposed emotion-specific finger movements map onto the interpersonal communication of emotion via touch.

MARCELLO MORTILLARO
AND KLAUS R. SCHERER

Harrigan, J.A. (2005). Proxemics, kinesics, and gaze. In: J.A. Harrigan, R. Rosenthal, and K.R. Scherer (eds), *The new handbook of methods in nonverbal behavior research*, pp. 137–98. New York: Oxford University Press.

bounded rationality There are three interpretations of the concept of bounded rationality (see RATIONALITY). The first defines it as a deviation of unbounded rationality due to external constraints, such as information and deliberation costs. This view, called *optimization under constraints*, is a standard modelling technique in economics and beyond (Arrow 2004). The second interpretation defines bounded rationality as a deviation from unbounded rationality because of internal constraints, notably limited information-processing capacities and lack of willpower. This *cognitive illusions* or *heuristics and biases* approach, as it is variously called, attributes the deviations to cognitive limitations (Kahneman 2003). The two interpretations appear diametrically opposed. By looking at the constraints in the world, the first emphasizes the rationality of human action; by focusing on the constraints in the mind, the second perceives irrationality.

The third interpretation is known as *ecological rationality*; it focuses on how *heuristics succeed in the real world rather than in comparison with unbounded rationality (Gigerenzer *et al.* 1999). The difference between the three interpretations can be explained in terms of two ideals underlying the concept of unbounded rationality: *optimization* and *universality*. Optimization under constraints retains both: It models how to find the optimal (best) action given constraints based on a universal calculus (such as maximizing expected utility). The cognitive illusions programme also retains the ideal of optimality, but attributes deviations to cognitive limitations rather than to optimization under constraints. Finding the optimal action is, however, usually impossible when it comes to real-world problems. For instance, the optimal sequence of moves in chess cannot be found, neither by Deep Blue nor Kasparov. Most interesting problems are computationally intractable (or NP-hard) or do not allow optimization for other reasons, such as when multiple goals compete, when the criterion cannot be precisely measured (with concepts such as happiness), and when the problem is ill-defined (finding the best wife or husband). Optimization under constraints deals with this problem by transforming complex real-world problems into 'small worlds' and introducing convenient mathematical assumptions that allow optimization. The hope is that the optimal behaviour determined for the small world might also be optimal in the messy real world.

In contrast, the programme of ecological rationality asks how real people make decisions when optimization is out of reach. It replaces optimizing by satisficing (finding an action that is good enough), and universality by modularity. The programme is threefold: (1) to describe the heuristics in the 'adaptive toolbox', their building blocks, and the evolved capacities they exploit; (2) to determine the social and physical environments in which a given heuristic is better than other strategies, that is, their ecological rationality; and (3) to design heuristics and environments in applied contexts, such as medicine, law, business, and engineering. Examples of heuristics include the recognition heuristic (e.g. relying on brand name recognition in consumer choice), one-reason decision-making (basing a complex decision on one good reason only), equality (dividing your assets equally, as in investment and food sharing), peer group imitation, advice taking (learning from the experience of others), and default (e.g. abiding by a legal default for organ donation, whether opt-in or opt-out). Examples of environmental structures that support one-reason decision-making include moderate to high uncertainty, redundancy, and variability of cue weights. In these situations, relying solely on one good reason and ignoring the rest can result in more accurate predictions than complex statistical methods, including multiple regression, neural networks, and classification and regression trees—while being faster and entailing less information cost. In an uncertain world, an intelligent mind needs to ignore part of the information available rather than combining everything. This insight poses a challenge to the ideal that more information and computation is always better; a beneficial amount of cognitive limitation can in fact be adaptive in the sense that we would fare worse without it (Hertwig and Todd 2003).

What is the role of affect in bounded rationality? A supernatural being with perfect knowledge, approximated by the ideal of unbounded rationality, can dispense with emotions. If you can predict the behaviour of others perfectly, then hope, trust, joy, surprise, or fear are redundant. Similarly, these feelings play little role in optimization under constraints. In the cognitive illusions programme, affect has been treated in the same way as cognitive limitations. The study of ecological rationality, in contrast, investigates the situations in which a given emotion or intuition would be good enough for making important decisions (see DECISION-MAKING) (Gigerenzer 2007). For instance, some emotions can function similarly to but more efficiently than the cognitive building blocks of heuristics. Love can stop the search for partners more effectively than an aspiration level, and

Brunswikian lens model

disgust can limit the choice set more consistently than a consideration set based on weighting of features. The challenge ahead is to incorporate emotions as search or stopping rules into the cognitive models of heuristics, and to analyse the environmental structures that make emotions rational.

GERD GIGERENZER

Gigerenzer, G. and Selten, R. (eds) (2001). *Bounded rationality: the adaptive toolbox*. Cambridge, MA: MIT Press.

Payne, J.W., Bettman, J.R., and Johnson, E.J. (1993). *The adaptive decision maker*. Cambridge: Cambridge University Press.

Brunswikian lens model Egon Brunswik (1903–55) formulated several innovative theoretical and methodological principles for the study of visual perception, which may be particularly suitable for the study of nonverbal communication of affect. Brunswik proposed a 'cue theory', according to which perceivers make 'inferences' about objects or states of affairs based on a number of uncertain but partly redundant cues in the environment. Brunswik (1952) recognized the importance of social perception in biological adaptation: 'Forced to react quickly or within reasonable limits of time (the organism) must respond before direct contact with the relevant remote conditions in the environment, such as . . . friends or enemies, can be established' (p. 22).

This evolutionary perspective on human behaviour implies a focus on the relationship between the organism and its environment. Brunswik argued that researchers should try to capture how organisms 'come to terms' with the inherent uncertainty in the environment. This requires that studies are designed in such a way that they represent the conditions to which the findings are intended to apply, Brunswik's notion of *representative design*. The above features—uncertain cues, focus on environment–organism relationships, and representative design—come together in Brunswik's (1952) symmetrical conceptualization of human behaviour, the lens model.

The lens model has been outlined in several variants by Brunswik and other authors. Figure B3 presents the version proposed by Hammond and colleagues in 1975 (see Cooksey 1996) for the study of social judgement. It shows the probabilistic relations between a physical or social object in the environment (left side of the model), a limited number of indicators (cues at the centre of the model), and the conscious perception (commonly called judgement or attribution in studies of interpersonal perception) of this object (right side of the model). Researchers have commonly used multiple regression to model each side of the lens, though other analytical methods can be used as well. A mathematical formulation of the relations among the different parts of the lens model (i.e. the lens model equation) was formulated by Hammond and colleagues (Cooksey 1996). It allows one to explain the validity of a judgement by decomposing it into different components (e.g. the consistency of cue utilization, the degree to which the cue utilization is 'matched' to the 'true' or 'ecological' validity of each cue). Ideally, the analysis should feature stimuli that vary freely, instead of being varied systematically by the investigator, to preserve the natural statistical characteristics of the environment. However, one can also design the experiment in such a way that it recreates the most relevant characteristics.

The Brunswikian lens model has been used in a number of different applications (e.g. Hammond and Stewart 2001). Scherer (1978) has repeatedly advocated

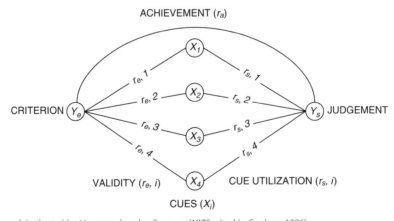

Fig. B3. Lens model adapted by Hammond and colleagues (1975; cited in Cooksey 1996).

the use of the lens model for the study of *nonverbal communication of affect, extending the approach from the study of fairly stable characteristics of an individual (e.g. personality traits, intelligence) to more transient characteristics (emotions). However, in the field of affective science, Brunswik's framework has so far been used in only two lines of research, involving musical (Juslin 2000) and vocal communication (Bänziger 2004).

Although the lens model might appear simple, it has a crucial implication for communications research: if the cues are redundant to some extent, more than one way of using the cues may lead to a similarly high level of decoding accuracy, because different cues can substitute for one another. Therefore, the Brunswikian lens model may explain why there is commonly accurate communication of affect even when the cues are used inconsistently. This is because multiple cues that are partly redundant yield a robust communicative system that is 'forgiving' toward deviation from optimal cue utilization. Researchers in nonverbal communication are sometimes frustrated because it is difficult to find patterns of cues that unequivocally indicate particular emotions. The lens model can help to explain why this is the case: the communicative system is so robust that perfect consistency is not required. However, robustness comes with a price: the redundancy of the cues means that the same information is conveyed by many cues. This limits the information capacity of the channel.

The characteristics captured by the Brunswikian lens model also have several implications for how research on communication of affect should preferably be conducted.

For instance, the model implies that valid inferences about affect depend equally on the encoder and the decoder (see ENCODING/DECODING OF EXPRESSION). For example, the extent to which a communicative signal features cues that reliably index emotion necessarily sets the upper limit on the accuracy with which perceivers may infer that emotion. Only an analysis of both aspects will allow the researcher to explain poor accuracy in terms of encoding or decoding. Also, researchers should strive to achieve a representative sampling of both encoders and decoders. Most studies of social perception have sampled decoders, but not the 'social objects' (e.g. faces, voices, gestures) to be judged. But unless stimuli are sampled representatively, almost any level of decoding accuracy may be obtained in a given study.

Ironically, Brunswik's ideas have had the least impact in the field where he made the largest effort (visual perception). Most studies inspired by him have focused on cognitive judgement. However, Brunswik's ideas could have some broader implications for emotion research as well. For instance, a better understanding of how emotions are evoked may require a serious effort to sample emotional situations in a representative manner.

PATRIK N. JUSLIN AND TANJA BÄNZIGER

Hammond, K.R. and Stewart, T.R. (eds) (2001). *The essential Brunswik: beginnings, explications, applications*. New York: Oxford University Press.

Juslin, P.N. and Scherer, K.R. (2005). Vocal expression of affect. In: J.A. Harrigan, R. Rosenthal, and K.R. Scherer (eds), *The new handbook of methods in nonverbal behavior research*, pp. 65–135. New York: Oxford University Press.

C

Cannon–Bard theory The Cannon–Bard theory of emotion refers to a theoretical framework developed by the psychologists and physiologists Walter Cannon and Philip Bard in the 1920s and 1930s. The development of the Cannon–Bard theory arose out of concerns about the validity of the *James–Lange theory of emotions which proposed that emotions were the perception of bodily changes in response to a stimulus. So, for example, you see a bear in the woods, you run, and the perception of the physiological changes associated with flight is the emotion of fear. Cannon and Bard reasoned that for the James–Lange theory to hold, emotions must require intact motor and sensory cortices to mediate perception of the physiological changes in the body in order to produce emotion. However, Cannon and Bard, in their seminal studies, showed that removing the cortex in cats did not eliminate emotional behaviour but in fact intensified it in the form of frequent ill-directed anger attacks that Cannon and Bard labelled sham rage.

On the basis of these studies, Cannon and Bard proposed an alternative theory in which encountering emotional stimuli leads directly to the onset of emotion via hypothalamic circuitry in the brain (see NEURAL ARCHITECTURE OF EMOTION). The role of more recently evolved cortical structures is then to modulate and control the emotion and to select appropriate responses. So, you see a bear in the woods, you feel afraid, and you choose to run. The Cannon–Bard theory was thus the first real brain model of emotion and was pioneering in drawing upon animal emotions as human homologues and in utilizing data from brain lesion data to understand affective processing in the intact brain.

Criticisms of the Cannon–Bard theory focus on the fact that the neuroanatomical mapping of process to brain region was probably wrong (Dalgleish 2004a) and that the direct relationship between stimulus (e.g. a bear) and emotion implies that there is no mechanism for the generation of emotion, an issue hotly disputed by later cognitive theorists.

TIM DALGLEISH

cardiovascular system The human cardiovascular system consists of the heart, blood vessels, and blood. The cardiovascular system works to deliver oxygen (O_2) and nutrients to the tissues of the body and to remove waste products from tissues for delivery to the lungs, kidneys, and liver. Blood circulates through the cardiovascular system in two parallel circuits. Deoxygenated blood containing carbon dioxide (CO_2) and other waste products returns from the body to the right side of the heart where it is pumped to the lungs for gas exchange. Carbon dioxide is delivered to the lungs for removal while O_2 is taken up by the haemoglobin molecule in red blood cells for transport to the rest of the body. This reoxygenated blood then returns to the left side of the heart from which it is pumped through the aorta to the rest of the body. In addition, nitrogenous wastes are delivered to the kidney and fats and carbohydrates and other nutrients and metabolites are circulated to the liver and remaining tissues.

Response to stress

A complex neurohormonal system directs adaptation to various environmental stimuli. For example, the physiological demands of exercise require an increase in cardiac output (volume of blood pumped per minute) to supply the muscles with oxygen and energy. This is accomplished through an increase in stress hormones such as epinephrine, norepinephrine, and cortisol. The beneficial effects of regular exercise over time include lowering of the blood pressure and weight loss. In addition to these positive effects of stress, it is well recognized that a parallel but unique response to psychological stressors may result in deleterious increases in blood pressure and heart rate (see STRESS; HEALTH AND EMOTION). In contrast to exercise, this response has been associated with an increase in clinical heart disease.

Cardiovascular disease

After more than 50 years of research in the 20th century, much is known about the causes, consequences, and treatment of cardiovascular disease. It is now well-recognized that maladaptive health behaviours such as physical inactivity, smoking, and dietary indiscretions result in the accumulation of the principal risk factors such as diabetes, high cholesterol, and high blood pressure. These risk factors and health behaviours work synergistically with genetic predispositions leading to clinical cardiovascular disease.

JARETT D. BERRY AND
DONALD M. LLOYD-JONES

Zipes, D.P., Libby, P., Bonow, R.O., and Braunwald, E. (2005). *Braunwald's heart disease: a textbook of cardiovascular medicine*, 7th edn. Philadelphia, PA: Elsevier Saunders.

childhood (emotional development)

Emotional competence (see COMPETENCE, EMOTIONAL) is central to children's ability to form relationships with others (see SOCIAL RELATIONSHIPS). Susanne Denham (1998) and Carolyn Saarni (1999) also assert that early emotional competence contributes to mental health throughout the lifespan. The building blocks of emotional competence include emotional expression (see EXPRESSION, PRINCIPLES OF EMOTIONAL) and experience (see FEELINGS (PSYCHOLOGICAL PERSPECTIVES)), understanding emotions of self and others (see INTELLIGENCE, EMOTIONAL), and emotion regulation (see REGULATION OF EMOTION). These skills develop throughout life, such that children become increasingly emotionally competent over time. Much of the variation in children's emotional competence derives from experiences within the family (Eisenberg *et al.* 1998). Components of emotional competence, developing through the preschool and elementary school periods, and bolstered or undermined by such experiences, are outlined here.

Expression and experience of emotions

The interpersonal function of emotion is central to its expression and experience; conversely, social interactions and relationships are guided, even defined, by emotional transactions. Emotions are inherently social, as follows: (1) others' behaviours often constitute antecedent conditions for emotions; (2) emotional expressiveness within a social setting is important information for oneself and for others; (3) one's expression of emotion may form the antecedent condition for others' experience and expression of emotions (Campos and Barrett 1984, Saarni 1990).

Emotions must be expressed while keeping one's *goals in line with the social context; that is, the goals of self and other must be coordinated. Thus, emotional competence includes expressing emotions in a way that is advantageous to moment-to-moment interaction and relationships over time (Halberstadt *et al.* 2001). First, emotionally competent individuals are aware that an affective message needs to be sent. But what affective message should be sent for successful interaction? Children slowly learn which expressions of emotion facilitate specific goals. Second, children also come to determine the appropriate affective message, one that 'works' in the setting or with a specific playmate. Third, children learn how to send the affective message convincingly. Method, intensity, and timing of an affective message are crucial to its meaning, and its eventual success or failure. When real affective messages are inappropriate (e.g. situationally but not contextually relevant, or irrelevant), 'false' messages must be managed.

Preschoolers express all the 'basic', self-conscious, and social emotions, and are also developing the aforementioned skills. After preschool, expression and experience of emotion become more sophisticated. Children learn that their goals are not always met by freely showing their most intense feelings. For example, older children regulate anger due to the negative consequences they expect in specific situations or from specific persons. In addition to the 'cool rule', which mandates more muted emotions within most social settings, older children's emotional messages can be more complex, with more blended signals and better-differentiated expressions of 'social' emotions. Much of the new ability to more clearly express and experience complex emotions (guilt, pride, and shame) is buttressed by comprehension of responsibility and other norms.

Understanding emotions

Knowledge of emotion predicts later social functioning, including social acceptance by peers (O'Neil and Parke 2000). By preschool, most children can infer basic emotions from expressions or situations, and understand the consequences of these emotions. Preschoolers tend to have a better understanding of happy situations compared with those that evoke negative emotions. They gradually come to differentiate among the negative emotions, and become increasingly capable of using emotional language. Furthermore, young children begin to identify others' emotions, even when they may differ from their own.

As children progress through elementary school, their awareness of emotional experience broadens to include the complexity of multiple emotions, and the realization that inner and outer emotional states may differ. By middle school, children comprehend the time course of emotions, display rules associated with emotional situations, and moral emotions. They now have an adult-like sense of how different events elicit different emotions in different people, and that enduring patterns of personality may impact upon individualized emotional reactions.

Emotion regulation

Emotion regulation becomes necessary when the presence or absence of emotional expression and experience interfere with one's goals. Negative or positive emotions can be regulated when they threaten to overwhelm, or need to be amplified. Children learn to retain or enhance those emotions that are relevant and helpful, to attenuate those that are relevant but not helpful, and to dampen those that are irrelevant. These skills help them to maintain satisfying relationships with others.

Early in the preschool period, most emotion regulation is biobehavioural (e.g. thumbsucking), and supported by adults. Important cognitive and attentional foundations of emotion regulation contribute to the changes observed in emotional competence from preschool to adolescence. Preschoolers gradually begin to use independent coping strategies for emotion regulation, such as problem solving, support-seeking, distancing, internalizing, externalizing, distraction, reframing/redefining, cognitive 'blunting', and denial. Older children refine these strategies.

Following preschool, older children learn that there are multiple strategies at their command, and know which are adaptive in specific situations. They also use more cognitive and problem-solving methods, and fewer support-seeking strategies.

SUSANNE A. DENHAM AND
HEATHER K. WARREN

Denham, S. (1998). *Emotional development in young children*. New York: Guilford Press.

Saarni, C. (1999). *The development of emotional competence*. New York: Guilford Press.

circumplex models For over a century, scientists have debated the basic building blocks of emotional life that a science of emotion should focus on (see EMOTION THEORIES AND CONCEPTS (PSYCHOLOGICAL PERSPECTIVES)). The 'discrete emotion' approach argues that certain categories (e.g. those described by such English words as anger, sadness, fear, happiness, and disgust) form the most basic elements of emotional life (see BASIC EMOTIONS; DIFFERENTIAL EMOTIONS THEORY). The 'dimensional' approach (see DIMENSIONAL MODELS) argues that anger, sadness, fear, and so on are words that name common sense categories that are grounded in more basic affective properties such as valence and arousal (Russell and Barrett 1999), valence and intensity (e.g. Lang *et al.* 1990), positive and negative activation (e.g. Watson and Tellegen 1985), or approach and withdrawal (see APPROACH/WITHDRAWAL) (e.g. Davidson 1992). Questions about the structure of emotion are important for the field to resolve, because the answers will dictate which constructs will best support scientific induction and allow for the accumulation of knowledge.

Dimensional models of affect

Dimensional models assume that, at their core, all affective phenomena are necessarily (but not sufficiently) described by two properties. Typically, these properties (i.e. the dimensions) do not represent higher-order conceptual groupings but are instead basic, psychological primitives that describe an affective state. A number of dimensional models of affect can be found in the existing literature. The oldest is the valence/arousal model. This model has theoretical roots in work by Wundt (1912/1924), who attempted to classify affective experiences along three dimensions (i.e. pleasant–unpleasant, calm–excited, relaxation–tension); Titchener (1909), who focused mainly on the valence dimension; Woodworth (1938), who attempted to similarly classify facial expressions of emotions; and Schlosberg (1952), who proposed a circular structure of emotion defined first by two dimensions (pleasantness–unpleasantness, attention–rejection), following which he added an intensity dimension (sleep–tension) to produce a cone-like structure (Schlosberg 1954). The valence/arousal model is also consistent with the semantic differential work by Osgood (Osgood *et al.* 1957) who demonstrated that there are three major components of meaning in natural language (evaluation, activity, and potency). Russell (1980) consolidated and elaborated this earlier work with the notion that the circular structure of emotion was actually a circumplex (a multipurpose, mathematical formalism for representing the mental structure for a group of stimuli through the geometry of the circle). Barrett (2004) demonstrated that the circumplex structure of emotion varies idiographically across people. According to the valence/arousal circumplex model of affect, all affective phenomena at their core are necessarily (but not sufficiently) described by two psychological properties: valence (or hedonic tone), which is distinct from desirability or value (Barrett 1996), and arousal (or a feeling of activation or quiescence), which is related to, but does not have a one-to-one correspondence with, peripheral nervous system activity (Barrett *et al.* 2004). The affective circumplex is presented in Fig. C1.

Other dimensional models of affect do not incorporate circumplex assumptions, although they often depict their models in a circular space. For example, the valence/intensity models (e.g. Lang *et al.* 1980, Larsen and Diener 1992, Reisenzein 1994) assumes that affective states can be described as a combination of quality (pleasure–displeasure) and the intensity, but do not suppose that these experiences relate to one another in circumplex fashion. Thayer's model of affect, where the dimensions represent different properties of arousal, also does not rely on circumplex assumptions (Thayer 1989). In addition, there are circular models of emotion that do not incorporate the affective dimensions (e.g. Plutchik 1980).

Dimensional models that assume pleasure and displeasure to be independent dimensions (rather than opposites along one bipolar dimension) also do not specify that affective experiences assume a circumplex structure (e.g. Cacioppo *et al.* 1997; Reich *et al.* 2003; Watson and Tellegen 1985). In fact, Watson and Tellegen's NA/PA model explicitly assumes that affective experiences conform to simple structure rather than to a circumplex structure (for a discussion see Russell and Barrett 1999), although they do depict their dimensions graphically in a circular space. Originally called 'negative affect' and 'positive affect', NA and PA dimensions

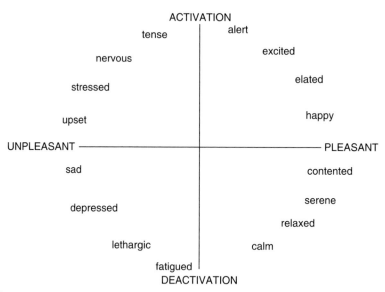

Fig. C1. The affective circumplex.

recently underwent a name change (Watson *et al.* 1999) to avoid conceptual confusions (for a discussion see Barrett and Russell, 1998). NA and PA dimensions are typically derived by orthogonally rotating the valence and arousal dimensions to simple structure using the varimax criterion (Watson and Tellegen 1985). A varimax rotation orients factors towards large clusters of variables, thereby trying to come as close as possible to a simple structure solution (i.e. items load on one factor but not the other). As a result, the NA/PA model has affect terms clustering together in particular portions of the affective space in a way that is more consistent with a simple structure than with a circumplex configuration (Watson and Tellegen 1985, p. 221). Although they can be thought of as rotational variants in cross-sectional analyses of self-reported affect, the NA and PA dimensions are conceptually distinct from valence and arousal. Whereas valence and arousal are each bipolar, NA and PA are defined as 'descriptively bipolar, but affectively unipolar' dimensions of affective experience (Watson and Tellegen 1985). Descriptively, the NA dimension is anchored by a cluster of negatively valenced, high-arousal emotions on one end (e.g. nervous, angry), and by positively valenced, low-arousal emotions on the other (e.g. calm, relaxed). Similarly, the PA dimension is anchored to a cluster of positively valenced, high-arousal emotions on one end (e.g. enthusiastic, excited), and by negatively valenced, low-arousal emotions on the other (e.g. tired, bored). NA and PA dimensions are thought to be affectively unipolar, however, in that the

low-arousal ends of each dimension are meant to refer to the absence of affective feeling. As a result, the self-report measure built to measure NA and PA dimensions, called the PANAS, capture only the high-end dimension markers (Watson *et al.* 1988).

What is a circumplex?

Circumplex models abound in psychology. Simply put, the circumplex model of affect is a circle and a set of axes. In the circumplex model of affect, the circle depicts the similarity or relatedness between any set of affect-related objects or items such as judgements of affect-related words, perceptual judgements of faces depicting emotion, or self-reports of affective experience. For example, the circle depicts the similarity between the words 'angry' and 'sad' when thinking about what the words mean, when using the words to describe someone else's facial behaviours, or when using them to self-report one's own momentary feeling state. The axes are the psychological properties that quantify what is similar and different about those affective items.

Mathematically speaking, the circumplex represents the relationship between any set of items through the geometry of a circle (Guttman 1957). (A circumplex structure is defined by formal, mathematical criteria and when items conform to a circumplex structure, they need not have perfect communality with the circular space, nor equally spaced elements around the circle; for a discussion see Fabrigar *et al.*, 1997). The term 'circumplex' literally means 'circular order of

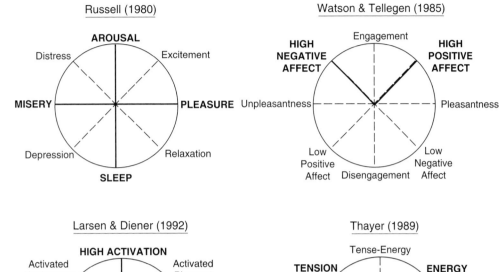

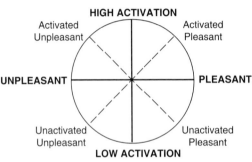

Fig. C2. Various dimensions to anchor the affective circumplex.

complexity' to indicate that the objects in question (in this case, affect-related items) are heterogeneous (can be decomposed into more basic psychological properties) and therefore cannot be easily ordered relative to one another in a simple linear fashion. Instead, their qualitative (or ordinal) similarity to one another is reflected in their proximity around the perimeter of the circle. The similarity between affect items is represented solely by their position in the circle—this similarity might be due to two properties, or three, or even four—the point is that there is more than one property.

The affective circumplex has additional properties, over and above the generic circumplex structure. First, items that are closer together are similar, whereas items separated by an arc distance of 180 degrees are maximally dissimilar. For example, as the minimal arc distance between items increases (e.g. 'happy' and 'enthusiastic'), the degree of similarity decreases (i.e. the correlation becomes smaller), suggesting that the items are experienced as qualitatively different. When affect items are separated by an arc distance of 90 degrees (e.g. 'happy' and 'surprised'), they are com-

pletely independent. When the arc distance increases to 180 degrees (e.g. 'happy' and 'sad'), the items represent opposite experiences. Past 180 degrees, the reports become increasingly similar again until the original starting point is reached.

Second, it is possible to discover the psychological primitives that anchor the affective circumplex, by statistically examining the circumplex within a two-dimensional Euclidean space (see Shepard 1978). Various sets of dimensions to anchor affective space have been proposed (see discussion of dimension models above, and Fig. C2), but the only set that are empirically associated with the circumplex structure are valence and activation (Russell and Barrett 1999). Both dimensions are bipolar (for a discussion, see Russell and Carroll 1999) independent from one another, meaning that arousal is not merely the intensity of pleasure or displeasure (Barrett and Russell, unpublished data).

Breadth of the affective circumplex
The affective circumplex model is highly robust and is the only dimensional model that has been empirically

identified across a range of affective stimuli. Circumplex-like structures have been found for judgements of emotion language from many cultures (see Russell and Barrett 1999). Circumplex-like structures have been identified in judgements of emotion as they are perceived in other people's faces by participants of different ages, and have been established in both nomothetic and idiographic self-reports of affective states (for a review see Russell and Barrett 1999). The affective circumplex can also incorporate other dimensions of affective experience (such as positive and negative activation, or PA and NA) and therefore is useful for integrating different models of affect into a single space (Carroll et al. 1999).

The psychological meaning of the affective circumplex

The generalizability of the circumplex model indicates that all affective stimuli (i.e. emotion-related language, judgements of facial behaviours, subjective ratings of emotional episodes such as anger, sadness, and fear, as well as nonemotional affective states like fatigue, sleepiness, and placidity) can be minimally characterized as a combination of these two independent properties. By this interpretation, when derived from similarity judgements (estimates of relatedness) of emotion-related words, multidimensional scaling solutions yield valence and arousal dimensions that represent the basic, semantic properties contained in our knowledge about those words, and the concepts that those words represent (Barrett and Fossum 2001). When derived from ratings of facial behaviours, the dimensions represent the affective perceptions of other people's behaviour. When derived from subjective ratings of experience, valence and arousal refer to the basic or core phenomenological properties of affective experience (Russell and Barrett 1999).

LISA FELDMAN BARRETT AND
JAMES A. RUSSELL

Barrett, L.F. (2004). Feelings or words? Understanding the content in self-report ratings of emotional experience. *Journal of Personality and Social Psychology*, **87**, 266–81.

Barrett, L.F. (2006). Valence as a basic building block of emotional life. *Journal of Research in Personality*, **40**, 35–55.

Carroll, J.M., Yik, M.S.M., Russell, J.A., and Barrett, L.F. (1999). On the psychometric principles of affect. *Review of General Psychology*, **3**, 14–22.

Russell, J.A. (1980). A circumplex model of affect. *Journal of Personality and Social Psychology*, **39**, 1161–78.

Russell, J.A. and Barrett, L.F. (1999). Core affect, prototypical emotional episodes, and other things called emotion: dissecting the elephant. *Journal of Personality and Social Psychology*, **76**, 805–19.

climate, emotional Emotional climate refers to the state of emotional relationships in a collective (such as a

nation, community, or organization). Thus, descriptions of emotional climate involve the extent to which people and groups within a collective trust and respect one another, and hence the degree to which a society is unified or polarized. Descriptions typically include the extent to which people are feeling secure or insecure; whether they are living in a climate of fear that isolates people from one another, or feel comfortable in sharing their beliefs; whether they experience a climate of anger and despair at the corruption in their government, or are hopeful in their country's future. Note that an emotional climate is not simply the sum of individual emotions. Theoretically, it is a collective affect that is generated by how people interact with one another as the collective responds to its economic, political, and social conditions.

Issues of conception and measurement

There are at least four different ways of conceptualizing and measuring emotional climate: (1) As the *perception* of how people relate to one another. This is usually measured by questionnaires asking people how they believe most *other* people feel. Questions phrased in this manner may be used to describe differences in national emotional climates that are relatively independent of a respondent's social class (de Rivera et al. 2007). (2) As the priming of choices about how to perceive situations and hence as the probability of the actual *experience* of specific emotions (or working to avoid them). This may be measured by reports of individual experiences or behaviours in social situations. (3) As social norms or convention about what is *appropriate* to feel, what ought to govern behaviour, or what can be used to justify behaviour, rather than what is actually experienced. This may be measured with simple counts of the usage of different emotion terms (see Fernandez-Dols et al. 2007). (4) As an abstract *emotional field* that is centred about a collective narrative, and related signs (such as the presence of armed guards). Such fields may be described by observing how people are behaving in relevant behaviour settings.

Distinguishing emotional climate from other collective affect

It is important to distinguish between emotional climate and emotional atmosphere and other sorts of collective affect. Emotional atmospheres occur when group members focus on a particular event. Group-based emotions in general occur when individuals are identified with a group, as when the fans of a team or citizens of a nation feel pride, sorrow, anger, etc. at what happens to their team or nation (see INTERGROUP EMOTIONS). Although climates may be influenced by atmospheres and group emotion, they are constituted by the longer-lasting relationships among members of the collective. In this aspect climates are more closely related to aspects of culture (see INDIVIDUALISM/COLLECTIVISM). However, emotional climates are relatively independent of culture and more attuned to the collective's pervasive situation. Thus, they are similar to a collective's emotional orientation to long-standing situations or to the emotional currents that may sweep through a society when people are caught up in historical events.

Usefulness of the concept

Since emotional climate is influenced by governmental policies, the measurement of changes in climate may allow us to assess the impact of these policies. For example, measurements suggest that the heightening of post 9/11 'national security' has not affected the national climate of security in the United States, but has increased the extent to which there is a fear of speaking.

Understanding the state of a collective's emotional climate probably helps explain significant aspects of the behaviour of the collective's members. Although we cannot yet be certain, emotional climate appears to affect the behaviour of individuals by making some things appear more sensible than others. Thus, the cooperative behaviour so essential for a culture of peace may appear much more sensible in a climate of social trust, while violence appears more reasonable in climates of hate and fear. Within a collective, subclimates may have mutual influences. Thus, Ruiz (2007) shows that prisons whose employees report more positive emotional climates have prisoners who report less negative climates, and that when a positive climate predominates amongst prisoners there is less negative climate amongst employees.

Individual differences in the perception of climate also appear to account for an important source of variance in behaviour. Conejero and Etxebarria (2007) show that perceptions of emotional climate are much more stable than reports of personal emotions or emotional atmospheres, and less affected by the extent of national identification. Measures of the perception of climate appear to increase our ability to predict the avoidant and altruistic behaviour of individuals as they respond to a terrorist attack. In a similar vein, Páez et al. (2007) show that the perception of climate predicts the degree of posttraumatic growth.

JOSEPH DE RIVERA

Bar-Tal, D., Halperin, E., and de Rivera, J. (2007). Collective emotions in conflict situations: societal implications. *Journal of Social Issues*, **63**, 441–60.

de Rivera, J. and Páez, D. (2007). Emotional climate, human security, and cultures of peace. *Journal of Social Issues*, **63**, 233–53.

clinical aspects (of affect) see HEALTH / CLINICAL ASPECTS (OF AFFECT).

cognitive behaviour therapy Cognitive behaviour therapy refers to a range of psychotherapeutic approaches based on cognitive and behavioural theories of the development and maintenance of emotional or functional problems. These theories propose that learned patterns of thinking and behaviour (including conditioned responses, overt thoughts, and deeply held assumptions and beliefs) make an important contribution to emotional problems (see LEARNING, EMOTIONAL (NEUROSCIENCE PERSPECTIVES); ASSOCIATIVE PROCESSING). The therapies aim to help people to identify thoughts and behaviours that may be contributing to their problems and to modify those thoughts and behaviours using a range of techniques.

The earliest examples of behaviour therapy focused on *anxiety as a conditioned response to certain stimuli or situations. Therapy aimed to reduce anxiety through exposure to the provoking stimuli and subsequent habituation of the anxiety response. Subsequently, more emphasis was placed on the role of negative biases (see COGNITIVE BIAS) in thinking in *depression and anxiety (e.g. Beck et al. 1979). Cognitive therapy aims to help people to alleviate these negative biases through viewing relevant situations in a more even-handed and realistic fashion. Within cognitive behaviour therapy, the therapist and patient collaborate actively in addressing agreed goals and the therapist uses a questioning style to guide the patient's process of discovery.

Originally developed as a brief (12–20 weeks) treatment for acute emotional disorders, cognitive behaviour therapy has recently been extended to address more enduring problems such as chronic depression, personality disorders, and psychosis. Such developments place greater emphasis on understanding the development of involuntary cognitive processes and long-standing cognitive schemas and use a more eclectic range of techniques for addressing these more enduring aspects of cognition.

From its outset, cognitive behaviour therapists have attempted to validate their methods empirically. Although efforts to substantiate cognitive behavioural theories have often obtained mixed results, the consistency of evidence supporting the efficacy of cognitive behaviour therapy for a wide range of disorders has been impressive, and the possibility that its benefits extend beyond the termination of therapy is most encouraging (Roth and Fonagy 2004).

RICHARD G. MOORE

cognitive bias A cognitive bias is any systematic deviation from a normative criterion that affects thinking, often leading to errors in judgement. Affect, in particular, may bias cognition, both by altering the depth of cognitive processing and by having an impact on the content of cognitions. A useful example of emotion altering the depth of processing appears in studies by Bodenhausen et al. (1994). Happy individuals demonstrated less depth of processing than individuals in a neutral affective state, as evidenced by their reliance on simple mental categories rather than on complex stimuli. A useful example of emotion altering the content of thought appears in studies on the *affect-as-information model. Individuals in a positive mood judged their overall life satisfaction more positively than did individuals in a negative mood. That is, their temporary positive mood altered the content of their thoughts about satisfaction as a whole.

Psychologists attempt to measure the existence and magnitude of a bias in different ways (Hastie and Rasinski 1988). Below are four ways that emotional biases have been demonstrated by researchers.

Judgement lacks correspondence with a criterion

The most direct way to measure a bias is to compare human judgement with a known normative criterion. For example, Bechara *et al.* (1997) examined the decision-making of patients with lesions in their prefrontal cortex—an area that integrates emotion with cognition. They compared patients' performance on the Bechara gambling task to an optimal (i.e. normative) strategy that maximized expected value. The patients consistently chose riskier options that failed to maximize expected value, and the patients also exhibited lower levels of galvanic skin conductance in response to risky choices. The patients' diminished skin conductance was used to argue for the idea that patients lacked emotional responses to the risky choices, and that emotions can be a necessary cue for making normatively rational decisions (see SOMATIC MARKER HYPOTHESIS).

Judgement lacks correspondence with the judgements of others

Another way to measure a bias is to compare the judgement of different groups on a task. If the groups' judgements fail to cohere then one can infer that at least one of the groups must be biased. When using this approach, it is especially useful to identify one group as expert, so it can serve as the standard for comparison. In a study by Wilson and Schooler (1991), individuals were randomly assigned either to generate a list of reasons for their ratings regarding different types of jam or else to simply list their ratings. Results revealed that the ratings among individuals who simply listed ratings more closely resembled the ratings of jam experts. The authors thus concluded that reason giving can bias judgements of one's preferences.

Judgement relies on bad information

The existence of cognitive bias can also be inferred from individuals' reliance on a bad judgemental cue. In this case, information used to make a decision does not correlate with good judgement on a task (where good judgement would be defined along some normative criterion). In a

study by Bodenhausen *et al.* (2000), for example, subjects made judgements about various domains of real-world knowledge after being exposed to an arbitrary anchor. For example, they were asked to estimate the length of the Mississippi after being asked if its length was above or below 5,000 miles. In this case, 5,000 miles was an arbitrary/bad cue. Sad individuals' responses were more strongly related to these arbitrarily high or low anchors. Therefore, sad individuals' increased reliance on these anchors was interpreted as evidence of cognitive bias.

Judgement fails to use good information

Finally, one can infer a bias if individuals fail to utilize a good judgemental cue. In Lerner *et al.*'s (1998) study of legal decision-making, participants were randomly assigned to an anger condition or a neutral condition. In addition, half of the participants in each condition were randomly assigned to be accountable for their legal decisions and half were not. Then they all read a series of fictional tort cases and assess the extent, if at all, to which the defendant should be punished. Results revealed that unaccountable participants in the anger condition failed to consider mitigating factors about the defendants. Instead, they relied on their own feelings of incidental anger over past, unrelated events (i.e. bad cues). By contrast, accountable participants in the anger condition showed a better pattern of cue utilization. They disregarded their personal feelings of incidental anger and instead focused on all the facts of the cases, including mitigating information. In sum, the failure to use mitigating information was used as evidence for a judgemental bias.

Summary

To recap, researchers use a variety of analytical methods to uncover cognitive biases—the above four forming the fundamental approaches. It is important to highlight the fact that none of these methods demonstrate that emotions, on average, have a detrimental effect on human judgement. Whereas an emotion can bias judgement in some cases (as in the Bodenhausen *et al.*, 2000, study), the lack of an appropriate emotion (as in the Bechara *et al.* study) can bias judgement in other cases. Thus, emotions do not have a consistent biasing influence on judgement. It is also important to highlight the fact that emotion and cognition can influence bias in a bi-directional fashion. Whereas intense emotion can bias thoughts (e.g. in studies by Lerner *et al.*), intense thought can bias affective responses (e.g. in studies by Wilson and Schooler).

PAUL M. LITVAK AND JENNIFER S. LERNER

Forgas, J.P. (2003). Affective influences on attitudes and judgments. In: R.J. Davidson, K.R. Scherer, and H.H. Goldsmith (eds) *Handbook of affective science*, pp. 596–618. New York: Oxford University Press.

Loewenstein, G. and Lerner, J.S. (2003). The role of affect in decision making. In: R.J. Davidson, K.R. Scherer, and H.H. Goldsmith (eds), pp. 619–42. *Handbook of affective science*. New York: Oxford University Press.

communication see EXPRESSION, FUNCTIONS OF EMOTIONAL; EXPRESSION, PRINCIPLES OF EMOTIONAL; INTERPERSONAL COMMUNICATION; INTERSUBJECTIVITY; MEDIA COMMUNICATION; NONVERBAL COMMUNICATION.

compassion Literally, compassion means feeling or suffering *with* another person (Latin: *com-*, together + *pati*, to suffer). However, both in common parlance and in psychology and philosophy, compassion typically means feeling *for* a person in distress. So defined, compassion serves as a less paternalistic and pejorative synonym for sympathy or pity, and a synonym for one meaning of *empathy. Compassion is not simply emotional *contagion or feeling the same emotion the other feels. Rather, it is an *other-oriented emotion* elicited by and congruent with the perceived welfare of another person (i.e. an emotional response to one's appraisal of the other's welfare, not one's own welfare). The antecedent conditions of compassion are (1) perceiving the other as in need (distress) and (2) valuing the other's welfare. Taking the other's perspective by imagining how he or she is affected by the need situation can increase compassion. Compassion is considered a likely source of altruistic motivation (see ALTRUISM (PSYCHOLOGICAL PERSPECTIVES)) to relieve the other's plight, and of a range of behaviours that promote this end. The Good Samaritan is said to have had compassion for the man who fell among thieves.

C. DANIEL BATSON

Haidt, J. (2003). The moral emotions. In: R.J. Davidson, K.R. Scherer, and H.H. Goldsmith (eds), *Handbook of affective sciences*, pp. 852–70. New York: Oxford University Press.

compatibility with standards Appraisal theorists (see APPRAISAL THEORIES) have recognized the important role of the social context of appraisal, particularly with respect to *norms, *values, and justice on the one hand, and the self and its social identity on the other. Evaluating the social consequences of a particular action is an important step before finalizing the appraisal process and deciding on appropriate behavioural responses. Several appraisal theorists have suggested dimensions such as *legitimacy, value relevance, or compatibility with external standards which are used to evaluate the compatibility of an action with the perceived norms of a salient reference group (Roseman and Smith 2001, Scherer 2001a). A discrepancy with regard to such norms results in states one could label 'righteous rejection' in evaluating another person, or 'shame' if it concerns one's own behaviour (see MORAL EMOTIONS). When, for example, the behaviours of others are judged to be in violation of social norms, anger often results. In consequence, appraisal on this 'moral' dimension is a powerful factor in socialization and in the maintenance of social order. A particularly important dimension in this respect is the evaluation of deservedness or justice (Mikula *et al*. 1998), as perceived injustice can provoke and increase the intensity of a number of different emotions, in particular anger. Appraisal theorists debate the utility of postulating a separate dimension for justice, or to subsume it under a general dimension of moral and normative standards.

Another eminently social aspect of the appraisal process is the evaluation of one's behaviour with reference to the self-ideal, one's social identity or self-concept. This dimension is central for the genesis of the so-called *self-reflexive emotions (see Tangney and Fischer 1995). The individual consistently evaluates the extent to which an action falls short of or exceeds internal standards, such as one's personal self-ideal or internalized moral code. While these internal standards generally reflect sociocultural values or moral standards, they can sometimes be at variance with cultural or group norms, (e.g. incompatibility between the norms or demands of particular reference groups or persons). Discrepancy with regard to internal standards can sometimes lead to feelings of contempt, resulting from judging the behaviour of others, and feelings of guilt in the case of one's own behaviour. On the other hand, exceeding internal or external standards may produce feelings of pride. Markus and Kitayama (1991) have highlighted the central role of the self-concept, and its cultural variation, in these processes.

KLAUS R. SCHERER

Ellsworth, P.C. and Scherer, K.R. (2003). Appraisal processes in emotion. In: R.J. Davidson, K.R. Scherer, and H.H. Goldsmith (eds), *Handbook of the affective sciences*, pp. 572–95. New York: Oxford University Press.

competence, emotional Research on emotional intelligence (EI) (see INTELLIGENCE, EMOTIONAL) has its roots squarely in the theoretical and methodological tradition of intelligence measurement, starting from ability scores defined by factor analytic procedures. Assessment of EI is focused on regulating, understanding, and manipulating emotion, with performance often being defined by self-ratings or in relation to expert or standardization group scores. In contrast, work on emotional competence starts from the function of emotion in human adaptation and its role in social interaction. Consequently, the roots of this research tradition are tied to social competence, and in particular to the development of this competence (Eisenberg and Fabes 1992, see CHILDHOOD (EMOTIONAL DEVELOPMENT)). Following this lead, Halberstadt *et al*. (2001) have defined affective social competence as the dynamic integration of three integrated and dynamic components: sending affective messages, receiving affective messages, and experiencing affect. They identify central and interconnected abilities within each component which include awareness and identification of affect, working within a complex, constantly changing social context, and management and regulation. They also review research with special populations of children to highlight the importance of affective social competence in social relationships. From a similar developmental vantage point, Saarni (1999) defined emotional competence as the capacity for self-efficacy in emotion-eliciting social transactions and suggested that its constituents include an awareness of one's emotions and those of others, a capacity to use emotion vocabulary and expressions, empathy, the differentiation of internal subjectivity from outward expression, emotion regulation and coping skills, and adaptive emotional communication within relationships.

From a more general, theoretical viewpoint, Scherer (2007) has criticized EI approaches with respect to two major problems: (1) an overemphasis on cognitive aspects of knowledge about emotion, and (2) an overemphasis on adaptive aspects of personality. Instead, it is suggested to define emotional competence as the ability to optimally use the emotion mechanism as *it has been shaped by evolution* (see FUNCTIONALIST THEORIES OF EMOTION; EVOLUTION OF EMOTION). Specifically, one can imagine that individuals will differ widely with respect to four major classes of competencies: *production, response preparation, regulation,* and *communication.* Production competence consists of generating appropriate emotional reactions to different types of eliciting events based on appropriate appraisals of internal goal states, available coping potential, and the probable consequences of events, as well as of efficient elicitation mechanisms (avoiding over- or underreaction). Response preparation competence involves a shaping of emotional reactions that fit the appraisal results and allow the preparation of adaptive action tendencies, as well as an appropriate monitoring of the unfolding response patterns. The latter is essential for regulation competence, which involves the absence of impulsiveness and the timely and context-specific use of regulation and coping mechanisms. Finally, communication competence in social interactions requires appropriate expression of one's own state (ability to adapt emotional expression to strategic interaction goals and authentic congruent expression in different modalities), a capacity for empathy, and a high ability to recognize the emotional states of others in different modalities, even if controlled or concealed. While much remains to be done in this area, a number of performance-based instruments are currently available (see Scherer 2007). A stronger investment by emotion researchers in this domain can help to raise the conceptual and methodo-

92

logical standards for different applications in the areas of work and organization, education, and health, currently mostly exploited by self-appointed 'experts' using dubious tests and training procedures.

KLAUS R. SCHERER

compliance Compliance refers to a particular kind of response, acquiescence, to a particular kind of communication, a request. The request may be explicit, as in the direct solicitation of funds in a door-to-door campaign for charitable donations, or it may be implicit, as in a political advertisement that touts the qualities of a candidate without directly asking for a vote. But in all cases, the target recognizes that he or she is being urged to respond in a desired way. Systematic scientific study of the compliance process has been under way for well over a half century, beginning in earnest with the United States government's public information and persuasion programmes of World War II (e.g. Hovland *et al.* 1949). As a consequence, the social science literature contains a substantial body of work on various factors that cause one individual to comply with another's request for action of some sort.

A review of that literature (Cialdini 2008) suggests that a set of six psychological principles accounts for the success of the majority of communications designed to produce compliance. Briefly, the principles involve pressures to comply because of tendencies to: (1) reciprocate a gift, favour, or service, (2) be consistent with prior commitments, (3) follow the lead of similar others, (4) accommodate the requests of liked others, (5) conform to the directives of legitimate authority, and (6) seize opportunities that are scarce or dwindling in availability.

ROBERT B. CIALDINI

componential theories Componential theories generally attempt to decompose the phenomenon or process to be explained into its essential elements or constituents and then predict the effect of the determinants on the components and their interaction. In the affective sciences, the term is used to refer to a family of emotion theories that define emotion as a process that involves changes in several subsystems—cognitive activity, motor expression, physiological arousal, action tendencies, and subjective feeling state—which are seen as components of the theoretical construct of 'emotion' (see Scherer, 2005, for an overview) (see APPRAISAL THEORIES). Most of these theories assume that these components are jointly driven by a set of common determinants and interact during the emotion process in a recursive fashion, resulting in a high degree of coherence or *synchronization. Componential theorists generally do not endorse the idea of a small number of tightly organized basic emotions (or affect programmes), but rather opt for the notion of a large number of highly differentiated emotions, assuming that some of these occur more frequently because of the ubiquity of certain situational outcomes (e.g. frustration) (see MODAL EMOTIONS). One of the major features of componential theories is an attempt to render the link between the elicitation of emotion and the response patterning more explicit and theoretically predictable than has been the case in earlier theories, developing detailed predictions of specific physiological, expressive, and motivational changes expected to occur as a consequence of specific appraisal results. Contrary to constructivist approaches, componential theorists postulate that, given the interrelatedness of all emotion components, the processes in emotion episodes need to be studied in a comprehensive fashion, attempting to measure all participating components and their interaction (see EMOTION THEORIES AND CONCEPTS (PSYCHOLOGICAL PERSPECTIVES)).

KLAUS R. SCHERER

component process model The component process model (CPM), proposed by Scherer (1982, 2001a) was one of the first *componential theories. It suggests that efferent effects of sequentially accrued appraisal results cumulatively constitute the unique, context- and individual-specific response pattern for a given emotion episode (see APPRAISAL THEORIES). The CPM is based on the idea that during evolution, emotion replaced instincts in order to allow for more flexible response to events in a complex environment, and it did so by introducing an interrupt for further processing into the stimulus–response chain. It also contends that emotion has been optimized to serve the following functions: (1) evaluation of objects and events, (2) system regulation, (3) preparation and direction of action, (4) communication of reaction and behavioural intention, and (5) monitoring of internal state and organism–environment interaction (see Scherer 2001a).

As shown in Fig. C3 (adapted from Sander *et al.* 2005), the appraisals (called stimulus evaluation checks, SECs) are expected to unfold sequentially over time. Each type of assessment receives input from other cognitive and motivational mechanisms, such as attention, memory, motivation, reasoning, and the self-concept, which provide stored information and evaluation criteria that are

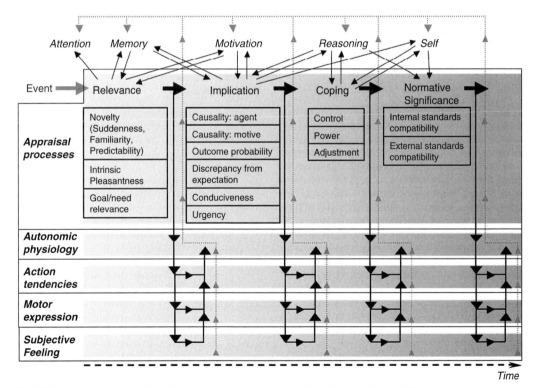

Fig. C3. Comprehensive illustration of the component process model of emotion (see Scherer 2001a).

essential for the appraisal process. For each sequential stage of assessment, there are two types of output: (1) a modification of the cognitive and motivational mechanisms that have influenced the appraisal process and (2) efferent effects on the periphery, in particular the neuroendocrine system and the autonomous and somatic nervous systems. In this model, emotion differentiation is predicted as the result of the net effect of all subsystem changes brought about by the outcome profile of the appraisal sequence. As part of the CPM, Scherer (2001a) has proposed a componential patterning theory, which predicts specific changes in the peripheral subsystems brought about by concrete patterns of SEC results. The central assumption of the componential patterning theory is that the different organismal subsystems are highly interdependent, and that changes in one subsystem will elicit related changes in other subsystems in a recursive fashion. In consequence, the result of each consecutive check will differentially and cumulatively affect the state of all other subsystems. The predicted patterning of the component states is specific to the unique evaluation history of the stimulus concerned. Each SEC result and the changes produced by it set the scene for the effects of the following SEC in the sense of 'added value' in a complex sequential interaction. The concrete predictions and their justification in the framework of a functional approach that views emotion as adaptation are described in Scherer (2001a). A sizable number of studies report empirical evidence that confirms many of these predictions, including the assumption of sequential processing (Grandjean et al. 2008, Grandjean and Scherer 2008).

KLAUS R. SCHERER

computational analysis of emotion Inspired by David Marr's levels of analysis, cognitive neuroscience defines computational analysis as a logical exercise aimed at determining what processing subsystems are necessary to produce a specific behaviour, given specific input (Kosslyn and Koenig, 1995). Computational analyses that are both biologically and psychologically constrained gave rise to a rich literature on perception—in particular vision—as well as memory, attention, or action. Computational analysis was also used to propose a functional architecture of emotion constituted of interacting specialized subsystems. For instance, a computational analysis of emotion led Sander and Koenig (2002) to further specify the model proposed by Kosslyn and Koenig (1995) by suggesting the following subsystems: (1) a *somatosensory buffer* that represents, as a somatic map, the actual state of one's body; (2) a *somatotopic mapping subsystem* that specifies the body localization where an internal state change has occurred on the basis of the information provided by the somatosensory buffer; (3) an *internal-state preprocessing subsystem* that extracts

distinctive information about one's internal state; (4) an *internal-state pattern activation subsystem* that stores in long-term memory representations of previous internal-state patterns; (5) a *stimulus–response connection subsystem* that implements 'processing reflexes'; (6) an *associative memory subsystem* that stores amodal representations, and may be involved in overlearnt appraisals of emotion-eliciting events; (7) an *emotion–instructions–generation subsystem*, that generates an initial specification of the brain / body profile that is appropriate when facing an emotional situation on the basis of information provided by associative memory and appraisal processes; and (8) *emotion–execution subsystems* that activate 'effector' subsystems in order to modulate the internal state and more generally the emotional expression.

An advantage of computational analysis of emotion is that it invites affective scientists to develop functional architectures that are sufficiently explicit to be tested using computational, neuroscientific, and psychological methods.

DAVID SANDER

computational models When addressing computational models of emotion, a first important consideration concerns their wide range of uses—comprising expression, recognition, simulation, and generation tasks—which go together with many widely differing uses of the word 'emotion' (see AFFECTIVE COMPUTING). To exemplify: in computer animation (or also more generally, in multimedia systems, which comprise other modalities instead of or in addition to the visual one), emotion is often reduced to perceivable behavioural expressivity (visual or otherwise). A generic computational approach to the expression of emotion is to train classifiers to capture causal relations between (e.g. dimensional) components of emotion (and personality) on the one hand and individual observable effects (e.g. volume or speed of speech) on the other: once configured, Bayesian networks, for instance, can be used to both express emotional states (by setting the values of components and reading the expressive parameters), and to recognize them (by setting the expressive parameters and reading out the values of emotional component nodes); methods such as sensitivity analysis have been proposed for the verification of the parameters learned. To ensure the 'believability' or 'engagingness' of extended performances of synthetic actors, more articulated supporting models of emotions are required. Given the vastness of the enterprise if synthetic actors were to be endowed with full autonomy (i.e. social, cultural, communicative, perceptual, motor, physiological, and deliberative, as well as memory and adaptivity competences, to name a few, along with a detailed model of the physical environment capable of supporting all these faculties), virtual reality systems typically employ numerous shortcuts and rely heavily on symbolic representations. The models employed for the control of virtual characters can then deliberately be kept at a shallow level of detail (which may well even include mere explicit sequencing of prerecorded material), with the adoption of a heterogeneous compositional engineering approach permitting selective coverage of the key aspects in broad application scenarios. Here, the primary contribution of the computational models of emotions is to ensure compliance with some minimum standard of consistency over time. The problem of inferring or simulating modal emotions in virtual environments is frequently solved by means of some sufficient rule-based categorization mechanism for discrete constellations of situations encountered (e.g. Ortony 2003).

Efforts towards increasing levels of detail and achieving a more encompassing scope of prescription of the emotional behaviour of virtual humans have led to increased interest in the development of operationalizations of psychological theories; cognitive appraisal theories (see APPRAISAL THEORIES) in particular have been found to provide a good match to the symbolic representations employed (e.g. Gratch and Marsella 2004), paving the way to the possibility of utilizing theoretically 'earlier' levels of emotion synthesis (i.e. preceding the hypothesized abstraction to modal emotions) for a more differentiated and flexible generation of overt and internal consequential effects as integration of numerous contributions computed in parallel (as well as including extensions to the vocabulary of numerical characteristics considered in classical decision theory). Even though fundamentally detached ('offline') characteristics and pervasive use of objectified conceptualizations of the world currently impose limits on the levels of resolution and scope achievable, such computational models of emotion have already proved to be amenable to verification using established psychological procedures. From the opposite view, the conceptual gap between lower-level and higher-level cognition is approached by, for example, modulation models of emotion; but it has to be noted that overall progress towards complete computational models of emotions is (significantly) constrained by the state of the art in the modelling of the manifold capabilities involved (as listed above) as well.

Within these limitations, but also providing contributions to efforts aimed at removing this latter obstacle, computational models have been successfully employed to evaluate the internal coherence and completeness of underlying theories in neuroscience, e.g. by mapping traditional functional components as established in control theory to hypothesized modular functional circuits (see CONNECTIONIST MODELS). As a final important example of the scientific relevance of computational models of emotion, since its advent, research in embodied artificial intelligence has been providing contributions to the critiquing of current psychological theorizing (e.g. Pfeifer 1994).

PAOLO PETTA AND JONATHAN GRATCH

Armony, J.L., Servan-Schreiber, D., Cohen, J.D., and LeDoux, J.E. (1997). Computational modeling of emotion: explorations through the anatomy and physiology of fear conditioning. *Trends in Cognitive Science*, 1, 28–34.

Fum, D., Missier, F.D., and Stocco, A. (2007). The cognitive modeling of human behavior: why a model is (sometimes) better than 10,000 words, *Cognitive Systems Research*, 8, 135–42.

Gratch, J. and Marsella, S. (2005). Lessons from emotion psychology for the design of lifelike characters. *Applied Artificial Intelligence*, 19, 215–33.

Grey, W.D. (ed.) (2007). *Integrated models of cognitive systems*. New York: Oxford University Press.

Trappl, R., Petta, P., and Payr, S. (eds) (2003). *Emotions in humans and artifacts*. Cambridge, MA: MIT Press.

conation Conation (from the Latin *conor*, to try or to attempt) refers to the impulse by which an agent acts towards an expected end (or away from an anticipated loss) (see MOTIVATION). Conative states include the various forms of desiring, emoting, intending, and willing, i.e. the propositional attitudes that represent states of affairs as being of interest to the self and thereby susceptible to trigger some form of action.

In contrast to epistemic attitudes, conative attitudes have a 'world-to-mind direction of fit' (Searle 1983): their contents are satisfied if the world acquires the properties which they represent the world as having. For example, a desire at t_1 to the effect that it rains at t_2 is satisfied if it rains at t_2. Some states, such as S regretting (or fearing) that P, are both epistemic and conative; accordingly their conditions of satisfaction have two directions of fit. They presuppose that S believes that P occurred—or might occur—(mind-to-world direction of fit), and that S would have been—or is—disposed to prevent P or P-type events from happening (world-to-mind direction of fit).

Philosophers of action and theologians have been debating for several centuries on the faculty (or faculties) involved in providing the impulse to act. Should *desire be conceived of as nonmotivated appetite and be distinguished from a motivated pro-attitude reached after deliberation? If such is the case, is the latter to be equated with a form of judgement? Or should it rather be understood as a second-order desire, i.e. in Harry Frankfurt's terms, the desire in virtue of which the desiring subject identifies himself with a first-order desire (Frankfurt 1988)?

Some contemporary philosophers of action, such as Donald Davidson, claim that the impulse to act is caused by the reason that the agent has to act. This reason to act combines beliefs and desires in an unconditional judgement that expresses the preferences of the agent in an 'absolute' way (Davidson 1980).

A third avenue consists in recognizing that the will to act derives from a separate capacity—irreducible both to judging and desiring. John Searle (1983) argued that an action can be triggered without any prior reasoning: 'intentions in action' can be formed impulsively and control behaviour without prior evaluation. The proponents of intentions as the main conative attitudes deny that desires can play a similar role. Although a desire may determine an action, it is not the case that each desire can trigger a corresponding action. Furthermore intentions have an important dual function in guiding conduct and in coordinating plans that desires cannot fulfil (Bratman 1987).

The ultimate nature of the executive force of intentions has, however, in turn been questioned. Suppose that S believes that her arm is paralysed. She may attempt to move it, to show that she cannot. In this case she does not believe that she can do it, nor does she intend to do it. She just forms the volition to move it (Ginet 1990). While intentions are needed to coordinate plans, volitions might ultimately be required to execute the intentions.

In contrast to desiring and emoting, willing and intending are often taken to include a reflexive condition emphasizing that the world should acquire a target property in virtue of the conative state itself. For example, an intention is *carried out* not only if a change in the world occurs as required by its conditions of satisfaction, but also if the intended change is caused by this very intention (Searle 1983). It can be objected, however, that it is not plausible that a young child should be able to represent the concept of having an intention (or wanting, or willing) in order to act intentionally, and that such reflexivity does not apply to various cases of intentional action (Mele 1992). A line of response consists in proposing that the form of reflexivity that is central to willing and intending may be grasped in nonconceptual representations.

JOËLLE PROUST

Mele, A.R. (1992). *Springs of action*. Oxford: Oxford University Press.

concerns 'Concern', in emotion theory, covers the dispositional sources of emotions: the major motives, interests, and affective sensitivities of an individual. The term thus refers to the dispositional and motivational background of emotions (see MOTIVATION). No concern, no emotion: only when an event is appraised as favouring or threatening satisfaction of at least one of an individual's concerns will an emotion arise. Such interconnection of motivation and emotion is a core tenet of most current emotion theories.

Concerns represent the link between emotions and *well-being. Lazarus (1991) pointed out that well-being largely consists of safeguarding or satisfying one's concerns.

The impact of an event on any particular concern can give rise to different emotions when events represent different kinds of impact (for instance, benefit or harm), or are appraised that way. By and large, events appraised as concern conducive lead to pleasant emotions, and events appraised as concern obstructive lead to unpleasant ones (see APPRAISAL THEORIES).

Humans have a multitude of concerns; a distinction can be made between general or 'source' concerns (e.g. security, affiliation) and particular or 'surface' concerns (e.g. attachment to a particular person). So far, little consensus exists on which human source concerns should be distinguished. See also MOTIVATION.

NICO H. FRIJDA

Frijda, N.H. (1986). *The emotions*. Cambridge: Cambridge University Press.
Lazarus, R.S. (1991). *Emotion and adaptation*. New York: Oxford University Press.

connectionist models Connectionist or neural network models are those *computational models that contain representations of neurons, in any form. The architecture of these neurons or nodes is (loosely) based on that of neurons in the brain, which means the neurons or nodes will usually transform an input signal into an output signal through input and output weights, potentially combined with a transfer function in the node itself. If the node represents a single neuron, it might be a spiking neuron, which means the output will consist of short bursts, analogous to the output of neurons. Nodes representing larger groups of neurons could output a graded response, thus providing a more continuous output stream. The goal of this kind of modelling is to produce a system with nodes that are analogous to a set of neurons with respect to their connections and their activations and thereby explain the associated behaviour. This does not necessarily mean that there is a defined neural correlate; the node can also represent an unidentified brain area representing a certain stimulus, response, or concept.

Conditioning

Conditioning is an emotion-related process that is very suitable for this kind of modelling, because its inputs and outputs are relatively straightforward and have been studied in great detail both by psychologists and neuroscientists, meaning that detailed knowledge is available of the timings and neural processed involved (see ASSOCIATIVE PROCESSING). Grossberg (1971) was the first to develop a neural network model of operant conditioning, mathematically describing drive, sensory (for unconditioned (US) and conditioned stimuli (CS)), and motor nodes in terms of their activations and excitatory/inhibitory connections. He assumed there is no direct association of an input CS with a motor response, but only with satisfaction of a drive (e.g. hunger). However, this model (and many elaborations of it that followed) did not take into account that the US and CS do not necessarily arrive at the same time and that conditioning is optimal when there is an interstimulus interval (ISI; a delay between onset of US and CS). Sutton and Barto (1981) introduced eligibility traces to solve this problem, later extended to temporal difference (TD) learning. Eligibility traces are activations representing the stimulus that are longer lasting than the stimulus presentation, a kind of short-term memory (but not to be confused with conscious stimulus representations). These eligibility traces allow for a representation of the stimulus and for weight changes after the stimulus is no longer present. This work was extended into the differential Hebbian learning rule (Klopf 1988), where connection weight changes are a function of activities of both connecting nodes. This allowed for simulation of a large number of conditioning phenomena, including secondary conditioning, extinction and reacquisition, and ISI effects. TD learning was developed in the actor–critic model (Suri and Schultz 1998) in order to incorporate the idea that emotional responses are largely dependent on whether or not a stimulus is in accordance with the expected reward or punishment, as well as to provide an analogy with activations of limbic dopaminergic neurons in, for example, striatum, ventral tegmentum, *amygdala, and nucleus accumbens, that are known to respond to an absence of predicted reward or punishment. One part of this model, the critic, produces a prediction error through TD learning (detected in the ventral tegmentum) which then allows the learning of a direct stimulus–response association in the other part of the model, the actor, as well as learning in the critic, thereby allowing for changes in the prediction. In a subsequent model of the dopamine data, Brown et al. (1999) created two different pathways for CS information, where one pathway receives primary reward information and the other contains adaptive timing. This allows for the learning of a range of ISIs, rather than one fixed ISI as in the actor–critic model.

Based on LeDoux's (1996) fear conditioning research, Armony et al. (1995) developed a range of models specific to fear, employing cortical and thalamic modulation of the amygdala, which produces behavioural output, reproducing many experimental results in great detail (see NEURAL ARCHITECTURE OF EMOTION).

Emotional bias/influence

In addition to the induction of emotion through reinforcement or punishment, neural networks have also been used to model the influence of emotions on other processes in the brain, most notably attention (see ATTENTION AND EMOTION) and *decision-making. In attention, we (Taylor and Fragopanagos 2004, Korsten et al. 2006) have extended the corollary discharge of attention movement (CODAM) model to incorporate an amygdaloidal module. This emotional module can bias attentional processing by either increasing activation of emotional stimuli in sensory areas, or in working memory or attention control command modules, where it can drag attention away from previous goals through mutual inhibition of the attentional modules, modelling quantitative results of several research paradigms.

Decision processes as induced by the extensively studied Iowa Gambling Task have been modelled, amongst others, by Frank and Claus (2006). The authors expand their model of Parkinsonism to encompass modules representing orbitofrontal cortex, nucleus accumbens, amygdala, globus pallidus, substantia nigra, and premotor cortex, showing a neurally realistic mechanism of retaining gain/loss information for the different decks of cards presented to the subject, and subsequently making a choice between them.

Depression

Many attempts have been made to model malfunctions in the brain, most notably by Siegle and Hasselmo (2002), who successfully constructed a neural network model that imitates the behaviour of depressive patients when mechanisms potentially indicative of depression (overlearning, reduced inhibition, and rumination) are invoked (see DEPRESSION). This model is behaviourally based, without neural correlates. We (Korsten et al. 2007) have recently created a neural model in which hyperactivation of the node representing subgenual cingulate (hyperactivation of which in the human brain is known to be correlated with depression) cause depression-like activations in other parts of the model.

In conclusion, neural network models can serve to formulate a clearer and/or more complex hypothesis about the neural processes underlying (emotional) behaviour, to combine different data sets or approaches into a single framework, and to generate predictions to guide future experimental research. As such, they are an essential tool in the search for knowledge about the emotions. We note in ending that there are as yet no neural network models of the popular appraisal approach to emotions (but see Sander et al., 2005, and also Korsten et al., 2007). This lacuna should be filled to build a suitable bridge between possible neural network models of emotions and the models of psychologists.

JOHN G. TAYLOR AND NIENKE KORSTEN

constructivism (philosophical perspectives)

Levine, D.S. (2007). Neural network modeling of emotion. *Physics of Life Reviews*, **4**, 37–63.

Korsten, N.J., Fragopanagos, N., Hartley, M., Taylor, N., and Taylor, N. (2006) Attention as a controller. *Neural Networks*, **19**, 1408–21.

constructivism (philosophical perspectives) Constructivism (or constructionism) is the controversial view, based on anthropological evidence of cross-cultural diversity in emotion concepts, that emotions are socio-cultural constructions. Emotions are considered to be complex structures, involving cognitions, appraisals, expressions, feelings, and action tendencies, and which are created and disseminated by sociocultural groups (see CULTURAL SPECIFICITY). While weak constructivism allows that a limited number of emotions remain untouched by culture, strong constructivism claims that all the emotions we feel depend on our sociocultural context (Armon-Jones 1986). The social function of emotion is taken to be essential. According to James Averill (1980), for instance, emotions are *transitory social roles* governed by rules which spell out what ought to cause an emotion experience (moral transgression, insults, etc.) and what behavioural response is required (aggressive behaviour, reprimands, etc.). These rules can be thought of as scripts or scenarios telling us what to feel and how to behave in given situations, and which are determined by the sociocultural environment. Emotions are felt as passively experienced, but they are in fact our own creatures. Strong constructivism is opposed to the view shared by evolutionary psychologists that at least some emotions are pan-culturally and universally shared by human beings (see UNIVERSALITY OF EMOTIONS).

CHRISTINE TAPPOLET

constructivism (psychological perspectives) In its broadest sense, constructivism refers to the tendency to make psychological wholes (*Gestalten*) (see GESTALT (AND FEELING)) when given only partial information. To take an extreme example, a person may vividly 'remember' being abducted by space aliens, thus lending coherence to fragmented recollections. Everyday emotional experiences are subject to constructive processes in this sense. As applied to the emotions, however, constructivism is typically used more narrowly, namely, to emphasize the role of society—as opposed to biology—in lending coherence to emotional experience. When emphasis is placed on social influence as the primary source of coherence, reference is sometimes made to 'social constructionism' (Harré 1986). In the present entry the simpler term, constructivism, will be used, the 'social' being implicit.

A (social) constructivist view of emotion rests on three assumptions: (1) emotions are complex syndromes comprising diverse, semi-autonomous components; (see COMPONENTIAL THEORIES); (2) no one component or class of components—physiological, behavioural, or cognitive—is essential to the whole; and (3) social *beliefs and rules are the primary principles by which the various components are organized into wholes. The first assumption (a componential approach) is becoming increasingly common among theorists of diverse persuasions (e.g. Scherer 2001b). The second assumption (nonessentialism) has ample empirical support (e.g. Barrett 2006b). The third assumption—that social beliefs and rules are the primary organizing principles—is perhaps the most controversial.

Beliefs about human behaviour can be self-confirming, provided that they are not too unrealistic. This is particularly true in the emotional domain, since emotional beliefs are highly value laden (see VALUES). (If you want to know what people hold dear, ask about their hopes and fears, what makes them angry, sad, or happy, and so forth.) Of course, emotional beliefs do not exist in isolation, but presume a network of ideas—a folk-theory of what it means to be emotional. Unlike scientific theories, folk-theories are linked to social rules—the *shoulds* and *should nots* of behaviour. All theorists recognize that emotions are regulated by *display rules; for example, that you should not laugh at a funeral. But many rules have a constitutive as well as regulatory function. To illustrate with a nonemotional example, the rules of English grammar help regulate how to speak properly. More fundamentally, English grammar helps constitute the language as English as opposed, say, to German or Chinese; simply put, without the rules of grammar there would be no English language to regulate. Similarly, without the rules of anger, say, there would be no anger to regulate, but only inarticulate rage reactions, or perhaps some other socially constructed emotional syndrome (cf. *liget* among the Ifaluk, a headhunting tribe in the Philippines; Rosaldo 1980).

In addition to studies of emotional development and socialization, support for a constructivist view comes from three main sources. (1) *Cross-cultural comparisons*: historical and cultural differences, as between anger in Western societies and *liget* (which can involve taking the head of a person who has committed no offence), illustrate the influence of social beliefs and rules in organizing and legitimating emotional syndromes (see CULTURAL SPECIFICITY). (2) *Within-cultural analyses*: a constructivist view assumes mutually transformative relations between emotions and social institutions; hence, in-depth analyses that demonstrate such dialectical relations also support a constructivist view. (3) *Personality variables*: what societies construct, individuals can reconstruct; additional support for a constructivist view thus comes from the ability of people to be emotionally creative, that is, to improvise and modify 'received' emotions to better meet personal and situational needs (Averill 2005). With this third way, we come full circle. If it were not for innovations on the individual level (3), and subsequent diffusion of adaptive variations through a society (2), historical and cultural differences in emotional syndromes would not emerge (1).

Constructivism does not deny the importance of biology. Some emotional components are innate (e.g. certain facial expressions), and some neural structures (e.g. the *amygdala) play a greater role in emotional than intellectual behaviour. More broadly, biological systems of behaviour—what used to be called *instincts*, such as aggression, sexual attraction, attachment, and flight from danger—may singly or in combination contribute to the formation of some emotions (e.g. sexual attraction and attachment in the case of romantic love). However, no one-to-one relation exists between biologically based elements and systems of behaviour, on the one hand, and specific emotions as experienced in everyday life, on the other.

Emotions form a heterogeneous category and no one formulation is equally applicable to all affective states. Constructivism is least applicable to (1) reflex-like reactions, such as fright to an immediate danger and lashing out at a source of pain, and (2) broad affective dispositions, such as states of undirected excitation, anxiety, and depression. The relevance of a constructivist view increases with the complexity of the emotion and the involvement of cognitive mediating mechanisms (cf. *appraisal theory). Thus, as important as the above exclusions may be, a constructivist view is applicable to the majority of discrete emotions recognized in ordinary language.

JAMES R. AVERILL

Mascolo, M.F., Fischer, K.W., and Li, J. (2003). Dynamic development of component systems of emotions: pride, shame, and guilt in China and the United States. In: R.J. Davidson, K.R. Scherer, and H.H. Goldsmith (eds), *Handbook of affective sciences*, pp. 375–408. New York: Oxford University Press.

Mesquita, B. (2003). Emotions as dynamic cultural phenomena. In: R.J. Davidson, K.R. Scherer, and H.H. Goldsmith (eds), *Handbook of affective sciences*, pp. 871–90. New York: Oxford University Press.

contagion Contagion has been defined as 'the spread of an attitude, doctrine, idea, mood, emotion, or activity from one person to another or throughout a group'. Scientists may speak of 'a contagion of mirth', or describe 'hysterical contagion' in groups—when one person imagines that, say, their workplace is infested with parasites, and suddenly, the entire factory is falling ill from this imaginary malady.

Emotional contagion has been defined as 'the tendency to automatically *mimic and *synchronize facial expres-

sions, vocalizations, postures, and movements with those of another person and, consequently, to converge emotionally' (Hatfield et al. 1994, p. 5) (see EXPRESSION, PRINCIPLES OF EMOTIONAL). The Emotional Contagion Scale was designed to assess people's susceptibility to 'catch' joy and happiness, love, fear and anxiety, anger, and sadness and depression, as well as emotions in general.

Theoretically, contagion can occur in several ways. Early investigators proposed that conscious reasoning, analysis, and imagination accounted for the phenomenon. More recently, social psychologists have assumed that primitive emotional contagion is a far more subtle, automatic, and ubiquitous process than theorists once thought. Neuroscientists, for example, have discovered that the same neurons (mirror neurons) may fire when primates merely *observe* another perform an action as when they themselves perform that same action. They propose that these brain structures may account for emotional contagion (see Iacoboni 2005.)

Many scientists argue that that the process of emotional contagion consists of three stages: mimicry→feedback→contagion: (1) People tend to mimic the facial expressions, vocal expressions, postures, and instrumental behaviours of those around them. (2) As people mimic their companions' fleeting facial, vocal, and postural expressions, they often come to *feel* pale reflections of their companions' actual emotions. (3) By attending to this stream of tiny moment-to-moment reactions, people can and do 'feel themselves into' the emotional lives of others (see EMPATHY (NEUROSCIENCE PERSPECTIVES)). It is this tripartite process that accounts for the ubiquitous process of emotional contagion.

ELAINE HATFIELD AND RICHARD L. RAPSON

contempt Contempt is generally elicited by the negative evaluation of others and their actions. Rozin et al. (1999) consider contempt to be part of the contempt–anger–disgust (CAD) triad of *moral emotions. Moral emotions, according to this view, are elicited by *norm violations, with different specific emotions being elicited depending on the type of norm that is violated. Thus, *anger is elicited by violations of autonomy (i.e. violations of individual rights), *disgust by violations related to divinity (i.e. violations of purity–sanctity), and contempt by violations related to community (i.e. violation of communal codes). This definition links contempt to what Price et al. (2002) refer to as punitive sentiments. Punitive sentiments are motivational adaptations that evolved specifically to address the cheater or free-rider problem in social groups. Free-riders are individuals who accept resources but do not reciprocate adequately, thus harming the group in the long run. Punitive sentiments towards free-riders motivate the punishment of these individuals, thereby discouraging free-riding in the long term, even if this punishment should involve some personal cost to the emoter in the short term (see ALTRUISM (ECONOMICS PERSPECTIVES); ECONOMICS (ROLE OF EMOTION IN)). Thus contempt is an inherently social emotion, elicited by social norm violations and its function is to enforce social norms (see SOCIAL EMOTIONS).

The view of contempt as part of an evolved system for managing the free-rider problem makes it plausible that there exists a specific facial expression of contempt and that this expression is universal across cultures. At the same time, contempt as a member of the CAD triad (Rozin et al. 1999) is closely related to both anger and disgust and hence may share considerable semantic overlap with these emotions, which may also result in overlap between expressions.

Putting forward the notion that contempt is a basic emotion, and hence associated with a specific universal expression, Ekman and Friesen (1986) described the unilateral lip raise and tightener as a universal prototypical expression of contempt. However, results of subsequent research have been more equivocal. In an overview of the literature, Matsumoto and Ekman (2004) note that specifically native English speakers from the USA, western Canada, and Great Britain show notably lower recognition rates for this expression compared with other expressions of basic emotions, i.e. anger, fear, sadness, disgust, and happiness. Based on this observation they suggest that the low recognition rates for this expression are specific to speakers of English, because of some linguistic feature of that language; they note the similarity between contempt and content. However, Hess et al. (unpublished) found a similar pattern of reduced recognition for the contempt expression for speakers of French from Quebec and Gabon. Interestingly, the two groups made different mistakes such that French speakers of Quebec tended to confuse contempt with anger, whereas French speakers from Gabon tended to confuse contempt with disgust. These findings match findings by Elfenbein et al. (2007) demonstrating a cultural dialect for contempt such that this expression resembled anger more when shown by Quebecois and disgust more when shown by Gabonese. None of the participants in that study chose the unilateral lip raise and tightener to portray contempt.

Thus, the evidence speaks more to the second hypothesis, i.e. the equivocal findings concerning the recognition of the contempt expression may be best explained if contempt is considered as a blend of anger and disgust, at least conceptually. The exact nature of the resulting emotion concept may then depend on the cultural context in which the emotion is experienced. Thus, in some cultural contexts contempt may be more closely related to anger, in others more closely to disgust.

This raises the question of whether to consider contempt a basic emotion (see BASIC EMOTIONS). If one uses

the criterion advanced by Ekman (1992a)—the universal recognition of the expression at above chance levels—it is clear that in most studies this not very stringent criterion is fulfilled.

Yet, in the discussions for adequate criteria for basic emotions, the issue of blended versus pure emotion has not been addressed. On the one hand, most emotional states only rarely occur unblended (happiness seems an exception); on the other hand, for the 'canonical' basic emotions instances of 'pure' emotion can be found. By contrast, contempt seems inherently a blend of two other emotions—rather than simply an emotion that frequently, or even usually, co-occurs with other emotions.

In addition, contempt, unlike the other basic emotions, is an exclusively social emotion that is used as a punishment for the violations of learned social norms rather than a biologically grounded reaction to goal obstruction or noxious stimuli, which may or may not occur in a social context. That a social species heavily dependent on cooperation should have evolved such a system is not contradictory to the notion that the target of the emotion is learned. Thus, the answer to the question as to whether contempt is a basic emotion rests with the definition that one is inclined to employ.

URSULA HESS

contentment Contentment refers to a pleasant emotional state that shares conceptual space with other *positive emotions such as serenity, peacefulness, satisfaction, tranquillity, and, to a lesser extent, relief. Some theorists (Izard 1977) identify contentment as a mild form of *joy. Contentment occurs in circumstances appraised as safe and familiar, and as requiring little personal effort. The *action tendency historically associated with contentment is 'do nothing'. More recent theorizing (Fredrickson 1998) suggests that the physical inactivity of contentment is accompanied by a mindful and receptive mental state poised to savour one's current circumstances and integrate them into new priorities for the self and new values. In this manner, repeated experiences of contentment are hypothesized to build people's self-knowledge and refine their value systems.

BARBARA L. FREDRICKSON

controllability Control or controllability (also referred to as *control potential* or *situational control* in the appraisal literature) is one of the appraisal dimensions that determine the elicitation and differentiation of an emotion (see APPRAISAL THEORIES). It is related to the evaluation of *coping potential, an individual's assessment of his or her capacity to deal with an event which might threaten the well-being of the person.

Control appraisal relates to the perception of how well an event or its outcomes can be influenced or controlled by known natural agents—not necessarily by the appraising individual him/herself (Scherer 2001a). For example, while the temperature inside a house is generally controllable, the weather conditions outside are not. Situations characterized by a lack of control might lead to emotions such as hopelessness.

Control is not the same as predictability. When an event is controllable, this necessarily means that it is predictable. However, this is not valid in reverse: one may be able to predict an event without being able to influence it (e.g. a rainstorm). It is furthermore important to differentiate between control and power (see POWER (IN APPRAISAL)). Control refers to the likelihood that an event or its outcomes can be influenced by any natural agent. Power, on the other hand, refers to the perceived potential of the appraising individual to influence a potentially controllable event (maybe with the help of others). When used in the literature, control and power are not always clearly distinguished; the use of 'controllability' often seems to imply both aspects.

TOBIAS BROSCH

cool cognition Cool cognition has been proposed as one of two central constructs for clarifying the interaction of cognition and emotion within the hot system/cool system framework (see HOT COGNITION).

The cool system is the basis of self-regulated behaviour. It is cognitive, emotionally neutral, contemplative, flexible, integrative, slow, and strategic. In contrast, the hot system is emotional, impulsive, rigid, simple, fast, and stimulus driven. The cool system is reflective rather than reflexive. Cool system functions, most likely enacted in hippocampal, frontal, and related cortical areas, encompass spatio-temporal and episodic memory, comprehension, semantic processing, working memory, metacognition, planning, control functions, problem-solving, and high-level thinking.

The cool system is thought to be the basis of willpower. It is crucial in overcoming hot-system stimulus control which could otherwise undermine efforts at self-control resulting in a failure of self-regulation. The costs of such failures are evident from crime and teenage pregnancy rates, alcoholism and drug addiction (see ADDICTION), to domestic violence (see VIOLENCE) and educational underachievement. The cool system is also thought to modulate primitive and sometimes dysfunctional hot-system responses leading to anxieties, fears, and phobias. The cool system continues to develop throughout middle and late childhood. High levels of *stress can also disrupt the cool system, while at the same time potentiating the hot system, with consequences ranging from a re-emergence of maladaptive fears or previously conquered addictions, to a reduction in rational, considered

thought. Overregulation, however, can itself be debilitating, preventing a person from being fully engaged by the pleasures of life.

JANET METCALFE AND W. JAKE JACOBS

Metcalfe, J. and Jacobs, W.J. (1998). Emotional memory: effects of stress on 'cool' and 'hot' memory systems. *Psychology of Learning and Motivation*, **38**, 187–221.

Metcalfe, J. and Mischel, W. (1999). A hot/cool system analysis of delay of gratification: dynamics of willpower. *Psychological Review*, **106**, 3–26.

coping The word 'coping' with reference to adversity has been in use in the English language since at least the 14th century (*Oxford English Dictionary*, 2nd edition, 1989). In its earliest usage, 'a coping' was a combat encounter. The idea of coping as a response to an attack has persisted over the centuries. Its modern usage developed during the early part of the 20th century hand in hand with the growing interest in what can be thought of as psychological encounters, or psychological *stress. Walter Cannon's research on the fight/flight syndrome and Hans Selye's conceptualization of the general adaptation syndrome helped establish stress as a phenomenon with measurable physiological responses, and the psychological traumas experienced by soldiers in World Wars I and II created very practical reasons for wanting to better understand ways to help people manage their responses to real-life stressful encounters. The literature on coping theory, measurement, findings, and intervention has grown rapidly since the mid-20th century.

Theoretical foundations of coping

Modern approaches to coping tend to fall within two major categories: psychoanalytic ego process approaches (see EGO) and cognitive approaches (see COPING POTENTIAL (APPRAISAL OF)).

The earliest of the modern 20th century approaches were based on psychoanalytic ego processes, which is consistent with the dominance of psychoanalytic thought during the later part of the 19th and the early part of the 20th century. Psychoanalytic ego process approaches emphasize ego processes that are hierarchically arranged with the highest and most advanced or mature ego processes representing coping. Lower on the hierarchy are defence mechanisms and the lowest levels represent fragmentation or ego failure or psychotic levels of ego functioning. Ego process approaches often focus on pathology, and two characteristic themes are the extent to which the person distorts reality and the regulation of anxiety. Although ego process approaches to defence and coping are often rich with clinically relevant material, they tend to be difficult to operationalize for the purposes of research.

In 1966 Richard Lazarus published a landmark book, *Psychological Stress and the Coping Process*, that presented a new theoretical formulation that has shaped the field ever since. Lazarus' formulation went beyond defence and an emphasis on pathology to include cognitive and behavioural responses that ordinary people use in their daily lives to cope with stressful situations. His formulation of coping was embedded in a cognitive theory of stress that defined stress as a relationship between the person and the environment that the individual cognitively appraises as personally significant and as taxing or exceeding his or her resources for coping. Within this framework, coping is viewed as a dynamic process that is initiated in response to the individual's appraisal (see APPRAISAL THEORIES) of a specific person–environment transaction as stressful, that is, as harming, threatening, or challenging personally meaningful *goals. The appraisal process is evaluative and it is inherently emotional. An appraisal of threat, for example, is likely to generate worry, anxiety, fear, or dread. Coping thoughts and behaviours are used to regulate distress emotions (see REGULATION OF EMOTION) (emotion-focused coping) and manage the problems causing the distress (problem-focused coping).

An important feature of this approach is that the definition does not imply that coping efforts have to be successful to be considered coping. Coping is what people try to do, regardless of the effect of the efforts on the outcome. This distinction is important for research because if coping is to be used to predict outcomes, it cannot have its definition confound coping with those outcomes.

A major contribution of Lazarus' model was its applicability across situations. Previously, studies of coping tended to be situation specific. The model Lazarus proposed could be used with reference to combat situations, divorces, and the ordinary events of daily life.

Coping comes of age

Coping emerged as a distinct field of psychological inquiry during the 1970s and 1980s. Empirical research that focused on the coping process *per se* such as *The Structure of Coping* (Pearlin and Schooler 1978) and *An Analysis of Coping in a Middle Aged Community Sample* (Folkman and Lazarus 1980) were published and other studies soon began to appear. Major books on coping were published including *Stress, Appraisal, and Coping* (Lazarus and Folkman 1984), *Stress, Coping and Development* (Aldwin 1994), and *The Handbook of Coping* (Zeidner and Endler 1996). Although defence-focused research continued throughout this period within psychology, cognitive approaches prevailed. There is now a vast list of publications on coping that numbers in the thousands.

Classifying coping

People use a wide range of thoughts and behaviours to cope with stressful situations that vary from the con-

crete to abstract, from short term to long term, and in their purpose. It is important to classify these myriad strategies to facilitate research as well as communication about clinical practice. A number of schemes are described in the literature, but three functions are common to most: problem-focused and emotion-focused coping, and more recently, meaning-focused coping.

Problem-focused coping refers to instrumental thoughts and behaviours directed at the problem causing distress, and *emotion-focused coping* refers to thoughts directed at regulating the negative emotions associated with the problem. Some examples of problem-focused coping are making a plan of action or concentrating on the next step. Some examples of emotion-focused forms of coping are engaging in distracting activities or using alcohol or drugs.

Although the theoretical distinction between problem- and emotion-focused types of coping is useful for classifying many specific coping strategies and is used extensively in the coping literature, the distinction between the two types of coping is not always clear. Problem-focused coping can also serve an emotion-focused function when it addresses the source of negative emotions. Thus, if the problem-focused efforts are successful, the negative emotions associated with the problem will also be reduced. There are also occasions in which emotion-focused types of coping can ultimately serve a problem-focused function. For example, anxiety related to an upcoming exam may interfere with studying. Reducing the anxiety, an emotion-focused objective, can facilitate studying, a problem-focused objective. Most people use a mix of problem- and emotion-focused responses in coping with the events of daily life.

Many types of life stress are ongoing and require sustained coping efforts over long periods of time. Examples include a loved-one's chronic illness or a difficult family situation. Over time, chronic stress can deplete psychological, social, physical, and material coping resources. In this context, *meaning-focused coping* becomes important.

Meaning-focused coping responses draw on deeply held values, goals, and beliefs. These responses help motivate and sustain coping efforts and restore coping resources over the long term. They are linked to *positive emotions, which reinforces their motivational and sustaining qualities. Meaning-focused coping encompasses a number of strategies. One example is to substitute new, meaningful, and realistic goals for goals that are no longer tenable. For example, the goal of restoring the health of a loved one with an illness that has become terminal may no longer be tenable; that goal needs to be relinquished. A new goal may be to ensure that the patient is well cared for and feels loved and looked after. The pursuit of these new, realistic goals increases the caregiver's sense of control, which increases the caregiver's positive affect, which, in turn, helps reinforce coping efforts. Another example is benefit-reminding, a form of positive *reappraisal in which the individual appraises benefit in a stressful situation such as improved personal relationships, appreciation of the little things in life, or greater sense of self-worth.

Assessing coping

The assessment of coping has been approached using both quantitative and qualitative methods.

During the 1980s several measures of coping were published that reflected the cognitive approach to coping. For the most part, the new measures were self-report checklists of specific coping thoughts and behaviours relevant to specific stressful situations. Two of the most widely used measures were developed during this period: *The Ways of Coping* (Folkman and Lazarus 1980, 1988) and *The COPE* (Carver *et al.* 1989). Both of these measures are relatively generic and appropriate for a wide range of situations. These measures, along with many others that have since appeared in the literature, usually assess diverse aspects of coping such as gathering information, making a plan of action, seeking social support, distancing, or escape avoidance. Context-specific coping measures have also been developed that are usually a blend of situation-specific and generic items.

Usually coping checklists ask the person to recall how he or she coped with a specific situation. The researcher usually specifies a recall period such as a day, a week, or a month. The shorter the recall period, the more accurate the report of coping is likely to be. Checklists are helpful because they allow multidimensional descriptions of situation-specific coping thoughts and behaviours that people can self-report but their length can be burdensome and the list of coping strategies may not be comprehensive.

Narrative approaches involve asking people to provide narratives about stressful events, including what happened, the emotions they experienced, and what they thought and did as the situation unfolded. Narrative approaches are helpful in understanding what the person is coping with and for uncovering ways of coping that are not included on inventories. Studies show that narrative and quantitative approaches overlap somewhat, but are not equivalent.

Effective coping

A central tenet of stress and coping theory is that coping effectiveness must be judged in the context of the stressful situation. A given form of coping may be effective in one situation but not in another. For example, problem-focused forms of coping are likely to be beneficial in situations where the individual has some control over the outcome, but are likely to be counterproduc-

tive in situations that are completely out of the hands of the individual. Furthermore, a given coping response can be beneficial in terms of one outcome but detrimental in terms of another. For example, a strenuous workout may be good for physical health goals but it could conflict with the time needed to rehearse a presentation for the following morning. Another consideration in judging coping effectiveness is proximity of the outcome. A particular coping strategy may be beneficial in the short run (e.g. confronting the person responsible for the problem may make you feel better), but detrimental in the long run (damage the potential for working with the person you confronted in the future).

Teaching coping

One of the reasons for interest in coping is that since it is a conscious response, it is potentially amenable to change. A growing body of evidence indicates people can be taught to cope more effectively with a variety of stressors. One approach is to help individuals identify whether a situation is changeable or not, then to match the form of coping to the situation so that the person uses problem-focused types of coping for changeable situations, emotion-focused types of coping for unchangeable situations, and meaning-focused coping in chronic situations. Traditional stress management interventions often emphasize training in emotion-focused coping.

SUSAN FOLKMAN AND
JUDITH TEDLIE MOSKOWITZ

coping potential (appraisal of) In its most general form, coping potential refers to the ability of an individual to successfully cope or deal with a situation that is potentially or actually threatening to the well-being of the person (see COPING). This could mean an adverse event to be mastered (such as a dangerous situation in traffic, or being attacked by a human or animal) or a debilitating emotional state that needs to be overcome to allow normal emotional functioning.

In appraisal theories of emotion (see APPRAISAL THEORIES), coping potential is used in the sense of an individual evaluating his or her capacity to deal with or master a particular event that is unfolding or expected to occur. A pioneering contribution by Lazarus (1991) was his insistence that emotion and stress depend not only on the evaluation of a situation's significance for our well-being (primary appraisal) but also on our assessment of our ability to deal with the situation (secondary appraisal). Appraisal is proactive, as it goes beyond the immediate situation and assesses the probability of different, possible outcomes by taking into account our ability to change the situation and its consequences. The major function of the coping appraisal is to determine the appropriate response to an event, given the nature of that event and the resources at one's disposal. For example, in the case of a threat by a predator, the power or coping appraisal evokes flight if the threatened being is weak or powerless or fight if there is a good chance of winning. In evaluating one's ability to deal with an event and its consequences, it is useful to know what caused the event. This is why some (but not all) appraisal theorists subsume the dimension of causation or responsibility (postulated by all appraisal theorists) under the general heading of power and control assessment. All appraisal theorists postulate a dimension called *agency, responsibility or causation, reflecting the determination of the agent (oneself, someone else, or circumstances) and the cause (e.g. intention, chance) of the event (see also Weiner 1982).

Scherer (2001a) has suggested distinguishing between control (see CONTROLLABILITY), power (see POWER (IN APPRAISAL)), and adjustment capacity as each accounts for separate aspects of coping ability. Control relates to the assessment of how well an event or its outcomes can be influenced or determined by people or if it is beyond human control, like the weather. If the situation is controllable, the outcome depends on one's own power to exert control or to recruit the help of others. Here, the organism evaluates the resources at its disposal for changing contingencies and outcomes according to its interests. Sources of power might be physical strength, money, knowledge, or social attractiveness, among others. The adjustment evaluation concerns the organism's potential to adapt to changing conditions in the environment. This is particularly important if the control and power appraisals suggest that it is not possible for the organism to change the outcome of an event. Here, the feasibility of changing goals or reducing their likelihood, and the cost of doing this, is established. The results of these three appraisal checks have a major impact on the type of emotion and the associated action that will emerge (e.g. anger and aggression if one believes one has high control and power versus fear and flight if one is convinced one lacks control and/or power). Lack of perceived adjustment potential may, on the other hand, lead to resignation, sadness, or despair.

KLAUS R. SCHERER

Ellsworth, P.C. and Scherer, K.R. (2003). Appraisal processes in emotion. In: R.J. Davidson, K.R. Scherer, H.H. Goldsmith (eds), *Handbook of the affective sciences*, pp. 572–95. New York: Oxford University Press.

Scherer, K.R. (1999a). Appraisal theories. In: T. Dalgleish, and M. Power (eds), *Handbook of cognition and emotion*, pp. 637–63. Chichester: Wiley.

core affect Core affect is defined as a neurophysiological state consciously accessible as a simple primitive nonreflective feeling most evident in mood and emotion but always available to consciousness (Russell 2003, Russell and Barrett 1999). Although one feeling, it can be characterized by two pan-cultural bipolar dimensions: pleasure–displeasure (*valence; feeling good versus bad) and activation (*arousal; feeling energetic versus enervated). The phrase 'core affect' was chosen because it (unlike *emotion, mood, anger*, etc.) is not an everyday lay concept.

Core affect can remain constant (as in *mood) or change rapidly (as in emotion). It is subject to many causes, some internal, some external, some obvious, some beyond human ability to perceive. Functionally, core affect is an aspect of the core self, a barometer of one's state and, as such, influences psychological processes from reflexes to complex cognitions. Individuals often attribute core affect to something, and they are often correct but also sometimes mistaken.

Although a person is always in some state of core affect, even when not conscious of it, interest in core affect stems partly from its role in our emotional lives. Core affect *per se* is free-floating (i.e. not about something). Strong free-floating core affect occurs in such object-free mood disorders as anxiety or depression. Core affect is the mental heat in an emotional episode. A rapid change in core affect perceived as due to something is a key ingredient in such object-directed emotions as anger: to be angry is, in part, to feel bad because of someone's offence. (Prototypically, anger also includes appraisal, action, and so on.) Core affect is part of, not the whole of, moods and emotions.

JAMES A. RUSSELL AND LISA FELDMAN BARRETT

core relational themes Core relational themes, as described by Lazarus and his colleagues (e.g. Smith and Lazarus 1990, Lazarus 1991, Smith *et al.* 1993), represent a higher-order, more categorical conceptualization of emotion-eliciting appraisals (see APPRAISAL THEORIES; ANTECEDENTS) than the appraisal dimensions, or appraisal components, included in most appraisal models (e.g. Smith and Lazarus 1990, Roseman 2001, Scherer 2001a). Whereas the appraisal components can be thought of as representing the important questions, or issues, to be evaluated in the immediate circumstances (e.g. 'Does this situation matter to me?', or 'Can I handle what is happening here?'), the core relational themes can be thought of as patterns of answers to these questions that have specific adaptational implications, and result in the elicitation of specific emotions. Each core relational theme implies a specific combination of answers to a set of appraisal questions, and each distinct emotion has its own distinct core relational theme, which represents a particular type of adaptational relationship with one's circumstances. For instance, in the model of Smith and Lazarus (1990), appraisals of high motivational relevance (importance), high motivational incongruence (undesirability), and other-accountability combine to define the core relational theme of 'other-blame', which evokes anger at the other who is held accountable. In contrast, the same appraisals of relevance and incongruence in combination with self-accountability define the core relational theme of 'self-blame' which elicits guilt. The combined appraisal components defining the theme take on a higher-order meaning that reflects more than the simple, additive sum of the individual appraisal components.

One notable point of theoretical controversy concerns whether such core relational themes represent emotion-antecedent appraisals as depicted by Smith and Lazarus (1990), or are subsequent, emergent properties of the emotional response itself, as argued by Frijda and others (e.g. Frijda and Zeelenberg, 2001).

If they are viewed as emotion-antecedent appraisals, the construct of core relational themes represents a potential theoretical bridge between dimensional appraisal models that have the capacity to predict an infinite variety of emotional states and discrete emotion theories that predict a relatively small number of qualitatively distinct emotional categories.

CRAIG A. SMITH AND LESLIE D. KIRBY

corrugator muscle The corrugator supercilii muscle is a small but forceful facial muscle in the upper part of the face. It is proximally attached to the frontal bone of the skull at the medial wall of the orbit and distally to the skin over the middle part of the eyebrow (Pernkopf *et al.* 1989). Its contraction results in frowning of the eyebrow, an expression that is characteristic of states of mental *distress in general, and specific negative affective states like sadness, fear, and anger in particular. In behavioural research, the electrical activity (electromyogram; see ELECTROMYOGRAPHY) of the corrugator is often used as an index of the subject's affective state. This activity is generally negatively related to affective *valence. Compared with the slight level of sustained activity that is habitually present in this muscle during neutral situations, negative emotional states are characterized by proportional increases in activity whereas activity is inhibited during positive emotional states.

Although corrugator activity may be a useful marker of emotional valence, it is not entirely determined by emotion. This muscle is also active during a wide range of nonemotional situations during which the subject is involved in more or less complex forms of cognitive information processing. In such situations, enhanced corrugator activity may be a sign of automatic orienting responses to unexpected changes in the environment, voluntary attention to external stimuli, or mental effort.

ANTON VAN BOXTEL

counterfactual emotions In his eulogy for his slain brother Robert, Ted Kennedy said that 'Some people see things the way they are and ask why; my brother saw things the way they never were and asked why not'. Without taking anything away from Robert Kennedy, the literature on counterfactual thinking and emotion suggests that he wasn't exceptional in this regard. Everyone evaluates events both as what they are and what they are not, and our thoughts of what did not happen influence our feelings about what did (Kahneman and Tversky 1982, Roese and Olson 1995).

The very essence of some emotions lies in counterfactual comparisons. The negative feelings associated with *regret, for example, stem from comparing outcomes obtained on a chosen path with those that would have been obtained on an alternative path (Gilovich and Medvec 1995). *Shame and *guilt derive from potent rumination about a path one should have taken but did not. Sometimes the counterfactual state can be anticipated, as when we know we'll regret eating an extra bowl of ice cream before going to bed or when we anticipate that we'll be disappointed (see DISAPPOINTMENT) if we don't fare well in a competition. At other times the counterfactual state is only apparent after the fact, as when a silver medallist contemplates a minor stumble that kept her from the gold.

Even emotions that are not inherently counterfactual are enhanced by salient comparisons to what 'almost happened', a phenomenon known as emotional amplification. A regrettable action that one almost didn't take is particularly regrettable. Film directors use this to enhance emotion in their audiences. When a character says 'This is my last mission', that character is not long for this world. His subsequent death is experienced as more poignant because of the irresistible thought that he was almost out of harm's way.

THOMAS GILOVICH

crying (evolutionary perspectives) We define crying as a multimodal behaviour consisting of tears, nonverbal vocalizations (wails, sobs), and facial expressions of distress. Being most frequent in infants, and arguably less subject to cultural display rules, we take infant crying as the prototypical form. Correspondingly, we take *distress (sadness, fear, anger, or pain) as the core condition expressed through crying since although adults sometimes cry in other circumstances (notably when happy), infants appear not to do so. Lastly, although tears are a uniquely human component of crying, distress vocalizations and corresponding displays occur in many mammals, again primarily present in infancy.

Compared with most affective displays, crying is intrinsically costly, particularly for human infants.

Full-fledged crying involves the contraction of large muscle groups, and hence is energetically more expensive than many displays. Moreover, cries of helpless human infants are easily detected by animals, increasing the risk of predation in ancestral populations. Finally, whether by design of the cries themselves, the design of listeners' auditory systems, or both, crying is irritating and distracting to adults (particularly nonkin), increasing the risk of infanticide. These costs must be considered in any functional analysis of crying.

Infant crying is traditionally considered an index of the need for succour (Zeifman 2001). The interests of parents who spread their resources over multiple offspring sometimes conflict with those of the infant, who would monopolize investment. Although infants might therefore profit by exaggerating signals of need, the intrinsic costs of crying may constrain such dishonesty, as natural selection would disfavour exaggeration beyond the point where added costs exceed additional benefits. Perhaps combining contextual information with assessments of intensity of the cry, caregivers often distinguish among 'types' of cries (hunger, pain, etc.) (Gustafson et al. 2000), suggesting that infants do not extensively exaggerate signals of need.

If crying honestly signals need, why do infants sometimes cry in the apparent absence of elicitors? Caregivers ought to be able to deduce the cause, yet infants can be inconsolable. Given the energetic costs of crying, this suggests that cries from so-called colicky infants serve as signals not of need but of vigour—advertising vigour could benefit the infant whenever parents must decide how much to invest in a given child (Soltis 2004). However, this argument remains controversial, as colicky crying often induces frustration or depression in parents rather than increased attachment and investment (Beck 1996); others have questioned whether colic is specific to patterns of childcare in industrialized societies where, unlike many hunter–gatherer societies, infants are often not in contact with caregivers (Fouts et al. 2004).

The propensity to cry in response to distress is preserved into adulthood. However, the honesty of the signal is degraded. Being less vulnerable to predation and aggression, crying adults pay lower costs than infants. Moreover, adults seem more capable of manipulating this signal—adults can suppress crying even in the face of stimuli, such as pain inducers, that invariably evoke crying in infants; conversely, some adults can spuriously cry in the absence of distress. Presumably, crying is maintained into adulthood because it continues to elicit supportive responses from others, yet the degradation of the honesty of the signal makes this puzzling—given that Machiavellian individuals cry strategically, why have recipients not stopped responding to adult crying, leading to the disappearance of

this pattern? One possibility is that the signal remains somewhat costly both because of its irritating nature and because crying is modestly incapacitating, leaving the crier more vulnerable to attack; this may explain why adults cry more freely in the presence of kin or friends (Zeifman 2001). Moreover, while kin and friends remain susceptible to manipulation, they have the advantage of fuller access to information regarding the frequency with which crying occurs and the eliciting circumstances, facilitating the detection of dissimulation. This suggests that solitary adult crying reflects the assessment that bonds with potential observers are sufficiently weak as to make it more likely that they would respond with hostility than aid. Likewise, the value of strategic deployment may account for a developmental shift in emphasis from the acoustic to the visual components of crying—whereas helpless infants are best served by broadcasting a vocalization detectable at a distance, adults profit more from tears, visible only to those in close proximity (Zeifman 2001).

In addition to the question of honesty, adult crying differs from infant crying in that adults occupy a symbolic world opaque to infants. This includes not only elicitors of distress, but also the meaning of crying itself. Perhaps because of its ease of detection, its association with infancy, or both, crying is highly subject to cultural *display rules that dictate behaviour as a function of social identity and context. Consistent with the notion that crying entails vulnerability and signals need for aid, a common pattern across cultures is for such rules to be highly gendered, with crying being less frequently acceptable among men (Becht and Vingerhoets 2002, Rosenblatt et al. 1976), who typically engage in more overt, and more violent, competition. With regard to context, while *grief and mourning are common circumstances in which adult crying occurs, the permissibility and expected duration of such crying varies greatly across cultures (Rosenblatt et al. 1976). Cultural display rules influence not only the outward manifestations of adult crying, but also the subjective consequences thereof, as nonnormative crying can induce shame while normative crying can be cathartic (Becht and Vingerhoets 2002). Finally, the expressive facets of crying are often institutionalized in ritual displays of crying and crying-like vocalizations, with mourning again being a common context for such behaviour (cf. Rosenblatt et al. 1976).

DANIEL M. T. FESSLER AND CRISTINA M. MOYA

Soltis, J. (2004). The signal functions of early infant crying. *Behavioral and Brain Sciences*, **27**, 443–90.

Vingerhoets, A.J.J.M. and Cornelius, R.R. (eds) (2001). *Adult crying. A biopsychosocial approach.* Hove: Brunner-Routledge.

crying (psychological perspectives) Crying in adults and children is characterized by the secretion of tears from the lachrymal glands in response to a variety of emotional stimuli (Vingerhoets and Cornelius 2001). Crying may be accompanied by vocalization, but need not be. To distinguish crying involving the secretion of tears from the distress cries of infants, which are primarily vocalizations that may not be accompanied by tears, some prefer the term weeping. Crying may take a variety of forms, from watery eyes, to tears running down the cheeks, to sobbing, which is characterized by convulsive movements of the upper body. Some include feeling pressure on the eyes and a 'lump in the throat' as either a precursor to crying or a stifled cry. Given the very different forms that crying may take, there is debate as to whether crying is one behaviour or many. The different forms of crying differ by experienced intensity and may also differ in terms of the kinds of situations in which they occur. Crying may be accompanied by a number of *coping behaviours, two of the most frequent being seeking comfort or attempting to conceal one's tears. Studies have consistently found that women cry more frequently than do men, but the size of the gender difference varies considerably across cultures. While nonhuman animals have been observed to tear in response to illness or injury, it is thought that crying in response to emotional stimuli is unique to humans. Charles Darwin held that the shedding of emotional tears was a by-product of the secretion of tears to protect the eyes during screaming or crying out in *pain or *distress. More recently, it has been argued that tears, like the distress vocalizations of infants, evolved to signal to others that one is in need of succour.

RANDOLPH R. CORNELIUS

cultural specificity The anthropological literature is full of examples of culture-specific emotions: Some cultures have emotions not recognized in other contexts and some cultures lack words that occur in most other cultures (Russell 1991). An example of a culture-specific emotion word is *hasham* among the Awlad Ali Bedouins, loosely translated as modesty or shame, which is related to threats or injuries to one's honour, but does not have a direct counterpart in English. Moreover, even if a translation of the emotion word itself can be approximated, the web of connotations in which it is embedded would get lost in translation (Abu-Lughod 1986). Honour in this Bedouin society is defined as autonomy and strength, and *hasham* is thus associated with any sign of weakness, including merely being in the presence of someone who is of higher status. Since men are considered higher up in the hierarchy than women, the women are supposed to feel *hasham* in the presence of men.

Emotions such as *hasham* are culture-specific and unfamiliar to English speakers, but they are not incomprehensible, as a description like the one provided above shows (see also Oatley 1991). Linguists have analysed the meaning of culture-specific emotion words in terms of semantic primitives, words that are shared by all languages (see LINGUISTICS AND EMOTION) (Wierzbicka 1999).

It is even possible that emotions can be experienced by a speaker when his or her language has no word for them (although it might be argued that the language has a concept for the emotion, even without a single word to describe it). One recent study showed that the experience of *amae*—a Japanese emotion word without English equivalent—was recognized and experienced by Americans (Niiya *et al.* 2006). The Japanese emotion *amae* has several connotations, but the research focused on the feeling of being close when indulging the unreasonable requests by an intimate other. Americans not only recognized this feeling, but they were also able to generate situations that Japanese recognized as instances of *amae*.

Even when two languages share a word for emotion (such as anger or happiness), this does not guarantee that the emotion is experienced in exactly the same way across cultures. Emotions such as anger and happiness are experienced in ways that fit the meanings and practices of being a person and having relationships, which can vary across cultures (Mesquita and Leu 2007). For example, when Americans get angry in offence situations, they blame the offender, feel betrayed, and want to aggress, but the modal Japanese anger response, in addition to blaming the offender, includes trying to understand the offender, and doing nothing as a way of avoiding conflict. The differences in the anger experience reflect the ways that relationships are practised and implemented. In an American independent context, it is important to be independent and feel good about yourself. Anger responses like blaming and aggression protect self-esteem and aim to remove obstacles to personal goals, but they also increase interpersonal distance. On the other hand, Japanese anger fits in with the interdependent cultural model of keeping relational harmony (Mesquita and Leu 2007) (see INDIVIDUALISM/COLLECTIVISM). The meaning of happiness also varies across cultures. Whereas happiness in American contexts means self-esteem and personal control, in Japanese contexts it means feeling connected with others (Mesquita and Karasawa 2002). Therefore, even if lexical equivalents exist across cultures, the experiences associated with them appear to vary according to the cultural meanings and practices of relationships in those cultures.

BATJA MESQUITA AND RYAN POWELL

Mesquita, B. and Leu, J. (2007). The cultural psychology of emotion. In: S. Kitayama and D. Cohen (eds), *The handbook of cultural psychology*, pp. 734–59. Guilford Press, New York.

cytokines

Niiya, Y., Ellsworth, P.C., and Yamaguchi, S. (2006). Amae in Japan and the United States: an exploration of a 'culturally unique' emotion. *Emotion*, **6**, 279–95.

cytokines The term 'cytokine' comes from the Greek *cytos*, cell, and *kinein*, move. This terminology refers to the fact that cytokines usually promote cell proliferation or differentiation. Most cytokines are soluble factors that are produced by cells of the immune system. However, they are also produced by other cells, including endothelial cells, muscle cells, adipocytes, and cells within the nervous system such as microglia and astrocytes. Cytokines can act in an autocrine manner by feeding back on the cells that produce them, in a paracrine manner by acting on nearby cells, and even in an endocrine manner when released into the blood reaching distant cell targets. In order to exert their effects on the target cells, cytokines must bind to specific membrane receptors.

Cytokines play an important role in immunity, inflammation, and haematopoiesis. Cytokines produced by cells of the innate immune system such as macrophages are classified as pro-inflammatory and anti-inflammatory, depending on whether they promote or suppress inflammation. Cytokine action is characterized by pleiotropism and redundancy. Pleiotropism refers to the multiplicity of action of a given cytokine because of its many cellular targets. For instance, the pro-inflammatory cytokine interleukin-1 acts on various cellular targets such as endothelial cells to promote prostaglandin E2 and nitric oxide production, on lymphocytes to support the activation and proliferation of B cells into immunoglobulin-secreting plasma cells, and on the bone marrow to increase mobilization of granulocyte progenitors and mature neutrophils (see Fig. C4) (Dinarello 2005). Redundancy refers to the fact that different cytokines share the same activity. For instance, fever can be

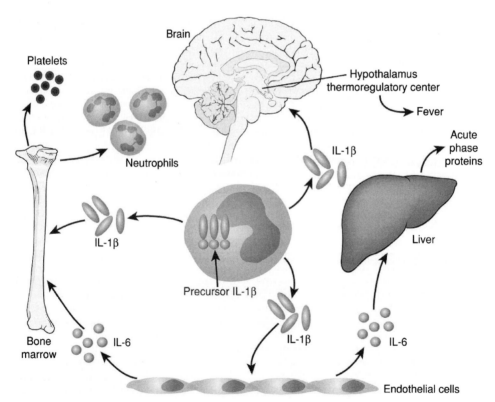

Fig. C4. Pleiotropic activities of interleukin-1-beta (IL-1β). This cytokine, that is mostly produced by activated macrophages and monocytes, acts on endothelial cells, bone marrow cells, hepatocytes, and brain cells. Reprinted with permission from Dinarello (2005).

induced by various cytokines including the inter-ferons, interleukin-1, tumour necrosis factor-alpha, and interleukin-6.

Cytokines are produced in the central nervous system (Dantzer 2007). During the course of a peripheral infection, brain macrophage-like cells and microglia produce the same cytokines as those that are produced at the periphery in response to activation of the immune-to-brain communication pathways. Peripheral immune signals reach the brain mainly via the circulation and the afferent nerves that innervate the bodily site at which the inflammatory response takes place. Brain cytokines regulate the subjective, behavioural, and metabolic components of the host response to pathogenic micro-organisms. Ill individuals typically feel sick and feverish, withdraw from their environment and eat less despite the increased metabolic demand associated with fever. The intensity and duration of these nonspecific signs of illness are enhanced in individuals whose innate immune system is chronically activated. This is the case for both obese and elderly subjects. In vulnerable individuals, the increased expression of brain cytokines that is associated with peripheral inflammation can lead to the occurrence of cognitive and affect disorders in addition to the clinical signs of sickness. Brain cytokines also play a major role in the pathophysiology of various neurodegenerative diseases by promoting astrocyte proliferation, demyelination, and neuronal death.

ROBERT DANTZER AND
KEITH W. KELLEY

Dantzer, R. (2007). Expression and action of cytokines in the brain: mechanisms and pathophysiological implications. In: R. Ader (ed.), *Psychoneuroimmunology*, Vol. 1, pp. 271–80. Amsterdam: Academic Press.

D

decision-making Classical theories of decision-making were cognitive in nature: they assumed that decision-makers dispassionately evaluated the consequences of alternative courses of action and chose the one that would yield the most positive consequences (for review see Loewenstein and Lerner, 2003) (see RATIONALITY). However, research in the last several decades has demonstrated powerful effects of emotion on decision-making. Moreover, understanding the effects of emotion has become an essential part of building descriptively valid theories of decision-making. Here we review some of the ways in which emotion enters into decision-making.

Broadly speaking, there are two types of affective influences: those of *expected emotions* and those of *immediate emotions* (Loewenstein and Lerner 2003).

Expected emotions

Expected emotions are cognitive predictions about the emotional consequences of decision outcomes. That is, expected emotions are not experienced as emotions *per se* at the time of decision-making; rather, as the label suggests, they are expectations about emotions that will be experienced when outcomes materialize in the future (see AFFECTIVE FORECASTING). For example, in deciding whether to invest in a high-risk and high-return commercial development project, a potential investor might attempt to predict whether she will feel regret (or relief) if she did not invest in the project and it yielded huge returns (or losses). Thus, her expectations for emotional outcomes constitute expected emotion.

We present this lengthy definition of expected emotion because theories of decision-making—to the degree that they incorporate emotions at all—have typically assumed that expected emotion is the only emotion that matters. For example, a standard expected utility model assumes that people attempt to predict the emotional consequences associated with alternative courses of action and then select an action that maximizes the net balance of future positive to negative emotions.

Although most economic models of expected emotion have historically been relatively naïve, incorporating unrealistic assumptions about emotion, a number of important innovations for modelling expected emotion have been introduced. Most notably, researchers now recognize that people: (1) respond emotionally to rela-

tive changes rather than to absolute consequences of their decisions (Kahneman and Tversky 1979, Markowitz 1952); (2) compare what happened against counterfactual scenarios and derive pleasure not only from concrete outcomes but also from other aspects, such as what the outcomes imply for one's competence (Bell 1982, Loomes and Sugden 1982, Mellers *et al.* 1997); and (3) care more about the same time delay if it occurs earlier than later (for review see Loewenstein and Lerner 2003).

Expected emotions clearly play an essential role in decision-making. However, two major factors limit the efficacy of decision-making based on expected emotions. First, people systematically mispredict their own affective reactions to outcomes of their own decisions (see Loewenstein and Schkade 1999, Gilbert and Wilson 2000). Second, expected emotions do not capture all the factors that decision-makers should care about, leaving key criteria out of the decision process (Loewenstein and Lerner 2003). For example, cognitive analysis of reasons for preferring a particular choice object to another was shown to reduce postchoice satisfaction with the chosen object, presumably by leaving out important considerations that cannot be captured by expected emotions (Wilson *et al.* 1993).

Immediate emotions

Whereas expected emotions fundamentally consist of cognitions, immediate emotions are real emotions experienced at the time of decision-making. That is, immediate emotions include not only a cognitive component but also somatic components such as facial expressions and changes in the autonomic nervous system. Immediate emotions exert influence on decision-making either by carrying information that people use as an input into the decision they face (Schwarz and Clore 1983) (see AFFECT-AS-INFORMATION MODEL), by overwhelming deliberative decision-making at high intensity (Loewenstein 1996), or by changing the nature and/or depth of processing (Tiedens and Linton 2001).

Broadly speaking, affective influences from immediate emotions fall into one of two categories: *anticipatory influences* and *incidental influences*.

Anticipatory influences (also known as *integral influences*) are the influences from immediate emotions that arise from contemplating the consequences of the decision itself. For example, while thinking about possible consequences of investing in a risky project, the investor might experience immediate anxiety at the thought of the project failing. This type of immediate emotion is also commonly called *integral emotion*.

Although arising from thinking about the consequences of a decision, integral emotions depend on a variety of factors that have little or no influence on expected emotions and are thus qualitatively different from expected emotions. First, unlike expected emotions, integral emotions are relatively insensitive to probabilities. For example, when decision outcomes are pallid (e.g. losing $20) decision-makers are quite sensitive to probability variations. But when decision outcomes are emotionally evocative (e.g. electric shock) decision-makers are insensitive to probability variations (Rottenstreich and Hsee 2001). Second, integral emotions are especially sensitive to the timing and vividness of outcomes. As an event approaches in time, integral emotions such as fear tend to intensify, even when evaluations of the event's probability, or likely severity, remain constant (Van Boven et al. 2005). As an event increases in vividness, a similar pattern of emotion intensification occurs. For example, people pay more for insurance protecting against death due to terrorism than for insurance protecting against any reason (Johnson et al. 1993), presumably because it is easier to vividly form a mental image of death by terrorism than it is to form an image of 'death by any reason'.

Taken together, integral emotions are qualitatively different from expected emotions and thus often propel behaviour in directions that are very different from those that would be dictated by a contemplation of expected emotions. For example, emotional reactions to risky situations often diverge from cognitive assessments of those risks, leading people to be afraid of flying but not driving even if objective risks are far greater for the latter (Loewenstein et al. 2001, Slovic and Peters 2006).

There is no simple dichotomy between good and bad influences of integral emotions. On one hand, integral emotions can be problematic for decision-making. As has been suggested, they often crowd out considerations of expected emotions and cause people to make decision that ignore or underweight important future consequences (Loewenstein and Lerner 2003) On the other hand, however, integral emotions provide intangible but important inputs into decision-making as well as impetus to execute the decision. Recent neuroscientific studies show that individuals with major emotional deficits lack 'somatic markers' and thus might have difficulty making good decisions (Bechara et al. 1997) (see SOMATIC MARKER HYPOTHESIS). However, well-reasoned studies dispute the evidence for somatic markers (Maia and McClelland 2004). Thus,

more research is needed to understand when and how integral emotions serve helpful or harmful roles in decision-making. Interested readers can find further discussion in Vohs et al. (2007).

Incidental influences are the influences from immediate emotions that arise from factors unrelated to the decision at hand. Such factors could include an individual's immediate environment or chronic dispositional affect. For example, if the weather is sunny, the conflicted investor might experience incidental happiness at the time she contemplates her choice. This type of immediate emotion is also commonly called *incidental emotion*. Influences from incidental emotions are difficult to justify because such emotions, by definition, arise from factors that are incidental to—that is, normatively irrelevant to—the decision. Nevertheless, numerous studies have revealed powerful effects of incidental emotions on decision-making.

The influences of incidental emotion are apparent in decision-making under risk. Generally speaking, it has been argued that people tend to be more optimistic when they are in good moods than whey they are in bad moods (Forgas 2003). Recent studies, however, have begun to reveal more nuanced effects of specific emotions. For example, whereas fearful individuals make relatively pessimistic and risk-averse choices, angry individuals make relatively optimistic and risk-seeking choices (Lerner and Keltner 2001). Moreover, the choices of angry individuals more closely resemble those of happy individuals than those of fearful individuals. Importantly, it has been shown that the appraisal patterns of each specific emotion carry over to a new situation and drive such emotion-specific effects.

Incidental emotions also affect other kinds of decisions, such as valuation of objects and decisions regarding prosocial behaviour. For example, sadness from past situations increases buying prices and decreases selling prices of an object. Disgust, on the other hand, decreases both buying and selling prices (Lerner et al. 2004). Incidental happiness induced by finding a dime in a phone booth or receiving free cookies increases people's willingness to help others (Isen and Levin 1972). Similarly, incidental gratitude also increases people's willingness to engage in costly helping behaviour (Bartlett and DeSteno 2006). Considering that these effects all held even when real outcomes were at stake, these studies demonstrate reliable and nonnegligible effects of incidental emotions. Fleeting feelings from one's past can systematically alter decisions in the present.

Conclusions

As the foregoing review indicates, emotions enter into decision-making in various ways. Decision-makers predict and take into account the emotional consequences of alternative decision outcomes. Such *expected emotions* are not experienced as emotion *per se* but influence decision-making as predictions about emotions that will be experienced when outcomes materialize in the future. Immediate emotions, on the other hand, are real emotions experienced at the moment of decision-making. Whereas *integral immediate emotions* are emotions that arise from contemplating the consequences of the decision itself, *incidental immediate emotions* are emotions that arise from factors unrelated to the decision at hand.

Many emotional experiences, however, span the categories reviewed here. For example, decisions that involve a choice between two core values, such as lives against money, may evoke negative integral and incidental emotion (Luce 1998).

Affective influences on decision-making cannot be dichotomized into good and bad influences. Emotions, both expected and immediate ones, clearly serve essential functions in decision-making. But they are also a potential source of biased choice and reckless action. More research is needed to fully elucidate how and why different kinds of emotions influence decision-making. Some of the most exciting research combines models from multiple disciplines, including psychology, economics, and neuroscience. In sum, what was once a neglected area of study (emotional influences in decision-making) has now become a dynamic field, forging an innovative path of interdisciplinary research.

SEUNGHEE HAN AND JENNIFER S. LERNER

Loewenstein, G. and Lerner, J.S. (2003). The role of affect in decision making. In: R.J. Davidson, K.R. Scherer, and H.H. Goldsmith (eds), *Handbook of affective science*, pp. 619–42. New York: Oxford University Press.

Vohs, K.D., Baumeister, R.F., and Loewenstein, G. (eds) (2007). *Do emotions help or hurt decision making?* New York: Russell Sage Foundation.

delay of gratification Delay of gratification in psychological science refers to the willingness and ability to postpone or forego immediate gratifications and temptations for the sake of anticipated delayed consequences and rewards. Difficulties with delay of gratification are a key aspect of diverse problems, including early school failure, conduct disorders, and addictive and antisocial behaviour patterns.

In psychological research, individual differences in delay of gratification and the mechanisms that underlie it are studied with a variety of methods used over the course of development, beginning in early childhood and infancy. In the most extensively studied *delay of gratification paradigm* (Mischel *et al.* 1989), typically a 4-year-old is shown some desired treats, for example tiny

marshmallows or little pretzel sticks, or small trinkets or toys. The child faces a conflict: Wait until the experimenter returns and get two of the rewards, or ring a bell, and the experimenter will come back immediately—but then the child gets only one. After the child chooses to wait for the larger outcome, the delay soon becomes difficult and frustration increases quickly. The number of seconds the child can wait without ringing the bell, touching or eating the rewards, or leaving the seat, is measured as an index of delay of gratification.

Long-term outcomes

In this method, some children fidget and squirm but keep waiting, some quickly ring the bell, and others self-distract, sing songs or talk to themselves, or make themselves fall asleep in order to persist for the delayed rewards. Such differences proved to be diagnostic of important outcomes years later. Those who waited longer at age 4 achieved higher scholastic aptitude test scores in adolescence and were rated by parents and teachers as more competent both socially and cognitively (Mischel and Ayduk 2004). In their late 20s, they reported themselves to be more highly goal-oriented, planful, and persistent, achieved high educational levels and exhibited more positive self-concepts and ego-resiliency. Furthermore, high delayers have been found repeatedly to be protected against a variety of maladaptive outcomes associated with vulnerability factors such as being highly sensitive to rejection (i.e. anxiously expecting interpersonal rejection) in early adulthood. For example, despite being rejection sensitive, high delayers tended to use drugs less often and had developed fewer features of borderline personality by their late 30s (Mischel and Ayduk 2004, Ayduk *et al.* 2008). Thus delay ability in early life may have some protective effects against potential long-term vulnerabilities.

Control mechanisms in delay of gratification

Given the long-term implications of the ability to delay gratification, the mechanisms that underlie it have been extensively analysed in experiments with young children.

Strategic distraction: Attention away from the rewards. Delay is much easier when the rewards are not available for attention. When the rewards are exposed, delay is facilitated by strategic self-distraction from the rewards (e.g. when the child is cued in advance that she can 'think of fun things while you wait').

Hot and cool representations—cooling the temptations: In experiments, delay behaviour and self-control can be changed dramatically by modifying how the desired objects are mentally represented or 'cognitively appraised' (see APPRAISAL THEORIES) (Mischel *et al.* 1989). The young child can exert self-control and wait for otherwise unbearable delay periods for a tempting treat such as a marshmallow by focusing on its non-consummatory 'cool' qualities (e.g. its shape) (see COOL COGNITION) or yield immediately to the temptation by focusing on its consummatory 'hot' or arousing features (e.g. its yummy, sweet, chewy taste) (see HOT COGNITION). A hot, arousing representation elicits behaviours associated with experiencing or consuming the reward by increasing the salience of the short-term goal and subsequently the temptation. When young children look at the actual rewards, or think about them, they tend to spontaneously form hot representations which increase their own frustration, making it more difficult to delay. In contrast, a cool, cognitive, more abstract representation reduces temptation and frustration, enhancing goal-directed waiting. While delay ability in early life is correlated with diverse positive outcomes in the course of development, the same individual who is able and willing to delay in some contexts and situations may be unwilling or unable to do so in others. Both ability and motivation are required for delay.

Hot/cool system interactions underlying delay of gratification: In theory, two interacting systems—an emotional 'hot' system and a cognitive 'cool' system—underlie the psychological dynamics of delay of gratification (Metcalfe and Mischel 1999). The hot 'go' system does fast, virtually reflexive, emotional processing of biologically significant cues (e.g. sex, food, threat) eliciting automatic approach or avoidance reactions. The cognitive, cool system is a 'know' system attuned to the informational features in the environment, and activates rational, reflective, strategic, and planful behaviour. The two systems are interconnected, interacting continuously, such that as one becomes accentuated the other becomes attenuated. In delay of gratification, a focus on the hot, arousing, consummatory features of the stimulus (e.g. the sweet, chewy taste of the marshmallows) accentuates the hot system, increasing impulsive behaviour. A focus on the cognitive, cool, abstract, informational features (e.g. shape, size, similarity to cotton balls) inhibits hot system activation, and enhances delay ability.

Implications

Taken collectively, experiments have identified basic cognitive, affective, and attention mechanisms that control delay ability and make it difficult or easy for the young child. Applications of these findings to educational and therapeutic interventions remain a major challenge for further work.

WALTER MISCHEL AND OZLEM AYDUK

Ayduk, O., Mendoza-Denton, R., Mischel, W., Downey, G., Peake, P.K., and Rodriguez, M. (2000). Regulating the interpersonal self: strategic self-regulation for coping with rejection sensitivity. *Journal of Personality and Social Psychology*, 79, 776–92.

Baumeister, R.F. and Heatherton, T.F. (1996). Self-regulation failure: an overview. *Psychological Inquiry*, 7, 1–15.

denial The psychological concept of denial is a type of defence mechanism within the psychoanalytic/psychodynamic tradition. Denial refers to the rejection of a fact (or associated features) about oneself or aspects of one's life, despite strong or overwhelming evidence to the contrary. The denied fact is invariably something that would be extremely painful for the individual to accept. Psychoanalytic theory argues that denial operates unconsciously such that individuals often deny any denial.

Although the concept of denial was first introduced by Sigmund Freud as a primitive defence mechanism serving to protect the *ego, the idea was more fully elaborated and researched by his daughter Anna Freud (1936). She conceptualized denial as a function of an 'immature mind' because it acts as a barrier between individuals and potential learning experiences afforded by painful realities. However, more recent psychoanalytic/psychodynamic theorists, such as Elisabeth Kübler-Ross and Mardi Horowitz (e.g. Horowitz *et al.* 1990), treat denial as an initial adaptive reaction to a traumatic experience or a negative and unexpected event (e.g. the death of a loved one), that allows individuals to titrate their exposure to the painful reality of the situation in a way that they are able to cope with emotionally (see COPING).

Different types of denial have been proposed in the literature. Denial of fact (sometimes called simple denial) is when the individual denies completely the reality of an unpleasant event. Denial of impact, or minimization, is where the fact is accepted but its import is significantly downplayed. Finally, denial of responsibility is where the fact and its impact are accepted but the person minimizes or refutes any personal responsibility for the fact.

TIM DALGLEISH AND NICOLA MORANT

depression The term 'depression' derives from the Latin *deprimere*, meaning 'to push down'. The term was rare before the 18th century, but it then started to appear in everyday parlance, in part following its use by Samuel Johnson (1709–84) who seems to have suffered from depression himself (Jackson 1986). 'Depression' was first introduced into medical terminology by influential 19th-century German psychiatrists such as Griesinger and Kraepelin, and this tradition has been largely incorporated into the modern psychiatric classification systems such as the American Diagnostic and Statistical Manual (DSM) (American Psychiatric Association 1994) and the World Health Organization's International Classification of Disease (ICD) (World Health Organization 1992). It should be noted, however, that the more common term from the time of Hippocrates (*c.*460–*c.*370 BC) up until the 19th century had been 'melancholia', deriving from the Greek for 'black bile', which was one of the four humours; 'melancholia' is still in occasional use. Influential works such as Robert Burton's *The Anatomy of Melancholy* (1621) and even Freud (1917) in *Mourning and Melancholia* continued this tradition, but it is extremely rare nowadays to see any formal use that does not refer to 'depression' rather than 'melancholia'.

The term depression has both a lay use and a more formal use in medico-psychological terminology. Everyday use tends to equate depression with something like the misery of returning to work on a Monday morning after a demandingly enjoyable weekend, but from which the sufferer has normally recovered by Monday afternoon. However, the lay use captures only a flavour of the severity and chronicity of the disorders of depression, which refer to a constellation of symptoms that typically include: low *mood, feelings of *sadness, *guilt, and *shame, feelings of suicidality, loss of physical and mental energy, inability to concentrate, withdrawal from normal activities, and changes in drives such as appetite, sleep, and libido (Champion 2000). When untreated, symptoms such as these can persist for 6 months or more and result in further losses in the individual's life such in relation to careers, education, and significant relationships. The psychiatric classification systems tend to classify types of depression according to atheoretical severity and chronicity criteria and are therefore of limited use other than for descriptive purposes. However, one distinction that appears to have some theoretical and clinical use is the distinction introduced by Carlo Perris (e.g. Perris 1974) and others between 'unipolar depression' and 'bipolar depression' (see BIPOLAR DISORDER). The latter is typified by the presence of episodes of *mania, which are not present in the former.

The epidemiology of depression reveals much of the complexity of the disorder (Bebbington 2004). A frequently quoted statistic is that twice as many women suffer from depression as men. Although this figure is largely true within the adult lifespan, below the age of puberty there are at least as many boys as girls who suffer from depression. The two-to-one ratio appears after puberty, but it is again modified by factors such as marital status (with marriage being good for men, but bad for women, at least in relation to depression), and the presence of children. Interestingly, the figures seem to suggest that in old age men and women are equally vulnerable to depression (Laidlaw 2004).

The complexity of the epidemiology of depression is reflected in the fact that there is no adequate theory of depression. Biological models are complicated by the preliminary studies of the genetics of depression; thus, unipolar depressions tend to have a small but on average low genetic contribution, whereas the bipolar disorders have been found to have a much higher genetic contribution (e.g. Kendler *et al.* 2001). There are a number of biological theories concerning hormones and neurotransmitters, none of which in themselves provide an adequate explanation. Nevertheless, the major form of treatment is with antidepressant medication, with more severe cases still sometimes treated with electroconvulsive therapy. There are a number of types of antidepressant medication that target different brain neurotransmitter systems, with the most popular of the new generation of antidepressants being the selective serotonin reuptake inhibitors (SSRIs) such as Prozac.

Psychological theories of depression start with Freud's (1917) theory in *Mourning and Melancholia* in which he argued that melancholia can sometimes include the type of loss seen in mourning of a significant other (though sometimes, Freud argued, the losses in depression can be more 'abstract'). However, melancholia includes an attack on the self or self-loathing, which is not found in mourning. This attack on the self, or 'retroflective anger', was seen as the basic aggressive drive being turned against the self. This aspect of the theory was later rejected by the psychoanalyst Bibring writing in the 1950s, in what has become one of the most influential statements on modern psychological approaches to depression, not just in psychoanalysis but in psychology more generally (e.g. Bibring 1953). Bibring argued that the person vulnerable to depression overinvests in a particular goal or role, such as in a career or in a marital relationship, the perceived loss of which leads to depression. The idea of an overinvested area is continued into the most popular modern psychological approach to depression, that of Beck's cognitive therapy (Beck *et al.* 1979). Beck's approach includes both a psychological model of depression and a treatment approach that has become increasingly widely used and that appears to show benefits over antidepressant medication in terms of the prevention of relapse in people who have recovered from depression.

Throughout history there have been many famous sufferers from depression such as Samuel Johnson, who largely popularized the term, so it seems fitting to conclude this entry with some comment on their suffering and on their contributions to humanity. One of the earliest records is that of Job in the Bible who clearly suffered from a period of depression 'My days are past, my purposes are broken off... the grave is mine house'. In more recent times, one of the most famous sufferers was Winston Churchill (1874–1965) who referred to depression as his 'black dog' (e.g. Storr 1988). Churchill's autobiography and his many biographies record a troubled and emotionally impoverished childhood followed by major episodes of depression when he felt he was underachieving such as before World War II when he thought his political career was over, and then after World War II when the public immediately voted him out of office despite his leadership during the war. He found a number of creative activities that he used to fight his 'black dog' with that included writing (for which he won the Nobel prize for literature), painting (and his paintings show some degree of talent), and brick-laying (for which there are huge brick walls around his former home in Kent). Indeed, there seems to be some evidence that a disproportionate number of famous writers, composers, and other talented people suffered from one or other type of depression, as Kay Redfield Jamison (1993) summarized in her excellent book *Touched With Fire*, which includes amongst others accounts of the lives of Byron, Van Gogh, Schumann, and Woolf.

MICHAEL J. POWER

Gotlib, I.H. and Hammen, C.L. (eds) (2002). *Handbook of depression*. New York: Guilford Press.

Power, M.J. (ed.) (2004). *Mood disorders: a handbook of science and practice*. Chichester: Wiley.

desire A desire is a propositional *attitude. That is, a desire is a mental state directed toward some perceivable or conceivable state of affairs (see, e.g., Searle 1983). For example, my father's being healthy is a conceivable state of affairs, and my attitude toward it is one of desire. I desire that he be healthy. Desiring an object, thus, is always desiring a perceivable or conceivable state of affairs involving that object. If Eve desires a mango, it must be the case that she desires that she eat the mango, or that she possess the mango, or something of that sort.

Desires have a number of characteristic effects. First, they combine with perception and belief to cause behaviour. My desire that my father be healthy and my belief that he has arthritis cause me to ask him about his health, to learn more about his form of arthritis, to carry his luggage in the airport, and so on. Second, desires cause felt impulses to behaviour. Even if I do not pick up my father's bag at the airport, I might feel an impulse to do so because I want to protect his health, and think the bag is a little too heavy given his arthritis. Third, desires cause feelings of pleasure and displeasure. Learning that my father's health has been in decline causes me displeasure, but learning that his new drug regimen is highly effective pleases me. Fourth, desires influence attention. Because I desire that my father be healthy, I pay more attention to advertisements for arthritis medication than I would otherwise. Fifth, desires determine what counts as a reward or a punishment. A doctor might reward me for doing her a favour by making sure

my father receives the very best care, since that is what I want, or she might punish me for being rude to her by dismissing my father's complaints, that being what I want not to happen.

Generally, researchers have emphasized the connections between desire and behaviour (e.g. Searle 1983, Berridge 1999), but there have been other efforts to connect it to pleasure (e.g. Strawson 1994) or reward (e.g. Dretske 1988).

A key distinction to make when thinking about desires is the distinction between intrinsic and instrumental desires. Intrinsic desires are desires for things for their own sake, whereas instrumental desires are desires for things merely as a means to some further end. Thus, I might desire to eat a walnut merely as a means to getting enough protein, and I might desire protein merely as a means to maintain my health, but I might desire to be healthy just for its own sake. Some researchers hold that only pleasure is desired for its own sake, while others hold a more ecumenical view on which many different things are intrinsically desired.

TIMOTHY SCHROEDER

Schroeder, T. (2004). *Three faces of desire*. New York: Oxford University Press.

despair Despair is a complex affective state. As Darwin observed (1872/1998, p.176): 'If we expect to suffer, we are anxious; if we have no hope of relief, we despair': hopelessness may describe it better than any other single concept. Although hopelessness may be central to despair, hopelessness itself may be a very complex experience. Neither despair nor the feeling of hopelessness that characterizes it is a unitary state caused by a unitary process.

Acute onset of distress may result from extreme intensities of any one of several different emotions, including *sadness/*grief, *fear, *anger, *disgust, or *shame and possible other complex emotion phenomena or emotion schemas (interacting emotion and cognition). The experience or feelings of despair may include one or more of these specific emotions, emotion schemas, or complex patterns of emotion schemas like *anxiety and *depression. Thus despair is often a cluster of feelings.

Perhaps the common denominator among the varieties of despair is the loss of *hope and the concomitant loss of interest (see INTEREST/ENTHUSIASM). One can lose hope and interest in one's relationships, one's work, or one's ability to cope effectively. In the gradual onset of more or less chronic despair, losing hope and losing interest are probably interacting processes and not a simple or linear cause–effect relationship. Loss of interest is as likely to initiate the process of despair as is a transient feeling of hopelessness. Loss of hope and loss of interest characterize depression, and severe depression is considered as another possible source of despair.

In any case, despair involves emotions of extreme intensity. Many emotions are associated with *action tendencies; thus, despair may lead to extreme behaviour including harm to self or others.

CARROLL E. IZARD

development (emotional) see ADOLESCENCE (EMOTIONAL DEVELOPMENT); AGEING (AND EMOTIONAL DEVELOPMENT); CHILDHOOD (EMOTIONAL DEVELOPMENT); INFANCY (EMOTIONAL DEVELOPMENT IN); MORAL DEVELOPMENT.

differential emotions theory Differential emotions theory (DET) draws from Darwin (1809–82) and more substantially from Silvan Tomkins (1911–91). It assumes that emotions constitute the primary motivational system for human behaviour and that each emotion has unique motivational and regulatory functions (see MOTIVATION). For example, the emotion of interest facilitates selective attention, exploration, learning, and constructive activities. An important distinction is made between evolutionarily derived *basic emotions and developmentally influenced emotion schemas. Emotion schemas derive from the learned association of any of a wide variety of evolved feelings on the one hand and cognition (appraisal and thoughts) on the other. This distinction is critical for understanding the functions of these types of emotions and their role in the relations between emotion, cognition, and action systems. The relations between these three broad systems and their subsystems change across different periods of development and in different life circumstances (Abe and Izard 1999). This distinction also has important implications for the relations between emotion processes, levels of consciousness, and the development of traits of personality and symptoms of psychopathology.

Basic emotions

In DET the basic emotions are interest (see INTEREST/ENTHUSIASM), *joy/*happiness, *sadness, *anger, *disgust, and *fear. This list is quite similar to those of basic emotion theorists (Ekman 1999, Panksepp 2005). They are considered basic emotions in DET because they are products of evolution and have a common set of properties. For example, each consists of neural, bodily/expressive, and experiential/feeling components and each has specific motivational and regulatory functions. Each typically, though not necessarily, involves at least a minimal appraisal process or perceptual activity (cf. Scherer et al. 2006). Evidence suggests that a brainstem (mesodiencephalic) neural arrangement through interconnection with other subcortical systems (e.g. *amygdala, hypothalamus) generates basic emotion processes (cf. Merker 2007). Children with anencephaly or hydra-

nencephaly (and hence with massive loss in the cerebral hemispheres and lack of a cerebral cortex) were observed displaying the expressive behaviour patterns of basic emotions as do normal infants and young children (Izard et al. 1995).

The *components* of a basic emotion consist of dedicated neural substrates, a unique subjective feeling or motivational state that derives from evolved neurobiological processes, and innate capacities to generate and recognize emotion-specific expressive behaviour and to execute a more or less prototypical response to the stimulus (see COMPONENTIAL THEORIES). In many instances, basic emotions include an action tendency even when there is no overt behaviour. However, there are considerable individual differences in the innate capacity to generate and recognize emotion-expressive behaviour and engage in automatic emotion-related behaviour (Izard 1977).

Several characteristics are common to all basic emotions. They can be activated by sensory detection or simple perception of a bio-evolutionarily prepared or ecologically valid stimulus. Basic emotions are activated and become motivational/functional and regulatory via rapid, automatic, subcortical information processing, independent of neocortical activity (Merker 2007). They are characterized by organizing, motivational, and regulatory functions (Izard and Ackerman 2000).

Basic negative emotions perform essential adaptive functions in response to serious loss and other threatening or aversively challenging stimuli. For example, the basic emotion of fear motivates protective behaviour. It always has minimal perceptual/cognitive content related to an ecologically valid stimulus such as a dangerous animal or strange large object looming toward one. However, the frequency of basic emotion activation is a function of the level and frequency of such ecologically valid stimuli in the environment. In nurturing and safe environments and peaceful cultures, basic negative emotions occur relatively infrequently and account for only a small portion of human motivation.

The *basic positive emotion* of interest occurs very frequently and endures for relatively long periods of time in safe and friendly environments. In such contexts, interest is activated by virtually any change in the sensory fields, particularly by novel stimuli, change, and motion. Interest more or less continually regulates other emotions, attention, and information processing. By virtue of its relative ubiquity and capacity to drive and regulate other emotions, attention, and information processing, basic interest and interest schemas are critical organizing factors in mental processes and in establishing and maintaining interaction of the individual with the social and physical environment (Izard 1977).

differential emotions theory

Basic emotions and early development

DET maintains that the evolved basic emotions emerge early in ontogeny and that their motivational and regulatory functions help explain many important aspects of socio-emotional development. For example, the interplay of the basic emotions of interest and joy during a young infant's expressive-behaviour play with a familiar adult has long been considered as a foundation to the normal infant's development of a sense of self as causal agent (see CHILD-HOOD EMOTIONAL DEVELOPMENT). Such mother–infant play may also contribute to the ability of 4-month-old infants to discriminate and respond differentially to discrete positive and negative emotion expressions of their mothers, a skill that will eventually facilitate empathic responding.

Expressive-behaviour play is also fundamental to the development of young children's *emotion schemas* or feeling-cognition structures that constitute emotion knowledge, the understanding of the expressions, feelings, and functions of emotions. Such emotion knowledge will eventually become critical in the development of interpersonal skills that mediate adaptive social behaviour and help prevent the emergence of precursors of psychopathology (Izard 2002, Denham and Burton 2003).

Emotion schemas emerge in synchrony with cognitive development, and the developmentally increasing complexity of some of them (e.g. those involving feelings of shame or guilt) is dependent on the emergence of a concept of self and relationships with others (Lewis and Brooks 1978). In terms of psychopathology, *anxiety and *depression are more or less coherent sets of genetically and environmentally influenced emotion schemas, involving fear and sadness, respectively, as the key emotion (Izard 1977). Emotion schemas vary across developmental periods, individuals, and cultures (Shweder 1993): in the 1970s, a Peace Corps volunteer who spent a hot summer's night with a rural Congolese family might sleep in a house with all doors and windows closed to keep out evil spirits.

Emotion schemas frequently, though not necessarily, involve appraisal processes (Ellsworth and Scherer 2003). Their feeling/motivational component evolved along with all other types of subjective feelings (Langer 1967, Edelman 2006). Their higher-order cognitive components are products of learning and experience and are heavily influenced by life circumstances and culture. The present distinction between basic emotions and emotion schemas is viewed as critical in understanding emotion–cognition–action relations in different contexts and across different periods of the lifespan. For example, the cognitive content in fear schemas may change from thoughts of monsters in young children, to bullies in older children, threats to self-identity and security in adolescents and young adults, to accidents and incapacitating diseases in old people.

Over the course of the lifespan a normal individual will develop countless emotion schemas. Many schemas consist of simply an emotion feeling component and a restricted set of memories and context-mediated perceptions and thoughts (e.g. sadness schemas and anger schemas). Some examples of more complex emotion schemas or coherent sets of emotion schemas are love, interest in constructive activities (including avocations, work, art, and science), envy, hatred, jealousy, and ideologies. An emotion schema may or may not have a characteristic expression or expressive-behaviour component. However, the feeling/motivational component of an emotion schema and its underlying neurobiological substrates are products of evolution (Langer 1967, Edelman 2006). The feeling component of an emotion schema can range across all levels of intensity. Emotion schemas are generally comparable to the 'emotions' described by appraisal theorists (see APPRAISAL THEORIES). Many appraisal theorists, though not all, consider cognitive appraisals as part of emotion (see Ellsworth and Scherer, 2003, for a review).

The development of emotion schemas

The talk of parents, caregivers/teachers, and peers about eliciting events and consequent emotion feelings provides the child with the opportunity to learn emotion-related language (Izard 2002). Through cognitive development, conditioning, and social learning, feelings that are characteristic of basic and later emerging emotions may become components of a large number of emotion schemas that include complex appraisals and thought. Thus different manifestations of the feeling that is associated with a basic emotion (e.g. interest) may emerge in different emotion schemas over developmental time. The labels or names that become associated with emotion experiences and the cognitive content of emotion schemas vary across individuals, families, and cultures (Izard 1971, 1992).

Developmental processes, particularly cognitive development, in interaction with emotion development, play a key role in the transition that makes emotion schemas (rather than basic emotions) predominant in human motivation when favourable circumstances and environments prevail. The developmental processes during this transition also build in more or less automatic systems for regulating basic emotions and relegating basic negative emotions to personal conditions or contexts that pose a serious loss, threat, or aversive challenge.

Emotion schemas, on the other hand, depend in part on the ability to symbolize things in awareness. A sharp developmental increase in the complexity of emotion schemas begins when the human infant achieves conscious awareness of objects and events and can demonstrate object recognition (recognition-memory). Most of the relevant developmental data suggest that children pass this milestone between the ages of about 9 and 18 months.

Young infants' ability to categorize discrete emotion expressions and discriminate among them (Nelson 1987) helps lay the foundation for learning emotion-relevant language and developing emotion schemas. After children acquire adequate language and sufficient cognitive ability for complex appraisals and emotion-related thought, they can utilize appraisal processes and related cognition in interaction with ongoing emotion (e.g. interest) to transform a basic emotion process into an emotion schema. Some emotion schemas may become quite complex. Eventually an emotion schema like jealousy may involve feelings of sadness, anger, or fear and the kinds of thoughts usually associated with these feelings. The feeling state of each emotion can eventually become associated with a virtually limitless variety of cognitive contents to form emotion schemas. Achievement goals (motivated mainly on the emotion of interest) are good examples.

The processes in the development of emotion schemas parallel the development of emotion regulation (Cole *et al.* 2004). Increased regulation of basic emotion processes and their associated action impulses, together with increased cognitive ability, enables two things: the child can inhibit or modify the automaticity of the basic emotion-action processes and at the same time enable more complex appraisals, thoughts, and adaptive actions relevant to the eliciting event. Thus the child can transform what would be a burst of basic emotion and a more or less automatic prototypical response (or basic emotion episode) into a more controlled emotion (feeling-thought) schema (Izard 2002). With further cognitive and moral development, an emotion schema may include in its cognitive component the consideration of the consequences of impulsive or basic emotion driven actions. Considering the feelings of others and substituting negotiation for aggressive actions depend on the development of empathy (Hoffman 2000).

Levels of consciousness in relation to levels of emotion

Philosophers and scientists who study consciousness have by no means reached consensus on its definition or number of levels, but there is considerable agreement that there is a clear distinction between reflective consciousness and phenomenal or primary consciousness (Edelman 2006). DET assumes that basic emotions involve no complex cognitive processes and can thus operate in phenomenal consciousness. Emotion schemas that include higher-order cognition operate as processes of reflective consciousness.

CARROLL E. IZARD AND KRISTEN A. KING

dimensional emotion models Whether variations in the emotion domain have to be conceptualized in terms of gradual differences on underlying dimensions, or in terms of discrete differences between emotion categories forms a theme cutting across much of emotion research (see EMOTION THEORIES AND CONCEPTS (PHILOSOPHICAL PERSPECTIVES); BASIC EMOTIONS). Like the categorical approach, the origins of the dimensional approach to emotions can be traced back to philosophy. Aristotle (384–322 BC) identified the hedonic tone (see VALENCE) as a major dimension of gradual differences in the emotion domain and the 18th-century Dutch philosopher Baruch Spinoza (1632–77) may have been the first to point out that emotions are more-dimensional entities. According to him, emotions are not just pleasant or unpleasant, they are also weak or strong, and they are also more or less persistent.

Right from the beginning of psychology as a science, the dimensional view has played an important role. In 1896, Wilhelm Wundt (1832–1920), on the basis of *intro-spection, proposed a polarity principle to structure the space of *feelings (Gefühle) and suggested three basic dimensions: pleasure–displeasure, arousal–calming, and tension–relaxation (*Lust–Unlust, Erregung–Hemmung,* and *Spannung–Lösung*). The real breakthrough of the dimensional emotion model can be attributed to Osgood. He (e.g. Osgood *et al.*, 1957) discovered in the 1950s that the affective meaning of words (the connotative meaning) is organized according to three dimensions, namely evaluation (later also labelled as *valence or pleasantness), potency (later also labelled as dominance), activity (later also labelled as *arousal or activation). Later, in the 1960s and 1970s he and his colleagues (Osgood *et al.*, 1975) would demonstrate that these three dimensions spanned the affective connotation of words across languages and cultural groups (see VOCABULARY OF EMOTION).

Osgood's work has been a point of reference for much research within the emotion domain, notably on the cognitive structure of the emotion words. Within both Western and non-Western groups similarities between emotion words, obtained by means of pairwise similarity ratings or similarity sorting tasks, can be represented in the three-dimensional space of pleasantness, potency, and arousal (e.g. Shaver *et al.* 1987).

The dimensional approach is probably the most widespread for the measurement of the subjective experience of emotions and moods. Participants have to indicate how well various words for feelings and emotions describe their own experience, or how intensely they experience the feelings and emotions these words are referring to. Four two-dimensional models have gained a good deal of popularity (e.g. Yik *et al.* 1999): the positive and negative affect model of Watson and Tellegen, the pleasantness versus unpleasantness and high-activation versus low-activation model of Larsen and Diener, the tension versus calmness and energy versus tiredness model of Thayer, and the pleasure versus misery and arousal versus sleep circumplex model of Russell (see CIRCUMPLEX MODELS). A vigorous debate has taken place between proponents of the first and the three other models on the bipolarity of the emotion domain. While the first model assumes two unipolar, uncorrelated factors of positive and negative affect, the other three models assume bipolar factors. By carefully controlling for methodological factors (mainly by a multimethod approach, by working with bipolar response scales, and by modelling unreliability via structural equation modelling) Russell and colleagues have given strong evidence for bipolarity in the emotion domain, at least in a psychometric sense. Moreover, they have shown that these four rather different models are psychometrically equivalent: they can be considered as rotations within the same two-dimensional representation (e.g. Yik et al. 1999). While it has been demonstrated that these four models are psychometrically interchangeable, the main discussion is now focused on the optimal rotation of the two dimensions. The valence–arousal proponents focus on the fundamental nature of the hedonic tone of the emotional experience. Proponents of the positive–negative affect rotation claim that these two dimensions best represent the underlying emotion architecture.

It has to be noted here that in each of these four models the potency or dominance dimension—which played a central role in the work of Osgood and in work on the similarity structure of emotions—is lacking. The Geneva emotion wheel (Scherer 2005), a circumplex model based on the underlying appraisal dimensions of pleasantness and control (with intensity/arousal represented as the distance to the central neutral origin) forms a notable exception here. Another exception is the nonverbal assessment procedure proposed by Bradley and Lang (1994) which captures the three dimensions of pleasantness, activation, and dominance.

Next to the measurement of the subjective experience of emotions, the dimensional approach has played an important role in research on the expressive component of emotions. Thus, Schlosberg (1952) demonstrated that facial expressions of emotions can be represented in a two-dimensional space with valence and arousal as the underlying dimensions. In the domain of vocal expression, the arousal dimension has been identified as the most important dimension distinguishing vocal expression. Although cues for the pleasantness and the dominance dimensions have been found, they are taken to be a less important in the vocal domain (Laukka et al. 2005). More generally, Mehrabian (1972) has related nonverbal expressive behaviour to Osgood's three dimensions. In his theorizing,

evaluation is related to signs of approach, such as making eye contact and leaning forward, while arousal is related to signs of activity, such as speech volume and facial activity. Potency is related to signs of control and dominance, which becomes clear in the relaxation of the posture.

It is now well established that the three dimensions of valence, potency, and activation can quite economically represent the variability in the emotion domain. The major question, however, is why these three dimensions keep popping up across studies, emotion components, and cultural groups (although not always in the same study). Recently, Fontaine et al. (2007) have argued and demonstrated for three Western languages, that these three dimensions refer to variation in *all* of the emotion components proposed by the componential emotion approach (see COMPONENTIAL THEORIES). According to this approach, emotions consist of variably interrelated changes in activity across a set of six components: (1) appraisals of events, (2) psychophysiological changes (bodily sensations), (3) motor expressions (face, voice, gestures), (4) action tendencies, (5) subjective experiences (feelings), and (6) emotion regulation. Most of the overlap of 140 emotion characteristics, which operationalized each of these six components, could be described by the three dimensions of pleasantness, potency, and activation. These three dimensions form the common denominator of a vast array of emotion characteristics.

JOHNNY R. J. FONTAINE

disappointment Disappointment is an emotional reaction following disconfirmation of the prospect of a desirable event (Ortony et al. 1988). Its intensity is affected by previous *hope, *desire, and promise: high hopes, strong desires, and promises all give rise to more intense disappointment when they are dashed (van Dijk and van der Pligt 1997).

In disappointment, an unexpected event suddenly arrests the process of desire and counteracts excessive *expectations, thereby suppressing confidence or optimism that is not well founded: 'Disappointment turns life from false dreams to stern realities: It prompts to an investigation of causes, and arouses cognition to a full understanding of the situation. Hope thereby, becomes more rational and realisable' (Stanley, cited in Shand 1914).

Disappointment also corrects anticipations; the maxim 'there is many a slip between the cup and the lip' teaches disappointment. Anticipation of disappointment prepares an individual for a possible negative outcome. It prompts one to intensify one's efforts to avoid this negative outcome, which can be achieved in at least three ways (Armor and Taylor 1998, Zeelenberg et al. 2000). First, by investing (extra) effort people can try to live up to their initial expectations. Second, people can lower their expectations about obtaining a desirable outcome. The lower one's initial expectation, the smaller the chance that this expectation exceeds an obtained outcome and hence the smaller the chance of being disappointed. Third, people can set very global expectations instead of specific ones. Setting global expectations has an advantage over specific expectations, in that the former are less easily disconfirmed and therefore less likely to lead to disappointment.

It is not always possible to avoid disappointment; and the best thing left to do then is to attempt to reduce the experience. Two basic strategies are applicable to these forms of disappointment regulation (Armor and Taylor 1998, Zeelenberg *et al.* 2000): (1) cognitively changing a negative outcome, and (2) dealing with a negative outcome. For example, people might reinterpret an obtained negative outcome by biasing their thinking about what happened and what might have happened in order to regulate how they feel, thereby mitigating their disappointment. One way of reinterpreting outcomes is by shifting the standard of comparison. First, people may select a worse-off *social comparison target, enabling them to maintain a belief that their current status is not as bad as other (more objective) standards might suggest. A second way of shifting standards involves the generation of downward counterfactuals. One can feel good about one's current (negative) outcome if one compares the outcome with an even worse situation that could have occurred.

Biasing the recall of what was initially expected might also help in regulating disappointment. Such biasing can be obtained by questioning the validity of one's initial expectation. For example, people may argue that their initial expectation was perhaps too optimistic, and adjust their expectation retrospectively in such a way that the discrepancy between the obtained outcome and their expectation is smaller. Or they may reappraise (see REAPPRAISAL) the decision process and outcomes, and how these match to their preferences, and come to the conclusion that the chosen option is actually the best.

Apart from trying to change or reinterpret a negative outcome people might also try to engage in psychological repair work in order to regulate their feelings of disappointment. For example, one may employ a 'silver lining' strategy (i.e. focusing on the beneficial aspects of a bad situation) in order to take of the edge off one's disappointment. Another way of dealing with a negative outcome is putting the outcome into perspective. When confronted with an outcome that was less than expected, one could argue that the outcome was not that important anyway. By derogating the importance of an outcome, any experienced emotion in reaction to this outcome is likely to be less intense.

Many of these strategies are related to processes of dissonance reduction, in the sense that people can experience dissonance between the desired outcome and the outcome that is obtained. These feelings may motivate people to 'distort' their thinking about what happened and what might have been in order to mitigate their negative emotional experiences and thus to regulate the disappointment they feel.

WILCO W. VAN DIJK

van Dijk, W.W. (1999). *Dashed hopes and shattered dreams: on the psychology of disappointment*. Doctoral thesis, University of Amsterdam, The Netherlands.

van Dijk, W.W. and van Harreveld, F. (2008). Disappointment and regret. In: N.M. Ashkanasy and C.L. Cooper (eds), *Research companion to emotions in organizations*, pp. 90–102. London: Edward Elgar Publishers.

disgust From Darwin (1809–82) onward, disgust has been considered one of the *basic emotions, along with *happiness, *fear, *anger, and *sadness. In its more primitive forms, disgust guards the body against dangerous foods and microbial infection. In its more elaborated forms, disgust protects the self or soul from nonphysical threats, such as moral violations. More than other emotions, disgust has been transformed in the evolution of human cultures.

Disgust has three distinctive characteristics: first, a facial expression, including closed nostrils, raised upper lip, and gaping jaw; second, a typical behaviour, which is withdrawal from the object that elicits disgust; and third, an accompanying physiological event, nausea. The presence of nausea and a facial expression involving oral rejection strongly suggest that disgust originated as a food rejection mechanism. Disgust is likely to have evolved from a distaste system, but differs in that disgust responses to food are centred not on their taste, but on their nature or origin. In a classic paper, Andras Angyal (1941) defined disgust as 'Revulsion at the prospect of (oral) incorporation of an offensive object'. As he points out, those offensive substances are almost always of animal origin.

A critical feature of disgusting substances is that they are so powerful that they render any edible food unacceptable if they merely touch it. This phenomenon is called *psychological contamination*, and seems to be universal in adult humans but absent in young children and animals. Contamination involves high-level cognition; it requires sensitivity to the contact history of an object in the absence of any stimulus trace of the contact. A cockroach contaminates a glass of milk without changing the taste.

This food-oriented disgust has been called *core disgust* (Rozin and Fallon 1987, Rozin *et al.* 2000). Elicitors include culturally variable 'bad foods', certain animals,

disinhibition

often those associated with these foods (maggots, rats), and every bodily product except tears. A disgust response to faeces is virtually universal for adults in every culture, but infants do not show aversion to faeces. Children develop aversion to faeces around toilet training, but, for a few years, faeces is still not contaminating. By about 5 years of age, children show a full disgust response.

There may be three other sets of elicitors of disgust that appear cross-culturally. Elicitors of *animal-nature disgust* include poor hygiene, inappropriate sex, gore or violations of body boundaries, and death. Disgust moves us away from reminders of our mortality, such as dead bodies and the odour of decay. Second, *interpersonal disgust* is elicited by contact with others, especially contact with strangers or other individuals or groups we are averse to. Third, *moral disgust* is elicited by some kinds of especially egregious moral violations (e.g. stealing from a blind person). In this context, disgust seems to function as one of three emotions that involve responses to the moral violations of others, along with anger and *contempt (see MORAL EMOTIONS).

The elicitors and meanings of disgust seem to have expanded in cultural evolution. The process through which this occurs may be the evolutionary mechanism of *pre-adaptation*, in which a system that evolved for one purpose is used for another (Rozin *et al.* 2008). Thus the mouth, teeth, and tongue evolved for eating, but are used in language expression. Individuals and societies profited by being able to produce a strong rejection of something by making it disgusting.

Within a culture, the Disgust Scale (Haidt *et al.* 1994) shows major individual differences in disgust sensitivity. At one extreme there are Americans who will eat insects and are not revolted by body products or touching dead bodies, and at the other extreme there are those who cannot even touch the doorknob of a public convenience or blow their nose in brand new toilet paper. Women are somewhat more disgust sensitive than men.

Cultures differ markedly in what they find disgusting. In the food domain, some of the animal foods of one culture (insects, cheese) are disgusting to others. Interpersonal and moral disgust are particularly variable across cultures. Psychological contamination plays an important role in the symbolic life of many cultures, especially in religious practices of purity and pollution and in ideas of desecration.

Disgust is an important component of some animal *phobias, blood/injury/injection phobias, and *obsessive–compulsive disorder. A few brain areas are particularly active when individuals experience disgust. One, the anterior insula, is closely connected to the taste system.

There remain important issues for future research. Psychologists do not yet understand in any detail the evolution or development of disgust, nor how the various types of disgust (core, animal reminder, interpersonal, moral) are related to one another. Psychologists are just beginning to explore the role of disgust in intergroup hostility. There are also puzzling features of disgust: even though it is a negative emotion, it is sometimes sought out and is often the subject of humour.

PAUL ROZIN, JONATHAN HAIDT, AND
CLARK MCCAULEY

Miller, W.I. (1997). *The anatomy of disgust*. Cambridge, MA: Harvard University Press.
Rozin, P., Haidt, J., and McCauley, C.R. (2008). Disgust. In: M. Lewis, J.M. Haviland-Jones, and L. Feldman Barrett (eds), *Handbook of emotions*, 3rd edn, pp. 757–76. New York: Guilford Press.

disinhibition Inhibition has become a central concept in numerous domains of psychology. In particular, deficient inhibition-related processes (or disinhibition) have been postulated in various psychopathological states and neuropsychological disorders. In addition, changes in inhibition have been hypothesized to explain the development and age-related decline of cognitive abilities. Finally, individual differences in inhibition have been proposed to explain variations in working memory capacity, language comprehension, *decision-making, long-term memory, emotion regulation, and social appropriateness. Recently, it has been suggested that inhibition should be conceived of as a multidimensional construct rather than a unitary one. Friedman and Miyake (2004), for example, examined the relationships between three inhibition-related functions. They found that prepotent response inhibition and resistance to external distracter interference were closely related and that both were unrelated to resistance to proactive interference. In addition, they showed that a latent variable combining prepotent response inhibition and resistance to external distracter interference was related to everyday cognitive failures while resistance to proactive interference was related to unwanted intrusive thoughts. These results underscore the importance of establishing a taxonomy of inhibition-related mechanisms, a theoretical refinement that should improve our understanding of the role of inhibition in psychological activities, as well as the contribution of disinhibition to psychopathology and neuropsychology. Nevertheless, some researchers have criticized the concept of inhibition, suggesting that many behavioural results could be interpreted just as well without using the concept of cognitive inhibition (Gorfein and MacLeod 2007). On the other hand, the view that an action can be initiated and then inhibited (motor response inhibition) is more widely accepted.

MARTIAL VAN DER LINDEN AND
LUCIEN ROCHAT

disorder (affective, emotional) There is a small but active literature which has dealt with the problems of defining mental disorder, participants being mainly psychiatrists, behavioural scientists, and philosophers. Much of the problem derives from the debates of the 1960s, from the so-called antipsychiatry critiques of Foucault, Laing, Szasz, Rosenhan, Goffman, and others. Foucault's (1965) main work has recently been published in an enlarged English translation (Foucault 2006); sociological critiques of psychiatry continue (Kutchins and Kirk 1997) and are excellently reviewed and updated in Horwitz (2002), and the present author has the only recent book on the general topic of defining mental disorder that includes some historical review (Bolton 2008). One of the key purposes of defining mental disorder is to help demarcate disorder from normal functioning (see Horwitz and Wakefield, 2007, for the demarcation problem in depression).

The critiques of the 1960s laid major charges against mainstream psychiatry and its medical model: that it medicalized and pathologized what were essentially socially defined and meaningful problems. At their most profound, as in Foucault, these criticisms were levelled not so much at psychiatry as at society at large. Most of the explicit debate about the concept of mental disorder since the 1960s revolved around the question of whether mental disorder attributions rest on some hard, natural, medical fact or whether they are merely an expression of social norms and values. Candidates for such a fact are, first, statistical abnormality, and second, failure of a psychological mechanism to function as it has been designed to do—selected for—in evolution. The biostatistical theory proposed by Boorse is interesting but has few adherents (Boorse 1976, 1997), while the evolutionary theoretic view proposed by Jerome Wakefield has dominated the field for the last 20 years (Wakefield 1992a,b, 1999a,b, 2003). The *Journal of Abnormal Psychology* published an impotant special section on the concept of mental disorder (Clark 1999), with most of the contributions being on Wakefield's analysis. Wakefield's analysis has come to be called the 'harmful dysfunction' analysis and it can be stated briefly along the following lines: 'A "mental disorder" is a harmful disruption of a natural function, where "natural function" is to be understood in terms of functioning in the way designed in evolution' (see FUNCTIONALIST THEORIES OF EMOTION; EVOLUTION OF EMOTION). According to this approach negative evaluation is necessary for a condition to be a disorder. This has the consequence that conditions can change from being (con-

sidered as) disorders to being (considered as) normal, and vice versa, depending on the prevailing social norms, and in this sense its inclusion in the definition is consistent with the social constructionist antipsychiatry critiques of the 1960s. On the other hand, Wakefield emphasizes that his approach puts a definite limitation on what legitimately counts as a mental disorder, namely that it has to involve, as a necessary condition, a failure of a natural function.

Criticisms of Wakefield's analysis include that it has a limited or oversimplified approach to evolutionary psychology (Cosmides and Tooby 1999, Richters and Hinshaw 1999, Jensen *et al.* 2006), that it implies modularity in mental architecture that may not apply for some mental disorders (Murphy 2006), and that it makes diagnosis of mental disorder a speculative and unreliable hypothesis that is unsuited for both clinical and research purposes (Bolton 2008).

Further criticism can be added specifically in relation to the emotions. In the theory of the emotions there are plausible candidates for natural, evolved functions, namely the *basic emotions each (or some) with characteristic objects and responses: *fear is about threat, and prompts escape or attack; *sadness is about loss, and prompts inactivity or help-seeking, for example. However, it is clear that how all this pans out— what counts as threat, loss, appropriate attack or help-seeking—is highly sensitive to cultural and personal norms, priorities, and values. In other words, the distinction between *natural* and *social*, which all parties took for granted in the 1960s, is probably no longer viable in current psychological theory set within an evolutionary theoretic framework (Cosmides and Tooby 1999, Mallon and Stich 2000, Bolton 2008). The importance of social and personal norms and values becomes still more evident as we shift from the 'basic' to the 'moral' emotions (see MORAL EMOTIONS) such as *guilt, *shame, and *pride, all of which are implicated in presentations of affective disorders.

ICD-10 (World Health Organization 1992) and DSM-IV (American Psychiatric Association 1994) have their own definitions of mental disorder, the latter being the longer of the two. Following caveats and qualifications, DSM-IV (pp. xxi–xxii) has the following (abbreviated here for reasons of space): 'In DSM-IV, each of the mental disorders is conceptualized as a clinically significant behavioral or psychological syndrome or pattern that occurs in an individual and that is associated with present distress . . . or disability. . . . In addition, this syndrome or pattern must not be merely an expectable and culturally sanctioned response to a particular event, for example, the death of a loved one. Whatever its original cause, it must currently be considered a manifestation of a behavioral, psychological or biological dysfunction in the individual. Neither deviant behavior (e.g. political, religious or sexual) nor conflicts that are primarily between the individual and society are mental disorders unless the deviance or conflict is a symptom of a dysfunction in the individual, as described above'.

What can been seen here is emphasis on the harm associated with mental disorders, distress and/or disability linked to the need to treat, the concern to distinguish mental disorder from social deviance, and the caveat that mental disorders should not be 'expectable' responses. This caveat may refer to statistical abnormality, or to the mind not working as it should, as 'intended' by evolution or as expected by the culture—the form of words is exquisitely ambiguous. Spitzer has written extremely helpful papers explaining the background and rationale of the definition of disorder which appeared first in DSM-III (Spitzer and Endicott 1978, Spitzer and Williams 1988), and which survives pretty much unchanged in DSM-IV, as above, and which will presumably survive in some form in the pending DSM-V.

It can be seen that much of the literature around the concept of mental disorder, and before that mental illness, has revolved around psychiatry, its medical model, and sociological critiques thereof. A different strand can be tracked through the behavioural sciences. Psychology has long rejected the medical model, specifically the categorical distinction between normality and abnormality, and the implication that mental illnesses or disorders necessarily lack meaning (strategy, function). Clinical psychology models, from psychoanalysis though behaviourism to cognitive behaviourism, emphasize continuity between normality and abnormality, the operation of learning principles even in problematic behaviour, and the understanding of problematic behaviour as being 'maladaptive'— meaning roughly, persistently failing to meet the needs or wishes of the agent. Psychological principles of these kinds are strengthened within an evolutionary framework (Richters and Hinshaw 1999, Cosmides and Tooby 1999).

As indicated above, affective disorder is typically understood in terms of its object being absent or inappropriate: sadness without loss, or without sufficient loss, anxiety without threat, or sufficient threat; anger without sufficient hurt, etc. This can be reconstrued in terms of maladaptation in various ways. For example, it is maladaptive to be anxious in the face of insufficient threat because anxiety involves costs (distress, resources, avoidance), and therefore anxiety without sufficient cause is maladaptive; and so on.

The notion of maladaptation in the behavioural sciences is not caught up in the same disputes as the medical model in psychiatry. Specifically, it is clear that maladaptive behaviour commonly involves meaning (strategy, function, etc.), and secondly, the appraisal that behaviour is maladaptive, that it leads on balance to no good, plainly involves personal and social values.

In both approaches, the medical and the psychological, it is becoming clear that attribution of psychological dysfunction, and the connected decision regarding need to treat, involve values that need negotiation between the clinician and the person involved.

DEREK BOLTON

Bolton, D. (2008). *What is mental disorder? An essay in philosophy, science and values*. Oxford: Oxford University Press.

Horwitz, A.V. and Wakefield, J.C. (2007). *The loss of sadness. How psychiatry transformed normal sorrow into depressive disorder*. New York: Oxford University Press.

Mallon, R. and Stich, S. (2000). The odd couple: the compatibility of social construction and evolutionary psychology. *Philosophy of Science*, **67**, 133–54.

display rules Coined by Ekman and Friesen (1969), the term display rules refers to sociocultural norms regarding regulation of expression in social contexts (see FACIAL EXPRESSION OF EMOTION). These are rules regarding what is appropriate to display on the face in any given social situation when emotions are elicited. They are complex; when an emotion occurs, individuals may: (1) express it as is; (2) deamplify it, expressing less than what is truly felt; (3) neutralize it, displaying nothing; (4) amplify it, expressing more than what is truly felt; (5) qualify it, by expressing it in combination with other emotions so as to comment on the original one; or (6) mask it, concealing it by showing something else altogether. Individuals can also simulate emotions, displaying them when they are not felt at all.

Display rules explain differences in emotional displays as a function of different contexts, and across cultures. The first study to document the existence of cultural differences in emotional expressions in different contexts, and thus highlight the existence of display rules, was Ekman and Friesen's classic study of Americans and Japanese viewing highly stressful films (Ekman 1972). Most recently, the nature of display rule norms has been examined across a wide range of cultures, demonstrating both pancultural universal and culture-specific aspects to them (Matsumoto *et al.* 2006).

Display rules are learned early in life; studies have documented children as young as preschool age as masking their negative emotions with smiles (Cole 1986, Matsumoto *et al.* 1986). They play a major role in every culture and society by aiding the regulation of individual behaviours in social contexts, allowing individuals to engage in normative behaviours prescribed by social roles in specific situations, and maintaining the culture-specific meaning of social relationships. Their importance to social regulation may be seen most dramatically, perhaps, when individuals express emotions that violate their culture's display rules, for example when a person smiles at a funeral or displays anger at a wedding. Display rules work to make sure things like that don't happen, and social interaction is regulated.

DAVID MATSUMOTO

distal factors (from the Latin *distare*, to stand apart, to be distant) The term distal comes from anatomy, where it refers to structures which are remote from some reference point. If unspecified, the latter is generally implied to be the centre or midline of the body. It is a relative term. The hand is more distal than the forearm and the fingers are more distal than the hand. But both the hand and fingers are distal structures (with implicit reference to the midline of the body). The term distal has been co-opted more broadly in psychology to refer to events, process, causes, or relations that are distant or indirect, as opposed to close or direct. For example, the immediate trigger of a 'road rage' incident may be a discourteous driver, but a more distal cause may lie in poor emotion regulation and anger management. See McVittie (2006) for the use of the terms distal and *proximal contexts which affect health, where distal contexts refer to factors such as poverty and lack of education and proximal contexts include more immediate causes such as poor nutrition, lack of medical care, and drug abuse.

GARY G. BERNTSON

distress In general terms, distress involves suffering, mental or physical or both. It is considered as a state of dire need or extreme misfortune. The suffering is described variously as *pain, *anxiety, or *sadness. Infants respond to the acute pain of inoculation with a prototypical facial expression of physical distress and loud crying (Izard *et al.* 1987).

The condition of distress always includes emotion feelings. In addition to the affective states mentioned above, it may also be associated with complex emotion states or emotion schemas (interacting emotion and cognition) relating to *embarrassment, *shame, or *anger.

Darwin (1872/1998) thought that mental distress could cause weeping (see CRYING (EVOLUTIONARY PERSPECTIVES)) and thus associated it with sadness and grief. He also maintained that when a person experiences distress, the brain always tends to activate the contraction of certain muscles, 'as if we were still infants on the point of screaming out' (Darwin 1872/1998, p. 190).

Perhaps taking a lead from Darwin but trying to make a somewhat more specific definition, Tomkins used distress and anguish to anchor the low and high ends of the intensity of a discrete emotion that corresponds reasonably well with what other theorists call *sadness (Tomkins 1963, Ch. 14).

Contemporary emotion theorists typically do not include distress on their lists of emotions. They do identify the distress-related emotions mentioned above. These emotions in older children and adults may be experienced differently depending on the accompanying appraisals and higher-order cognition (Ellsworth and Scherer 2003).

CARROLL E. IZARD

Duchenne smile The Duchenne smile is characterized by the simultaneous contractions of the *zygomaticus major muscle (which pulls the lip corners up and back) and the inferior part of orbicularis oculi muscle (surrounding the eyes and that raises the cheeks to produce slight squinting and 'crow's feet'). It was so named in honour of the pioneering work of the 19th-century French neurologist Guillaume Duchenne de Boulogne (1806–75) (Ekman 1989) who first proposed distinct functional interpretations for morphologically different types of smiles using the technique of localized electrical stimulation of facial muscles (Duchenne 1862/1990). Duchenne suggested that, contrary to a 'fake smile' that involves only the muscles around the mouth, a 'genuine smile' expresses the experience of joy by recruiting the contraction of muscles around the eyes (see SMILING).

Modern research has corroborated the heuristic value of the morphological and functional distinctions between the Duchenne smile and the other forms of smiling. Several studies have reported evidence that, compared with other types of smiling, the Duchenne smile is consistently correlated with the subjective report of *positive emotions (*happiness, *amusement, *enjoyment), and occurs more often during success than failure and during mother–infant play as well as when the mother rather than a stranger approaches an infant. Compared with other smiles, the Duchenne smile has also been found to be associated with greater left frontal EEG activation (see FRONTAL BRAIN ASYMMETRY; a cortical asymmetry presumed to reflect 'approach' emotions) in infants in response to approach of the mother or in adults watching pleasant films.

ROBERT SOUSSIGNAN

dynamic systems theory A particular meta-theoretical view of the behaviour of complex systems has come to be identified with such terms as dynamic systems, complexity, and chaos. This view holds that the behaviour of a system reflects the multiplicity of forces operating on (and within) it. Because all the forces operating can never be known, and because the relations between and among forces are often nonlinear (Brown 1995,

Kelso 1995, Vallacher and Nowak 1997), the behaviour of a complex dynamic system is hard to predict over anything but the very short term. Thus, though the behaviour of the system is fully determined it can give the appearance of randomness. This determinism in principle but unpredictability in practice underlies the label *chaotic*.

Dynamic-systems models focus on how systems change in their configurations, or their 'behaviour', over time. The behaviour of a system is often portrayed as a continuous tracing of a line in a two-dimensional space. Time is represented in the continuing trace, and other variables are embodied in the *x* and *y* axes. (Sometimes this means that only two influencing variables are being modelled; sometimes it means instead that multiple variables have been condensed to two.) The term *phase space* refers to the set of states the system can take. As the system changes states over time, it traces a *trajectory* in its phase space—a path of the successive states it occupies.

Attractors

Discussions of dynamic systems rely heavily on a set of metaphors. When a system's behaviour is observed over an extended period, in the way just described, it sometimes happens that certain regions of the phase space are occupied often, others occasionally, and others never. An area of phase space the system occupies or approaches more frequently than others is called an *attractor*. An attractor exerts a kind of metaphorical pull on the system, bringing the system's behaviour close to it. There can in principle be many attractors in a phase space. A system that has several attractors is said to display *multistability*, because there is a temporary stability in the vicinity of each attractor.

Each attractor has a *basin*, its region of attraction. Trajectories that enter the basin move toward that attractor. A shift from one attractor to another is called a *phase transition* or phase change. In systems with more than one attractor, the system's trajectory typically approaches each one periodically but is never fully captured by any of them. Plotting the behaviour of such a system over time shows a tendency to approach the various attractors, but often unpredictably. Shifts from one attractor to another are typically abrupt, and may seem random.

A phase space may also contain regions called *repellers*, regions that are hardly ever occupied. Indeed, these regions seem to be actively avoided. That is, forcing the system near the focal point of a repeller would lead to a rapid escape from that region of phase space. Indeed, it can appear very much as though the forces that are in operation on and within the system normally prevent the system from ever entering that region.

There are many ways to apply these concepts to human behaviour. One simple application is to suggest that *goals represent attractors for behaviour over time (Pribram 1991, Vallacher and Nowak 1997, Carver and Scheier 1998). People spend much of their time trying to keep their behaviour in line with their goals (of which they generally have several). In the same way, dynamic systems spend much of their time near attractors (of which there may also be several).

Dynamic-systems jargon includes a variety of labels for parameters of the system's behaviour. For example, one can talk of a system's degree of resistance to perturbation when in an attractor basin (a psychological example might be a person's resistance to distraction when in pursuit of a particular goal). One might also describe the width of a given attractor basin (which might reflect the ease with which the person is induced into pursuit of this goal when not currently doing so).

Dynamic systems ideas are easy to apply to psychological phenomena, in their general form. It should be recognized, however, that the picture of causal processes in dynamic models is very different from that often assumed to underlie behaviour. In particular, the notion of attractor regions does not include assumptions about top-down management of behaviour, as is usually the case in discussions of goals. Rather, attractors are said to arise from the intrinsic dynamics of the system as it operates in its world over an extended period of time. Complex systems are said to have a *self-organizing* character (Prigogene and Stengers 1984, Kelso 1995). The various forces in play interweave in ways that are not determined by any one of them alone, but rather by their mutual influences on each other. Patterns emerge spontaneously. It is fairly intuitive to apply that idea to weather systems, but it is more challenging to see people's attitudes, or social behaviours, as coalescing in that way. Nonetheless, precisely such arguments have been made.

Oscillation

Chaotic systems have been characterized as 'irregular oscillatory processes' (Brown 1995). An oscillatory process is a process that has recurrences (e.g. movements of a pendulum). A surprising number of events are oscillatory. Some oscillations are fairly regular (the waking–sleeping cycle, the inspiration–expiration cycle, the start of the American major league baseball season). Other events cycle, but do so more irregularly (putting fuel in the car, doing laundry). Other events oscillate with an even more irregular pattern (the love life of an avoidant introvert).

Chaotic events have a high degree of irregularity. Thus, although they do recur, their occurrence is hard to predict. Why the irregularity? One reason is that the forces underlying their recurrence are sometimes nonlinear. Another is that small differences now sometimes make a huge difference later. These ideas are addressed further, below.

Coupling

Oscillators can exist independently, but they can also be coupled to one another. That is, they can be linked in such a way that each has an influence on the other. Once two systems are linked, the potential for diversity in events becomes even greater. A lot depends on how well synchronized the oscillators are.

It is possible for two oscillators to be perfectly in phase with each other. For example, a father pushing his son on a swing can step back, catch, step forward and push rhythmically, exactly in phase with the swing's period of motion. But oscillators can also be out of phase (the father can step back and forth faster or slower than the swing's period of motion). Being a little out of phase has effects on both of the oscillators (if the father backs up too fast and starts his push before the swing has come back all the way, the result is a jerky start to the next swing cycle). Being a lot out of phase can have larger influences on both systems (if the father pushes forward just as the swing is coming back, he may knock the son off the swing and sprain his own wrist).

Thus, how systems relate to each other is often as important as what the system is doing itself. Keep in mind that coupling of oscillators is an extremely general concept. It is applicable to many different kinds of links between and among systems.

Nonlinearity

An idea that has come up a couple of times already, and an important theme in dynamic systems thinking, is that many relationships between variables are nonlinear. Nonlinearity occurs when the effect of a variable differs across different parts of its range. For example, the effect of temperature on the behaviour of water is nonlinear. At a low temperature, this substance is a solid: ice. As the temperature rises, ice doesn't gradually lose viscosity to become water. If the temperature is below the melting point, ice remains ice. If the temperature rises to the melting point, though, all the ice becomes water (not instantly, but without further rise in temperature).

In line with concepts outlined earlier, one might think of ice and water as two attractors in the phase space of water. The change from one form to another is a *phase transition* within that space.

Several kinds of psychological phenomena reflect nonlinearities (Vallacher and Nowak 1997). Examples are *threshold* effects and *ceiling* effects. Nonlinearity is also illustrated when two predictor variables interact to create an outcome. In an interaction the effect of one predictor on the outcome differs as a function of the level of the second predictor. Thus the effect of the first predictor on the outcome is not linear. Many developmental psychologists now think developmental changes are often dynamic rather than linear (Bertenthal *et al.* 1994, Thelen 1995). There is also evidence that physical development in the brain follows a pattern of discontinuous growth spurts (Fischer and Rose 1994).

Sensitive dependence on initial conditions

Another theme in the dynamic systems literature is identified with the phrase *sensitive dependence on initial conditions* (e.g. Ruelle 1991). That is, a very small difference between two conditions of a system can lead to divergence in the system's behaviour, and ultimately the absence of any correlation between the paths the system takes. The small initial difference causes a difference in what is encountered next, which yields slightly different influences, producing slightly different outcomes (Lorenz 1963). Through repeated iterations of small differences, the paths diverge, eventually leading them to form very different trajectories.

A phrase identified with this phenomenon is the *butterfly effect*, reflecting the idea that the flapping of a butterfly's wings changes local air conditions slightly, setting into motion a series of small, then potentially larger, changes that ultimately might create a storm in another part of the world (Lorenz 1963). The idea is apocryphal, but many embrace it as a way of thinking about sensitivity to small differences. It is the sensitivity of nonlinear systems to small differences at any given moment that makes long-term prediction of them next to impossible. For that reason, for example, it appears that accurate prediction of weather more than a week or so ahead is not a realistic goal.

Catastrophe theory

Catastrophe theory is a topological model that focuses on the creation of discontinuities, bifurcations, or splittings (Zeeman 1977, Stewart and Peregoy 1983, Brown 1995). A catastrophe occurs when a small change in one variable produces an abrupt and usually large change in another variable. The fact that the change is abrupt implies nonlinearity or discontinuity.

As can be seen from that brief description, catastrophe theory shares several themes with dynamic systems theory, though the two have quite different origins and purposes. The focus on nonlinearity is one similarity. The discontinuity that is the focus of catastrophe theory can easily be viewed as reflecting two attractors. A catastrophe in a surface could be seen as representing 'the sudden disappearance of one attractor and its basin, combined with the dominant emergence of another attractor' (Brown 1995, p. 51). Indeed, there are several other parallels between dynamic systems theory and catastrophe theory, though some view the two as quite different (e.g. Kelso 1995, Ch. 2)

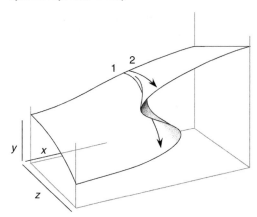

Fig. D1. Three-dimensional surface of a cusp catastrophe.

Several types of catastrophe exist (Brown 1995), each reflecting the operation of a specific number of control parameters. Control parameters are variables that change the dynamics of a system's behaviour. A figure portraying a catastrophe has one dimension corresponding to each control parameter, and another showing the 'behaviour' of the system in response to changes in control parameters. The simplest catastrophe (i.e. with one control parameter) can be shown in a two-dimensional figure. A catastrophe with two interacting predictors requires a three-dimensional figure. Beyond that, visualization becomes increasingly difficult.

The catastrophe that is used most frequently for illustrations is the *cusp catastrophe*, in which two control parameters influence an outcome. Figure D1 portrays its three-dimensional surface. The control parameters are x and z, the outcome is y. Figure D2 displays three cross-sections of this surface, slices made at three different values of variable z (moving from back to front of the surface in Fig. D1). At lower values of z, the surface of the catastrophe expresses a roughly linear relationship between x and y (as x increases, so does y). As z (the second control parameter) increases, the relationship between x and y gradually becomes less linear. It first shifts toward something like a step function. With further increase in z, the x–y relationship becomes even more discontinuous, with the upper and lower surfaces now overlapping. Thus, changes in z cause a change in the way that x relates to y.

As noted earlier, the theme of nonlinearity is one link from catastrophe theory to dynamic systems. Another is the idea of sensitive dependence on initial conditions. The cusp catastrophe displays this characteristic quite clearly (Fig. D1). Consider the portion of Fig. D1 where z has low values and x has a continuous relation to y, the system's behaviour. Points 1 and 2 on x are nearly identical, but not quite. As z increases and the move-

ment from these points is followed forward on the surface, for a while they track each other closely until suddenly they begin to be separated by the emerging fold. At even higher levels of z, one track ultimately goes to the upper region of the surface and the other to the lower region. Thus, a very slight initial difference results in a substantial difference farther along.

Hysteresis

Another interesting feature of a catastrophe is a phenomenon called *hysteresis*. A simple way to characterize hysteresis is that, at some levels of z, a 'foldover' exists in the relationship between x and y. A region of x exists in which there is more than one value of y. The unstable area is illustrated in Fig. D3, which shows the same cross-section as was shown earlier in Fig. D2. The dashed-line portion of Fig. D3 that lies between values a and b on the x-axis—the region where the fold is going backward—repels trajectories (Brown 1995), whereas the areas near values c and d attract trajectories.

The system's behaviour in this region depends on its recent history (Brown 1995). For example, as it moves into the zone of variable x that lies between points a and b in Fig. D3, it matters which side of the figure it is coming from. If the system is moving from point c into the zone of hysteresis it stays on the bottom surface until it reaches point b, where it abruptly jumps to the

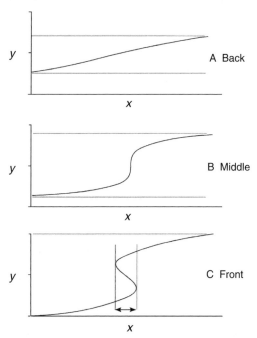

Fig. D2. Three cross-sections through the cusp catastrophe shown in Fig. D1.

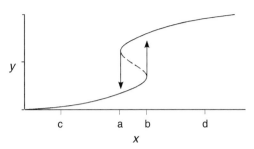

Fig. D3. The region of hysteresis.

top surface. If the system is moving from *d* into the zone of hysteresis it stays on the top surface until it reaches point *a*, where it jumps to the bottom surface. The greater the foldover, the farther along the *x* variable the system maintains its previous trajectory before jumping.

Perhaps the best-known illustration of the cusp catastrophe is the perceptual phenomenon in which ambiguous images are perceived in different ways in different contexts (Stewart and Peregoy 1983). Viewers see a series of drawings in which a relatively clear depiction of one figure gradually becomes more ambiguous then transforms to a different figure. The initial perception is retained as the stimulus shifts toward the alternative image, until suddenly the perception reorganizes.

The reorganization illustrates the nonlinearity of the transition, because there is no in-between. The viewer sees one image or the other. This example also illustrates hysteresis, because the most ambiguous stimuli are perceived differently, depending on which end of the series was the starting point (i.e. depending on the person's history). This example can also be used to illustrate the thematic similarity between catastrophe theory and the ideas of dynamic systems. One could easily characterize the reorganization as a phase change from one attractor region to another.

For further discussion of issues pertaining to dynamic systems and catastrophe theory as they relate to issues in psychology in particular see Carver and Scheier (1998), Kelso (1995), and Vallacher *et al.* (2002). More detailed discussions of the principles themselves can be found in Morris *et al.* (2003) and Ott (2002).

CHARLES S. CARVER

Kelso, J.A.S. (1995). *Dynamic patterns: the self-organization of brain and behavior*. Cambridge, MA: MIT Press.

Morris, W., Hirsch, M.W., Smale, S., and Devaney, R. (2003). *Differential equations, dynamical systems, and an introduction to chaos*. San Diego, CA: Academic Press.

Vallacher, R.R., Read, S.J., and Nowak, A. (eds) (2002). The dynamical perspective in personality and social psychology. (Special issue). *Personality and Social Psychology Review*, **6**(4).

dysphoria The term dysphoria is applied generically to negative *mood states—states of feeling unhappy or displeased. Infrequently, it occurs in the literature on clinical psychology in reference to both manic and depressive states associated with *bipolar disorder. A specialized term, gender dysphoria, refers to a state of discomfort with assigned gender identity. The most prevalent use of the term, however, is to characterize a category of research participants in cognitive and social psychology experiments. Dysphoric participants are typically those who score above a certain cut-off on the Beck Depression Inventory (Beck *et al.* 1996) or other similar questionnaires designed to screen participants for depression. Similarly, nondysphoric participants are those who score below a sometimes lower cut-off score. The choice of the term dysphoria in place of depression makes it clear that formal diagnostic procedures have not been used to categorize participants. Although subclinical depression is used as a synonym for dysphoria in some studies, clinical levels of depression cannot be ruled out; typically, researchers do not know the clinical status of the participants.

PAULA T. HERTEL

E

economics (role of emotion in) Throughout most of the 20th century, economics ignored emotions. With a few minor exceptions, such as John Maynard Keynes' (1883–1946) famous reference to the role of 'animal spirits' in markets or Adam Smith's (1723–90) less familiar reference to the influence of the 'passions', economic theory was largely derived from rational, consequentialist assumptions about *decision-making (see RATIONALITY). Standard economic theory assumes that people choose between alternative courses of action based on the desirability or 'utility' of their consequences, and that *preferences can be inferred from choices. While not explicitly denying a role for emotions in the formation of preferences, the very concept of revealed preference was intended to distance economics as much as possible from the need for any involvement in the messy details of human psychology, including emotions.

This situation changed dramatically with the emergence of behavioural economics, a subfield of economics that came of age in the early 1980s and imported research findings and insights from psychology. Behavioural economists identified a wide range of anomalies—common patterns of individual and market behaviour that violated the assumptions and predictions of standard theory—and showed how these could be explained by more realistic accounts of human behaviour. For example, the anomalous tendency for real estate markets to 'dry up' (i.e. for volume to plummet) during market downturns can be explained by 'loss aversion'—the observation that people dislike losses more than they like comparable gains—which causes owners of houses that lose value to hold out for unrealistically high prices to avoid selling at a loss.

Behavioural economics has stimulated two waves of research on, and theorizing about, the role of emotions in economic behaviour. To understand the difference between the two waves, it is important to distinguish two types of emotions that can influence behaviour: expected emotions and immediate emotions (cf. Loewenstein *et al.* 2001, Rick and Loewenstein 2008).

Expected emotions are emotions that are anticipated to occur as a result of outcomes associated with different possible courses of action. For example, in deciding whether to purchase a house, a potential home-buyer might attempt to predict the pleasure he or she would experience from living in the house, as well as the disappointment he or she would feel if the house declined in price. Immediate emotions, by contrast, are experienced at the moment of choice, and could arise from thinking about the consequences of the decision, though such thoughts are not necessarily the sole cause. For instance, the anxiety experienced while contemplating buying a house may be the result of imagining signing on the dotted line, or lingering thoughts about a loved one's impending surgery. Though only one cause is related to the decision at hand, both could lead to anxiety at the moment of choice.

That expected emotions might influence decision-making is perfectly consistent with the idea that people seek to maximize expected utility. For example, one might assign greater utility to a holiday in San Diego than to a holiday in Death Valley because one anticipates greater happiness while surfing than while melting. However, any influence of immediate emotions on decision-making poses a critical challenge to consequentialist economic theory. In particular, if emotions that arise from factors unrelated to the decision at hand ultimately affect the decision at hand, then the fundamental consequentialist assumption that decisions are based on the utility of possible outcomes must be called into question.

Economists have made tremendous progress in understanding how expected emotions influence decision-making. Research on decision-making under risk, for example (see RISK-TAKING), introduced the idea that emotional reactions to the outcomes of risky decisions might depend on gains and losses rather than final levels of wealth (Kahneman and Tversky 1979). Combined with the notion of *loss aversion, this can explain a wide range of otherwise anomalous phenomena, such as the aforementioned drop in housing volume when prices decline. Other research played on the observation that people experience disappointment when outcomes fail to meet *expectations, and regret when what they chose ends up being inferior to what they could have chosen. These insights about expected emotions, it turns out, can help to explain why people sometimes make choices that are intransitive (i.e. choose A over B, B over C, *and* C over A; Loomes and Sugden 1982, Mellers *et al.* 1997).

131

Research on intertemporal choice introduced the idea that people derive positive and negative emotions not only from outcomes themselves, but also from the anticipation of future outcomes. Taking emotions associated with anticipation (e.g. savouring, dread) into account can explain the otherwise anomalous propensity for people to get unpleasant outcomes over with quickly instead of deferring them as much as possible, as predicted by standard economic theory (Loewenstein 1987, Berns *et al.* 2006).

Research on decision-making in social contexts proposed that people derive strong negative emotions from outcomes that are perceived as inequitable or unfair (see FAIRNESS). The desire to avoid situations in which they will experience such emotions can potentially explain a wide range of social phenomena, from reciprocal *altruism to rejections of lucrative but unfair offers in one-shot games.

More recently, economists have begun to investigate how *immediate* emotions influence decision-making. Casual empiricism and intuition suggest that immediate emotions play an important role in economic behaviour. For example, people gamble in part because they derive immediate pleasure from the activity, not just because the expected utility of winning exceeds the expected disutility of losing. Negotiations break down not only because people believe they can get more from the other side through intransigence, or even because they want to avoid experiencing unfair outcomes that will make them miserable, but also because anger sometimes 'blinds' them to their own self-interest. In fact, a very wide range of self-destructive actions occur under the influence of strong emotions, from binge-eating to road rage, 'flaming' in response to an offending e-mail, failing to use contraception in the 'heat of the moment', and many other phenomena.

Research on immediate emotion and risky decision-making has revealed that the inability to experience fear (due to lesions in brain regions involved in the processing of emotion) can lead brain-damaged subjects to perform worse (Bechara *et al.* 1997) or better (Shiv *et al.* 2005) than non-brain-damaged subjects on a gambling task, depending on the parameters of the task. This research strongly suggests that emotions experienced at the moment of choice are not merely epiphenomenal, but rather that immediate emotions influence decision-making. More recent work has found that stock market returns are sensitive to incidental emotions caused by sunshine (Hirshleifer and Shumway 2003) and World Cup outcomes (Edmans *et al.* 2007).

Walter Mischel (1974) and colleagues found that children faced with the choice between a small immediate reward (e.g. one marshmallow) and a larger delayed reward (two marshmallows) crave the immediate reward more when it is proximal and thus tend to behave more

impatiently (see DELAY OF GRATIFICATION). Giordano *et al.* (2002) find that addicts discount both money and drugs more steeply when they are craving than when they are not.

Social preferences are also not immune to the influence of immediate emotions. Blount (1995), for example, found that people were more willing to accept unintentionally (randomly generated) unfair offers in one-shot games than intentionally unfair offers. Intentional unfairness is a source of anger, but unintentional unfairness is merely disappointing. Moreover, differential sympathy towards identifiable victims (e.g. Baby Jessica, whose rescue after falling into an abandoned well gained worldwide media coverage) and statistical victims (e.g. thousands dead in a distant country) probably underlies the tendency to give more to the former than to the latter (Small and Loewenstein 2003, Kogut and Ritov, 2005).

In general, research on the role of emotions has yielded a number of important insights. One is that people are effectively transformed by emotions; the same person in different emotional states is likely to behave as differently as two people in the same emotional state. For example, studies that have examined the effect of sexual arousal on decision-making have found that sexual arousal dramatically changes people's preferences, moral behaviour, risk-taking, and their time preference (Wilson and Daly, 2004). Other studies have found that immediate emotions, whether induced by the nature of the decision at hand or by incidental factors, tend to make people less sensitive to the probabilities of potential outcomes (Rottenstreich and Hsee 2001). One study by Ditto *et al.* (2006) had subjects choose whether to spend additional time in an unpleasant experiment in exchange for either a small or large chance of winning cookies. When the aroma of freshly baked cookies filled the laboratory, subjects were insensitive to the probability of winning—they were just about as likely to agree to spend the extra time whether the likelihood of getting cookies was small or large. However, subjects were highly sensitive to the probability of winning when the cookies were merely described, without the accompanying aroma.

Other research shows that people are not very accurate in predicting the impact of emotional states on their own behaviour; when in one emotional state, they tend to underappreciate the impact of other states on the actions they will take. This 'hot–cold empathy gap' (Loewenstein 1996) has diverse ramifications for judgement and behaviour (see, e.g. Nordgren *et al.* 2006). For example, the failure to predict the motivational force of drug craving when one is not currently craving may help to explain why people first take addictive drugs despite full knowledge of the consequences of addiction (Badger *et al.* 2007).

Research on the role of immediate emotions in behaviour has been bolstered by a new development in economics called neuroeconomics. One of the major insights of neuroeconomics has been that decision-making is driven by a combination of deliberation (corresponding, roughly, to preference satisfaction) and emotion (Cohen 2005). Research by neuroeconomists and their colleagues has found that brain regions associated with deliberation and regions associated with emotion are activated in diverse tasks, including moral judgements (Greene *et al.* 2001), behavioural responses to fair and unfair offers in the 'ultimatum game' (Sanfey *et al.* 2003), intertemporal choice (McClure *et al.* 2004), and decision-making under risk (Tom *et al.* 2007).

Research on immediate emotions is key to understanding when the economic model, which assumes rational self-interested behaviour, is valid and when it is not—when people behave in a self-destructive or otherwise irrational fashion. In some cases the cause of irrationality seems to be strong emotions that cause people to lose control, meaning they make decisions on the basis of immediate rather than expected emotions. In other cases, however, adverse patterns of behaviour can be caused by a failure to accurately anticipate future emotional states.

GEORGE LOEWENSTEIN AND SCOTT RICK

efference The value of Santiago Ramón y Cajal's (1852–1934) contribution to the development of modern concepts in the neurosciences is incalculable: 'He solved at a stroke the great question of the direction of nerve-currents in their travel through brain and spinal cord' (Sir Charles Sherrington, 1857–1952). One of his most revolutionary contributions was the notion of 'dynamic polarization of the neuron', amply described in his *Textura del Sistema Nervioso* (Ramon y Cajal 1899–1904). Even though this concept seems rather simple, it has been a cornerstone of our understanding of the physiology of the central nervous system. Briefly, the concept of dynamic polarization states that 'the currents collected in the dendrites and the cell bodies of neurons are polarized toward the axons'. In other words, the flow of information within the neurons has a unique directionality.

A second remarkable notion pioneered by Ramón y Cajal was the principle of 'connection specificity'. This principle states that a particular neuron does not connect at random with other neurons, but rather forms specific connections. With this principle, Cajal focused attention on brain networks as the actual basis of information flow.

It is no surprise that the consequent link between the dynamic polarization theory and the principle of connection specificity provided the foundation for expanding the directionality of flow of information from single neurons to pathways. However, Cajal did not describe the cellular mechanisms by which such pathway polarization is implemented in the central nervous system. It was Sherrington's remarkable description of the unidirectionality of the synapse that provided the basic mechanism for the reliability of the dynamic polarization theory as applied to brain pathways.

Based on these ideas, the concept of 'efference' can be defined in two complementary ways. (1) At an individual neuronal level, an efferent describes the element (typically the axon) carrying flow of information away from a neuron or group of neurons. (2) At a systems level, efferent describes pathways carrying a flow of information away from the central nervous system, eventually reaching an effector (muscle or gland). The efferent system has two components: the first component innervates skeletal muscles; the second, smooth muscles.

Control of skeletal musculature

Neurons acting on (or affecting) skeletal muscles exert their influence through major descending pathways that originate not only in motor (primary motor cortex, lateral premotor region, supplementary motor region, cingulate motor cortex) and sensory (primary sensory cortex) cortical regions (Lemon *et al.* 2004), but also in several subcortical regions (cerebellum, reticular nuclei, and midbrain). The individual pathways from these cortical and subcortical areas converge and synapse on interneuronal and motor neuronal groups located in the spinal cord and brainstem motor nuclei. Motor neurons in turn innervate skeletal muscles. Because of this convergence of descending inputs from a variety of regions, motor neurons are considered the 'final motor pathway' to the muscles. This skeletal efferent system has several important functions related to motor control. Although one of the primary functions is the control and production of voluntary movements, it is also concerned with the control of posture, eye movements, and rhythmic motor behaviours such as locomotion and swimming (Lackner and DiZio 2000).

Control of smooth musculature

In contrast to the innervation of skeletal muscles, normal body functions in the internal organs are maintained by the autonomic nervous system (Shields 1993). The activity of internal organs is managed in part by reflexes regulated by autonomic centres located in the medulla and spinal cord (e.g. respiration). These autonomic centres receive descending control mostly from the hypothalamus, but also from the *amygdala and limbic cortices (infralimbic Brodmann's area 25 and cingulate cortex). These supraspinal networks are essential in the integration of autonomic, endocrine, and somatomotor (skeletal) functions, important in behaviours such as temperature regulation, emotional behaviour, feeding and drinking, sleep and wakefulness, circadian rhythms, pain processing, and memory.

Although the usefulness of the notion of efferent systems has not been inconsequential, it is important to remember that it represents an oversimplification. János Szentagothai highlights this issue with his critique on 'downward causality' to caution about unidirectional, hierarchical models of information flow (Szentagothai 1984). He supports the paradigm proposed by Mountcastle and Edelman, among others, who consider that 'neuronal functions be envisaged as dynamic patterns of neuronal network activity' that take into account 're-entrant dynamic circuits'. He suggests further that these re-entrant circuits are particularly important in the study of mind–brain relationships.

ANA SOLODKIN

Cannon, W.B. (1932). *The wisdom of the body.* New York: Norton.
Dunn, R.P. and Strick, P.L. (1996). The corticospinal system: a structural framework for the central control of movement. In: L.B. Rowell and J.T. Sheperd (eds), *Handbook of physiology. exercise: integration and regulation of multiple systems,* pp. 217–54. New York: Oxford University Press.

effort The construct of *effort* can be defined as the mobilization of resources to carry out behaviour. Effort refers to two aspects of *goal pursuit: persistence and intensity. The former involves resource mobilization extending across time; the latter involves resource mobilization at a point in time. Effort is generated to overcome behavioural impediments, that is, factors that make it more difficult to attain goals. For this reason, effort is believed to be proportional to the difficulty of instrumental behaviour so long as success is

perceived to be possible and worthwhile (Brehm and Self 1989). When success is perceived as impossible or excessively difficult, given the benefit it could accrue, effort is expected to be low. The preceding view assumes that the allocation of both mental and physical effort is guided by a conservation principle that calls for resources to be expended only to the degree that they are useful. It conflicts with popular notions that effort directly increases with need, incentive value, and perceived ability, or efficacy.

A distinction has been made between *fixed* and *unfixed* performance challenges. Fixed challenges allow people to secure a benefit or set of benefits by attaining a particular performance standard. Thus, for example, a saleswoman who has to sell two houses per month to earn her salary would be confronted with a fixed challenge. Unfixed challenges allow people to secure different degrees of benefit by attaining different performance standards. Thus, a saleswoman provided with the chance to earn increasingly generous salary bonuses by reaching increasingly difficult sales goals would be confronted with an unfixed challenge. When confronted with fixed challenges, people should expend effort to the degree it is needed if success is possible and justified, and low effort if success is impossible or excessively difficult (see Fig. E1). When confronted with unfixed challenges, people should expend the effort required to attain the highest standard that is possible and justified. If it is unclear what is required to secure a benefit or set of benefits, effort should be the maximum justified, given the value of the benefit or benefits and the performer's state of need.

There is convergent support for the view that subjectively experienced difficulty determines the intensity

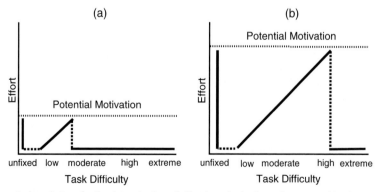

Fig. E1. The theoretical predictions for the determination of effort intensity in dependence on subjective difficulty and maximally justified effort (i.e. potential motivation). Panel (a) shows the predictions for low justified effort. Panel (b) shows the predictions for high justified effort.

of effort. The importance of success defines only the maximum effort justified, referred to as the level of *potential* *motivation. Experienced difficulty is determined by various factors, including performance standards, belief in one's ability, and mood states. The value of success is influenced by need, incentive value, and variables referring to the evaluation of the self (see Wright and Kirby 2001).

Effort has been measured in many ways (Gendolla 2004). Two common measures of effort are *self-report* and *achievement*. A limitation of self-report measures is that they are vulnerable to self-presentational influences. For example, there is evidence that people sometimes underreport effort to protect their self-esteem if failure is possible. Another limitation of the measures is that they assume conscious awareness of effort, which may not always be present. A limitation of achievement measures is that they can be affected by a variety of noneffort factors, including ability, task complexity, and strategy use (Locke and Latham 1990). Noneffort factors can not only impact upon achievement, but can also interact with effort in doing so. In considering achievement measures, it is important to bear in mind that achievement is an outcome associated with effort, not effort itself. A third measure of effort is length of engagement. This can be useful, but only as a measure of persistence; the measure is silent about effort intensity at a point in time.

Investigators are increasingly employing psychophysiological indices of effort, which are direct, objective, and unobtrusive. Two such indices are oxygen and blood glucose consumption. Others are adjustments in the *cardiovascular system (Obrist 1981). Cardiovascular adjustments are of special interest; these apply to both mental and physical effort and are mediated by arousal of the sympathetic nervous system. Mental effort appears to be closely associated with activity of the prefrontal cortex, which is involved in executive cognitive functions. Given the function of effort to facilitate behaviour, it is hardly surprising that the motivational impetus of specific emotions becomes visible in the impact of these states on effort mobilization and its physiological correlates.

GUIDO H. E. GENDOLLA AND REX A. WRIGHT

Gendolla, G.H.E. and Wright, R.A. (2005). Motivation in social settings: studies of effort-related cardiovascular arousal. In: J.P. Forgas, K. Williams, and W. von Hippel (eds), *Social motivation*, pp. 71–90. New York: Cambridge University Press.

Hockey, G.R.J. (1997). Compensatory control in the regulation of human performance under stress and high workload: a cognitive-energetical framework. *Biological Psychology*, **45**, 73–93.

Wright, R.A. (1996). Brehm's theory of motivation as a model of effort and cardiovascular response. In: P.M. Gollwitzer and J.A. Bargh (eds), *The psychology of action*, pp. 424–53. New York: Guilford Press.

ego In ordinary language, the ego is the *self. In psychoanalysis, it generally refers to an aspect of the self. It is that part of Freud's tripartite structural theory of the mind that stands between the pressing instinctual demands of the id and the constraining social and moral requirements of the superego. It is the agency which attempts to use reason, in accordance with the reality principle, to achieve the desires of the self in the face of an unyielding world. 'Ego' is the Latin translation for Freud's '*das Ich*' (which is the ordinary German word for 'I'). See also ID; SUPEREGO.

JEROME NEU

electrodermal response system Electrodermal activity (EDA) literally refers to electrical changes in the skin. The most common method of measuring EDA involves passing a very small current across a pair of metal electrodes placed on the skin and then measuring the electrical conductance of the skin for that current. The typical anatomical placements of the electrodes are on the fingertips or palm of the hand. The peripheral effectors mediating skin conductance are the eccrine sweat glands, which are most prominently found on the palms and fingertips. These sweat glands, which are innervated by the sympathetic nervous system (see AUTONOMIC NERVOUS SYSTEM), are highly responsive to psychological processes.

Figure E2 shows tracings of two hypothetical skin conductance recordings during a 20-second rest period followed by three presentations of a simple stimulus (e.g. mild tone). The upper trace represents a higher arousal state than the lower trace. Several important aspects of skin conductance are illustrated in this figure. First, the ongoing tonic skin conductance level (SCL) begins at 10 microsiemens (μS) in the upper trace and 5 μS in the lower trace. Tonic SCL can vary widely between individuals and within individuals depending on their psychological state. SCL is higher during states of high *arousal. In other words, the skin is a better conductor of electricity when participants are aroused.

Second, it can be seen in Fig. E2 that the SCL slowly declines in the bottom trace from 5 to 4 μS. It is common for the SCL to gradually decrease as participants adapt to their surroundings. This is more likely in a low or moderately aroused subject as depicted in the lower trace than a highly aroused subject as depicted in the upper trace.

Third, momentary phasic increases in skin conductance occur even while participants are at rest and no external stimuli are presented. These are referred to as 'spontaneous' or 'nonspecific' skin conductance responses (SCRs). Nonspecific SCRs are more common in highly aroused states; thus there are two such

electromyography

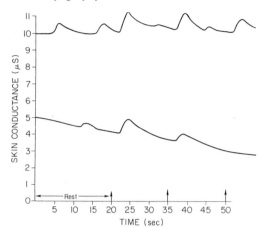

Fig. E2. Two hypothetical skin conductance recordings during 20 seconds of rest followed by three repetitions of a simple discrete stimulus. Arrows represent the presentation of a stimulus. Reprinted with permission from Dawson and Neuchterlein (1984).

responses in the top trace and only one in the lower trace. Nonspecific SCRs are usually measured as frequency (per minute).

Fourth, when stimuli are presented, represented in Fig. E2 by arrows along the abscissa, SCRs are often elicited. Novel, unexpected, emotional, or significant stimuli usually elicit SCRs that are considered a component of the orienting response associated with attention to the stimuli. Aversive stimuli will also elicit SCRs that are considered a component of the defensive response. It should be noted that SCRs are not sensitive to emotional *valence, as they will respond equally to positive and negative valence stimuli that are equally arousing. The most frequently measured aspect of the elicited SCR is its amplitude, measured as the increase in conductance from response onset to its peak.

Orienting responses in particular will habituate with repeated stimulation, and habituation is usually faster in states of low to moderate arousal. Thus, the lower trace in Fig. E2 shows complete habituation of SCRs after three stimulus presentations, whereas the participant represented by the top trace continues to respond to each stimulus presentation.

In summary, electrodermal activity is commonly measured as skin conductance. Tonic skin conductance level and the frequency of nonspecific SCRs are used as indexes of sympathetic nervous system arousal. Phasic SCRs to mild innocuous stimuli are considered to index orienting and attention, whereas phasic SCRs to highly aversive stimuli are thought to index the defensive

response. Both orienting and defensive responses habituate, although habituation is much faster with orienting responses, and is generally faster in states of low arousal.

EDA is widely used in affective science to index levels of arousal, attention, and emotion associated with environmental conditions or individual differences. For instance, SCRs have been used to study classical conditioning, and more recently in investigating the role of consciousness in fear conditioning with biologically prepared fear-relevant conditioned stimulus–unconditioned stimulus relationships (Öhman *et al.* 2000a). SCL and the frequency of nonspecific responses have been used along with other autonomic measures to index sympathetic activation when studying the effect of emotional regulation on physiological responses to aversive stimuli (Gross 2002). SCL and frequency of nonspecific responses have also been used to index hyperarousal in patients with schizophrenia and the relationship of hyperarousal to symptomatic and functional outcome (Schell *et al.* 2005). SCRs elicited by stimuli, on the other hand, have frequently been used to test for impaired response to distress signals and impaired conditioned fear in psychopaths (see discussion by Newman and Lorenz 2003).

MICHAEL E. DAWSON AND ANNE M. SCHELL

Boucsein, W. (1992). *Electrodermal activity*. New York: Plenum Press.

Dawson, M.E., Schell, A.M., and Filion, D.L. (2000). The electrodermal system. In: J.T. Cacioppo, L.G. Tassinary, and G.G. Berntson (eds), *Handbook of psychophysiology*, 2nd edn, pp. 200–223. New York: Cambridge University Press.

electromyography Electromyography is a technique for recording the electrical activity of a skeletal muscle (Basmajian and De Luca 1985). Surface electromyographic activity is generally of interest in behavioural research and is recorded using two small sensors that are applied on the skin over the muscle. An electromyogram is a signal with a semi-stochastic wave pattern that fluctuates in amplitude. The amplitude of the signal bursts corresponds well with the mechanical force exerted by the muscle. An electromyogram is a summation of elementary signals, the so-called motor unit action potentials. A motor unit is a group of muscle fibres whose activity is controlled by a single motor neuron in the central nervous system. Each discharge of the neuron generates a motor unit action potential in the muscle fibres belonging to the motor unit that is accompanied by a brief contraction of these fibres. The compound force response of the muscle is a summation of the contractions of the elementary motor units.

Electromyography enables an objective measurement of muscular activity in the human face and other parts of the body. Due to its sensitivity, weak responses that do not result in visible movements of the skin, and that therefore would be unobservable to the human eye, can also be recorded. Nevertheless, it may sometimes be difficult to discriminate between the responses of muscles that are overlaying each other or located in close proximity.

ANTON VAN BOXTEL

elicitation of emotion see ANTECEDENTS (OF EMOTION).

eliciting stimulus sets (for emotion research) If scientists wish to study the effects of background noise on decision-making, it is fairly easy for them to control the type of noise by using accepted physical scales for determining loudness and frequency. Because these established scales are widely used, results can be exactly evaluated by retest in another laboratory, confirming or disconfirming the original results, and effects of the same background noise in other contexts determined. In this systematic manner, science progresses in its many fields of endeavour.

For scientists who study emotion, a similar need exists to specify the emotionality of stimuli used to elicit affect in the laboratory. On the other hand, there are no obvious physical parameters that can be used to organize emotional stimuli. Stimuli that are visually similar, for example, such as a snake and a garden hose, differ widely in emotional impact. Moreover, whereas one person may fear dogs, her neighbour loves them. There is great diversity of emotional reactions to physically equivalent events.

Nonetheless, in recent years efforts have been made to address the seemingly intractable problem of standardizing emotional stimuli. Clearly, a critical issue concerns the parameters used in defining the affective characteristics of potential inducing stimuli. Beginning with Wilhelm Wundt's (1832–1920) early studies of feeling states, it has been recognized that although there are hundreds of words that describe different affects in every language, emotional differences among stimuli—words, objects, events—can be succinctly described by a relatively few affective dimensions. Using factor analysis of evaluative reports (e.g. Osgood et al. 1957), two dimensional factors of *pleasure* (see VALENCE) and *arousal were shown to be central in organizing emotional judgements, together with a third, weaker dimension (variously called *strength*, *control*, or *dominance*). Because of their conceptual simplicity and reliability, these three dimensions are ideal for the standardization of different affective stimuli (see DIMENSIONAL EMOTION MODELS).

The Self-Assessment Manikin (SAM; Lang 1980, Bradley and Lang 1994) is illustrated along the *x* and *y* axes in Fig. E3 and is a graphic instrument that measures the pleasure, arousal, and dominance dimensions without requiring language. SAM ranges from a smiling, happy figure to a frowning, unhappy figure when representing the pleasure dimension. For arousal, SAM ranges from an excited, wide-eyed figure to a relaxed, sleepy figure. For dominance (not pictured), SAM ranges from a large figure (in control) to a small figure (completely controlled).

Using SAM, a large set of pictures, words, sounds, and texts have been rated for pleasure, arousal, and dominance by both men and women, and these ratings, together with the affective stimuli, are distributed by researchers at the Center for the Study of Emotion and Attention at the University of Florida to scientists around the world for use in the study of emotion. Currently, these stimulus sets include the International Affective Picture System (IAPS), the International Affective Digitized Sounds (IADS), Affective Norms for English Words (ANEW), and Affective Norms for English Text (ANET). The goal of distributing these sets of materials is to encourage standardization, selection, and replication in emotion research within and across research sites, and to date, hundreds of laboratories throughout the world have received these materials for use in all areas of psychology and neuroscience.

Figure E3 (top) illustrates the distribution of pictures in a two-dimensional 'affective space' defined by plotting each picture as a function of its mean pleasure and arousal rating, with the distributions of words, sounds, and texts illustrated below. These distributions are quite similar across stimulus modalities: for all materials, an overall boomerang-shaped distribution suggests two arms that extend from a common neutral, nonarousing base towards either a highly arousing pleasant or highly arousing unpleasant quadrant. All sets include stimuli that elicit judgements ranging from extremely unpleasant to extremely pleasant, and from calm to arousing. Using the ratings distributed with each set of materials, scientists are able to select materials that are equated for level of arousal and differing in hedonic valence, allowing one to determine independent effects of pleasure and arousal on emotional reactions, evaluative judgements, and behaviour. Taken together, the standardization of emotional materials encourages replication and extension of psychological and neuroscience studies of emotion by allowing scientists to control stimulus emotionality, to use the same or similar stimulus materials as in previous studies, and to explore new questions, promoting a cumulative increase in scientific knowledge regarding emotion and affect.

MARGARET M. BRADLEY AND PETER J. LANG

Bradley, M.M. and Lang, P.J. (2000). Measuring emotion: behavior, feeling, and physiology. In: R. Lane and L. Nadel

International Affective Picture System (IAPS)

Lang, Bradley, & Cuthbert, 2005

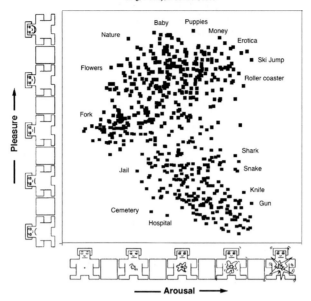

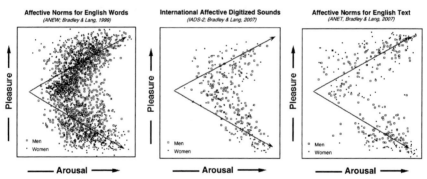

Fig. E3. Plots of stimulus sets in the affective space defined by mean ratings of pleasure and arousal using the Self-Assessment Manikin (SAM; Lang 1980). Top: SAM ratings for pictures. Bottom: SAM ratings for words (left), sounds (centre), and text (right). Trajectories in the bottom plot illustrate the hypothetical underlying systems of appetitive and defensive motivation that are indexed by ratings of pleasure and arousal.

(eds), *Cognitive neuroscience of emotion*, pp. 242–76. New York: Oxford University Press.

Bradley, M.M. and Lang, P.J. (2007). The International Affective Picture System (IAPS) in the study of emotion and attention. In: J.A. Coan and J.J.B. Allen (eds), *Handbook of emotion elicitation and assessment*, pp. 29–46. Oxford University Press.

embarrassment Embarrassment is one of the self-conscious emotions (see SELF-REFLEXIVE EMOTIONS), which are characterized by an evaluation of the self in comparison with social and personal standards or *goals. Embarrassment often follows from socially awkward, clumsy, or conspicuous behaviour. The phenomenology of embarrassment includes feelings of exposure, high levels of self-awareness, bodily sensations (e.g. increased heart rate or blushing), and tendencies to look away or smile.

Embarrassment makes people aware of the social consequences of their actions and may prompt them to engage in remedial or ameliorative behaviours that reaffirm the social relations within a group. Embarrassment also has an appeasement function in the sense that its expression can reduce potential aggression by others or elicit helping behaviour (Keltner and Buswell 1997).

Although experiences of embarrassment are unpleasant, behaviours that are motivated by the emotion tend to have positive consequences for interpersonal relations.

Embarrassment is closely related to *shame, another self-conscious emotion. There is some debate as to whether embarrassment represents a distinct emotion or is just a mild form of shame. Embarrassment results more often from violations of social or conventional standards, whereas shame results more often from violations of moral standards. In contrast to shame, people who are embarrassed do not experience their concept of 'self' as profoundly flawed. Some studies have even found that the phenomenological experience of shame is more similar to experiences of guilt than to experiences of embarrassment (Tangney et al. 1996). In addition, nonverbal displays of embarrassment include elements, such as smiling, that are absent with shame. Interestingly, the clear lexical distinction between emotions of embarrassment and shame that is found in the English language appears to be absent in several other languages (e.g. Dutch, Indonesian Malay, and Spanish).

SEGER M. BREUGELMANS

embodied conversational agents Embodied conversational agents (ECAs) are software entities capable of autonomously communicating with users by verbal and nonverbal means (see AUTONOMOUS AGENTS; INTERPERSONAL COMMUNICATION). As such, ECAs are endowed with the ability to display human-like nonverbal behaviours in order to convey information reflecting their mental and emotional states (Cassell et al. 2000). ECAs can smile, nod, show iconic gestures, and even display emotional expressions. Being autonomous creatures, they can plan what to say, know when to start a conversation, when to answer, and when to take their conversational turn. They can adopt several roles, such as being a teacher, a museum guide, a real-estate agent, or a companion.

Their cognitive and expressive capabilities simulate human capabilities and their models (see COMPUTATIONAL MODELS; AFFECTIVE COMPUTING) are based on theories from human studies, particularly in the domains of linguistic, phonetics, cognitive science, emotion, psychology, and sociology. While computational models of ECAs are far from being comparable to even pale reproductions of human communication, several models have highlighted some of the core capabilities that ECAs need to have in order to be truly interactive, communicative, emotional, and social.

To endow ECAs with a rich repertoire of behaviours, a first step is to develop a behaviour representation language. Several languages have been proposed (Prendinger and Ishizuka 2004). Recently an attempt to build a unified language has been initiated (Vilhjálmsson et al.

2007) where the aim is to create a behaviour description scheme independent of the model specification and the animation player's technology. These languages describe a behaviour by its form and movement in space. A scheme is also being provided to anchor temporal points for synchronization purposes between the verbal and nonverbal streams. Another aspect of behaviour is its expressivity, representing the manner in which a behaviour is executed, according to strength, speed, spatial extend, and so forth. Expressive behaviours make the ECA more lively and emotionally believable.

Having access to a behaviour description is not enough to provide an animated ECA. One must also build a behaviour planner and a behaviour scheduler. The former selects behaviours to be displayed according to modality so that a given meaning can be transmitted (Vilhjálmsson et al. 2007). The latter instantiates these behaviours and synchronizes within and across modalities (Cassell et al. 2000).

However, before being able to show behaviours the agent has to plan what to say. As for behaviour, representational languages encoding high-level functions such as communication, semantics, and emotion are being developed (Prendinger and Ishizuka 2004). The agent's discourse is enriched by high-level functions. Different theories among categorical, dimensional, or appraisal ones have been considered and implemented. The resulting models permit one to derive subtle facial expressions of emotion, or to simulate how the agent manages its emotion, taking into account the agent's reasoning about the events in the world as well as its interpretation of the world.

Communication involves at least two partners, a sender and a receiver. Both partners should be able to perceive each other visually and acoustically, namely they should not only be able to receive raw signals but should also be able to create meaning out of them. ECAs are also context aware, that is they are able to consider content (persons or objects) in the virtual and/or real world. If the ECA can perceive the environment in which it is placed or the environment of the partner(s) with whom it is conversing it can pay attention to someone, show its interest in an object or a person, and show its engagement in the conversation. These properties (Wachsmuth and Knoblich 2008) give the ECA the basis to be an active, emotional, and social participant in the conversation, either as a sender or as a receiver.

ECAs have been placed into dialogue systems where they determine, autonomously and in real-time, what to say and how to say it, for example using facial, vocal, and bodily emotional expressions (Wachsmuth and Knoblich 2008). These systems are complex and include modules specialized for handling a diverse range of functions, including intention and behaviour planning as well as emotional modelling in terms of expression and recognition.

CATHERINE PELACHAUD

Cassell, J., Sullivan, J., Prevost, P., and Churchill, E. (eds) (2000). *Embodied conversational characters*. Cambridge, MA: MIT Press.

Wachsmuth, I. and Knoblich, G. (eds). (2008). *Modeling communication with robots and virtual humans* (Lecture Notes in Artificial Intelligence Vol. 4930). Berlin: Springer-Verlag.

embodiment Embodiment is the major theme in European phenomenology, some versions of which distinguish between the objective body, or the body as physical entity, and the phenomenal body, which is the personal experience of one's own body. These physical and phenomenal bodily entities are held to be a necessary precondition for subjectivity, emotion, language, thought, and social interaction. Embodiment is similarly a major theme in the writings of William James (1842–1910) about emotion (see JAMES–LANGE THEORY). He suggested that an emotion is the conscious perception of the state of the body. The perception of this state, the embodied emotion, motivates specific adaptive actions. Classically, then, the concept of embodiment refers to the body as an important vessel for introspection, providing information about the state of the self and the environment.

More recently the concept of embodiment has been used to refer to the processes by which information, including emotionally significant information, is perceived, stored, and used in higher-level cognition (Niedenthal *et al.* 2005a). Classical models of information processing assume that sensory, motor, and emotional stimuli retain no perceptual or experiential basis in thought or memory. In such models, which reveal a strong influence of the metaphor of mind as computer, information encoded by the sense modalities is stored in memory as abstract symbols that are functionally separated from the original neural systems—those involved in vision, olfaction, and audition, for example—that encoded them. Theories of embodied cognition, in contrast, hold that thought and language use partial reactivations of states in sensorimotor and affective systems to perform their tasks. From this latter perspective, information processing requires embodiment in the sense that it requires essentially reliving past experience in all of its sensory, motor, and affective modalities—events that take place in the body.

Here is how an emotionally significant stimulus might be perceived and recalled from the perspective of theories of embodied cognition. The perception of an emotional event, such as a rabid dog, involves, among other responses, seeing, hearing, and feeling consciously afraid of the dog. The active populations of neurons in the sensorimotor and affective systems that support these responses are highly interconnected, and by this fact support the multimodal experience of the dog. Later, in thinking about dog, the neural states that represented the visual impression of the dog, for example, can be reactivated. reinstating a pattern of neurons in one system can then complete the full pattern in its other components in the other sensory systems, yielding something that approximates the state of activation of the original experience (but is never identical to it).

In embodiment theories of information processing, using knowledge—as in recalling memories, drawing inferences, and making plans—is thus called 'embodied' because an admittedly incomplete but cognitively useful re-experience is produced in the originally implicated sensorimotor systems *as if* the individual were there in the very situation, the very emotional state, or with the very object of thought (Barsalou 2005). The concept of re-enactment, also called simulation, resonance, reinstatement, and emulation, is widely accepted in theories of embodied cognition, but many different mechanistic neural accounts of it have been proposed (see MIMICRY, SENSORIMOTOR ASPECTS).

Embodiment in the current psychological literature refers more to the brain's modality-specific systems, and not exclusively to the muscles and viscera, which were at the heart of the earlier use of the term embodiment. The circuits in modality-specific brain systems are fast and subtle and are able to flexibly represent a very large number of entities and experiences. Moreover, these states can be reactivated without their output being observable in overt behaviour, so that embodiment need not be associated with an observable bodily re-enactment of a stimulus. Nevertheless, actual embodied states may arise under many circumstances, as when the motor system becomes primed or actually begins to execute facial expressions, head motions, postures, arm actions, etc. Thus, embodiment refers to re-enactments that can span the range from cortical reactivation of modality-specific areas, to internal bodily activity associated with arousal, heart rate, and breathing, to actions in the musculature.

PAULA M. NIEDENTHAL AND
LAWRENCE W. BARSALOU

emotion classification A number of researchers in the emotion area have adopted classification systems for emotions that suggest that there are typological differences, including hierarchical organization, for different kinds of emotions. The most widely used typology orders emotions into primary, secondary, and tertiary emotions (see Griffiths 2003, Zinck and Newen

2008). The nature of the criterion varies between researchers. Often the distinction between primary and secondary emotions is based on the notion that primary emotions consist of the evolutionarily continuous *basic emotions which represent fundamental and universal adaptive mechanisms based on affect programmes. They are considered to often be elicited in an automatic fashion and require little or no cognitive processing (if any, of the automatic, schematic kind; see AUTOMATIC APPRAISAL). In contrast, secondary emotions are described as requiring much more cognitive investment (especially of an effortful, propositional kind) in terms of antecedent appraisal and regulation. They are sometimes also called 'complex emotions' as distinct to the supposedly simpler basic emotions. The term 'tertiary emotions' is more rarely used to refer to even more complex emotions, often those linked to social values and norms such as *moral emotions. It has also been suggested that emotions that are linked in some way to the self-concept or to self-esteem (such as pride and shame) should be treated as a separate class, using terms such as self-referential emotions or *self-reflexive emotions.

A serious problem with the use of such classification schemes for emotions is that there is no agreement on the definition for each class or on the criteria to be used for differentiation. Often, these issues are not even addressed and the categories are used in a rather unreflective fashion. This may be appropriate if one wants to refer descriptively to a group of emotions that seem to have a readily apparent feature in common, like self-reflexive emotions. However, frequently the underlying assumption in using such typologies is that each type or class of emotions has specific characteristics that make it a class of its own, often even implicitly or explicitly suggesting that different mechanisms and neural architectures may be involved. Such speculations in the absence of clearly defined theoretical constructs and criteria can be quite counterproductive, especially given the lack of pertinent empirical evidence. Facile classifications of entire emotion families into a specific class also tend to obscure the fact that members of a given emotion family can involve more or less complex, and more or less propositional, processing, which makes a categorization of emotion types on the basis of these criteria highly questionable. Another example of the dangers involved in typological emotion classifications is the widely used, and apparently intuitively plausible, distinction between positive and negative emotions. It is automatically assumed that *joy is good and *fear is bad, but the basis for the distinction is not clear. In terms of adaptation, fear is also a good, and maybe a better emotion than joy (see FUNCTIONALIST THEORIES OF EMOTION). A classification in

terms of how the person feels when having the emotion is problematic in that individuals may have rather different ideas of what feels good and what bad—righteous anger may feel very good and boastful pride slightly bad to certain individuals in certain cultures. See also POSITIVE EMOTIONS.

KLAUS R. SCHERER

emotion definitions (neuroscience perspectives)

From the perspective of neuroscience, emotion is a fundamental property of the brain and is instantiated in distributed circuitry that enables emotion to interact with other major mental functions such as attention and memory (see NEURAL ARCHITECTURE OF EMOTION). In the psychological literature on emotion, there is debate about the existence of so-called *basic emotions such as *happiness, *anger, *fear, and *disgust. Of concern in this literature is the number of such emotions, whether they are invariant across cultures, and whether they are associated with unique expressive signs. From the perspective of neuroscience (see AFFECTIVE NEUROSCIENCE), affective processes are probably ubiquitous and present throughout all other psychological processes and context, including sleep. This suggestion is advanced in part based upon the fact that emotion-relevant processing regions of the brain are active across many different psychological processes and states (e.g. the *amygdala, insula, and sectors of the anterior cingulate cortex and prefrontal cortex).

An alternative to the view of basic discrete emotions is one that is based more on dimensions such as *valence or *approach/withdrawal processes (see DIMENSIONAL MODELS). There is some evidence that these dimensions are encoded in activation patterns, in specific patterns of activation in emotion-relevant brain circuitry (see, e.g., Davidson et al. 2000). Other evidence points toward specific patterns of neural activity associated with different discrete, basic emotions (e.g. Kipps et al. 2007). It is likely that both positions contain some truth, and that different neural systems will be found for both emotion dimensions and discrete emotions.

Another important issue regarding emotion in humans from the perspective of neuroscience is the fact that emotion in humans is represented at multiple levels of the neuraxis and includes a major cortical contribution. Different sectors of the prefrontal cortex are recruited in various emotion subcomponents (see Rolls 2000, Davidson 2004a). These different zones of the prefrontal cortex are probably involved in several different functions, including the representation of basic value, the subjective experience of emotion, and the regulation of emotion including both automatic and voluntary aspects.

The brain regions implicated in different aspects of emotion processing are not exclusively dedicated to emotion and are probably responsible for the interaction between emotion and other related functions including learning, memory, and attention. Affect is crucial for each of these domains, and in turn these domains affect emotional processing. The brain circuits that include the prefrontal cortex, anterior cingulate cortex, amygdala, and insula are crucial for affective function and for the integration between emotion and other relevant behavioural processes.

RICHARD J. DAVIDSON

Davidson, R.J., Putnam, K.M., and Larson, C.L. (2000). Dysfunction in the neural circuitry of emotion regulation—possible prelude to violence. *Science*, **289**, 591–4.

Dolan, R.J. (2002). Emotion, cognition, and behavior. *Science*, **298**, 1191–4.

emotion definitions (philsophical perspectives)

The general term 'the emotions' is a relatively recent arrival, first gaining prominence in the 19th century, long after terms such as *fear, *shame, and *joy, and roughly synonymous terms in other languages, were in common use. Its introduction was an attempt to bundle together states that were supposedly marked by a degree of 'emotion', a metaphorical extension of the original sense of the word, namely agitated motion, or turbulence. Only the vagueness of the metaphor allows it to stretch far enough to cover typically quiescent 'emotions' such as being pleased or sad about something.

Among the features associated with particular emotions are involuntary physiological changes, including the overt 'expression' of emotions (see EXPRESSION, PRINCIPLES OF EMOTIONAL) that Darwin (1809–82) called attention to; also, the subjective *feeling of these changes, which William James (1842–1910) took to be 'the emotions themselves'. However, people commonly distinguish emotions partly by what they are *about*, such as the possibility of something bad (fear) or the exposure of something one would wish to remain hidden (*embarrassment), and thus by the types of cognitions and attitudes that give rise to the emotion. The aboutness, or intentionality, of emotions also distinguishes them from *moods, which are general response templates that are not about anything in particular, even though they may have been precipitated by the awareness of particular facts or events.

It is arguable that much if not all of our everyday conception of the emotions, including our diverse taxonomies, must be laid aside in biological explanations of the behaviour commonly attributed to emotions (see AFFECTIVE NEUROSCIENCE). However, certain elements of the everyday conception appear to be indispensable to normal human engagement. The evidence from autism suggests that someone who is fully knowledgeable about the biology of emotional behaviour but incapable of conceiving emotions as intentional states of mind-endowed entities would be seriously impaired in social perception and understanding. These biologically irrelevant elements of our everyday conception may themselves be biologically ordained. See also PASSION.

ROBERT M. GORDON

Gordon, R. (1987). *The structure of emotions*. Cambridge: Cambridge University Press.

Oatley, K. (2004). *Emotions: a brief history*. Oxford: Blackwell Publishing.

Prinz, J. (2004). *Gut reactions: a perceptual theory of emotion*. Oxford: Oxford University Press.

de Sousa, R. (2003). Emotion. In: E. N. Zalta (ed.), *The Stanford encyclopedia of philosophy*, Spring 2003 (http://plato.stanford.edu/archives/spr2003/entries/emotion/).

emotion definitions (psychological perspectives)

The term 'emotion' may be one of the fuzziest concepts in all of the sciences. This seems somewhat paradoxical as, on the one hand, everyone would agree that the type of mental and bodily states we call *anger, *joy, *fear, or *sadness are indeed emotions, whereas on the other hand, it has been virtually impossible to arrive at an agreed-upon definition of the category and what states or processes are to be included in it. One of the problems may be that both laypeople and scientists use the term quite abundantly, often in a rather loose and inconsistent fashion. Another problem may have to do with the fact that emotions have been studied by many different disciplines ever since antiquity, each often defining their object of investigation in a somewhat different fashion. The crucial problem is probably intrinsic to the subject: whatever one might designate as emotion is a multicomponential phenomenon (Scherer 1984b, Frijda 2007b) in which the relationships between the component phenomena and the role of each component as a constituent (necessary or sufficient) criterion are far from clear (see COMPONENTIAL THEORIES).

The frustration over the impasse of defining emotion in a consensual way has led some psychologists to doubt the utility of even trying to formally do so, as this enterprise would be doomed to failure and might actually hamper and constrain research (see Frijda 2007c). However, closing one's eyes to the problems generated by the lack of minimal consensus on how to circumscribe the object under study hardly seems a solution, given the fruitless debates due to a lack of a differential definition of emotion and *feeling, or cognition and emotion (Leventhal and Scherer 1987), not to mention the danger this poses to the cherished values of replication and cumulation of research findings. In consequence, it seems useful here to at least make an inventory of those aspects of a definition of emotion that are relatively uncontroversial.

The following features of emotion are of central importance to the understanding of the phenomenon:

(1) Emotions are elicited when something happens that the organism considers to be of *relevance*, by being directly linked to its sensitivities, *needs, *goals, *values, and general well-being (see CONCERNS). Organisms need to constantly scan external and internal stimulus input to check whether the occurrence of stimulus events (or the nonoccurrence of expected ones) requires the deployment of attention, further information processing, and possibly adaptive reaction, or whether the status quo can be maintained and ongoing activity pursued. Most importantly, given the constant barrage of stimulation, the organism must decide which stimuli are sufficiently relevant to warrant more extensive processing and instrumental or social action (see RELEVANCE DETECTION). Among the chief criteria for appraisal of relevance are the novelty or unexpectedness of a stimulus or event, its intrinsic pleasantness or unpleasantness, and its motivational consistency, i.e. its conduciveness to respond to a sensitivity, satisfy a need, reach a goal, or uphold a value, or its 'obstructiveness' to achieving any of those (Scherer 2001c). Emotion intensity appears to be mainly determined by the degree of relevance, itself a result of the importance and number of the needs, goals, or values involved.

(2) In most cases emotion-evoking events require the organism to react, which often implies suspending ongoing behaviour and engaging in a new course of action. Therefore, emotions have a strong motivational force, they produce states of *action readiness (Frijda 2007b) that help the organism to adapt to or deal with important events in their lives. Action readiness refers to a motive state pertinent to one's relationship to some object. The motive state aims at establishing, maintaining, or modifying one's relationship with the world—with the external world as a whole, with an object in that world, or with an object of thought or imagination. Emotions basically pertain to interaction, most of them to interpersonal interaction, and they do not so much involve readiness for a specific behaviour as readiness for a particular aim in an interaction. The overall goal defines the state of action readiness. Several different actions may be appropriate paths toward reaching the aim and thus, during the state of readiness, further processing can go on to determine the optimal alternative under the given situation.

(3) Because of the importance of the event, the action readiness engages the entire person—it urges action and/or imposes action suspension and is, in consequence, accompanied by preparatory tuning of the somatovisceral and motor systems. This in turn means that emotions involve several *components*, subsystems of the organism that tend to cohere to a certain degree in emotion episodes, sometimes to the point of becoming highly synchronized (Scherer 2005; see SYNCHRONIZATION). This does not mean that emotions represent a limited number of rigid prototypical patterns. Rather it means that the components mutually call, shape, and reinforce each other, and together contribute to emerging patterns in the emotional episode.

(4) Emotions bestow *control precedence* on those states of action readiness, in the sense of claiming priority in the control of behaviour and experience. They tend to take control of all emotion components: action planning, action, attention, cognition, somatovisceral changes, and feeling—the synchronization referred to above. They manifest persistence over time, regardless of obstacles or interruptions. They also block the access of other concurrent claims for attention and considerations of propriety and possible unwanted consequences of the instigated actions. However, even though emotions claim priority, they do not always get it, as overriding concerns, strategic considerations, or social norms and conventions may require emotion regulation. It could be argued that most everyday emotions are weak and do not consistently interrupt or change behaviour. However, even in these cases some measure of control precedence tends to remain. Even weak emotions cause intrusive thoughts. They disturb concentration, or demand effort to keep one's mind on the task. A fleeting emotion still makes one pensively glance out of the window for a second or two. Control precedence reveals priority settings of current action readiness, and thereby underlines the appraised importance of whatever led to the emotion.

It can be argued that it is these four determining features that jointly define what is generally meant by *emotion*, both in lay and scientific terminology. These features also allow us to distinguish emotions from other affective states such as *preferences, *moods, *attitudes, interpersonal stances, or affective dispositions or traits (see PERSONALITY). Using a system proposed by Scherer (2005), one can argue that emotions (1) are focused on specific events, (2) involve the appraisal of intrinsic features of objects or events as well as of their motive consistency and conduciveness to specific motives, (3) affect most or all bodily subsystems which may become to some extent synchronized, (4) are subject to rapid change due to the unfolding of events and reappraisals, and (5) have a strong impact on behaviour due to the generation of action readiness and control precedence. As a consequence of these features, emotions are generally more intense than other affective states and have a shorter duration. While this leaves us short of a formal definition, it at least provides a framework that allows researchers to agree more readily on the nature of the phenomena under study, allowing greater comparability and cumulation of research, as well as avoiding fruitless confusion and debate. The history of the field shows that it is quite counterproductive if preferences, attitudes, or moods are called emotions, and vice versa. Similarly, defining emotion as a multicomponent process allows one to distinguish the process as a whole from its individual components, such as feeling, rather than using these terms as synonyms.

NICO H. FRIJDA AND KLAUS R. SCHERER

Frijda, N.H. (2007). *The laws of emotion.* Mahwah, NJ: Lawrence Erlbaum Associates.

Scherer, K.R. (2005). What are emotions? And how can they be measured? *Social Science Information,* 44, 695–729.

emotion theories and concepts (philosophical perspectives)
Careful conceptual labour may often be viewed as the bailiwick of philosophers, but in fact it is a part of the infrastructure of any fruitful cross-disciplinary research. Sometimes it is possible to conceive of something with quite definite linguistic boundaries. Such concepts have strict definitions. Thus we can all agree that the definition of a triangle is 'any three-sided polygon'. However, in other fields, where the subject matter is more disputable, we can only generate soft-edged concepts and quasi-definitions. The concept of emotion is of the latter sort.

Over the last 100 years or so, what is to count as an emotion has been heavily dependent upon the dominant methodology in psychology and, to a lesser extent, philosophy. One of the founding figures of scientific psychology, William James (1842–1910), argued that the proper field of enquiry for psychology was consciousness, for that was what the mind was, and its appropriate method was introspection. So, in turn, he defined emotion in terms of that conscious state we call a feeling: 'Bodily changes follow directly the perception of the exciting fact (stimulus), and ... our feeling of the same changes as they occur IS the emotion' (James 1890) (see JAMES–LANGE THEORY). The founder of behaviourism, J. B. Watson (1878–1958), deeming introspection to be unreliable and unscientific, conceived of an emotion as 'an hereditary "pattern reaction" involving profound changes of the bodily mechanism as a whole, but particularly of the visceral and glandular systems'. However, a later behaviourist, B. F. Skinner (1904–90), felt that a pure behaviourist should not refer to any 'inner states', even physiological ones, but only to clearly observable behaviour. So he conceived of an emotion as 'a predisposition to act in a certain way' triggered by 'specific features of the environment'. The behaviourist account of emotion was eventually destroyed by its own god, science. Experimental work made clear

that, apart possibly from the case of *fear and *anger, one could not reliably distinguish emotions physiologically or behaviourally. Indeed, from a purely behaviourist standpoint, one could not even convincingly distinguish emotions from, say, stomach upsets or behavioural tics.

In recent decades there has been something like agreement that a richer concept of emotion is needed to distinguish emotions from nonemotions and to distinguish one emotion from another (see EMOTION THEORIES AND CONCEPTS (PSYCHOLOGICAL PERSPECTIVES)). The best known of these accounts is sometimes called a cognitive account of emotion, and is a revival and modification of an ancient Aristotelian concept (see Aristotle 1941, Bedford 1956–7, Arnold 1960, Kenny 1963, Lazarus 1966, Wilson 1972, Solomon 1976, Thalberg 1977, Lyons 1980, Scherer and Ekman 1984, Nussbaum 1990, Oakley 1992, Neu 2000). Strictly speaking the phrase, cognitive account of emotion, is highly misleading. For it embraces not merely the *cognitive attitudes* in the subject of an emotional state (such as knowing and believing that something has happened) but also the *evaluative attitudes*, usually called *appraisals* (see APPRAISAL THEORIES) in psychology (such as judging, for example, that what has happened is dangerous, or else insulting) as well as the *physiological reactions* to those attitudes, the internal conscious *feelings generated by those physiological reactions, as well as the resulting manifestations of all of the foregoing in facial expressions, gestures, posture, and behaviour (see EXPRESSION, PRINCIPLES OF EMOTIONAL).

This new and richer concept of emotion can distinguish emotions from nonemotional states in the following way. A stomach upset is a visceral reaction caused by ingesting, say, a lamb chop that is 'a bit off'. This is not an emotional upset because the physiological changes in question have not been initiated and shaped by a cognitive cum evaluative attitude. Contrariwise a sinister neuroscientist might give someone an injection of a drug that induces in him a belief that he is in grave danger, even though he is not. Nevertheless the resulting physiological reactions, feelings, facial expressions, and so on, arising in the recipient of the injection, do constitute a real emotional state of fear precisely because they resulted from his 'believing that he is in danger'. The cognitive component can also readily distinguish one emotion from another. Though, after careful examination, a physiologist might pronounce that both subjects' physiological reactions are similar, the one who believes he is *in danger* is undergoing an emotional reaction of *fear*, while the one who believes she has been *deeply insulted* is undergoing an emotional reaction of *anger*. It also became clear that a cognitive theory was best able to make sense of the fact that we sometimes judge emotions as *appropriate* (his being afraid of the growling slavering

Rottweiler) or *inappropriate* (his fear of the butterfly), and *justified* (she was right to be angry at his racist remark) or *unjustified* (she was wrong to be angered by his absence—he was gravely ill).

But then, perhaps inevitably, this new 'orthodoxy' was criticized, most often as portraying emotions as too cerebral, sophisticated, and rational. Certain versions of the cognitive theory, for example, seemed to imply, wittingly or unwittingly, that only language users, and fairly sophisticated ones at that, could generate genuine emotional states. This, of course, precluded animals and infants from having genuine emotional states—a conclusion that seemed to be a *reductio ad absurdum* of any thesis from which it was derived. And so more subtle, hybrid accounts emerged (Rorty 1980, de Sousa 1987, Greenspan 1988, Stocker and Hegeman 1996, Elster 1999, Goldie 2000). Others distanced themselves from cognitive theories as a result of a growing interest in evolutionary theories of emotion (see EVOLUTION OF EMOTION) where the emphasis was on a small number of fundamental *affect programs hard-wired by evolution at the nonconscious physiological level and subserving evolutionary functions (Plutchik 1980, Frank 1988, Ekman 1989, Damasio 1994, Griffiths 1997, Panksepp 1998, DeLancey 2002).

The demand for careful conceptual work extends throughout the whole field of emotion research. Thus researchers find that they need to make viable conceptual distinctions between emotions viewed as *dispositions* (one's long-term liability or proneness to exhibit an occurrent state of a particular sort of emotion when aroused by relevant circumstances, e.g. Fred's being an irascible person (see PERSONALITY)) and as comparatively short-term *occurrent states* of a particular emotion (e.g. Fred now being in a rage), as well as distinctions between the *cause* of an emotion (his taking LSD caused him to be afraid) and the *object* of an emotion (he was afraid of the shadow on the wall). Researchers also find it useful to make conceptual distinctions between *basic emotions* (emotions, such as fear and *aggression, that do not depend upon any understanding of underlying concepts and clearly extend to the other primates and beyond) and nonbasic *sophisticated emotions* (emotions such as awe and nostalgia, that only humans, who are capable of the underlying concepts of reverence and time, can exhibit). Researchers also argue, rightly, that there is a conceptual category of *moral emotions* (such as guilt and remorse) that only humans with a prior concept of moral responsibility can exhibit. They also point out that there are *culture-related emotions* (see CULTURAL SPECIFICITY) as well as *universal emotions* (see UNIVERSALITY OF EMOTIONS). Since emotions are generated by attitudes, it is inevitable that there will be emotions that are exhibited in one culture but not in another. Thus is it often claimed that

only people in certain oriental countries could have emotions associated with the concept of 'loss of face'. By now it will be clear that a host of conceptual distinctions, and the debates concerning them, have become essential to any sophisticated approach to emotion research. Many of those distinctions discussed above, as well as others not mentioned, will have their own separate entries in this volume.

WILLIAM LYONS

emotion theories and concepts (psychological perspectives) This entry covers the major current theories of emotion in psychology, although precursors may be found in other disciplines, particularly philosophy. Therefore philosophical theories (see EMOTION THEORIES AND CONCEPTS (PHILOSOPHICAL PERSPECTIVES)) and approaches proposed by neuroscientists (see AFFECTIVE NEUROSCIENCE; EMOTION DEFINITIONS (NEUROSCIENCE PERSPECTIVES)) are not discussed. Coverage is limited to theories that claim to provide a comprehensive explanation of the whole range of emotions and their underlying mechanisms, rather than those limited to a specific component or a particular emotion. Following a brief overview of the basic elements of emotion episodes, three major theoretical traditions or orientations are described, along with their historical development. The positions of these three orientations on central theoretical issues are then systematically compared. To conclude, some criteria for the choice of a theory as a framework for research in the affective sciences are proposed. Given space restrictions, not all theorists can be covered nor can their work be extensively referenced (a wider selection of theories can be found in Scherer and Ekman 1984, Scherer and Peper 2001, Moors, 2009).

Emotion has been a particularly difficult concept to define in psychology, and while there has been some convergence in recent years there is no consensus on a unified theoretical framework to guide cumulative research. This is all the more surprising as the basic facts have been quite uncontroversial from the dawn of human thinking about emotion: (1) There are certain types of events or situations (such as loss, frustration, danger, success) that seem to produce somewhat special reactions and behaviours in humans. (2) The latter consist of physiological changes (in cardiovascular activity, blood flow, respiration, temperature, and muscle tension), expressions in voice, face, and body (such as laughing, crying, shouting, gesticulating, cringing), and of shifts in behavioural intention and direction. (3) These episodes generally (but not always) give rise to a conscious feeling of a particular quality in the person concerned that constitutes a unitary experience over a certain period of time. (4) These episodes and the associated experiences can be, and often are, labelled with a specific word, a brief expression, or a metaphor, both by the experiencing person and by observers. Such expressions exist in all languages of the world and show a remarkable degree of semantic overlap.

Major theoretical positions and their history
As one might expect, all current emotion theories are rooted in historical traditions, often in a complex fashion. Yet one can make a reasonable case for three major currents which emerged out of different schools of thought. One such tradition, *basic emotion theories*, with its roots in antiquity, has received a strong impetus from Darwin's (1872/1998) work on the expression of emotion (see FACIAL EXPRESSION OF EMOTION) in which he described the appearance of characteristic expressions for eight families of emotions and the functional principles underlying their production (*serviceable associated habits*) (see EXPRESSION, FUNCTIONS OF EMOTIONAL). Despite its pioneering nature, Darwin's book was long neglected by psychologists until Tomkins (1962) proposed a new psychobiological theory postulating a list of basic affects (interest/excitement, enjoyment/joy, surprise/startle, distress/anguish, fear/terror, shame/humiliation, contempt, and disgust) with underlying neuromotor expression programs (see the chapter by Tomkins in Scherer and Ekman, 1984). Inspired by Tomkins, Ekman (in Scherer and Ekman 1984; see BASIC EMOTIONS) and Izard (1992; see DIFFERENTIAL EMOTIONS THEORY) developed theories respectively known as basic or discrete emotion theories. The fundamental assumption is that a specific type of event triggers a specific *affect program corresponding to one of the basic emotions and producing characteristic expression patterns and physiological response configurations. Very much in line with Darwin's early concerns, much of this research has centred on the issue of prototypical expressions for each emotion, particularly in the face. However, in more recent versions of their theories, both Ekman (1999) and Izard (2007) have emphasized the flexibility of the emotion system, the difference between basic and complex (or primary and secondary) emotions, the influence of sociocultural context, and the interactions of different emotion components. While acknowledging the existence of complex social and self-reflective emotions requiring elaborate cognitive processing, these theorists continue to focus on the most elementary emotional reactions to stimuli of overriding importance, likely to be largely universal. Importantly, all basic emotion theorists stress the coherence between different components of the emotion systems.

The second tradition, *constructivist emotion theories*, started with a bang in 1884 when William James (1842–1910) proposed 'that the bodily changes follow directly the perception of the exciting fact, and that our feeling

of the same changes as they occur *is* the emotion' (James, 1884/1968, p. 19) (see JAMES–LANGE THEORY). This claim, and the reaction by Cannon (1927b) (see CANNON–BARD THEORY), led to a century of debate (Ellsworth 1994c) which is still not quite settled. The difficulty of empirically demonstrating response specificity and the fascination with unspecific sympathetic arousal in the 1960s even led to the claim that emotions are nothing but variations in sympathetic *arousal (Duffy 1941). In order to solve the specificity problem, Schachter and Singer (1962) proposed a two-factor theory in which increased arousal (the first factor) is perceived by an individual as requiring an explanation (see SCHACHTER–SINGER THEORY). This is achieved by a cognitive analysis of context features (the second factor) resulting in a differentiated feeling state. In a clever and hugely influential experiment the authors induced arousal through adrenalin injections and systematically varied situational factors to manipulate feelings. The data were equivocal and have not been replicated. In addition, Schachter and his collaborators were aware that this experimental situation had little ecological validity, stating: 'In nature, of course, cognitive or situational factors trigger physiological arousal, and the triggering stimulus usually imposes the label we attach to our feelings' (Nisbett and Schachter 1966, p. 228). Yet this tradition (also referred to as *peripheralist* in comparison with Cannon's emphasis on the *central* nervous system) continued unabated and took a strongly constructivist turn. Proponents of this position generally argue that, except for the origin of increased arousal, no specific determinants for emotion differentiation are required: the individual is free to *construe* situational meaning, and thus to identify the felt emotion, on the basis of motivational or situational factors. Thus Mandler (1990) argued that arousal serves as a signal to construe situational meaning. Constructivist accounts have also been proposed by scholars concerned with the social role of emotion and the influence of culture (see CONSTRUCTIVISM) (e.g. Averill 1980; see also Keltner and Haidt 2001).

More recently the theoretical current started by Schachter and Mandler has been revived by Russell (2003) who has suggested that the first factor is not just arousal but a *valence by arousal composite (see CORE AFFECT; CIRCUMPLEX MODELS), with the second factor, as in Schachter and Singer's case, consisting of cognitive categorization. Barrett (2005) adopted the same position but proposed a variant which assumes that core affect is differentiated by a *conceptual act* which is in part driven by embodied representations.

The third tradition, *appraisal theories of emotion*, represents both one of the most ancient as well as one of the most recent theoretical traditions: Ancient because many leading philosophers, in particular Aristotle (384–322 BC),

Descartes (1596–1650), Spinoza (1632–77), and Hume (1711–76), have assumed that the major emotions (as indexed by the respective words in the language) are differentiated by the type of evaluation or judgement a person makes of the eliciting event; recent because the term appraisal was first used in this specific sense by Arnold (1960) and Lazarus (1968), and only produced active theoretical development in the early 1980s (see the historical reviews by Schorr, 2001, and Scherer, 1999a). Ellsworth and her students (Smith and Ellsworth 1985, Roseman 1991, Roseman and Smith 2001) and Scherer (1982, 2001a) independently developed theories that, despite some differences in terminology, share many essential features (see APPRAISAL THEORIES). They assume an emotion architecture that is based on people's subjective evaluation or appraisal of the significance of events for their well-being and goal achievement. While Lazarus (1991) postulated a primary (valence) and a secondary (coping) appraisal step, later theorists specified the appraisal criteria in greater detail (e.g. novelty, intrinsic pleasantness, goal conduciveness or motive consistency, agency, responsibility, coping, legitimacy, compatibility with self and societal standards), and detailed predictions are made about the emotional experiences generated by specific appraisal combinations. All appraisal theorists stress the fact that the process of evaluation or appraisal can occur at different levels of processing, ranging from simple sensorimotor links or primitive associations, over conscious and unconscious schemata, to effortful propositional analysis (Leventhal and Scherer 1987; see LEVELS OF PROCESSING; AUTOMATIC APPRAISAL). In addition these theories highlight the dynamic character of the emotion process (an episode rather than a state) as well as the organized nature of the emotion components (see COMPONENTIAL THEORIES), assuming some degree of coherence or *synchronization across the emotion episode driven by appraisal results. Conscious emotional experience or feeling is seen as a central representation of the unfolding emotion process in all components, producing a rich variety of dynamically changing feeling *qualia which can ultimately be bounded, categorized, and labelled, especially when the emotional experience is shared via verbal communication (Scherer 2004). Despite large conceptual overlap, different appraisal theorists have proposed somewhat divergent accounts of the temporal organization of appraisal checks and the nature of the underlying mechanism, as well as the nature of valence appraisal, the number and nature of emotion categories, including emotion blends (see MIXED EMOTIONS; MODAL EMOTIONS), and the role of consciousness (Grandjean et al. 2008).

There are a number of theories stemming from somewhat different traditions that share some of the major assumptions of appraisal theories but differ in scope, focus, or underlying architecture. Thus, Weiner (1982), a major proponent of social psychological attribution theory, stressed the role of agency and control in appraisal, and empirically showed their powerful effects on ensuing emotions (see ATTRIBUTIONAL THEORY). Also, Ortony et al. (1988) focused on the cognitive or situational structure of emotions as implied by emotion concepts. As most other appraisal theorists, they postulated that all aspects of specific emotions, including their characteristic response patterning, is dictated by the psychologically significant situation as determined by the characteristic appraisals. They see the underlying structures for different emotions as an analogy to grammar in language, a rule system that describes speech and emotion but that is not consciously evoked when speaking or emoting.

Not all psychological emotion theories fit easily into the three traditions outlined above. Some theorists focus on a specific aspect or component of emotion, such as *motivation or action preparation (see ACTION READINESS), and combine features from the three major orientations. Some theorists, embracing the general notion of discrete emotions, strongly focus on their *motivational* underpinnings. Thus, Plutchik (1980) proposed a set of basic emotions based on fundamental, phylogenetically continuous classes of motivation as identified by ethological research. Like Russell (2003), he also argued for an arrangement of these emotions in a two-dimensional affect space, but adding intensity as a third dimension. In a similar fashion, Oatley and Johnson-Laird (1996) stressed the evaluation or appraisal of current goal states on two levels of representation, nonpropositional and propositional (awareness of causes and targets). As for the elaboration of differentiated feelings, they adopted a constructivist approach.

Other theorists have focused on the output side of the emotions, the preparation of action tendencies or even specific emotional behaviours. This is particularly true for Frijda (1986, 2007) who considers 'action readiness' and the meaning and function of motor response processes as the defining core of emotional response. Specifically, he identifies a set of defined action tendencies as characteristic for certain emotions. He sees appraisal as the natural precursor of these action tendencies, highlighting the important role of an individual's concerns, and stresses the importance of dispositional appraisal propensities such as personality. He places major emphasis on the behaviour control exerted by emotions through the action readiness and adaptive action tendencies they generate. Panksepp (2005), coming from a neuroscience background, reached similar conclusions to basic emotion theorists, postulating the existence of core emotional networks in mammals and humans through which significant sensory stimuli can unconditionally access emotion systems which in turn generate appropriate adaptive motor output and modulate sensory input. Finally, Lang's theoretical approach to emotion (Lang and Davis 2006), in the tradition of information processing networks (see Moors, 2009), focuses on reflex patterns, the change from attention to action mobilization, evoked by arousing appetitive/pleasant, dangerous, or important/interesting stimuli, and highlights the response physiology of the brain's evolved motivational systems—appetitive and defensive. While the approach identifies some individual emotions like interest and fear, much of the emphasis is placed on affective dimensions (valence, arousal, dominance; see DIMENSIONAL MODELS).

Systematic comparison of the major theoretical traditions

The scope of emotion theories: Theorists often diverge in their basic assumptions about how emotion should be defined and what an emotion theory should attempt to explain (the *explanandum*). For basic emotion and appraisal theorists the term emotion denotes all of the components of emotion: elicitation processes, physiological symptoms, motor expression, motivational changes, and subjective feeling. In contrast, ever since James, constructivist theorists have tended to define the subjective feeling component as emotion. Using these two terms synonymously has been, and continues to be, a major source of confusion and debate. If William James had said 'our becoming aware of the bodily changes that are generated by an exciting event *is the emotional feeling*' (instead of emotion—which is probably what he meant because he later said that the nature of the bodily changes was determined by the overwhelming 'idea' of the significance of an event; James 1894, p. 518) and that the perception of these bodily changes would have a strong impact on the resulting emotional feeling, the history of emotion psychology might have taken a different course.

The underlying process—components and their relationships: While most scholars agree that the essential elements or components of emotion must somehow be linked to the theoretical construct, dissent reigns with respect to how this is to be achieved and how the emotion mechanism should be best described. Proponents of the three traditions described above differ greatly in their accounts of the underlying representation of the concepts or constructs, their observable manifestations, and the interrelationships among these. These differences are partly explained by (1) fundamental beliefs about the nature of emotion and (2) assumptions about the causal structure and the temporal unfolding of emotion processes.

On one extreme we find the notion of a limited number of evolutionarily continuous adaptive emotion systems (held by many basic emotion theorists) and on the other, that of fuzzy, unpredictable state

changes that achieve coherence only by their place in a valence/arousal space and by conceptual classification, espoused by some constructivists. In this debate, appraisal theorists are somewhere in the middle—they neither accept the idea of a limited repertoire of basic, homogeneous emotions with highly prototypical characteristics nor that of emotions being individually labelled points in two-dimensional affect space. Rather, while assuming that there are widely varying types of emotions they postulate the existence of modal emotion families with frequently occurring appraisal profiles that have adaptive functions in dealing with quintessential contingencies in animal and human life (similar to the *core relational themes* postulated by Lazarus, 1991). As to labels, they assume sizable variability across individuals, situations, and cultures, but interpret the similarity of emotion labels over languages as a sign of universality of these modal categories (even though cultures may differentially emphasize different modal emotions).

As to the organization of the components, both basic emotion and appraisal theorists suggest that these are organized in a lawful fashion. The former focus on a small number of fundamental, evolutionarily continuous emotions, assuming prototypical *affect programs* which are expected to generate relatively fixed configurations of response patterns on the level of each basic emotion (although these may be executed only partially; Ekman 1999). In contrast, appraisal theorists suggest that response patterns are functionally organized on the level of appraisal results rather than emotions, being generated (very much in the sense of Darwin) in the service of facilitating information search (e.g. raising the eyebrows), or implementing action tendencies (e.g. clenching one's teeth; Frijda 2007, Scherer 2001a). According to these models, then, the response patterning in physiological symptoms and motor expression is an emergent phenomenon determined by changes in appraisal profiles over time that may vary greatly across as well as within specific emotion families. Scherer (2001a) has suggested that to the extent that certain emotions show partially consistent profiles of appraisal and response patterning they belong to the same modal emotion family, even though there are potentially as many different emotions as there are appraisal-generated response configurations.

Constructivist theorists do not share the assumption that there is a link between unfolding appraisal results as part of the emotion process and the temporal organization of the responses in different emotion components. Importantly, this is not true for James—claimed as a precursor by many constructivists—as he believed that the perception of bodily symptoms causally determines feelings. Modern constructivists are mostly interested in the process of the individual's construction of emotional meaning on the basis of a primitive core affect, constituted by valence and arousal, through cognitive categorization (Russell, 2003) or (partially embodied) conceptual acts (Barrett 2005). In consequence, they do not attempt to propose specific hypotheses for component organization. Thus, Barrett's (2005) conceptual act model assumes that core affect and conceptualization are always in play and continually shaping one another as they combine like ingredients to produce a variety of mental states, some of which individuals may then label with a specific emotion term. In this model, attributions and appraisals are some of the factors that lead to core affect but are considered as 'mental contents' that contribute to the process of constructing a conceptualized emotional feeling following the logic of constraint satisfaction.

To summarize these differences, shown in a highly simplified form in Fig. E4, one could argue that the basic emotion model (here illustrated by Ekman's 2003 model) is deterministic on a macro level—a given stimulus or event will determine the occurrence of one of the basic emotions (through a process of largely automatic appraisal). In contrast, appraisal theorists (here illustrated by Scherer's, 2001a, 2004 *component process model) are deterministic on a micro level—specific appraisal results or combinations thereof are expected to determine, on a more molecular level, specific action tendencies and the corresponding physiological and motor responses. Most importantly, appraisal theorists espouse *emergentism* (in the sense of John Stuart Mill, 1806–73) assuming that the combination of appraisal elements in a recursive process unfolding over time and the ensuing reactions will form emergent emotions that are more than the sum of their constituents and more than instantiations of rigid categories, namely unique emotional experiences in the form of qualia. This assumption demonstrates that appraisal theorists also engage in mild constructivism in that the categorization and labelling of the nonverbal representation of an emotion episode, including the somatosensory proprioceptive feedback, allows for the active search and construction of individual, cultural, or situational meaning. In comparison, modern constructivist theorists (here illustrated by Barrett's 2005 model) are generally antideterminist and define constructivism in a strong sense, i.e. the study of how individuals search to meaningfully understand their worlds and experiences. While they admit that core affect is produced by a large number of different factors including appraisal, they have not elaborated specific hypotheses about the mechanisms that determine the position of core affect in valence/ arousal space or about the organization of components over time. However, the criterion that seems to organize constraint satisfaction processes between different types of mental contents seems to be existence of culturally learned

concepts, and one could argue that the existence of a concept and/or its momentary salience for an individual actually *determines* the emotion.

Criteria for the choice of a research-guiding theory for the affective sciences

The following definition of a scientific theory (quoted from the English language Wikipedia) is useful to define the criteria to be used in choosing between the competing theories outlined above: 'In scientific usage, a theory does not mean an unsubstantiated guess or hunch, as it can in everyday speech. A theory is a logically self-consistent model or framework for describing the behaviour of a related set of natural or social phenomena. It originates from or is supported by experimental evidence. In this sense, a theory is a systematic and formalized expression of all previous observations, and is predictive, logical, and testable. In principle, scientific theories are always tentative, and subject to corrections, inclusion in a yet wider theory, or succession. Commonly, many more specific hypotheses may be logically bound together by just one or two theories. . . . Of several competing theories, one theory may be superior to another in terms of its approximation of reality. Scientific tests of the quality of a theory include its conformity to known facts and its ability to generate hypotheses with outcomes that would predict further testable facts.'

The litmus test for emotion theories with respect to the criteria outlined above remains to be done. Does Theory X originate from known facts and is it supported by experimental evidence? To what extent is it a systematic and formalized expression of all previous observations? Is it predictive, logical, and testable? Empirical research on emotion in all of the affective sciences is hampered by the absence of a systematic evaluation of theories that could guide research in a systematic fashion, allow falsification, and promote the accumulation of knowledge. Often, particular theories are chosen with a relative ignorance of what alternatives are available and what the advantages and disadvantages of each of these are. Another problem is the perseverance of misconceptions and the inability to see convergence, aggravated by the popularity of purely semantic debates (such as the enduring cognition–emotion debate; see Leventhal and Scherer 1987). Thus, there is widespread acceptance, by protagonists from different traditions, of the idea that emotions can be produced by many different mechanisms on several levels of information processing, involving different structures of the brain. Similarly, there is some convergence on the need for emotions to be defined by different components which show some coherence during the course of an emotion episode and that emotions are processes rather than states. If one accepts

1. Basic emotion theories (<u>Ekman</u>, Izard)

2a. Early constructivist theories - <u>Schachter</u>, Mandler

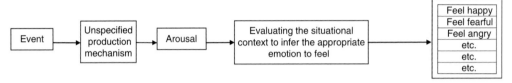

2b. Current constructivist theorists - <u>Russell</u>, Barrett

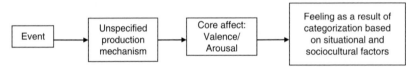

3. Appraisal theories (<u>Scherer</u>, Ellsworth, Roseman, Smith)

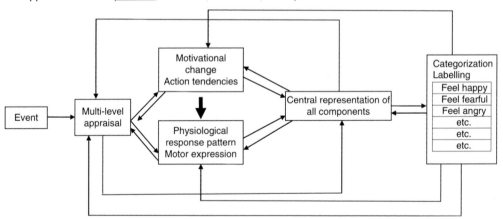

Fig. E4. Synthesis of three traditions of emotion theories (diagrams correspond to models proposed by underlined authors).

the latter, and accepts the important role of recursivity and of dynamic nonlinear systems (Sander *et al.* 2005), the simplistic conception of causality and temporal unfolding which has dominated so much of the theoretical debate during the last century should be seriously questioned. Finally, given the increasing realization of the need for greater interdisciplinarity in emotion research, it may be necessary to develop integrative theories that can accommodate the needs of several disciplines. This should not pose insurmountable problems as most theories reviewed above do not fundamentally contradict each other; rather, they differ in the degree of emphasis they place on elicitation, response organization, action preparation, or conceptualization.

KLAUS R. SCHERER

Moors, A. (2009). Theories of emotion causation: a review. *Cognition and Emotion*, **23**, 209–37.

Scherer, K.R. and Ekman, P. (eds) (1984). *Approaches to emotion*. Hillsdale, NJ: Lawrence Erlbaum Associates.

Scherer K.R. and Peper, M. (2001). Psychological theories of emotion and neuropsychological research. In: F. Boller and J. Grafman (eds), *Handbook of neuropsychology*, Vol. 5, pp. 17–48. Amsterdam: Elsevier.

empathy (neuroscience perspectives) Philosophers, biologists, and psychologists have long debated the nature of empathy, and whether this capacity sets humans apart from other species (see de Waal 2006). Developmental psychologists argue that empathic behaviour is essential to human social and moral development (Eisenberg *et al.* 2006a). For example, empathy and perspective-taking are associated with the development of *prosocial behaviour in children. Furthermore, social psychologists are concerned with the situational and dispositional factors that can trigger empathic concern (Batson *et al.* 2006). More recently, however, there has been an increasing interest in neurophysiological investigations of empathy. This is primarily due to newly available neuroimaging methods that allow exploration of the anatomical circuits involved in empathy-related tasks using diverse and sophisticated paradigms. These methods support the goals of *social neuroscience, which is an interdisciplinary science devoted to understanding how biological systems implement social processes and behaviour.

Most scholars agree that empathy can be characterized by two primary components: (1) an affective response to another person, which often (though not always) entails sharing that person's emotional state, and (2) a cognitive capacity to take the subjective perspective of the other person. The affective component is hypothesized to be phylogenetically older than the cognitive component, emerging in its simplest form as the automatic ability to detect the affective state of another person. This affective response to a conspecific's distress is a widespread phenomenon in the animal kingdom, especially in species that live in social groups (Preston and de Waal 2002). The second component of empathy, perspective-taking, is likely to be a more recent development in evolutionary history, and is specific to great apes, or perhaps solely to humans, although this is still a matter of debate. This cognitive component of empathy relies to a much greater extent on effortful, controlled processes. The basic mechanism for empathy rests on the ability to recognize that the self and other are similar, but also on an ability to separate the two (Decety and Hodges 2006).

The two-component view of empathy accounts for the sense of similarity in the feelings experienced by self and other (such translations go both ways), while allowing the subjective experience of two individuals to remain distinct. This experience of empathy can lead to sympathy (concern for another based on the apprehension or comprehension of the other's emotional state or condition) when the self is clearly distinguishable from the other, or personal distress (i.e. an aversive, self-focused emotional reaction to the apprehension or comprehension of another's emotional state or condition) when there is confusion between self and other.

Social neuroscience research indicates that the experience of empathy emerges from an interaction between two major neural and computational mechanisms. These mechanisms are: (1) 'shared neural representations' common to the self and other, including the capacity to implicitly imitate actions, emotions and affect, and (2) meta-cognitive processes that modulate this sharing (Decety and Lamm 2006). The former mechanism, underpinned by perception–action coupling, is automatic (bottom-up), and occurs unconsciously, effortlessly, and without intention. By contrast, its modulation is a controlled (top-down) process. Evidence suggests that automatic processes are often subtle and vulnerable to being overridden by more controlled mechanisms.

The results of a number of studies suggest that similar neural circuits are active when humans experience emotions and when they perceive others expressing emotions. For instance, the anterior insula is activated in response to the sight of the disgusted facial expressions of others as well as by the first-hand experience of *disgust (Wicker *et al.* 2003). One functional magnetic resonance imaging (fMRI) experiment demonstrated that when participants were required to observe or to imitate facial expressions of various emotions, increased neurodynamic activity was detected in the superior temporal sulcus, the anterior insula, and the *amygdala, as well as in areas of the premotor cortex corresponding to the representation of faces (Carr *et al.* 2003). Another study showed that the observation of everyday hand and face actions performed with an emotion recruited regions involved in the perception and the experience of emotion and/or in communication (Grobras and Paus 2006). Thus it seems that, in addition to inducing resonance in the motor program necessary to execute an action, watching an action performed with emotion induces a resonance in the emotional system responsible for the affective modulation of the motor program. Such a mechanism plays a key role in understanding how the other person feels as well as his or her likely intentions.

It appears that this same action–perception coupling mechanism also underlies our ability to perceive and understand the pain of others. A handful of fMRI studies revealed that the brain areas implicated in processing the affective and motivational aspects of pain also mediate the observation of pain in others. In one study, participants undergoing a fMRI scan either received painful stimuli or observed a signal that their partner, who was present in the same room, would receive painful stimuli (Singer *et al*. 2006). The first-hand experience of pain resulted in activation of the somatosensory cortex, which encodes the sensory–discriminative dimensions of a noxious stimulus such as its bodily location and intensity. In both conditions, the anterior medial cingulate cortex (ACC), the anterior insula, and the cerebellum were activated. Interestingly, these regions contribute to the affective and motivational processing of noxious stimuli (i.e. aspects of pain that pertain to desires, urges, or impulses to avoid or terminate a painful experience). These patterns were also observed in participants who were asked to imagine the level of pain involved while watching photographs depicting right hands and feet in painful or neutral everyday-life situations, or facial expression of pain (Jackson *et al*. 2005). Significant activation in the regions involved in the affective aspect of pain processing, notably the ACC, the thalamus, and the anterior insula were detected.

Social psychological studies have documented the distinction between imagining the other and imagining oneself (Batson *et al*. 1997). These studies indicate that the former may evoke empathic concern (defined as an other-oriented response congruent with the perceived distress of the person in need), while the latter induces both empathic concern and personal distress (i.e. a self-oriented aversive emotional response such as anxiety or discomfort). Social neuroscience research supports this distinction. In one fMRI study, when participants were asked to imagine the painful situations from a first-person perspective (i.e. imagine you are this person) as compared with a third-person perspective (i.e. imagine how that person feels), additional activation was detected in regions involved in the sensori-discriminative aspect of pain, including the middle insula, the somatosensory cortex, and the amygdala (Jackson *et al*. 2006). One recent study further demonstrates that, depending upon the adopted perspective, observing other people in pain triggers either empathic concern or personal distress, and that this other- versus self-oriented responding engages distinct neural networks (Lamm *et al*. 2007). In this study, participants were asked to watch a series of video clips featuring patients' facial expressions of pain while undergoing painful medical treatment either with the instruction to put themselves explicitly in the shoes of the patients ('imagine self'), or to focus their attention on the feelings and reactions of the patients ('imagine other'). Behavioural measures replicated previous social psychology

findings. Specifically, results showed that projecting oneself into an aversive situation led to higher personal distress and lower empathic concern, while focusing on the emotional and behavioural reactions of another's plight was accompanied by higher empathic concern and lower personal distress. The neuroimaging data were also consistent with these findings. The self-perspective evoked stronger haemodynamic responses in brain regions involved in coding the motivational–affective dimensions of pain, including bilateral insular cortices and anterior medial cingulate cortex. In addition, the self-perspective was associated with stronger activation in the amygdala (see Fig. E5). This limbic structure plays a critical role in fear-related behaviours, such as the evaluation of actual or potential threats. Interestingly, the amygdala receives nociceptive information from the spino-parabrachial pain system and the insula, and its activity appears to be closely tied to the context and level of aversiveness of the perceived stimuli. Imagining oneself to be in a painful and potentially dangerous situation thus triggers a stronger fearful and/or aversive response than imagining someone else to be in the same situation. Alternatively, and less specifically, the stronger involvement of the amygdala might also reflect a general increase of arousal evoked by imagining oneself to be in a painful situation.

The sharing mechanism between self and other can be modulated by various variables, such as disposition toward others. For instance, it would not be adaptive to respond the same way to a friend or a foe in distress. Singer *et al*. (2006) engaged participants in a sequential Prisoner's Dilemma game with confederate targets, who would either play the game in a fair or an unfair way. Following this behavioural manipulation, participants' brains were scanned while they observed 'fair' and 'unfair' confederates receiving painful stimulation to their hands. Observing fair players replicated earlier findings of increased activation in brain areas coding the affective aspect of pain, such as the anterior insula and medial/anterior cingulate cortex. However, activation in these brain regions was significantly reduced when participants observed unfair players in pain. Interestingly, this effect was detected in male participants only, who also showed a concurrent increase of activation in reward-related areas (i.e. nucleus accumbens and ventral striatum).

In sum, current evidence from social neuroscience clearly indicates that we come to understand others' emotion and pain by using the same neural machinery that we would use to produce similar states in ourselves. Such a neural mechanism provides a basis on which the experience of empathy stems. Modulation due to situational and dispositional factors may have an effect on this sharing mechanism. A deeper understanding of empathy, intersubjectivity, and related

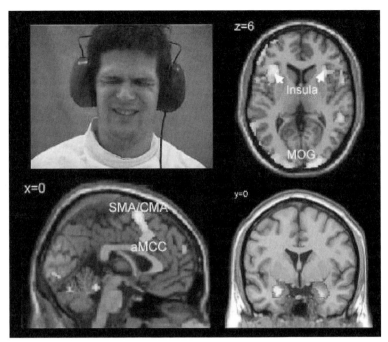

Fig. E5. When individuals are watching a patient expressing pain as a result of a medical treatment involving sound, neurohaemodynamic activation is detected in the anterior insula, thalamus, anterior cingulate cortex, and supplementary motor area. Signal increase was also detected in the amygdala. Adapted from Lamm *et al.* (2007).

emotions will be fostered by integrative analyses that span the biological and social levels of organization. However, one should remain aware of the ecological validity of findings from social neuroscience. Indeed, it is difficult to reproduce in the laboratory, especially in the environment of a fMRI scanner, experimental paradigms that match the complexity of real-life interaction involving the combination of situation and personality variables. Thus, future neuroscience investigations of empathy should strive towards methodologies that simulate realistic intersubjective transactions.

JEAN DECETY

Decety, J. and Lamm, C. (2006). Human empathy through the lens of social neuroscience. *The Scientific World Journal*, **6**, 1146–63.

de Waal, F. (2006). *Primates and philosophers: how morality evolved* (ed. S. Macedo and J. Ober). Princeton, NJ: Princeton University Press.

empathy (philosophical perspectives) The word 'empathy' is surprisingly young, having entered the English language only in the early 1900s as a translation of the German term *Einfühlung*. That concept was coined in German aesthetics to refer to a postulated kind of response to art, in which the observer first engages in some involuntary bodily mimicry of the work, then projects onto the work an emotional response that somehow fits with his acquired bodily posture (see AESTHETIC EMOTIONS (PHILOSOPHICAL PERSPECTIVES)). Theodor Lipps (1851–1914) eventually came to think that the phenomenon could occur in interpersonal cases as well, when people come through unconscious *mimicry of another's behaviour to feel some emotional response which they then project onto the observed subject. An influential treatment of empathy within this tradition, which emphasized and expanded the social role of empathy, was Edith Stein's *On the Problem of Empathy* (Stein 1989/1916).

Empathy should be distinguished from 'sympathy', a much older term with a number of different meanings. 'Sympathy' was widely used by 18th-century British philosophers such as Lord Shaftesbury (1671–1713), Frances Hutcheson (1694–1746), David Hume (1711–76), and Adam Smith (1723–90) to refer both to mechanisms of emotional transmission or acquisition and to various feelings and benevolent motives which those mechanisms can produce. 'Empathy' is similarly ambiguous. It can stand for any of a variety of ways in which one person may be brought to respond emotionally to the circumstances or the emotions of another; or it can be used to refer to an affective response in an observer that is congruent with the emotion experienced by an observed model. Most recent work by philosophers and psychologists focuses on the former sense of the term, whereby empathy is held not to be itself an affective state (for instance, it is not the same thing as pity), but a way of acquiring an affective state in response to another person's affect. So understood, empathy is widely thought to be important to socialization, to prosocial motivation, and to the integration of evaluative beliefs with patterns of emotional response.

A central distinction among varieties of empathy is between simulation and *contagion. Simulation involves one person (the 'observer') imaginatively putting him- or herself into another's (the 'model's') position, and then reacting emotionally to the imagined position. Much of the recent empirical work on empathy has taken such simulation (or 'perspective-taking', or 'role-taking' as it is sometimes called) as the paradigmatic empathic process (a useful survey is Strayer, 1987). Researchers have been interested in the role of such simulation in allowing subjects to gain knowledge of the mental states of others, including but not limited to their emotions. The general idea that such simulation is a means of learning about how others feel goes back at least to Adam Smith, who held that 'we can form no idea of the manner in which (other men) are affected, but by conceiving what we ourselves should feel in the like situation'.

The other important category of empathy is contagion, in which an emotional response is transmitted from the model to the observer without active simulation. What is striking about this kind of empathy is the apparently noncognitive nature of the mechanism. Without any reflection on the model or the emotional state that the model is in, an observer can acquire an emotion that matches the model's (a useful survey is McIntosh et al., 1994.) One hypothesized mechanism of contagion (Adelman and Zajonc 1989) involves involuntary mimicry of the model by the observer, followed by emotional feedback from the vicariously acquired facial expressions and bodily behaviours.

JUSTIN D'ARMS

D'Arms, J. (2000). Empathy and evaluative inquiry. Symposium on Law, Psychology and the Emotions. *Chicago-Kent Law Review*, **74**, 1467–500.

Preston, S. and de Waal, F. (2002). Empathy: its ultimate and proximate bases. *Behavioral and Brain Sciences*, **25**, 1–20.

encoding/decoding (of expression) Encoding and decoding refer, respectively, to the processes whereby people send (express) and receive (make judgements, attributions, or inferences about) nonverbal cues such as those embodied in facial expressions, vocal qualities, and body movements. Researchers ask questions such as: How are different states and traits manifested in nonverbal cues (see NONVERBAL COMMUNICATION)? What cues do perceivers use in drawing inferences about someone's states and traits? How accurately can states and traits be judged on the basis of nonverbal cues? And, what are the characteristics of persons who are more or less easy to judge (i.e. have higher or lower encoding accuracy), and of persons who are more or less accurate in judging others? Although a great many characteristics of people can be examined for their accuracy of being encoded and decoded, most research is concerned with affective states and personality traits.

Encoding

Nonverbal cues can convey information on emotions, intentions, attitudes, physical conditions, sociodemographic information, personality traits, mental health, and intelligence, among others. Encoding occurs on a continuum from totally spontaneous to totally deliberate, according to the encoder's awareness of his/her behaviour, intention to control its form, and ability to do so (see PUSH/PULL EFFECTS). Once criteria for establishing the state or trait are established, it is possible to measure the nonverbal cues that are associated with a given state or trait, for example how the facial muscles move for different felt emotions (see FACIAL EXPRESSION OF EMOTION), or how gestural animation and loud speech are related to the trait of *extraversion.

Accuracy of encoding is typically measured in terms of how accurately decoders can judge the state or trait based on samples of the encoders' nonverbal behaviour that can be less than one second in duration, though typically exposures range from seconds to a few minutes. The term 'thin slices of behaviour' is sometimes used to describe samples of less than five minutes in length (Ambady and Rosenthal 1992). Encoding accuracy is typically defined as the average accuracy of a group of perceivers. Thus, an encoder who is accurately judged by perceivers is considered to have high encoding accuracy. Correlates of high encoding accuracy include female gender, dominance, extraversion, high self-monitoring, and social competence.

Decoding

To measure decoding accuracy, perceivers are asked to make judgements about encoders' states or traits from samples of nonverbal behaviour such as described above. Cue channels and modalities vary, and may include, for example, photographs of posed facial expressions, videotapes of people in conversation, or content-masked voice samples. Judgements can also be made by perceivers who are (or were) also interactants, as when members of interacting dyads make judgements about the meaning of each other's cues.

Judgements can be analysed in terms of both judgement policies and accuracy. A judgement policy is the implicit or explicit rule by which a perceiver draws an inference based on nonverbal cues—for example, inferring submissive personality in a person who smiles a great deal. Judgement policies that are shared by many perceivers can be considered nonverbal stereotypes. Many nonverbal stereotypes have been documented, for example for power and dominance (Hall et al. 2005a), and for differences between men and women (Briton and Hall 1995). Brunswik's (1956) lens model (see BRUNSWIKIAN LENS MODEL) is often used as a device for understanding the nonverbal communication process. The lens model allows identification of cues that are validly diagnostic of the construct in question, cues that are incorrectly utilized by perceivers (i.e. inaccurate judgement policies), and cues that perceivers use appropriately in order to achieve accuracy. Lens model analyses have contributed greatly to an understanding of the process of nonverbal communication (e.g. for intelligence, extraversion, interpersonal rapport, and deception).

Decoding accuracy refers to correct identification of the criterion variable. Methods for scoring accuracy vary with different testing formats, with the most common being the percentage correct based on multiple-choice judgements, used mainly in research on judging affective states, and correlations between judgements and criteria when both are continuous in nature, used mainly in research on judging personality (Hall et al. 2005b). Researchers should be cautioned to account for possible judgement biases in their scoring algorithms; when tests have a multiple-choice format, presentation of confusion matrices (i.e. cross-tabulation of criterion values against responses) is advised.

There is a great deal of research on individual differences in decoding accuracy. Several standard tests are in use (e.g. Rosenthal et al. 1979, Nowicki and Duke 1994), but many investigators create their own stimuli to measure the specific constructs they wish to measure. Some correlates of higher decoding accuracy—also called nonverbal sensitivity—include female gender, better mental health, positive personality traits including more internal locus of control, and better social adjustment. Theorists of the emotional intelligence construct include accuracy of judging emotional nonverbal cues as a component of emotional intelligence (see INTELLIGENCE, EMOTIONAL). Higher general cognitive ability is associated with higher decoding accuracy, but only slightly.

JUDITH A. HALL

Hall, J.A. and Bernieri, F.J. (eds) (2001). Interpersonal sensitivity: theory and measurement. Mahwah, NJ: Lawrence Erlbaum Associates.

Hall, J.A., Bernieri, F.J., and Carney, D.R. (2005). Nonverbal behavior and interpersonal sensitivity. In: J.A. Harrigan, R. Rosenthal, and K.R. Scherer (eds), The new handbook of methods in nonverbal behavior research, pp. 237–81. Oxford: Oxford University Press.

enjoyment Enjoyment is an emotional response to the experience of *pleasure. Its phenomenology varies depending on levels of consciousness. At the level of first-order experience, enjoyment can be inferred from 'acceptance wriggles', such as trembling whiskers in rats, or from attribution of a 'niceness' gloss to external objects (Frijda 2007). At the level of second-order awareness, enjoyment is a reportable pleasure derived from the awareness of pleasure. At the tertiary level of consciousness, enjoyment can take the form of savouring (Bryant and Veroff 2007), which may be defined as a self-initiated emotion action that extends enjoyment beyond pleasure (Frijda and Sundararajan 2007). This transition from the hedonically based action of relishing a positive experience to an intrinsically pleasurable evaluation of experience is made possible by three main factors: higher-order self-reflexive consciousness, detachment, and cognitive processing competence. Savouring, as the Chinese traditional formulations (Frijda and Sundararajan 2007) made clear, capitalizes on the intrinsically self-reflexive nature of experience—the object of our pleasure is the experience, not the stimulus per se. With savouring, the self-reflexive turn from the stimulus to the experience takes another recursive loop to situate pleasure in the pleasure process itself, which monitors the unimpeded functioning and competence of any function (Frijda 2007). Thus savouring finds intrinsic pleasure in certain processing strategies that evince an effort after meaning. Cognitive processing competence is enhanced in savouring by detachment and action restraint, mental attitudes which cast processing in a nonanalytic, mindful mode, and which also expand the temporal dimension of experiences (Frijda and Sundararajan 2007).

LOUISE SUNDARARAJAN

Bryant, F. B. and Veroff, J. (2007). Savoring a new model of positive experience. Mahwah, NJ: Lawrence Erlbaum.

Frijda, N. H. (2007). The laws of emotion. Mahwah, NJ: Erlbaum.

Frijda, N. H. and Sundararajan, L. (2007). Emotion refinement: a theory inspired by Chinese poetics. Perspectives on Psychological Science, 2, 227–41.

envy Envy refers to an unpleasant emotional state that is aroused by another person who is perceived as possessing a desired object, advantage, or superiority. It is typically resentful and hostile in nature, although it can involve other emotional components. Envy has been the topic of legend and literature since antiquity; it was analysed extensively by the ancient Greek and Roman philosophers, and has figured prominently ever since in accounts of politics, psychology, sociology, anthropology, philosophy, and theology (Schoeck 1969/1966). Envy's significance derives from its being one of several possible emotional reactions to human inequality. It therefore figures importantly in accounts of social harmony, justice, social comparison, self-worth, motivation, and ethics (see SOCIAL EMOTIONS; SOCIAL COMPARISON).

To become envious, a person must compare himself or herself with another person and find that person to be advantaged in some way. Anything can serve as the basis of the superiority: possessions, rewards, talent, beauty, reputation, family, friends, personality, comfort, happiness—the list is endless. The envied person may acquire the quality by effort or by luck. The quality may be one-of-a-kind (e.g. winning first prize), but need not be (e.g. having friends). The only requirement for the envied quality is that it must be something that the envious person lacks, desires, and seems unlikely to obtain (see DESIRE). The envious person yearns for what the envied person has, and may even desire that the envied person no longer have it. It is that latter desire that has given envy its reputation as an immoral emotion and that earned it a place on the 6th-century Christian list of seven deadly sins. Some authors make a distinction between *malicious* and *nonmalicious* envy on the basis of the presence or absence of a wish to deprive the envied person of the desirable thing (Parrott 1991).

Envy is best thought of as an episode that unfolds in time, and it is in that context that the interrelations of its characteristic features can be seen most clearly (Parrott 1991). A clue to the genesis of envy is found in Aristotle's observation (in *Rhetoric*, Book 2) that the envied person is usually a peer or competitor of the envious person. The superiority of a peer seems to provide proof of what a person of that sort can achieve, and to demonstrate what the envious person might have had but does not. Because this demonstration influences public perceptions and private *self-esteem, what may start as mere longing can lead to feelings of inferiority. Yet, in many cases, the envious person is not to blame for his or her inferiority, so there may arise a sense that the outcome is unfair (see FAIRNESS), which in turn can give rise to resentment of the circumstances. In the final and most distinctive step, *blame may be directed at the envied person, if only for being the source of the envious person's unhappiness. Such blame, and the hostility and *hatred it rationalizes, may be motivated by the envious person's desire to boost his or her own self-esteem or public reputation (Smith *et al.* 1994, Smith 2003).

Envy involves a particularly subtle combination of objective and subjective criteria. Hostility due to another's superiority is considered to be envy only when that superiority is objectively fair but subjectively seems unfair. If there is objective unfairness, the hostility is considered to be resentment or anger not envy. Labelling a person's emotion as *envy* therefore has a pejorative quality, implying that the envious person does not have a genuine grievance but is merely attempting to buttress his or her diminished self-esteem and public standing by undercutting another person's achievement or excellence. The dissonance between objective fairness and subjective unfairness also explains why envious people may deny that they are envious: confessing to envy amounts to admitting the unjustified and self-serving nature of their hostility.

Because of the possibility of being envied, a person who possesses desirable qualities has reason for concern. People in enviable circumstances frequently try to placate others' envy so as to minimize symptoms ranging from strained relationships to overt aggression (Parrott and Rodriguez Mosquera, 2008). Societies differ in the extent to which envious hostility is sanctioned or circumvented. These differences may be associated with cultural differences in emphasis on competition or cooperation, concern for reputation, or norms for pursuing or displaying excellence (Schoeck 1966/1969).

In modern English, the word *jealousy can be used to refer both to envy as well as to the quite different emotional state that typically occurs when a person's place in an important relationship is threatened by a third party (Parrott 1991).

W. GERROD PARROTT

Konstan, D. and Rutter, N.K. (2003). *Envy, spite and jealousy: the rivalrous emotions in ancient Greece*. Edinburgh: Edinburgh University Press.

Smith, R.H. and Kim, S.H. (2007). Comprehending envy. *Psychological Bulletin*, **133**, 46–64.

episode (emotional) An episode of emotion usually has a clear starting point that is recognized by the person who experiences it. This helps to distinguish episodes from *moods and *sentiments, which may have no clear onset. A definition of the following kind is useful: an episode of emotion can be recognized when there occurs: some bodily sensation such as the heart beating faster, and/or thoughts coming to mind that are hard to stop, and/or an urge to act emotionally, so that the person experiencing such an occurrence can give it an emotion name such as *happiness, *sadness, *anger, etc. (see Oatley and Duncan 1994). The important concept of appraisal (see APPRAISAL THEORIES) in research on emotion draws implicitly on the idea that the typical occurrence of an emotion is an episode, elicited by an event on the basis of how that event is appraised.

Research on episodes of emotion is often conducted by asking participants to keep a diary, structured like a questionnaire. In modern times the study that laid out how such research was to be done was conducted by Averill (1982) who asked people to make diary entries of episodes in which either they were angry at someone or were the targets of someone's anger. Most episodes of anger were directed not at enemies but at people the angry person knew and liked. Usually they had the function of renegotiating some aspect of the relationship with that person.

Using a comparable method, Oatley and Duncan (1994) asked people to record emotions of any kind, and found that most emotions occurred in relation to other people. Typically an episode was caused when a social goal that the participant was aware of was either furthered (giving rise to happy emotions) or impeded (giving rise to emotions of anger, fear, or sadness). Frijda *et al.* (1991) found that whereas emotions recorded by analysing facial expressions or monitoring skin conductance last no longer than a few seconds, 53% of episodes of self-recognized emotion lasted between ten minutes and six hours, with 8% lasting for three days or more, some with alternating phases of waning and intensification.

An important series of studies of emotional episodes has been conducted by Rimé and colleagues (see, e.g., Zech *et al.* 2004). They found that whenever an episode of emotion is salient enough to be remembered at the end of the day, it is very likely to have been shared (confided) (see SOCIAL SHARING OF EMOTION) with least one other person. Emotional episodes are not only our most intimate indices of how we are getting along in the world, but, when shared, their discussion lets us understand them more deeply and in letting us know how we are seen by our intimates, the discussion allows us to coordinate our selfhood with our social world.

KEITH OATLEY

ethical issues (in affective science research) Like any area of inquiry that engages in research with human subjects, research in *affective science must meet existing canons for the ethical conduct of research. This includes observing existing international, national, and local ethical codes and guidelines, and following due process in such areas as informed consent, confidentiality, and the storage of data. However, as the field of affective science grows and interdisciplinary partnerships and stakeholders multiply, new areas of ethical concern are emerging.

One such issue is the possible intrusion of market-driven forces into basic scientific research in affective science (see MARKETING (ROLE OF EMOTION IN)). Medical research on the nature of affective disorders and their treatment has already been radically and irreversibly transformed by the profit-oriented research priorities of the pharmaceutical industry (Healy 1997). There is no reason to believe that basic research in the affective sciences on mood, emotion, and temperament is immune from such influences. Such a commercialization of research is both ethically worrisome and compelling. It is worrisome because it may represent a potential threat to academic freedom and scientific impartiality, but it is also compelling because it may offer much needed financial support and incentives for research.

A related issue is cosmetic psychopharmacology. Supporters argue that the ability to pharmaceutically enhance and alter moods, emotions, temperament, and even personality should be considered a positive liberating advance (Kramer 1997). Critics worry that this promise of enhancement represents a pernicious tendency that sends many individuals on an endless search for personal fulfilment and improvement (Elliott 2003). As our ability to understand and regulate the affective domain evolves, decisions will have to be made about which enhancements are ethically permissible and which are not. What sorts of moods, emotions, temperaments, and personalities do we want? And should such enhancements be prescribed by doctors or be freely available to consumers?

Not to be forgotten among the novel ethical issues that affective science must confront is the ethics of animal research. Affective science is itself partly responsible for renewed attention to this topic, as leading scientists in the area argue they have found homologous brain systems in humans and many animals that are responsible for the processing of affect (Panksepp 1998) (see ANIMAL EMOTIONS). The fact that such animals 'feel' and have rich affective lives is said to limit the amount of suffering and even inconvenience we can ethically impose on them. Our improved understanding of the affective lives of animals may have deleterious ethical consequences depending on how it is put to commercial use. A happy cow may produce better milk. But suppose a depressed one produces better meat. Should we then regulate the desired affective states accordingly? Such commercially driven practices in the regulation of animal affect raise important ethical questions.

The rise of affective science as a distinct domain of inquiry is itself a phenomenon with ethical implications. Behaviourism banished the mind from the scientific concept of the person only to be superseded by cognitivism which returned it. But both behaviourism and cognitivism ignore subjective feelings of affect in their scientific model of the person. Affective science is correcting that omission. The point is ethically important, since science influences how we think of ourselves and the scope and limits of our agency. As affective science continues to evolve, we may learn we have new powers or limitations we did not previously know of, which is sure to give rise to new ethical issues.

LOUIS C. CHARLAND

eustress The concept of eustress was introduced by Selye (1964) to refer to the ensemble of positive adaptive reactions of the organism to beneficial stressors, as opposed to *distress, which he viewed as a specific syndrome that was triggered by unspecific harmful stimuli or activities (general adaptation syndrome). For Selye, eustress represents the pleasant *stress of fulfilment, without the harmful consequences of damaging distress. This concept includes properties of the stressor (beneficial stressor), the effort (positive valence), and the effects (without damaging outcomes). Stressors are seen as beneficial when they do not exceed the capacity for maintaining or restoring homeostasis.

Selye's initial concept of eustress received an alternative theoretical interpretation in Lazarus' stress theory. Lazarus (1966) distinguished different types of stress, differentiating the modalities of *primary appraisals (harm/loss, threat, and challenge), which depend on the goal relevance and goal congruence, and ego involvement. Challenge is related in some way to Selye's eustress. The appraisal of challenge may occur under the following conditions: goal relevance and goal congruence are given, ego involvement enhances positive self-esteem and social esteem, environmental demands, and the internal and external resources for meeting the demands are balanced. With regard to the motivational and affective state, individuals faced by a challenge are strongly motivated to cope with obstacles in the sense of problem-oriented coping. They feel expansive or even joyous about struggle on the way. At the micro-stressor level, Lazarus and Launier (1978) suggested that the 'uplifts' generated by successfully negotiating situations act as antistressors to daily hassles.

According to Selye's (1987) later research, which may be influenced by the work of Lazarus, the eu- or distressful quality of a stressor depends on the subject's interpretation of the situation.

The positive affective states that characterize eustress can be theoretically related to the assumptions of the broaden-and-build theory (Fredrickson and Branigan 2005), suggesting that positive affects enlarge an individual's gamut of thoughts and actions, and predicts long-term positive effects for the person (see POSITIVE EMOTIONS).

MEINRAD PERREZ

evaluative processing Evaluative processing refers to the cognitive and emotional appraisal (see APPRAISAL THEORIES) of the value or *valence (good or bad, positive or negative) of an object, event, or context. It typically entails a cognitive judgement as to desirability, value, or significance; an affective reaction or disposition along the dimensions of reward/aversion, pleasure/pain, and goodness/badness; and a behavioural component along the dimension of approach/avoidance (see APPROACH/WITHDRAWAL). Evaluative processes are multiple, extending from genetically endowed approach/avoidance reactions to positive and negative stimuli, respectively. Examples include positive approach/ingestion responses to palatable flavours and the negative avoidance/withdrawal reactions to pain stimuli. Other evaluative judgements may be acquired and based on mid-level associative processes and higher-level cognitive processes. Examples include the positive rewarding effects of money (which may have no intrinsic value, in and of itself) or fear, anxiety, or avoidance reactions to things like snakes or the sound of a dentist's drill. Evaluative processes also entail social judgements about the desirability, friendliness, 'goodness', or worthiness of others or groups of others. A classic view has been that evaluative processes are organized along a bipolar continuum extending from good to bad or positive to negative, with the midpoint being neutral. Recently, however, attention has been given to bivariate models of evaluation, in which positive and negative dimensions are seen to vary independently (Cacioppo et al. 2004). Examples are ambivalence or approach–avoidance conflicts, in which one may harbour both positive and negative evaluations of an object (e.g. cigarettes to a smoker) (see AMBIVALENT EMOTIONS). The bivariate conceptualization represents a more comprehensive model of affect space, which can subsume the bipolar model as one dimension.

GARY G. BERNTSON AND JOHN T. CACIOPPO

evolutionary and proximate explanations The most fundamental distinction in biology is between proximate and evolutionary explanations. Proximate explanations are about a trait's mechanism (see PROXIMAL FACTORS). Evolutionary explanations are about how the mechanism came to exist. These two kinds of explanation do not compete. They are fundamentally different. Both are essential for a complete explanation.

Ernst Mayr (1904–2005) did the most to promote the basic distinction (Mayr 1982). He emphasized that a complete proximate explanation requires description of a trait at all levels, from DNA to development, to protein structure, to the levers and pulleys, and how they are regulated by internal and external cues. For emotions research, this means everything from genes to brain scans, to psychological structures. An evolutionary explanation, by contrast, is a description of how a trait came to exist—the precursor traits, their variations, and the environmental forces that gave a selective advantage to individuals with certain variations instead of others (see EVOLUTION OF EMOTION).

One can think of the evolutionary explanation as the 'function' that the trait serves (see FUNCTIONALIST THEORIES OF EMOTION), but this is tricky because evolutionary functions benefit genes, not necessarily individuals. Also, one trait may serve several functions, some traits are epiphenomena of other useful traits, and it can be difficult to determine what advantages shaped a trait. Some readers may be aware of the unfortunately politicized controversy about the difficulty in testing evolutionary hypotheses, especially those about mechanisms that regulate human behaviours. Testing evolutionary hypotheses is indeed sometimes challenging, and many ludicrous hypotheses get proposed, but a great deal of science involves finding creative ways to test slippery hypotheses.

Confusion has resulted on occasion because Mayr often used the term 'ultimate' instead of evolutionary. Also confusing is his tendency to talk about function in terms of how a mechanism works, while most people think about a functional explanation as one aspect of an evolutionary mechanism. Nonetheless, he showed over and over again that biology consists of two only sometimes intersecting threads, one the study of how things work, the other of how they got to be the way they are (Mayr 2004).

Tinbergen (1963) proposed a more differentiated approach in his famous article arguing that four questions need to be asked about every trait:

Tinbergen's Four Questions
1. What is the mechanism?
2. What is the ontogeny of the mechanism?
3. What is the phylogeny of the mechanism?
4. What selection forces shaped the mechanism?

The first two are proximate questions. An answer to the first question describes every aspect of the mechanism from its chemical constituency to its regulation by environmental cues. The second question is the other half of a proximate explanation; it traces the ontogeny of the mechanism in the individual, from DNA to cell migrations to the final trait under examination. The other two questions are evolutionary: question (3) is about the development of the trait over evolutionary history, the precursors, and the forces that shaped them and question (4) is about function. How does this trait offer a selective advantage? Why do individuals with this trait on average have more offspring than others?

These four questions are now nearly universal as a foundation for the study of animal behaviour (Dewsbury 1999). Textbooks all begin by explaining the need for all four kinds of explanation (Alcock 2001). Emotions

research is increasingly keeping these questions separate and trying to answer each of them.

RANDOLPH M. NESSE

evolution of emotion Evolution explains why emotions are so difficult to explain. Emotions research has been transformed by recent recognition that natural selection shaped emotions and the mechanisms that regulate them, but agreement remains elusive on exactly how evolutionary principles can best advance our understanding. This entry begins by noting that the scope of a modern evolutionary approach is much wider than Darwin's work on the expression of emotions. It proceeds to emphasize that some of evolutionary biology's most useful contributions are so simple that their profound implications are easy to overlook. One of the most profound implications is also disturbing; many long-standing difficulties in understanding emotions may result because we have been seeking simple well-structured explanations, while what selection has shaped is a jury-rigged jumble.

Darwinism and emotions, old and new
Darwin's *The Expression of Emotions in Man and Animals* (1872/1998) is the beginning of an evolutionary theory of emotions, but in several respects it is surprisingly anti-Darwinian (Fridlund 1992). Darwin had good reasons for emphasizing the phylogenetic continuity of emotions between species, the constraints on their evolution, and their utility for communication. As a result, he says little about other functions of emotions or about how selection acts on individual variations to shape emotions fine-tuned for a specific species (see FUNCTIONALIST THEORIES OF EMOTION).

A more modern Darwinian view instead emphasizes how special states give advantages in certain situations, how natural selection differentiated more general states into subtypes, and how selection shaped regulation mechanisms that express emotions in the situations in which they are useful (Nesse 1990, Plutchik 2003, Keltner et al. 2006b). The emphasis is on finding evolutionary explanations for why emotions are the way they are, as distinct from the completely separate proximate explanation needed for how they work. Recognition that both evolutionary and proximate explanations are essential has proved essential for biology in general (Mayr 1982) as well as emotions in particular (Nesse 1999) (see EVOLUTIONARY AND PROXIMATE EXPLANATIONS). Growing recognition that emotions need both kinds of explanation is advancing emotions research (Gross and Keltner 1999, Keltner et al. 2006b); however, recent progress in understanding the psychological and brain mechanisms of emotions has only begun to be synthesized with progress in the evolutionary understanding of emotions (see NEURAL ARCHITECTURE OF EMOTION) (Panksepp 1998, LeDoux 2000).

Some simple implications

Perhaps the most fundamental contribution of an evolutionary perspective is clarifying what emotions are, based on how they came to exist. Emotions are specialized states, shaped by natural selection, that adjust many aspects of an individual in ways that increase the ability to succeed in situations that have posed consistent adaptive challenges over evolutionary time (Nesse 1990, Tooby and Cosmides 1990). Individuals who express an appropriate emotion in the relevant situation get a selective advantage. Success and selective advantage, from this evolutionary point of view, refers to the individual's Darwinian fitness, best summarized as the number of surviving offspring. For instance, when chased by a predator, individuals who have the coordinated response of panic will be more likely to survive to have more children, thus making their genes, and the capacity for panic, more common in future generations.

A related simple principle, already widely accepted, is that no one component of an emotion is primary; physiology, behaviour, expression, and motivation are all coordinated parts of a special mode of operation (see COMPONENTIAL THEORIES). There is not much point in arguing which comes first. An evolutionary view carefully distinguishes useful from nonadaptive aspects of emotions. For instance, faster breathing can be useful in anxiety, but tingling fingers offer no advantage, they are just an epiphenomenon of other changes. An evolutionary perspective by no means suggests that every aspect of an emotional state will be useful, and it emphatically does not imply that every instance of emotion expression will be useful.

A related implication is that the utility of an emotion depends entirely on the context. When expressed in the wrong situation, emotions tend to be harmful. Panic is useful when a lion looms, but not in response to a lover's gentle touch. Sexual arousal is useful in response to a lover's touch, but not a lion's.

Note that the mechanisms selection shapes to regulate emotions may use any cue correlated with the relevant situation, even if it is not reliably or causally connected. For instance, an approaching shadow arouses anxiety because that cue has sometimes been associated with danger, even if only occasionally. Emotional reactions are often not sensible, because the mechanisms that regulate them are products of selection, not design.

An evolutionary perspective emphasizes the utility of both positive and negative emotions. Positive emotions seem valuable and negative emotions seem harmful, but this is an illusion that arises from their associations with beneficial and harmful situations. In situations of threat

or loss, negative emotions are useful and positive emotions can be harmful. Positive emotions may now be more often useful than negative ones because life is safer than it was. Also, the smoke detector principle implies that many individual instances of negative emotion will be normal but useless (Nesse 2005). In general, however, the costs of positive emotions and the benefits of negative emotions have been neglected; both areas are ripe for exploration.

Implications for psychopathology are closely related. Emotional disorders are now diagnosed with checklists of symptom severity and duration. With the single exception of grief, diagnostic criteria for depression ignore context. This is biologically nonsensical. To determine if an emotional response is normal requires knowing what situations it was shaped for, and the details of the current situation. Psychiatric diagnosis of emotional disorders remains confused because it has utilized only the proximate half of biology. Progress will come as knowledge about the biological origins and functions of emotions is incorporated (Nesse and Jackson 2006, Wakefield and Horwitz 2007) (see DISORDER (AFFECTIVE, EMOTIONAL)).

An evolutionary perspective has related implications for psychopharmacology. It warns against using drugs to mindlessly block potentially useful negative emotions. However, it also explains why many normal expression of emotion are useless or harmful for this individual in this situation, and they can therefore be blocked safely (Nesse 2005).

Carving emotions at nature's joints

Different emotions were shaped by selection because different situations posed different sets of adaptive challenges (Nesse 1990, Tooby and Cosmides 1990, Plutchik 2003). Each emotion corresponds to some situation that has occurred again and again over evolutionary time. Some such situations are defined by external cues, such as an attacking animal. However, most situations are created from interactions of the internal and external environments; for instance, the emotional reaction to a bowl of ice cream depends on one's appetite, while the emotional impact of a sly wink depends entirely on the motives of the winker, the recipient, and who is watching.

Emotions exist because they offered advantages in situations that recurrently influenced survival and reproduction over evolutionary time. This has major implications for classification. Emotions can be arrayed on dimensions because diverse situations have certain adaptive challenges in common (see DIMENSIONAL MODELS). Two relevant characteristics of all situations are whether they are significant or insignificant to fitness (*arousal), and whether they pose threats of possible loss or offer opportunities to gain useful resources (*valence). Emphasis on valence as a primary characteristic of emotions is well placed (Barrett 2006a). Special states originated in single-celled animals that were capable of only two actions—move forwards (towards resources or away from dangers) or tumble to proceed in some random new direction. This history has left its mark in the separation of neural mechanisms for positive and negative emotions (Gray 1987), and the psychological separation of promotion and prevention states (Higgins 1997).

A third dimension is not a really continuous dimension at all, but the various categories of resources at issue. Food, shelter, status, mates, the security of offspring, allies—the challenges of dealing with possible gain or loss are somewhat different for each different kind of resource (Nesse 1990, Tooby and Cosmides 2000). Opportunities to gain or lose each resource create naturally opposed pairs of states for each domain that can be arrayed on a circumplex (see CIRCUMPLEX MODELS) (Russell and Barrett 1999, Plutchik 2003).

*Basic emotions exist (Ekman 1992b) because organisms have repeatedly encountered consistent situations that posed significant adaptive challenges. Each basic emotion corresponds to such a situation. However, neither the situations nor the corresponding emotions are completely differentiated from each other; different emotions have much in common and merged boundaries. They are not natural kinds in the philosophical sense (Barrett 2006c), but they are states partially differentiated by natural selection whose differences and similarities make sense in light of their origins. This is perhaps the most substantial implication of evolution of emotion research. It is also disturbing, because it implies that much emotions research has been in pursuit of a nonexistent Holy Grail. No clear framework to categorize and describe emotions can be accurate. The emotions are jury-rigged patchworks of neural connections that often succeed in getting the job done. They emerge not from any plan or design that would give them a neat structure, but from slight modifications of previous patchworks.

Emotions are fuzzy sets that adjust many parameters in an N-dimensional space, so they cannot be accurately represented by any metaphor our minds can grasp. However, our minds demand metaphors. How can we represent emotions in a way that gets beyond discrete categories arrayed on just two or three dimensions? Basic emotions are perhaps most similar to the preprogrammed settings on an electronic keyboard. Each mode—classical, rock, jazz, thrash rock, weddings, salsa, etc.—adjusts the presence or absence of various instruments, the volume of each frequency band, the amount of distortion, the background rhythm, the reverberation, the separation, and a host of other parameters. Each mode is separate, but they are built from the same mechanisms and any two modes will have many overlapping characteristics. The analogy is not entirely accurate because emotions are not distinctly separate states, their components are not distinctly separate modules, and individuals differ genetically while keyboards of the same model are all the same.

Individual variations in emotional tendencies are problematic for theories of emotion (see PERSONALITY; APPRAISAL STYLES) (Davidson 2004a). Some people rarely experience anger, others are consumed by it. Some die of unrequited love, others never experience love. Much of this variation arises from genetic differences (Bouchard and Loehlin 2001) that persist for the simple reason that no one genotype is consistently superior (see GENETICS OF AFFECT). The correlation of a given allele with Darwinian fitness varies substantially even within one lifetime, to say nothing of the variations across diverse genetic, physical, and social environments across millions of years. An evolutionary perspective offers the only scientific foundation for studying the generic core of behavioural regulation mechanisms, but this same perspective severely challenges any essentialized view of human nature.

Of course, variations in emotions also arise from different environments. Some result from adaptive systems shaped by selection to monitor environmental cues and adjust emotions accordingly. Other variations arise from cultural influences on schemas that shift appraisals. Finally, much variation in emotions arises from random differences in neuronal migration and receptor expression that will differ even in identical twins, but that can never be measured as the effects of any specifiable environmental factor.

An evolutionary approach implies neither that emotions are genetically determined nor that they should be exactly the same in different individuals. It instead recognizes that variations in emotions arise from complex interactions of genes and environment that create individuals with personal values, goals, and strategies, to say nothing of a sense of self. Much difficulty in emotions research results because a full causal understanding requires idiographic approaches that utilize all the information in personal narratives. Behavioural ecology may eventually better connect idiographic and nomothetic approaches.

Much evolutionary psychology has emphasized the modular structure of mind, proposing that each adaptive challenge shapes the equivalent of a tiny computer specialized to deal with that challenge and emotions as superordinate states that coordinate the actions of thousands of such modules (Tooby and Cosmides 2000). However, an evolutionary approach to emotions by no means requires a commitment to massive modularity. Controversies about modularity (Fodor 2001) should

Fig. E6. Phylogeny of the emotions. From Nesse (2004).

not distract from more general agreement that emotions coordinate many parameters to create special modes of operation well suited to cope with the challenges of certain situations (see SYNCHRONIZATION).

Studying partially differentiated emotions

If emotions are a tangled bank of poorly differentiated entities that are difficult to define and measure, how should we proceed? The same logic that explains why emotions lack a crisp structure also provides a foundation for studying the structure that they do have in terms of the evolutionary histories that shaped them. Beyond the fundamental dichotomy of threat and opportunity, the situations that shape emotions get complicated fast. Different combinations of opportunities

and threat arise in pursuit of each major resource—safety, food, mates, territory, status, etc. Promotion and prevention systems are reunited to deal with situations that involve both opportunities and risks. For instance, the opportunity to get a wonderful partner has involved risks of humiliation so routinely that we expect special states of arousal to deal with that situation.

Figure E6 offers a rough sketch of how selection could have differentiated specific emotions from more general precursor states. The illustration is not entirely accurate—the tree will be different for different species, the actual pathways would have many dead-ends, and selection can undifferentiate specific emotions to deal with more general situations. Also, of course, the diagram

162

Table E1. Emotions for situations that arise in goal pursuit

	Domain	Before	Usual progress	Fast progress	Slow progress	Success	Failure
Opportunity	Physical	**Desire**	**Engagement**	**Flow**	**Frustration**	**Pleasure**	**Pain**
	Social	**Excitement**	**Friendship**	**Pride**	**Anger** **Low mood**	**Happiness**	**Sadness**
Threat	Physical	**Fear**	**Coping**	**Confidence**	**Despair**	**Relief**	**Pain**
	Social	**Anxiety**	**Defensive arousal**	**Confidence**	**Anger**	**Pride**	**Shame** **Embarrassment**

should be in about twenty dimensions. Nonetheless, it represents a step towards a biologically accurate depiction of the relationships among the emotions as overlapping states shaped to deal with situations that have recurrently posed adaptive challenges.

The emphasis on situations does not imply crude fixed responses to simple cues. Far from it. For instance, the pursuit of *goals in general gives rise to situations that have shaped specific emotions (Klinger 1975, Nesse 1990, Carver and Scheier 1998, Keltner *et al.* 2006b). Goal pursuit starts with the detection of opportunity or threat, creating excitement or anxiety. In the midst of goal pursuit there is confidence, and even flow, when things are going well, while obstructions arouse fear and frustration. Rapid progress improves *mood, while lack of progress lowers mood. Reaching the goal results in pleasure or happiness. Failure to reach the goal results in disappointment or sadness. Persisting in pursuit of an unreachable goal arouses depression which eventually disengages all *motivation (Klinger 1975, Nesse 2000). This general model has been recognized at least since Plato (*c.*427–*c.*347 BC). What is new is recognition of why emotions should exist for the situations that arise during goal pursuit. Table E1 categorizes situations in terms of valence (opportunity or threat), global domain (physical or social), and the sequence of situations that often arise in goal pursuit.

Different individuals not only have somewhat different brain mechanisms, they also have different *values and current *concerns. Thus, emotions depend profoundly on culture and cognitive appraisals of the implications of new information for the likelihood of reaching personal goals (see APPRAISAL THEORIES) (Ellsworth and Scherer 2003). Recognition of a pregnancy brings excitement and joy to a woman who wants children, but anxiety and sadness to a woman who finds herself accidentally pregnant. If the capacity for pursuit of personal long-term goals is exclusively human, other species may not have comparable emotions, and some self-conscious emotions may emerge

only after consciousness (Sullivan *et al.* 2003). Looking from a historical perspective, this also means that the emotions we humans experience about future possibilities were derived from precursor emotions in organisms with no capacity for internal representations of the future. The emotions we experience in response to our thoughts about the future must be severely constrained by their origins.

Emotions shaped to cope with generic goal pursuit have been partially specialized to deal with the exigencies of pursuing goals in specific domains; for instance, *jealousy is useful in pursuit of the goal of not losing a partner, *panic makes escape from a predator more likely. However, the evolutionary pathway goes both ways. Specialized emotions can be co-opted for other or more general uses. For instance, it appears that observing moral violations excites the same brain regions as disgust. It is tempting to think of evolution as a planful and progressive process, but it is neither. In the grand sequence things tend to become bigger and more complex because they necessarily started from simple, but in any lineage the direction may be towards increased or decreased specialization and complexity.

Social situations give rise to recurrent situations with important consequences for Darwinian fitness. So, not surprisingly, selection shaped specialized emotions to cope with those situations, especially those that

Table E2. Emotions for situations that arise in social exchanges

You	Other	Before	After
Cooperate	Cooperate	Trust	Gratitude
	Defect	Suspicion	Anger
Defect	Cooperate	Anxiety	Guilt
	Defect	Disgust	Rejection

recurrently arise in personal relationships (Nesse 1990, Keltner and Haidt 1999, Keltner *et al.* 2006a) (see SOCIAL EMOTIONS). Table E2 illustrates some situations that can arise in exchange relationships as they are often portrayed using the Prisoner's Dilemma. These are just a few social emotions, however. Of particular interest are emotions whose expressions have been shaped to extremes because of their signalling function in situations of conflict or commitment (Nesse 2001a). Basic evolutionary theory to deal with such phenomena is still developing. Also of major interest are new insights about how partner choice creates selection for emotions that facilitate cooperation and empathy (Hammerstein 2003, Nesse 2007).

Conclusion

An evolutionary perspective offers a foundation for describing and categorizing emotions in terms of the processes that shaped them. This perspective helps to resolve some long-standing questions about emotions. However, it also implies the disquieting conclusion that much controversy in emotions research has arisen from attempts to discover clear categories and causal pathways that do not exist. Selection shaped emotions with amorphous boundaries and substantial individual variations to deal with imperfectly defined situations. This conclusion could well elicit denial, frustration and anger, but acceptance of the untidy nature of evolved emotions should foster faster progress.

RANDOLPH M. NESSE

Keltner, D. and Haidt, J. (1999). Social functions of emotions at four levels of analysis. *Cognition and Emotion*, **13**, 505–21.

Nesse, R.M. (1990). Evolutionary explanations of emotions. *Human Nature*, **1**, 261–89.

Plutchik, R. (2003). *Emotions and life: perspectives from psychology, biology, and evolution*. Washington, DC: American Psychological Association.

Wakefield, J.C. and Horwitz, A.V. (2007). *The loss of sadness: how psychiatry transformed normal sorrow into depressive disorder*. New York: Oxford University Press.

expectation An expectation is a mental construct generated from past and current experience that serves to disambiguate the future. An expectation is a 'subjective probability linking the future with an outcome at some level of probability ranging from merely possible to virtually certain' (Olson *et al.* 1996, p. 211). Expectancies can concern the self, others, events, and any other global or specific future state of affairs. Expectancies refer to a subset of beliefs that are specific to future occurrences. Expectancies fulfil the important evolutionary function of allowing organisms to make predictions about future contingencies. By utilizing information gathered from experience, an organism has reduced error in predicting and responding to future events. The more accurate the expectation, the better one's forecast.

Sources of expectancies

Expectancies have three primary sources of origin (Wilson and Klaaren 1992). First, an expectation can arise from direct experience with one's own environment. Examples include expectancies derived from classical and operant conditioning. Second, expectancies develop based on communication with others about their experiences. Examples include expectancies gleaned from specific discussions with friends and family, as well as expectancies that are passed along via cultural norms. Finally, an expectation can be constructed by the combination and extrapolation of one's existing knowledge. For example, in a relatively novel experience, an individual may logically deduce what to expect in the novel situation from their knowledge of related situations. Similarly, an individual may conduct mental simulations of an approaching event which can result in the generation of a new expectation.

Dimensions of expectancies

Expectancies vary on at least six dimensions. The position of an expectation on these dimensions determines how it will relate to subsequent thought, affect, and behaviour. First, expectancies differ in the certainty with which they are held. That is, the subjective probability of an expectation can vary (at least theoretically) from 0 to 100. Second, expectancies differ in their level of accessibility. At any given moment, some expectancies have a greater potential for activation than others. Third, expectancies differ in explicitness, with some consciously recognized and openly discussed whereas others have an influence without ever surfacing into conscious awareness. Fourth, expectancies differ in specificity. Some relate to a particular future outcome and others relate to a generalized future outlook or overall anticipated life experience (Bandura 1986). Fifth, expectancies differ temporally, with some expectancies pertaining to proximal events and others pertaining to very distal events. Finally, expectancies differ in their affordance for volitional responding (Kirsch 1999). Many expectancies are volitional expectancies in that they provide information that is valuable for one's future intentional behaviour. Other expectancies are nonvolitional expectancies (also called response expectancies) and concern future events over which an individual anticipates no control (e.g. pain after a surgical procedure).

Consequences of expectancies

Expectancies are a primary conduit by which knowledge and experience are used in managing future activities. As such, expectancies have a wide array of influences and have been a pivotal variable in psychological theories ranging from learning theories, self-regulation theories, expectancy × value models, and theories on stereotyping and health (Rotter 1966, Carver and Scheier 1998). Expectations are important determinants of performance, learning, and memory, as they connect past events and future events. Expectancies also serve as an interpretive frame. They guide attention, encoding, interpretation, and storage of information (Bruner 1957). In addition to influencing the aforementioned variables, expectations have a causal role in the generation of affective reactions, attributions, anxiety, and depression, as well as neurological, physiological, and somatic responding. Typically, expectations produce expectation-consistent, or assimilation, effects. In other words, expectations tend to be self-confirming. Although expectations generally result in assimilation effects, research has revealed that under conditions in which a violation of an expectation is detected, responses can be contrasted with an expectation (Geers and Lassiter 1999).

ANDREW L. GEERS AND JUSTIN A. WELLMAN

expression, emotional see AFFECT BURSTS; ANIMAL EMOTIONS; ANIMAL VOCALIZATIONS; BODILY EXPRESSION OF EMOTION; CORRUGATOR MUSCLE; DISPLAY RULES; DUCHENNE SMILE; ENCODING/DECODING (OF EXPRESSION); EXPRESSION, FUNCTIONS OF EMOTIONAL; EXPRESSION, PRINCIPLES OF EMOTIONAL; ACIAL ACTION CODING SYSTEM; FACIAL EXPRESSION (NEURAL ARCHITECTURE OF); FACIAL EXPRESSION OF EMOTION; FACIAL FEEDBACK HYPOTHESIS; FACIAL IMAGE ANALYSIS AND SYNTHESIS; GESTURAL EXPRESSION OF EMOTION; LAUGHTER; MULTIMODAL EXPRESSION OF EMOTION; PUSH/PULL EFFECTS; RECOGNITION OF EMOTION (NEURAL SYSTEMS FOR); VOCAL EXPRESSION OF EMOTION; VOCAL SYNTHESIS; VOICE PRODUCTION AND ACOUSTICS; ZYGOMATIC MUSCLE.

expression, functions of emotional It is indisputable that facial expressions are instrumental as outward signs communicating the contents of one's internal emotional state (see FACIAL EXPRESSION OF EMOTION). Despite their communicative utility, emotional facial signs, however, do not easily fit with models of language and social communication. The semiotics of verbal language critically distinguishes the sign or signifier (symbol) from the signified (meaning) (see INTERPERSONAL COMMUNICATION). Sign and signified occupy distinct domains, sharing only an arbitrary relationship, with the surface features of the sign having no inherent meaning. By contrast, facial expressions may not be arbitrarily configured, demonstrating significant stereotypy across cultures. Defying linguistic conventions, evidence from facial semiotics suggests that facial signs not only denote associated underlying meaning but that the sign itself may have intrinsic value.

Charles Darwin (1809–82) in his work on emotional expression in human and nonhuman animals suggested that emotional expressions not only serve as social signposts, but originated as functional adaptations for other purposes (Darwin, 1872/1998). The skeleto-motor actions underlying facial expressions were argued to more closely align with physiological expressions of autonomic response—akin to changes in the homeostatic functions of blood flow and respiration. Facial expressions would then not only 'express' emotions but originate in adaptive functions for the sender beyond their well-established signal value. In investigating the evolutionarily older origins of emotionally expressive behaviour, Darwin proposed three evolutionarily derived principles, two of which are directly related to the form of expression: (1) the principle of *serviceable associated habits*—whereby specific facial expressions originate in reflexive patterns of movement serving adaptive functions for the sender—and (2) the principle of *antithesis*—whereby emotions with opposite functions are opposites in physical configuration. For instance, Darwin's fanciful observations in cats and dogs suggested that the reflexive convex arching of the back during fight or flight activation is evolutionarily selected, serving the function to render the animal's appearance larger and more threatening. The opposite or antithetical action—the concave arching of the back—would serve to make the animal appear smaller and submissive. Applying this logic to facial expressions, emotions should have systematic structural relations reflecting their underlying function and associated meaning (Scherer 2001a). The precise form of modern day social–emotional expressions should then be intrinsically significant, bearing some vestige or residue of their underlying functional origin (see PUSH/PULL EFFECTS).

While basic emotions theory implies that distinct emotions should be associated with distinct facial expressions, Darwin's notions of form and function would suggest that different emotional states have specific relationships in their appearance. Examinations of the perceived emotional content of prototypical facial expressions reveals a classic *circumplex structure, where expressions convey not only unique meaning but also *proximal (e.g. fear and surprise) and *distal relations (e.g. fear and disgust) (Fig. E7a) to other expression types. We examined whether these relations between expressions reflect shared deeper meaning or surface form, being read directly off the face itself (Susskind et al. 2007). To examine the role of expression meaning and structure, we compared the performance of human and machine (support vector machine, SVM) in the recognition of facial expression. Six independent SVMs were trained to develop optimal recognition of one of six basic emotional expressions based on inputs similar to that of primary visual cortical receptive fields. With

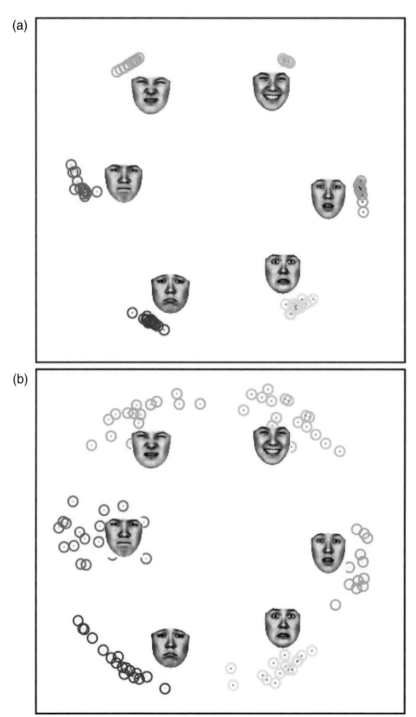

Fig. E7. Comparison of recognition of emotional expression by (a) humans and (b) support vector machines. Multidimensional scaling of ratings (e.g. disgust, fear content) of each of six expression prototypes were projected on two-dimensional space to form an expression circumplex. The similarity between human and machine circumplexes reveals that meaning of an expression is reflected in its form. Open circles represent the locations of each facial expression exemplar. Faces represent the location of the mean of each type of facial expression. Data are from Susskind *et al.* (2007).

no explicit training on similarity or distinctiveness of expressions, the magnitude of activation across emotion-specific SVMs nearly perfectly captured human judgements of the proximal and distal relations among expressions (Fig. E7b). That a mindless, bodiless machine with only access to visual features can capture human perception of facial expressions demonstrates that the meaning of an expression is strikingly mirrored in the expression's appearance. The semiotics of emotional facial expressions suggests that, unlike verbal language, sign and signified are highly correlated as Darwinian models would predict. A close correspondence between facial expression form and meaning suggests that the precise form that facial signs take has intrinsic importance, and thus the origins of facial expressions are unlikely to be in communication alone.

Why then do facial expressions of emotional states appear as they do? It has long been argued that facial expressions contribute to an emotion's unique phenomenological experience. However, linked to emotional experience, the role of facial and bodily efference to emotional phenomenology is likely to be a secondary by-product of more primary adaptations associated with different emotional states. According to a Darwinian adaptionist programme, the origin of facial expressions may lie most directly in serving to alter the sensory systems whose receptors reside on the face, altering exposure to environmental stimulation. In addition to the signal value they confer, the origin of certain facial expressive actions would then be in the service of regulating sensory intake. As depicted in the circumplex model, evidence for the sensory regulation hypothesis can be seen in the similarity and opposition in meaning (Figure E7a) and form (Figure E7b) of expression. Consistent with the principles of antithesis and associated habits, close inspection of the circumplex reveals the expression form and meaning are associated with an opposing dimension of relative eye opening (fear and surprise) and closure (disgust and anger) that may underlie a primitive sensory regulatory function. This notion is consistent with the *component process model of emotions (Scherer 2001a), whereby emotions are thought of as constellations of overlapping subcomponents that represent distinct stimulus evaluation checks or appraisals by the organism. Increased eye opening, for instance, would be an *action tendency related to increased orienting toward a novel or unexpected stimulus. If the stimulus is an impending threat, this would evoke an opposing action tendency of closing off the senses, as indicated by eye closure, and rejection of and protection from the stimulus.

Following Darwin's logic of looking for cross-species continuities for the functional origin of emotional ex-

pressions, eye closure–opening has both special functional and signal value across primates. Nonhuman primates close their eyes and flatten their ears as part of the startle defensive reflex, which serve as a set of innate protective actions to reduce exposure of the sensory organs. Such innate reflexes also serve as important communicative functions, signalling looming threats to conspecifics (Andrew 1963b). In humans, comprehension of expression and the role of the *amygdala therein are specifically related to the critical signal value of the eyes (Adolphs et al. 2005a). Whereas the amygdala is important for learning to recognize the importance of the eyes for social communication, patients with lesions of the amygdala demonstrate remarkably intact production of facial expressions (Anderson and Phelps 2000), suggesting that facial actions associated with sensory regulation may depend on innate, evolutionarily older, motor programmes. Thus, signal value probably follows functional value. Facial actions originally serving primarily as functional adaptations come to serve secondarily as a preadaptation for social communication, only later acquiring significance as 'facial expressions'.

In sum, the form of a facial expression may be specifically shaped by forces from our hominid evolutionary past as functional adaptations for the sender. One such original role may have been to regulate sensory exposure and intake. The capacity for nonverbal emotional communication is likely to have piggy-backed on such primitive functional origins of forms of facial expression. The significant utility of facial expressions in the present day may reflect this dual role—to promote greater fitness in navigating both the social and the physical environment.

ADAM K. ANDERSON

Marsh, A.A., Adams, R.B., Jr, and Kleck, R.E. (2005). Why do fear and anger look the way they do? Form and social function in facial expressions. *Personality and Social Psychology Bulletin*, **31**, 73–86.

expression, principles of emotional As the etymology of the term 'expression' implies, there has always been a fundamental assumption that internal thoughts and feelings are externalized, literally pushed out, in the form of sounds, words, or facial and bodily movements. In a pioneering book, Darwin (1872/1998) reviewed earlier work and provided, in addition to a rich inventory of observational evidence, a functional theory of expression based on comparative, developmental, and cross-cultural considerations. His claim that there were emotion-specific patterns of expression that served important functions in the adaptation of the organism to the eliciting situation was revived by Tomkins (1962) and in turn by Ekman (1972) and Izard (1971), whose work on facial expression had a central impact on the development of modern emotion psychology (see FACIAL EXPRESSION OF EMOTION). Darwin also mentioned the voice as an important modality of expression and communication, and much of the recent work on vocal expression is based on his functional approach (Scherer 1985) (see VOCAL EXPRESSION OF EMOTION).

While widely accepted in many different disciplines studying emotional expression, this functional view has been challenged by sociobiologically oriented researchers (e.g. Dawkins and Krebs 1978) who deny the role of expressive displays as signs of underlying emotions and adaptive reactions to eliciting events and argue for a view that considers these displays as exclusively social signals or messages, intentionally produced for strategic and often deceptive purposes. While protagonists of the dominant functional view also predict that expressive signals will often be strategically manipulated and thus provide false signals of underlying emotions, they consider the success of such a strategy to be entirely dependent on the fact that the expression often *is* a true signal of actually existing emotion reactions and behaviour intentions— and thus of central importance for the regulation of social interaction (Scherer 1985). In addition, we now have the first evidence for some of Darwin's functional explanations (see EXPRESSION, FUNCTIONS OF EMOTIONAL) (e.g. Susskind *et al.* 2008) as well as indirect

evidence from recognition studies that an emotion view of expression is more plausible than a social message view (Scherer and Grandjean 2008).

Most importantly, proponents of an extreme social message view fail to explain why the assumption that expression reveals something about the underlying emotional reaction is incompatible with the notion that the same mechanism serves communicative purposes. Indeed, expression is *multifunctional*. Bühler (1934/1990) postulated that any sign always has three facets: it functions as a symptom (of the sender's state), as a symbol (of a socially shared meaning category), and as an appeal (a social message toward others). Bühler insisted that a sign is all of these things at the same time. As shown in Fig. E8, this conceptualization can be directly applied to expressions of emotion which function as a symptom (of the sender's underlying cognitive and emotional state), as a symbol (an emotion concept), and as an appeal (signalling reaction, behaviour tendencies, and action requests) (see Scherer 1992). As the ethological evidence suggests (e.g. Leyhausen 1967), there is strong pressure exerted by impression (pull) factors on expression (push) factors (see PUSH/PULL EFFECTS) during the course of the evolution of communication in socially living species. Concretely, signal production that was originally determined by internal,

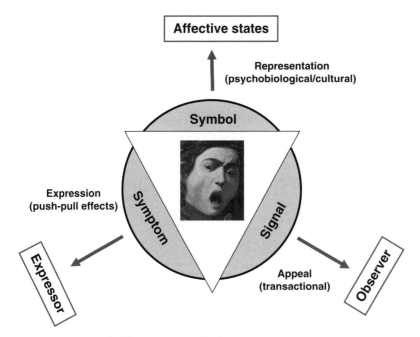

Fig. E8. A revised version of Bühler's Organon model of signs.

physiological factors may be increasingly shaped by criteria linked to impression, perception by the observer, in the direction of greater easy and accuracy of recognition (Scherer 1985). Bühler's model reminds expression researchers that: (1) expressive behaviours, while variable over contexts, individuals, and cultures, do have a symbolic, representational function which is directly linked to the question of the categorization of diffuse emotional feelings and the use of verbal labels to refer to such categories, and (2) that the process of expression should be studied as a process which includes transmission and impression, as suggested by the *Brunswikian lens model.

Except for Darwin, there has been surprisingly little concern about the nature of the presumed mechanism underlying expression. With respect to emotion, there are two major competing positions specifying testable predictions: (1) Discrete or basic emotion theories (Tomkins 1962, Izard 1971, Ekman 1972), postulating that affect programmes for *basic emotions, such as anger, fear, sadness, and joy, produce prototypical response configurations that include emotion-specific patterns of expressions. (2) *Componential emotion models (Scherer 1985, 2001a, Smith and Scott 1997), postulating that the individual elements of facial expression are determined by appraisal results and their effects on motor behaviour (see APPRAISAL THEORIES). While both models adopt a functional approach based on Darwin, they differ with respect to the scope and level of predetermination of the predicted expression patterns. Past research has shown little evidence for frequent occurrence of the well-formed, prototypical, and highly emotion-specific expression patterns or configurations that would be expected as the result of affect programmes (see Scherer and Ellgring 2007a). Importantly, there are modality-specific factors to be taken into account for facial, vocal, and gestural expessions (see GESTURAL EXPRESSION OF EMOTION).

KLAUS R. SCHERER

externalizer An externalizer tends to show greater overt emotional expression (see FACIAL EXPRESSION OF EMOTION), but lower *electrodermal responses. Generally, the externalizer–internalizer dimension refers to the degree to which individuals inhibit their expressive behaviour at the cost of increased physiological arousal. The dimension was originally explored in the 1930s by H. E. Jones and studied further by Jack Block in the 1950s (Block 1957), who studied individual differences in electrodermal responsiveness. Block's scale has been developed into the Affect Expression Rating Scale (AERS) by Buck and colleagues (Buck and Powers 2005).

Compared with internalizers, externalizers are more expressive and less conforming; but also more impulsive (see IMPULSIVITY) and attention seeking. In most emotion-arousing situations, adult females generally tended to show the externalizing pattern of more overt expression, but less electrodermal response. This sex difference is not observed in preschool children and may result from sex-role related differences in emotion socialization.

The externalizer–internalizer dimension has connections to theories across a number of psychological domains. It also has important implications for socio-emotional development, emotional education, and the development of emotional competence. Emotional communication may be disrupted at both extremes of the externalizer–internalizer dimension: while the extreme internalizer fails to display emotion, the extreme externalizer may show complex and uncoordinated displays which are difficult for others to understand. In either case, coherent feedback from others about emotion (social biofeedback) is disrupted, potentially leading to problems in emotion labelling and understanding (*alexithymia). This disruption relates to the classification of psychopathology into externalizing and internalizing categories, which may be associated with hyperexpressive and hypoexpressive alexithymia, respectively.

Generally, externalizers should have less reactive physiological responses; have higher self-esteem and be less susceptible to punishment; show fewer stress-related physiological effects; and should be more likely to suffer from antisocial personality and substance abuse disorders. See also INTERNALIZER.

ROSS BUCK AND R. THOMAS BOONE

extraversion and introversion Extraversion and introversion typically appear together as a pair of words. They describe the opposite poles of a dimension of human personality variation. This dimension is often referred to as a trait; that is, a tendency towards certain feelings and behaviours. The words have origins in Jung's psychology, but the present-day scientific usage is different.

The extraversion–introversion dimension is most commonly measured in humans using a personality inventory. There are many such inventories, and most of them contain this dimension or something akin to it. Many of the inventories are self-reported. This means that individuals answer questions about how they typically feel and act. Some inventories also have forms which can be completed by other people, in which they report how some person known to them tends to feel and behave.

The extraversion–introversion dimension is a broad dimension of personality. This means that it comprises a number of constituent, narrower traits, all of which tend to correlate in a population. Two of the best known personality theories, each of which has its own measurement instrument (personality inventory), are those of H. J. Eysenck and of Costa and McCrae. The constituent, intercorrelated traits thought by Eysenck to comprise extraversion–introversion are: sociable, venturesome, lively, surgent, sensation-seeking, carefree, active, dominant, and assertive. Eysenck devised several personality scales. One widely used instrument is the Eysenck Personality Questionnaire—Revised (Eysenck et al. 1985). In addition to a measure of extraversion–introversion, it has measures of the personality traits of *neuroticism and psychoticism. It also has a Lie scale, which can be used to identify people who tend to make socially desirable responses. There are full (100 items) and shorter (48 items) forms of the questionnaire. The personality instrument devised by Costa and McCrae has a dimension of extraversion that has six facets: warmth, gregariousness, assertiveness, activity, excitement seeking, and positive emotions. The questionnaire associated with this model of human personality variation is the Revised NEO–Personality Inventory (Costa and McCrae 1992). It has both self-rated and other-rated forms. It has 240 questions: 48 for each of five broad personality dimensions and, within the 48, eight questions for each of the six facets that comprise each dimension. The five dimensions in the Costa and McCrae model are extraversion, neuroticism, openness, agreeableness, and conscientiousness. A shorter questionnaire, the NEO–Five Factor Inventory, has 60 questions, with twelve for each of the five broad dimensions. The shorter questionnaire does not measure the facets.

There are two broad, though connected, research streams that led to a general consensus about the dimensional structure of human personality and the prominent and especially well-agreed place of extraversion–introversion within that. The first stream is the lexical research on personality (Saucier and Goldberg 2001). From the 1930s onwards, psychologists have gone through the English, and now many other, language lexicons, looked for personality descriptors, and have studied how these are related to each other. That is, they look for groups of words within the dictionary whose usage about a person's personality tends to be correlated. Thus, for example, in the work of Goldberg (2006), the following are closely correlated English trait terms related to extraversion–introversion: vivacious, extroverted, quiet, reserved, introverted, daring, gregarious, shy, talkative, timid, and unexcitable. Which of these terms occur at the two poles of the dimension should be obvious. In what is called emic research on personality trait terms, the lexicons of other culture's languages have been analysed and, although the same number and types of personality factors do not always

appear, the extraversion–introversion factor is one of the most reproducible. Most languages encode this dimension of human variation prominently and importantly.

The second stream of research that leads to the conclusion that extraversion–introversion is a prominent human personality dimension is work on personality questionnaires. This stream is related to the first because some of the early personality questionnaires, such as Cattell's, can be traced back to early work on the lexicon. A substantial proportion of the research on this topic was done by Costa and McCrae (1992) and McCrae and Costa (2005). They and others have taken numbers of different personality questionnaires, administered them to large samples, and studied their correlations. Even where questionnaires do not explicitly identify a dimension of extraversion–introversion by name, they often contain a dimension that relates strongly to it. Other work on personality questionnaires in different cultures is called etic research. This involves translating widely used inventories, such as those of Eysenck and Costa and McCrae, into many different languages (McCrae and Costa 1997). In almost all cases the dimensions, especially extraversion–introversion, can be measured effectively in different cultures. This work and the emic work point to extraversion–introversion being a human universal; a dimension of human variation found across human cultures. Even beyond that, extraversion–introversion, or similar dimensions, appear as prominent personality traits in different species, including chimpanzees, rhesus macaques, dogs, and horses (Gosling 2001).

The distribution of people's extraversion–introversion scores in most samples is normal, or bell-shaped. Most people have an intermediate score on the dimension, with relatively few people who are very extraverted or very introverted. People's own scores on extraversion–introversion find moderately strong agreement when they are rated by other people who know them (McCrae et al. 2004). Almost by definition, a personality trait should show some stability; it should not be unpredictable. A person's traits should be something quite lasting about them. Stability in personality can mean two things. First, whether the mean level of the trait changes with age: extraversion tends to decline from young to old adulthood (McCrae and Costa 2005). The other type of stability is the stability of individual differences; whether people who tend to be extraverted, intermediate, or introverted are still in their respective positions when studied again some years later. The finding is that there is high stability of extraversion–introversion differences over several years (Roberts and Del Vecchio 2000). Even within children, when appropriate instruments are used, the extraversion–introversion dimension shows the stability of individual differences. Part of the difference in extraversion–introversion, perhaps between a third and a half, is caused by genetic factors (Matthews *et al.* 2003). Most of the rest of the variation appears to be due to people's unique environmental experience, that which has not been shared by members of their rearing family.

Does the extraversion–introversion personality dimension matter? People who score more toward the extraversion side of the dimension tend to be happier, and report less low mood (Diener and Seligman 2002). This greater happiness is partly the result of their taking part in more social activities, and partly due to their social competence.

IAN J. DEARY

McCrae, R.R. and Costa, P.T. (2005). *Personality in adulthood*, 2nd edn. New York: Guilford Press.

Matthews, G., Deary, I.J., and Whiteman, M.C. (2003). *Personality traits*, 2nd edn. Cambridge: Cambridge University Press.

eye blink The eye blink is largely due to contraction of the orbicularis oculi facial muscle which is innervated by the facial nerve (cranial nerve VII), the nucleus of which receives input from various locations in the brainstem and midbrain. This means that the blink response can be used to quantify activity in the central nervous system. Measures of the blink response include lid movement (using a lid potentiometer, photocell, or electro-oculogram (EOG)) and muscle contraction (electromyogram (EMG)) (see ELECTROMYOGRAPHY) of the orbicularis oculi (Blumenthal *et al.* 2005). The EMG measure is the most sensitive, since it can be seen at levels of activation too low to overcome the inertia of the eyelid and can provide more precise information about *startle elicitation and modulation. The EMG can also be used to measure blinking when the eyes are closed or during sleep. Blinks can be spontaneous, voluntary (on demand or intentional), or reflexive (elicited by a sudden sound, light, puff of air, electrical pulse, or mechanical tap to the face). The spontaneous blink rate can be increased by social anxiety, and increasing cognitive load in an information processing task can delay blinking until the end of the task. Voluntary blinks can be used as a communication tool by 'locked-in' patients who are unable to speak or move muscles below the face. Reflexive blinks can be used to evaluate a variety of physiological and psychological phenomena, such as the application of modulation of the startle response as a measure in emotion and clinical research. Modulation of the startle response involves a short-latency eyeblink which is larger when the individual is processing unpleasant (negatively valenced) than pleasant (positively valenced) stimuli, such as pictures, sounds, smells, or imagined situations (Bradley *et al.* 2006). This means that modulation of the blink response is useful in evaluating affective motivation, differences within and across individuals in the emotional impact of stimuli, and changes in emotional reactivity as a function of clinical intervention.

TERRY D. BLUMENTHAL

F

Facial Action Coding System The Facial Action Coding System (FACS) is a comprehensive, anatomically based system to measure facial behaviour. Created by Ekman and Friesen in 1978, the FACS identifies over 40 functionally independent actions of the facial muscles known as *action units (AUs). FACS coding allows for each AU to be coded for its occurrence, singly or in combination with other AUs. Depending on the level of complexity and the research questions, FACS coding can also involve coding of the timing characteristics of each innervated AU, including its beginning (onset), peak (apex), and disappearance (offset). FACS coding can also involve coding of each AU's laterality (unilateral, bilateral, or asymmetrical) and intensity on a five-point scale.

Although it was originally created on the basis of research examining facial expressions of emotion (see FACIAL EXPRESSION OF EMOTION), FACS coding can be used to measure any facial behaviour, not just those limited to emotional displays. Facial behaviours can serve many purposes—to illustrate speech, as conversation regulators, as emblematic gestures, and as emotional signals. The facial muscles are also used for speech and chewing. FACS coding can describe the muscles used in any and all of these functions of the facial muscles. For this reason, the FACS has been used in many different types of studies of facial behaviour, not limited to those examining emotional expressions (Ekman and Rosenberg 2005).

In creating the FACS, Ekman and Friesen electrically stimulated individual muscles in their faces and observed the changes in appearance that were produced. They noted that the facial mimetic muscles were different from other muscles in the body, as they are often attached on one side to bone and the other side to skin. Some are not attached to bone at all (e.g. the orbicularis oris, the muscle in the lips). Thus, these muscles may be specialized for social communication. Also, some muscles can move in multiple ways despite the fact that they are anatomically a single muscle. The frontalis muscle across the forehead, for example, can move only in the middle, raising the inner corners of the eyebrows, and on the outside, raising the outer corners of the eyebrows. The *corrugator muscle group, however, comprises three muscles, and when one is innervated they are all innervated, lowering the brows down and

together. For these reasons, facial measurement systems based on structural anatomy cannot accurately describe human facial behaviour, which is why the FACS is based on functional, not structural, anatomy.

Because FACS coding is comprehensive, it can be time-consuming and costly. For this reason, Ekman and colleagues have developed the Emotion FACS (EMFACS), in which coding is limited specifically to facial movements related to discrete emotion signals (Ekman and Friesen 1982, Matsumoto *et al.* 1991). There is also an emotion dictionary that is available to researchers who have FACS data and would like to obtain predictions of emotional states associated with their data (Levenson 2005).

FACS coding is based on the appearance changes in the face that occur when specific action units are innervated. Because the faces of infants are different, especially in the amount of fatty deposits, adjustments to FACS for use with infants led to the creation of BabyFACS (Oster 2004). Likewise, because the facial anatomy and appearance changes are different in chimpanzees, adjustments to FACS has led to the creation of a ChimpFACS that can be used in studies of the facial behaviours of chimps (Burrows *et al.* 2006). FACS and all of its related tools—EMFACS, BabyFACS, ChimpFACS—offer researchers reliable, comprehensive tools to study all of the functions of the face.

DAVID MATSUMOTO

facial expression (neural architecture of) Although the psychological and neural mechanisms involved in the *recognition* of facial expressions of emotion are starting to be elucidated (see RECOGNITION OF EMOTION (NEURAL SYSTEMS FOR)), much less is known about the mechanisms responsible for the *production* of facial expressions (see ENCODING/DECODING (OF EXPRESSION)). Understanding the neural architecture of the production of facial expression is particularly critical, because it opens windows on the functions of emotion in terms of social communication, display of underlying cognitive processes, and direct interaction with the physical environment (see FACIAL EXPRESSION OF EMOTION) (Susskind *et al.* 2008).

In terms of anatomy, most facial muscles attach to the facial skin or fascia, and are innervated by the seventh cranial nerve (also called the facial nerve). Although other muscles, such as the masseter and the eye muscles, are innervated by the third, fourth, fifth, or sixth cranial nerves, we will focus here on the activity of the muscles innervated by the facial nerve.

Facial expressions take their origin in motor neurons of the nuclei of the facial nerves (the facial nuclei), located in the ventrolateral region of the inferior pons. Neural motor impulses reach the facial muscles via the fibres of the facial nerves, which leave the skull from a hole called the stylomastoid foramen, before dividing into five major branches. The facial nucleus is similar across human and nonhuman primates, and lower mammals (e.g. rabbits, dogs, cats), except for the fact that it contains more neurons innervating muscles of the mouth and lower face in humans than in lower mammals (allowing for a high degree of fine and controlled movement, as required for speech). In lower mammals, compared with humans, it also contains more neurons innervating the upper face and auricular muscles (which allow ear movements as part of the orienting response). Five cortical areas send motor impulses to the facial nuclei via a direct and an indirect corticobulbar tract. Direct fibres synapse directly onto the motor neurons of the facial nucleus, whereas indirect fibres pass through inter-neurons of the brainstem reticular formation. It is interesting to note that the primary motor cortex (MI) and the lateral premotor cortex (LPMC), as well as the medially lying caudal cingulate motor cortex (CMCc), innervate primarily the contralateral facial nucleus, and here mainly the motor neurons of the lower-face muscles (see Fig. F1). In contrast, the supplementary motor area (SMA) and rostral cingulate motor cortex (CMCr), both located on the medial wall of each hemisphere, project bilaterally onto ipsi- and contralateral upper-face motor neurons of both facial nuclei. Thus, cortical innervation is rather unilateral for the lower face but bilateral for the upper face. In parallel, a bilateral indirect corticobulbar pathway passes through interneurons of the brainstem reticular formations, and thus allows for subcortical (e.g. from the basal ganglia, *amygdala, hypothalamus, periaqueductal grey) modulation of cortical motor commands. Facial movements may also directly originate subcortically, and reach the facial nucleus via the reticular formation. Interestingly, these indirect pathways influence mainly motor neurons of the facial nucleus innervating the upper face (Rinn 1984).

Importantly, emotional and voluntary facial expressions seem to arise from partly different neural circuitries. This hypothesis stems mainly from the observation in neurological patients of a double dissociation between emotional facial paresis (EFP) and volitional facial paresis (VFP) (Hopf *et al.* 1992). The former is a neuro-

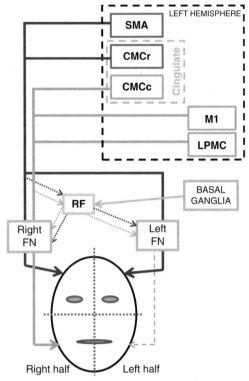

Fig. F1. The main corticobulbar and subcortical projections. The facial nuclei receive inputs from cortical motor areas via a direct and an indirect corticobulbar tract. Along the direct corticobulbar tract (plain lines) the muscles of the lower face are mainly innervated contralaterally, whereas the muscles of the upper face receive bilateral cortical input. The indirect corticobulbar pathway (dotted lines), passing through interneurons of the brainstem reticular formation, carries cortical motor commands to upper- and lower-face motor neurons of both facial nuclei. It allows for subcortical motor impulses and for subcortical modulation of cortical motor commands, but influences mainly facial nucleus motor neurons projecting to the upper face. Spontaneous expressions may at least partly depend on motor areas of the cingulate cortex (CMCr and CMCc), in addition to subcortical areas. CMCc, caudal cingulate motor area; CMCr, rostral cingulate motor area; FN, facial nucleus; LPMC, lateral premotor cortex; M1, primary motor cortex; RF, reticular formation; SMA, supplementary motor area.

logical disorder leading to the loss of the capacity to show emotional facial expressions (e.g. smiling at a joke), often only on one side of the face, in the absence of any impairment of the ability to contract facial muscles voluntarily. EFP can occur due to lesions of the thalamus, the striatocapsular area, the frontal subcortical white matter, the insula, the medial frontal lobe including the SMA, or the dorsolateral pontine tegmentum area. The more commonly observed VFP leads to difficulties in moving facial muscles of the lower face voluntarily, but does not affect a person's emotional facial expressions. VFP is commonly observed with lesions of contralateral M1 and/or LPMC or along the corticobulbar tract descending to the facial nucleus.

Recent neuroimaging studies have partly confirmed this emotional/voluntary dissociation. For example, Iwase *et al.* (2002) employed positron emission tomography (PET) and Wild *et al.* (2006) used functional magnetic resonance imaging (fMRI) together with amusing film clips and cartoons to investigate spontaneous smiling/laughter. Lateral somatomotor areas including M1 were found to be more active during voluntary smiles. In contrast, spontaneous smiling led to activation of more rostral and medial cortical structures, such as the pre-SMA and the cingulate motor areas, as well as of subcortical structures including the basal ganglia and amygdala.

In conclusion, the precise anatomical substrates of spontaneous versus voluntary facial expressions in humans remain unclear to date. Voluntary and spontaneous facial movements have long been thought to originate in cortical and subcortical structures, respectively. However, as newer studies suggest, areas of the cingulate cortex may be relevant for spontaneous facial movements as well. Providing higher temporal resolution than PET and fMRI, event related potentials (ERPs)—in particular if combined with facial electromyography—constitute a further valuable technique, which may allow the investigation of the temporal dynamic and neurophysiological underpinnings of the preparation and execution of facial expressions (Korb *et al.* 2008).

SEBASTIAN KORB AND DAVID SANDER

Morecraft, R.J., Stilwell-Morecraft, K.S., and Rossing, W.R. (2004). The motor cortex and facial expression: new insights from neuroscience. *Neurologist*, **10**, 235–49.

Rinn, W.E. (1984). The neuropsychology of facial expression: a review of the neurological and psychological mechanisms for producing facial expressions. *Psychological Bulletin*, **95**, 52–77.

facial expression of emotion Many theories of emotion suggest that when emotions are elicited, they recruit a host of responses, which include expressive behaviours, physiological reactions, certain types of cognitions, and subjective experience (Ekman 1993, Levenson 1999). The expressive behaviours involve many types of nonverbal behaviours, including facial expressions, voice, and posture. Darwin (1872/1998) claimed, in his principle of serviceable habits, that facial expressions are the residual actions of more complete behavioural

responses. Thus, we express anger by furrowing the brow and tightening the lips with teeth displayed because these actions are part of an attack response; we express disgust with an open mouth, nose wrinkle, and tongue protrusion as part of a vomiting response. Facial expressions, then, are elements of a coordinated response involving multiple response systems.

Although there is general agreement concerning the link between emotion and facial expression, there are controversies concerning the exact nature and strength of this linkage, and its source. On the one hand, a large number of studies in which emotions were actually elicited and immediate facial behaviours were actually measured in precise, moment-to-moment fashion have demonstrated that discrete facial expressions of emotion are produced when emotions are aroused (Matsumoto *et al.* 2008). The facial configurations that have been found correspond to the universal facial expressions of emotion originally posited by Darwin (with some exceptions), and later documented by Ekman and his colleagues, and the available studies have involved individuals from a wide range of cultures. More recent studies have documented that blind individuals, as well as nonhuman primates, display the same facial configurations when emotions are aroused, suggesting a biologically innate source for them (see UNIVERSALITY OF EMOTIONS).

On the other hand, there are also a fair number of studies that report that facial expressions do not necessarily occur when emotions are aroused. They highlight the fact that people can have emotions without producing any facial expression, and they can fabricate facial expressions without any emotion. These studies point to the need for the field to identify the circumstances under which facial expressions will or will not occur when emotion is aroused.

When they do occur, facial expressions have both intra- and inter-personal functions. The intrapersonal functions of emotion and expressive behaviour suggest that select facial expressions will co-vary with emotional experience, physiological responses, certain types of cognitions. And this is generally what has been found (Matsumoto *et al.* 2008). Facial expressions that accompany actual emotional experience are more reliable signals; they act as commitment devices to likely courses of action that are momentarily beyond the individual's volitional control. They are part of a package of coherent responses that prepare an individual to deal with the emotion-eliciting stimulus.

Facial expressions of emotion are more than simple readouts of internal states; they coordinate social interactions through their informative, evocative, and incentive functions (Keltner and Kring 1998). They provide information to perceivers about the individual's emotional state, behavioural intentions, relational status *vis-à-vis* the target of the expression, and objects and events in the social environment. Thus, an individual's emotional expression serves as a 'social affordance' which evokes 'prepared' responses in others. *Anger, for example, might have evolved to elicit fear-related responses and the inhibition of inappropriate action (Dimberg and Ohman 1996). Distress calls might have evolved to elicit sympathetic responses in observers (Eisenberg *et al.* 1989). Through these processes, emotional communication helps individuals in relationships—parent and child, mates, boss and subordinates—respond to the demands and opportunities of their social environment. They are basic elements of social interaction, from flirtatious exchanges to greeting rituals.

DAVID MATSUMOTO

facial feedback hypothesis Tracing its inspiration to Charles Darwin (1809–82) and William James' (1842–1910) statements that advocate the role of expressive behaviour in the experience of emotion (see FACIAL EXPRESSION OF EMOTION), this hypothesis asserts that facial muscular activity provides sensory feedback (proprioceptive, cutaneous, or vascular signals) that influence emotional experience. A strong version of the facial feedback hypothesis (FFH) states that appropriate patterns of facial activity can generate emotional experience even without eliciting stimuli (initiation hypothesis). According to a weaker version, facial action can strengthen or attenuate people's emotional experience in response to eliciting emotional stimuli (modulation hypothesis). An additional distinction has been made between dimensional (e.g. negative–positive dimension) and categorical (e.g. *basic emotions, such as happiness, sadness, anger) perspectives of the FFH. Empirical tests of the FFH have usually employed facial simulation (i.e. the simulation of facial expressions that represent particular emotions) or exaggeration–suppression procedures. More recently, new paradigms (e.g. oral pencil-holding technique) have been developed to take into account the flaws in standard procedures which were potentially contaminated by experimental demands and cognitive mediation (e.g. recognition of the emotional meaning of facial behaviour, self-perception). Although the facial action effects have been shown to be moderate, the experimental literature has generally provided evidence that voluntary facial activity may influence self-reported emotional experience, and to some extent, autonomic response patterns (McInstosh 1996). For example, *Duchenne smiles were found to increase positive experience and autonomic reactivity in adults exposed to video clips of pleasant stimuli and funny cartoons (Soussignan 2002).

ROBERT SOUSSIGNAN

facial image analysis and synthesis Facial expression (see FACIAL EXPRESSION OF EMOTION) has been central to the study of emotion for over 100 years (Darwin 1872/1998). Much of what we have learned was made possible by technological breakthroughs: photography in the 19th century and film and later video in the 20th. Today, two new technologies are just beginning to make their potential felt. These are automated facial image analysis and facial image synthesis. A recent review of the former can be found in Cohn and Kanade (2007). Here we summarize major approaches to facial image synthesis of identity and static and dynamic changes in facial expression. Synthesis of dynamic sequences is referred to as animation.

The anatomical structure of the face consists of layers of bone, muscle, subcutaneous fat, and skin. Facial expression results from complex, nonlinear interactions among these layers. For the animator attempting to simulate facial appearance or expression, the question is how best to represent these layers and model interactions between them.

These questions can be approached from three perspectives. One utilizes computer graphics, a second image processing, and a third integrates both. Graphics-based approaches offer a high degree of flexibility, are computationally inexpensive, and can be integrated easily into animation systems for full-bodied avatars. Most commercial systems use this approach. Image-based approaches are computationally more expensive, more limited in the range of facial expression, and cannot animate full-body avatars. They can, however, produce stunning realism. Hybrid approaches that combine computer graphics and image processing are just emerging.

Computer graphics-based synthesis

Graphics-based approaches represent the surface of the face as vertices in a three-dimensional (3D) space. The vertices are connected to form a triangulated mesh that approximates the skin. By manipulating the position of the vertices, changes in facial appearance and expression result. Early systems adopted a *keyframe* approach, in which the animator painstakingly specified the movement of each vertex at set points in time. The vertex positions were then interpolated to generate the *in-between* frames (a technique known as *tweening*). A breakthrough occurred when animators learned to control groups of vertices using a single control parameter. All graphics-based approaches synthesize images by acting on the facial mesh either directly or indirectly.

Directly parameterized models make no attempt to represent the detailed anatomical structure of the face. Instead, a collection of meshes, known as morph-targets, is defined that specify changes in a mesh relative to a default

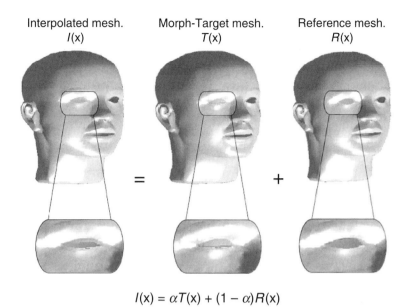

Interpolated mesh.
$I(x)$

Morph-Target mesh.
$T(x)$

Reference mesh.
$R(x)$

$$I(x) = \alpha T(x) + (1 - \alpha)R(x)$$

Fig. F2. Illustration of directly parameterized facial animation. Each image consists of 5,828 vertices in a 3D space, connected to form 11,370 triangles. The image on the right is a reference face model in a default pose. The central image illustrates a morph-target, where the right (from the point of view of the model) eye-lid has closed. The image on the left is a weighted average of the vertices of the reference and morph-target meshes. A complete facial animation system would contain a sufficient number of morph-targets to define all facial actions of interest. The greater the number of morph-targets, the more subtle the animation produced. Adapted from (Pighin, Hecker, Lischinski, Szeliski, and Salesin, 1998).

pose (Fig. F2). Interpolating the morph-targets and combining the resultant facial gestures produces facial expressions. Each parameter of a directly parameterized model controls the amount of interpolation between the reference mesh and a morph-target. An advantage of this approach is that the parameters have a direct, physical, intuitive meaning (e.g. lip-rounding or eye-blinking), which makes them attractive for non-experts in facial kinematics.

Whereas the directly parameterized approach models only the changes visible on the surface of the face, the *indirectly parameterized approach* models interactions among all layers of the face. For this reason, they are often referred to as physically based models. They have two advantages over directly parameterized models: (1) Because the parameters do not act directly on the mesh, the model is not tied to a particular mesh topology. The mesh can be modified without the cost of updating parameters, and any number of meshes can be animated using a single parameterization. (2) Face models can be defined in terms of the *Facial Action Coding System (FACS) (Ekman *et al.* 2002). Parameters can be designed to have a one-to-one mapping to FACS *action units. Disadvantages include: (1) Because knowledge of facial

kinematics is assumed, nonexperts may require trial-and-error to generate realistic expressions. (2) While muscle vectors are not tied to a particular mesh topology, they must be *married* to a mesh before they can be used. The location of each muscle within the model must be defined, and errors can produce unexpected results. (3) Physically based animation is more computationally expensive than directly parameterized animation, although with advances in hardware this difference fades.

For both directly parameterized and physically based animation, long sequences of realistic and complex expression are difficult to generate. Key-framing, even for groups of vertices, can quickly become tedious as each parameter must be manually specified in all key-frames. A more efficient but less flexible alternative is to capture motion data from the face of an actor and then use a predefined correspondence between points on the actor's face and the vertices of the mesh model.

Computer graphics-based models are usually adopted when video-realism is not required or when an application must be computationally efficient. They are particularly suited to web-based applications as they require a relatively low bandwidth. When video-realism is required, image-based methods are usually preferable.

facial image analysis and synthesis

Image-based synthesis

In contrast to graphics-based approaches, image-based synthesis uses images of real faces rather than a geometric model. Image-based animation uses a number of images to capture subtle variation in facial shape and appearance. The key is how to create a realistic transition from one expressive image to another. Two main approaches are *image morphing* and *image concatenation*.

Image morphing is similar to traditional graphics-based key-frame animation using morph-targets. However, rather than representing key-frames as mesh poses, static images of prespecified facial expressions are selected. The pixel values within key-frames are interpolated to create the in-between frames.

The pixels in the key-frames are interpolated using optical flow. This approach involves a dense pixel-wise morph between the images. Alternatively, the approach can be area based, where a coarse mesh is divided into triangles, and the pixels in one triangle in one image are mapped to the corresponding triangle in a second image.

Image morphing has been extended to 3D with great effect. One example (Pighin *et al.* 1998) successfully synthesized facial expression by capturing eight expressions in five different poses, recovering the 3D geometry, then interpolating the static expressions. The image quality was greatly improved by blending the original image from the different viewpoints.

The idea underpinning *image concatenation* is to mimic flip-book animation, where each page of a book has a picture of an object in a slightly different position. Flipping the pages quickly enough gives the illusion that the object is moving seamlessly around the pages. Animation based on image concatenation is similar. Images from a video sequence are reordered to generate new sequences. The challenge is to select images that match the desired expression at each point in time while maintaining a smooth transition from one to the next.

The main advantage of image-based synthesis is photorealism—images of real faces are used. However, image-based synthesis has several limitations: (1) The range of expressions is limited to those available in a database or video sequence. While the expression space can be extended by capturing new images, acquisition conditions (e.g. the lighting) must be identical to those of the original recording. (2) To animate a new person's face requires the capture of complete training data for that person. (3) Animation is generally limited to full-frontal views.

Hybrid graphics and image synthesis

With suitable hardware for capturing the shape and reflectance properties of the face, stunning animated sequences can be generated by coupling image-based and graphics-based animation. An essentially image-based face model can be viewed in different poses and under a number of lighting conditions.

Two such hybrid approaches are 3D morphable models (3dMMs) (Blanz 2006) and active appearance models (AAMs) (Xiao *et al.* 2004). The idea behind both approaches is to model both the shape (graphics-based synthesis) and appearance (image-based synthesis) of the face.

Morphable models are learned from Cyberware scans of human faces. The scan provides both an image and the vertices of a dense mesh sampled at tens of thousands of points on the face surface. Faces are represented as a linear combination of training faces; new faces are synthesized by applying a weighted combination of faces from the training faces. 3dMMs can synthesize photorealistic images of faces that have altered lighting, pose, identity, and expression. Figure F3 shows examples of variation in face characteristics.

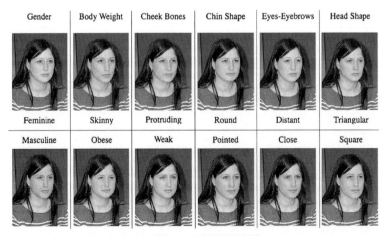

Fig. F3. Example of image synthesis by 3dMM. From (Blanz, 2006) (©2006 IEEE).

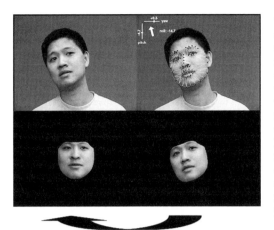

Re-Rendered	Reconstructed
Frontal Pose	Same Pose

Fig. F4. Example of image synthesis by AAM. The image on the upper left is the original image. Upper right: 3D shape overlaid onto the original image. The bottom row shows reconstructed (i.e. synthesized) views. From Xiao, Baker, Mathews, and Kanade, 2004). (©2004 IEEE).

AAMs lack the photorealism of 3dMMs but have two important advantages: they use normal video rather than special-purpose scanning, and AAMs process video at frame rate, which makes real-time applications possible. Recent uses include synthesis of the visual aspects of speech production (Theobald *et al.* 2009) and pose normalization and expression synthesis (see Fig. F4).

Conclusion

Approaches to facial animation include graphics-based, image-based, and hybrid. Modern graphics-based systems are attractive as they are able to animate a wide range of facial identities and expressions, are computationally efficient, and can animate the face of a full-bodied virtual character. Their major limitation is lack of photorealism. Image-based techniques can produce sequences that approach real video but lack the efficiency and flexibility of graphics-based approaches. Commercial packages tend to be graphics-based. Hybrid techniques may offer improved realism, efficiency, and flexibility.

With recent developments in facial animation, exciting possibilities emerge for research on the facial expression of emotion: (1) It becomes possible for the first time to separate stable characteristics of a facial image, such as those associated with sex, race, or attractiveness, from the dynamics of facial expression. Faces with a different appearance, such as those of men and women, may all be animated using the same dynamics. Stable and dynamic characteristics no longer need be confounded. (2) Also for the first time, hypotheses about rapid facial actions can be experimentally tested. Because facial action parameters can be manipulated on the fly, in real time, expressive behaviour can be scaled to exaggerate or attenuate actual behaviour. One could, for instance, experimentally manipulate the occurrence, amplitude, and timing of the Duchenne marker (see DUCHENNE SMILE), micro-expressions, or incongruent facial actions to discover their influence on social dynamics. Until now, such questions could be addressed only by using quasi-experimental approaches or static images. These are only some of the topics that may prove fruitful to investigate with these new tools.

BARRY-JOHN THEOBALD AND JEFFREY F. COHN

Blanz, V. (2006). Computing human faces for human viewers: automated animation in photographs and paintings. *ICMI '06. Eighth International Conference on Multimodal Interfaces* (Banff, Canada, 2–4 Nov. 2006), pp. 249–56. New York: The Association for Computing Machinery.

Cohn, J. F. and Kanade, T. (2007). Use of automated facial image analysis for measurement of emotion expression. In: J.A. Coan and J.B. Allen (eds), *The handbook of emotion elicitation and assessment*, pp. 222–38. New York: Oxford University Press.

Massaro, D.W. (1998). *Perceiving talking faces*. Cambridge, MA: MIT Press.

Parke, F.I. and Waters, K. (1996). *Computer facial animation*. Wellesley, MA: A. K. Peters.

fairness Fairness implies that people care about how well they fare compared with relevant others. Theoretical models of inequality aversion capture such basic fairness best. They pose that in addition to their own monetary payoffs, people either also care about the differences between their own payoffs and those of others or their relative share of the pie. Considerations of fairness differ from other social preferences such as, for example, *altruism, where a person's utility increases by increasing someone else's utility.

Basic models of fairness assume that people only care about outcomes, not about how and why those outcomes came to be. In contrast, *attribution theory models assert that people have a need to infer causes and to assign responsibility for why outcomes occur. More complex theories of fairness, i.e. models of reciprocity, take this into account. They pose that in addition to their own monetary payoffs, people care about how kindly they have been treated (relative to their own kindness), i.e. their counterparts' intentions. At a cost to themselves, people are willing to reward kindness with kindness or punish unkindness with unkindness. Reciprocity helps explain why people respond to above-market clearing wages with above-standard effort, are more willing to pay their taxes in return for good service, and more generally, perform a contract in response to a generous offer. Fehr and Schmidt (2002) and Meier (2007) provide excellent summaries of the research on fairness in behavioural economics.

Outcome-based models best capture interactions in which intentions play no role. Examples include the dictator game, which measures people's willingness to voluntarily give money away to another person, and games involving third parties not taking any action. If such third parties belong to people's reference group, people will be concerned about social comparisons and will dislike, for example, income disparity between themselves and their referents.

Intention-based models of fairness are best suited to help understand people's behaviour in strategic interactions, such as in bargaining contexts (e.g. the ultimatum game), in social dilemmas (e.g. public goods games), and in trust interactions (e.g. investment or gift exchange games). In the latter context, Bohnet et al. (2008) showed that people are willing to pay more to avoid experiencing intentional harm than accidental harm. This indicates betrayal aversion.

To better understand what might motivate the dislike of inequality, unfair treatment, or betrayal, neuroscientific studies are searching for its neural locus. In Sanfey et al.'s (2003) functional magnetic resonance imaging study of ultimatum bargaining, very unfair offers activated three regions of the brain, the insula cortex, dorsolateral prefrontal cortex, and anterior cingulate. The insula is an area typically activated when negative emotions like pain and disgust are experienced. The prefrontal cortex is associated with deliberate decisions and executive control. Knoch et al. (2006) experimentally disrupted the dorsolateral prefrontal cortex. As a result, subjects in the treatment group made the same fairness judgements as the control group; however, they did not behave according to them but acted more selfishly. Camerer et al. (2005) provide an excellent review of the relationship between neuroscience and economics.

IRIS BOHNET AND STEPHAN MEIER

family (role of emotion in) Emotions inside the family are characterized by the specific, intimate social setting in which they occur. Sociologists see the family as the only system within modern society that is specialized to meet emotional needs. Emotions have the same function in the family as in other contexts, i.e. individual and social adaptation. Their (1) *valence, intensity, and frequency, (2) transmission, and (3) the modalities by which they are regulated have a strong impact on the development of the family and its members.

Valence, intensity, and frequency

Until now, only a few studies have explored the frequency and distribution of different emotions in the family (see Scherer et al., 2004, and commentaries in the same issue).

A positive family climate can be interpreted as a preponderance of positive rather than negative affective states. Gottman (1994) found a ratio of five positive interactions to one negative during conflict resolution in stable marriages, compared with a ratio of 0.8 to one in unstable ones. Frequent displays of positive emotion in the family support cohesion and interaction, and evaluative conditioning enhances the positive valence of the family as a consequence. How young children experience parental expressiveness is one factor that facilitates the emergence of emotional schemas in social situations (Nixon and Watson 2001). Negative family expressiveness and low maternal acceptance of child emotion are related to a reduced ability of children to regulate their emotions with respect to aggressiveness (Ramsden and Hubbard 2002).

The occurrence of frequent negative emotions in the family is a risk factor for the probability of relapse of some mental disorders in adults (schizophrenia and depressive disorders). The oft-quoted assumption that *violence against women is concentrated in the family and intimate partnerships has been challenged by international studies (Killias et al. 2005). In Switzerland, Denmark, and the Czech Republic, the prevalence for violence against a partner over a lifetime varies from 10–38%, compared with a range from 35–42% for non-partner violence (Killias et al. 2005). Nevertheless, it remains true that the intimate family setting is the most common place for strong emotional (positive and negative) events to occur, sometimes with violence as a consequence. Violence by parents against their children is often produced by stressful anger situations, and reduced tolerance for disobedient child behaviour, or a tendency for cognitive avoidance (due to defensive attitudes) (Schoebi et al. 2006).

Transmission

Larson and Almeida (1999) define emotional transmission (the crossover effect) as the positive or negative emotions of one family member showing a consistent predictive relationship to subsequent emotions in another family member. Transmission of emotions to another member of the family may be due to *contagion (Hatfield et al. 1992), such as when a husband's anger 'contaminates' the emotional state of his wife (Thompson and Bolger 1999).

*Empathy represents an alternative road for emotional transmission in and outside the family, and may be a core process for positive interpersonal family

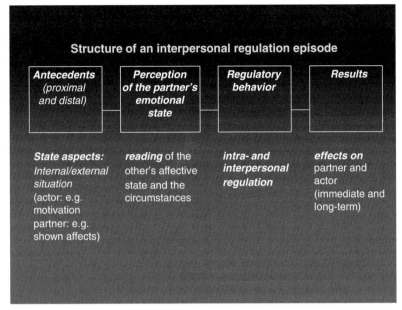

Fig. F5. Structure of an interpersonal emotion regulation episode.

behaviour. An episode of interpersonal emotion regulation starts with reading the partner's emotional state. Empathic accuracy depends on the actor's own emotional state, their competence and motivation to perceive their partner's emotion, and on their partner's emotional expressiveness (see Fig. F5).

The term 'spill-over effect' refers to the intrapersonal transfer of an emotional state from one situation to another, e.g. a conflict between partners spills over into parental behaviour toward a child (Krishnakumar and Buehler 2000). Spill-over is related to the mechanisms by which parents with high levels of partner conflict have a dysfunctional effect on the *emotional development of their children (see CHILDHOOD EMOTIONAL DEVELOPMENT). Negative emotions emerging from partner conflicts generate their noxious effects on the child's development by aggressive parental behaviour characterized by a lack of empathy.

Interpersonal regulation of emotion in the family

It is well known that mammals, and especially humans, have evolved with capacities to regulate emotions via interpersonal behaviour and relationships (Bowlby 1969). We understand interpersonal emotion regulation—analogous to intrapersonal emotion regulation (see REGULATION OF EMOTION) (Eisenberg and Spinrad 2004)—as the regulatory process referring to *other people's* affective states (rather than our own), i.e. initiating, avoiding, inhibiting, or maintaining interactions, or modulating

the occurrence, form, intensity, or duration of other people's emotions. Empathy, an accurate sympathetic reading of the partner's affective state, is considered as an antecedent for functional regulation (see Fig. F5).

Functional regulation facilitates the tuning of negative affective states of family members toward neutral or positive states, and contributes to the maintenance of positive emotions, while not impairing the self-esteem of those people who are involved in the regulation episode. Functional interpersonal emotion regulation is assumed to enhance prosocial behaviour, coherence, and intimacy within both couples and families. Gilbert (2005) has pointed to various underlying mechanisms for how soothing, caring, and supportive interactions operate on a particular type of positive affect system that is linked to opiate and oxytocin activity. Compassionate focused interactions—a variant of functional interpersonal emotion regulation which has soothing qualities—are those that focus on the care/well-being of the other with sensitivity, empathy, disclosing and sharing of emotions (see SOCIAL SHARING OF EMOTION), and ability to tolerate distress and conflict. Compassionate relationships provide experiences of safety which set the emotional tone for the achievement of positive health and well-being.

Computer-aided diary studies show that in conflict situations in families with adolescents, the probability of dysfunctional regulatory responses (such as expression of anger to control a partner's behaviour, or social withdrawal) is higher if they are addressed to family members than if they focus on people outside the family (Perrez *et al.* 2005). Families facilitate the expression of negative emotions, and also provide an environment in which dysfunctional social behaviour can be tolerated more easily than in other social settings. The replicated finding that the interpersonal coping behaviour of family members is significantly more dysfunctional within family settings than outside the family suggests the existence of something like 'display rules' for regulating interpersonal emotion that are similar to the display rules for emotional expression.

MEINRAD PERREZ

fear Fear is an activated, aversive emotional state that motivates attempts to cope with events that provide threats to the survival or well-being of organisms. As an experience, fear is characterized by feelings of threat and impending doom, and by an urge to get out of the situation. It has a quite distinct expressive signature: wide-open eyes, raised drawn-together eyebrows, an opened mouth with tense lips, and a withdrawing posture. Behaviourally, it is centred on coping attempts, related to biologically evolved defensive manoeuvres shared among mammals, such as immobility, escape, or attack.

Fear behaviour

Immobility or 'freezing', to be 'paralysed by terror', involves an ancient defence response marked by a quiescent body associated with marked cardiac deceleration, but also by an active mind scanning the environment for possible escape routes. In contrast, active, effortful defence related to escape or attack involves recruitment of the body's metabolic resources through activation of the sympathetic branch of the *autonomic nervous system.

The imminence of the threat determines which type of behavioural defence is exhibited. When threat is distant, the organism orients attention toward it (see ATTENTION AND EMOTION), and when it is identified as a potential threat the initially preferred defence is typically immobility accompanied by facilitation of defensive reflexes such as *startle. Immobility may prevent discovery by a threatening agent and allows time to evaluate the situation. A close or approaching threat increases the readiness to respond and elicits attempts to escape, and eventually defensive attack. The imminence of the threat is an important determinant of the patterning of psychophysiological responses diagnostic of fear (Öhman and Wiens 2003; see Fig. F6).

Fear stimuli

Adaptive action is favoured by quick and rapid identification of threatening stimuli. Indeed, research shows that we need not be aware of threatening stimuli before responses are activated.

Orienting	Freezing	Fight-or-Flight
SCR↗, HR↘, startle↘	SCR↗, HR↘, startle↗	SCR↗, HR↗
PNS dominance		SNS dominance

Threat Imminence

Fig. F6. Effects of imminence of a threat on fear activation (adapted from Lang *et al.* 1997a). When imminence of a threat increases, the response changes from orienting to the threatening stimulus, to freezing, to fight-or-flight. Orienting is mainly associated with skin conductance responses (SCRs), but also with decreases of heart rate (HR) and startle inhibition. Freezing is mainly associated with startle potentiation and HR decreases. Fight-or-flight is mainly associated with HR increases. The parasympathetic nervous system (PNS) dominates in orienting and freezing, and the sympathetic nervous system (SNS) dominates in fight-or-flight. (Reprinted by permission from Öhman and Wiens, 2003.)

Humans fear innumerable events and situations. Clearly most fear stimuli are learned, but nevertheless there are a number of recurrent themes in human fears, which suggest that we more easily learn to fear some things rather than others. First and foremost, fear is a vehicle for survival, and thus we fundamentally fear death, injury, and illness. Second, humans evolved among awesome predators (e.g. poisonous snakes, sabretoothed tigers), and hence we have a readiness to develop fear of animals (see EVOLUTION OF EMOTION). Third, we often fear social situations and events (e.g. dominating individuals, encountering strangers, being evaluated, embarrassed, or humiliated by others). Finally, we fear situations (e.g. closed and crowded places, forests, public transportation) that lack an escape route to a safe haven, which reflects our preoccupation with safety.

Fear and avoidance

The most effective way of dealing with fear is by anticipating fear stimuli in order to avoid actual exposure to dangers. Learning what signals the likely occurrence of a dangerous episode, therefore, improves the odds for successfully coping with them, and it has an early evolutionary origin. The exquisite cognitive apparatus of humans fosters the development of elaborated associative networks between a multitude of events that eventually converge on representing threats to the wellbeing and survival of oneself, one's kin, and one's social group. These (often socially shared) networks are useful for avoiding danger. Avoidance also has its costs, however. For example, in *phobias, the primary fear disorder, pervasive avoidance of specific fear stimuli (e.g. public speaking) interferes with normal adjustment.

Furthermore, acting by avoidance on the belief that something signals danger prevents one from testing the belief that danger will follow, as well as closer scrutiny of the danger itself. Thus, avoidance insulates phobic fear from the exposures that have proven to be curative.

The fear network of the brain

A neural network centred on the *amygdala in the anterior temporal lobe controls fear (LeDoux 2000) (see NEURAL ARCHITECTURE OF EMOTION). The amygdala evaluates brain input in terms of whether it represents a potential threat. It receives both fully processed sensory information from the cortex and merely preliminarily processed information from a subcortical pathway via the thalamus. The latter route may activate fear responses after only a crude and nonconscious analysis of the stimulus, which results in very quick defence recruitment that improves the odds of escaping the threatening circumstances. This rapidly available information is supplemented by consciously accessible information via the cortical route, allowing more cognitively elaborated defence strategies.

Neural pathways from the amygdala to structures in the hypothalamus and brainstem activate autonomic and endocrine responses, as well as overt motor responses (freezing, fight–flight) and defence reflex facilitation (see Fig. F6). Facial expressions of fear are activated through the facial motor nucleus in the brainstem. This circuit accounts both for the independence of conscious recognition and fear activation, and the complex efferent organization of the fear response.

ARNE ÖHMAN

Öhman, A. (2008). Fear and anxiety: overlaps and dissociations. In: M. Lewis, J.M. Haviland-Jones, and L. Feldman Barrett (eds), *Handbook of emotions*, 3rd edn., pp. 709–29. New York: Guilford Press.

feelings (philosophical perspectives)

William James (1842–1910) thought that bodily feelings were essential to emotion, and also that no other feelings were involved. So, James said, the perception of some arousing event would cause certain bodily changes, and an emotion is 'nothing but' the feeling of these bodily changes (James 1890/1983, p. 1065). This is known as the *James–Lange theory, also after Carl Lange (1834–1900), who developed a similar theory at about the same time. Recently, Antonio Damasio (1994) has followed James in arguing that the feelings in emotion are bodily, although he allows that emotional feelings can arise where there is no bodily change yet somatic brain states are aroused (see SOMATIC MARKER HYPOTHESIS). This kind of view is gaining considerable popularity, not only amongst empirical psychologists but also amongst philosophers. Ironically, those other philosophers who rejected the James–Lange theory in favour of the view that emotions are some kind of judgement or cognition also used to hold that the only feelings in emotion were of the body (see, for example, Lyons, 1980). The James–Lange theory has been questioned in a famous experiment by Stanley Schachter and Jerome Singer (see SCHACHTER-SINGER THEORY). They argued that how participants in the experiment 'labelled' their feelings was significantly determined by the context in which they found themselves (Schachter and Singer 1962). Participants who were given an adrenalin injection labelled their emotion anger in an anger-inducing context and elation in an elation-inducing context. It is not clear, however, that this experiment successfully refutes the James–Lange theory (for helpful discussion see Griffiths, 1997).

Some psychologists are inclined to understand emotional feelings more widely than the James–Lange theory would suggest, including, for example, hedonic states of pleasantness or unpleasantness, or some kind of felt *valence, positive or negative, in varying degrees of intensity (e.g. Russell 1980). Recently, some philosophers have sought to show first, and against the James–Lange theory, that emotional feelings are not only bodily feelings but that they also can be feelings that are bound up with cognition and directed towards things in the world beyond the bounds of the body; and secondly that emotional feelings are *sui generis* and not reducible to some simpler kind of hedonic state (Goldie 2000).

PETER GOLDIE

Robinson, J. (2005). *Deeper than reason: emotion and its role in literature, music, and art*. New York: Oxford University Press.

Scherer, K.R. (2005). What are emotions? And how can they be measured? *Social Science Information*, 44, 693–727.

feelings (psychological perspectives)

There is a widespread tendency, based on lay terminology and folk theories, to treat *emotion* and *feeling* as synonyms. This seemingly innocent terminological blur is responsible for decades of debate between peripheralists in the Jamesian tradition and centralists in the tradition of Cannon (see EMOTION THEORIES AND CONCEPTS (PSYCHOLOGICAL PERSPECTIVES)). If one replaces the term 'emotion', as used by William James (1842–1910), by 'feeling', defined as subjective experience as one component of emotion (see COMPONENTIAL THEORIES), his peripheral theory becomes much more compatible with modern theories (see Scherer 2005). Most likely this is what James meant when he wrote 'that the bodily changes follow directly the *perception* of the exciting fact, and that our feeling of the same changes as they occur *is* the emotion' (James 1884/1968, p. 19, emphases in the original), using the term 'feeling' in the sense of proprioceptive sensations (see JAMES-LANGE THEORY). In most modern theories bodily changes are considered as an independent component of the emotion, the proprioceptive representations of which become part of an integrated subjective experience or feeling component. In contrast to James, this experiential component reflects not only bodily changes but also cognitive evaluation of events, motivational tendencies, and attempts at regulation.

While even today theorists and researchers continue to use the terms emotion and feeling interchangeably, it seems advisable, to avoid confusion, to use these terms as separate constructs with emotion comprising feeling as one component. The feeling component has a special status in the emotion process, because it integrates and regulates the component processes in the emotion episode. If subjective experience is to serve a monitoring function, it needs to integrate all information about the continuous patterns of change in all other components, as well as their coherence. Thus, feeling is an extraordinarily complex conglomerate of information from very different systems.

Scherer (2004) has suggested conceptualizing this component as a Venn diagram (see Fig. F7), in which a set of overlapping circles represents different aspects of feeling: (A) reflection or representation of changes in all components through cortical integration of central, somatosensory, and motor information; (B) that part of the integrated representation that enters awareness and thereby becomes available to consciousness, constituting the experienced feeling qualities (qualia); and (C) the categorization and verbal labelling of a consciously experienced feeling. The nonoverlapping parts of circles B and C symbolize the fact that (1) during the process of

entering awareness, schemata, scripts, or social representations and (2) in the process of verbalization, categories and labels can add surplus meaning. Automatic and reflexive regulation processes occur on the unconscious and conscious levels, respectively (see UNCONSCIOUS EMOTIONS). Much of this account remains hypothetical, however, as the role of consciousness of feelings is still ill-defined and underresearched (Niedenthal *et al.* 2005b).

KLAUS R. SCHERER

fiction and emotion Most, though certainly not all, novels, plays, films, poems, and representational paintings are fictional, offering to our appreciation characters and events we know to be unreal. And among the chief reasons why we value such artworks is the intense emotional engagement that we have with their fictions (see LITERATURE AND EMOTION; MUSIC (EMOTIONAL EFFECTS); MEDIA COMMUNICATION). However uncontroversial these two claims may seem, together they bring to light something deeply puzzling about our experience of art, in fact so puzzling that modern aesthetics has baptized it—note the definite article—the paradox of fiction.

There are nearly as many ways of setting up the paradox as there are strategies for resolving it, but a few basic reflections on the nature of emotion suffice to give shape to the problem. It is commonly thought that emotions are cognitively rich, in the sense that they have as a constitutive component a propositional attitude toward some state of affairs. Whether this attitude should be construed as '*belief' or a cognitively thinner state such as 'construal' is a matter of debate. But at the

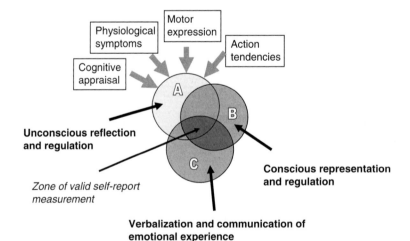

Fig. F7. Venn diagram of three hypothetical types of central representation of the emotion components and the emergence of feeling.

very least it seems that an emotion must include a cognitive commitment to the *existence* of its object: my pitying you on account of your suffering requires a commitment to your existence and hence the existence of your suffering. Yet strictly speaking we do not have such cognitive commitments when emoting over fictions: it is essential to our appreciating something *as a work of fiction* that we understand and acknowledge the described characters and events to be fictional.

This generates a number of questions. First, how do we tell an appropriate *causal* story of the emotions we experience toward fictions, absent a belief (or however one conceives the cognitive element) in the very object of these emotions? What generates them, what so much as gets them afoot? Second, even if we can tell a convincing causal story, how can such emotions be regarded as *rational*, since it would seem odd, even silly, to emote over what we know to be unreal and untrue? The resolution of the paradox thus requires showing that our emotional engagements with fictions are both rational and genuine (what philosophers mean by 'genuine' is often unclear, though it usually at least means that the cognitive and affective profile of, say, the pity we feel for a fictional character is in most relevant respects of a piece with the profile of the pity we would feel for an actual person).

Three approaches to the paradox have been especially prominent in recent philosophical aesthetics. The *idea* or *thought-content* approach begins by pointing out that simply entertaining, rather than believing, a description is often sufficient for generating an emotion (for example, a gruesome description of a human body being dismembered or the mere idea of a 'vomit sandwich') and then attempts to assimilate the object of emotions in the context of art to entertained ideas of this sort. The *simulation* approach explores our capacity to run our emotions 'off-line' when appreciating fictions, either by (1) simulating the experience of someone reading a true report (or witnessing actual events, in the case of theatre and cinema), as the 'report' model casts it, or (2) imaginatively projecting ourselves into the shoes of fictional characters and taking on their experiences as our own, as the 'experiential' model casts it. Lastly, the *startle* approach argues that many emotions simply do not require cognitive or existential commitments at all (for example fright after an unexpected noise or a sudden movement in the dark) and models emotions toward fictions on noncognitive emotions of this variety.

However promising, all these approaches raise worries. The startle approach has done much to dispel the sense of paradox about a class of the emotions we experience toward fictions—for example the class characterized by our experience of works of horror and suspense—but the traditional 'tragic' emotions of pity

and fear (at least fear of a certain stripe) do seem to be sufficiently cognitively complex to refuse assimilation to the kinds of emotion the startle theorist has in mind. The thought-content approach and the 'experiential' model of the simulation approach each seem to avoid the paradox rather than resolve it, implying as they do that we do not really emote over fictions but rather mental 'ideas' or imagined versions of ourselves in situations like those of fictional characters. And it is unclear how the 'report' model of the simulation approach can resolve the paradox, since it seems to repeat, just in a novel way, the very aspect of our emotional involvement with much art that seems paradoxical: our emoting over that which we know to be unreal.

For these reasons, and quite a few more, the paradox of fiction remains one of the central debates in modern aesthetics (see AESTHETIC EMOTIONS (PHILOSOPHICAL PERSPECTIVES)).

JOHN GIBSON

Choi, J. (2003). Fits and startles: cognitivism revisited. *Journal of Aesthetics and Art Criticism*, **61**, 149–57.

Levinson, J. (1997). Emotion in response to art: a survey of the terrain. In: M. Hjort and S. Laver (eds), *Emotion and the arts*, pp. 20–34. Oxford: Oxford University Press.

Matravers, D. (2005). The challenge of irrationalism, and how not to meet it. In: M. Kieran (ed.), *Contemporary debates in aesthetics and the philosophy of art*, pp. 254–64. Oxford: Blackwell.

flashbulb memories The term flashbulb memory was introduced by Brown and Kulik (1977). Their interest had been stimulated by a 1973 magazine article in which celebrities recalled the moment at which they had first learned the news of the assassination of the American President John F. Kennedy in November 1963. They noticed that all those interviewed were able to recall detailed personal circumstances, i.e. who, what, where, when, and some rather indiscriminate, idiosyncratic, highly specific details, such as the 'feel' of a new pair of shoes, the name on a discarded pack of cigarettes, the headline chalked on a board, etc. Brown and Kulik became curious because this degree of specificity is rarely found in any memories, let alone memories of an event that occurred over a decade earlier. Moreover, recall of one's personal circumstances, termed the *reception event*, when learning of an item of public news is also rare—most items of news and circumstances in which they were first encountered are rapidly forgotten. Thus, these memories had a 'flashbulb' quality to them, as though the brain had taken a photograph of the moment when the news was announced and kept it in long-term memory in pristine quality never fading or distorting (as so many memories do) over long retention intervals.

Kennedy's assassination was not, however, the first public event to trigger the formation of these unusual memories. A memory survey in 1890s reported a detailed flashbulb memory for the assassination of Abraham Lincoln half a century earlier. The English writer Thomas Hardy described the flashbulb memory of a relative for the guillotining of the French Queen during the French Revolution. We can assume that there are in fact many events throughout history that have led to the widespread formation of such memories. Indeed, since Brown and Kulik's seminal article there have been many studies of flashbulb memories encompassing murders and attempted murders of leading figures, deaths and departures of public figures, natural and human-made disasters, and even of the announcement of scientific discoveries. It seems that there may be two classes of flashbulb memories: those that are of events for which many people have flashbulb memories, e.g. the death of Princess Diana, 9/11, and those that are shared by members of a group, e.g. a sports team winning a competition, an unexpected breakthrough in a scientific area. Whatever the precipitating event it seems that one of the functions of flashbulb memory is to connect personal history with the history of one's times. As Neisser (1982) pointed out, flashbulb memories allow one to say, with authority, 'I was there'. Flashbulb memories define, in memory, the historical time of one's life and they may also help define *generation identity*, that is public events that were the defining events of an individual's generation.

Researchers do not doubt that there are flashbulb memories and that they appear to play an important role in the self. However, many questions and controversies remain about the accuracy and origins of flashbulb memories. Brown and Kulik originally suggested that a special brain mechanism responding to the perceived consequentiality of an experience became activated and caused the brain to keep, in an unchanging form, a detailed record of that experience. But this now seems increasingly unlikely. The brain mechanisms that mediate the encoding and retrieval of memories are complex and interact together in dynamic ways during the formation and later reconstruction of memories (see MEMORY (EMOTIONAL)). The other candidate theory, that flashbulb memories are a product of rehearsal which occurs naturally when people talk to each other about these unusual events, also seems unlikely as measures of rehearsal have not been found to be consistently associated with the formation of flashbulb memories. There are also reports of flashbulb memories which individuals claim to have rarely or even never recounted previously. If this is the case then rehearsal is unlikely to account for these memories. Instead it seems that flashbulb memories are a product of complex processes both at the level of the brain and cognition that respond to the personal meaning of an event, public or private, and create a memory representation that reflects the impact upon the individual. This meaning-making process may continue for long intervals, even over the whole period of retention, e.g. a lifetime.

Given this complex, dynamic, and continuing construction of flashbulb memories it seems reasonable to ask 'Are flashbulb memories accurate?'. Research has found that flashbulb memories, and trauma memories more generally, are prone to distortions and errors. Additionally, as Brown and Kulik pointed out, although they have a 'flashbulb' or 'live' quality they are also, unlike photographs, incomplete records of an event. Yet, and most importantly, they have also been found to contain highly accurate details over periods measured in decades. They are then peculiar psychological representations which can be simultaneously accurate and inaccurate—yet still true to a person's life and experience. Flashbulb memories tie us into the history of our times and with their accurate and inaccurate details link personal experience with public events; because of this thay are of high importance to the self.

MARTIN A. CONWAY

Conway, M.A. (1994). *Flashbulb memories*. Hillsdale, NJ: Lawrence Erlbaum Associates.

focal events Culturally focal events embody culturally central concerns: they can be either consistent or inconsistent with culturally important *values, *goals, and practices. Focality implies that cultural representations of these events are extensive and detailed, and that the event is evaluated as highly positive, in the case of consistency with culturally central concerns, or as highly negative, in the case of inconsistency. Focality of an event makes the event salient to an individual, and its meaning unambiguous. Salience and certainty of interpretation render certain emotional responses extremely likely (Mesquita and Frijda 1992, Frijda and Mesquita 1994, Mesquita 2003).

For example, in many cultures where social connections are at the core of one's self definition, events that threaten to compromise one's social status are focal. Very detailed knowledge exists on the situations that might compromise status, the situations never remain unnoticed, and they would thus invariably lead to feelings of shame. Although loss of status may at times also become salient in Western contexts, and in those cases may be associated with shame, individuals in these cultures are less expert in interpreting the meaning of these situations, making these situations less salient, and rendering them less likely to elicit shame.

Focality of events explains certain patterns of emotions that emerge at the cultural level. It can explain why some cultures have a propensity to see threats to one's status everywhere and to experience shame, as in the example above (see CULTURAL SPECIFICITY). Similarly, it can explain why in other cultures (e.g. middle class North Americans) success and happiness appear to be prevalent.

On the other hand, focality of events can also explain why certain other emotions are nearly absent in particular cultures. Among the Utku Inuits, who live in small groups under coarse weather conditions, and are thus highly dependent on each other, conflict is a focal event. Social life among the Utku is geared towards the avoidance of conflict, or any situation that could disturb interpersonal harmony. As a consequence there is a striking absence of *anger, and anger itself is met with disapproval, shame, or fear (Briggs 1970). Focality of events can thus underlie the conspicuously low and high prevalence of certain emotions in given cultures.

The concept of focality is similar but not identical to the concept of hypercognition as proposed by the anthropologist Levy (1984a). Hypercognition, like focality, supposes that there is cultural expertise on the emotions that are central to a culture. However, hypercognition implies that this expertise is reflected in a differentiated lexicon. This suggestion, that hypercognition of emotions is marked by a large number of emotion words, appears to be contradicted by the data (e.g. Keeler 1983). Focal emotions are in many cases expressed by one word that covers a wide range of related emotional states. For example, in cultures where shame-eliciting events are focal, there is often only one word that corresponds with a wide range of terms in Western languages, such as shame, modesty, shyness, and embarrassment.

BATJA MESQUITA AND ISHANI BANERJI

Mesquita, B. (2003). Emotions as dynamic cultural phenomena. In: R.J. Davidson, K.R. Scherer, and H.H. Goldsmith (eds), *Handbook of affective sciences*, pp. 871–90. New York: Oxford University Press.

frontal brain asymmetry (and emotion) The idea that the two hemispheres of the prefrontal cortices make a differential contribution to positive versus negative or to approach versus withdrawal-related emotion (see APPROACH/WITHDRAWAL) was first introduced in the early 1980s (see Reuter-Lorenz and Davidson 1981, Davidson and Fox 1982). This proposal was derived from lesion data suggesting that patients with damage to the left hemisphere, particularly anterior cortical zones, were likely to exhibit a depressive reaction to their brain injury while those with the opposite lesion pattern were more likely to display indifference to their medical condition, or inappropriate euphoria (see, e.g. Gainotti 1972).

Most of the extant research on frontal brain asymmetry and emotion has used measures of brain electrical activity to make inferences about asymmetric hemispheric activation. In adult participants such inferences are typically made on the basis of differential alpha power from homologous electrodes over prefrontal scalp regions. Decreased relative alpha power in these measures is taken to indicate increased activation (see, e.g. Davidson et al. 1990b, Oakes et al. 2004). Using these measures, researchers have investigated two different components of frontal brain asymmetry. One component represents task-elicited changes and the other represents baseline individual differences. The former reflects changes in electrical asymmetry of the brain in response to specific task conditions. The latter refers to baseline individual differences in asymmetric prefrontal activation. This type of measure is obtained during trials in which a 'resting baseline' electroencephalogram (EEG) is recorded while the participant is simply instructed to 'rest, with no specific mental activity'. It turns out that the test–retest reliability of EEG measures of frontal asymmetry during a resting period are remarkably stable over time with test–retest correlations over a three-week period in the 0.6–0.7 range (Tomarken et al. 1992a). Moreover, these baseline individual differences are associated with an interesting nomological network of associations including association with childhood temperament (Davidson and Fox 1982, Pfeifer et al. 2002), self-report measures of dispositional mood (Tomarken et al. 1992b), immune function (Rosenkranz et al. 2003), and well-being (Urry et al. 2004). In addition, there are task-elicited changes in frontal asymmetry produced by emotion-eliciting stimuli (e.g. Wheeler et al. 1993).

Of particular interest is just what the prefrontal cortex is 'doing' in emotion (see Davidson 2004b). This question has not yet been systematically addressed since studies have not been explicitly conducted to test this question. However, it is clear that the function of the prefrontal cortex in emotion is not unitary and depends importantly on the specific sector of prefrontal cortex under consideration. Secondly, it is also clear that portions of the prefrontal cortex that have historically not been featured in emotion circuitry (e.g. dorsolateral prefrontal cortex) nevertheless play some role in emotion. An important component of some emotion, particularly approach-related positive emotion, is the *goal orientation of the emotion. We often experience positive emotion as behaviour is guided to the acquisition of a goal. It is likely that the dorsolateral prefrontal cortex is engaged during this process of appetitive goal instantiation, and in this case evidence suggests that it would be more left-sided. Data from nonhuman primates are consistent with this suggestion (e.g. Wallis and Miller 2003).

RICHARD J. DAVIDSON

Davidson, R.J. (2004). What does the prefrontal cortex 'do' in affect: perspectives in frontal EEG asymmetry research. *Biological Psychology*, **67**, 219–34.

frustration The term frustration refers either to a particular set of external circumstances preventing the satisfaction of a desire or to reactions to these circumstances. Laboratory-oriented investigators are especially apt to employ the former usage, whereas discussions based primarily on more naturalistic observations are more likely to speak of frustration as an emotional reaction. This entry regards frustration as the blocking of an expected *goal attainment.

Investigators have differed in which frustration-produced reaction they singled out for attention. As some classic examples, Barker *et al.* (1941) were concerned with children's regression, their reverting to a 'less mature state' that they had previously outgrown; Maier (1956) emphasized a fixation on the behaviour that had been ongoing just before; and Amsel (see Amsel 1992) postulated a sequence of consequences, chiefly the increased drive (*arousal) resulting in more vigorous responses and the learning that can arise. Amsel also recognized the occurrence of aggressive reactions, but Dollard *et al.* (1939) provided the best known formulation of the relation between frustration and aggression.

Dollard and colleagues held that every frustration produces an instigation to *aggression, although other kinds of response may initially be more dominant. If the frustration continues, they said, overt aggression becomes more likely. Many critics have insisted that the thwarting will not lead to aggression unless it is appraised as an intentional misdeed. However, a good number of studies have found that aggression can occur even in the absence of the particular conditions that critics argued were necessary for aggression to appear. In Berkowitz's version of the original frustration-aggression hypothesis (Berkowitz 1989), it is the aversiveness of the frustration and not the thwarting in itself that creates the instigation to aggression.

The few studies that have inquired about the specific feelings that are experienced when a frustration occurs suggest, consistent with the frustration–aggression thesis, that the thwarting-induced bodily reactions are similar to those associated with anger. As one example, Shields (1984) found that anger is often linked to feelings of muscular tension, restlessness, and even stomach sensations, much the same bodily feelings reported by many of Davitz's research participants when they were frustrated (Davitz 1969).

A good many problems remain in the study of frustration effects: for example, under specifically what conditions do thwartings give rise to the passivity of learned helplessness and just when do they generate more active responses including overt aggression?

LEONARD BERKOWITZ

functionalist theories of emotion Functionalist theories of emotion are not concerned with what emotions are, but with why they exist. A central assumption is that emotions evolved (see EVOLUTION OF EMOTION) to motivate behaviour fitting the demands of the physical and social environment (Keltner and Gross 1999), and the goal of these theories is to discover the adaptive functions of emotions in general, or of particular emotions. Evolutionary theories of emotion are the most obvious example of functionalism (Cosmides and Tooby 2000, Plutchik 2003, Nesse 2004), but in fact most modern theories—*appraisal theories, *basic emotions theories, *circumplex theories, and social constructionist theories—share the assumption that emotions are adaptive, in contrast to previous theories that conceived of emotions as maladaptive and disruptive of rational thought.

In order to survive and flourish, an organism must be sensitive to potential threats and opportunities in its environment, and must be motivated to react appropriately. According to most functionalist theorists, emotions contribute to adaptive responses in several ways. First, emotions direct attention to changes in the environment that have implications for the organism's well-being and away from irrelevant information (see ATTENTION AND EMOTION). Emotions tell us what matters to us, and how it matters (Schwarz and Clore 1988, Lerner and Keltner 2001) (see RELEVANCE DETECTION). Second, emotions motivate the organism to respond in an appropriate way (see MOTIVATION). Simple versions of this motivation involve basic approach–avoidance tendencies, or fight-or-flight responses, but the *action tendencies associated with emotion are far more varied, especially in human beings, including approach, freezing, attack, nurturance, exploration, and many other behaviours (Frijda 2007). Third, emotions connect the perceptions of changes in the environment to the relevant behavioural motivations; in Scherer's terms, emotions function as an 'intelligent interface that mediates between input and output' (Scherer 1994b, p. 127). Finally, when there are several threats and opportunities in the environment, or when the organism has several potentially competing goals, emotions set priorities, directing attention and action to whatever is most important for its survival or well-being.

Functionalist theorists do not claim that every time an emotion occurs it is adaptive. Emotions may be calibrated to motivate action when action is unnecessary: a rabbit runs away whenever a person come too close, wasting energy, even though 99 times out of 100 the person intends no harm. A functionalist might argue that this overreaction is actually adaptive, because ignoring the possible danger when it really is a danger could be fatal, whereas running away 99 times unnecessarily is merely tiring (Ellsworth 1994b, Nesse 2005) Examples of specific occasions when emotions are dysfunctional are common: in a moment of anger people ruin relationships they value, are paralysed by unrealistic fears, spend more money than they have in a burst of euphoria. But functionalist theorists believe that the benefits of having emotions greatly outweigh the occasional costs.

In addition to contributing to individual survival, emotions also have important functions in social relations. Their expression communicates people's feelings to others, helping them to understand each other, and to respond appropriately (see EXPRESSION OF EMOTION). An expression of fear alerts a person's companions to possible danger; an expression of anger puts them on their guard. Children's survival depends on their ability to communicate distress and contentment, and on their parents' strong emotions motivating them to protect and nurture them (see ATTACHMENT). Members of the opposite sex communicate attraction and availability, or distance and distaste, facilitating mate selection without undue awkwardness. Friendships are fostered by recognition of sympathy and trustworthiness, blocked by feelings of hostility and distrust.

At the larger group level, shared emotions can create a sense of belonging and cohesiveness, increasing loyalty and cooperation (Keltner and Haidt 1999). People who violate social norms are subjected to shaming, a temporary ostracism that serves as a reminder of the dire possibility of permanent exclusion, and motivates the offender to apologize and make reparations, strengthening group solidarity. Emotions are also important in reinforcing social hierarchies in groups and maintaining social orders based on status: high-status people express anger, contempt, and benevolence, while low-status people express embarrassment, humility, and gratitude (Tiedens et al. 2000). Ingroup emotions emphasize group boundaries and the social structure.

Thus, according to functionalist theories, emotions evolved to cope with situations that were relevant to survival at the individual, interpersonal, and group levels.

PHOEBE C. ELLSWORTH

Frijda, N.H. (2007). *The laws of emotion*. Mahwah, NJ: Lawrence Erlbaum Associates.

Keltner, D. and Gross, J. (1999). Functional theories of emotions. *Cognition and Emotion*, 13, 467–80.

Keltner, D. and Haidt, J. (1999). Social functions of emotions at four levels of analysis. *Cognition and Emotion*, 13, 505–21.

Plutchik, R. (2003). *Emotions and life: perspectives from psychology, biology, and evolution*. Washington, DC: American Psychological Association.

G

gender differences (and emotion) Understanding the complexities of gender differences in everyday emotional functioning requires a consideration of multiple emotional processes (e.g. perception, decoding, expression, experience, communication) which differ in the extent to which gender differences exist. Moreover, within each process gender differences may exist for some emotions and not others, and may also differ depending on how emotion is measured, for example *self-report versus observational data. Gender differences in each process and emotion are invariably qualified by sociocultural and demographic factors.

The strongest evidence for gender differences consists of self-reports of emotional expression, especially emotional intensity. Females report greater intensity when describing global affect; *empathy and sympathy; positive experiences such as *joy, affection, warmth, well-being, and love; and *dysphoric experiences such as *sadness, *depression, *shame, *disgust, *anxiety, *fear, hurt, and *embarrassment. Across 37 different countries, women report more intense emotions that last longer and are expressed more overtly than do men. Only *contempt, loneliness, *pride, confidence, excitement, and *guilt are sometimes reported to be more intensely expressed by males than by females. Although men often express more *anger in their vocal, facial, and behavioural modalities than women, they do not do so on self-report measures (Brody 1999).

Gender differences in self-reports may be affected by gender differences in stereotypes, self-presentation biases, and memory-encoding abilities. Gender differences may be minimal or absent when self-reported in the moment, rather than retrospectively. However, the existence of behavioural differences suggests that the self-report differences are not due entirely to bias or stereotype. Women express more frequent or more intense emotions when observed in social interactions and when verbalizing emotion, and they are more facially expressive (both when posing deliberately and when being observed unobtrusively). Women smile more frequently and more expansively than men, and are also more accurate in identifying the meanings of nonverbal affective cues of face, body, and voice (Hall 2006). Women report a higher likelihood of 'catching' the emotions of others than do men, and their self-reports of emotional *contagion are sometimes corroborated when facial muscle activity is recorded through *electromyography. Women report a greater tendency to pay attention to their emotions and display more complex emotion knowledge than men when asked to describe emotional reactions in hypothetical scenarios. Finally, standardized tests of emotional intelligence (see INTELLIGENCE, EMOTIONAL) consistently find higher scores among women than men (Brody and Hall 2008).

Gender differences in physiological arousal (e.g. heart rate and blood pressure) are specific to particular physiological measures and emotions, as well as to particular tasks and circumstances (Brody 1999). Patterns in the data suggest that men are more often '*internalizers' (showing physiological arousal with no overt emotional expressions) or 'low responders' (showing no or low levels of expression across modalities). Women are more often '*externalizers' (showing overt emotional expressions with no corresponding physiological arousal) or 'generalizers' (showing concordance in physiological and overt expression of emotion, especially at high levels of physiological reactivity).

Gender differences in emotional functioning are both mediated and moderated by sociocultural, cognitive, biological, behavioural, situational, and demographic variables. For example, gender differences in the intensity of joy, shame, disgust, and guilt are greater in individualistic than in collectivistic countries (see INDIVIDUALISM/COLLECTIVISM) (Fischer and Manstead 2000).

The pattern of gender differences noted above in expression, decoding, and emotional awareness mirror stereotypes and cultural values about the desirability of emotional expression for each gender. Across 48 countries, adults report that happiness is more desirable for girls and that fearlessness and anger suppression are more desirable for boys, and stereotypes generally hold that women express emotions more than men do. These values and stereotypes may shape the reality of gender differences by generating expectancies that influence and elicit behaviours and emotional expressions, becoming self-fulfilling prophecies. People may be motivated to conform to stereotypes because violating stereotypic display rules can lead to negative social consequences, such as social rejection and discrimination.

Complex biopsychosocial interactions or feedback loops may contribute to the aetiology of gender differences, both in specific situations and across development. In particular, cultural values as well as differential emphases on interdependence and independence for each gender may shape caretakers' and peers' elicited and reactive responses to gender differences in infant *temperament. Differences in temperament include higher activity and arousal levels in males and faster maturation rates for effortful control processes in females. Early temperament may influence and be influenced by sociocultural values, contributing to the development of gender differences in emotional functioning over the lifespan. Similarly, gender differences in social roles and cultural values, social knowledge, self-construals, social attributions, and developmental history probably interact with proximal factors, including characteristics of the situation and of social partners, facial feedback processes, and emotional contagion, in determining the nature of affective expression in immediate situations (Brody and Hall 2008).

LESLIE R. BRODY AND JUDITH A. HALL

Eagly, A.H., Beall, A.E., and Sternberg, R.J. (eds) (2004). *The psychology of gender*, 2nd edn. New York: Guilford Press.

genetics of affect The genetics of affect begins with the realization that individual differences in affect are central to some fundamental personality traits, which are highly heritable (see PERSONALITY; TEMPERAMENT) For example, personality traits that are associated with individual differences in affect include harm-avoidance, sensation-seeking, and agreeableness. A personality trait specifically associated with positive affect is *extraversion (or extroversion). Individuals who are highly extraverted tend to enjoy socializing and having fun. They are strongly reactive to positive mood induction procedures and report more positive emotional experiences than individuals who are much less extraverted, i.e. introverted. On the other hand, a personality trait specifically associated with negative affect is *neuroticism. Individuals who score high in neuroticism tend to experience or display negative emotions related to *anxiety, *sadness, or *anger. They are strongly reactive to negative mood induction procedures and report more negative emotional experiences than individuals who are much less neurotic. A high degree of neuroticism *per se* is not indicative of psychopathology, but may be a predisposing factor for later psychopathology if other risk factors come to bear on the individual.

These personality traits, like physical traits, have a strong heritability, suggesting that individual differences in personality traits may be linked to specific genes. This association is not believed to be influenced by a single gene having a large effect but rather by multiple genes

of small effect size. This model of genetic transmission is known as a multigenic or polygenic mode of transmission, and the genes that contribute in small ways to genetic variance of complex, continuous traits are known as quantitative trait loci (QTLs).

In the past decade, many genes have been identified that exhibit common (greater than 1%) variations (polymorphisms) within their nucleotide sequence across individuals. These polymorphisms may be located within promoter or intron regions of the DNA that can lead to alterations in protein levels, or within exon regions of the DNA that can lead to changes in the protein sequence. There are different kinds of polymorphisms. For example single nucleotide polymorphisms (SNPs; pronounced 'Snips'), in which one nucleotide is exchanged for another. Another example is the variable number of tandem repeats (VNTR) polymorphism, in which a sequence of nucleotides is repeated variable numbers of times. A third example is the insertion/deletion polymorphism, in which a sequence of nucleotides is present in one variant, but absent in another.

To investigate the possible effect of a QTL on a trait of interest, association studies examine the correlation between a phenotype of interest and a candidate polymorphism. The following will illustrate such a line of research, using the serotonin transporter polymorphism as a case study.

Case study: the serotonin transporter polymorphism
To date, the most-studied polymorphism related to affect is the serotonin (5-HT) transporter (5-HTT), which is a key regulator of serotonergic neurotransmission as it removes 5-HT released into the synaptic cleft. 5-HTT contains several polymorphisms, including the *5-HTT*-linked polymorphic region (5-HTTLPR), which comprises an insertion/deletion polymorphism that results in a long (L) and a short (S) variant. This polymorphism is functional: presence of the S variant leads to levels of transporter 40% lower than with the L variant. The polymorphism is also quite common: amongst Caucasians, 32% are homozygous for the L variant, 49% are heterozygous, and 19% are homozygous for the S variant (any individual will carry two copies of the gene, one from each parent).

The first association study reported that individuals with either one or two copies of the 5-HTTLPR S variant have significantly higher scores of neuroticism than those who are homozygous for the 5-HTTLPR L variant (Lesch et al. 1996). Several meta-analyses based on this and subsequent replication studies concluded that there is evidence for a small but significant effect of 5-HTTLPR on neuroticism (Schinka et al. 2004, Sen et al. 2004, Munafo et al. 2005).

To begin to identify the underlying neural mechanisms, investigators have turned to measures of brain function in dependence on 5-HTTLPR genotype. The first such example was a study in which investigators used a cognitive response control (Go–NoGo) task and measured event-related potentials (ERPs) to find a significant association between 5-HTTLPR genotype and excitability of prefrontal cortex–limbic system (Fallgatter *et al.* 1999). The first functional magnetic resonance imaging (fMRI) study to investigate affect-related processes as a function of 5-HTTLPR variation was conducted by Hariri and colleagues (Hariri *et al.* 2002). In this seminal study, these investigators found that carriers of the 5-HTTLPR S variant, compared with noncarriers, exhibited significantly greater activation of the *amygdala during an emotion-related task (matching of emotional facial expressions of anger and fear) relative to a neutral control task.

Later studies have confirmed and expanded this initial observation. For example, functional connectivity analyses have revealed increased coupling between the amygdala and the ventromedial prefrontal cortex in healthy carriers of the S variant (Heinz *et al.* 2005). This is of interest because the S variant is a risk factor for depression, and depressed patients exhibit elevated activation in the amygdala and ventromedial prefrontal cortex, suggesting a biological vulnerability marker. Another study reported decreased functional connectivity between the amygdala and the subgenual *anterior cingulate cortex (ACC), both of which are implicated in depression, in healthy carriers of the S variant (Pezawas *et al.* 2005). Furthermore, these investigators discovered a reduced volume of grey matter in both of these structures as a function of the S variant. Based on these functional and structural data, these investigators proposed a model of dysregulation of the amygdala, in which developmental mechanisms, possibly in interaction with environmental variables, could differentially affect structural and functional connectivity within a circuit that is critical for affect processing, and thus render some individuals vulnerable for depression.

The interaction between 5-HTTLPR genotype and environmental variables has been well-documented for life stress experiences. Caspi and colleagues (Caspi *et al.* 2003), in the course of a 23-year longitudinal study, discovered that presence of the S variant moderated and greatly amplified the adverse effects of life stress on depression and depression-related symptoms. An imaging study showed that this interaction is also observed at the level of neural activation (Canli *et al.* 2006). For carriers of the S variant, more life stress was associated with greater activation in the amygdala and other regions, whereas for noncarriers (i.e. homozygous carriers of the L variant) more life stress was associated with *lesser* activation in the amygdala and elsewhere. These neural activation patterns were mirrored by self-reported rumination: life stress correlated positively with rumination in carriers of the S variant, but correlated negatively with rumination in noncarriers.

The commonly held view is that presence of the S variant increases reactivity of the amygdala to negative stimuli (see Fig. G1). This model offers an intuitive explanation for why the S variant is associated with negative affect and vulnerability to depression or other mood disorders. An alternative explanation has been put forward (Canli *et al.* 2005b, 2006), named the *tonic activation model*, according to which carriers of the S variant are characterized by tonic activation of the amygdala which may cause these individuals to be in a constant state of emotional arousal, heightened vigilance, or enhanced emotional affective encoding. In support of this alternative model, these investigators reported greater blood flow in the amygdala of carriers of the S variant, compared with noncarriers, at rest, which was independently confirmed by Rao *et al.* (2007). However, it is possible that this elevated level of activation reflects the response of carriers of the S variant to an undefined, and therefore possibly threatening, environment (Heinz *et al.* 2007), rather than an intrinsic level of emotional arousal. Thus, the two models of 5-HTTLPR function remain to be examined in future work.

Other polymorphisms related to affect

Another polymorphism of interest related to affect is the gene that regulates the production of monoamine oxidase A (MAO-A). This gene is critical for neurotransmission because MAO-A regulates the catabolism of monoamines, particularly serotonin. The gene contains a functional VNTR polymorphism: variants with three and a half or four repeat sequence copies are transcribed two to ten times more efficiently ('high-expression alleles') than variants with three or five repeat sequence copies ('low-expression alleles'). Caspi and colleagues reported that presence of the low-expression *MAOA* variant, in interaction with childhood maltreatment, is associated with later *antisocial behaviour in adulthood (Caspi *et al.* 2002). A recent neuroimaging study suggests that the low-expression *MAOA* variant is associated with dysfunctional neural activation in a circuit involved in emotion regulation during a cognitive inhibition task (Meyer-Lindenberg *et al.* 2006), suggesting that aggression in these individuals may be moderated, at least in part, by *MAOA* genotype.

Another candidate polymorphism is the tryptophan hydroxylase-2 gene, which codes for the rate-limiting enzyme during serotonin synthesis in the brain. For example, a SNP leading to a G-to-T substitution has been linked to differential response of the amygdala to angry and fearful facial expressions (Brown *et al.* 2005), but more likely moderates reactivity of the amygdala to

"Standard" (Phasic) Model

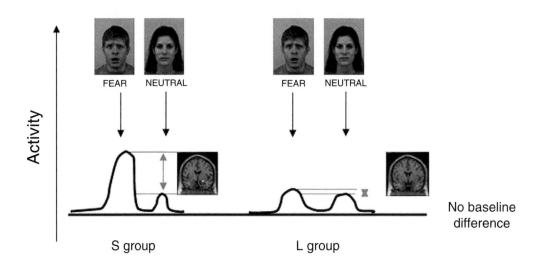

No baseline
difference

Tonic Model

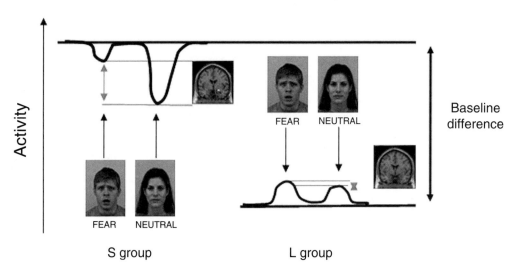

Baseline
difference

Fig. G1. The standard 'phasic' versus 'tonic' model of modulation of brain activity by 5-HTTLPR. The phasic model explains greater negative emotionality in carriers of the 5-HTTLPR S variant, compared with noncarriers, in terms of greater reactivity of the amygdala to negative stimuli. The tonic model explains greater negative emotionality in carriers of the 5-HTTLPR S variant, compared with noncarriers, in terms of greater baseline activation of the amygdala. (From Canli and Lesch 2007.)

emotional signals regardless of valence (Canli *et al.* 2005a). Furthermore, this genetic polymorphism interacts with the 5-HTTLPR polymorphisms. Individuals who carry the variant associated with greater emotional reactivity for both genes exhibit the greatest neural response to emotionally arousing stimuli, whereas individuals who carry the variant associated with least emotional reactivity for both genes exhibit the least neural response to emotionally arousing stimuli (Herrmann *et al.* 2007).

From candidate genes to large-scale genomics

With the arrival of large-scale SNP gene chips it is now possible to obtain information about hundreds of thousands of gene variations simultaneously from a single subject. Although it is widely believed that complex affective traits involve dozens, if not hundreds, of genetic polymorphisms, current methods for analysing and interpreting such huge amounts of data are lacking. Therefore there will be much interest in developing novel computational and analytical tools to integrate large-scale genomics data with complex phenotype measures, particularly those obtained from neuroimaging studies.

TURHAN CANLI

Canli, T. and Lesch, K.P. (2007). Long story short: the serotonin transporter in emotional regulation and social cognition. *Nature Neuroscience*, **10**, 1103–9.

Hariri, A.R. and Holmes, A. (2006). Genetics of emotional regulation: the role of the serotonin transporter in neural function. *Trends in Cognitive Sciences*, **10**, 182–91.

Hariri, A.R., Drabant, E.M., and Weinberger, D.R. (2006). Imaging genetics: perspectives from studies of genetically driven variation in serotonin function and corticolimbic affective processing. *Biological Psychiatry*, **59**, 888–97.

Meyer-Lindenberg, A. and Weinberger, D.R. (2006) Intermediate phenotypes and genetic mechanisms of psychiatric disorders. *Nature Reviews Neuroscience*, **7**, 818–27.

Gestalt (and feeling) The distinctive claim of the Gestalt psychologists is that we are typically aware of wholes which have 'Gestalt qualities', such as being a melody, and that these qualities could not be properties of mere sums, for example of sums of tones. A common, stronger claim is that the wholes we are aware of are themselves 'Gestalten', the parts of which are inseparable from each other and from the wholes they belong to. The Gestalt psychologists took themselves to be opposing associationalistic and atomistic assumptions in psychology. The notion of a Gestalt is applied primarily in their accounts of perception and to a much lesser extent in their accounts of feelings (*Gefühle*), aesthetic and nonaesthetic, of their objects, of our awareness of the feelings of others, of our attributions of emotions, of our grasp of value, and of the relations between affective phenomena and perception.

A *feeling is itself a complex whole, an episode consisting of at least four parts: (1) an affective aspect—being pleased, admiration—which is distinct from any sort of affective sensation (*Gefühlsempfindung*) such as a localized pain (Stumpf 1928) and depends on its (2) basis or presupposition, a perception, judgement, phantasy etc. The basis consists of two parts, (3) a mode or quality—a seeing, a judging, visual imagining—and (4) a content, for example a presentation of Sam or of an imaginary woman or the propositional content that it is raining. The affective aspect of an emotion depends one-sidedly on its basis: displeasure based on the *belief that it is raining may disappear while the belief survives. Alexius Meinong (1853–1920) and Witasek (1904) argue that the affective aspect of a feeling may depend directly or predominantly on either the mode or on the content of its presupposition. In the first case, the feeling is an act-feeling, in the second, a content-feeling. Aesthetic feelings are content-feelings, indeed aesthetic pleasure in a melody may be pleasure based on hearing the melody or on remembering the melody (see AESTHETIC EMOTIONS (PHILOSOPHICAL PERSPECTIVES)). But consider someone who wants to know whether it is raining and succeeds in finding out. His pleasure in his discovery is an act-feeling. But displeasure based on the belief that it is raining is a content-feeling; it depends directly on the content of the emotion's basis—that it is raining—and indirectly on the mode or quality of the basis—belief. Where a content is complex the affective aspect of a feeling may directly depend on or 'colour' part of a content rather than the whole content: there is a pleasure based on listening to a melody which is pleasure in the way the melody is played and which may coexist with dislike of the melody itself.

Feeling may be based on 'serious' acts and states, judgements, beliefs, perceptions etc. but also on visual imaginings or on suppositions, that is, on phantasy seeings and phantasy judgements. Are there phantasy feelings? The affirmative answer to this question, given by Meinong and then by Edmund Husserl (1859–1938), has it that in a phantasy feeling (what is now often called a 'make-believe emotion') the affective aspect itself is a phantasy act or state. Witasek disagrees. The state that feels like fear when one watches the monster on the screen really is fear but fear based on visual make-believe and perception of the screen. Phantasy feelings have a serious affective aspect and a make-believe presupposition.

The most ambitious account of feelings as Gestalten is that explored by Robert Musil (1995) or rather by Ulrich, the hero of Musil's *The Man without Qualities*. Ulrich rejects the view that feelings are merely one-sidedly dependent on ideas, thought, or perceptions in favour of an interdependence between feelings and thoughts or perceptions, and between these, stimuli, and the subject's situation and history. He describes the forms of the different ways in which affective phenomena can develop (their *Ausgestaltung*) and locates these on a continuum between two extremes: feelings which culminate in action (processes) and feelings for which the best term seems to be 'moods' (states). Musil's analysis is in some respects an application of the framework developed by Kurt Lewin (1925c) in his account of intentions, the will and behaviour (an account Lewin applies in passing to affective phenomena and which is developed further by Dembo, 1931). Musil's narrator notes that the concept of love is a family resemblance concept: the different types of love are related to each other merely by overlapping, partial similarities.

Karl Bühler (1927; Duncker 1941) gives a pioneering account of pleasure in activity (*Funktionsfreude*) and of its relation to the products of activity and uses this account to criticize Freud's psychology.

Husserl and then Max Scheler (1973) argue that values and goods require (*fordern*) or demand certain affective reactions: danger demands fear and fear in the face of danger forms a whole in which the fear 'fits' its object. The idea is developed by Wolfgang Köhler (1935) and by Lewin, who claims that practical objects may display demand, prohibition, or permission characters (*Aufforderungscharaktere*), what has come to be called *valence, as when the use-value of tools requires or allows certain practical and affective attitudes.

Felix Krueger (1874–1948) argued that feelings are more or less deeply rooted in a person. Scheler (1973) attempts to unpack the metaphor of depth in terms of the extent to which feelings are more or less indirectly subject to the will: sensory pleasure is more easily controlled than feelings of exhaustion or health, the latter are easier to influence than admiration. But felicity and despair (Musil's states), love and hate are more difficult to manipulate than any of these.

KEVIN MULLIGAN

Mulligan, K. (1995). Musil's *Analyse des Gefühls*. In: B. Böschenstein and M.-L. Roth (eds), *Hommage à Robert Musil*, pp. 87–110. Berne: Lang.

Reisenzein, R. (2003a). Stumpf's kognitiv-evaluative Theorie der Emotionen. In: L. Sprung and W. Schönpflug (eds), *Zur Geschichte der Psychologie in Berlin*, pp. 227–74. Frankfurt am Main: Lang.

Reisenzein, R. (2003b). Die Emotionstheorie von Meinong. In: R. Reisenzein, W.-U. Meyer, and A. Schützwohl (eds), *Einführung in die Emotionspsychologie, Band III: Kognitive Emotionstheorien*, Ch. 1. Bern: Huber.

Smith, B. (1994). *Austrian philosophy. The legacy of Franz Brentano*, Chs 5, 8, 9. Chicago: Open Court.

Smith, B. (ed.) (1988). *Foundations of Gestalt theory*. Munich: Philosophia Verlag.

gestural expression of emotion Gestures form a specific group of body actions performed by the hands, arms, and sometimes the head. They usually, but not exclusively, occur during speech interaction and form an integral part of the system of symbolic expression (see INTERPERSONAL COMMUNICATION). A crucial distinction from other types of hand, arm, and other body movement lies in the fact that gestures are voluntary actions that arise from the deliberative attempt to convey certain semantic and pragmatic information, and are recognized as such by the viewer (Kendon 2004). Waving goodbye or hand movements when explaining directions are some typical examples, whereas self-manipulative movement like scratching is usually not considered a gesture.

Research on gestures is found in cognitive science, particularly psycholinguistics. The integration of nonverbal signalling in verbal communication has not only revealed a way to understand functions of gesture in relation to speech, it is also used as a means to investigate processes such as thought and mental imagery (McNeill 2005). However, while touching on pragmatic-affective aspects of speech, this tradition does not centrally include issues such as the expression and communication of emotion.

In contrast, starting from early observations on the use of hand movements and gestures in affectively laden psychiatric interviews, scholars of nonverbal communication have investigated the bodily expression and perception of emotion (see BODILY EXPRESSION OF EMOTION). In this area (sometimes referred to as kinesics; see Harrigan 2005), gesture is rarely treated as an autonomous expressive system but is usually included in a broad range of communicative and regulatory body actions with varying degrees of communicative intention and connection to the verbal utterance.

Based on the seminal work of David Efron, Ekman and Friesen (1969) developed a functional classification system that includes hand and arm gestures such as illustrators (movements which accompany, illustrate, or accentuate the verbal content) and emblems (conventialized movements with a culturally shared and fixed meaning). Their typology has been widely cited and various extensions (Scherer and Wallbott 1985) provided a first platform for gestural studies on emotion (see survey in Harrigan 2005). For example, Wallbott (1998) reported the first evidence for links between certain emotions and types of hand movement and dynamic features (e.g. illustrators being used more frequently during active emotions such as hot anger and elated joy).

In general, hand actions, intentional or not, are a relevant but thoroughly understudied means of emotion communication. Their expressive or signalling value for emotion can be examined via both categorical and dynamic approaches. Thus one can investigate which *types* of gestures are used to display emotion, such as certain illustrators or gestures as part of affect emblems (e.g. raising the arms above the head with hand in fists for pride). Alternatively, one can focus on *dynamic performance* of gestural movements in time and space. Spatial and dynamic qualities of movement, such as velocity and fluency, tension and force, path and manner of hand action, are important cues that are actively used by people in their attribution of emotion to others (e.g. Atkinson *et al.* 2004). How these cues are actually shaped by emotion in their production, how they are related to physiological underpinnings and other expressive modalities, and how they influence emotion perception and attribution are important questions for future research.

NELE DAEL AND KLAUS R. SCHERER

Harrigan, J.A. (2005). Proxemics, kinesics, and gaze. In: J.A. Harrigan, R. Rosenthal, and K.R. Scherer (eds), *The new handbook of methods in nonverbal behavior research*, pp. 137–98. New York: Oxford University Press.

goals Goals are the major motivational source (see MOTIVATION) for human behaviour; they compel us to act in a way intended to help us achieve a desired objective. As with other organisms, one of the fundamental motives for humans is to approach things that benefit us and avoid things that will harm us (see APPROACH/WITHDRAWAL). However, goals allow humans to go beyond reflexes and drives to make individualized, contextualized evaluations of what our current circumstances imply for our well-being, rather than having to rely only on the properties of the stimulus itself (see RELEVANCE DETECTION). According to many, but not all, theorists, one could not have emotions without goals. Goals are related to emotions and emotional processes in at least two distinct ways.

First, goals (along with closely related motivational constructs such as *needs, *values, and *concerns) play an essential role in the elicitation of emotion. In fact, the theoretical link between goals and emotions is so strong that emotions can, in part, be conceptualized as a read-out of how one is faring in relation to one's goals and values (e.g. Smith and Ellsworth 1985, Frijda 1986, Smith and Lazarus 1990, Lazarus 1991, Roseman 2001, Scherer 2001a). In general, benign emotions signal that one has achieved or is making progress toward achieving one's goals, whereas stress-related emotions signal that one's progress has in some way been slowed or thwarted.

According to most emotion theories, emotion involves a direct evaluation of the relation of one's circumstances to one's goals and values (sometimes referred to as *primary appraisals due to their import-

ance in eliciting emotion; see Lazarus, 1991). For example, Smith and Lazarus (1990) propose two such evaluations. One, motivational relevance, reflects the extent to which one's circumstances are relevant to one's goals and values, and is hypothesized to determine the intensity of the emotional response. The second is an evaluation of motivational congruence, which reflects the degree to which what is happening is consistent versus inconsistent with one's goals. This evaluation distinguishes benign from stress-related emotions. Scherer (2001a) includes similar evaluations of concern relevance and goal/need conduciveness in his model, and Roseman (2001) includes an evaluation of *motive consistency.

One point of controversy regarding the relations between goals and emotions concerns the link between the content or type of goal and the emotional response. Both Scherer (2001a) and Smith (see Smith and Lazarus 1993) consider the evaluation of a goal in relation to one's circumstances to be all that is directly relevant to the emotion, and would argue that, if appraised appropriately, any goal could contribute to any emotional reaction. Both Roseman (2001) and Lazarus (1991) argue that the nature or type of goal implicated in a situation contributes directly to the emotions elicited. For Roseman (2001), holding other appraisals constant, different emotions sometimes result depending on whether the goal or motive is appetitive or aversive. For example, the inability to obtain something desired (an appetitive motive) will produce sadness, whereas the inability to avoid something undesired (an aversive motive) will result in distress. Lazarus (1991, 2001) and most evolutionary theorists take the specificity idea a step further and argue that at least some emotions *always* involve specific goals; for example, self- and/or social esteem is always threatened in anger, whereas moral values are always implicated in guilt, and so on.

Beyond the important links between goals and the elicitation of emotion, there is a second important relation between emotions and goals: According to virtually all emotion theories, an important component of emotional responses is motivational urge to act on the situation in a particular way—to attack in anger, to flee in fear, to celebrate in happiness, and to withdraw and cry in sadness, etc. A number of theorists have discussed this motivational component of emotion (e.g. Scherer 1984a, 2001a), sometimes referring to its products as *action tendencies or modes of *action readiness (e.g. Frijda 1986). One theorist who has explicitly linked this motivational aspect of the emotional response to goals is Roseman (Roseman *et al.* 1994, Roseman 2001), who describes emotivational goals as the 'characteristic goals that people want to attain when the emotion is experienced' (2001, p. 75). For instance,

gratitude

he lists the emotivational goal of sadness as wanting to 'recover', of fear as wanting to 'get to safety, prevent', and of anger to 'hurt' (Roseman 2001, pp. 70–71).

Emotions arise in the service of one's goals and values, and once elicited these emotions provide the person with more immediate, situated goals and urges that push the person to respond to the emotion-eliciting situation, but to do so in a way that allows for considerable flexibility and behavioural plasticity.

CRAIG A. SMITH AND LESLIE D. KIRBY

Ellsworth, P.C. and Scherer, K.R. (2003). Appraisal processes in emotion. In: R.J. Davidson, K.R. Scherer, and H.H. Goldsmith (eds), *Handbook of affective sciences*, pp. 572–95. Oxford: Oxford University Press.

Roseman, I.J., Wiest, C., and Swartz, T.S. (1994). Phenomenology, behaviors, and goals differentiate discrete emotions. *Journal of Personality and Social Psychology*, **67**, 206–21.

gratitude Gratitude is a commonly experienced affect. Chipperfield *et al.* (2003) reported that feeling grateful was the third most common discrete positive affect experienced in a sample of older adults, reported by nearly 90% of their sample. Gratitude can also represent a broader attitude toward life—the tendency to see all of life as a gift. Gratitude thus has various meanings, and can be conceptualized at several levels of analysis ranging from momentary affect to long-term dispositions (McCullough *et al.* 2002). Gratitude defies easy classification. It has been conceptualized as an emotion, an attitude, a moral virtue, a habit, a personality trait, and a coping response. The word gratitude is derived from the Latin *gratia*, meaning grace, graciousness, or gratefulness. All derivatives from this Latin root 'have to do with kindness, generousness, gifts, the beauty of giving and receiving, or getting something for nothing' (Pruyser 1976, p. 69).

Although a variety of life experiences can elicit feelings of gratitude, prototypically gratitude stems from the perception that one has received a gift or benefit from another person. Grateful emotions and behaviours typically result from the perception that another person has intended to promote one's *well-being. Most existing theoretical treatments concur that gratitude is greatest under a specific set of attributions: (1) when a benefit is evaluated positively; (2) when the benefit that one has encountered is not attributed to one's own effort; and (3) when the benefit was rendered intentionally by the benefactor. Existing research suggests that gratitude is a typically pleasant experience that is linked to *contentment, *happiness, and *hope. There is consensus that gratitude can be regarded as a *moral emotion in that it leads to behaviour intended to benefit others. The experience of gratitude results from acknowledging the

'gratuitous' role that sources of social support may play in propagating beneficial outcomes in our lives. Gratitude aids in reciprocating kindness towards those who have been kind to us.

Considerable research has examined the ability of gratitude to produce positive psychological, interpersonal, and physical outcomes. Gratitude interventions, by increasing the intensity and frequency of grateful emotions, have been shown to have sustainable effects on emotional and interpersonal well-being, as well as physical health. Emmons and McCullough (2003) found that those who kept gratitude journals on a regular basis exercised more regularly, reported fewer physical symptoms, felt better about their lives as a whole, and were more optimistic about the upcoming week compared with those who recorded hassles or neutral life events. They also reported higher levels of high-engagement positive emotions, such as interest, excitement, enthusiasm, and vitality.

Gratitude is also measured at the trait level. These measures of individual difference emphasize the emotional component of gratitude more so than the moral component of reciprocity. At the dispositional level, grateful people report higher levels of positive emotions, life satisfaction, vitality, and optimism and lower levels of depression and stress (McCullough *et al.* 2002). The positivity of gratitude is not limited to self-reports. Grateful people are seen by others as being more empathic, forgiving, agreeable, and altruistic (McCullough *et. al.* 2002) such that it may be reasonable to conclude that expressions of gratitude and appreciation are essential to successful, vital, and thriving long-term relationships.

Over the years, mainstream social science has been somewhat neglectful of the concept of gratitude. Negative psychological states such as anger, depression, or anxiety have generated literally thousands of scientific research studies. Research that has specifically focused on gratitude, on the other hand, is limited to fewer than a score of high-quality rigorous scientific studies. Therefore, much is still unknown. Basic issues, such as the emotional structure of gratitude, its uniqueness from other positive emotions, the consequences of its experience and expression for emotional, physical, and relational well-being, and the cognitive mechanisms that sustain gratitude over time require further study.

ROBERT A. EMMONS

Emmons, R.A. and McCullough, M.E. (eds) (2004). *The psychology of gratitude*. New York: Oxford University Press.

grief Grief is the reaction of intense suffering following a *bereavement (i.e. the loss of a significant person, e.g.

a partner, child, parent, sibling, or close friend, through that person's death). In the current scientific literature grief is typically distinguished from mourning, the latter referring to the public display, the social acts expressive of grief that are shaped by the (religious) beliefs and practices of a given society or cultural group (clearly, there is mutual impact between grief and mourning). Grief is understood to be primarily an emotional (affective) reaction but it also incorporates diverse psychological (cognitive, social-behavioural) and physical (physiological-somatic) components. It is a complex syndrome, featuring a variety of manifestations, such as loneliness, *anger, *despair, and *guilt feelings. Reactions vary from one bereaved person to another, across cultures, and over the course of time for a single grieving person. Grief is associated with mental and physical health deficits and even with higher rates of mortality compared with nonbereaved persons (Stroebe et al. 2007). A minority of bereaved individuals suffer complicated forms of grieving and are in need of therapeutic intervention (Schut and Stroebe 2005). A variety of risk factors for increased vulnerability to various health consequences have been identified among bereaved persons, including violent, traumatic causes of death, prior susceptibilities to mental health problems or personality characteristics such as neuroticism (see Stroebe et al. 2007). The majority of bereaved people are, however, able to cope, and come to terms with their loss without professional intervention.

MARGARET S. STROEBE AND
WOLFGANG STROEBE

guilt There is substantial disagreement in the psychological literature about the definition of guilt and its differentiation from related emotions such as shame (see SHAME). At least four major theoretical approaches to guilt can be identified. They all agree that guilt is a self-conscious emotion (see SELF-REFLEXIVE EMOTIONS) that occurs when a person brings about a negative outcome by acts of commission or omission. The four approaches disagree, however, on the specific appraisals, subjective experiences, and *action tendencies that are typical of guilt.

According to the first approach (the *internal standards* approach), guilt is activated when people perceive that they have done something that violates their own internalized standards. In the *internal standards* approach it makes no difference whether or not anyone else is aware of the violation (e.g. Ausubel 1955). According to the second approach (the *moral transgression* approach), the sole criterion of guilt is that the behaviour violates a *moral* standard (e.g. Lazarus 1991). In the third approach (the *behavioural focus* approach), the person focuses on his or her unacceptable behaviour and

its consequences (e.g. Tangney and Dearing 2002). The final approach (the *interpersonal approach*) emphasizes the interpersonal nature of guilt. Here guilt is seen as a communal emotion that functions to restore interpersonal harmony when someone has hurt another person or the group as a whole (e.g. Baumeister et al. 1994).

In the internal standards and moral transgression approaches, rumination and pangs of conscience are central to the experience of guilt. One is acutely aware of the discrepancy between one's behaviour and one's own internal standards or the moral standards of one's group. This awareness can lead either to intrapunitive behaviour or to behaviour aimed at repairing the negative consequences of the behaviour (atonement). This means that guilt can elicit either destructive (intrapunitive) or constructive (restorative) action tendencies. In the behavioural focus approach appraisals of *agency and control are central to the experience of guilt, leading to proactive attempts to undo the offensive behaviour and repair the consequences. Thus, from the behavioural focus approach guilt always results in constructive action tendencies. The sense of agency and control is a necessary feature of guilt in this approach, but not in any of the other approaches. In the internal standards and moral transgression approaches, the wrongdoing may be beyond one's own personal control. It may be the results of intrinsic defects or of an inherently sinful nature, as in some Judaeo-Christian religious traditions. In the interpersonal approach, the experience of empathy plays a central role. The wrongdoer experiences the suffering he or she has caused to someone else, and is motivated to restore good interpersonal relations. Guilt is not seen as internal, but as interpersonal. Moreover, it is often actively provoked in close relationships by the person who feels hurt; by reproaching the person who has caused the harm, one can use induction of guilt as a way to correct imbalances in the relationship.

Two other emotions closely related to guilt are embarrassment (see EMBARRASSMENT) and shame. Embarrassment occurs when there is a disruption of normal social functioning, and in awkward social situations. Unlike guilt, it does not implicate important internalized or moral standards. Smiling is common in embarrassment, but not in guilt. The distinction between guilt and shame is the central focus of three of the four major approaches. According to the internal standards view of guilt, the difference between shame and guilt is that shame involves a violation of external standards. Guilt is a matter of one's personal conscience, independent of the evaluations of others, whereas the disapproval of others (real or imagined) is considered essential for shame. In the moral transgression approach, guilt is produced by violation of moral imperatives, whereas shame results from a discrepancy between one's goals, standards, and aspirations and one's actual accomplishments. In the behavioural focus approach, guilt is differentiated from shame by a focus on a particular behaviour, rather than on the self in general. In guilt, the focus is on the specific act of wrongdoing. The person takes responsibility for the blameworthy behaviour, and is motivated to repair the damage caused. In shame, however, the negative emotion encompasses the whole self. The wrongdoing is seen as a manifestation of fundamental, uncontrollable defects in the self.

Recent cross-cultural research suggests that all four perspectives are valid, but for different kinds of situations or different phenomena related to guilt (Fontaine *et al.* 2006). While the internal standards, moral transgression, and interpersonal approaches describe emotional reactions to different kinds of situations the behavioural focus perspective describes individual differences that generalize across situations. The internal standards perspective applies to situations that may or may not involve moral deficiency but that primarily affect one's own outcomes, such as failing a course because of insufficient commitment to studying. Typical responses to this type of guilt are rumination and self-reproach. In the moral transgression approach, the situation may or may not involve other people, but always involves a violation of moral standards. The interpersonal perspective best describes situations in which a person unjustifiably causes someone else to suffer. Typical responses are a strong tendency to empathize and to attempt to undo the harm done. Unlike the other three approaches, the behavioural focus approach is not specific to any kind of guilt-inducing situation, but is a general personality disposition involving a sense of control, a focus on specific behaviour rather than on the self in general, and a tendency to take an active approach to reparation.

JOHNNY R. J. FONTAINE

gut feelings The term gut feelings has two meanings: one physiological and the other psychological. The more physiological meaning of the term refers to interoceptive (see INTEROCEPTION) perception of sensations emanating from the gut or internal visceral organs. These sensations can be caused by any number of conditions including acute illnesses such as food poisoning, chronic diseases of the intestines such as ulcerative colitis, or even cramps caused by dehydration.

Gut feelings also refer to various psychological states related to affect and emotion. The term is often used synonymously with intuition or the sense that good or bad consequences will come from a particular deci-

sion or event. When individuals feel that they possess intuitions about upcoming events they will often indicate that they have a 'feeling in their gut' even though they cannot put into words exactly how they know that something will come to pass.

There is a large literature that has tried to determine whether intuitions and gut feelings tend to be accurate or inaccurate. The answer is somewhat complex. On the one hand, doctors' and nurses' intuitions, and those of various other studied groups, do not seem to be nearly as accurate as their own confidence would suggest. Research on *decision-making suggests a whole range of biases that lead to systematic errors in judgement while producing feelings of intuitive correctness (Tversky and Kahneman 1974). On the other hand, there are various phenomena in which individuals are much more accurate than chance while relying only on their gut feelings. For instance, after being shown two-second video clips, without sound, of college teachers teaching, individuals were able to tell with a remarkable degree of accuracy how those teachers were rated by students who had finished a semester long course with the same teachers (Ambady and Rosenthal 1993). In these 'thin slice' studies, subjects often report that they do not know how they answered and simply went with their gut feelings.

The fact that there are both physiological and psychological meanings of gut feelings could be a result of the way these processes interact with one another. The *James–Lange theory of emotion suggests that the experience of emotion, psychologically, was dependent on the perception of bodily signals, including those of the interoceptive variety. Similarly, cognitive dissonance theory (Festinger 1957) proposes that individuals change the way they feel about various things when they experience physiological discomfort caused by the conflict between their current attitudes and other conflicting beliefs.

Neuroscientists have also explored the links between the physiological and psychological aspects of gut feelings. One general finding of interest is that serotonin, one of the two neurotransmitters most commonly associated with affective processes in the brain, is more prevalent in the gut than any other region of the body. In fact, about 95% of the body's serotonin is found in the gut and is thought to transmit information to the brain (Gershon and Tack 2007).

Neuroimaging studies have also examined how the brain might incorporate information from the gut in its processes (see Fig. G2). These are complex processes that are just beginning to be understood. One prominent theory (Damasio 1994) has argued that the ventromedial prefrontal cortex learns, with practice, to predict

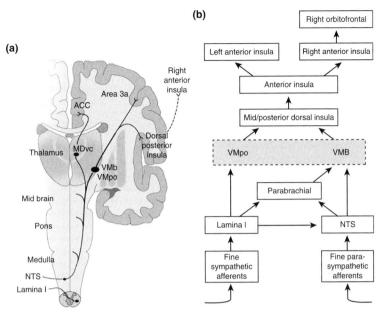

Fig. G2. Ascending projections of homeostatic afferents. (a) Organization of interoceptive pathways. Small-diameter afferents that travel with sympathetic and with parasympathetic efferents provide input to lamina I and nucleus tractus solitarius (NTS), respectively. In mammals, the activity of both types of afferents is integrated in the parabrachial nucleus (PBN), which projects to insular cortex. In nonhuman and human primates there exists a direct projection from lamina I and from the NTS to the ventromedial thalamic nuclei (VMpo and VMb, respectively). Neurons in these nuclei project in a topographical fashion to the mid/posterior insula. In humans, this cortical image of the homeostatic state of the organism is re-represented in the anterior insula on the same side of the brain. These re-representations provide the substrate for a subjective evaluation of interoceptive state. (b) Spino-thalamo-cortical system. Summary diagram illustrating the projections in primates of homeostatic afferent pathways from lamina I (spinal) and NTS (vagal) to thalamic nuclei, and the two cortical regions involved in the sensory (insula) and motivational (anterior cingulate cortex, ACC) dimensions of homeostatic emotions. Reprinted from Mayer *et al.* (2006)

how the body would respond to particular situations so that the brain can respond more efficiently to those situations without waiting for relatively slow feedback from bodily responses (see SOMATIC MARKER HYPOTHESIS). Work by Craig (2002), Critchley (2004), and others points to a neural network including the *anterior cin- gulate cortex, insula, thalamus, and orbitofrontal cortex in the detection of gut feelings.

MATTHEW D. LIEBERMAN

Mayer, E.A., Naliboff, B.D., and Craig, A.D. (2006). Neuroimaging of the brain–gut axis: from basic understanding to treatment of functional GI disorders. *Gastroenterology*, **131**, 1925–42.

H

happiness The emotion of happiness is a subjective, valenced reaction to a positive experience or event (Ortony et al. 1988). Happiness can be conceptualized as an umbrella term that encompasses a variety of positive feelings, ranging from the low-intensity states of *contentment, *enjoyment, serenity, and *amusement to the high-intensity states of elation, *joy, and euphoria. These positive states are typically experienced when a person is making progress towards the realization of *goals (Carver and Scheier 1998), and, notably, signal that the environment is benign and safe for both relaxation and exploration (Schwarz and Clore 1983). As such, researchers had originally conceptualized a happy emotion as producing a form of 'free activation' that is conducive to creativity and divergent thought (Frijda 1986, Isen et al. 1992). Extending this idea, Fredrickson's (2001) broaden-and-build model argued that feelings of happiness are functional, such that they open people up to creative endeavours and novel approaches to problem-solving, as well as building social, physical, and intellectual resources that prepare them for future challenges (see POSITIVE EMOTIONS). Consistent with this reasoning, the frequency of happy emotions has been found to be positively related to approach-related motivation, effective coping, physical health and longevity, strong social support, satisfaction with social relationships, prosocial behaviour, productivity in the workplace, and other markers of success (Lyubomirsky et al. 2005a). In short, happiness is more than a hedonically pleasant state. It is the means to a variety of positive ends that have value for both the individual and the society at large.

In the light of these benefits, it is natural to wonder whether the frequency with which people experience happy emotions can be increased and maintained. Some cite evidence suggesting that people have a genetically determined set point for experiences of happiness—namely, a baseline to which they gravitate following triumphs or setbacks (Lykken and Tellegen 1996). In addition, temporally stable and cross-situationally consistent personality traits such as *extraversion and *neuroticism are highly predictive of a person's reports of happiness (Costa and McCrae 1980). Although these observations highlight the futility of pursuing lasting improvements in the frequency of happy emotions, there are also reasons

for optimism. Recent research has found that an individual's experiences of happiness can be significantly bolstered by the regular, committed practice of activities such as counting blessings, expressing optimism, and performing acts of kindness (Lyubomirsky et al. 2005b). In sum, frequent happiness is a highly valued goal that is partially a function of *temperament, but can also be attained through effortful intentional activity.

SONJA LYUBOMIRSKY AND JAIME L. KURTZ

hatred Hatred, the noun, and to hate, the verb, do not completely coincide in their semantic ranges. Hatred carries with it more intensity and greater seriousness than many of our most common uses of the verb. Hatred is unlikely to apply aptly to one's feelings about broccoli, though it would be perfectly normal to register one's aversion to it by saying 'I hate broccoli'. In daily speech, hate can be used to indicate a fairly strong but not very serious aversion to a film, novel, or food, all the way to desiring, with varying seriousness, the extermination of an entire people. The word hate can thus mark a powerful moral/immoral *sentiment, or merely register a negative *preference. In this it tracks Latin usage, where the verb, odi, and the noun odium, can be used to register both simple aversion and also an intense passion of all-consuming detestation.

Attempts to get at the substance of hatred in the philosophical tradition focus mostly on how to distinguish it from *anger. Both anger and hatred accompany and inform relations of hostility, but not in quite the same way. Following Aristotle, the usual view is that anger is tied up with claims for redress against a particular person for particular wrongs, whereas hatred need no personal involvement; we can hate a person for what or who he or she is even without knowing them. Thus whole groups can be hated. Aristotle (384–322 BC) gives thieves and informers as examples. The grim history of the 20th century would add whole peoples based on religion, ethnicity, or race. Anger, Aristotle says, is curable and can be repaired via compensation, revenge, or apology. Unlike anger, which can exhaust itself within moments, hatred decays slowly if at all; it endures. The angry man might feel pity, says Aristotle, but not the hater; for the angry man wants the person he is angry at to suffer, while the hater wants him not to exist. Roughly then, anger is about acts, hatred about the mere existence of the hated.

Folk wisdom, not incorrectly, sees a link between *love and hate, each tied up with the other, not just as opposites but also as marking the roil and turmoil of close relations. It is disputed whether both can be co-experienced, though a good portion of the world's best known literature and not a little of our own experience would be incomprehensible if they could not be. Their relation is not symmetrical: hatred does not bring about the conditions for love, though love (spurned, betrayed) can readily supply the conditions for hatred. Both hatred and love share a focused intensity; both, strangely, involve caring. Both love and hatred are held to be character defining for those who feel them, with hatred maybe beating out love in this regard, for it seems we derive as much (or more) of our sense of who we are from our hatreds as from our loves. Thus it may be that though haters want their objects dead, they may find they need to resurrect them or reinvent them in order to maintain their own sense of self: to wish, in Othello's idiom, the hated one a thousand lives so he can keep on killing him.

Many of the distinctions between anger and hatred break down on closer inspection. We can hate individuals no less than groups. Consistently being angered by someone can lead to hate, and hate can easily trigger anger.

Darwin (1809–82), with his usual perspicuity, recognized that hatred mixes and mingles with other closely related sentiments depending on the relative status of the parties. Hatred for the lowly is not just tied up with disgust and contempt but disgust and contempt may in fact be the form hatred of the low takes. Hatred of the high by the low, he says, is closely annexed to fear, if not also a form of it. Nietzsche's (1844–1900) well-known account is that morality itself owes its very being to a particular form of hatred the weak have for the strong: *ressentiment*. But the genocides of the 20th century have shown that hatred has an even more remarkable transformative power: it allows the strong to invest the weak with magical and phantasmal powers of control, insinuation, infection, and pollution. A true history of hatred would have to come to terms with anti-Semitism.

Much routine hatred is experienced less as an emotion than as a quasiformal attitude of opposition, of obligatory enmity. And, when experienced as an emotion, hatred may never exist uncoloured variously by anger, disgust, contempt, fear, envy, competitiveness, and all-consuming love. For this reason too it has not been studied systematically in the scientific way anger has; it encompasses too many disparate inner states and outer settings for traditional psychological experimentation to get at. Even the most brilliant of philosophers despair. Thus David Hume's (1711–76) observation: 'Tis

altogether impossible to give any definition of the passions of love and hatred'.

WILLIAM IAN MILLER

health and emotion According to the World Health Organization health is defined as 'a state of complete physical, mental and social well-being and not merely the absence of disease or infirmity'. While the regulation or dysregulation of emotion has clearly been identified as a key factor in mental health (see DISORDER (AFFECTIVE, EMOTIONAL)),123 whether or not emotion plays a role in determining physical health outcomes is more controversial. References to the idea that emotions influence physical health can be found in the Bible and repeatedly throughout history. While many aspects of early ideas about *how* emotion influences physical health have been refuted, there is sufficient evidence of linkage that the relationship continues to be actively investigated (Kubzansky 2005). As research methods and technologies have improved, investigators have been able to explore the question with more compelling and methodologically rigorous studies than was previously possible.

Emotion might be related to physical health in a variety of ways. Emotions might influence the development of disease. Alternatively, emotions may exacerbate symptomatology or trigger acute disease-related events. Additionally, emotion may affect the progression of disease. Emotions may also affect compliance with medical regimen and disease management. Disease may also influence emotion states, since being ill is distressing.

To understand how or why emotions influence health, it is important to know how the term 'emotion' is conceptualized. Specific emotions are considered to be biologically based, and mediate between continually changing situations and the individual's behaviour (Frijda 1986). A major task of early childhood is developing the ability to regulate emotions (see CHILDHOOD EMOTIONAL DEVELOPMENT), and both the social environment and *personality play an important role in shaping regulatory capacity and the resulting emotional experiences. Positive and negative feeling states represent distinct emotional forces, and effective emotion regulation (see REGULATION OF EMOTION) is probably related to the achievement of some form of balance between positive and negative emotion (Rozanski *et al.* 2005). Thus, emotions may be considered to be adaptive and functionally appropriate processes which have dysfunctional consequences when the frequency, strength, or duration with which they occur is excessive (see FUNCTIONALIST THEORIES OF EMOTION). Failure to learn appropriate strategies for emotion regulation in childhood may set up a chain of risk, whereas effective regulation may lead to accruing resilience in relation to physical health.

Emotions have identifiable cognitive, neurobiological, and behavioural components. The experience of most emotions occurs along a continuum ranging from normal to pathological, and the components of emotion are essentially similar regardless of where on the continuum an emotion reaction lies (Clark and Watson 1994). As a result, effects of emotion on physical health may occur across the emotion continuum. Interestingly, studies using symptom measures of negative emotion have not suggested a threshold at which damaging effects are more likely to occur; rather risk appears to increase with each additional symptom (Kubzansky and Kawachi 2000).

Most emotions may be seen either as transitory *states* brought on by specific situations, or as *traits*, i.e. stable and general dispositions to experience particular emotions (Frijda 1994). Thus, emotions may directly affect the development of disease via biological alterations that occur as a result of either cumulative effects of repeated emotion experiences or an acute emotion episode. For example, negative emotions activate a 'stress response'. This involves a cascade of hormonal and neural activity whereby stored energy is converted to a usable resource, and growth and repair functions are inhibited (see STRESS). Emotions may also indirectly influence the development of disease via behavioural, cognitive, and social processes. For example, emotions motivate health-related behaviours and influence the availability of coping resources. Negative emotions have been linked to smoking, excessive alcohol consumption (see ADDICTION), and lower physical activity, and in turn these processes are risk factors for an array of diseases. Emotions influence cognitive and decision-making processes like symptom perception and healthcare use, and may also disrupt or promote social relationships, which are themselves associated with health outcomes.

Findings from experimental, prospective observational, and animal studies have converged to suggest that emotions significantly influence physical health outcomes (Everson-Rose and Lewis 2005, Kiecolt-Glaser *et al.* 2002). The best evidence has been provided in relation to cardiovascular diseases. However, evidence has also been presented in relation to numerous other outcomes including diabetes, cancer, infectious diseases, lung function, disability, and mortality. While most studies have focused on the harmful effects of negative emotions, limited work has also found positive emotions to have a protective effect.

Although evidence increasingly supports the role of emotion in determining health outcomes, we have not yet reached a detailed understanding of this relationship. For example, we have not established the duration or intensity of emotion experience that is needed to influ-

ence health, nor determined whether such effects are reversible. The importance of the social environment in shaping and modifying emotional processes and their subsequent health effects needs to be considered, with attention given to how these experiences unfold and accumulate across the life course. Additional understanding may be used to develop strategies for preventing disease and promoting health.

LAURA D. KUBZANSKY

Everson-Rose, S.A. and Lewis, T.T. (2005). Psychosocial factors and cardiovascular diseases. *Annual Review of Public Health*, **26**, 469–500.

Rozanski, A., Blumenthal, J.A., Davidson, K.W., Saab, P., and Kubzansky, L.D. (2005). The epidemiology, pathophysiology, and management of psychosocial risk factors in cardiac practice: the emerging field of behavioral cardiology. *Journal of the American College of Cardiology*, **45**, 637–51.

health/clinical aspects (of affect) see ADDICTION; ALEXITHYMIA; ANHEDONIA; ANTISOCIAL BEHAVIOUR; ANXIETY; APATHY; AUTISM; BIPOLAR DISORDER; COGNITIVE BEHAVIOUR THERAPY; COGNITIVE BIAS; DENIAL; DEPRESSION; DISINHIBITION; DISORDER (AFFECTIVE, EMOTIONAL); DYSPHORIA; EUSTRESS; HEALTH AND EMOTION; HYPOMANIA; ILLNESS COGNITIONS AND EMOTION; IMPULSIVITY; INFLAMMATION (AND MOOD); MANIA; MOOD DISORDERS; NARCISSISM; OBSESSIVECOMPULSIVE DISORDER; PAIN (BIOLOGICAL PERSPECTIVES); PAIN (PHILOSOPHICAL PERSPECTIVES); PANIC DISORDER; PARANOIA; PHOBIAS; POSTTRAUMATIC STRESS DISORDER; PSYCHONEUROENDOCRINOLOGY; PSYCHONEUROIMMUNOLOGY; PSYCHOPATHY; PSYCHOSOMATIC DISORDERS; REPRESSION; RESILIENCE; RISK FACTORS FOR EMOTIONAL DISORDERS; RISK-TAKING; RUMINATION; SEPARATION ANXIETY; STRESS; UNIPOLAR DISORDER; VIOLENCE; VULNERABILITY; WELL-BEING.

heuristics A heuristic is any procedure which simplifies a calculation, choice, or judgement, either by restricting the amount of information that is considered or the complexity of ways in which it is combined (see BOUNDED RATIONALITY). For example, the rule of thumb for converting degrees Celcius to degrees Fahrenheit ('double and add 30') is a heuristic; it replaces a more difficult operation (multiplying by 1.8 and adding 32) with something simpler. Like many other heuristics, this causes predictable errors (overestimating temperature when it is cool and underestimating temperature when it is hot), but it approximates the correct calculation and is often close enough (Simon 1978).

Many heuristics are designed to simplify choices among multidimensional alternatives (for reviews see Payne *et al.*, 1993, and Gigerenzer *et al.*, 1999). For example, a lexicographical (or 'take the best') heuristic selects the alternative that is superior on the most important attribute, neglecting all other information.

Such choice heuristics are degraded versions of optimal procedures which have, by necessity and design, been stripped down to accommodate cognitive limitations in short-term memory and computational capacity. These heuristics are viewed as heuristics by the people who use them, who will readily describe what they are doing as a simplifying strategy.

Not all heuristics, however, are best conceived as *deliberate* simplifying strategies. Some reflect differences in the fluency of mental operations required to process the different types of information relevant to the requested judgement (Kahneman *et al.* 1982). For example, when asked to predict the future outcome of a woman with a history of political activism, people generally considered it more likely that she turned out to be both a bank teller *and* an active feminist than that she became 'just' a bank teller (Tversky and Kahneman 1983). This reflects the fact that one piece of information relevant to such predictions (the similarity between her history and her life's outcome) is 'computed' much more readily than the other key piece—the statistical incidence of feminists, bank tellers, and feminist bank tellers. Although basing probability judgements on a computation of similarity has the effect of conserving effort (because the presence of a plausible answer terminates the judgmental process), people do not generally regard their judgement as resulting from a simpler version of another procedure they might instead perform.

Kahneman and Frederick (2002, 2005) proposed a general model of heuristic judgement called *attribute substitution*. They argued that people frequently answer a slightly different question from the one they were asked without being aware of the substitution. This can occur whenever the attribute being judged (e.g. probability) is less readily accessible than some conceptually related attribute (e.g. similarity). These intuitive judgements can be overridden when people are cued to consider other inputs or search for logical flaws, but often are not. Moreover, the power of intuitions remains and continues to compete with more careful and deliberate analyses, and even a thorough understanding of the logic does not always dislodge a contrasting intuitive impression. When reflecting on the bank teller problem, Stephen Jay Gould (1991) remarked: 'I know (the right answer), yet a little homunculus in my head continues to jump up and down, shouting at me—"But she can't just be a bank teller; read the description".'

SHANE FREDERICK

history of emotion The history of emotion refers here not to the emergence of emotion in the course of human evolution (see EVOLUTION OF EMOTION) but to how emotions and the concept of emotion may have changed over historical time. The topic borders on the cross-cultural variation of emotion (see CULTURAL SPECIFICITY), from which it differs in that history involves a certain chronological continuity; but a single society at diverse stages may well exhibit greater disparities than contemporary but apparently unrelated cultures. To the extent that emotions vary in response to new historical conditions, they will appear to be culturally constructed (see CONSTRUCTIVISM). But change presupposes a substrate that undergoes modification, which suggests that there are some transhistorical constants, although these may be at the level of emotional components rather than emotions themselves (see COMPONENTIAL THEORIES). The history of emotion is thus a site at which constructivist and universalist (see UNIVERSALITY OF EMOTION) theories of emotion may fruitfully intersect.

'Emotion' is a relatively recent term in English, having won out over '*passion*', 'affection', and 'sentiment' only in the past 200 years. These words vary in meaning and in the range of responses they cover. Still greater discontinuities are to be expected over longer periods of time and across languages. The ancient Greek term *pathos* (plural *pathê*), which most closely corresponds to 'emotion', can refer to almost any experience, but even in the affective sphere it embraces, in one list, pleasure, pain, desire, and contempt and in another love, anger, drunkenness, and ambition (*Rhetoric to Alexander*). Aristotle (384–322 BC) in his *Rhetoric* analyses anger and the allaying of anger, love, hatred, fear, confidence, shame, gratitude, pity, indignation, envy, emulousness, and contempt, which are nearer to modern inventories; still, only two of these figure among Ekman's *basic emotions.

Individual emotions may also change over time. *Jealousy, for example, has evolved over the past two centuries in the United States in tandem with the conception of romantic love (Stearns 1989), and no term in classical Greek or Latin exactly corresponds to it (the Greek root *zêlos* means something like 'competitive zeal'; Konstan 2006). English '*envy' derives from Latin *invidia*, but in ancient Rome *invidia* signified not just malicious spite but also righteous indignation (Kaster 2005). The conception of pity has shifted over time from a positive emotion to a religious duty to a negative attitude bordering on contempt. Even so fundamental an emotion as *anger may vary. A modern dictionary defines anger as 'a strong feeling of displeasure and usually of antagonism' (Merriam-Webster, http://www.merriam-webster.com/), whereas Aristotle defines *orgê*—the closest analogue to anger—as 'a desire, accompanied by pain, for a perceived revenge on account of a perceived slight'. Aristotle's view that insult is the sole cause of anger corresponds to a society highly conscious of status and honour; subsequent centuries witnessed a greater emphasis on anger control (Harris 2001). Attitudes toward expressions of grief and weeping (male and female) have also varied considerably; ancient Rome legislated the length of time allowed for mourning—less for newborn than for older children. But change does not necessarily imply progress or a 'civilizing process', in Norbert Elias' phrase, according to which ostensibly primitive emotions are refined over time (cf. Harris 2001, Rosenwein 2006). Recent research, for example, has emphasized the intensity of familial affection in the early modern period despite high infant mortality rates.

A historical perspective on emotion can help attune investigators to the provisional or transient nature of modern categories. It may also enrich modern theoretical approaches (see EMOTION THEORIES AND CONCEPTS (PHILOSOPHICAL PERSPECTIVES)). Aristotle's treatment of emotions depends crucially on appraisal (for example, an insult that arouses anger must be intentional), and his definition of *pathê* as 'those things on account of which people change and differ in regard to their judgements, and upon which attend pain and pleasure' is highly cognitive in character (see APPRAISAL THEORIES). In classical antiquity emotions were often assumed to be subject to persuasion and were discussed in treatises on rhetoric, like Aristotle's, but it is only recently that experimental psychologists have begun to examine how emotions motivate beliefs. Emotions were often expressly related to status and relations of power—Romans denied that slaves experienced shame, and anger was a prerogative of royalty for some medieval writers; power, however, is often elided in modern analyses. Emotions were also conceived principally as reactions to the behaviour of morally responsible agents; but the central role of *agency is a relatively new theme in modern treatments of emotion.

Understanding how the emotions of past societies may have differed from ours and how they evolved requires the meticulous interpretation of sources, both scientific and literary, together with a thorough acquaintance with modern emotion research. The fruits are of more than antiquarian interest; but the work is still only beginning.

DAVID KONSTAN

Gross, D.M. (2006). *The secret history of emotion: from Aristotle's Rhetoric to modern brain science*. Chicago: University of Chicago Press.
Reddy, W.M. (2001). *The navigation of feeling: a framework for the history of emotions*. Cambridge: Cambridge University Press.

hope Hope has figured in Western discourse at least since the myth of Pandora, and the reader may remember that hope was housed with other evils, implying that it could be as dangerous as greed or sorrow. However, hope also kept humanity from being filled with *despair, and so had considerable value. A later meaning of hope is found in Christian theology, which groups it with faith and charity as theological virtues and defines hope as the desire and search for a future good. With God's help, even a difficult good could be attained. The current meaning of hope is similar but secular: a wish or *desire accompanied by some *expectation of its fulfilment.

Although a much more recent arrival on the lexical scene, *optimism* is a close cousin of hope, and research psychologists may use the terms interchangeably. If one is careful about meanings, though, hope is more emotional and carries connotations of perseverance, whereas optimism is more cognitive and purely expectational.

The best-known psychological work on hope was done by C. Rick Snyder, who created several version of a Hope Scale, a brief, face-valid, self-report survey that measures two components of hope as he conceived it. The first component is *agency* (someone's determination that goals can be achieved) and the second *pathways* (someone's beliefs that successful plans can be generated to reach these goals). Studies show that hope thus measured has a variety of desirable correlates and consequences, including *well-being, *happiness, and general *life satisfaction.

CHRISTOPHER PETERSON

Peterson, C. (2000). The future of optimism. *American Psychologist*, **55**, 44–55.
Snyder, C.R. (ed.) (2000). *Handbook of hope: theory, measures, and applications*. San Diego, CA: Academic Press.

hot cognition Hot cognition has been proposed as one of two central constructs for clarifying the interaction of emotion and cognition within the hot system/cool system framework (see COOL COGNITION). The hot system is the basis of emotionality—fears as well as passions. It is impulsive, rigid, simple, and fast. Initially responsive to innate releasing stimuli, with experience it becomes responsive to conditioned stimuli. It is fundamental for classical conditioning and is thought to centre on the *amygdala. Characterized by stereotypy and affective primacy, it is triggered selectively by fear-provoking and appetitive stimuli, generating feelings of *fear or of *desire, and impulsive urges. The hot system contributes the feeling components to the phenomenology. The contrasting cool system, which is emotionally neutral, flexible, strategic, and slow, constrains the hot system.

If unconstrained, the hot system can give rise to an inability to delay gratification, explosive temper, unbridled violence, and unchecked sexual impulses, with their obvious personal and social consequences. It may also produce unwanted emotional states including cravings and anxieties. The crucial balance between the hot and cool systems is determined by stress, developmental level, and the individual's self-regulatory dynamics, and may be influenced by disease, pharmaceutical interventions, priming, or learning. While the hot system, if poorly controlled, can produce negative emotional or social behaviours, this system is, nevertheless, necessary for appropriate motivations, contributes affective value to our mental life, and is at the heart of human vitality.

JANET METCALFE AND W. JAKE JACOBS

LeDoux, J.E. (2000). Emotion circuits in the brain. *Annual Review of Neuroscience*, **23**, 155–84.

Metcalfe, J. and Jacobs, W.J. (1998). Emotional memory: effects of stress on 'cool' and 'hot' memory systems. *Psychology of Learning and Motivation*, **38**, 187–221.

hypomania Hypomania is defined as a period of elevated or irritable *mood which lasts for at least four days and which represents a significant change from the individual's typical mood state. The symptom criteria for hypomania (bipolar II) are identical to those for *mania (bipolar I) but the time criterion is shorter (four days instead of a week). Additional differences are that hypomanic symptoms are associated with a clear change in functioning (as opposed to marked impairment in functioning or the need for hospitalization characteristic of mania) and that unlike some forms of mania there are no accompanying psychotic symptoms. Bipolar II disorder criteria are met when an individual has experienced one episode of hypomania and at least one episode of major depression (American Psychiatric Association 2000). Bipolar II disorder has a prevalence rate of around 3% in population studies. There is evidence that hypomania may be missed in routine clinical practice, with some researchers arguing that 40–50% of individuals diagnosed with unipolar depression have actually also experienced diagnosable hypomanic episodes (Hantouche *et al.* 1998, Ghaemi *et al.* 2000).

STEVEN JONES

I

id The id is that 'cauldron full of seething excitations' that drives the individual to seek instinctual satisfaction in accordance with what Freud called the pleasure principle. In his tripartite model of the psychic apparatus, the id stands beside the ego and the superego as 'the dark, inaccessible part of our personality' (Freud 1933). The distinction between the conscious and the unconscious, however, cuts across all three components, each having both conscious and unconscious aspects. There remains something primordial about the id and it is governed by primary process mental functioning. 'Id' is the Latin for 'it'. Freud's *'das Es'* was a term he borrowed from Georg Groddeck's *Das Buch vom Es* (*The Book of the It*). See also EGO; SUPEREGO.

JEROME NEU

ideal self For decades, social scientists have written about and studied how people think about themselves (see SELF). The term 'self-concept' is typically used to refer to what people believe is currently true about themselves. That is, however, not the total of ideas people have about themselves. The ideal self is another relevant concept of self, but it refers to how the self might be or what it might become, as opposed to what people think of their current selves.

The ideal self is typically contrasted with the actual self. Both involve concepts of the person, but as the adjectives imply, the actual self refers to current status and the ideal self refers to a favourable, possibly future version of what the self might become. The ideal self typically differs from the actual self by having fewer faults and more good qualities (or better versions of the same good qualities).

Two uses of ideal self have been emphasized. One is motivational: the ideal self is seen as the self that one wants to become. The current or actual self might be regarded as an intermediate, temporary version on a journey to achieve or become the ideal self. Hence people's efforts to change and improve may be guided by the ideal self, and the ideal itself may serve to inspire the person to strive to improve.

The other usage involves measurement of *self-esteem. For a time, it was popular to measure self-esteem by having people furnish two ratings of self, one for the actual self and one for the ideal self, and then computing the difference. The assumption was that the greater the disparity between someone's actual and ideal selves, the lower the person's self-esteem. This idea resurfaces periodically, reflecting its intuitive appeal, but it is usually abandoned again because of empirical and theoretical shortcomings. People with high self-esteem might hold higher ideals than people with low self-esteem, and holding high ideals should not cause researchers to classify them as having low self-esteem. Also, how people rate their actual selves is usually sufficient for measuring their self-esteem, and the ratings of ideal selves add little or no useful information while introducing statistical problems common to all measures that employ difference scores.

ROY F. BAUMEISTER

identity The term identity refers literally to who you are, but its application in psychology has changed repeatedly. The notion of identity first came into widespread usage when Eric Erickson (1968) coined the term 'identity crisis', though its rapid adoption in psychology as well as in everyday society indicated that it referred to a problem or concern that was already quite familiar. Erickson's theory proposed that there was a particular stage in life (between childhood and adulthood) at which the formation of identity was often, though not always, a major concern. Some people seemed to skip this stage by remaining with the identities their parents and society had assigned them. Others, however, would go through an 'identity crisis', which meant rejecting some of the *values, *goals, and self-images (see SELF) they had been taught and replacing these with others that they chose for themselves. Erickson proposed that although an identity crisis was often somewhat unpleasant and stressful, in the long run it made for a more mature self and a healthier identity, as opposed to remaining 'foreclosed' in the identity one had acquired from family and background. Later research mostly supported this view, although there were some signs that remaining foreclosed led to worse outcomes for men than for women.

By the late 1970s, identity had become the focus of considerable theory and research across multiple social sciences. This may have reflected the rebellion against straitlaced conformity that had swept through Western society in the 1960s and inspired many young people to seek to find themselves (a term that was common then) by questioning the values and goals they had been taught. The idea of identity crisis as a normal and healthy stage resonated with the Zeitgeist.

After Erickson, the most influential person in identity theory may have been James Marcia. He developed an interview method that classified people according to four identity statuses, depending on whether they had a firm and clear identity and whether they had gone through an identity crisis. (Gradually the term 'crisis' came to be regarded as overly melodramatic, and Marcia campaigned for replacing it with the more modest term 'exploration'.) The optimal outcome was to have a clear sense of self that was partly the result of a crisis or exploration, and this was called 'achieved identity'. Having a firm identity without the crisis period was classified as 'foreclosed'. A currently ongoing crisis or exploration was classified as 'moratorium'. And having neither a firm identity nor an active exploration was called 'identity diffusion'. In most studies, people with achieved identity came out as very well adjusted, whereas the diffusion category generally fared the worst.

The many interdisciplinary threads of work relevant to identity were summarized in Baumeister's book (Baumeister 1986). From philosophy, the concept of identity was understood as based on two criteria: continuity and differentiation. That is, one's identity marks one out as different from other people and entails being the same person across time, and so the core of identity is one's stable, distinctive attributes. Psychological research has furnished an understanding of how a person's identity is formed and changed. Historical and sociological analyses reflected how changes in Western culture had made identity more flexible and hence more difficult to achieve and sustain. For example, Erickson emphasized that adult identity starts with occupation and marriage, but in modern society many people go through multiple jobs and even multiple occupations, as well as multiple marriages—and, crucially, they have to choose most of these themselves, as opposed to being assigned them by external circumstances. Hence the problem of identity is in many ways uniquely modern.

In the 1990s, the rise of identity politics has gradually insinuated itself into psychological theory and co-opted the term. Today, when psychologists speak of identity, they typically refer less to the individual sense of self than to membership in a group or category of persons. Ethnic identity, gender identity, sexual identity, and other such usages have become the predominant usages and connotations of identity. Much of what Erickson and his successors discussed under the rubric of identity is now discussed in terms of self.

ROY F. BAUMEISTER

illness cognitions and emotion Studies of illness cognition have raised three sets of questions about affective processes (Leventhal et al. 2008): (1) How do an individual's emotional reactions and cognitive representations—which are processed in separate, parallel systems—interact to form the emotionally charged representations of illness and the procedures for illness management (see HEALTH AND EMOTION)? (2) Since representation of illnesses are combinations of experiential (what we have felt and seen) and conceptual (what we label and talk about; Leventhal 1984) memory traces, what are the processes that integrate experiential and abstract memories into organized prototypes? (3) How do the processes involved in the integration of prototypes affect emotional reactions?

Possible answers to these questions are emerging from studies of the way in which experiences (specific and diffuse symptoms or dysfunctions such as fatigue, memory difficulties, etc.) are compared to and integrated with abstract, conceptual structures or prototypes; for example, an individual inferring that her or his headache and cough (symptoms) are due to a cold or due to stress, or that fatigue and swollen feet are due to age rather than congestive heart failure. The ongoing process of comparing and integrating experience with existent prototypes appears to be involved in the construction of illness prototypes and in the revision of prototypes over successive iterations. We have labelled the cognitive elements active in the constructive process as 'prototype assembly and appraisal checks' (prototype checks, or PCs) (see APPRAISAL). These units integrate the flow of somatic experience (changes in symptoms and physical and mental function), with prototypes and construct and revise them over time (see Leventhal and Scherer 1987). The primary PCs that every one of us use, either consciously or implicitly, to interpret changes in somatic experience and physical and mental function include: *sensory pattern* (sharp, dull, throbbing), *location* (head, chest, legs), *duration* (hours, days), *intensity, trajectory* (getting worse, declining, fluctuating), and *control* (e.g. did an antacid stop gastrointestinal distress?). Negative emotions, such as disgust and nausea (feeling sick), and positive emotions such as feeling happy and good, complete the primary PC set. For most people, the prototype checking process creates prototypes for acute illness; the upper respiratory cold, stress headache, stomach flu, etc, that are time-limited and perceived to be distressing but 'safe'. Although acute prototypes are the default models in the check process that generate the perception that a symptom is time-limited and safe (a cold or an episode of gastrointestinal distress), the somatic experience may be the result of physiological processes associated with a potentially life-threatening condition. For example, if you are in your late 60s and feel chronic (duration) fatigue (sensory feel) that changes little or slowly (flat trajectory) and notice swelling in your feet and legs (location; heat as cause) and you have no chest pain (negative, sensory feel at a defining location), you may conclude that your symptoms are signs of normal ageing when they are characteristic signs of heart failure. In short, interpretations generated by the check process may be incorrect, physiologically.

PCs are not just involved in processing information intrapersonally; they are key players in conversations about illness symptoms with family, friends, and doctors. PCs based upon perceptions of shared life experience, similarity of temperament, physical build, and shared genes are specific elements in the social comparison process.

PCs affect the relationship between emotion and cognition in multiple ways: uncertainty and fear may arise when: (1) the check process fails to match experience of symptom and functional changes to an acute (safe) model; (2) experience proves fallible, as when PCs fail to detect a disease (e.g. you feel great—positive affect—when diagnosed with cancer; positive emotions are unreliable checks for most chronic illnesses); and (3) PCs match symptoms to a threatening model (e.g. chest pain matches heart attack prototype).

PC's also test the efficacy of actions for controlling both experience-based and conceptually framed *goals; they check whether an action reduced symptoms and/or improved function in a time frame appropriate to an illness prototype (e.g. aspirin should reduce a stress headache in an hour). Actions that fail to produce an expected ameliorative effect in an anticipated time frame, and actions that generate disruptive and unexpected side-effects, can create uncertainty, apprehension, and fear.

Effective management of chronic conditions (e.g. asthma, diabetes) requires representations of an illness as a state that is stable, internal, undetectable, and manageable by specific actions, e.g. taking medication, dieting, and exercise. Successful management of most chronic illnesses is best guided by objective indicators (glucometer for assessing blood sugar levels in diabetes, blood pressure cuff for assessing hypertension). When patients find themselves unable to monitor and act to effectively regulate a chronic disease because they are using subjective, 'on-line' cues that are invalid guides to action, they can experience uncertainty and loss of control which can set the stage for depression (Vileikyte et al. 2005). A key task for research is to identify the sequences of response-based checks that can generate representations for illnesses as chronic states that permit full participation in activities of daily life, i.e. functional chronic models versus dysfunctional models associated with affective distress and depression.

Our view of the bidirectional interplay among multi-level cognitive and affective processes in the regulation of health threats has led us to view emotions such as fear and depression as 'embedded' in dynamic, multi-level cognitive representations. Clustering multiple experiences under a specific concept can reduce uncertainty and fears if action plans that alleviate symptoms are available can be enacted. The conceptual envelope can blend the emotions associated with each of these formerly discrete experiences creating a new illness-based emotional state.

In sum, understanding the relationship of emotion to cognition and behaviour seems better accomplished by treating emotions as embedded in cognitive-affective scripts or roles, such as self with cancer, heart disease, ageing, or self as terminal and dying (Maher et al. 2006). Although the typical emotions embedded in these roles—fear, depression, pleasure in mastery of tasks, etc.—are in some sense the 'same' across roles, the cues and behaviours that define the script will create a blend of affects that are no longer a set of discrete emotions the behavioural consequences of which can be understood independent of the cognitive behavioural framework in which they are embedded (Maher et al. 2006). The intra-and interpersonal activity of the PCs that construct and conduct the ongoing tests to validate representations provide a view of the processes underlying the building and maintenance of the roles in which typical emotions are embedded. PCs test, interpret and connect experience to representations that support action, inaction, problem-solving, distraction, and denial and the feedback from these actions can confirm or disconfirm the prototypes (cancer; heart attack) embedded in the roles (cancer survivor; cardiac cripple) and emotions of fear, anger, and depression that are associated with these.

HOWARD LEVENTHAL

immunity and emotion Although still controversial, there is evidence that psychological events, including emotions, can and do influence the outcome of infectious, autoimmune, and neoplastic diseases (see PSYCHO-NEUROIMMUNOLOGY). A surprising finding has been that inflammation arising in the periphery also affects a variety of events in the central nervous system, such as activation of the hypothalamic–pituitary axis, affect, and cognition. The original discovery that activation of the innate immune system in the periphery causes clinical signs of sickness that are processed in the brain is now being extended to the involvement of the immune system in depressive disorders (see DEPRESSION). This new information has consolidated the idea that *cytokines, hormones, and nerves are the minimum essential elements that permit the immune system and the brain to communicate with one another. Thus, the immune system is likely to be involved in not only how emotions affect health (see HEALTH AND EMOTION) but also how immune events may regulate the development and expression of emotions.

Physiological basis for emotions affecting health

Emotions are well known to be associated with *arousal, as identified by activation of a variety of physiological systems. These regulatory events contribute to homeostasis, which was originally defined by Claude Bernard (1813–78) as aiming at the maintenance of a constant 'milieu interieur', by maintenance of blood pressure and body temperature, for example, in the face of changing environmental stimuli. Since the days of Hans Selye (1907–82), the father of the *stress concept, and the American physiologist Walter Cannon (1871–1945), who consolidated the concept of homeostasis, it has been well-appreciated that the *autonomic nervous system and the *neuroendocrine system are key participants in homeostasis. All emotions involve some form of arousal, with an expressive behaviour and a conscious experience. For this reason, the study of emotions is inherently complex. There are at least three major issues that limit progress in understanding relationships between emotions and immunity.

(1) Animal models of either positive (e.g. happiness, optimism) or negative (e.g. disgust, hate) emotions are difficult to develop and validate. The adaptive value of negative emotions, like fear causing animals to run from a predator, is easy to reconstitute in the laboratory. However, the undesirable effects of emotions, such as when negative emotions cause subjects to fail to adhere to medication or to adopt unhealthy lifestyles like smoking and substance abuse (see ADDICTION), are more difficult to model in the laboratory situation. These behaviours lead to extensive comorbid conditions that increase costs for the entire healthcare system (Kopnisky et al. 2007). Although there are limitations, some progress has been made in developing animal models of psychopathology, e.g. depression (McArthur and Borsini 2006) and rage (Zalcman and Siegel 2006). When coupled with the relatively new approach of characterizing endophenotypes and neuroimaging studies with humans, these animal models have the potential of enhancing the acquisition of new knowledge about these disorders.

(2) Different emotions elicit different patterns of arousal. An example is a report where the brain and the immune and endocrine systems were simultaneously evaluated in three novel environmental situations that were all designed to subject humans to pleasant stimuli (Watanuki and Kim 2005). However, even though all the stimuli provided pleasant experiences, only comic story telling increased secretory immunoglobulin A and decreased salivary cortisol (see SALIVATION). Pleasant odours and emotional pictures activated different physiological arousal systems. These data are consistent with the idea that at least some aspects of positive emotions are correlated with relatively specific changes in the immune system. However, the relevant emotions and pathways by which this occurs remain a daunting task to unravel.

(3) A given emotion can have different effects on immunity depending on the context in which it takes place. Perhaps the best example of this issue is *optimism. Suzanne Segerstrom has demonstrated that when stressors are brief and can be controlled, greater optimism is associated with enhancement in some immune events (Segerstrom 2005) (see Fig. I1). However, in situations where the stressors are prolonged and uncontrollable, optimism is negatively related to immunity.

In the mid-1980s it was proposed that the immune system is simply another regulatory system that is actively involved in homeostasis following exposure to pathogens (Kelley 1985). It is now known that neurotransmitters from both the sympathetic (Kin and Sanders 2006) and parasympathetic (Pavlov and Tracey 2005) systems regulate a variety of immune events in the periphery. The latter system has now been coined the 'cholinergic anti-inflammatory reflex'. Activation of the hypothalamic–pituitary axis following emotional stimuli, as well as by pituitary hormones like growth hormone and prolactin, is well known to regulate a variety of immune events (Malarkey and Mills 2007). Regulation of cells of the immune system by nerves and hormones provides a rational physiological basis for the notion that arousing events associated with emotions can affect health (Koh 1998). These early ideas have been extended by others who have concluded that clinical depression is reproducibly associated with reductions in three immune events: activity of natural killer cells, mitogen-induced proliferation of both T and B cells, and cytotoxic T-cell activity (Irwin and Miller 2007). Treatment of depressive disorders normalizes these reductions in natural killer activity and lymphocyte proliferation. Central corticotrophic releasing hormone (CRH), acting via the sympathetic nervous system rather than the hypothalamic–pituitary–adrenal axis, is responsible for the reduction in natural killer activity in animal models. CRH within in the central nervous system may therefore be responsible for the reduced tumour cell lysis by natural killer cells in clinically depressed patients.

Out with the old, in with the new

The concept elaborated in most medical textbooks is that the brain is 'immune' to the immune system. This

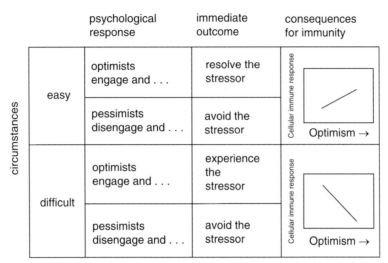

	psychological response	immediate outcome	consequences for immunity
easy	optimists engage and . . .	resolve the stressor	
	pessimists disengage and . . .	avoid the stressor	
difficult	optimists engage and . . .	experience the stressor	
	pessimists disengage and . . .	avoid the stressor	

Fig. I1. Summary of the relationship between optimism and immunity. The effects on cellular immune response that are shown in the right column are drawn from effects of optimism or pessimism on the intensity of delayed type hypersensitivity skin testing with mumps and candida antigens in first-year law students who are faced with the conflict that arises between the time demands of law school and their engagement in other domains. Reprinted with permission from Segerstrom (2005).

idea is wrong and must be updated. It is true that survival of histoincompatible tissue, when grafted into the brain, is prolonged when compared with grafting this same tissue in the periphery. It is also true that the brain is encased by an impervious sheet of capillary endothelial cells with no fenestrations and extensive tight junctions. However, the concept that the blood–brain barrier's only function is to protect the brain from blood-borne soluble substances and immune cells is wrong. Instead, the blood–brain barrier actively transports specific substances from the blood to the brain and synthesizes a number of proteins that were originally identified in the immune system (Banks 2006). The blood–brain barrier should therefore be considered as another one of the important physiological systems that form part of the communication system between the brain and the immune system. Furthermore, both T and B cells migrate through the brain, and resident macrophages of the brain, microglia, are actively involved in brain function and repair (Carson et al. 2006). The brain and the immune system share an active dialogue with one another, and this communication system is critical for homeostasis.

The isolation, cloning, and expression of proinflammatory cytokines and their receptors in the late 1980s, coupled with the discovery of pathogen-associated molecular patterns (PAMPs) and their pathogen recognition receptors (PRRs), are two of the major advances in immunology that set the stage for defining brain–immune communication pathways. A prototypical proinflammatory cytokine that is released from activated macrophages following activation of some PRRs is interleukin-1 (IL-1). One of the more surprising discoveries in psychoneuroimmunology is that injection of IL-1, either systemically in the form of intraperitoneal administration or centrally via an intracerebroventricular route, causes clinical signs of sickness, as determined by motivational deficits in both eating and social behaviours (Kent et al. 1992a). The amount of IL-1 required to induce similar amounts of sickness is approximately 100 to 200 times less when injected into the brain than when injected systemically. Both of these effects can be significantly blocked by injection via the same route of a pure antagonist of IL-1 receptor (IL-1Ra). The most significant finding in these experiments was that pretreatment of rats with the IL-1Ra in the lateral ventricles of the brain significantly impaired the ability of systemic IL-1 to cause behavioural deficits. These data, more than any other at that time, showed clearly that inflammatory events in the periphery somehow communicate that message to the brain and lead to a change in social and eating behaviour. We termed this and other behavioural events associated with acute inflammation 'sickness behaviour' (Kent et al. 1992b).

The robustness of cytokine-induced sickness behaviour has provided a very useful framework for beginning to understand and dissect brain–immune communication pathways (Dantzer and Kelley 2007). For example, it is now known that the afferent vagus nerves form a fast route of communication from the periphery to the brain in response to an inflammatory event taking place in the peritoneal cavity. It is also now clear that proinflammatory cytokines in the periphery induce cytokine synthesis in the brain, thus forming a mirror image of systemic inflammation. Once an infection, and therefore cytokine synthesis, resolves over the time course of a few days, behavioural symptoms of sickness normally disappear. However, if the infection does not resolve, or if there is an ongoing autoimmune inflammatory process of a chronic nature, such as rheumatoid arthritis, the synthesis of cytokines and their downstream products continues to be elevated. The chronic action of proinflammatory cytokines acting in the brain has now led to the hypothesis that these very same proteins are somehow involved in affective disorders such as depression and this, in turn, is likely to affect a variety of emotions. A leading candidate protein for this effect is a cytokine-activated enzyme known as indoleamine 2,3 dioxygenase (IDO) (Capuron et al. 2001), which can be expressed by microglial cells in the brain. This enzyme degrades tryptophan, an essential amino acid that is required for the synthesis of the mood-regulating neurotransmitter serotonin. Increased degradation of tryptophan associated with inflammation results in a relative deficit in serotonin neurotransmission in the brain that can precipitate depression.

Concluding comments

A few years ago, scientists who proffered the idea that depressive disorders could be induced by an infective process were considered heretical. That view has changed considerably with the discovery that cytokines from the immune system act as elements that permit active communication between the brain and the rest of the body. In 1984 a pioneering scientist in psychoneuroimmunology, J. Edwin Blalock, proposed that the immune system is really a sixth sensory system (Blalock 1984). Humans cannot see, smell, touch, hear, or taste pathogenic micro-organisms. However, cells of the immune system, whether they be T cells, B cells, macrophages, microglial cells, or dendritic cells, are uniquely endowed with the molecular machinery to detect an endless array of pathogens. One way that the immune system informs the brain that a pathogen has entered the body is by immune cells recognizing these invaders. These leucocytes respond by releasing proinflammatory cytokines, which act as messengers to alert the brain that something is amiss in the periphery. The foundation for this conceptual system has strengthened during the last 20 years. It forms the intellectual basis for the

notion that emotions are regulated by the immune system, and the immune system affects expression of emotions.

KEITH W. KELLEY AND ROBERT DANTZER

Ader, R. (ed.) (2007). *Psychoneuroimmunology*, 4th edn. Amsterdam: Elsevier.

impulsivity Impulse control is an important aspect of self-regulation and constitutes a core concept in almost all major personality theories. Impulsivity (problems with impulse control) is also associated with various psychopathological states and problematic behaviours such as alcoholism, gambling, compulsive buying, attention deficit/hyperactivity disorder, *bipolar disorder, bulimia nervosa, conduct problems, and risky sexual activities. Nevertheless, impulsivity may be appropriate in contexts or tasks requiring any sort of spontaneous behaviour. Despite the widespread use of the concept of impulsivity in almost every domain of psychology, its definition and measurement are still a matter for debate.

Some authors have recently underscored the need to consider impulsivity as a multifaceted construct. Whiteside and Lynam (2001) conducted a factor analysis on several widely used measures of impulsivity and identified four components: *urgency*, defined as 'the tendency to experience strong impulses, frequently under conditions of negative affect'; *premeditation (lack of)*, defined as 'the tendency to think and reflect on the consequences of an act before engaging in that act'; *perseverance (lack of)*, defined as 'the ability to remain focused on a task that may be boring or difficult'; and *sensation seeking*, defined as 'a tendency to enjoy and pursue activities that are exciting, and an openness to trying new experiences'. They also developed the UPPS Impulsive Behavior Scale, which specifically assesses these facets. Multitrait, multimethod matrix results demonstrated clear convergent and discriminant validity among these facets (Smith et al. 2007). In addition, the four constructs had different correlates with different aspects of risky and problematic behaviours, thus supporting the value of drawing distinctions among them. More recently, it has also been proposed that two aspects of urgency be distinguished (Cyders et al. 2007), corresponding to the tendency to engage in rash actions while in a negative mood (negative urgency) and while in a positive mood (positive urgency). There have also been proposals to relate the facets of impulsivity to specific cognitive and emotional mechanisms (Bechara and Van der Linden 2005). More specifically, urgency may be associated with the ability to deliberately inhibit automatic, dominant, or prepotent responses, whereas lack of perseverance may be linked to the ability to inhibit recurrent and irrelevant thoughts or memories, or, in other words, the ability to resist proactive interference. Lack of premeditation may, at least partly, correspond to *decision-making processes in which a choice is made after taking into account the emotional consequences of that choice. This suggestion has been supported by data showing that high scores on the lack of premeditation subscale of the UPPS questionnaire are significantly related to risky and disadvantageous decisions on the Iowa Gambling Task (Zermatten *et al.* 2005). In contrast to the first three dimensions of impulsivity, which involve executive and decision-making capacities, sensation seeking seems to involve motivational aspects of impulsivity that rely on a system that exaggerates the impact of reward and underestimates the impact of punishment. Further studies are clearly needed to explore in more detail the cognitive and affective processes underlying the different facets of impulsivity and to discover their neural correlates.

MARTIAL VAN DER LINDEN AND
JOËL BILLIEUX

Chamberlain, S.R. and Sahakian, B. (2007). The neuropsychiatry of impulsivity. *Current Opinion in Psychiatry*, **20**, 255–61.

individual differences (and emotion) see AFFECTIVE STYLE; ALTRUISM (ECONOMICS PERSPECTIVES); ALTRUISM (PSYCHOLOGICAL PERSPECTIVES); APPRAISAL STYLE; COGNITIVE BIAS; EXTERNALIZER; EXTRAVERSION/INTROVERSION; GENDER DIFFERENCES (AND EMOTION); IMPULSIVITY; INTERNALIZER; NARCISSISM; NEUROTICISM; OPTIMISM/PESSIMISM; PERSONALITY (AND EMOTION); TEMPERAMENT.

individualism/collectivism Individualism refers to a set of cultural beliefs and practices characterized by a sharp separation and independence of the *self from others, which can be traced back to Western European cultural traditions (Markus and Kitayama 1991). Research has shown that individualistic cultures value a strong drive for self-uniqueness and self-enhancement, are concerned with personal (rather than relational or collective) aspects of self in general and *self-esteem in particular, favour a justice principle in moral judgement, and reveal a dispositional bias in social perception and an analytic mode of reasoning and attention, among other tendencies. Today, individualism is assumed to characterize social institutions, practices, and psychological tendencies common to North America (Hofstede 1980, Triandis 1995).

Individualism is often contrasted with 'collectivism', which refers to a set of cultural beliefs and practices that are characterized by a fundamental connectedness and interdependence of the self with others (Markus and Kitayama 1991). Research has shown that collectivist cultures tend to value the maintenance of social harmony, are concerned with relational (rather than personal) aspects of self, show lesser self-enhancement tendencies than in other cultures, place an emphasis on a caring principle in moral judgement, demonstrate a lesser dispositional bias in social perception, and rely on a holistic mode of reasoning and attention, among other tendencies. Today, collectivism is assumed to characterize social institutions, practices, and psychological tendencies common in many societies outside of the West including East and Southeast Asia, the Middle East, Africa, and much of Latin America (Triandis 1995). At present much existing scientific knowledge is based on research on East Asians. Collectivism is often contrasted with individualism, which is a set of cultural beliefs and practices more prevalent in Western cultures.

These two cultural ethos can be understood in terms of their social–historical contexts. North American individualism has important roots in Western European civilization. Among the factors implicated in the emergence of individualism are Protestantism, a variety of Enlightenment philosophies, a traditional emphasis on debate and rhetoric, democratic political systems, and national wealth, especially during the last several centuries. Furthermore, in combination with these factors, certain ecological and social factors relatively unique to North America probably played important roles in fostering a strongly individualistic ethos. These factors include low population density, high social mobility, and voluntary settlement. Depending on specific characteristics of particular locales and populations of interest, individualism can take different forms. Even within the United States, working-class culture is characterized by self-reliance, self-control, and maintenance of personal integrity (e.g. Snibbe and Markus 2005). Social relations may be limited largely to family relations. In contrast, middle-class or upper middle-class individualism is defined more by self-actualization, personal choice, and instrumental use of nonfamilial relations. The latter form of individualism therefore tends to be more socially expansive.

By comparison, East Asian collectivism has important roots in Chinese civilization. Among the factors implicated in the emergence of collectivism are Confucianism, traditional emphasis on avoiding conflict and finding the 'Middle Way', and hierarchical political systems. Furthermore, in combination with these factors certain ecological and social factors, such as high population density and low social mobility, are likely to have played important roles in fostering a strongly collectivistic ethos.

The type of cultural ethos has been shown to have important influences on emotional experience (see CULTURAL SPECIFICITY). First, in an individualistic ethos there is a strongly held belief that there exists a tight correspondence between internal sensations and expressed emotions. When asked to rate the intensity of felt emotions of stimulus persons displaying different emotional expressions, Americans have been found to estimate the intensities to be much higher than do Asians (Matsumoto and Ekman 1989). The most intriguing finding that is likely to be grounded, in part, on this cultural belief is the facial feedback effect (see FACIAL FEEDBACK HYPOTHESIS). Specifically, when Americans pose facial expressions of different emotions such as anger and happiness they report feeling states that correspond to the posed emotions. Evidence exists that this effect is difficult to obtain in cultures that are more interdependent or collectivistic, where emotional experiences are considered inseparable from relational contexts (Levenson et al. 1992).

Second, in individualistic cultures some emotions are particularly salient in subjective experience. For example, given the important role of self-esteem in North America, pride in self is likely to be very salient. Similarly, frustration, anger, and aggression have formed a central theme of North American social psychology. All these emotions may be closely linked to individualism. Whereas pride and other so-called 'socially disengaging' positive emotions are experienced when one succeeds in tasks of independence (e.g. personal achievement and standing out), anger, frustration, and other socially disengaging negative emotions are experienced when one fails in such tasks and thus feels motivated to restore the compromised independence. These emotions may be contrasted with the so-called 'socially engaging' positive (e.g. friendly feelings and communal feelings) and negative (e.g. guilt and shame) emotions, which are more closely linked to interdependence and collectivism. A recent diary study shows that Americans experience socially disengaging emotions more than socially engaging emotions, whereas Japanese experience socially engaging emotions more than socially disengaging emotions (Kitayama et al. 2006a).

Third, there is an important cross-cultural difference in the normative desirability of high-arousal (e.g. excited) versus low-arousal (e.g. calm) emotions (see AROUSAL) (for review see Tsai, 2007). High-arousal emotions tend to be more highly valued in individualist cultures, and low-arousal emotions are more highly valued in collectivist cultures. This has been demonstrated in ratings of normative desirability of different emotions and in content coding of storybooks for children in the United States in comparison with those in China, as well as religious texts of Christianity in comparison with those of Buddhism. Moreover, such differences in the normative desirability of emotions are partially explained by cultural differences in tendency to influence or adjust to others. In their daily lives, Americans report influencing others more than adjusting to others, whereas Japanese report adjusting to others more than influencing others (Morling et al. 2002). Influencing others involves action and thus requires high physiological arousal, whereas adjusting to others involves suppression of action and thus requires low physiological arousal. In fact, when experimentally induced to influence others, both Americans and Chinese tend to value high-arousal emotions more and low-arousal emotions less than when they were induced to adjust to others (Tsai et al. 2007).

Fourth, cultural ethos influences the relationship between positive and negative emotions. Cross-cultural studies on dialectical thinking have suggested that East Asians are more likely than European Americans to recognize and accept the contradiction and duality (Peng and Nisbett 1999). Reflecting such cultural differences in dialecticism, the correlation between positive and negative emotions tends to be negative for Americans but positive or weaker for Asians (e.g. Bagozzi et al. 1999). In addition, the relationship between positive and negative emotions can be moderated by the immediate cultural context to which one is exposed: bicultural Asian Canadians showed a negative association between positive and negative emotions when they had recently spoken in English but not when they had recently spoken in an Asian language (Perunovic et al. 2007).

Finally, predictors of psychological *well-being seem to vary across cultures. Aspects of the self that highlight and foster independence (e.g. self-esteem, independent goal pursuit, and positive disengaging emotions) are found to be stronger predictors of well-being in individualistic countries than in collectivistic countries. In contrast, aspects of the self that highlight and promote interdependence (e.g. social harmony, interdependent goal pursuit, and positive engaging emotions) are found to be stronger predictors of well-being in collectivistic countries than in individualistic countries (Kwan et al. 1997, Oishi and Diener 2001, Kitayama et al. 2006a). For example, American happiness is better predicted by the experience of positive disengaging emotions (e.g. pride in self) than by positive engaging emotions (e.g. friendly feelings). These patterns are reversed for Japanese (Kitayama et al. 2006a).

In sum, individualism exerts important influences on emotion in general and emotional experience in particular. Future work utilizing physiological measures and neuroimaging techniques may shed new light on the cultural shaping of emotion.

YURI MIYAMOTO AND SHINOBU KITAYAMA

Kitayama, S., Duffy, S., and Uchida, Y.K. (2007). Self as cultural mode of being. In: S. Kitayama and D. Cohen (eds), *The handbook of cultural psychology*, pp. 136–74. New York: Guilford Press.

Mesquita, B. and Leu, J. (2007). The cultural psychology of emotion. In: S. Kitayama and D. Cohen (eds), *The handbook of cultural psychology*, pp. 734–59. New York: Guilford Press.

infancy (emotional development in) The study of emotional development at one time focused on identifying the earliest age at which specific emotions such as fear, anger, joy, shame, pride, guilt, etc., are first observed—i.e. when they 'emerge'. Until the late 1970s, the focus on emergence was reasonable because emotion was deemed coterminous either with discrete patterns of facial expression (see FACIAL EXPRESSION OF EMOTION) or with the onset of effectiveness of prototypic eliciting circumstances. Thus, 'joy' was said to emerge between 1 and 2 months of age because newborns do not smile to faces in waking states, but 6-week-olds do. Similarly, 'fear' was believed to appear at 7 to 8 months of age because infants typically do not show avoidant or distressed reactions to maternal separation or to the approach of a stranger in the first 6 months of life, but do after 7 months. Similar considerations were applied to the development of anger, sadness, and other emotions. Bridges' (1932) influential differentiation theory of emotion instantiated the 'emergence' approach.

The view of emotional development as the study of emergence is no longer held. Emotions are not seen as having a 'gold standard', whether in facial or vocal expressions or in any single factor. Instead, emotions are construed as the organization of a multiplicity of components (appraisal, expressive, autonomic, central nervous system, instrumental reactions, etc.; see COMPONENTIAL THEORIES), some of which become observable at a different age from others. For example, although newborns do not smile, neonates do show behavioural evidence of avidity—a member of the joy family—in response to hedonically positive stimuli such as sucrose. Similarly, although most 3-month-olds do not show expressions of fear, some do if they are reared under abusive circumstances. As a result, the study of emotional development has become the investigation of changes with age in each component of emotion, and the description and explanation of the growing interweaving of components into ever more complex wholes.

Consider the development of anger. When construed relationally, anger involves a reaction to obstruction of the goals of an individual. Newborns can react to frustrations such as the removal of a nipple or arm restraint, but they do not show patterns of facial and vocal behaviour such as those described by Ekman (1992a) and Scherer (1986a). Those patterns, though, are evident by 4 months of age, after which further developments take place. At 4 months, the expressions are not targeted at the source of the frustration, but at 7 months, they are targeted and in addition instrumental behaviours linked to anger can also be seen. Eventually, with the development of symbolic processes and language, nonverbal expressions are conjoined with words, and still later in age, words can replace the paralinguistics, creating even higher levels of organization of anger. The coordination approach was first described by Campos *et al.* (1983).

The so-called *basic emotions of anger, fear, sadness, surprise, disgust, and joy are evident in reasonably coordinated fashion by 8 months of age, if not earlier. However, emotions such as embarrassment, shame, pride, jealousy, and guilt (see SELF-REFLEXIVE EMOTIONS) become organized at later ages, typically after 15 to 18 months of age. Like joy and fear, they often show components much earlier. One reason proposed for the late manifestation of these emotions is the necessity for the infant to acquire a sense of 'self', which comes about between 15 and 18 months of age (hence the designation of these later-appearing states as 'self-conscious emotions'). In support of the link between 'self' and these emotions, some studies show that embarrassment and pride are evident only after an infant can recognize him/herself by using a mirror to rub off a spot of rouge on his/her nose (Lewis 2008). Others, though, consider these emotions as 'other conscious' because the emotions depend on the infant's appreciation that another person is evaluating his or her behaviour (Campos 2007). Most likely, both self-consciousness and other-consciousness play a role in the construction of these later-appearing emotional reactions. More specifically, emotions such as embarrassment, shame and pride depend on the coordination of component factors such as: (1) the attribution by the infant of importance to other persons, especially the parent, (2) appreciation by the infant of the importance of emotional cues such as sadness, anger, scorn, disappointment, etc., in the other, and (3) understanding that the important person's signals are targeted toward oneself, and not to another person. There is considerable research to suggest that it is not until the early part of the second year of life that these components are within the capacity of the typical infant.

From this brief narrative, then, what can we say develops with emotional development? (1) As noted, emotional development is, above all else, the progressive coordination of components identifiable as belonging to a given emotional state into better organized and more flexibly manifested ensembles. (2) Eliciting circumstances previously ineffective in generating discrete affect become functional with age, while others (e.g. peek-a-boo games), once functional, lose their prior effectiveness. (3) Facial, vocal, autonomic (e.g. facial blushing, blanching, flushing), and instrumental behaviours become patterned when a given emotion is elicited. (4) The targeting of emotions to specific objects in the environment (i.e. the 'aboutness' of an emotion) comes online, both receptively and productively, coincident with or subsequent to the acquisition of social attentive or spatial cognitive skills. (5) The perception of the affective meaning of another person's emotional expressions or signals begins to regulate behaviour. (6) Emotional responses become equipotential; that is, any one of several quite different responses can be deployed in the service of a specific emotional state. (7) Emotion regulatory or coping skills begin to be deployed by the infant to prevent an elicitor from arousing undesired emotions, or to foster the manifestation of desired reactions (see REGULATION OF EMOTION). (8) The acquisition of a system of values resulting from the child's immersion and acculturation into a society affects all emotions, but especially leads to pride, guilt, shame, scorn, jealousy, and envy.

JOSEPH J. CAMPOS

Saarni, C., Campos, J., Camras, L., and Witherington, D. (2006). Emotional development: action, communication and understanding. In: N. Eisenberg (ed.), *Handbook of child psychology: social, emotional, and personality development*, 6th edn, pp. 226–99 (series editors W. Damon and R. Lerner). New York: John Wiley.

inflammation (and mood) Recent theories have proposed that proinflammatory cytokines participate in the pathophysiology of *mood disorders, especially *depression, given their potent effect on brain neurotransmitters, the *neuroendocrine system, and behaviour (Dantzer *et al.* 1999). Behavioural changes induced by proinflammatory *cytokines include the induction of a syndrome referred to as 'sickness behaviour' that has many overlapping features with major depression. Recent advances have been made in the understanding of the relationship and connections between *mood and inflammation, notably using the model of cytokine therapy in clinical populations (Raison *et al.* 2006). Cytokine-induced neuropsychiatric symptoms represent two distinct behavioural syndromes or sets of symptoms, with different phenomenology and responsiveness to antidepressants. The neurovegetative syndrome is characterized by symptoms of fatigue, psychomotor slowing, anorexia, and altered sleep patterns. This syndrome develops rapidly in almost every individual exposed to cytokines. In contrast, the mood and cognitive syndrome is characterized by the typical symptoms of depression, including depressed mood, anxiety, irritability, memory, and attentional disturbance. The mood and cognitive syndrome develops only in vulnerable patients and involves chronic exposure to proinflammatory cytokines and/or chronic activation of the innate immune system. Whereas the mood and cognitive syndrome is

highly responsive to treatment with antidepressants, the neurovegetative syndrome is minimally responsive to these drugs. In terms of underlying pathophysiological mechanisms, neuroendocrine hyperreactivity together with impaired serotonin metabolism/function is likely to contribute to the pathophysiology of inflammation-related mood symptoms. Neurovegetative symptoms including fatigue probably involve other neurochemical systems, particularly dopamine.

The discovery that depression can be associated with inflammation has introduced a paradigmatic revolution in the consideration of the relationship between psychological factors and physical illness in psychosomatic medicine. The high prevalence of mood disorders in diseases with an inflammatory component (e.g. atherosclerosis, asthma, cancer, autoimmune disorders) together with the correlation between depression scores and inflammatory biomarkers indicates that apart from psychological factors (see PSYCHONEUROIMMUNOLOGY; IMMUNITY AND EMOTION), such as the loss of a spouse or unresolved conflicts (Steptoe 1997), biological aspects of the disease itself can contribute primarily to mood disorders in physically ill patients.

LUCILE CAPURON AND ROBERT DANTZER

Dantzer, R., Wollman, E.E., Yirmiya, R. (eds) (1999). *Cytokines, stress and depression*. New York: Kluwer Academic.
Raison, C.L., Capuron, L., and Miller, A.H. (2006). Cytokines sing the blues: inflammation and the pathogenesis of depression. *Trends in Immunology*, **27**, 24–31.
Steptoe, A. (ed.) (2007). *Depression and physical illness*. Cambridge: Cambridge University Press.

intelligence, emotional Emotional intelligence (EI) refers to the processes involved in the recognition, use, understanding, and management of one's own and others' emotional states to solve emotion-laden problems and to regulate behaviour (see COMPETENCE, EMOTIONAL) (Mayer and Salovey 1997). EI in this tradition refers to an individual's capacity to reason about emotions and to process emotional information in order to enhance reasoning. EI is a member of an emerging group of mental abilities alongside social, practical, and personal intelligences.

Research on EI is an outgrowth of two areas of psychological investigation that emerged toward the end of the 20th century. In the 1980s psychologists and cognitive scientists began to examine in laboratory experiments how emotion interacts with thinking, and vice versa. For instance, researchers studied how mood states can assist and influence autobiographical memory and personal judgement. At the same time, there was a gradual loosening of the concept of intelligence to include a broader array of mental abilities. Howard Gardner, for instance, advised educators and scientists to place a greater emphasis on the search for multiple intelligences (e.g. interpersonal intelligence, body-kinaesthetic intelligence).

The term 'emotional intelligence' was introduced to the scientific literature in 1990. Peter Salovey and John (Jack) D. Mayer formally defined EI as 'the ability to monitor one's own and others' feelings and emotions, to discriminate among them and to use this information to guide one's thinking and actions' (Salovey and Mayer 1990). Daniel Goleman popularized the construct in a best selling 1995 book, *Emotional Intelligence: Why it can Matter more than IQ*. EI quickly captured the interest of the media, the general public, and researchers. In subsequent years, educators, psychologists, and human resource professionals began to consult and write about EI. Many of these individuals used the term more broadly to represent the traits and skills related to character and achieving 'success' in life. So, for example, other investigators described EI in terms of a set of dispositions or traits, such as *happiness, *self-esteem, *optimism, and self-management rather than more focused abilities (Schutte *et al.* 1998, Petrides and Furnham 2001, 2003, Bar-On 2004, Boyatzis and Sala 2004, Tett *et al.* 2005).

Mayer, Salovey, and their collaborators, however, focused their definition of EI on a set of four abilities: (1) accurately perceiving and expressing emotion, (2) using emotion to facilitate cognitive activities, (3) understanding emotions, and (4) managing emotions for both emotional and personal growth. *Perceiving emotion* refers to the ability to perceive and identify emotions in oneself and others, as well as in other stimuli including people's voices, stories, music, and works of art. *Using emotion* refers to the ability to harness feelings that assist in certain cognitive enterprises such as problem-solving, *decision-making, and *interpersonal communication, as well as focused attention and possibly creative thinking. *Understanding emotions* involves knowledge of both emotion-related terms and of the manner in which emotions combine, progress, and transition from one to the other. *Managing emotions* includes the ability to employ strategies that alter feelings, and the assessment of the effectiveness of such strategies.

There are a number of published tests to measure EI. Many of the investigators who define EI in terms of dispositions and traits, cited above, have also developed ways of assessing these attributes through either self-judgement scales or '360-degree' assessments. The only ability-based (rather than self-report) measure of EI currently available is the Mayer–Salovey–Caruso Emotional Intelligence Test (MSCEIT) for adults and the Mayer–Salovey–Caruso Emotional Intelligence Test, Youth Version (MSCEIT-YV) for adolescents (ages 12 to 17). These tests are performance-based measures of EI because they require individuals to solve tasks pertaining to each of the four abilities that are part of the theory (i.e. the perception, use, understanding, and management of emotion) (Mayer *et al.* 2003).

There is growing evidence that the self-judgement tests of EI do not correlate highly with ability-based tests of EI, and that the self-judgement tests show substantial overlap with traditional (i.e. Big Five) measures of personality (Brackett and Mayer 2003, Brackett *et al.* 2006). A substantial review of the literature conducted by a group of investigators not associated with any of these measurement instruments concluded that the ability-based approach was likely to prove most fruitful in terms of not sharing substantial overlap with well-defined constructs such as analytical intelligence and *personality as well as in accounting for incremental variance in significant outcomes (Matthews *et al.* 2002).

EI, measured by the MSCEIT, is related to a range of important social behaviours in multiple life domains (reviewed by Mayer *et al.* 2008a,b). For example, individuals with higher MSCEIT scores report better quality friendships, and dating and married couples with higher MSCEIT scores report more satisfaction and happiness in their relationship. In addition, EI is associated (negatively) with maladaptive lifestyle choices. For example, college students with lower MSCEIT scores report higher levels of drug and alcohol consumption and more deviant acts, including stealing and fighting. Moreover, among adolescents, lower MSCEIT scores are associated with higher levels of anxiety and depression. Finally, EI is associated with a number of important workplace outcomes. For example, business professionals with high EI both see themselves and are viewed by their supervisors to effectively handle stress and to create a more enjoyable work environment. Future research will expand upon the theory of EI, and new tasks will be developed to measure the construct.

PETER SALOVEY AND MARC BRACKETT

Brackett, M.A., Rivers, S.E., Shiffman, S., Lerner, N., and Salovey, P. (2006). Relating emotional abilities to social functioning: a comparison of self-report and performance measures of emotional intelligence. *Journal of Personality and Social Psychology*, **91**, 780–795.

Mayer, J.D., Roberts, R.D., and Barsade, S.G. (2008). Human abilities: emotional intelligence. *Annual Review of Psychology*, **59**, 507–36.

Salovey, P. and Grewal, D. (2005). The science of emotional intelligence. *Current Directions in Psychological Science*, **14**, 281–5.

intentionality (and emotion) Mental states, such as thoughts, memories, perceptions, beliefs, desires and emotions, are said to exhibit *intentionality* because they are directed towards or are *about* the world: I think *about* horses; I believe *that* Port-Au-Prince is the capital of

Haiti; I am afraid *of* the bear. The concept was first employed by medieval philosophers, but the modern discussion of intentionality is due to Franz Brentano (1838–1917). Because I can think about unicorns, believe that Atlantis is the capital of Haiti, and be afraid of the Abominable Snowman, Brentano (1874/1973) thought that 'mental acts' such as beliefs and emotions are not relations between mental states and things in the world, but rather between mental states and special irreducible 'intentional objects', which are neither in the mind nor the world. In recent decades, most philosophers have argued that there are no such irreducible entities and that there are straightforward causal connections between objects in the world and mental states ('concepts') that signify them, although how this signification is accomplished is a matter of dispute. Some (e.g. Fodor 1987) have argued that mental states are simply brain states that have semantic properties and thereby represent actual or possible states of affairs.

In emotion theory the concept of intentionality has been cited in defence of the view that emotions are or entail some kind of belief, judgement, or cognitive appraisal of the world. According to appraisal theorists (see APPRAISAL THEORIES), emotions are necessarily intentional: if I am in love, there must be somebody with whom I'm in love (even if it is a fictional character in a movie); if I am angry, I am angry with somebody about something. For this very reason emotions cannot merely be bits of behaviour, dispositions or tendencies to act or behave in certain ways, or patterns of bodily change. Nor can they be merely bodily feelings like itches and tickles, which are not 'about' anything.

Solomon (1976), following in the phenomenological tradition of Brentano, argued that beliefs and emotions are 'noncontingently', rather than *causally* related to their 'intentional objects'. If I am angry that Jones stole my car, the 'intentional object' of my anger is an offence; if I am pleased that he stole my car the object of my pleasure is a boon. On this view the actual fact in the world—Jones' stealing my car—is not the 'object' of either emotion. Solomon claims that emotions constitute our 'surreality'—the way the world appears to each one of us—rather than the world as it actually is.

Naturalistic philosophers have rejected the idea of special 'intentional objects'. Gordon (1987) specifies what an emotion is 'about' simply by describing its causal structure, the desires, wishes, beliefs, and other epistemic states that *cause* it.

Others reject the view shared by Solomon and Gordon that the intentionality of emotions can be explained solely in terms of the intentionality of beliefs and/or desires. According to de Sousa (1987), there are intentional objects of emotion distinct from the objects of belief or desire. These are defined by 'axiological properties', such as the offensive, the disgusting, or the threatening, which are learned by exposure to 'paradigm scenarios'.

William James (1842–1910) denies that emotions essentially require cognitive appraisals (James 1884). Emotions are a certain kind of mental awareness: an awareness *of* bodily changes (see JAMES–LANGE THEORY). This conception of emotion endures in Schachter and Singer's (1962) idea that emotions consist in a combination of arousal and 'cognition', where 'cognition' is understood as labelling one's state of arousal (see SCHACHTER–SINGER THEORY). What's intentional here, i.e. what one's consciousness is directed towards, is not the content of a thought but a state of bodily arousal. Jesse Prinz's (2004) theory of emotion brings about a rapprochement between James' theory and older appraisal theories: he argues that emotions are indeed appraisals, but 'embodied appraisals' (see EMBODIMENT). Drawing on Fred Dretske's (1981) theory of mental representation, and Damasio's (1994) theory of somatic markers (see SOMATIC MARKER HYPOTHESIS), he argues that emotions are perceptions of patterns of somatic change that *represent* threats, losses, and so on by virtue of the fact that they are *reliably caused* by these things. Emotions are, then, intentional in the sense that they represent the world via changes in the body.

JENEFER ROBINSON

interest/enthusiasm Interest has been a controversial emotion in the history of affective science. Silvan Tomkins (1962), believing that interest was the 'affect which has been most seriously neglected' (p. 337), included *interest–excitement* as one of his basic positive emotions. Tomkins proposed that the function of interest was to motivate learning, exploration, and curiosity. Unlike *enjoyment, which motivates the forming of attachments to familiar sources of reward, interest motivates trying new actions and exploring new things. Interest and enjoyment can thus oppose each other, such as when people must choose between a new, intriguing thing and a familiar, enjoyable thing. In his model of emotion, Carroll Izard (1977) contended that interest is the most frequently experienced emotion. He emphasized the role of interest in human development, from cultivating knowledge and competence in infants to motivating learning and creativity in adults. Although emotion theories disagree over whether interest is an emotion, a large body of work suggests that interest has the expressive, physiological, motivational, and developmental features typical of emotions (see Silvia 2006b).

Feelings of interest, according to most theories, stem from a class of *novelty variables, such as novelty, complexity, uncertainty, conflict, and unfamiliarity. In his landmark work on curiosity, Berlyne (1971) showed that the interestingness of pictures, poems, music, and films stemmed from their novelty and complexity. Consistent with Tomkins' distinction between interest and enjoyment, many of Berlyne's experiments found that interest came from unfamiliar, arousing stimuli, whereas enjoyment came from familiar, calming stimuli. Recent appraisal research has recast the sources of interest in terms of appraisal components. In this model, interest's appraisal structure has two components: (1) a *novelty–complexity* check (an appraisal of the event's novelty, complexity, and unfamiliarity), and (2) a *coping potential* check (an appraisal of one's ability to comprehend the complex, unfamiliar event). Events appraised as complex but comprehensible are interesting (Silvia 2006b).

A wide body of research supports the notion of interest as an emotion associated with learning, exploration, and intrinsic motivation. Research in education, for example, shows that people pick interesting texts to read, process interesting texts more deeply, and remember interesting texts more easily. For classes that they find interesting, students use deeper study strategies, earn better grades, and report feeling more engaged (see Silvia 2006b). When struggling to achieve an important *goal, people will boost their motivation by using interest-enhancing strategies (e.g. turning a tedious task into a game). Making a task more interesting, in turn, increases persistence and performance (Sansone and Thoman 2005). In the long term, interest fosters expertise in a domain by motivating sustained practice and learning.

PAUL J. SILVIA

Renninger, K.A., Hidi, S., and Krapp, A. (1992). *The role of interest in learning and development*. Hillsdale, NJ: Lawrence Erlbaum Associates.

Silvia, P.J. (2006b). *Exploring the psychology of interest*. New York: Oxford University Press.

intergroup emotions Most theories of emotion, even those that emphasize its social aspects (such as the cultural shaping of emotions or their communicative functions), assume that emotions are experienced when events or objects become relevant to the individual (see RELEVANCE DETECTION). In contrast, current research finds that people can experience emotions when events impinge on their important social groups, even if the events do not directly affect the individual at all. Such groups can include a wide range of social categories and affiliations, such as a committee, a sports team, or a national, ethnic, or religious identity. In research demonstrating this point, Yzerbyt *et al.* (2002) manipulated whether or not participants categorized themselves in a common ingroup with someone who was victimized by an event that had absolutely no implications for the participants as individuals. Those who categorized themselves with the victim tended to feel more anger and less happiness—emotions that are clearly mediated by the shared group membership. Cottrell and Neuberg (2005) offer one conceptual framework for group-based emotions, an evolutionary analysis postulating specific emotional responses to group-based threats (e.g. threats to boundary clarity or territorial integrity) as well as individual-level threats (e.g. physical harm).

Our own model, intergroup emotions theory (Smith 1993, Mackie *et al.* 2004) rests on the idea, derived from the tradition of social identity theory (Tajfel 1978), that when an individual identifies with a social group the group membership attains emotional significance by becoming part of the self. Identification with a group is especially likely in what is termed an *intergroup situation*, one in which social comparisons, competition, or conflict between groups are salient—hence the name of the theoretical model. When people think of themselves as members of a group, they appraise events and objects for their implications for the group—not only implications for the individual self (Smith 1993). Appraisals of the event as positive or negative, deserved or undeserved, intentional or not (and so forth) in turn lead to the experience of distinct intergroup emotions, such as anger, pride, guilt, happiness, or fear. Finally, like any emotions these intergroup emotions are linked to tendencies or desires for action; often, these actions will be at the group level rather than the individual level. Thus, anger at a rival group may lead to a desire to attack that group or to oppose governmental policies perceived as favouring the rival. Fear of another group may lead to the desire to avoid that group and perhaps to support for restrictions on immigration of group members into the country.

Evidence reviewed in Mackie *et al.* (2004) supports many of the assumptions and predictions of intergroup emotions theory. First, as noted above, when a particular group membership is made salient, people report experiencing emotions appropriate to the situation of a fellow group member, even though the situation has no implications for the perceiver as an individual. Second, people feel differentiated emotions toward outgroups, depending on how the groups are appraised, rather than just experiencing a general negative reaction to any outgroup (see also Cottrell and Neuberg 2005). Third, the more closely individuals identify with a group the more intensely they feel positive emotions about the ingroup and anger toward rival outgroups. Fourth, the intergroup emotions experienced when people think of themselves in terms of membership of a particular group are meaningfully distinct from those they experience as individuals. Fifth, the intergroup emotions reported by members of a particular group tend to be socially shared, to converge toward a group-typical profile of emotions. And finally, it is intergroup, rather than individual, emotions that are more powerful predictors of desires for group-relevant actions (such as affiliating with fellow ingroup members or confronting a rival group).

Intergroup emotions are of practical importance because they are significantly related to prejudice against outgroups, and, potentially, can be part of processes that reduce prejudice as well. For example, friendly contact with members of a racial outgroup has been shown to reduce prejudice against that group, and several recent studies demonstrate that this effect is mediated by changes in the positive and negative emotions that people feel toward the outgroup (rather than by changes in inaccurate stereotypes of the outgroup). Future research on the role of group-based emotions may reveal additional ways in which they contribute to the reduction of prejudice and intergroup conflict.

ELIOT R. SMITH AND DIANE M. MACKIE

Mackie, D.M., Maitner, A.T., and Smith, E.R. (2009). Intergroup emotions theory. In: T.D. Nelson (ed.), *Handbook of prejudice, stereotyping, and discrimination*. New York: Psychology Press.
Smith, E.R. and Mackie, D.M. (2008). Intergroup emotions. In: M. Lewis, J.M. Haviland-Jones, and L. Feldman Barrett (eds), *Handbook of emotions*, 3rd edn, pp. 428–39. New York: Guilford Publications.

internalizer An internalizer tends to show less overt emotional expression (see EXPRESSION, FUNCTIONS OF EMOTIONAL; EXPRESSION, PRINCIPLES OF EMOTIONAL), but higher *electrodermal responses. The externalizer–internalizer dimension was originally explored by H. E. Jones (1935) in the Berkeley Growth Study; he found that children who express their emotions overtly show smaller electrodermal activity. This may reflect the degree to which expressive behaviour is inhibited, with the inhibition associated with increased physiological *arousal. It can reflect *temperament—trait inhibition—or conditioned inhibition in a specific situation—state inhibition. Compared with externalizers, internalizers are generally more reserved, more deliberate, and less animated; but also more anxious and solitary, and more likely to be high in denial.

Developmentally, the degree to which a person is an internalizer or externalizer is thought to be the result of the individual's temperament and social learning with respect to emotional expression. These patterns are influenced by sex-role-related social learning experiences: in most emotion-arousing situations, adult males tend to show an internalizing pattern, but this is not the case in preschool-aged children. Typically boys are punished for being expressive in most emotion-arousing situations, and as a result they tend to become more inhibited. In contrast, girls are typically punished for aggressive behaviour and tend to become more inhibited in aggressive situations.

The externalizer–internalizer dimension has connections to several theories across a number of psychological domains, including theories of emotional communication; theories of behavioural activation and inhibition proposed by Eysenck, Gray, and Rolls; Kagan's theory of reactive temperamental style; the underlying mechanisms of stress-related illnesses; and the broader classification of psychopathology into categories of externalizing and internalizing disorders. Internalizers should have more reactive physiological responses, should be more susceptible to punishment, should show greater immune dysfunction as a result of stress, and be more likely to suffer from *depression and *anxiety disorders. See also EXTERNALIZER.

ROSS BUCK AND R. THOMAS BOONE

interoception Interoception is the transmission and representation in the central nervous system of stimuli that impinge on interoceptors. Interoceptors are the sensory source of the vegetative infrastructure of higher animals. They include mechano-, thermo-, and chemoreceptors of the gut; stretch receptors of the atria, carotid arteries, and aorta; chemoreceptors of the carotid sinus; lipid receptors in the circulation of the liver and intestines; and metaboreceptors (metabolic state receptors) in the skeletal muscles. Most are situated within the body cavities, and are the basis of visceral reflexes and the central neural representation of the blood vessels and visceral organs. More broadly, within an organ or tissue there are sensory elements that serve special host organ functions, such as photoreceptors in the eye, hair cells in the cochlea, the spindles of the skeletal muscles, or the stretch and mucosal chemoreceptors of the intestine, and others that subserve more general tissue maintenance functions, such as the metaboreceptors of the skeletal muscles. To be complete, interoceptors should include all sensory receptors in visceral organs, plus other receptors, wherever located, that subserve local tissue metabolic functions. Anatomically, nearly 90% of the fibres of the vagus and more than 50% of the fibres of all autonomic nerves are afferent (Norgren 1985, p. 145), and these fibres convey extensive information from interoceptors to the brain.

Conscious perception of non-noxious stimuli via interoceptors is probably restricted to special functions, such as hunger, or to special structures, such as the bladder or rectum. There is a possibility that conscious perception in special structures, especially those which communicate with the external environment, is not direct, and that perception exists, at least to a large degree, because of learned associations with proprioceptive and exteroceptive stimuli. Conscious perception of visceral stimuli is probably unimportant to the regulation of normal physiological function.

The best studied and most generally accepted role of interoceptors is as afferent components in control loops that regulate the viscera. In fact, interoceptors are the first element of the feedback path of all reflex mechanisms of physiological regulation. These mechanisms do not involve conscious perception. Adaptation, or loss of response to constant stimuli, is an established feature of all interoceptors which have been adequately studied. Receptor adaptation is a key theoretical problem in understanding the role of interoceptors in the steady-state in physiological regulation.

Interoceptive stimuli can function as conditioned stimuli for visceral and somatic Pavlovian conditioned reflexes, and these interoceptive–exteroceptive, or interoceptive–interoceptive reflexes may coordinate various visceral–visceral and visceral–somatic relationships.

For an interoceptive–exteroceptive conditioned reflex, an interoceptive stimulus, such as distension of the small intestine, carotid sinus, or renal pelvis, is associated with an externally produced skeletal motor reflex, such as shock-induced limb withdrawal. The usual goal in elaborating such reflexes is to estimate the detectability and discriminability of particular interoceptive stimuli. The conditioned response is a substitute for verbal behaviour in infrahuman species, and, in certain special cases, with humans (Àdàm 1967).

For an interoceptive–interoceptive conditioned reflex, an interoceptive stimulus, such as distension of the small intestine, carotid sinus, or renal pelvis, thermal stimulation of the stomach, or osmotic stimulation of the liver, is associated with a visceral reflex, such as food-induced gastric secretion or fluid load-induced renal secretion, or activation of the baroreflex.

Separate from conscious perception, there are well-established effects of non-noxious interoceptive stimuli on higher functioning of the central nervous system and on behaviour. Appropriate interoceptive stimulation can affect satiety, modify reflex activity or pain perception, and produce electroencephalogram synchronization and sleep. The best-studied examples of these interoceptor mechanisms involve the inhibitory effects of the baroreceptors and of the afferent fibres of the vagus nerve (Dworkin et al. 1994).

BARRY R. DWORKIN

interpersonal communication Interpersonal communication conveys affect, but does more than express a state of mind/feeling. Although interpersonal communication entails the transfer of meaning from one person to another (assuming three basic elements: sender, message, and receiver), this idea is simplistic (see ENCODING/DECODING (OF EXPRESSION)). It *presumes* a system of shared meaning between sender and receiver represented symbolically in the message. Furthermore, communication theorists debate the role of *intentionality in communicative behaviour (some messages are unintended; some intended messages are not received).

These disagreements suggest three ways of portraying interpersonal communication. First as action, such that all behaviour intended as communication is termed communication, whether or not the intended target receives and understands the message. Second, communication as interaction requires that the message be both sent and received. Third, communication as transaction (the most widely accepted view) recognizes interactants as simultaneous senders and receivers of messages, but also notes that there is 'value added'. For instance, communication could result in trust, love, respect, or a legal contract over and above the simple exchange of messages: this would be transaction.

The transactional view sees communication as more than merely movement of 'messages' from one mind to another, however imperfectly. Instead, it allows that additional meaning is actually created through the transaction. The shift here is significant, for it externalizes the forces which shape self and other, such as affect.

Krauss and Fussell (1996) provide an overview of interpersonal communication theory offering four categories to illuminate the shift in emphasis from a focus on interior representations to the process of making meaning which occurs between people. They first describe encoder–decoder models of interpersonal communication which entail the encoding of a perception into a symbolic message, which is expressed and then decoded by a target. A second category of models are the intentionalist models which acknowledge that people make choices of what to encode, how to encode it, and the manner in which the message is decoded.

Perspective-taking models are the third category of theories. The idea that any given message has both a content and a relational component is now widely accepted. Perspective-taking models build on these twin components by acknowledging the human capacity for *empathy and the role it plays in establishing and maintaining affect-laden relationships through communication.

The fourth category of interpersonal models is dialogic models. These models have only recently gained attention amongst communication theorists and they face resistance from adherents to the traditional view of communication as the expression of aspects of *self. A dialogic view, by contrast, holds that individuals exist in a world of multiple discourses. We privilege some discourses by incorporating them in our communication and over time these discourses transact both individual identity and also relational identity. Dialogism rejects the traditional idea of an essential self that is simply expressed through communication (for instance, through self-disclosure). A dialogic approach instead holds that the expression actually creates or reinforces characteristics by offering them as a discourse to be accepted and maintained (transacted) by the partner.

Other theorists dispute whether an assumption of intentionality is a necessary or sufficient condition for communication. Guerrero and Floyd (2006) addressed the issue by distinguishing various types of communication. *Successful communication* is sent intentionally and decoded accurately. *Miscommunication* is sent intentionally but decoded inaccurately. *Accidental communication* is sent without intent but decoded accurately. *Attempted communication* is sent intentionally but not received. The echoes of action, interaction, and transaction are evident, but communication theorists are far from unanimous on the role of intention.

In addition, scholars also dispute the *personal* aspect of interpersonal communication. Some claim that impersonal interactions which through technology or habit are rendered mechanical should not be termed interpersonal. Both perspective-taking and dialogic models tend toward this interpretation in that they hold that communication is always engaged with an expectation of how a specific or general other will respond.

Underlying much of the research to date is a bias assuming that disclosive communication is necessarily good communication. Many affective outcomes such as intimacy, self-disclosure, trust, and empathy are viewed as essentially positive. A growing number of researchers, including Spitzberg and Cupach (2007), have turned attention to the negative or 'dark side' of interpersonal communication. The first recognition was that negative affect could be produced in open interpersonal communication (e.g. hostility, conflict, and slander). More recent research upholds a dualism in darkness: too much 'good' communication can be bad (individuals may be too intimate or too empathetic). Second, 'bad'

communication such as conflict, secrecy, and deception can generate positive functions (such as relationship growth, or politeness). No simple relationship exists between affect and communication.

BRENDAN YOUNG AND STEVE DUCK

intersubjectivity Although the term 'intersubjectivity' is used in a variety of senses, common to most formulations is the coordination or reciprocal influence of the experiences of two or more individuals. Examples include states of empathic communion, and the sense of mutual engagement in tasks (see EMPATHY (NEUROSCIENCE PERSPECTIVES); EMPATHY (PHILOSOPHICAL PERSPECTIVES)). For some theorists, subjective experiences of all kinds derive from prior participation in intersubjective processes (e.g. Baldwin, 1906, Vygotsky, 1934/1986). Correspondingly, some theorists believe that emotions are primarily events that occur between rather than (or in addition to) inside people's minds (e.g. de Rivera and Grinkis 1986), whereas others simply acknowledge the obvious fact that some of our emotions can sometimes affect other people as well as ourselves.

From the perspective of developmental psychology, Trevarthen and Hubley (1978) introduced an influential distinction between primary and secondary intersubjectivity. According to them, infants enter the world with genetic predispositions to engage with other humans, and engage in direct active communion with caregivers from the start of their lives (primary intersubjectivity). Secondary intersubjectivity usually emerges before the age of one year and involves the capacity to calibrate perspectives with others on objects of mutual activity or attention.

These two forms of intersubjectivity are associated with distinctive emotional processes. For example, primary engagement with caregivers is infused with affection- and attachment-related emotions (see ATTACHMENT) (as well as more negative affective responses to disruptions of interpersonal coordination; e.g. Murray and Trevarthen 1985, Tronick et al. 1978). Following the onset of secondary intersubjectivity, infants' emotions become oriented not only to other humans, objects, or activities, but also to relations between other humans and objects in the shared field of activity. It may be that the precursors of supposedly cognitively complex emotions such as *jealousy and *guilt emerge at this stage (Draghi-Lorenz et al. 2001).

The ontogenetic origins of intersubjectivity are disputed. Some developmentalists dismiss innate capacities for human engagement, arguing instead that infants simply respond to other people as they would to any other complex and contingently changing physical object (e.g. Watson, 1979). Regardless of one's position in this debate, it seems clear that an active infant coupled with a continually responsive caregiver provides a dynamic system out of which intersubjective experience should inevitably coalesce (Fogel *et al.* 1992). More generally, there can be little doubt that many infant as well as adult emotions can act upon and adjust to the active and adjusting emotions and unfolding conduct of others.

BRIAN PARKINSON

Hobson, P. (2002). *The cradle of thought: exploring the origins of thinking*. London: Macmillan.

Stern, D.N. (1985). *The interpersonal world of the infant*. New York: Basic Books.

intrinsic pleasantness The intrinsic pleasantness of a stimulus indicates whether the effect of a stimulus on an organism is likely to be pleasant or painful/unpleasant (in the widest sense), independent of the current state of the organism (Scherer 2001a). Intrinsic pleasantness is a fundamental, very basic appraisal dimension (see AP-PRAISAL THEORIES) which can be observed across many species (Schneirla 1959). The assessment of intrinsic pleasantness—with an outcome along a *valence dimension (pleasant–neutral–unpleasant)—determines the fundamental reaction of the organism toward a stimulus by engaging basic motivational systems. Stimuli high in intrinsic pleasantness/liking encourage approach behaviour, whereas high unpleasantness leads to withdrawal or avoidance (see APPROACH/WITHDRAWAL).

Concepts such as pleasure, reward, and reinforcement play a central role in many psychological theories; nevertheless it is not well understood which critical features of a stimulus generate liking/pleasure/preference or dislike/distress/aversion. Some potentially contributing factors are (1) stimulus characteristics related to stimulus processing, (2) phylogenetic innate evaluation templates, and (3) the individual's ontogenetic learning history.

Stimulus characteristics

Several dimensions of stimulus characteristics related to the processing of the stimulus have been shown to influence intrinsic pleasantness. One such factor is stimulus intensity, with hedonic tone becoming more positive with the increase of stimulus intensity up to a certain point and then becoming negative as intensity increases further (Berlyne 1960). Similar effects can be observed in animals, in which low stimulus intensity tends to elicit approach responses whereas high stimulus intensity tends to produce adjustment responses and withdrawal (Schneirla 1959). As demonstrated by research on the *mere exposure effect*, frequency of stimulus exposure also has an effect on intrinsic pleasantness (Zajonc 2001). Stimulus complexity seems to be a further relevant factor, with some optimal intermediate level of stimulus complexity resulting in pleasantness. Moreover, stimuli which are both novel and highly interpretable are evaluated as pleasant. This has been linked to findings of opioid receptors in visual pathways. The processing of stimuli that are highly interpretable and thus activate many associations may lead to release of endorphins, which is experienced as pleasant (Yue *et al.* 2007).

Phylogenetic innate evaluation templates

In addition to general stimulus characteristics such as intensity or interpretability, it is rather probable that evolution has developed specific innate evaluation templates for environmental patterns and stimuli which are relevant for survival and reproduction and which are thus evaluated as intrinsically pleasant or unpleasant (Buss 1995). 'Innate templates' does not necessarily imply that these templates are 'coded in the genes' or 'present at birth'; instead the organism might be biologically prepared (Seligman 1971) to rapidly develop these evaluations after birth, taking into account environmental information that the genes cannot predict (see Dellarosa Cummins and Cummins, 1999, for a discussion). Comparative and developmental work suggests that innate evaluation templates exist for a number of different stimuli. While some of these templates might be universal and phylogenetically continuous, others are probably species-specific. Some examples of innate evaluation templates are preferences for sweet tastes and aversions for bitter tastes, which have been found in many species, in infants and adults, and across cultures. Similar patterns have been found for different kinds of odours. Facial features and expressions can be detected and evaluated by newborn infants, possibly serving as innate releasing mechanisms for approach or avoidance responses (Lorenz 1981). In adults, the *Kindchenschema* (baby schema; Lorenz 1943), a configuration of perceptual features found in newborns across species, elicits positive emotions and behaviour patterns of parental care such as increased attention to the infant (Brosch *et al.* 2008). Preferences guiding human mate selection are known to be related to a number of morphological criteria promoting reproductive success. Furthermore, specific kinds of landscapes are consistently evaluated as pleasant—in particular places that provide nourishment, safety, and protection from hazards, or landscapes that provide a hidden vantage point with multiple views for surveillance of the adjacent environment. Such location preferences might result from an innate need to find the optimal location for settlement, indicating that intrinsic pleasantness might reflect the likely survival value of a scene (Kaplan and Kaplan 1982).

Individual ontogenetic learning history

Humans and many animals furthermore have many different object preferences that are unlikely to be based on innate evaluation templates. Conditioning (see ASSOCIATIVE PROCESSING) is a straightforward way to rapidly acquire likes and dislikes (De Houwer *et al.* 2001); via generalization those preferences may even extend to stimuli which have not yet been encountered. The evaluation of intrinsic pleasantness must include, then, the evaluation of stimulus input with regards to acquired preferences or aversions. Due to different learning histories, this evaluation will produce different results for each individual organism. A role of innate templates can also be found in individual learning processes, as primates seem to be biologically prepared to rapidly learn fears toward specific stimuli such as spiders, snakes, or heights, which have been associated with dangerous situation during the phylogenetic development of primate species (Seligman 1971).

The intrinsic pleasantness or unpleasantness detected by an organism is a characteristic of the stimulus, and even though the preference may have been acquired, it is independent of the current *goal state of the organism. It is important to distinguish between intrinsic pleasantness appraisal and the appraisal of *motive consistency. The evaluation of whether a stimulus helps the organism to reach goals or satisfy needs may also evoke positive or negative feelings. However, in contrast to intrinsic pleasantness, which refers to the hedonic tone of a stimulus and is independent of the organism's goal state, the motive consistency appraisal depends on the relationship between the stimulus and the organism's current motivational state. The difference is obvious in cases where an inherently pleasant stimulus blocks goal achievement in a particular situation and thus generates negative feelings (like a tasty chocolate cake encountered during a diet).

TOBIAS BROSCH

introspection Introspection is the forming of *beliefs about one's mind through direct awareness of it. I know that I feel tired because I am directly aware of my feelings of tiredness: this is a paradigmatic case of introspection. If I only infer that I must feel tired (perhaps on the basis of observing that I am cranky, and recalling that I get cranky when I feel tired), then I am not introspecting. Many researchers hold that introspection is not wholly reliable (e.g. Schwitzgebel 2002, Wegner 2002).

TIMOTHY SCHROEDER

irrationality There are many varieties of irrationality of emotion (see also RATIONALITY). Here are four. (1) *Epistemic*

irrationality. Whether it is correct to say that an emotion is epistemically irrational depends in part on the person's evidential grounds for her taking things to be a certain way. It could be epistemically rational to fear something if there is good evidence that it is dangerous, even if, in fact, it turns out not to be dangerous. Conversely, it could be epistemically irrational to fear something if there is no evidence that it is dangerous, even if, in fact, it turns out to be dangerous (see REASON). (2) *Prudential irrationality*. It may be prudentially irrational to be angry (and to act out of anger) at someone who has power over you, for it might not serve you own best interests, even if you think it does at the time. (3) *Conflicting emotions*. A person's emotion can conflict with her *beliefs or with her other emotions, as one might be afraid of something that one believes not to be dangerous. Some consider this to be *eo ipso* irrational, but arguably this will depend on the circumstances. (4) *Weakness of the will*. This, like (3), is another kind of internal conflict. Known by the Greeks as *akrasia*, this often arises where one's emotions lead one to act against what one knows at the time to be in one's own best interests; thus this kind of irrationality is distinct from that in (2). Weakness of the will can also be epistemic, arising in relation to evidence, where because of an emotion one chooses to ignore what one knows at the time to be good evidence about something. For discussion, see Ronald de Sousa, *The Rationality of Emotion* (de Sousa, 1987); and the locus classicus for *akrasia* is Aristotle's *Nicomachean Ethics* Book VII.

PETER GOLDIE

de Sousa, R. (2007). *The Rationality of Emotion*. Cambridge, Mass. MIT Press.

irritation The term irritation is used to refer to both an emotional state ('I feel irritated') and to the object or act that causes it ('That noise is a real irritation'). As an emotional state, irritation is closely related to *anger.

Two different views exist about what determines feelings of irritation and how it relates to the emotion of anger. According to one view, irritation differs from anger in quantity, that is, in intensity. In this view, irritation consists of relatively mild feelings of anger. Irritation would differ from anger in intensity because the events that cause irritation are characterized by lower levels of personal relevance (see CONCERNS) or consequences in comparison with the events that elicit anger. In the other view, irritation is considered to differ from anger in qualitative ways, characterized by a qualitatively different appraisal of events as compared to anger (see APPRAISAL THEORIES). According to Averill (1982), unlike anger, irritation is characterized by the appraisal of low seriousness and without the moral dimension (of blame and injustice) that often is implicated in feelings of anger. According to Scherer (2001a), unlike anger, irritation is less sudden and does not involve a specific assignment of blame. Relatively stable dispositional individual differences in irritability are assumed to exist, and are related to a higher tendency to experience irritation and anger and to aggressive responding (see AGGRESSION).

PETER KUPPENS

J

James–Lange theory The James–Lange theory was developed in the late 19th century and refers to a seminal hypothesis concerning the nature of emotion that was developed independently by the American William James (1842–1910) and the Danish physiologist Carl Lange (1834–1900). The essence of the theory is that physiological changes mediated by the *autonomic nervous system, such as increased muscular tension, perspiration, accelerated heart rate, butterflies in the stomach, and so forth, are a direct response to experiences in the world, such as unexpectedly encountering a bear in the woods. Emotional *feelings arise as a result of these physiological changes, rather than being their cause. As James (1884) stated in his paper 'What is an emotion?': 'My theory . . . is that the bodily changes follow directly the perception of the exciting fact, and that our feeling of the same changes as they occur IS the emotion'. Within the James–Lange theory, therefore, our experience of different emotions such as fear, sadness, and anger is simply a function of different repertoires of physiological response to the environment.

The first significant challenge to the James–Lange theory was posed in the 1920s by the psychologists Walter Cannon (1871–1945) and Philip Bard (1898–1977) (see CANNON–BARD THEORY). Cannon and Bard pointed out that total surgical separation of the viscera and the brain in animals did not impair emotional behaviour, that bodily or autonomic states could not reliably distinguish different emotions, that bodily changes are typically too slow to generate emotions, and that artificial hormonal stimulation of the body is insufficient to generate emotion. Cannon and Bard claimed that these findings were fundamentally incompatible with the James–Lange theory and, in its place, they proposed the Cannon–Bard theory of emotions—the first substantive hypothesis about the brain mechanisms involved in emotion.

More recent research has undermined some of Cannon and Bard's criticisms of the James–Lange theory. Emotional responses, at least in part, can be distinguished on the basis of autonomic activity (Ekman *et al.* 1983); emotional intensity diminishes when the brain is disconnected from the viscera, even in Cannon's original studies; and some artificial manipulations of bodily activity can induce emotions—for example, intravenous administration of a particular gastric peptide can bring about panic attacks.

The James–Lange theory remains influential due to an increasing emphasis in current thinking on the *embodiment of emotion. Indeed, many current theories would endorse some modulatory role of the body in determining the intensity of experienced emotion (see Izard 1990a). Other theories, such as Damasio's *somatic marker hypothesis (see Dunn *et al.* 2006), go further in proposing a critical role for bodily signals (somatic markers) as emotional tags linked to regularities in past experience that have emotional consequences. New encounters with tagged stimuli elicit somatic marker activation and this serves to direct decision-making in situations of uncertainty.

Interestingly, there exists some modern debate about the exact nature of the James–Lange theory (Ellsworth 1994c, Reisenzein *et al.* 1995). For instance, Ellsworth has proposed that James later advocated a more cognitive theory of emotion (James 1894) whereby the interpretation of the experience is also essential in the genesis of emotion. However, Reisenzein *et al.*, among others, dispute Ellsworth's reading of the later literature, suggesting that it remains consistent with the traditional interpretation of James–Lange theory.

TIM DALGLEISH

Dalgleish, T. (2004a). The emotional brain. *Nature Reviews Neuroscience*, **5**, 582–9.

Izard, C.E. (1990a). The substrates and function of emotion feelings: William James and current emotion theory. *Personality and Social Psychology Bulletin*, **16**, 626–35.

jealousy Jealousy is aroused when a person feels threatened by a rival in his or her relationship with another individual, in particular an intimate partner. Jealousy may involve feelings of threat, fear, suspicion, distrust, anxiety, anger, betrayal, and rejection. Jealousy has clear cognitive aspects (such as paranoid thoughts and worries about the behaviour of one's partner) as well as behavioural aspects (such as spying on one's partner or rummaging through his or her belongings). Jealousy has been found to be more pronounced in individuals with an anxious ambivalent attachment style (see ATTACHMENT), a high dependency on the relationship, a high degree of neuroticism, and, especially among women, a low *self-esteem. In response to a partner's infidelity, women are more likely to think that they are 'not good enough' and become depressed, whereas men are more likely to get drunk and use violence. Indeed, jealousy is among men an important cause of homicide. Among women, it is evoked more by physically attractive rivals, and among men by physically and socially dominant rivals. In addition, individuals tend to report more jealousy as their rival is better on self-relevant attributes, such as intelligence, popularity, athleticism, and particular professional skills.

From an evolutionary perspective it has been argued that males have in the course of evolution faced the problem of confidence in paternity, and females of securing the partner's investment of resources (see EVOLUTION OF EMOTION) (Buss 2000). Therefore, males will experience more sexual jealousy, focusing upon the sexual aspects of the partner's involvement in extramarital relationships, and women will experience more emotional jealousy, focusing on the emotional involvement of one's partner in such relationships. There is increasing evidence for this sex difference, although the debate on the theoretical interpretation and on the methodological aspects of the supportive research is still continuing. In general emotional infidelity is more likely to evoke feelings of insecurity and threat, whereas sexual infidelity is more likely to evoke feelings of betrayal, anger, and repulsion.

ABRAHAM P. BUUNK

joy Joy is a pleasant state that shares conceptual space with other *positive emotions such as gladness, elation, happiness, and, to a lesser extent, amusement. Feelings of joy arise in circumstances appraised as safe, familiar, and requiring little personal effort. Joy is the pleasant state experienced when people have made progress toward important personal *goals, especially when that progress is better than expected (Lazarus 1991). Phenomenologically, joy feels bright and light. Colours seem more vivid. Physical movements become more fluid. Smiles become difficult to suppress. Joy broadens people's attention and thinking. Such broadened thinking is thought to support the playful 'do anything' action tendency associated with joy. Even though the playfulness inspired by joy is often aimless, it has reliable outcomes. Ethologists have long held that play promotes the acquisition of skills. Physical skills are developed and practised in rough-and-tumble and chasing play, manipulative–cognitive skills are developed and practised in object play, and social–affective skills are developed and practised in social play. In this manner, repeated experiences of joy are thought to build people's resources for survival.

BARBARA L. FREDRICKSON

Fredrickson, B.L. (1998). What good are positive emotions? *Review of General Psychology*, **2**, 300–319.

justice (procedural) The procedural justice literature highlights the notion that individuals are affected not only by *what* they get, but *how* they get it. Specifically, procedural justice refers to the extent to which the decision-making procedures used to determine outcomes or resource distributions are fair (see FAIRNESS) or just.

Elements of fair procedures

Decision-making procedures can be formal, codified, and enacted by groups or committees, or informal, unrecorded, and enacted by individual agents. While decision-making procedures can vary on a considerable number of dimensions, there are some characteristics that are consistently associated with procedural justice.

Fair procedures are those which: (1) are consistently applied across people and situations, (2) suppress the potential influence of biases, (3) use accurate information, (4) incorporate mechanisms for correcting flawed decisions, (5) consider the concerns of all relevant parties, and (6) meet ethical standards (Leventhal 1980). In addition, the provision of 'voice', or a channel by which constituents can express their concerns or provide input into the decision-making process, greatly contributes to the sense that procedures are fair (Thibaut and Walker 1975). Procedures lacking these components are thought to be less fair, or even unfair. Though these features contribute to mean level differences in the extent to which procedures are thought to be fair, there is still individual variation in perceptions of fairness. While the fairness of a given set of procedures is, to some degree, in the eye of the beholder, some types of procedures are generally viewed as fairer than others.

Reactions to procedural justice and injustice

One's thoughts, feelings, and behaviours are powerfully affected by the experience of fair or unfair procedures (Colquitt *et al.* 2001). For instance, people think that decisions that are made fairly are more appropriate, they feel enhanced commitment to organizations and institutions that use fair procedures, and they voluntarily comply with decisions that are made fairly. In contrast, unfair decisions-making procedures are more likely to lead to devaluations of the resulting outcomes, dissatisfaction and distrust of the decision-making bodies, and more group undermining behaviours (such as employee theft). Being treated unfairly can also evoke strong emotional reactions, including sadness and anger. Positive reactions to fair procedures, and negative reactions to unfair procedures, are apparent whether the outcomes they lead to are desirable or undesirable to the individual.

The use of fair procedure has largely beneficial consequences for those in positions of authority as well as the groups that they represent. Being treated fairly allows members to maintain a positive image of the group, feel committed to the group, and buy in to group goals. By eliciting *trust and commitment, a climate of procedural justice serves as a foundation for fostering social coordination (Tyler and Blader 2000). Group members feel free to move beyond protecting individual interests to promoting group interests.

Psychological concerns addressed by procedural justice

Several theoretical perspectives consider the motivations behind the widespread effects found for procedural justice. Initial work on procedural justice was based on the understanding that procedures were afforded importance as they led to more desirable outcomes or resources. People were thought to care about, and react to, variations in the fairness of procedures because procedures could determine the quality of outcomes. But this notion was challenged by findings demonstrating that people prefer fair to unfair procedures even when these procedures have no bearing on outcomes. For instance, being afforded the opportunity to voice an opinion, even after decisions have already been made, contributes to the perception of fairness and produces related positive reactions (Lind *et al.* 1990). If decision control does not motivate interest in procedural justice, what does?

Several more recent theoretical approaches have been put forth which move beyond instrumental explanations for procedural justice. In one influential framework, relational models of procedural justice argue that procedural justice is valued due to its capacity to convey one's standing within the group in which the procedures are enacted. People are concerned about their place within social groups, and use procedural justice as a means of gauging their status. Other psychological drivers, such as the desire to reduce uncertainty, and concern about adherence to moral principles (including fairness and justice), have also been hypothesized to underlie interest in procedural justice.

CELIA M. GONZALEZ AND TOM R. TYLER

Blader, S.L. and Tyler, T.R. (2005). How can theories of organizational justice explain the effects of fairness? In: J. Greenberg and J.A. Colquitt (eds), *Handbook of organizational justice*, pp. 329–54. Mahwah, NJ: Lawrence Erlbaum Associates.

van Prooijen, J.W., van den Bos, K., and Wilke, H.A.M. (2004). The role of standing in the psychology of procedural justice: toward theoretical integration. In: W. Stroebe and M. Hewstone (eds), *European review of social psychology*, pp. 33–58. Hove: Psychology Press.

L

language and culture see CULTURAL SPECIFICITY; DISPLAY RULES; EVOLUTION OF EMOTION; HISTORY OF EMOTION; INDIVIDUALISM/COLLECTIVISM; INTERGROUP EMOTIONS; LANGUAGE AND EMOTION; LINGUISTICS AND EMOTION; NORMS; PUSH/PULL EFFECTS; RELIGION AND EMOTION (HISTORICAL PERSPECTIVES); UNIVERSALITY OF EMOTIONS; VALUES; VOCABULARY OF EMOTION.

language and emotion Emotion and language represent our two principal systems of communication, yet if one were to ask adults 'How do you communicate?' they would generally respond that language is their primary communication system (see INTERPERSONAL COMMUNICATION). However, in daily interaction, any utterance is expressed and interpreted in an emotional context. One's emotional state can influence language production, as in 'She was stunned, speechless', but more commonly, we simultaneously use both systems in interpreting and expressing our message.

Accompanying a spoken utterance, emotion can be expressed paralinguistically, for example using vocal prosody or emotional facial expression (see FACIAL EXPRESSION OF EMOTION; VOCAL EXPRESSION OF EMOTION). In this case the emotional expression can add supplementary information, colouring or adding nuance to a neutral utterance. A sentence such as 'John arrives tonight' can be produced with neutral, angry, or joyful prosody to convey the speaker's response or attitude to this event. In contrast, prosody or facial expression that is dissonant in meaning with the linguistic message yields an ironic or sarcastic message. Emotion can also be explicitly expressed lexically, as in 'She was delighted to learn that John arrives tonight' or, somewhat more indirectly, 'She sobbed piteously'. And of course the lexical and prosodic can be combined, as in 'She was sooooooooo excited to see him!'. Similarly, in languages such as English, we can use the modal verb system to subtly convey our attitude, as in: 'I am going to New York'; 'I could go to New York'; 'I may go to New York'; or 'I *will* go to New York'.

For adults, these two systems of language and emotion are successfully integrated, working together so smoothly that it can be difficult to untangle the contributions of the individual components to communication. However, if we look at children and trace the emergence

and development of these systems, we gain a clearer understanding of how the systems interact. During the first year of life, infants begin to produce and interpret various affective vocalizations and emotional facial expressions (see INFANCY (EMOTIONAL DEVELOPMENT IN)). By their first birthday, as they begin to produce their first words, infants are already very effective emotional communicators. They can convey their needs using vocalizations, facial expressions, and *gestures, and they can use adult affective responses both to guide their own behaviour and to learn new information (Tomasello 2001). Language *per se* emerges in this established social–communicative context, but young children have difficulty integrating the systems expressively (Bloom 1993). As language develops, children begin producing two-word utterances (at the end of their second year). Between about 18 and 24 months of age, words for emotional states and behaviours emerge, e.g. 'Joey crying. Joey sad', suggesting that children are explicitly attending to emotion signals. Interestingly, whereas infants are sensitive to affective prosody, preschool aged children give priority to the lexical or linguistic content of the message, especially if the prosody and content are inconsistent. It is not until about the age of 7 or 8 years that children are able to address both aspects of the message.

Children acquiring a sign language as their first language provide a unique window to understanding the developmental relations of language and emotion—in American Sign Language (ASL) facial behaviours not only convey emotion, but certain facial movements also constitute obligatory grammatical signals. Thus children acquiring ASL face the challenge of using similar facial behaviours, e.g. furrowed brows, for both affective and linguistic purposes (e.g. asking 'WH' questions). Our studies (Reilly 2006) have shown that deaf signing children, similar to hearing children, use emotional facial expression competently in infancy. However, rather than recruiting such apparently pertinent prelinguistic knowledge for acquiring grammatical facial structures, these same children exploit an alternative, but ungrammatical, manual strategy (using a manual sign) and only later acquire the facial markers. The findings suggest a functional bifurcation of facial expression for emotion and language as children move from the single word/sign stage into the grammar and syntax of the language. Broadly, it is not until about preschool age that children successfully integrate the co-expression of emotion and language.

For more than a century, we have had evidence that, for adults, formal aspects of language (e.g. morphology and syntax) are mediated by the left hemisphere of the brain and that emotional facial expression is a right-hemisphere function. Similar to adults, infants show a right-hemisphere advantage for faces and emotional expression (Reilly *et al.* 1995); however, early language is bilaterally distributed (e.g. Mills, *et al.* 1997). It is only with the successive mastery of each formal aspect of language that we see left lateralization for language functions. The question then arises: how does the brain organize ASL grammatical facial behaviours? Consonant with the proposed bifurcation in acquisition, recent evidence (Corina *et al.* 1999) suggests that the two different functions of facial expression in sign language (grammatical versus affective) can break down independently in lifelong deaf signers with brain lesions to the left versus right hemisphere.

JUDY S. REILLY

Reilly, J. and Seibert, L. (2003). Language and emotion. In: R.J. Davidson, K.R. Scherer, and H.H. Goldsmith (eds), *Handbook of affective sciences*, pp. 535–59. New York: Oxford University Press.

laughter Spontaneous laughter is a universal human vocal signal that has only recently begun to receive systematic empirical attention as an acoustic, emotion-related, and social communication event (e.g. Provine 2000) (see VOCAL EXPRESSION OF EMOTION). Restricting the focus to emotion-triggered rather than volitional laughter, emerging findings are contradicting a number of the common conceptions held about these sounds. Such results suggest that there may be much more to be learned about the mechanisms and functions of laughter than is actually known so far.

Recent findings

Spontaneous laughter is commonly believed to proto-typically consist of vowel-like sounds, for instance occurring as a series of 'ha-ha-ha' or 'hee-hee-hee' bursts (see VOICE PRODUCTION AND ACOUSTICS). The particular acoustic form of any given laugh is furthermore taken to convey coded information concerning details of the vocalizer's affect. In other words, states such as positive *enjoyment, derisive pleasure, nervousness, and *embarrassment are assumed to each be associated with distinctive laugh sounds. However, an extensive study on the acoustics of laughter (Bachorowski *et al.* 2001) has provided contrary evidence on both counts. First, the work suggests that distinct vowel-qualities like 'ah', 'ee', 'oh', and the like are relatively infrequent in spontan-

eous laughter, which instead more resembles neutral, unarticulated sounds. In addition, while the expected, 'voiced' laughs (produced with regular vocal-fold vibration) were indeed abundant in the analysed sample, laughs were just as often 'unvoiced' (lacking vocal-fold vibration), for instance resulting from turbulent air flow in the vocal tract. A last important aspect was that while all the laughs had been recorded from participants experiencing positive affect, acoustically the sounds were extremely variable (see also Kipper and Todt 2003). While evidence is not available to allow systematic comparison of laughter occurring across affectively dissimilar circumstances, the high degree of variability found within this one, affectively homogeneous, context argues against the possibility that laugh sounds are in fact nuanced, well-differentiated, and state-specific.

Contrasting theoretical interpretations

These kinds of evidence suggest that understanding the mechanisms and functions of spontaneous laughter will require careful assessment of its acoustic form under varying conditions of *arousal and *valence of the laugher. On the one hand, the occurrence of valenced emotion is incontrovertibly a critical mechanism for triggering spontaneous laughter. Further, these sounds are clearly deeply grounded in human biology, emerging very early in life even in congenitally hearing-impaired and deaf infants (Scheiner *et al.* 2004). On the other hand, it does not necessarily follow that the function of laughter is to convey information about that internal state. Instead, as for any communication signal, the function of spontaneous laughter as a form of social communication must be that the laugher can benefit from exerting some influence on the person hearing these sounds. From this broader perspective, there are probably a number of avenues by which that influence can occur, including, but certainly not limited to, conveying coded representational information about one's own affect.

An alternative is that spontaneous laughter may instead have its most important effects by inducing learned, affective responses in listeners (Owren and Bachorowski 2003). In this view, while spontaneous laughter is triggered by vocalizer affect, it evolved as an unconscious strategy for eliciting positive responses in others. This approach argues that while spontaneous *production* of laughter is grounded in human biology, affective *responses* to laughter are specifically learned—for instance through emotional conditioning. That process probably begins very early in life, for example when an infant engages in mutually positive, often face-to-face, interactions with caregivers and others. Here, the child will be consistently hearing laughter and simultaneously experiencing positive affect, while the laughter that this emotion triggers will be reinforcing the partner's behaviour. Continuing throughout life, episodes of shared positive affective responses with others are proposed to produce both modest positive responses to laughter in general, and significantly stronger learned responses to the particular sounds produced by friends and loved ones—the individuals with whom mutually positive interactions occur most frequently. The well-known 'contagion' of laughter (Provine 2000) can thereby be understood as a simple, associative learning effect (see CONTAGION).

Looking to the future

Given that rigorous scientific work on laughter has only recently begun, the future promises to bring important new empirical discoveries and insightful interpretations. To date, for example, one of the most intriguing emerging findings is that the notable positive response that listeners experience when hearing voiced laughter does not extend to unvoiced versions—even when both are produced under positive circumstances. While unexpected, this result is also robust, having been independently documented in various guises by multiple investigators. At present, this outcome remains a puzzle—and emblematic of the paradox that a human behaviour as ubiquitous and seemingly mundane as spontaneous laughter may not be so familiar after all.

MICHAEL J. OWREN AND
JO-ANNE BACHOROWSKI

Bachorowski, J.-A. and Owren, M.J. (2008). Vocal expression of emotion. In: M. Lewis, J.M. Haviland-Jones, and L. Feldman Barrett (eds), *Handbook of emotions*, pp. 196–210. New York: Guilford Press.

Makagon, M.M., Funayama, E.S., and Owren, M.J. (2008). An acoustic analysis of laughter produced by congenitally deaf and normally hearing college students. *Journal of the Acoustical Society of America*, **124**, 472–83.

law and emotion Human societies developed systems of law for reasons that are deeply intertwined with emotions. The rule of law strives to satisfy emotional needs for *fairness, *justice, and honour with a system of rules, adjudication, and punishment rather than with feuds, vigilantism, and cycles of revenge. Human emotions arise in many legal contexts, including interpersonal conflicts, *social relationships, and judgments of responsibility, culpability, and morality. Emotions are therefore foundational to law.

A person's emotional state while engaged in potentially criminal activity can profoundly influence perceptions of his or her culpability. Consider, for example, the act of killing another person. In Anglo-American law, this act, depending in part on the killer's emotional state, could lead to a conviction for first-degree murder (either because the act was 'cold-blooded' or because it was hateful), for second-degree murder (because callous

disregard for human life suggested a 'depraved heart'), or for manslaughter (because it was committed in the 'heat of passion'), as well as to a judgement of not guilty by reason of insanity (because delusional emotions gave rise to an 'irresistible impulse'), or, if the killing is ruled to be self-defence, to acquittal (because the defendant's fear was deemed justifiable).

A coherent account of such distinctions has proved elusive. In Anglo-American law there exists a long-standing tradition of attempting to define crimes objectively in terms of the actions (*actus reus*) and intentionality (*mens rea*) present at the moment of the act. When applied to emotions, this approach has led to the proposal of objective criteria, such as the amount of time passed since provocation, for determining the relevance of emotion to culpability. Such rules, however, are fraught with inconsistencies and do not match the intuitions of real-life jurors. A better explanation of jurors' perceptions of culpability must consider contextual factors extending beyond the objectivity of the law and narrow temporal focus. These factors would include the defendant's subjective point of view, the interpersonal history between the defendant and victim, the opportunities for self-control, and social standards and customs (Finkel 1995, Spackman *et al.* 2002). Real-life judgements of culpability are neither completely objective nor completely subjective; they take the defendant's subjective appraisals into account, but only when they are judged reasonable in light of prevailing social norms (Finkel and Parrott 2006).

Research on emotions can inform public policy and the law in a variety of ways. Research on emotion regulation (see REGULATION OF EMOTION) is quite relevant to legal judgements of emotional self-control. Research on the accuracy of folk theories of emotion is helpful for evaluating assumptions about emotion that have crept into the legal code. Research on narratives and mental representations of emotions can inform accounts of juror decision-making (Finkel and Parrott 2006).

Research on specific emotional states can illuminate a variety of legal issues. Actions that cause others to become angry, feel disgust, be humiliated, or feel grief are often those that are considered wrong and that may be criminalized. Emotions such as concern, sympathy, remorse, disgust, and compassion can influence judgements of culpability by affecting how people perceive those who are accused of crimes or are the victims of crimes. Emotions such as fear, envy, anger, and jealousy not only motivate actions but can also help to justify, mitigate, or condemn these very actions (Oakley 1992, Finkel and Parrott 2006).

General theories of emotion have implications for the law as well. Theories that characterize emotions as primitive, mechanical, or noncognitive imply a different conception of the relation of emotions to culpability than do theories that characterize emotions as evaluative, cognitive, or a matter of choice (see EMOTION THEORIES AND CONCEPTS (PHILOSOPHICAL PERSPECTIVES); EMOTION THEORIES AND CONCEPTS (PSYCHOLOGICAL PERSPECTIVES)). Some approaches to personal accountability, such as voluntarism and consequentialism, tend to assume a mechanical theory of emotions, whereas other approaches, such as those based on relative valuations, tend to rely on a more cognitive theory of emotions (Kahan and Nussbaum 1996). Social constructionist theories of emotion can aid understanding of how emotions can be treated quite differently in the legal systems of different cultures (Averill 1982), as well as how the legal treatment of emotions can influence the degree to which people are able to control their behaviour when under the influence of emotional states (Finkel and Parrott 2006).

These connections between emotions and legal judgements are not without controversy (see Bandes 1999). Disgust can be considered either an essential part of our moral intuition and a valuable guide to blameworthiness or a problematic source of prejudice and bias. The emotions of victims may or may not be relevant to how a criminal should be punished, depending in part on how one construes the relation between justice and vengeance, retribution, and retaliation. The relation between vengefulness and such emotions as disgust and hatred, or between culpability and remorse, are subtle and open to debate. In all, the relation between emotion and law should continue to stimulate theory, research, and public policy.

W. GERROD PARROTT

Bandes, S.A. (ed.) (1999). *The passions of law.* New York: New York University Press.

Finkel, N.J. and Parrott, W.G. (2006). *Emotions and culpability: how the law is at odds with psychology, jurors, and itself.* Washington, DC: American Psychological Association.

learning, emotional (neuroscience perspectives)

Investigations of the neuroscience of emotional learning have often focused on fear due to the relative ease of eliciting fear in the laboratory and the similarity of fear expression across species (see FEAR). As a result, fear provides the most thoroughly examined neurobiological mechanism of emotional learning. Laboratory studies of fear learning typically use a procedure called classical conditioning, which has been established as a central model for affective learning across species (Phelps and LeDoux 2005). In this procedure, an animal is exposed to a meaningless stimulus, such as a tone (conditioned stimulus, CS), together with a harmful stimulus, such as a mild electric shock (unconditioned stimulus, US). After very few pairings, or even a single pairing, of these

stimuli the presentation of the tone itself is now capable of eliciting a characteristic pattern of behavioural and physiological stress responses, such as freezing, increased sweating, changes in heart rate and respiration, and stress hormone release. In other words, the animal has come to fear the stimulus that was, just moments ago, meaningless.

Studies of the neural substrates underlying fear learning have highlighted a brain region called the *amygdala. The initial observation, back in the late 1930s, was that damage to the temporal lobe, where the amygdala is situated, resulted in profound emotional changes in monkeys. This phenomenon, termed the Kluver–Bucy syndrome (Kluver and Bucy 1937), set the stage for a substantial amount of research revealing the neural circuitry of fear in detail. The amygdala is not a unified structure but rather an assemblage of subnuclei (Amaral *et al.* 1992). A subset of these nuclei was identified with specific roles in fear conditioning. The principal region is the lateral nucleus, where sensory inputs conveying information about the CS and the US converge. This convergence leads to synaptic plasticity, such that when the CS later occurs alone it can sufficiently trigger these potentiated synapses. Information from the lateral nucleus flows into two key output regions, the central and basal nuclei, controlling fear reactions and fear-motivated actions (LeDoux and Gorman 2001). More specifically, the central nucleus controls emotional reactions and associated physiological responses via connections with the hypothalamus and the brainstem. These target regions generate passive fear responses such as sweating in humans or freezing in rats. The basal nucleus influences instrumental behaviours, such as active avoidance, through connections with motor circuits (LeDoux 2000).

Although the amygdala is a critical region for the acquisition and expression of conditioned fear responses (Phelps and LeDoux 2005), it is in essence a component of a greater circuitry underlying fear learning (see NEURAL ARCHITECTURE OF EMOTION). This circuitry includes sensory input and motor output systems, but also regions that participate in the control and regulation of fear. For example, the hippocampus, a region adjacent to the amygdala in the temporal lobe, encodes contextual information relevant to the fear learning setting. Consequently, this region exerts contextual control over the expression of fear, and is required for the recall of fear memories evoked by a particular context (see MEMORY (EMOTIONAL)) (Anagnostaras *et al.* 2001, LaBar and Phelps 2005, Kalisch *et al.* 2006). Another important modulatory region is the prefrontal cortex. The ventral-medial portion of this region is critical for the top-down regulation of fear responses by way of inhibitory connections with the amygdala (Quirk *et al.* 2000, Phelps *et al.* 2004).

The orchestrated activation of this circuitry results in adaptive fear learning, which is rapid and persistent on the one hand but also flexible and appropriately controlled on the other. However, this well-organized learning mechanism is not always efficient, as learning by direct aversive experience might come with a high price, namely being hurt. An alternative means to learn about stimuli in the environment that might predict danger or an aversive outcome is through social communication. By either watching or talking to others we can learn about situations and stimuli that might predict danger without directly experiencing aversive consequences ourselves. The social environment provides a safer and more economical means to learn how to predict potential danger.

Social means of emotional learning include observation and verbal instruction. Although learning through observing conspecifics has been reported in a number of species, observational fear learning has primarily been investigated in primates. Laboratory raised nonhuman primates demonstrate a robust fear response to an unfamiliar neutral stimulus, such as a plastic snake, after observing a conspecific react fearfully to the same stimulus (Öhman and Mineka 2001). Similarly, humans will exhibit fear to a neutral stimulus after watching the same stimulus predict the administration of a mild electric shock to another person (Olsson and Phelps 2007). In contrast, learning through verbal instruction, which requires language and symbolic representation, is unique to humans. Simply being told that a neural stimulus, such as a coloured square, predicts the possibility of a mild electric shock will elicit a robust fear response (Phelps *et al.* 2001). These basic laboratory paradigms demonstrate what we have all experienced outside the laboratory, that is we will fear and avoid situations that we know from others are potentially dangerous.

Laboratory studies of social fear learning demonstrate that in most circumstances these fears are indistinguishable from those acquired through direct aversive experience. One exception is with subliminal presentation. Studies of classical fear conditioning have shown that for certain classes of stimuli, which are proposed to be prepared through evolution to elicit more robust fear learning, a conditioned fear response will be observed even when the CS is presented subliminally (Öhman and Mineka 2001). In a study comparing the expression of fear learning through classical conditioning, observation, and verbal instruction it was found that learning through social observation also results in expression with subliminal presentation, but learning through verbal instruction does not (Olsson and Phelps 2004). This suggests some similarity in the mechanisms underlying fears acquired through classical conditioning and social

observation, in contrast to the abstract representation of instructed fear. Studies of the neural systems of socially acquired fears have found that they overlap with classical fear conditioning in that all types of fear learning seem to depend on the amygdala for expression (Funayama *et al.* 2001), although learning through social observation and instruction also require other, unique neural circuits (Olsson and Phelps 2007). It is not possible to investigate the neurobiological mechanisms of social fear learning in humans with the same level of detail as conditioned fear in other species. However, we can take advantage of the similarity of fear learning through social and nonsocial means to help understand the neuroscience of social means of emotional learning.

Both brain imaging and lesion studies in humans have shown that the left, but not the right, amygdala is important in the expression of instructed fear. The left lateralization of amygdaloidal involvement is unique to instructed fear and is probably due to the fact that language is localized to the left hemisphere in most individuals. In classically conditioned fear, the representations of the CS and US converge in the lateral nucleus of the amygdala where neural plasticity establishes a link between these stimuli. It is not possible to investigate the subnuclei of the amygdala in humans with standard brain imaging techniques, but it is unlikely that the linguistic, symbolic representation of potential threat conveyed in instructed fear is localized within the amygdala. It is more likely that this abstract representation does not require the amygdala for acquisition and is stored elsewhere in the left hemisphere, but projects to the central nucleus of the left amygdala, which then mediates the physiological expression of instructed fear. The lack of expression of instructed fear with subliminal presentation may be a reflection of the different mechanisms underlying the acquisition and symbolic representation of threat, in contrast to conditioned fear.

Observational fear appears to be more similar to classically conditioned fear in both its underlying neural circuitry and its expression. Unlike learning through language, observing another experience an aversive event often elicits an emotional response in the perceiver (Olsson and Phelps 2007). This empathic emotional response may be similar to a US that is directly experienced in both its expression and underlying neural circuitry (Singer *et al.* 2004). In this way, the neural systems of observational fear may mirror conditioned fear. Consistent with this, a study examining observational fear learning reported robust involvement of the amygdala, both when participants observed another person during a fear conditioning procedure and when they expected the same stimulus might predict the delivery of a mild shock themselves (Olsson and Phelps 2007). These findings suggest that the amygdala may play a central role in the acquisition and expression of observational fear, similar to fear conditioning. In addition, observational fear may also take advantage of neural circuits thought to be involved in mentalizing about the state of another person. We may learn more effectively from those similar to us, who are shown to engage the neural circuits of mentalizing more strongly (Mitchell *et al.* 2005).

Learning the stimuli in the environment that predict potential danger is one of most critical functions for survival. All species can do this, but humans have adapted the fear learning circuitry, and the systems mediating its control, for the unique and flexible ways in which we communicate. Although emotional learning entails more than learning about fear, this model system provides a starting point for understanding the complex means by which emotional responses can be acquired.

DANIELA SCHILLER AND ELIZABETH A. PHELPS

LeDoux, J.E. (2000). Emotion circuits in the brain. *Annual Review of Neuroscience*, 23, 155–84.

Öhman, A. and Mineka, S. (2001). Fears, phobias, and preparedness: toward an evolved module of fear and fear learning. *Psychological Review*, 108, 483–522.

Olsson, A. and Phelps, E.A. (2007). Social learning of fear. *Nature Neuroscience*, 10, 1095–102.

legitimacy In modern emotions research, legitimacy refers to an appraisal (see APPRAISAL THEORIES) of whether something is morally right (legitimate) or morally wrong (illegitimate).

Different theorists have conceptualized legitimacy in different ways, for example whether an event is deserved versus undeserved, just versus unjust (see JUSTICE (PROCEDURAL)), fair versus unfair (see FAIRNESS), or compatible versus incompatible with norms (see NORMS).

Appraisals of legitimacy are prominent in most or many instances of some emotions (e.g. *anger, *guilt, and 'elevation'); some instances of other emotions (e.g. *pride, *shame, *disgust, *contempt, *schadenfreude); and relatively few instances of still other emotions (e.g. *joy, *sadness, *surprise, *fear). With the exception of elevation and pride, these emotions are associated with perceived *illegitimacy*.

Some theorists have proposed that legitimacy with regard to different norms is associated with different emotions. For example: Aristotle (384–322 BC), in his *Rhetoric* (1941), claimed that anger is caused by offences to honour; Scherer (2001a) proposed that shame results from incompatibility with external standards, whereas guilt results from incompatibility with either internal or external standards; and Rozin *et al.* (1999) proposed and found evidence that anger is elicited by violations of autonomy norms, contempt by violation of community/hierarchy norms, and disgust by violation of purity/divinity norms. However, there is no consensus yet on these proposals, and it is possible that they represent typical rather than necessary relationships.

As with other appraisals, there has been debate about whether appraisals of legitimacy are causes, components, or consequences of emotions (perhaps they are all three); and, if causes, whether they are distal or proximal causes. For example, Roseman *et al.* (1996) suggested that appraisals of legitimacy influence appraisals of control potential (see CONTROLLABILITY), which in turn affect emotions.

Controversies aside, available evidence indicates that some emotions at least sometimes influence and/or are importantly influenced by moral judgements (see Haidt 2003).

IRA J. ROSEMAN

levels of processing (and emotion) *Appraisal theories contend that cognitive processes give rise to emotion. This cognitive-mediational framework is consistent with the basic premise of cognitive psychology, namely that information processing is required to represent stimulus meaning. Yet there continue to be critics of this cognitive perspective on emotion. According to Murphy and Zajonc (1993), for example, affective processing is faster, cruder, and less cortical than cognitive processing, exerting its effects prior to cognitive processing of stimuli (see UNCONSCIOUS EMOTIONS). There has been much controversy in this area, but it is clear that Murphy and Zajonc follow an intellectual tradition in which cognition is largely equated with conscious, effortful, controlled processing.

This view of cognition is limited, and fails to capture many of the processing achievements of the mind recognized by cognitive psychologists. For example, processing within later stages of the visual cortex can be characterized as cognitive because it is at this neural level that object categorization and identification occur. Importantly, such achievements occur prior to affective evaluation, and this neural perspective therefore suggests that meaning-related processing precedes affect retrieval (Storbeck *et al.* 2006).

Nevertheless, such criticisms of appraisal theory have been important in clarifying the nature of emotion-antecedent cognitive processing, and one relevant line of thought relates to levels-of-processing frameworks (for a review see Teasdale, 1999). The contention of such frameworks is that cognition is too monolithic an entity to describe the nuances of emotion-antecedent processing. For this reason, it is necessary to distinguish multiple forms of cognition, variously described as pre-attentive versus attentive, unconscious versus conscious, automatic versus controlled, reflexive versus reflective, associative versus rule-based, schematic versus propositional, and so on. The important point is that much of emotional appraisal is likely to rely on simplified forms of information processing rather than the sort of conscious, effortful processes highlighted by Murphy and Zajonc (1993) (see AUTOMATIC APPRAISAL).

Although theory on levels of processing abounds in the literature, data are preliminary and of paramount importance (van Reekum and Scherer 1997). In this connection, two recommendations are offered for further developments. First, it is important to focus on levels of processing that can be operationalized. Included in this category are distinctions between unconscious and conscious processes and between pre-attentive and postattentive processes. By contrast, other distinctions, such as that between propositional and implicational meaning (Teasdale 1999), seem to us to lend themselves to no clear operational definitions. Secondly, it is important to build on findings in the literature. For example, Neumann (2000) reported that procedural priming of attribution tendencies influenced subsequent reactions to emotional provocation. Yet, to our knowledge, this promising line of investigation has yet to be followed up to a sufficient extent. Many other findings in the literature suffer from the same fate of isolation. It is therefore paramount that promising lines of inquiry receive further empirical study so that we can build upon them in a more complete manner. In part, this means that advocates of the appraisal perspective should collect more data of a cognitive nature so that process-related views of appraisal are systematically developed.

By way of illustration, we highlight developments related to facial and posture-related effects on emotional experience. Early reports in the literature suggested that such effects were somewhat invariant and potentially noncognitive. However, recent research suggests that this is a mistaken view, in that such expression-related effects appear to be exquisitely sensitive to manipulations of context, and therefore consistent with a cognitive view of such effects (Tamir *et al.* 2004). Although we do not claim that Tamir *et al.*'s study is definitive, what we do claim is that this sort of sustained empirical effort seems necessary to better understand the benefits and limitations of 'low routes' to emotion.

MICHAEL D. ROBINSON

Tamir, M., Robinson, M.D., Clore, G.L., Martin, L.L., and Whitaker, D.J. (2004). Are we puppets on a string?: The contextual meaning of unconscious expressive cues. *Personality and Social Psychology Bulletin*, **30**, 237–49.

van Reekum, C.M. and Scherer, K.R. (1997). Levels of processing for emotion-antecedent appraisal. In: G. Matthews (ed.), *Cognitive science perspectives on personality and emotion*, pp. 259–300. Amsterdam: Elsevier Science.

life satisfaction Life satisfaction is a component of *well-being; it is assessed with questions like, 'Taking all things together, how satisfied are you with your life as a whole these days?' accompanied by a rating scale. Respondents' answers do not reflect stable inner states of well-being but temporary evaluations relative to some standard, based on information that is chronically or temporarily accessible at that point in time.

In affluent countries, 85 to 90% of the respondents in representative samples report that they are either satisfied or very satisfied. The relationship between reported satisfaction and the objective conditions of life is weaker than lay intuitions would suggest.

How do people evaluate their lives?

Like other evaluative judgements (see EVALUATIVE PROCESSING), evaluations of one's life require a mental representation of the object of judgement (one's life) and a standard against which it is evaluated (Schwarz and Strack 1999). Which aspects of their lives people consider is highly context sensitive; some information is likely to come to mind in most circumstances (e.g. information bearing on current concerns, like serious illness), whereas other information may only come to mind because it was addressed earlier in the questionnaire. For example, dating frequency figures prominently in students' life satisfaction when it is brought to mind by a preceding question ($r = 0.66$), but not otherwise ($r = -0.12$). The selection of standards is similarly variable and depends on current concerns as well as contextual influences. Potentially relevant standards include *goals and expectations, previous living conditions or events, and the situation of relevant others. People are more satisfied when their living conditions meet or exceed expectations and when they make progress towards their goals than when they fail to do so. Because high goals and expectations are motivating as well as difficult to meet, they can simultaneously facilitate factual achievement and subjective dissatisfaction. For example, people with high financial goals at college entry earn higher salaries two decades later, but are less satisfied with them. Similarly, people are more satisfied with their lives when they compare their own situation with that of others who are less well off than with others who are better off. However, the latter comparison may provide more useful information for attempts to improve one's circumstances. Hence, the selection of goals and standards can exert opposite influences on factual achievement and on subjective satisfaction.

Complicating things further, the same information can serve as a relevant feature of one's life and as a standard, resulting in opposite influences. For example, a recent negative life event will decrease life satisfaction when it is thought of as a feature of one's current life, but will increase life satisfaction when it serves as a standard against which one's current conditions are evaluated. Variables like the temporal distance of the event, the salience of life transitions, and the vividness of the memory influence how information about one's past is used.

Finally, people may bypass feature-based evaluation processes by drawing on their current affect as an indicator of their overall well-being (see AFFECT-AS-INFORMATION MODEL). This results in reports of higher satisfaction with one's life as a whole (as well as any other object) under happy rather than sad *moods, unless people are aware that their current feelings are due to an irrelevant influence (like rainy weather or finding a dime).

Given these dynamics, it is not surprising that the relationship between objective conditions and reported life satisfaction is usually weak in cross-sectional surveys.

Correlates of life satisfaction

As one would expect from a judgement perspective, cross-national comparisons show that average life satisfaction is low in societies in which daily needs of food and shelter are not met or in which the material standard of living has undergone a pronounced recent downward change; under both conditions, material concerns are likely to be on people's minds, resulting in the observed relationship. In contrast, gradual improvements in the material standard of living over time are less likely to capture attention and are not accompanied by increased life satisfaction in affluent societies. For example, the material standard of living in the United States and Japan improved profoundly since the 1950s, whereas life satisfaction remained flat (Easterlin 1974). Moreover, gradual improvements give rise to upward shifts in expectations and aspirations, which undermine favourable intrapersonal comparisons; similarly, the simultaneous improvement in the conditions of others implies that one's relative position does not change, which undermines favourable interpersonal comparisons.

Within a society, the rich, well-educated, healthy, and married individuals report somewhat higher satisfaction than their less fortunate counterparts (for an overview see Argyle, 1999). However, the observed long-term impact of favourable as well as unfavourable circumstances and events is far more limited than lay intuition would suggest.

DANIEL KAHNEMAN AND NORBERT SCHWARZ

Kahneman, D. (1999). Objective happiness. In: D. Kahneman, E. Diener, and N. Schwarz (eds), *Well-being: the foundations of hedonic psychology*, pp. 3–25. New York: Russell Sage Foundation.

linguistics and emotion Although rarely posited as such in the main theories of emotion, language plays a crucial role in the conceptualization and expression of emotion (cf. Barrett 2006b, Fiedler 2008). Language is *de facto* an integral part of the affective sciences' endeavour For instance, much psychological research relies on free *self-report and the use of verbal labels for emotion. Some models explicitly state the importance of language in assessing emotional awareness (Lane and Schwartz 1987) or representing emotion (Norman 2004). Influential dimensional approaches (see DIMENSIONAL MODELS) derive their dimensions from the connotative structure of lexical items (Osgood *et al.* 1957). In addition, affective neuroscience investigates how emotional language primes cognitive processes (Kissler *et al.* 2006), and substantial evidence is available of the influence of language on the facial perception of emotion (Barrett *et al.* 2007a).

Given that linguistics as a discipline concerns itself with the study of language, its relevance for the affective sciences is apparent. In the following, some of its contributions will be discussed. First, we review some linguistic approaches to emotion, and then we discuss the extent to which linguistic findings have bearings for emotion theorizing itself.

The study of emotion in linguistics

Since affect pervades language (see LANGUAGE AND EMOTION), the linguistics of emotion comprises all levels of linguistic analysis (phonetic, morphological, syntactic, semantic, etc.) and a variety of methodological approaches (cognitive, anthropological, diachronic, comparative, etc.). This vast body of linguistic literature on emotion can be seen as instantiating two main research orientations: one concerned with *conceptual/semantic* representation and another with *performance*. Sweeping as it is, this differentiation accounts for both the research on *emotion concepts* (e.g. Johnson-Laird and Oatley 1989, Wierzbicka 1999) and the study of *emotion talk* as a socioculturally-, age-, gender-, and personality-specific practice (e.g. Bamberg 1997, Weigand 2004). A comprehensive account of all these contributions exceeds the scope of this entry, but a few examples from different disciplines can briefly illustrate the field.

A straightforward case is (evaluative) *morphology*, where diminutive suffixes (like English -y in *doggy*) have been shown to communicate affection, while pejorative suffixes (like Spanish -*ucha* in *casucha*, from *casa* 'house') convey contempt. Within *syntax*, the alteration of the canonical word order of a language motivates topicalization effects that can be related to affect (e.g. *and he went out* versus *and out he went*). Similarly, different grammatical configurations reflect greater or lesser degrees of agency, responsibility, or control in the construal of the emotion-eliciting event, and they can manipulate an audience's affective response (e.g. a passive construction like *Baghdad was bombarded last night*, conceals the agency that would have been present in the active voice). In *phonetics*, sound symbolism has been found to interplay with affect. For example, back vowels, like the (*u*) sound in *ugh*, are often found in words expressing disgust or dislike in English (e.g. *blunder*, *dull*, *muck*) (Jespersen 1922). Within *discourse*, research has been conducted on specific emotion communication patterns, like children's narrative accounts of emotional situations (Bamberg 2001), or cultural varieties of mother–child emotion talk. Discourse analysis also studies the power of framing to invite inferences leading to specific cognitive-emotional responses. Within *semantics*, connotation is crucial in the study of linguistic affective expression (e.g. Pavlenko 2005) and affective response (as when we use euphemisms to manipulate aversion-acceptance in our interlocutors).

Another important area in semantics for the study of affect is figurative language (see METAPHORS). Beyond specific linguistic expressions, the study of 'conceptual' metaphors and metonymies (Lakoff 1993, Panther and Radden 1999) has gained popularity. These are basic cognitive phenomena underlying novel *and* conventionalized linguistic expressions, as well as gesture, ritual, art, and abstract reasoning at large. Many emotion concepts have been analysed cross-culturally using this approach (cf. Kövecses 2000). The concept of 'emotion' is metaphorically construed itself: an emotion is frequently represented as a person, an object, a force, or a location. These seem to be fairly universal conceptualizations, while different cultures specify in different manners what sorts of tokens instantiate those types, and what sorts of metaphors/ metonymies are more salient. The use of metaphor seems to be universal, as is our resorting to physiological experience (either literal or metaphorically elaborated) to refer to emotional episodes (Wierzbicka 1999), which many scholars see as an instance of the conceptual metonymy THE EFFECTS FOR THE CAUSE.

The most relevant area of semantics for emotion research is probably the study of emotion terms. The emotion vocabularies (see VOCABULARY OF EMOTION) of the natural languages vary significantly in the way they categorize the emotional continuum. Quantitatively, the reported body of emotion terms of a language varies considerably both intra- and cross-culturally. For instance, the number of reported emotion terms in English fluctuates between 525 and 2000, depending on the criteria used to define 'emotion term'. Somewhere in between is Taiwanese Chinese, reported to have 750 emotion lexemes, while some languages have extremely scarce emotion lexicons, like the two Ghanaian languages Fante and Dagbani, with 14 and 9 emotion terms, respectively (e.g. Dzokoto and Okazaki 2004). Qualitatively, a distinct line of research in lexical seman-

tics has focused on culture-specific emotion terms that cannot be easily translated into other languages (see CULTURAL SPECIFICITY). This is the case of Russian *sočuvstvie* and *sostradanie*, Portuguese *saudade*, or German *Angst* and *Schadenfreude* (e.g. Wierzbicka 1999). Like the universalists from psychology, linguists in the quest for universal emotion terms have failed to arrive at a consensual list of basic emotions with respect to both their number and their phenomenological characteristics. Recent overviews of universals in semantics maintain that no *lexical* item in natural languages is universal in an absolute sense (von Fintel and Matthewson 2008), the very term 'emotion' being a cultural artefact of the English language.

Despite abundant lexical variation, not everything is culture-specific in the semantics of emotion. In response to the problem that English is used as *tertium comparationis* in most contrastive studies, an inventory of semantic universals has been proposed as metalanguage in the cross-linguistic description of emotion terms (e.g. Wierzbicka 1999). Additionally, nine putative linguistic emotional universals have been proposed, which include the mere existence of emotion terms, the possibility of evaluating emotions as *good* or *bad*, and the existence of emotive interjections and verbs similar to *feel*, *smile* or *cry* (Wierzbicka 1999, pp. 275–86). In spite of the cultural specificity of any emotion term, 'anger-like', 'fear-like', and 'shame-like' words are also stated to be universal (Wierzbicka 1999, pp. 286–94). This means that at least three superordinate semantic categories, as instantiated by the English terms *anger*, *fear*, and *shame*, are thought to be common to all languages, even if the specific configuration of each domain varies from language to language, or if other superordinate categories emerge to account for the emotional space.

Finally, recent dimensional studies on the semantics of emotion *terms* (Fontaine *et al.* 2007) have shown a considerable degree of overlap with dimensional studies of emotional *experience*, suggesting the existence of certain pancultural dimensions, such as pleasantness, potency, or arousal (also found in event-related potential studies; Chapman *et al.* 1978), capable of accounting for variation in the emotional domain.

Emotion: the verbal and the conceptual

A pertinent question at this point is whether linguistic descriptions like the above provide any insights into emotional cognition. Do semantic differences reflect conceptual differences? More generally, are semantic content and concepts the same?

The two most widespread traditions in linguistics nowadays would answer this question differently. Within the generativist school, linguistic representation and conceptual representation are independent and need not coincide. In this view, language is disembodied and modular, categories are discrete, subject to minimal and sufficient conditions, syntax is central, and its rules universal and innate.

Cognitive linguistics, on the contrary, advocates an embodied view of language, with scalar (i.e. continuous) categories and no hard-bound distinction between syntax and semantics. Linguistic meaning is seen as a form of conceptual representation largely governed by the same principles as nonlinguistic cognition (prototypicality effects, *gestalt or holistic perception, profile-base construal, basic-level categorization, etc.). Within this tradition, the way we talk about emotions reveals something about the way we mentally represent them. Semantic content is thought to be encyclopaedic (i.e. to encompass everything we know about the domain), and both embodied and socially construed. In this paradigm the distinction between semantic and conceptual representation fades.

If semantic representation is not independent of conceptual representation, the issue of whether linguistic categorization (1) merely reflects, (2) completely determines, or (3) partially influences conceptual representation still needs to solved.

For (1) to be true, we would have to assume that the use of language is purely referential and language practices cannot change conceptual representation. However, considerable evidence is available nowadays suggesting the contrary (cf. Fiedler 2008). In the case of emotions, recent works acknowledge that emotion language plays a role in creating or transforming emotional experience, as opposed to merely representing it (Barrett 2006b, Barrett et al. 2007a). Besides, there is research in psychotherapy emphasizing the role of linguistic manipulation in construing new conceptual representations for people with disorders like depression (Caro 2001).

A position like (2) exemplifies a strong linguistic relativity stance: the idea that we can only think, and even perceive, according to the linguistic categories provided by our language, because they tap on the basic phenomenon of categorization ('We dissect nature along lines laid down by our native language'; Whorf 1956, p. 213). This is frequently assumed to mean that we cannot think of entities for which we lack a 'name' (e.g. the concept behind the Portuguese emotion term *saudade*). However, all human beings are capable of *feeling* any emotional configuration, and they are also capable of *expressing them verbally*, either with a readily available lexical term or through other means (paraphrase, creative metaphor, analogy, etc.) (cf. von Fintel and Matthewson 2008).

A more moderate position is exemplified in (3): the potential for conceptual representation of emotion is likely to go beyond what salient categories language

provides us with; but linguistic differences bias towards preferred, default ways of categorizing and processing emotional reality in a linguistic community.

Within this view there is space for both culture-specific and pancultural traits in emotion semantics. It is also highly compatible with a cognitive view of meaning. If emotion concepts are not organized according to sufficient and necessary conditions, but around a prototype, and they encompass world knowledge about the category, great variability is to be expected cross-culturally in the specific meaning structure of any given term. At the same time, the model predicts that the prototype of semantically close terms across cultures will share some features that are not sufficient to define each emotion (and maybe none of them is individually necessary to do so), but which render the basis for a superordinate category that makes it possible for us to ascribe emotional experiences to the same semantic 'foci'. Those semantic/conceptual foci can be said to be embodied if their features arise out of frequently activated emotion appraisal patterns relevant for humans as a species.

CRISTINA SORIANO AND ANNA OGARKOVA

Kövecses, Z. (2005). *Metaphor in culture: universality and variation.* New York and Cambridge: Cambridge University Press.

Pavlenko, A. (2005). *Emotions and multilingualism.* Cambridge: Cambridge University Press.

Wierzbicka, A. (1999). *Emotions across language and cultures: diversity and universals.* Cambridge: Cambridge University Press.

literature and emotion Since stories were first written some 5000 years ago, emotions have been salient in them. For instance, the first phrase of the *Iliad*—which can be taken as the beginning of Greek literature—is 'Of rage sing, goddess'. The poet invokes the muse to sing of the anger of Achilles against the commander of the Greek army at Troy. Similarly, in the opening of the Bible: Eve and Adam eat of the tree of the knowledge of good and evil, and with the dawning of their consciousness they become self-consciously ashamed. Nor are emotions just the subject matter of stories. As readers, we would no more wish to read a short story, novel, play, or poem that did not move us emotionally (see BEING MOVED) than we would wish to read an empirical article that did not offer a validly drawn conclusion.

Worldwide, Hogan (2003) has shown that certain stories are universals, each based on a certain kind of emotion. Most common is the love story: two lovers long to be united, but their union is impeded. Such stories may have happy or unhappy endings. The second most common story worldwide is of anger. One prototype is of two brothers, one of whom is a rightful ruler. His place is usurped by the other brother. Now occurs a battle of good (the displaced brother) against evil (the usurper), often with immoderately angry vengeance. The third most common universal story is of sacrifice; one may call this the sad story. Society enters a torturing or difficult passage, and a protagonist—representing society as a whole—sacrifices herself or himself for the benefit of the community.

In the West, emotions came explicitly to be regarded as central to literature during the Romantic era. The preface to the second edition of *Lyrical Ballads* is often seen as a manifesto: Wordsworth (1802/1984, p. 611) wrote: 'Poetry is the spontaneous overflow of powerful feelings: it takes its origin from emotion recollected in tranquillity: the emotion is contemplated till by a species of reaction the tranquillity disappears, and an emotion, kindred to that which was before the subject of contemplation, is gradually produced and does itself actually exist in the mind'.

In the current era of psychological experimentation, the emotions of readers of short stories and poetry have been measured in various ways (see, e.g., Miall and Kuiken 2002). Even under the empirical eye, such emotions are seen to be present, sometimes very forcefully so while reading literary works. A review and theory of the psychology of emotions in literature can be found in Oatley (2004b), and a recent collection of articles on emotions in the literature of the early modern period is in the book by Paster *et al.* (2004).

KEITH OATLEY

longing The state of longing is one that people in studies of everyday conceptions of emotion often mention as being an 'emotion'. It is often, but not always, viewed as part of a cluster of love-related emotions (see LOVE), because longing for love itself, or a particular lost love, or a lover from whom one is separated (e.g. by war or distance) is a familiar theme in songs, poems, and narratives about romantic pining, wishing, hoping, wistfully daydreaming, and so on.

It is interesting that love and longing are seen as closely related in modern studies of emotion language in English, Spanish, Basque, Indonesian, and Chinese, because the ancient Greeks viewed Pothos, or longing, as one of three brother gods, sons of the west wind (Zephyros or Zephyr)—the other two being Eros (love) and Himeros (desire). Himeros represented *desire toward something within reach, whereas Pothos referred to yearning for an unattainable goal. This unattainability was eventually generalized by the neo-Platonist Plotinus (AD 205–70) to describe the passion for beauty, the thirst for knowledge or truth, and the longing for a higher, better reality, including God.

Viewed scientifically as a possible emotion, longing is quite complex. Like certain other complex emotions,

such as nostalgia and poignancy, it includes both hedonically positive and hedonically negative feelings, whereas most scientifically bona fide emotions are easy to classify as one or the other. This mixed quality makes longing a popular subject of sad but beautiful poems, popular songs, and pieces of classical music. Longing is also complex by virtue of combining aspects of 'emotion' and 'motivation', two separate categories in modern psychology. In general, emotions are scientifically conceptualized as reactions to appraisals of events in relation to motives, needs, or *goals. But longing has no simple 'cognitive' appraisal (unless an absence or a lack or a sense of incompleteness is viewed as 'cognitive'), and longing itself seems to be the expression of a need or of reaching toward a distant goal. It seems to arise when a goal is mentally portrayed as utterly wonderful, highly desirable, extremely significant, almost literally 'out of this world', yet temporarily or permanently unattainable.

There is almost no research on longing, although there are relevant studies of physical hunger, drug-related craving, and various other psychological motives (e.g. for achievement, power, or affiliation). If there is a brain state that uniquely corresponds to romantic longing, no one has yet identified it.

PHILLIP R. SHAVER

loss Loss is a central concept in the social and behavioural sciences (Harvey and Miller 1998). Loss can be defined as a reduction in a person's resources that involves a degree of emotional involvement. For example, people may not feel loss when they lose a few strands of hair; however, if they lose large chunks of hair (as can happen in chemotherapy) such an event may be perceived as emotionally debilitating, and as a major loss. The continuum of loss phenomena is vast, including chronic illness, death and dying, dissolution of relationships, injuries of various types, and a variety of types of assaults on the *self. Loss is a core idea in the aetiology of many forms of mental illness and underlies people's stressful reactions to traumatic events. One of the most important concepts in this field pertains to how people cope (see COPING), and a key approach to coping is that of account-making (story-telling to a trusted confidant about one's loss and its implications; see EMOTIONAL SHARING) or emotional expression (Harvey 2002).

J. H. HARVEY

love In all cultures, people seem to distinguish between passionate love and companionate love. Passionate love (sometimes called 'obsessive love', 'infatuation', 'love-sickness', or 'being in love') is a powerful emotional state. It is defined as 'a state of intense longing for union with the other...' and may be associated with a confusion of feelings: elation and pain, tenderness and sexuality (see SEXUALITY AND EMOTION), anxiety and relief, altruism and jealousy. Companionate love is a far less intense emotion. It has been defined as 'the affection and tenderness we feel for those with whom our lives are deeply entwined', and is characterized by affection, commitment, intimacy, and a concern for the welfare of others (Hatfield, Rapson, and Martel 1993).

Researchers have proffered other, more fine grained, definitions and typologies of love (Fisher 2004, Frijda 2007, Sternberg 1998) but for the purposes of this entry we will concentrate on love (in general) and on passionate and companionate love.

In recent years, social psychologists have attempted to understand the cultural, cognitive, emotional, neurohormonal, and evolutionary processes that give love its distinct emotional flavour (Aron and Aron 1986, Buss 1994, Fisher 2004, Hatfield and Rapson 2005, Frijda 2007).

Anthropological and evolutionary perspectives

Anthropologists and historians generally agree that passionate and companionate love are 'cultural universals'—existing in all cultures and during all historical eras. Cultural psychologists point out, however, that culture is an important determinant as to whether the culture idealizes love or depicts it as sinful, how passionately young people love, whether they confess feelings of love to family and friends, whether love is assumed to be a precursor to marriage (or if marriages are arranged), and how long love lasts (Jankowiak 1995, Hatfield et al. 2007).

Since Darwin (1809–82), of course, evolutionary psychologists have argued that love and sexual selection are of critical importance in shaping the evolution of humans and animals. Today, evolutionary psychologists argue that passionate and companionate love evolved to solve different problems in pair-bonding. Passionate love—which is associated with romantic *attraction*—is designed to assist lovers in identifying (and selecting) suitable candidates for mating and in motivating them to attempt to attract the other's interest, and to attempt to solidify the relationship. Companionate love—which is associated with attachment, intimacy, trust, and caring—is designed to assist couples in maintaining close relationships over time (Buss 1994, Fisher 2004)—at least for long enough that children can be nurtured until they are old enough to survive on their own.

Genetic and biological perspectives

Recently, social psychologists, neuroscientists, and physiologists have begun to explore the links between love, sexual desire, and sexual behaviour. Bartels and Zeki (2000, 2004), for example, studied the neural bases of passionate love using functional magnetic resonance imaging techniques. They interviewed young men and women from eleven countries who claimed to be 'truly, deeply, and madly' in love. They discovered that passionate love leads to an increase of activity in the areas of the brain associated with euphoria and reward and decreased levels of activity in the areas associated with distress and depression.

Scientists interested in the chemistry of passionate love have found that a variety of neurochemicals spark passionate love and sexual desire. Fisher (2004), for example, found that passionate love is associated with the natural stimulant dopamine (and perhaps norepinephrine and serotonin). *Lust is associated primarily with the hormone testosterone (oestrogen may decrease desire). *Attachment is produced primarily by the hormones oxytocin and vasopressin (Regan and Berscheid 1999, Fisher 2004). Psychologists' opinions may differ on whether romantic and passionate love are emotions (Regan and Berscheid 1999, Fisher 2004, Hatfield et al. 2007) and whether passionate love, *sexual desire, and sexual motivation are closely related constructs (neurobiologically and/or physiologically) or are very different in their nature (Hatfield and Rapson 1993, Bartels and Zeki 2000, 2004, Diamond 2003, Fisher 2004). Nonetheless, this pathbreaking research has the potential to answer age-old questions about the nature of culture, love, and human sexuality.

Love: how long does it last?

When asked 'How long does love last?' most social psychologists would counter with 'What kind of love?'. According to most theorists, the passage of time has a very different impact on passionate versus companionate love. In general, passionate love is assumed to decline fairly quickly, while companionate love is assumed to remain stable (or actually increase) over time.

Social psychologists have interviewed dating couples, newlyweds, and older couples (ranging in age from 18 to 82), who have been dating or married for varying lengths of time. They asked about couples' love for their partners and the extent to which their partners returned their love. Scholars find that time *does* have a corrosive effect on love—but that effect is equally strong for passionate *and* companionate love. Both forms of love tend to decline slightly, and equally, over time. How do scholars interpret this surprising finding? One can draw an optimistic conclusion or a pessimistic one. On the positive side, even after several years of marriage, men and women were still reporting high levels of both passionate and companionate love. Contrary to what is often portrayed by the mass media, older persons, married for several years, can still experience passionate and companionate love in their relationships. However, if one wants to interpret the results pessimistically, one can point to the fact that time tended to produce a deterioration in both kinds of love.

ELAINE HATFIELD AND RICHARD L. RAPSON

Buss, D.M. (1994). *The evolution of desire*. New York: Basic Books.

Fisher, H.E. (2004). *Why we love: the nature and chemistry of romantic love*. New York: Henry Holt and Company.

Hatfield, E. and Rapson, R.L. (1993). *Love, sex, and intimacy: their psychology, biology, and history*. New York: HarperCollins.

Hatfield, E., Rapson, R.L., and Martel, L.D. (2007). Passionate love and sexual desire. In: S. Kitayama and D. Cohen (eds), *Handbook of cultural psychology*, pp. 760–779. New York: Guilford Press.

Sternberg, R.J. (1998). *Cupid's arrow: the course of love through time*. Cambridge: Cambridge University Press.

lust Lust has been defined as 'an intense passionate or sexual craving' (see SEXUALITY AND EMOTION). Passionate *love, *sexual desire, and lust are as old as humankind. The Sumerian love fable of Inanna and Dumuzi, for example, was spun by tribal storytellers in 2000 BC (see Hatfield *et al.* 2007).

Given the controversial nature of sexuality, however, it is not surprising that scholars disagree as to the nature of such passion. Many modern scholars consider passionate love, sexual desire, and lust to be positive experiences (equating them with a 'lust for life'). (They prefer the term 'lusty' to 'lust' because of its more positive connotations.) Other, more traditional scholars have distinguished between 'pure, chaste love' and 'decadent lust and lechery': in fact, religious leaders once classified lust as one of the seven deadly sins.

Today, many dictionaries still describe lust as a sinful, illicit, excessive, improper, and degrading passion. It is assumed that lust must be restrained, lest it otherwise destroy a person's sanity, *well-being, and health and a society's stability and integrity.

Recently, social psychologists, neuroscientists (using functional magnetic resonance imaging techniques), and physiologists have begun to explore the neural and chemical substrates of passionate love, lust, and sexual mating. They find that passion produces increased activity in the brain areas associated with euphoria and *reward and decreased levels of activity in the areas associated with distress and depression (Regan and Berscheid 1999). Lust appears to be associated primarily with the hormone testosterone in both men and women (Fisher 2004).

Psychologists may differ on whether passionate love is an emotion and whether passionate love, sexual desire, and sexual motivation are closely related constructs (neurobiologically and/or physiologically) or are very different in their nature. The new neuroscientific techniques, combined with more traditional methods, have the potential to extend our knowledge about age-old questions about the nature of love and human sexuality.

ELAINE HATFIELD AND RICHARD L. RAPSON

Bartels, A. and Zeki, S. (2000). The neural basis of romantic love. *Neuroreport*, **11**, 3829–34.

Carter, C.S. (1998). Neuroendocrine perspectives on social attachment and love. *Psychoneuroendocrinology*, **23**, 779–818.

Hatfield, E. and Rapson, R.L. (1993). *Love, sex, and intimacy: their psychology, biology, and history*. New York: HarperCollins.

Hatfield, E. and Rapson, R.L. (2005). *Love and sex: cross-cultural perspectives*. Lanham, MD: University Press of America.

M

mania Mania (bipolar I) is defined as a period of persistently elevated (or irritable) *mood continuing for a period of at least a week associated with significant disturbances in the day to day functioning of the individual. One episode of mania is sufficient to meet US DSM-IV criteria for bipolar I disorder (American Psychiatric Association 1994). European diagnostic criteria require that the individual has at least one other affective episode before the bipolar disorder diagnosis can be met. Mania is distinguished from *hypomania (bipolar II) by its longer duration, greater interference with day to day functioning (marked impairment versus clearly different from normal mood), and the possible presence of psychotic symptoms during the episode. Around 1% of the population experience mania, with onset typically in the period of late adolescence to early adulthood (Bebbington and Ramana 1995) with similar rates in men and women. In clinical studies individuals rarely experience mania as a single episode, with half of patients experiencing a relapse of mood disorder within a year going on to experience multiple episodes of mania and *depression, with recent studies commonly reporting lifetime histories of twenty or more affective episodes (e.g. Judd et al. 2003). Community-based studies have confirmed the recurrent nature of mania but identify about one-fifth of individuals as not experiencing any diagnosable depressive episodes. In addition to discreet episodes of mania, most individuals also experience significant levels of subsyndromal mood symptoms (depressive and hypomanic) during the course of their illness course. A recent study reported from symptom data over a twenty-year period that bipolar I patients spent 10% of weeks during that period with symptoms of mania and 31% of weeks with depression, with an additional 6% of weeks spent with mixed (depression and mania relevant) symptoms (Judd et al. 2003). Individuals who experience mania commonly experience other problems including substance abuse and anxiety disorders. The risk of self-harm and suicide is significantly elevated in individuals with a clinical history of mania, often during associated periods of depression, but *risk-taking behaviour during mania is also associated with elevated mortality rates.

Although mania is therefore associated with multiple difficulties for many individuals there is also evidence for associations with creativity and achievement. There are numerous individuals who have achieved prominence in the fields of arts, science, and education reported to have a history of mania including the musician Ray Davis (1944–), the actor Richard Dreyfuss (1947–), the novelist Hermann Hesse (1877–1962), and the businessman Ted Turner (1938–). In many cases people report periods of heightened output and creativity associated with more mildly elevated mood; as this turns into a specific manic episode, however, the capacity to function effectively rapidly deteriorates.

There is evidence that the tendency to experience mania runs in families, with recent evidence from twin studies suggesting heritability rates of 85% (McGuffin et al. 2003); however, no gene or group of genes for mania has been identified. Researchers are beginning to explore the relationships between genes and the psychological and neurochemical processes that are associated with mania.

Drugs which ameliorate acute mania typically serve to reduce dopamine functioning, which has led to proposals that overactivity of brain dopamine function is a neurochemical cause of mania (Depue and Iacono 1989). There is also evidence for manic states occurring in individuals who recreationally consume stimulants which promote dopamine turnover, although direct evidence for this hypothesis is less consistent.

Psychological theories are currently being explored with respect to mania. One such is that a fundamental motivational system governing the individual's sensitivity to signals of reward (the *behavioural activation system) is dysregulated in individuals who become vulnerable to mania, leading to high levels of *goal-driven behaviour (Depue and Iacono 1989). Patterns of sleeping and waking are disrupted in manic episodes, but sleep disturbance often also precedes the onset of mania. There is evidence for disturbance in the 24-hour (circadian) rhythms across a range of behavioural and physical parameters in mania. Increasing evidence is also accruing for disturbance in the circadian patterns of sleep and activity in manic individuals in between episodes and in individuals at risk of mania. Investigations of cognitive aspects of manic individuals indicate a high tendency towards goal achievement and similar rigid inflexible standards for self to those observed in depression. Biases in how people interpret disturbance in mood and behaviour also seem to be relevant, with greater risk of mania being associated with greater tendency to explain early changes in mood and energy in terms of aspects of the self rather the environment and reduced sensitivity to appropriate social feedback (Jones *et al.* 2006).

Drugs prescribed in acute mania include lithium, carbamazepine, and antipsychotics (including olanzepine and haloperidol). Most individuals who have experienced mania will also be prescribed more long-term medication in an effort to reduce the risk of further episodes. Drugs which are associated with reduced risk of relapse include lithium, sodium valproate, lamotrigine, and olanzepine.

There is recent evidence for promising psychological treatments to reduce the risk of mania relapse. In particular, cognitive behavioural and psycho-educational approaches which focused on teaching the individual and/or a relative more about how to cope effectively with both elevated and depressed episodes have been associated with reduced risk of future episodes of mania.
STEVEN JONES

Johnson, S.L. (2005). Mania and dysregulation in goal pursuit: a review. *Clinical Psychology Review*, **25**, 241–62.
Jones, S.H. and Bentall, R.P. (2006). *The psychology of bipolar disorder*. Oxford: Oxford University Press.

marketing (role of emotion in) At its core, marketing strives to accomplish three broad goals related to three critical phases of the consumer decision-making process: problem recognition, evaluation-choice, and the post-choice phases (see DECISION-MAKING). The first goal is to trigger problem recognition and, thereby, convert dormant consumers in a specific product category into active potential buyers in that category. The second goal is to create a competitive advantage for the marketer's brand so that the consumer who becomes active ends up choosing the marketer's brand rather than a competitor's brand. The third goal is to ensure that the consumer who chooses a marketer's brand is happy with the choice so as to ensure positive word-of-mouth, repeat purchases, and a reduced likelihood of product returns. The paragraphs below elaborate on the three phases of the consumer decision-making process and highlight the crucial role that emotion can play in each of these phases.

Emotion and the problem recognition phase

Viewed as the perceived gap between the consumer's desired state and his/her actual state, problem recognition is the crucial first step that needs to occur for the marketer to have a chance of making a sale. Emotion plays a critical role in triggering problem recognition. Common triggers of problem recognition include frustration and/or anger

toward the product or service currently in use (actual state), feelings of distress at not being in pace with changing fashions (actual state), and emotions elicited by chic design elements in products (e.g. Apple iPod; desired state). Distress-related emotions could also be engendered by current visceral drive states such as hunger, which, in turn, could be triggered by environmental cues (e.g. in grocery stores) such as the taste, sight, or smell of food. Recent research shows that the effects of taste and odour-related cues are not restricted to just hunger or thirst but can extend to a desire for a whole range of products as long as they are rewarding (e.g. a foot massager; Wadhwa *et al.* 2008). Factors that can dampen problem recognition include negative emotion related to the prospect of losing accumulated incentives from loyalty programmes (e.g. frequent flier miles).

Emotion and the evaluation-choice phase

Once a consumer becomes active, it becomes imperative for the marketer that (1) the consumer considers the marketer's brand and (2) the overall evaluation of the marketer's brand is greater than that of the competition so that the consumer ends up choosing the marketer's brand. Overall evaluation, in turn, can be construed as an integration of three components, namely brand emotion (E), the value proposition arising from the tangible and intangible benefits (Vb) and the value proposition arising from price (Vp), including momentary incentives such as price-discounts, rebates, etc. Thus viewed, the power of emotion in creating a competitive advantage becomes apparent. While audio-visual (e.g. television) advertising has been the *de rigueur* among marketers as a means of shaping brand emotions, other tactics such as product placements in emotion-eliciting television shows has been gaining in popularity in recent years.

Recent research on the role of E in the evaluation-choice phase has focused on two broad areas. First, research has focused on factors that enhance the impact of E on evaluations and choice. Factors that have been identified include situations in which evaluating Vb is difficult or ambiguous (e.g. when expertise is lacking), where the consumer is distracted or under cognitive load (Shiv and Fedorikhin 1999, Pham *et al.* 2001), and where the consumer has experiential rather than instrumental motives. A second area of research has focused on the potential for E to 'drive the consumer out of the decision-making process'. Specifically, research shows that aversive emotions arising from trade-off conflicts have the potential to cause consumers to eschew the trade-offs altogether by choosing the status quo or deferring the choice (Luce 1998).

Emotion and the post-decision phase

As stated earlier, a third goal of marketing is to ensure that the consumer is satisfied post-choice, since a satisfied consumer is likely to yield positive future revenue streams for the marketer both through repeat purchases as well as through positive word-of-mouth. One factor that has been found to hamper post-choice satisfaction is cognitive elaboration, which results in unpleasant feelings associated with the perceived loss of foregone options in the choice set (Carmon *et al.* 2003). Also, decisions that are made more cognitively rather than emotionally seem to hamper post-choice satisfaction and prompt consumers to change their minds about their choices.

Conclusion

The paragraphs above have highlighted the various ways in which emotion can play a crucial role in the three phases of the consumer decision-making process. The study of emotion is currently one of the hottest areas of research in marketing and has been yielding rich insights into the critical role that emotion plays in the consumer decision-making process.

BABA SHIV

Cohen, J.B., Pham, M.T., and Andrade, E.B. (2008). The nature and role of affect in consumer behavior. In: C.P. Haugtvedt, P. Herr, and F. Kardes (eds), *Handbook of consumer psychology*, pp. 297–348. Mahwah, NJ: Erlbaum.

Loewenstein, G. and Lerner, J.S. (2003). The role of affect in decision making. In: R.J. Davidson, K.R. Scherer, and H.H. Goldsmith (eds), *Handbook of affective sciences*, pp. 619–42. New York: Oxford University Press.

media communication The study of media and media effects has integrated affect and affect-related constructs in numerous ways to help explain message selection, emotional responses to the media, and the processing and effects of mediated messages. Focusing on *selection*, Zillmann's (1988) mood management theory (MMT) asserts that people use the media to modulate their affective states (see REGULATION OF EMOTION). Specifically, Zillmann argues that people, driven by hedonistic desires, strive to alter negative moods as well as maintain and prolong positive ones. Consequently, they will arrange their environments to adjust their moods by consciously or unconsciously selecting media messages they expect to meet their affective needs at that moment. Much research supports the predictions of MMT. However, its boundaries have been challenged by paradoxes of media selection, like the enjoyment of horror movies or tearjerkers that are designed to evoke negative affect, seemingly in contradiction to MMT's assumption of hedonistic motivation. The most recent research on affect and media selection has moved to consider *goals other than those related to hedonism (e.g. information-seeking, *coping, retaliation, self-actualization) to explain these seemingly counter-hedonistic media choices.

Affect has also been studied as an *outcome* of media exposure. Most prominent in this domain are the fright reactions of children to the media. Cantor's extensive work in this area (see Cantor 2002) documents the pervasive and sometimes debilitating effects of fright reactions to both fictional portrayals and news accounts. As viewers generally realize that the media content is either not real or not a direct personal threat (the bases for *fear responses), Cantor argues that these media-based fright reactions result from stimulus generalization, or the recognition that the frightening event is similar to one that could actually happen to the viewer. Cantor's work focuses especially on the developmental differences in children's fright reactions, which in sum suggests that as children age they are more likely to find dangers that are conceptual, abstract, and/or realistic to be more frightening than more fantastic images and scenarios (see CHILDHOOD EMOTIONAL DEVELOPMENT). Cantor has further considered how to help children cope with media-induced fright. Though fright has dominated the literature, other emotional reactions specific to entertainment fare, like horror, suspense, humour, and the like, have also been of interest to media scholars (see Bryant *et al.* 2003).

Beyond the simple evocation of an affective state, two processes have been examined to explain the intensity of emotional reactions to the media: excitation transfer and desensitization. Zillmann's (1983) excitation transfer theory (ETT) addresses increases in the intensity of emotional reactions to media messages. According to ETT, the physiological *arousal associated with emotional experiences adjusts more slowly than the cognitive processes related to those experiences. Thus whether that arousal comes from another activity (e.g. exercise) or from media viewing (e.g. a frightening scene), the lingering physiological arousal enhances the emotional reaction to subsequent media scenes or messages. Desensitization, on the other hand, suggests that repeated exposure to certain media images (e.g. violence or sex) reduces their ability to arouse the same degree of affect as the initial exposures (see Bryant *et al.* 2003).

Finally, a growing body of literature considers the role of affect in the *processing and effects* of media messages. For example, Lang's (2000) limited capacity model focuses on how arousing features of media messages—those related to either message structure (e.g. edits, screen size) or content (e.g. sex, violence)—influence how people's limited cognitive resources are allocated to the encoding, storage, and retrieval of information during message exposure. She specifically argues that emotionally arousing media messages demand that resources be directed toward both message encoding and storage, thus increasing one's ability to store the emotionally arousing content but reducing one's ability to encode details of that message.

Further, there is a large and growing body of research on the persuasive effect of emotion-based media messages (see Nabi 2007). This research area generally concentrates on the emotions aroused by media content and their effects on information processing, attitudes, and behaviours. Within this context, there has been an overwhelming focus on so-called fear appeals, with the most current thinking suggesting that a message that evokes perceived severity and susceptibility to a threat will evoke fear. A message that then also contains response and self-efficacy information will be more likely to generate adaptive responses than one that does not. In recent years, attention to other discrete emotions, like *anger and *guilt, has prompted the development of broader frameworks through which to understand the persuasive effects of emotion (e.g. the cognitive functional model, the emotion-as-frames model), but research in these areas is still in its infancy.

ROBIN L. NABI

memory (emotional) Emotional memory refers to the acquisition, retention, and retrieval of life experiences that have biological or personal relevance (see RELEVANCE DETECTION). These experiences form the basis of an individual's autobiographical record and are often shared with kin or other members of a culture. Emotional memories are mediated by the interaction of at least two systems in the brain: a collection of emotion-processing regions that are sensitive to the *arousal and/or *valence properties of stimuli, and distributed networks of memory-processing regions that establish long-lasting representations of events. By influencing the learning parameters, forgetting rates, or other operating characteristics of memory systems, emotional experiences can be preferentially retained over time relative to other mundane experiences that are inconsequential to the individual (see LEARNING, EMOTIONAL (NEUROSCIENCE PERSPECTIVES)). Emotional memories in humans build upon survival mechanisms in other species that help organisms remember the locations and quality of food sources, social interactions with mates and offspring, and situations leading to threat and predation.

Memories can be either explicit (declarative) or implicit (nondeclarative) in nature. Explicit memories are accessible to consciousness and critically depend on the integrity of brain structures in the medial temporal lobe. Explicit memories can be further subdivided into episodic memories (memories for events) and semantic memories (memories for facts). Episodic memories correspond to the everyday experience of personal memories in life and are the most well-characterized in terms of the influence of emotion. Implicit emotional memories, by contrast, are nonconscious and do not depend on the medial temporal lobe memory system. For instance,

one may develop an aversion to a particular food without recalling any specific instance in which ingesting the food led to getting sick. In this case, the memory is inferred by a change in behaviour or physiology (e.g. avoiding eating aubergine or increased heart rate when presented with the sight or smell of aubergine) in the absence of conscious recollection. Implicit memories are mediated by a variety of brain systems that have different specializations, many of which have direct connections with emotion-processing structures. Emotional effects on episodic memory are described below.

Behavioural mechanisms
Emotion typically facilitates memory, although sometimes emotion can have a detrimental impact. Emotional triggers can be internal (e.g. readout of visceral changes indicating a sad mood state) or external (e.g. evaluation of the emotional nature of a stimulus in the environment such as a snake), and both sources can influence the formation and retrieval of memories. Memory can be modulated by the valence (pleasantness) or arousal (intensity) properties of an emotional experience, although most findings suggest that arousal is the critical dimension. The impact of emotional arousal is best described as an inverted-U effect, in which a moderate degree of arousal benefits memory but too much arousal can impair memory, particularly at retrieval (see YERKES–DODSON LAW). Emotion influences all stages of memory processing: the initial encoding of events into memory, the stabilization and consolidation of memory traces over time, and the retrieval of memory traces from long-term storage.

Several cognitive and physiological processes contribute to emotional influences on memory. Emotional stimuli capture attention more readily during encoding (see attention and emotion) and cause a narrowing of attentional focus on the central emotionally salient features of the environment at the expense of other peripheral features (Heuer and Reisberg 1990). For example, memories of crime scene witnesses tend to focus on the weapon at the expense of peripheral details, such as the clothing of an accomplice (Steblay 1992). Such attentional effects alter both short- and long-term memory for the episode. Once encoded, emotional events undergo enhanced consolidation, which leads to prolonged retention in long-term memory (Kleinsmith and Kaplan 1964, Sharot and Phelps 2004). Consequently, when memory is tested across multiple time points, neutral events have steeper forgetting curves than emotional events (see Fig. M1). Consolidation is facilitated in part by the activation of physiological arousal systems and the release of stress hormones into the bloodstream, which provide feedback signals onto central brain sites to promote the storage of

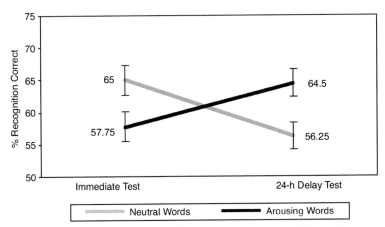

Fig. M1. Emotionally arousing words are selectively consolidated in long-term memory. Words high in arousal are initially recognized somewhat more poorly than neutral words on an immediate memory test. As time progresses, memory for the arousing words improves whereas memory for the neutral words declines. This time-dependent retention advantage shows that emotionally arousing information undergoes selective consolidation into long-term storage. Adapted from Sharot and Phelps (2004).

emotionally salient events (McGaugh 1995). Emotional events tend to be more distinctive and are rehearsed to a greater extent than neutral events, which further promotes greater storage in long-term memory.

Emotion also biases the retrieval of prior memories, even long after the traces have been consolidated. Emotional events tend to be organized in memory such that recall of one type of emotional experience (such as one fearful episode) triggers others that are similar. A *spreading activation model* has been postulated to describe such effects, whereby different nodes in memory represent different emotions, and activation of a particular node will facilitate retrieval of similar emotions but inhibit the retrieval of opposing emotions (Bower 1981). Spreading activation models have been used to explain *mood-congruent memory* in which depressed individuals tend to retrieve sad or stressful personal memories consistent with their depressed mood state. In addition, emotional memories are associated with specific retrieval operations that promote *recollection* rather than *familiarity* (Ochsner 2000). Recollection refers to memories that are retrieved with contextual details and a sense of travelling back in time to relive the event. In contrast, familiarity refers to a memory that lacks such details but the individual simply knows that the event occurred. When recalling an episode from the personal past, emotional arousal alters the subjective experience of remembering such that the memory is associated with greater vividness, is accompanied by perception of physiological changes, and has a more coherent narrative structure,

although it is not necessarily more accurate (Talarico et al. 2004) (see FLASHBULB MEMORIES).

Neural mechanisms

The *amygdala is a critical brain structure that mediates the effects of emotional arousal on memory (see Fig. M2). Neurological patients with damage to the amygdala show less focusing of attention on central details of emotional stories (Adolphs et al. 2005b), exhibit less memory consolidation for emotionally arousing stimuli (Cahill et al. 1995, LaBar and Phelps 1998), and are impaired in recalling some aspects of autobiographical memories (Buchanan et al. 2005). Neuroimaging studies in healthy adults indicate that the amygdala interacts with regions of the prefrontal cortex and other medial temporal lobe structures, including the hippocampus and entorhinal cortex, to promote the long-term retention of emotionally arousing material (Dolcos et al. 2004, Richardson et al. 2004). The same brain regions participate in the retrieval of emotional events from long-term storage, particularly for those that are rated high in emotional intensity and retrieved with a vivid sense of recollection (Sharot et al. 2004, Dolcos et al. 2005, Greenberg et al. 2005). The amygdala exerts its influence through direct interactions with memory-processing regions of the frontal and temporal lobes as well as the release of noradrenaline and stress hormones that enhance memory consolidation (Cahill et al. 1994). The amygdala works in consort with other limbic and paralimbic regions of the brain, including the insula, anterior

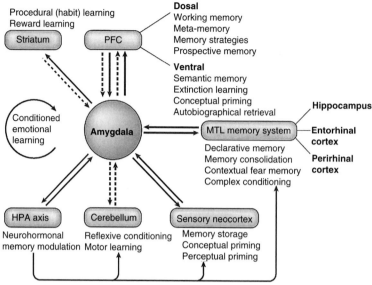

Fig. M2. Schematic of interactions between the amygdala, a structure in the temporal lobes important for processing emotionally arousing stimuli, and memory systems of the brain. Through direct effects on distributed networks that process different types of memories, the amygdala facilitates encoding and retrieval processes. In addition, through indirect effects on the hypothalamic–pituitary–adrenal (HPA) axis, stress hormones released in the periphery feed back onto various regions of the cortex to consolidate emotional memories. PFC, prefrontal cortex; MTL, medial temporal lobe. Adapted from LaBar and Cabeza (2006).

cingulate gyrus, and ventromedial and orbital prefrontal cortex, to integrate sensory–visceral evaluation functions with other cognitive operations recruited during the stages of memory formation, consolidation, and retrieval. In contrast, memory benefits for valenced emotional stimuli that are low in arousal are not mediated by the amygdala (Phelps *et al.* 1997) but instead reflect the engagement of strategic and semantic processes in frontotemporal networks of the brain (Kensinger and Corkin 2004). These multiple cognitive and neural routes to emotional remembering collectively ensure that individuals retain information about experiences that are most salient to their livelihood.

KEVIN S. LABAR

LaBar, K.S. and Cabeza, R. (2006). Cognitive neuroscience of emotional memory. *Nature Reviews Neuroscience*, **7**, 54–64.
McGaugh, J.L. (2004). The amygdala modulates the consolidation of memories of emotionally arousing experiences. *Annual Review of Neuroscience*, **27**, 1–28.
Uttl, B., Ohta, N., and Siegenthaler, A.L. (eds) (2006). *Memory and emotion: interdisciplinary perspectives*. Malden, MA: Blackwell Publishing.

metaphor (and emotion) Metaphor (typically a linguistic phenomenon; see LINGUISTICS AND EMOTION) is a communicative device, three main aspects of which are generally studied (see Ortony 1993): (1) what metaphors are, (2) the processes involved in their comprehension, and (3) the processes involved in their production (see INTERPERSONAL COMMUNICATION). Here, these will be discussed primarily as they relate to affect and emotion.

The standard account of metaphors, deriving from Aristotle (384–322 BC), views them as covert comparisons between essentially dissimilar things. Richards (1936), elaborating Aristotle's account, defined the terms of a metaphor as the 'tenor' (today often called the topic) and the 'vehicle'. That which they have in common he called the 'ground', and their essential dissimilarity he viewed as responsible for metaphorical 'tension'. While proponents of other views (e.g. Black's, 1962, interaction view and Glucksberg's, 2001, categorization view) have argued against such 'comparison' theories, it is clear that metaphors always embody some kind of incongruity which is the source of Richards' notion of tension. Although this incongruity often resides within the metaphorical assertion itself, as in literally false assertions such as 'An army of bees attacked him' or 'Einstein was a giant', it does not necessarily reside there. It can also derive from presuppositions, as with the literally true, yet metaphorical statement 'No man is an island', or from the relation between the metaphorical assertion and the context, usually by virtue of co-reference, as with the second sentence in 'John had boundless energy. Yet few people appreciated this dynamo' (where 'John' and 'dynamo' are co-referential).

Metaphor comprehension is influenced by how conventional and metaphorical the metaphors are. Highly conventional, or 'frozen' or 'dead' metaphors (usually having an explicit or underlying genitive structure as in 'head of state'), are so rigidly embedded in the language that for native speakers they function like literal language, thus raising few interesting questions relating to affect and emotion. On the other hand, unfamiliar unconventional metaphors place a burden on comprehension mechanisms, especially when they are highly metaphorical—that is, when the metaphorical tension is high. There is reason to believe that when people reach an interpretation of such metaphors, the insight or 'click of comprehension' that results has affective correlates. Activation of the *amygdala during 'Aha!' experiences has been found in positron emission tomography studies of logical reasoning (Parsons and Osherson 2001), and in functional magnetic resonance imaging studies (Jung-Beeman et al. 2004) of people solving remote associates problems (e.g. find a word that is related to the triple pine, crab, sauce). In interpreting their findings, Parsons and Osherson speculate that in their tasks, there might have been a 'pleasurable release from tension as the subject suddenly perceives the logical status of an argument' (p. 962). It may well be that the same thing happens when the solution to a remote associates item (e.g. apple) suddenly dawns on a person, or when people suddenly realize what is meant by an unfamiliar and nonobvious metaphor that they encounter.

When people produce metaphors, they generally do so because of the difficulty of expressing themselves in literal language, the resources of which are quite inadequate to express the huge range and subtlety of affective (and other) feeling states that we experience. Consequently, characterizations of affective states are replete with metaphorical language—some, novel and created 'on the fly', and others embedded in the language as underlying 'conceptual' metaphors (e.g. Lakoff and Johnson 1980). This latter idea has become very influential amongst those studying the relation between cognition and metaphor more generally. In the context of emotion, the idea is that an underlying metaphor such as 'Love is a journey' or 'Anger is a heated fluid in a container' is the source of a variety of idiomatic expressions that characterize various aspects of the target concept. For example, with respect to love, the argument is that these conceptual metaphors give rise to expressions such as 'the relationship is at a crossroads', 'the marriage is on the rocks', and for anger, 'blowing (one's) top', 'letting off steam',

'getting all steamed up', 'exploding with anger', 'fuming', and so on. Certainly these are interesting observations, although it might be objected that there is a certain ad hoc quality to the analysis. First, how do we decide what the underlying metaphor really is—why not 'Anger is a volcano', which seems to fit better, and additionally explains 'erupting in anger'? More problematically, some metaphors even run counter to restricted categorizations like 'Anger is a heated fluid'—for instance, 'icy stares' and 'cold spite' surely connote angry interactions. These and other expressions, such as 'fly off the handle', that don't easily fit predetermined categories of conceptual metaphors appear to demand the postulation of a new underlying metaphor. Nevertheless, the point remains that at least as far as emotions are concerned, given the limited resources of literal language, the ability to talk about them vividly is vastly enhanced by the expressive affordances provided by metaphor.

ANDREW ORTONY AND DAVID N. RAPP

Glucksberg, S. (2001). *Understanding figurative language: from metaphor to idioms*. New York: Oxford University Press.
Jung-Beeman, M., Bowden, E., Haberman, J., Frymiare, J.L., Arambel-Liu, S., Greenblatt, R., et al. (2004). Neural activity when people solve verbal problems with insight. *PLoS Biology*, **2**, 500–510.

mimicry (psychological perspectives) Mimicry refers to the imitation of the nonverbal behaviour of others (see NONVERBAL COMMUNICATION). These others may be people we interact with, but also people we see in photos, films, and so forth. Mimicry is ubiquitous. The mimicking of nonverbal behaviours includes the adoption of similar bodily postures (see Fig. M3), foot tapping, face touching, but also increased forearm muscle tension when watching arm wrestling, or speech accommodation, as well as the imitation of emotional expressions such as facial expressions, tone of voice, or wincing when observing the pain of others (see FACIAL EXPRESSION OF EMOTION). Mimicry is found in babies as early as several hours after birth; they tend to imitate aspects of facial expressions such as the protrusion of the tongue (see INFANCY (EMOTIONAL DEVELOPMENT IN)). Mimicry is typically difficult to suppress, and most of the time people are not aware that they are mimicking others or that they are being mimicked themselves (see Hess et al. 1999).

At least three functions of mimicry have been proposed. Thus, mimicry has been described as (1) part of the emotion recognition process, (2) a means to establish rapport (affiliation), (3) a communicative signal.

Mimicry and emotion recognition

This function of mimicry, as the name indicates, applies only to the imitation of emotional behaviours and has been formulated specifically with regard to

mimicry (sensorimotor aspects)

Fig. M3. Postural mimicry.

facial expression. Simulationist accounts of face-based emotion recognition posit that people use their own mental mechanisms to comprehend the mental states of others; that is, they attempt to replicate, mimic, or impersonate the mental life of the other person in order to recognize or comprehend his or her emotions. One such model involves the activation via mirror neurons of facial expressive mimicry, which in turn provides information about the emotion process that otherwise activates those facial expressions (see MIMICRY (SENSORIMOTOR ASPECTS)). In response to findings by Blairy and colleagues (e.g. Blairy *et al.* 1999) that mimicry is not directly related to emotion recognition, this model has been reformulated to involve an 'as if' processing loop rather than actual imitation (see Goldman and Sripada 2005).

Mimicry as a means to establish affiliation

Chartrand and Bargh (1999) refer to mimicry as the 'chameleon effect' and include it under the general heading of automatically primed social behaviours. That is, they hold that people's behaviour passively and unintentionally changes to match that of others in their current social environment. The function of this process is to foster affiliation or to serve as 'social glue'. A series of studies by Chartrand and colleagues support this function of nonemotional mimicry (see Lakin and Chartrand 2003).

All forms of mimicry have the potential to increase rapport and establish *affiliation. However, in the case of emotional behaviours one should note that emotion expressions *per se* already signal affiliation. Thus, smiling signals affiliation goals, whereas anger and disgust signal the absence of affiliation goals. This leads to the contention, as affiliation goals cannot reasonably be signalled by the imitation of nonaffiliative behaviours, that these latter emotion expressions are not mimicked in contexts in which the social signal value of the emotion expression is salient.

Mimicry as a communicative signal

Bavelas *et al.* (1986) contend that the main function of mimicry is to 'show (you) how you feel.' That is, mimicry serves to signal to interaction partners that we understand how they feel. To the degree that a social signal of understanding is a sign of positive rapport, mimicry then also fosters affiliation. In turn, such clearly visible mimicry behaviours as congruent postures signal to others that the interaction partners like each other.

Mimicry and social context

Both simulationist accounts of face-based emotion recognition and the chameleon effect posit that mimicry is automatic and cannot be suppressed (albeit, according to Lakin and Chartrand, 2003, amplified by pre-existing affiliation goals). However, it has been shown that the social relationship between expresser and observer moderates mimicry reactions. Thus, mimicry may be absent when the relationship is competitive or some other reason to not affiliate is present. Moreover, when affiliation goals are not only not present, but in fact a non-affiliation goal exists, counter-mimicry effects, that is, facial reactions incompatible with the observed reaction (e.g. smiling when observing someone who winces in pain) have been observed (see Hess *et al.* 1999).

URSULA HESS

mimicry (sensorimotor aspects) There is plenty of evidence showing that humans tend to communicate and share emotions by imitating each other and by synchronizing their bodies. For instance, young couples were videotaped while teaching one another made-up words. The couples that demonstrated the greatest motor synchrony also had the strongest emotional rapport with each other. Also, warm interviewers—who lean forward, smile, and nod—elicit leaning forward, smiling, and nodding in the interviewees (Hatfield *et al.* 1994).

This motor mimicry even has a role in the perception of other people's emotions (see MIMICRY (PSYCHOLOGICAL ASPECTS)). Subjects were asked to detect changes in facial expressions. Some subjects could not move their face because they were holding a pencil between their lips and teeth. These subjects were much worse in detecting changes in emotional facial expressions than subjects who mimicked the observed expressions (Niedenthal *et al.* 2005a). Thus, by mimicking others we better perceive the expressions of other people.

This seems to reverse the traditional logic according to which one needs to recognize an emotion first in order to imitate it. This apparent paradox can be explained by the role of mirror neurons in *empathy. Mirror neurons are cells that fire when we perform an action or when we make a facial expression, and when we see somebody else performing the same action or the same facial expression. Thus, mirror neurons create an automatic simulation—or inner imitation, if the imitation is not overt—of the facial expressions of other people. By sending signals to the emotional brain centres in the limbic system, mirror neurons may allow us to feel the emotions associated with those facial expressions (see Fig. M4). Only after we feel those emotions internally are we able to explicitly recognize them.

If mimicry helps the recognition of emotions, then good imitators should also be good at recognizing emotions in other people and at empathizing with them (see RECOGNITION OF EMOTION (NEURAL SYSTEMS FOR)). Indeed, the tendency to imitate others correlates with the ability to empathize with them (Chartrand and Bargh 1999). Mirror neuron areas and limbic areas are connected through a brain region called the *insula*. Functional brain imaging has demonstrated activation of mirror neuron areas, insula, and the limbic system during observation and during imitation of facial emotional expressions. The observed pattern of neural activity suggested that mirror neurons indeed send signals to limbic areas through the insula, thus supporting the idea that these cell areas help us understanding the emotions of other people by implementing some form of *inner imitation*, when we do not overtly imitate. According to the 'mirror neuron hypothesis of empathy', when we see others expressing their emotions by facial expres-

sions, our mirror neurons fire as if we were making those facial expressions ourselves. Through their firing, mirror neurons would also send signals to emotional brain centres in the limbic system to make us feel what other people feel (Carr *et al.* 2003). Indeed, activity in mirror neuron areas during imitation and observation of the actions and facial expressions of other people correlates with the tendency to empathize with others (Kaplan and Iacoboni 2006).

MARCO IACOBONI

Iacoboni, M. and Dapretto, M. (2006). The mirror neuron system and the consequences of its dysfunction. *Nature Reviews Neuroscience*, **7**, 942–51.

Rizzolatti, G. and Craighero, L. (2004). The mirror-neuron system. *Annual Review of Neuroscience*, **27**, 169–92.

mind–body problem Aristotle (*c.* 330 BCE) took it that basic intrinsic purposes govern changes in all physical things. A rock, he claimed, has the purpose of heading to the centre of the earth; a plant, the purpose of growing; a chipmunk, the purpose of feeding. A human rationally contemplates and acts.

Since the 17th century, physicists have been basing central theories on purposeless mathematical interactions of tiny-scaled physical things. Simultaneously, chemistry has become physicalized, and biology, chemicalized.

By about 1970 just about all workers in mind–body philosophy and the philosophy of science took it that biological changes are sums of (typically inaccessible) smaller-scale physiochemical changes, and that such changes are sums of (typically inaccessible) smaller-scale microphysics-based changes, and call this physics-through-biology relationship 'physical completeness' (note: this relationship does not include psychology).

Most philosophers of religion, and a tiny handful of other theorists, ignored the development of physical completeness: they retain the notion that there are some nonphysical mental elements (or only subtly physical elements, or physical configurations) that purposefully govern some of the biological changes, overturning

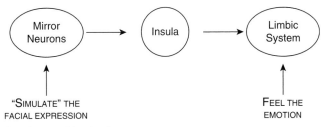

Fig. M4. Neural mechanisms for empathic mirroring.

the (typically inaccessible) sums of the ordinary physics-only changes.

It was within the consensus accepting physical completeness that the main debates in mind–body philosophy have occurred in the last few decades. The central question is: Given that all the fundamental forces objectively governing the changes in a human body are nonpurposive forces of physics, how do we explain the way states such as beliefs, desires, fears, and hopes, work?

There are many answers. One answer asserts that a type of mental-affective state is identical with a type of physical state in a brain. But what if a silicon-based thing works just like a carbon-based brain? Then that type-identity wouldn't obtain. What remains, however, is physical completeness, and that yields a token-identity. (To explain: suppose there are four tables in a room. Two are exactly alike, Edwardian, and four-legged; two are exactly alike, Victorian, and three-legged. There are two table types. And, there are four tables, or four table tokens. Being a table is not being an easy-to-state sum of parts. But each token table would be the sum of its token parts including their relations.)

In the token-identity theory yielded by physical completeness, any token biological or artificial item is identical with the sum of the smaller tokens that compose it, including their relations; and the sum of the physics-based changes (however inaccessible) is the sum of changes taking place in the large item.

Under this umbrella token-identity theory, a variety of nontype-identity theories arose for mental states (equivalently, mental-affective states): *Eliminativism* claims that mental states (beliefs, desires, fears, etc.) do not map onto brain states, and do not exist. *Anomalous monism* states that although physical completeness obtains, and so monism for objects in spacetime is true, still, the psychological terms are not theoretically reducible. *Functionalism* states that analysis of the causal–functional relations between mental states yields analysis of mentality. *Property dualism* holds that functions do not embrace the *qualia of mental states. There are both properties that, in combination, become qualitative mental properties and nonmental physical properties. *Mysterianism* maintains that the relation between qualitative experience and merely physical items will be forever a mystery.

These views, and others, too, including some top-down causal theories and some revised type-identity theories, accept physical completeness. Religious philosophers have ignored the last 400 years of natural science. Ignoring natural science seems untoward. Still, both groups—the group accepting physical completeness, and the group (arbitrarily) rejecting it—may be, to some extent, sidestepping a central problem, namely: What is the philosophically genuine body that underlies a person?

LEONARD ANGEL

Angel, L. (2005). Compositional science and religious philosophy. *Religious Studies*, 41, 125–43.

Guttenplan, S. (1994). An essay on mind. In: S. Guttenplan (ed.), *A companion to the philosophy of mind*, pp. 1–107. Oxford: Blackwell.

McLaughlin, B. (1995). Philosophy of mind. In: R. Audi (ed.), *Cambridge dictionary of philosophy*, pp. 597–606. Cambridge: Cambridge University Press.

Ruse, M. (1995). Reductionism. In: T. Honderich (ed.), *Oxford companion to philosophy*, pp. 750–1. Oxford: Oxford University Press.

<http://consc.net/mindpapers/4/all> For a vast bibliographical resource see 'Metaphysics of mind', Part 4 of MindPapers: a bibliography of the philosophy of mind and the science of consciousness, D. Chalmers (ed.) and D. Bourget (assistant ed.) (accessed 21 November 2008).

mixed emotions While many emotion theorists admit the existence of *mixed emotions, emotion blends,* or *ambivalent emotions* (Plutchik 1980, Izard 1994), this theoretical acceptance has so far had little effect on research practice. A large majority of studies attempt to identify and measure pure emotions. Even in those cases where subjects are asked to indicate the relative intensity of several discrete emotions, often neither the data analyses nor the discussion of the results explicitly address the issue of emotion blends and their nature. This is all the more surprising as field studies examining realistic emotion experiences generally find a large proportion of emotion blends, often, but not always, of the same positive or negative *valence (e.g. Scherer and Tannenbaum 1986, Ellsworth and Smith 1988, Larsen *et al.* 2001, Scherer *et al.* 2004).

How do different theoretical traditions account for the occurrence of mixed emotions? Most basic or discrete emotion theories can be described as 'palette theories' implying a blending of basic emotions, like that of an artist mixing basic colours on a palette, or adjoining colours on the colour wheel being perceived as a unique colour combination (e.g. Plutchik 1984, pp. 204–5). Izard (1992) suggests basic emotion–cognition interactions that result in a wide variety of affective-cognitive structures. However, the presumed mechanisms remain unclear and there has been little direct empirical research on the matter in this tradition.

In dimensional theorizing there is debate on whether valence consists of a single, bipolar dimension in affective space (which makes blends impossible) or rather of two independent unipolar dimensions for positive and negative affect (which could explain *ambivalent emotions) (see CIRCUMPLEX MODELS). While the debate is ongoing, there is now growing evidence that feelings can be both positive and negative simultaneously and that situational and individual factors may moderate the probability of ambivalent feelings occurring (Rafaeli et al. 2007). In addition, there may be strong cultural differences in the attitudes toward duality, contradiction, and ambiguity (Williams and Aaker 2002), suggesting that ambivalent emotions are more frequent in some cultures (e.g. in Asia) than in others (e.g. in Anglo-American countries).

Mixed emotions can be best explained in the *appraisal theory tradition. Based on the notion that there are as many different emotions as appraisal outcome configurations, it has been suggested that the *component process model could be called a 'kaleidoscope theory'. Just as a unique pattern of colour and light results from the way in which kaleidoscope pieces rearrange themselves when shaken, appraisal outcomes may result in 'hybrid' emotions sharing elements of the typical profiles for different modal emotions (Scherer 1984a; see MODAL EMOTIONS). This may be due to conflicting *goals or *values (Weigert 1991), or to vacillating evaluations of event consequences or *coping potential. A number of studies have addressed this issue directly. Thus, a majority of students describing their cognitive appraisals and emotional states before taking a college examination and after receiving their grades reported experiencing complex blends of two or more emotions, which could be accounted for by the reported appraisal patterns (Smith and Ellsworth 1987). Similarly, airline passengers whose baggage was lost upon arrival, reported mixed emotions, containing various elements of anger, resignation, worry, and good spirits in almost all cases. These complex reactions could be statistically accounted for as a consequence of differential appraisal of the personal importance and implications of the loss, and of general attitudes toward the airlines and their employees (Scherer and Ceschi 1997).

The understanding of the mechanisms underlying mixed, and in particular ambivalent emotions (both positive and negative), is central to the understanding of underlying emotion mechanisms and has important implications for the critical testing of theories. Precise measurement and more sophisticated self-report assessment is needed, as the distinction between different events and different facets (or meanings) of the same event is not always easy to draw (due to the rapid dynamic unfolding of events and the continuous changes in appraisal; see Scherer and Tannenbaum 1986). Furthermore, as different groups of individuals may show different patterns of emotional experiences (e.g. anger and resignation versus sadness, after failing an exam), sophisticated multivariate analysis methods may be required to understand the wide variety of responses to the same event (e.g. latent class analysis; see Eid 2001, pp. 322–4).

KLAUS R. SCHERER

modal emotions The idea that there are a number of fundamental categories of emotions—basic emotions—like *anger, *joy, *disgust, *fear, and *sadness, that represent evolutionarily old modes of adaptation to specific situations and have specific response patterns, has strongly influenced the field of emotion research (see BASIC EMOTIONS; EMOTION THEORIES AND CONCEPTS (PHILOSOPHICAL PERSPECTIVES); EMOTION THEORIES AND CONCEPTS (PSYCHOLOGICAL PERSPECTIVES)). However, it has been puzzling researchers over the last decades that the prototypical profiles of expressive and physiological responses associated with basic emotions are rather difficult to demonstrate empirically (Cacioppo et al. 2000, Scherer and Ellgring 2007a) and that there seem to be many different varieties of the standard basic emotions (often described as *families*), as well as *mixed or blended* emotions, often subject to strong individual differences (see MIXED EMOTIONS). The extraordinary variability and multifacetedness of many emotion episodes has led proponents of alternative theories, especially appraisal theorists, to question the notion of basic emotions as rigid *affect programs and to propose that, because many different combinations of appraisal outcomes are possible, the number of potential emotional reaction profiles and corresponding subjective experiences is virtually infinite (Scherer 2001a) (see FEELINGS (PHILOSOPHICAL PERSPECTIVES); FEELINGS (PSYCHOLOGICAL PERSPECTIVES); QUALIA).

However, the so-called 'basic emotions', such as anger and happiness (see Scherer et al. 2004), clearly occur more frequently, and even when rare (like fear), they are more memorable than the myriad of other, less prominent, emotion varieties. From an appraisal perspective, one can assume that there are some major patterns of adaptation in the life of animate organisms which reflect frequently recurring patterns of results of environmental evaluation. Thus, all individuals, at all stages of ontogenetic development, encounter situations in which the path to satisfying their needs or attaining their goals is blocked, resulting in *frustration. Thus, frustration in a very general sense is universal and ubiquitous. Equally universal are the two major reaction patterns *fight* and *flight*. Consequently, it is not surprising that the emotions which often elicit these behaviours, anger and fear, seem universal and in some sense basic. Scherer (1994c) has suggested the use of the term *modal emotions* for the response patterns and experiences resulting from the predominant outcomes of these stimulus-evaluation checks due to general conditions of life, constraints of social organization, and similarity of innate equipment. Just as certain appraisal outcomes in response to certain types of situations are more frequent, the patterning of elements in the other emotion components would also occur more frequently. Modal emotions are characterized, then, by a

models (of emotion)

prototypical pattern of appraisals and the corresponding patterning of expression, autonomic arousal, *action tendencies, and feeling states. This accounts for the predominance of certain types of emotions. However, it is important to highlight the central difference of the *modal emotion* concept from the postulate of *basic emotions* in the sense of affect programs—no effort is made to find or define a definite number of homogeneous, integral categories or mechanisms that justify their a priori definition as basic or fundamental. Instead, it is proposed to empirically study the frequency with which certain patterns of sequential, synchronized changes in the different components of emotion episodes occur.

Given the prominence and frequency of occurrence of these episodes of highly similar emotional experiences, it is not surprising that they have been labelled with a short verbal expression, mostly a single word, in most languages of the world (see VOCABULARY OF EMOTION). This would be predicted on the basis of a principle of economical verbal coding for objects of communication (see Clark and Clark 1977, pp. 552–7). Thus, discreteness is—at least in part—bestowed by linguistic categorization and the cultural prototypes these categories reflect (see Shaver *et al.* 1987). Linguistic categories conceptually order the world for us in many domains, and they do so for emotion too. Among the many advantages of this categorical organization are cognitive economy and the communicability of the underlying referents. One can venture rather specific theoretical predictions as to the appraisal profiles that are likely to produce such modal emotions, labelled in a similar fashion in many different languages (see Scherer 1997, 2001a).

KLAUS R. SCHERER

Scherer, K.R. (1994). Toward a concept of 'modal emotions'. In: P. Ekman and R.J. Davidson (eds), *The nature of emotion: fundamental questions*, pp. 25–31. New York: Oxford University Press.

models (of emotion) see THEORIES AND MODELS (OF EMOTION).

mood Moods are affective reactions distinct from emotions. Emotions are usually considered responses to a distinct event. They are intentional states: they are 'about' some object or event (see INTENTIONALITY). 'Mood', by contrast, is the appropriate designation for affective states that are about nothing specific or about everything—about the world in general (Frijda 1993).

Mood is often defined as an affective state of long duration, low intensity, and a certain diffuseness. The longer duration is presupposed in current methods of mood measurement that employ questions like 'How did you feel over the last days?'. Emotions, however, can likewise last for a long time, such as apprehension

during prolonged threat. Low intensity is characteristic of fleeting affective responses without much overt reaction. However, some states that are generally considered moods can be very intense, as for instance depression and anxious restlessness.

'Diffuseness', however, does fit affective states that are not about a particular object or event. Even when a particular event has precipitated the mood—as when loss of a partner precipitates depressed mood—the state is not felt as 'about' that loss, even while knowing that it was the loss that caused it: 'Man delights me not, nor woman for that matter'. Nor does it specifically induce behaviour and thought related to that cause. Depressed mood, whatever its cause, tends to induce generalized listlessness, loss of initiative, and *apathy (Thayer 1989). Elated mood tends to establish fleeting contacts, interests, and initiatives, and renders the individual more sociable, friendly, and creative (Isen 2000). Moods render one susceptible to emotion arousal by a large range of events that match the mood's affective tone. In depressed mood, few events cause *joy and many events cause *sadness; in irritated mood, trifles cause *irritation.

Moods, therefore, appear to lower thresholds for mood-congruent event-elicited appraisals and emotions. Mood-consonant appraisals are facilitated; there is faster detection of mood-consonant events. These generalizations stem from clinical observations on depressed and elated patients, as well as from findings in normal subjects after experimental mood inductions. These various effects appear largely independent of awareness of mood (e.g. Bargh 1997). Moods are not necessarily tied to *feelings, when defined by the effects of mood inductions; the notion of nonconscious moods is not incoherent.

Cognitive mood effects

The last-mentioned aspects of moods are usually discussed as cognitive effects of moods (Forgas and Vargas 2004). There is evidence for a number of such effects. One of these is mood-consonant encoding facilitation. Others are mood-congruent recall, judgement biasing, and attentional selectivity (see ATTENTION AND EMOTION) (mood-congruent features are noticed more easily). There also is some evidence of mood-dependent processing: pleasant moods often lead to more superficial processing in precision tasks, and to more mental flexibility when there is opportunity for that (Isen 2000); unpleasant moods tend to lead to deeper processing (Forgas 1999) The underlying mechanisms are interpreted from two different viewpoints. In one view they result from affect priming (see PRIMING (AFFECTIVE)): mood serves as a cue that primes matching contents and not others. In the other view, mood serves as information used in solving decisions under uncertainty (the affect-as-information perspective; see AFFECT-AS-INFORMATION MODEL). Both interpretations are probably valid, and applicable to different situations.

The findings on most of these effects show major inconsistencies, though, and divergences between positive and negative mood effects. The inconsistencies are probably due to different processing strategies (Forgas and Vargas 2004), and to features of the cognitive situations. One of those features concerns the possibility for and desirability of mood-management processes that seek to maintain positive and attenuate unpleasant moods (see REGULATION OF EMOTION).

Mood determinants

Moods can be the after-effect of pleasant and unpleasant emotional events. Other mood changes are due to endogenous rhythms, to changes in organismic state such as fatigue and ill-health, and to biochemical influences, including alcohol and drugs (Thayer 1989). The overall sense of *well-being also influences mood, as it is in turn influenced by mood. Mood is significantly moderated by specific attributes of personality such as *extraversion and *neuroticism.

The variety of determinants of mood has led to functional interpretations. Mood is being interpreted as a 'resource index', a hedonic summary of the sensed relationship between momentary resources and past, present, and expected future *coping demands. Unpleasant mood results when demands have exceeded sensed resources, or are expected to do so; pleasant moods reflect the converse (Morris 1989).

NICO H. FRIJDA

Forgas. J.P. (ed.) (1999). *Feeling and thinking: the role of affect in social cognition.* Cambridge: Cambridge University Press.

Frijda, N.H. (1993). Moods, emotion episodes, and emotions. In: M. Lewis and J.M. Haviland (eds), *Handbook of emotions,* 1st edn, pp. 381–403. New York: Guilford Press.

mood disorders Whether ascribed to elemental (earth, air, fire, water), physiological (black bile, blood, yellow bile, phlegm), or astrological (Saturn, Jupiter, Sun, Moon) causes, the basic rendering of variations in emotional tone among humans is as old as history itself. Such descriptions capture and celebrate the fact that our lives are enriched by the diversity of emotions we experience, ranging from powerful surges of feeling to subtle, nuanced sensitivities, each of which may, in themselves, be pleasant, neutral, or aversive. This capacity allows us to respond to the demands of our surroundings and to feel that our lives are deep and vibrant. Yet, these same moods can be marked by an unrelenting intensity, a severity that impedes other mental functions and disrupts an individual's social and occupational investments. In this case, the consensus, at least within the

framework of psychiatric nosology, is of mood as the basis of a mental disorder, one, as it turns out that entails significant costs for both its sufferers and society as a whole (Wells *et al.* 1996) (see MOOD).

Close to a century ago, Emil Kraepelin's (1856–1926) observation of little overlap between the symptoms of manic-depressive illness and dementia praecox supported the view of mood disorders as a distinct diagnostic category. Within this category, change in the polarity of a patient's feeling states has permitted further discrimination. Episodes of lowered mood or *depression followed by a return to normal mood with recovery are diagnosed as a *unipolar mood disorder, whereas if a patient at any time experiences episodes of depression and mood elevation or mania, then they are suffering from a *bipolar mood disorder (Perris 1966).

Even within this bipartite approach, some patients experience chronic but relatively mild levels of depressive symptomatology. The protracted nature of dysthymic disorder or dysthymia can undermine many areas of the sufferer's life. Patients with episodic disorders may mobilize their adaptive capacities and try to cope with an acute depression, but as dysthymia drags on, the patient's coping responses may gradually wear down and subtle changes in personality may occur. In a similar vein, patients with cyclothymic disorder or cyclothymia, experience the symptoms of bipolar disorder in a less severe form. During periods of mild depression, patients often feel worthless, but when they are hypomanic their view of themselves is inflated (see HYPOMANIA). This type of shift between contrasting personality styles, combined with mood volatility, can have a negative impact on interpersonal relationships. Some may be drawn to the traits exhibited by the patient in the hypomanic phase, but find the person less appealing when his or her mood starts to drop, thereby eroding social support when it is most needed. Seasonal cycling of depressive episodes and the cluster of hyperphagia, hypersomnia, and leaden paralysis are other features that have defined mood disorder subtypes.

Rates of comorbidity in mood disorders are high, with the most frequent co-occurring disorder being anxiety (Kessler *et al.* 1998). As there is considerable symptom overlap between these two conditions—poor concentration, irritability, sleep difficulties, and worry—it is likely that *anxiety and depression share a common neurobiological substrate, although the actual basis for this is still unknown.

Selective serotonin reuptake inhibitors (SSRIs) are currently the first-line treatment for unipolar depression (Rush *et al.* 2006) while lithium and mood stabilizers such as valproic acid are used to treat acute manic and mixed episodes. Psychotherapies designed specifically to address the psychological impairments and challenges faced by patients with a mood disorder have been shown to be of equal efficacy to antidepressants (Hollon *et al.* 2005). The means of achieving effective prophylaxis for these chronic and recurrent conditions remains an enduring treatment challenge. In light of the high rates of relapse associated with treatment discontinuation, practice guidelines recommend extending treatment into and well beyond episode remission.

While genetic heritability is higher for bipolar than for unipolar disorder it is unlikely that a single gene for mood disorders will be located. Most researchers agree that a stress-diathesis formulation holds the greatest promise of modelling the presumed multifactorial origins of the problem. Of interest is the recent finding that a polymorphism in the gene encoding the serotonin transporter (5-HTTLPR) may moderate the relationship between stress and depression by altering the processing of negative affect (Jacobs *et al.* 2006) (see GENETICS OF AFFECT).

ZINDEL V. SEGAL

Klein, D., Shankman, S., and McFarland, B. (2006). Classification of mood disorders. In: D. Stein, D. Kupfer, and A. Schatzberg (eds), *Textbook of mood disorders*, pp. 171–232. Arlington, VA: American Psychiatric Publishing.

McGuffin, P., Rijsdijk, F., Andrew, M., Sham, P., Katz, R., and Cardno, A. (2003). The heritability of bipolar affective disorder and the genetic relationship to unipolar depression. *Archives of General Psychiatry*, **60**, 497–502.

Power, M.J. (ed.) (2004). *Mood disorders: a handbook of science and practice*. Chichester: John Wiley.

Segal, Z.V., Kennedy, S., Gemar, M., Hood, K., Pedersen, R., and Buis, T. (2006). Cognitive reactivity to sad mood provocation and the prediction of depressive relapse. *Archives of General Psychiatry*, **63**, 750–55.

moral development Despite the fact that numerous philosophers and psychologists have minimized the role of emotion in moral development, many theorists and researchers view emotion as an important correlate or causal agent in moral development and moral behaviour. Perhaps the most frequently discussed aspect of emotion in this literature is the role of *empathy-related responding and *guilt in moral behaviour, moral values (e.g. conscience), and sometimes moral reasoning. However, investigators have also argued that people's initial *gut emotional reactions, such as *disgust and revulsion, play an important role in guiding our evaluations of moral issues (Haidt 2001) (see MORAL EMOTIONS). In addition, *mood appears to influence whether or not people are helpful in many situations and *anger has been linked to behaviours that harm others. In this entry, research findings on empathy-related responding, guilt, mood states, and links of emotion to *aggression and externalizing problems is briefly summarized.

Empathy-related responding

Although definitions of empathy vary somewhat in subtle (and sometimes not so subtle) ways, *empathy* is sometimes defined as an affective response that stems from the apprehension or comprehension of another's emotional state or condition, and that is similar to what the other person is feeling or would be expected to feel in the given situation (Eisenberg *et al.* 2006b). Thus, if a person views someone else who is sad and consequently also feels sad, that person is experiencing empathy. True empathy is typically believed to involve at least minimal differentiation between *self and other and the recognition that the vicariously induced emotion is associated with another person, not the self.

Some theorists have argued that, especially after infancy, empathy is likely to lead to sympathy, personal distress, or perhaps both sequentially. *Sympathy* is an emotional response stemming from the apprehension of another's emotional state or condition that is not the same as the other's state or condition but consists of feelings of sorrow or concern for the other. In contrast, *personal distress* is a self-focused, aversive affective reaction to the apprehension of another's emotion (e.g. discomfort, anxiety; Batson 1991). Personal distress may often stem from empathic overarousal—that is, high levels of vicariously induced aversive emotion (see Eisenberg *et al.* 1996).

Relations of empathy-related responding to moral development

Empathy-related responding has been linked with a variety of aspects of moral development. For example, empathy, and especially sympathy, are believed to motivate altruistic behaviour—voluntary behaviour intended to benefit another that is motivated by relatively pure moral values or sympathy rather than self-gain or the desire for approval (see ALTRUISM (PSYCHOLOGICAL PERSPECTIVES)). Specifically, psychologists have argued that feelings of empathic concern or sympathy are associated with the desire to help the target of one's concern, whereas feelings of personal distress are associated with the desire to alleviate one's own distress. Thus, people experiencing personal distress are expected to help another person only if that is the easiest way to alleviate their own distress (e.g. when they cannot escape the situation; Batson 1991). In fact, research findings with both adults and children are consistent with the idea that higher levels of sympathy are associated with more helping or sharing behaviour, whereas more personal distress is negatively related or unrelated to such prosocial behaviour (Batson 1991, Eisenberg *et al.* 2006b).

Sympathy also appears to be related to the level of individuals' moral reasoning, at least when people reason about moral dilemmas in which one person's needs conflict with another. For example, when children are asked to reason about hypothetical situations in which a person can assist another but at a cost to the self (e.g. assist an injured peer rather than go to a birthday party), sympathetic children tend to orient more to the other person's needs and often use more mature reasoning (Eisenberg *et al.* 2006b). Sympathy may help people to access cognitions related to others' welfare; it also has been argued that children who are prone to sympathy are more likely to be concerned with others' needs and justice and, hence, develop more mature moral reasoning (Hoffman 2000).

Individual differences in empathy and sympathy also are associated with relatively low levels of aggression in both children and adults (Miller and Eisenberg 1988, Eisenberg *et al.* 2006b). If a person experiences a second individual's distress or pain, the former may often find it difficult to cause pain or harm to the latter. Indeed, a lack of empathy and sympathy appears to be a defining characteristic of *psychopaths. Such individuals seem to have some difficulty identifying the emotions of others and are relatively unlikely to experience either empathy or sympathy for others (Blair *et al.* 2001).

Relations of empathy-related responding with emotion and emotion-relevant self-regulation

Empathy/sympathy tends to be associated with the dispositional differences in the tendency to experience emotions such as *sadness, but is negatively related to emotions such as *anger (Rothbart *et al.* 1994, Eisenberg *et al.* 2006b). In addition, there is some evidence that whether children experience empathy is associated with emotion-related self-regulation; moreover, self-regulation and emotionality may jointly predict sympathy. Unregulated children are low in sympathy regardless of their level of emotional intensity, whereas for moderately and highly regulated children the level of sympathy increases with the level of emotional intensity (Eisenberg *et al.* 1996). Well-regulated children seem able to modulate their vicarious arousal and therefore focus their attention on the emotions and needs of others rather than on their own aversive vicarious emotion (Eisenberg *et al.* 2006b). In contrast, individuals who are prone to frequent negative emotions tend to be especially prone to personal distress, as are individuals who are relatively unregulated (Eisenberg *et al.* 1994a, 2006b).

Guilt and shame

Guilt has been defined in a variety of ways. In developmental and social psychology, guilt often refers to regret over wrongdoing. The guilty actor tends to accept responsibility for behaviour that violates internalized standards or causes another's distress and desires to make amend or punish the self (Tangney 1991).

Sometimes *shame has been differentiated from guilt. Shame is generally viewed as a more helpless, severe emotion that involves the dejection of the entire self, self-consciousness, the experience of the self as fundamentally flawed, and causes one to want to avoid others (Ferguson and Stegge 1998). When a person experiences shame, the entire self feels exposed, inferior, and degraded; guilt is generally less painful than shame, and the primary concern is with a particular behaviour, somewhat distinct from the self (Ferguson *et al.* 1991, Tangney 1998). Guilt is generally seen as involving feelings of tension, remorse, and regret, but not as affecting one's core identity, as does shame. Thus, guilt is more important than shame as a moral motive.

Adults report that shame and guilt both involve a sense of responsibility and the feeling that one has violated a moral standard. However, probably because guilt is focused on the transgression than on the self, guilt appears to motivate restitution, confession, and apologizing rather than avoidance and is associated with empathy or sympathy for others (Tangney 1991, 1998). Moreover, there is some evidence that shame is more consistently and highly correlated than is guilt with externalizing problems, including aggression. Similar results have been obtained for children in some studies, although even shame-free guilt has been associated with externalizing problem for girls (see Eisenberg, 2000, and Tangney, 1998, for reviews).

There is some evidence that individuals high in guilt are actually better at perspective taking compared with individuals high in shame (Leith and Baumeister 1998). Unlike empathy, when experiencing guilt an individual does not have to experience the same emotion as the other person—the individual must merely perceive him/herself as having caused distress in someone else. Nonetheless, empathy may often be the basis of guilt in that it alerts children to the effects of their behaviour on others (Hoffman 2000).

Guilt and shame have been linked to fear, hostility, anxiety, and sadness in adulthood. However, some researchers have found that guilt is less associated with various negative emotions than is shame (see Eisenberg, 2000, for a review). Thus, shame may be more closely linked to temperament or personality than is guilt.

As already discussed, guilt is closely associated with empathy and perspective taking (Hoffman 2000) and empathy and guilt often co-occur (Tangney 1991). In young children, empathic distress (e.g. sadness and various indicators of bodily distress when someone is hurt) and guilt form one component of conscience, with rule-compatible behaviour being a second, related aspect of conscience (Aksan and Kochanska 2005). Moreover, relatively young fearful children are prone to develop a conscience (e.g. Kochanska 1997), probably because they are more sensitive to negative evaluations and to socialization pressures.

Moods

Research on moods has typically focused on the effects of mood across individuals rather than on individual differences in the effects of mood. Moreover, in the moral domain, mood has most often been studied in relation to *prosocial behaviour. In general, researchers have found that people in a positive mood are relatively likely to offer help. Findings support the view that people in positive moods often help to maintain their positive mood, although other processes may also contribute to this pattern of association (see Carlson et al. 1988). In contrast, people in a negative mood are sometimes more prone to help, and sometimes not. In a meta-analytic review, Carlson and Miller (1987) found an association between negative emotion and helping, which varied as a function of the degree to which attention was focused on the self versus others (people help more when attention is focused on the self), with helpers' feelings of responsibility for the mood-lowering event, and with a high level of objective self-awareness (i.e. the focusing of attention on the self as an object). Although it has been argued that people (including older children) often help when they are in a sad mood to make themselves feel better, support for this argument is mixed.

Externalizing/aggression and directly experienced emotions

In addition to empathy-related responding, directly experienced emotions have been related to aggression and externalizing problems. For example, anger/frustration has frequently been associated with externalizing problems such as aggression and other problem behaviours (Arsenio et al. 2006). In addition, proneness to anger in childhood has been correlated with aggression in the preschool or early school years (e.g. Rothbart et al. 1994, Frick and Morris 2004), and individual differences in typical intensity of anger reactions have been related to the degree to which young children's reactions to anger are constructive rather than hurtful (Eisenberg et al. 1994b). Moreover, self-reported anger among high-school seniors predicts delinquency nine months later, even controlling for earlier levels of delinquency (Colder and Stice 1998), whereas frustration in the workplace is associated with adults' antisocial behaviour (Spector 1997). Moreover, among younger children, there is some evidence that aggression is associated with happiness—that victimizers often feel happiness following successful victimization of others (Arsenio et al. 2006).

In contrast, some emotions other than anger are negatively related to aggression. Children prone to anxiety and fear or negative emotionality, as reflected in

cortisol (physiological responding), tend in novel contexts to be low in aggression (see Eisenberg 2000). Negative emotions such as fear or anxiety may serve to inhibit externalizing behaviour because individuals prone to these emotions are less likely to find the stimulation and emotion associated with externalizing behaviour pleasurable and are likely to experience more negative emotion (anxiety, guilt, and perhaps empathy) than other people when they engage in problem behaviour.

Summary

Both directly and vicariously experienced emotions have been linked to a range of moral behaviours, sometimes positively and sometimes negatively. For example, morally relevant emotions such as empathy and sympathy tend to be positively associated with moral reactions, whereas anger and personal distress are sometimes associated with low levels of moral responding. There are also associations between individual differences in dispositional emotionality and the tendency for individuals to experience morally relevant emotions. Finally, individual differences in, as well as the experience of, emotions such as anger and anxiety tend to be related to morally relevant behaviours such as aggression.

NANCY EISENBERG

Eisenberg, N. (2000). Emotion, regulation, and moral development. *Annual Review of Psychology*, 51, 665–97.

Tangney, J.P. and Dearing, R.L. (2002). *Shame and guilt*. New York: Guilford Press.

moral emotions Emotions are said to be moral, as opposed to nonmoral, by virtue of their objects. They are also said to be moral, for example morally good, as opposed to immoral, for example morally bad or evil, by virtue of their objects, nature, motives, functions, or effects. The definition and content of moral matters is even more contested and contestable than the nature of emotions and of other affective phenomena. At the very least we should distinguish moral *norms (one ought to keep one's promises, one ought not to tell lies), moral obligations (to look after one's aged parents), moral right and wrong (murder), moral *values (goodness, evil), and moral virtues (courage). And different accounts of morals and of morality understand norms, values, and virtues and their interrelations in different ways. For example, such accounts disagree (1) about the relation between moral and nonmoral oughts (the norms of prudence and rationality), the relation between moral and nonmoral values (cognitive and aesthetic values, the values of *pleasure and *well-being, vital values such as health), and the relation between moral and intellectual virtues (accuracy, open-mindedness); and (2) about the moral weight to be attached to self-regarding attitudes and behaviour (see SELF) (egoism, egotism, self-love, self-respect, *self-esteem, amour propre) and other-regarding attitudes and behaviour (*altruism, *empathy, sympathy, intolerance). Thus we may expect the range of putative moral emotions to display a bewildering variety.

Are there emotions which are moral, as opposed to nonmoral, simply by virtue of the nature of their objects? The question is ambiguous. It may be understood as a question about *types of emotions* or about *instances* of types of emotions.

Is there an emotion every instance of which is moral by virtue of its object? A favourite candidate is *guilt feelings. The object of a feeling of guilt is some action of the agent which he or she takes to involve an infringement of some moral ought or obligation, an action which may simply be an omission, a failure to do the right thing. But are guilt-feelings really emotions (Ortony 1987)? Unlike emotional episodes of shame, pride, and remorse they are often long-lasting. Guilt weighs on one, it is a burden. *Shame, *pride, and remorse may recur regularly (in the shame-, pride-, or remorse-prone) but do they last like guilt? Guilt, once triggered, is an enduring affective state. But if enduring affective states are merely dispositions and emotions are either episodes or dispositions, then guilt feelings are indeed moral emotions. They are also, it may be thought, morally valuable: someone who is incapable of guilt feelings is morally defective. On the other hand, novelists such as Fyodor Dostoevsky (1821–81) and Sigmund Freud (1856–1939) and Martin Heidegger (1889–1976) report guilt feelings which have objects quite different from infringements of moral norms or which have no objects at all.

Instances of many types of emotions have as their objects moral features of people, actions, and situations. Lies, corruption, or betrayal may trigger moral disgust. One may hope that one will do one's duty. Indignation or resentment may be triggered by the injustice of an action or of a situation; shame by the sudden realization that one has failed to live up to some moral ideal. One may take pride in one's moral goodness or virtue. Although such indignation, shame, and pride are reactions to (what seem to be) moral properties and are therefore moral (as opposed to nonmoral) emotions, one may think that whereas the indignation and shame described are morally valuable or morally indifferent, pride in or admiration of one's moral goodness or moral excellence is immoral, a bad thing, or evil. (In some languages there is a clear distinction between morally bad prides and a pride which is not morally bad and may be, for one reason or another, morally positive: 'orgueil' versus 'fierté', 'Hochmut' versus 'Stolz'; Kristjánsson 2006). In some traditions affective pro-attitudes towards one's moral goodness or excel-

lence count as pharisaical. The Pharisee is a man who not only admires his own generosity or political commitments but admires these because they are morally good. He admires what he takes to be his moral superiority and glows with self-righteousness (Ranulf 1938).

The distinction between instances of an emotion which are moral and instances which are nonmoral is closely related to the distinction between the natural and nonnatural instances of a kind of emotion, for example between natural shame (the shame of the woman who does not have red hair) and moral shame (Rawls 1971). The latter distinction is in its turn closely related to the traditional distinction between virtues which are natural (benevolence) and artificial (justice).

One important difference between the objects of shame and of guilt indicates a possible difference between the moral scope of these emotions. Shame and guilt, like pride and remorse, are always *self-reflexive emotions. The object of shame and of guilt is always a self and something else—a failure to live up to or to exemplify some ideal or value of a subject in the case of shame, the infringement of a norm by the subject in the case of guilt. But the self does not play the same role in shame and in guilt. The exclamation or question of the guilty woman is 'How could I have done *that*?'. The exclamation or question of the ashamed man is 'How could *I* have done that, had those feelings or beliefs, have been a such and such?'. The primary object of guilt is the infringement of a norm, that of shame a self. The secondary object of guilt is the self, of shame some feature or action of a self and one of its values, moral or nonmoral (Taylor 1985; Tangney *et al.* 2007).

Guilt-feelings are morally valuable, it is sometimes claimed, because they are essential to being a morally autonomous person: consider one difference between shame, according to a very old and popular view, and guilt. Shame, it is argued, whether its object is a moral or a nonmoral failing, is typically, centrally, or essentially triggered by the presence of a real or imagined observer or judge. Since shame is social it is not the reaction of a morally autonomous person. (It is also argued by psychologists that differences between the effects of shame and the effects of guilt show that shame, in contrast to guilt, hinders moral development.) Against this it has been argued that moral matters are basically social matters and that the moral significance of guilt is not greater than that of shame, the object of which is moral failings. A very different objection simply denies that shame is essentially social: there is shame before oneself and shame before others. A stronger version of this objection adds that shame before oneself with respect to one's moral failings is just the sort of reaction which characterizes a morally autonomous person (Rawls 1971, Williams 1993, Wollheim 1999).

moral emotions

So far we have considered the relation between moral emotions, on the one hand, and values and norms, on the other. What is the relation between moral emotions and virtues and vices? On most accounts of virtues and vices, emotions and other affective phenomena are essential to them. Virtues and vices are habits. It is therefore not surprising that it is emotional dispositions, sentiments, and the will rather than emotional episodes which go to make up vices and virtues. Perhaps the single most important feature of these dispositions and sentiments is that they are the motives out of (or from) which the vicious or virtuous person acts. Sometimes they are referred to indirectly: the 'feelings of benevolence' of someone who has the virtue of benevolence (Zagzebski 1996, pp. 77–136). Sometimes they can be directly characterized as features or qualities of a person's loves, hates, preferences, and will: kindness, tenderness, affection, vindictiveness, vengefulness, distrustfulness, trustfulness, gratitude. Sometimes they are said to contribute to a person's character, sometimes they are held to be more fundamental than mere character traits (Goldie 2004). Thus a person who has the virtue of justice acts out of a concern for fairness, and this concern underlies the disposition to feel indignation when confronted with examples of injustice. If this sort of claim is correct, then the emotional dispositions and sentiments which help to constitute moral virtues such as courage and justice are morally valuable and the affective components of moral vices such as cowardice and injustice are morally bad.

Many sentiments and emotions are often held to be (at least prima facie) morally valuable in virtue of their nature—for example, respect, remorse, *love, and *joy. In some but by no means all moral traditions, pity and compassion would belong here too. Similarly, envy and *ressentiment* (sour grapes) are often held to be morally speaking a bad thing, like our earlier example of pharisaical pride or self-admiration. But there is a view of morality which denies that emotions and sentiments are morally valuable or significant. According to this 'deontological' view, the heart of morality is the rightness and wrongness of actions, our obligations, and what we ought and ought not to do. Actions are subject to the will. They are what we are responsible for. Emotions and sentiments are only indirectly subject to the will. So emotions and sentiments are not morally significant although they may be moral by virtue of their objects. Another consequence of the deontological conception of morality is that values and virtues, whether moral or not, are not central to morality (Strawson 1974, Oakley 1992, Wallace 1994, Haidt 2003, Nichols 2004).

One reaction to such views is to: (1) distinguish between matters ethical and matters moral; (2) assign moral obligations, norms, duties, and, for example, guilt, remorse, and resentment to the latter category and values, virtues, and, for example, shame, love, and hate to the former; and (3) argue for the priority of what belongs to ethics. Versions of this reaction are to be found in the writings of three anti-Kantians—Max Scheler (1874–1938), the Austrian novelist Robert Musil (1880–1942), and Bernard Williams (1993). Perhaps the simplest sort of argument in favour of the priority of values is to be found in those utilitarian and consequentialist philosophies which argue that what makes an action morally right or wrong is just the consequences it has for the realization of the values of human well-being, welfare, or happiness. This claim can be considered a special case of a more general type of claim which involves no endorsement of utilitarianism or consequentialism: what makes actions morally binding is their relation to values, not just the values of happiness and of the useful but vital, aesthetic, political, cognitive, and other values; what makes a preference ethically valuable or good is that it is a preference for higher over lower nonethical values (Scheler 1973).

Two influential 18th century candidates for the role of what were then called moral sentiments are certain types of (dis)approval and of respect or reverence. Adam Smith (1723–90) argued that there are different sentiments or feelings of moral approval the objects of which are character, action, and virtue. Amongst the sources of moral approval are sympathy, gratitude, the impression that the approved behaviour is part of a system of behaviour which tends to promote happiness, and an impression of the beauty of this utility (Smith 1982/1759, VII. iii. 3 326–7). Such approval, then, is moral and aesthetic in virtue of its objects and is also morally good or a moral good.

David Hume (1711–76) at one point says that 'the proper *guardian* of every kind of virtue, and a sure preservative against vice and corruption' is one type of modesty, 'that tenderness and nicety of honour, that apprehension of blame, that dread of intrusion or injury towards others', which he also calls 'Pudor' (Hume 1970, p. 213; my emphases). The Latin word 'pudor' is one possible translation of the Greek term 'aidôs'; another is 'sense of shame', yet another is 'reverence'. And Hume goes on to say that: '(The) constant habit of surveying ourselves, as it were, in reflection, keeps alive all the sentiments of right and wrong, and begets, in noble natures, a certain *reverence* for themselves as well as others, which is the surest *guardian* of every virtue' (Hume 1970, p. 225; my emphases).

Reverence of this kind is a moral sentiment and *'pudor'* a moral sentiment or affective disposition. Both can motivate. Their objects are others, their opinions about us and ourselves: 'our regard to a character with others seems to arise only from a care of preserving a character with ourselves; and in order to attain this end, we find it necessary to prop our tottering judgement on the correspondent approbation of mankind' (Hume 1970, p. 225). Reverence and 'pudor' are moral sentiments by virtue of their objects, which include virtues and vices, and morally valuable by virtue of their functions.

According to Immanuel Kant (1724–1804) there is exactly one moral emotion or feeling (*Gefühl*): respect (*Achtung*), which Kant sometimes seems to regard as the same as reverence (*Ehrfurcht*), the object of which is the moral law. Of this emotion Kant says that it can motivate us, that every good ethical (*sittlich*) disposition or sentiment (*Gesinnung*) can be grafted on to it and that it functions as a *guardian* (Kant 1986, I.3. pp. 127, 130, 252–4). It is therefore moral by virtue of its object and morally valuable in itself and by virtue of its function.

Hume's reverence bears on moral *virtues*, Kant's reverence or respect on moral *oughts*. There is thus a third possible view: self-reverence, self-respect, and care for oneself (*cura sui*) bear on one's *individual values* or on what one takes or makes these to be. This sort of view has been eagerly embraced ever since the 19th century, for example by Friedrich Nietzsche (1844–1900), personalist philosophers such as Scheler and John McTaggart (1866–1925) and psychologists such as C. H. Cooley (1864–1929) (Rawls 1971, Roland and Foxx 2003). Self-reverence and self-respect presumably should not involve taking oneself to be morally good or valuable, for then they would be pharisaical. Similarly, the self-love which is often put forward as a fundamental ethical sentiment along with self-reverence by supporters of the latter should not have as its object any actual valuable feature of the self-lover, for then it would merely be amour propre, self-esteem, or self-admiration. Self-reverence and self-love so conceived bear on the individual values or 'better self' which constitute what one really is and may, with luck, become.

KEVIN MULLIGAN

Haidt, J. (2003). The moral emotions. In: R.J. Davidson, K.R. Scherer, and H.H. Goldsmith (eds), *Handbook of affective sciences*, pp. 852–70. New York: Oxford University Press.

Nichols, S. (2004). *Sentimental rules*. Oxford: Oxford University Press.

de Sousa, R. (2001). Moral emotions. *Ethical Theory and Moral Practice*, **4**, 109–26.

Tangney, J.P., Stuewig, J., and Mashek, D.J. (2007). Moral emotions and moral behavior. *Annual Review of Psychology*, **58**, 345–72.

motivation If one were to choose a single term for what is meant by motivation, it would be the verb 'to want'. This one term captures in everyday language a wide variety of relevant meanings: to have or feel need of; to be necessary (require); to wish or demand the presence of; to desire to come, go, or be; to have a strong desire for or inclination to (like); to fail to possess (lack); to hunt or seek in order to seize (see NEEDS). The study of motivation is concerned with *the nature and functions of wanting and their relation to knowing and doing*. Wanting is not only a process but also a structure within which a vast gamut of experiences unfolds. Different kinds of wants involve different kinds of experience (e.g. hunger versus thirst versus belonging). Different experiences accompany trying to get what one wants (e.g. easy versus difficult; eagerness versus vigilance). Getting or not getting what one wants produces different emotions (e.g. happy versus sad; relaxed versus tense). Motivation is concerned not only with behaviour but also with personal experiences, with the experiences of pleasures and pains that underlie the quality of life (see Kahneman *et al.* 1999) (see LIFE SATISFACTION). The study of motivation extends not only across the various areas of psychology, such as social–personality, abnormal–clinical, developmental, organizational, animal learning, and physiological, but also beyond psychology to other disciplines encompassing law, business, education, and health. Three classic questions in motivation are: What are the basic wants? How does wanting bridge the gap between knowing and doing? How do actors get what they want? Answers to each of these questions will be considered in turn.

A science of wanting must consider whether there are basic wants and, if so, what they are. This can be a daunting task. When wants were conceptualized as instincts, some theorists described a small number of basic wants, such as Freud's (1915/1957) life and death instincts, whereas others proposed a very large number of instincts. Because instincts could be postulated as propelling each specific end state, there were only weak constraints on how many could be postulated. The original concept of drive (Woodworth 1918) provided greater constraints by relating basic wants to basic physiological deficits. However, this physiological equilibrium notion of drive is too constraining. Although all basic wants have some biological underpinnings, these underpinnings need not be directly related to physiological disequilibria. Moreover, it is possible to consider basic wants in relation to general survival without postulating specific physiological substrates.

Not surprisingly, basic survival wants that relate to getting along in the social world have received special attention. There is a basic human need to form and maintain strong and stable interpersonal relationships (see Baumeister and Leary 1995). In an undifferentiated social environment that provides few guidelines for action, there is a motivation for intergroup categorization that can provide order and coherence to the social situation (see Tajfel *et al.* 1971). Consistent with *Gestalt notions of 'good form' or 'good fit', there is a basic human need for coherence among beliefs, feelings, and actions, for a social world that makes sense (Festinger 1957).

An important general question is: Are there distinctly *human* motives, and, if so, what are they? More than anyone else, Darwin (1809–82) had a revolutionary effect on scientists' approach to answering these questions. If humans *evolved* from other animals, would it not make sense to use the motives of nonhuman animals to discover the motives of the human animal (see EVOLUTION OF EMOTION)? If sex, aggression, hunger, and thirst are basic motives in other animals, then they are likely to be basic motives in humans. If instincts or drives underlie the behaviours of animals, then they are likely to underlie human behaviour as well. If the pleasure principle is the central motivational concept for explaining animal behaviour, then it should be central when explaining human behaviour as well. This is not the only implication of Darwin's work, however. Evolution means 'develop from' as well as 'derive from'. What distinguishes humans from other animals is their social consciousness—their awareness that it is the inner states of people, i.e. their feelings, hopes, expectations, *beliefs, *goals, and so on, that determine how they respond to one another. People want to understand what other people are feeling and thinking. They want to manage how other people feel and think about things, and especially how others feel and think about them and the groups to which they belong. They want to share with others their feelings and thoughts about the world, and especially the social world. Humans are distinct in these motives to comprehend, manage, and share inner states (Higgins and Pittman 2008).

Another basic question in motivation has been whether it is just a by-product of cognition. Edward Tolman's (1886–1959) influential expectancy theory was criticized as leaving actors 'lost in thought'. What is it about motivation that is different from cognition but works together with cognition? Given that the root of the term 'motivation' is 'to move', it is not surprising that a classic way of thinking about motivation has been in terms of *approach/avoidance* (see APPROACH/WITHDRAWAL) as found in theories of regulatory anticipation that concern expectancies of pleasant versus painful outcomes (e.g. Atkinson 1964), theories of regulatory reference that concern desired end states versus undesired end states as the reference point for self-regulation (e.g. Carver and Scheier 1990), and in regulatory focus theory that concerns approach and avoidance as strategic means for goal attainment (see Higgins 1997). The reason that actors are not left 'lost in thought' is because they have needs and goals; they take action because there is something they want to approach or want to avoid.

But what is the nature of the bridge that wants provide between knowing and doing? One approach to bridging the gap between knowing and doing is to reconsider the nature of knowing itself. James (1890) stated: 'Primarily then, and fundamentally, the mental life is for the sake of action of a preservative sort' (p. 4). The first step, then, in bridging the gap between knowing and doing is to recognize that individuals' mental life has fundamental survival value through its contribution to adaptive action. Social category knowledge can be understood as serving social interaction goals, such as allowing for rapid responses (see Fiske 1992). The second step is to recognize that the motivated nature of cognition is intertwined with its social functions. When people enter into association with others their mental life is transformed, which in turn transforms their associations with others. People do not learn how the world works all on their own. They learn in association with others. Such learning is shared with others and the shared reality aspect of the knowledge is one of its critical properties. It is critical that people learn what matters to others about some activity or object. Children are motivated to learn how their appearance and behaviours influence caretakers' responses to them in order to increase the likelihood that the caretakers will provide them the nurturance and security they need to survive (see Bowlby 1969). From this functional perspective, people learn what they need to know to make the world work for them. The gap between knowing and doing is bridged by connecting knowing to wanting.

A different way to bridge the gap between knowing and doing is to link knowing what you are doing to the means and ends of goal attainment. Roger Brown (1958), for example, proposed that people name objects and events, such as calling a dime 'money', 'a coin', or 'a dime', at whatever level of categorization is most useful for a current objective. It should also be noted that the relation between knowing and doing need not involve the kinds of controlled, effortful processing discussed thus far. Knowing can translate into action in more automatic ways as well. Beliefs and encodings can be affectively laden so that they are themselves 'hot' cognitions (see HOT COGNITION) (see Metcalfe and Mischel 1999). These 'hot' cognitions can be activated preconsciously and effortlessly (see Bargh 1996). *Attitudes also function as a bridge between knowing and action. By knowing that one likes or dislikes some object, one is motivated to approach or avoid it; attitudes can be used to make action decisions with less effort than conscious reasoning (see Fazio 1990).

Finally, how *do* actors get what they want? Although habits can bridge the gap from cognition to action (see

Bargh 1996), the bridge from cognition to action usually involves activating specific wants where the action to be taken is *not* specified. The bridge says *what* is wanted but not *how* to get it. The most general answer to the 'How?' question is that people approach pleasant end states and avoid painful end states. It is not enough, however, to want to approach or avoid something (Higgins 1997). It is also necessary to monitor or evaluate where one is in relation to where one wants to be. For desired end states, the monitoring system provides feedback about whether there is a need to reduce any perceived discrepancy. For undesired end states, the monitoring system provides feedback about whether there is a need to amplify any perceived discrepancy (Carver and Scheier 1990).

Another question concerns how an *intention* to do something effectively produces the intended action. People can intend to lose weight by eating only healthy food and then nibble candy bars all day. What strategies underlie effective self-control? Effective tactics include distracting oneself by thinking about other things, or symbolically transforming the alternative in ways that make it less tempting (see Metcalfe and Mischel 1999). People need strategies not only for self-control but also to assign sufficient resources to a task and proceed smoothly with its execution. Effective action requires appropriate mind-sets at the different phases (see Gollwitzer 1996). For example, a deliberative mind-set is most appropriate in the predecisional phase in which potential goals are considered and a decision to pursue one of them is made, whereas an implemental mind-set is most appropriate for the postdecisional–pre-actional phase in which the execution of goal-directed actions is planned and strategic alternatives for goal attainment are selected.

The process of mobilizing effort itself involves strategic decisions. For example, it is important to mobilize no more and no less *effort (or motivational energy) than is required by the difficulty of the task (e.g. Brehm and Self 1989). Positive illusions about how much control one has in life can serve the function of mobilizing effort and maintain effort in the face of setbacks (see Taylor and Brown 1988). There are also general strategic preferences for how to attain desired end states (Higgins 1997). When individuals have a promotion focus on accomplishment or advancement, they are eager to act in ways that facilitate goal attainment. When they have a prevention focus on safety or responsibility, they are vigilant to act in ways that avoid goal impairment. What has become increasingly clear is that humans and other animals are not motivated simply by outcomes, simply to approach pleasure and avoid pain. They are also motivated by *how* they

approach pleasure and *how* they avoid pain. Indeed, people will forsake better outcomes for the sake of their preferred ways of getting what they want, and offering outcome incentives to engage in some activity can even undermine people's interest in that activity because it changes the manner of their engagement (Deci and Ryan 1985, Higgins 1997).

E. TORY HIGGINS

motivational aspects of emotion see ACHIEVEMENT MOTIVATION; ACTION READINESS; ACTION TENDENCIES; AFFILIATION; AGGRESSION (PSYCHOLOGICAL PERSPECTIVES); ANHEDONIA; APPETITIVE MOTIVATIONAL SYSTEM; BEHAVIOURAL ACTIVATION SYSTEM; BEHAVIOURAL INHIBITION SYSTEM; CONCERNS; DELAY OF GRATIFICATION; DESIRE; FRUSTRATION; GOALS; MOTIVATION; MOTIVE CONSISTENCY; NEEDS.

motive consistency Motive consistency (also referred to as *goal/need conduciveness* or *perceived obstacle* in the appraisal literature) is a central appraisal dimension reflecting whether a stimulus event is unwanted or wanted by the person, taking into account the current goal/need state of the individual (Roseman, 1984) (see APPRAISAL THEORIES). The motive consistency appraisal evaluates to what extent the current stimulus event is perceived as conducive or obstructive to the motivational concerns of the individual (see MOTIVATION). Motive consistency thus indexes the adaptive value of a stimulus for an organism in a given situational state. Linking needs to behaviour, stimuli appraised as motive consistent bring about approach behaviour in order to get more of the stimulus and to maximize benefits, whereas motive-inconsistent stimuli generate avoidance behaviour in order to get less of the stimulus and thus to minimize harm.

Many psychological theories suggest that organisms have hierarchies of very disparate types of motivational concerns that they try to satisfy. Empirical data from a cross-cultural study of emotional experience revealed three major types of motives or concerns (Scherer 1986b): person concerns (survival, bodily integrity, fulfilment of basic needs, *self-esteem), relationship concerns (establishment, continued existence and intactness of relationships, cohesiveness within social groups), and social order concerns (sense of orderliness, predictability in the social environment including phenomena such as *fairness and appropriateness). To conceptually cover the whole range of motivational concerns, it seems useful to distinguish between *needs, motivation, *goals, and plans, even though such a distinction is rarely explicitly made in the motivation literature (Austin and Vancouver 1996). *Needs*, be they basic or acquired, reflect a deficiency that requires replenishment in order to restore homeostasis, for example food deprivation. This need state triggers *motivation*, which energizes the organism's behaviour toward restoring a state of homeostasis. For the present example, motivation refers to the urge to exit the hunger state. Needs or extrinsic states of motivation can lead to the formation of a *goal*, the internal representation of a desired end state, in this case finding something to eat. A goal can be transformed into a concrete *plan*, the reflected intention of how to implement the goal to reach the desired outcome and satisfy the need (in the example developed here, going to the kitchen and foraging in the fridge).

The motive consistency appraisal has been proposed to differentiate positive from negative emotions (Roseman 1984). Other appraisal theorists suggest a further differentiation, separating appraisals of the *intrinsic pleasantness* of a stimulus, referring to the general hedonic tone of the stimulus, and appraisals of the *goal/need conduciveness* (Scherer 2001a) or the *perceived obstacle* of a stimulus to the current purposes (Smith and Ellsworth 1985). Both appraisals can lead to positively or negatively valenced evaluations (see VALENCE): in the case of goal/need conducive stimuli or stimuli low in perceived obstacle, positive feelings can result when a goal has been reached or goal attainment furthered, whereas intrinsically pleasant stimuli may generate positive feelings in the organism due to their general hedonic tone, independent of the current goal state of the organism. The difference between the two appraisal dimensions becomes more obvious in cases where an intrinsically pleasant stimulus blocks goal achievement in a particular situation and thus generates negative feelings (like a beautiful summer's day when a conference paper is due).

TOBIAS BROSCH

multimodal expression of emotion While the fact that humans use many different modalities of expression to express emotions and attitudes, often in highly coherent packages of facial, vocal, and bodily features that are inextricably intertwined, has been widely acknowledged (Argyle 1988, Scherer and Ekman 2005), most empirical research has been conducted on specific modalities such as facial and vocal expression (see EXPRESSION, PRINCIPLES OF EMOTIONAL; FACIAL EXPRESSION OF EMOTION; VOCAL EXPRESSION OF EMOTION; BODILY EXPRESSION OF EMOTION; GESTURAL EXPRESSION OF EMOTION). Recently, multimodality has gained popularity as a key issue for understanding emotional communication, in both recognition (decoding) and production (encoding) processes, especially in the context of efforts to construct emotionally competent virtual agents (see ENCODING/DECODING (OF EXPRESSION); AFFECTIVE COMPUTING).

Recognition studies (*decoding*) have demonstrated that many emotions can be recognized with a better-than-chance accuracy in each of the different modalities of communication alone, although recognition rates differ between them (facial expression studies generally yield higher accuracy rates, e.g. Hess *et al.* 1998; see overview in Scherer *et al.*, 2003, p. 444). Nevertheless, when several expressive channels are available, observers seem to base their judgements of the sender's affective states on all of these, and there is no single channel which consistently prevails over the others (Ekman *et al.* 1980). Several studies have suggested the existence of an integration of cues from different modalities in emotion recognition whenever multiple modalities are available (de Gelder and Vroomen 2000a, Van den Stock *et al.* 2007). According to these authors, observers are somehow compelled to use multimodal information. This aspect is important because it stresses that emotional perception is multimodal in itself. In addition, evidence from neuroscience research is increasingly supporting the notion of multisensory integration in emotional perception, and specific cortical regions as well as subcortical structures are under investigation as areas potentially responsible of this integrative process (de Gelder and Bertelson 2003).

Multimodal *encoding* of emotions is studied much more infrequently than decoding—essentially because of the considerable time and effort required as well as sizable methodological difficulties—but the multimodal integration process assumed to underlie recognition seems to be present at the production or encoding stage as well (Siegman and Feldstein 1985). According to Scherer (2001a) the appraisal process at the basis of the emotional experience triggers multimodal efferent patterns of features in the service of adaptive action and communication strategies (see COMPONENT PROCESS MODEL). Vocal, facial, and bodily cues are used in a coordinated and synchronized fashion during an emotional experience driven by the outcomes of the ongoing, recursive appraisal process (see SYNCHRONIZATION).

The degree of synchronization and congruency among modalities is the result of the joint effects of *push and pull effects. Multimodal synchronization can be expected to be especially pronounced when the expression is the result of purely physiologically driven push effects, as in the cases of *affect bursts and *laughter. In these cases there is a gradual onset of expression as efferent effects of appraisal sequentially cumulate across different modalities and synchronize the changes. In contrast, multimodal synchronization is least pronounced when the expression is the result of pure pull effects, so that highly conventional displays are shown and different aspects of the expression need to be produced by deliberate motor commands. In these cases information is essentially multimodal, but each modality is controlled independently, consciously regulated, and often somewhat uncoordinated.

Most emotional experience falls between these two extremes, showing various degrees of synchronization and differential use of the different modalities. Empirical evidence is rare, but the results available so far confirm the existence of multimodal patterns. However, these do not seem to be specific to discrete or basic emotions, but rather tied to appraisal-generated information search and *action tendencies (Scherer and Ellgring 2007b).

Adopting a multimodal perspective thus does not imply the need to combine expressive channels in an additive fashion, but rather to examine emotional expression as an integrated, coherent process that is manifested in several modalities at the same time, and of which the total meaning can—at least in some cases—be inferred only when cues of different modalities are simultaneously present (for example, a prototypical expression of pride consists of both facial and bodily features, with both single-modality cues necessary but not sufficient condition for recognition; Tracy and Robins 2004). One of the major challenges for future expression research is to find the underlying driving mechanism; looking at synchronized multimodal expressions adds to the complexity but greatly increases the chances of understanding what expression expresses.

MARCELLO MORTILLARO
AND KLAUS R. SCHERER

Scherer, K.R. and Ekman, P. (2005). Methodological issues in studying nonverbal behavior. In: J.A. Harrigan, R. Rosenthal, and K.R. Scherer (eds), *The new handbook of methods in nonverbal behavior research*, pp. 471–512. New York: Oxford University Press.

Siegman, A.W. and Feldstein, S. (eds) (1985). *Multichannel integrations of nonverbal behavior*. Hillsdale, NJ: Lawrence Erlbaum Associates.

music (emotional effects) Music is often defined as that one of the arts that is concerned with combining sounds with a view to producing beauty and expression of emotions, though definitions of music vary according to culture (see AESTHETIC EMOTIONS (PHILOSOPHICAL PERSPECTIVES); AESTHETIC EMOTIONS (PSYCHOLOGICAL PERSPECTIVES)). Music has been linked to the emotions at least since the time of ancient Greece, and emotions do figure prominently in people's reported motives for listening to music. While philosophers, musicologists, and aestheticians have written much about musical emotions (see Budd 1985), psychologists have been slow to catch up.

Modern research has mostly neglected music, even though pioneers like Charles Darwin (1809–82) and William James (1842–1910) recognized the peculiar role of music in our emotional life. Contributing to the slow progress have been various methodological and conceptual problems, largely shared with the emotion field as a whole. Since the 1990s, the field has seen increasing interest, with valuable contributions coming from several disciplines, such as philosophy, musicology, psychology, biology, anthropology, and sociology.

It is generally believed that music may both express emotions that are perceived by listeners and induce emotions in listeners. These are different processes that have been mostly studied separately. The majority of studies have focused on the perception of emotion. Numerous studies have revealed that listeners usually agree about the broad character of the emotions expressed in music and that virtually all musical factors (e.g. tempo, loudness, mode) may contribute to the perceived expression. A summary of factors associated with various emotions is presented in Table M1. Following Darwin (1872/1998), it has been suggested that vocal expression and musical expression share a common code, based on emotion-related physiological effects on the voice (see VOCAL EXPRESSION OF EMOTION; VOICE PRODUCTION AND ACOUSTICS). Empirical evidence tends to support this hypothesis (Juslin and Laukka 2003).

Although most musicians and listeners would seem to take the emotional powers of music for granted, it has been a matter of some controversy whether music really can evoke emotions. Strong evidence has been fairly slow to emerge, though an increasing number of studies have reported evidence in terms of different emotion components such as self-reported experience, physiological response, activation of brain areas similar to those of other emotional responses, emotional expression, *action tendencies, and emotion regulation. There is further preliminary evidence of synchronization among these components. While most studies have relied on self-report, which may be subject to demand characteristics (i.e. cues that convey the researcher's hypothesis to the participant and might affect the participant's behaviour), music has also been found to influence a number of so-called implicit measures (e.g. word association).

Consequently, the primary issue is rather to explain *how* music induces emotions in listeners. One problem with musical emotions is that the conditions for eliciting emotions appear to be different from those in everyday life: in the paradigmatic case, an emotion is evoked when an event is appraised as having the capacity to influence the *goals of the perceiver somehow (see APPRAISAL THEORIES). Because

music (emotional effects)

Table M1. Summary of factors correlated with various emotions in musical expression.

Emotion	Musical factors
Happiness	Fast tempo, small tempo variability, major mode, simple and consonant harmony, medium–high sound level, small sound level variability, high pitch, much pitch variability, wide pitch range, ascending pitch, perfect 4th and 5th intervals, rising micro intonation, raised singer's formant, staccato articulation, large articulation variability, smooth and fluent rhythm, bright timbre, fast tone attacks, small timing variability, sharp contrasts between 'long' and 'short' notes, medium–fast vibrato rate, medium vibrato extent, microstructural regularity
Sadness	Slow tempo, minor mode, dissonance, low sound level, moderate sound level variability, low pitch, narrow pitch range, descending pitch, 'flat' (or falling) intonation, small intervals (e.g. minor 2nd), lowered singer's formant, legato articulation, small articulation variability, dull timbre, slow tone attacks, large timing variability (e.g. rubato), soft contrasts between 'long' and 'short' notes, pauses, slow vibrato, small vibrato extent, ritardando, microstructural irregularity
Anger	Fast tempo, small tempo variability, minor mode, atonality, dissonance, high sound level, small loudness variability, high pitch, small pitch variability, ascending pitch, major 7th and augmented 4th intervals, raised singer's formant, staccato articulation, moderate articulation variability, complex rhythm, sudden rhythmic changes (e.g. syncopations), sharp timbre, spectral noise, fast tone attacks/ decays, small timing variability, accents on tonally unstable notes, sharp contrasts between 'long' and 'short' notes, accelerando, medium–fast vibrato rate, large vibrato extent, microstructural irregularity
Fear	Fast tempo, large tempo variability, minor mode, dissonance, low sound level, large sound level variability, rapid changes in sound level, high pitch, ascending pitch, wide pitch range, large pitch contrasts, staccato articulation, large articulation variability, jerky rhythms, soft timbre, very large timing variability, pauses, soft tone attacks, fast vibrato rate, small vibrato extent, microstructural irregularity
Tenderness	Slow tempo, major mode, consonance, medium–low sound level, small sound level variability, low pitch, fairly narrow pitch range, lowered singer's formant, legato articulation, small articulation variability, slow tone attacks, soft timbre, moderate timing variability, soft contrasts between long and short notes, accents on tonally stable notes, medium–fast vibrato, small vibrato extent, microstructural regularity

music would not appear to have any capacity to further or block life goals, researchers have been forced to come up with an alternative explanation that makes more sense in a musical setting. Proposed mechanisms include brainstem responses, affective conditioning, *contagion, episodic memory, and imagery. One especially popular theory is that music gives rise to musical expectations that are rejected, delayed, or confirmed, thus evoking various emotions, as described in Meyer's (1956) seminal book (arguably the most cited book on the topic ever). None of these mechanisms have yet been systematically tested in regard to music, though preliminary findings suggest that there is no single mechanism that can account for all emotional responses to music. Consistent with the notion that there are many induction mechanisms are findings from an increasing number of neurophysiological studies sug-

gesting that emotional responses to music involve several different and widely distributed parts of the brain (e.g. Blood and Zatorre, 2001).

The study of music and emotions is fraught with considerable controversy and disagreement. Current debates in the field revolve around such questions as which emotions music typically induces, whether there are uniquely 'musical' emotions, and what the relationship is between perceived and induced emotions. It is increasingly recognized that key to an understanding of musical emotions is to capture the complex interplay between the music, the listener, and the situation. Thus, a significant trend has been to study music in everyday life, using experience sampling methods, surveys, and interviews. Results reveal that music is intentionally used by listeners to regulate their moods and emotions, and that positive emotions tend to dominate in their responses (see REGULATION OF EMOTION). The latter result has stimulated interest in the effects of music on physical health and subjective *well-being. The study of emotions in music might offer novel perspectives on emotions in general. Possible applications of music–emotion research include music therapy, film music, marketing, health care, and the games industry.

PATRIK N. JUSLIN

Gabrielsson, A. and Juslin, P.N. (2003). Emotional expression in music. In: R.J. Davidson, K.R. Scherer, and H.H. Goldsmith (eds), *Handbook of affective sciences*, pp. 503–34. New York: Oxford University Press.

Juslin, P.N. and Sloboda, J.A. (eds). (2010). *Handbook of music and emotion: Theory, research, application*. New York: Oxford University Press.

N

narcissism The term narcissism was first coined in a psychological context by Freud (1914/1957) in his essay 'On narcissism: an introduction'. It refers to a set of personality traits revolving around self-admiration, self-love, and egocentrism. Narcissism tends to manifest itself as overconfidence in one's own abilities, craving for regard and attention, resistance to criticism, over-absorption in one's own affairs, and lack of self-blame and empathy for others. The term narcissism derives from the Greek myth of Narcissus who, legend has it, fell in love with his own image reflected in a pool of water as a punishment for rejecting the advances of the beautiful nymph, Echo.

Narcissistic traits can be regarded as a continuous individual differences variable, with everyone possessing some degree of narcissism. At the extreme end of this continuum it has been proposed that narcissism manifests itself pathologically in the form of narcissistic personality disorder (NPD). Individuals with NPD have a grandiose sense of self-importance, lack empathy with others, seem to require excessive admiration, and are often preoccupied by fantasies of success, beauty, or power (American Psychiatric Association 1994) (see ADMIRATION/AWE; EMPATHY (NEUROSCIENCE PERSPECTIVES); EMPATHY (PHILOSOPHICAL PERSPECTIVES)). NPD is a chronic condition associated with interpersonal and social dysfunction. Although it may engender distress in the individual concerned and those close to him or her, a characteristic of NPD is a lack of awareness of the condition or its manifestations, such that those diagnosed rarely seek treatment or come to the attention of service providers.

TIM DALGLEISH AND NICOLA MORANT

needs Needs are internal sources of *motivation, which are frequently, but not always, elicited by deprivation. Together with other factors, like incentive value or accessibility, they can determine which goal objects an organism seeks to approach or to avoid for need satisfaction (see APPROACH/WITHDRAWAL). This frequently happens in the service of a basic hedonic need to maximize *pleasure and to minimize *pain.

The relation between needs and *goals—i.e. mental representations of desired end states—had already been considered in the psychoanalytic theory of motivation. Freud distinguished between objective deprivation—

need (e.g. hunger)—and its psychological representation—wish (e.g. food)—which motivates behaviour (e.g. eating). In contrast, behaviourism conceptualized needs merely as states of biological deprivation (Hull 1943), such as the need for food (hunger), the need for water (thirst), or the need to avoid tissue injury (pain) without any reference to their mental representation. Unlike instincts, which supply action-specific energy, needs were supposed to contribute to an unspecific motivational force that energizes any behaviour—described with the concept of drive. However, outside behaviourism researchers also considered psychological, non-biological needs.

Murray (1938) has posited 'viscerogenic needs' (e.g. hunger, thirst) and about twenty 'psychogenic needs' (e.g. affiliation, recognition, autonomy), forming personality. Individuals experience 'press' to those objects in the environment that promise satisfaction of needs, resulting in motives to engage in action. Murray posited that the majority of psychogenic needs operate outside consciousness. Also, according to field theory (Lewin 1935), all behaviour is finally based on biological or psychological needs, which are associated with tension states urging the organism to act to re-establish a state of equilibrium by means of need satisfaction. Internal needs furnish external objects with *valence (i.e. subjective value) in dependence of their potential for need satisfaction. The resulting magnitude of goal valence is determined together with the incentive aspects of the objects themselves (e.g. delicious food versus regular food). Motivational strength is finally determined by the proportion of goal valence to goal distance.

Behaviourists have determined need strength simply by the duration of deprivation. However, needs are usually assessed via introspective, explicit self-report or with implicit, projective measures, like the Thematic Apperception Test (TAT), which was introduced by Henry Murray and elaborated by David McClelland and colleagues. McClelland (1987) has also proposed a comprehensive theory about the development, function, and structure of three of Murray's psychogenic, unconscious needs—so-called implicit motives. These are the approach-oriented needs for achievement, power, and affiliation plus an avoidance motive resulting in the need to avoid failure, control, or affiliation. Motives are regarded as the result of learning during childhood when positive (e.g. challenge) or negative (e.g. fear) affective responses are associated with sign stimuli (e.g. a moderately difficult task) and a consummatory response (e.g. effort mobilization or avoidance). As a result, learned sign stimuli can later directly activate motives and their behavioural and affective correlates.

The strongest emphasis on the significance of psychogenic needs is articulated in humanistic psychology, which claims that human behaviour and development are guided by different needs from animal behaviour (see Cloningner 2004): Humans strive for self-actualization and self-esteem. Rather than only responding to 'homeostatic crises' individuals are proposed to seek autonomy and competence, want to experience the freedom of choice, and strive for self-determination. In a popular (though empirically hardly supported) model by Abraham Maslow (1908–70), human motivation changes during development because needs are organized in a hierarchy. Persons first seek to satisfy physiological and safety needs, followed by love and belonging needs, and esteem needs. Once these so-called 'deficiency needs' are more or less satisfied, behaviour is guided by so-called 'being needs', referring to self-actualization, such as beauty, truth, and justice. Being needs are associated with the experience of psychological freedom and creativity.

Still another class of proposed human need states are those related to information processing, like the need for consistency, the need to understand and explain (in the service of control motivation), or the needs for cognition and closure, which are claimed to determine how much mental effort individuals mobilize for the resolution of epistemic problems (see Pittman 1998).

GUIDO H.E. GENDOLLA

Hall, C.S. and Lindzey, G. (1970). *Theories of personality*, 2nd edn. New York: Wiley.

McClelland, D.C. (1987). *Human motivation*. Cambridge: Cambridge University Press.

negativity bias The affect system has been sculpted in complex environments where the opportunity for reward and the threat of punishment often go hand in hand (see REWARD; PUNISHMENT). In the savanna, for instance, prey animals must come to drink at the same waterholes where their predators come to dine. Errors in such situations can be costly. Whereas avoidance can leave animals without water, approach can expose them to predators. Noting that failing to secure even critical resources is less harmful in the long run than debilitating or fatal injury, Cacioppo and Berntson (1994) contended that a negativity bias evolved to promote survival. Consistent with this proposition, researchers have uncovered negativity biases in a wide variety of domains.

Extensive reviews of research on the negativity bias have been provided by Baumeister *et al.* (2001) and Rozin and Royzman (2001). In the domain of relationships, Baumeister *et al.* note that negative acts have more impact on the quality of relationships than positive acts. Thus, for instance, it may take as many as five compliments to undo the damage done by a single insult. They also review evidence that levels of distress among spouses, but not affection, predict subsequent divorce. Rozin and Royzman note the asymmetry between purification and contamination. Most individuals, for instance, refuse to eat food touched just once by cockroaches or any number of other aversive objects. Yet there exists no 'anticockroach', no object that can purify aversive objects by coming into contact with them. Similarly, Rozin and Royzman note that whereas negative attitudes that are resistant to extinction can be acquired through single-trial learning, positive attitudes take much longer to develop.

People's conscious choices are also more sensitive to negative than positive information. Prospect theory (Kahneman and Tversky 1979), the most influential descriptive model of *decision-making, features a value function that is steeper for losses than gains. Consistent with prospect theory, decision-making tends to be characterized by loss aversion. For instance, individuals are only indifferent to a prospect involving a 50% chance of losing $50 if it also affords a 50% of winning roughly $100. Loss aversion has also been invoked to explain the endowment effect (e.g. Rozin and Royzman 2001), whereby individuals who have been endowed with, for instance, a mug demand far more money to part with the mug than individuals who have not been endowed with a mug are willing to pay for one.

A great deal of evidence indicates that the negativity bias emerges, at least in part, because negative stimuli garner more attention than positive stimuli. In an event-related potential (i.e. brainwave) study, for instance, Smith *et al.* (2003) measured the amplitude of the P1 elicited by pleasant and unpleasant pictures. (The P1 is a positive-going brainwave originating within 120 ms of stimulus onset that reflects neural activity in the extrastriate area of the visual cortex.) Smith *et al.* found that unpleasant negative pictures elicit larger P1s than pleasant pictures, indicating that negative stimuli garner greater attention than positive stimuli extremely early in the evaluative process. Indeed, the P1 arises prior to stimulus identification, so these results indicate that negative stimuli receive preferential processing before they have even been identified.

The findings reviewed here represent a mere fraction of the field and laboratory studies that have demonstrated that negativity has greater effect on affect, cognition, and behaviour than does positivity. Indeed, though human behaviour is nuanced and subject to any number of moderating factors, the negativity bias appears to represent a fundamental psychological law (Baumeister *et al.* 2001). As Baumeister *et al.* conclude, 'bad is stronger than good' (p. 323).

JEFF T. LARSEN

Baumeister, R.F., Bratslavsky, E., Finkenauer, C., and Vohs, K.D. (2001). Bad is stronger than good. *Review of General Psychology*, **5**, 323–70.

Rozin, P. and Royzman, E.B. (2001). Negativity bias, negativity dominance, and contagion. *Personality and Social Psychology Review*, **5**, 296–320.

negotiation (the emergence of affect in negotiations research) Research on negotiation has blossomed over the last 25 years. Key to this surge has been a shift in focus from how individual differences and situations affect negotiation to how negotiator cognition affects negotiation. Specifically, researchers have embraced the behavioural decision perspective as they have examined how systematic cognitive biases affect the decision-making and behaviour of negotiators.

As this research focus has shifted, so too has the institutional home of the negotiation field. Before the rise of this cognitive approach, negotiation research rested principally in psychology departments. As the cognitive approach took root, negotiation research arguably became the fastest growing area of research in business schools (see Bazerman *et al.* 2000). The appeal of this research to business theorists and practitioners was its eminently prescriptive punch: it identified systematic cognitive barriers to optimal negotiation outcomes and subsequently proposed solutions to overcoming them. Over time, though, the behavioural decision perspective on negotiation has faced criticisms. Notably, it has been accused of neglecting what many believe to be the most obvious factor affecting negotiation outcomes: the strong emotions experienced by negotiators at the negotiating table.

A first wave of research on negotiator affect tended to broadly characterize emotions as positive and negative, and did not generally distinguish between fleeting *feelings and more stable moods. In one of the earliest examples of this work, Carnevale and Isen (1986) showed that positive mood increases the likelihood of negotiators finding integrative agreements and makes them less likely to behave contentiously. Another example of this research showed that negative emotions can make negotiators less concerned about the interests of other parties and less willing to make sacrifices for the sake of equality in the negotiated outcome (Loewenstein *et al.* 1989). While this first wave furthered negotiation research by documenting the importance of affect, it lacked two critical pieces. First, it lacked conceptual precision concerning how various human emotions af-

fect cognition and behaviour. Second, it did not substantially advance the prescriptions that educators could convey to negotiation practitioners.

The next wave of research on negotiator affect, made possible by critical conceptual developments in affective science, is just beginning. The publication of the Handbook of affective sciences (Davidson *et al.* 2003a) is one reflection of recent discoveries. First, the development of appraisal-tendency theory (Lerner and Keltner 2001) provides a useful—and badly needed—framework for categorizing emotions and predicting differential cognitive effects arising from similarly valenced emotions. For example, anger and fear could both be classified as generally negatively valenced, but anger evokes appraisals of increased certainty and individual control while fear evokes appraisals of decreased certainty and loss of individual control (Lerner and Keltner 2001). As a result of these different appraisals, different risk preferences arise from these two negatively valenced emotions (see RISK-TAKING). Specifically, research has shown that anger makes people more risk-seeking, while fear makes people more risk-averse. A well-known result is that risk aversion leads to greater concession-making and higher settlement rates in negotiation.

A second critical conceptual development in affective science in recent years has been the distinction between incidental and integral affect. In negotiation, integral affect arises in direct response to stimuli related to the negotiation, while incidental affect arises from ostensibly unrelated stimuli that carry over into the negotiation. Normatively, incidental affect should have no effect on negotiated outcomes, but recent research has shown that it can have important effects. For example, Lerner *et al.* (2004) have looked at how incidental sadness and disgust, both negatively valenced emotions, affect the endowment effect—the tendency for people to require more compensation to sell an item that is in their possession (selling price) than they would be willing to pay to acquire the item if it were not in their possession (buying price). Lerner and colleagues found that both sadness and disgust reduced people's selling prices for an item compared with neutral emotions. However, with regard to buying prices, the two emotions had opposite effects: sadness increased people's buying prices, while disgust decreased them. Lerner and colleagues argue that appraisal-tendency theory predicts this difference. The theory suggests that sadness will increase one's buying price and decrease one's selling price because sadness evokes a desire to change one's circumstances. At the same time, appraisal-tendency theory suggests that disgust will decrease both buying and selling prices because it increases people's desire to 'expel' what they currently have and to 'avoid taking in' anything new.

As negotiation research moves beyond the focus of the behavioural decision perspective on cognitive biases, we look forward to learning how different emotions affect negotiators' abilities to create and claim value, how incidental and integral emotions differently affect negotiated outcomes, and how these insights can be used prescriptively.

TODD ROGERS AND MAX H. BAZERMAN

Barry, B., Fulmer, I.S., and Van Kleef, G.A. (2004). I laughed, I cried, I settled: the role of emotion in negotiation. In: M. Gelfand and J. Brett (eds), *The handbook of negotiation and culture*, pp. 71–94. Palo Alto, CA: Stanford University Press.

Loewenstein, G. and Lerner, J.S. (2003). The role of affect in decision making. In: R.J. Davidson, K.R. Scherer, and H.H. Goldsmith (eds), *Handbook of affective science*, pp. 619–42. New York: Oxford University Press.

neural architecture of emotion The modern debate on the nature of emotions began with William James's famous paper 'What is an emotion?' (James 1884). James answered this question by asking two others: does the conscious feeling of being afraid cause us to act afraid or does that act itself account for the feeling? In choosing the latter as the answer, James redefined the question of what an emotion is as the question of what a *feeling is. But it's important to realize that underlying James's two questions were two others: what causes us to act afraid and what causes us to feel afraid? Psychology largely followed James's lead and has focused on the nature of feelings. But in neuroscience, where the subjects have often been animals, it is difficult to study feelings and the emphasis has been on how the brain controls emotional responses on the basis of evaluating the emotional implications of the stimulus (see AFFECTIVE NEUROSCIENCE; EMOTION DEFINITIONS (NEUROSCIENCE PERSPECTIVES)). Below, I will summarize some historical aspects of research on emotions in the brain, and then turn to a modern approach to the neural architecture of emotion. I focus primarily on animal research, since this work has led the way in providing a detailed understanding of the brain circuits of emotion, but also present human findings where relevant.

Historical aspects of the emotional brain

The study of emotions and the brain has a rich and complex history (LeDoux 1996). A brief overview of the past will help us understand the present.

James not only had a psychological theory but also a brain theory of emotion. He proposed that the bodily responses during emotions occur by way of the perception of the emotional stimulus in the sensory cortex and the expression of emotional responses through outputs of the motor cortex. Feelings, on the other hand, result when sensory cortex perceives body sensations arising from the responses (see JAMES–LANGE THEORY).

Walter Cannon (1871–1945), on the basis of findings from lesion studies, questioned James's view that sensory and motor cortex are involved in detecting and responding to emotional stimuli and instead proposed that the hypothalamus plays this role. He then argued that the experience of emotion, the feeling, occurs via connections from the hypothalamus to the cortex (see CANNON–BARD THEORY). James Papez (1883–1958) later added circuitry to Cannon's model, describing structures that directly communicate between the hypothalamus and cortex, and identifying the cingulate cortex as the specific cortical region for feelings.

Building on the work of Cannon, Bard, and Papez, Paul MacLean (1913–2007) proposed the influential limbic system theory of emotion, arguing that emotional responses and feelings are both mediated by an evolutionarily old set of cortical structures located in the medial wall of the hemisphere and connected with the hypothalamus either directly or via several subcortical structures, such as the *amygdala and other regions. Like his predecessors, MacLean proposed that the hypothalamus mediates the expression of emotion and the cortex the conscious experience of emotion. In contrast to Papez, for MacLean the hippocampus, rather than the cingulate cortex, was responsible for the experience of emotion.

The limbic system theory has been criticized on numerous grounds over the years (LeDoux 1991). First, the evolutionary basis of the limbic system concept was weakened by the discovery of neocortical like structures in reptiles and birds, thus challenging the crisp distinction between old and new cortex that MacLean proposed. Second, there are still no criteria that define what constitutes a limbic area. Third, the hippocampus, the centrepiece of the limbic system theory, turned out to be more involved in memory and cognition than in emotion. In spite of these criticisms, the limbic system theory is still a powerful force in neuroscience.

A modern neural architecture of emotion

In recent years an alterative, empirically based understanding of the emotional brain is emerging. This goal of this approach is to account for the brain mechanisms of specific emotions rather than 'emotion' in general (LeDoux 1996). In this view, an understanding of the emotional brain will come from the bottom up rather than from top-down concepts like the limbic system that attempt for impose a conception of emotion on specific emotions.

Research has been conducted on emotions such as *fear, *aggression, *attachment and separation, *pleasure and *reward, and *disgust, among others (LeDoux 1996, Balleine and Dickinson 1998, Panksepp 1998, Damasio 1999, Cardinal *et al.* 2002, Holland and

Gallagher 2004, Rolls 2005, Siegel *et al.* 2007). Because fear is the emotion that is best understood I will use it as a paradigmatic example for the purpose of illustrating how the neural architecture of emotion can be approached.

Fear is a particularly useful emotion to focus on for several reasons. First, it is a universal emotion related to survival. Second, there are good tasks for studying it in animal models. Third, it is very closely tied to the psychopathology of *anxiety disorders, the most common set of psychiatric conditions afflicting humans today.

In describing the neural basis of fear, I will first discuss the mechanisms by which the brain evaluates fear-arousing stimuli and controls the expression of fear responses. Although past work in neuroscience has relied heavily on animal studies, the emergence of new tools for imaging the brain has allowed the exploration of the circuits of emotional expression in humans as well as animals, and has also allowed new insights into the nature of conscious feelings in people.

The expression of fear reactions involves inputs and outputs of the amygdala. The neural circuitry of fear has been known for some time to involve the amygdala (LeDoux 1996). In 1937, Kluver and Bucy discovered that damage to the temporal lobes led to alterations in emotional behaviour, such as the loss of fear responses in the face of threatening stimuli. This is one of the main findings that prompted MacLean to update the Cannon–Bard and Papez theories. Later, Weiskrantz showed that damage to the amygdala accounted for the emotional changes seen by Kluver and Bucy with large lesions of the temporal lobe. In the following decades much research focused on the role of the amygdala in emotion. In fact evidence that the amygdala contributed to emotion was viewed as evidence in support of the limbic system theory. However, the exact manner in which the amygdala participated was unclear.

Part of the difficulty was that the behavioural tasks used to study the role of the amygdala in fear involved complex avoidance conditioning procedures that were carried out in different ways by different labs, making it difficult to build up a systematic understanding of the underlying circuits. Starting in the late 1970s, researchers began to turn to a simpler task, Pavlovian fear conditioning (see LEARNING, EMOTIONAL (NEUROSCIENCE PERSPECTIVES)). This task allowed rapid progress to be made.

Fear conditioning studies in animals have mapped the circuits for emotional reactions. In fear conditioning, the subject receives a neutral conditioned stimulus (CS), usually a tone, followed by an aversive unconditioned stimulus (US), typically footshock. After one or at most a few pairings, the CS comes to elicit emotional responses that naturally occur in the presence of threatening stimuli. It is important to note that avoidance conditioning involves a Pavlovian phase, and the emotional learning that occurs in avoidance conditioning occurs during this phase. Pavlovian conditioning is thus a more direct means of studying emotional processing.

The simpler approach allowed progress to be made in mapping the fear circuitry because it involves a specific stimulus that is under the complete control of the investigator, and the stimulus, when presented, leads to the expression of a coordinated reaction involving emotional behaviour (freezing) and corresponding changes in autonomic nervous system activity and endocrine responses.

Not surprisingly, research using fear conditioning implicated the amygdala in the acquisition and expression of the fear reaction (LeDoux 2000, Fanselow and Poulos 2005, Maren 2005, Lang and Davis 2006). The amygdala consists of a number of distinct nuclei (LeDoux 2007). Convergence of CS and US takes place in the lateral nucleus of the amygdala (LA). This convergence leads to synaptic plasticity and the formation of a CS–US association. When the CS later occurs, the associative memory formed by CS–US convergence in LA is retrieved and leads to activation in the central amygdala, which then connects to hypothalamic and brainstem areas that control behavioural, autonomic, and hormonal responses that help the organism cope with the threat. Thus, the lateral amygdala can be thought of as the threat detector or appraiser and the central amygdala as the reaction control region. This simplified description of the fear conditioning circuitry omits many details.

The amygdala does not function alone. One important additional region is the medial prefrontal cortex (mPFC). Damage to this region interferes with the ability to regulate emotion, as assessed in extinction tests where the subject is exposed to the CS repeatedly until the fear reaction weakens. Connections between the mPFC and amygdala are believed to mediate extinction (LeDoux 1996, Quirk *et al.* 2006).

Lesion and imaging studies implicate the human amygdala in fear and show that the amygdala is an unconscious emotional processing system. Research in humans has confirmed the essential role of the amygdala in fear conditioning (Damasio 1994, LeDoux 1996, 2002, Dolan and Vuilleumier 2003, Phelps 2006). Thus, damage to the amygdala in humans prevents fear conditioning from occurring and functional imaging studies show that activity increases in the amygdala during fear conditioning. Further, fear conditioning can occur in the absence of awareness of the CS and its relation to the US in humans. Other studies showed that emotional faces, which are thought to be unconditioned emotional stimuli, elicit activity in the amygdala, and that these responses can occur in the absence of any conscious awareness of the stimulus. Thus, both conditioned and unconditioned emotional stimuli elicit activity in the amygdala and autonomic nervous system responses independent of conscious awareness of the stimulus.

Recent studies have added additional dimensions to the role of the amygdala in fear processing (Phelps 2006). For example, instructed fear conditioning involves telling subjects that a CS may be followed by a shock. Even if the shock is never delivered, the CS comes to elicit Galvanic skin responses. Function imaging studies show that the amygdala is activated by such instructed stimuli. Galvanic skin responses can also be conditioned by watching others be conditioned and the amygdala is also involved in this social fear learning.

Just as fear extinction in rats involves the mPFC, so does fear extinction in humans (Phelps 2006). Although it is difficult to precisely equate areas of the prefrontal cortex in humans and rats, functional magnetic resonance imaging studies in humans show changes in activation in the mPFC associated with extinction and other forms of emotion regulation.

Thus, emotional processes that control emotional responses involve the same basic circuits in humans. Studies have also made it possible to explore mechanisms that may be uniquely human, such as fears based on verbal instruction. Human studies have also shown that emotional processing by the amygdala occurs unconsciously. At the same time, under normal conditions people will often be consciously aware of the stimulus that is eliciting emotional arousal. As we see below, this involves additional circuits.

Brain mechanisms of other emotions have also been studied. Besides fear, emotions that have been studied include aggression, attachment and separation, pleasure and reward, and some social emotions (Damasio 1994, 1999, LeDoux 1996, Balleine and Dickinson 1998, Panksepp 1998, Cardinal *et al.* 2002, Holland and Gallagher 2004, Rolls 2005, Siegel *et al.* 2007, Everitt *et al.* 2003). However, the neural mechanisms of these are understood in less detail than in the case of fear. For illustrative purposes we will consider some aspects of the neural basis of positive emotions, especially in the context of reward-based *motivation and *addiction.

Just as a CS paired with shock acquires aversive properties, a CS paired with tasty food or addictive drugs acquires appetitive properties. The appetitive properties of a CS are evident from the fact that a rat will orient to and approach a stimulus that has been paired with a positive US. Further, just as rats will work to avoid a CS paired with shock, they will work to obtain a CS paired with a positive stimulus. Through this kind of learning,

cues associated with drug use are believed to trigger relapse.

Much work on appetitive conditioning has examined the role of dopamine inputs to the nucleus accumbens. Release of dopamine in this region leads to the invigoration of behaviour, guiding behaviour towards goal objects. The amygdala also plays a key role in processing a CS during appetitive conditioning. In contrast to aversive conditioning, appetitive conditioning seems to involve the central amygdala. The basal and lateral amygdala seem to be especially important in the ability of a CS to function as a second-order or conditioned reinforcer that supports new learning. Another brain region involved is the *orbitofrontal cortex, which evaluates the incentive or motivating properties of a CS through interactions with the amygdala and nucleus accumbens.

Conscious feelings involves prefrontal working memory circuits. Research in cognitive science has begun to explain how the conscious experience of external stimuli occurs (see FEELINGS (PHILOSOPHICAL PERSPECTIVES); FEELINGS (PSYCHOLOGICAL PERSPECTIVES)). Most proposals centre on the concept of a multipurpose workspace (working memory) that (1) is regulated by attention, (2) holds onto attended stimuli temporarily, (3) integrates information from multiple sensory modalities, (4) integrates currently processed events with long-term memories, and (5) uses these temporary multisensory, memory-integrated representations in the control of thought (decision-making, planning, imagining, monitoring) and action.

Considerable research has indicated that areas in the prefrontal cortex play a key role in working memory. Functional imaging studies show that when subjects are consciously aware of external stimuli posterior cortical areas that process sensory modality-specific information and prefrontal areas are active, whereas when awareness is prevented by masking or other techniques posterior sensory but not prefrontal activation occurs. While these studies have used nonemotional stimuli, a similar pattern of results occurs when emotional stimuli are used. Sensory processing regions in the cortex and/ or thalamus and the amygdala are active when emotional stimuli are prevented from entering awareness but when subjects are consciously aware of emotional stimuli prefrontal activation also occurs.

To be consciously aware of an emotional stimulus is not the same as consciously feeling the emotional impact of a stimulus. Antonio Damasio has proposed that a feeling involves the awareness of bodily responses (see SOMATIC MARKER HYPOTHESIS). This is an update of the James–Lange theory. Damasio's somatic maker hypothesis assumes that conscious feelings are based on emotional responses initiated by the unconscious processing of emotional stimuli. Damasio has amassed evidence for his theory showing that so-called body-sensing areas of the cortex (somatosensory and insular areas) are active when people consciously feel emotions (Damasio 1994, 1999). However, these findings are largely correlational rather than causal. It remains to be determined that information about the bodily response (either in the form of actual feedback or in the form of memory) determines what one feels.

Even if information about the bodily expression of emotions turns out to be necessary, in some situations, for feelings, the question would arise as to the sufficiency of such information. In particular, feelings are associated not only with the activation of body-sensing areas, but also of working memory circuits. It seems likely that the conscious experience of a feeling occurs in the same way as the conscious experience of a stimulus—by the representation of the relevant information in working memory.

More specifically, the working memory hypothesis of feelings (LeDoux 1996, 2001, 2008b) proposes that a feeling occurs when several kinds of information are simultaneously processed in working memory: information about the stimulus and the context (social and physical) in which it is occurring; long-term memories (semantic and episodic memories) that provide meaning to the stimulus and its physical and social context; and information about emotional arousal. There are several sources of emotional information that can influence working memory. First, connections from emotion-processing regions such as the amygdala to cortical areas provide a means by which emotional processing can directly affect cortical processing. Second, connections from the amygdala to brainstem arousal systems that release neuromodulators throughout the brain. These change signal to noise processing, emphasizing the salience of stimuli being processed and memories being activated during the aroused state. Third, connections from the amygdala to brainstem areas that control emotional responses allow such responses to be expressed and their effects to feed back to the brain. The extent to which all of these must be present is not known but is testable.

A theory by Panksepp (1998) emphasizes the commonality of conscious feelings in humans and other animals. In this view if a rat and a human express similar behavioural responses to a fear-arousing stimulus they experience similar conscious feelings. While there may be a primitive core feeling that is similar, it seems unlikely that human conscious feelings and rat conscious feelings will be isomorphic. Given that the prefrontal cortex seems to be involved in human conscious experience this alone suggests that nonprimate mammals are likely to have different kinds of experiences. Add to this the importance of language, and human consciousness takes on an unparalleled dimension.

Conclusion

After decades of neglect, emotion is again a flourishing area of research in neuroscience. Much progress has been made in understanding the expression of emotion in behavioural and physiological response systems through studies of fear. This work implicates sensory inputs transmitted to the lateral amygdala in the processing of the emotional significance of threats and in learning about novel dangers and motor outputs of the central amygdala in the expression of emotional responses. Imaging studies in humans confirm the importance of the amygdala, and show that the amygdala performs its functions independent of conscious awareness. While the amygdala is implicated in positive emotions as well, its role may differ. However, these other emotions have been studied in less detail than fear. Both historically and in modern times, cortical areas have been proposed to play a crucial role in the conscious experience of emotions. The somatic marker theory of conscious feelings argues that body-sensing areas of the cortex play a key role, while the working memory theory argues that conscious feelings, like other aspects of conscious awareness, involve areas of the prefrontal cortex.

JOSEPH LEDOUX

Damasio, A. (1994). *Descartes' error: emotion, reason, and the human brain.* New York: Putnam.

LeDoux, J.E. (1996). *The emotional brain.* New York: Simon and Schuster.

neuroendocrine system The neuroendocrine system is composed of peripheral endocrine glands that release hormones into the general circulation in response to regulation by the central nervous system (CNS) (see PSYCHONEUROENDOCRINOLOGY). Part of the influence of the CNS is mediated by activating or inhibitory brain chemicals that are produced by specialized neurons in an area of the brain known as the hypothalamus. These proteins are released by nerve terminals directly into a specialized vascular system, the hypophyseal portal venous system, that drains into the anterior pituitary gland (adenohypophysis). These small protein factors from the hypothalamus regulate the production and release of hypophyseal hormones that are produced by specialized endocrine cells in the anterior pituitary, an organ that is located at the basis of the brain.

A well-identified part of this neuroendocrine system is the hypothalamic–pituitary–adrenal axis. Many external stimuli (e.g. pain and fear) and internal stimuli (e.g. hypoglycaemia) release corticotropin-releasing hormone (CRH) into the portal venous blood from terminals of small (or parvocellular) neurons that are located in the paraventricular nucleus of the hypothalamus (Herman et al. 2003). CRH acts on the corticotrophic cells of the anterior pituitary to increase the production and release of adrenocorticotropic hormone (ACTH) into the systemic circulation. ACTH induces the production and release of cortisol from the adrenal cortex. Besides its many functions in metabolism and physiology, cortisol negatively feeds back on the production of ACTH at the pituitary level and also on the production of CRH at the hypothalamic level, although to a lesser extent. A similar organization exists for a number of pituitary hormones including thyroid-stimulating hormone (TSH) that acts on the thyroid gland, luteinizing hormone (LH) and follicle-stimulating hormone (FSH) that act on gonads, prolactin that stimulates the production of milk from the breast, and growth hormone (GH) that ultimately acts on bones and muscles to stimulate growth and cell proliferation via insulin-like growth factors produced in the liver and locally at the level of the target organ. Activation of the hypothalamic–pituitary–adrenal axis is an essential component of the stress response. The gonadotropic axis triggers puberty and regulates activity of male and female gonads. The somatotropic axis regulates growth. The thyrotropic axis plays an essential part in metabolism and heat production. The gonadotropic axis is critical for sex and successful reproduction in both men and women.

The neuroendocrine system also comprises two hypothalamic hormones, vasopressin and oxytocin, that are produced by relatively large (or magnocellular) neurons in the paraventricular and supraoptic nuclei of the hypothalamus. In contrast to proteins that are transported from the hypothalamus to the adenohypophysis via a portal capillary system, posterior pituitary hormones are directly released by nerve endings into the neurohypophysis in response to relevant stimuli. Vasopressin acts on the kidneys as an antidiuretic hormone to reduce the loss of fluids into the urine. It is released into the general circulation in response to a reduction in plasma volume and increase in plasma osmolality. Oxytocin is released from the posterior pituitary at the end of pregnancy to trigger labour by its contracting effect on uterine muscles. It is also released by suckling and promotes the release of milk stored in the breast. Finally, there is an intermediate lobe in the pituitary gland in many species. This small group of cells produces melanocyte-stimulating hormone (MSH) in humans.

Complex interactions exist between the different neuroendocrine axes. For instance, activation of the hypothalamic–pituitary–adrenal axis inhibits the production and release of hormones of the somatotropic axis and hormones of the gonadotropic axis. Hypothalamic neurons produce gonadotrophin-releasing hormones (GnRH) in a pulsatile manner. This pulsatory aspect of

the GnRH signal is more important than the amount of GnRH for triggering the release of pituitary gonadotropins (FSH and LH) (Moenter et al. 2003). The pulsatility of GnRH-producing neurons is very sensitive to energy balance (Fernandez-Fernandez et al. 2006) and in some species to duration of light, which explains delayed puberty and/or inhibition of the menstrual cycle in anabolic conditions (e.g. during intense exercise in young female athletes) and in short-day light conditions (e.g. restriction of oestrus to long-day light in female sheep; Malpaux et al. 1999).

In addition to their effects on peripheral tissues, hormones act in the brain to modulate behaviour, mood, and cognition. For example, adrenal-derived glucocorticoids easily cross the blood–brain barrier to modulate the memory of stressful events (Het et al. 2005). Glucocorticoids also increase appetite and decrease sleep. Gonadal hormones play a key role in the sexual differentiation of the brain (Swaab 2007). Peripherally produced peptide hormones cannot enter the brain in the absence of a transport system. However, many peptides are produced and released in the brain where they function as neurotransmitters or neuromodulators at the same time as they are released at the periphery (e.g. CRH). See also NEUROPEPTIDES; NEUROTRANSMITTERS.

ROBERT DANTZER

Larsen, P.R., Kronenberg, H.M., Melmed, S., and Polonsky, K.S (2003). *Williams textbook of endocrinology*, 10th edn. Philadelphia, PA: Saunders.

Nelson, R.J. (2005). *An introduction to behavioral neuroendocrinology*, 3rd edn. Sunderland, MA: Sinauer.

neuropeptides Neuropeptides are peptide communication signals that are produced by neurons and other cells and act as neurotransmitters or neuromodulators (see NEUROTRANSMITTERS; NEUROENDOCRINE SYSTEM). The two pituitary peptides, adrenocorticotropic hormone (ACTH) and vasopressin (also known as antidiuretic hormone), were the first neuropeptides to be discovered. They were identified on the basis of their ability to modulate learning and memory in laboratory animals. Fragments of these peptides that were devoid of their original hormonal activity were found to maintain the behavioural activity of the full sequence peptide. This finding indicated that the amino acid sequence that codes for the neuronal activity of a neuropeptide is not necessarily the same as the sequence that codes for hormonal activity. Opioid neuropeptides, including endorphins and encephalins, were discovered later and derive from the precursor peptide pro-opiomelanocortin that encodes ACTH. They were initially identified on the basis of their ability to bind opioid receptors and their functionality was described later. More than 100 neuropeptides have now been described in the brain.

Some neuropeptides have very specific actions. For instance, vasopressin and oxytocin act on social memory and bonding. Corticotropin-releasing hormone (CRH) induces in the brain the various behavioural, physiological, and metabolic facets of the stress response. Many neuropeptides are found in the gut as well as in the brain. They include neuropeptide Y, agouti-related protein, cholecystokinin, ghrelin, and alpha-melanocortin, all of which have potent influences on the regulation of food intake.

Neuropeptides are often colocalized with classical neurotransmitters in presynaptic terminals. They are released at the same time as neurotransmitters but since they are not regulated by the same inactivation systems their activity usually lasts longer. Neuropeptides interact with specific neuronal receptors that can lead to different activities of the neuropeptide. For instance, CRH and other related neuropeptides including urocortins bind to two types of receptor, CRH receptor 1 and 2. The neuroanatomical localization and functions of these receptors often differ, so that it is possible to design specific synthetic antagonists that block only one type of receptor. For instance, CRH receptor 1 is claimed to be a target for designing new anti-anxiety or antidepressant drugs. However, a complicating factor is that neuropeptides are often expressed together with their receptors both in the central nervous system and peripheral tissues, so that it is difficult to ensure tissue-specific activity of a synthetic molecule that mimics or opposes the effect of a given neuropeptide.

ROBERT DANTZER

McEwen, B. (2004). *Roles of vasopressin and oxytocin in memory processing.* Advances in Pharmacology, Vol. 50, Amsterdam: Elsevier.

Nelson, R.J. (2005). *An introduction to behavioral neuroendocrinology*, 3rd edn. Sunderland, MA: Sinauer.

Steckler, T., Kalin, N.H., and Reul, J.M.H.M. (2005). *Handbook of stress and the brain*, Vols 1 and 2. Amsterdam: Elsevier.

neuroticism Neuroticism is a personality dimension that was popularized by Hans Eysenck (e.g. Eysenck 1981). There are substantial differences in neuroticism, with high scorers being individuals who experience negative emotional states such as *anxiety and *depression relatively frequently and intensely.

According to Hans Eysenck, there are three major personality factors. Neuroticism is one of those factors, *extraversion (closely related to sociability) and psychoticism (involving hostility and coldness; see PSYCHOPATHY) being the other two. Of crucial importance, these three factors are orthogonal to each other, and so an individual's scores on one dimension cannot be predicted from his/her scores on the other two. Neuroticism is also regarded as one of the major personality dimensions within the very influential 'Big Five' factor approach, in which the five

factors of neuroticism, agreeableness, conscientiousness, extraversion, and openness are often identified (e.g. Costa and McCrae 1992).

There are various reasons why individuals differ in their level of neuroticism. However, there is convincing evidence from twin studies that genetic factors account for approximately 30–40% of individual differences in neuroticism (Eysenck 1981).

MICHAEL W. EYSENCK

neurotransmitters Neurotransmitters are molecules that are synthesized by neurons and released into the synaptic cleft between a presynaptic neuron and a postsynaptic cell to ensure the transmission of neural activity between these two elements. The postsynaptic element can be either a neuron or another type of cell, such as muscle or endocrine cells. Transmission of neural activity to the postsynaptic element requires binding of the neurotransmitter to high-affinity receptors that are usually localized on the postsynaptic membrane. The excess of neurotransmitter that is released into a synapse is normally opposed by reuptake mechanisms and/or enzymatic degradation on the presynaptic neuron. In addition, the amount of neurotransmitter that is released into the synapse can be regulated by presynaptic receptors.

The discovery of neurotransmitters and the description of their anatomical localization in the central nervous system has permitted an understanding of a functional representation of the central nervous system in terms of neurotransmitter systems. This system complements the structural organization of the central nervous system in terms of fibre tracts and nuclei that regroup neuronal cell bodies. The two main neurotransmitters are glutamate, which is excitatory, and gamma-amino butyric acid, which is inhibitory in the adult mammalian brain. Other neurotransmitters include acetylcholine and monoamines such as noradrenalin, dopamine, and serotonin. Adenosine triphosphate (ATP) also functions as a neurotransmitter in the central nervous system. Gases such as nitric oxide and carbon dioxide function as neurotransmitters, especially between neurons and nonneuronal elements such as endothelial cells of blood vessels.

Although it has been tempting to attribute different functions to different neurotransmitters, the exact function of a given neurotransmitter is very much dependent on the neuronal network in which the neurotransmitter exists. For instance, dopamine codes the rewarding properties of stimuli in the limbic system, but it regulates the fine control of movement by basal ganglia. This fact explains why degeneration of dopaminergic neurons that project from the substantia nigra to the striatum leads to the development of Parkinson's disease.

Serotonin is a potent regulator of mood in the cortex and limbic system, but it controls sleep and appetite in the hypothalamus and brainstem. Degeneration of acetylcholinergic neurons that project from the nucleus basalis in the basal forebrain to the cortex is responsible for the cognitive deficits that are characteristic of Alzheimer's disease.

ROBERT DANTZER

Cooper, J.R., Bloom, F.E., and Roth, R.H. (2002). *The biochemical basis of neurochemistry.* Oxford: Oxford University Press.

nonverbal communication Nonverbal communication (also referred to as nonverbal behaviour or nonverbal cues) includes all aspects of behaviour and appearance aside from verbal content (SEE INTERPERSONAL COMMUNICATION). Visual nonverbal cues include facial expressions, head movements, posture, body and hand movements, self- and other-touching, leg positions and movements, interpersonal gaze, directness of interpersonal orientation, interpersonal distance, and synchrony or *mimicry between people. Auditory nonverbal cues include discrete vocal sounds (e.g. sighs), mean levels and variations in pitch, loudness, and speed, and tonal qualities (e.g. nasality, breathiness). Several additional speech-related behaviours are often included: interruptions, pauses, listener responses (such as 'uh-huh' uttered while another is speaking), dysfluencies in speech, and amount of speech. Clothing, hairstyle, and adornments, as well as physiognomy (such as height or facial features) are also considered to be nonverbal cues.

Uses and meanings of nonverbal communication
Nonverbal cues emitted by a person are likely to be interpreted by others, whether correctly or not, allowing for misunderstandings to occur. The process of drawing inferences from nonverbal cues is often not in conscious awareness; similarly, encoders (expressors) may or may not be aware of the cues they are sending. The unintentional conveyance of veridical information through nonverbal cues is called leakage.

Nonverbal cues often accompany spoken words, and when they do the nonverbal cues can augment or contradict the meanings of the words as well as combine with the words to produce unique messages, as in sarcasm, which involves the pairing of contradictory messages through verbal and nonverbal channels.

Some nonverbal behaviours have distinct meanings, most notably the hand gestures called emblems that have direct verbal translations (such as the 'A-okay' sign or the 'thumbs up' sign in North American usage). However, most nonverbal cues have multiple and often ambiguous meanings that are dependent on other information for correct interpretation (associated words, situational context, antecedent events, other

nonverbal cues, etc.). Some nonverbal behaviours are discrete (i.e. have distinct on–off properties), examples being nodding, blinking, pausing, and gestural emblems. Others are continuous, such as the fluid movements of the hands while speaking, vocal qualities, and movement style.

The face, body, and voice have been extensively studied in terms of emotional expression, with at least six basic emotions having characteristic configurations of movements and/or of acoustic correlates (see FACIAL EXPRESSION OF EMOTION; VOCAL EXPRESSION OF EMOTION; GESTURAL EXPRESSION OF EMOTION). Prototypical displays are most likely to occur when the expressor is deliberately attempting to convey certain feelings. In naturalistic interaction, facial expressions often lack some of the prototypical muscle movements, and there is an imperfect correspondence between the experience of emotion and the display of predicted corresponding expressions. Nonverbal cues can also contribute to a person's emotional experience and self-regulation via physiological feedback processes; engaging in certain behaviours (e.g. extending the *zygomatic muscle, sitting upright) can intensify or produce the associated emotions (e.g. positive affect, feelings of pride).

Conveying emotions is only one of several important functions of nonverbal behaviour. Nonverbal cues convey information about attitudes, personality traits, intelligence, intentions, mental and physical states, physical characteristics, identity, deception, and roles. Nonverbal cues of the face, eyes, voice, and hands are used in the regulation of turn-taking in conversation, and also for purposes of providing feedback regarding comprehension and interest to a speaker. Face and hand movements serve dialogic functions, for example to illustrate, comment, refer, and dramatize. Speech-dependent gestures also contribute to fluent speech by facilitating word retrieval; speakers lose fluency and complexity if they are constrained from gesturing while speaking. Nonverbal cues can also arise from cognitive activity, as when hard thinking produces a furrowed brow or averted gaze.

The coordination of nonverbal behaviour between people helps to produce and maintain desired levels of arousal and intimacy. People (including infants) often mimic, reciprocate, or synchronize their movements with others. Such behaviour matching can contribute to rapport. However, behavioural compensation is also a common occurrence; one person adjusts his or her behaviour to compensate for another's behaviours, for example by gazing less or backing up if the other person is standing too close.

Another important function of nonverbal behaviour is self-presentation, that is, representing oneself in a desired way (e.g. as nice, brave, or competent). Related to self-presentation are societal *display rules, which are conventions regarding what kinds of expressions are appropriate at what times and by whom. Nonverbal cues play a role both in the intention to appear honest and in the actual differences between truthful and deceptive communications.

Nonverbal cues play a role in social influence, for example persuasion and interpersonal expectancy effects, also called self-fulfilling prophecies. In the latter, one person's beliefs or expectations for another person can be fulfilled in a process that can be out of the awareness for both parties. For example, a teacher may be especially warm and nonverbally encouraging to a student believed to be a high achiever; the expected high performance will actually be produced if the student responds with heightened motivation and effort, thus confirming the teacher's belief even if it was initially unfounded and the teacher was unaware of his/ her role in producing such an effect.

Individuals differ in the accuracy with which they convey information via nonverbal cues (called encoding, or sending accuracy) and interpret others' nonverbal cues (called decoding, or receiving accuracy) (see ENCODING/DECODING (OF EXPRESSION)).

JUDITH A. HALL

Harrigan, J.A., Rosenthal, R., and Scherer, K.R. (eds) (2006). *The new handbook of methods in nonverbal behavior research*. Oxford: Oxford University Press.

Knapp, M.L. and Hall, J.A. (2010). *Nonverbal communication in human interaction*, 7th edn. Belmont, CA: Wadsworth.

Manusov, V. (ed.) (2005). *The sourcebook of nonverbal measures*. Mahwah, NJ: Lawrence Erlbaum Associates.

Manusov, V.L. and Patterson, M.L. (eds) (2006). *The handbook of nonverbal communication*. Thousand Oaks, CA: Sage.

Russell, J.A. and Fernández-Dols, J.M. (eds) (1997). *The psychology of facial expression*. Cambridge: Cambridge University Press.

norms Neither the ordinary uses of the term norm nor its technical uses allow for an easy characterization of what the phenomenon covers. Although often employed loosely to refer to mere regularities of behaviour, norms, in a stricter sense, are rules for behaviour or attitudes the departure from which entails sanctions. There are legal norms, moral norms, epistemic norms, linguistic norms, norms of etiquette, etc., and perhaps also sentimental norms, i.e. rules pertaining to what emotions should be felt in what circumstances. The sanctions associated with these types of norms take very different forms, from physical punishment to mere sneering; they can be explicitly tied to the norm or only implicitly so. Beyond this initial formulation, the best entry point for approaching the phenomenon is to explore the language in which it is couched. Norms are typically expressed in a language containing expressions such as 'one ought to', 'it is forbidden to', 'it is obligatory

to', etc., followed by a proposition commanding a certain behaviour. Because of this commanding character (1) norms are often talked about in relation to *values, and (2) both norms and values are said to contrast with *facts*.

Values, like norms, appear to share at least the following dimensions: (1) *appreciative*—they both focus on what is good or correct to do, think or feel; (2) *prescriptive*—they both have intimate links with what should be done, thought or felt. While the language of norms is primarily concerned with the prescriptive dimension, it also contains an appreciative component which allows for the distinction between norms on the one hand and other types of rule-like phenomena, such as the laws of nature or the rules of chess. The latter types of rules also dictate behaviour, but as opposed to norms there is nothing good or commendable about them. Value language, on the other hand, focuses on the appreciative dimension, but also has obvious links with what should be done. If killing is bad, then perhaps one ought not to kill. Beyond these commonalities and variations in emphasis, values and norms differ in interesting respects. Generally, the study of value properties can be viewed as being the study of the good and the bad and all their determinates. Good and bad would be determinables of which the courageous, the elegant, the honest, etc., on the one hand, the cruel, the ugly, the pernicious, etc. on the other, are respectively determinates. Value properties can be arranged in a tree-like hierarchy and can in principle be applied indifferently to objects, persons, situations, etc. This fact reflects important differences between values and norms. First, values admit of degrees, norms do not. Thus, it makes sense to ascribe more of a given value to one object than to another, whereas it makes no sense to speak of degrees with respect to norms. Living up to a value is thus a matter of degree, whereas one either flouts a norm or one doesn't. Second, there are *thick* (e.g. the courageous) and *thin* (e.g. the good) values, i.e. values that depend on descriptive content and values that do not, but no thick and thin norms (Williams 1985, pp. 141–2). Although norms can be hierarchically ordered, this does not mirror the internal relations between thick and thin values as they figure in the tree-like structure. Third, supererogatory acts (e.g. 'John jumped in the stormy waters at the risk of his life to save the baby') are best understood as acts that are *good* (value) but not *required* (norm). Finally, and perhaps most importantly, the domain of application of values is infinitely vaster than that of norms. While the latter apply to actions, and perhaps thoughts and attitudes, values might apply to almost anything. The thorny question of which from values or norms is ontologically prior is one of the most debated issues in modern practical philosophy and might depend on claims regarding the *source* of the respective phenomena.

novelty

While reason is often cited as the source of our norms and values (Kant 1785/1959, Korsgaard 1996), it is *emotions* that are thought by most psychologists and philosophers to be at the root of both phenomena (Hume 1751/1975, Gibbard 1990). This helps us to understand why many have thought that evaluative and normative judgements should be contrasted with *factual* judgements to the extent that the former, as opposed to the latter, do not have correctness conditions. For example, while it is clear that the fact that Sam killed Maria makes the sentence 'Sam killed Maria' true, it is much less clear what fact makes the sentence 'One should not kill' true. The injunction contained in such statements—their normative force—does not square well with the idea that norms refer to facts and can thus be made true or false by them. Norms, according to *prescriptivism*, for example Hare (1952), would only be the sophisticated linguistic expression of what are mere emotional responses to salient facts in the environment. But such a claim depends on the further thesis that emotions do not have any content, that by their very nature they are not in any way reactions to states of the environment. If, on the contrary, they are reactions to or perceptions of values then two things follow: there are many senses in which it can said that emotions are governed by norms and it remain a totally open question whether norms have factual bases. If sadness is sensitivity to loss, then perhaps sadness has *correctness conditions* involving loss and loss constitutes a *reason* for sadness, two notions that are governed by norms.

JULIEN A. DEONNA

novelty The concept of 'novelty' has two different components. One refers to familiar events that are unexpected (a clap of thunder at midnight) whereas the second refers to events that are unfamiliar and not immediately assimilated (seeing the hijacked planes strike the World Trade Center on 11 September 2001). Both classes of experience are often called novel. Both unexpected and unfamiliar events are inherently quantitative, even though individuals usually treat them as primary categories. It is important to distinguish between an unexpected event that alters a person's immediate experience but does not engage the person's long-term store of knowledge, and an unexpected event that does engage that knowledge. Many laboratory experiments present participants with a series of identical sounds or visual stimuli in which a deviant sound or visual stimulus occurs only 15% of the time (called an oddball procedure). This category of novelty creates a brain state that can be distinguished from the one that occurs when the unexpected event bears some relation to the person's understanding of the world (for example, seeing a face with one eye or hearing the sentence 'The boy wore a sleeveless mountain'). Most unfamiliar events are also unexpected, but there are exceptions. An unfamiliar odour presented in a laboratory setting in which the investigator told the participants they would experience novel stimuli would be expected but unfamiliar.

Unexpected or unfamiliar events replace the usual activity of thalamic neurons with an interval of burst firing that creates a special form of excitation in sensory areas of the cortex and often leads to an increase in brain dopamine (Rolls *et al.* 2005, Bunzeck and Duzel 2006). Unfamiliar events usually activate the right hemisphere more extensively than the left and, in addition, alter neuronal firing patterns in the prefrontal cortex which often interrupt ongoing thought and activity (Horstmann 2006).

The emotion that the English language calls *uncertainty, which is associated with unexpected or unfamiliar events, has two origins, each with distinct brain and psychological profiles. The state of uncertainty generated by an unfamiliar event, called *stimulus uncertainty*, recruits activity in the *amygdala, parahippocampal region, and prefrontal cortex. The uncertainty produced by unsureness over what decision or behaviour an individual should make when alternatives are available is called *response uncertainty* and activates different brain circuits.

Although both unexpected and unfamiliar events activate many brain sites, the amygdala invites special attention because of its contribution to the acquisition and expression of behavioural signs of fear in animals. Many investigators interpret increased activity of the amygdala to any event that is aversive or symbolic of threat as reflecting a state of fear. The problem with this inference is that most of the time aversive or threatening events are also unexpected, unfamiliar, or both. The amygdala is activated by the unexpected occurrence of events that have no relation to fear or anxiety, including neutral or happy faces, pleasant pictures, erotic scenes, musical chords, and vignettes that attribute to a person the intentional commission of an act that violated a community *norm. Thus activation of the amygdala does not always imply a state of fear. The corpus of evidence suggests that a primary function of the amygdala is to respond to initial encounters with unexpected or unfamiliar events whether they are safe or potentially dangerous (Chen *et al.* 2006). Scientists who rely on measures of brain activity as the primary referents for emotions would profit from acknowledging the importance of unexpected or unfamiliar events. See also NOVELTY (IN APPRAISAL).

JEROME KAGAN

Kagan, J. (2007). *What is emotion?*. New Haven, CT: Yale University Press.

Rolls, E.T. (2005). *Emotion explained*. New York: Oxford University Press.

novelty (in appraisal) The appraisal of a stimulus event by the organism starts with the assessment of stimulus *novelty* and the resulting effects on the attention system: something in the environment (external or internal) happens/changes, the organism's attention is drawn to it, and consequently further processing takes place in order to evaluate the relevance of the event for the organism (novelty appraisal is alternatively referred to as *attentional activity* in the appraisal literature). In this sense, stimulus novelty acts as a gateway to the appraisal process (see APPRAISAL THEORY).

At the least complex level of processing, any stimulus characterized by abrupt stimulus onset and high intensity is likely to be appraised as novel and will trigger allocation of attention and further processing. The literature on attention (Wolfe and Horowitz 2004) and the orienting reflex (Siddle and Lipp 1997) suggests a large number of factors that influence novelty detection at this early level, related to both the nature of the stimulus and the prior state of the organism. Beyond the basic level of stimulus novelty, more complex types of novelty exist. Novelty as opposed to *familiarity* depends on prior experiences with a given stimulus: novelty detection in this sense is triggered by a non-match of the stimulus with memory templates. Novelty as opposed to *probability* and *predictability* depends on conceptual representations of the lawfulness or regularity of the occurrence of certain events: novelty detection in this sense is triggered by the violation of expectations which are based on those regularities. Any intense, unfamiliar, or unexpected event—including the nonoccurrence of expected events—needs to be prioritized by the attention system in order to determine possible causes and consequences, as the event may signal potential threats or opportunities. Thus, novelty-triggered stimulus appraisal serves as an interrupt to ongoing behaviour in order to draw the organism's attention toward potentially relevant environmental stimuli (Corbetta and Shulman 2002) (see ATTENTION AND EMOTION). Further processing then determines whether adaptive actions are required. See also NOVELTY.

TOBIAS BROSCH

O

obsessive–compulsive disorder According to the *Diagnostic and statistical manual of mental disorders*, fourth edition, text revision (DSM-IV-TR; American Psychiatric Association 2000), obsessive–compulsive disorder (OCD) is characterized by recurrent obsessions and/or compulsions that interfere with daily functioning. Obsessions are 'persistent ideas, thoughts, impulses, or images that are experienced as intrusive and inappropriate and cause marked anxiety or distress' (p. 418) (see ANXIETY; DISTRESS). Compulsions are 'repetitive behaviors . . . or mental acts . . . the goal of which is to prevent or reduce anxiety or distress' (p. 418). Strong emphasis is placed in DSM-IV-TR on the functional relationship between obsessions and compulsions, i.e. compulsions are performed in order to decrease distress associated with obsessions. Notably, although obsessions are always mental events, compulsions may be either overt, observable behaviours (e.g. handwashing) or covert, intentional mental actions (e.g. replacing repugnant images with pleasant, neutralizing ones). A continuum of 'insight' or 'strength of belief' best captures the clinical picture of OCD in that there is a range of recognition by individuals with OCD regarding the senselessness of their obsessions and compulsions, which led to the inclusion of a subtype of OCD in DSM-IV-TR known as OCD 'with poor insight'. Low insight has been found predictive of poor treatment response, so its evaluation prior to initiating treatment is important.

Multiple studies estimate the prevalence of OCD at approximately 1–2% in the United States, with similar rates cross-culturally. Age of onset typically ranges from early adolescence to young adulthood, with earlier onset in males; modal onset in males is between the ages of 13 and 15 years compared with between 20 and 24 in females. Associated functional impairment is considerable in affected adults and in youth, and clinical OCD symptoms tend to persist throughout a person's life. Given these data, developing and disseminating treatments to help OCD patients lead more productive and high-quality lives are important public health priorities.

The neurobiological underpinnings of OCD have received considerable research attention in the past two decades, but a detailed account of these findings and neurobiological theories of OCD more generally is beyond the scope of this entry. Neurobiological theories implicating serotonin deficiencies in OCD led to the development of pharmacotherapies that prevent serotonin reuptake; these medications include the tricyclic antidepressant clomipramine (CMI) and the selective serotonin reuptake inhibitors (SSRIs). Multisite randomized controlled trials of CMI and SSRIs in adults, and now several such large studies in youth, have indicated the acute efficacy of these medications in reducing OCD symptoms, although these studies also collectively suggest that clinically significant residual impairment is the norm.

As applied to OCD, learning theory would suggest that compulsions and avoidance behaviour produce temporary relief from obsessional distress and hence are negatively reinforcing; this has led to the development of behavioural treatments for OCD. In the 1960s Meyer introduced a treatment known as exposure and response prevention (EX/RP; Meyer 1966) in which individuals with OCD were encouraged to intentionally confront situations and thoughts that evoked obsessional distress (exposure) while simultaneously refraining from compulsions and other avoidance behaviours. Emotional processing theory was later invoked to explain how such exposure-based treatments worked in reducing anxiety, with the theory suggesting that individuals with pathological levels of anxiety were essentially exposed to corrective information, i.e. they learned via exposure that their distress diminished without resorting to rituals or other avoidance behaviours and that the consequences that many feared did not occur (Foa and Kozak 1986). Many randomized controlled trials support the efficacy and durability of EX/RP for adults with OCD. Further, developmentally sensitive EX/RP protocols have also been created for youth with OCD, and the efficacy of these protocols has also been supported in several randomized controlled trials.

Cognitive theories emphasizing the role of OCD-specific irrational beliefs in the psychopathology of the disorder have also emerged; these beliefs are then specifically targeted in the cognitive therapies that have followed from these cognitive theories. Specifically, Salkovskis (1985) proposed that intrusive obsessional thoughts may provoke certain types of negative automatic thoughts that would lead to mood disturbances through interaction between the unacceptable intrusion and the individual's belief system (e.g. only bad people have sexual thoughts). According to Salkovskis, an exaggerated sense of responsibility and self-blame are central themes in the belief systems of individuals with OCD. Neutralization, in the form of behavioural or cognitive compulsions, can be understood as an attempt to reduce this sense of responsibility and to prevent blame. In addition, frequent intrusive thoughts or images of engaging in unacceptable actions (e.g. stabbing a loved one with a carving knife) may be perceived by the person with OCD as equivalent to having actually committed such actions. Several formal cognitive therapy protocols have been found to be efficacious in reducing OCD relative to control conditions. Moreover, discussions of mistaken beliefs and the ultimate futility of thought suppression are routinely incorporated into behavioural protocols that emphasize EX/RP. The efficacy of cognitive therapies for paediatric OCD has yet to be examined in randomized studies.

MARTIN E. FRANKLIN AND EDNA B. FOA

Foa, E.B., Liebowitz, M.R., Kozak, M.J., Davies, S.O., Campeas, R., Franklin, M.E., et al. (2005). Treatment of obsessive compulsive disorder by exposure and ritual prevention, clomipramine, and their combination: a randomized, placebo-controlled trial. *American Journal of Psychiatry*, **162**, 151–61.

Pediatric OCD Treatment Study Team (2004). Cognitive-behavioral therapy, sertraline, and their combination for children and adolescents with obsessive-compulsive disorder: a randomized controlled trial. *Journal of the American Medical Association*, **292**, 1969–76.

odour and emotion In Marcel Proust's novel *Swann's way* (1913), the smell of a madeleine biscuit dunked in tea brings the author back to his childhood, sparking off a vivid emotional experience. This example—which is frequently used to illustrate the privileged link between olfaction, memory, and emotion—is referred as the 'Proust phenomenon' (see MEMORY (EMOTIONAL)). Consistent with this example, empirical research has shown that odour-evoked memories are indeed particularly emotional, vivid, specific, and relatively old compared with memories cued by verbal, visual, or auditory stimuli (e.g. Herz et al. 2004). This privileged effect of odours on emotion and other affective phenomena goes beyond memory, and has been established in the scientific literature using not only self-reports but also physiological indicators and behavioural measures. For example, there is evidence that the affective tone of odours has an influence on human voice pitch, reaction time, resolution of logical or reasoning tasks, alertness, mood, and motivation.

Past research has also shown the remarkable extent of individual differences in the emotional responses to the same types of fragrance (e.g. Hudson and Distel 2002). Moreover, affective reactions to odours are often dependent on the familiarity of the odour (see Delplanque et al. 2008) as well as contextual factors, including environmental variables, type of activity, and the nature of relationships or social interactions (e.g. Chrea et al. 2005). The origin of the strong affective effects of odours is debated, with some scholars arguing that the acquisition of the affective tones of odours is driven by associative learning processes (Herz et al. 2004), while others suggest the existence of innate mechanisms involved in odour preferences (see Schaal et al., 2002, for discussion). Even if the specific processes involved in odour-elicited emotions are not yet fully understood, the scientific literature confirms the popular view that olfaction is a very 'emotional' sense.

This privileged link between odour and emotion might be subserved by neuroanatomical specificities of the olfactory system. Indeed, to put it simply, olfactory information is conveyed from the olfactory bulb first to the primary olfactory (piriform) cortex and then to the *amygdala and the orbitofrontal cortex without going through the thalamus, unlike the case for the other sensorial modalities. Thus, these unique direct anatomical connections between the olfactory system and the amygdala—a structure known to be critical for both emotion elicitation and emotional memory (Rolls 2005)—are certainly involved in this privileged link.

Most scientific studies on olfaction and emotion relations embrace one of two dominant theories: discrete emotion theories or bidimensional theories of emotion. Discrete emotion theories applied to olfaction typically focus on response patterning of basic emotions such as *disgust, mainly via both self-report and physiological indicators, but rarely explore the causal mechanisms underlying differences in emotion elicitation (often implying schema-driven response selection by emotion-specific neuromotor programs) (see BASIC EMOTIONS; DIFFERENTIAL EMOTIONS THEORY). However, odour stimuli produce a rich set of highly differentiated response patterns and feeling states that typically do not match basic emotions categories (see Sander 2008). On the other hand, research using bidimensional models of emotion has allowed the measurement of physiological differences associated with verbally reported pleasantness and arousal produced by odours, as well as the investigation of underlying brain structures associated with emotional odour pleasantness and intensity (see Winston et al., 2005, for discussion) (see DIMENSIONAL MODELS; CIRCUMPLEX MODELS). Concerning the elicitation of emotional response, dimensional theorists make little attempt to present an explanatory framework that predicts the occurrence of specific responses in a consistent manner. Moreover, projecting the odour-elicited emotions onto a bidimensional grid of pleasantness by arousal fails to capture most of the important qualitative differences between the effects of different types of fragrance. According to this view, recent findings (Chrea et al. 2009) highlighted that the subjective affective experiences or feelings induced by odours are structured around a small group of dimensions that reflect the role of olfaction in well-being, social interaction, danger prevention, arousal or relaxation sensations, and conscious recollection of emotional memories. This findings point to a structure of affective responses to odours that differs from the classical taxonomies of emotion such as posited by discrete or bidimensional emotion theories.

Given the role of the subjective evaluation of odours—and not only their inherent properties—in the elicitation of emotion, a helpful theoretical approach might be the use of appraisal models (see APPRAISAL THEORIES). According to these models, odour-elicited emotions are driven by the interpretation of the personal significance of the odour for the individual, in particular as a function of his or her current needs, goals, values, and concerns. These models might therefore offer a more satisfactory theoretical framework suggesting mechanisms involved in the appraisal-driven emotional response to odours (Delplanque et al. in press), thereby accounting for the extraordinary intra- and interindividual changeability and high degree of qualitative differentiation of emotional experiences induced by odours.

SYLVAIN DELPLANQUE AND DAVID SANDER

Herz, R.S., Schankler, C., and Beland, S. (2004). Olfaction, emotion, and associative learning: effects on motivated behavior. *Motivation and Emotion*, **284**, 363–83.

Rolls, E.T. (2005). *Emotion explained*. New York: Oxford University Press.

Schaal, B., Soussignan, R., and Marlier, L. (2002). Olfactory cognition at the start of life: the perinatal shaping of selective odor responsiveness. In: C. Rouby, B. Schaal, D. Dubois, R. Gervais, and A. Holley (eds), *Olfaction, taste, and cognition*, pp. 421–40. Cambridge: Cambridge University Press.

optimism/pessimism The term optimism is a relatively recent arrival on the historical scene, as is pessimism. In the 1700s, Leibniz (1646–1716) characterized optimism as a mode of thinking, and Voltaire (1694–1778) popularized the term in his 1759 novel *Candide*, which was critical of the shallowness of an optimistic perspective. Pessimism appeared a century later, independently introduced by Schopenhauer (1788–1860) and Coleridge (1772–1834). In their original forms, optimism and pessimism were not symmetric. Optimism was cognitive, reflecting a reasoned judgement that good would predominate over evil, even if goodness was associated with suffering. In contrast, pessimism was emotional: the pessimistic individual was one for whom suffering outweighed happiness. Someone can be optimistic in the cognitive Leibniz sense yet pessimistic in the emotional Schopenhauer/Coleridge sense.

The original definitions of optimism and pessimism introduced distinctions still worth taking seriously. An optimistic person, as described by Leibniz, is one who has arrived at the conclusion that eventually good will outweigh bad. Optimism is not accepted on blind faith; it is not happiness; it is not freedom from disappointments. A pessimistic person, as characterized by Schopenhauer and Coleridge, was simply one who suffered. By these views, optimism and pessimism are not opposites. One can attempt to alleviate pessimism without urging optimism. At least theoretically, one can encourage optimism but leave pessimism in place.

More recent discussions of optimism by social scientists tend to take two forms. In the first, it is regarded as an inherent part of human nature, and either praised or decried. Early approaches to optimism as part of human nature were critical. This negative view of positive thinking lies at the heart of Freud's influential writings on the subject. Freud (1928) argued that optimism was widespread but illusory. For Freud, optimism makes civilization possible but requires the denial of our instinctual nature and hence the denial of reality. As psychodynamic ideas became popular, Freud's formula equating optimism and illusion had widespread impact. Although no mental health professional asserted that extreme pessimism should be the standard of health, most theorists pointed to the accurate perception of reality as the epitome of good functioning.

Matters began to change in the 1960s and 1970s in the light of research evidence showing that most people are not strictly accurate in how they think. Another turning point was a review of research by Shelley Taylor and Jonathan Brown (Taylor and Brown 1988) of what they called positive illusions. They concluded that people are biased toward the positive and that the only exceptions are individuals who are anxious or depressed.

Perhaps the strongest statement that optimism is an inherent aspect of human nature is found in Lionel Tiger's 1979 book *Optimism: the biology of hope*. He located optimism in the biology of our species and argued that it is one of our defining and adaptive characteristics. For Tiger, optimism was selected for in the course of evolution, developing along with our cognitive abilities and indeed the human capacity for culture.

At the same time that optimism as general human nature was being discussed in positive terms, other psychologists interested in individual differences began to address optimism as a characteristic which people possess to varying degrees. These two approaches are compatible. Our human nature provides a baseline optimism, of which individuals show more versus less, and our experiences influence the degree to which we are relatively optimistic or pessimistic *vis-à-vis* this baseline.

Today's best known approach to optimism is the work by Charles Carver and Michael Scheier (Carver and Scheier 1981) on dispositional optimism: the global expectation that good things will be plentiful in the future and bad things scarce. Carver and Scheier's overriding perspective is in terms of how people pursue *goals, defined as desirable values. They refer to their approach as a self-regulatory model. Optimism enters when people ask themselves about impediments to the achievement of the goals they have adopted. In the face of difficulties, do people believe that goals will be achieved? If so, they are optimistic—if not, pessimistic. Optimism leads to continued efforts to attain the goal, pessimism to giving up.

The correlates and consequences of optimism (and pessimism) have been extensively studied. Investigations using a variety of methods and designs show that when people are placed along a continuum from pessimistic to optimistic and examined with respect to measures of adaptation drawn from a variety of domains—cognition, mood, behaviour, physical health, and social relations—optimism is usually associated with good outcomes and pessimism with bad outcomes. The notable exception, not surprisingly, is that optimistic people may underestimate the risks of future dangers.

CHRISTOPHER PETERSON

orbitofrontal cortex The orbitofrontal cortex is a key brain region in emotion. It represents the *reward (and *punishment) or affective value (see VALENCE) of many stimuli, and because it is rewarding or punishing stimuli that lead to affective behaviour and feelings, it has a key role in emotion (Rolls 2004, 2005).

The (primate and human) orbitofrontal cortex receives taste, olfactory, visual, somatosensory, and auditory inputs from cortical regions which are towards the end of the unimodal cortical processing streams that build representations of what stimulus is present in each of these sensory modalities, in most cases independently of whether the stimulus is rewarding or punishing (see Fig. O1) (see NEURAL ARCHITECTURE OF EMOTION).

Neuronal recording studies in primates show that it is the reward value of taste, olfactory, oral texture, and visual stimuli that is represented, as shown for example by the reduction to zero of the neuronal responses after feeding to satiety on a particular food (Rolls 2006). Facial expression (which is a cue for emotional responses) and facial identity are represented by neuronal activity in the orbitofrontal cortex (see FACIAL EXPRESSION OF EMOTION).

Visual and olfactory stimuli become rewarding by learned association in the orbitofrontal cortex with a primary (unlearned) reinforcer such as the taste of food (see ASSOCIATIVE PROCESSING). This learning can be

reversed (in as little as one trial for visual stimuli), and may be facilitated by error neurons that respond when an expected reward is not obtained (Rolls 2005).

Complementary neuroimaging studies in humans show not only that rewards such as pleasant odours, touch, and the flavour of food are represented in the orbitofrontal cortex, but also that abstract reinforcers, such as winning or losing money, and facial beauty, are also represented in the orbitofrontal cortex (Kringelbach and Rolls 2004, Rolls 2005). In studies in neuroeconomics, it has been shown that the expected value of a reward may be represented in the orbitofrontal cortex (Rolls 2008). The orbitofrontal cortex is also activated when an expected reward is not obtained, and behaviour should change (see ECONOMICS (ROLE OF EMOTION IN)).

A number of the symptoms of frontal lobe damage in humans appear to be related to the functions of representing primary (unlearned) reinforcers and of altering behaviour when stimulus–reinforcement associations alter. For example, lesions of the orbitofrontal cortex can impair reward-related (reversal) learning (Hornak et al. 2004), identification of facial and vocal expression (Hornak et al. 2003), and can produce impulsive behaviour (Berlin et al. 2004) and disinhibited emotional behaviour (Hornak et al. 2003).

Some of the personality changes that can follow frontal lobe damage may be related to a similar type of dysfunction in processing rewards and punishers. For example, the euphoria, irresponsibility, lack of affect, and lack of concern for the present or future that can follow frontal lobe damage may be related to a dysfunction in altering behaviour appropriately in response to a change in reinforcement contingencies. Indeed, in so far as the orbitofrontal cortex is involved in the disconnection of stimulus–reinforcer associations, and such associations are important in learned emotional responses (Rolls 2005), then it follows that the orbitofrontal cortex is involved in emotional responses by correcting stimulus–reinforcer associations when they become inappropriate (see below).

It is of interest that frontal patients may be able to verbalize the correct rules yet may be unable to correct their behavioural sets or strategies appropriately, implying separate implicit emotional and rational (reasoning) routes to action and *decision-making (Rolls 2005, 2008).

The most anterior, pregenual, cingulate cortex receives from the orbitofrontal cortex, and may be one route by which the orbitofrontal cortex can influence behaviour, as shown by its activation in similar functional neuroimaging tasks and the effects of lesions to it (Hornak et al. 2003, Rushworth et al. 2004, Rolls 2005, 2009). Indeed, the perigenual cingulate cortex may be part of an executive, output, response selection system

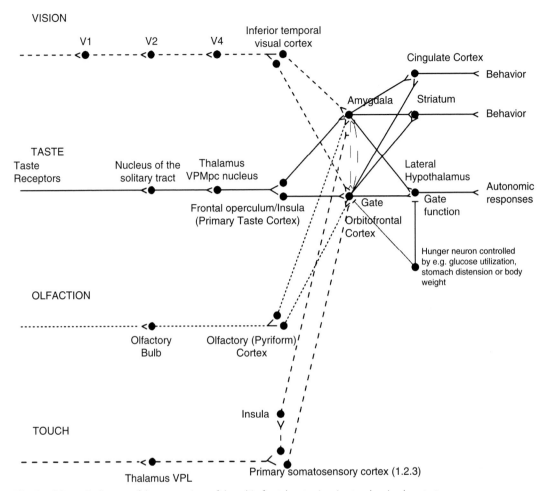

VISION

Fig. O1. Schematic diagram of the connections of the orbitofrontal cortex in primates showing how taste, olfactory, somatosensory, and visual pathways converge in the orbitofrontal cortex. The gate functions shown refer to the finding that the responses of taste, olfactory, visual, and oral somatosensory neurons in the orbitofrontal cortex and the lateral hypothalamus are modulated by hunger, and thus represent reward value. VPMpc, ventralposteromedial thalamic nucleus; V1, V2, V4, visual cortical areas.

for some emotional states, where the responses can include autonomic responses. Part of the basis for this suggestion is its inputs from somatosensory cortical areas including the insula, and the orbitofrontal cortex and *amygdala (see Fig. O2), and its outputs to brainstem areas such as the periaqueductal (or central) grey matter in the midbrain, the ventral striatum, and the autonomic brainstem nuclei. Lesions of the *anterior cingulate cortex in humans can produce apathy, autonomic dysregulation, and emotional instability. We have shown that patients with circumscribed, even unilateral, surgical lesions of the anterior/perigenual cingu-

late cortex may be impaired in identification of vocal and facial expression, have impaired subjective emotional states, and show some changes in social behaviour, including being less likely to notice when other people were angry, not being close to his or her family, and doing things without thinking (Hornak et al. 2003).

In conclusion, the orbitofrontal cortex and the most anterior part of the anterior cingulate cortex appear to be key brain systems involved in computing affect, in producing emotional behaviour, and in decision-making (Rolls 2005, 2008).

EDMUND T. ROLLS

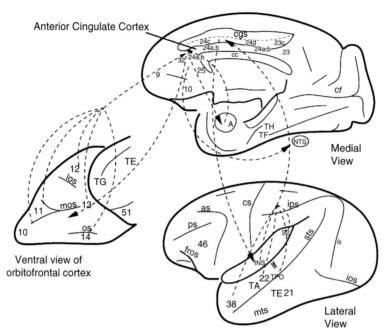

Anterior Cingulate Cortex

Medial View

Ventral view of orbitofrontal cortex

Lateral View

Fig. O2. Connections of the perigenual and midcingulate cortical areas (shown on views of the primate brain). The cingulate sulcus (cgs) has been opened to reveal the cortex in the sulcus, with the dashed line indicating the depths (fundus) of the sulcus. The cingulate cortex is in the lower bank of this sulcus, and in the cingulate gyrus which hooks above the corpus callosum and around the corpus callosum at the front and the back. The perigenual cingulate cortex extends from cingulate areas 32, 24a and 24b to subgenual cingulate area 25. (The cortex is called subgenual because it is below the genu (knee) formed by the anterior end of the corpus callosum, cc.) The perigenual cingulate cortex tends to have connections with the amygdala and orbitofrontal cortex, whereas area 24c tends to have connections with the somatosensory insula (INS), the auditory association cortex (22, TA), and with the temporal pole cortex (38). The midcingulate areas include area 24d, which is part of the cingulate motor area. Abbreviations: as, arcuate sulcus; cc, corpus callosum; cf, calcarine fissure; cgs, cingulate sulcus; cs, central sulcus; ls, lunate sulcus; ios, inferior occipital sulcus; mos, medial orbital sulcus; os, orbital sulcus; ps, principal sulcus; sts, superior temporal sulcus; lf, lateral (or Sylvian) fissure (which has been opened to reveal the insula); A, amygdala; INS, insula; NTS, autonomic areas in the medulla, including the nucleus of the solitary tract and the dorsal motor nucleus of the vagus; TE (21), inferior temporal visual cortex; TA (22), superior temporal auditory association cortex; TF and TH, parahippocampal cortex; TPO, multimodal cortical area in the superior temporal sulcus; 38, TG, temporal pole cortex; 12, 13, 11, orbitofrontal cortex; 51, olfactory (prepyriform and periamygdaloid) cortex.

orienting response The orienting response (OR) describes an integrated system of physiological responses which are said to promote information processing through the direction of attention to novel stimuli (see NOVELTY) and a lowering of sensory thresholds accompanied by increases in processing efficiency and *arousal. Although first coined as the 'what it is' reflex by Pavlov (1849–1936) in the early 20th century, Sokolov in his seminal work *Perception and the conditioned reflex*

(1963) described a body of research which identified both central (i.e. electroencephalogram (EEG) activation) and peripheral (i.e. electrodermal and peripheral vascular) response components, together with studies of the effects of stimulus novelty, modality, intensity, complexity, and repetition on the elicitation and habituation of these response components (see Siddle 1983). A theoretical model of the OR is based on a 'comparator system', whereby the stimulus novelty is assessed relative to existing neuronal models and the detection of novelty results in response elicitation. Subsequent repetition results in decline of the response or habituation which reflects decreases in novelty and the progressive elaboration of the neuronal model, unless another novel stimulus is introduced which reinstates the response and a process of dishabituation to subsequent stimuli.

The OR has been a ubiquitous concept in psychophysiology for understanding the relationship between physiological responses and information processing. The range of relevant responses has been extended to include heart rate responses and associated changes in various evoked potential components of the EEG. Recent research has focused around the unitary nature of the response, the effects of stimulus omission and significance, the impact of intense and aversive stimuli, and the relationship between the orienting and conditioned autonomic responses. Öhman *et al.* (2000a) provide a recent review of theories of the orienting response. Applications of the OR have included its use in the study of attentional dysfunction in psychopathology and also its relationship to emotional processing (Lang *et al.* 1997b).

GRAHAM TURPIN

outcome expectancies It is a central tenet of appraisal theories of emotion that it is not a stimulus event itself but the perceived outcomes for the individual that determine the ensuing emotion (Scherer *et al.* 2001a) (see APPRAISAL THEORIES). Especially in the case of events that might be relevant to the *needs and *goals of the organism, the likelihood of possible effects needs to be predicted.

This is particularly important for events where (1) it is not certain whether the event will occur at all and (2) the consequences of the event cannot be predicted with certainty, as in the case of prospective emotions such as *hope or *fear which may be elicited by signal events (e.g. communication acts such as a threat). But even when an event has already occurred, the organism needs to estimate the outcome and the likely consequences of the event for itself.

In order to produce an approximate estimation, an individual needs to know more about the event and its causation. In addition to attributions about the cause of an event (who caused it and why), inferences about the further development of a situation and possible consequences of the event are of high importance for the appraising organism, in particular the probability of different outcomes and the organism's ability to cope with them, i.e. to modify or adapt to possible consequences (What will happen next? Can I deal with this?).

Thus, the appraisal of a situation by an organism will include different outcome expectancies with regards to: (1) the development of the situation without any action or response by the organism; (2) the contingencies between potential responses and outcome (outcome expectations in the sense of Bandura, 1977); (3) the controllability of the situation; (4) the power of the organism to control or influence the situation (efficacy expectations in the sense of Bandura, 1977); and (5) the capacity of the organism to adapt to the situation (see CONTROLLABILITY; POWER (IN APPRAISAL); COPING POTENTIAL (APPRAISAL OF)).

TOBIAS BROSCH

P

pain (biological perspectives) In 1979, the Taxonomy Committee of the International Association for the Study of Pain (IASP 1979) produced a definition of pain: 'Pain is an unpleasant sensory and emotional experience associated with actual or potential tissue damage, or described in terms of such damage'. This definition makes the point that pain is due to physical causes but is also a subjective experience with psychological components.

The physical cause of pain is a peripheral high-intensity nociceptive stimulus triggering a cascade of physiological events that leads to integration of the information encoding the various facets of pain. Alterations in these events can prolong the pain-inducing process, leading to the development of chronic pain. The pain then loses its meaning as a warning signal and develops into a chronic syndrome that is usually responsible for disability. Research on this chronic pain pattern is recent and in most cases few effective treatments are available. Chronic pain may result from prolonged nociceptive input, due for instance to inflammation or nociceptor sensitization, and from a lesion of the nervous system, leading to neuropathic pain, related either to lesions in peripheral sensory nerves or to lesions in relay structures located in the central nervous system.

Pain is a word which refers to different states. Each type of pain enriches the understanding of other pains by similarities but also differences. In its present concept, pain seems to be a multidimensional phenomenon, also combining social elements, in a so-called 'biopsychosocial model'. To make reference to a multidimensional aspect of pain helps to better understand the differences between various kinds of pains and, in a day to day approach, promotes an overview for the relief of chronic pain.

As previously defined, pain is a subjective experience perceived as an unpleasant emotional experience. The components of this experience vary in intensity according to the characteristics of the stimulus, those of the patient, and those of the setting in which the stimulus is applied. The conventional model distinguishes four hierarchically arranged components that interact, modulating one another so closely that none can be considered separately: (1) The sensory-discriminative component involves neurophysiological mechanisms that lead to pain caused by an excessive number of nociceptive signals; these mechanisms translate nociceptive signals into information on the intensity, duration, location, and quality of the nociceptive stimulus. (2) The emotional-affective component makes pain unpleasant, burdensome, or unbearable and may lead to differentiated emotional disorders such as *anxiety or *depression, most notably when the pain is chronic. This component is called into play by the nociceptive stimulus itself via activation of the limbic system and by the environmental conditions surrounding the stimulus (e.g. the nature of the disease causing the pain, uncertainty about its outcome, and social and family support). (3) The cognitive component encompasses all the processes that modulate pain perception. Examples of these processes include attention (a neutral task that deflects the patient's attention away), meanings ascribed to pain by the patient's culture, religion, or social group, and the influence of recollections of former pain. (4) The behavioural component is composed of the verbal and non-verbal behaviours of the patient in response to pain, such as complaints, moaning postures, and facial expressions, which constitute in large part a means of communication with others. These behaviours assist in the diagnosis in clinical practice.

From a physiological point of view, the cascade of events that leads to the integration of pain signals first involves nociceptors (mechano-, thermo- and chemo-nociceptors) which are nerve endings of primary sensory nerves disseminated through the skin, muscles, joints, and organ walls. Peripheral nociceptors may be activated by direct stimulation or by various molecules released at a site of inflammation (Coutaux et al., 2006). Nerve signals encoding the nociceptive stimulus travel along primary afferent small-calibre fibres of sensory nerves which are either myelinated (Aδ fibres) or unmyelinated (C fibres). These fibres are peripheral branches of axons of primary sensory neurons, the cellular bodies of which are located in dorsal root ganglia, and their central branches reach the spinal cord via the dorsal roots of the spinal nerves. Their central branches end in the grey matter (located centrally with two symmetrical dorsal and ventral horns) within the dorsal horn of the spinal cord. Ten layers have been classically described within the grey matter, six in the dorsal horn, three in the ventral horn, and one (layer X) around the ependyma or central canal. Afferent primary sensory fibres form synapses with postsynaptic nociception-relay neurons: (1) Specific nociceptive neurons which are located mainly in the outermost layers of the dorsal horn (layer I and to a lesser extent layer II) but are also found in deeper layers (layer V as well as layers VI, VII, and X). They respond only to high-intensity peripheral stimuli coming from a variety of sites (skin, joints, and organs). (2) Nonspecific nociceptive neurons (also known as wide dynamic range (WDR) neurons) which are located mainly in layer V but are also found in the outermost layers (layers I and II, but also VI, VII, and X). They respond to both low- and high-intensity peripheral stimuli, and their firing frequency increases with stimulus intensity, thereby coding stimulus intensity. A single neuron receives afferent fibres from the skin, organs, muscles, and joints. (3) Non-nociceptive-specific neurons that respond only to low-intensity peripheral stimuli and play no role in integrating nociceptive information.

The axons of dorsal horn nociceptive neurons constitute the ascending spinal cord pathways, travelling in the contralateral side of the spinal cord white matter, chiefly in the ventrolateral quadrant; consequently they project their information at various supraspinal levels contralaterally to the stimulus.

Supraspinal projection sites for spinal specific and nonspecific nociceptive neurons constitute brain relay stations that integrate the pain signals. They can be divided roughly into four main categories: (1) The ventro-postero-lateral (VPL) thalamus composed of nuclei which are specific for touch and nociception. Their neurons promptly receive nociceptive signals conveyed by the axons of the spino-thalamic tract originating mainly from neurons in layers I, II, and V. These thalamic neurons are somatotopically organized and present electrophysiological properties suggesting a role in the sensory-discriminatory component of pain. (2) Projection sites in the reticular formation relay nociceptive information conveyed by the spino-reticulo-thalamic tract to the median thalamus, a nonspecific thalamic relay. These relay stations also contribute to cardio-respiratory alert responses, to the development of motor and emotional responses, and to alertness mechanisms involved in behavioural responses to painful stimuli. (3) The hypothalamus receives axon endings directly from the spino-hypothalamic tract or indirectly from the spino-parabrachial–hypothalamic tract, both originating in spinal neurons mainly located in the superficial layers of the dorsal horn. The hypothalamus is involved in controlling responses of the *autonomic nervous system to pain and in releasing hormones that contribute to stress control. (4) The amygdaloid complex (see AMYGDALA), part of the limbic system, receives information relayed by the lateral parabrachial nucleus and originating from specific nociceptive neurons located in layer I of the dorsal horn, conveyed by the spino-parabrachial–amygdaloid tract. This pathway may be involved in the emotional-affective component of pain.

The terminal segment of the pathways involved in the integration of nociceptive stimuli consists of neurons located in the two different parts of the thalamus: neurons in the VPL thalamus project on the somatosensory areas (S1, S2) of the parietal cortex, where the characteristics of the nociceptive information are integrated, leading to the genesis of pain perception (quality, location, intensity, and duration); neurons in the median thalamus project on the frontal cortex, insular cortex, and *anterior cingulate cortex, which generate the more complex emotional responses to pain.

Pain is a sensation whose perception can be modulated by the environment, in the broadest meaning of the term (affective, sociocultural, geographical, and other factors), and by the individual's psychological status. This modulation is mediated by controls (inhibitory as well as facilitatory) coming from spinal and supraspinal structures.

Spinal segmental influences are the most extensively studied pain control mechanisms. Melzack and Wall (1965) modelled the effects of these influences in their 'gate control theory'. There is a balance between two types of influences exerted on spinal WDR nociceptive neurons: activating influences from peripheral segmental neurons via nociceptive $A\delta$ and C fibres and inhibitory influences from peripheral segmental neurons via non-nociceptive $A\alpha$ and $A\beta$ fibres and from supraspinal neurons (see below). Thus, pain is perceived only when WDR neurons are activated, i.e. when the balance tips in favour of excitatory influences, either because of excessive activity of nociceptive fibres or because of deficient inhibitory influences. According to 'the gate-control theory', activation of $A\alpha$ and $A\beta$ fibres inhibits the responses of WDR neurons to nociceptive stimuli via mechanisms involving activation of segmental inhibitory interneurons located in dorsal horn layer II, thereby closing the gate and blocking the transmission of nociceptive signals to supraspinal structures (leading to analgesia). These interneurons activated by non-nociceptive fibres may be inhibited by $A\delta$ and C nociceptive fibres, opening the gate and facilitating transmission of the nociceptive signals to supraspinal structures (leading to pain). This spinal regulation mechanism is controlled by descending influences from supraspinal structures. However, this model fails to explain all experimental and clinical data and additional findings partially contradict some of its components, whereas the existence of other components has never been demonstrated. In the light of these additional data, Wall (1978) modified the model by assuming the existence of two families of inter-neurons modulating the activity of WDR neurons: one WDR-inhibiting family activated by non-nociceptive fibres, and one WDR-activating family activated by noci-ceptive fibres. Both families are controlled by descending influences coming from supraspinal structures.

Supraspinal influences concern descending inhibitory as well as facilitating controls. Activation of the descend-ing inhibitory influences from brainstem structures (the peri-aqueducal grey matter (PAG) in the mesencephalon and the rostral-ventromedial medulla (RVM) which comprises the nucleus raphé magnus (NRM) and the paragigantocellular and gigantocellular nuclei) induces analgesia related to inhibitory effects of descending ser-otoninergic tracts on spinal WDR neurons, the result being blockade of the transmission of nociceptive sig-nals. The axons of serotoninergic neurons in the RVM (most notably in the NRM) project, at each spinal seg-ment, directly on the dorsal horn of the spinal cord. Based on these data, and on the fact that the reticular formation in the medulla and PAG (two relay stations in the transmission of nociceptive signals) project on RVM neurons, the PAG and NRM have been implicated in a spinal–medullary–spinal negative feedback loop under-pinning an endogenous analgesic system called into play by nociceptive stimuli (Basbaum and Fields 1984).

Activation of facilitating descending influences from the brainstem exacerbates the effects of nociceptive stimulation at the spinal cord level. High-intensity stimulation of the RVM produces analgesic effects (see above), whereas stimulation of the same region with intensities four to ten times lower has a facilitating effect on pain production, and inhibitory analgesic sites can be differentiated from strictly facilitating pain-potentiating sites. Most of the information available on RVM cells was obtained by Fields (1992).

In sum, the balance between the two descending control systems described above may ultimately deter-mine the overall level of excitability of the neuronal network in the dorsal horn, which in turn may modu-late the transmission of pain signals to the supraspinal central nervous structures (modulation of WDR neuron activity, but via supraspinal influences, which were part of the initial 'gate control' concept).

From a psychological point of view, the affective com-ponent of pain results from unpleasant feelings which can be evoked as two kinds of emotions: primary emo-tions combined with secondary emotions that may play a role in the future, both in the short term (such as anxiety, fear, or distress) and in the long term (such as suffering). Secondary emotions are often determined by the personal history of each patient, the difficulties encountered in coping with pain over time, and the impact these difficulties may have in the future. Experi-mental and clinical studies have identified interactions involving pain intensity, the unpleasant feeling that accompanies pain, and secondary emotions (Price 2000).

In conclusion, the description of pain involves far more than a network of neurons connected by ascend-ing and descending tracts and located in spinal segments or in supraspinal structures. Such pathways have been identified in animal experiments, and have been de-scribed here briefly (for more details see Calvino and Grilo, 2006). However, a far more complex picture emerges when one considers chronic pain, which is the main focus of concern for clinicians and patients, as it frequently fails to respond to treatment. The in-ability of a simple model involving signal transmission within the above-mentioned neuronal network to ex-plain chronic pain can be ascribed to the neuroplasticity of the central nervous system. Manifestations of neuro-plasticity occur when nociceptive stimuli are repeated over a long period (such as in a chronic inflammatory state) or when neurons are injured. Modulation of pain-inhibiting or pain-activating influences generated by supraspinal areas undoubtedly occurs in disease states as a result of neuroplasticity, resulting in chronic pain.

BERNARD CALVINO

pain (philosophical perspectives) Our common-sense conception of pain is that each pain, which has very specific sensible qualities, occurs at a particular place and time (see PAIN (BIOLOGICAL PERSPECTIVES)). Pains appear to track tissue damage in our body. Under normal conditions, when we feel a pain we know that damage has occurred or is occurring where the pain is. We should think of pain, therefore, as a perceptual experience, just like seeing objects or hearing sounds. Under normal conditions, when we see a red apple, we know that a red apple is located there.

However, there are two important differences be-tween pain experiences and (other) perceptual ones. First, under normal conditions, objects of perception are available to others. If I see a red apple on the table before me, then, properly oriented, you can see the same thing I do. But you cannot feel the pain of my tissue damage. Pains are private in a way that other perceptions are not. Second, unlike perception, if we feel a pain when there is no tissue damage—which turns out to happen quite often—we do not dismiss the pain as something hallucinatory or otherwise mistaken. Pains appear to have an incorrigibility that we do not ascribe to our other perceptual states.

Notice that our commonsense conceptions describe pain in two very different ways. On the one hand, pain is a kind of *experience*. On the other, it is an *object* of experience. Our loose folk conception of pain can switch between these two ways of understanding pain in almost the same breath.

In the 1950s, philosophers developed an indirect realism analysis of pain perception that tried to accommodate both conceptions. On this analysis, perception of an object is an experience in which the subject categorizes the object by applying concepts to it and to its attributes. Perception is thus always indirect; we actually perceive or experience our world through our categories and concepts. Some philosophers argued that phenomenal experience can be an object in its own right and that therefore we categorize and conceptualize the experience as we experience it (e.g. Broad 1959). If they are correct, then that explains why pain can be both an experience and an object of experience. The problem with this approach is that it describes and codifies the peculiarities of pain more than it actually explains them. It just shifts the problem of understanding pain to that of understanding categorization, conceptualization, and mental objects.

In response to this difficulty, Armstrong (1962) and Pitcher (1970) put forth a rather simple direct realism view of pain: To feel a pain is to be aware of tissue damage. (More modern versions of this view are representationalist: the experience of pain represents tissue damage.) The problem with this view stems from the disconnection between what pains feel like and tissue damage. What is it, exactly, that we are perceiving when we feel pain? Unlike when we see a red apple, we cannot articulate the physical properties of the object associated with the experience on the basis of our pain. Our concept of pain does not seem to refer to a physical object or event in the world in the same way our concept 'red apple' does. Indeed, given the disassociation between actual tissue damage and pain experiences, it would seem that simple versions of this view at least are a non-starter.

Modern philosophers are trying a new approach to get around these difficulties: pain is not a perception at all; instead, it is a sort of emotional experience (e.g. Clark 2005). The most basic component of pain is its unpleasantness, which is an affective, not a cognitive response (see VALENCE). It remains to be seen how successful this new approach will be.

VALERIE GRAY HARDCASTLE

Aydede, M. (ed.) (2005). *Pain: new essays on its nature and the methodology of its study.* Cambridge, MA: MIT Press.

panic disorder A panic attack is a discrete episode of terror or discomfort that begins suddenly and is associated with intense physiological sensations and thoughts of impending harm, despite the absence of genuine danger. Panic attacks usually reach peak intensity within 10 minutes, and often much sooner than that. For an episode to count as a panic attack, at least four of thirteen symptoms must occur: palpitations, pounding heart, or accelerated heart rate; sweating; trembling or shaking; sensations of shortness of breath or smothering; feeling of choking; chest pain or discomfort; nausea or abdominal distress; feeling dizzy, unsteady, lightheaded, or faint; derealization (feelings of unreality) or depersonalization (being detached from oneself); fear of losing control or going crazy; fear of dying; paraesthesias (numbness or tingling sensations); and chills and hot flushes (American Psychiatric Association 2000, p. 432). An episode characterized by these features, but less than the requisite four symptoms, is called a limited-symptom attack.

Types of panic attack
There are three categories of panic attack. An unexpected (uncued) attack is the classic 'spontaneous' one whereby the person experiences it as erupting 'out of the blue' (Klein 1981). A situationally bound (cued) panic attack is one that nearly always occurs when the person either anticipates or encounters a feared stimulus. For example, individuals phobic of snakes will probably experience a cued panic whenever a snake slithers across their path (see PHOBIAS). A situationally predisposed panic attack is similar to a cued one except that the cue does not invariably trigger an attack. Thus, a person afraid of enclosed spaces is more likely to panic in a crowded elevator than in open spaces, but elevators do not inevitably make the person panic.

This tripartite taxonomy, however, depends on the ability of individuals to identify either internal (e.g. skipped heartbeat) or external (e.g. crowded places) stimuli as cues. The less astute a panicker is in terms of identifying a cue, the more often his or her attacks will seem 'spontaneous'. Moreover, it is often difficult to tell whether an identified cue figured causally in the genesis of the attack or merely preceded it.

Panic disorder
Panic disorder is an *anxiety disorder characterized by recurrent, uncued panic attacks accompanied by at least one month of concern about experiencing further attacks, about their possible consequences, or by marked change in behaviour in response to the attacks. Panic disorder, then, is a psychobiological syndrome comprising episodes of physiological *arousal accompanied by a *fear of the symptoms of arousal. Most individuals with the disorder experience many situationally predisposed attacks as well as the requisite uncued ones. They may also awaken from sleep in the midst of (nocturnal) panic attacks. Panic attacks occur among people with no mental disorder, and in people with other disorders

(e.g. major *depression). Although panic attacks seldom last for more than a few minutes, the abiding dread of further attacks can produce marked functional impairment and suffering.

Individuals with panic disorder may avoid situations and activities associated with the possibility of panic, especially those from which ready escape may be difficult or embarrassing. If avoidance is extensive, a diagnosis of panic disorder with agoraphobia is warranted. Although agoraphobia has often been misconstrued as a fear of open or public spaces, the individual with agoraphobia does not fear these places *per se*. The agoraphobic person fears them as settings where panic may strike.

Epidemiology, sex ratio, and course of panic disorder

According to the National Comorbidity Survey Replication (Kessler *et al.* 2006), 28.3% of Americans have had either a cued or uncued panic attack at least once in their lives. The lifetime prevalence of panic disorder without agoraphobia is 3.7%, whereas the lifetime prevalence of panic disorder with agoraphobia is 1.1%. About twice as many women as men develop panic disorder with or without agoraphobia.

The age of onset for panic disorder appears bimodal, with one peak in late adolescence and the other in the mid-30s. Panic attacks seldom begin before puberty or during middle or old age. About 80% of patients with panic disorder report having experienced major stressors prior to the onset of panic (e.g. divorce, death of a parent). Attacks vary greatly in their frequency. Sometimes people will experience them several times a day, yet these same people may go for months without having an attack. Most people with panic disorder experience a fluctuating course marked by periods of remission and relapse, whereas about 20% experience a chronic course, at least if untreated (Katon 2006).

Approximately 90% of people with panic disorder will have another comorbid condition, such as depression, generalized anxiety disorder, or alcohol abuse (Katon 2006). Some epidemiological studies suggest that a history of panic attacks is associated with increased risk for attempting suicide, but this effect seems driven by the presence of comorbid conditions not by panic disorder alone (Vickers and McNally 2004).

Panic disorder runs in families. The rate of panic disorder among first-degree relatives with the illness is about eight times as high as among relatives of healthy control subjects (Crowe *et al.* 1983). Individuals characterized by elevated *anxiety sensitivity*—fear of anxiety-related symptoms based on beliefs about their possible harmfulness (Reiss and McNally 1985)—are at heightened risk of experiencing spontaneous panic attacks (Schmidt *et al.* 1999) and panic disorder (Schmidt *et al.*

2006). Hence, both genetic and cognitive variables are implicated in the aetiology of panic disorder.

Theories of panic disorder

Most theorists distinguish panic from extreme anxiety. Anxiety, for example, concerns more distant threats than panic, does not have a paroxysmal onset, is marked by less intense physiological responses, and is probably mediated by different neurobiological circuits. But theorists disagree about whether panic is distinct from extreme fear. According to Klein (1993), intense dyspnoea characterizes spontaneous panic, but not fear, thereby implying a respiratory abnormality in panic. According to Barlow (2002, pp. 106–7), panic constitutes intense fear—a false alarm involving the misrelease of the otherwise adaptive fight/flight response.

Psychopathologists have advanced theories about the mechanisms of panic disorder. Klein's (1993) suffocation false alarm theory holds that panic arises from dysfunction in the brain system monitoring possible asphyxiation. When this system incorrectly signals an excess of carbon dioxide, the person experiences a sense of suffocation, thereby inciting panic.

In contrast, Clark's (1986) cognitive theory locates the problem elsewhere. According to Clark, panic occurs when a person catastrophically misinterprets a certain bodily sensation as a harbinger of immediate harm. For example, a person might appraise a harmless heart palpitation as a sign of an impending heart attack, thereby amplifying fear and worsening the palpitations. This seeming confirmation of the catastrophic misappraisal leads to a vicious circle that spirals upward into full-blown panic.

In one of the most comprehensive theories, Bouton *et al.* (2001) draw on modern learning theory to explain the emergence of panic disorder, arguing that the false alarms of uncued panic attacks function as conditioning events heightening the fear of bodily sensations. They also incorporate vulnerability factors into their model (e.g. early experiences with lack of control over important events; neuroticism; anxiety sensitivity).

Treatment of panic disorder

There are several efficacious treatments for panic disorder. Randomized controlled trials confirm the efficacy of five classes of medication relative to pill placebo (Katon 2006): selective serotonin reuptake inhibitors (SSRIs; e.g. fluoxetine (Prozac)), serotonin–norepinephrine reuptake inhibitors (SNRIs; e.g. venlafaxine (Effexor)), high-potency benzodiazepines (BZDs; e.g. alprazolam (Xanax)), tricyclic antidepressants (TCAs; e.g. imipramine (Tofranil)), and monoamine oxidase inhibitors (MAOIs, e.g. phenelzine (Nardil)). In terms of their efficacy in panic disorder, the similarities among these drug classes exceed their differences, and hence other factors figure in treatment choice. Most psychopharmacologists prefer SSRIs as the treatment of choice because the safety and side-effect profile is more favourable for these drugs than for TCAs and MAOIs, and there is less chance of dependence than with the BZDs.

Cognitive behaviour therapy (CBT) is at least as effective as pharmacotherapy (e.g. Barlow *et al.* 2000, Clark *et al.* 1994), and it does not present problems with side-effects or dependence. Despite slight differences in emphasis, most CBT protocols include the following elements. Therapists begin by providing education about panic symptoms, designed to reduce the patient's misconceptions and to attenuate their sensitivity to anxiety. Patients often harbour mistaken beliefs that probably maintain their disorder, such as fears that dizziness will lead to fainting, pounding heart rate portends cardiac arrest, or that anxiety can cause one to go insane. Patients are taught that panic reflects an adaptive, evolved fight/flight response that fires inappropriately when there is no danger. Accordingly, panic itself is not dangerous, but rather an evolved mechanism for defending against danger.

Some CBT clinicians teach patients skills for managing anxiety symptoms, such as applied muscle relaxation and respiratory control to counteract hyperventilation. These methods may restore a sense of control over their bodies, often lacking in panic sufferers. Other CBT clinicians dispense with these methods because they are concerned about conveying the wrong message (i.e. that bodily sensations are potentially harmful and thus must be controlled).

Given that panic disorder is a kind of 'fear of fear', therapists endeavour to desensitize fear via systematic exposure to feared bodily sensations. They may have the patient hyperventilate to induce derealization, breathe through a straw to induce breathlessness, spin in a chair to induce dizziness, and run up stairs to elevate heart rate. Graduated, systematic exposure to feared bodily sensations demonstrate their harmlessness, especially when such exposure is conducted within the context of behavioural experiments designed explicitly to test and refute the patient's problematic beliefs, framed as testable hypotheses. For example, a patient who believes that dizziness leads to collapse may be asked to spin in a chair, and then stand up quickly. The patient's failure to collapse disconfirms the catastrophic prediction, and supports the alternative, benign hypothesis that dizziness may cause unsteadiness, but not collapse.

Many patients have retained their catastrophic beliefs because they have never been tested. More specifically, they have engaged in safety behaviours that have protected the beliefs from testing and hence refutation. For example, if patients also sit down or lean against a wall whenever they get dizzy, they will never learn that they will not collapse.

Finally, many panic disorder patients have developed agoraphobic avoidance, and hence therapists often need to urge them to do *in vivo* (i.e. real-life) exposure exercises, whereby they enter situations they had hitherto been avoiding for fear of panicking.

The authors of a systematic meta-analysis recommended psychological treatment either alone or in combination with medication as the first line of treatment (Furukawa *et al.* 2006). Most studies involved either behavioural or cognitive behavioural treatment, and combined psychological and pharmacological treatment was more effective than medication alone, but not more effective than psychological treatment alone.

RICHARD J. MCNALLY

Barlow, D.H. (2002). *Anxiety and its disorders: the nature and treatment of anxiety and panic*, 2nd edn. New York: Guilford Press.

McNally, R.J. (1994). *Panic disorder: a critical analysis*. New York: Guilford Press.

McNally, R.J. (2002). Anxiety sensitivity and panic disorder. *Biological Psychiatry*, **52**, 938–46.

Roth, W.T., Wilhelm, F.H., and Pettit, D. (2005). Are current theories of panic falsifiable? *Psychological Bulletin*, **131**, 171–92.

paranoia The term paranoia is used to describe a mental state characterized by extreme suspicion and fear of the malevolent intentions of others. Historically, the term has also been used as a name for a type of psychotic disorder in which delusions are the primary symptom, although the name 'delusional disorder' is now more often used instead. Paranoid (or persecutory) delusions—irrational *beliefs that concern the expectation of harm from others, which are resistant to evidence or counter-argument, and which do not simply reflect the individual's cultural background—are often held by patients with this diagnosis, but also by patients diagnosed as suffering from other psychotic conditions. They are also common in patients with *bipolar disorder and psychotic *depression.

Patients with paranoid delusions and ordinary people with subclinical paranoia have often experienced genuine victimization at some point in their lives Animal studies show that the repeated experience of social defeat can lead to sensitization of the midbrain dopamine system (Selten and Cantor-Graae 2005), which is thought to be abnormal in acute psychosis. At the psychological level a number of mechanisms have been implicated. It has been shown that deluded patients in general tend to 'jump to conclusions' when reasoning about sequentially presented probabilistic information Some studies also suggest that 'theory of mind' deficits (impairments in the ability to understand the mental states of others) are implicated in paranoia, although the specificity of this finding remains contentious. Other studies have pointed to abnormal causal inferences and beliefs about the *self in paranoid patients, leading some to argue that their delusions arise from dysfunctional efforts to regulate *self-esteem. However, at present there is no consensus about how these findings can be integrated, although several psychological models have been proposed (Bentall et al. 2001, Freeman et al. 2002).

RICHARD P. BENTALL

passion Like the term *emotion*, *passion* may be used as a mass noun, designating something one may have or exhibit a lot of or a little of at a particular time, usually 'strength' of emotion or *desire, particularly of felt emotion or desire (see FEELINGS (PHILOSOPHICAL PERSPECTIVES); FEELINGS (PSYCHOLOGICAL PERSPECTIVES)). Although in some cases passion, or 'strong' emotion or desire, seems to act as a constraint on a person's will, in other cases it embodies or represents a person's will. To be passionate about politics, for example, is not, typically, to be drawn unwillingly to politics.

The term may also be used as a count noun, as in *the passions*, an archaic term that refers to approximately what we call *the emotions* (see HISTORY OF EMOTIONS). To understand why emotions might have been called *passions*, it helps to note that in many languages nearly all emotion adjectives are derived from participles: for example the English words 'amused', 'annoyed', 'ashamed', 'astonished', 'delighted', 'embarrassed', 'excited', 'frightened', 'horrified', 'irritated', 'pleased', 'terrified', 'surprised', 'upset', and 'worried'. ('Afraid' was originally a participle of the verb 'to affray', and 'sad' descends from the etymological forebear of 'sated'. Colloquial and slang emotion descriptions suggest that the participial model remains a compelling one: 'tickled', 'ticked off', 'burned up', 'bent out of shape', and so on.) When we are, for example, embarrassed, something acts on us, that is, *embarrasses* us: typically, some situation or fact of which we are aware, such as our having tripped on the way to the podium. Not only situations and facts but also persons may 'do' something to us, as in love and hate, and mere possibilities may have an effect on us, as in fear and hope. However, from the assumption that these are all 'passions', in the sense of ways of being acted upon, it does not follow that we are passive with respect to them. Although it is our situation that embarrasses us, we may nevertheless exercise control over whether it does or not.

There is another sense in which the emotions might be described as passions. Unlike intentional actions, emotions do not originate as implementations of our desires. In the case of actions, some of our *beliefs (or rather, their contents) constitute *reasons for* so acting, premises of an *argument in favour*, given our desires: for example, beliefs that the action might be conducive to a particular (desired) end. This is not true of emotions.

Although emotions may depend on desires, wishes, or other pro-attitudes, as well as on beliefs or other epistemic states, the beliefs do not lead to, say, being angry, by operating as premises of an argument in favour of being angry, showing anger to be conducive to a particular (desired) end. For this reason, anger appears to originate independently of our will. Even so, anger, fear, disgust, and several of the social and moral emotions tend to produce new desires of characteristic types, usually pressing, urgent (perhaps insula-based) desires with accompanying arousal, which then may be implemented in intentional actions (see SOCIAL EMOTIONS; MORAL EMOTIONS; AROUSAL). Again, this is not to deny that we (or the relevant cortical areas) may dampen or inhibit the emotions, desires, or actions as they emerge.

ROBERT M. GORDON

Gordon, R. (1987). *The structure of emotions*. Cambridge: Cambridge University Press.
Griffiths, P.E. (1997). *What emotions really are: the problem of psychological categories*. Chicago: University of Chicago Press.

peripheral psychophysiology Psychophysiology is the study of the relationship between psychological states and processes and biological systems. Formally, peripheral psychophysiology is the branch of psychophysiology that focuses on measurements of peripheral physiological processes, in contrast to central psychophysiology where the measures are more focused on the brain. In practice, researchers rarely honour this formal distinction, and peripheral psychophysiology is generally pursued as it derives from, relates to, or impacts on central processes. Peripheral psychophysiology may centre around a specific organ system, such as the *cardiovascular system, *electrodermal system, gastrointestinal system, *neuroendocrine system, neuromuscular system, or others. Typically, however, research interest lies more in patterns or interactions among systems, their relations to neural, endocrine or immune functions, and their implications for behavioural processes, health, and disease (see PSYCHONEUROENDOCRINOLOGY; PSYCHONEUROIMMUNOLOGY).

Below we detail a few general classes and specific examples of peripheral psychophysiological measures and their applications (see Table P1).

Autonomic control: the cardiovascular system
The heart and vascular system are essential for life and are highly regulated by local, hormonal, and neural controls. The heart is dually innervated by the sympathetic and parasympathetic branches of the *autonomic nervous system (see Berntson et al. 2007). Activation of the sympathetic branch increases heart rate, whereas parasympathetic activation slows the beat of the heart. In contrast, the sympathetic branch is largely responsible for the control of myocardial contractility, which

peripheral psychophysiology

Table P1. Some illustrative peripheral organ systems and measures.

Organ	Method	Measure	Application/significance
Heart	Electrocardiography	Heart rate	Measure of autonomic control, arousal
		Heart rate variability	Index of parasympathetic activity
	Impedance cardiography	Pre-ejection period	Index of cardiac contractility/sympathetic control
		Stroke volume	Measure of cardiac output function
Vasculature sphygmomanometry, tonometry		Blood pressure	Studies of determinants of hypertension
Dermal system	Electrodermography	Skin conductance	Index of sympathetic activity
		Skin potential	Marker of arousal and stress
			Detection of deception
Adrenal medulla	Chemical assay	Epinephrine levels	Marker of stress
		Norepinephrine levels	Surrogate for sympathetic activation
Adrenal cortex	Chemical assay	Cortisol levels	Index of stress and hypothalamic–pituitary–adrenal activation
Immune system	Chemical assay	Lymphocyte mobilization	Marker of specific cellular immune responses
		Cytokine release	Marker of humoral immune responses

determines the strength of the contraction and the expulsion of blood. Common psychophysiological measures of cardiovascular function include the electrocardiogram (ECG), which is the recording of the electrical signature of the heartbeat, generally from skin electrodes. From this electrical signal, beat by beat changes in heart rate can be determined and measures of heart rate variability can be derived. Heart rate has been used extensively as a measure of *arousal or activation, but it is ambiguous with regard to its autonomic origins. An increase in heart rate, for example, could arise from sympathetic activation or parasympathetic withdrawal, and these distinct sources of heart rate change may have different implications from a psychophysiological or health perspective. The pattern of heart rate variability (change in heart rate over time), however, can be more informative. Respiratory sinus arrhythmia is a periodic variation in heart rate associated with respiration, with inspiration yielding an increase in heart rate and expiration a decrease. This is attributable to respiratory reflexes which modulate activity in the autonomic branches. This relatively high (respiratory) frequency heart rate variability is mediated solely by the parasympathetic branch of the autonomic nervous system. This is due to the fact that parasympathetic control of the heart is sufficiently fast to follow the respiratory rhythms in parasympathetic control whereas sympathetic cardiac control cannot change sufficiently rapidly to track respiratory fluctuations. Con-

sequently, measures of respiratory sinus arrhythmia (RSA, or high-frequency heart rate variability) are commonly used as an index of vagal control of the heart (Berntson *et al.* 2007).

Another common measurement approach, impedance cardiography, entails recording of the changes in electrical impedance in the chest throughout the cardiac cycle. These electrical changes reflect the movement and distribution of blood, and together with the ECG allow derivation of systolic time intervals, such as the pre-ejection period (PEP). The PEP is the time between the electrical excitation of the ventricular myocardium and the opening of the aortic valve and ejection of blood. The PEP is a function of myocardial contractility, and because the sympathetic system modulates contractility, the PEP has been used as an index of sympathetic control of the heart.

Autonomic control: the electrodermal system

Electrodermal responses are electrical signatures of sympathetic innervation of eccrine sweat glands, and have been used widely as an index of sympathetic control, arousal, attention, and even deception. In the late 1800s, Charles Féré (1852–1907) found that the electrical resistance to a small external current passed across electrodes on the skin was diminished on presentation of sensory stimuli, and shortly thereafter, Jean de Tarchanoff (1857–1927) reported that the skin itself was electrically polarized and this skin potential can be measured by surface electrodes (for a review see Bloch, 1993). These early studies spearheaded a now extensive literature on skin potential levels (SPLs) and responses (SPRs) and on skin conductance levels (SCLs) and responses (SCRs), which are the reciprocal of skin resistance and are used more commonly than resistance measures for technical reasons.

Electrodermal responses are variously applied in studies of stress, which tends to increase SCL and increase the rate of phasic SCRs (*spontaneous* or *nonspecific* responses). In addition to SCL, transient SCRs evoked by explicit stimuli (*specific* SCRs), especially surprising or noxious stimuli, have been used to index arousal, emotional response, and the *orienting (attentional) response (see Dawson *et al.*, 2007, for review).

Peripheral hormonal measures: adrenal medullary hormones

In addition to direct or indirect measures of autonomic neural control, such as those addressed above, peripheral psychophysiology may entail measures of hormonal control. This might include assays for circulating adrenomedullary 'stress' hormones—epinephrine (adrenaline) and norepinephrine. These hormones are secreted by the adrenal medulla under the control of the sympathetic branch of the autonomic nervous system, and have been used as markers of stress and sympathetic activation (see STRESS).

Peripheral hormonal measures: adrenal cortical hormones

Another stress-related hormone, cortisol, is secreted by the adrenal cortex. Secretion of cortisol is under the control of adrenocorticotropic hormone (ACTH) from the pituitary gland, which in turn is under the control of corticotropin-releasing hormone (CRH) from the hypothalamus. The hypothalamus is important in neuroendocrine control and in the integration of autonomic and endocrine systems. Consequently, it figures prominently in stress, and circulating levels of ACTH and cortisol have been among the most widely used hormonal markers of stress (Kaltsas and Chrousos 2007).

The immune system—psychoneuroimmunology and peripheral psychophysiology

Psychophysiologists have long been concerned with the relations between psychology, physiology, health and disease. Historically, this interest has centred around autonomic or hormonal measures. More recently, however, it has become clear that autonomic and humoral systems affect immune functions and the immune system can in turn modulate behavioural, autonomic, and hormonal states (Cohen and Kinney 2001). This interaction represents a potential pathway by which autonomic and hormonal systems can affect health outcomes. Often, the attention has focused on the pathway from brain→auto-

nomic/neuroendocrine system→immune functions. Examples include the effects of cortisol on *cytokines (immune signalling molecules) or the effects of epinephrine and norepinephrine on the selective mobilization of immune cells (Dhabhar and McEwen 2001, Bosch *et al.*, 2005).

An interesting and equally important direction of influence has also been identified, from immune system→autonomic/neuroencorine system→brain. Immune cytokines can influence diverse neurobehavioural processes such as sickness response, pain perception, and *mood, in part via ascending projections of the vagus (parasympathetic) nerve (Watkins and Maier 2005). That is, not only can brain/behavioural states affect immune functions, but immune states can affect brain/behavioural functions. This reciprocal interaction, as depicted in Fig. P1, is of pivotal importance.

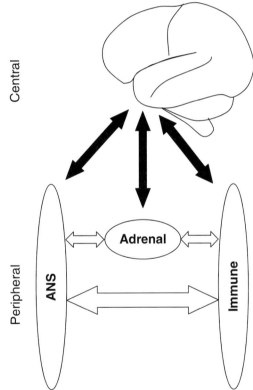

Fig. P1. Illustration of the multiple interactions between peripheral and psychophsyiological systems and central neural mechanisms. Open arrows indicate interactions among the autonomic, endocrine, and immune systems at a peripheral level. Solid arrows indicate interactions among these peripheral systems and the brain. ANS, autonomic nervous system.

personality (and emotion)

Reciprocal interactions among central and peripheral systems

Researchers in peripheral psychophysiology have often focused on the efferent control of organ systems. As noted above, however, it is now clear that reciprocal influences from the periphery can affect the brain and behaviour. Autonomic sensory feedback, for example, has been shown to enhance memory and foster attention and cortical processing (for reviews see Berntson et al., 2003, and McGaugh and Cahill, 2003). Moreover, stimulation of ascending vagal afferents is being explored as a method for treating intractable pain, epilepsy, and depression (Groves and Brown 2005). The ultimate understanding of peripheral psychophysiology will require further work on each of the pathways of interaction depicted in Fig. P1.

GARY G. BERNTSON AND JOHN T. CACIOPPO

Ader, R., Felton, D.L., and Cohen, N. (2001). *Psychoneuroimmunology.* San Diego, CA: Academic Press.

Berntson, G.G., Cacioppo, J.T., and Sarter, M. (2003). Bottom-up: implications for neurobehavioral models of anxiety and autonomic regulation. In: R.J. Davidson, K.R. Scherer, and H.H. Goldsmith (eds), *Handbook of affective sciences,* pp. 1105–16. New York: Oxford University Press.

Cacioppo, J.T., Tassinary, L.G., and Berntson, G.G. (eds) (2007). *Handbook of psychophysiology,* 3rd edn. Cambridge: Cambridge University Press.

personality (and emotion) Personality is the coherent patterning of affect, behaviour, cognition, and desires (goals) over time and space. Just as a full-blown emotion represents an integration of feeling, action, appraisal, and wants at a particular time and location so personality represents integration over time and space of these components (Ortony et al. 2005). A helpful analogy is to consider that personality is to emotion as climate is to weather. That is, what one expects is personality, what one observes at any particular moment is emotion.

To understand the personality–affect link it is necessary to consider the ways in which personality may be described. Since Theophrastus' (371–c.287 BC) discussion of characters and Galen's (c.AD 129–200) theory of temperament (Stelmack and Stalikas 1991), dimensional models of individual differences in personality have consistently identified three (the Giant Three; e.g. Eysenck and Eysenck 1985) to five (the Big Five; e.g. Digman 1990) broad dimensions of personality. Two of these dimensions, in particular, extraversion (E) and neuroticism (N; sometimes referred to by the other end of the dimension as emotional stability) have been associated with individual differences in affective level and environmental responsivity (Revelle 1995, Corr 2008) (see EXTRAVERSION; NEUROTICISM).

Ever since antiquity, starting with Galen's classification of the four different humours, it has been assumed that individuals differ in their predisposition to experience certain emotions. Extrapolating from animal studies, E and N have been associated with the *behavioural activation system (BAS) and the *behavioural inhibition system (BIS), respectively, while distinctions between trait fear and trait anxiety have been associated with the fight/freeze/flight system (FFFS) (Gray and McNaughton 2000, Corr 2008). Indeed, the basic assumptions of reinforcement sensitivity theory (Corr 2008), perhaps better labelled as the three systems theory, are that the stable personality traits reflect individual differences in reactivity to emotional and affectively valenced environmental cues.

Descriptively, there is much literature on hysteric, neurotic, or anhedonic personalities (Kellerman 1990), or, in more recent terminology, on trait anger, trait anxiety, or trait positive–negative affect (Spielberger et al. 1999, Tellegen et al. 1999) (see AFFECTIVE STYLE). These trait differences in emotionality increase the odds of experiencing trait-congruent emotions. In other words, individuals high on trait anxiety run an increased risk of experiencing anxiety bouts, individuals high on trait anger get irritated more often, and so forth.

Thus, in a quasirepresentative survey of everyday emotion experiences Scherer et al. (2004) showed that the emotionality dispositions may significantly increase the risk of experiencing certain emotions. Concretely, the more frequently respondents habitually experienced a particular kind of emotion (trait emotionality), the more likely they experienced an exemplar of that emotion category yesterday. Thus, respondents high on trait anxiety were almost three times as likely to have experienced anxiety yesterday compared with those who are low on this trait. In the case of trait sadness and trait despair, the likelihood is about two times higher. Respondents high on trait irritation are about 1.5 times more likely to have experienced anger yesterday. Similarly, respondents reporting frequent habitual pleasure, surprise, or pride experiences are also 1.5 times more likely to have experienced joy or happiness. Because some emotions occur less frequently than expected for respondents with certain habitual emotion dispositions, some types of trait emotionality might inoculate, or shield, against particular emotions. The results seem to indicate that trait pleasure may reduce the risk of despair, and that trait surprise may reduce the risk of anxiety.

These results do not just reflect common responses to questionnaires, but rather reflect basic neural processes. Using functional brain mapping (e.g. functional magnetic resonance imaging), trait extraversion and neuroticism were associated with differential activation to rewarding or positive slides (extraversion) and to threat cues (neuroticism). Extraversion was correlated with amount of activation in widely distributed brain regions (*amygdala, caudate, medio-frontal gyrus, right fusiform gyrus) in response to positively valenced slides but unrelated to activation to negatively valenced slides. Neuroticism, on the other hand, was correlated with amount of activation to negatively valenced slides, but unrelated to activation to positively valenced slides (Canli 2004).

Taken together, these results seem to strongly confirm the notion of habitual or trait emotionality; that is, an individual difference variable consisting of a disposition to experience certain types of emotions more frequently than other people. While this notion is widely accepted for trait anxiety and trait anger (Spielberger et al. 1999), as well as trait positive affect (Tellegen et al. 1999), other types of trait emotionality have rarely been investigated. Nor is the relationship of affect to the other three of the 'Big Five' as well established.

To some, extraversion is just trait positive affect and neuroticism is just trait negative affect. Although trait extraversion is associated with trait positive affect in many cultures (Lucas and Baird 2004) and has been proposed to have the tendency to experience positive affect at its core (Watson and Clark 1997), extraversion is more than positive affect, for it also represents differences in behaviour, cognition, and desires (Wilt and Revelle in press). Extraversion is related to general activation and behavioural approach as well as ways of categorizing words in terms of their semantic associates (Rogers and Revelle 1998). Similarly, neuroticism is not just negative affect, for it has cognitive and behavioural components as well. Other non-affective components of extraversion and neuroticism include differences in desires, with extraversion associated with a need for social contact, power, and status and neuroticism associated with needs for acceptance, tranquillity, order, vengeance, and savings (Olson and Weber 2004).

One of the issues that remains difficult to assess is the origin of such affect dispositions. While clearly sharing a large genetic component (Bouchard 2004), some of these dispositions may in fact be already prepared at birth or early childhood (Durbin et al. 2005) while others may develop through learning and socialization, often in interaction with innate dispositions (Caspi et al. 2005) (see GENETICS OF AFFECT; TEMPERAMENT). Of course, many other individual factors may also play a role.

Recently, attribution and appraisal theorists have suggested that specific styles of causal attribution or appraisal styles in a very general sense can lead certain people to be more or less prone to experience certain types of emotions because of differences in *goals, *values, and *coping potential (van Reekum and Scherer 1997) (see ATTRIBUTIONAL STYLE; APPRAISAL STYLE). This is

particularly salient when a person demonstrates an appraisal bias which may lead to dysfunctional and unrealistic appraisals and, in consequence, to maladaptive emotions or even emotional disturbances (Kaiser and Scherer 1998, Roseman and Kaiser 2001). An appraisal bias would be exhibited if a person has a tendency to always over- or underestimate the responsibility of self or another person for a failure experience, or to systematically, irrespective of circumstances, over- or underestimate his or her coping potential. Like the question of the origin of affect dispositions, it will be important to examine to what extent these biases are effects of individual learning or socialization careers or whether cultural or social group factors may play a major role in sensitizing individuals to certain appraisal possibilities or to privilege certain types of appraisal style.

Although representing different research traditions, normal and abnormal personality may be integrated into a common framework with respect to individual differences in affective processes (Markon et al. 2005, Krueger and Tackett 2006). Extreme levels of activation of the BIS, BAS, or FFFS have been used as explanations of many of the personality disorders, particularly those associated with uninhibited behaviours, 'externalizing' disorders, overly inhibited anxious behaviours, and 'internalizing' disorders. The search for a common core to normal and abnormal personality has emphasized the study of affective and cognitive deficits in psychopathology as they relate to multiples levels of processing, from the reactive, to the routine, to the reflective (van Reekum and Scherer 1997, Ortony et al. 2005).

In that personality represents the integration over time of feelings, actions, thoughts, and desires, theoretical developments in personality benefit from a greater understanding of emotional processes. At the same time, research in emotion can take advantage of individual differences in sensitivities to situational cues and predispositions to emotional states. The questions of why some people become angry while others become frightened or depressed in response to threats, and why some become elated while others seem unaffected when given rewards will be better understood by jointly studying the problem of long-term coherence (personality) with short-term fluctuations in affect, behaviour, cognition, and desire (emotion).

WILLIAM REVELLE AND KLAUS R. SCHERER

perspective taking Perspective taking is a broad topic, a central component of which concerns people's intuitive understanding of others' affective states (see EMPATHY). Research makes clear that such affective perspective taking is egocentrically biased: People project onto others their own reactions to affective situations. One way that affective perspective taking is egocentrically biased is that people predict others would react as they themselves do to the affective situations they are in (Krueger, 1998). For instance, when people were asked whether they were willing to wear a sign saying "Repent," the 50% of willing people estimated that 61% of others would also be willing whereas the 50% of unwilling people estimated that only 39% of others would be willing. The difference between 61% and 39% reflects projection of people's own behavior onto others. One important reason for egocentrically biased perspective taking of this type is that people assume they experience reasonable, natural reactions to reality, and that other reasonable people will therefore react similarly (Ross and Ward 1995).

A different kind of social projection occurs when people in a relatively neutral situation estimate others' reactions to being in an affectively arousing situation. Such affective perspective taking across situations entails two distinct judgments (Van Boven & Loewenstein, 2005). First, people in relatively neutral situations predict what their own reactions would be to an affectively arousing situation; for instance, when people predict how others would react to an embarrassing situation by predicting how they themselves would react to the embarrassing situation (see AFFECTIVE FORECASTING). Second, people moderate their self-predictions to accommodate perceived similarity between themselves and others. For instance, people may adjust their self-predicted reaction to an embarrassing situation based on an intuitive belief that others are generally less influenced than themselves by embarrassment. Because of these dual judgments their biased self-predictions may cause people to exhibit egocentrically biased perspective taking even if people have perfectly calibrated perceptions of interpersonal similarity. Specifically, because people tend to underestimate the impact of affective arousal on themselves (Loewenstein, 1996), they tend to underestimate the impact of being in an affectively arousing situation on others. For instance, people faced with a relatively neutral, purely hypothetical choice underestimated how reluctant they would be to engage in an embarrassing public performance (dancing) in exchange for money, which led them to underestimate other people's reluctance to perform (Van Boven, Loewenstein, & Dunning, 2005).

Egocentric biases in affective perspective taking can have important implications for social judgment and behavior. People's tendency to underestimate the impact of affective arousal on others can lead people to interpret others' behavior as stemming from their underlying dispositions rather than from transient affective states. For instance, people who were in a neutral state, but not those who were fatigued, attributed the aggressive behavior of a temporarily exhausted and stressed individual to that person's underlying aggression rather than to a natural reaction to a transient

affective situation (Nordgren, van der Pligt, and van Harreveld 2007). People's tendency to underestimate the impact of affective arousal on others can also lead people to behave in costly ways toward each other. For instance, people who do not fully appreciate how attached others are to the objects they happen to own may offer too little to purchase those objects, thereby preventing otherwise mutually beneficial transactions from taking place (Van Boven, Dunning, and Loewenstein 2000 ; see ECONOMICS AND EMOTION).

LEAF VAN BOVEN

Krueger, J. (1998). On the perception of social consensus. In M. Zanna (Ed.), *Advances in experimental social psychology*. San Diego, CA: Academic Press.

Loewenstein, G. (1996). Out of control: Visceral influences on behavior. *Organizational Behavior and Human Decision Processes*, **65**, 272–292.

Nordgren, L. F., van der Pligt, J., and van Harreveld, F. (2007). Evaluating Eve: Visceral states influence evaluation of impulsive behavior. *Journal of Personality and Social Psychology*, **93**(1), 75–84.

Ross, L., and Ward, A. (1995). Psychological barriers to dispute resolution. In M. P. Zanna (Ed.), *Advances in experimental social psychology*. San Diego, CA: Academic Press.

Van Boven, L., Dunning, D., and Loewenstein, G. (2000). Egocentric empathy gaps between owners and buyers: Misperceptions of the endowment effect. *Journal of Personality and Social Psychology*, **79**, 66–76.

Van Boven, L., and Loewenstein, G. (2005). Cross-situational projection. In M. D. Alicke, D. Dunning & J. Krueger (Eds.), *The self in social perception*. New York: Psychology Press.

Van Boven, L., Loewenstein, G., and Dunning, D. (2005). The illusion of courage in social predictions: Underestimating the impact of fear of embarrassment on other people. *Organizational Behavior and Human Decision Processes*, **96**, 130–141.

pheromones Most animals use odorous substrates originating from their bodies to communicate. Beyond reliance on common olfactory cues, many species have evolved specialized chemosignals to orchestrate behaviour in critical phases of social interactions and reproductive physiology. Karlson and Lüscher (1959) called these latter signals 'pheromones', a concept referring to biologically active compound(s) externalized by one individual and prompting a response in a receiving conspecific. Key characteristics of such pheromones are well-identified, chemically simple stimuli (one or a few compounds in a given ratio) which, at infinitesimal concentration, elicit species-specific stereotyped responses that are minimally dependent on learning. Depending on measurable outcomes, the pheromone is qualified as a 'releaser', for compounds affecting immediate behaviour, or as a 'primer', for compounds affecting more progressive neuroendocrine or developmental processes (these effects not always being exclusive).

From the original definition in insects, the concept was extended to mammals and humans with profuse debates and redefinitions to fit to the complexities of mammalian behaviour (Doty 2003). Although numerous chemosensory effects have been described as pheromonal, only few pheromones have been effectively identified in nonhuman mammals (the best-known examples being androstenone, the boar attractant triggering a sow's mating posture, 2-dimethylbut-2-enal releasing sucking in newborn rabbits, and a set of urinary volatiles eliciting intermale aggression or acceleration of female puberty in mice). In humans, the pheromone concept remains even more contentious, some espousing it uncritically while others rebuff it as devoid of strong empirical evidence. Pheromonal effects have been reported, for example ovarian cyclicity entrained by female or male axillary sweat, but so far no convincing evidence is available for a pheromonal compound that invariably elicits these effects. This does not mean that body substrates are informationally empty to humans. Their odours do play a part in recognition and evaluative assessment of others, in mate choice, sexual attraction, and regulation of mother–infant relations. Some steroid derivates in body secretions are also known to modulate mood and affective states, often without conscious odour percept. When used in brain imaging studies such steroid chemosignals activate areas involved in attentional, emotional, and olfactory processing. But as the results hardly overlap across studies, and as considerable interindividual differences and strong contextual effects appear, the pheromonal nature of these stimuli remains equivocal (Wysocki and Preti 2004). Thus, although odours have deep and ubiquitous influences on human affect, cognition, and actions, pheromones remain to be scientifically ascertained in humans, beyond any pressure from what has also become a marketing catchword. See also ODOUR AND EMOTION.

BENOIST SCHAAL

phobias There are three forms of phobia: specific phobia (sometimes called 'simple phobia'), social phobia, and agoraphobia. This section will focus mainly on simple/specific phobia. The American Psychiatric Association *Diagnostic and statistical manual of mental disorders* (DSM-IV) (American Psychiatric Association 1994) characterizes specific phobias as follows: (1) A marked and persistent fear that is excessive or unreasonable, cued by the presence or anticipation of a specific object or situation. (2) Exposure to the phobic stimulus almost invariably provokes an immediate anxiety response. (3) The person recognizes that the fear is excessive or unreasonable. (4) The phobic situation in avoided or else endured with intense distress. (5) The avoidance, anxious antici-

pation, or distress in the feared situation interferes significantly with the person's normal routine, occupation (or academic) functioning, or social activities or relationships, or there is marked distress about having the phobia. (6) For those under 18 years of age, there must be a minimum duration of 6 months. (7) The symptoms are not better accounted for by another diagnosis. See FEAR; ANXIETY.

Social phobia is similarly diagnosed, but the trigger has to be one or more social or performance situations in which the person is exposed to unfamiliar people or possible scrutiny by others. In agoraphobia, anxiety and panic attacks would be triggered by a variety of public situations including walking along the street, travelling on public transport, and visiting shops and shopping malls (see PANIC DISORDER).

Prevalence and course of phobias
Estimates of the prevalence of specific phobias vary markedly. However, specific phobias are generally accepted to be one of the most common psychological disorders. In one large and well-conducted British study, 1.8% of adults had a diagnosis of a phobia (Jenkins *et al.* 1997). In children, reported prevalence rates for specific phobias also vary substantially, but a large, well-conducted British epidemiological survey reported that about 1% of children had a phobia (Ford *et al.* 1999) and a number of other studies have reported rates that are not much higher (Bergeron *et al.* 1992, Briggs-Gowan *et al.* 2000). Indeed, it appears that most phobias develop during childhood (Craske *et al.* 1996) and, in the absence of treatment, these disorders are highly chronic, meaning that the prevalence rates are probably similar in adults and children.

As is often the case in the emotional disorders, research shows that adult women are consistently more likely to suffer from phobias than men. In the study described above (Jenkins *et al.* 1997) 2.5% of women reported phobias, compared with 1.2% of men.

Using DSM-IV criteria for specific phobias, Fredrikson *et al.* (1996) reported that the most common phobias in a sample of adults were heights (7.5%), snakes (5.5%), and enclosed spaces (4.0%).

Theories
There is compelling evidence that there are 'fear-relevant' stimuli that more readily acquire fear-evoking properties (for example snakes and spiders) compared with fear-irrelevant stimuli (e.g. flowers and mushrooms). One influential model suggests that humans have evolved a 'fear module' in the brain, which gives rise to selective associations being formed between certain prepared stimuli and negative outcomes. Indeed, biological research has identified specific brain regions that process fear information: for example, lesions to the

central *amygdala interfere with fear responses (LeDoux 1998b) and this area is well connected to regions of the brainstem and hypothalamus that have been implicated in specific symptoms of fear (see NEURAL ARCHITECTURE OF EMOTION). These systems affect learning and processing of fear-relevant events.

Consistent with this evidence, phobic humans have several biases in the way they process threat information. For example, a spider phobic would be slower to name the colour of spider-related words compared with non-anxious controls (the emotional Stroop task); social phobics show selective attention to angry faces; and animal phobics show selective attention towards their fear-evoking stimuli (see ATTENTION AND EMOTION). These biases appear to occur even when stimuli are presented subliminally, although the effect is around half that of supraliminal exposures (see Bar-Haim et al., 2007 for a thorough meta-analysis of this literature). Genetic research suggests that about 44% of the variance in specific fear is explained by genetics, with 37% attributable to nonshared environments (Eley et al., 2003) (see GENETICS OF AFFECT). The genetic component is supported by models of phobias that suggest that *temperament is major factor in vulnerability to phobias. The *behavioural inhibition system (BIS) is a nervous system circuit, or set of circuits, the anatomical substrate of which is the septo-hippocampal system (SHS). This system is thought to control the experience of anxiety in response to anxiety-relevant cues (see Gray and McNaughton 2000). The BIS is believed to underpin a core temperamental trait important in the acquisition of fear, which Gray and McNaughton labelled 'trait anxiety'. Other theorists concur (broadly speaking) on the importance of the BIS but the trait it underlies has been labelled variously as 'negative emotionality', 'negative affect', 'fear', and 'neuroticism/negative affect'. Despite the differing nomenclature, there is agreement that the BIS underlies a core temperament that either lies on a continuum with anxiety disorders or acts as diatheses for anxiety disorders (see PERSONALITY).

In terms of nonshared environment, direct traumatic experiences, vicarious learning, and verbal information are experiences implicated in the development of phobias (see Field, 2006a, for a review) (see LEARNING, EMOTIONAL (NEUROSCIENCE PERSPECTIVES)). Early learning models of phobias explained them in terms of a stimulus coming to evoke fear through association with a traumatic event. For example, Watson and Rayner (1920) famously 'conditioned' fear of a rat into a 9-month-old infant 'little Albert' by banging a claw hammer on an iron bar every time the rat was proximal (see Field and Cartwright-Hatton, in press for details). Although this simple and elegant model explained a variety of unusual fears, not all phobics remember experiencing such trau-matic events. This can be explained in part by the subtler pathways to fear. Fears can be acquired simply by watching someone else's fearful reaction to something (vicarious learning): laboratory-reared rhesus monkeys rapidly learn to fear snakes after witnessing wild-reared monkeys acting fearfully toward real and toy snakes, and this fear is still present three months later (e.g. Mineka et al. 1984). Also, children acquire behaviours and responses consistent with fear simply through hearing threat information about stimuli: children given threat information about animals they had previously not encountered showed changes in their long-term self-reported fears, their avoidance of these animals, and attentional biases towards these animals, similar to those described (Field 2006a, b). Temperament (trait anxiety) appears to mediate the effect of fear information on avoidance and attentional biases too (Field 2006b).

Although all of these theories could broadly be applied to social phobia, models of social phobia are more recent and have yet to unpick the developmental causes of the disorder. However, like specific phobias, social phobics have often had negative social experiences, or memories of such experiences, exhibit cognitive biases to socially relevant cues, and are more at risk of developing social anxiety if they have an anxious temperament (see Field and Cartwright-Hatton, in press for a review).

Treatment of phobias

Although phobias are often considered to be one of the least serious psychological disorders they can be extremely distressing, and can cause substantial interference in the sufferer's life. Without treatment, phobias will very often run a chronic course.

Most of the extant research on treatment has examined behavioural approaches, which rely on exposure to the feared stimulus (see COGNITIVE BEHAVIOUR THERAPY). Exposure may take place either imaginally or in vivo. In 1993, the American Psychological Association task force on specific phobias concluded that both were effective treatments for simple phobias (American Psychological Association 1997). However, research seems to suggest that, where possible, in vivo exposure might be preferable (Choy et al. 2007). Stern and Marks (1973) concluded that anxiety levels during exposure have little effect on the outcome, but in general, prolonged exposure is more effective than brief exposure.

Recently, attention has turned to how cognitive approaches might be employed in treatment. Cognitive techniques are used to challenge distorted negative *beliefs about the feared stimulus, and have been shown to be a useful adjunct to behavioural approaches. These approaches have been particularly useful for social phobia, in which, for example, video feedback can be used to challenge beliefs about how the person looks in social situations.

A very recent and promising addition to the clinician's armoury is the use of virtual reality technology to provide exposure to the feared stimulus. Early results of trials demonstrate high efficacy and high acceptability to clients.

A range of other techniques are reported in the literature, in particular eye movement desensitization (EMDR), hypnotherapy, and psychodynamic approaches, but there is a dearth of high-quality outcome research to support their use in the treatment of specific phobias. However, 'applied tension', which has been used to treat blood-injury phobia (where in contrast to other phobias, heart rate and blood pressure fall to the point where the individual may faint), does have good empirical support (Öst et al. 1991).

ANDY P. FIELD AND SAM CARTWRIGHT-HATTON

Bar-Haim, Y., Lamy, D., Pergamin, L., Bakermans-Kranenburg, M.J., and van Ijzendoorn, M.H. (2007). Threat-related attentional bias in anxious and nonanxious individuals: a meta-analytic study. *Psychological Bulletin*, **133**, 1–24.

Choy, Y., Fyer, A.J., and Lipsitz, J.D. (2007). Treatment of specific phobia in adults. *Clinical Psychology Review*, **27**, 266–86.

Field, A.P. (2006a). Is conditioning a useful framework for understanding the development and treatment of phobias? *Clinical Psychology Review*, **26**, 857–75.

Platonism

Plato (*c*.427–*c*.347 BC) has no formal theory of affectivity. His importance for the field consists largely in having initiated the philosophical analysis of human motivations in the context of theories, both implicit and explicit, about the nature of the human soul and its relationship to the body (see MOTIVATION; MIND–BODY PROBLEM). He developed different views in his various dialogues and it is not to be expected that a single view on motivation, the emotions, or affectivity can be constructed from them. For example, in the *Phaedo* the soul is sharply opposed to the body and most emotions, desires, fears, etc. are located in the body—that is, it is implicitly denied that these are psychological states or events (see EMBODIMENT). In the *Republic* (especially in Book 4) Plato's Socrates purports to prove that the soul consists of three quasi-autonomous 'parts' or aspects, each with its own dispositions and motivations and each able in principle to oppose the others. The appetitive aspect of the soul (*epithumētikon*) is tied most closely to the body and is the locus of a wide variety of sexual, alimentary, and acquisitive motivations. The spirited aspect (*thumos*) is associated with a variety of aggressive, self-assertive motivations. The reasoning or calculative aspect (*logistikon*) plans for itself and for the whole person and also focuses its attention

on abstract intellectual endeavours. In the *Timaeus* these three 'parts' are given spatial location by being associated with regions of the body: the reasoning part in the head, the spirited part in the upper midriff, the appetitive part in the lower abdomen.

Plato's exploration of the idea of parts of the soul (which is developed somewhat differently in the *Phaedrus*) has many problematic aspects. It does, however, allow for important reflections on the nature of mental conflict and on the challenges of self-control (both mental and physical). Although Plato had no consistent doctrine on affectivity (notoriously, the views taken about physical pleasure vary across the dialogues), his model for psychological partition became a framework for much subsequent analysis of motivations, virtues and vices, and affective response. From Aristotle to Freud and beyond, Plato's direct and indirect influence on psychological theory has been overwhelming—a considerable accomplishment for a philosopher with no settled theory on the matter.

BRAD INWOOD

pleasure

Dictionaries commonly define pleasure as a feeling of happiness, enjoyment, and satisfaction. In empirical research, these components have received separate attention (see POSITIVE EMOTIONS; HAPPINESS; JOY; ENJOYMENT). Rozin's (1999, p. 12) definition of pleasure as 'a positive experienced state that we seek and that we try to maintain or enhance' highlights pleasure's positive hedonic value, and its motivational force and role in behaviour regulation, in particular when juxtaposed with a similarly inclusive definition of pain (see APPROACH/WITHDRAWAL; PAIN). Pleasure is often assumed to provide a common currency that allows for comparable valuations of different sources of experience. While these assumptions are widely shared in psychology, they are the topic of centuries of controversy in philosophy (Katz 2006).

Typologies of pleasure usually distinguish between the sensory pleasures of smell, taste, touch, and vision; pleasures derived from mastery, including the experience of flow; pleasures of social contact; and pleasures of the mind, like aesthetic appreciation (see AESTHETIC EMOTIONS). Sexual pleasure may involve any or all of these. Throughout, pleasure is intensified by attention to the enjoyable activity or object, but impaired by introspective attention to the experience of pleasure itself.

Prospective, concurrent, and retrospective reports of pleasure often diverge, indicating that expectations and memories are sometimes poorly related to actual experience. Moreover, a growing body of findings suggests that desire and experienced pleasure are frequently dissociated (Berridge 1999) (see WELL-BEING; LIFE SATISFACTION). Hence, choice (based on expectations and desires) is a poor indicator of the actual experience of pleasure (Kahneman 1999).

DANIEL KAHNEMAN AND NORBERT SCHWARZ

Frijda, N.H. (2007). Pleasure. *The laws of emotion*, Ch. 7. Mahwah, NJ: Lawrence Erlbaum Associates.

positive emotions Positive emotions include a range of distinct pleasant states (e.g. *joy, *interest, *contentment, *gratitude, *pride, and *love). Such feelings frequently arise when organisms appraise their current circumstances as safe and their current *needs as satiated. Distinct appraisals further characterize distinct positive emotions. Most positive emotions are marked by smiles as well as the urge to continue doing whatever it is that brings on the pleasurable feeling (see DUCHENNE SMILE).

Positive emotions had long been a puzzle for evolutionary accounts of emotion (see EVOLUTION OF EMOTION). Most accounts rested on the assumption that all emotions—both pleasant and unpleasant—were adaptive to our human ancestors because they produced urges to act in particular ways, by triggering *specific* *action tendencies (Frijda 1986). Fear, for instance, is linked with the urge to flee, anger with the urge to attack, disgust the urge to expel, and so on. A core idea within the concept of specific action tendencies is that having these particular actions spring to mind made emotions evolutionary adaptive because these were the actions that worked best in getting our ancestors out of specific situations that threatened life and limb. Another core idea is that specific action tendencies are *embodied thoughts* (see EMBODIMENT): as they overtake conscious thought, they also trigger rapid changes in *cardiovascular and neuroendocrine activity to support the actions called forth (see PSYCHONEUROENDOCRINOLOGY). The concept of specific action tendencies, then, explained why emotions infuse both mind and body and how the forces of natural selection might have shaped and preserved emotions to the extent that they aided quick and decisive action in life-or-death circumstances.

Difficulties arose when past theorists tried to pinpoint the specific action tendencies for positive emotions. Joy was linked to the urge to *do anything*. Contentment was linked to the urge to *do nothing*. Although fitting, these tendencies are vague and nonspecific. Positive emotions, then, did not fit the same theoretical mould that worked so well for the negative emotions.

The broaden-and-build theory was developed to provide a new evolutionary account for the existence of positive emotions (Fredrickson 1998). The theory holds that unlike negative emotions, which narrow people's ideas about possible actions (through their associated specific action tendencies), positive emotions *broaden* people's ideas about possible actions, opening their awareness to a wider range of thoughts and actions than is typical for them. Joy, for instance, sparks the urge to play and be creative, interest sparks the urge to explore and learn, contentment sparks the urge to savour current circumstances and integrate them into new self-views and world views. Experimental studies confirm that positive emotions broaden attention and thinking (Fredrickson and Branigan 2005) (see ATTENTION AND EMOTION).

Whereas narrowed mindsets sparked by negative emotions were adaptive in instances that threatened our human ancestors' survival, broadened mindsets sparked by positive emotions were adaptive in different ways, over longer timescales: broadened mindsets were adaptive because, over time, such expansive awareness served to build our human ancestor's resources, spurring on their development. For instance, the play inspired by joy can build physical, intellectual, and social skills. The exploration inspired by interest can build knowledge and intellectual complexity. The savouring and integration inspired by contentment can build and refine self-views and world views. With repeated experiences of positive emotions, these resources accumulated and compounded, better equipping our human ancestors to respond to subsequent and inevitable threats to their survival. Indeed, several well-controlled longitudinal studies have found a link between expressed positive emotions and longevity (e.g. Danner *et al.* 2001). To the extent that the capacity to experience positive emotions was genetically encoded, this capacity would have been shaped by natural selection in ways that explain the form and function of the positive emotions experienced by modern-day humans.

BARBARA L. FREDRICKSON

posttraumatic stress disorder Posttraumatic stress disorder (PTSD) is an *anxiety disorder comprising three clusters of signs and symptoms that develops after a person has experienced a traumatic event (DSM-IV-TR, American Psychiatric Association 2000, pp. 463–8) (see STRESS). Canonical stressors include combat, natural disasters, rape, and confinement to a concentration camp. To qualify for the diagnosis, a victim must experience the following symptoms for a least a month following the trauma: at least one symptom from the re-experiencing cluster (e.g. intrusive thoughts, nightmares); at least three symptoms from the avoidance/numbing cluster (e.g. avoiding reminders of the trauma, difficulty experiencing positive emotions toward others); and at least two symptoms from the increased arousal cluster (e.g. exaggerated startle, insomnia). Finally, the symptoms must produce clinically significant distress or impairment in important areas of functioning.

Unlike most syndromes in DSM-IV-TR, the definition of PTSD incorporates an aetiological event—exposure to a trauma—as part of the criteria set. That is, the memory of the trauma provides the aetiological core from which the other symptoms originate. As Breslau *et al.* (2002, p.574) emphasized: 'It is their connection to a specific stressor that transforms the list of PTSD symptoms into a distinct DSM disorder'. Some PTSD symptoms are intentional in Brentano's (1889/1984) sense (see INTENTIONALITY). They are *about* the traumatic event, not merely *caused* by it. Hence, the content of intrusive thoughts and nightmares is the traumatic event, and when someone avoids thoughts, feelings, and activities it is because they are reminders of the trauma. Although other syndromes, such as major *depressive disorder, can be described without reference to any triggering event, this is impossible for PTSD. PTSD without reference to criterion A (the trauma) is nonsensical.

Other symptoms of PTSD lack intentional content, and most overlap with other disorders (e.g. insomnia, loss of interest in activities, irritability, concentration impairment, feeling of detachment from others). The only thing that unites this symptomatic goulash into a syndrome is the assumption that the trauma caused the emergence of these otherwise nonspecific symptoms.

What qualifies as a traumatic stressor?
Implicit in the original concept of PTSD is the assumption that a certain category of stressors possessed the capacity to produce this distinctive syndrome. Unlike the mundane stressors of everyday life, these stressors were deemed traumatic. There are two complexities embedded in this assumption. First, most people exposed to qualifying stressors do not develop PTSD (Yehuda and McFarlane 1995, Breslau and Kessler 2001). This implies that people vary in terms of their *vulnerability to succumb to the disorder following exposure to trauma. The study of risk factors for PTSD was once deemed politically incorrect because it partly shifted the causal burden from the stressor to the person, leading some to argue (incorrectly) that this amounts to 'blaming the victim'. Today, however, the study of risk factors has become a very active area of research in the trauma field (Bowman and Yehuda 2004).

Second, some individuals exposed to subtraumatic stressors report enough postevent symptoms to qualify for the diagnosis if the definition of traumatic stressor were broader. Accordingly, in DSM-IV-TR the definition of trauma expanded. Not only do qualifying stressors include being the victim or witness to trauma, but also experiencing fear, helplessness, or horror after being 'confronted with' (American Psychiatric Association 2000, p. 467) a threat to the physical integrity of another person. Hence, a horrified person in Idaho watching television

coverage of New Yorkers fleeing the collapsing World Trade Center counts as a trauma victim even though he or she was not directly threatened. This conceptual bracket creep in the definition of trauma (McNally 2003a) means that the vast majority of Americans now qualify as trauma survivors. For example, Breslau and Kessler (2001) found that 89.6% of adults in south-eastern Michigan had been exposed to a qualifying traumatic event, but only 9.2% had developed PTSD.

Broadening the definition of trauma decreases the likelihood of false negatives—people who truly have PTSD but who would fail to receive the diagnosis because their trauma was insufficiently severe. Yet broadening the definition of trauma threatens to undermine any chance we might have of identifying the psychobiological mechanisms generating the symptoms of the illness. Indeed, a person whose disorder results from a fender bender will be unlikely to have much in common with someone whose disorder results from being confined to a Nazi concentration camp. Moreover, the more we broaden the concept of traumatic stressor, the less plausibly we can assign causal significance to the stressor itself, and the more we must emphasize pre-existing vulnerability factors. However, shifting the causal emphasis away from the stressor undermines the very rationale for having a diagnosis of PTSD in the first place.

Epidemiology, sex ratio, and course of PTSD
According to the National Comorbidity Survey Replication (Kessler *et al.* 2005), the lifetime prevalence rate of PTSD in the United States is 6.8%. Although men are exposed to traumatic events more than women are, the rate of PTSD is about twice as great in women than in men. Even when one controls for type of traumatic stressor (e.g. rape), sex differences in the severity and prevalence of PTSD remain (Tolin and Foa 2006).

Military personnel are among the groups most likely to be exposed to trauma. Correcting problems in the National Vietnam Veterans Readjustment Study dataset (Kulka *et al.* 1990), Dohrenwend *et al.* (2006) found that the current (late 1980s) prevalence of PTSD dropped by 40% (i.e. from 15.2% to 9.1%). Requiring that symptoms be associated with at least moderate impairment results in a drop of 65% (i.e. to 5.4%; McNally 2007).

In those developing PTSD, symptoms almost always begin within hours or days of the trauma; delayed-onset PTSD is extremely rare (Jones and Wessely 2005, p. 184). Epidemiological data indicate that the median time to remission is 36 months for those who sought help for any mental health problem (not necessarily PTSD) and about 64 months who never sought help for a mental health problem (Kessler *et al.* 1995). About one-third of those who qualify for PTSD will have a chronic course (Kessler *et al.* 1995).

311

Risk factors

Among people exposed to trauma, certain variables are associated with risk for PTSD. Prospective longitudinal studies indicate that above average intelligence is not only associated with decreased risk of trauma exposure, it is associated with decrease risk of PTSD among the trauma-exposed (Breslau et al. 2006). Other variables associated with heightened risk of PTSD include smaller hippocampi (Gilbertson et al. 2002), elevated *neuroticism, and a family or personal history of anxiety disorders (Bowman and Yehuda 2004).

Psychobiological correlates of PTSD

About two-thirds of patients with PTSD exhibit psychophysiological reactivity when listening to audiotaped scripts of their traumatic experiences (Orr et al. 2004). Several neuroimaging studies suggest that PTSD is characterized by a hyperresponsive *amygdala, hyporesponsive prefrontal cortical regions, or both (Shin et al. 2004, McNally 2006). Other correlates include selective processing of threat-related cues in the emotional Stroop paradigm (a quantitative index of intrusive cognition) and a tendency to experience difficulties retrieving specific memories from one's past—perhaps reflecting a tendency to avoid thinking about disturbing material.

Treatment

Attempts to prevent the emergence of PTSD by conducting psychological debriefing procedures requiring cathartic expression of one's trauma days after it has occurred have failed (McNally et al. 2003). However, clinical researchers have been reasonably successful treating PTSD via *cognitive behaviour therapy (CBT) methods, especially in civilian survivors of trauma (Keane 2006). Core elements include correction of misconceptions about symptoms (e.g. flashbacks mean impending insanity; symptoms signify moral weakness); provision of anxiety management skills; prolonged imaginal exposure to traumatic memories until distress wanes; and in vivo (real life) exposure to avoided activities and situations reminiscent of the trauma. One recent study, however, indicated that cognitive restructuring added to prolonged exposure to traumatic memories was no more efficacious than prolonged exposure alone (Foa et al. 2005b). Finally, selective serotonin reuptake inhibitors are modestly efficacious in PTSD, but apparently less so than CBT (Keane et al. 2006).

RICHARD J. MCNALLY

Brewin, C.R. (2003). Posttraumatic stress disorder: malady or myth? New Haven, CT: Yale University Press.

Dalgleish, T. (2004). Cognitive approaches to posttraumatic stress disorder: the evolution of multirepresentational theorizing. Psychological Bulletin, 130, 228–60.

McNally, R.J. (2003). Remembering trauma. Cambridge, MA: Belknap Press/Harvard University Press.

McNally, R.J. (2006). Cognitive abnormalities in post-traumatic stress disorder. Trends in Cognitive Sciences, 10, 271–7.

power Power is one of the appraisal dimensions that determine the elicitation and differentiation of an emotion (see APPRAISAL THEORIES). It is related to the evaluation of *coping potential, an individual's assessment of his or her capacity to deal with an event which might threaten the *well-being of the person.

The appraisal of one's power to deal with such an event and its consequences corresponds to an assessment of one's resources to change a situation and its outcomes according to one's interests (Scherer 2001a). This implies that a situation is controllable, and that the outcome depends on one's own power to exert control (see CONTROLLABILITY). Power can be derived from many different sources, such as physical strength, money, knowledge, or attractiveness (French and Raven 1959). Perception of one's power in a given situation will critically influence the selection of action alternatives. For example, in situations of aggressive conflict, the comparison between the estimate of one's own power and the power of the opponent is likely to decide between anger/fight and fear/flight behaviour.

It is important to distinguish between power and control. Control refers to the likelihood that an event or its outcomes can be influenced by any natural agent. Power, on the other hand, refers to the perceived potential of the appraising individual itself to influence a potentially controllable event (maybe with the help of others). Assessments of control and power may lead to different ensuing emotions: situations characterized by a lack of control be associated with emotions such as hopelessness, whereas a lack of power might lead to feelings of helplessness. When used in the literature, control and power are not always clearly distinguished; 'controllability' often seems to imply both aspects.

TOBIAS BROSCH

preferences The expression of preference reflects the influence of two broad modes of judgement—intuition and deliberation (Kahneman and Frederick 2002). The intuitive mode includes emotional reactions (e.g. Loewenstein 1996), but it also includes heuristic process which are largely perceptual or cognitive in nature. Intuitive processes occur early in a judgement process; they are fast and largely automatic. This is in contrast with deliberative processes which tend to occur later in a judgement process, are slower, and are more controlled. Intuitive and deliberative processes interact with each other, although they are often in conflict, and there is some evidence that they are anatomically separated in the brain.

Many intuitive systems are emotional in nature. These include *fear and *disgust responses, as well as reward responses. In the brain, fear and disgust responses are closely linked to the *amygdala and anterior insula. These areas show increased activity when people are exposed to frightening stimuli, but also when they are exposed to unpleasant flavours, or when they make moral judgements of condemnable acts. *Reward responses are mediated by the nucleus accumbens (NAcc) and ventromedial prefrontal cortex (VMPFC). These areas universally coactivate to rewards. While reward responses appear to occur largely automatically, they may be altered by category information. In one study, Plassmann *et al.* (2008) found that the VMPFC responds more strongly when participants thought they were tasting a higher-quality beverage (i.e. a more expensive wine), suggesting that categorical knowledge (in this case pertaining to pricing) can affect the raw reward experience.

Another set of processes commonly described as 'intuitive' are cognitive heuristics. Several such heuristics were posited by Tversky and Kahneman (reviewed in Kahneman and Frederick, 2002) in their demonstrations that many human judgements showed systematic deviations from rationality (see BOUNDED RATIONALITY). Specifically, such heuristics have been shown to lead to inconsistencies in risk preferences and temporal preferences. There are some situations in which such heuristics can be overridden by deliberative processes, and there are individual differences in the likelihood of recruiting such deliberative processes.

Deliberatively derived preferences are believed to be mediated by a network of brain areas, principal among which is the dorsolateral prefrontal cortex (DLPFC). The DLPFC supports basic cognitive processes such as working memory and the initiation of behaviours based on long-term *goals (Miller and Cohen 2001). Damage to the prefrontal cortex in humans causes behaviour to be abnormally dependent on immediate environmental stimuli and leaves people unable to consider or maintain long-term goals.

While intuition- and deliberation-related brain areas can be separately identified, brain anatomy also indicates that they are not independent. The DLFPC is directly connected to the regions previously mentioned to be implicated in emotions. Some data indicate that regions in the medial prefrontal cortex appear to mediate between emotion and cognition. Patients with lesions in the medial prefrontal cortex show evidence of producing both emotional and rational valuations, but are unable to apply emotion in making decisions (Bechara *et al.* 1999) (see DECISION-MAKING).

It is not necessarily the case that preferences derived from deliberative processes are superior to those derived from intuitive processes. An early demonstration of this was by Wilson and Schooler (1991), who found that people were happier with product choices when they relied on first impressions (i.e. 'intuition'), rather than taking the time to think about reasons why one item might be better than another (i.e. 'deliberation').

At the same time, however, there is considerable evidence that more rational choices (i.e. those that maximize a person's utility) are derived through deliberative processing in the DLPFC. For example, Sanfey *et al.* (2003) found that choices to accept small awards in the ultimatum game we accompanied by greater DLPFC activation than were choices to reject equivalent offers. Rejections were predicted by greater activity in the insula, suggesting that these responses were based on an intuitive anger response rather than on a deliberative calculation of utility.

Deliberative choice processes are not triggered in all situations, and there is evidence that there are individual differences in the tendency for such processes to trigger. One anatomical region thought to be involved in this triggering is a brain region known as the *anterior cingulate cortex (ACC). Botvinick *et al.* (2001) suggested that the ACC is a conflict monitor, responsible for recognizing situations when decisions include conflicting response options. Upon detection of conflict, the ACC is believed to recruit deliberative decision processes of the DLPFC.

The 'systems' account of decision-making and preference has a long history in philosophy and psychology, and it is beginning to find support from neurobiology, but this latter effort is still in its infancy.

SAMUEL M. MCCLURE AND JASON RIIS

Plassmann, H., O'Doherty, J., Shiv, B., and Rangel, A. (2008). Marketing actions can modulate neural representations of experienced pleasantness. *Proceedings of the National Academy of Sciences USA*, **105**, 1050–4.

Sanfey, A.G., Rilling, J.K., Aronson, J.A., Nystrom, L.E., and Cohen, J.D. (2003). The neural basis of economic decision-making in the ultimatum game. *Science*, **300**, 1755–8.

pride Pride is the experience of one's positive social worth, a signal that one is likely to be socially accepted. Pride does not require the actual presence of approving others. It ensues from a favourable comparison between one's behaviours and one's self-standards (Lewis 2000a) (see IDEAL SELF). Self-standards are derived from internalized social standards.

The experience of pride is cognitively complex. It requires objective self-awareness, or the realization that you are being evaluated as a social object. Not surprisingly, the ability to experience pride occurs relatively late in development, as it coincides with the development of the self-concept. Children are about 2½ to 3 years of age when they show behaviours that are characteristic of pride (Lewis 2000a). While proto-typic instances of pride do not occur until the preschool years, even infants are aware of instances where the approval of the caregiver (my mother smiles) is contingent on a positive outcome (having built a tall tower), and these instances may be conceived of as an early form of pride (Mascolo et al. 2003).

There is some evidence for a unique facial and postural configuration that is associated with pride. North American university students recognized two sets of facial behaviour as pride at above chance levels (about 75% identified pride as intended), and distinguished it from facial behaviours associated with happiness and surprise. The most prototypical facial configuration for pride involves a small smile, the head tilted slightly back, a fully visible expanded posture (upper body), and arms on the hips or raised (Tracy and Robins 2004). The posture may well be seen as an expression of dominance. At the age of 4, American children start identifying the behaviour as pride at a level above chance. The same facial behaviours were identified as pride at above chance by the members of an illiterate culture, suggesting that pride expressions may be pan-cultural (see UNIVERSALITY OF EMOTIONS).

That pride is associated with a unique set of facial behaviours and posture does not preclude cultural differences in the experience of pride, or its behavioural concomitants. In fact, there is growing evidence that the content of pride feelings varies according to differences in cultural models of *self—or what it means to be a good person (Mesquita and Karasawa 2004). Because self-standards differ across cultures, the experience of pride does too. Pride in Western contexts with independent cultural models of self is associated with the accomplishments of a competent and independent individual. Pride comes with a sense of personal worth, efficacy, and conveys value to others. Pride *action tendencies include self-celebration, and showing others one's worth (Mascolo et al. 2003). In contrast, pride in East Asian and Mediterranean cultures does not as much reflect the internal qualities of the person, but rather confers honour on one's ingroup, parents, or nation (Mesquita 2001, Mascolo et al. 2003) (see INDIVIDUALISM/COLLECTIVISM). Furthermore success is often attributed to a group of people (e.g. one's family), rather than to an individual by him- or herself. Individual pride in these interdependent cultures is neither valued nor communicated (Mesquita and Karasawa 1994, Mascolo et al. 2003). Consistently, the experience of individual pride in American groups predicted general *well-being, whereas it did not in groups of Japanese students (Kitayama et al. 2006b).

BATJA MESQUITA AND SUSAN POLANCO

314

Mascolo, M.J., Fischer, K.W., and Li, J. (2003). Dynamic development of component systems of emotions: pride, shame, and guilt in China and the United States. In: R.J. Davidson, K.R. Scherer, and H.H. Goldsmith (eds), Handbook of affective sciences, pp. 375–408. New York: Oxford University Press.

Tracy, J.L. and Robins, R.W. (2007). The nature of pride. In: J.L. Tracy, R.W. Robins, and J.P. Tangney (eds), The self-conscious emotions: theory and research, pp. 263–82. New York: Guilford Press.

primary appraisal Primary appraisal along with its counterpart secondary appraisal comprise the two basic types of emotion-antecedent appraisal defined by Lazarus and his colleagues (e.g. Lazarus, 1966, 1991, Lazarus and Folkman 1984, Smith and Lazarus 1990) (see APPRAISAL THEORIES). In general, appraisal consists of an evaluation of what one's circumstances imply for personal *well-being. The outcome of this evaluation determines and organizes one's emotional state.

Within this framework, primary appraisal consists of evaluations of whether, to what degree, and how the circumstances are personally relevant to well-being (see RELEVANCE DETECTION). For instance, the model of Smith and Lazarus (1990) includes two components of primary appraisal. The first, motivational relevance, is an evaluation of whether and to what degree the circumstances touch upon the person's *goals or *concerns, or how important the situation is to the individual. This component is hypothesized to determine the overall intensity of the resulting emotional reaction. Situations appraised as irrelevant to one's goals evoke little or no emotion, whereas those appraised as highly relevant evoke strong emotions. The second component, motivational congruence, is an evaluation of the degree to which the circumstances are consistent (desirable) or inconsistent (undesirable) with one's goals (see MOTIVE CONSISTENCY). This evaluation differentiates between benign (motivationally congruent) and stressful (motivationally incongruent) states.

As conceptualized by Lazarus (e.g. 1991), primary appraisal is considered 'primary' because these evaluations determine whether or not an emotion will be evoked in an encounter. However, the term 'primary' does not imply that these evaluations necessarily precede other (e.g. secondary) appraisal components in time. The appraisal models advanced by Lazarus and colleagues do not assume that appraisals occur in a fixed sequence. In contrast, other appraisal theorists (e.g. Scherer 1984a, 2001a), propose that appraisals are made in a fixed sequence, and typically in such models appraisal components corresponding to primary appraisal precede other appraisal components in the sequence. See also SECONDARY APPRAISAL.

CRAIG A. SMITH AND LESLIE D. KIRBY

priming (affective) The term 'priming' can be used to refer to a procedure or an effect of this procedure. As a procedure, priming most often entails that participants are asked to respond to a target stimulus that is preceded by a prime stimulus. In some trials, the prime and target are somehow related, whereas in others they are not related in the same way. Different priming procedures can be distinguished on the basis of the type of relation that is manipulated. For instance, in associative priming studies the prime and target are associatively related (e.g. DOC-TOR–NURSE) or unrelated (ROAD–NURSE). In affective priming studies, on the other hand, the affective match between the prime and target is manipulated. In some trials, they have the same *valence (e.g. HAPPY–FLOWER) whereas in others they differ in valence (e.g. SAD–FLOWER). Priming procedures can vary on a host of other variables such as the task of the participant, the time between the onset of the prime and the target, the duration of the prime presentation, and so on.

When defined as an effect, priming refers to the observation that responses to target stimuli are influenced by whether the target is preceded by a related or unrelated prime. Associative priming studies, for instance, showed that participants need less time to determine the lexical status of a target word (i.e. word or nonword) when it is preceded by an associatively related prime than when it is preceded by an unrelated prime. This observation is called an associative priming effect. Likewise, affective priming studies showed that participants need less time to determine the valence of a target (i.e. good or bad) when it is preceded by a prime with the same valence compared with a prime with a different valence. Such a finding is most often referred to as an affective priming effect, although other expressions such as evaluative priming effect or attitude activation effect have also been used.

Affective priming is an interesting tool for studying affective processing because, given the proper controls, affective priming effects can occur only if the valence of the prime has been processed. Hence, if an affective priming effect is found under certain conditions, one can infer that the valence of the prime was processed under those conditions. Interestingly, affective priming effects have been found under a wide range of conditions, including when participants are asked to ignore the prime stimuli, when there is little time to process the prime stimuli, when valence is not task relevant, when participants are engaged in an effortful secondary task, and when participants are unaware of the presence of the prime stimuli. Such findings suggest that the processing of stimulus valence can occur automatically in the sense of unintentionally, quickly, goal-independently, efficiently, and unconsciously (see Klauer and Musch, 2003, for a review).

In other studies affective priming has been used to not to examine affective processing in general but to assess whether particular individuals like or dislike particular stimuli or concepts. The logic underlying these studies is as follows: because positive prime stimuli facilitate response to positive targets whereas negative stimuli facilitate responding to negative targets, one can infer the valence of a prime stimulus by examining whether it facilitates responding to positive or negative targets. Based on this logic, affective priming effects have been used to assess the valence of a wide range of objects including the self (i.e. *self-esteem), racial stimuli, foods, and conditioned stimuli (see Fazio and Olson, 2003, and Hermans et al., 2003; for reviews).

It is important to realize that priming effects have been attributed to a range of processes. One of the many possible processes is spreading of activation. This entails that activation in a semantic network that is due to the presentation of the prime will spread to the representation of the target which will facilitate the processing of the target and thus responding. Although models based on the spreading of activation are well known and seem intuitively plausible, evidence suggests that many kinds of priming effects are not due to such processes. Affective priming effects, for instance, most often seem to be due to mechanisms of response conflict rather than to spreading of activation. However, research on which processes underlie which kind of priming effect is still ongoing (see Klauer and Musch, 2003, for a review).

JAN DE HOUWER

Klauer, K.C. and Musch, J. (2003). Affective priming: findings and theories. In: J. Musch and K.C. Klauer (eds), *The psychology of evaluation*, pp. 7–50. Mahwah, NJ: Lawrence Erlbaum Associates.

prosocial behaviour Prosocial behaviour refers to a broad category of actions defined by society as generally beneficial to other people and to the ongoing political system (Piliavin *et al.* 1981) (see ANTISOCIAL BEHAVIOUR). This category includes behaviours intended to benefit others, such as helping, sharing, comforting, donating, and volunteering, and mutually beneficial behaviours such as cooperation.

Psychological research on prosocial behaviour developed in several stages. Work in the early and mid-1960s typically focused on *norms, such as social responsibility and reciprocity, which seemed to govern prosocial behaviour. In the 1980s, research questions moved primarily from *when* people help to *why* people help. Researchers attempted to understand the fundamental motivational processes that underlie prosocial actions. Research in the 1990s provided a clearer link between prosocial motivations and general personal, social, and intergroup orientations. This work also focused on a variety of planned forms of helping, such as volunteering, and helping within established personal relationships, such as social support. In the last decade, the study of prosocial behaviour expanded to include exploration of underlying biological processes as well as interdisciplinary questions shared by economists, sociologists, anthropologists, and psychologists.

The organizational scheme for this discussion of prosocial behaviour follows the one proposed by Penner *et al.* (2005), who argued that empirical and theoretical interest in such phenomena can be placed at one of three nonmutually exclusive levels: (1) the mesolevel, which is the study of helper–recipient dyads in the context of a specific situation; (2) the microlevel, which involves the study of the origins of prosocial tendencies and the sources of variation in these tendencies; and (3) the macrolevel, which represents the study of prosocial actions that occur within the context of groups and large organizations.

Mesolevel analysis

The initial emphasis of mesolevel research was on the role of social norms and models in spontaneous prosocial activity between strangers. Interest in the topic was subsequently stimulated by lay reactions to the 'Kitty Genovese incident' (Dovidio 1984). In this infamous episode, at least 38 people heard Ms Genovese's cries for help but did nothing to prevent her brutal murder. Intrigued by the bystanders' inaction, psychologists sought to answer two mesolevel questions: (1) when will people help? and (2) why do they help?

Answering the first question involved identifying the features of situations that increase or decrease the probability of helping. Extensive laboratory and field research investigated factors such as the attributes of the person in need, the rewards and costs that are associated with helping and not helping, and the relationship between helpers and their beneficiaries (see Dovidio *et al.* 2006).

One influential model (Latané and Darley 1970) characterized the process of bystander intervention as the outcome of a series of decisions about the person's need for assistance and bystanders' responsibility and ability to help. This model emphasized the importance of the social context of helping in emergency situations. The presence of other, unresponsive, bystanders can lead people to interpret a potential emergency as one in which helping is not needed. In addition, when people believe other bystanders can help, they may *diffuse* responsibility, assuming that they are not personally responsible for helping because others will provide assistance. The process of diffusion of responsibility was used to explain the inaction of bystanders in the Kitty Genovese incident.

In addressing the question of why people help, or the motivational processes that underlie helping, research focused on *empathy. Empathy is a person's emotional response caused by and congruent with another person's emotional state (Eisenberg and Fabes 1990). Although there was consistent evidence that empathy facilitated prosocial action, a major debate developed concerning whether the motivation for helping was exclusively egoistic (i.e. self-oriented) or could ever be altruistic (i.e. other-oriented) (see ALTRUISM (PSYCHOLOGICAL PERSPECTIVES)). Egoistic models included the arousal: cost–reward model (Piliavin *et al.* 1981), which proposed that people help others primarily to reduce their own distress, and the negative state relief model (Cialdini *et al.* 1982), which posited that people help to alleviate personal feelings of *guilt or *sadness. The major altruistic model was Batson's (1991) empathy-altruism hypothesis, which held that specific empathic responses related to feelings of sympathy and concern (termed 'empathic concern') could lead to truly altruistic behaviours, defined as actions primarily directed at improving another person's welfare.

One resolution was that empathy can produce different emotions depending on the context. In severe emergency situations, bystanders may become upset and distressed; in less critical, less intense problem situations, observers may feel sad or sympathetic (Batson 1991). How empathic arousal is interpreted, in turn, elicits either egoistic or altruistic motivation. Yet, the issue has still not been fully resolved. Some researchers contend that what appear to be altruistically motivated behaviours, directed at benefiting another person, can still be explained parsimoniously in terms of self-interest. Nevertheless, there is now considerable agreement that under certain, relatively restricted and rare conditions, humans appear capable of acting primarily for the benefit of another person (Dovidio *et al.* 2006). With the integration of various perspectives, research at the mesolevel continues today, but not nearly at its earlier pace, nor at the same rates as research at the microlevel or macrolevel.

Microlevel analysis

Research at the microlevel of analysis focuses on mechanisms that occur at genetic and biological levels, as well as on processes that produce different prosocial tendencies over time (that is, developmentally) and individual differences in prosocial orientations. Much of this work has been the product of evolutionary theorists, biologists, geneticists, and developmental and personality psychologists trying to explain the origins of prosocial behaviours in humans.

Among evolutionary theorists, the critical question was how a tendency for self-sacrifice, which often puts the actor's life at peril, could be passed on to successive generations. The answer to this question began with the post-Darwinian realization that it was the survival of an individual's genes, rather than the individual, that was the key to evolutionary success (Hamilton 1964). From this perspective, a behaviour that increased the probability these genes would be present in subsequent generations (Hamilton's concept of 'inclusive fitness') was an adaptive action.

This insight gave rise to several theories accounting for the evolution of prosocial orientations. Kin selection theory (Smith 1964) argues that organisms are most predisposed to help fertile members of their species with whom they have the greatest genetic overlap. The theory of reciprocal altruism (Trivers 1971) posits that prosocial actions toward unrelated individuals will also increase the likelihood the actor's genes will survive and be passed on to subsequent generations if such actions are reciprocated. Group selection theory proposes that tribes or groups that were more cooperative or less competitive towards other members of the same collective had an evolutionary advantage over less cooperative and altruistic tribes (Sober and Wilson 1998). Observational studies with nonhuman species, computer simulations, laboratory simulations with humans, and experimental tests of the implications of these approaches have provided some support for each of these hypothesized evolutionary mechanisms, although less so for group selection than for the other two theories.

Recent findings in neuroscience also yield evidence consistent with evolutionary and biologically based theories of prosocial behavior (see ECONOMICS (ROLE OF EMOTION IN)). For instance, brain scans reveal that punishing someone who had not been cooperative in an economic exchange is associated with increased activity in the region of the brain associated with experiencing personally rewarding activities (de Quervain et al. 2004). However, it is not possible to know whether this is an innate or a learned reaction.

Within the microlevel approach, the origins of empathy have also been studied. The capacity to experience empathy appears to have been present in the earliest mammals over 180 million years ago. Although humans may be generally inclined to empathize with and offer aid to distressed others, considerable variation can be found in prosocial affective responses. Studies of twins suggest a genetic basis for individual differences in empathy either as specific behavioural tendencies or, more likely, as broader differences in *temperament. These innate tendencies interact with and are shaped by environmental factors to produce enduring developmental differences among people in prosocial tendencies (Eisenberg et al. 2000).

Other individual differences in general prosocial tendencies are related to fundamental dimensions of *personality. People high in agreeableness, which is associated with trust and tender-mindedness, and conscientiousness, which is associated with competence and reliability, tend to be more prosocial (Graziano and Eisenberg 1997). Other work suggests the existence of a general 'prosocial personality orientation', comprising a combination of several different personality attributes, including empathy and a sense of social responsibility (Penner 2002). These dispositions combine with specific contextual factors (e.g. the clarity of another's need) to affect the likelihood of prosocial actions.

Macrolevel analysis

Prosocial behaviour studied at the macrolevel focuses primarily on two distinct aspects of prosocial actions. The first is the behaviour of individuals who engage in prosocial behaviours within an organizational context; the second is cooperation, in which the outcomes of individuals' actions are jointly determined. Most of the research on prosocial behaviour within an organizational context concerns volunteering. Volunteering differs from interpersonal helping in many ways. Volunteering is typically a less spontaneous action than helping, involves more sustained commitment, is less likely to result from a sense of personal obligation, and is less sensitive to the immediate reactions of recipients.

Because of these fundamental differences, explanatory models of volunteering are quite different from explanatory models of mesolevel helping. Two of the most prominent models are the volunteer process model (Omoto and Snyder 1995) and the role identity model (Piliavin et al. 2002). The volunteer process model focuses first on the motives that initially cause a person to volunteer, which are typically other-oriented, and then on the motives or needs that maintain volunteering over an extended period of time, which are often less selfless motives, such as advancing one's career or developing social relationships. The more sociologically oriented role identity model proposes that volunteering over time can cause people to incorporate the volunteer role into their self-concept, which produces sustained volunteering.

Other research on volunteering has focused on the correlates of sustained volunteering (Wilson 2000). In general, as income, education, and age increase, so does the incidence of volunteering. Social institutions, particularly family and church, also play vitally important roles. People are more likely to volunteer if their parents were volunteers and if they have a strong affiliation with a religion. In addition, personality characteristics, such as empathy and self-efficacy (which also relate to spontaneous helping), and personal motivations, such as motives to strengthen social relationships and to grow and develop psychologically, relate to the decision to volunteer and the maintenance of this behaviour (Penner 2002).

In recent years, there has been interest in the consequences of volunteering for the individual volunteer. The available evidence suggests that being an active volunteer has benefits for volunteers ranging from higher occupational prestige (Wilson and Musick 2003) to better psychological and physical health (Thoits and Hewitt 2001).

Turning to cooperation, the primary topics of interest are the factors that foster increased cooperation within the same group and between different groups. The causal variables for both within- and between-group cooperation include many of the same variables that have been used to explain prosocial behaviours at the mesolevel, namely empathy, reciprocity, cost–reward considerations, and social influence (Dovidio et al. 2006). However, because people are typically more fearful and mistrustful of members of other groups than members of their own group, cooperation between groups is more difficult to attain and sustain than is cooperation within groups.

Conclusion

Predictions about future directions of research always carry some risk. However, it is likely that research on prosocial actions will continue to grow. At the microlevel, neuroscientists are exploring the neurological substrata of prosocial actions, while behavioural geneticists examine the reciprocal effects of genes and environment on prosocial tendencies. Macrolevel research on ways to increase both volunteering and intergroup cooperation has substantial theoretical and applied value. Finally, mesolevel research offers great promise as a means to better understand the basic dynamics of human dyadic interactions.

LOUIS A. PENNER AND JOHN F. DOVIDIO

Dovidio, J.F., Piliavin, J.A., Schroeder, D.A., and Penner, L.A. (2006). The social psychology of prosocial behavior. Mahwah, NJ: Lawrence Erlbaum Associates.

Eisenberg, N., Losoya, S., and Spinrad, T. (2003). Affect and prosocial responding. In R.J. Davidson, K.R. Scherer, and H.H. Goldsmith (eds), Handbook of affective sciences, pp. 787–803. New York: Oxford University Press.

Penner, L.A., Dovidio, J.F., Piliavin, J.A., and Schroeder, D.A. (2005). Prosocial behavior: multi-level perspectives. Annual Review of Psychology, 56, 365–92.

proximal factors The term proximal (from the Latin prope, near) comes from anatomy, where it refers to structures which are near or close to some reference

point. If unspecified, the latter is generally implied to be the centre or midline of the body. Proximal is a relative term. The neck is a proximal structure, and is more proximal than the shoulder. But both the neck and the shoulder could be considered proximal structures (with implicit reference to the midline of the body). The thumb could also be considered proximal to the index finger. The term proximal has been coopted more broadly in psychology to refer to events, process, causes, or relations that are direct or close in time or space, as opposed to indirect or distant. For example, the proximal trigger of a 'road rage' incident may be a discourteous driver, but a more remote cause may lie in poor emotion regulation and anger management. McVittie (2006) discusses the use of the terms distal and proximal contexts which impact health, where proximal contexts include immediate causes such as poor nutrition, lack of medical care and drug abuse, while distal contexts refer to more remote factors such as poverty and lack of education. See also DISTAL FACTORS.

GARY G. BERNTSON

psychoneuroendocrinology Psychoneuroendocrinology is an interdisciplinary field of research that is at the interface of endocrinology, neuroscience, and psychology. It is concerned with both psychological influences on the *neuroendocrine system and the effect of hormones and *neuropeptides on behaviour, cognition, and affect.

Psychological influences on bodily functions in general and endocrine glands in particular have been known for centuries. Who has not felt one's heart pounding in the face of fear or one's neck hot with anger? The sympathetic nervous system that innervates the viscera, the *cardiovascular system and the sweat glands in the skin, and the hypothalamic–pituitary–adrenal axis, are the most important pathways of communication from the brain to the rest of the body. The *stress response mobilizes both pathways, resulting in the release of catecholamines (noradrenaline and adrenaline) and cortisol from the adrenal gland. These responses are not always the same in the face of a threat. Their nature, intensity, and duration depend on the way the organism copes with the situation (see COPING). Efforts to control the stressor are associated with a predominant activation of the sympathetic nervous system, whereas lack of control and predictability are associated with a predominant activation of the hypothalamic–pituitary–adrenal axis (Henry 1982) (see Fig. P2). Social factors also exert strong influences on the neuroendocrine system. The most striking illustration of this phenomenon is the inhibition of puberty and hormonal cycling that occurs in young female cottontop tamarins (Saguinus oedipus) as long as they remain in the parental group (Ziegler et al. 1987) (see Fig. P3). In a

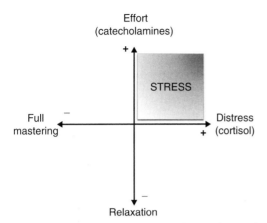

Effort
(catecholamines)

Fig. P2. Influence of coping strategies on the stress hormonal response. Efforts to actively control the situation are associated with activation of the sympathetic nervous system, leading to the release of catecholamines (adrenaline and noradrenaline). Distress induced by lack of controllability and predictability is associated with activation of the hypothalamic–pituitary–adrenal axis, leading to the predominant release of cortisol. Relaxation decreases activation of the sympathetic nervous system whereas full mastering of the situation with high social support decreases activity of the hypothalamic–pituitary–adrenal axis. Modified from Henry (1982).

Fig. P3. Cotton-top tamarin. From <http://creativecommons.org/licenses/by-sa/2.0/>.

dominance–subordination hierarchy, individuals of low social rank do not always display heightened activity of the pituitary–adrenal axis compared with high-ranking individuals. The hormonal pattern of subordinates depends on the behavioural strategies which dominants need to use in order to maintain the social hierarchy, and the social support they receive from congeners (Abbott *et al.* 2003).

Hormones that are released by endocrine glands feed back on the brain to modulate behaviour. Historically, the observations by Arnold Berthold (1803–61) at the University of Göttingen in the mid-1800s that castration caused the disappearance of aggressive behaviour in young cockerels and implantation of testes made it reappear was the first scientific demonstration of the influence of hormones on the brain (Freeman *et al.* 2001). Since these pioneering studies, many hormones produced by peripheral endocrine glands have been found to influence neuronal circuits underlying behaviour not only in a baseline manner but also in a retroactive manner. As a typical example, glucocorticoids produced by the adrenal cortex modulate development of the submissive responses of intruder mice to attacks by resident mice. The higher the corticosterone response, the faster the intruder mouse displays submis-

sive behaviour (Leshner 1980). This type of hormonal action is typical of a feedback process in which the hormonal response, the nature of which depends on the way the situation is perceived and represented and the individual behaves, influences—by its effect on the brain—the way in which the individual will adapt to the same situation on further occasions. Neuropeptides that are produced in the brain to regulate endocrine systems also have profound effects on the brain. For example, the hypothalamic corticotropin-releasing hormone (CRH) was initially characterized on the basis of its ability to upregulate the production of adrenocorticotropin (ACTH) by the pituitary gland. Later, it was found to trigger a generalized state of *arousal that can culminate in anxiety (de Kloet 2003). These behavioural effects of hormones do not depend solely on the level of their production; characteristics of hormone receptors are also important. A typical example is the pair-bonding behaviour of voles, commonly known as field mice. Prairie voles (*Microtus ochrogaster*) are highly social and monogamous whereas montane voles (*Microtus montanus*) are solitary and polygamous. Both species have similar levels of the circulating neurohypophyseal hormone vasopressin. However, montane voles lack vasopressin receptors in some critical areas of their brains in contrast to prairie voles (see Fig. P4). Artificial insertion of the gene for this receptor into the brains of montane voles causes them to change their phenotype from promiscuity to monogamy and behave like prairie voles (Lim *et al.* 2004).

The study of possible alterations in the bidirectional relationships between hormones and behaviour over the lifespan is becoming an important theme of modern research in psychoneuroendocrinology. In particular, there is currently much interest in understanding how activation of the stress hormonal systems early in life

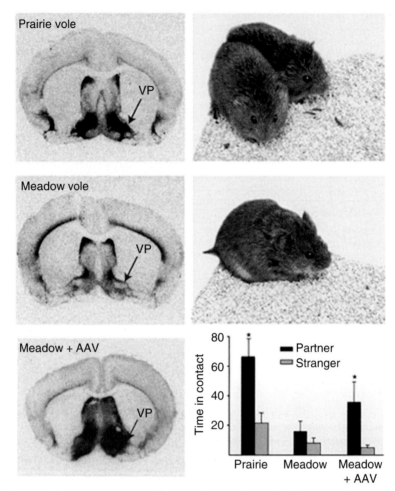

Fig. P4. Autoradiograms of vasopressin receptors of the V1a subtype in the ventral pallidum (VP) of socially monogamous prairie voles and polygamous meadow voles. When V1a receptors levels are artificially increased within the VP of meadow voles using adenoassociated viral vector (AAV) gene transfer (meadow + AAV), they display social behaviour that is reminiscent of that of monogamous prairie voles, preferring social contact with their partner over a stranger (right lower part of the graph). Error bars indicate standard errors; asteriks indicate $P < 0.05$. Times in contact is given in minutes. From Donaldson, Z.R. and Young, L.J. (2008). Oxytocin, vasopressin, and the neurogenetics of sociality. *Science*, **322**, 900–904. Reprinted with permission from the AAAS.

can shape coping strategies and physiological response to adversity in adulthood.

ROBERT DANTZER

Becker, J., Breedlove, M., Crews, D., and McCarthy, M. (eds) (2002). *Behavioral endocrinology*, 2nd edn. Cambridge, MA: MIT Press.

psychoneuroimmunology Psychoneuroimmunology is an interdisciplinary field of research that is at the interface between immunology, neuroscience, and psychology. By studying the bidirectional communication network between the brain and the immune system, psychoneuroimmunology aims to understand the way in which psychological factors influence immune function and how the immune system affects behaviour, all of which can ultimately affect resistance to infectious, autoimmune, and neoplastic diseases (see IMMUNITY AND EMOTION).

Immune cells express intracellular steroid and membrane *neuropeptide receptors, which explains why the proliferation and differentiation of these cells are sensitive to variations in concentrations of hormones. Growth hormone and prolactin, for instance, stimulate the phagocytic activity of macrophages and neutrophils in a manner similar to interferon-gamma (Kelley *et al.* 2007). Both hormones are actually produced by T-lymphocytes in an autocrine manner when they are stimulated with nonspecific mitogens, and both peptides contribute to lymphocyte proliferation. In addition, fully functional noradrenergic branches of the sympathetic nervous system innervate the primary (thymus, bone marrow) and secondary (lymph nodes, spleen) lymphoid organs and terminate in zones of lymphocyte maturation and differentiation. Although *stress is often described as immunosuppressive because of the negative effects of glucocorticoids on proliferation of T-lymphocytes and the cytotoxic activity of natural killer cells, it can stimulate the immune response in certain conditions. For instance, acute restraint stress stimulates delayed-type hypersensitivity reactions in the skin of rats. This immunoenhancement is mediated by an increased trafficking of leucocytes to the skin in response to low doses of glucocorticoids and adrenaline (Dhabhar and McEwen 1999). In contrast to the acute pro-inflammatory effect of stress, chronic activation of the major stress hormones, glucocorticoids and catecholamines, induces a shift in the balance between different classes of T-helper (Th) lymphocytes, resulting in a predominance of Th2-humoural immunity over Th1-cellular immunity. As a typical example of this shift in the Th1/Th2 balance, mice that are exposed for 24 hours to the odour of another stressed mouse display a decrease in proliferation of T-lymphocytes and a reduction in natural killer cell activity. However, they synthesize more antibodies against a T-cell-dependent antigen. This type of result is difficult to extrapolate to clinical conditions. The possible consequences of stress-induced immune alterations on the resistance of the host to infection or the progression of tumour cells are still largely speculative. In most cases, the impact of stress is indirect via alterations in life habits (e.g. sleep disorders), addictive behaviour (e.g. smoking and drinking alcohol), and illness behaviour (symptom awareness, adherence to medication, and use of health services).

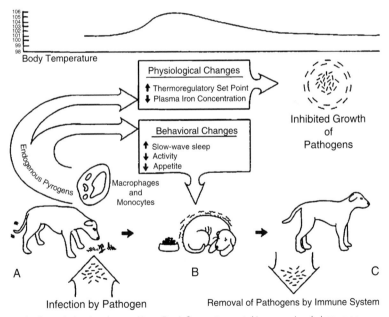

Fig. P5. Induction of sickness behaviour by cytokines. Pro-inflammatory cytokines, previously known as endogenous pyrogens, are released by activated macrophages and monocytes in response to infection. They act on the brain to induce physiological changes, including fever and decreased plasma iron concentration, and behavioural changes such as increased sleep and decreased activity and appetite. These changes converge to facilitate eradication of the infectious agent by the feverish organism and promote recovery. Reprinted from Hart (1988) with permission.

psychopathy

The study of immune influences on brain functions has been the object of intense research efforts during the last three decades that has drastically changed our understanding of the behavioural and affective components of physical illness. It has long been known that factors elaborated by the immune system are responsible for the fever and activation of the pituitary–adrenal axis that develop during an infection. Characterization of *cytokines and their receptors has been responsible for a surge in this research. During the course of an infection, the brain forms a molecular and cellular representation of the peripheral immune response that makes use of the same type of cells and cytokines that are mobilized in the periphery. This is possible because of several immune-to-brain communication pathways including the humoral route via the systemic circulation and the neural route via the afferent nerves that innervate the part of the body in which the infection occurs. The cytokines that are produced in the brain reorganize the priorities of the organism and trigger a newly identified motivational system, the expression of which is sickness behaviour (Dantzer 2001). This accounts for why one feels sick and behaves in a sick way during the course of an infection. This is normally a temporary adaptive response to infection (Hart 1988) (see Fig. P5) but it can become prolonged and ultimately culminate in mood disorders such as *depression when the immune system is chronically activated. See also INFLAMMATION AND MOOD.

ROBERT DANTZER AND KEITH W. KELLEY

Ader, R. (ed.) (2007). *Psychoneuroimmunology*, 4th edn. Amsterdam: Elsevier.

psychopathy Psychopathy involves two core components: emotional dysfunction and *antisocial behaviour. The emotional dysfunction involves reduced *guilt and *empathy as well as reduced *attachment to significant others. The antisocial behaviour component involves a predisposition to antisocial behaviour from childhood. The classification of psychopathy in adulthood is usually given on the basis of the empirically derived Psychopathy Checklist–Revised (Hare 2003). Comparable measures have been developed to index psychopathy in childhood (see relevant chapters in Patrick, 2006). It is a developmental disorder in that the classification can be used with children by the age of 10.

The disorder of psychopathy is not equivalent to the psychiatric diagnoses of conduct disorder or antisocial personality disorder (DSM-IV; American Psychiatric Association 1994). These psychiatric diagnoses concentrate on the antisocial behaviour shown by the individual rather than any form of functional impairment that might lead to its development, such as the emotional dysfunction seen in psychopathy. These diagnoses are far more commonly applied than psychopathy. Rates of diagnosis of antisocial personality disorder can be over 80% in forensic institutions while those of psychopathy are typically a third of this (Hare 2003).

In the early 1950s, pre-dating the American Psychiatric Association's use of the label antisocial personality disorder, the term sociopathy was frequently used clinically. This term denoted the then prevalent belief that the disorder was exclusively social in origin. More recently, the term has been revitalized by Damasio and colleagues when they described the personality changes sometimes seen in patients with acquired ventromedial frontal cortex lesions as demonstrating 'acquired sociopathy' (Damasio 1994).

Commonly proposed social causes for the emergence of the disorder, such as physical/sexual trauma or neglect, are associated with an increased risk for *aggression. However, this aggression is *reactive* (frustration/threat based) in nature and associated with heightened emotional responding, rather than the reduced emotional responding seen in psychopathy. Indeed, it is now believed that there is a considerable genetic contribution to the emergence of psychopathy. The behavioural manifestation of this genetic contribution is then thought to be under considerable socio-environmental influence (Blair *et al.* 2005).

Neural regions that appear to be implicated in the development of psychopathy include the *amygdala, ventromedial frontal cortex, and possibly the *anterior cingulate cortex. These regions are crucial for emotional learning (particularly the amygdala) and the use of reinforcement information to guide behaviour (particularly the ventromedial frontal cortex) (see LEARNING, EMOTIONAL (NEUROSCIENCE PERSPECTIVES)). The moral socialization of the typically developing child involves the child learning to avoid actions that harm others (see MORAL DEVELOPMENT). When others are harmed, particularly in childhood, they display expressions of fear and sadness. These expressions activate the amygdala and, by doing so, initiate emotional learning (guiding others away from actions that caused this harm). The deficits in psychopathy are thought to interfere with this emotional learning, increasing the probability that individuals with psychopathy will choose to commit actions which harm others to achieve their goals (Blair *et al.* 2005).

While there are treatments available to reduce antisocial behaviour in other forensic populations, psychopathy itself is currently regarded as untreatable (Hare 2003).

R. J. R. BLAIR

psychosomatic disorders Psychosomatic (or somatoform) disorders are a group of psychological problems where an individual experiences marked physical (e.g.

gastrointestinal, respiratory, or cardiovascular) symptoms despite the absence of an underlying medical condition that can adequately explain their development. Psychosomatic disorders represent the severe end of a continuum of 'medically unexplained' symptoms seen in the general population, ranging from mild and transient aches and pains to chronic and severe physical symptoms, which are believed to come about by a process of somatization (whereby mental states and experiences are expressed as bodily symptoms). Somatization symptoms are often precipitated by stressful life events (see STRESS). They are associated with increased use of medical and mental health services, so place a considerable burden on the healthcare system. Further, they can lead to psychosocial difficulties, including depression, relationship breakdown, and protracted absences from work.

Prevalence

While formally diagnosed psychosomatic disorders are relatively rare (a lifetime prevalence rate of less than 1%; Creed and Barsky 2004), milder presentations involving somatization symptoms are common. It is estimated that up to 30% of new outpatient visits involve medically unexplained symptoms. Somatization is more common in children, and has been linked to a range of risk factors including female gender, family dysfunction, older age, disability, minority race, lower levels of education, and psychiatric disturbance (particularly depression and personality disorders).

Diagnosis

The *Diagnostic and statistical manual of mental disorders* (DSM-IV; American Psychiatric Association 1994) identifies six somatoform disorders. *Somatization disorder* (historically known as Briquet's syndrome) is where an individual presents with a wide variety of physical complaints over several years, with first onset before the age of 30. The symptoms cannot be accounted for by an underlying medical condition and result in impairment of functioning and/or unnecessary medical intervention. The physical symptoms need to include at least four different pain sites or functions, and have at least two gastrointestinal symptoms, one sexual symptom, and one pseudoneurological symptom. *Undifferentiated somatoform disorder* is a less stringent diagnosis, requiring only one or more unexplained physical complaint and/or functional impairment, lasting for at least six months. *Conversion disorder* is characterized by unexplained symptoms or deficits affecting voluntary sensory or motor function (e.g. blindness or paralysis). *Pain disorder* is diagnosed instead of a conversion disorder in instances where pain symptoms dominate the presentation (e.g. recurring abdominal pain). *Body dysmorphic disorder* is a marked preoccupation or excessive concern with an imagined defect in appearance or a minor physical anomaly (e.g. minor flaws of the face). Finally, *hypochondriasis* is an anxious preoccupation about having a serious disease based on misinterpretation of bodily symptoms (e.g. fearing cancer). It is important to distinguish psychosomatic disorders from instances where a medical cause has been missed or where an individual is intentionally simulating (e.g. malingering) or generating (e.g. ingesting poison) their symptoms. Psychosomatic disorder can of course also be comorbid with physical disorders which account for a subset of the presenting symptoms.

The DSM-IV classification system of somatoform disorders has been extensively criticized (Mayou *et al.* 2005), including that the terminology is unacceptable to patients, that the disorders do not form a coherent conceptual category and lack clearly defined thresholds, that the concept is incompatible with non-Western cultures holding a less dualistic model of disease, and that the existing criteria focus too much on 'symptom counting' rather than understanding the development of somatization symptoms.

Causes

Despite the prevalence and cost of psychosomatic disorders, relatively little is understood about their cause. It is increasingly accepted that there are strong reciprocal body–brain connections. Perception of changes in the body has been linked to how individuals experience emotions (the *James–Lange theory) and make intuitive decisions (Damasio's *somatic marker hypothesis) (see INTEROCEPTION). Similarly, how we think, feel, and behave is believed to change responses in the body. Somatizing individuals may have subtle differences in the neural machinery that represents and regulates activity in the body (Kirmayer *et al.* 2004). Early Freudian accounts of 'hysteria' understood psychosomatic symptoms as a consequence of 'splitting off' of unwanted thoughts and feelings. More recently, suppression of emotions has been linked to immune system problems (Pennebaker 1997), making individuals vulnerable to physical illness and sometimes early death. Prompting emotional disclosure (e.g. via writing) has been shown to reduce psychosomatic complaints and improve functioning of the immune system. Somatizing individuals are more likely to have grown up in a family with a high rate of parental physical illness and to show insecure attachments in relationships. This has led some to suggest that somatization is in part an interpersonal behaviour motivated to elicit care, which has developed via parental modelling and/or reinforcement of illness behaviours (Stuart and Noyes 1999). Somatization may also be maintained by the abnormal behaviours patients display when they become ill (Rief and Sharpe 2004), including consulting multiple doctors and requesting unnecessary investigations in an attempt to verify a physical cause, socially withdrawing, and taking time off from work. Further, somatization may be maintained by an information processing style characterized by hypervigilance towards the body and a tendency to make catastrophic interpretations of physical complaints.

Treatment

Psychosomatic disorders are challenging to manage (Mai 2004). The exclusion of medical or neurological conditions that could underlie the symptoms is initially the major diagnostic focus. Once a psychosomatic diagnosis is made, it is important to build a lasting relationship with the patient, striking a balance between avoiding unnecessary and potentially iatrogenic medical interventions whilst investigating and treating physical symptoms where appropriate. It is also helpful to explain nonperjoratively the presenting problem to the patient, to avoid them feeling dismissed or neglected. The key point to get across is that the symptoms are viewed as real and genuine, even if they may have a biopsychosocial rather than a medical cause. There is encouraging early evidence that psychological interventions, principally *cognitive behaviour therapy, can be effective in the treatment of certain somatization disorders (Kroenke and Swindle 2000).

BARNABY D. DUNN

Mai, F. (2004). Somatization disorder: a practical review. *Canadian Journal of Psychiatry*, **49**, 652–62.

Rief, W. and Sharpe, M. (2004). Somatoform disorders—new approaches to classification, conceptualization, and treatment. *Journal of Psychosomatic Research*, **56**, 387–90.

punishment Punishment is the presentation of an aversive stimulus following a target behaviour, for example an insulting comment after failing an exam. As for *reward or reinforcement, there are two types of punishment. Positive punishment reduces behaviour by means of the presence of an aversive stimulus (e.g. an electric shock following a bar press), while negative punishment works by means of the elimination of an appetitive stimulus (e.g. time out after shouting at the dinner table). Punishment is the functional opposite of reward or reinforcement—it aims at reducing the probability of executing a target behaviour (cf. Terry 2003).

In psychological research various types of punishment have been applied and tested. Animal researchers have most frequently administered electric shocks or loud noises—types of positive punishment. In human research, education, and the law, both positive punishment (e.g. verbal critique) and negative punishment (e.g. losing money, social isolation) are frequently applied. In general, punishment can vary in its intensity, duration, and delay after a target behaviour—variables that influence the punishment's efficiency. Punishment most effectively reduces the probability of a target behaviour when it is intense and immediately delivered. Moreover, the effectiveness of punishment depends—like the effectiveness of reward—on its schedule, which can be fixed or variable and with reference to time intervals or response ratios (see Skinner 1938, Ferster and Skinner 1957): Fixed delivery of punishment is faster in reducing the execution of a target behaviour, but variable delivery is more effective in maintaining the reduction of response during extinction—when no further punishment is delivered. However, although it is clear that punishment can reduce the probability of repetition of a target behaviour, it has long been discussed which process underlies this effect. Can punishment *eliminate* an unwanted behaviour or can it only *suppress* it?

Suppression or elimination?

Skinner (1938) was very sceptical that punishment can eliminate unwanted behaviour. He found that positive punishment did not reduce the execution of a target behaviour more effectively than mere extinction, i.e. the elimination of a previously administered reward for the target behaviour. This finding was later qualified in a well-known study by Estes, one of Skinner's doctoral students, in 1944: rats first learned to press a lever by means of positive reinforcement. Next, one group of these rats underwent extinction, i.e. reward was no longer delivered upon bar pressing. In the other group, bar pressing was now punished with a mild electric shock. As presented in Fig. P6, the positive punishment immediately reduced the target behaviour (bar pressing). Thus, punishment seemed to be very effective. However, subsequently both groups of rats experienced extinction in four successive sessions. As presented in Fig. P6, the omission of punishment led to a recuperation of the bar pressing behaviour in the formerly punished group and the bar pressing rate equalled that of the previously unpunished group. That is, the target behaviour was *suppressed* by the punishment, but not *eliminated*. This suggests that punishment can only control or suppress behaviour in the short run. Moreover, punishment is more expensive than extinction and punishment can lead to secondary learning: a punished child learns that (ab)using social power over others is legitimate for attaining one's goals. And finally, there is a problem of contingencies: Punishment can work as an unconditioned aversive stimulus that is associated with the punishing person due to classical conditioning: A punishing parent becomes associated with the punishment and thus disliked by his or her child.

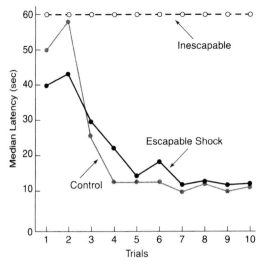

Fig. P6. The effects of positive punishment and extinction on behavior in the experiment by Estes (1944). Figure taken from Terry WS (2003). Learning and memory (2nd ed.). Allyn and Bacon, Boston, MA, p. 135.

Contingent punishment, escape, and avoidance

Punishment is central for both escape and avoidance learning (see ASSOCIATIVE PROCESSING; LEARNING, EMOTIONAL (NEUROSCIENCE PERSPECTIVES)). In both cases the repetition of a behaviour becomes more probable because an organism removes itself from an aversive stimulation—which functionally corresponds to negative reinforcement. In escape learning an organism is negatively reinforced for escaping an aversive stimulation (e.g. pain/harm stops after running away). Escape learning is explicable with one process—operant or instrumental conditioning. Avoidance learning is more complex. Here an organism learns that a conditioned sign stimulus signals danger in terms of the probable *onset* of pain (e.g. running away as soon as a red light is illuminated, but before the shock is delivered). Avoidance learning needs the consideration of two processes: (1) classical or Pavlovian conditioning to explain the acquisition of the association between the sign stimulus and punishment and (2) operant or instrumental conditioning to explain why the organism actively avoids. According to Mowrer (1956), avoidance learning occurs because the feeling of relief rewards the avoidance of stimuli or situations that elicit fear because they have been associated with pain.

Noncontingent punishment

What happens when punishment is delivered noncontingently upon a target behaviour? One well-known effect can be so-called 'learned helplessness'. In the learned helplessness paradigm, an organism first receives uncontrollable (i.e. noncontingent) punishment. Subsequently, it is tested whether the organism shows deficits in avoidance and escape learning in a new situation. In a famous study by Maier *et al.* (1969) dogs received uncontrollable (i.e. noncontingent) electric shocks. One group could escape the shocks while another group was harnessed and could not escape. Additionally, there was a control group that did not receive shocks. In the second phase of the study the dogs were placed in a 'shuttle box'—an experimental device that is frequently used in escape and avoidance learning experiments (Miller 1948). The box consists of two compartments with a barrier between them. The bottom of each compartment consists of a grill via which electric shocks can be delivered. The research subject can escape from the shock by jumping to the other, safe, side. In the Maier *et al.* experiment the light in one compartment was dimmed 10 seconds before the shock was delivered, i.e. the light became a conditioned stimulus signalling shock onset. As presented in Fig. P7, there were strong differences between the experimental conditions. The dogs in the control condition and the dogs that had been able to escape the shocks in the study's first phase learned to escape and even avoid the shock by jumping over the barrier. But the dogs that had previously not been able to escape the shocks did not. They remained in the compartment and took the shock for the whole sixty seconds of its delivery. These dogs were helpless because they had learned that they could not control the shock delivery and generalized that expectancy of having a lack of control to the new situation in the shuttle box (Seligman 1975). Learned help-

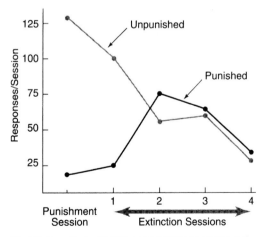

Fig. P7. The effects of helplessness training on escape and avoidance learning in the experiment by Maier et al. (1969). Figure taken from Terry WS (2003). Learning and memory (2nd ed.). Allyn and Bacon, Boston, MA, p. 149.

lessness due to uncontrollable exposure to noise or failure has also been demonstrated for humans (e.g. Hiroto and Seligmann 1975). These findings suggest that aversive stimulation that is noncontingently delivered is even more harmful than behaviour-contingent and thus controllable punishment.

GUIDO H.E. GENDOLLA AND
MICHAEL RICHTER

Campbell, B.A. and Church, R.M. (eds) (1969). *Punishment and aversive behavior*. New York: Appleton-Century-Crofts.

Terry, W.S. (2003). *Learning and memory*, 2nd edn. Boston, MA: Allyn and Bacon.

push/pull effects There is an ongoing debate about whether emotional expression expresses some internal state or whether it is largely determined by strategic message intentions and/or attempts to induce certain states in the receiver (*impression*) (see INTERPERSONAL COMMUNICATION). Scherer has suggested that both factors typically play a role, and has proposed the distinction of internal push effects and external pull effects on expression (Scherer *et al.* 2003). Push factors are defined as those changes in the states of organismal subsystems which directly affect the production of vocal or bodily expression (see EXPRESSION, PRINCIPLES OF EMOTIONAL). For example, increased muscle tension produced by sympathetic arousal can affect breathing patterns, the shape of the vocal tract, and facial features. In other words, internal factors 'push' motor behaviour in a certain direction (such as an adaptive action) but do not necessarily program specific target configurations. External pull factors, on the other hand, are in the service of specific communication intentions or of culturally defined *norms or expectations which require the production of specific expressive features in terms of a specific signal structure. The sender needs to produce this pattern to achieve a particular effect. In this case the outcome or target is fixed, but the processes by which it is brought about are variable. Examples of such pull factors are self-presentation—the kind of impression the sender 'wants' to create in the receiver, for example trying to give the impression of a big, powerful body through loud, low-frequency vocalization. Often, pull factors are based on underlying push effects, since big vocalizers naturally phonate with a lower pitch and small vocalizers with a higher vocal pitch. Thus, impressions of infant helplessness as created by the high-pitched harmonic sounds in fear, submission, and friendliness make the vocalizer appear smaller. One of the most common types of pull effect is associated with conventionalized social signals, stereotyped expression patterns that have a shared meaning for the group. In general, any formalized and conventionalized signal, particularly if it involves iconic or arbitrary referencing, will be the result of pull effects.

The relationship between the structure of the signal and the nature of the referent is frequently similar for both push and pull effects, with the former having developed out of the latter. The difference between the two types of effect is the actual presence or strength of the referent—the referent being an affective or motivational state—at the time when the signal is produced. As motor expression is often used with a strategic communicative intent, even if there is already a push from inside (e.g. exaggerating one's anger in a negotiation situation), push and pull effects are very frequently interacting with each other, except in the cases of pure push (*affect bursts) or pure pull (a polite smile directed at an aggravating superior—imposed by sociocultural *display rules).

KLAUS R. SCHERER

Q

qualia The term 'qualia' is a technical philosophical term used to refer to the introspectible phenomenal subjective character of conscious experience. It denotes the special 'what it's like' to be in a particular mental state. (Latin, *qualis*, of what kind.) Perceptions and emotions are typical examples of mental states that are said to have distinct qualia. Seeing the redness of an apple, sensing the hardness of a table, and feeling angry or delighted, are examples of qualia on this sense (see FEELINGS (PHILOSOPHICAL PERSPECTIVES)); FEELINGS (PSYCHOLOGICAL PERSPECTIVES)).

The topic of qualia is currently the subject of intense debate in modern analytic philosophy of mind (Tye 2003). The reason for this is that qualia occupy a strategic place in philosophical disputes over competing approaches to the *mind–body problem (Crane 2000). Those who argue that the mental cannot be reduced to the physical often do so by appealing to the fact that there are qualia and that these are irreducibly mental. Conversely, those who argue that the mental can be reduced to the physical often do so by attempting to show that qualia are reducible or eliminable. Qualia play an especially important role in efforts to assess 'functionalist' theories of mind in modern cognitive science (Block 1980).

The philosophical literature on qualia is extremely technical and speculative, which may deter some outsiders. However, it is also rich with provocative and vivid 'thought experiments' that are sure to excite interest in others. In one case, we are asked to imagine the case of a woman imprisoned in a black and white room who learns everything there is to know about colour and then all of a sudden is exposed to colour (Jackson 1982). In another, we are asked to imagine two individuals who are alike in all respects except for the fact that their experiences of colour are inverted (Shoemaker 1982). There is also the amusing example of philosophical zombies who are identical in their physical configuration except for the qualitative component of their experience (Dennett 1991). In each case, we are asked to consider whether the alleged qualitative dimension of experience really makes a difference and whether it can or should be philosophically jettisoned or retained.

As far as affective science is concerned, perhaps the most glaring feature of the philosophical literature on qualia is the manner in which it largely ignores the affective dimensions of consciousness. It is true that emotions and moods often figure in the examples of qualia provided by philosophers. Moreover, there have been some philosophical attempts to address the importance of the affective dimension of qualia (Charland 1995, Tye 1995). One especially interesting proposal is that all qualia probably have an affective dimension (Campbell 2000). Nevertheless, philosophical disputes about qualia, like philosophical discussions of the mind in general, invariably take place against the backdrop of cognition. It is as if affective science did not exist. Apparently, philosophical discussions of qualia still have a long way to go before they catch up with the latest scientific discussions on the affective dimensions of consciousness experience (e.g. Colombetti and Thompson 2005, Barrett *et al.* 2005).

LOUIS C. CHARLAND

R

rationality The chaotic history of human affairs may incite scepticism about the traditional definition of our species as the 'rational animal'. But possession of the implied capacity for correct reasoning, effective deliberation, and judicious planning does not entail that it is always exercised. The characterization can be safely endorsed if we take 'rational' in a categorial rather than an evaluative sense. In the categorial sense, the term includes contrasts with 'arational', and includes both rationality and *irrationality. In the evaluative sense, we can distinguish three domains. Two of these, epistemic and practical or strategic rationality, have been extensively studied. A third, axiological rationality, is most pertinent to emotions but remains underexplored.

Both epistemic and strategic rationality embody a common idea, namely the quest for ways to maximize the probability of success in enterprises that aim at different sets of *goals. Strategic rationality seeks the best ways of attaining practical goals, while epistemic rationality aims at truth, the avoidance of falsehood, and other epistemic values such as explanatory power (see BOUNDED RATIONALITY). Deductive rationality is the object of logic: it identifies forms of inference guaranteed to preserve truth and consistency. Inductive rationality, as David Hume (1711–76) pointed out, affords no such guarantee since no logical rule could warrant the reliability of inferences from past to future observations (Hume 1888/1978). Inductive rationality therefore aims not at certainty but at maximizing the likelihood of correctness. Despite some unconvincing carpings from post-modernist sceptics and relativists, the consensus is that the theory of rationality ultimately merges with the complexities of scientific method (Brown 2001). Complications, however, beset the relation between epistemic and strategic rationality. Maximizing true belief is not logically equivalent to avoiding false ones. The need to balance these two epistemic aims, as well as other considerations arising from a pragmatic view of truth, supports a strategic view of epistemic rationality itself (Levi 1967). Furthermore, epistemic rationality can conflict directly with strategic rationality. A notorious example is Blaise Pascal's (1623–62) wager: assuming a possibility of infinite gain or loss, belief in God might be the better strategic choice despite its extreme improbability. Those complications highlight the problem of whether the choice of goals can itself be subject to rational principles. Aristotle (382–322 BC) seems to have thought that choice of goals should be brought under the aegis of *phronesis* (a species of rationality usually rendered as 'practical wisdom') (Aristotle 1984, 1144b 14–17). Hume, on the contrary, notoriously thought that reason could only be the 'slave of the passions' (Hume 1888/1978, 2.3.3.4).

One crucial role of emotions in rationality is therefore that of defining the goals of action, to which reason then calculates the means. Emotions are thus directly pertinent to the third domain of axiological rationality, so named after the Greek word for value. In that perspective, emotions are perceptions of *values, or at least normative responses to values (Tappolet 2000). Although the principles of axiological rationality—that domain of rationality which assesses appropriateness of emotions and attitudes—remain obscure, it may be that it alone can arbitrate in those cases where epistemic and strategic rationality conflict.

R. DE SOUSA

Longino, H. (2006). The social dimensions of scientific knowledge. In: E.N. Zalta (ed.), *Stanford encyclopedia of philosophy*, Fall 2006 edn <http://plato.stanford.edu/archives/fall2006/entries/scientific-knowledge-social/>.

de Sousa, R. (1987). *The rationality of emotion*. Cambridge, MA: MIT Press.

reappraisal Reappraisal is a cognitive form of emotion regulation (see REGULATION OF EMOTION). It involves altering the meaning of a situation so that the emotional response to that situation is changed. Reappraisal may be used to increase, decrease, or qualitatively change an emotional response, although it is perhaps most frequently used to decrease negative emotion.

Interest in reappraisal dates back thousands of years to philosophers such as the Stoics, who emphasized that the way we think determines the emotions we have (see STOICISM). Within psychology, the notion of reappraisal is linked to *appraisal theory, which holds that our evaluation (or appraisal) of a situation—rather than the situation itself—determines our emotional response. Reappraisal also is a key element in *cognitive behavioural therapy, where maladaptive appraisals are altered in order to decrease negative emotion.

Empirical support for the idea that reappraisal can alter our emotions is provided by modern studies of re-appraisal. Often, these studies involve eliciting negative emotions in the laboratory using slides or films and then asking participants to think about the stimulus from the perspective of a detached observer. Findings from such studies indicate that reappraisal decreases explicit (e.g. self-reports, behaviour) and implicit (e.g. startle responses) indicators of emotion (Gross 2002). Using functional magnetic resonance imaging (fMRI), researchers have found that regions of the prefrontal and *anterior cingulate cortices—implicated in cognitive control—show increased activation during reappraisal, whereas brain regions associated with emotion generation, such as the *amygdala and insula, show decreased activation (Ochsner et al. 2004). Researchers are currently investigating the role that reappraisal plays in normal and abnormal functioning. The evidence to date suggests that reappraisal can be an effective strategy for regulating the experiential, physiological, and neural responses to emotional situations.

NICOLE R. GIULIANI AND JAMES J. GROSS

reason Our ordinary language can lead to a general confusion of two different uses of the term 'reason', and this is relevant when considering emotion. Although the uses are not the same, they are connected. One use concerns a person's *subjective* reason, the reason which justifies from the point of view of the agent. For example, if Peter ran away from Paul, he might explain his action by saying that he was afraid of Paul, and he was afraid because he thought he was being threatened by Paul. But there is another sense of reason, namely *objective* reason, in which we might say that Peter had *no* reason to be afraid of Paul, and thus no reason (no *good* reason) to run away from him, simply because, in fact, Paul was not threatening him. Empirical psychology is generally only concerned with subjective reasons. Ethics is concerned with both subjective and objective reasons.

PETER GOLDIE

Dancy, J. (2000). *Practical reality*. Oxford: Oxford University Press.

recognition of emotion (neural systems for)

Charles Darwin (1809–82) highlighted one aspect of emotions that is prominent in mammals, especially primates: their social communication (see INTERPERSONAL COMMUNICATION). We infer how other people feel by observing their face and their gestures, and by listening to their tone of voice (see VOCAL EXPRESSION OF EMOTION). Such expressions are often regulated by cultural *display rules; sometimes they can be deceptive and used to manipulate others—at least in adult humans. Given this complexity of possible expressions it is not surprising

to find complexity in recognition as well. A baby's smile evokes an immediate sense of joy in the viewer; a posed smile can be cognitively matched to the label 'happy'; and the complex, fleeting, and highly regulated emotions we typically see on the faces of those around us often require for their recognition a mixture of empathic response, cognitive deduction, and inferences that take into account the person and their situation.

What happens in the brain when we recognize emotions? The psychological complexity notwithstanding, findings from cognitive neuroscience have begun to shed some light on this question, and have begun to inform psychological models in the process. In prosopagnosia, often following bilateral damage to occipito-temporal cortex, recognition of the identity of a face (who the person is) can be impaired yet recognition of the emotion (how they are feeling) remains largely intact. Conversely, bilateral damage to the *amygdala impairs recognition of the emotion but leaves recognition of identity intact. Double dissociations such as these suggest that information about the emotional expression of a face is processed differently by the brain, and by somewhat separate regions, than is information about its identity. These data are consistent with earlier models of face processing that cleanly separated identity and emotion processing, although current models argue for a more sophisticated view in which identity recognition and emotion recognition arise from partly different combinations of more abstract underlying component processes (Calder and Young 2005).

What is 'recognition'?

Detection and discrimination of emotions (e.g. judging whether two simultaneous facial expressions are the same or different) depends on sensory cortices, and can occur without recognition or naming (as in category-specific agnosias). Perception of faces involves processing of their static configuration, which draws on cortex in the fusiform gyrus, and processing of their dynamic changes, which draws on cortex in the superior temporal gyrus and sulcus. These regions are most important for perception related to identity and expression, respectively (see Fig. R1) (Haxby et al. 2000). In monkeys, cells have been recorded near these regions that respond best to faces as stimuli.

Recognition requires more than just basic perception; it requires association of a perceptual representation of the stimulus with its meaning (with some kind of memory). The simplest form of recognition is re-identification of a previously seen stimulus. More commonly, recognition involves matching a stimulus onto a category—for instance, recognizing that a given facial expression shows happiness. There is some evidence that facial expressions show categorical perception: they

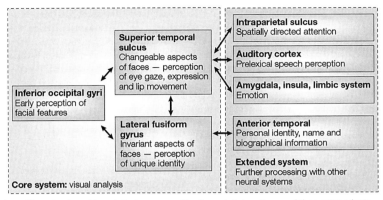

Fig. R1. Processing of faces begins with early feature perception in occipital cortices, and then proceeds via multiple, parallel streams that decode different kinds of information. From Haxby *et al.* (2000), reproduced in Calder and Young (2005).

cannot be discriminated any more accurately than they can be recognized (Young *et al.* 1997). In real life, recognition usually involves generating many other inferences as well—such as judging what the relevance and importance of the emotion is, and what it is that oneself should do in response to it.

What are the 'emotions'?
The interpretation of performance on emotion recognition tasks is limited by the list of possible emotion categories provided as response options. Typically, subjects are provided with a list of word labels, such as the list of *basic emotions (*happiness, *surprise, *fear, *anger, *disgust, *sadness) and asked to choose the label that best matches the emotion shown in the stimulus. If the stimuli are selected so that most subjects agree on their emotion labels, this can be a relatively straightforward way to measure emotion recognition. The pattern of errors (confusions) produced can be informative as well, as some patients may consistently mistake one emotion for another, whereas others may simply produce the same confusions as normal subjects, only more of them (e.g. confusing surprise with fear, or confusing anger with disgust). Yet it seems likely that most, if not all, brain structures participate in emotion recognition in more abstract ways that do not map cleanly onto our preconceived emotion categories. For instance, the amygdala has been hypothesized to be important for recognizing fear, for processing most facial expressions, or for processing related to any highly relevant, salient, or ambiguous expressions.

Other tasks ask subjects to rate the intensity of different emotions expressed by a stimulus, or ask them to make similarity judgements between two stimuli. Data from such tasks have shown that the similarity structure

of the emotion categories that are commonly recognized shows certain regularities. For instance, surprise and happiness are judged to be more similar to one another than are sadness and happiness. Some psychological theories have taken such data to support dimensional theories of emotion (such as a two-dimensional space of valence and arousal), and some kinds of brain damage show disproportionate impairments along certain dimensions in this space (see DIMENSIONAL MODELS).

Recognition of 'basic' emotions
The evidence that a particular brain structure is important for the recognition of a particular emotion is clearest for two basic emotions. Fear recognition can be disproportionately impaired by damage to the amygdala. Disgust recognition can be impaired by damage to the insula, the basal ganglia, or in Huntington's disease (a genetic neurodegenerative disease that preferentially damages cells in the basal ganglia early in its course) (Calder *et al.* 2001). Yet in both cases, the dependency is not absolute (there are cases of patients with damage to these structures whose recognition is relatively intact) and not completely specific (there are usually also impairments in the recognition of other emotions, and activation in imaging studies showing complex patterns across all emotions (Fitzgerald *et al.* 2006)). The amygdala is known to be involved in a variety of processing related to fear, such as Pavlovian fear conditioning, and appears to be important for recognizing fear from faces as well as perhaps other cues, such as body postures and tone of voice (although the evidence is most clear for faces). Responses of the amygdala to emotional faces are modulated by the context in which the face occurs, and by the direction of eye gaze in the face (Adams *et al.* 2003). The insula is known to be involved in processing

331

interoceptive information, including taste and nausea, and appears to be important for recognizing disgust from all stimuli, including facial expressions.

Across lesion studies, and especially across neuroimaging studies, it is generally clear that emotion recognition draws on a quite distributed set of brain structures, as is the case for emotion experience. Moreover, there are probably strong individual differences, and effects of gender (Wager *et al*. 2003). Recognition of happiness appears to be least susceptible to brain damage, whereas recognition of negatively valenced emotions is more easily impaired. One reason for this finding may be that there are more negative than positive emotion categories, and so distinguishing among the negative ones is just more difficult because it requires more subordinate-level categorization (Adolphs 2002).

Lesion data suggest that structures in the right hemisphere are more important for emotion recognition than structures in the left hemisphere, although this is less well supported by neuroimaging studies. The story is also complicated by the finding that right-hemisphere lesions may disproportionately impair the recognition of negatively valenced emotions, or of highly arousing emotions. Lesion studies have suggested that right somatosensory cortices, including insula and supramarginal gyrus, are especially important for recognizing emotion from faces (Adolphs *et al*. 2000), whereas right premotor and prefrontal cortices may be most important for recognizing emotion from prosody (Adolphs *et al*. 2002). Other studies have found activation of the right middle superior temporal sulcus in response to angry prosody in voice stimuli (Grandjean *et al*. 2005), and there is evidence that parts of the right prefrontal cortex may also be most engaged by stimuli that signal anger.

Social emotions and theory of mind
*Social emotions include those focused on the *self (such as *embarrassment, *guilt, *pride, and *shame) and those focused on the fortunes of others (such as *empathy, *envy, and *schadenfreude). Much less is known about the neural substrates for recognizing these emotions, and they usually require more complex cues and context in order to be recognized (they are difficult to recognize from facial expressions alone). Some imaging and lesion studies suggest that medial prefrontal cortices are especially important for recognizing these emotions (Shamay-Tsoory *et al*., 2007), perhaps because these regions of the brain are necessary for reasoning about minds more generally.

'Theory of mind' refers to the ability to conceive of mental states, which are inferred from observed behaviour (see THEORY OF MIND AND EMOTION). There are debates about whether nonhuman primates have a theory of mind, and about the age at which it arises in human

development. Theory of mind appears to draw on medial frontal and inferior parietal cortex, among other structures, and is important for attributing thoughts, intentions, and complex mental states to others, in addition to social emotions. It is impaired in people with *autism, who also have difficulty judging social emotions from faces, especially from the eye region.

Mechanisms behind emotion recognition
Some emotion recognition tasks can be performed simply with a combination of normal perception, semantic knowledge, and reasoning: for instance, deducing that a smiling face signals happiness. Others that require more subtle judgements, or that require judgements on the basis of cues that are not so obvious, may rely on simulating aspects of the emotion in the viewer. The theory that simulation and empathy play a role in emotion recognition has received considerable attention, and is in line with the observation that impairments in the ability to experience emotions often correlate with impairments in the ability to recognize them in others (Goldman and Sripada 2005). One structure important for experience, recognition, and empathy is the insula, an interoceptive somatosensory cortex activated by pain, anger, empathy, and disgust (see Fig. R2). A recent study found that the perceived sadness of faces was enhanced by large pupils, involved an empathic pupillary response in the viewer, and activated the insula (Harrison *et al*. 2006).

It would seem important for the brain to be able to extract some information about the emotional meaning of certain cues very rapidly when they can be related to life-and-death situations—such as wide eyes signalling fear, or bared teeth signaling anger, for instance. There is evidence for rapid processing of emotional expressions via subcortical routes to the amygdala, and there is evidence that the amygdala can be engaged, and emotional responses evoked in the viewer, even for stimuli that are presented subliminally (Jiang and He 2006). Subcortical processing proceeds via the superior colliculus and pulvinar thalamus. Such processing may underlie attentional pop-out effects in visual search for certain facial expressions, such as anger. However, it falls short of what we normally call recognition, but may be an accompaniment of normal recognition and may help to guide slower cognitive processing by providing an immediate bias (see ATTENTION AND EMOTION). Subcortical processing routes may also be the predominant mode of face processing available to many other animals, especially nonmammals, and the predominant mode available early in human development (Johnson 2005).

Finally, it is of interest to ask what it is about an emotional expression that allows the brain to decode the emotion. Responses in the brain to faces or voices have been found to decode emotion from complex

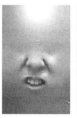

Fig. R2. Features in facial expressions that distinguish the different basic emotions. By showing viewers small, randomly sampled pieces of faces, it was possible to extract which features are the most effective in allowing them to discriminate between different emotions. The classification images shown in the figure show the regions of the face that, when revealed, are most effective in allowing viewers to discriminate that emotion from all the other basic emotions. From left to right: happiness, surprise, fear, anger, disgust, sadness, neutral. Note that the eyes are most important for distinguishing fear. From M.L. Smith *et al.* (2005).

configurations of stimulus cues that are not reducible to a single feature. Certain spectrotemporal components of the voice or of music signal emotional information, and certain feature configurations in faces are used to distinguish among different emotions (see Fig. R3). Recent studies have extracted the cues from faces that signal basic emotions, and have found that the amygdala is most important for processing information about the eyes, which distinguish fear from the other basic emotions. A patient with lesions of the amygdala was found to be impaired in fear recognition because she failed to fixate and process the eye region of facial expressions (Adolphs *et al.* 2005a).

Summary

(1) Many brain structures participate in recognizing any emotion. (2) Emotion recognition is always relative to the task used and the emotions presumed to exist. (3) Recognition of fear and disgust relies substantially on the amygdala and the insula, respectively. (4) Simulation may be one important mechanism for recognizing emotions.

RALPH ADOLPHS

Adolphs, R. (2002). Recognizing emotion from facial expressions: psychological and neurological mechanisms. *Behavioral and Cognitive Neuroscience Reviews*, **1**, 21–61. A comprehensive review on recognizing emotion from faces.

Harrison, N.A., Singer, T., and Rothstein, P. (2006). Pupillary contagion: central mechanisms engaged in sadness processing. *Social Cognitive and Affective Neuroscience*, **1**, 5–17. A study showing that empathic pupillary responses in the viewer influence recognition of emotion, and providing evidence for the role of simulation in emotion recognition.

Adolphs, R., Gosselin, F., Buchanan, T.W., Tranel, D., Schyns, P., and Damasio, A.R. (2005). A mechanism for impaired fear recognition after amygdala damage. *Nature*, **433**, 68–72. A study showing that the amygdala impairs fear recognition, at least in part, by impairing the processing of a feature in faces that is normally important to signal fear: the eyes.

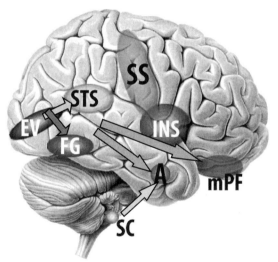

Fig. R3. Some of the brain regions important for recognizing emotions. Arrows show the predominant feedforward flow of information, but there are known feedback connections as well. Rapid subcortical information about faces can reach the amygdala (A) via the superior colliculus (SC) and provide a bias for emotion recognition, even for stimuli that cannot be consciously perceived. Cortical input to the amygdala is conveyed via early visual cortex (EV) and then regions in the fusiform gyrus (FG) and superior temporal sulcus and gyrus (STS); such information is also conveyed to regions of medial prefrontal cortex (mPF), which is connected with the amygdala. The amygdala and medial prefrontal cortex can trigger emotional responses to stimuli. Regions involved in empathy and simulation, and important for emotion recognition, at least in the right hemisphere, are somatosensory cortex (SS) and insula (INS). Most of the structures indicated are situated deep in the brain and would not be visible on the surface view shown here. Modified from Adolphs (2002).

refined emotions Emotions with refinement, or 're-fined emotions' for short, form a contrast to what William James (1842–1910) referred to as 'coarse emotions'. They do not constitute a subset of emotions but, rather, pertain to a potential for every emotion to be refined. Refined emotions can be described as emotions that show little or no expressions or other behavioural manifestations, are focused on *feelings, and contain expansion of appraisal of the emotional object or event. Emotion refinement appears to rest on three conditions: detachment, higher-level second-order awareness, and self-reflexivity. This will be examined in terms of three interrelated components of emotion: *action readiness, appraisal, and pleasure processes.

Refined action readiness

Refined emotions are more felt than acted upon. They are marked by absence of conspicuous expression behaviour, by definition, and by absence of pronounced physiological arousal, but still involve strong feeling. Self-report indicates that they contain virtual or incipient states of action readiness, manifest in feeling and thought only. Merely felt action readiness appears possible thanks to the mental set of detachment. Detachment results from a mental set for, on the one hand, not engaging in actual interaction with the object or event and, on the other hand, adopting a state of receptive observation and unfocused attention that lets information come in from outside and lets associated meanings come up from within. Detachment entails a shift from operating in pragmatic action space to operating in the virtual space of mental imagery and simulation. Reflexive second-order awareness facilitates imagining action readiness of greater complexity than readiness for actual actions would allow.

Refined appraisal

In comparison to standard or coarse emotions, emotion refinement involves a shift from implicit to explicit appraisal, and from simple and immediate to complex and extended appraisal (see APPRAISAL THEORIES). For instance, when the beloved is perceived not merely as endearing, but also as vulnerable, one may savour the event with its subtle aspects, in which endearment and appraised vulnerability are felt by tracing or sketching one's action tendencies of caring for and handling with care. Second-order elaboration of appraisal may invest the appraised events with meanings far beyond their immediately given aspects.

Refined appraisals open up, and are fostered by, extra dimensions in mental space and time. In addition to capitalizing on the mental distance of detachment, second-order appraisals make explicit appropriation of temporality. Savouring involves lingering that slows down or halts pragmatic progress, and, in the Chinese trad-

ition, entails processing that focuses on the incipient as well as the poststimulus phases of the event.

Refined pleasure processes

Refined emotions include refined pleasure or pain. Refined pleasure and pain may be understood as involving a competence of feeling more fully: feelings of *pleasure and *pain or the felt hedonic glosses of objects and events are brought centre stage. They may also lead to being aware of pleasure and pain at a more abstract level: awareness of what aesthetics refers to as 'harmony'. Harmony represents a holistic integration of multiple hedonic components, along with second-order awareness of that integration. Harmony results from successful integration that has proceeded well without effort.

This entails the further competence of reflexive second-order awareness. It allows the derivation of pleasure from one's awareness of pleasure. With sufficient acuity, it allows awareness of subtle distinctions in the phenomena, and of subtle shifts in balance between calls for letting go and restraint. It allows simultaneous experience of pain and pleasure as, for instance, in the Chinese Buddhist notion of emptiness (Sundararajan 2008): experiencing emptiness is an achievement that, as achievement, entails a certain pleasure.

Emotion refinement and the conduct of life

Emotion refinement does not merely appear in savouring and other forms of contemplation or dealing with pleasure. It can be a mode of handling painful emotions such as grief and suffering humiliation. It can form a mode of confronting everyday emotional situations, deepening their meaning and the scope of their sensed impact. It can be one of the ways in which conflicting emotional impacts are dealt with, such as combining self-esteem and regard for others. Refining one's emotions is capable of entering one's style of life, and become an aspect of a cultural conception of dignity.

Emotional refinement is a universal phenomenon. Yet it shows important cultural and individual variations in prominence, in the forms it takes, and in being or not being valued.

LOUISE SUNDARARAJAN

Frijda, N.H. and Sundararajan, L. (2007). Emotion refinement: a theory inspired by Chinese poetics. *Perspectives on Psychological Science*, **2**, 227–41.

Sundararajan, L. (2008). *Kong* (Emptiness): A Chinese Buddhist emotion. In W. Lemmens and W. Van Herck (eds), *Religious emotions/some philosophical explorations*: pp. 183–97. Cambridge: Cambridge Scholars Publishing.

reflexes (emotional) Emotional reflexes are physiological or behavioural reactions evoked automatically in humans by affectively evocative stimuli. They resemble reflexes prompted in mammals by appetitive/rewarding or threatening/punishing events or by associated conditioned cues. In this reflex view, emotions are founded on brain circuits old in phylogenetic history that mediate survival actions. These reflex actions evolved because they helped preserve or protect the lives of organisms, ensuring propagation of their genetic inheritance. Schneirla (1959), for example, suggested that *approach* to moderate stimulation (and thus, possible nutrients), and *withdrawal* from high-intensity stimulation (potentially dangerous input), are basic reflexes 'applicable to *all* motivated behavior in *all* organisms' (see APPROACH/WITHDRAWAL). Konorski (1967), a student of Pavlov, proposed a functional typology that considered a wider range of unconditioned reflexes and related them to human affect. In this view, reflexes are either preservative (e.g. ingestion, copulation, nurture of progeny) or protective (e.g. escape, rejection of noxious agents): Preservative emotions underlie such affects as sexual passion, joy, and nurturance; fear and anger were considered protective affects. Dickinson and Dearing (1979) developed Konorski's dichotomy into a theory of two opponent motivational systems, aversive and attractive, each activated by a different, but equally wide, range of unconditioned stimuli. Masterson and Crawford (1982) further elaborated the concept of aversion reactions, noting that threat stimuli occasioned a variety of context-based reflexive behaviours—such as fleeing, freezing, fighting, and defensive burying—that were organized in the brain by a general 'defense motivation system'. He proposed, furthermore, that unpleasant emotions in humans could be construed as a phylogenetic mammalian development that involved the same underlying defence system circuitry.

In this motivational reflex view, the *hedonic valence* of a stimulus is determined by the dominant motive system: stimuli that activate the appetitive system are pleasant (preservative/attractive) and mediate positive affects; stimuli that activate the defence system (protective/aversive) are unpleasant and mediate negative affects (see VALENCE). Human emotions often occur, of course, in the absence of overt action—reflecting an evolved greater ability to delay or inhibit behaviour and to plan ahead. Although the insult of a boss may inflame, the wise employee does not throw the punch. Nevertheless, the physiology is reflexively mobilized for action, and in the hiatus of a withheld response, emotions are strongly experienced (see ACTION READINESS).

Measuring emotional reflexes

In response to threatening or attracting stimuli, a variety of somatic and autonomic reflexes, similar to those in other mammals, can be measured bioelectrically in human beings. For example, when prey animals first observe a predator at a distance, the animal stops moving ('freezes'), and orients to the predator. In this context, the prey animal's cardiac rate decelerates profoundly. A similar 'fear bradycardia' is found in humans looking at unpleasant pictures (e.g. mutilated bodies, threat to the viewer). Such unpleasant pictures also prompt reflexive contraction of the *corrugator ('frown') muscle of the face, and a phasic increase in skin conductance at palmar and plantar sites. The changes in heart rate and facial muscles during picture viewing covary significantly with reports of unpleasant feelings, and skin conductance increases reliably with higher self-ratings of emotional arousal (Bradley and Lang 2007b) (see PERIPHERAL PSYCHOPHYSIOLOGY).

Reflex-eliciting stimuli have also been used to probe emotional states, and to explore the neural circuits that mediate emotion. In animal studies, fear conditioning—a neutral cue (e.g. a light) repeatedly followed by a painful shock—is used to establish an emotional state. At extinction, when the neutral cue is presented alone, an abrupt, startling stimulus is introduced that was not previously part of the procedure. The magnitude of the evoked *startle reflex is significantly greater in this context than when measured in the absence of the conditioned cue or during the same cue without the prior conditioning. Comparable startle potentiation findings have been obtained in fear conditioning studies with humans. Furthermore, in studies probing natural emotional cues (e.g. pictures, sounds) in human participants, systematic modulation of the startle reflex has been shown, i.e. increasing potentiation for more arousing unpleasant stimuli and relative inhibition for pleasant stimuli. These effects have been interpreted as an effect of motivational priming, i.e. the foreground stimulus generates a defensive state in the participant, which primes (enhances) activation of defensive reflexes such as startle.

Considering that emotional language (as reports of feelings) can be culturally shaped and that individuals learn to use emotional language instrumentally for reasons unrelated to their affective experience, the measurement of emotional reflexes has become an increasingly important tool in the study of emotion. These measures have the advantage of a clear neural provenance, providing a link between studies of human affect and its neuroscience base. Thus, research has established that fear potentiation of the startle response is directly attributable to activation of the *amygdala, a central structure in the older limbic brain, that projects signals directly to the pontine centre of the normal startle circuit. The amygdala also projects to the facial nucleus and the lateral hypothalamus, mediating facial muscle and cardiovascular and other autonomic reflexes in emotion.

335

In summary, the activation of emotional reflexes is a fundamental feature of affect. The function of these reflex actions is to heighten sensory intake, as in the extra widening of the pupil to threat or attractive stimuli, and through a range of autonomic and somatic changes to direct and mobilize the body for survival actions.

PETER J. LANG AND MARGARET M. BRADLEY

Lang, P.J. (1995). The emotion probe. Studies of motivation and attention. *American Psychologist*, **50**, 372–85.
Lang, P.J. and Davis, M. (2006). Emotion, motivation, and the brain: reflex foundations in animal and human research. *Progress in Brain Research*, **156**, 3–29.

regret Regret is the negative emotion that we experience when realizing or imagining that our present situation would have been better had we decided or acted differently (see COUNTERFACTUAL EMOTIONS). It is a comparison-based emotion that reflects on our own causal role in the current, suboptimal situation (Van Dijk and Zeelenberg 2005). The emotion of regret is accompanied by feelings that one should have known better, by having a sinking feeling, by thoughts about the mistakes one has made and the opportunities lost, by tendencies to kick oneself and to correct one's mistake, by desires to undo the event and get a second chance, and by actually doing this if given the opportunity.

Regret is the prototypical decision-related emotion (see DECISION-MAKING). One only experiences regret when at some point in time one could have prevented the regretted outcome from happening. Of course, other emotions can also be the result of decisions; for example one may be disappointed with a decision outcome, or happy about the process by which one made a choice (see DISAPPOINTMENT; HAPPINESS). But all other emotions can also be experienced in situations where no decisions are made. For example, one can be disappointed with a birthday present, but one cannot regret it (unless, of course, the disappointing present was suggested by oneself).

Experiences of regret can be the result of a decision to act or a decision not to act. Early regret research indicated that people tend to regret their actions (commissions) more than their inactions (omissions). Later research showed that time is crucial (Gilovich and Medvec 2005). In the short run people tend to feel more regret over their actions (the stupid things they did or bought), but in the long run they tend to feel more regret over their inactions (the school they never finished, the career or romance never pursued). This temporal pattern to regret is due to a number of factors that decrease the regret for action over time (e.g. we take more reparative action and engage in more psychological repair work for action regrets than for inaction regrets), and to factors that increase the regret for inaction over time (e.g. over time we may forget why we did not act on opportunities, making the inaction inexplicable). An additional factor producing this temporal pattern is that we forget regrettable actions more easily than regrettable failures to act, resulting in a greater cognitive availability for our failures to act.

Regret is not only a passive emotional reaction to bad decisions but also a major influence in our day-to-day decision-making. This influence can take two forms. First, the experience of retrospective regret may produce a behavioural inclination to reverse one's decision or undo the consequences. For example, after buying a product which proves to be suboptimal, regret can motivate us to ask for our money back, or it may result in apologies in the case of interpersonal regrets. Second, decision-makers may anticipate possible future regret when making decisions, and choose in such a way that this future regret will be minimal.

This latter idea has some history in research on decision-making, starting with economists studying rational choice (Loomes and Sugden 1982). We now know that the influence of anticipated future regret on current decision-making can take several forms. First, people may avoid deciding in order to avoid making the wrong decision. People may also avoid or delay their decisions because they want to gather more information in order to make a better decision. Research has shown that anticipated regret influences many real-life decisions, such as salary negotiations, stock market investments, the prescription of medical testing, condom use, lottery play, and others (for a review see Zeelenberg and Pieters, 2007).

Regret is a functional emotion that can protect us from wasting money and help us to maintain good social relationships. Additionally, it makes bad decisions and wrong choices stand out in our memory and helps us to make better decisions in the future. This is also shown by the finding that we tend to feel most regret about things that we can still improve in the future, sometimes referred to as the opportunity principle (Roese and Summerville 2005).

Taken together, regret is an aversive emotional state that is related to counterfactual thoughts about how the present situation would have been better had one chosen or acted differently and people are motivated to avoid or minimize this emotion.

MARCEL ZEELENBERG

Landman, J. (1993). *Regret: the persistence of the possible*. New York: Oxford University Press.
Zeelenberg, M. and Pieters, R. (2007). A theory of regret regulation 1.0. *Journal of Consumer Psychology*, **17**, 3–18.

regulation of emotion Oscar Wilde (1854–1900) once noted that a 'man who is master of himself can end a sorrow as easily as he can invent a pleasure' (Wilde 1890/1988, p. 85). This quote nicely captures the idea that although emotions seem to come and go as they please, they can in fact be regulated. Present-day emotion regulation research builds upon prior work on psychological defences, *stress and *coping, and self-regulation (Ochsner and Gross 2005). To set the stage for our analysis of emotion regulation, we first outline a 'modal model' of emotion. We then distinguish emotion regulation from related processes, and present a process model that organizes the many different types of emotion regulation strategies.

The 'modal model' of emotion
Emotions involve a person–situation interaction that engages attention, has meaning to an individual, and causes a coordinated yet malleable multisystem response to the interaction. We believe that this conception of emotion—which we refer to as the 'modal model' of emotion—satisfies lay intuitions about emotion, and represents some of the major points of convergence among those concerned with defining and studying emotion (see EMOTION DEFINITIONS (PSYCHOLOGICAL PERSPECTIVES)).

In Fig. R4 we present the modal model of emotion. This model outlines how an emotion arises over time. The first element is a psychologically relevant situation, which is commonly external. However, relevant 'situations' can also be internal, taking the form of mental representations. These external or internal situations must be attended to in some way, which allows the individual to assess (or appraise) the situation's familiarity, *valence, and value relevance (Ellsworth and Scherer 2003). The emotional responses that follow from these appraisals are reflected in loosely coupled changes in experiential, behavioural, and physiological response systems (see SYNCHRONIZATION) (Mauss et al. 2005). Like other responses, emotions often change the situations that prompted them. This change is represented by the recursive arrow from one emotional response to the next eliciting situation in Fig. R4.

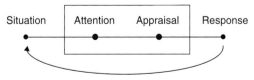

Fig. R4. The 'modal model' of emotion. From Gross and Thompson (2007).

Defining emotion regulation
Emotion regulation refers to influencing which emotions one has, when one has them, and how one experiences and expresses these emotions. This includes attempts to change the magnitude and/or duration of behavioural, experiential, and/or physiological aspects of the emotional response. Emotion-regulatory processes may be automatic or controlled, conscious or unconscious, and may dampen, intensify, or maintain positive or negative emotion, depending on an individual's goals. Emotions may be regulated by oneself (intrinsic regulation) or by others (extrinsic regulation). Although extrinsic regulation of emotions (e.g. by a parent) is crucial for the development of emotion regulation (Thompson 1991), our focus here is on the intrinsic regulation of emotions.

Emotion regulation is closely related to several other psychological constructs. Just as emotion is one of many types of valenced reaction classified as *affect, we see emotion regulation as one of several types of *affect regulation*. In addition to emotion regulation, affect regulation encompasses coping, mood regulation, and psychological defences. Emotion regulation is distinct from these processes in that it targets emotion rather than other forms of affect (for a fuller analysis see Gross and Thompson, 2007).

Given the goal of modulating one's own emotions, there are many different strategies one can employ. Regulation strategies have been categorized by the target of regulation (situation-focused or problem-focused coping: Lazarus and Folkman 1984), the way in which regulation is implemented (behavioural or cognitive interventions), or whether they involve engagement with or distraction from emotion (Parkinson and Totterdell 1999). Our approach has been to organize regulation strategies according to when in the emotion-generative process the strategy has its primary impact.

The process model of emotion regulation
The modal model of emotion (Fig. R4) provides a framework for representing the major points in the emotion-generative process at which individuals may intervene to shape the trajectory of an emotional response. In Fig. R5, the modal model is redrawn, highlighting five points at which regulation can occur. These five points represent five loose-knit families of emotion regulation strategies: situation selection, situation modification, attentional deployment, cognitive change, and response modulation. Everyday actions often involve multiple regulatory processes. Nonetheless, we believe that this process model provides a conceptual framework that is useful for understanding the causes, consequences, and mechanisms underlying various forms of emotion regulation.

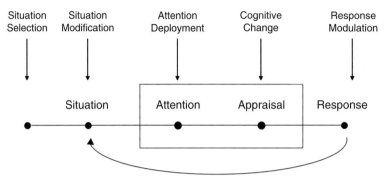

Fig. R5. A process model of emotion regulation that highlights five families of emotion regulation strategies. From Gross and Thompson (2007).

Situation selection is the most forward-looking emotion regulation strategy. This type of emotion regulation involves forming expectations about the emotional consequences of future situations and choosing between situations according to one's own emotional goals. Situation selection requires an understanding of remote situations, and of the expected emotional responses to these situations. It also involves balancing the short-term emotional effects of situations with their forecasted longer-term effects.

Consider a young professional who is faced with a considerable daily commute to work. Although factors that do not involve emotion may influence his choice of transportation, this particular young man gets so frustrated with traffic congestion that he's noticed that it interferes with his productivity. Therefore, he may opt to take a commuter train to decrease his anticipated agitation in the short term. In addition, this choice may coincide with longer-term emotional goals, such as the joy that arises when one sacrifices personal convenience for a societal cause, such as decreasing pollution.

Situation modification refers to the fact that, after selecting a situation, individuals can continue to tailor aspects of their environment to meet their emotional goals. Situation modification may require that individuals view situations as malleable, and see themselves as effective agents of change in those situations. As previously noted, situations can be external or internal, but situation modification—as defined here—has to do with acting upon the external, physical environment.

Our young professional from the previous example may modify aspects of his morning train ride that have the potential to cause him anger or fear. For example, he may change seats when he notices a heated disagreement arising between two passengers in his usual carriage or section. He may even attempt to break up or

338

mediate the disagreement to avoid causing widespread fear or discomfort for other passengers, thereby engaging in intrinsic and extrinsic emotion regulation at the same time.

In addition to situation selection and modification, it is possible to regulate emotions without affecting the external environment. *Attentional deployment* occurs when individuals direct their attention in order to influence their emotions. In some cases, attentional deployment may be conceived of as situation modification performed upon an internal situation. Three major attentional manipulations are distraction, concentration, and rumination. Distraction focuses attention on unemotional aspects of the situation, or on another situation entirely. By contrast, concentration directs attention towards the emotional features of a situation. Rumination refers to the perseverative redirection of attention towards one's feelings and their consequences. Rumination on sad events has been shown to lengthen and worsen depressive symptoms (Nolen-Hoeksema 1993).

When our commuting professional reseats himself in another carriage, he might find himself next to a teenager engaged in a deeply personal conversation on her mobile phone. He may then choose to avoid his discomfort and embarrassment at overhearing her conversation by physically blocking the sound of her voice with earphones, or by attempting to become engaged in whatever reading material he has at his disposal.

Even after a situation has been selected, modified, and attended to, an emotional response requires an evaluation of the situation's meaning and one's capacity to handle the situation. *Cognitive change* exploits the flexible nature of appraisal, changing how one evaluates the situation to alter its emotional significance, either by changing how one views the situation or one's capacity to handle it. One form of cognitive change that has received particular attention is *reappraisal (Gross 2002). Several studies have shown that the use of reappraisal can successfully modulate self-reported negative affect, startle *eye blink response, and blood flow to the *amygdala (Gross 1998, Jackson *et al.* 2000, Ochsner and Gross 2005).

Our commuting protagonist has made it through most of his morning commute when the train unexpectedly slows and an announcement is made that the train will be delayed by thirty minutes. Instead of getting angry, the young professional can choose to remind himself that he was dreading his first morning meeting, and be thankful that the delay didn't occur on another day, when he has a more desirable morning appointment.

Response modulation is a last-ditch effort to change the way an emotional response is manifested. Response modulation refers to attempting to change physiological, experiential, or behavioural responding directly, once the emotion is under way. Food, drugs, and alcohol are often used to regulate the physiological and experiential aspects of the emotional response. Another typical and relatively well-studied type of response modulation is the regulation of emotion-expressive behaviour. Studies have shown that generating emotion-expressive behaviour can increase the experience of that emotion (Izard 1990b). Decreasing emotion-expressive behaviour has mixed effects on emotion experience (decreasing positive but not negative experience) and actually increases activation of the *cardiovascular system (Gross 1998).

Just as our professional thinks his morning adventure is over, he runs into a close colleague on the train platform. This is the first time that he's seen her since she has earned a promotion for which they were both considered. Although he may feel disappointed, hurt, or angry that he was not promoted, he can choose to override his urge to scowl, pout, or curse at his colleague and instead smile and offer polite congratulations.

Directions for future research
It bears emphasizing that any one emotion-regulatory processes may be helpful in some settings and harmful in others. Although there are some data on the positive and negative ramifications of employing different emotion-regulatory strategies (Parkinson and Totterdell 1999, Gross and John 2003), no strategy is likely to be more adaptive than others across all possible contexts. Consistent with a functionalist perspective, regulatory strategies may accomplish a person's own goals but be perceived by others as maladaptive. Imagine the outcome if the commuter in the example above attempted to use situation selection and avoided going to work whatsoever in order to sidestep friction with his recently promoted colleague. Successful regulation most likely involves the flexible application of a range of context-appropriate emotion-regulatory processes. Future research is needed to investigate not only an individual's skill at implementing individual strategies, but at selecting the appropriate place and time to use each strategy.

One point of debate is over the extent to which emotion regulation can be separated from emotional responding (Campos *et al.* 2004, Gross and Thompson 2007). Most research on emotion regulation has reported the effects of regulation on measures of the emotional response (experience, behaviour, expression, physiology). A recent approach to the separation of response and regulation has been to adopt a dual-process cognitive neuroscience approach which makes contact with the cognitive control literature (Ochsner and Gross 2005). This approach has most commonly taken the form of functional magnetic resonance imaging studies investigating the neural basis of reappraisal. These studies have identified a network of prefrontal regions that are more active when participants are actively reappraising than when they are passively viewing negative stimuli. Activity in some of these prefrontal regions has been shown to predict reappraisal-related changes in self-reported negative affect (Ochsner *et al.* 2002) and activity in emotion-generative regions such as the amygdala (Urry *et al.* 2006). Future studies will clarify the relationship between emotion-generative and emotion-regulatory processes.

KATERI MCRAE AND JAMES J. GROSS

Gross, J.J. (ed.) (2007). *Handbook of emotion regulation*. New York: Guilford Press.

relevance detection Cognitive theories of emotion posit that emotions result from an evaluation of cognized objects (typically events or states of affairs) as good or bad (see APPRAISAL THEORIES). But what does it mean to evaluate an event as good versus bad? Most proponents of cognitive emotion theory in psychology (e.g. Arnold, Frijda, Lazarus, Ortony and colleagues, Roseman and colleagues, and Scherer; see Scherer *et al.* 2001a) answer this question as follows: to evaluate an event as good versus bad means to appraise the event as congruent versus incongruent with what one *desires, wants, wishes, has as one's *goal, or is motivated to obtain (as a general term for these various motivational states, Frijda (1986) proposed '*concern') (see MOTIVATION). However, this assumption implies that emotions are not only caused by cognitive states (perceptions, *beliefs, judgements), but also, at least indirectly, by motivational states: emotions occur if an event (1) is believed to be certain or at least possible and (2) is evaluated as congruent or incongruent with one's concerns.

Lazarus combined these two appraisals into a single process termed *primary appraisal. The emotionally significant information provided by primary appraisal is that *a good or bad event—and hence, the satisfaction or frustration of a concern—is certain or possible*. Appraising an event in any of these ways means to appraise it as concern-relevant; otherwise it is concern-irrelevant. Primary appraisal is thus the process that detects concern-relevant changes in the world as well as, simultaneously, in the 'fate' of the concerns affected by the world changes. In both of these senses, primary appraisal is the process of relevance detection. Accordingly, emotions can be characterized as responses to the detection of concern-relevant events (Frijda 1986).

Being caused by the detection of concern-relevant events, emotions (emotional experiences) *carry information* about the occurrence of these events and the fate of the concerns affected by them. This information is undoubtedly of high importance to the individual. One may therefore speculate that the signalling of concern relevance is the (or at least one important) evolutionary function of emotions. This has indeed been proposed by several theorists (e.g. Frijda; Oatley and Johnson-Laird). However, one may ask, why is the information about concern-relevant events 'broadcast' in the form of emotional experiences (e.g. feelings of pleasure or displeasure)? A partial answer is probably that consciousness is needed to make this information available system-wide, presumably because this is a precondition for it to exercise global control (i.e. to influence cognition and action).

Thus far, relevance detection was discussed assuming a system of mental representations suited to support beliefs and desires (i.e. propositional attitudes). Such a representation system probably exists, at least in elaborated form, only in humans and higher mammals. On the other hand, the behaviour of even the simplest systems appears to be controlled by feedback mechanisms that can be described, metaphorically, as involving the comparison of 'believed (or perceived)' states of the world with 'desired states'. This being the case, it is reasonable to ask whether any of these 'lower level' analogues of the concern-relevance detection mechanism can give rise to emotion analogues in humans, as well as in other creatures (including artificial agents; Allen 2001). Both questions have been answered affirmatively by some theorists. Concerning humans, for example, Frijda (1986) proposed that an extended concept of desire—the concept of a *set-point*—is both necessary and sufficient to bring sensory pleasures and displeasures (the hedonic tone of sensations of colour, sound, taste, etc.) within the reach of appraisal theory (see also Arnold 1960). Scherer and Leventhal (see Scherer 2001a, c) have gone further to propose that emotion-producing relevance

detectors exist on each of three representational–computational levels in humans: the conceptual (propositional) level, the schematic level, and the sensorimotor level (see LEVELS OF PROCESSING). A problem of multilevel models is to specify how the different levels are related, that is, if (and if yes how) they communicate with each other (Allen 2001). Independent of this issue, it is conceivable that *analogues* of the human concern-relevance detection mechanism are responsible for *analogues* of human emotional reactions in animals, even those low on the evolutionary scale (see ANIMAL EMOTIONS). If so, the concern-relevance detection mechanism responsible for human emotions may only be the manifestation of an old evolutionary principle in a highly developed representational system.

For a discussion of some of the issues involved in constructing *computational models* of concern-relevance detection, and of appraisal processes more generally, readers are referred to Allen (2001) and Reisenzein (2001).

RAINER REISENZEIN

relief Relief is a positive emotion that is felt when a negative outcome did not materialize (see POSITIVE EMOTIONS; OUTCOME EXPECTANCIES; COUNTERFACTUAL EMOTIONS). It is a prospect-based emotion (Ortony *et al.* 1988), and closely linked to *disappointment (felt when a positive outcome did not materialize) and satisfaction (felt when a positive outcome did materialize). Relief may be felt in comparison to a prior expectation, but also in comparison to a counterfactual outcome that was never anticipated (If only I had taken that plane, I would have been dead as well). This makes relief a cognitively complex, comparison-based emotion that is relevant in *decision-making situations. As such, the experience of relief will often produce negative emotions as a by-product. Realizing that one missed out on something very negative also causes one to be aware of the possibility of these negative outcomes, eliciting sadness, anger, and fear (Oliver 1996).

Relief can be considered an end state in the sense that it does not have clear motivational properties associated with its experience. However, in the consumer behaviour literature, relief has been described as something that consumers may strive for in products or services that eliminate something aversive (medication, prophylactics, insurances, legal defence, etc.)

MARCEL ZEELENBERG

religion and emotion (historical perspectives)
Religious experience is emotional by definition. William James (1902) introduced it as an instinctive impulsion, comparable with love, anger, ambition, and jealousy. Religion gives to life an enchanted and inexplicable

perspective. James observed that one has it, or not. It is a gift to be considered as an organic endowment according to physiologists, or something due to divine grace according to theologians. Some individuals can be deprived of religion. But no society exists without such unexplained *values, *beliefs, and ritual behaviours. The affirmation or the denial of these symbolic foundations produces strong emotional reactions, as everybody knows. Harvey Whitehouse (2004) has shown how the use of emotion in initiation rituals (especially through rites of terror) may have, in certain cultures, a cognitive function. Emotion appears as a mnemonic device, intended to set firmly in the mind of initiates some religious teaching of important social value.

Maybe the best expression of the emotional characteristic of religion is found in the concept of sacredness. The classic study on sacredness is Rudolph Otto's (1917) *The idea of the holy*. Written by a Lutheran theologian specializing in comparative mysticism, this book tries to define the basic religious experience as an encounter with God, before any theological construction of this experience. Otto's approach lies on the assumption of a universal experience of the holy (the *numinosum*) as being the evidence of a contact, or even a seizure. The creature would be suddenly confronted by the Creator. This approach may be described as a phenomenology of theophany (or epiphany). It is focused on the description of a variety of emotions considered as human reactions to the mysterious presence of a transcendent reality. According to Otto the basic category of such affective, emotional, and religious reactions, before any knowledge of God, is what he calls the experience of the numinous. This numinous (*numinosum* in Latin, from *numen*) is conceived by him as an impersonal power, perceived through a feeling of terror, of fear. He calls this feeling *mysterium tremendum*. It is manifested by tremor, trembling, and quivering. The *tremendum* implies and induces humility in front of the *mysterium*. The awareness of the radical alterity (otherness) of this *mysterium* induces the feeling of its *majestas*. From *fear, one is conducted towards admiration (see ADMIRATION/ AWE). The *mysterium tremendum* becomes *mysterium fascinans*. Fear and admiration, terror and veneration coincide.

Considered on a very large scale, this experience of awe, or (in German) *Ehrfurcht*, may look universal. But this type of phenomenon should be contextualized, and analysed more precisely. In religious life, as far as scientific observation is concerned, the worshipper pretends very rarely to be confronted by the divinity without mediation. Such encounters would normally be considered as real transgressions, to be avoided.

Considered by Otto as being the stimulus of every religious emotion, this meeting face to face with the

Unknown is an ethnocentric and Judeo-Christianizing occasional concept, not a universal one. As a common experience, the holy or the sacred are better understood in terms of hesitation, scruple, restraint, and caution, in front of an object which does not necessarily have to be a god. This object could be a person (human or nonhuman), something inanimate, a natural landscape, a building such a temple, a special space or a special time, and so forth. The main characteristic of this object is its supposed remoteness. It has to be conceived of as being separated from common, banal, experience.

The emotion tied to sacredness actualizes the essential values of a person, those which relate her to a precise culture and give her a social identity. But even if the experience of the sacred is emotional by nature, most religions are most of the time disdainful of emotion. They feel uneasy in front of any potential disturbance. They strive to attain ideal calm, order, and serenity. The ritualization of emotions, in many religious ceremonies, has as its function not to teach something, but to purify emotions: in the Eleusinian mysteries, for example, the initiate had to go through nocturnal experiences of fear and agitation. A dramatized exaltation guided him from this trouble towards a comforting luminous revelation. Ritualization induces a cathartic effect, by mastering and controlling emotions. Nothing more than a ritual is harmoniously assembled and susceptible to be reproduced. Even when it is concerned by violence and emotion, as for example in some Christian stagings of the Passion at Easter.

Emotion may be part of the religious ritual, or result from it. But it may also appear as soon as normal ritual performance is jeopardized. It is therefore important not to oppose pretended emotional religions and pretended less emotional religions. The institutional dimension of religion assures the control of emotions. This process of ritualization may be compared with the techniques of dramatization of trance as they were described by ethnologists (Leiris 1958). Emotion, in the context of religion, has to be perceived first of all in relationship with the regular, scrupulous, and harmonious performance of the rite. This implies that the mastering of affects is a preliminary condition to a peaceful relationship with the gods.

PHILIPPE BORGEAUD

Borgeaud, P. (2007). Rites et émotions. Considérations sur les mystères. In: J. Scheid (ed.), *Rites et croyances dans les religions du monde Romain* (Entretiens sur l'antiquité classique, tome LIII), pp. 189–229. Genève-Vandoeuvres: Fondation Hardt.

religion and emotion (psychological perspectives) At the outset, a distinction needs to be made between religion and spirituality. When Nietzsche (1889/2003) called for 'spiritualizing the passions' he was not advocating religion, for he had already declared that 'God is dead'. Even if we limit consideration to religion, emotionally relevant distinctions can be made, for example, between authoritarian versus humanistic religions (Fromm 1950), intrinsic versus extrinsic religious orientations (Allport 1950), and religion as an open-ended quest for meaning versus a single-minded commitment, whether intrinsically or extrinsically oriented (Batson *et al.* 1993). In this brief entry such distinctions can only be noted, not discussed. Rather, the focus is on five ways in which religion, as an institutionalized set of *beliefs and practices, not only influences the emotional lives of individuals but can also serve as a resource for the study of emotion.

Religious practices are elicitors of emotion

Religious rites are common triggers for profound emotional experiences, from mystical bliss and awe to the throes of anxiety and despair. Closer to everyday experience are the sense of belonging, hope, and joy that spread through a congregation as they worship together (see CONTAGION). Of course, not all religiously inspired emotions are benign: self-mortification and self-righteous aggression against others have been commonplace, today as well as historically.

Religion helps regulate emotions that are elicited in nonreligious contexts

Good examples are the seven deadly sins of traditional Christianity: anger, pride, lust, greed, sloth, gluttony, and envy. By definition, 'sinful' emotions are regulated down; other emotions, those considered virtuous (e.g. love, compassion, humility), may be regulated up. Significantly, religiously inspired regulation applies not only to behaviour but also to thoughts and feelings. This, in turn, implies higher-order or multiple levels of consciousness, as when a person feels guilty about being proud of becoming angry at, say, an offensive but disadvantaged colleague (see REGULATION OF EMOTION).

Religion is an agency for the socialization of emotion

Einstein observed that 'a man's worth is not measured by what his religious beliefs are but rather by what emotional impulses he has received from Nature during his lifetime' (letter to Sister Margrit Goehner, February 1955, Einstein archive). The sentiment expressed by Einstein may be unassailable; nevertheless, to speak of emotional impulses as he does is misleading, for it implies greater unity to emotions than actually exists. Emotions are complex syndromes, the components of which can be acquired independently, only later to be integrated into a whole, if at all. For an instructive analysis of this process as it involves the socialization of trance among the Balinese, see Bateson (1976).

Religion provides the blueprints (beliefs and rules) for the creation of emotions unique to a creed

Einstein's observation, quoted above, is misleading in another respect, namely, it implies too strict a division between religious beliefs and related emotional states. Some emotions can be divorced from the beliefs and rules involved in their creation, but others cannot. The Balinese variety of trance, for example, could not exist outside its religious context. Other examples of emotions specific to a creed are easily found, such as stigmata (suffering accompanied by bodily marks or sensations in imitation of Christ's crucifixion), and the Chinese Buddhist emotion of *kong*, a sense of emptiness that is yet full of meaning (Sundararajan 2008).

The above four ways in which religion influences emotion (elicitation, regulation, socialization, and blueprints for construction) are not independent, nor do they differ in principle from related nonreligious influences. The crucial point is that religion offers an important but underutilized resource for natural experiments. The fifth way that religion can help us understand emotion is more conjectural.

Religion is a rich source for thought experiments

One of the earliest works on anger was by the early theologian Lactantius (*c*.240–*c*.320). How can God—an unembodied, omniscient, and beneficent being—become angry, as portrayed in the Old and New Testaments of the Bible? In order to answer such a question, Lactantius had to analyse anger in its most abstract and fundamental form. Similar questions could be asked about other emotions, as they might be postulated to occur, or not occur, in an afterlife. A naturalistic counterpart to such hypothetical questions might be: how can a supercomputer be programmed not just to express emotion (by sending an error message, say, with swear words and invectives) but actually to be in an emotion-like state (Fellous and Arbib 2005)? Gods and computers differ, of course, in their architectural requirements, but conjectures about each force us to think creatively about the meaning and functions of emotions.

To summarize, the potential contribution of religion to emotion is not limited to phenomenological analyses of religious experiences, nor to possible ameliorating benefits of certain religious practices (e.g. prayer, meditation, yoga). As an institutionalized set of beliefs and practices, religion offers a rich resource for the study of the elicitation, regulation, socialization, and construction of emotional syndromes, and for the analysis of emotional concepts.

JAMES R. AVERILL

Haidt, J. (2003). The moral emotions. In: R.J. Davidson, K.R. Scherer, and H.H. Goldsmith (eds), *Handbook of affective sciences*, pp. 852–70. New York: Oxford University Press.

Watts, F. (2007). Emotion regulation and religion. In: J.J. Gross (ed.), *Handbook of emotion regulation*, pp. 504–22. New York: Guilford Press.

repression Throughout his life Sigmund Freud (1856–1939), the founder of psychoanalysis, claimed that the purpose of psychoanalytic therapy was to lift the repression that excluded unacceptable mental contents from awareness and to 'make the unconscious conscious'. In 1893 he and Josef Breuer (1842–1925) argued that repression operated on memories of traumatic events and that allowing these memories back into consciousness could bring about a permanent cure for hysteria. By the beginning of the 20th century Freud preferred to believe that repression operated primarily on infantile drives and wishes rather than on memories of actual events.

Repression sometimes refers to a process whereby unwanted material is turned away before it reaches awareness at all (Freud's 'primary repression'). This material, Freud argued, re-enters awareness in disguised ways, such as slips of the tongue. Repression can also mean that a person becomes aware of unwanted mental contents and then deliberately attempts to exclude them from consciousness (Freud's 'repression proper' or 'after-expulsion'). Although there is little empirical evidence for 'primary repression', many memory researchers would have little problem with 'after-expulsion'. It is widely believed that everyday mental functioning depends on flexible excitatory and inhibitory mechanisms that select relevant material and exclude unwanted material from entering consciousness.

Do people first forget and later remember significant traumatic incidents? Numerous studies have found that many clients in therapy for the effects of childhood sexual abuse report having periods in their lives when they could not remember that the abuse had taken place. People have reported forgetting of nonsexual as well as sexual traumas, and many of the incidents have received some corroboration. These findings strongly suggest that it is possible to forget traumatic incidents but do not indicate whether repression is involved or rule out the likelihood that some 'recovered memories' are not accurate.

CHRIS R. BREWIN

Brewin, C.R. (2003). *Posttraumatic stress disorder: malady or myth?* New Haven, CT: Yale University Press (see chapter 7, Myths, memory wars, and witch-hunts, and chapter 8, The return of repression?).

resilience Resilience is variously defined as the absence of a psychopathological outcome or successful adaptation following exposure to stressful or potentially traumatic life events or life circumstances (see STRESS). Thus, it involves both the capacity to maintain a healthy outcome following exposure to adversity as well as the capacity to rebound after a negative experience (see VULNERABILITY). Early work in this area developed out of the recognition that some children exposed to extreme conditions of poverty or neglect nonetheless maintained psychological health and effective functioning and even thrived under these conditions. Recent work has noted that a substantial number of individuals who are exposed to traumatic events (physical assault, violence, sudden and tragic loss) do not succumb to the negative experience by developing mental disorders or exhibiting extreme distress and instead maintain a healthy emotional and psychological stance. Most scholars resist seeing resilience as a single personality trait or individual attribute. Instead, resilience is seen as a process that is facilitated by the presence of individual protective factors (e.g. high *self-esteem or social skills) as well as environmental ones (e.g. a supportive family or peer network). Emerging work seeks to identify psychobiological factors that may also play a role in the development or maintenance of resilience.

ROXANE COHEN SILVER

Bonanno, G.A. (2004). Loss, trauma, and human resilience – have we underestimated the human capacity to thrive after extremely aversive events? *American Psychologist*, **59**, 20–28.
Luthar, S.S., Cicchetti, D., and Becker, B. (2000). The construct of resilience: a critical evaluation and guidelines for future work. *Child Development*, **71**, 543–62.

respiration Respiration is a crucial and often-overlooked physiological process that is closely associated with emotionality. While much of the literature on respiration is devoted to either clinical problems, such as apnoea or asthma, or the physiological processing of gasses, other breathing phenomena can be potent indicators of emotional activity. Sighing, for instance, has a characteristic pattern of long inspiration followed by a shorter and often forceful expiration and is indicative of stress reduction even in rats (Soltysik and Jelen 2005). Respiration is also physiologically coupled to cardiac activity (see CARDIOVASCULAR SYSTEM; PERIPHERAL PSYCHOPHYSIOLOGY). Respiratory sinus arrhythmia (RSA) is a change in the pattern of heart rate as a function of breathing cycle and is closely associated with responses to stress and emotional reactivity. RSA is primarily mediated by vagal influences and respiration affects vagal activity through both central nervous system mechanisms and feedback networks related to carbon dioxide metabolism (Berntson *et al.* 1993). Recent technological advances have made noninvasive measurement of breathing much easier. As an example, Van Diest *et al.* (2006) used both inductive plethysmography and nasal air sampling to measure breathing changes in persons engaging in emotional imagery and found changes in both ventilatory behaviour and carbon dioxide utilization. Interestingly, a major component of their findings indicated that anxiety reduced variability in breathing patterns.

TYLER LORIG

Berntson, G.G., Cacioppo, J.T., & Quigley, K.S. (1993). Respiratory sinus arrhythmia: autonomic origin, physiological mechanisms, and psychophysiological implications. *Psychophysiology*, 30, 183–196.

Soltysik, S. & Jelen, P. (2005). In rats, sighs correlate with relief. *Physiology and Behavior*, **85**, 598–602.

Van Diest, I., Thayer, J.F., Vandeputte, B, Van de Woestijne, K.P., & Van den Bergh, O. (2006). Anxiety and respiratory variability. *Physiology and Behaviour*, 30, 189–95.

reward Reward is a desirable outcome that is obtainable in dependence on behaviour. That is, reward differs from other desirable or pleasant stimuli, like gifts, in terms of its contingency upon achievement and an organism's implicit or explicit knowledge about this contingency. In general, psychological researchers have attributed two functions to reward—the first is 're-inforcement' for learning new behaviours, the second is 'incentive' for motivating behaviour (Beck 2004) (see PUNISHMENT).

Reward is probably the most powerful variable that influences learning in terms of a relatively stable change of behaviour in dependence on experiences (see LEARN-ING, EMOTIONAL (NEUROSCIENCE PERSPECTIVES); ASSOCIA-TIVE PROCESSING). According to the 'law of effect' (Thorndike 1911)—the fundamental basis of instrumental or operant conditioning—behaviour is shaped in dependence on its contingent consequences. Consequences that are *satisfying* (rewarding) will augment and consequences that are *annoying* (punishing) will reduce the probability of repeating a certain behaviour in the future. Interestingly, Thorndike referred to the affective characteristics of reward—an aspect that was later neglected and even rejected in American behaviourism and that is still a topic of discussion in modern psychology.

Reward as reinforcement
The idea that reward functions as reinforcement was most strongly stressed and defended by C. L. Hull (1884–1952) and B. F. Skinner (1904–90). Both researchers were eminent and radical behaviourists and thus committed to the idea of discovering the mechanistic laws of behaviour without considering intervening cognitive or affective processes. Around 1940, both Hull and Skinner published highly influential ideas and discoveries about the effects of reward on behaviour. While Skinner's research on operant conditioning was primarily concerned with elaborations of the law of effect and the question of *how* reinforcement affects learning, Hull was more interested in explaining *why* learning occurs at all.

For Hull (1943), in his drive-reduction theory, any behaviour is the product of an organism's actual energetic state and its learning history. Energetic state was described as 'drive' and quantified as the duration of deprivation of satisfaction of biological need. Learning history was described as 'habit', with the assumption that habit strength augments with increasing numbers of past reinforcements an organism has received for executing a certain behaviour. Although Hull avoided terms like satisfaction or pleasure, he proposed that the reason *why* reward can reinforce behaviour was that reward reduces drive. As a consequence, drive motivates an organism to do something, and its reward history will determine which behaviour is carried out for drive reduction.

Skinner's perspective on how reward affects learning and behaviour was more reductionist (e.g. Skinner 1938). Accordingly, organisms continuously emit behaviours. If any behaviour is by chance followed by a reinforcing stimulus—Skinner avoided the term reward—the probability of repeating that behaviour increases. There are two types of reinforcement—positive and negative. A positive reinforcer operates on behaviour by means of its presence (e.g. receiving a food pellet as consequence of a bar press), while a negative reinforcer functions by its elimination (e.g. a reduction of noise as consequence of a bar press). The effects of reinforcement on the effectiveness of the acquisition and the extinction of behaviour are significantly influenced by reinforcement schedules—a topic to which Skinner devoted much of his research with his famous 'Skinner box' that has revealed very detailed knowledge about the effects of reward on behaviour (see Fig. R6).

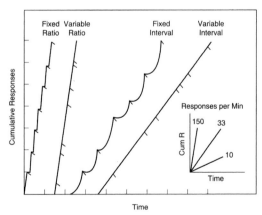

Fig. R6. Effects on cumulative responses as a function of different reinforcement (reward, respectively) schedules. From Beck (2004, p. 186).

As the basic rule, compared with intermittent reinforcement, continuous reinforcement results in faster acquisition but also faster extinction when reinforcement is no longer provided. Moreover, reinforcement schedules can be distinguished as a function of the contingency rule—reward for proportions of correct responses or for a correct response after a certain time interval. A discriminative stimulus that is learned according to stimulus learning—which is the same as Pavlovian or classical conditioning—can signal if such a contingency between behaviour and reward exists or not. To give an example, a pigeon in a Skinner box can learn that each fifth bar press is reinforced with a food pellet, but only in the presence of a green light and not in the presence of a red light. Skinner was sure that reward (reinforcement, respectively) is much more efficient in learning than *punishment, because punishment can only suppress behaviour but not eliminate an existing behaviour-reinforcer contingency.

Reward as incentive

The conceptualization of reward as incentive is closely connected with two important experimental observations—*latent learning* and *motivational shifts*. A famous study by Tolman and Honzik (1930) demonstrated that rats who could explore a labyrinth for ten days without finding any reward in the labyrinth's goal chamber outperformed rats who had been continuously rewarded, when the previously nonrewarded group found a reward on the eleventh day of the experiment. That is, the formerly nonrewarded group had learned the way to the goal chamber—according to Tolman, the rats had formed a *cognitive map* of the labyrinth—but did not use their 'knowledge' until it was purposeful to do that. Together with other groundbreaking observations in Tolman's laboratory, this discovery led to an important distinction: learning is not the same as behaviour. Learning depends on experience, while behaviour depends on *motivation—especially in terms of the expectancy of finding a valuable reward or incentive to reduce drive by applying what has previously been learned. This distinction led to the development of social-cognitive theories of motivation and learning that further highlighted the role of expectancies for obtaining reward as a motivational variable (see Hergenhan and Olson 2005).

Another observation that challenged the view that reward is nothing but reinforcement was the observation of 'motivational shifts'. In a well-known study by Crespi (1942), one group of rats was always rewarded with 256 food pellets for running through a straight-alley maze. The important manipulation was that from the twenty-first trial on the reward was reduced from 256 to only sixteen food pellets. As the result, the rats reduced their running speed by about 50%.

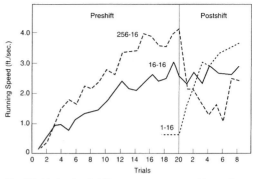

Fig. R7. Motivational shifts as a consequence of increasing (positive contrast) or decreasing (negative contrast) reward. From Beck (2004, p. 203).

Another group of rats first received only one pellet as reward and than sixteen pellets, with the result that this group ran three times faster than before. In still another group, the rats always found sixteen pellets. This group did not show significant motivational shifts manifested in running speed (see Fig. R7). These performance effects are compatible with new evidence that the magnitude of reward directly determines effort intensity when task difficulty is unclear (e.g. Richter and Gendolla 2007).

Similar effects can be obtained by modifying the quality of reward—children work harder for getting ice cream than for getting a slice of dry bread. These observations challenged the view that reward influences behaviour because it merely reduces drive or need strength. Rather, the incentive value of reward significantly changes behaviour, and organisms actively seek reward rather than merely getting reinforcement.

Outside American behaviourism, these effects had already been considered, as for instance in the concept of *goal valence* in Kurt Lewin's (1890–1947) field theory, where the subjective value of a reward depends on the organism's need state *and* the attractiveness of a goal object (Lewin 1926). But also within animal psychology, it became more accepted that hedonic experiences play an important role in learning and motivation and that incentive is largely determined by anticipated or experienced *pleasure. This led to the formulation of more complex models of learning (see Berridge, 2001, for a discussion). However, despite this evidence that reward works as an incentive due to its affective aspects, it should not be forgotten that need states can significantly moderate the experience of pleasure, as evident in the phenomenon of 'alliesthesia' (Cabanac 1971): a piece of chocolate cake tastes better when one is hungry than when one is satiated.

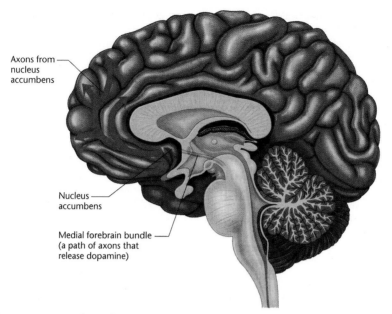

Axons from
nucleus
accumbens

Nucleus
accumbens

Medial forebrain bundle
(a path of axons that
release dopamine)

Fig. R8. The dopamine system and reward. From Kalat (2007, p. 72).

Reward and affect

Within experimental psychology, the first considerations of affective experiences as reward may be found in Young's (1959) idea of conditioned, anticipatory affective arousal as incentive to execute behaviours and in Mowrer's (1956) two-factor theory of learning. According to the latter idea, which was developed to explain avoidance learning, the feeling of relief rewards the avoidance of stimuli or situations that elicit fear because they have been associated with pain by classical conditioning; for example a box chamber where electric shocks are delivered, a shaky bridge, or a crowd of people. That is, phobic individuals manifest avoidance behaviour because avoidance is rewarded by the positive feeling of relief. An even more hedonic perspective can be found in Atkinson's (1964) achievement motivation theory, according to which the primary reward for achievement behaviour is strictly affective—experiencing pride following success (positive incentive) and avoiding shame following failure (negative incentive).

Other research has even shown that organisms prefer pleasure over drive reduction. In a famous study by Olds and Milner (1954), rats that had learned to electrically stimulate their hypothalamic brain area by means of a bar press developed addictive-like behaviour and stimulated their brains up to 2,000 times per hour. Those rats also preferred the electrical stimulation to direct drive reduction after longer periods of deprivation. These findings support the view that reward works as incentive because it provides pleasure—the most direct way to experience pleasure was the most preferred. This idea is also compatible with the finding that the behavioural effects of reward significantly depend on the neurotransmitter dopamine, which seems to be the substance leading organisms to learn (i.e. to repeat) behaviours. Dopamine secretion is associated with the experience of pleasure, and blocking dopamine reception in the brain significantly reduces the establishment of behavioural preferences—learning and approach motivation dramatically decrease (see Hoebel *et al.* 1999). A brain structure that is strongly involved in the regulation of dopamine outflow is the nucleus accumbens, which is close to the hypothalamus—the brain area where Olds and Milner placed their electrodes (see Fig. R8).

Still more observations are of note regarding the role of the hedonic aspects of reward. Frequently executed (i.e. preferred) behaviours can function as reward for other behaviours that are less attractive (Premack 1959)—a principle that is frequently applied in education—'first you tidy your room, then you can watch TV'. Moreover, individuals execute many behaviours for the sake of self-reward. For instance, people actively search levels of optimal stimulation, which is associated with *well-being. Examples are behaviours like exploration and sensation-seeking instead of resting in a state of equilibrium. In fact, boredom and understimulation have been found to be highly aversive (see Silvia 2006b).

Moreover, individuals self-regulate their mood states by executing those behaviours that promise well-being, especially when they are in intense positive or negative moods (Gendolla 2000).

Boundary conditions of reward effects

In contrast to the evidence discussed so far that reward increases performance, there are also indications that reward can reduce performance—especially when it corrupts interest or intrinsic motivation (see Deci 1975). However, this corruption effect of reward seems to depend on the important boundary condition that obtaining reward is not under the control of the performing individual. When reward is perceived to be contingent upon performance, and therefore regarded as a signal of competence, it has no detrimental effect on performance (Harackiewicz et al. 1984). If, by contrast, individuals feel controlled by a reward, reactance is likely to occur, leading to diminution of both interest and performance (Brehm 1966). Furthermore, a prominent example of reduced reward effects pertains to *depression. Evidence from self-report, behavioural, and physiological data suggests that rewards frequently lose their motivating effects under conditions of depression or related negative affect phenomena (see Gotlib and Hammen 2002).

GUIDO H.E. GENDOLLA AND KERSTIN BRINKMANN

Beck, R.C. (2004). *Motivation: theories and principles*, 5th edn. Upper Saddle River, NJ: Pearson.

Berridge, K.C. (2001). Reward learning: reinforcement, incentives, and expectations. In: D.L. Medin (ed.), *The psychology of learning and motivation*, Vol. 40, pp. 223–78. San Diego, CA: Academic Press.

Hergenhan, B.R. and Olson, M.H. (2005). *An introduction to theories of learning*, 7th edn. Upper Saddle River, NJ: Pearson.

risk factors for emotional disorders Epidemiological data indicate that over half of all people will experience a significant emotional disorder at some point in their lives (see DISORDER (AFFECTIVE, EMOTIONAL)). Not surprisingly, therefore, across both industrial and developing countries, emotional disorders exact a heavy economic and societal toll. Depressive disorders, for example, are the fourth leading cause of global disease burden and the leading cause of disability worldwide (Hyman et al. 2006) (see DEPRESSION). The chronicity and recurrence of emotional disorders, combined with their significant prevalence and costs, makes it imperative that we identify factors involved in their onset. Research examining risk factors for the development of emotional disorders has the potential to elucidate their underlying mechanisms and to inform efforts to prevent their occurrence, in addition to providing important information about normal regulatory processes.

The term 'risk factor' is used to describe variables that statistically increase the probability of experiencing a disorder (see VULNERABILITY). Thus, risk factors for emotional disorders can include such demographic variables as gender, education, and income, as well as variables that are more closely related to theoretical formulations of the disorders and, consequently, more likely to inform us about why people develop such disorders. In this context, there is converging evidence that having a parent with an emotional disorder is one of the most important risk factors for emotional disorders in children (see GENETICS OF AFFECT). For example, the offspring of a parent who is diagnosed with unipolar depression has a three- to five-fold increased risk of developing a significant emotional disorder (Goodman and Gotlib 1999) (see UNIPOLAR DISORDER). It is not yet clear, however, *why* these children are at risk. While genetic factors certainly contribute to the risk, it is becoming increasingly clear that the adverse effects of parental psychopathology are transmitted through multiple mechanisms, including innate dysfunctional neuroregulatory mechanisms, exposure to, and modelling of, negative cognitions, behaviours, and affect, the stressful context of the children's lives, and an inability to deal effectively with stress and to regulate negative emotions (Goodman and Gotlib 1999) (see COPING; REGULATION OF EMOTION).

In particular, difficulties in regulating negative emotions in the face of *stress appear to represent a broad and important class of risk factors for emotional disorders. The construct of emotion regulation involves the utilization of behavioural and cognitive strategies in efforts to modulate intensity and duration of affect. For example, theorists have recently postulated that individuals who are vulnerable to developing depression are characterized by a compromised ability to control their affect in response to life stressors. From this perspective, therefore, in attempting to understand risk for emotional disorders it is critical to examine psychological and biological responses to stress as well as the course of recovery from these negative affective states. Recent work in this area has clearly highlighted the importance of examining and integrating diverse domains involved in emotion dysregulation, including cognitive functioning, hypothalamic–pituitary–adrenocortical (HPA) axis activity, and patterns of neural activation in response to stress.

For example, many theorists have posited that individuals who are at high risk for the onset of an emotional disorder are characterized by negative biases in their processing of environmental information, selectively attending to negative stimuli, and demonstrating better memory for negative than for positive experiences (see APPRAISAL STYLE). These processing biases are hypothesized to maintain negative affective states and hinder recovery from stressful events. Although a large body of literature has documented the operation of these negative cognitive styles in people who are experiencing emotional disorders, most notably *anxiety and depression, only a few investigators have explicitly assessed their role as risk factors for disorder. In particular, Joormann et al. (2007) recently demonstrated that the young offspring of depressed mothers exhibit an attentional bias to negative faces despite not yet having experienced an emotional disorder themselves (see ATTENTION AND EMOTION).

A growing literature is also beginning to elucidate the biological foundations of difficulties in emotion regulation by examining neuroendocrine and neural functioning in response to stressors (see PSYCHONEUROENDOCRINOLOGY). The HPA system is activated when organisms are exposed to stress, producing cortisol as a means of mobilizing the resources necessary to sustain appropriate physical and psychological activity; indeed, investigators have posited that levels of cortisol produced under stress reflect the ability of individuals to regulate and cope (Gunnar et al. 1989). It is not surprising, therefore, that atypical cortisol secretion has been found in people experiencing various forms of emotional disorder. Importantly, there is also now evidence that high levels of cortisol production in response to stress may be a risk factor for the development of emotional disorders (e.g. Gotlib et al. 2008). Finally, investigators have begun to delineate the neural aspects of emotion regulation and dysregulation. In particular, researchers have implicated relations among medial and dorsolateral prefrontal brain areas and emotion-processing areas, such as the *amygdala and the orbitofrontal cortex, in the regulation of affect. Here, too, investigators are now presenting initial evidence that sustained activation of the amygdala, already found to characterize individuals with depression, may represent a critical risk factor for the experience of emotional disorders (e.g. Gotlib et al. 2006).

Although important, this literature is developing in relative isolation. It is clear that we must work to integrate the study of psychological and biological variables in order both to gain a more comprehensive understanding of risk factors and to be able to prevent the onset of debilitating emotional disorders.

IAN H. GOTLIB AND JUTTA JOORMANN

Gotlib, I.H., Joormann, J., Minor, K.L., and Cooney, R.E. (2006). Cognitive and biological functioning in children at risk for depression. In: T. Canli (ed.), *Biology of personality and individual differences*, pp. 353–81. New York: Guilford Press.

Gotlib, I.H., Joorman, J., Minor, K.L., and Hallmayer, J. (2008). HPA-Axis reactivity may underlie the associations among the 5-HTTLPR polymorphism, stress, and risk for depression. *Biological Psychiatry*, **63**, 845–51.

Kessler, R.C., Berglund, P., Demler, O., Jin, R., Merikangas, K.R., and Walters, E.E. (2005). Lifetime prevalence and age-of-onset distributions of DSM-IV disorders in the National Comorbidity Survey Replication. *Archives of General Psychiatry*, **62**, 593–602.

risk-taking Risk-taking generally means taking an action with the possibility of a worse consequence than not taking the action, for example sky-diving with the possibility of death. In the decision literature, risk-taking often refers to choosing an option with probabilistic outcomes over an option with a sure outcome of the same (or higher) expected value; for example, choosing a gamble with a 50% chance of winning $1000 or nothing, over a sure gain of $500 (see DECISION-MAKING). In this sense, risk-taking is one of three types of risk preferences, the other two being risk aversion and risk neutrality. Most existing models of choice under risk explain risk preference in cognitive terms, assuming that decision-makers assess the desirability and probabilities of possible outcomes of choice options and integrate the information multiplicatively to arrive at a decision. Among these models, the best-known descriptive model is Kahneman and Tversky's (1979) prospect theory, according to which people are generally risk-taking when faced with losses and risk averse when faced with gains. More recent research suggests that risk preference is often dictated by the decision-maker's emotional reactions (e.g. fear and anxiety) toward the risks in the decision situation, and such emotional reactions often diverge from cognitive assessments of the risks (e.g. Loewenstein et al. 2001, Slovic et al. 2002).

CHRISTOPHER K. HSEE AND YANG YANG

Kahneman, D. and Tversky, A. (1979). Prospect theory: An analysis of decisions under risk. *Econimetrica*, **47**, 313–27.

Loewenstein, G.F., Weber, E.U., Hsee, C.K. and Welch, N. (2001). Risk as feelings. *Psychological Bulletin*, **127**, 267–86.

Slovic, P., Finucanea, M.L., Petersa, E. and MacGregora, D.G. (2002). The affect heuristic. In Gilovich, T., Griffin, D., Kahneman, D. (ed.) *Heuristics and Biases: The Psychology of Intuitive Judgement*. pp. 397–420. New York, Cambridge University Press.

rumination Rumination refers to recurrent, profound, and prolonged thinking about matters of personal concern and interest, although there are a number of distinct conceptualizations within this general definition. Within the clinical field, rumination has been conceptualized relatively narrowly as a learnt response style characterized by repetitive thinking about the symptoms, meanings, and consequences of depressed mood (Nolen-Hoeksema 1991). Such depressive rumination is found to be elevated in patients with major *depression and to predict the onset and maintenance of depressed symptoms in prospective longitudinal studies. Experimental manipulations demonstrate that ruminative self-focus exacerbates negative mood and negative thoughts compared with distraction, indicating a causal effect of rumination on mood and cognition. Depressive rumination is found to be elevated in women compared with men, and provides a partial explanation for the 2:1 ratio of depression in women compared with men. Taken together, this evidence suggests that depressive rumination is a key pathological process in the onset and maintenance of depression. Nonetheless, recent research has suggested that even depressive rumination has distinct subtypes, each with distinct functions, some of which can be constructive. The most unhelpful form of rumination is characterized by abstract and evaluative brooding about problems and difficulties, e.g. 'Why do I have problems that other people don't have?'.

More broadly within social cognition, rumination has been conceptualized as recurrent instrumental thinking about an unresolved *goal, which is triggered by a perceived discrepancy between the current state and the desired goal, which focuses on the perceived discrepancy, and which persists until the unresolved goal is achieved or abandoned (Martin and Tesser 1996). Within this definition, rumination has the potential to be constructive or unconstructive, depending, respectively, on whether it focuses on how to reduce the perceived discrepancy through active problem-solving or passively makes the unattained goal more salient.

EDWARD WATKINS

S

sadness Sadness tends to be felt when an event is appraised as unpleasant, obstructive to one's goals and concerns, typically caused by others or circumstances, and one feels unable to cope with it or to modify it (e.g. Scherer 1997). Its most typical *antecedent* is the (partial, temporary, or absolute) *loss of a valued object, often *interpersonal* in nature: a loved one is dead, a friend moves away; one has conflicts (misunderstandings, quarrels, etc.) with family, friends, colleagues, or the partner (e.g. Shaver *et al.* 1987); the loss impinges negatively on attachment and social bonding motives (Bowlby 1980). Sadness is likewise felt, empathically, when losses occur to significant others, even by early childhood (e.g. Eisenberg *et al.* 1988). Disruption of *personal* goals and beliefs (e.g. good health, economic security, a positive self-concept) may also elicit it.

The expression of sadness, and its perception

The facial expression of sadness, for example furrowed eyebrows, lip corners stretched and turned down, tends to be similar across cultures (e.g. Keltner *et al.* 2003) (see FACIAL EXPRESSION OF EMOTION). Sadness is also often expressed by, and recognized on the basis of, a pattern of vocal parameters that includes voicing irregularities, low intensity and decreased speaking rate, low fundamental frequency (F_o), and narrow F_o variability (Scherer *et al.* 2003) (see VOCAL EXPRESSION OF EMOTION; VOICE PRODUCTION AND ACOUSTICS). Interestingly, similar structures, for example low pitch level, slow tempo, soft timbre and loudness, minor mode, characterize music pieces perceived as sad (Zammuner *et al.*, 2006) (see MUSIC (EMOTIONAL EFFECTS)). Expression, and recognition of, sadness is already present in the first few months of life—caregivers or onlookers can correctly detect it in infants. Sadness may also be expressed by *crying: in addition to possibly being a mode to alleviate tension, crying may be conceived as an attachment behaviour, a signal to others that one is suffering and needs attention or support. Expressed sadness—crying especially—tends to elicit *empathy, facilitating *prosocial behaviours in observers—who may act out of egoistic motives (e.g. to reduce their own distress in the presence of a sad person) as well as for altruistic reasons (e.g. Dovidio *et al.* 1990). From childhood on, sadness may also be associated with behavioural withdrawal and analytical

cognitive style, with the function of allowing the person to slow down, reappraise the causes and implications of the event, and motivate him or her to restore optimal conditions (e.g. strengthen existing social bonds).

Appraisals and (personal and sociocultural) factors influencing sadness

As already mentioned, appraisal processes are responsible for the felt feeling, its intensity and duration, and for changes therein. For instance, events perceived as avoidable (e.g. a separation due to a quarrel) or due to self-agency might elicit self-blame, guilt, remorse, or regret in addition to, or instead of, sadness; if someone else, or the circumstances, caused the event, then anger might be prominent. If the loss touches central concerns of the individual, and its anticipated consequences stretch long into the future (e.g. a partner's death), then depression might be experienced, with associated apathy or lethargy, sleep disturbances, fatigue, pessimism, cognitive negativity biases, etc. How the event is appraised (e.g. its degree of goal disruptivity), the intensity of felt sadness, what coping strategies the individual is able or willing to employ, and the extent to which sadness is expressed tend to vary with age (e.g. as a function of developmental level; Dunn 2003), gender, personality variables, and situational and sociocultural factors (e.g. culturally based beliefs and norms) (Barr-Zisowitz 2000). The same variables in turn modulate empathic and social responses to sad displays. For instance, less sadness is reported by men than by women living in highly individualistic and masculine cultures (e.g. Fischer and Manstead 2000). Seeking socioemotional support (typically a more positive coping strategy than either *rumination, isolation, and denial, all of which may characterize responses to loss) is more likely if the person enjoys a supportive social network, as typically is the case for females rather than males and for younger rather than older people, but is less likely if loss-agency is attributed to the self—as in performance failures or in gambling losses. Likewise, the probability of a given kind of loss and its potential disruptivity vary with age and/or culture. For example, loss of one's job might occur to young and mature adults, and be more likely in cultures with high rates of job instability, whereas loss of an attachment figure is possible at all ages, in all cultures. Adolescents, typically more sensitive than adults to negative evaluation of themselves by others, are more likely to be afraid of, and saddened by, loss of face or social rejection. Selective exposure to events, in order to avoid anticipated aversive consequences, is greater in older than younger people. Boys more than girls are socialized to attenuate or suppress sad displays, especially crying and in front of males, fathers included. Only a somewhat elaborate knowledge and understanding of emotions, i.e. emotional competence, itself related to socialization processes, allows children, as much as adults, to intentionally try and change their sad feelings: this could be done by changing their respiratory pattern to calm down, by recalling a positive experience, or by social sharing (see REGULATION OF EMOTION; COMPETENCE, EMOTIONAL). Competence, coupled with the motivation to do so, is likewise necessary to regulate expressive reactions so that they fit sociocontextual requirements—for example smiling upon receiving a disliked gift; attenuating one's sadness in the work setting; intensifying one's sadness in order to achieve (inter)personal goals, such as getting attention; avoiding saddening the interactant, making social acceptance of self more likely. Finally, personality variables such as low self-esteem and/or self-efficacy make certain kinds of appraisals more likely (e.g. self-blame, failure), and thus enhance the likelihood of sad experiences—in turn, sad mood may enhance negative self-evaluations.

'Sadness' as a constellation

In sum, sadness—as a felt experience, and as expressed and coped with—is best conceived of as an often complex constellation of features whose values are modulated by several factors, both personal and sociocultural.

VANDA L. ZAMMUNER

Barr-Zisowitz, C. (2000). 'Sadness': is there such a thing? In: M. Lewis and J.M. Haviland-Jones (eds), *Handbook of emotions*, 2nd edn, pp. 607–22. New York: Guilford Press.

Dunn, J. (2003). Emotional development in early childhood: a social relationship perspective. In: R.J. Davidson, K.R. Scherer, and H.H. Goldsmith (eds), *Handbook of affective sciences*, pp. 332–46. New York: Oxford University Press.

salivation Salivation is the process of releasing saliva from the salivary glands. Saliva is primarily water (approximately 98%) with small amounts of electrolytes, proteins, mucins, nitrogenous substances, and immunoglobulins. Saliva is secreted primarily by acinar cells in the salivary glands and helps to lubricate, protect, and maintain the oral cavity, aids in taste and digestion, and fights pathogens. The flow rate and composition of saliva can vary depending on neural input from the sympathetic and parasympathetic divisions of the *autonomic nervous system. Parasympathetic input leads to

relatively more fluid and less protein release whereas sympathetic input leads to relatively larger concentrations of protein. Mechanical and taste signals arising from the mouth are the primary determinants of salivation, but other variables can affect the flow and composition of saliva. Variables such as physical and psychological *stress that lead to broad sympathetic activity increase the concentration of alpha-amylase (a primary salivary protein) in saliva. In addition to the functional components of saliva produced by the acinar cells, saliva also contains many blood-borne substances because certain substances pass readily from blood plasma to saliva. Assessing the concentrations of these substances in saliva is a noninvasive means of estimating their active concentrations in the blood. One example is cortisol, a hormone secreted by the adrenal cortex in response to stress.

STEPHEN L. CRITES JR

Humphrey, S.P. and Williamson, R.T. (2001). A review of saliva: normal composition, flow, and function. *Journal of Prosthetic Dentistry*, **85**, 162–9.

Rohleder, N., Wolf, J.M., Maldonado, E.F., and Kirschbaum, C. (2006). The psychosocial stress-induced increase in salivary alpha-amylase is independent of saliva flow rate. *Psychophysiology*, **43**, 645–52.

Schachter–Singer theory Proposed by social psychologists Stanley Schachter and Jerome Singer in 1962, the Schachter–Singer theory of emotion is also known as the 'two-factor', 'cognitive-physiological' or 'cognition-arousal' theory of emotion. As these names suggest, its central claim is that emotion (i.e. feelings of anger, joy, and so forth) is a function of the interaction of two factors: perceived physiological *arousal and 'a cognition appropriate to this state of arousal' (see APPRAISAL THEORIES). Although proposed in a similar form by previous authors (e.g. by Marañon in 1924; see Cornelius 1991), the theory had no significant impact until the publication of Schachter and Singer (1962; Reisenzein 1983), which reported an apparently supportive experiment. In this more empirically grounded version, cognition-arousal theory rapidly became popular. In fact, during the 20 years following its publication, it was probably the most influential emotion theory in academic psychology (Reisenzein 1983).

Schachter and Singer's theory of emotion can be read as a revision of William James's (1842–1910) theory of emotion proposed some 80 years earlier (James 1884) (see JAMES–LANGE THEORY). James's theory is that emotions are a special kind of sensation: the sensations caused by the bodily, in particular visceral, changes elicited by emotional events (e.g. an increase in heart and respiratory rate). In this account, feelings of physiological arousal (or 'arousal' for brevity) are both *necessary* and *sufficient* for the experience of emotion. Schachter and Singer agreed with James that arousal is necessary, but disagreed that it is sufficient. For an emotion to occur, they argued, a second factor is also required. The second factor is a cognition; more precisely, it is an interpretation of the arousal by the one experiencing it. This interpretation consists in a *causal explanation* of the experienced arousal, namely its attribution to the appraisal of an object or event as concern-relevant (see CONCERNS; RELEVANCE DETECTION).

To illustrate, imagine that William, while wandering in the forest, is confronted by a bear. To feel afraid, it is not sufficient that William feels how his heart is racing, his mouth is dry, his fingers are clammy, and so forth, as proposed by James. Rather, to feel fear, William must also believe that his physiological arousal is caused by his (possibly unconscious) appraisal of the bear's approach as threatening. In Schachter and Singer's (1962) words, the emotion is 'a function of the interaction' of arousal and cognition, with the arousal determining the emotion's intensity and the cognition—the kind of appraisal to which the arousal is attributed—determining its quality (e.g. fear versus anger). One can interpret this as meaning that the emotion is an emergent mental state that results from an *integration* of felt arousal with the appraisal of the object, with this integration being effected by the causal attribution of the arousal. The attribution is usually correct because appraisals of objects as concern-relevant typically *do* cause arousal. However, misattributions of arousal (e.g. of emotional arousal to a nonemotional source, or vice versa) can occur in special cases. This can cause a reduction or an increase in the intensity of the emotion relative to the case of correct attribution (see below).

The Schachter–Singer theory stimulated much empirical research. The research mainly tested three central predictions of the theory and found varying amounts of support for them. The first prediction is that physiological arousal from an extraneous source intensifies an experienced emotion if it is misattributed to the source of this emotion. This prediction received limited support. The second prediction is that misattribution of arousal stemming from an emotional source reduces the intensity of emotion. This prediction was prima facie supported in many studies; however, subsequent research suggested that the observed reduction of emotionality may have been due to other factors such as the provision of accurate information about to-be-expected physiological symptoms conveyed as part of the misattribution manipulation (see Reisenzein 1983). The third prediction is that the reduction of physiological arousal or its feedback causes a proportional reduction of the intensity of experienced emotions. To test this idea, researchers examined the effects of arousal-reducing

drugs on the emotions of healthy participants and the emotional experience of spinal-cord injured people (who suffer reduced physiological feedback). In most such studies, no reduction of the intensity of emotional experience was reported. Also, correlational studies found that the intensity of emotion is often only weakly related to physiological arousal parameters (e.g. changes in skin conductance; see Barrett *et al.* 2007b).

The available evidence suggests that—contrary to the emotion theory of Schachter and Singer, as well as that of James—peripheral physiological arousal is (1) most likely not necessary for emotional experience and (2) if present, has only a weak and context-dependent effect on emotion. These conclusions are relevant for neo-Jamesian and neo-Schachterian theories of emotion (e.g. Damasio 1994, Niedenthal *et al.* 2005a, Barrett *et al.* 2007b). Cognition-arousal theory also suffers from a theoretical problem in that it fails to explain how two mental states that are intrinsically nonemotional (cognition and feelings of arousal) produce an emotion when appropriately combined.

Although the Schachter–Singer theory of emotion appears to many theorists to be no longer tenable, its fundamental idea—that emotional experience consists of cognitive and noncognitive components—lives on in a number of more recent theories of emotional experience (see Barrett *et al.* 2007b).

RAINER REISENZEIN

schadenfreude The German word *Schadenfreude* describes the pleasure that is experienced at others' misfortune. Many languages, including English, lack a specific term for this emotion; this possibly indicates a social reluctance to admit that this emotion, which is perceived to be highly immoral, is in fact quite common.

Two features of schadenfreude are indisputable: our pleasure and the other's misfortune. The conflict here between our positive evaluation of the situation and the other person's negative evaluation of the same situation indicates the importance of *social comparison. A major reason for our pleasure at the misfortune of another person is that his or her misfortune may somehow benefit us; it may, for example, emphasize our superiority. In calculating our comparative position, the misfortune of others appears on the credit side. In *envy the comparison of our fortune with that of another person is also crucial, but only in schadenfreude do we occupy the superior position.

Three additional significant aspects of schadenfreude are: (1) the other person is perceived to deserve the misfortune; (2) the misfortune is perceived to be relatively minor; and (3) we are not responsible for it (van Dijk *et al.*, 2005). These features reduce the negative impact of the above two undisputable features of schadenfreude: pleasure at the other's misfortune is not so immoral, and in a sense even appears justified, when the other person deserves the misfortune, when the misfortune is minor, and when we are not responsible for it. People tend to experience pleasure when misfortune befalls the villain.

The very fact that we are pleased at someone's misfortune implies our belief that this misfortune is not fully undeserved. In some circumstances the other's misfortune may be grave, but it does not appear to be significantly graver than that caused by this person to other people—in particular, to ourselves and those related to us. One may be pleased by the murder of a brutal dictator, but this murder is not too grave in comparison with what the dictator did to other people. Schadenfreude may also refer to what seems to be an insignificant or irrelevant misfortune of others, such as someone haughty or proud slipping on a banana skin (without seriously hurting themselves) or when we see a stranger getting what we consider to be a well-deserved traffic ticket. Although these cases do not contain an improvement in our comparative position, they do have symbolic importance in demonstrating some failure on the part of the other person and hence our satisfaction in occupying a better situation. Such insignificant and irrelevant failures may not justify elation, but it is not to be denied that they afford us some pleasure. This is a pauper's joy. Joy over insignificant misfortune may also express humour rather than the emotion of schadenfreude. Also humour often involves punishing those who lay claim to greater status than they deserve.

As in other emotions, typical cases of schadenfreude consist of a subtle equilibrium of different features. When the relative weight of one of them is changed, changes in the weight of other characteristics may be expected as well. If a cruel criminal suffers a substantive misfortune, we may feel pleasure at this misfortune if we consider that the criminal deserves it. Similarly, we may somehow be responsible for a mild misfortune to befall a person whom we consider deserving of such a misfortune, and still feel pleasure at that misfortune.

Typical cases of schadenfreude are fundamentally different from cases of sadism, hatred, or cruelty. Unlike schadenfreude, sadism is a personality trait and not an emotional experience. Social comparison, which is central to schadenfreude, has no place in sadism. The three additional characteristics of schadenfreude—namely, the dominant role of deservingness, the minor nature of the misfortune, and the lack of responsibility—are absent from sadism.

It is generally assumed that schadenfreude is a mean-spirited, nasty emotion and is less acceptable than many other emotions, including envy. Such severe moral criticism can be challenged when the importance of social comparison in schadenfreude is taken into account and the distinction between schadenfreude and sadism is made. In contrast to sadism, the delight we feel in schadenfreude does not stem from the suffering of another person, but from our advantageous comparative position. When the subtle equilibrium involving social concern is violated, for example when the misfortune is severe or the person does not deserve it, other emotions rather than schadenfreude are likely to appear, for example pity or sadness.

Schadenfreude may not be a virtuous emotion, but nor is it wicked. It is a natural expression of human nature to which issues of comparative and just deserts are central.

AARON BEN-ZE'EV

Ben-Ze'ev, A. (2000). *The subtlety of emotions*. Cambridge, MA: MIT Press.

van Dijk, W.W., Ouwerkerk, J.W., Goslinga, S., and Nieweg, M. (2005). Deservingness and Schaderfreude, *Cognition and Emotion*, **19**, 933–9.

Portmann, J. (1999). *When bad things happen to other people*. London: Routledge.

secondary appraisal Secondary appraisal and its counterpart, primary appraisal, comprise the two basic types of emotion-antecedent appraisal defined by Lazarus and his colleagues (e.g. Lazarus 1966, 1991, Lazarus and Folkman 1984, Smith and Lazarus 1990) (SEE APPRAISAL THEORIES; PRIMARY APPRAISAL). In general, appraisal consists of an evaluation of what one's circumstances imply for personal well-being. The outcome of this evaluation determines and organizes one's emotional state.

Within this framework, secondary appraisal consists of evaluations of a person's options and resources for coping with the situation (see COPING POTENTIAL). Secondary appraisals are hypothesized to shape and differentiate the emotional reactions evoked by primary appraisals. For example, in the model of Smith and Lazarus (1990) (and see Smith, 1991), the secondary appraisal of accountability (self versus other) determines who is to be held responsible for the situation, and thus provide a target for a person's coping efforts. Under stressful conditions such evaluations differentiate between anger (other-accountability) and shame or guilt (self-accountability); whereas under beneficial conditions these evaluations differentiate between gratitude (other-accountability) and pride (self-accountability). Similarly, evaluations of problem-focused coping potential represent an assessment of the degree to which a person can act to improve the situation, and, under stress, these evaluations differentiate between states of challenge/determination (high coping potential) and sadness/resignation (low coping potential).

Although these examples focus exclusively on appraisal components proposed by Smith and Lazarus (1990), it should be noted that the Smith and Lazarus model includes two additional secondary appraisal components—emotion-focused coping potential and future expectancy—that are not illustrated here, and other appraisal models include different components that would also be considered secondary appraisal under Lazarus's definition, including norm/self-compatibility (Scherer 2001a) and probability (Roseman 2001).

CRAIG A. SMITH AND LESLIE D. KIRBY

self Self is a simple everyday word that also has come to signify a complex, powerful, and important psychological structure. Self has resisted precise definition and specification, partly because selfhood is elusive yet seemingly ubiquitous. It seems impossible to be specifically and precisely aware of one's self, to describe or know it fully, or to give a complete list of its properties. Likewise, researchers have thus far been unable to associate it with a specific location in the brain or a single definition. Yet human social life depends heavily on selves. The self is the entity who owns your possessions, carries on your relationships, experiences your body, and keeps your promises, among other functions (see IDENTITY; IDEAL SELF).

The modern adult human self is a product of evolutionary and individual development, and understanding these processes is vital. Such research makes it clear that adult human selves are quite unusual among all the creatures of the world. Functionally, this probably reflects the unique demands of human social life. The self is not 'in' the brain or mind, nor is it just a name on a door or bank account. It is probably best understood as an interface between the animal body and the cultural society. Selfhood thus serves to transfer information in both directions. That is, a self enables the social system to guide, keep track of, and communicate with each individual, such as knowing where to send your tax return. It also enables the animal to operate in society, as is revealed in how people introduce themselves, make decisions, and occupy social roles.

Challenged to provide an integrative review of psychological research on self, Baumeister (1998) strove to find the basic root phenomenon or experience from which all selfhood could be seen to derive. He was, however, unable to identify one, and instead he concluded that three basic experiences reflected three aspects of self that can serve as a conceptual framework for understanding the self. Regardless of whether one agrees that the self consists of these three parts, the framework provides a useful heuristic for understanding how psychologists understand, study, and use the concept of self. The following sections will examine each of these three aspects: self-knowledge, the interpersonal self, and the agent or executive function.

Self-knowledge

Selfhood begins with self-awareness, indeed most likely with being able to distinguish one's own body from other objects (and bodies). The experience of reflexive consciousness—that is, when awareness turns back toward its source—is an important foundation of self and a focus of research attention. Human self-awareness, in particular, has been found to be generally evaluative (Duval and Wicklund 1972). Self-aware people typically compare themselves with various standards, such as norms, values, ideals, and expectations. Many emotional reactions stem from these self-aware evaluations, and in particular the entire category of self-conscious emotions (including shame, guilt, embarrassment, and pride) are precisely about how well the self is meeting its goals and other standards (Tangney and Dearing 2002, Higgins 1987) (see SELF-REFLEXIVE EMOTIONS).

Awareness of self plus inference creates self-knowledge: what kind of person is the self? The term *self-concept* has been used for decades to refer to accumulated self-knowledge. Recently, that term has come under fire for its seeming implication that there is a single self-concept and that all self-knowledge fits together into a coherent structure. Instead, it appears that self-knowledge contains a large amount of information that is at best loosely connected. Moreover, at any given time only a small part of self-knowledge is active in the person's mind, and self-awareness is typically awareness of only one part of self. Some self-knowledge may be specific to situations or relationships, and parts of it may even contradict other parts. The term *self-schema* (Markus 1977) has become fashionable because it refers to specific, interconnected sets of ideas about the self, and because it accommodates the idea that each person may have many self-schemas. Some researchers have taken this a step further and proposed that people have multiple selves, but others think this violates the very idea of selfhood. After all, for the animal body to interact with the social system, it is vital to have a single identity so that others will know who will fulfil your social obligations, collect your salary, and sleep with your romantic partner.

*Self-esteem is the evaluative component of self-knowledge: How favourably does the person evaluate self? Increases in self-esteem tend to bring pleasant emotions, while threats to or decreases in self-esteem bring unpleasant ones. Despite decades of research, experts still disagree as to whether self-esteem should be studied in specific domains or as a general attitude about self, about how much of self-esteem is emotion and how much is cognition, and about what benefits derive from high self-esteem (see Baumeister *et al.* 2003). It is clear, however, that people are reluctant to accept reductions in their self-esteem.

In Western culture, at least, self-esteem tends to be high, indeed implausibly so (e.g. the average person regards himself or herself as above average). More generally, researchers accept that self-knowledge is not fully accurate. Full-blown delusions (e.g. thinking oneself to be Napoleon) may be rare, but mild distortions are common, especially in the direction of making the self seem more competent, more in control, and more likely to experience positive outcomes than is objectively warranted. Although accurate self-knowledge would have the greatest pragmatic utility, well-adjusted people seem to exhibit many of these mild positive distortions in self-knowledge (Greenwald 1980, Taylor and Brown 1988).

Interpersonal being
Self-knowledge may seem like a solitary phenomenon based on introspection, but in fact selves develop, exist, and operate in interpersonal settings and relationships. Even self-knowledge is heavily dependent on interpersonal interactions, insofar as people learn about themselves from others, and changes in self-knowledge often depend on interpersonal validation (Shrauger and Schoeneman 1979, Tice 1992, Wicklund and Gollwitzer 1982).

One well-studied aspect of the interpersonal self is self-presentation. A great deal of behaviour is shaped by the goal of communicating some information about the self to others, as indicated by how much behaviour changes when people think others are present as opposed to solitary behaviour (Schlenker 1980, Baumeister 1982). As stated earlier, the self is essentially an interface between the animal body and the social system or group, and human success is heavily dependent on how one is perceived by others—so it is vitally important to ensure that one is perceived favourably.

The concern with reputation may even address the seeming paradox of self-esteem, which is that people strive to think well of themselves even though such favourable self-views seem to have fairly little in the way of direct benefits. The explanation may be that people are concerned with how others perceive them, and the seeming concern with self-esteem is based on esteem by others. The so-called sociometer hypothesis holds that self-esteem is simply an inner measure (meter) of actual or anticipated approval by others (Leary and Baumeister 2000).

Executive function
Agency, also called executive function, has been the least studied aspect of self. Yet without it, the self could not do anything. The executive function is the aspect that makes choices, exerts control (over the en-

vironment and the self), and takes initiative instead of responding passively.

The most studied aspect of executive function is self-regulation, which involves efforts by the self to exert control over itself, including controlling thoughts, controlling emotions, impulse control, and performance management. Indeed, the primary function of self-awareness may be to facilitate self-regulation (Carver and Scheier 1981), insofar as being aware of self in comparison with goals or standards is essential for enabling the person to change for the better. Emotion is also vitally involved in self-regulation: *positive emotions come from making progress toward goals and reaching them, while *negative emotions stem from failing to make suitable progress (Carver and Scheier 1990).

Self-regulation appears to depend on a limited resource, akin to the folk concept of willpower (and like glucose in the bloodstream). After use, it is depleted, so that subsequent acts of self-control are impaired (Baumeister *et al.* 1998). Making decisions and exerting initiative also appear to involve this resource. Thus, the self is partly made of energy.

The self-regulation of emotion is a special case. Unlike the self-regulation of thoughts or actions, it seems largely impossible to change one's emotional state by direct acts of will. Hence people rely on many indirect strategies for regulating their emotions, such as changing their cognitions (e.g. reframing a conflict, or seeking distraction) or their bodily state (e.g. reducing arousal) (Gross 2007) (see REGULATION OF EMOTION). It is not entirely clear why the self cannot dictate its emotions as well as its thoughts or behaviours, though one theory is that emotions function to control the self (e.g. as a feedback system; see Baumeister *et al.* 2007) and this system would be unworkable if the self could control emotions. For example, if people could stop feeling guilty by deciding not to feel guilty, then guilt would lose its power to shape behaviour. Guilt is, moreover, one vital emotion by which the cultural system can shape the behaviour of the individual, and so it is vital for the interface between the individual and society.

Conclusion
The self is too complex to be reduced to a single formula or explanation. It consists of information, interpersonal behaviours, and energy. Minimal selfhood might be sufficient for solitary existence, but the elaborate social worlds that humans construct and inhabit require comparably elaborate and multifunctional selves.

ROY F. BAUMEISTER

Baumeister, R.F. (ed.) (1999). *The self in social psychology.* Philadelphia, PA: Psychology Press.

Baumeister, R.F. and Vohs, K.D. (eds) (2004). *Handbook of self-regulation: research, theory, and applications.* New York: Guilford Press.

self-esteem Self-esteem is defined as the evaluative component of the self-concept, the extent to which people view themselves as likeable and worthy, good or bad (see SELF). It reflects an emotional response as people contemplate and evaluate different character-istics about themselves. As a self-reflexive attitude, self-esteem comprises cognitive and affective components. It influences personal beliefs about skills, abilities, and future outcomes, as well as the strategies that people use to gain self-knowledge. Feelings of low self-esteem are associated with poor mental health and have been implicated in a number of disorders ranging from *de-pression to eating disorders.

Self-esteem is generally measured through self-report questionnaires that assess either an overall evaluation of the self (i.e. global self-esteem) or self-esteem within specific domains (i.e. social, performance, or appearance self-esteem). Researchers also differentiate between en-during levels of self-esteem that are consistent across time and situation (i.e. trait self-esteem) and momentary fluctuations that are influenced by situational events (i.e. state self-esteem). There appears to be a gender difference in the development of self-esteem, with girls more influenced by relationships and boys more influ-enced by objective success. In other words, males gain self-esteem from getting ahead whereas females gain self-esteem from getting along.

In North America there is a widespread belief that low self-esteem is an important cause of a number of societal problems, ranging from drug abuse to teenage pregnancy to poor school performance. However, the objective evidence does not support this view. A review of several hundred studies indicates that although people with high self-esteem report being much happier with their lives, self-esteem is only weakly related to objective life out-comes (see LIFE SATISFACTION). That is, many people with high self-esteem are successful in their careers, but so are many people who have low self-esteem. Indeed, to the extent that there is a small relationship between self-esteem and life outcomes, it is possible that success causes high self-esteem. Moreover, some recent research has found that people with high self-esteem can be de-fensive when they feel threatened, thereby causing them interpersonal difficulties. Ultimately, the essential feature of self-esteem is that it shapes how individuals interpret and respond to their social worlds.

TODD F. HEATHERTON

self-reflexive emotions In the literature, emotions have been distinguished on a continuum ranging from basic to self-reflexive or self-conscious emotions (see BASIC EMOTIONS; EMOTION CLASSICATION). All emotions are triggered by a match or, more frequently, a mis-match between the concerns of the organism and the event the organism is confronted with. The two poles of the continuum are differentiated by the type of *con-cerns that are involved. At the basic pole emotions are characterized by a (mis)match in survival concerns. For basic emotions a quick onset of the emotion process is essential. The emotion process often takes place in an automatic and unconscious way. At the self-conscious pole the person's self is at stake (see SELF). Self-reflexive emotions are cognitively more complex than basic emo-tions; they require the cognitive capabilities of self-awareness and self-representation, and complex self-evaluative processes.

Ontogenetically, basic emotions develop earlier than self-conscious emotions (e.g. Lewis 2000b) (see CHILD-HOOD EMOTIONAL DEVELOPMENT). Developmental re-search shows that basic emotions emerge during the first year of life. Whereas some self-reflexive emotions, such as *embarrassment, start to develop in the second year of life, most self-reflexive emotions, including *guilt, only emerge the third year. The ontogenetic difference in development is mirrored by a different phylogenetic development. Basic emotions have a long phylogenetic history and are shared by many organisms. As self-conscious emotions require self-awareness and self-representation, they emerge much later in phylo-genesis. Furthermore, their phylogenetic development has been linked to the submissiveness–dominance di-mension, which plays an important role in organisms living in socially and hierarchically organized groups (e.g. Keltner and Buswell 1996). The function of submis-sive behaviour is to promote acceptance and avoid exclusion by the social group. The function of dominant behaviour is to indicate high social status and to signal that one merits increased group attention. This phylo-genetic interpretation is supported by the study of ex-pressive behaviour of self-conscious emotions. Although these emotions cannot be identified by particular facial expressions, as is the case for basic emotions, there is a growing body of evidence that these emotions can be identified on the basis of gestural expressive behaviour that is comparable across cultural groups. For instance, an expanded posture and head tilted slightly back have been found to be characteristic of *pride, whereas low-ered eyelids, head tilted slightly forward, and a crouched upper body are characteristic of embarrassment and *shame (see GESTURAL EXPRESSION OF EMOTION). The former expressions have been related to dominant be-haviour, while the latter have been interpreted as sub-missive appeasement behaviour. The ashamed person signals compliance with others or with the social norms in general, thereby reducing the probability of open conflict with or exclusion by the social group.

The link with the submissiveness–dominance dimen-sion points to the intricate relationships of the self-reflexive emotions with the social context. While consciousness of the self is an essential ingredient, these emotions are supposed to contribute to the attainment of complex social goals. There has been a vigorous debate in the literature about whether the evaluation by others, real or imagined, is a precondition for experiencing self-reflexive emotions. On the one hand it has been amply demonstrated that the mere involvement of a personal standard is sufficient for eliciting self-conscious emotions (e.g. Tangney and Dearing 2002). On the other hand it has been found that these emotions play a central role in our social life. Some even claim that our social life is geared towards the avoidance of negative self-conscious emotions (e.g. Scheff 1988). The intricate relationships between the personal and the social aspects of self-reflexive emotions can be explained from a developmental perspective. During development, the focus is first on the negative or positive evaluation by others, especially the attachment figures. Gradually, the standards, *norms and *values espoused by these attachment figures become internalized to the extent that the evaluation of these figures is neither a necessary nor a sufficient trigger. Hence, the emotions elicited by the reactions of others become self-reflexive emotions. Once internalized, the mere self-evaluation of a behaviour or a displayed characteristic with respect to the personal standards forms a sufficient trigger.

Historically, self-reflexive emotions have received scant research attention in comparison with the basic emotions. With the rise of the affective sciences, the advent of the componential emotion approach, and more specifically the *appraisal theories, scientific attention to self-reflexive emotions has gathered momentum. Until now most studies have focused on two families of self-reflexive emotions, namely the pride family (authentic pride and hubris) and the shame family (embarrassment, shame, and guilt) (e.g. Tangney and Fisher 1995, Tangney and Dearing 2002, Tracy et al. 2007). There is broad consensus in the literature that these two families of particular emotions are triggered when a person meets (for the pride family) or violates (for the shame family) a competence, a conventional or a moral standard. Depending on whether a standard has been met or violated, very different action tendencies follow. Meeting norms and standards relates to a tendency of showing off and putting oneself at the centre of attention, while violating these norms leads to a tendency of compliance, be it in the form of appeasement as in embarrassment, hiding or withdrawal as in shame, or reparation as in guilt.

There are ongoing debates about how the emotions within each family have to be differentiated. The most important distinction is related to the attribution of the behaviour or displayed characteristic to a global, stable, and uncontrollable cause versus a specific, unstable, and controllable cause (e.g. Tangney and Dearing 2002). From this perspective, shame is the result of a norm violation that is attributed to a global, stable, and uncontrollable cause. Shame is characterized by a global negative self-focus. Guilt is the result of a norm violation attributed to a specific, unstable, and controllable cause. In guilt the focus is on the specific norm-violating behaviour and setting right the wrong that is caused by that behaviour. Based on the same differentiation, two forms of pride have been distinguished. One type of pride, called authentic pride, is caused by a personal achievement that is specific, unstable, and controllable. The other type of pride, called hubris, is characterized by a presumed characteristic of the person that is global, stable, and uncontrollable. Three more criteria have been proposed to differentiate the emotions within the shame family. First, the type of violation is proposed to distinguish between emotions in the shame family. The violation of a conventional standard would be central to embarrassment. The violation of a competence standard (and more generally not meeting an ego-ideal) would be characteristic of shame. The violation of a moral standard (which is supposed to related to *superego functioning) would be typical of guilt. The evidence for these distinctions is at best mixed. A second source of differentiation is the intensity of the emotion. It has been suggested that shame is a much more intense emotion than embarrassment. Although differences in intensity between embarrassment and shame have been found, it is debatable whether all differences between these two emotions—such as smiling, which is reported during embarrassment episodes but not during shame episodes—can be accounted for by a mere difference in intensity. The third distinction is the presence or absence of an audience. While the presence of a real or even imagined audience does not form a precondition for shame or guilt, it plays a central role in embarrassment.

Recently, humiliation has begun to receive attention as a self-conscious emotion (e.g. Elison and Harter 2007). The differentiation of humiliation from shame and embarrassment lies in the intentionality of the reactions of the other. If the other is merely observing a norm violation, or if the other is reacting emphatically, embarrassment or shame is likely. However, if the other is perceived as intentionally using the norm violation to degrade, ridicule, or put down the person, humiliation is likely to result. Like humiliation, the other complex emotions of *gratitude, *envy, *jealousy, and being hurt (e.g. Lazarus 1991) can be considered to fall under the scope of self-reflexive emotions. They all have in common that another person's behaviour or characteristic is affecting the self. In gratitude, the other is not just facilitating goal attainment, but profoundly supporting the person's self. If the other is perceived as supportive for the self, an *action tendency of commitment and affiliation is induced. Envy is elicited when the other achieves something or possesses characteristics that the person wants to achieve or possess her- or himself. In jealousy, the other has an affective and/or sexual relationship with someone the person would want to have an affective and/or sexual relationship with. During hurt feelings, the person feels her or his inner self (intentionally) attacked by the other. Both hurt feelings and humiliation share the perception of a negative intentionality of the other vis-à-vis the self. If the other is perceived as depriving or (intentionally) attacking the self, opposing and even aggressive action tendencies are elicited.

In sum, the concept of self-reflexive or self-conscious emotions is an umbrella concept for all emotions in which the self rather than a particular (survival) concern is at stake. While focused on the self, the main function of self-reflexive emotions is to contribute to the attainment of complex social goals.

JOHNNY R. J. FONTAINE

self-report The subjective (first-person phenomenological) nature of self-report continues to polarize opinion in the literature. Advocates argue that no other method better captures the subjective *feelings associated with emotion, whereas detractors worry that self-reports cannot be verified by outside observers and therefore may be of uncertain validity. Both views may have some truth to them and yet a further nuanced perspective is desirable.

Consider self-reports of body symptoms. If it is assumed that such reports should correspond with actual bodily functioning, then this correspondence can be checked. Such correspondence is very low to almost nonexistent for mainstays of psychophysiological research such as heart rate, breathing rate, and blood pressure (for a general overview, see Stone et al. 2000) (SEE PERIPHERAL PSYCHOPHYSIOLOGY). Self-reports of fatigue, dizziness, hot and cold spells, and other signs of sickness are only moderately correlated with actual sickness, although these correlations are sufficiently large to guide medical decision-making (Stone et al. 2000). The arousal level of emotional states would presumably relate to bodily arousal processes, but such links have been difficult to establish.

The *valence and *arousal of emotional stimuli have robust effects on self-reported, physiological, and expressive channels. Yet concordance among the channels is poor. What this means, concretely, is that knowledge of physiology and expressive behaviour allows almost no prediction concerning the individual's self-reported reac-

tions to an emotional stimulus (Lang 1994). The reasons for such dissociations are probably multiple, but a simple consequence is that it may be naïve to assume that concordance among emotion channels is the default rule.

Self-reports of emotion could potentially be validated in other ways. It is often thought that mood states bias cognitive processes, and that emotion states bias *action tendencies. Therefore, it is possible to correlate self-report measures of *mood and emotion with these other criterion measures. In the case of mood, there has been some work linking mood states to implicit cognitive tendencies such as those involving mood-congruent processing (Kihlstrom et al. 2000). However, the correlations are not large, rendering it uncertain what one would conclude if self-reported mood and a cognitive processing measure disagree on the state of the individual.

Turning to a different issue, what do people report on when they report on their emotions? This simple question is a surprisingly difficult one to answer. As a broad heuristic framework, Robinson and Clore (2002) contrasted reports of emotion based on momentary experience versus beliefs about one's emotions. It is important to distinguish these sources of emotion knowledge because people have beliefs about their emotions that are demonstrably false when compared with their online emotional reactions (Robinson and Clore 2002).

Studies of online emotional reactions can be done in the laboratory or in real life. In the laboratory, prototypic stimuli are often used, such as pictures of roller-coaster rides or of dangerous animals. Individuals report fairly strong and uniform reactions to such stimuli (Lang 1994). Still, it is not entirely clear whether individuals are reporting on their emotional reactions (e.g. fear) or on their interpretation of the emotional stimulus (e.g. fearful picture). The distinction is worth considering, although it is not obvious how one would distinguish the two possibilities. Such issues are less relevant in experience-sampling studies because the vast majority of life involves mild and nonprototypical emotion elicitors.

Self-reports rely on language, which may or may not be synonymous with experience. Along these lines, it has been proposed that rats and mice have very strong and genuine emotional reactions despite their inability to conceptualize or verbalize such experiences in linguistic terms (Panksepp 1998). Although this position is somewhat controversial, it is not without merit. More important, it forces us to consider the possible manner in which language may be insufficient for capturing some of the nuances of emotional experience. If this is true, self-report can only be an imperfect reflection of experience, even among human beings.

In sum, of all the measures of emotion, self-report probably does have some unique claim to be measuring the subjective experiences of the individual. However, self-reports should not be viewed as synonymous with experience, at least not under all circumstances or reporting conditions. Therefore, further progress on two fronts may be desirable. One front involves developing and validating implicit measures of emotional experience (Kihlstrom *et al.* 2000). A second front involves clarifying the sources of information that are retrieved to make self-reports of emotion (Robinson and Clore 2002). With more knowledge in both areas, we may then be better able to make important advances concerning the question of when self-reports are, and are not, likely to reflect emotional experiences.

MICHAEL D. ROBINSON

Kihlstrom, J.F., Mulvaney, S., Tobias, B.A., and Tobis, I.P. (2000). The emotional unconscious. In: E. Eich, J.F. Kihlstrom, G.H. Bower, J.P. Forgas, and P.M. Niedenthal (eds), *Cognition and emotion*, pp. 30–86. New York: Oxford University Press.

Robinson, M.D. and Clore, G.L. (2002). Belief and feeling: evidence for an accessibility model of emotional self-report. *Psychological Bulletin*, **128**, 934–60.

sentiment (philosophical perspectives) Sentiment as it is understood today is very different from its sense in the 18th century (see HISTORY OF EMOTION). Today, sentiment is often taken to be related to, or the same as, sentimentality. Taken in this sense it is often denigrated as being necessarily wrong-headed or ethically suspicious in some way, although this has been disputed (see Solomon 1990). In the 18th century, for writers such as Adam Smith (1723–90) and David Hume (1711–76), sentiment neither meant sentimentality nor was it simply coextensive with our modern sense of emotion or with their own sense of *passion. Sentiment was understood as something like a felt reason or thought, which could be in conflict with a stronger and more violent passion (see Smith 1976; for a helpful historical perspective see Dixon, 2003).

PETER GOLDIE

sentiment (psychological perspectives) The word 'sentiment' has been used in English for much longer than the word 'emotion', which became its synonym. It was used by Chaucer (1379–1383/1912), for instance: 'Ye in my naked harte sentement/Inhelde . . .' (*Troilus and Cressida*, III, 43–44). It derives from the Latin *sentire*, to feel, and although the term has changed somewhat in meaning during the last 600 years, this root of 'feeling' has persisted, usually with a cognitive aspect in relation to a specific object, and often with a connotation of approval or disapproval (see APPRAISAL THEORIES). Adam Smith (1759/1976) called sympathy a 'moral sentiment' and regarded it as the glue that held society

360

together. In the days of phrenology, the propensities concerned with emotion such as veneration and benevolence were called 'sentiments'. A celebrated philosophical work was Scheler's (1912/1961) *Ressentiment*, in which the motivational qualities of resentment are discussed. Around the same time, the term 'sentiment' was used in psychology by Shand (1914) to mean a system of emotions organized around a common goal.

In ordinary language the adjective 'sentimental' means pertaining to emotion, more specifically to love. Flaubert (1869/1964) called his second-most-famous novel *Sentimental education* (*L'Education sentimentale*), with this implication and with irony, but without sarcasm. More recently, the term 'sentimental' came to be used to imply insincerity. To be sentimental came to mean to bask in emotion without regard for truth or for other people. And if a novel were described as sentimental, this meant it was soppy.

Perhaps affected by currents of ordinary usage, 'sentiment' fell somewhat out of favour in psychology until it was revived by Frijda *et al.* (1991) to denote an emotional process that lasts longer than a *mood but not so long as a personality trait. They say 'sentiment' serves: 'to explain the emergence of emotions that are not warranted by an eliciting event *per se*' (Frijda *et al.* 1991, p. 207). Examples are protracted affections and aversions towards individuals, groups, or political issues, as well as grudges, jealousies, and phobias. The term has been used with these implications by Oatley (2000) to fill a gap in psychological thinking about emotional phenomena, because although there has been much research on how emotions are elicited by events that affect goals there has been insufficient about how emotional processes—sentiments—sustain goals and commitments, particularly in relation to other people.

KEITH OATLEY

sentimentalism Sentimentalist theories of *value attempt to explain evaluative properties, concepts, or judgements in terms of emotional responses. This serves only as a rough characterization, and two potential misunderstandings need to be averted. First, sentimentalists need not take evaluations to be mere expressions of emotion. Second, the central claim cannot merely be that some sort of intimacy exists between sentiment and value, since this should be granted on all sides. Surely fear is sensitive to danger, for example, and amusement to the funny—albeit imperfectly. According to sentimentalism, however, emotions play more than just an epistemological role as a form of sensitivity to some independently characterized value (or disvalue). Rather, the sentiments serve partly to constitute certain values. But just how to understand this constitutive relationship, and which values are amenable to such treatment, are matters of controversy among sentimentalists.

The classical British sentimentalists of the 18th century focused primarily on moral judgement, especially of virtue and vice, which they founded in sentiments of moral approbation and disapprobation. According to David Hume (1711–76) 'when you pronounce any action or character to be vicious, you mean nothing, but that from the constitution of your nature you have a feeling or sentiment of blame from the contemplation of it' (Hume 1978, p. 469). Although he is more circumspect elsewhere, Hume here seems to be claiming that to judge something vicious simply is to express one's disapprobation of it. But this proposal fails because emotions can be *recalcitrant*, in that they can fail to correspond to the agent's considered judgement. We sometimes find ourselves disgusted or amused by things we don't really deem disgusting or funny. One might instead try putting Hume's claim in metaphysical rather than metaethical terms—that is, about value properties not evaluative judgements—by claiming that vicious traits and actions are those commonly disposed to arouse the sentiment of disapprobation. But this proposal founders on the observation that emotional responses often fail to track the values they purport to descry. It is all too common for people to admire what fails to be genuinely admirable. These responses are not recalcitrant, because they accord with the agent's judgement, but we must be allowed to criticize them nonetheless. Hence, a sentimentalist account of virtue should focus not simply on what people actually approve of but on what justifies that response: the virtuous is what makes approbation *fitting*.

Classical sentimentalism reached its apex with the work of Adam Smith (1723–90), who held that an emotion is directed toward what he called its proper object whenever an impartial spectator to the scene would feel it sympathetically (Smith 1982). This proposal can easily be read as an attempt to develop a theory of emotional fittingness, but that idea would not receive anything like full development until recently, when philosophers such as Allan Gibbard (1990) differentiated more clearly between the various forms of rational appraisal given to emotions. While David Wiggins (1987) focuses on evaluative properties rather than judgements, he too associates values with specific emotional responses, holding that for a value to be instantiated is for its associated response to be fitting. Though both Gibbard and Wiggins propose to explicate almost all evaluation by way of the emotions, sentimentalism need not be put forward as a global theory of value. Another recent approach, developed by Justin D'Arms and Daniel Jacobson (2003), limits the theory's application to those values that seem most intimately connected to emotions plausibly

claimed to belong to the general human mental economy, such as shameful and enviable, as well as some value concepts that lack any corresponding term in English, including that which befits guilt, pride, joy, sorrow, or jealousy.

Of course, psychologists and philosophers differ over how many such pancultural sentiments exist, with some theorists recognizing only a handful and others willing to posit almost indefinitely many. While sentimentalism is compatible with either answer, it finds certain theories of the emotions more congenial than others. In particular, cognitivist theories of emotion, which type-identify the emotions via supposedly 'constitutive thoughts', threaten to render sentimentalism circular. Gibbard proposes (roughly) to analyse wrongness in terms of fitting guilt, for example, but cognitivists claim that guilt essentially involves the concept *wrong*. Although Wiggins insists that such circularity is not vicious, precisely because 'one would not . . . have sufficiently elucidated what value is without this detour' through the sentiments (Wiggins 1987, p. 189), most sentimentalists aspire to give a noncircular account. One of the outstanding challenges to sentimentalism is to meet the objection that even basic emotions already contain judgements in terms of the very concepts the theory seeks to explain.

Furthermore, sentimentalists must explain in more detail how to distinguish those reasons to feel a *sentiment that count towards its fittingness, and hence bear on evaluative judgement, from those that do not. This challenge has been termed the 'wrong kind of reasons' problem. Contrast the consideration that a vicious-looking dog will respond more aggressively if you are afraid (which doesn't make it any less dangerous), and the consideration that the dog only looks vicious but is in fact quite friendly (which does). Although both considerations provide good reason not to be afraid, only the latter speaks to whether the object of one's fear is truly fearsome. These two challenges are related. In order for sentimentalism to make good on its ambitions, it must be able to explain how the relevant sentiments can be subject to norms of fittingness without being even partly constituted by judgements made in terms of exactly those evaluative concepts that the theory seeks to explicate.

DANIEL JACOBSON

D'Arms, J. and Jacobson, D. (2006). Sensibility theory and projectivism. In: D. Copp (ed.), *The Oxford handbook of ethical theory*, pp. 186–218. Oxford: Oxford University Press.

separation anxiety Separation anxiety is a developmentally normal affective response typically displayed by infants and toddlers when proximity to their caretakers is inadequate (see CHILDHOOD (EMOTIONAL DEVELOPMENT);

ADOLESCENCE (EMOTIONAL DEVELOPMENT)). Infants show signs of separation anxiety as early as 7 months, but separation anxiety usually intensifies during early childhood, then subsides gradually between the ages 3 and 5 years. According to Bowlby (1973), separation anxiety is a biologically adapted response, not reducible to other terms (e.g. need for food), serving to protect the child from harm when a threat to the child's protective *attachment relationship with the primary caregiver occurs.

When separation anxiety persists beyond the developmentally typical phase or when it is unusually intense, the presence of a separation anxiety disorder may be diagnosed (Silverman and Dick-Niederhauser 2004). Separation anxiety disorder is a common psychiatric disorder of childhood and early adolescence, characterized by an unrealistic and excessive fear of separation from an attachment figure, usually the parent. The key clinical features include excessive distress when separation from home or from the attachment figures occurs or is anticipated, persistent worry about losing the attachment figures or about possible harm befalling them, worry about getting lost or being kidnapped, reluctance or refusal to go to school, fear of being alone at home, reluctance or refusal to go to sleep without being near the parents, repeated nightmares involving the theme of separation, and repeated complaints of physical symptoms (e.g. headaches, nausea) when separation occurs or is anticipated.

Separation anxiety disorder is prevalent in approximately 3–5% of children and adolescents. Peak age onset appears to be around 7–9 years of age, but the disorder may develop during adolescence as well. Family processes (i.e. insecure mother–child attachment, parental overprotection), parental psychopathology, and temperamental factors in the child (i.e. shy, withdrawn) seem to be related to the risk of developing separation anxiety disorder.

WENDY K. SILVERMAN AND
ANDREAS DICK-NIEDERHAUSER

sequence of appraisal processes Appraisal theories suggest that emotions are elicited and differentiated through the appraisal of events that are highly pertinent to the individual, postulating a set of criteria or checks such as relevance (novelty, intrinsic pleasantness, and goal relevance), implications (goal conduciveness, urgency), coping potential, and self/norm compatibility of the event (see APPRAISAL THEORIES; RELEVANCE DETECTION). The results of this evaluation are expected to determine the nature of the ensuing emotion. While most appraisal theorists do not conceptualize the dynamics of the appraisal process, in his *component process model Scherer (1984, 2001a) proposed that appraisal

checks occur in a sequential, serial fashion, and in an invariant order in which the different stimulus evaluation checks are processed in a repetitive and recursive fashion. This assumption specifies that the appraisal operations, namely the checks, while based on parallel processing, are unfolding in time and yield results in a sequential manner. The appraisal process is seen to unfold in an overlapping fashion on several levels of processing, from automatic, schematic, and largely unconscious, to effortful, symbolic, and highly conscious. The assumption that the different appraisal checks produce efferent results in a fixed sequence (see Fig. S1), rather than in parallel and simultaneously or in a sequence determined by the context (Smith and Lazarus, 1990) is based on phylogenetic, ontogenetic, and microgenetic considerations (Scherer 1984, 1999b) as well as recent neuroscience findings (see Grandjean and Scherer, 2008, for details),

A growing corpus of empirical evidence supports the sequential view of appraisal processes. Thus, indirect evidence from a timed scenario recognition task showed that sequential information of appraisal results in the predicted order of checks increases speed and accuracy of emotion recognition (Scherer 1999b). More direct experimental evidence has been obtained in studies that focus on the efferent reactions that are predicted to follow outcomes of appraisal checks, using peripheral as well as central measures. Using facial electromyography (EMG), Lanctôt and Hess (2007) demonstrated that *zygomaticus innervation, an established index of intrinsic pleasantness, precedes corrugator innervation, a putative signature of consternation and goal 'obstructiveness'. Similarly, Aue et al. (2007) have demonstrated that, as predicted, the facial EMG effects of manipulations of goal relevance and goal conduciveness appraisal occurred in subsequent time windows, arguing again for the sequential nature of these checks. Grandjean and Scherer (2008) have investigated the sequential nature of appraisal by monitoring brain electrical activity, using electroencephalography event-related potential (EEG-ERP) methods to tap central traces of appraisal processing. In this study, several hypotheses were tested: (1) the occurrence of brain activity modulations related to specific appraisal checks, (2) their processing on different levels, and (3) the unfolding of the appraisal process in a fixed sequence. Using visual paradigms, *novelty, goal relevance (see MOTIVE CONSISTENCY), and *intrinsic pleasantness were manipulated. The results showed early modulations of EEG related to novelty (~50–90 milliseconds), followed by intrinsic pleasantness (~100–200 milliseconds), and finally goal relevance (~130–250 milliseconds). In a second experiment the effects related to intrinsic pleasantness occurred earlier (~100–250 milliseconds) than those related to goal conduciveness

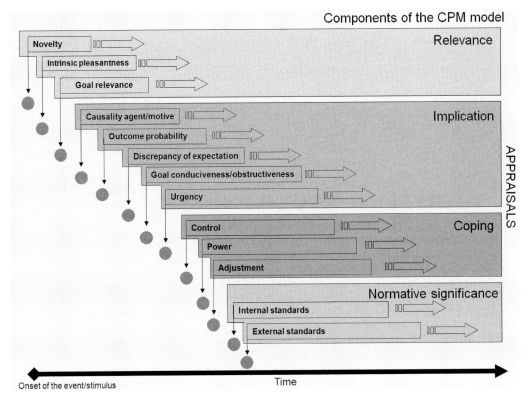

Components of the CPM model

Relevance

- Novelty
- Intrinsic pleasantness
- Goal relevance

Implication

- Causality agent/motive
- Outcome probability
- Discrepancy of expectation
- Goal conduciveness/obstructiveness
- Urgency

Coping

- Control
- Power
- Adjustment

Normative significance

- Internal standards
- External standards

APPRAISALS

Onset of the event/stimulus   Time

Fig. S1. Theoretical predictions of the component process model (CPM) concerning the sequence of appraisals in emotion elicitation. The solid circles show the theoretically predicted sequential effects of preliminary closure of the different appraisal results on the different subsystems of the organism (e.g. autonomous nervous system, motor expression).

(~250–600 milliseconds). These two studies using central measures, with high temporal resolution, have demonstrated that appraisal checks reach first preliminary closure (and trigger efferent effects) in a sequential fashion, even though processing of the different checks is ongoing in a parallel fashion. The empirical findings reported above confirm that the different appraisal checks have specific peripheral and brain state correlates, occur rapidly in a brief time window after stimulation, and generate efferent effects in sequential rather than parallel fashion. Furthermore, the results show that the duration of processing varies over checks and situations, as they achieve preliminary closure at different points in time.

DIDIER GRANDJEAN AND KLAUS R. SCHERER

Grandjean, D. and Scherer, K.R. (2008). Unpacking the cognitive architecture of emotion processes. *Emotion*, **8**, 341–51.

serenity Serenity belongs to a cluster of emotions denoting low arousal with pleasant feeling tones, such as calmness and tranquillity. But it is not a 'coarse' emotion of calmness so much as a refined one (Frijda and Sundararajan 2007) (see REFINED EMOTIONS). This point can be illustrated by the Chinese Buddhist notion of *kong*, which is serenity *par excellence*. *Kong* is the Chinese rendition of the Buddhist term '*sunyata*', meaning 'nothingness' or 'emptiness'. Differences between *kong*/serenity and the coarse emotions of calmness may be marked on three registers: levels of consciousness, appraisal, and valence.

At the level of consciousness, *kong* is an experience with second-order awareness. Whereas coarse emotions of calmness can be immersed experiences of first-order consciousness, *kong* is always accompanied by a second-order awareness that lends itself to savouring (Frijda and Sundararajan 2007). As for appraisal, coarse emotions of calmness entail a world-focus appraisal of a safe environment or absence of threat. *Kong* in contrast has a self-reflexive focus. *Kong* names that existential shudder when one scrutinizes the very foundation of one's goals and concerns—what Buddhists call 'attachment'—and finds it wanting: 'vanity, vanity, all is vanity'. The pain of disillusionment may find its consolation in detachment, which helps to recode experiences in such a way as to prompt, in response to loss and grief, a set of action readiness that consists of acceptance, but not resignation; letting be, but not giving up; savouring rather than coping. Lastly in contrast to coarse emotions of calmness that are univocal in valence, *kong* is complex and nuanced in valence—it is loss with a consolation; an interdigitation of disillusionment on the one hand, and a contemplative appreciation (savouring) of things from a new perspective, on the other (Sundararajan 2008).

LOUISE SUNDARARAJAN

Frijda, N.H. and Sundararajan, L. (2007). Emotion refinement: a theory inspired by Chinese poetics. *Perspectives on Psychological Science*, **2**, 227–41.

Sundararajan, L. (2008). *Kong* (emptiness): a Chinese Buddhist emotion. In W. Lemmens and W. Van Herck (eds), Religious emotions/some philosophical explorations pp. 183–97. Cambridge: Cambridge Scholars Publishing.

sexual desire According to the 'plain sex' account of Alan Goldman (1977), sexual desire is desire for contact with another person's body and for the pleasure which such contact produces (see DESIRE; PLEASURE). Contact and pleasure are inseparable: sexual desire is the desire for physical-contact pleasure, not for a sensation that might be produced apart from contact (see SEXUALITY AND EMOTION). It follows that if a person desires pleasure without contact (e.g. wanting only to look at another's body), or desires contact not for its own sake, or not for its pleasure (e.g. the person is pursuing a mugger), then the desire is not sexual. It also follows that if a person desires contact-pleasure, with nothing else present, for example expressing *love or trying to procreate, the desire is sexual. This implies that an infant's desire to be cuddled by a parent and the parent's desire to cuddle the infant are sexual, if contact-pleasure is what is sought. Goldman is in this respect Freudian, but his analysis would benefit from a distinction between sexual and other somatic pleasures.

Goldman assumes that the identification of a desire as sexual is accomplished by referring to its goal. If so, it is unclear what *kind* of desire the voyeur has, since he desires pleasure but deliberately eschews contact. Goldman, however, implies both that voyeurism is not sexual (it lacks desire for contact) and that it is sexual, but a perversion of desire (it deviates from desire's statistically normal form). If the latter, the voyeur must desire contact in *some* sense. A person who desires only to smell—at a distance, without 'immediate' contact—the genitals of another person for pleasure exhibits (atypical) sexual desire. If so, looking, too, involves vicarious contact and hence *is* sexual. Whether fetishism is a

sexual perversion or not sexual to begin with remains unclear. To appeal to the fetishist's unconscious desire for contact (the stroked shoe is the mother's penis) threatens to make all our desires sexual.

Perhaps Goldman has chosen the wrong goal to identify sexual desire. In a 'plainer', more Freudian account, sexual desire aims at pleasure *simpliciter*, no matter how caused. Then any desire for pleasure, whether sought through heterosexual coitus, looking, or fondling shoes, is sexual. This account also benefits from distinguishing between sexual and other pleasures.

Jerome Shaffer (1978) has argued, however, that the deeper problem (for both views) is that sexual desire cannot be identified at all by referring to its goal, because it is unlike other desires in not being a desire *that* something happen or a desire *for* something. For Shaffer, 'what makes desire ... *sexual* is ... sexual arousal', that is, identifying a desire as sexual depends on specifying the physiological processes with which it is associated. 'Sexual desire is a state ... such that, if it is followed by sexual arousal, then certain subsequent events will be felt as constituting the satisfaction or frustration of that ... state'. These satisfying events frequently, but need not, include orgasm.

Shaffer argues that sexual desire is not an ordinary desire, or is not a desire at all but a 'state'. It is like an *emotion* (an attitude that involves beliefs, feelings, and behaviours), although there are differences (emotions, not sexual desire, can be evaluated as 'appropriate'). Horniness is a *mood*, like being sad or bored, and is not sexual desire—which, for Shaffer, focuses on a particular person. This thesis is defended by Roger Scruton (1986), for whom 'individualizing intentionality' is a distinctive mark of sexual desire. This partially means that sexual desire is nontransferable: if James experiences desire for Jill and later experiences desire for Jane, these are two distinct sexual desires, not the transfer of the same desire from Jill to Jane. Were it a transfer, it would be mere lust or horniness. Thus sexual desire is experienced only by beings having sophisticated cognitive equipment, not by animals who are doomed by Nature to be horny.

ALAN SOBLE

Giles, J. (2004). *The nature of sexual desire*. Westport, CT: Praeger.

Jacobsen, R. (2006). Desire, sexual. In: A. Soble (ed.), *Sex from Plato to Paglia: a philosophical encyclopedia*, pp. 222–9. Westport, CT: Greenwood Press.

Morgan, S. (2003). Dark desires. *Ethical Theory and Moral Practice*, **6**, 377–410.

Primoratz, I. (1999). *Ethics and sex*. London: Routledge.

sexuality and emotion Sexual reproduction in humans has evolved as a complex interplay of behavioural and brain systems that support attraction, sexual excitement, *desire, *lust, and *love (see SEXUAL DESIRE). Reproduction is a remote consequence of sexual interaction. Although the conscious pursuit of reproduction is unlikely to be the proximal cause of such interaction, it is possible. Combined with lowered fertility because of ageing or medical reasons, however, the conscious pursuit of reproduction may compromise the quality and intensity of the emotions involved. Interpersonal attraction, sexual interaction, and the complicated emotions that are associated with these behavioural processes depend on the presence of immediate reinforcing consequences. Attraction and sexual interaction are thus driven by emotions.

Sexuality has always been associated with emotions: 'Engaging in sexual intercourse, making love, lusting, being in love, always involve complex emotions. All of the intricate behaviours concerned result from arousal, through brain processes, hormones, external stimulation, imagery and thought in massive interaction, all tempered by learning and experience' (Strongman 1987, p. 221). For a long time, however, sexuality was classified with motivations, as excitement, desire, and other sexual phenomena were considered to depend on a hypothalamic imbalance, similar to the mechanism of thirst and hunger. The idea of an inborn drive for sex is consistent with male sexual experience and the historically accepted dominance of men. Prominent sexologists from the early 1900s proposed that men have a sex drive and women do not. Since the introduction of the concept of incentive motivation in the 1960s, however, the drive hypothesis has lost its heuristic value.

Incentive motivation theory states that, in and of itself, a central motive state does not activate sexual motivation; an incentive stimulus is required. Gonadal hormones modify the sensitivity of sensory systems, and their relative presence or absence may enhance or decrease the impact of incentive stimuli (Ågmo 1999, Ågmo et al. 2004). Incentive motivation connects emotion and motivation like two sides of the same coin, with emotion as the perceptual side and motivation as the action or motor side. In other words, as real or imagined incentive stimuli are processed, emotions generate approach tendencies. These tendencies may activate motor programmes and, under certain social circumstances, actions (Panksepp 1998, Frijda 2007). Once the existence of sexual emotions has been accepted, it becomes necessary to determine what they are. In a list of 18 incentives, Kagan (2003) provides parenthetical suggestions for a number of sexual emotion names. The following are two examples: 'Number 13: The individual experiences sexual arousal to a person, surrogate symbol or thought (sexual desire). Number 14: The individual experiences sexual arousal

combined with a feeling of admiration for the qualities for another (love)'.

How do stimuli acquire sexual meaning?

In primates, sexual attractiveness is determined by characteristics of secondary sexual features, such as sexual skin swelling and genital odours, which signal reproductive status in females. In humans, some of the secondary sexual features may have evolved as signals of reproductive fitness. The macho appearance of men, fat deposits in breasts and buttocks in women, and gender-specific movements are examples of such features in humans. The possible effect of body-fat distribution on *attractiveness has been determined by measuring waist circumference and the circumference of the hips at the point at which the buttocks are largest, and then calculating a ratio between the two measures. This measurement is known as the waist-to-hip (WHR) ratio. When men were asked to rate the sexual attractiveness of line drawings of female body shapes, they consistently preferred drawings representing normal weight and low WHR (0.7). The normal range of WHR in men is 0.85–0.95 (Dixon 1998). Attractiveness in humans has been enhanced by cultural constructions that prescribe female attire, which may provide a signal of marital status, or fashion codes that amplify secondary features or allow the visibility of attractive body parts.

In humans, the experience of lustful touch (including the genitals) and smell precedes the transformation of tactile and olfactory stimuli into sexual stimuli. In early adolescence, pubertal hormones amplify these experiences and make them more specific genitally, as well as cognitively through fantasies and daydreams about lustful experiences. Conditioning and cultural instruction may cause other stimuli to acquire the capacity to elicit lustful experiences as well. In some permissive educational environments, people are taught to identify certain classes of stimuli that evoke lustful experiences as sexual stimuli; others learn to recognize these stimuli through moral instruction (e.g. lists of dos and don'ts).

The extent to which sexual stimuli signal or predict lust depends on characteristics of the specific stimulus. For example, many consider kissing less exciting than genital caressing. The signalling capacity of sexual stimuli also depends on many neurobiological characteristics, however, including sex steroids and a variety of transmitters. Recent literature suggests that a polymorphism in the dopamine D4 receptor gene may contribute to individual variation in human sexual desire and arousal (Ben Zion et al. 2006). Dopamine invigorates approach responses and enables stimulus representations to acquire incentive properties (Ikemoto and Panksepp 1999). The study by Ben Zion and colleagues suggests that variation in dopaminergic activity may influence the incentive value of stimuli and the tendency to approach such stimuli. These authors conclude that both hyperactive and hypoactive sexual desire and arousal may have a genetic component; both high and low levels of desire are thus adaptational and should not in themselves be considered cause for guilt or treatment.

Sexual stimuli are commonly associated with lust and other *positive emotions. For some individuals, however, the positive valence can change into a negative one, or it may never acquire a positive valence. The experience of sexual abuse may transform sexual stimuli into predictors of violence, threat, and degradation. When love withers away in a relationship, sexual acts that were once positive may become negative and associated with aversion or disgust.

Sex differences in the processing of sexual information

When men and women are presented with emotion scales in connection with their experiences of sex, women report more and more varied emotions than men do (Dekker and Everaerd 1988). This result implies that the appraisals of women are more elaborate than are those of men, and that women may attribute more meaning to their sexual experiences. The finding that women and men may use different brain circuits to process sexual–emotional information can help explain differences between the outcomes of women and men (see GENDER DIFFERENCES).

Several studies have compared brain activation in both men and women in reaction to sexual stimuli. For example, Karama et al. (2002) presented heterosexual men and women with emotionally neutral film excerpts and with erotic film excerpts during functional magnetic resonance imaging (fMRI) analysis. Both sexes showed increased activation in the *anterior cingulate, medial prefrontal, orbitofrontal, insular, and occipito-temporal cortices, as well as in the *amygdala and the ventral striatum. The amount of increased activation was different for men and women, however, and only men showed significant increases in activation in the thalamus and hypothalamus. For men, these increases correlated with self-reported sexual arousal; men also reported higher levels of arousal than women did. Such findings suggest that the experience of sexual response is different for men and women, as both the subjective reports and the difference in brain activation (thalamus and hypothalamus) have implications for sexual awareness. In a related fMRI study, Hamann et al. (2004) used sexually arousing pictures to induce brain activation in men and women. Their results corroborated a finding of Karama et al. (2002) that demonstrated a link between activation of the amygdala and activation of the nucleus

accumbens/ventral striatum. Because the ventral striatum has been implicated in the reward process, its coactivation in both men and women suggests that the sexual stimuli were similarly rewarding for each sex (see REWARD). This assumption was supported by the participants' subjective reports about the attractiveness of the stimuli. As the study by Hamann et al. further demonstrated, however, visual sexual stimuli resulted in greater activation of the amygdala for men than it did for women, confirming the link between the amygdala and the ventral striatum. Such findings may indicate that the expectation and experience of 'sexual' reward may be more prominent for men than it is for women.

In a study of intense sexual arousal and orgasm, Holstege's group (Georgiadis and Holstege 2005) proposed that brain activation and deactivation vary across the spectrum of intensity and orgasm. In men, they observed deactivation of the thalamus, the genital substrate of the primary somatosensory cortex, the hypothalamus, and the amygdala during orgasm (Georgiadis and Holstege 2005). Although similar deactivations were observed in women as well, they were more intense in men. Holstege speculates that the emotional circuit is activated for survival reasons (for instance anxiety), thus enhancing alertness and attention to the environment, but that it is switched off for reproductive reasons (Le Page 2005, as reported in New Scientist). These findings appear to indicate a switch in attentional focus and fading of the role of situational appraisal in emotional experience. They clearly reinforce the complexity of the information-processing patterns that are likely to underlie this process.

There is additional evidence to suggest that men and women experience sex differently. One finding that consistently surfaces relates to the correlation between genital measures of sexual arousal and subjective reports about arousal or excitement (Laan and Everaerd 1995). In general, a low correlation between genital response and subjective sexual arousal is found in women. In reaction to visual sexual stimuli, women tend to report fewer or less intense feelings of arousal or excitement than men do. Furthermore, women seem to be less aware of the initial stages of genital sexual arousal than men are, and to be less specific in their preference for sexual stimuli. In contrast to those of men, the genital responses of women to sexual stimuli that do not match their sexual orientation are just as strong as those that are elicited by stimuli that are consistent with their orientation (Chivers and Bailey 2005).

The automatic genital response of women may have evolved as an adaptive mechanism. More specifically, an increase in vasocongestion produces vaginal lubrication, thus facilitating sexual interaction. Given the adaptive nature of the response, the explicit sexual stimuli that are used in psychophysiological studies could represent a class of unlearned stimuli to which women are innately prepared to respond. This automatic genital response may also be a preparatory response for sexual contact. This preparatory response could facilitate conception in fecund women more cost-efficiently than would a genital response that required wilful intention. From a strictly evolutionary perspective, a highly automated response mechanism is adaptive; the species would not survive without a genital response to sexual stimuli. Nevertheless, such observations again point to gender differences in the experience of sex, which may subsequently explain differences in the experience of sexual emotions.

Control of sexual emotions and actions

The ability to regulate sexual emotions and actions is an important aspect of social relations. In their seminal paper on sexual motivation, Singer and Toates (1987) referred to what they called the final ingredient in the (incentive) motivational pie: species-typical access behaviour toward the incentive class; in this case, sexual and relational incentives. Birnbaum *et al.* (2006) report associations between *attachment orientation and sexual experience for couples who were either married or romantically involved. Attachment anxiety was associated with ambivalent perceptions of sexual experience, whereas attachment avoidance was associated with more aversive feelings and cognitions. Access to sexual incentives and sexual function is deeply influenced by nonsexual emotional reactions to potential partners (Kaplan 1995).

There are many cultural and religious rules for access to sexual partners; access may be prescribed as a privilege that is reserved solely for married people, sometimes only for reproductive reasons. Other rulings are more permissive, incorporating and allowing traffic in sexual incentives; in other words, they may allow for the exchange of sexual rewards for monetary rewards. Power and aggression can also be used to gain access, as in the case of rape and other forms of sexual abuse.

Conclusion

The study of sexuality and emotions is interesting because it may help to explain the complex emotions that are involved in sexuality, as well as the negative and positive experiences that are associated with it. Sexual health and the global impact of problems related to sexuality provide an important practical justification for further studies of sexuality and emotions.

WALTER EVERAERD, STEPHANIE BOTH,
AND ELLEN T. M. LAAN

Ågmo, A. (1999). Sexual motivation—an inquiry into events determining the occurrence of sexual behavior. *Behavioural Brain Research*, **105**, 129–50.

Singer, B. and Toates, F.M. (1987). Sexual motivation. *Journal of Sex Research*, **23**, 481–501.

shame There is considerable disagreement about the definition of shame and its differentiation from related emotions such as *embarrassment and *guilt. Three major theoretical approaches can be distinguished. According to the first approach (the *external standards* approach), shame is elicited by being the focus of others' attention, and often of their disapproval or *contempt. Thus shame essentially serves to socialize the person to behave appropriately. In eliciting shame the social group promotes conformity and adherence to the group's *norms, practices, and moral standards (e.g. Ausubel 1955). According to the second approach (the *discrepancy with aspirations* approach), shame is an emotion that is triggered by the discrepancy between one's ideals and aspirations and one's actual behaviour and accomplishments. Shame, from this psychoanalytically based perspective, is related to ego-ideal functioning (e.g. Lazarus 1991). According to the third approach (the *negative self-focus* approach), shame stems from a global negative perception of the *self. In this approach, shame is not triggered by situation-specific violations of social norms or expectations, nor by a discrepancy between one's behaviour and one's aspirations, but by a heightened consciousness of the self as incompetent or even fundamentally flawed (e.g. Tangney and Dearing 2002).

Although the three approaches disagree about the specific elicitors of shame, they agree that shame is essentially a self-conscious emotion (see SELF-REFLEXIVE EMOTIONS). Shame involves a negative perception of the self. Even in the external standards approach, one sees oneself as deficient through the eyes of others. The shame experience is a painful, negatively valenced experience in which the person feels weak, inferior, and submissive.

A characteristic expression of shame is a lowering of the eyelids in order to avoid eye contact with others. From an evolutionary point of view this expressive reaction is interpreted as an appeasement response. Blushing, especially in the face, is often thought to be associated with shame; however, the empirical evidence for blushing in shame is mixed.

The three approaches also agree that shame triggers a desire to disappear from view, but the precise form and function of this *action tendency differ according to the approach. From the *external standards* perspective, the action tendency is primarily meant to display submissiveness, as indicated by the behaviour of cringing with shame. By displaying submission, the person acknowledges the social norms of the situation and the recognition that he or she has violated them. Moreover, the submissive response moderates the negative reactions of others, reducing the risk of escalation. It strengthens group ties and serves as a signal of propitiation in tense social situations. According to the *discrepancy with aspirations* approach, the motivation to disappear is a direct response to the unpleasant situation. The person is acutely aware that she or he falls short, and wants to avoid public exposure of the failure. By the experience of not wanting to be in the particular situation, shame motivates one to improve oneself. According to the *negative self-focus* approach, the essence of shame is the awareness of deep flaws in the self which are beyond one's control. Therefore, the motivation to disappear is part of a broader action tendency of withdrawal from social situations.

Two emotions that are closely related to shame are guilt and embarrassment. Embarrassment is distinguished from shame by its less serious and painful nature. Embarrassment occurs in awkward situations and in situations where one unintentionally disrupts the normal flow of social interaction. Unlike shame, it does not imply a general weakness or flaw in the person, nor does it imply a violation of important social or moral standards. Smiling is often observed in experiences of embarrassment, but not in experiences of shame.

The distinction between shame and guilt is one of the major theoretical differences between the three approaches. According to the *external standards* approach, shame involves external norms while guilt involves internal, personal standards. In the *discrepancy with aspirations* approach, shame involves a failure to live up to one's ideals, while guilt involves moral transgressions. In psychoanalytic terms, guilt is related to *superego functioning. From the *negative self-focus* perspective, guilt is focused on a specific behaviour and its consequences, while shame is focused on the self as a whole. Guilt is about what the person does and shame is about who the person is.

Recent cross-cultural research indicates that all three theoretical perspectives are valid, but for different kinds of situations or different phenomena related to shame (Fontaine *et al.* 2006). The *external standards* and *discrepancy with aspirations* approaches involve emotional reactions that are activated by specific situational cues, whereas the *negative self-focus* approach involves individual differences that are independent of any specific situation. In situations where one is the focus of other people's attention, the emotional response corresponds to the one proposed by the *external standards* approach. In situations where one is confronted with a discrepancy between one's behaviour and one's aspirations, respondents report a somewhat different emotional process that corresponds to the one proposed by *discrepancy* theories.

The *negative self-focus* approach does not involve emotional responses to specific situations, but a generalized tendency to feel powerless and incompetent to deal with a wide range of situations.

JOHNNY R. J. FONTAINE

shyness Shyness is a term deeply rooted in everyday language that refers to an affective state in social situations, characterized by reserved, inhibited, anxious, or withdrawn behaviours, feelings of uneasiness and discomfort, and an excessive self-focus. It may vary from mild social awkwardness to totally inhibiting social phobia (see PHOBIAS).

State shyness is experienced in three types of situations: when meeting strangers; in large groups, particularly if one is the centre of attention; and in social-evaluative situations such as meeting valued authorities, applying for a job, oral examinations, or meeting a dating partner. Because most large groups imply unfamiliarity and/or social evaluation, these three situational factors can be reduced to two: unfamiliarity and social evaluation.

Nearly everybody reacts shyly once in a while; both excessive shyness and the complete lack of shyness indicate problems with social-emotional adaptation. Interindividual differences in the frequency and intensity of shyness are moderately stable from the second year of life onwards; thus, shyness can be considered as a temperamental personality trait (see TEMPERAMENT). In adulthood, interindividual differences in shyness are quite consistent across unfamiliar and social-evaluative situations, but shyness with strangers and social-evaluative shyness are clearly separable in early childhood (Asendorpf 1990) and become only gradually associated later on.

Cross-cultural studies show that approximately 40% of the general population describe themselves as shy; thus, trait shyness is frequent and considered as socially undesirable only if it is excessive. Because trait shyness is often associated with an unassuming, modest demeanour, it is less valued in cultures favouring assertiveness such as current Western cultures, and more valued in cultures favouring modesty such as traditional eastern Asian cultures.

Asendorpf (1989, 1990) proposed a two-factor theory of shyness, based on the *behavioural inhibition system (Gray 1982). According to Gray, this system mediates reactions to both novel stimuli and conditioned cues for punishment and frustrative nonreward, leading to inhibited behaviour, increased arousal, and increased attention to the stimuli. Thus, in social situations, this system is assumed to mediate reactions to strangers and to conditioned cues for negative or insufficiently positive evaluation, i.e. cues for being rejected or ignored by others (see Fig. S2). The independent contribution of

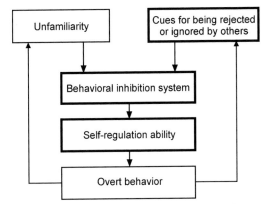

Fig. S2. A three-factor model of shyness. Bold lines indicate sources of interindividual differences. Reprinted with permission from Asendorpf (2007, Fig. 1).

unfamiliarity and social-evaluative concerns to state shyness was experimentally confirmed by Asendorpf (1989).

Interindividual differences in the strength of the behavioural inhibition system (threshold for and intensity of response) *and* interindividual differences in prior experiences of being socially rejected or ignored might therefore contribute to trait shyness. Although strangers are principally evaluatively neutral, increasing experiences of social neglect or rejection are expected to generalize to strangers. Thus, this two-factor model explains both the independence of stranger shyness and evaluative shyness in early childhood and their later association in adolescence and adulthood.

Asendorpf's (1989) two-factor model of shyness describes only the reactivity component of temperament. In line with more recent theories of temperament (Rothbart and Bates 1998), the initial reactions are increasingly moderated by effortful self-regulation with increasing age. Therefore, Asendorpf (2007) included self-regulation ability as an additional third factor into the model.

This three-factor model explains why observed inhibition to unfamiliar situations, a much studied temperamental trait in infants and children (Kagan and Snidman 2004), shows only a moderate to low stability from early to middle childhood. A proper understanding of shyness in older children, adolescents, and adults requires us to consider not only the reactivity component of temperament but also individual experiences of being neglected or rejected by parents or peers, and the ability to effortfully control one's reactions to shyness-inducing situations. This may be also true for extreme forms of shyness such as social phobia.

JENS B. ASENDORPF

Asendorpf, J.B. (2007). Shyness. In: M.M. Haith and J.B. Benson (eds), *Encyclopedia of infant and childhood development*. San Diego, CA: Elsevier.

Crozier, A. and Alden, L.E. (eds) (2001). *International handbook of social anxiety: concepts, research and interventions relating to the self and shyness*. London: Wiley.

sleep and emotion There is a bidirectional relationship between daytime emotion/mood and nighttime sleep; an escalating vicious cycle of emotional and *mood disturbance during the day interferes with nighttime sleep and the effects of sleep deprivation contributes to emotion/mood disturbance the subsequent day (Dahl 1996). This vicious cycle is depicted in Fig. S3.

Evidence that emotion/mood during the day disturbs sleep (the dashed line in Fig. S3) includes that presleep mood and *stress delay sleep onset (see Harvey, 2005, for review) and influence the content of dreaming, the emotion within a dream, the latency to rapid eye movement (REM) sleep as well as REM density (see Perlis and Nielsen, 1993, for review). These effects reflect that emotion/mood and sleep are opponent processes. Physiologically, going to sleep requires turning off awareness and responsiveness to threats in the external environment. Because of this loss of vigilance and responsiveness, sleep is naturally restricted to safe times and places (e.g. animals and birds tend to sleep in safe burrows, nests, or niches that minimize dangers). Hence, individuals experiencing presleep emotional and mood states often have difficulty getting to sleep. While these tendencies potentially have adaptive advantages (inhibiting sleep in dangerous environments) they also have costs; they can lead to chronic sleep difficulties (Dahl 1996). Note that the above specifically implicates the emotion of *fear and raises an as yet unanswered empirical question as to whether sleep is perturbed by other emotions, both positive (e.g. elation) and negative (e.g. sadness).

Evidence that sleep disturbance contributes to emotion/mood disturbance the following day (the dotted line in Fig. S3) includes that one adverse consequence of sleep deprivation is increased negative mood (see Pilcher and Huffcutt, 1996, for meta-analysis) and, at the neural systems level, circuits involved in emotion/mood regulation and sleep interact in bidirectional ways (Saper *et al.* 2005). Recent studies are defining the specifics of the relationship between sleep deprivation and mood/emotion the following day. Clinical studies of children and adolescents have shown an association between sleep deprivation and irritability/aggression (Dahl 1996). A recent study by Zohar *et al.* (2005) showed that context is important for determining the effect of sleep disturbance on mood/emotion. These researchers examined the relationship between sleep

Fig. S3. Graphical depiction of the bidirectional relationship between daytime emotion/mood and nighttime sleep.

loss and emotion reactivity in 78 medical residents who were monitored for 5–7 days every 6 months over a 2-year period. The results indicated that sleep loss not only intensified negative emotions following a goal-thwarting event but also, following a goal-enhancing event, diminished positive emotions.

The mechanism by which sleep impacts upon mood/emotion the next day is thought to be via REM sleep (Stickgold *et al.* 2001). Supportive evidence includes the emerging neuroscience literature demonstrating the presence of *amygdala activity during REM sleep (e.g. Maquet *et al.* 1996). The amygdaloid structures have been implicated in the acquisition of emotional memories (see MEMORY (EMOTIONAL)). Hence, the presence of activity in this region is consistent with the possibility that REM sleep has a role in emotion-related regulation (see REGULATION OF EMOTION). Also implicating REM sleep is the study reported by Cartwright *et al.* (1998) who investigated 61 people recently separated from a marital partner. Each participant was assessed for depression at baseline and 1-year follow-up, and sleep was monitored for three nights at each assessment point. At baseline, 39 of the participants were classified as suffering from *depression. One year later, 72% of these people could be classified correctly as remitted or not remitted based on the presence of negative/unpleasant dreams during awakenings from REM at baseline. The direction of the relationship was that the *more* expression of negative affect in dream reports arising from REM awakenings during the first half of the night, the *less* likely the person suffered from depression a year later. Presumably, unpleasant dreams diffuse the impact of the emotion and reflect effective processing and resolution of the emotional issues surrounding the separation. The participants in this study were not in treatment for the year of the study.

Another type of 'emotional' dream is a nightmare. Nightmares are associated with exposure to trauma and are a symptom of posttraumatic stress disorder. Why don't nightmares also promote habituation and recovery of emotional/traumatic memories? Rothbaum and Mellman (2001) suggest that: (1) nightmares are not long enough in duration for processing and resolution to

occur; (2) following a nightmare the person will often wake feeling highly anxious this may sensitize them to the trauma memory; (3) the perception and meaning of the trauma is unlikely to be altered in dreams; and (4) a sense of control is not promoted.

Given the bidirectional relationship between daytime emotion/mood and nighttime sleep, it is not surprising that sleep disturbance is transdiagnostic (i.e. characteristic of most psychiatric disorders). An important hypothesis currently being tested is that symptoms of psychiatric disorders not only contribute to sleep disturbance but that sleep disturbance also contributes to core symptoms of psychiatric disorders the subsequent day.

ALLISON G. HARVEY

Hu, P., Stylos-Allan, M., and Walker, M.P. (2006). Sleep facilitates consolidation of emotional declarative memory. *Psychological Science*, **17**, 891–8.

smiling Smiling is a ubiquitous behaviour. People smile in public and in private, when they are happy and when they are distressed, during conflict and as a sign of intimacy. Chapell (1997) counted smiles in public places for 15,824 individuals across all ages and found that 35.3% of the men and 40.3% of the women smiled. People who smile are perceived as more pleasant, sincere, sociable, competent, carefree, relaxed, polite, and attractive. The two most prominent functions of smiles are as a sign of *happiness and as an appeasement/dominance display. Smiling is also strategy for concealing negative emotions and reducing tension and conflict.

Generally, smiles vary along two dimensions, the intensity of the activity of the *zygomaticus major muscle that pulls the corner of the mouth up and the presence of activity of other muscles, in particular, action of the orbicularis oculi muscle (which produces wrinkles around the corners of the eyes). This so-called *Duchenne smile is considered to be a marker of enjoyment.

Smiling can be considered a 'female' activity. Women report smiling more and are considered by others to smile more, yet this difference only emerges slowly in the course of childhood. Conversely smiling individuals are perceived as more female. The fact that women are expected to smile more has been attributed to the female gender role of being nurturing and affiliative as well as to power differences (appeasement). In line with both of these suggestions, Hess *et al.* (2007) reported evidence that smiling is not strictly a feminine activity, nor is it an activity that individuals with objective low power are obliged to perform. Rather, observers expect more smiling from those individuals whom they perceive as less dominant and more affiliative.

URSULA HESS

Abel, M. (2002). *An empirical reflection on the smile.* New York: The Edwin Mellen Press.

social aspects of emotion *see* ALTRUISM ANTISOCIAL BEHAVIOUR; ATTACHMENT; FAMILY (ROLE OF EMOTION IN); INTERPERSONAL COMMUNICATION; INTERSUBJECTIVITY; MORAL EMOTIONS; NORMS; PROSOCIAL BEHAVIOUR; SOCIAL COGNITION; SOCIAL COMPARISON; SOCIAL EMOTIONS; SOCIAL NEUROSCIENCE; SOCIAL REFERENCING; SOCIAL RELATIONSHIPS; SOCIAL SHARING OF EMOTIONS; SOCIAL STRUCTURE OF EMOTION.

social cognition Social cognition describes how people make sense of people, both self and others (Fiske and Taylor 2008). Social cognition includes processes ranging from automatic to controlled, as well as the functions that determine when each occurs. Social cognition operates through attention, mental representation, and response.

Affect interplays with all aspects of social cognition, each inevitably influencing the other. Research on affect and cognition reveals the different directions simultaneously, some focusing on physiology and neuroscience, some on cognition influencing affect, and some on affect influencing cognition. Some of theoretical efforts are supported by considerably more empirical evidence than others. Nevertheless, central themes direct research and theory.

Definitions of affect in social cognition
In social cognition, affect is a generic term encompassing all kinds of evaluations, *moods, and emotion (see EVALUATIVE PROCESSING). *Preferences include relatively mild subjective reactions that are essentially either pleasant or unpleasant; the preferences most frequently studied by social psychologists are *attitudes and interpersonal evaluations. Moods typically do not have a specific target, are considered as simply positive or negative, and have some duration. Emotions are more complex and differentiated affects, often include physiological responses, and can be relatively brief.

Social cognition research identifies two common ways of distinguishing among emotions: (1) Russell's (2003) two dimensions of pleasantness and arousal or (2) Cacioppo and Berntson's (1999) two independent dimensions of positive and negative emotions (see DI-MENSIONAL MODELS). Positive emotions, analysed separately, have a simpler structure than negative emotions.

People have cognitions about emotions. Prototypes (i.e. mental representations of the average or ideal case) describe people's culturally shared concepts of specific emotions and the idea of emotion in general. Emotions might also represent social roles enacted according to cultural rules.

Theories of emotion, physiology, and cognition
Early theories of emotion posed the question of whether physiological responses precede (*James–Lange theory) or follow (*Cannon–Bard theory) the cognitive experience of differentiated emotions. Following this debate, many physiological theories of emotion assumed that autonomic arousal in particular was undifferentiated and that other mechanisms must account for the complexity of emotional experience.

Facial feedback theory, as one solution, posits that the complex and subtle musculature of the face provides the detailed patterns of feedback that underlie different emotions (see FACIAL FEEDBACK HYPOTHESIS). The face does reliably express basic dimensions of emotion, particularly *valence and intensity. Also, manipulated facial expressions influence the experience of affect. Although this evidence has sparked considerable debate, it is gaining status as embodied cognition (see EMBODIMENT).

Excitation transfer theory posits that autonomic arousal from emotions or exercise decays slowly, and that people often cannot consciously distinguish the source of their arousal. Consequently, prior excitation can transfer or spill over to intensify new affective responses, even those of a different valence; considerable research supports this premise.

Neural signatures of specific emotions have so far proved elusive (see NEURAL ARCHITECTURE OF EMOTION). Meta-analyses combining multiple independent neuroscience studies agree that the *amygdala is involved in *fear at least, and the insula in *disgust (Phan *et al.* 2002, Murphy *et al.* 2003). Human neuroscience has identified global hemispherical asymmetries between positive (approach) and negative (avoidance) reactions, as well as brain areas recruited in emotion processing generally, but especially for intense emotions (amygdala) and negative ones (insula) (see FRONTAL BRAIN ASYMMETRY).

All these approaches tend to neglect cognition in emotional responses, compared with the theories covered next, but they increasingly recognize that emotions include components: conscious, unconscious, cognitive, affective, social, peripheral, subcortical, and cortical configurations (see COMPONENTIAL THEORIES). The brain is not divided up neatly, with separate social, cognitive, and affective areas. Instead these processes all intertwine in form and function.

Social cognition influences affect

Social cognition research and theory identify a central role for cognition in emotion. One major set of work has examined how cognition might contribute to affect, focusing on cognitive structures and on cognitive appraisals (see APPRAISAL THEORIES).

Some research shows how social cognitive structures—either interrupted or successfully applied—influence affect. This work includes interruption theories, matching theories, outcome theories, and monitoring theories (see Fiske and Taylor, 2008, for a longer review).

Interruption theories. One set of approaches examines the interplay between arousal and cognition, building on Schachter's two-component theory of emotion; this theory states that unexplained arousal leads people to search their environment for cognitive labels for their emotions (see SCHACHTER–SINGER THEORY).

Mandler's theory of mind and emotion extends this analysis in several respects: first, it explains the origins of the unexplained physiological arousal in the interruption of perceptual schemas or complex goal sequences. The degree of disconfirmation of a perceptual schema determines its experienced pleasantness; a small interruption being pleasant but a significant one being unpleasant. The interruption of a goal sequence similarly prompts cognitive interpretation that determines the nature of the experienced emotion.

Berscheid's theory of emotion in close relationships extends this analysis to complex goal sequences in which people are interdependent: the more intimate the relationship, the more interdependence, and the more potential for interruption, and consequently emotion. This theory explains various phenomena in relationships (e.g. the initial excitement and the mellowing over time), and research is beginning to provide further support.

Matching theories. Other social cognition theories focus more specifically on cognitive structures and their impact on affect. A variety of work has examined social schemas and affect. Keltner has posited a simple matching theory, whereby high-power expectancy leads to positive affect and low-power expectancy to negative affect.

Fiske's more general theory of schema-triggered affect posits that affective values are stored at the top level of a schema (an abstract mental representation). Affect is accessible immediately upon categorization of an instance as matching the affect-laden schema; research supports this idea with self-report and neuroimaging data. Attitude research showing accessibility of attitudes upon immediate perception of the target reflects a related process.

Considerable research has examined Linville's analysis of how a category's informational complexity influences affect; more complex knowledge structures often

moderate affect, whereas simple ones allow more extreme affect. Over time, however, thought polarizes affect. In Tesser's analysis this occurs to the extent that thought organizes the relevant schema, the schema contains correlated dimensions, and the person has made a public commitment to the initial affective response: research also supports these points.

Outcome theories. Another set of theories examines people's emotional reactions to outcomes they or others have obtained. Weiner's theory focuses on dimensions of attribution (inferences about causes of people's outcomes) (see ATTRIBUTIONAL THEORY). Configurations of attributions—involving internal and external locus, stability over time, and controllability—result in specific emotional and behavioural responses to self and others. For example, person-caused negative outcomes elicit anger, whereas situation-caused negative outcomes elicit pity. This perspective has garnered a considerable research support.

Besides already obtained outcomes, some social cognition theories of emotion have emphasized alternative outcomes: what might have been or what might yet be. Kahneman and Miller's norm theory describes the process of deciding how surprising an outcome was, compared with the alternatives. The ease of imagining alternatives determines the amount of surprise and the intensity of emotional response; again research supports these ideas. These theories of obtained outcomes and alternative outcomes, as well as the theories of interruption as a basis for arousal, all posit that interruptions cause emotion.

Monitoring theories. Emotions also in turn cause interruptions. Several theories describe emotions as managing goal priorities; in these views, emotions interrupt goals to suggest changes in priorities. In Simon's view, emotions serve as alarm signals providing arousal and interruption that alert the organism to an unmet need that has shifted its urgency while the organism has been pursuing another goal. In Oatley and Johnson-Laird's related view, emotions provide transitions between plans with changes in the estimated success of the plan. Although not yet tested directly, some data are consistent with these views. A third approach, based on Carver and Scheier's cybernetic model, posits an affective feedback system that senses and regulates the rate at which the organism pursues the goal; a number of studies support these ideas.

Cognitive appraisals underlie affect

Another set of theories examines ways in which cognition generates affect. The appraisal theories describe how people assess the environment to ascertain its significance for their concerns, based on older work by Arnold and

Lazarus. The appraisal of personal meaning involves preconscious and conscious cognitive assessments of, first, personal relevance and, second, coping options; research on stress and coping is consistent with this view. Cognitive appraisal assesses particular dimensions of the current situation, determining particular emotional responses, and several studies of appraisal and emotions support this theory. Other theories have identified similar dimensions of appraisal leading to emotion, in particular pleasantness, agency, certainty, and attention.

Cognitive appraisals not only evaluate the present, but also possible future events. *Affective forecasting tends to overestimate the impact of future events on happiness. People underestimate their own ability to cope, the competing influence of other events, and the pull of their own emotional set-point.

Affect influences social cognition

In addition to the consideration of the various influences of cognition on affect in the last section, a considerable body of research has considered the influences of affect on cognition, and in particular the influences of mood. Even small manipulations of mood influence a variety of cognitive processes.

Positive mood effects. The effects of positive mood are more clear-cut than the effects of negative mood in general (Isen 1993). Positive moods lead to more *prosocial behaviour (Penner et al. 2005). These robust effects may be explained by the cheerful person's sensitivity to positive reinforcement; helping in a good mood is enhanced by focus of attention on oneself, requests emphasizing the rewards of helping, an emphasis on a positive social outlook, and the opportunity to maintain one's positive mood. People in a negative mood may or may not be helpful, depending on the circumstances.

Mood and memory. Mood reliably increases people's memory for mood-congruent material, due to both automatic and controlled processes. Effects for positive moods are stronger than those for negative moods, with the exception of people who are chronically depressed, who also show strong mood-congruent memory. Another mood-memory phenomenon, mood-state-dependent memory, posited that people would best recall material that was learned and retrieved in the same mood state; this hypothesis has little support.

Mood and judgement. Mood generally influences judgement in a mood-congruent direction as well. Arousal similarly creates arousal-congruent judgements. Again, the effects of positive mood are more reliable than the effects of negative moods.

Specific emotions have specific effects on relevant judgements, beyond simple positive–negative valence.

Moreover, the effects on adults are more reliable than the effects on children. Various explanations for these effects have been proposed but, for the most part, remain to be tested.

Mood also affects people's style of *decision-making, with positive moods making people more expansive, inclusive, impulsive, and perhaps creative. Positive moods also make people more compliant toward attempts at persuasion, at least under low involvement. Emotion also drives ethical judgements.

Cheerful people have a variety of advantages that culminate in a wide array of general life outcomes: Being happy improves health, friendships, marriage, income, and performance.

Affect versus cognition The contrast between affect and cognition has been hotly debated, leading to a proposal that they are separate systems, with affect being primary (Zajonc 1998). Evidence from mere exposure and person perception research is cited in support of this perspective; people report liking frequently encountered stimuli they cannot discriminate as familiar, and people's evaluative judgements are often made on-line, without recall of the data on which they were based. Objections to this perspective have focused on the possibility of nonconscious cognitive processes, the role of affect within broader (cognitive) representational systems, the problems of defining both affect and cognition, and empirical tests of the differences. The most constructive course seems to be to examine the bases of each and to investigate the multiple ways in which they do relate, as reviewed here.

SUSAN T. FISKE

Barrett, L.F., Mesquita, B., Ochsner, K.N., and Gross, J.J. (2007). The experience of emotion. *Annual Review of Psychology*, **58**, 373–403.

Cacioppo, J.T. and Gardner, W.L. (1999). Emotions. *Annual Review of Psychology*, **50**, 191–214.

Fiske, S.T. and Taylor, S.E. (2008). *Social cognition: from brains to culture*, Chs 13, 14. New York: Wiley.

Phelps, E.A. (2006). Emotion and cognition: insights from studies of the human amygdala. *Annual Review of Psychology*, **57**, 27–53.

social comparison Social comparison involves thinking about the self in relation to one or more other people. It is believed to be a ubiquitous aspect of social life. People compare themselves with others both automatically (e.g. Am I as good-looking?) and deliberately to serve various motives, including self-evaluation (e.g. Am I a good dancer?), self-improvement (e.g. I'd like to learn to cope as well as she does), and self-enhancement—to feel better (e.g. I did not get a raise, but I earn more than co-workers). Social comparisons affect such outcomes as self-esteem, self-descriptions, motivation, and satisfaction with pay.

Comparisons with others who are superior to oneself or more advantaged are referred to as 'upward', whereas comparisons with others who are inferior or less fortunate are called 'downward'. People often compare themselves with others who are similar to themselves, either on the dimension of comparison or on other dimensions. For example, pianists may compare their playing ability with others who are similar in piano-playing ability, or with others who are similar on dimensions related to piano-playing, such as how long they have played, or even on unrelated dimensions, such as birthplace. Comparisons with similar others have more psychological impact than comparisons with dissimilar others.

Social comparisons figure into people's affective experience in a number of important ways. First, they affect people's specific emotions. An upward comparison, for example, can make one feel envious (see ENVY) or sad (Salovey and Rodin 1984). Secondly, people make social comparisons so as to understand their emotional states (Cottrell and Epley 1977). For example, in a novel situation they may seek others' company to learn which emotions are appropriate. Third, emotions may determine which comparisons people make, through either of two routes: mood-congruent priming and motivation (Wood et al. 2000). For example, when one is sad, one may be biased to see oneself as inferior to others, but one's desire to feel better can motivate one to deliberately seek downward comparisons.

JOANNE V. WOOD AND JUSTIN V. CAVALLO

social emotions Many theorists distinguish a specific subset of emotions, usually including emotions such as *shame, *embarrassment, *jealousy, *admiration, *guilt, *gratitude, *schadenfreude, and *pity, as social emotions (Hareli and Weiner 2002, Parkinson et al. 2005). A variety of approaches have been taken to the questions of what should count as a social emotion and what criteria imply membership of that category (see EMOTION CLASSIFICATION). While some writers assume that only certain emotions count as social, others tend to view all emotions as social emotions (see SOCIAL COGNITION). Despite the variety of criteria used to define social emotions and the divided opinions about which emotions belong in this category, a few characteristics are widely accepted to characterize social emotions.

Many writers agree that social emotions serve important social functions. Some of these functions are said to be grounded in evolutionary roots. According to this perspective, social emotions serve the purpose of motivating actions, both of the self as well as of others whose goal is of a social nature. The social goals

thought to be served by actions motivated by social emotions are general goals such as *affiliation or dominance, or more specific goals that often can be seen as subserving them. For example, social emotions may serve the goal of affecting others' reactions or of outwardly communicating one's own intentions and attitudes.

Some social emotions are thought to be devices aimed at achieving such goals. For example, anger may be seen as an attempt to gain or maintain a superior social status, embarrassment as a way of deflecting undue attention from someone else, and guilt as a means of restoring relationships damaged by one's undesirable acts. Specific actions or *action tendencies associated with each of these emotions serve to shape the social environment in a way that is conducive to the particular emotion's goal. The bodily and behavioural manifestations of *anger may serve as signals warning others to desist from undesired actions, as well as exerting a more direct punitive effect. Similarly, presentations of embarrassment may communicate discomfort about interpersonal attention as well as constituting an intrinsically unpleasant stimulus configuration for observers. Expressions of guilt demonstrate commitment to a fractured relationship and *empathy towards the wronged party in addition to motivating reparatory actions from the wrongdoer (Baumeister et al. 1994).

These distinctive social goals can be seen as the concerns that lie at the heart of the associated social emotions. Such concerns are best conceived as aspects of one's life that bear social significance and that the person cares about. Because emotions are evoked when events or situations impinge on *concerns, social emotions can be seen as emotions that arise when a socially relevant event is perceived to occur. That is, social emotions arise from appraising situations as relevant to specific social concerns. Certain appraisals weigh up specific types of social information. Consistent with this idea, several appraisal theorists have proposed appraisal dimensions which are of a social nature. Appraisals such as *fairness, responsibility, or deservingness involve orientation towards issues that are only important in the context of social life and hence can be considered social appraisals (see APPRAISAL THEORIES).

Thus social emotions can be characterized as emotions that are closely tied to social aspects of the environment. This idea is reflected in various views in the literature that define social emotions by referring to the typical objects of such emotions or their eliciting conditions. Thus, some have defined social emotions as emotions that are aroused by real, imagined, anticipated, or recalled encounters with others. A similar perspective assumes that a common characteristic of many social emotions is their dependence on perceptions of others' actual or imagined view of the self. Still others consider social emotions to always involve others and be related to socialized goals.

These features characterize the category of social emotions as a whole. However, a few discussions in the pertinent literature further divide social emotions into a few subcategories. Notable among such analyses are those concerning *moral emotions and self-conscious emotions (see SELF-REFLEXIVE EMOTIONS) (e.g. Lewis 1993, Haidt 2002). Moral emotions are defined as emotions that are intrinsically linked to the interests or welfare either of society as a whole or of persons other than the agent. As such, moral emotions are readily evoked by the perception of moral violations in the context of interpersonal events and guide moral behaviour. Included in this category are emotions such as shame, guilt, or *regret. Self-conscious emotions, on the other hand, are seen as emotions that arise when an individual becomes aware that a certain event or situation impinges on his or her self-evaluation or personal welfare. Frequently mentioned examples are shame, guilt, *pride, and embarrassment.

In sum, social emotions can be defined as emotions that arise from social appraisals impinging on social concerns. Such emotions serve significant social functions by motivating relevant social behaviours.

SHLOMO HARELI AND BRIAN PARKINSON

Buck, R. (1999). The biological affects: a typology. *Psychological Review*, **106**, 301–36.

Leary, M.R. (2000). Affect, cognition, and the social emotions. In: J.P. Forgas (ed.), *Feeling and thinking*, pp. 331–56. Cambridge: Cambridge University Press.

social neuroscience Social neuroscience is an interdisciplinary field of science that deals with the biological mechanisms underlying social processes and behaviour (see SOCIAL COGNITION) and uses biological concepts and methods to develop and refine theories of complex human behaviour in the social and behavioural sciences.

In 20th-century biological sciences the architects of development and behaviour were conceived of as anatomical entities (e.g. genes) sculpted by the forces of evolution and located within living cells far from the reaches of the social world. The brain was treated as a rational information-processing machine. Social factors, such as early family environment or social isolation later in life, were thought to have minimal implications for the basic development, structure, or processes of the brain, which meant that social factors need not be considered in understanding the human mind and behaviour. And, even if relevant, the notion was that considering social factors made the study of the human mind and behaviour too complicated to sustain scientific progress.

The embrace of the neurosciences by cognitive and social scientists throughout most of the 20th century was no less antagonistic. World wars, the Great Depression, and civil injustices made it clear that social and cultural forces were too important to address to await the full explanation of cellular and molecular mechanisms. Given the antagonism between biological and social sciences which characterized psychology throughout most of the 20th century, research crossing social and biological levels of analysis was relatively rare.

By the dawn of the 21st century, neuroscientists, cognitive scientists, and social scientists began to collaborate more systematically, joined by the common view that complex human behaviour must consider both biological and social factors and mechanisms. The research in social neuroscience has quickly grown to be broad and diverse. Investigations in the field include genetic studies of social recognition and affiliation in mice, research on social perception in stroke patients, animal studies of nurturance and affiliation, autonomic (e.g. neural pathways to and from internal organs) and neuroendocrine (e.g. hormones) research of social stressors and morbidity, and brain imaging studies of racial prejudice, social cognition, decision-making, and interpersonal processes to name but a few. The meteoric growth in research crossing social and biological levels of analysis over the past decade is testimony that the gap between the neurosciences and social sciences can be bridged, that the mechanisms underlying complex human behaviour will not be fully explicable by a biological or a social approach alone, and that a common scientific language grounded in the structure and function of the brain and biology can contribute to this endpoint.

Current work has demonstrated that theory and methods in the neurosciences can constrain and inspire social psychological hypotheses, foster experimental tests of otherwise indistinguishable theoretical explanations, and increase the comprehensiveness and relevance of social psychological theories. That is, social neuroscience improves our scientific understanding of complex human behaviour. Several principles from social neuroscience indicate why this might be the case.

The principle of *multiple determinism* specifies that human behaviour can have multiple antecedents within or across levels of organization. For instance, one might consume a considerable quantity of pizza in an effort to remedy a condition of low blood sugar (biological determinant) or win a food-eating contest (social determinant). If either the biological or social level of analysis is regarded as inappropriate for their science, then that science will be ignoring an entire class of determinants and, therefore, will not be able to provide a comprehensive explanation for such behaviours.

The principle of *nonadditive determinism* specifies that properties of the whole are not always readily predictable from the properties of the parts. In an illustrative study, the behaviour of nonhuman primates was examined following the administration of amphetamine or placebo. No clear pattern emerged until each primate's position in the social hierarchy was considered. When this social factor was taken into account, amphetamine was found to increase dominant behaviour in primates high in the social hierarchy and to increase submissive behaviour in primates low in the social hierarchy. A strictly physiological (or social) analysis, regardless of the sophistication of the measurement technology, may not have unravelled the orderly relationship that existed.

Finally, the principle of *reciprocal determinism* specifies that there can be mutual influences between microscopic (e.g. biological) and macroscopic (e.g. social) factors in determining behaviour. For example, it is well known that the level of testosterone in nonhuman male primates promotes sexual behaviour; however, it has also been shown that the availability of receptive females increases the level of testosterone in nonhuman primates. That is, the effects of social and biological processes can be reciprocal.

JOHN T. CACIOPPO AND GARY G. BERNTSON

Adolphs, R. (2003). Cognitive neuroscience of human social behaviour. *Neuroscience Reviews*, 4, 165–78.

Cacioppo, J.T. and Berntson, G.G. (2005). *Social neuroscience*. New York: Psychology Press.

Cacioppo, J.T., Berntson, G.G., Adolphs, R., Carter, C.S., Davidson, R.J., McClintock, M.K., et al. (2002). *Foundations in social neuroscience*. Cambridge, MA: MIT Press.

Decety, J. and Jackson, P.L. (2006). A social neuroscience perspective of empathy. *Current Directions in Psychological Science*, 15, 54–8.

social referencing Social referencing is a dual process involving (1) seeking information from another person to disambiguate an uncertain situation and (2) the consequences for behavioural regulation that result from the emotional expressions or actions observed in another person. Social referencing occurs throughout life, but has been studied primarily in infancy where there is considerable interest in identifying at what age different emotional signals affect the infant's approach or avoidance behaviours as well as other *action tendencies (see INFANCY (EMOTIONAL DEVELOPMENT IN)).

The most successful investigation on social referencing to date was a study identifying what happens when a 12-month-old infant encounters a modest dropoff the size of a stairstep. Almost all infants showed information-seeking toward their mothers when encountering the virtual stairstep. Moreover, almost all infants whose mothers posed a fear or anger face avoided the stairstep, whereas those whose mothers posed a happy or interest face continued onward to approach the mother (Sorce et al. 1985).

Social referencing has acquired a second, less strict, usage. It has been applied to situations in which the emotional signal is imposed on the child without any evident information-seeking by the child, or indeed any uncertainty. For instance, the mother's vocalizations of fear and anger powerfully inhibited the approach of 8.5-month-olds to an ambiguous toy, whereas joyful vocalizations did not (Campos et al. 2003).

Studies of social referencing have revealed several important findings about infant emotional regulation stemming from the emotional signals of others (Saarni et al. 2006). Among these are: (1) Positive emotional signals elicit approach behaviours and avoidance behaviours follow negative emotional signals, especially after 8 months of age. (2) Different negative emotions do not seem to bring about differential behavioural regulatory effects in infants younger than 15 months of age. (3) Persons other than the mother or father can bring about emotion regulation (see REGULATION OF EMOTION). (4) Infants begin to appreciate the target of the emotional signal between 11 and 14 months (i.e. is my mother angry at me or at the dog or the sibling?); before this age emotional signals produce only a general change in hedonic tone. (5) Recent speculations link social referencing to the generation of so-called 'self-conscious' emotions, such as *pride, *shame, and *guilt (see SELF-REFLEXIVE EMOTIONS).

JOSEPH J. CAMPOS

social relationships Human beings are highly social animals, spending much of their time living, working, and interacting with others. Evidence suggests that people have a strong and pervasive need to maintain a minimum number of lasting, positive, and significant relationships with other people and that a great deal of human thought, emotion, and behaviour is devoted to establishing and maintaining these relationships (Baumeister and Leary 1995).

Theorists have distinguished between at least five fundamental types of social relationships that differ in terms of their functions, features, and expectations, as well as the criteria by which people are included in and excluded from these relationships (Kirkpatrick and Ellis 2001). The fundamental types include: kin relationships that are based on genetic relatedness; task-oriented coalitions (such as hunting parties, teams, and committees) in which people work directly together to achieve mutually desired goals; friendships that develop on the basis of a communal commitment to provide companionship and mutual support that span time, roles, and tasks; mating relationships for the purpose of producing and raising offspring; and collectives (such as tribes, villages, communities, and nations) in which people may not have direct contact with all other members of the collective but nonetheless identify themselves as members of the group because membership offers benefits such as access to resources and defence against other groups.

Recent social functionalist analyses of emotions have outlined the importance of emotion in the development, quality, and disintegration of social relationships (see SOCIAL EMOTIONS). *Love and *compassion, for instance, motivate and maintain romantic relations, *guilt and *embarrassment may motivate people to repair relationships that they have damaged, and *anger directed toward those who violate group *norms may contribute to the cohesion of groups.

MARK R. LEARY

social sharing of emotion After 80–95% of emotional episodes, affected persons evidence a process of social sharing of emotion. This means that they talk with selected members of their social network about the emotional circumstances and their experienced feelings (e.g. Rimé *et al.* 1998). Experimental studies have confirmed emotional exposure to cause the social sharing of emotion.

Basic observations

People first share an emotional event on the day it happened (in some 60% of cases). Modally, sharing is repetitive and addresses several successive recipients. More intense emotions are shared more recurrently, with more addressees, and the urge to share them extends for longer. Progressive extinction is the normal fate of sharing. For instance, whereas in the first week back home from the maternity ward, 97% of young mothers in a sample had shared their delivery-related emotions, this was the case for 55% of them in the third week, and for only 32% in the fifth week. The length of the extinction period depends upon the intensity of the emotion. To illustrate, in the first week following the loss of a close person, 100% of bereaved respondents had shared their loss-related emotions; one month later, the corresponding figure was of 87%; three months after the loss, it still reached 79%. Steeper extinction slopes characterize less intense emotional events. When the propensity to share an episode persists, it is generally associated with a failure to recover and predicts poor recovery in the future.

Generality

The social sharing of emotion is manifested independently of age and gender. Neither the type of *basic emotion

involved nor the emotional *valence affected the proportion of shared episodes. *Fear, *anger, and *sadness are shared as widely as *happiness or *love. However, *shame and *guilt are shared to a lesser degree. The propensity to share emotions was evidenced at comparable levels whether people held a university degree or had only an elementary school education. It was also observed with comparable importance in Asian, North American and European countries. Every emotion thus tends to be socially shared but the way people share them fluctuates broadly. Parameters of the social sharing of emotion such as latency, recurrence, or target vary considerably as a function of respondents' gender, education, culture, and of the characteristics of the involved emotions.

Targets

Sharing targets are chosen among intimates (parents, brothers/sisters, friends, spouse/partner). However, within this circle, gender and age differences in elected partners occur. Males and females have a comparable sharing network at adolescence. Later, their respective networks evolve quite differently. Among females, even if the spouse/partner is a privileged target, a differentiate network is maintained. Among males, the sharing network vanishes with adulthood so that the spouse/partner becomes exclusive listener.

Social responses

Observation of targets' responses revealed that a typical interpersonal dynamic develops in emotional sharing (Christophe and Rimé 1997). First, targets evidenced a marked interest for shared emotional episodes. Second, hearing an emotional story is emotion-eliciting. Listeners' manifested emotions which varied in intensity as a function of intensity of the shared episode, thus favouring *empathy and emotional communion. Third, for low-intensity episodes, listeners displayed mostly verbal responding. However, the more the intensity of shared episodes increased, the more verbal responses were replaced by nonverbal ones (touching, body contact, taking into the arms, kissing . . .). Thus, sharing emotion brings interactants closer to one another. As sharing addresses predominantly intimates, it is instrumental in maintaining, refreshing, and strengthening important social bonds. Yet there are notable exceptions to this general trend. For instance, interactions between patients suffering from a severe illness and healthy members of their social network totally diverged from this sharing–intimacy model.

Propagation

As the social sharing of emotion arouses emotion in the target and as emotion elicits social sharing, targets tend to share with third persons what they heard. In other words, a secondary social sharing develops. As for pri-

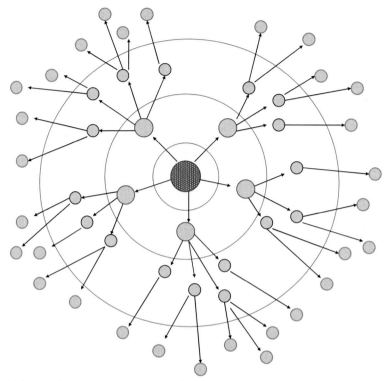

Fig. S4. The social sharing of emotion. Propagation wave after a private emotional episode: at the center of the figure someone experienced an emotion and shared it with a number of intimates. Each of the recipients then shared the episode with some of their intimates in a secondary social sharing process. The latter in their turn propagated the narrative in a tertiary social sharing. From Rimé (2005).

mary social sharing, frequency of secondary sharing was related to emotional intensity, with more intense episodes eliciting more frequent repetitions of secondary sharing and with more partners (Christophe and Rimé 1997, Curci and Bellelli 2004). Social consequences of sharing an emotion do not end there. Data have confirmed that episodes heard in a secondary sharing were also shared (Harber and Cohen 2005). Emotional episodes thus open upon a spreading of emotional information across social networks (see Fig. S4).

Emotional regulation

It is commonly assumed that verbalizing an experience can reduce its emotional load (see REGULATION OF EMOTION). Correlative and experimental tests of this assumption yielded unsupportive conclusions, but sharing participants generally reported important personal benefits from sharing. These benefits result largely from the fact that sharing situations respond particularly well to socioaffective regulation needs elicited by emo-

tional experiences, such as need for comforting, concrete support, social integration, validation, esteem support. Social sharing thus naturally regulates the *collateral effects* of emotional experiences (destabilization, anxiety, insecurity, helplessness, estrangement, alienation, lowering of *self-esteem ...) and brings people emotional relief. By contrast, naturally developed sharing generally falls short of bringing emotional recovery because it fails to address a number of cognitive needs borne with the emotion: reorganization of motives, modification of schemas, re-creation of meaning, and reframing. Emotional recovery indeed presupposes regulation of the *central effects* (automatic meaning analysis) of emotional experiences. Natural social sharing does not generally have this effect and professional intervention may be needed to improve regulation capacity.

BERNARD RIMÉ

Rimé, B. (2005). *Le partage social des émotions* (The social sharing of emotion). Paris: Presses Universitaires de France.

Rimé, B. (2007). Interpersonal emotion regulation. In: J.J. Gross (ed.), *Handbook of emotion regulation*, pp. 466–85. New York: Guilford Press.

Rimé, B. (2009). Emotion elicits the social sharing of emotion: Theory and empirical review. *Emotion review*, 1, 60–85.

social structure of emotion Emotional experiences typically arise through the emoting subject's relationship with the world, which for humans is essentially social (see SOCIAL RELATIONSHIPS). Human emotions, then, may be conceptualized in terms of interactions or relations between persons (see SOCIAL EMOTIONS; AFFILIATION). When these relations are stable and enduring they constitute social structure. Participation in social relations generates and requires a sense of involvement which may be positive or negative, strong or weak, but always includes an evaluation of both the other and the relationship that registers in the person's physical and dispositional processes. This is what is meant by emotion. The connection between social structure and emotion has been conceived in two forms: causal and consequential.

Social structure as cause of emotion

Social relationships can be characterized as power or status forms. Coercion and domination in relationships is the assertion of one participant over another. This is the dimension of power. Another relates to support, sympathy, and regard between persons such that one participant accords a certain standing or status to the other. This is the status dimension. These formal properties of social relationships are the basis of a comprehensive account of a large range of particular emotions (Kemper 1978). The outcome of any social relationship will be an increase, decrease, or absence of change in the power of each participant and similarly for their status. On this basis there are twelve possible outcomes of any episode of a social relationship between self and other, each of which is associated with a particular emotional experience: if a person's own power decreases in an interaction or the power of the other increases, then it is likely that person will experience *fear. An increase in status is likely to produce *happiness, while a decline is likely to lead to *depression. This simple model can be made more complex by including responsibility for the outcome of social relationships, whether the power or status is appropriate to the relationship, and by adding complexity to the interactions, so that while subordination to another's power may provoke fear, through patronage or alliance another's power may provoke feelings of security. Power and status as formal properties of social relationships are ubiquitous, thus this account has universal application.

The social world has local or cultural variation as well as universal properties. This leads to an alternative causal account, namely that emotional experiences depend on cultural cues and interpretations. Thus, linguistic practices, *values, *norms, and currents of belief constitute the substance of experience of emotions (McCarthy 1994). A corollary is that persons can determine the emotions they experience, that the cultural construction of emotions entails management of emotions. The strength of this perspective is in the fact that many emotions are integrated into the broader conceptual repertoire of a culture and prevailing cultural values and beliefs are infused into the meaning of named emotions (Russell 1991). But by treating emotions as strategic evaluations derived from local meaning systems the constructionist approach is arguably itself captive of cultural preferences. Emotions that escape cultural tagging are not thereby without consequence. Indeed, socially important emotions may be experienced below the threshold of conscious awareness and cannot be fully accounted for in only cultural terms (Scheff 1990).

Social structure as consequence of emotion

Radical microsociology holds that social structure arises out of 'interaction ritual chains' that begin with any momentary encounter in which the participants mutually focus their emotions (Collins 2005). During the course of interaction these originating, disruptive, or transient emotions become intensified and transformed into long-term emotions that Collins calls 'emotional energy' (EE). Successful interactions, such as religious rites as described by Durkheim (1995) (see RELIGION AND EMOTION (PSYCHOLOGICAL PERSPECTIVES)), produce high levels of EE which in turn are consolidated as group solidarity, social symbols which crystallize the collective experience of group membership, and a moral order.

There are difficulties with this approach: no emotion has an intrinsic time frame so the distinction between transient and long-term emotions can only relate to particular emotional episodes and is not a meaningful theoretical distinction between types of emotions. Also, the idea that transient emotions are disruptive is a misunderstanding of how to formulate *intentionality, a quality common to all emotions, their goal-setting propensity. If an emotion is experienced in a setting that offers imperatives at odds with the intentions or purposes implicit in the emotion it may be described as disruptive, but that is contingent upon the setting and not intrinsic to the emotion. Finally, while Collins acknowledges that EE has affective tone—high EE is confidence, low EE is depression—he operatively defines it quantitatively, as high, moderate, or low, and the quantitative energizing form of EE is held to be stored in the symbolic output of interaction rituals. But what symbols convey is invariably the affect not the energy.

JACK BARBALET

Barbalet, J.M. (2001). *Emotion, social theory and social structure: a macrosociological approach*. Cambridge: Cambridge University Press.

somatic marker hypothesis The somatic marker hypothesis (SMH) was originally proposed by Antonio Damasio (1994) to address the problems of *decision-making encountered in patients with certain kinds of prefrontal damage and with compromised emotions. Damasio proposed that '...somatic markers (SM) are a special instance of feelings generated from secondary emotions. Those emotions and feelings have been connected by learning to predicted future outcomes of certain scenarios. When a negative SM is juxtaposed to a particular future outcome the combination functions as an alarm bell. When a positive SM is juxtaposed instead, it becomes a beacon of incentive. This is the essence of the SMH...'. Thus the centrality of emotion to the SMH is evident from this and other (earlier and later) texts, as is the notion that SMs are emotion-related signals, which are either conscious or unconscious.

The Iowa Gambling Task (IGT) was developed by Bechara and colleagues (Bechara *et al.* 1994) to assess and quantify the decision-making defects of neurological patients by simulating real-life decision in conditions of reward and punishment and of uncertainty; and to investigate the SMH further. In one experiment (Bechara *et al.* 1997) the task was interrupted by questioning regarding the conscious knowledge of the situation (but not that of SMs), in both normals and patients, while skin conductance responses (SCRs) were monitored, both before and after decisions, as an index of SMs. Normal participants began to trigger anticipatory SCRs when they pondered risky decisions, and began to prefer the good decks before having adequate conscious knowledge of the situation. Patients with lesions in the ventromedial prefrontal cortex (VMPC) failed to generate anticipatory SCRs, and played deficiently. Even after several realized which decks were bad, they still made the wrong choices. It was concluded that conscious knowledge of the situation alone is not sufficient for implementing advantageous decisions, and that its absence does not preclude them. This was one of the primary findings providing empirical evidence for the SMH.

Although the SMH has achieved prominence, it is not without critics. One chief criticism is that the behavioural decisions on the IGT need not be accounted for by the SMH (Maia and McClelland 2004). This view has been rebutted, however (Bechara *et al.* 2005, Maia and

McClelland 2005), and a later independent study revealed that the criticism is a questionable one (Persaud *et al.* 2007).

ANTOINE BECHARA

somatic nervous system For many years, a principal focus of neurobiologists has been to elucidate the relationship between brain and behaviour. One particular aspect of this philosophical and scientific problem has been how the central nervous system represents perceptions of the external and internal environments.

It is clear that the nervous system is primed to capture subtle changes in the environment. Initial sensory information is processed through several stages, from peripheral receptors to spinal cord and brainstem, to thalamus, and finally to the cerebral cortex, the site of complex information processing prior to ultimate perceptual experience. This sensory information is processed in parallel for the different sensory modalities, but in higher centres it is integrated to form complex perceptions of the internal and external worlds (Amaral 2000).

Due to the intricate nature of this sensory integration, the traditional approach to the study of these afferent sensory systems has been to segregate one from the other according to the type of sensory modality involved (visual, auditory, etc.). Based on this, the somatic sensory system (Greek, *somatikos* (σωματικόσ), of the body), in its most traditional definition, refers to sensory processing that originates in the body, excluding information coming from the viscera. However, since the general role of the somatic sensory system is to transform information from the external and internal state of the body, and since visceral afferents tend to converge with somatic afferents in several regions (Strigo *et al.* (2003), the concept of somatic sensations has been amplified (to include visceral input) and classified according to their particular functions as follows: (1) *Exteroceptive*: these include sensations from the surface of the body originating in the external environment. They can be mechanoreceptive (touch) or receptive to temperature and pain. (2) *Proprioceptive*: these include the kinesthetic sensations originating in muscles and tendons that provide information on the position and movement of the body (Kaas 1990). (3) *Interoceptive*: these sensations originate in the internal organs and provide information about the health of the viscera. Most, but not all, convey pain information (Cervero and Foreman 1990) (see INTEROCEPTION; PAIN (BIOLOGICAL PERSPECTIVES)).

The anatomical organization of the networks that processes the different functions of the somatic sensory system, albeit not identical, follows the same general pattern throughout the central nervous system.

Although each somatic submodality is associated with specific receptors, the cell bodies of all afferents are found in the dorsal root ganglia along the spinal cord. They all enter the spinal cord through the dorsal roots, where they either synapse with spinal cord neurons located in various laminae (touch and proprioception, III–IV; pain/temperature and visceral, I–II, V, and X), or ascend directly to the medulla, where they synapse with second-order neurons found in the *nucleus gracilis* and *nucleus cuneatus* (touch and proprioception). The next stage for all of these pathways is at the level of the thalamus where most of them make synaptic connections with neurons located in the ventroposterior complex (VPL and VPM). The thalamic neurons in turn project to the primary (SI) and secondary (SII) somatosensory cortices (exteroceptive information in Brodmann's areas 3 and 1; proprioceptive information in Brodmann's area 2; visceral information in SII). Hence, SI and SII constitute the first cortical relay in the integration of somatosensory perception. In turn, these cortices exert powerful influence on cortical and subcortical regions through a large variety of efferent projections: (1) Cortico-fugal: these fibres terminate in spinal cord, medulla, pons, tectum, thalamus, and striatum. (2) Commissural: these terminate in homotypical and heterotypical contralateral cortices. (3) Cortico-cortical: these fibres terminate either in motor cortices or in a variety of regions determined by the somatic submodality they convey. For instance, whereas the flow of mechanoreceptive and proprioceptive information is integrated in the superior parietal lobule, visceral and pain information flow towards limbic (*anterior cingulate and insular) cortices.

The differences in organization across the somatic submodalities allow the system to form perceptual experiences specific for each sensation. By contrast, the anatomical similarities facilitate their convergence, thereby allowing the formation of complex, more complete perceptual experiences.

The integration and ecological validity of the notion of somatic integration is perhaps best illustrated in a concept originally proposed by William James (see JAMES–LANGE THEORY) and later expanded by Antonio Damasio (Damasio 1994). Damasio suggests that integrated somatic states, associated with previous emotional experiences, serve as markers to aid individuals in the evaluation and efficient response upon current emotional situations. This has become known as the *somatic marker hypothesis.

ANA SOLODKIN

Mountcastle, V.B. (1958). Somatic functions of the nervous system. *Annual Review of Physiology*, **20**, 471–508.

Yates, B.J. and Stocker, S.D. (1998). Integration of somatic and visceral inputs by the brainstem: functional considerations. *Experimental Brain Research*, **119**, 269–75.

somatovisceral feedback Proprioception is a general class of sensory processes that conveys information to the brain and spinal cord from receptors in somatic (body) muscles and joints. Proprioceptive signals contribute to simple reflexes and motor control, and support our general awareness of limb position and body movement. *Interoception refers to the class of sensory processes that conveys information concerning the internal state of the body from receptors in internal visceral organs (heart, gut, etc.). These interoceptive signals are transmitted to peripheral autonomic ganglia and to the central nervous system, where they participate in autonomic reflexes and otherwise report visceral status to the brain. More generally, proprioception and interoception provide critical *somatovisceral feedback* which can guide external (skeletal) and internal (visceral) regulation. Although we often cannot precisely report the perceptions related to proprioception and interoception, these perceptions do rise to some level of awareness. For example, we can recognize the position of our limbs, even without looking, although it is difficult to describe the sensations that support this ability. Similarly, we may be unable to readily describe many internal organ states, but we certainly can become aware of our heart beat and can recognize and report states such as nausea or stomach cramps.

Somatic and visceral feedback has long been recognized by physiologists as important in motor and organ regulation. These sensory signals, however, may play a much broader role in behaviour and cognition. In the late 19th century, William James (1842–1910) proposed that perception of somatovisceral feedback may constitute emotional experience (see JAMES–LANGE THEORY). Considering the fear reaction to a bear, he suggested that we do not run from a bear because we are afraid, but that we are afraid of the bear because we run (and show autonomic arousal). Although the strong form of James's theory (independently proposed by Carl Lange (1834–1900)) has not been supported by recent evidence, it is increasingly recognized that somatovisceral feedback may indeed prime or bias emotional expression and may have an impact on other psychological processes as well. Visceral activation by adrenaline (epinephrine), for example, has been shown to enhance emotional memories in animals and humans and may play a role in the establishment of *posttraumatic stress disorder. Visceral activation has also been shown to alter pain sensitivity and potentiate the cortical processing of threat-related stimuli. These effects appear to be mediated by visceral signals carried by the vagus nerve (a major autonomic nerve), and the central systems by which these signals affect psychological processes (including the *amygdala, basal forebrain cholinergic system, and medial prefrontal cortex) are increasingly being elucidated. More generally, somatovisceral feedback has been suggested to serve as the basis for the regulation and guidance of behaviour and choice by rewards and punishments (see SOMATIC MARKER HYPOTHESIS).

Although proprioceptive and interoceptive feedback certainly plays an important role in lower-level motor and visceral regulation, the more recent findings discussed above suggest a much broader role for somatovisceral feedback in behavioural and cognitive processes.

GARY G. BERNTSON AND JOHN T. CACIOPPO

Bechara, A., Damasio, H., and Damasio, A.R. (2003). Role of the amygdala in decision-making. *Annals of the New York Academy of Sciences*, **985**, 356–69.

Berntson, G.G., Sarter, M., and Cacioppo, J.T. (2003). Ascending visceral regulation of cortical affective information processing. *European Journal of Neuroscience*, **18**, 2103–9.

Cacioppo, J.T., Berntson, G.G., and Klein, D.J. (1992). What is an emotion? The role of somatovisceral afference, with special emphasis on somatovisceral 'illusions'. *Review of Personality and Social Psychology*, **14**, 63–98.

startle The startle response is a brainstem reflex found in humans and many other species, serving as a defensive response to sudden stimulation. In humans, startle is sensitive to variations in stimuli, pharmacology, personality, social situation, and clinical condition. The most common and sensitive measure of startle in humans is the electromyogram (EMG) of the orbicularis oculi facial muscle, a minimally invasive surface recording measure (Blumenthal et al. 2005) (see ELECTROMYOGRAPHY).

The startle response can be modified by stimuli that are presented before or during the eliciting stimulus, and this has resulted in startle being used to measure the impact of affective (emotionally valenced) stimuli, as well as fear potentiation following conditioning (see VALENCE; LEARNING, EMOTIONAL (NEUROSCIENCE PERSPECTIVES)). A startle response can be modulated by the visual, acoustic, tactile, or olfactory stimuli that are present when the startle stimulus is presented. The startle response is larger when the individual is processing unpleasant (negatively valenced) than pleasant (positively valenced) background stimuli, such as pictures, sounds, smells, or imagined situations (Bradley et al. 2006). This effect of facilitated startle in the presence of unpleasant stimuli is limited to background stimuli that are relatively highly arousing, and the picture must be present for at least 500 milliseconds before the startle stimulus is presented for affective modulation of startle

to occur. Startle has also been shown to be facilitated in the presence of stimuli that have been conditionally paired with painful shocks, an example of fear-potentiated startle. Since the startle response modulation is similar across species, a great deal of information about the physiological mechanisms underlying emotion and *fear can be gleaned by the application of this response measure.

TERRY D. BLUMENTHAL

stoicism The ancient Stoics were the first Greek philosophers to develop an articulated scheme of and terminology for affective and motivational states. They were often formalizing distinctions implicit in earlier philosophical analyses, but they also deployed an innovative set of normative claims about human experience.

There is no distinct Stoic term for 'emotion' as such; affective and motivational states are classified according to their normative standing. Idealized wise people have only correct states and all other people have states characterized as wrong and vicious. Hence the treatment of 'emotion' and affectivity is bifurcated. *Pathos* (plural *pathē*) is the term reserved for vicious states, which makes 'emotion' a misleading translation. 'Passion' is preferable in some respects, but the word *pathos* also has important overtones of disease and dysfunction (see PASSION). Wise people have the 'good' counterparts of such passions, called *eupatheiai* (singular *eupatheia*). Since wise and vicious people exhaust the class of rational (i.e. adult) humans, human affective and motivational states will either be *pathē* or *eupatheiai*. A *pathos* is defined as a particular kind (irrational and excessive) of *hormē*, which is a psychological event triggered by a cognitive assessment of stimuli and circumstances; hence the Stoics often claimed that passions are forms of judgement. *Hormē* is the basic term in a complex theory which explains human actions in terms of discriminating responses to stimuli. Accordingly, affectivity and motivation are treated as kinds of *rational action* and hence as voluntary, in the sense that they are determined by the dispositions of the agent and not by external causes. There are no involuntary passions; some involuntary affective responses are recognized (and sometimes labelled *propatheiai* or preliminary passions) but these are sharply distinguished from affective reactions in the sense of passions.

Passions are divided into four high-level types: *fear (phobos), *desire (epithumia), *pleasure (hēdonē), and *pain (lupē). Pleasure and pain are cognitive assessments rather than bodily conditions. The physical pain of an injured foot is quite distinct from the 'pain' one feels as the result of a judgement that something bad is happening. Fear and desire are oriented towards future states of affairs, attempts to avoid what is (erroneously) judged to be bad for the agent or to acquire what is (erroneously) judged to be good for it. Pain is a reactive passion; a judgement that something bad for the agent is present leads to a 'contraction' of the mind, a kind of withdrawal or cramping. Pleasure is the counterpart; a judgement that something good is present leads to an 'expansion' of the mind, a sense of uplift or elation. There is a clear attempt here to incorporate the subjective 'feeling' of a mental state into the definition of pain and pleasure alongside the cognitive component (compare Aristotle *De Anima* 403a29-b1), but there is no such component in the definitions of the future-oriented passions.

Each passion has many subtypes (anger is a kind of desire, for example, and shame is a fear of ill-repute), the classification and definition of which was a major contribution of Stoic theory. Each passion except *lupē* has a virtuous counterpart or *eupatheia*. Rational 'fear' is termed *eulabeia* or caution and is an attempt to avoid what is truly bad. Rational 'desire' is *orexis*, an attempt to acquire the genuine good. Rational pleasure is *chara*, usually translated 'joy', an elation at the presence to the agent of something correctly assessed as good (that is virtue). There is no rational counterpart of 'pain', since virtuous agents are (in Stoic theory) immune to anything bad.

Such a highly normative classificatory analysis of human experience cannot properly be called a theory of affectivity as such, even when one includes the theory of preliminary passions. But its sophisticated analytical foundation, its technical terminology, and its complex classification of experience, not to mention its uncompromisingly cognitive approach, have made it influential. All the more reason, then, to avoid treating it as a general theory of human affectivity. Its own more limited achievements are sufficiently impressive.

BRAD INWOOD

Inwood, B. (1985). *Ethics and human action in early Stoicism*, Ch. 5. Oxford: Oxford University Press.

Principal ancient sources at Diogenes Laertius *Lives of the philosophers*, 7.110–117; Stobaeus *Eclogae* 2, pp. 88–93, ed. C. Wachsmuth; Cicero *Tusculan disputations* books 3–4 (esp. in the translation by M. Graver (2002), *Cicero on the Emotions*. Chicago, IL: Chicago University Press).

stress Stress has long been a central concept across disciplines. Researchers in psychology, sociology, anthropology, medicine, and the neurosciences have emphasized its importance in explaining significant physical health outcomes (see HEALTH AND EMOTION). Moreover, recent interdisciplinary perspectives are beginning to shed light on multilevel mechanisms. Such mechanistic accounts are important for the development of informed interventions aimed at helping individuals manage their stress and promote positive health outcomes. In this entry, we first discuss frameworks for examining stress, followed by a brief review of research linking stress to physical health. Recent integrative perspectives are then reviewed, along with future research directions.

Conceptualization of stress

The concept of stress is often used ubiquitously in the research literature to refer to either acute or chronic strains. The focus of researchers has historically emphasized stress as a stimulus (stressor), a response (biological changes), or a transactional process in which perceptions of stress are emphasized (Lazarus and Folkman 1984). A classic distinction is also usually drawn between more acute (or time-limited) versus chronic (long-term) stressors. Chronic stress is generally regarded as being more consequential for health and usually results from long-term exposure to stressors. However, chronic stress may also be a result of lasting perceptions of stress that are driven by ruminative thinking (Baum *et al.* 1990) (see RUMINATION). Thus, chronic stress may be defined as long-term exposure, lasting perceptions, or both (e.g. caregiving for a family member with Alzheimer's disease).

Although the time course and associated perception of stress have traditionally been emphasized in past research, more recent models are attempting to separate component processes associated with stress. Such perspectives are important because a strict focus on general perceptions of stress does less to elucidate the mechanisms operating to influence health outcomes. Cacioppo and Berntson (2007) have argued that stress may have at least four health-related components: exposure, reactivity, recovery, and restoration. Exposure refers to the number of stressors that an individual experiences, reactivity refers to the strength of an individual's physiological reaction to any given event, whereas recovery refers to how long it takes an individual to return to 'baseline' following stressful events. A unique (and understudied) aspect of this perspective is on restoration that focuses on anabolic processes that refresh or repair the organism because stress may directly impede our ability to perform these functions (e.g. disturbed sleep, impaired wound healing). Of course, it should be noted that the activation of these component processes may be adaptive in the short term (e.g. energy mobilization), but over the long term can lead to physiological changes that place healthy individuals at risk for disease (McEwen 1998).

Stress and physical health

The major causes of morbidity and mortality are cardiovascular disease (e.g. coronary artery disease, hypertension), cancer, and infectious diseases (see CARDIOVASCULAR SYSTEM; PSYCHONEUROIMMUNOLOGY). Is there evidence that stress can influence these diverse disease outcomes? Currently there is strong epidemiological and clinical/laboratory evidence linking stress to cardiovascular and infectious diseases (Krantz et al. 2000; Kiecolt-Glaser et al. 2002), with more controversial links to cancer outcomes (Fox 1998).

Theoretically, stress processes may play a role in the development and/or the exacerbation of cardiovascular disease. Animal models clearly suggest a role for stress in the development of cardiovascular disease (Manuck et al. 1983). Human epidemiological studies on the incidence of cardiovascular disease provide further evidence for this point (e.g. Rosengren et al. 2004), in addition to studies linking stress to plaque build-up in the carotid arteries (Kamarck et al. 2004). Finally, prospective studies suggest a role for stress in the clinical course of diagnosed cardiovascular disease (Sheps et al. 2002).

There is also strong evidence linking stress to risk for infectious disease. These studies suggest that life stress, and chronic stress in particular, is related to increased susceptibility to infectious disease (Kiecolt-Glaser et al. 2002). For instance, the important work by Sheldon Cohen and colleagues using a common cold paradigm (i.e. consenting adults exposed to a cold virus) is providing strong evidence for a link between stress and susceptibility to infectious illnesses (Cohen et al. 1998). There have also been a handful of studies examining the link between stress and the progression of HIV infection. Although some inconsistencies arose in early research, a study that followed HIV-positive populations for a longer time frame found that faster progression to AIDS was predicted by stressful events (Leserman et al. 1999). Although more research is needed, there is preliminary evidence linking stress to the progression of HIV infection (Kopnisky et al. 2004).

As noted above, the overall evidence linking stress to cancer outcomes is controversial. Animal models provide a stronger case for stress influencing some types of cancer (Fox 1998). However, human studies have provided inconsistent findings linking stress to overall cancer outcomes (Fox 1998). Some researchers have argued that given the heterogeneity of different cancers an examination of specific cancer types may provide a stronger test of the role of stress. In one meta-analysis, significant effects of stress on breast cancer development were found (McKenna et al. 1999). Moreover, these associations were not moderated by various methodological factors such as type of control group and sample size. More consistent evidence for links between stress and the course of cancer comes from the small number of available intervention studies (Fawzy and Fawzy 1998). Such interventions usually include an educational/stress management component and appear to have beneficial influence on health outcomes. However,

given the state of this area, future research will be needed to shed light on the apparent inconsistencies.

An important emphasis of the literature linking stress to disease is also to understand potential mechanisms. The focus has generally been on direct and indirect pathways (Baum and Posluszny 1999). The direct pathways include physiological responses as stress may influence the cardiovascular, neuroendocrine, and immune systems in health-relevant ways (e.g. reactivity hypothesis of cardiovascular disease) (see PSYCHONEUROENDOCRINOLOGY). More indirect pathways include the negative influence of stress on health behaviours (e.g. exercise, smoking) that then have an adverse influence over time in healthy and clinical populations. A broader perspective on mechanisms is needed, however, and such a view is highlighted below.

Integrative and cutting edge issues

Most prior research on stress and health has focused on links to a specific disease process. However, there are several trends emerging from the social, biomedical, and neuroscience literature that hold the potential to model greater integration in understanding risk for disease. These trends relate to the role of inflammation on cardiovascular disease, central nervous system (CNS) coordination of health-relevant physiological responses, and integrative multilevel analyses of the influences of stress.

Inflammation and disease. Traditionally, the immune system has been linked to infectious diseases and cancer. Cardiovascular disease can now be added to that list of disease processes with an immunological component as immune processes are implicated in just about every stage of atherogenesis (Libby 2002). Importantly, stress can lead directly to the release of inflammatory cytokines (e.g. interleukin-1, tumour necrosis factor (TNF)-alpha) which are crucial mediators of the cardiovascular inflammatory response (Kiecolt-Glaser et al. 2002). Moreover, *cytokine production may be mediated by the release of stress-related neuroendocrine hormones (e.g. catecholamines) because cells of the immune system have functional neuroendocrine receptors (Kiecolt-Glaser et al. 2002). In fact, the links between neuroendocrine and inflammatory processes are reciprocal, as chronic stress can lead to a state of glucocorticoid resistance. In such cases, proinflammatory cytokines such as TNF-alpha and macrophage inhibitory factor can modulate important isoforms of glucocorticoid receptors on cytokine-producing cells (Webster et al. 2001).

CNS coordination of health-relevant biological responses. Evidence for coordinated central pathways potentially linking stress to disease provides further impetus for a more integrative view (Chrousos and Gold

1992). Animal models suggest that one promising integrating mechanism may involve the activation and release of central corticotropin-releasing hormone (CRH) in emotion-based areas of the brain including the *amygdala, hypothalamus, and locus coeruleus (Dunn and Berridge 1990). Central administration of CRH mimics many of the physiological (e.g. autonomic activation, cortisol release) and behavioural states (e.g. freezing behaviour) seen during stress and the CRH receptor antagonist antalarmin attenuates such biological and behavioural responses (Habib *et al.* 2000). It is also important to emphasize, however, that there are critical afferent (ascending) pathways to brain structures that may be activated in stressful circumstances. For instance, Berntson *et al.* (2003b) have reviewed evidence for the role of the basal forebrain cholinergic system that can potentiate stress responses via such afferent connections.

Recent work in brain imaging (e.g. functional magnetic resonance imaging (fMRI), and positron emission tomography (PET)) is starting to provide converging evidence to animal models for the coordinated CNS structures responsible for more peripheral physiological activation in humans. Indeed, fMRI data across a variety of domains suggest that the amygdala may play an important role in emotional learning, emotional memory, and emotional influences on attention and perception (Phelps 2006). Recent research is also focusing on blood oxygen level-dependent (BOLD) fMRI activation of the prefrontal cortex and *anterior cingulate cortex as correlates of stress appraisals. These structures appear to modulate stress-induced activation of the amygdala with subsequent influences on more peripheral physiological activity (Ochsner *et al.* 2002, Gianaros *et al.* 2005). A model of the role of stress processes, basic CNS structures, and inflammatory processes discussed above is detailed in Fig. S5.

Integrative multilevel analysis of pathways. An examination of multilevel pathways responsible for stress effects on health is an emerging area of inquiry (see Fig. S6). Accordingly, the CNS and peripheral biological pathways depicted in Fig. S5 could be influenced by complementary social, personological, psychological, and behavioural levels of analyses (Cacioppo and Berntson 1992). An important aspect of Fig. S6 is that the different functional levels are embedded, and hence processes at more macrolevels can influence the more microlevel processes, and vice versa. An examination of such multilevel pathways can complement physiological approaches and provide a more integrative analysis of how stress may ultimately influence physical health. In fact, such multilevel approaches are highlighting the important role of social and contextual factors in the study of stress. For instance, social stressors (e.g. conflict) and dyadic processes (e.g. support/conflict within established couples) appear particularly important in explaining variations in health outcomes (Kiecolt-Glaser and Newton 2001).

Conclusions

The study of stress is evolving to emphasize more specific component processes in order to understand disease-relevant mechanisms. The modelling of such pathways is one of the most pressing issues in this literature. A second important trend relates to recent work on integrative processes (i.e. inflammation, CNS processes, multilevel analysis) that are starting to promote a more complete understanding of the influences of stress across disciplines. In fact, the future of stress research may hinge on our ability to bring these conceptual approaches together in order to advance

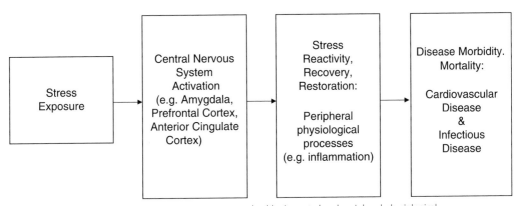

Fig. S5. Basic model linking stress component processes to health via central and peripheral physiological activation.

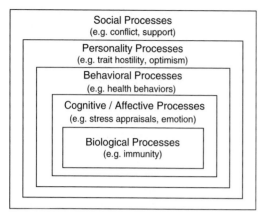

Fig. S6. Integrative multilevel perspective on factors influencing the links between stress and health.

basic models and highlight unique intervention approaches.

BERT N. UCHINO, JOHN M. RUIZ,
AND JULIANNE HOLT-LUNSTAD

Cacioppo, J.T. and Berntson, G.G. (2007). The brain, homeostasis, and health: balancing demands of the internal and external milieu. In: H. Friedman and R. Cohen Silver (eds), *Foundations of health psychology*, pp. 73–91. New York: Oxford University Press.

McEwen, B.S. and Seeman, T. (2003). Stress and affect: applicability to the concepts of allostasis and allostatic load. In: R.J. Davidson, K.R. Scherer, and H.H. Goldsmith (eds), *Handbook of affective sciences*, pp. 1117–38. New York: Oxford University Press.

Phan, K.L., Wager, T., Taylor, S.F., and Liberzon, I. (2002). Functional neuroanatomy of emotion: a meta-analysis of emotion activation studies in PET and fMRI. *NeuroImage*, **16**, 331–48.

Uchino, B.N., Smith, T.W., Holt-Lunstad, J.L., Campo, R., and Reblin, M. (2007). Stress and illness. In: J. Cacioppo, L. Tassinary, and G. Berntson (eds), *Handbook of psychophysiology*, 3rd edn, pp. 608–32. New York: Cambridge University Press.

superego In Freud's tripartite structural model of the mind, the superego is distinguished by the functions of self-observation and self-criticism (Freud 1923). It contains an ego-ideal, derived from early social and familial influences, towards which the individual strives. As the agency of conscience, it judges and punishes the self for failing to meet ideals or for transgressing boundaries (the fundamental conditions for shame and guilt). According

to psychoanalytic theory, it can operate unconsciously. See also EGO; ID.

JEROME NEU

surprise Common-sense psychology conceptualizes surprise as a peculiar state of mind, usually of brief duration, caused by encountering unexpected events of all kinds. Subjectively, surprise manifests itself in a characteristic phenomenal experience or 'feeling' (Reisenzein 2000a). Objectively, it may reveal itself—depending on the circumstances—in any of a number of behavioural indicators, including interruption or delay of ongoing motor activities, orienting of the sense organs to the surprising event, investigative activities such as visual search and questioning others, spontaneous verbal exclamations ('Oh!') and proclamations of being surprised, and a characteristic facial expression consisting, in full-blown form, of eyebrow-raising, eye-widening, and mouth-opening/jaw drop. Research has shown, furthermore, that surprising events may elicit various physiological changes, commonly subsumed under the so-called *orienting response*, such as a temporary slowing of heart rate and an increased activity of the eccrine sweat glands (Sokolov *et al.* 2002). It must be emphasized, however, that the behavioural manifestations of surprise occur by no means in all situations and are in general only loosely associated with one another (Reisenzein 2000b).

Theories of surprise seek to describe the mechanism(s) that underlie the feeling of surprise and surprise-related behaviours, and thereby to elucidate the causal generation of surprise, its nature, and its functional role in the architecture of the mind. To illustrate, we describe the outlines of the cognitive-psychoevolutionary model of surprise proposed by Meyer *et al.* (1997), which is intended as an integration and elaboration of the modal views of previous surprise theorists within the framework of schema theory. According to this model, the mental processes elicited by (ultimately) surprising events begin with (1) the appraisal of a cognized event as schema-discrepant or unexpected (see EXPECTATION; NOVELTY). If unexpectedness exceeds a threshold, it causes (2) the occurrence of a feeling of surprise and, simultaneously, the interruption of ongoing information processing and the reallocation of processing resources to the unexpected event. This is typically followed (3) by the analysis and evaluation of the unexpected event plus—if the results of this analysis indicate so—the updating of the relevant schemas (beliefs). The first two steps in this series of mental processes are identified with the workings of the surprise mechanism proper, which is taken to be a 'hardwired' schema-discrepancy detector that continuously compares—at a preconscious level of information processing—activated cognitive schemas with newly acquired information. It is assumed that the evolutionary function of the surprise mechanism is to *detect* schema-discrepant events and, if they are detected, to *enable and prepare* the processes of event analysis and schema update by interrupting ongoing processes and reallocating processing resources. The behavioural manifestations of surprise are interpreted as being either adaptive processes that, in one way or another, subserve the function of surprise (e.g. as argued by Darwin, eyebrow-raising may facilitate visual search); or as functionless side-effects of the mental surprise processes (e.g. behavioural interruption is a side-effect of mental interruption).

Meyer *et al.* (1997) assume that the immediate output of the schema-discrepancy detector is a nonpropositional signal (see Reisenzein 2000b) whose intensity codes the degree of schema discrepancy or unexpectedness. The subjective experience or 'feeling' of surprise may simply consist in the conscious awareness of this nonpropositional signal; however, it may also include other elements, such as a direct phenomenal awareness of mental interruption (see Reisenzein 2000b). In any case, the schema-discrepancy signal is the direct or indirect cause of all subsequent mental processes postulated by the cognitive-psychoevolutionary model of surprise (the feeling of surprise, interruption and attentional shift, event analysis, and schema revision), as well as of the various external manifestations of surprise—it is the causal hub in the wheel of surprise. Because of its central role, the discrepancy signal suggests itself as the best candidate for the scientific referent of surprise. That is, the *theoretical definition* of surprise suggested by the cognitive-psychoevolutionary model is: surprise is a nonpropositional signal that is the immediate output of the schema-discrepancy detector.

The cognitive processes involved in the detection of schema-discrepancies and the updating of schemas have recently been elucidated further in several computational models of surprise (e.g. Lorini and Castelfranchi 2007, Macedo and Cardoso, 2001, cited in Lorini and Castelfranchi, 2007).

In contrast to paradigmatic emotions such as joy or fear, surprise does not presuppose the appraisal of the eliciting event as positive (motive-congruent) or negative (motive-incongruent), and the feeling of surprise is *per se* hedonically neutral rather than pleasant or unpleasant (see MOTIVE CONSISTENCY). Mainly because of these differences from paradigmatic emotions, some emotion theorists refuse to classify surprise as an emotion. Note, however, that surprise is a component of several unquestioned emotional states, such as disappointment, relief, and shock; and that the intensity of most emotions is enhanced if their eliciting events occur unexpectedly. Furthermore, the cognitive mechanism that produces surprise (the *schema-discrepancy detector*)

and the mechanism that produces valenced emotions (the *concern-relevance detector*) may be partly integrated (e.g. they could work in parallel on the same inputs; Reisenzein 2000b) (see RELEVANCE DETECTION). For these and other reasons, surprise needs to be considered in theories of emotion, even if it is not itself classified as an emotion.

RAINER REISENZEIN AND WULF-UWE MEYER

synchronization (and emotion) In the affective sciences, the term 'synchronization' is mainly used to refer to the following two phenomena: (1) the establishment of some degree of coherence or synchronization of the different components of emotion during an emotional episode, organized as temporal and functional emergent patterns (see COMPONENTIAL THEORIES) and (2) the synchronization of neuronal assemblies at the central nervous system level, brought about by functional coupling of different close or distant neuronal populations. These two different phenomena are described below.

The main assumption of the component synchronization hypothesis is that emergent emotional processes and the concomitant feelings or emotional experience emerge as a function of a multilevel appraisal-driven response synchronization. Scherer (2001a, 2004) has proposed a componential patterning theory which attempts to predict specific changes in the peripheral subsystems that are brought about by concrete patterns of stimulus evaluation check (SEC) results (see COMPONENT PROCESS MODEL). The central assumption of the componential patterning theory is that the different organismal subsystems are highly interdependent and that changes in one subsystem will tend to elicit related changes in other subsystems in a recursive fashion. In consequence, the result of each consecutive check will differentially and cumulatively affect the state of all other subsystems. Due to the temporal organization of the appraisal processes, their efferent impact on peripheral, motivational, and motor components is likely to induce some degree of synchronization in these different subcomponents (see SEQUENCE OF APPRAISAL PROCESSES). This is functionally meaningful, as all resources of the organism are recruited to deal with the event that elicited the emotion. The central integration and representation of these synchronized patterns defines the feeling component, which has an important regulatory function. Subjective experience serves a monitoring function, integrating all information about the continuous patterns of change in all other components, as well as their coherence, and then building an integrative conscious representation. The feeling component can be described by a Venn diagram in which a set of overlapping circles represent its different aspects. It has been suggested that the degree of synchronization of the different components might be one of the factors that determines the emergence of consciousness in the emotion process (Grandjean *et al*. 2008).

At the cerebral level, the different neuronal assemblies underlying the processes related to the different components must continuously interact to be able to exchange information and to integrate the multiple representations related to the different components. Several pieces of evidence indicate that the neuronal synchronization of electrical activity between two or more neuronal assemblies is necessary to allow the communication between distant or local neuronal networks. In particular, Fries (2005) has proposed the communication through coherence (CTC) model, which implies that phase coherence underlies neuronal communication: neuronal assemblies have to be in synchronization to exchange information. Based on this model one can predict that central neuronal regions in emotional processes like the *amygdala and orbitofrontal areas have to be synchronized during an emotional episode to exchange information and thus contribute to the organization of the emotional reaction and its representation in terms of feeling. Previous findings suggest that neuronal synchronization may indeed be necessary to process emotional information. For example, Luo *et al*. (2007) report synchronization between the thalamus/hypothalamus and the amygdala in response to facial threat. Distant synchronization between hippocampus and amygdala has also been shown during various stages of fear memory (Narayanan *et al*. 2007). These empirical findings of neuronal synchronization in the human brain in response to emotional stimuli highlight the importance of the functional coupling between different distant and local neuronal assemblies and suggest continuous cross-talk between different brain regions during the processing of emotional stimuli (see NEURAL ARCHITECTURE OF EMOTION). The results of these studies can be interpreted as evidence that different neuronal assemblies, representing different levels of processing in the brain, work in conjunction to assess input of high significance for an individual. This suggestion is reminiscent of the assumption of massive parallel processing in neural network models, and is consistent with a recent proposal of a neural network model of emotional consciousness in which emotional coherence through interactions among multiple brain areas needs to be achieved for emotional consciousness to emerge (Thagard and Aubie, 2008). These synchronizations could occur at different levels, including local and distant neuronal synchronies. In this context it can be assumed that local synchronies, in a specific neuronal network, are necessary to achieve preliminary closure and send information to another neuronal network. For example, to process information relative to the state of the body during an emotional episode, the synchronization of neuronal assemblies inside the insula would be necessary. When a stable representation emerges from this neuronal network, the information might be sent to another part of the brain, for example to prefrontal brain areas (inducing a specific body representation in working memory). In this example, local synchronization is required to build a stable representation, and distant neuronal synchronization is required to exchange this information with another functional unit, in this case the body consciousness state in working memory. The local synchronies of the electrical activity of neuronal assemblies are expected to occur at a higher frequency range compared with the distant synchronies, which should occur at a lower frequency range (Fries 2005).

DIDIER GRANDJEAN AND KLAUS R. SCHERER

T

temperament Temperaments are usually defined as biologically based biases favouring particular feelings and actions observed during infancy and early childhood and shaped by the child's environment into a large, but nonetheless limited, number of personality profiles. Some primary qualities nominated as temperaments include the variation in the susceptibility to select feeling states, the intensity of those states, and the ability to regulate them (see PERSONALITY). It is generally believed that most temperamental biases are the result of heritable variation in brain chemistry, although some biases could be the result of variation in anatomy or prenatal events that were not strictly genetic. For example, a female embryo developing next to a male sibling is subject to the masculinizing effect of testosterone secreted by her brother between weeks 8 and 24 of gestation. As a result, the girl's style of play at the age four will resemble the play of boys rather than girls for they are usually more active and dominating than the average girl (Collaer and Hines 1995). Because the number of possible heritable brain profiles is large, there will necessarily be a very large number of temperamental biases and most remain undiscovered at the present time.

Two primary temperamental dimensions observed among infants are called reactivity and self-regulation (Rothbart 1999). Reactivity refers to the ease of arousal of motor activity, emotions, or brain systems. Self-regulation refers to processes that either facilitate or inhibit the infant's reactivity and include forms of attention, approach, or withdrawal to objects or people as well as a capacity for self-soothing.

The most extensive research on temperamental biases refers to the variation among infants and young children in their approach to or avoidance of unfamiliar people, objects, or situations (see ATTACHMENT). Similar variation has been noted in many animal species, including mice (Crabbe et al. 1999) and various breeds of dog (Scott and Fuller 1965). There is now a great deal of evidence indicating that variation in these classes of behaviour in the first or second year of life is preserved, to a modest degree, through adolescence (Kagan and Snidman 2004).

Many different chemical systems could influence these two temperamental biases, including serotonin, norepinephrine, opioids, and gamma-aminobutyric acid (GABA). However, the month in which conception occurs might have a subtle influence on these qualities. Melatonin, secreted by the pineal gland, is inhibited during daylight and secreted during darkness. Thus, if conception occurs at the end of summer (late July to September in the Northern Hemisphere), the mother will be secreting increasing amounts of melatonin as the embryo's brain is developing. Infants conceived during this season are more likely to be shy during the pre-school years compared with others (Gortmaker et al. 1997).

The *amygdala is an important structure that contributes to these temperamental biases because a basic property of the amygdala is a preparedness to receive information from the parahippocampal region indicating that a current event deviates from the immediate stimulus surround, the individual's long-term store of representations, or the context in which the event normally appears. These events create a state we might call 'alerted surprise' or 'vigilance'. States of *fear or *anxiety in humans are interpretations imposed on the thoughts provoked by unfamiliar events and accompanying bodily sensations. Fear and anxiety are not brain states but interpretations of the psychological products of those brain states. Because the amygdala reacts to unfamiliar events and sends projections to centres controlling motor activity and crying, infants with an excitable amygdala should show a great deal of vigorous thrashing of limbs and distress to unfamiliar events. These infants are called high-reactive, and about 20% of healthy, middle-class infants are classified as high-reactive. About 40% of infants show little motor activity and no distress to the same set of unfamiliar events, and they are called low-reactive.

A longitudinal study followed a large group of infants who were first classified at 4 months of age as high- or low-reactives, and then assessed many times until they were 15 years old (Kagan and Snidman 2004). At the age of 15 more high-reactive, compared with low-reactive, adolescents were emotionally subdued when interacting with unfamiliar adults and more likely to describe themselves as less happy and more serious than low-reactives. The two groups also differed in several biological measures that implicate an excitable amygdala. For example, the adolescents who had been high-reactive were more likely to show greater activation of the right, compared with the left, hemisphere, a larger brainstem auditory evoked potential in the inferior colliculus, greater sympathetic tone in the cardiovascular system, and a larger event-related potential waveform at 400 milliseconds to discrepant and unfamiliar scenes (Kagan and Snidman 2004).

An interesting difference between the two groups is that adolescents who had been classified as high-reactive at 4 months reported more serious concern over future events that were unpredictable and for which they believed they had no coping response. More high-reactives than low-reactives also had unrealistic worries and concerns, compared with the more realistic worries over academic performance or quality of extracurricular skills characteristic of low-reactives. The high-reactives were more vulnerable to spontaneous visceral feedback from targets in the autonomic nervous system which pierces consciousness to create uncertainty because its origin is ambiguous. This feeling resembles the state that occurs when young children encounter unfamiliar people or situations.

It is likely that research over the next 20 years will uncover three new sets of facts. First, we will learn of many more infant temperamental biases and begin to understand how the rearing environment shapes each bias into an envelope of personality types. Second, scientists will discover the genetic foundations for some of the temperaments and the neurophysiological signs that are derivatives of the person's genome (see GENETICS OF AFFECT). Finally, it is likely that following the expansion of the Human Genome Project to diverse populations reproductively isolated groups, such as Asians, Europeans, South Americans, and Africans, will have distinctive profiles of temperamental biases.

JEROME KAGAN

Kagan, J. and Fox, N.A. (2006). Biology, culture, and temperamental biases. In: N. Eisenberg (ed.), *Handbook of child psychology: social, emotional, and personality development*, 6th edn, pp. 167–225 (series editors W. Damon and R. Lerner). New York: John Wiley.

Kagan, J. and Snidman, N. (2004). *The long shadow of temperament*. Cambridge, MA: Harvard University Press.

tension A recent psychology dictionary (Corsini, 2002) defines tension in part as 'a feeling of physical and psychological strain accompanied by discomfort, uneasiness, and pressure to seek relief...'. Another dictionary (Reber 1985) speaks of 'An emotional state characterized by restlessness, anxiety, excitement, and a general, diffuse preparedness to act'. In general, definitions deal with both muscular and subjective tension. Tension has a long history in psychology, dating back to Wilhelm Wundt (1832–1920), Kurt Lewin (1890–1947), and Sigmund Freud (1856–1939) among others.

My own approach to understanding tension (e.g. Thayer 1989) focuses particularly on tense arousal and energetic arousal, the two most basic dimensions of mood (similar to negative and positive affect) (see AROUSAL; MOOD). Tense arousal is a broadly inclusive mood system that includes biochemical and physiological systems of arousal at various levels, including systems of the brain and conscious awareness at the highest level. The conscious experience of tension, including *anxiety and *fear and related feelings, reflects the underlying physiological arousal. Tense arousal is a kind of 'stop system' denoting caution or inhibition as opposed to energetic arousal which is a 'go system' predisposing directed action or engagement.

When considering tension on the physiological level one of the most important elements of arousal is skeletal-muscular tension (especially as differentiated from energetic arousal). In times of danger, real or imagined, we experience what I call the 'activated freeze response'. This generalized muscular inhibition occurs before the well-known 'fight or flight' response and often accounts for chronic bodily discomforts including back, neck, and jaw pain that occurs from persistent muscle tension.

Tense and energetic arousal are sometimes thought to be orthogonal or independent based on psychometric studies that sample the full range of states, but actually the two arousal systems are positively and negatively correlated at different levels of activation. For example, as tension increases from low to moderate levels, energy also increases (positive correlation), but at some point if tension increases further energy begins to decline (negative correlation). When tension and energy are both at high levels, the mood state is called 'tense energy' and this is a moderately pleasant and somewhat productive condition that is quite prevalent in a culture involving stress. But when tension is high and energy is low through depletion of resources, a state called 'tense tiredness' is experienced. The mood of tense tiredness is unpleasant (cf. *depression) and people often try to self-regulate the feelings, sometimes in undesirable ways including by overeating and using drugs of choice, but a wide variety of other behaviours also are commonly used to self-regulate this state (Thayer et al. 1993, Thayer 2001) (see REGULATION OF EMOTION). Compared to the unpleasant mood of tense tiredness, the most optimal mood state is 'calm energy', and this occurs when tension is low and energy is high.

On a cognitive level, tension often results in distracted as opposed to directed attention. It predisposes a kind of wide-ranging *vigilance as if searching for the source of the danger, and when the source of danger is not apparent (as in generalized anxiety) attention to anything other than the danger appears distracted. Energetic arousal, on the other hand, predisposes focused and directed attention for the task at hand. In the tense tired state, problems appear more serious and pessimism about the future prevails, but in a calm energetic state the same problems may appear more solvable and a general optimism prevails (Thayer 1987).

ROBERT E. THAYER

Thayer, R.E. (1989). *The biopsychology of mood and arousal.* New York: Oxford University Press.

theories and models of emotion see AFFECT PROGRAMS; APPRAISAL THEORIES; ATTRIBUTION THEORY; BASIC EMOTIONS; BRUNSWIKIAN LENS MODEL; CANNON–BARD THEORY; CIRCUMPLEX MODELS; COMPONENT PROCESS MODEL; COMPONENTIAL THEORIES; COMPUTATIONAL MODELS; CONNECTIONIST MODELS; DIFFERENTIAL EMOTIONS THEORY; DIMENSIONAL MODELS; DYNAMIC SYSTEMS THEORY; EMBODIMENT; EMOTION THEORIES AND CONCEPTS (PHILOSOPHICAL PERSPECTIVES); EMOTION THEORIES AND CONCEPTS (PSYCHOLOGICAL PERSPECTIVES); FUNCTIONALIST THEORIES OF EMOTION; JAMES–LANGE THEORY; SCHACHTER–SINGER THEORY.

theory of mind and emotion Research on theory of mind accelerated rapidly in the 1980s. The initial focus was on when children start to realize that someone's actions can be guided by a false belief as well as by a true belief (see BELIEFS). Early experiments established that this insight emerges at around 4 years of age. Thus, 4- and 5-year-olds typically understand that a person who has not witnessed the movement of an object to a new location will mistakenly search for it where they last put it. By contrast, 3-year-olds ignore the key role of the searcher's false belief. They predict that the person will search at the new location even though he or she has not seen the object's displacement. This developmental change is now well established, even if its interpretation remains controversial (Wellman *et al.* 2001). Indeed, an understanding of false beliefs probably typically emerges among all normal children, irrespective of culture, provided they suffer from no developmental psychopathology, such as *autism. There is also considerable evidence that most children arrive at an understanding of *desires and *goals in advance of an understanding of beliefs. For example, 2- and 3-year-old children understand that people vary in their desires, and they talk explicitly about such variation before they acknowledge comparable variation in beliefs.

Desires and beliefs determine people's emotions as well as their actions. Research in the 1990s showed that preschool children also understand these causal links. Thus, 3- and 4-year-olds realize that the same situation can make one person happy but another person sad, depending on the particular desires that each individual brings to that situation. In addition, 5- and 6-year-olds realize that beliefs, true or false, determine a person's emotion. For example,

they correctly predict that Little Red Riding Hood, knocking on the door of her grandmother's cottage, will feel happy rather than afraid; they take into account her mistaken belief that she will find her grandmother inside the cottage even though they themselves know that a wolf awaits her (Harris *et al.* 1989).

Preschoolers also come to understand the connection between memory, thinking, and emotion. They realize that an encounter that reminds a person of a past event is likely to re-evoke the emotion associated with that event. Indeed, 5- and 6-year-olds not only anticipate the particular emotion that a reminder will evoke, they can explain that emotion in light of the thoughts that are triggered by the reminder (Lagattuta and Wellman 2001). They also realize, conversely, that the gradual waning of many emotions is associated with forgetting about, or not thinking about, the event that originally gave rise to them.

Other insights into the mental determinants of emotion are less likely to be mastered in the preschool period. For example, it is only in the elementary school period that children show a systematic understanding of the way in which the same situation can elicit more or less concurrent and conflicting feelings, given that it can be appraised from different perspectives. Similarly, an understanding of the self-appraisal processes that underlie the *social emotions (e.g. pride and guilt) is rarely attained by preschoolers (Pons and Harris 2005).

Current research on children's understanding of mind and emotion has increasingly focused on individual differences among normal children. A provocative pattern of findings has emerged (Harris *et al.* 2005). Several lines of evidence suggest that children's facility at, and access to, verbal communication plays a key role in helping children to understand the mental processes that determine emotion (see LANGUAGE AND EMOTION). First, children with superior language skills perform better on tests of mental state understanding. Second, deaf children display either a delayed understanding of mental states if they are deprived of early access to normal communication (as a result of being born into a nonsigning, hearing family) but a normal understanding if they have access to such communication (as a result of being born into a fluently signing family). Third, mothers who are prone to engage in discussion of mental states are more likely to have children with an advanced understanding of mind and emotion. Finally, recent short-term training studies have shown that verbal intervention can promote children's understanding of mental states.

PAUL L. HARRIS

Harris, P.L. (2006). Social cognition. In: W. Damon, R. Lerner, D. Kuhn, and R, Siegler (eds), *Handbook of child psychology, volume 2: cognition, perception and language,* 6th edition, pp. 811–58. New York: John Wiley.

trust

Harris P.L. (2008). Children's understanding of emotion. In: M. Lewis, J. Haviland-Jones, and L. Feldman Barrett (eds), *Handbook of emotions*, 3rd edn, pp. 320–31. New York: Guilford Press.

trust Trust is an elementary component of social and economic life (see ECONOMICS (ROLE OF EMOTION IN)). Trust is indispensable in friendship, love, families, and organizations; it plays a decisive role in economic transactions and politics. In general, trust is valuable 'as it saves a lot of trouble to have a fair degree of reliance on other people's word' (Arrow 1974, p. 23). With regard to economics, the importance of trust derives from the fact that it reduces transaction costs and enhances efficiency if third parties' (courts) enforce contracts imperfectly. If institutions cannot guarantee compliance with contractual agreements, trust among trading partners allows for an efficient processing of economic transactions. The absence of trust, in contrast, forces people to take costly precautions and may therefore inhibit trade.

Definition of trust

There is a lingering ambiguity in the literature with regard to the formal definition of trust. The uncontested opinion is that trust refers to a subclass of decisions under risk (see RISK-TAKING), where the distinct feature is that the risk of the decision depends on another actor's performance. However, while some authors define trust as the trustor's expectation about whether the potential trustee will exploit his or her vulnerability, others define trust as the behaviour that follows from this belief. Since the belief-oriented definition refers to a person's internal state that is hard to measure, most empirical studies concentrate on the behavioural definition of trust. Coleman (1990) provides four points that characterize a trust decision: (1) The trustor's placement of trust allows an action on the part of the trustee that would not have been possible otherwise. (2) If the trustee is trustworthy, the trustor who places trust is better off than one who does not do so, whereas if the trustee is not trustworthy, the trustor is worse off than one who had not trusted. (3) The action placing trust involves the trustor's voluntary commitment of resources to the trustee's disposal, without any real commitment from that other party. (4) There is a time lag between the extension of trust and the consequence of the trusting behaviour.

Measurement of trust

For a long time, empirical studies on trust exclusively relied on questionnaires. The typical measurement of trust was obtained by analysing responses to the following question: 'Generally speaking, would you say that most people can be trusted or that you can't be too careful in dealing with people?'. This question is taken from the National Opinion Research Center's General Social Survey (GSS). The same or slightly modified versions of the question are, however, also used in many other surveys (see, for example, the World Bank's Integrated Questionnaire for the Measurement of Social Capital). However, although the survey approach is widely applied, its validity in measuring trust has been challenged in the literature. One drawback of the GSS trust question is that the responses are very hard to interpret (see also Glaeser *et al.* 2000). The question not only leaves the definition of 'other people' open, it also fails to specify what kind of trust is addressed in which situations. It has therefore been argued that variations in responses do not necessarily reflect differences in the exhibited amount of trust but can also be due to different perceptions of the question itself. Furthermore, as questionnaires do not provide any incentives for answering truthfully, there is always the danger that people's responses are biased.

More recently, economists and psychologists have started measuring trust in controlled laboratory experiments such as the gift exchange game (Fehr *et al.* 1993) and the trust game (Berg *et al.* 1995), where the participants' choices determine their monetary income. In a gift exchange game, the trustor offers a fixed payment (a 'wage') to the trustee, who can then choose among several actions ('effort levels') that are costly for him or her and yield a benefit for the trustor. Typically, a higher effort level is associated with higher costs for the trustee and larger benefits for the trustor, while the effort cost of any effort level is much lower than the associated benefit for the trustee. However, the trustor's receipt of the benefit in exchange for his or her wage payment is not guaranteed, as effort is costly. A typical trust game has the following structure: At the beginning of the experiment both the trustor and the trustee receive an endowment of E units of money. Trustor's must decide how much of their endowment they want to transfer to the trustee. The experimenter triples any amount $x \in (0, E)$ transferred and passes the ensuing amount to the trustee. The trustee is then free to return any amount $y \in (0, 3x)$ to the trustor. The trustor's payoff is therefore calculated as $E - x + y$, while the trustee earns $E + 3x - y$. These games have several advantages: First, despite their simplicity, they capture Coleman's four constituting characteristics of trust precisely. Second, in contrast to questionnaires, they provide a behavioural measure of trust in terms of the trustors' wage payments or transfers to the trustee. Third, the games provide the participants with salient incentives to reveal their true preferences.

In general, the evidence from gift exchange and trust game experiments reveals that most trustors exhibit some trust by transferring money to the trustee and expect the trustees to reciprocate by choosing positive effort levels or

392

back-transfers; many trustees meet this expectation and choose positive effort levels or send back a positive amount. Moreover, the trustors' actions and the trustees' back-transfers are often correlated positively. In the meantime, many variations of the gift exchange and the trust game have been played in various places around the world. An extensive survey of how cultural differences and modifications of the design affect the results in these games can be found in Camerer (2003).

Biological basis of trust

Most recently, the trust game was also used to investigate the biological basis of trust among humans. Kosfeld *et al.* (2005) show that the administration of oxytocin, a neuropeptide that plays a key role in social attachment and affiliation, causes a significant increase in trust among humans.

ERNST FEHR AND
CHRISTIAN ZEHNDER

U

uncertainty The *appraisal dimension of uncertainty* is a cognitive appraisal dimension that represents the extent to which individuals perceive situations as predictable, understandable, and assured (Ellsworth and Scherer 2003). Some emotions (e.g. *anger and *happiness) are associated with greater certainty, whereas other emotions (e.g. *fear and *surprise) are associated with greater uncertainty (Smith and Ellsworth 1985). Emotions with high levels of uncertainty have been linked with increased depth of information processing (see LEVELS OF PROCESSING) and increased perception of risk. By contrast, emotions with high levels of certainty have been linked with decreased depth of information processing (Tiedens and Linton 2001) and decreased perception of risk (Lerner and Keltner 2001).

Judgement under uncertainty can be defined as a judgement circumstance in which the probabilities associated with potential outcomes are unknown (see Knight 1921). Judgement under uncertainty is commonly distinguished from judgement under risk, which describes a circumstance in which the probabilities associated with potential outcomes are known. In a classic paper, Daniel Ellsberg (1961) argued that people prefer to avoid uncertain situations (in which probabilities of potential outcomes are unknown) in favour of risky situations (in which probabilities of potential outcomes are known) and that the desire to avoid uncertainty can lead to inconsistent preferences. This pattern of inconsistent preferences, termed the 'Ellsberg paradox', received great attention in economics and psychology because it highlighted a preference pattern that violates rational economic standards.

CYNTHIA E. CRYDER AND JENNIFER S. LERNER

unconscious emotions An emotion is many splendid things, but more technically, it is an orchestrated response to a significant event across several systems—perceptual, cognitive, motivational, expressive, bodily, and experiential (Barrett *et al.* 2005) (see COMPONENTIAL THEORIES). The question of which components of the response can be unconscious has a long history in emotion research. It goes back to Darwin (1809–82), who described several 'instinctive' (fast, rigid, involuntary) emotional behaviours and speculated about their origins in nonconscious creatures. On the other hand, William

James (1842–1910) emphasized that a conscious *feeling (a change in a subjective state) is essential for calling a state an emotion (see JAMES–LANGE THEORY). So, can an emotion be unconscious? There are several reasons why modern researchers are inclined to consider this possibility (Kihlstrom *et al.* 2000, Winkielman and Berridge 2004).

Evolutionarily speaking, the original function of emotion was to simply allow appropriate reactions to positive or negative events (see EVOLUTION OF EMOTION). Accordingly, basic emotional reactions are widely shared by animals, including reptiles and fish. The evolutionarily old neurocircuitry and neurochemistry underlying basic emotional reactions (fear, liking) is contained primarily in subcortical brain structures, such as the *amygdala, nucleus accumbens, hypothalamus, and even brainstem parabrachial nucleus and pons (Berridge 2003b). In fact, the most effective neural manipulations of basic emotional reactions involve physical or chemical interventions into subcortical structures. For example, in animal studies, brain microinjections of drug droplets that activate opioid receptors in subcortical nucleus accumbens cause increased 'liking' responses for sweetness (Berridge 2003b). Importantly, these effects do not depend on 'higher-order' neural machinery. For example, in anencephalic infants, whose brains lack nearly all of the forebrain including the entire neocortex, sweet tastes still elicit positive facial expressions whereas bitter tastes elicit negative facial expressions (Berridge 2003b). In short, affective neuroscience highlights the role of subcortical structures in basic emotional reactions. This raises the possibility that even in humans some causes of emotion, and perhaps even some emotional reactions themselves, might not be accessible to conscious awareness.

The data from psychological experiments with typical participants support this possibility. Regarding unconscious elicitation of emotion, there is now extensive evidence that affect, and perhaps even emotion-like states, can be triggered with subliminal stimuli such as geometric shapes in a mere-exposure paradigm (Zajonc 2000), fear-related images, such as snakes, spiders, or aversively conditioned faces and symbols (Öhman *et al.* 2000b). Some of these effects may require nothing more than low-level pattern-matching and associative processes with minimal computational requirements (Zajonc 2000). But other phenomena of unconscious elicitation may in fact reflect some form of unconscious appraisals, though there is a debate to what extent novel, meaning-based computations can occur without awareness (see AUTOMATIC APPRAISAL).

But can an emotional reaction itself be unconscious? Evidence suggests that, at least under some circumstances, people are unable to report a conscious feeling at the same time a consequential behaviour reveals the presence of an affective reaction. For example, in one series of studies, participants were unobtrusively exposed to several happy or angry subliminal emotional facial expressions (Winkielman *et al.* 2005b). Immediately after the subliminal elicitation of affect, participants reported their conscious feelings (mood and arousal) and also consumed and rated a novel drink. The ratings of conscious feelings were unaffected by subliminal faces. However, participants consumed more drink after happy rather than after angry faces, and rated it more favourably. Not only was their overt behaviour indicative of affective change, but follow-up studies using psychophysiological measures, such as *startle and facial *electromyography, revealed that responses of participants' low-level approach/avoidance systems were influenced in an affect-congruent way by the subliminal faces. In short, these results suggest the possibility of genuinely unconscious affect, in the sense of a valenced (positive/negative) reaction that is strong enough to alter behaviour and physiology, but of which people are not subjectively aware.

Of course, many questions remain. Current research in several laboratories is investigating whether the crucial property of unconscious states is simply positive–negative *valence (unconscious affect), or whether there are unconscious states that drive behaviour in differentiated fashion associated with specific emotions (fear, anger, disgust, sadness, etc). The current research also examines what exact psychological and neural mechanisms determine whether an emotional reaction remains unconscious or is accompanied by conscious feelings.

Finally, it is worth emphasizing the enormous role of conscious feelings in emotion research and clinical practice. For example, few patients complain of unconscious sadness, and few addicts take drugs to become unconsciously happy. On the other hand, clinicians know that, for example, pharmacological interventions into affective neurochemistry can sometimes influence emotional behaviour even before they influence conscious emotional experience. In sum, it appears that behavioural, physiological, and cognitive components of emotion can be, at least occasionally, separate from conscious feelings. Future research in human and animal affective

neuroscience will help us better understand the relation between conscious and unconscious components of emotion.

PIOTR WINKIELMAN AND KENT C. BERRIDGE

Barrett, L.F., Niedenthal, P.M., and Winkielman, P. (eds) (2005). *Emotion and consciousness.* New York: Guilford Press.
Winkielman, P. and Berridge, K.C. (2004). Unconscious emotion. *Current Directions in Psychological Science,* **13**, 120–123.

unipolar disorder The term unipolar disorder refers to one half of a distinction that has proven of use in the classification of disorders of *depression, in which the second half of the distinction is referred to as *bipolar disorder. A distinction between 'monopolar and bipolar disorders' was first made by the German psychiatrist Karl Leonhard (1904–88) in the 1950s, but was renamed by the Italian psychiatrist Carlo Perris (1928–2000) and others as 'unipolar and bipolar disorders' and it is the term 'unipolar disorder' that has now come into widespread use.

The distinction refers primarily to whether or not someone who suffers from episodes of depression also suffers from episodes of *mania or *hypomania. That is, in the unipolar disorders there is an absence of the extreme mood swings that are seen in the bipolar disorders. Evidence in favour of the distinction comes from a number of sources: from studies of the genetics of the disorders, with there being a significantly lower genetic contribution to unipolar than to bipolar disorders; the course and outcome of the disorders tends to be more severe in the bipolar disorders; the epidemiology of unipolar disorders shows considerable variation across the lifespan and across gender in contrast to the epidemiology for the bipolar disorders; and the disorders tend to respond to different types of pharmacotherapy.

The distinction between unipolar and bipolar, although it has proven of some use both clinically and in research, is nevertheless a descriptive rather than theoretically based distinction. As such, it may be susceptible to future revisions in the psychiatric classification systems as further developments are made in genetics and the affective neurosciences that allow for theoretically based classification.

MICHAEL J. POWER

Perris, C. (1992). The distinction between unipolar and bipolar mood disorders. A 25-years perspective. *Encephale,* **18**, 9–13.

universality of emotions Emotions are neither completely universal nor completely variable across cultures and individuals, and the question of universality involves several different issues: (1) the events that give rise to emotions, (2) the appraisal or evaluation of these events, (3) the emotional reactions, and (4) the communication of feelings. It is important to distinguish between *potential* or capacity and competence on the one hand, and *practice* or performance on the other (Mesquita *et al.* 1997). *Potential* is part of the capacity of the human organism, and thus concerns perceptions of events and patterns of response that are available to all individuals. However, only some of this potential is actually realized, due to lack of opportunity or normative control. *Practice* refers to the actual occurrence of particular emotional reactions in a particular culture or individual and may be shaped by experience, values, norms, habits, or environmental constraints that elicit certain appraisals of events, and subsequent emotional reactions (see APPRAISAL THEORIES). The issue of culture-dependent *regulation* of emotion expression and communication is of central importance in this respect (see DISPLAY RULES). Cross-cultural research in psychology has frequently focused on the potential for certain correlates of emotion (e.g. the ability to recognize facial expressions produced by members of another culture; Ekman 1993), leaving aside questions about the use of such skills in particular social contexts, the frequency of observed expressions, or the importance assigned to such signals. In contrast, anthropologists and ethnologists have generally concentrated on the particular practices of emotion in the people they have studied, i.e. the actual occurrence of emotional reactions and their social meaning (Briggs 1970, Abu-Lughod 1985), being less concerned with potential. Psychologists have generally looked for universals, anthropologists for cultural differences. Cultural differences often concern practice rather than potential. Thus, Levy (1984b) has suggested that they often result from under- or overemphasizing the cognitions that are related to certain antecedent events and the resulting emotions.

In most cross-cultural research on emotion, the existence of individual differences in emotional experience and expression *within* a given culture is neglected. People from small tribal societies are compared with Western city dwellers, without regard for the possible existence of similar—albeit less pronounced—differences between rural villages and major urban centres in Western countries, or between different socioeconomic strata. Furthermore, much evidence for cross-cultural differences is based on informant reports rather than on objective assessments. As languages differ in the way in which they cut up the emotional semantic space, one must beware of interpreting differences in emotion words across languages as evidence for underlying differences in reactions or feelings (see LANGUAGE AND EMOTION). Also, some emotions may be unacceptable in a particular culture, so that informants may be reluctant to admit that they recognize them.

Antecedent events

Emotions are generally considered to be elicited by specific events (Scherer 2005). Thus, it is important to examine differences in the frequency with which particular types of event actually occur in particular cultures: cultural differences in emotional reactions may be due to the differential occurrence of certain types of events rather than to fundamental differences in the process of elicitation. Cross-cultural studies have shown similarities and differences in the nature and frequency of certain emotion-eliciting situations across cultures living in dangerous or comparatively safe environments, for example (see also Scherer 1997).

The 'same' event (e.g. winning a contest, leaving home) may not have the same meaning in different cultures, and may have different consequences for the individual and elicit different *action tendencies. Situations that seem highly similar can be interpreted differently across cultures, and thus elicit different emotions. For example, 'being alone' may be interpreted as social isolation in cultures in which social contact is essential for survival, whereas city dwellers often see it as a welcome opportunity for privacy and contemplation. Similarly, a child's illness may be seen as an instance of bad luck, or as the work of evil spirits, or as a sign of one's own carelessness, producing sorrow, fear, or guilt. The determining factor for the emotion evoked is the subjective interpretation (appraisal) of the event.

Appraisal processes

Appraisal theories of emotion suggest that people interpret, evaluate, or appraise an event with respect to a number of criteria or dimensions related to the significance of the event to them and their ability to cope with its consequences. Theorists in this tradition predict, in a highly convergent manner, different profiles of appraisal outcomes as necessary conditions for the occurrence of specific emotions. For example, a person who is warned that someone intends to hurt him or her will feel anger if the chances of successful retaliation are high, but fear if they are low.

One way to study appraisal cross-culturally is to ask respondents to remember powerful emotional experiences and to describe the appraisals that accompanied the emotion. Scherer and Wallbott (1994) and Scherer (1997) asked nearly three thousand respondents from 37 countries to recall episodes for each of seven major emotions. The results show strong similarities for emotion-specific appraisal profiles across geopolitical regions, suggesting that the appraisal process—as a capacity—may indeed be universal. Furthermore, the profiles empirically found by this study largely correspond to the theoretical predictions made by appraisal theorists.

According to the hypothesis of *universal contingency* (Ellsworth 1991), if people in different cultures appraise an event in the same way, they will feel the same emotion: differences in emotional experience are due to differences in appraisal. Consistent with this hypothesis, in addition to the evidence for common appraisal–emotion links across cultures, the study by Scherer and colleagues also found sizable differences across geopolitical regions with respect to *practice* (e.g. in the way in which appraisal dimensions are used). For example, respondents in African countries tended to appraise events as being more immoral, more unfair or unjust, and more externally caused than the respondents in all other countries, which Scherer (1997) tentatively explained by the prevalence of sorcery and witchcraft beliefs in the African countries studied. Anthropologists have shown that in these countries misfortunes are commonly attributed to witches, who are morally reprehensible external agents. Other studies have confirmed that appraisal processes in general show a high degree of similarity, except for socially significant appraisal dimensions such as agency, morality, or justice—where considerable cultural differences are found. Thus, Mauro *et al.* (1992) found few differences between the United States, Japan, the People's Republic of China, and Hong Kong for the more 'primitive' dimensions, such as pleasantness, certainty, coping ability, and goal/need conduciveness, but quite pronounced differences for more complex appraisal dimensions such as responsibility. It is possible to explain these cultural differences in appraisal—at least partly—as differences in practice (i.e. the propensity to use certain appraisal dimensions). Thus, there is evidence that in some cultures (e.g. Japan) the assignment of responsibility for an event to a person is used sparingly (Solomon 1978, Matsumoto *et al.* 1988, Scherer *et al.* 1988, Mauro *et al.* 1992). In a survey of the role of culture in appraisal, Mesquita and Ellsworth (2003) concluded that the mediation of cultural differences in emotion by differences in patterns of appraisal is an important direction for further research, in particular the existence of culture-specific appraisals and the salience or accessibility of specific appraisal dimensions.

Reaction patterns

One of the major issues of debate is whether there are prototypical neurophysiological changes, motor expressions, motivational tendencies, and subjective feelings for different emotions, and whether these are universal or culture dependent. Unfortunately, there still is very little empirical research that examines intense real-life emotions with respect to these response patterns and compares them across cultures.

Theories of *basic emotions postulate specific, unique patterns of responses for each of a small number of emotions. Levenson (2003) strongly advocates this position, hypothesizing that the typical physiological response patterns in the peripheral or autonomic nervous system are universal. Levenson *et al.* (1992) tested this hypothesis with young Minangkabau men in West Sumatra. While the results did not completely replicate earlier findings with American college students, the researchers interpret the overall pattern as support for the existence of pancultural physiological differentiation in the basic emotions. However, Mesquita *et al.* (1997) pointed out that, even if physiological response mechanisms are cross-culturally similar, there may be differences with respect to practice (e.g. in the degree to which certain responses are suppressed or amplified in accordance with cultural *norms). For example, among the Bedouins in the Egyptian desert anger is considered to be a sign of strength and masculine honour, whereas it may be seen as a sign of immaturity or lack of control in some Western cultures. In some studies respondents are asked to describe the physiological symptoms that accompanied a remembered emotional experience. The available evidence suggests a high degree of similarity across cultures in emotion-specific physiological symptom reports, although this may be, at least in part, an effect of shared stereotypes (Scherer and Wallbott 1994). Cultural differences might reflect the likelihood that specific symptoms are noticed more, and therefore talked about more, in some cultures than in others. Another influence may be the existence of cultural norms that regulate the reporting of such bodily symptoms.

Expression has been by far the most frequently studied component of emotion in cross-cultural research (see EXPRESSION, PRINCIPLES OF EMOTIONAL). While all other emotion components are often difficult to discern, facial and vocal expression are readily observable and can be analysed objectively. One can also obtain an indirect test of the universality hypothesis by studying whether people in different cultures can recognize expressions produced by members of other cultures (from photographs of facial expressions or sound recordings of vocal expressions). The vast majority of cross-cultural research on expression since the 1960s has indeed been concerned with the pancultural recognition of emotion. While there are differences in the degree of accuracy with which members of Western and non-Western (particularly preliterate) cultures recognize emotional experiences, the general level of accuracy across cultures greatly exceeds what would be expected if the responses were due to chance (i.e. guessing). Elfenbein and Ambady (2002) showed via a meta-analysis of studies on emotion recognition within and across cultures that emotions were universally recognized at better-than-chance levels but that accuracy was higher when emotions were both expressed and recognized by members of the same national, ethnic, or regional group, suggesting an in-group advantage. On the whole, this strongly suggests the existence of a universal potential for emotion communication. Again, the practice of expression may well differ across cultures, and various culture-specific bodily expressions have been documented by ethologists and anthropologists (Eibl-Eibesfeldt 1989, Menon and Shweder 1994).

Thus, the available evidence points to the existence of a universal core of emotional expressions in face, voice, and body that may be based on a combination of the appraisal of emotion-eliciting situations, psychophysiological adaptations, action tendencies or behavioural intentions, and communicative signalling. However, there is an extraordinary flexibility in this expressive system, allowing for a large number of individual, contextual, and cultural variations in expressive behaviour. Part of this variability is due to the fact that expressions are influenced by both 'push effects'—the spontaneous psychophysiological changes occurring in a situation—and 'pull effects'—the social and cultural rules guiding personal behaviour in a specific context (see PUSH/PULL EFFECTS).

One of the major components of emotion is motivational change, the emergence of a particular action tendency or action readiness (e.g. approach, withdrawal and avoidance, rejection, help-seeking, hostility, breaking contact, dominance, and submission; Frijda 1986). There are very few cross-cultural studies of action readiness patterns, but they confirm the general findings of other approaches—there is a solid core of universality with a number of interesting cross-cultural differences (Scherer and Wallbott 1994, Frijda et al. 1995). For example, more than other groups, Japanese report a wish to depend on someone else, as well as apathy, feelings of helplessness, and urges to protect themselves. Markus and Kitayama (1994) proposed that these findings reflect the value placed on interdependence and acceptance by others in Japan.

Subjective emotional experience (*feelings) can be defined as a reflection of the changes in all of the other emotion components (i.e. appraisal of the situation, physiological changes, motor expression, and action tendencies). Using verbal report, one can attempt to assess some of the major aspects or dimensions of subjective experience and to determine their similarities and differences across cultures. Among the most readily measurable aspects are the perceived duration and intensity of different types of emotions. The large-scale study conducted by Scherer and his collaborators found that most of the variance in these aspects is due to differences among emotions, but that a sizable amount of the variation is also accounted for by cultural differences. Thus, people in poorer countries (particularly those located close to the equator) report longer durations for all emotional experiences. One possible ex-

planation is that because of a slower pace of life and fewer external diversions, emotion processes in those countries are less likely to be interrupted or superseded by new events (Scherer 1997).

Other dimensions are experienced valence or hedonic tone (pleasure versus pain), activity or arousal, and degree of tension. The first two of these dimensions have been reliably found across cultures in people's responses to emotion words, similarities of facial expressions, and emotional experiences (Russell et al. 1989) (see CIRCUMPLEX MODELS). This provides evidence that subjective experience can be mapped onto two or three comparable dimensions across different cultures. Fontaine et al. (2007) confirmed the intercultural stability, but suggested that four dimensions (valence, power/control, arousal, unpredictability) are needed to define the emotional space.

Affect dimensions are very general and do not represent the richness and detail of subjective emotional experience. Subjective experience or feeling is nonlinguistic much of the time—often people try to find the word for a feeling only when they are required to talk about it. Although there are rather close synonyms for many emotion words across languages, many languages have names for emotions that other cultures do not label, such as the famous example of Japanese 'amae'. In consequence, an important area of cross-cultural comparison concerns emotion words or expressions, including metaphors (see METAPHOR; LANGUAGE AND EMOTION).

Conclusion

It seems reasonable to assume that emotions consist of psychobiological building blocks that constitute a universally shared potential to react in specific ways to important life events. In practice, these building blocks are assembled according to rules and practices that can be highly culture specific, particularly with respect to how the subjective experiences are verbally communicated to others. Although the research shows that all components of emotion can show strong cross-cultural variations, researchers have only begun to study the cultural factors that determine these variations. Socioeconomic variables, history, demographic factors, social structure, norms, values, expectations, socialization, personality, linguistic background, and patterns of interpersonal interaction are all potential determinants of cultural differences in emotion practice. Only a more systematic exploration of the role that these factors play in emotion will allow researchers to understand the sources of cross-cultural variations in emotional processes.

KLAUS R. SCHERER AND PHOEBE C. ELLSWORTH

Mesquita, B., Frijda, N.H., and Scherer, K.R. (1997). Culture and emotion. In: J.E. Berry, P.B. Dasen, and T.S. Saraswathi (eds),

Handbook of cross-cultural psychology: Vol. 2. Basic processes and developmental psychology, pp. 255–97. Boston, MA: Allyn and Bacon.

Scherer, K.R. and Wallbott, H. (1994). Evidence for universality and cultural variation of differential emotion response-patterning. *Journal of Personality and Social Psychology*, **66**, 310–28.

urgency Urgency is a feeling about impending actions and events. This feeling reflects the imminence, likelihood, and importance of changes in the state of the self and the world. It is experienced intensely when our prospects hinge on the performance or suppression of time-critical actions, such as arriving at the day-care centre before closing time or remaining motionless while hiding within earshot of approaching footsteps.

Urgency is rooted in both implicit and explicit predictions about events, opportunities, and threats. Implicit predictions do not require awareness or mental imagery; they are derived from unconditioned stimuli, such as a rustling in the tall grass, from learned relationships between cues, from contextual conditioning, and from the elapsing of internally timed intervals. Humans, and perhaps certain other species, can engage in mental time travel, projecting themselves into an imagined future, thus making predictions and attendant expectations explicit.

The approach of a decisive moment is accompanied by an escalating sense of urgency as well as by changes in attentional focus, priorities, choices, autonomic responses, and overt behaviour. A prominent theory of interval timing (Gibbon 1977) posits that expectancy grows hyperbolically, increasing gradually when an anticipated event is far off but building quickly when it is imminent. Thus, events in the near future acquire disproportionate influence in comparison to more remote ones. Sudden reversals in preference and shortsighted choices may ensue. McClure *et al.* (2004) proposed that a quasihyperbolic trajectory of expectancy growth emerges from conflict between two brain modules; an impatient, affective processor struggles for control with a cooler deliberative processor that discounts future payoffs less steeply. On this view, a sense of urgency emerges as the affective processor gains the upper hand in the run-up to an imminent event. Thus, we make an extravagant bid at a hotly contested auction despite having sworn frugality and having initially assigned a lower value to the now tantalizing object.

PETER SHIZGAL

V

valence The term valence is used to describe the positive or negative character of emotions, of components of the emotional response such as subjective feelings or behavioural responses, and of emotion-eliciting stimuli (see Charland 2005b, Colombetti 2005). Valence derives from the Latin word *valentia*, which means power or capacity. It was first introduced into psychology by Edward Tolman (1886–1959) who used it to translate Kurt Lewin's (1890–1947) concept of *Aufforderungscharakter*, referring to the attracting or repulsive forces in a stimulus that determine the direction of the behaviour of an organism (see ACTION TENDENCIES).

In the affective sciences, valence is used as a dimensional variable with the poles positive and negative. There is some disagreement, however, about whether valence should be considered a single bipolar dimension (ranging from negative over neutral to positive) or a composite of two unipolar dimensions (one ranging from neutral to negative, the other ranging from neutral to positive; see, for example, Russell and Carroll 1999) (see CIRCUMPLEX MODELS; DIMENSIONAL MODELS).

Most frequently, the valence concept is used to characterize the hedonic quality (positive–negative quality, pleasant–unpleasant quality) of the subjective feeling component of an emotion, usually assessed via self-report. The pleasantness–unpleasantness dimension is a fundamental dimension of emotion experience: Aristotle (384–322 BC) wrote in his *Rhetoric* that emotions are 'those things through which, by undergoing change, people come to differ in their judgements and which are accompanied by pain and pleasure, for example, anger, pity, fear, and other such things and their opposites'. Some form of positive–negative dimension exists in virtually all models and theories of emotion, this dimension has also been shown to be one of the three primary dimensions of meaning in natural language (next to arousal and potency; see Osgood *et al.* 1957) (see EMOTION THEORIES AND CONCEPTS (PHILOSOPHICAL PERSPECTIVES); EMOTION THEORIES AND CONCEPTS (PSYCHOLOGICAL PERSPECTIVES)).

In the affective neurosciences in particular, valence is often defined in terms of the behavioural response of an organism to an emotion-eliciting stimulus (Davidson and Irwin 1999), approach being considered as positive and withdrawal or antagonism as negative, or in terms of the reinforcement contingencies of a stimulus (reward = positive, punishment = negative) (see APPROACH/WITHDRAWAL). This operationalization of valence reflects the motivating function of emotion, which consists in directing the organism toward meaningful, adaptive responses that preserve its well-being, especially by avoiding (or antagonizing) negative, harmful stimuli and approaching positive, beneficial ones.

Based on the valence of emotional components such as subjective feeling of behavioural responses, individual emotions can also be assigned a valence and classified as positive or negative, examples of positive emotions being *happiness or *pride, examples of negative emotions being *anger, *fear, *shame, or *guilt. However, emotions can also be classified as positive or negative in relation to their role in social interactions and ethical *norms, rendering shame and guilt positive emotions, whereas pride can in this sense be a negative emotion.

Valence has also been directly assigned to stimuli, apparently describing inherent stimulus properties. For example, standardized collections of emotion-eliciting stimuli usually come with normative lists where the stimuli are ranked according to a valence score (see ELICITING STIMULUS SETS (FOR EMOTION RESEARCH)). These lists are based on studies in which participants are asked to rate stimuli on valence scales, each score then represents a mean value across many participants. When using the term valence as a predicate of stimuli, this does not necessarily imply that stimuli have this valence independent of an organism that evaluates these stimuli. More likely, the valence attributed to a stimulus refers to the content of the representations that the stimulus elicits in the observer, including valenced feelings and responses or response tendencies. The assumption that a stimulus can be intrinsically attractive or aversive, pleasant or unpleasant, regardless of whether there is an evaluator who engages in an evaluation process, seems problematic. In the context of an evaluation of a stimulus by an observer, what is positive or negative always depends on the current concerns, needs, and goals of the observer. However, there exist certain stimuli or attributes of stimuli which elicit highly similar evaluations in most observers most of the time (e.g. angry faces or baby faces), and might in this sense be considered to possess intrinsic valence or (un)pleasantness (see INTRINSIC PLEASANTNESS). In addition to these rather universal factors, the valence of a stimulus for an observer is influenced by the degree to which the stimulus is conducive to the current motivational hierarchy of the individual (see MOTIVE CONSISTENCY; GOALS).

TOBIAS BROSCH AND AGNES MOORS

Colombetti, G. (2005). Appraising valence. *Journal of Consciousness Studies*, **12**(8–10), 103–27.

values Values, like *norms, are often considered to be importantly different from bare facts. In any case, values, whether moral or nonmoral, seem to be related, be it directly or indirectly, to *oughts*. It is useful to distinguish between judgements about what a person values, as expressed by 'S values x', and value judgements (or appraisals) proper, of which the paradigmatic expression can be considered to be 'x is valuable'. Sometimes, the term 'value' also refers to whatever is taken to be valuable, such as when we say that knowledge or peace are important values. It is generally believed that there is a great variety of value predicates. In addition to 'value', there is for instance 'good', 'admirable', 'kind', 'generous', but also 'bad', 'disgusting', 'cruel', or 'mean'.

Most would agree that values and emotions are closely related. This appears particularly obvious when one thinks of value concepts that are lexically derived from emotion terms, such as *admirable*, *disgusting*, *regrettable*, or *shameful*. There are deep disagreements, however, as to what the relation between values and emotions is. This is the debate between *value realism* and *value antirealism*. The basic question is analogous to the one Euthyphro put to Socrates in Plato's dialogues: do we love what is good because it is good, or is something good because we love it (de Sousa 1987). Strong value realism claims that our responses to values are sensitive to a completely independent evaluative reality. A realist who considers that this reality is reducible to what physics posits embraces *naturalism*, whereas a realist who denies this is a nonnaturalist. By contrast, value antirealism maintains that our responses constitute values, values being constructions or even projections of our reactions onto a neutral world. One extreme subjectivist view holds that something has value just in case it causes a positive reaction in whoever claims that the thing has value. One problem, obviously, is that things would keep acquiring and losing values, depending on the mood we are in. Another problem is that this view does not leave room for real disagreement about the value of things. This is why subjectivists usually claim that the person whose responses are relevant satisfy a number of conditions, such as normality, complete information, or lack of biases. This is the essence of so-called *ideal observer* theories. In general, most theories try to accommodate the subjective and objective aspects of values.

The debate about the status of values is related to a number of different questions. One important set of questions concerns the meaning of evaluative sentences. One famous but controversial view, dubbed the 'boo–hurray theory', claims that 'x has value' simply expresses our emotions and is thus not truth-assessable in any standard way (Gibbard 1990, Blackburn 1998). Value epistemology tries to determine how value judgements could be justified and what knowledge of values would consists in. One view, which has recently attracted quite a number of followers, claims that our emotions play a crucial role in our epistemic access to values: emotions would be *perceptions* of values (Tappolet 2001, Prinz 2004). Consider fear. Fear, like colour perception, has correctness conditions. Fear is correct (or appropriate) insofar as what one fears is really dangerous (or frightening). As philosophers would put it, danger (or the property of being frightening) is the *formal object* of fear. Thus, one could say that when we feel fear, we perceive the danger of a situation. Though controversial, this account meshes well with an evolutionary story: if we have the disposition to fear wild animals, it is because we are descendants of ancestors whose fears of wild animals helped them to survive.

CHRISTINE TAPPOLET

vigilance The English term 'vigilance' originates from the Latin term *'vigilantia'* meaning to 'keep awake'. For the purposes of psychology, the term can be defined as a heightened state of alertness in response to a stimulus that predicts or could predict some biologically relevant outcome. The purpose of such a state could be to protect oneself from danger, to increase the likelihood of discovering a reward, and/or to clarify some changing environmental circumstance. While the entire brain ultimately participates in these activities in the service of survival, the *amygdala, a brain region located within the medial temporal lobe, is critically involved in the instantiation of a heightened level of vigilance upon the detection of a stimulus that has proven to have at least some value in predicting biologically relevant outcomes (see RELEVANCE DETECTION). The fact that the amygdala has been shown to be sensitive to stimuli that predict both positive and negative outcomes makes it particularly well suited for this role.

The efferent and afferent connectivity of the amygdala underscores its fundamental role in modulating vigilance states. First, the amygdala directly projects to brainstem autonomic and somatomotor control regions, and can thus set the level of peripheral autonomic and motor tone. In addition, the amygdala can influence the detection of environmental stimuli through its direct reciprocal connections with primary and association sensory cortices (see ATTENTION AND EMOTION). The amygdala is also reciprocally connected with prefrontal cortical regions that regulate the organism's responses to detected sensory stimuli. Finally, the amygdala projects to all major neuromodulatory centres and in this way can change the number of transmitters delivered to cortical regions, thereby globally and instantaneously changing their response thresholds. This change in the *readiness* of sensory cortical neurons to fire to detected stimuli, together with the potentiation of prefrontal circuits that will coordinate the organism's response, constitutes a neural definition of 'vigilance'.

PAUL J. WHALEN

violence Violence is a topic of research interest for a variety of scientific disciplines because of its prevalence. Indeed, an atypically high level of *aggression is one of the most common reasons for referral to psychiatrists, particularly when it is shown by children.

An important division is frequently made between reactive (also termed affective, impulsive, or defensive) aggression and proactive (also termed instrumental, predatory, and premeditated) aggression (Crick and Dodge 1996). In reactive aggression, a frustrating (see FRUSTRATION) or threatening event triggers the aggressive act which is often accompanied by *anger; the aggression is 'hot'. The aggression is initiated without regard for any potential *goal. In contrast, proactive aggression is purposeful and goal directed (e.g. to obtain the victim's possessions); the aggression is 'cold'. Considerable data strongly support the existence of two relatively separable populations of aggressive individuals: individuals who present with mostly reactive aggression and individuals who present with high levels of proactive *and* reactive aggression (Crick and Dodge 1996).

It has been suggested that reactive aggression in humans is mediated by the same neural circuitry that mediates the basic response to threat in other animals (Gregg and Siegel 2001, Blair 2004). Animals tend to freeze when they are exposed to low levels of danger from a distant threat. At higher levels of danger, from a closer threat, they attempt to escape. At higher levels still, when the threat is very close and escape is impossible, reactive aggression is displayed (Blanchard *et al.* 1977). This progressive response to threat is mediated by a basic threat system that runs from medial amygdaloidal areas downward, largely via the stria terminalis to the medial hypothalamus, and from there to the dorsal half of the periaqueductal grey (Gregg and Siegel 2001). It is regulated by orbital, medial, and ventrolateral frontal cortex. Atypically increased levels of reactive aggression probably reflect an increased sensitivity of the basic threat response, perhaps due to prior physical/sexual abuse, and/or dysfunction in the regions of

frontal cortex responsible for emotional regulation (Davidson *et al.* 2000, Blair 2004). Various psychiatric and neurological conditions are associated with an increased risk for reactive aggression. These include *posttraumatic stress disorder, childhood *bipolar disorder, and 'acquired sociopathy' following orbital frontal cortex lesions.

Most individuals rarely show instrumental aggression, i.e. they rarely use aggression to achieve their goals. Usually, instrumental aggression is not considered as an option, the individual has learnt other behavioural options to achieve his or her goals. Even if it is considered, for most people the personal/social costs of *antisocial behaviour typically outweigh the benefits associated with achieving the goal. Parental and peer moral socialization helps the developing child appropriately represent the costs of antisocial behaviour. Given the role of socialization in specifying the costs of antisocial behaviour to the developing child, inappropriate parenting or dysfunction in the neural systems underlying socialization (the *amygdala and ventromedial frontal cortex; see PSYCHOPATHY) could lead to an increased risk of instrumental antisocial behaviour. The 'punishment' that best achieves moral socialization is the victim's distress: *empathy induction, focusing the transgressor's attention on the victim, particularly fosters moral socialization. Poor empathic responding has been linked to the development of psychopathy, a disorder particularly associated with heightened levels of instrumental aggression (Blair 2004).

R. J. R. BLAIR

vocabulary of emotion 'Some people would never have fallen in love if they had never heard of love': this maxim by La Rochfoucauld (1665/1959, no.136) contains an important insight: words, and the concepts they represent, help shape the realities they denote (see CONSTRUCTIVISM (PHILOSOPHICAL PERSPECTIVES); LANGUAGE AND EMOTION). In recognition of the distinction between words, concepts, and realities, the following convention is adopted for this entry: when reference is to words, italics are used (e.g. *love*); when reference is to concepts, quotation marks are used (e.g. 'love'); and when reference is to the realities denoted, no marks are used (e.g. love).

A distinction can also be made between the denotation of a word (its referent) and its connotation (associated thoughts and feelings); for example, the word *home* conveys pleasant, comfortable feelings, whereas the word *dungeon* conveys the opposite, although neither word denotes an emotional state. Most words in a language have connotations that can be mapped on to three main dimensions: evaluation (good–bad), potency (strong–weak), and activity (fast–slow). The *semantic* *differential*, a widely used technique for the assessment of affective states, is based on this feature of language (Snider and Osgood 1969). The dimensions of connotative meaning, it might be noted, are an empirical issue distinct from *dimensional theories of emotion, although the former is sometimes offered as support for the latter.

Words that refer specifically to emotional states vary considerably in meaning and number—from a few to hundreds—from one language to another (see LINGUISTICS AND EMOTION). To overcome this linguistic diversity, Wierzbicka (1999) has identified a small set (50 to 60) of cultural primitives—self-explanatory concepts such as 'good', 'bad', 'think', 'feel', 'know', and 'do', which retain their meaning across language groups. Wierzbicka illustrates how ostensibly similar emotion words (e.g. *anger* in English, *liget* in Ilangot, and *song* in Ifaluk) have different meanings when analysed in terms of these conceptual universals.

Wierzbicka wisely admonishes us not to privilege one language over another; if we do, we subtly bias our views of what emotional experience is or can be. Recognizing this limitation, our concern here is not with the meaning of emotion words, but with the way emotional vocabularies are organized.

Starting with everyday English words for emotion, Storm and Storm (1987) constructed a folk taxonomy of 525 terms. Adopting a more theoretical approach, Ortony et al. (1988) developed a taxonomy based on the cognitive principles underlying emotional *appraisals and *action tendencies. Storm and Storm emphasize that theirs is a taxonomy of emotion words; Ortony et al. are equally emphatic that theirs is a taxonomy of emotional states, with everyday English words serving as inexact labels for points in the structure. In spite of this difference in orientation, both studies illustrate two features of emotional vocabularies, and by implication of emotional concepts and states.

First, vocabularies are hierarchically organized, with some words more basic (useful and informative) than others. For example, *anger* is a more basic term than *chagrin* (too specific) or *hurt* (too general). It is important not to confuse basic-level words and associated concepts with so-called *basic emotions: simply because *anger* is a basic term in a lexical hierarchy, does not mean that anger is more fundamental (e.g. biologically) than are other emotions.

Second, the same word may be used to refer to emotions at different levels in a hierarchy. A word so used is known as a synecdoche. Take *anger*: as a generic term, *anger* may refer to a class of emotions that includes anger as a specific emotion, along with frustration, annoyance, irritation, fury, contempt, envy, jealousy, and the like. It is important to distinguish the

generic and specific uses of a word, for what is true of emotions referenced at a broad level of generality (e.g. *anger* as referring to a class of related emotions) need not be true of emotions referenced at a lower level (e.g. *anger* as referring to a culturally specific emotion). The reverse is also true; that is, *anger* as the name of a specific emotion may have implications that do not apply to *anger* as the name of a superordinate category.

The way emotional vocabularies are organized is one issue; another is the way emotion words are processed and used (Dewaele and Pavlenko 2002). For example, bilinguals may use their second rather than first language to 'distance' themselves from emotionally threatening topics; similarly, monolinguals may find it easier to express emotions in 'low' (slang, dialect) rather than 'high' (cultivated, standard) speech. Also, people suffering from *alexithymia may be unable to 'name' their own emotional experiences, even though they have the relevant vocabulary. A major question for research is whether emotion words are simply used differently (e.g. due to motivational and personality dynamics), or whether—and, if so, how—emotion words are cognitively encoded and accessed (e.g. to and from working memory) differently than affectively more neutral words.

Emotional vocabularies provide material for one of the major dependent variables used in research, namely *self-reports. Because self-reports are complexly related to emotional experience (Robinson and Clore 2002), the theoretical and practical implications of emotional vocabularies have tended to be neglected. The assumption seems to be that ordinary language is too imprecise for scientific purposes, that we should develop instead a technical vocabulary that is not tied to any particular language or culture. That is a reasonable goal with ample precedence in the history of science. It does not mean, however, that we can neglect the vocabularies of natural languages. As La Rochfoucauld recognized, the words we use in everyday speech not only reflect but also help determine what it means to be emotional.

JAMES R. AVERILL

Reilly, J. and Seibert, L. (2003). Language and emotion. In: R.J. Davidson, K.R. Scherer, and H.H. Goldsmith (eds), *Handbook of affective sciences*, pp. 535–58. New York, Oxford University Press.

vocal expression of emotion Speakers consistently modulate their speech, intentionally or unintentionally, to express different emotions and listeners are sensitive to these modifications and use vocal cues consistently to infer the emotional experience or message intention of the speaker. Emotional vocalizations range from nonverbal interjections or *affect bursts and *laughter to linguistically complex spoken utterances with important suprasegmental and prosodic features such as pausing, rhythm, and intonation. This reflects the fact that vocalization is an evolutionary old device for emotion expression and signalling, used both in animal and human communication, as well as the carrier of human speech (see INTERPERSONAL COMMUNICATION). In consequence, the effects of linguistically determined speech motor commands and physiologically driven emotional voice modulations are inextricably intertwined in speech production. The emotional and attitudinal aspects of speaking are semiotically designated as pragmatics as compared with syntax and semantics. Emotional communication is an inherently multimodal phenomenon and emotional vocalizations are not independent of the other modalities (de Gelder and Vroomen 2000b) (see MULTIMODAL EXPRESSION OF EMOTION).

The study of vocal emotion expression involves the entire chain from voice production and *encoding* in the speaker via acoustic wave *transmission* to the listener's perception and inference (*decoding*).

Encoding

There are several ways to study the encoding process (Scherer 2003): spontaneous portrayals, laboratory-induced emotions, and acted emotional expressions. Spontaneous portrayals have been the favoured approach in speech technology; journalists covering disasters, call-centre conversations, sporting events, and reality television provide a rich source of spontaneous emotional material. This approach, however, has serious drawbacks: most media appearances are most likely not completely spontaneous, and determining which emotion is displayed is a difficult task. In many cases it is impossible to obtain systematic sampling of different expressions by the same speakers, which is absolutely essential given the importance of interindividual differences (Scherer 2003).

Inducing emotional expression by means of experimental manipulations has been the favoured approach of laboratory psychologists because of the degree of control it affords (Johnstone *et al.* 2005). As with the previous approach, there are serious drawbacks: the ethical considerations in inducing emotions like fear or sadness in naïve participants and, in consequence, the fact that, generally, only rather weak affective responses can be elicited.

To avoid the disadvantages of these two methods, portrayals of emotional vocalizations by actors are often used to obtain purer and more intense expressions as well as to systematically sample different emotions for the same speaker, generally using standard utterances (to control for semantic and phonetic content). Common approaches to provoke relatively realistic and authentic expressions by actors are the Stanislawski technique (method acting; recalling past emotional experiences from memory) and the Velten technique (repeating a highly emotionally charged sentence several times to induce consistent changes in emotional state). A common critique of acted emotional expressions is that they might result in more stereotypical portrayals. While most likely true, this is also an interesting source of information as stereotypical expressions can shed light on the evolutionary and societal origins of vocal emotional expression (Scherer 2003) (see PUSH/PULL EFFECTS).

Encoding studies pursue two major aims: (1) to produce systematic stimuli for listener judgement studies (see below), and (2) to allow systematic acoustic analyses (generally using digital parameter extraction procedures from the recorded speech waves) of emotion-specific voice and speech feature profiles. The relevant acoustic properties for emotional speech can be grouped into four categories (see VOICE PRODUCTION AND ACOUSTICS): time related (utterance duration, speech rate), intensity related (loudness, dynamic range), fundamental frequency related (mean pitch, frequency perturbations) and complex time–frequency–energy related measures (voice quality and timbre, mainly visible in the speech spectrum). Research over the past decades has revealed a number of fairly reliable configurations of acoustic cues related to specific emotional expressions. Table VI contains a compilation of acoustic patterning over emotions based on the empirical data reported in several studies (see also Juslin and Scherer 2005).

Transmission

This part of the process concerns the transmission of the speech waves from the speaker's mouth to the listener's ear through the medium of wave propagation in the air. Transmission properties are important, as ambient noise and the amplitude and frequency composition of the speech signal can strongly affect the efficiency of the communication in the vocal/audio channel. However, this is rarely studied, although one might expect that emotions can be differentially affected (e.g. low, soft sadness vocalizations travelling less well than loud, strident fear utterances).

Decoding

Listener decoding studies are used to examine the auditory discriminability of vocally expressed emotions and individual differences in recognition ability in the vocal modality. The major dependent variable, recognition accuracy, measures how well emotions can be identified from vocal cues alone in categorical forced choice or free response paradigms. Recent reviews of the literature (Juslin and Laukka 2003, Scherer 2003) indicate that the average percentage of emotions correctly classified based on vocal cues alone lies at around 60%. While far from perfect, and lower than that found in recognizing

Table V1. Compilation of the review of empirical data on acoustic patterning of basic emotions (based on Johnstone and Scherer 2000).

	Stress	Anger/rage	Fear/panic	Sadness	Joy/elation	Boredom
Intensity	↑	↑	↑	↓	↑	
F_0 floor/mean	↑	↑	↑	↓	↑	
F_0 variability	↑			↓	↑	↓
F_0 range	↑	↑(↓)	↑(↓)	↓	↑	↓
Sentence contours	↓			↓		
High-frequency energy	↑		↑	↓	(↑)	
Speech and articulation rate	↑		↑	↓	(↑)	↓

facial expression, this recognition accuracy is far above the a priori chance level and equals the maximum accuracy of sophisticated statistical classification methods (Banse and Scherer 1996) (see UNIVERSALITY OF EMOTIONS; FACIAL EXPRESSION OF EMOTION). This indicates that quite specific patterns of acoustic parameters are used to infer different emotional states.

There are consistent differences in vocal recognition accuracy between emotions, with sadness and anger being recognized best, followed by fear. Disgust, joy, and despair are recognized least well vocally, although these emotions are often better recognized when nonverbal affect bursts rather than standard speech are used. In addition to simple accuracy percentages, the reporting of confusion matrices is considered state of the art as these provide information on the decoding process and the cues that are used by listeners. For example, most confusion occurs within emotion families (anger is confused more readily with fear than with sadness), suggesting that similar cues are involved for the former pair. These differences can be explained by evolutionary considerations linked to transmission. Vocal information is well suited for communication over larger distances, allowing the warning all conspecifics (fear) or the threatening of foes (anger) in hearing range. In contrast, disgust (provoked by unsavoury food) need only be communicated over a short distance to those likely to want to share the food and is efficiently communicated by facial expression visible to interaction partners at close range.

As with the recognition of emotions in the facial modality, vocal expressions of emotion are accurately recognized across cultures (Johnstone and Scherer 2000, Elfenbein and Ambady 2002), although there may be an in-group advantage: recognition of vocal emotion is easier in one's own language and culture (Scherer et al. 2001b).

In some cases, the *Brunswikian lens model, an integrative model of the complete vocal communication process, is used to study the relative weight of particular acoustic cues for listener inferences (Scherer 2003). Sev-

eral methods can be used: (1) correlating subjective ratings of unaltered portrayals with the extracted acoustic parameters; (2) using cue *masking* (or subtractive synthesis) to remove or mask specific cues from the original speech material (e.g. low-pass filtering, randomized splicing, backward replay, pitch inversion)—subsequent listener judgements of the resulting masked speech samples then reveal the relative contribution of different cues; and (3) cue *manipulation*, using rule or copy (re-)synthesis, to artificially create or modify specific acoustic parameters and measure their impact on decoding.

MARTIJN GOUDBEEK AND KLAUS R. SCHERER

Juslin, P.N. and Scherer, K.R. (2005). Vocal expression of affect. In: J.A. Harrigan, R. Rosenthal, and K.R. Scherer (eds), *The new handbook of methods in nonverbal behavior research*, pp. 65–135. New York: Oxford University Press.

Scherer, K.R. (2003). Vocal communication of emotion: a review of research paradigms. *Speech Communication*, 40, 227–56.

Scherer, K.R., Johnstone, T., and Klasmeyer, G. (2003). Vocal expression of emotion. In: R.J. Davidson, K.R. Scherer, and H.H. Goldsmith (eds), *Handbook of affective sciences*, pp. 433–56. New York: Oxford University Press.

vocal synthesis Vocal synthesis of emotion is the generation of emotionally expressive utterances by a computer program (see FACIAL IMAGE ANALYSIS AND SYNTHESIS). Two main types can be distinguished: (1) generation of expressive speech, where the emotional expression accompanies a verbal spoken utterance, and (2) generation of nonverbal vocalizations.

Synthesis of expressive speech

Since the first attempts to convey emotions in synthetic speech, at the end of the 1980s, a considerable range of approaches have been explored. Three fundamentally different approaches for modelling the acoustical correlates of emotions have been proposed (see VOCAL EXPRESSION OF EMOTION).

Playback approaches. The synthesis technology which currently yields the most natural-sounding speech, unit selection synthesis, generates speech by resequencing short audio snippets from a large database recorded with one speaker. The technique preserves the speaking style used during recordings. In particular, by recording a full database in a given emotion, it is possible to generate quite natural-sounding speech expressing that emotion (Iida and Campbell 2003). No knowledge about the link between an emotion and its acoustic correlates is needed to express emotions with this technique. Its major limitation, however, is its lack of flexibility: for each new expression, a new database needs to be recorded.

Explicit modelling approaches. Older synthesis technologies, such as formant synthesis and diphone synthesis, allow for a more flexible control of the acoustic parameters. Formant synthesis generates the speech acoustics entirely by rule; diphone synthesis uses a small speech database and applies signal processing techniques to impose a given intonation and rhythm onto the speech. Due to the limited quality of existing speech models, both techniques provide a speech quality which is inferior to unit selection synthesis.

The expression of emotions using formant or diphone synthesis requires an explicit model of the link between an emotional state and its acoustic correlates. Such a model can be established by means of systematic perception tests (Burkhardt and Sendlmeier 2000) or by analysing emotional speech data. The emotional state to express is often modelled as disjunctive categories, but has also been modelled in terms of emotion dimensions (Schröder 2006). Because of the difficulty of identifying, measuring, and generating exactly those acoustic variables which lead to the intended perceptual impression, the explicit models used are usually overly simple, thus leading to synthesized expressions which tend to be exaggerated in order to be interpretable.

Implicit modelling approaches. A recent extension of the playback approach has the potential to overcome some of the limitations of both the playback and the explicit modelling approaches. This 'implicit modelling' approach analyses recordings of emotion-specific databases, building an acoustic model for each emotional dataset using machine learning techniques. The resulting models cannot easily be interpreted by humans. A new synthesis technology based on hidden Markov models—statistical models usually applied in speech recognition technology—can generate expressive speech from these implicit models. Furthermore, it is possible to interpolate between the models, thus generating intermediate expressions between the ones recorded (Masuko *et al.* 2004). The full potential of this technique remains to be explored: by recording suitable 'landmark' databases, it may be possible to cover the expression of relevant subsets of emotion space in a continuous way.

Synthesis of nonverbal vocalizations

In addition to expression accompanying speech, a powerful means for expressing emotions in the voice is the use of nonverbal vocalizations, including high-intensity affect bursts but also more subtle vocalisations such as the feedback emitted by a listener in a dialogue.

Nonverbal vocalizations have started to appear in commercial speech synthesis products (Loquendo 2007), where a range of emotional expressions such as laughter and crying are provided in a playback paradigm. However, only a very limited amount of research has been carried out to date on the generation of such expressions in conjunction with synthetic speech.

MARC SCHRÖDER

Campbell, N., Hamza, W., Höge, H., Tao, J., and Bailly, G. (eds) (2006). *IEEE Transactions on Audio, Speech, and Language Processing*, **14**(4), 1097–178 (special section on expressive speech synthesis).

Schröder, M. (2008). Approaches to emotional expressivity in synthetic speech. In: K. Izdebski (ed.), *Emotions in the human voice, Volume 3: Culture and perception*, pp. 307–21. San Diego, CA: Plural.

voice production and acoustics Vocal sounds result from, and hence reflect movements of, structures contained in the vocal organ. In this sense, the voice can be said to translate movements into changes in sound properties. As moods and affects tend to manifest themselves also in terms of movement patterns, the voice reflects such aspects rather efficiently (see VOCAL EXPRESSION OF EMOTION). Hence, measurements of vocal properties are often used in the documentation of changes of emotional states.

Mechanism

The functioning of the vocal organ, illustrated in Fig. V1, is similar in speech and singing. As the respiratory system compresses air, it produces an overpressure of air in the lungs. If the airways are open and the slit between the vocal folds, or the *glottis*, is appropriately narrowed, this pressure, called the *subglottal pressure*, generates an air-stream that brings the vocal folds to vibration. As a result a pulsating airflow, the *voice source*, is produced.

The voice source is a sound comprising a series of harmonic partials with amplitudes which in flow units decrease by about 12 decibels (dB) per octave. The frequency of the lowest partial, the *fundamental frequency* (F_o), equals the vibration frequency of the vocal folds and determines the pitch we perceive.

The voice source is controlled by three main physiological parameters: (1) subglottal pressure, controlling vocal loudness, (2) vocal fold length and stiffness,

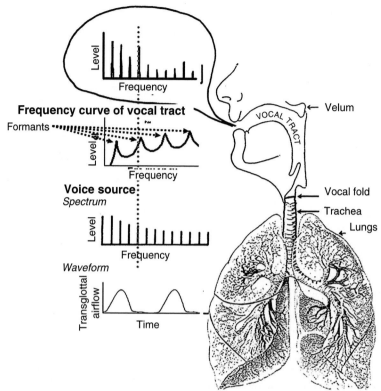

Fig. V1. Illustration of vocal function. The voice source is a pulsating transglottal flow containing a series of harmonic partials, as illustrated in the two bottom left inserts. These partials travel through the vocal tract, the frequency curve of which is characterized by peaks at the resonance (or formant) frequencies and valleys between them. Partials lying close to a formant are radiated from the mouth opening with greater amplitudes than other partials.

controlling F_o, and (3) the degree of glottal adduction, controlling the type of phonation.

The voice source propagates through the vocal tract and is thereby filtered in a manner determined by its resonance or *formant frequencies*. These frequencies are determined by the shape of the vocal tract. The two lowest formant frequencies are decisive to vowel quality, while the higher formant frequencies determine the personal vocal characteristics.

Breathing

Breathing behaviour is affected by many factors. In neutral as opposed to emotional speech subglottal pressure is mostly rather constant during a phrase (Abrahamson and Sundberg 2007). In singing, by contrast, it is constantly varied, not only to vary vocal loudness so as to mark the musical phrase structure, but also with F_o. Thus, higher pitches are sung with higher subglottal pressures than lower tones.

Subglottal pressure is determined by active forces produced by the breathing muscles and passive forces produced by gravity and the elasticity of the breathing apparatus. As the elasticity forces change from exhalatory at high lung volumes to inhalatory at low lung volumes, they reach an equilibrium at a certain lung volume, the *resting expiratory level* (REL). This lung volume is called the *functional residual capacity* (FRC). In normal breathing, inhalations are mostly started from the REL, such that inhalations result from muscle activation while recoil forces produce the exhalations. Phonation at lung volumes below FRC feels uncomfortable.

Voice source

The waveform of the voice source is characterized by quasitriangular airflow pulses, produced when the vocal folds open the glottis. Between the pulses horizontal portions near or at zero airflow occur, produced when

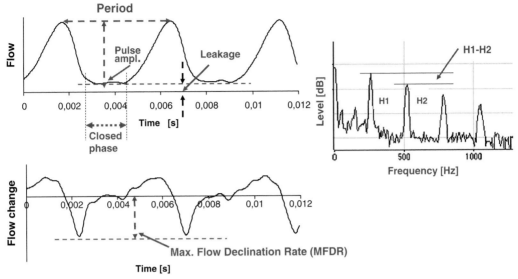

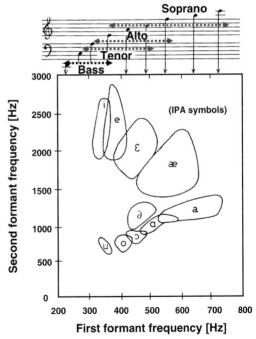

Fig. V2. Typical waveform, time derivative, and spectrum of the transglottal airflow (upper and lower left panels and right panel, respectively).

the folds have closed the glottis more or less completely (see Fig. V2).

Phonation with exaggerated glottal adduction is generally referred to as *hyperfunctional* or *pressed*. The opposite extreme, i.e. adduction that is too faint, is called *hypofunctional* or *breathy*. In the latter type of phonation the vocal folds fail to close the glottis completely during the vibratory cycle. As a result, airflow escapes the glottis during the quasiclosed phase, which generates noise. The pulse amplitude is high, so the fundamental is strong, and the higher overtones of the source spectrum are weak or buried in noise. The degree of glottal adduction during phonation is often influenced by the speaker's mood.

In speech an increase in vocal loudness is generally accompanied by an increase of the mean F_0. The increase is around 0.4 semitones per dB increase in vocal loudness (Gramming and Sundberg 1988). Also, an increase in vocal loudness increases the amplitudes of the higher spectrum partials more than the amplitudes of the lower partials, as mentioned. In other words, many differences between recordings of a given voice made on different occasions may be caused by differences in vocal loudness.

Resonance

The two lowest formant frequencies are vowel specific, such that each vowel is characterized by a particular combination of F_1 and F_2 (see Fig. V3). Moreover, since children have shorter vocal tracts than adults, and since female adults have shorter vocal tracts than male adults,

Fig. V3. Frequencies of the first two formants in the indicated vowels. At the top the first formant frequency is represented on a note staff. The arrows show the F_0 ranges of the main voice classifications.

voice production and acoustics

the formant frequencies of a given vowel vary depending on the speaker. Patterns of formant frequency transitions define consonants, even though these patterns are affected by syllable rate and phonetic context. Since the shape of the vocal tract determines the formant frequencies, this implies that each vowel is produced by a specific vocal tract shape. Likewise, each consonant is associated with a movement pattern of the articulators, i.e. the lips, the jaw, the tongue body and tip, the velum, and the larynx. In singing, however, F_o is often well above the normal value of F_1. In such cases the singers modify the vocal tract shape such that F_1 is kept higher than F_o (Sundberg 1987).

Voice measurements

The classical method for analysing speech and voice characteristics is the spectrogram (see Fig. V4). It shows frequency on the vertical axis and time on the horizontal axis, sound level being reflected along a grey scale. Thus, vowel formants appear as dark bands (because they are reflected in terms of spectrum partials of higher amplitudes). This allows examination of timing and rate of change, two aspects of speech production closely related to expression. Also F_o, reflecting a salient aspect of speech prosody, tends to form characteristic patterns.

As subglottal pressure has strong effects on the acoustic properties of voice, it is important to keep track of vocal loudness when recording voices. Sound level decreases by 6 dB with each doubling of the distance to the sound source, so the microphone–mouth distance is crucial as well as the gain in the recording equipment.

The sound pressure level (SPL) shows a strong correlation with perceived degree of vocal loudness under certain conditions only. The reason is that it mainly reflects the

sound level of the strongest spectrum partial, which, in turn, is strongly affected by the frequency distance between the first formant and the partials closest to this formant (Gramming and Sundberg 1988). Therefore, the SPL of a sustained vowel varies substantially if the F is changed. In soft phonation, the fundamental is the strongest partial and is thus reflected in the SPL, but in louder phonation the strongest partial is normally the overtone that is closest to F. Perceived loudness of vowel sounds is more closely related to subglottal pressure than to SPL (Ladefoged 1967).

In pathological dysphonic voices in particular, the period varies more or less from pulse to pulse. This variation is commonly measured in terms of *jitter*, which reflects the mean cycle-to-cycle variation of period duration, and *shimmer*, which reflects the mean cycle-to-cycle variation of amplitude. The harmonic-to-noise ratio (HNR) is a measure of the amplitude relations between the harmonic partials and the noise between them.

Many voice measures are averages over time. Vocal loudness during reading is sometimes measured as the time average of the SPL. However, this average is heavily influenced by the durations of silent intervals in the reading. The equivalent sound level, L_{eq}, represents a better alternative. This measure is the time average of the linear pressure amplitude, however expressed in the logarithmic dB unit.

The time average of F_o in running speech reflects a vocal characteristic that tends to vary depending on mood. Measuring it in a logarithmic unit such as semitones improves the possibility of meaningful comparisons between children and male and female adults. The mean time derivative of F_o, reflecting the average rate of pitch change, seems quite relevant to the affective colouring of speech (Nilsonne 1987).

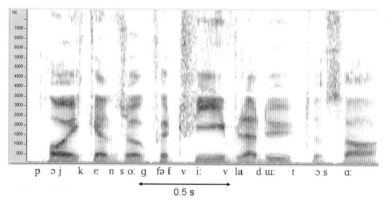

Fig. V4. Spectrogram of a male speaker uttering the sentence (IPA SYMBOLS).

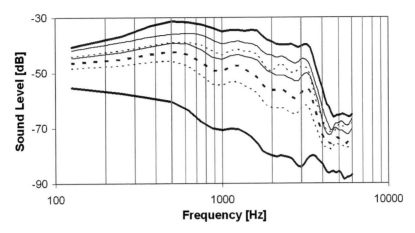

Fig. V5. Long-term-average spectrum of a male speaker reading the same text at seven different degrees of vocal loudness. After Sundberg and Nordenberg (2006).

The long-term-average spectrum (LTAS) is another time average measure. It shows the spectrum averaged over time. If the LTAS is taken over 40 seconds or more of running speech it becomes basically independent of the phonetic content and thus representative of the voice analysed. It shows the mean sound level of the partials in the various frequency bands. Figure V5 shows LTAS curves for a voice speaking at different degrees of vocal loudness. Constant spectrum characteristics such as the singer's formant produce high peaks in an LTAS.

Voice source characteristics are reflected in a LTAS. Hypo- and hyperfunctional voices produce high and low LTAS peaks near their mean F_o, respectively. Also spectral balance differs. This can be reflected in the ratio between the mean LTAS amplitude below and above 1000 Hz, the so-called alpha-ratio (Sundberg and Nordenberg 2006). However, this ratio also varies within a voice, depending on the vocal loudness.

JOHAN SUNDBERG

Juslin, P.N. and Scherer, K.R. (2005). Vocal expression of affect. In: J.A. Harrigan, R. Rosenthal, and K.R. Scherer (eds), *The new handbook of methods in nonverbal behavior research*, pp. 65–135. New York: Oxford University Press.

Sundberg, J. (1987). *The science of the singing voice*. DeKalb, IL: Northern Illinois University Press.

Titze, I. (1994). *Principles of voice production*. Englewood Cliffs, NJ: Prentice Hall.

vulnerability Vulnerability reflects an increased susceptibility to the onset, relapse, or recurrence of a disorder or dysfunctional emotional state that impairs normal functioning (see DISORDER (AFFECTIVE, EMOTIONAL)). Although often used interchangeably with the concept of 'risk',

vulnerability and risk in fact refer to different concepts (see RISK FACTORS FOR EMOTIONAL DISORDERS). Risk is any variable that is correlated with the development of a disorder, whereas vulnerability addresses the mechanisms that bring about the disorder. As a mechanism of disorder, vulnerability refers to an internal state of the individual that can be located in biological factors, neuroanatomical factors, genetic factors, or psychological factors. There is no reason to believe that disorders are caused by individual vulnerabilities. Instead, multiple vulnerability factors spanning different levels of analyses (e.g. biological and psychological) are believed to be implicated in the development of disorders.

Vulnerability is frequently conceptualized within a diathesis–stress model where the occurrence of stress activates vulnerability processes which then initiate the disorder or emotional state. For example, cognitive theories of depression propose that vulnerable individuals possess negative self-schemas that, when activated by stressful life events, bring about a downward spiral of negative information processing and affect that eventuate in a state of depression (Ingram et al. 1998). In line with diathesis–stress models, vulnerability is frequently seen as a latent process that is not easily observable in the absence of a triggering environmental event. Whereas the occurrence of a disorder reflects a state that waxes and wanes, vulnerability is typically seen as a stable trait of the individual. Some models theoretically allow for the possibility that vulnerability can be modified or attenuated, whereas other models view vulnerability as a permanent condition with no chance for modification. These latter models usually locate vulnerability in genetic or neuroanatomical factors.

RICK E. INGRAM

411

W

well-being Subjective well-being (SWB) refers to people's cognitive and affective appraisals of the quality of their lives; the most common measures are self-reports of *life satisfaction and positive and negative affect. One approach to SWB focuses on how people experience their lives moment-to-moment, as reflected in positive or negative affective responses to events, activities, and circumstances. From this perspective, a day filled with enjoyable and engaging activities is preferable to a day filled with dull or painful ones; measures of time use and hedonic experience are central to this approach (e.g. Kahneman 1999) (see POSITIVE EMOTIONS). A second approach focuses on how people evaluate their lives relative to some standard, as reflected in judgements of overall or domain specific standards. From this perspective, a satisfying life is one that meets one's standards. There is wide consensus that high SWB is characterized by both components, i.e. high life satisfaction and a preponderance of positive over negative affect.

Correlates of SWB

Most people report being satisfied and happy with their lives as a whole, with more than 90% of most representative samples reporting values above the neutral point of the respective scales. Similarly, positive affect exceeds negative affect for most people most of the time. Empirically, measures of momentary affect capture primarily the hedonic quality of current activities and immediate contexts, which can be aggregated and duration weighted to arrive at assessments of SWB over extended periods of time; measures of evaluation (life satisfaction) capture primarily comparisons of one's current conditions with standards and expectations (Kahneman et al. 2006). Hence, different measures highlight different aspects of SWB and are related to somewhat different predictors; here we focus on shared themes.

Objective conditions of life

Most people believe that they would be happier and more satisfied if they were richer, younger, or lived in a more favourable climate; they also make choices based on these and similar beliefs. However, the objective conditions of life exert less influence than expected; the conditions in a dozen domains of life rarely account for more than 10% of the variance in reported life satisfaction and their influence on momentary measures

of affect is even more limited. For example, in a study of American women, household income correlated $r = 0.32$ with reported life satisfaction but only $r = 0.06$ with moment-to-moment affect throughout the day (Kahneman et al. 2006). Moreover, many lay theories do not survive empirical testing. For example, life satisfaction and positive affect increase over the lifespan, except for a decline in the final years; in affluent societies, the rich are somewhat more satisfied than the poor, but do not experience more frequent positive affect; and the chronically ill and disabled are not as unhappy as expected (for a summary of well-documented relationships see Argyle, 1999). Such discrepancies between intuitions and observations are due to errors of prediction and processes of adaptation.

When predicting the likely impact of higher wealth or poorer health, people evaluate the change rather than the new steady state. They focus on the aspects that are likely to change while ignoring the numerous aspects that will not change (giving rise to focusing illusions) and fail to take likely adaptation into account. In contrast, actual changes are more limited than our focusing illusions suggest; as time passes, new aspects receive less attention, attenuating their impact; unanticipated aspects of change will emerge; and new activities will be substituted for previous ones. As a result, nothing has as much impact as expected. However, looking back at the change will usually reinstate the focusing illusion, resulting in corresponding errors in the reconstruction of the prechange past.

Whereas our discussion emphasizes differences in prospective, retrospective, and concurrent appraisals, much of the literature attributes the observed discrepancies to a number of *adaptation processes, including *coping strategies that involve changes in one's daily routines and the self-regulation of emotion (see REGULATION OF EMOTION). Moreover, observed shifts in judgement over time have been conceptualized in many different terms, ranging from models of sensory adaptation to shifts in expectations and standards. These possibilities are not mutually exclusive and their relative contributions remain to be determined.

Personality

Personality differences account for a large proportion of variance in SWB (for a review see Diener and Lucas,

1999). *Extraversion is moderately related to positive affect and *neuroticism strongly related to negative affect. Differences in *temperament have a substantial genetic component and twin studies indicate that genes may account for up to 80% of the variance in self-reports of affect aggregated over multiyear periods (SEE GENETICS OF AFFECT). Such observations gave rise to models that assume that the variation of SWB in response to life events and objective conditions is limited by genetically determined set points.

DANIEL KAHNEMAN AND NORBERT SCHWARZ

Diener, E., Suh, E.M. Lucas, R.E., and Smith, H.L. (1999). Subjective well-being: three decades of progress. *Psychological Bulletin*, **125**, 276–302.

Kahneman, D. (1999). Objective happiness. In: D. Kahneman, E. Diener, and N. Schwarz (eds), *Well-being: the foundations of hedonic psychology*, pp. 3–25. New York: Russell Sage Foundation.

work setting (role of emotion in) Affect in organizations was widely studied in the 1930s, but then fell out of fashion. After a period of relative neglect it was taken up so enthusiastically towards the end of the 20th century that an 'affective revolution' in organizational psychology research has been proclaimed (Barsade *et al.* 2003). The revolution involves a growing interest in emotional dynamics in work and organizations, and recognition that emotions are relevant to multiple facets and levels of organizational life (Brief and Weiss 2002).

There are two notable exceptions to the long neglect of 'feelings at work'. First, job satisfaction, historically an important topic in organizational psychology, has been regarded as an affective reaction of people towards their work. However, there are good arguments for regarding job satisfaction as a cognitive rather than an emotional response as it is known to involve an evaluation of working conditions and characteristics, such as work autonomy, variety or feedback, supervision, promotion opportunities, and social relationships at work. Job satisfaction involves assessments that weigh the pros and cons of these features in a process far less spontaneous than the idea of immediate, situation-based feelings and emotions at work. The spontaneous nature of affect at work is clearly and powerfully delineated by affective events theory (see Brief and Weiss 2002).

A second exception is research on *stress at work, where negative emotions are key (Lazarus and Cohen-Carash 2001). Pertinent research often does not focus on specific emotions but on negative emotions and feelings in general, or on families of negative emotions. In many studies, however, these emotions are not measured directly; rather, stress research focuses on more trait-like aspects of affect such as *depression, irritability, or generally negative affect (see Semmer 2003), assuming negative emotional states as mediators of more gener-

alized reaction tendencies. Only recently have stress researchers started to investigate stressful events and the immediate emotional reactions they evoke. Such investigations sometimes use rather general emotional reactions (e.g. Grebner *et al.* 2004), and at other times address specific emotions, such as *anger (Keenan and Newton 1985).

The study of emotion in organizations focuses primarily on the antecedents and consequences of individual affect, drawing on research in the psychology of emotion, with a small subset of research focusing on emotion beyond the individual, including emotion in work groups (e.g. Kelly and Barsade 2001) or in organizations (Huy 2005). To discuss current state of research on emotion at work one needs to address four questions: (1) What emotions do people feel? (2) Why do people feel these emotions? (3) What are the effects of experiencing these emotions? (4) What is the relationship between emotions felt and emotions expressed?

What emotions do people feel at work?

Work is associated with a wide range of affective reactions, including general feeling states that can be positive (*pleasure, *happiness) or negative (displeasure, *frustration), but also specific emotions (anger, frustration, *joy, excitement). Little research is available about general, everyday emotions at work (Scherer *et al.* 2004), and estimations about the frequency of different distinct emotions felt depend on the methodology used. For example, Fisher (2002), who asked people to rate the occurrence of distinct emotions, observed more positive than negative emotions at work. However, when other researchers asked participants to report every event that elicited *strong* feelings at work, they reported slightly more negative than positive emotions, with frustration being the most intense negative, and liking the most intense positive emotion (Grandey *et al.* 2002).

Disturbingly, it appears that people experience a higher proportion of negative emotions at work than in private life. Experience sampling studies showed that people enjoy activities related to working less than most other activities, with the exception of commuting from and to work and housework (Stone 2006). More generally, moods are lower on working days than on days off. On the other hand, experiences of 'flow' (described as 'optimal experience' characterized by feeling active, alert, concentrated, happy, and satisfied) are three times more likely to be experienced at work than in other settings (Csikszentmihalyi and LeFevre 1989).

In the work setting, anger seems to be an often experienced negative emotion (Scherer *et al.* 2004), most often caused by interactions with clients, colleagues, and superiors. *Pride is also an important emotion at work, as it was associated with 25% of events reported in one study (Grandey et al. 2002).

Why do people feel these emotions?

Generally speaking, the instigators of specific emotions at work are the same as outside work. Thus, injustice promotes anger (Barclay et al. 2005), success promotes pride, and internal attributions of stressful events promote shame or embarrassment. Research on specific emotions at work and their triggers at work are sparse (Lazarus and Cohen-Charash 2001), with Basch and Fisher (2000) representing a notable exception. Their data show, for instance, that goal achievement was one of the most important instigators of positive emotions, including pleasure, happiness, enthusiasm, relief, optimism, and power. Receiving recognition was second, being associated with pleasure, happiness, pride, enthusiasm, and affection. For negative emotions, acts of colleagues and acts of management were by far the most frequent events (representing 37% and 28%, respectively) of all events recalled; they were associated with all negative emotions measured. Making mistakes, on the other hand, was associated with only one emotion, that is, *embarrassment.

Dasborough (2006) asked for open descriptions for positive and negative interactions between supervisors and employees, deriving such categories as 'awareness and respect', 'motivation and inspiration', 'empowerment', 'communication', or 'reward/recognition'. The bulk of emotions reported referred to 'happy/pleased' and 'comforted/calm/relaxed', which together constituted 421 of the 520 positive emotional reactions. Admiration and excitement/enthusiasm occurred less frequently. The positive emotions are predominantly in the low–middle arousal domain, according to the well-known emotional circumplex (see CIRCUMPLEX MODELS). Negative emotions appear to be experienced in a more differentiated way than positive ones, and are typically triggered by communication that is ineffective (e.g. failing to inform) or inappropriate (yelling, blaming), by lack of awareness and respect, and by lack of empowerment. The most typical emotional negative reactions reported to Dasborough (2006) were annoyance/anger and frustration.

Research on stress at work also points to social situations, such as interpersonal conflict, as key negative events. Also frequently reported as negative is 'waste of time and effort', which refers to work that is done in vain (for instance, because the specified requirements were changed and then reverted to the original again), and work overload. Similar to Dasborough's (2006) results, emotional reactions to such negative events are anger, annoyance, and frustration. Importantly, however, participants often cannot recall a negative event that happened during the last two weeks (Keenan and Newton 1985), implying either that none occurred or that they were not serious enough to be remembered.

Thus, *social relationships, both with colleagues and supervisors, appear to be frequent triggers of emotions, both positive and negative. A topic repeatedly surfacing is respect and appreciation, or lack thereof (see Semmer et al. 2005), which points to the importance of justice and fairness in determining emotions (see Weiss et al. 1999).

What are the effects of the emotions that people feel?

Emotions felt at work can have a wide range of implications (Weiss and Cropanzano 1996). Strong affect may lead to 'intrusions', which compete for cognitive capacity and may interfere with performance. Although (mild) negative affect sometimes has positive consequences (Forgas 2002), positive mood is a more likely source of positive impact on social interactions, helping behaviour, creativity, decision-making, and dealing with difficult situations (Brief and Weiss 2002). These effects are, however, not uniform and depend on a variety of personal and contextual characteristics (Forgas 2002).

Experiencing negative affect is typically associated with poor social interaction and negotiating behaviours, reduced motivation and performance, lower creativity, and increased withdrawal behaviour, such as turnover (Brief and Weiss 2002). In the longer term affect is also related to health consequences (Semmer 2003). Less is known with regard to specific emotions, but anger mediates between perceptions of injustice and retaliatory behaviour (Barclay et al. 2005), and is related to health consequences such as coronary heart disease (Semmer 2003). Fostering positive emotions, and avoiding great amounts of stress, can therefore pay off both for organizations and their employees.

Emotion work: being obliged to express or hide certain emotions

Work requirements often specify the emotions that employees are expected to display, independent of how they actually feel, an idea discussed as emotion work or emotional labour (Rafaeli and Sutton 1987, 1989). For instance, bill collectors and criminal interrogators must display negative emotions (Rafaeli and Sutton 1991), and employees in sales or customer service roles must display happiness and good cheer as part of their work, because such emotion displays are presumed to improve sales. Some research has shown that the displaying positive emotions by service providers positively influences customers presumably through an emotion *contagion process (e.g. Pugh 2001). But managerial presumptions about role-appropriate emotions are rarely challenged, and there is evidence of invalid assumptions regarding the precise emotional displays that can promote organizational effectiveness; for example, the requirements and effect of emotional displays on customers can depend on situational factors, such as busy stores or crowded restaurants (Sutton and Rafaeli 1988). Employee selection, and especially training and socialization, appear to be key determinants of emotion displayed in organizations, though there also appear to be contextual influences such as how busy an individual is, or how demanding a particular task is (Rafaeli and Sutton 1990).

If an emotion that has to be displayed is not genuinely felt, emotion regulation processes are required (see REGULATION OF EMOTION). Hochschild (1983) suggested two main emotion regulation strategies: *surface acting* involves hiding the emotions actually felt and displaying the required emotion; the regulation effort consists of hiding the spontaneous expression of the felt emotion and 'faking' the desired emotion. *Deep acting* involves a reappraisal of the situation, for example in empathizing with a difficult customer. After such a reappraisal, the display of the required emotion is authentic, because the underlying feeling has been changed. A third possibility is to show 'deviance from the required emotion' (Tschan *et al.* 2005), that is, to display the felt emotion despite the requirement to the contrary.

Emotion work requirements *per se* have been found to have negative effects on well-being, including burnout and other stress symptoms (Hochschild 1983, Grandey 2003), although some authors report or suggest there may be positive effects of display rules, especially if there is a requirement to display positive emotions (Zapf and Holz 2006). The most straining aspect related to emotion work is experiencing emotional dissonance—dissonance between emotions felt and display rules, and thus having to regulate one's emotional display (see DISPLAY RULES). Especially for surface acting, the relationship to impaired well-being has been well established. These negative effects could be due to suppression of the emotion *per se* but also to its effects on interaction behaviour, which may carry the risk of being detected as inauthentic (Grandey 2003, Coté 2005).

Further research on emotions at work should focus on both situational and more permanent aspects, trying to integrate within-person and between-person approaches (Beal *et al.* 2005). Furthermore, it should better connect the various fields involved, such as the psychology of emotions, occupational stress research, research on emotional labour, and research on justice.

ANAT RAFAELI, NORBERT SEMMER, AND
FRANZISKA TSCHAN

Ashkanasy, N.M., Härtel, C.E.J., and Zerbe, W.J. (eds). (2000). *Emotions in the workplace: research, theory, and practice.* London: Quorum Books.

Beal, D.J., Weiss, H.M., Barros, E., and MacDermid, S.M. (2005). An episodic process model of affective influence. *Journal of Applied Psychology,* **90,** 1054–68.

Brief, A.P. and Weiss, H. (2002). Organizational behavior: affect in the workplace. *Annual Review of Psychology,* **53,** 279–307.

Lord, R.G., Klimoski, R.J., and Kanfer, R. (eds). (2002). *Emotions in the workplace.* San Francisco, CA: Jossey Bass.

Payne, R.L. and Cooper, C.L. (eds) (2001). *Emotions at work: theory, research and applications for management.* New York: Wiley.

Sutton, R.I. and Rafaeli, A. (1988). Untangling the relationship between displayed emotions and organizational sales: the case of convenience stores. *Academy of Management Journal,* **31,** 461–87.

Y

Yerkes–Dodson law First proposed by Robert M. Yerkes and John D. Dodson in 1908, the Yerkes–Dodson law describes a curvilinear relationship between *arousal and performance, often depicted as an inverted U-shaped curve (see Fig. Y1). Performance improves as arousal increases up to a certain point, after which it deteriorates. At levels of arousal that are too low, the organism may lack the *motivation for optimal performance. Very high levels of arousal are debilitating, causing disorganized behaviour or excessive focus on a narrow range of stimuli or responses (typically the most well-learned, dominant response). 'Arousal' may be purely physiological, or it may be emotional. 'Performance' has been interpreted very broadly to include information processing, learning, memory, thinking, problem-solving, skilled behaviour, and adaptive responses.

PHOEBE C. ELLSWORTH

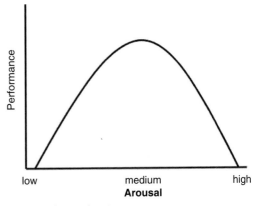

Fig. Y1. Yerkes–Dodson Law.

Z

zygomatic muscle The zygomaticus major muscle is located in the lower part of the face. It is proximally attached to the lateral surface of the zygomatic bone of the skull and distally to the skin lateral to the upper lip and the corner of the mouth (Pernkopf *et al.* 1989). The muscle is located directly under the skin, overlying several other muscles surrounding the mouth. Its contraction moves the corner of the mouth in an upward and lateral direction, which constitutes the most typical component of *smiling. Although other muscles may contribute to this action, and a real smile (see DUCHENNE SMILE) is also characterized by narrowing of the eye aperture due to activity of the ciliary muscle around the eye, the role of zygomaticus major in producing a real smile may be considered predominant. In behavioural research, the electrical activity (electromyogram) of this muscle is often used as an index of the subject's affective state (see ELECTROMYOGRAPHY). In comparison with the minimum level of activity during a neutral affective state, zygomaticus activity is proportionally increased during states of increasing positive *valence. This relationship is not perfectly linear as the activity is also somewhat increased during extremely negative states.

Although zygomaticus activity may be a useful marker of emotional valence, changes in activity may also be determined by nonemotional aspects of cognitive information processing. Inhibition of zygomaticus activity may occur during automatic *orienting responses to unexpected changes in the environment, or during voluntary attention to external stimuli.

ANTON VAN BOXTEL

References

Aarts, H. (2007). Unconscious authorship ascription: the effects of success and effect-specific information priming on experienced authorship. *Journal of Experimental Social Psychology*, **43**, 119–26.

Abbott, D.H., Keverne, E.B., Bercovitch, F.B., Shively, C.A., Mendoza, S.P., Saltzman, W., *et al.* (2003). Are subordinates always stressed? A comparative analysis of rank differences in cortisol levels among primates. *Hormones and Behavior*, **43**, 67–82.

Abe, J.A. and Izard, C.E. (1999). The developmental functions of emotions: an analysis in terms of differential emotions theory. *Cognition and Emotion*, **13**, 523–49.

Abel, M. (2002). *An empirical reflection on the smile.* New York: The Edwin Mellen Press.

Abrahamsson, M. and Sundberg, J. (2007). Subglottal pressure variation in actors' stage speech. In: M. Rees (ed.), *Voice and gender*, pp. 343–7. Cincinnati, OH: Voice and Speech Trainers Association.

Abramson, L.Y., Seligman, M.E.P., and Teasdale, J.D. (1978). Learned helplessness in humans: critique and reformulation. *Journal of Abnormal Psychology*, **87**, 49–74.

Abu-Lughod, L. (1985). Honor and the sentiments of loss in a Bedouin society. *American Ethnologist*, **12**, 245–61.

Abu-Lughod, L. (1986). *Veiled sentiments.* Berkeley, CA: University of California Press.

Ackerknecht, E.H. (1974). The history of the discovery of the vegatative (autonomic) nervous system. *Medical History*, **18**, 1–8.

Àdàm, G. (1967). *Interoception and behavior: an experimental study* (transl. R. Chatel and R. Slucki). Budapest: Akademiai Kiado.

Adams, R.B., Gordon, H.L., Baird, A.A., Ambady, N., and Kleck, R.E. (2003). Effects of gaze on amygdala sensitivity to anger and fear faces. *Science*, **300**, 1536.

Adelman, P.K. and Zajonc, R.B. (1989). Facial efference and the experience of emotion. *Annual Review of Psychology*, **40**, 249–80.

Ader, R. (ed.) (2007). *Psychoneuroimmunology*, 4th edn. Amsterdam: Elsevier.

Ader, R., Felton, D.L., and Cohen, N. (eds) (2001). *Psychoneuroimmunology*, 3rd edn. San Diego, CA: Academic Press.

Adolphs, R. (2002). Recognizing emotion from facial expressions: psychological and neurological mechanisms. *Behavioral and Cognitive Neuroscience Reviews*, **1**, 21–61.

Adolphs, R. (2003). Cognitive neuroscience of human social behaviour. *Neuroscience Reviews*, **4**, 165–78.

Adolphs, R., Russell, J.A., and Tranel, D. (1999). A role for the human amygdala in recognizing emotional arousal from unpleasant stimuli. *Psychological Science*, **10**, 167–71.

Adolphs, R., Damasio, H., Tranel, D., Cooper, G., and Damasio, A.R. (2000). A role for somatosensory cortices in the visual recognition of emotion as revealed by 3-D lesion mapping. *Journal of Neuroscience*, **20**, 2683–90.

Adolphs, R., Tranel, D., and Damasio, H. (2002). Neural systems for recognizing emotion from prosody. *Emotion*, **2**, 23–51.

Adolphs, R., Gosselin, F., Buchanan, T.W., Tranel, D., Schyns, P.G., and Damasio, A.R. (2005a). A mechanism for impaired fear recognition after amygdala damage. *Nature*, **433**, 68–72.

Adolphs, R., Tranel, D., and Buchanan, T.W. (2005b). Amygdala damage impairs emotional memory for gist but not details of complex stimuli. *Nature Neuroscience*, **8**, 512–18.

Ågmo, A. (1999). Sexual motivation—an inquiry into events determining the occurrence of sexual behavior. *Behavioural Brain Research*, **105**, 129–50.

Ågmo, A., Turi, A.L., Ellingsen, E., and Kaspersen, H. (2004). Preclinical models of sexual desire: conceptual and behavioral analysis. *Pharmacology, Biochemistry and Behavior*, **78**, 379–404.

Ainsworth, M.D.S., Blehar, M.C., Waters, E., and Wall, S. (1978). *Patterns of attachment: a psychological study of the strange situation.* Hillsdale, NJ: Lawrence Erlbaum Associates.

AISB '05 (2005). *Social intelligence and interaction in animals, robots and agents. University of Hertfordshire, Hatfield, UK, 12–15 April 2005. Proceedings of the Symposium on Agents that Want and Like: Motivational and Emotional Roots of Cognition and Action* (available at: http://www.aisb.org.uk/publications/proceedings/aisb05/2_Agents_Final.pdf).

Aksan, N. and Kochanska, G. (2005). Conscience in childhood: old questions, new answers. *Developmental Psychology*, **41**, 506–16.

Alcock, J. (2001). *The triumph of sociobiology.* New York: Oxford University Press.

Aldwin, C.M. (1994). *Stress, coping, and development: an integrative perspective.* New York: Guilford Press.

Alexander, R.D. (1987). *The biology of moral systems.* New York: Aldine De Gruyter.

Allen, S.R. (2001). *Concern processing in autonomous agents.* PhD Thesis, University of Birmingham (available at: http://citeseer.ist.psu.edu/allen01concern.html).

Allport, G.W. (1950). *The individual and his religion: a psychological interpretation.* New York: Macmillan.

Amaral, D.G. (2000). The anatomical organization of the central nervous system. In: E.R. Kandel, J.H. Schwartz, and T.M. Jessell (eds), *Principles of neural science*, 4th edn, pp. 317–36. New York, McGraw-Hill.

Amaral, D.G., Price, J.L., Pitkanen, A., and Carmichael, S.T. (1992). Anatomical organization of the primate amygdaloid complex. In: J.P. Aggleton (ed.), *The amygdala: neurobiological aspects of emotion, memory, and mental dysfunction*, pp. 1–65. New York: Wiley-Liss.

Ambady, N. and Rosenthal, R. (1992). Thin slices of expressive behavior as predictors of interpersonal consequences: a meta-analysis. *Psychological Bulletin*, **111**, 256–74.

References

Ambady, N. and Rosenthal, R. (1993). Half a minute: predicting teacher evaluations from thin slices of nonverbal behavior and physical attractiveness. *Journal of Personality and Social Psychology*, **64**, 431–41.

American Psychiatric Association (1994). *Diagnostic and statistical manual of mental disorders* (DSM-IV). Washington, DC: American Psychiatric Association.

American Psychiatric Association (2000). *Diagnostic and statistical manual of mental disorders*, 4th edn, text revision (DSM-IV-TR). Washington, DC: American Psychiatric Association.

American Psychological Association (1997). *Task force on promotion and dissemination of psychological procedures. A report to the Division 12 board of the American Psychological Association*. (Available from the Division 12 of the American Psychological Association, 750 First Street, NE, Washington, DC 20002–4242, USA.)

Amodio, D.M. and Frith, C.D. (2006). Meeting of minds: the medial frontal cortex and social cognition. *Nature Reviews Neuroscience*, **7**, 268–77.

Amsel, A. (1992). Frustration theory—many years later. *Psychological Bulletin*, **112**, 396–9.

Anagnostaras, S.G., Gale, G.D., and Fansleow, M.S. (2001). Hippocampus and contextual fear conditioning: recent controversies and advances. *Hippocampus*, **11**, 8–17.

Anderson, A.K. and Phelps, E.A. (2000). Expression without recognition: contributions of the human amygdala to emotional communication. *Psychological Science*, **11**, 106–11.

Anderson, A.K. and Phelps, E.A. (2001). Lesions of the human amygdala impair enhanced perception of emotionally salient events. *Nature*, **411**, 305–9.

Anderson, C.M. and Putterman, L. (2006). Do non-strategic sanctions obey the law of demand? The demand for punishment in the voluntary contribution mechanism. *Games and Economic Behavior*, **54**, 1–24.

Andreoni, J. (1990). Impure altruism and donations to public goods: a theory of warm glow giving. *Economic Journal*, **100**, 464–77.

Andreoni, J. and Miller, J. (2002). Giving according to Garp: an experimental test of the consistenca of preferences for altruism. *Econometrica*, **70**, 737–53.

Andrew, R.J. (1963a). The origin and evolution of the calls and facial expressions of the primates. *Behaviour*, **20**, 1–109.

Andrew, R.J. (1963b). Evolution of facial expression. *Science*, **142**, 1034–41.

Angel, L. (2005). Compositional science and religious philosophy. *Religious Studies*, **41**, 125–43.

Angyal, A. (1941). Disgust and related aversions. *Journal of Abnormal and Social Psychology*, **36**, 393–412.

Archer, J. (1999). *The nature of grief: the evolution and psychology of reactions to loss*. London: Routledge.

Argyle, M. (1988). *Bodily communication of emotions*. London: Methuen.

Argyle, M. (1999). Causes and correlates of happiness. In: D. Kahneman, E. Diener, and N. Schwarz (eds), *Well-being: the foundations of hedonic psychology*, pp. 353–73. New York: Russell Sage Foundation.

Aristotle (1941). *Rhetoric*. In: R. McKeon (ed.), *The basic works of Aristotle*. New York: Random House.

Aristotle (1984). Nicomachean ethics. In: J. Barnes (ed.), *The complete works of Aristotle: the revised Oxford translation*, Bollingen series. Princeton, NJ: Princeton University Press.

Aristotle (1987). *Poetics*, transl. R. Janko. Indianapolis, IN: Hackett.

Armon-Jones, C. (1986). The thesis of constructionism. In: R. Harré (ed.), *The social construction of emotions*, pp. 32–56. Oxford: Blackwell.

Armony, J.L., Servan-Schreiber, D., Cohen, J.D., and LeDoux, J. E. (1995). An anatomically constrained neural network model of fear conditioning. *Behavioral Neuroscience*, **109**, 246–57.

Armony, J.L., Servan-Schreiber, D., Cohen, J.D., and LeDoux, J.E. (1997). Computational modeling of emotion: explorations through the anatomy and physiology of fear conditioning. *Trends in Cognitive Science*, **1**, 28–34.

Armor, D.A. and Taylor, S.E. (1998). Situated optimism: specific outcome expectancies and self-regulation. In: M.P. Zanna (ed.), *Advances in experimental social psychology*, pp. 309–79. New York: Academic Press.

Armstrong, D. (1962). *Bodily sensations*. London: Routledge and Kegan Paul.

Arnold, M.B. (1960). *Emotion and personality*. New York: Columbia University Press.

Aron, A. and Aron, E.N. (1986). *Love and the expansion of self: understanding attraction and satisfaction*. New York: Hemisphere Publishing.

Arrow, K.J. (1974). *The limits of organization*. New York: W. W. Norton and Co.

Arrow, K.J. (2004). Is bounded rationality unboundedly rational? In: M. Augier and J.G. March (eds), *Models of a man: essays in memory of Herbert A. Simon*, pp. 47–55. Cambridge, MA: MIT Press.

Arsenio, W.F., Gold, J., and Adams, R. (2006). Children's conceptions and displays of moral emotions. In: M. Killen and J.G. Smetana (eds), *Handbook of moral development*, pp. 581–609. Mahwah, NJ: Lawrence Erlbaum Associates.

Asendorpf, J.B. (1989). Shyness as a final common pathway for two different kinds of inhibition. *Journal of Personality and Social Psychology*, **57**, 481–92.

Asendorpf, J.B. (1990). Development of inhibition during childhood: evidence for situational specificity and a two-factor model. *Developmental Psychology*, **26**, 721–30.

Asendorpf, J.B. (2007). Shyness. In: M.M. Haith and J.B. Benson (eds), *Encyclopedia of infant and childhood development*. San Diego, CA: Elsevier.

Ashkanasy, N.M., Härtel, C.E.J., and Zerbe, W.J. (eds).(2000). *Emotions in the workplace: research, theory, and practice*. London: Quorum Books.

Atkinson, A.P., Dittrich, W.H., Gemmell, A.J., and Young, A.W. (2004). Emotion perception from dynamic and static body expressions in point-light and full-light displays. *Perception*, **33**, 717–46.

Atkinson, J.W. (1964). *An introduction to motivation*. New York: Van Nostrand.

Aue, T., Flykt, A., and Scherer, K.R. (2007). First evidence for differential and sequential efferent effects of goal relevance and goal conduciveness appraisal. *Biological Psychology*, **74**, 347–57.

Aureli, F. and van Schaik, C.P. (1991). Post-conflict behaviour in long-tailed macaques (*Macaca fascicularis*): II. Coping with the uncertainty. *Ethology*, **89**, 101–14.

Austin, J.T. and Vancouver, J.B. (1996). Goal constructs in psychology: structure, process, and content. *Psychological Bulletin*, **120**, 338–75.

Ausubel, D.P. (1955). Relationships between shame and guilt in the socializing process. *Psychological Review*, **62**, 378–90.

Averill, J.R. (1980). A constructivist view of emotions. In: R. Plutchnik and H. Kellerman (eds), *Emotion: theory, research and experience*, Vol. I. *Theories of emotion*, pp. 305–39. New York: Academic Press.

Averill, J.R. (1982). *Anger and aggression. An essay on emotion*. New York: Springer.

Averill, J.R. (2005). Emotions as mediators and as products of creative activity. In: J. Kaufman and J. Baer (eds), *Creativity across domains: faces of the muse*, pp. 225–43. Mahwah, NJ: Lawrence Erlbaum Associates.

Axelrod, R. and Hamilton, W.D. (1981). The evolution of cooperation. *Science*, **211**, 1390–1396.

Aydede, M. (ed.) (2005). *Pain: new essays on its nature and the methodology of its study*. Cambridge, MA: MIT Press.

Ayduk, O., Mendoza-Denton, R., Mischel, W., Downey, G., Peake, P.K., and Rodriguez, M. (2000). Regulating the interpersonal self: strategic self-regulation for coping with rejection sensitivity. *Journal of Personality and Social Psychology*, **79**, 776–92.

Ayduk, O., Zayas, V., Downey, G., Cole, A.B., Shoda, Y., and Mischel, W. (2008). Rejection sensitivity and executive control: joint predictors of borderline personality features. *Journal of Research in Personality*, **42**, 151–68.

Bach, D.R., Schachinger, H., Neuhoff, J.G., Esposito, F., Salle, F.D., Lehmann, C., Herdener, M., Scheffler, K., and Seifritz, E. (2008). Rising sound intensity: an intrinsic warning cue activating the amygdala. *Cerebral Cortex*, **18**, 145–50.

Bachorowski, J.-A. and Owren, M.J. (2008). Vocal expression of emotion. In: M. Lewis, J.M. Haviland-Jones, and L. Feldman Barrett (eds), *Handbook of emotions*, 3rd edn, pp. 196–210. New York: Guilford Press.

Bachorowski, J.-A., Smoski, M.J., and Owren, M.J. (2001). The acoustic features of human laughter. *Journal of the Acoustical Society of America*, **110**, 1581–97.

Badger, G.J., Bickel, W.K., Giordano, L.A., Jacobs, E.A., and Loewenstein, G. (2007). Altered states: the impact of immediate craving on the valuation of current and future opioids. *Journal of Health Economics*, **26**, 865–76.

Bagby, R.M., Parker, J.D.A., and Taylor, G.J. (1994). The 20-Item Toronto-Alexithymia-Scale. 1. Item selection and cross-validation of the factor structure. *Journal of Psychosomatic Research*, **38**, 23–32.

Bagozzi, R.P., Wong, N., and Yi, Y. (1999). The role of culture and gender in the relationship between positive and negative affect. *Cognition and Emotion*, **13**, 641–72.

Baldwin, J.M. (1906). *Social and ethical interpretations in mental development: a study in social psychology*, 4th ed. London: Macmillan.

Balleine, B.W. and Dickinson, A. (1998). Goal-directed instrumental action: contingency and incentive learning and their cortical substrates. *Neuropharmacology*, **37**, 407–19.

Bamberg, M. (1997). Emotion talk(s). The role of perspective in the construction of emotions. In: S. Niemeier and R. Dirven (eds), *The language of emotions*, pp. 209–25. Amsterdam: John Benjamin.

Bamberg, M. (2001). Why young American English-speaking children confuse anger and sadness: a study of grammar in practice. In: K. Nelson, A. Aksu-Koc, and C. Johnson (eds), *Children's language*, Vol. 10: *Language in use, narratives and interaction*, pp. 55–72. Mahwah, NJ: Lawrence Erlbaum Associates.

Bandes, S.A. (ed.) (1999). *The passions of law*. New York: New York University Press.

Bandura, A. (1977). Self-efficacy: toward a unifying theory of behavioral change. *Psychological Review*, **84**, 191–215.

Bandura, A. (1986). *Social foundations of thought and action*. New York: Prentice Hall.

Banks, W.A. (2006). The blood–brain barrier in psychoneuroimmunology. *Neurology Clinics*, **24**, 413–19.

Banse, R. and Scherer, K.R. (1996). Acoustic profiles in vocal emotion expression. *Journal of Personality and Social Psychology*, **70**, 614–36.

Bänziger, T. (2004). *Communication vocale des émotions: perception de l'expression vocale et attributions émotionelles*, PhD thesis. School of Psychology, University of Geneva.

Bar, M. (2004). Visual objects in context. *Nature Reviews Neuroscience*, **5**, 617–29.

Barbalet, J.M. (2001). *Emotion, social theory and social structure: a macrosociological approach*. Cambridge: Cambridge University Press.

Barclay, L.J., Skarlicki, D.P. and Pugh, S.D. (2005). Exploring the role of emotions in injustice perceptions and retaliation. *Journal of Applied Psychology*, **90**, 629–43.

Bargh, J.A. (1992). The ecology of automaticity. Toward establishing the conditions needed to produce automatic processing effects. *American Journal of Psychology*, **105**, 181–99.

Bargh, J.A. (1996). Automaticity in social psychology. In: E.T. Higgins and A.W. Kruglanski (eds), *Social psychology: handbook of basic principles*, pp. 169–83. New York: Guilford Press.

Bargh, J.A. (1997). The automaticity of everyday life. In: R.S. Wyer (ed.), *Advances in social cognition*, Vol. 10, pp. 1–61. Mahwah, NJ: Lawrence Erlbaum Associates.

Bar-Haim, Y., Lamy, D., Pergamin, L., Bakermans-Kranenburg, M.J., and van Ijzendoorn, M.H. (2007). Threat-related attentional bias in anxious and nonanxious individuals: a meta-analytic study. *Psychological Bulletin*, **133**, 1–24.

Barker, R., Dembo, T., and Lewin, K. (1941). *Frustration and regression*. Iowa City: University of Iowa Studies in Child Welfare.

Barlow, D.H. (2002). *Anxiety and its disorders: the nature and treatment of anxiety and panic*, 2nd edn. New York: Guilford Press.

Barlow, D.H., Gorman, J.M., Shear, M.K., and Woods, S.W. (2000). Cognitive-behavioral therapy, imipramine, or their combination for panic disorder: a randomized controlled trial. *Journal of the American Medical Association*, **283**, 2529–36.

Bar-On, R. (2004). The Bar-On Emotional Quotient Inventory (EQ-i): rationale, description and summary of psychometric properties. In: G. Geher (ed.), *Measuring emotional intelligence: common ground and controversy*, pp. 115–45. New York: Nova Science Publishers.

Baron, R.A. and Richardson, D.R. (1994). *Human aggression*, 2nd edn. New York: Plenum.

Baron-Cohen, S. and Belmonte, M.K. (2005). Autism: a window onto the development of the social and the analytic brain. *Annual Review of Neuroscience*, **28**, 109–26.

Baron-Cohen, S., Knickmeyer, R.C., and Belmonte, M.K. (2005). Sex differences in the brain: implications for explaining autism. *Science*, **310**, 819–23.

References

Barrett, L.F. (1996). Hedonic tone, perceived arousal, and item desirability: three components of affective experience. *Cognition and Emotion*, **10**, 47–68.

Barrett, L.F. (2004). Feelings or words? Understanding the content in self-report ratings of emotional experience. *Journal of Personality and Social Psychology*, **87**, 266–81.

Barrett, L.F. (2005). Feeling is perceiving: core affect and conceptualization in the experience of emotion. In: L.F. Barrett, P. Niedenthal, and P. Winkielman (eds), *Emotion and consciousness*, pp. 255–84. New York: Guilford Press.

Barrett, L.F. (2006a). Valence as a basic building block of emotional life. *Journal of Research in Personality*, **40**, 35–55.

Barrett, L.F. (2006b). Solving the emotion paradox: categorization and the experience of emotion. *Personality and Social Psychology Review*, **101**, 20–46.

Barrett, L.F. (2006c). Are emotions natural kinds? *Perspectives on Psychological Science*, **1**, 28–58.

Barrett, L.F. and Fossum, T. (2001). Mental representations of affect knowledge. *Cognition and Emotion*, **15**, 333–64.

Barrett, L.F. and Russell, J.A. (1999). The structure of current affect: controversies and emerging consensus. *Current Directions in Psychological Science*, **8**, 10–14.

Barrett, L.F., Quigley, K., Bliss-Moreau, E., and Aronson, K.R. (2004). Arousal focus and interoceptive sensitivity. *Journal of Personality and Social Psychology*, **87**, 684–97.

Barrett, L.F., Niedenthal, P.M., and Winkielman, P. (eds) (2005). *Emotion and consciousness*. New York: Guilford Press.

Barrett, L.F., Lindquist, K.A., and Gendron, M. (2007a). Language as context for perception of emotion. *Trends in Cognitive Sciences*, **11**, 327–32.

Barrett, L.F., Mesquita, B., Ochsner, K.N., and Gross, J.J. (2007b). The experience of emotion. *Annual Review of Psychology*, **58**, 373–403.

Barry, B., Fulmer, I.S., Van Kleef, G.A. (2004). I laughed, I cried, I settled: the role of emotion in negotiation. In: M. Gelfand and J. Brett (eds), *The handbook of negotiation and culture*, pp. 71–94. Palo Alto, CA: Stanford University Press.

Barr-Zisowitz, C. (2000). 'Sadness': is there such a thing? In: M. Lewis and J.M. Haviland-Jones (eds), *Handbook of emotions*, 2nd edn, pp. 607–22. New York: Guilford Press.

Barsade, S.G., Brief, A.P., and Spataro, S.E. (2003). The affective revolution in organizational behavior: the emergence of a paradigm. In: J. Greenberg (ed.), *Organizational behavior: the state of the science*, pp. 3–52. Mahwah, NJ: Lawrence Erlbaum Associates.

Barsalou, L.W. (1999). Perceptual symbol systems. *Behavioral and Brain Sciences*, **22**, 577–660.

Barsalou, L.W. (2005). Situated conceptualization. In: H. Cohen and C. Lefebvre (eds), *Handbook of categorization in cognitive science*, pp. 619–50. St Louis, MO: Elsevier.

Bar-Tal, D., Halperin, E., and de Rivera, J. (2007). Collective emotions in conflict situations: societal implications. *Journal of Social Issues*, **63**, 441–60.

Bartels, A. and Zeki, S. (2000). The neural basis of romantic love. *Neuroreport*, **11**, 3829–34.

Bartels, A. and Zeki, S. (2004). The neural correlates of maternal and romantic love. *Neuroimage*, **21**, 1155–66.

Bartlett, M.Y. and DeSteno, D. (2006). Gratitude and prosocial behavior: helping when it costs you. *Psychological Science*, **17**, 319–25.

Barton, R.A., Aggleton, J.P., and Grenyer, R. (2003). Evolutionary coherence of the mammalian amygdala. *Proceedings of the Royal Society B: Biological Sciences*, **270**, 539–43.

Basbaum A.I. and Fields H.L. (1984). Endogenous pain control systems: brainstem spinal pathways and endorphin circuitry. *Annual Review of Neuroscience*, **7**, 309–38.

Basch, J. and Fisher, C. (2000). Affective events-emotions matrix: a classification of work events and associated emotions. In: N. Ashkenasy, C. Hartel, and W. Zerbe (eds), *Emotions in the workplace: theory, research and practice*, pp. 36–49. Westport, CT: Quorum Books.

Basmajian, J.V. and De Luca, C.J. (1985). *Muscles alive: their functions revealed by electromyography*, 5th edn. Baltimore, MD: Williams and Wilkins.

Bateson, G. (1976). Some components of socialization for trance. In: T. Schwartz (ed), *Socialization as cultural communication*, pp. 51–63. Berkeley, CA: University of California Press.

Batson, C.D. (1991). *The altruism question: toward a social-psychological answer*. Hillsdale, NJ: Lawrence Erlbaum Associates.

Batson, C.D., Schoenrade, P.A., and Ventis, W.L. (1993). *Religion and the individual*. New York: Oxford University Press.

Batson, C.D., Early, S., and Salvarini, G. (1997). Perspective taking: imagining how another feels versus imagining how you would feel. *Personality and Social Personality Bulletin*, **23**, 751–8.

Batson, C.D., van Lange, P.A.M., Ahmad, N., and Lishner, D.L. (2006). Altruism and helping behavior. In: M.A. Hogg and J. Cooper (eds), *The Sage handbook of social psychology*, pp. 279–95. New York: Sage Publications.

Baum, A. and Posluszny, D.M. (1999). Health psychology: mapping biobehavioral contributions to health and illness. *Annual Review of Psychology*, **50**, 137–63.

Baum, A., O'Keefe, M.K., and Davidson, L.M. (1990). Acute stressors and chronic response: the case of traumatic stress. *Journal of Applied Social Psychology*, **20**, 1643–54.

Baumeister, R.F. (1982). A self-presentational view of social phenomena. *Psychological Bulletin*, **91**, 3–26.

Baumeister, R. (1986). *Identity: cultural change and the struggle for self*. New York: Oxford University Press.

Baumeister, R.F. (1998). The self. In: D.T. Gilbert, S.T. Fiske, and G. Lindzey (eds), *Handbook of social psychology*, 4th edn, pp. 680–740. New York: McGraw-Hill.

Baumeister, R.F. (ed.) (1999). *The self in social psychology*. Philadelphia, PA: Psychology Press.

Baumeister, R.F. (2005). *The cultural animal: human nature, meaning, and social life*. New York: Oxford University Press.

Baumeister, R.F. and Heatherton, T.F. (1996). Self-regulation failure: an overview. *Psychological Inquiry*, **7**, 1–15.

Baumeister, R.F. and Leary, M.R. (1995). The need to belong: desire for interpersonal attachments as a fundamental human motivation. *Psychological Bulletin*, **117**, 497–529.

Baumeister, R.F. and Vohs, K.D. (eds) (2004). *Handbook of self-regulation: research, theory, and applications*. New York: Guilford Press.

Baumeister, R.F., Stillwell, A.M., and Heatherton, T.F. (1994). Guilt: an interpersonal approach. *Psychological Bulletin*, **115**, 243–67.

Baumeister, R.F., Bratslavsky, E., Muraven, M., and Tice, D.M. (1998). Ego depletion: is the active self a limited resource? *Journal of Personality and Social Psychology*, **74**, 1252–65.

Baumeister, R.F., Bratslavsky, E., Finkenauer, C., and Vohs, K.D. (2001). Bad is stronger than good. *Review of General Psychology*, **5**, 323–70.

Baumeister, R.F., Campbell, J.D., Krueger, J.I., and Vohs, K.D. (2003). Does high self-esteem cause better performance interpersonal success, happiness, or healthier lifestyles? *Psychological Science in the Public Interest*, **4**, 1–44.

Baumeister, R.F., Vohs, K.D., DeWall, C.N., and Zhang, L. (2007). How emotion shapes behavior: feedback, anticipation, and reflection, rather than direct causation. *Personality and Social Psychology Review*, **11**, 167–203.

Bavelas, J.B., Black, A., Lemery, C.R., and Mullett, J. (1986). 'I show how you feel': motor mimicry as a communicative act. *Journal of Personality and Social Psychology*, **50**, 322–9.

Baxter, M.G. and Murray, E.A. (2002). The amygdala and reward. *Nature Reviews Neuroscience*, **3**, 563–73.

Bazerman, M.H., Curhan, J.R., and Moore, D.A. (2000). The death and rebirth of the social psychology of negotiation. In: M. Clark and G. Fletcher (eds), *Blackwell handbook of social psychology*, pp. 196–228. Cambridge, MA: Blackwell.

BBC News (2006). *Bad behaviour 'worst in Europe'*, 8 May. http://news.bbc.co.uk/1/hi/uk/4751315.stm (accessed 10 december 2008).

Beal, D.J., Weiss, H.M., Barros, E., and MacDermid, S.M. (2005). An episodic process model of affective influence. *Journal of Applied Psychology*, **90**, 1054–68.

Bebbington, P. (2004). The classification and epidemiology of unipolar depression. In: M.J. Power (ed.), *Mood disorders: a handbook of science and practice*, pp. 3–27. Chichester: Wiley.

Bebbington, P. and Ramana, R. (1995). The epidemiology of bipolar affective disorder. *Social Psychiatry and Psychiatric Epidemiology*, **30**, 279–92.

Bechara, A. and Van der Linden, M. (2005). Decision-making and impulsive control after frontal lobe injuries. *Current Opinion in Neurology*, **18**, 734–9.

Bechara, A., Damasio, A.R., Damasio, H., and Anderson, S.W. (1994). Insensitivity to future consequences following damage to human prefrontal cortex. *Cognition*, **50**, 7–15.

Bechara, A., Damasio, H., Tranel, D., and Damasio, A.R. (1997). Deciding advantageously before knowing the advantageous strategy. *Science*, **275**, 1293–5.

Bechara, A., Damasio, H., and Damasio, A.R. (1999). Role of the amygdala in decision-making. *Annals of the New York Academy of Science*, **985**, 356–69.

Bechara, A., Damasio, H., and Damasio, A.R. (2003). Role of the amygdala in decision-making. *Annals of the New York Academy of Sciences*, **985**, 356–69.

Bechara, A., Damasio, H., Tranel, D., and Damasio, A.R. (2005). The Iowa Gambling Task (IGT) and the somatic marker hypothesis (SMH): some questions and answers. *Trends in Cognitive Sciences*, **9**, 159–62.

Becht, M. and Vingerhoets, A. (2002). Crying and mood change. *Cognition and Emotion*, **16**, 87–101.

Beck, A.T., Rush, A.J., Shaw, B.F., and Emery, G. (1979). *Cognitive therapy of depression: a treatment manual.* New York: Guilford Press.

Beck, A.T., Emery, G., and Greenberg, R.L. (1985). *Anxiety disorders and phobias.* New York: Basic Books.

Beck, A.T., Steer, R.A., and Brown, G.K. (1996). *Manual for the Beck Depression Inventory.* San Antonio, TX: Psychological Corporation.

Beck, C.T. (1996). A meta-analysis of the relationship between postpartum depression and infant temperament. *Nursing Research*, **45**, 225–30.

Becker, J., Breedlove, M., Crews, D., and McCarthy, M. (eds) (2002). *Behavioral endocrinology*, 2nd edn. Cambridge, MA: MIT Press.

Beck, R.C. (2004). *Motivation: theories and principles*, 5th edn. Upper Saddle River, NJ: Pearson.

Bedford, E. (1956–7). Emotions. *Proceedings of the Aristotelian Society*, **57**.

Bell, C. (1914). *Art.* London: Chatto and Windus.

Bell, D. (1982). Regret in decision making under uncertainty. *Operations Research*, **30**, 961–81.

Bentall, R.P., Corcoran, R., Howard, R., Blackwood, N., and Kinderman, P. (2001). Persecutory delusions: a review and theoretical integration. *Clinical Psychology Review*, **21**, 1143–92.

Ben-Ze'ev, A. (2000). *The subtlety of emotions.* Cambridge, MA: MIT Press.

Ben Zion, I.Z., Tessler, R., Cohen, L., Lerer, E., Raz, Y., Bacher-Melman, R., *et al.* (2006). Polymorphisms in dopamine D4 receptor gene (DRD4) contribute to individual differences in human sexual behavior: desire, arousal and sexual function. *Molecular Psychiatry*, **11**, 782–6.

Berg, J., Dickhaut, J., and McCabe, K. (1995). Trust, reciprocity and social history. *Games and Economic Behavior*, **10**, 122–42.

Bergeron, L., Valla, J., and Breton, J. (1992). Pilot study for the Quebec Child Mental Health Survey: Part 1. Measurement of prevalence estimates among six to 14 year olds. *Canadian Journal of Psychiatry*, **37**, 374–80.

Berkowitz, L. (1983). Aversively stimulated aggression. *American Psychologist*, **38**, 1135–44.

Berkowitz, L. (1989). The frustratration–aggression hypothesis: examination and reformulation. *Psychological Bulletin*, **106**, 59–73.

Berkowitz, L. (2000) *Causes and consequences of feelings.* Cambridge: Cambridge University Press.

Berkowitz, L. and Harmon-Jones, E. (2004). Toward an understanding of the determinants of anger. *Emotion*, **4**, 107–30.

Berlin, H., Rolls, E.T., and Kischka, U. (2004). Impulsivity, time perception, emotion, and reinforcement sensitivity in patients with orbitofrontal cortex lesions. *Brain*, **127**, 1108–26.

Berlyne, D.E. (1960). *Conflict, arousal, and curiosity.* New York: McGraw-Hill.

Berlyne, D.E. (1971). *Aesthetics and psychobiology.* New York: Appleton-Century-Crofts.

Berns, G.S., Cohen, J.D., and Mintun, M.A. (1997). Brain regions responsive to novelty in the absence of awareness. *Science*, **276**, 1272–5.

Berns, G.S., Chappelow, J., Cekic, M., Zink, C.F., Pagnoni, G., and Martin-Skurski, M.E. (2006). Neurobiological substrates of dread. *Science*, **312**, 754–8.

Berntson, G.G. and Cacioppo, J.T. (2007). Integrative physiology: homeostasis, allostasis, and the orchestration of systemic physiology. In: J.T. Cacioppo, L.G. Tassinary, and G.G. Berntson (eds), *Handbook of psychophysiology*, 3rd edn, pp. 433–52. Cambridge: Cambridge University Press.

Berntson, G.G., Cacioppo, J.T., and Quigley, K.S. (1991). Autonomic determinism: the modes of autonomic control, the doctrine of autonomic space, and the laws of autonomic constraint. *Psychological Review*, **98**, 459–87.

References

Berntson, G.G., Cacioppo, J.T., and Quigley, K.S. (1993). Respiratory sinus arrhythmia: autonomic origins, physiological mechanisms, and psychophysiological implications. *Psychophysiology*, **30**, 183–96.

Berntson, G.G., Sarter, M., and Cacioppo, J.T. (2003a). Ascending visceral regulation of cortical affective information processing. *European Journal of Neuroscience*, **18**, 2103–109.

Berntson, G.G., Cacioppo, J.T., and Sarter, M. (2003b). Bottom-up: implications for neurobehavioral models of anxiety and autonomic regulation. In: R.J. Davidson, K.R. Scherer, and H.H. Goldsmith (eds), *Handbook of affective sciences*, pp. 1105–16. New York: Oxford University Press.

Berntson, G.G., Quigley, K.S., and Lozano, D. (2007). Cardiovascular psychophysiology. In: J.T. Cacioppo, L.G. Tassinary, and G.G. Berntson (eds), *Handbook of psychophysiology*, 3rd edn, pp. 182–210. Cambridge: Cambridge University Press.

Berridge, K. (1999). Pleasure, pain, desire, and dread: hidden core processes of emotion. In: D. Kahneman, E. Diener, and N. Schwarz (eds), *Well-being: the foundations of hedonic psychology*, pp. 525–57. New York: Russell Sage Foundation.

Berridge, K.C. (2001). Reward learning: reinforcement, incentives, and expectations. In: D.L. Medin (ed.), *The psychology of learning and motivation*, Vol. 40, pp. 223–78. San Diego, CA: Academic Press.

Berridge, K.C. (2003a). Comparing the emotional brain of humans and other animals. In: R.J. Davidson, H.H. Goldsmith, and K.R. Scherer (eds), *Handbook of affective sciences*, pp. 25–51. New York: Oxford University Press.

Berridge, K.C. (2003b). Pleasures of the brain. *Brain and Cognition*, **52**, 106–28.

Bertenthal, B.I., Campos, J.J., and Kermoian, R. (1994). An epigenetic perspective on the development of self-produced locomotion and its consequences. *Current Directions in Psychological Science*, **3**, 140–145.

Bibring, E. (1953). The mechanism of depression. In: P.Greenacre (ed.), *Affective disorders*. NewYork: International Universities Press.

Birnbaum, G.E., Reis, H.T., Mikulincer, M., Gillath, O., and Orpaz, A. (2006). When sex is more than just sex: attachment orientations, sexual experience, and relationship quality. *Journal of Personality and Social Psychology*, **91**, 929–43.

Bishop, S.J. (2007). Neurocognitive mechanisms of anxiety: an integrative account. *Trends in Cognitive Sciences*, **11**, 307–16.

Black, M. (1962). Metaphor. In: M. Black (ed.), *Models and metaphors*, pp. 25–47. Ithaca, NY: Cornell University Press.

Blackburn, S. (1998). *Ruling passions*. Oxford: Clarendon Press.

Blader, S.L. and Tyler, T.R. (2005). How can theories of organizational justice explain the effects of fairness? In: J. Greenberg and J.A. Colquitt (eds), *Handbook of organizational justice*, pp. 329–54. Mahwah, NJ: Lawrence Erlbaum Associates.

Blair, R.J.R. (2004). The roles of orbital frontal cortex in the modulation of antisocial behavior. *Brain and Cognition*, **55**, 198–208.

Blair, R.J.R., Colledge, E., Murray, L., and Mitchell, D.G.V. (2001). A selective impairment in the processing of sad and fearful expressions in children with psychopathic tendencies. *Journal of Abnormal Child Psychology*, **29**, 491–8.

Blair, R.J.R., Mitchell, D.G.V., and Blair, K.S. (2005). *The psychopath: emotion and the brain*. Oxford: Blackwell.

Blairy, S., Herrera, P., and Hess, U. (1999). Mimicry and the judgment of emotional facial expressions. *Journal of Nonverbal Behavior*, **23**, 5–41.

Blalock, J.E. (1984). The immune system as a sensory organ. *Journal of Immunology*, **132**, 1067–70.

Blanchard, D.C. and Blanchard, R.J. (2005). Stress and aggressive behaviors. In: R. Nelson (ed.), *Biology of aggression*, pp. 275–94. Oxford: Oxford University Press.

Blanchard, R.J., Blanchard, D.C., and Takahashi, L.K. (1977). Attack and defensive behaviour in the albino rat. *Animal Behavior*, **25**, 197–224.

Blanchard-Fields, F. (1999). Social schematicity and causal attributions. In: T.M. Hess and F. Blanchard-Fields (eds), *Social cognition and aging*, pp. 219–36. San Diego, CA: Academic Press.

Blanz, V. (2006). Computing human faces for human viewers: automated animation in photographs and paintings. *ICMI '06. Eighth International Conference on Multimodal Interfaces* (Banff, Canada, 2–4 Nov. 2006), pp. 249–56. New York: The Association for Computing Machinery.

Bless, H., Bohner, G., Schwarz, N., and Strack, F. (1990). Mood and persuasion: a cognitive response analysis. *Personality and Social Psychology Bulletin*, **16**, 331–45.

Bloch, V. (1993). On the centennial of the discovery of electrodermal activity. In: J.C. Roy, W. Boucsein, D.C. Fowles, and J.H. Gruzelier (eds), *Progress in electrodermal research*, pp. 1–6. New York: Plenum Press.

Block, J.A. (1957). A study of affective responsiveness in a lie-detection situation. *Journal of Abnormal and Social Psychology*, **55**, 11–15.

Blood, A.J. and Zatorre, R.J. (2001). Intensely pleasurable responses to music correlate with activity in brain regions implicated in reward and emotion. *Proceedings of National Academy of Sciences USA*, **98**, 11818–23.

Block, N. (1980). Troubles with functionalism. In: N. Block (ed.), *Readings in philosophy of psychology*, Vol. 1, pp. 268–306. Cambridge, MA: Harvard University Press.

Bloom, L. (1993). *The transition from infancy to language; acquiring the power of expression*. Cambridge: Cambridge University Press.

Blount, S. (1995). When social outcomes aren't fair: the effect of causal attributions on preferences. *Organizational Behavior and Human Decision Processes*, **63**, 131–44.

Blumenthal, T.D., Cuthbert, B.N., Filion, D.L., Hackley, S.A., Lipp, O.V., and van Boxtel, A. (2005). Committee report: guidelines for human startle eyeblink electromyographic studies. *Psychophysiology*, **42**, 1–15.

Bodenhausen, G.V., Kramer, G.P., and Süsser, K. (1994). Happiness and stereotypic thinking in social judgment. *Journal of Personality and Social Psychology*, **66**, 621–32.

Bodenhausen, G.V., Gabriel, S., and Lineberger, M. (2000). Sadness and susceptibility to judgmental bias: the case of anchoring. *Psychological Science*, **11**, 320–323.

Bohnet, I., Greig, F., Herrmann, B., and Zeckhauser, R. (2008). Betrayal aversion: evidence from Brazil, China, Oman, Switzerland, Turkey, and the United States. *American Economic Review*, **98**, 294–310.

Bolton, D. (2008). *What is mental disorder? An essay in philosophy, science and values*. Oxford: Oxford University Press.

Bonanno, G.A. (2004). Loss, trauma, and human resilience—have we underestimated the human capacity to thrive after extremely aversive events? *American Psychologist*, **59**, 20–28.

Boorse, C. (1976). What a theory of mental health should be. *Journal of the Theory of Social Behaviour*, **6**, 61–84.

Boorse, C. (1997). A rebuttal on health. In: J.F. Humber and R.F. Almeder (eds), *What is disease?*, pp. 1–134. Totowa, NJ: Humana Press.

Booth, W.C. (1961). *The rhetoric of fiction*. Chicago: University of Chicago Press.

Borgeaud, P. (2007). Rites et émotions. Considérations sur les mystères. In: J. Scheid (ed.), *Rites et croyances dans les religions du monde Romain* (Entretiens sur l'antiquité classique, tome LIII), pp. 189–229. Genève-Vandoeuvres: Fondation Hardt.

Borkovec, T.D. and Inz, J. (1990). The nature of worry in generalized anxiety disorder: a predominance of thought activity. *Behaviour Research and Therapy*, **28**, 153–8.

Bosch, J.A., Berntson, G.G., Cacioppo, J.T., and Marucha, P.T. (2005). Differential mobilization of functionally distinct natural killer subsets during acute psychological stress. *Psychosomatic Medicine*, **67**, 366–75.

Botvinick, M.M., Braver, T.S., Barch, D.M., Carter, C.S., and Cohen, J.D. (2001). Conflict monitoring and cognitive control. *Psychological Review*, **108**, 624–52.

Bouchard, T.J. (2004). Genetic influence on human psychological traits: a survey. *Current Directions in Psychological Science*, **13**, 148–51.

Bouchard, T.J. and Loehlin, J.C. (2001). Genes, evolution, and personality. *Behavior Genetics*, **31**, 243–73.

Boucsein, W. (1992). *Electrodermal activity*. New York: Plenum Press.

Bouton, M.E., Mineka, S., and Barlow, D.H. (2001). A modern learning theory perspective on the etiology of panic disorder. *Psychological Review*, **108**, 4–32.

Bower, G.H. (1981). Mood and memory. *American Psychologist*, **36**, 129–48.

Bowlby, J. (1969). *Attachment and loss: Vol. 1. Attachment*. New York: Basic Books.

Bowlby, J. (1973). *Attachment and loss: Vol. 2. Separation: Anxiety and anger*. New York: Basic Books.

Bowlby, J. (1979). *The making and breaking of affectional bonds*. London: Tavistock.

Bowlby, J. (1980). *Attachment and loss: Vol. 3. Loss*. New York: Basic Books.

Bowlby, J. (1982). *Attachment and loss*, 2nd edn. New York: Basic Books.

Bowman, M. and Yehuda, R. (2004). Risk factors and the adversity-stress model. In: G.M. Rosen (ed.), *Posttraumatic stress disorder: issues and controversies*, pp. 15–38. Chichester: Wiley.

Boyatzis, R.E. and Sala, F. (2004). The Emotional Competence Inventory (ECI). In: G. Geher (ed.), *Measuring emotional intelligence: common ground and controversy*, pp. 147–80. New York: Nova Science Publishers.

Boyd, R.T. and Richerson, P. (2005). *The origin and evolution of cultures*. Oxford: Oxford University Press.

Brackett, M.A. and Mayer, J.D. (2003). Convergent, discriminant, and incremental validity of competing measures of emotional intelligence. *Personality and Social Psychology Bulletin*, **29**, 1147–58.

Brackett, M.A., Rivers, S.E., Shiffman, S., Lerner, N., and Salovey, P. (2006). Relating emotional abilities to social functioning: a comparison of self-report and performance measures of emotional intelligence. *Journal of Personality and Social Psychology*, **91**, 780–795.

Bradley, M.M. and Lang, P.J. (1994). Measuring emotion— the self-assessment mannequin and the semantic differential. *Journal of Behavior Therapy and Experimental Psychiatry*, **25**, 49–59.

Bradley, M.M. and Lang, P.J. (2000). Measuring emotion: behavior, feeling, and physiology. In: R. Lane and L. Nadel (eds), *Cognitive neuroscience of emotion*, pp. 242–76. New York: Oxford University Press.

Bradley, M.M. and Lang, P.J. (2007a). The International Affective Picture System (IAPS) in the study of emotion and attention. In: J.A. Coan and J.J.B. Allen (eds), *Handbook of emotion elicitation and assessment*, pp. 29–46. Oxford University Press.

Bradley, M.M. and Lang, P.J. (2007b). Emotion and motivation. In: J.T. Cacioppo, L.G. Tassinary, and G. Berntson (eds), *Handbook of psychophysiology*, 2nd edn, pp 581–607. New York: Cambridge University Press.

Bradley, M.M., Codispoti, M., and Lang, P.J. (2006). A multi-process account of startle modulation during affective perception. *Psychophysiology*, **43**, 486–97.

Bratman, M.E. (1987). *Intentions, plans, and practical reason*. Harvard, CT: Harvard University Press.

Breazeal, C. and Picard, R. (2006). The role of emotion-inspired abilities in relational robots. In: Parasuraman, R. and Rizzo, M. (eds), *Neuroergonomics: the brain at work*, pp. 275–92. Oxford: Oxford University Press.

Brehm, J.W. (1966). *A theory of psychological reactance*. New York: Academic Press.

Brehm, J.W. and Self, E.A. (1989). The intensity of motivation. *Annual Review of Psychology*, **40**, 109–31.

Brennan, P.A., Raine, A., Schulsinger, F., Kirkegaard-Sorensen, L., Knop, J., Hutchings, B., Rosenberg, R., and Mednick, S.A. (1997). Psychophysiological protective factors for male subjects at high risk for criminal behavior. *American Journal of Psychiatry*, **154**, 853–5.

Brenner, S.L., Beauchaine, T.P., and Sylvers, P.D. (2005). A comparison of psychophysiological and self-report measures of BAS and BIS activation. *Psychophysiology*, **42**, 108–15.

Brentano, F. (1874/1973). *Psychology from an empirical standpoint* (transl. A.C. Rancurello, D.B. Terrell, and L.L. McAlister). London: Routledge and Kegan Paul.

Brentano, F. (1889/1984). On the origin of our knowledge of right and wrong. In: C. Calhoun and R.C. Solomon (eds), *What is an emotion?*, pp. 205–14. New York: Oxford University Press. (Original work published 1889.)

Breslau, N. and Kessler, R.C. (2001). The stressor criterion in DSM-IV posttraumatic stress disorder: an empirical investigation. *Biological Psychiatry*, **50**, 699–704.

Breslau, N., Chase, G.A., and Anthony, J.C. (2002). The uniqueness of the DSM definition of post-traumatic stress disorder: Implications for research. *Psychological Medicine*, **32**, 573–6.

Breslau, N., Lucia, V.C., and Alvarado, G.F. (2006). Intelligence and other predisposing factors in exposure to trauma and posttraumatic stress disorder: a follow-up study at age 17 years. *Archives of General Psychiatry*, **63**, 1238–45.

References

Brewin, C.R. (2003). *Posttraumatic stress disorder: malady or myth?* New Haven, CT: Yale University Press.

Brickman, P. and Campbell, D.T. (1971). Hedonic relativism and planning the good society. In: M.H. Appley (ed.), *Adaptation-level theory: a symposium*, pp. 287–302. New York: Academic Press.

Brickman, P., Coates, D., and Janoff-Bulman, R. (1978). Lottery winners and accident victims: is happiness relative? *Journal of Personality and Social Psychology*, **36**, 917–27.

Bridges, K. (1932). Emotional development in early infancy. *Child Development*, **3**, 324–41.

Brief, A.P. and Weiss, H. (2002). Organizational behavior: affect in the workplace. *Annual Review of Psychology*, **53**, 279–307.

Briggs, J.L. (1970). *Never in anger: portrait of an Eskimo family.* Cambridge, MA: Harvard University Press.

Briggs-Gowan, M., Horwitz, S., Schwab-Stone, M.E., Leventhal, J., and Leaf, P. (2000). Mental health in pediatric settings: distribution of disorders and factors related to service use. *Journal of the American Academy of Child and Adolescent Psychiatry*, **39**, 841–9.

Briñol, P., Petty, R.E., and Barden, J. (2007). Happiness versus sadness as a determinant of thought confidence in persuasion: a self-validation analysis. *Journal of Personality and Social Psychology*, **93**, 711–27.

Briton, N.J. and Hall, J.A. (1995). Beliefs about female and male nonverbal communication. *Sex Roles*, **32**, 79–90.

Broad, C.D. (1959). *Scientific thought.* Paterson, NJ: Littlefield Adams.

Brody, L.R. (1999). *Gender, emotion, and the family.* Cambridge, MA: Harvard University Press.

Brody, L.R. and Hall, J.A. (2008). Gender and emotion in context. In: M. Lewis, J.M. Haviland-Jones, and L. Feldman Barrett (eds), *Handbook of emotions*, 3rd edn, pp. 395–408. New York: Guilford Press.

Brosch, T., Sander, D., and Scherer, K.R. (2007). That baby caught my eye . . . attention capture by infant faces. *Emotion*, **7**, 685–9.

Brosch, T., Sander, D., Pourtois, G., and Scherer, K.R. (2008). Beyond fear: rapid spatial orienting towards positive emotional stimuli. *Psychological Science*, **19**, 362–70.

Brown, C. (1995). *Chaos and catastrophe theories*, Quantitative Applications in the Social Sciences, no. 107. Thousand Oaks, CA: Sage.

Brown, C.H. and Waser, P.M. (1984). Hearing and communication in blue monkeys (*Cercopithecus mitis*). *Animal Behaviour*, **32**, 66–75.

Brown, J., Bullock, D., and Grossberg, S. (1999). How the basal ganglia use parallel excitatory and inhibitory learning pathways to selectively respond to unexpected rewarding cues. *Journal of Neuroscience*, **19**, 10502–11.

Brown, J.R. (2001). *Who rules in science? An opinionated guide to the wars.* Cambridge, MA: Harvard University Press.

Brown, R. and Kulik, J. (1977). Flashbulb memories. *Cognition*, **5**, 73–99.

Brown, R.W. (1958). How shall a thing be called? *Psychological Review*, **65**, 14–21.

Brown, S.M., Peet, E., Manuck, S.B., Williamson, D.E., Dahl, R.E., Ferrell, R.E., and Hariri, A.R. (2005). A regulatory variant of the human tryptophan hydroxylase-2 gene biases amygdala reactivity. *Molecular Psychiatry*, **10**, 884–8, 805.

Bruner, J.S. (1957). On perceptual readiness. *Psychological Review*, **64**, 123–52.

Brunswik, E. (1952). *The conceptual framework of psychology.* Chicago: Chicago University Press.

Brunswik, E. (1956). *Perception and the representative design of psychological experiments.* Berkeley, CA: University of California Press.

Bryant, F.B. and Veroff, J. (2007). *Savoring/a new model of positive experience.* Mahwah, NJ: Lawrence Erlbaum Associates.

Bryant, J., Roskos-Ewoldsen, D., and Cantor, J. (2003). *Communication and emotion: essays in honor of Dolf Zillmann.* Mahwah, NJ: Lawrence Erlbaum Associates.

Buchanan, T.W., Tranel, D., and Adolphs, R. (2005). Emotional autobiographical memories in amnesic patients with medial temporal lobe damage. *Journal of Neuroscience*, **25**, 3151–60.

Buck, R. (1975). Nonverbal communication of affect in children. *Journal of Personality and Social Psychology*, **31**, 644–53.

Buck, R. (1999). The biological affects: a typology. *Psychological Review*, **106**, 301–36.

Buck, R. and Powers, S.R. (2005). The expression, communication, and regulation of biological emotions: sex and cultural differences and similarities. *Psychologia*, **XLVIII**, 335–53.

Budd, M. (1985). *Music and the emotions: the philosophical theories.* London: Routledge.

Bühler, K. (1927). *Die Krise der Psychologie*, Sections 10, 14–16. Jena: Fischer.

Bühler, K. (1934/1990). *Sprachtheorie. Die Darstellungsfunktion der Sprache.* Jena: Fischer. (Translated as Bühler, K. and Goodwin, D.F. (1990) *Theory of language: the representational function of language.* Amsterdam: John Benjamins.)

Bullough, E. (1977). 'Psychical distance' as a factor in art and an aesthetic principle. In: *Aesthetics: lectures and essays* (reprint). Westport, CT: Greenwood Press.

Bunzeck, N. and Duzel, F. (2006). Absolute coding of stimulus novelty in the human substantia nigra/VTA. *Neuron*, **51**, 369–79.

Burkhardt, F. and Sendlmeier, W.F. (2000). Verification of acoustical correlates of emotional speech using formant synthesis. In: R. Cowie, E. Douglas-Cowie, and M. Schröder (eds), *Proceedings of the ISCA Workshop on Speech and Emotion: a conceptual framework for research*, pp. 151–6. Belfast: Textflow.

Burleson, W., Picard, R.W., Perlin, K., and Lippincott, J. (2004). In: *Workshop on Empathetic Agents, International Conference on Automonous Agents and Multiagent Systems*, pp. 69–78. New York: Columbia University.

Burrows, A.M., Waller, B.M., Parr, L.A., and Bonar, C.J. (2006). Muscles of facial expression in the chimpanzee (*Pan troglodytes*): descriptive, comparative and phylogenetic contexts. *Journal of Anatomy*, **208**, 153–67.

Burton, R. (1621/2001). *The anatomy of melancholy.* New York: New York Review of Books.

Bush, G., Luu, P., and Posner, M. (2000). Cognitive and emotional influences in anterior cingulate cortex. *Trends in Cognitive Sciences*, **4**, 215–22.

Bushman, B.J. (2002). Does venting anger feed or extinguish the flame? Catharsis, rumination, distraction, anger, and aggressive responding. *Personality and Social Psychology Bulletin*, **28**, 724–31.

Bushman, B.J. and Anderson, C.A. (2001). Is it time to pull the plug on the hostile versus instrumental aggression dichotomy? *Psychological Review*, **108**, 273–9.

Buss, D.M. (1994). *The evolution of desire*. New York: Basic Books.

Buss, D.M. (1995). Evolutionary psychology: a new paradigm for psychological science. *Psychological Inquiry*, **6**, 1–30.

Buss, D.M. (2000). *The dangerous passion. Why jealousy is as necessary as love and sex*. New York: The Free Press.

Buss, K.A., Malmstadt, J.R., Dolski, I., Kalin, N.H., Goldsmith, H.H., and Davidson, R.J. (2003). Right frontal brain activity, cortisol, and withdrawal behavior in 6-month-old infants. *Behavioral Neuroscience*, **117**, 11–20.

Buunk, A.P. and Dijkstra, P. (2006). The threat of temptation: extradyadic relationships and jealousy. In: D. Perlman and A.L. Vangelisti (eds), *The Cambridge handbook of personal relationships*, pp. 533–56. New York: Cambridge University Press.

Cabanac, M. (1971). Physiological role of pleasure. *Science*, **173**, 1103–7.

Cabanac, M. (1999). Emotion and phylogeny. *Journal of Consciousness Studies*, **6**, 176–90.

Cacioppo, J.T. and Berntson, G.G. (1992). Social psychological contributions to the decade of the brain: doctrine of multilevel analysis. *American Psychologist*, **47**, 1019–28.

Cacioppo, J.T. and Berntson, G.G. (1994). Relationship between attitudes and evaluative space: a critical review, with emphasis on the separability of positive and negative substrates. *Psychological Bulletin*, **115**, 401–23.

Cacioppo, J.T. and Berntson, G.G. (1999). The affect system: architecture and operating characteristics. *Current directions in psychological science*, **8**, 133–7.

Cacioppo, J.T. and Berntson, G.G. (2005). *Social neuroscience*. New York: Psychology Press.

Cacioppo, J.T. and Berntson, G.G. (2007). The brain, homeostasis, and health: balancing demands of the internal and external milieu. In: H. Friedman and R. Cohen Silver (eds), *Foundations of health psychology*, pp. 73–91. New York: Oxford University Press.

Cacioppo, J.T. and Gardner, W.L. (1999). Emotions. *Annual Review of Psychology*, **50**, 191–214.

Cacioppo, J.T., Petty, R.E., and Geen, T.R. (1989). Attitude structure and function: from the tripartite to the homeostasis model of attitudes. In: A.R. Pratkanis, S.J. Breckler, and A.G. Greenwald (eds), *Attitude structure and function*, pp. 275–309. Hillsdale, NJ: Lawrence Erlbaum Associates.

Cacioppo, J.T., Berntson, G.G., and Klein, D.J. (1992). What is an emotion? The role of somatovisceral afference, with special emphasis on somatovisceral 'illusions'. *Review of Personality and Social Psychology*, **14**, 63–98.

Cacioppo, J.T., Gardner, W.L., and Berntson, G.G. (1997). Beyond bipolar conceptualizations and measures: the case of attitudes and evaluative space. *Personality and Social Psychology Review*, **1**, 3–25.

Cacioppo, J.T., Berntson, G.G., Larsen, J.T., Poehlmann, K.M., and Ito, T.A. (2000). The psychophysiology of emotion. In: R. Lewis and J.M. Haviland-Jones (eds), *Handbook of emotions*, 2nd edn, pp. 173–91. New York: Guilford Press.

Cacioppo, J.T., Berntson, G.G., Adolphs, R., Carter, C.S., Davidson, R.J., McClintock, M.K., *et al.* (2002). *Foundations in social neuroscience*. Cambridge, MA: MIT Press.

Cacioppo, J.T., Larsen, J.T., Smith, N.K., and Berntson, G.G. (2004). The affect system: what lurks below the surface of feelings. In: A.S.R. Manstead, N. Frijda, and A. Fischer (eds), *Feelings and emotions*, pp.221–40. Cambridge: Cambridge University Press.

Cacioppo, J.T., Tassinary, L.G., and Berntson, G.G. (eds) (2007). *Handbook of psychophysiology*, 3rd edn. Cambridge: Cambridge University Press.

Cahill, L., Prins, B., Weber, M., and McGaugh, J.L. (1994). Beta-adrenergic activation and memory for emotional events. *Nature*, **371**, 702–4.

Cahill, L., Babinsky, R., Markowitsch, H.J., and McGaugh, J.L. (1995). The amygdala and emotional memory. *Nature*, **377**, 295–6.

Calder, A. and Young, A. (2005). Understanding the recognition of facial identity and facial expression. *Nature Reviews Neuroscience*, **6**, 641–51.

Calder, A.J., Lawrence, A.D., and Young, A.W. (2001). Neuropsychology of fear and loathing. *Nature Reviews Neuroscience*, **2**, 352–63.

Calvino B. and Grilo R.M. (2006). Central pain control. *Joint Bone Spine*, **73**, 10–16.

Camerer, C.F. (2003). *Behavioral game theory*. Princeton, NJ: Princeton University Press.

Camerer, C., Loewenstein, G., and Prelec, D. (2005). Neuroeconomics: how neuroscience can inform economics. *Journal of Economic Literature*, **43**, 9–64.

Campbell, A. (1981). *The sense of well-being in America*. New York: McGraw-Hill.

Campbell, A., Converse, P.E., and Rodgers, W.L (1976). *The quality of American life*. New York: Russell Sage.

Campbell, B.A. and Church, R.M. (eds) (1969). *Punishment and aversive behavior*. New York: Appleton-Century-Crofts.

Campbell, N. (2000). Physicalism, qualia inversion, and affective states. *Synthese: an International Journal for Epistemology, Methodology and Philosophy of Science*, **124**, 239–55.

Campbell, N., Hamza, W., Höge, H., Tao, J., and Bailly, G. (eds) (2006). *IEEE Transactions on Audio, Speech, and Language Processing*, **14**(4), 1097–178 (special section on expressive speech synthesis).

Campos, J. (2007). Foreword. In: J.L. Tracy, R.W. Robbins, and J.P. Tangney (eds), *The self-conscious emotions: theory and research*, pp. xiii–xv. New York: Guilford Press.

Campos, J.J. and Barrett, K.C. (1984). Toward a new understanding of emotions and their development. In: C.E. Izard, J. Kagan, and R.B. Zajonc (eds), *Emotions, cognition, and behavior*, pp. 229–63. New York: Cambridge University Press.

Campos, J., Barrett, K., Lamb, M., Goldsmith, H., and Stenberg, C. (1983). Socioemotional development. In: M. Haith and J. Campos (eds), *Handbook of child psychology. Infancy and developmental psychobiology*, 4th edn, Vol. 2, pp. 783–915 (series editor P. Mussen). New York: John Wiley.

Campos, J., Thein, S., and Owen, D. (2003). A Darwinian perspective on emotional development. In: P. Ekman, J. Campos, R. Davidson, and de Waal, F. (eds), *Emotions inside out: one hundred and thirty years after Darwin's Expression of emotions in man and animals*, pp. 110–134. New York: New York Academy of Sciences Press.

Campos, J.J., Frankel, C.B., and Camras, L. (2004). On the nature of emotion regulation. *Child Development*, **75**, 377–94.

References

Cañamero, L. (2005). Emotion understanding from the perspective of autonomous agents research. *Neural Networks*, **18**, 445–55.

Cañamero, L., Blanchard, A., and Nadel, J. (2006). Attachment bonds in human-like robots. *International Journal of Humanoid Robotics*, **3**, 301–20.

Canli, T. (2004). Functional brain mapping of extraversion and neuroticism: learning from individual differences in emotion processing. *Journal of Personality*, **72**, 1105–32.

Canli, T. and Lesch, K.P. (2007). Long story short: the serotonin transporter in emotional regulation and social cognition. *Nature Neuroscience*, **10**, 1103–9.

Canli, T., Sivers, H., Whitfield, S.L., Gotlib, I.H., and Gabrieli, J.D. (2002). Amygdala response to happy faces as a function of extraversion. *Science*, **21**, 2191.

Canli, T., Congdon, E., Gutknecht, L., Constable, R.T., and Lesch, K.P. (2005a). Amygdala responsiveness is modulated by tryptophan hydroxylase-2 gene variation. *Journal of Neural Transmission*, **112**, 1479–85.

Canli, T., Omura, K., Haas, B.W., Fallgatter, A., Constable, R.T., and Lesch, K.P. (2005b), Beyond affect: a role for genetic variation of the serotonin transporter in neural activation during a cognitive attention task. *Proceedings of the National Academy of Sciences USA*, **102**, 12224–9.

Canli, T., Qiu, M., Omura, K., Congdon, E., Haas, B.W., Amin, Z., Herrmann, M.J., Constable, R.T., and Lesch, K. P. (2006). Neural correlates of epigenesis. *Proceedings of the National Academy of Sciences USA*, **103**, 16033–8.

Cannon, W.B. (1927a). *Bodily changes in pain, hunger, fear, and rage*. New York: Appleton-Century-Crofts.

Cannon, W.B. (1927b). The James–Lange theory of emotions: a critical examination and an alternative theory. *American Journal of Psychology*, **39**, 106–24.

Cannon, W.B. (1932). *The wisdom of the body*. New York: Norton.

Cantor, J. (2002). Fright reactions to mass media. In: J. Bryant and D. Zillman (eds), *Media effects: advances in theory and research*, pp. 287–306. Mahwah, NJ: Lawrence Erlbaum Associates.

Capuron, L., Ravaud, A., Gualde, N., Bosmans, E., Dantzer, R., Maes, M., and Neveu, P.J. (2001). Association between immune activation and early depressive symptoms in cancer patients treated with interleukin-2-based therapy. *Psychoneuroendocrinology*, **26**, 797–808.

Carberry, S. and de Rosis, F. (eds) (2008). *User Modeling and User-Adapted Interaction*, **18**(1–2) (special issue on affective modeling and adaptation).

Cardinal, R.N., Parkinson, J.A., Hall, J., and Everitt, B.J. (2002). Emotion and motivation: the role of the amygdala, ventral striatum, and prefrontal cortex. *Neuroscience and Biobehavioral Reviews*, **26**, 321–52.

Carlson, M. and Miller, N. (1987). Explanation of the relation between negative mood and helping. *Psychological Bulletin*, **102**, 91–108.

Carlson, M., Charlin, V., and Miller, N. (1988). Positive mood and helping behavior: a test of six hypotheses. *Journal of Personality and Social Psychology*, **55**, 211–29.

Carlston, D.E. and Skowronski, J.J. (2005). Linking versus thinking: evidence for the different associative and attributional bases of spontaneous trait transference and spontaneous trait inference. *Journal of Personality and Social Psychology*, **89**, 884–98.

Carmon, Z., Wertenbroch, K., and Zeelenberg, M. (2003). Option attachment: when deliberating makes choosing feel like losing. *Journal of Consumer Research*, **30**, 15–29.

Carnevale, P.J. and Isen, A.M. (1986). The influence of positive affect and visual access on the discovery of integrative solutions in bilateral negotiations. *Organizational Behavior and Human Decision Processes*, **37**, 1–13.

Caro, I. (2001). The linguistic therapy of evaluation: a treatment plan for Silvia. *Journal of Psychotherapy Integration*, **11**, 165–85.

Carpenter, J. (2007). The demand for punishment. *Journal of Economic Behavior and Organization*, **62**, 522–42.

Carr, L., Iacoboni, M., Dubeau, M.C., Mazziotta, J.C., and Lenzi, G.L. (2003). Neural mechanisms of empathy in humans: a relay from neural systems for imitation to limbic areas. *Proceedings of the National Academy of Sciences USA*, **100**, 5497–502.

Carroll, J.M., Yik, M.S.M., Russell, J.A., and Barrett, L.F. (1999). On the psychometric principles of affect. *Review of General Psychology*, **3**, 14–22.

Carson, M.J., Doose, J.M., Melchior, B., Schmid, C.D., and Ploix, C.C. (2006). CNS immune privilege: hiding in plain sight. *Immunological Reviews*, **213**, 48–65.

Carstensen, L.L. and Mikels, J.A. (2005). At the intersection of emotion and cognition: aging and the positivity effect. *Current Directions in Psychological Science*, **14**, 117–21.

Carter, C.S. (1998). Neuroendocrine perspectives on social attachment and love. *Psychoneuroendocrinology*, **23**, 779–818.

Carter, C.S., Lederhendler, I.I., and Kirkpatrck, B. (1999). *The integrative neurobiology of affiliation*. Cambridge, MA: MIT Press.

Carter, R.M., Hofstötter, C., Tsuchiya, N., and Koch, C. (2003). Working memory and fear conditioning. *Proceedings of the National Academy of Sciences USA*, **100**, 1399–404.

Cartwright, R., Young, M.A., Mercer, P., and Bears, M. (1998). Role of REM sleep and dream variables in the prediction of remission from depression. *Psychiatry Research*, **80**, 249–55.

Carver, C.S. (2004). Negative affects deriving from the behavioral approach system. *Emotion*, **4**, 3–22.

Carver, C.S. and Scheier, M.F. (1981). *Attention and self-regulation: a control-theory approach to human behavior*. New York: Springer-Verlag.

Carver, C.S. and Scheier, M.F. (1990). Origins and functions of positive and negative affect: a control-process view. *Psychological Review*, **97**, 19–35.

Carver, C.S. and Scheier, M.F. (1998). *On the self-regulation of behavior*. New York: Cambridge University Press.

Carver, C.S. and White, T.L. (1994). Behavioral inhibition, behavioral activation, and affective responses to impending reward and punishment: the BIS/BAS scales. *Journal of Personality and Social Psychology*, **67**, 319–33.

Carver, C.S., Scheier, M.F., and Weintraub, J.K. (1989). Assessing coping strategies: a theoretically based approach. *Journal of Personality and Social Psychology*, **56**, 267–83.

Carver, C.S., Lawrence, J.W., and Scheier, M.F. (1996). A control-process perspective on the origins of affect. In: L. L. Martin and A. Tesser (eds), *Striving and feeling: interactions among goals, affect, and self-regulation*, pp. 11–52. Mahwah, NJ: Lawrence Erlbaum Associates.

Casey, J. (1990). *Pagan virtues*, pp. 21–4. Oxford: Clarendon.

Caspi, A., McClay, J., Moffitt, T.E., Mill, J., Martin, J., Craig, I. W., Taylor, A., and Poulton, R. (2002). Role of genotype in the cycle of violence in maltreated children. *Science*, **297**, 851–4.

Caspi, A., Sugden, K., Moffitt, T.E., Taylor, A., Craig, I.W., Harrington, H., McClay, J., Mill, J., Martin, J., Braithwaite, A., and Poulton, R. (2003). Influence of life stress on depression: moderation by a polymorphism in the 5-HTT gene. *Science*, **301**, 386–9.

Caspi, A., Roberts, B.W., and Shiner, R.L. (2005). Personality development: stability and change. *Annual Review of Psychology*, **56**, 453–84.

Cassell, J., Sullivan, J., Prevost, P., and Churchill, E. (eds) (2000). *Embodied conversational characters*. Cambridge, MA: MIT Press.

Cervero, F. and Foreman, R.D. (1990). Sensory innervation of the viscera. In: A.D. Loewy and K.M. Spyer (eds), *Central regulation of autonomic functions*, pp. 104–25. New York: Oxford University Press.

Chaiken, S., Liberman, A., and Eagly, A. (1989). Heuristic and systematic information processing within and beyond the persuasion context. In: J.S. Uleman and J.A. Bargh (eds), *Unintended thought: limits of awareness, intention, and control*, pp. 212–52). New York: Guilford Press.

Chaiken, S., Pomerantz, E.M., and Giner-Sorolla, R. (1995). Structural consistency and attitude strength. In: R.E. Petty and J.A. Krosnick (eds), *Attitude strength: antecedents and consequences*, pp. 387–412. Mahwah, NJ: Lawrence Erlbaum Associates.

Chamberlain, S.R. and Sahakian, B. (2007). The neuropsychiatry of impulsivity. *Current Opinion in Psychiatry*, **20**, 255–61.

Champion, L.A. (2000). Depression. In: L.A. Champion and M.J. Power (eds), *Adult psychological problems: an introduction*, 2nd edn, pp. 29–53. Hove: Psychology Press.

Chapell, M.S. (1997). Frequency of public smiling across the life span. *Perceptual and Motor Skills*, **85**, 1326.

Chapman, R.M., McCrary, J.W., Chapman, J.A., and Bragdon, H.R. (1978). Brain responses related to semantic meaning. *Brain Language*, **5**, 195–205.

Charland, L.C. (1995). Feeling and representing: computational theory and the modularity of affect. *Synthese: an International Journal for Epistemology, Methodology and Philosophy of Science*, **105**, 273–301.

Charland, L.C. (2005a). Emotion experience and the indeterminacy of valence. In: L.F.Barrett, P.M. Niedenthal, and P. Winkielman (eds), *Emotion and consciousness*. pp. 231–54. New York: Guilford Press.

Charland, L.C. (2005b). The heat of emotion: valence and the demarcation problem. *Journal of Consciousness Studies*, **12** (8–10), 82–103.

Charles, S.T. and Carstensen, L.L. (2007). Emotion regulation and aging. In: J.J. Gross (ed.), *Handbook of emotion regulation*, pp. 307–27. New York: Guilford Press.

Chartrand, T.L. and Bargh, J.A. (1999). The chameleon effect: the perception–behavior link and social interaction. *Journal of Personality and Social Psychology*, **76**, 893–910.

Chaucer, G. (1912). *Complete works of Geoffrey Chaucer*. Oxford: Oxford University Press. (Original works published 1379–83).

Chen, K., Cases, O., Rebrin, I., Wu, W., Gallaher, T.K., Seif, I., and Shih, J.C. (2007). Forebrain-specific expression of monoamine oxidase A reduces neurotransmitter levels, restores the brain structure, and rescues aggressive behavior in monoamine oxidase A-deficient mice. *Journal of Biological Chemistry*, **282**, 115–23.

Chen, S.W.C., Shamyakin, A., and Wiedenmayer, C.P. (2006). The role of the amygdala and olfaction in unconditioned fear in developing rats. *Journal of Neuroscience*, **26**, 233–40.

Childress, A.R., Ehrman, R.N., Wang, Z., Li, Y., Sciortino, N., *et al.* (2008). Prelude to passion: limbic activation by 'unseen' drug and sexual cues. *PLoS ONE*, **3**, e1506 (doi:10.1371/journal.pone.0001506).

Chipperfield, J.G., Perry, R.P., and Weiner, B. (2003). Discrete emotions in later life. *Journal of Gerontology: Psychological Sciences*, **58B**, 23–34.

Chivers, M.L. and Bailey, J.M (2005). A sex difference in features that elicit sexual response. *Biological Psychology*, **70**, 115–20.

Choi, J. (2003). Fits and startles: cognitivism revisited. *Journal of Aesthetics and Art Criticism*, **61**, 149–57.

Choy, Y., Fyer, A.J., and Lipsitz, J.D. (2007). Treatment of specific phobia in adults. *Clinical Psychology Review*, **27**, 266–86.

Chrea, C., Valentin, D., Sulmont-Rossé, C., Nguyen, D.H., and Abdi, H. (2005). Semantic, typicality and odor representation: a cross-cultural study. *Chemical Senses*, **30**, 37–49.

Chrea, C., Grandjean, D., Delplanque, S., Cayeux, I., Le Calvé, B., Aymard, L., *et al.* (2009). Mapping the semantic space for the subjective experience of emotional responses to odors. *Chemical Senses*, **34**, 49–62.

Christophe, V. and Rimé, B. (1997). Exposure to the social sharing of emotion: emotional impact, listener responses and the secondary social sharing. *European Journal of Social Psychology*, **27**, 37–54.

Chrousos, G.P. and Gold, P.W. (1992). The concepts of stress and stress system disorders: overview of physical and behavioral homeostasis. *Journal of the American Medical Association*, **267**, 1244–52.

Cialdini, R.B. (2008). *Influence: science and practice*. Boston, MA: Allyn and Bacon.

Cialdini, R.B., Kenrick, D.T., and Baumann, D.J. (1982). Effects of mood on prosocial behavior in children and adults. In: N. Eisenberg (ed.), *The development of prosocial behavior*, pp. 339–59. New York: Academic Press.

Clark, A. (2005). Painfulness is not a quale. In: M. Aydede (ed.), *Pain: new essays on its nature and the methodology of its study*, pp. 177–97. Cambridge, MA: MIT Press.

Clark, D.M. (1986). A cognitive approach to panic. *Behaviour Research and Therapy*, **24**, 461–70

Clark, D.M., Salkovskis, P.M., Hackmann, A., Middleton, H., Anastasiades, P., and Gelder, M. (1994). A comparison of cognitive therapy, applied relaxation and imipramine in the treatment of panic disorder. *British Journal of Psychiatry*, **164**, 759–69.

Clark, H.H. and Clark, E.V. (1977). *Psychology and language*. New York: Harcourt Brace Jovanovich.

Clark, L.A. (ed.) (1999). Special section on the concept of disorder. *Journal of Abnormal Psychology*, **108**, 371–472.

Clark, L.A. and Watson, D. (1994). Distinguishing functional from dysfunctional affective responses. In: P. Ekman and R. J. Davidson (eds), *The nature of emotion*, pp. 131–7. New York: Oxford University Press.

References

Clark, M.S. (2002). We should focus on interpersonal as well as intrapersonal processes in our search for how affect influences judgments and behavior. *Psychological Inquiry*, **13**, 32–7.

Clark, M.S. and Fiske, S.T. (1982). *Affect and cognition. The 17th Annual Carnegie Symposium on Cognition*. Hillsdale, NJ: Erlbaum.

Clark, M.S. and Isen, A.M. (1982). Toward understanding the relationship between feeling states and social behavior. In: A.H. Hastorf and A.M. Isen (eds), *Cognitive social psychology*, pp. 73–108. New York: Elsevier.

Cloninger, S. (2004). *Theories of personality*. Upper Saddle River, NJ: Pearson.

Clore, G.L. and Storbeck, J. (2006). Affect as information about liking, efficacy, and importance. In: J. Forgas (ed.), *Affect in social thinking and behavior*, pp. 123–42. New York: Psychology Press.

Clynes, M. (1973). Sentics: biocybernetics of emotion communication. *Annals of the New York Academy of Sciences*, **220**, 55–131.

Cohen, J.B., Pham, M.T., and Andrade, E.B. (2008). The nature and role of affect in consumer behavior. In: C.P. Haugtvedt, P. Herr, and F. Kardes (eds), *Handbook of consumer psychology*, pp. 297–348. Mahwah, NJ: Erlbaum.

Cohen, J.D. (2005). The vulcanization of the human brain: a neural perspective on interactions between cognition and emotion. *Journal of Economic Perspectives*, **19**, 3–24.

Cohen, N. and Kinney, K.S. (2001). Exploring the phylogenetic history of neural-immune system interactions. In: R. Ader, D.L. Felton, and N. Cohen (eds), pp. 21–54. *Psychoneuroimmunology*. San Diego, CA: Academic Press.

Cohen, S., Frank, E., Doyle, W.J., Skoner, D.P., Rabin, B.S., and Gwaltney, J.M. (1998). Types of stressors that increase susceptibility to the common cold in healthy adults. *Health Psychology*, **17**, 214–23.

Cohn, J.F. and Kanade, T. (2007). Use of automated facial image analysis for measurement of emotion expression. In: J.A. Coan and J.B. Allen (eds), *The handbook of emotion elicitation and assessment*, pp. 222–38. New York: Oxford University Press.

Colder, C.R. and Stice, E. (1998). The moderating effect of impulsivity on the relationship between anger and adolescent problem behavior: cross-sectional and prospective findings. *Journal of Youth and Adolescence*, **27**, 255–74.

Cole, P.M. (1986) Children's spontaneous control of facial expression. *Child Development*, **57**, 1309–21.

Cole, P.M., Martin, S.E., and Dennis, T.A. (2004). Emotion regulation as a scientific construct: methodological challenges and directions for child development research. *Child Development*, **75**, 317–33.

Coleman, J.S. (1990). *Foundations of social theory*. Cambridge, MA: Harvard University Press.

Collaer, M.L. and Hines, A. (1995). Human behavioral sex differences. *Psychological Bulletin*, **118**, 55–107.

Collingwood, R.G. (1963). *The principles of art*, Oxford: Clarendon.

Collins, R. (2005) *Interaction ritual chains*. Princeton, NJ: Princeton University Press.

Colombetti, G. (2005). Appraising valence. *Journal of Consciousness Studies*, **12**(8–10), 103–27.

Colombetti, G. and Thompson, E. (eds) (2005). Emotion experience. *Journal of Consciousness Studies* **12**(8–10; special triple issue).

Colquitt, J.A., Conlon, D.E., Wesson, M.J., Porter, C.O.L.H., and Ng, K.Y. (2001). Justice at the millennium: a meta-analytic review of 25 years of organizational justice research. *Journal of Applied Psychology*, **86**, 425–45.

Compton, R.J. (2003). The interface between emotion and attention: a review of evidence from psychology and neuroscience. *Behavioral and Cognitive Neuroscience Reviews*, **2**, 115–29.

Comte, I.A. (1875). *System of positive polity*, Vol. 1. London: Longmans, Green and Co. (original work published 1851).

Conejero, S. and Etxebarria, I. (2007).The impact of the Madrid bombing on personal emotions, emotional atmosphere, and emotional climate. *Journal of Social Issues*, **63**, 273–88.

Conway, M.A. (1994). *Flashbulb memories*. Hillsdale, NJ: Lawrence Erlbaum Associates.

Cooksey, R.W. (1996). *Judgment analysis. Theory, methods, and applications*. New York: Academic Press.

Cooper, J.R., Bloom, F.E., and Roth, R.H. (2002). *The biochemical basis of neurochemistry*. Oxford: Oxford University Press.

Corbetta, M. and Shulman G.L. (2002). Control of goal-directed and stimulus-driven attention in the brain. *Nature Reviews Neuroscience*, **3**, 201–15.

Corina, D., Bellugi, U., and Reilly, J. (1999). Neuropsychological studies of linguistic and affective facial expressions in deaf signers. *Language and Speech*, **42**, 307–31. (Special issue on prosody in spoken and signed languages, ed. W. Sandler.)

Cornelius, R.R. (1991). Gregorio Marañon's two-factor theory of emotion. *Personality and Social Psychology Bulletin*, **17**, 65–9.

Corr, P.J. (2004). Reinforcement sensitivity theory and personality. *Neuroscience and Biobehavioral Reviews*, **28**, 317–32.

Corr, P.J. (2008). Reinforcement sensitivity theory (RST): introduction. In: P.J. Corr (ed.), *The reinforcement sensitivity theory of personality*, pp. 1–43. Cambridge: Cambridge University Press.

Corsini, R. (2002). *The dictionary of psychology*. New York: Brunner-Routledge.

Cosmides, L. and Tooby, J. (1999). Toward an evolutionary taxonomy of treatable conditions. *Journal of Abnormal Psychology*, **108**, 453–64.

Cosmides, L. and Tooby, J. (2000). Evolutionary psychology and the emotions. In: M. Lewis and J.M. Haviland-Jones (eds.) *Handbook of emotions*, 2nd edn, pp. 91–115. New York, Guilford Press.

Costa, P.T. and McCrae, R.R. (1980). Influence of extraversion and neuroticism on subjective well-being: happy and unhappy people. *Journal of Personality and Social Psychology*, **38**, 668–78.

Costa, P.T. and McCrae, R.R. (1992). *Revised NEO Personality Inventory and NEO Five Factor Inventory*. Odessa, FL: Psychological Assessment Resources.

Coté, S. (2005). A social interaction model of the effects of emotion regulation on work strain. *Academy of Management Review*, **30**, 509–30.

Cottrell, C.A. and Neuberg, S.L. (2005). Different emotional reactions to different groups: a sociofunctional threat-based approach to 'prejudice'. *Journal of Personality and Social Psychology*, **88**, 770–789.

Cottrell, N.B. and Epley, S.W. (1977). Affiliation, social comparison, and socially mediated stress reduction. In: J.M. Suls and R.L. Miller (eds), *Social comparison processes: theoretical and empirical perspectives*, pp. 43–68. Washington, DC: Hemisphere.

Coutaux A., Adam F., Willer J.C., and Le Bars D. (2006). Hyperalgesia and allodynia: peripheral mechanisms. *Joint Bone Spine*, **72**, 359–71.

Crabbe, J.D., Wahlsten, D., and Dudek, B.C. (1999). Genetics of mass behavior. *Science*, **284**, 1670–1672.

Craig, A.D. (2002). How do you feel? Interoception: the sense of the physiological condition of the body. *Nature Reviews Neuroscience*, **3**, 655–66.

Crane, T. (2000). The origins of qualia. In: T. Crane and S. Patterson (eds), *The history of the mind–body problem*, pp. 169–95. London: Routledge.

Craske, M.G., Barlow, D.H., Clark, D., Curtis, G., Hill, E.M., Himle, J., *et al.* (1996). Specific (simple) phobia. In: T.A. Widiger, A. Frances, H. Pincus, R. Ross, M. First, and W. Davis (eds), *DSM-IV sourcebook*, Vol. 2, pp. 473–506. Washington, DC: American Psychiatric Association.

Creed, F. and Barsky, A. (2004). A systematic review of the epidemiology of somatisation disorder and hypochondriasis. *Journal of Psychosomatic Research*, **56**, 391–408.

Crespi, L.P. (1942). Quantitative variation of incentive and performance in the white rat. *American Journal of Psychology*, **55**, 467–517.

Crick, N.R. and Dodge, K.A. (1996). Social information-processing mechanisms on reactive and proactive aggression. *Child Development*, **67**, 993–1002.

Critchley, H.D. (2004). The human cortex responds to an interoceptive challenge. *Proceedings of the National Academy of Sciences USA*, **101**, 6333–4.

Crites, S.L., Jr, Fabrigar, L.R., and Petty, R.E. (1994). Measuring the affective and cognitive properties of attitudes: conceptual and methodological issues. *Personality and Social Psychology Bulletin*, **20**, 619–34.

Croce, B. (1992). *The aesthetic as the science of expression and of the linguistic in general*, transl. C. Lyas. Cambridge: Cambridge University Press.

Crowe, R.R., Noyes, R., Pauls, D.L., and Slymen, D. (1983). A family study of panic disorder. *Archives of General Psychiatry*, **40**, 1065–9.

Crozier, A. and Alden, L.E. (eds) (2001). *International handbook of social anxiety: concepts, research and interventions relating to the self and shyness*. London: Wiley.

Csikszentmihalyi, M. and LeFevre, J. (1989). Optimal experience in work and leisure. *Journal of Personality and Social Psychology*, **56**, 815–22.

Curci, A. and Bellelli, G. (2004). Cognitive and social consequences of exposure to emotional narratives: two studies on secondary social sharing of emotions. *Cognition and Emotion*, **18**, 881–900.

Cyders, M.A., Smith, G.T., Spillane, N.S., Fischer, S., Annus, A.M., and Peterson, C. (2007). Integration of impulsivity and positive mood to predict risky behaviour: development and validation of a measure of positive urgency. *Psychological Assessment*, **19**, 107–18.

Dahl, R.E. (1996). The regulation of sleep and arousal: development and psychopathology. *Development and Psychopathology*, **8**, 3–27.

Dahl, R.E. (2004). Adolescent brain development: a period of vulnerabilities and opportunities. In: R.E. Dahl and

L.P. Spear (eds), *Adolescent brain development, vulnerabilities and opportunities*, pp. 1–22. New York: New York Academy of Sciences.

Dalgleish, T. (2004a). The emotional brain. *Nature Reviews Neuroscience*, **5**, 582–9.

Dalgleish, T. (2004b). Cognitive approaches to posttraumatic stress disorder: the evolution of multirepresentational theorizing. *Psychological Bulletin*, **130**, 228–60.

Damasio, A. (1994). *Descartes' error: emotion, reason, and the human brain*. New York: Putnam.

Damasio, A. (1999). *The feeling of what happens: body, emotion and the making of consciousness*. London: Heinemann.

Dancy, J. (2000). *Practical reality*. Oxford: Oxford University Press.

Danner, D.D., Snowden, D.A., and Friesen, W.V. (2001). Positive emotions in early life and longevity: findings from the nun study. *Journal of Personality and Social Psychology*, **80**, 804–13.

Dantzer, R. (2001). Cytokine-induced sickness behavior: where do we stand? *Brain, Behavior, and Immunity*, **15**, 7–24.

Dantzer, R. (2007). Expression and action of cytokines in the brain: mechanisms and pathophysiological implications. In: R. Ader (ed.), *Psychoneuroimmunology*, Vol. 1, pp. 271–80. Amsterdam: Academic Press.

Dantzer, R. and Kelley, K.W. (2007). Twenty years of research on cytokine-induced sickness behavior. *Brain, Behavior, and Immunity*, **21**, 153–60.

Dantzer, R., Wollman, E.E., Yirmiya, R. (eds) (1999). *Cytokines, stress and depression*. New York: Kluwer Academic.

D'Arms, J. (2000). Empathy and evaluative inquiry. Symposium on Law, Psychology and the Emotions. *Chicago-Kent Law Review*, **74**, 1467–500.

D'Arms, J. and Jacobson, D. (2003). The significance of recalcitrant emotion (or, anti-quasijudgmentalism). In: A. Hatzimoysis (ed.), *Philosophy and the emotions*, pp. 127–46. Cambridge: Cambridge University Press.

D'Arms, J. and Jacobson, D. (2006). Sensibility theory and projectivism. In: D. Copp (ed.), *The Oxford handbook of ethical theory*, pp. 186–218. Oxford: Oxford University Press.

Darwin, C. (1872/1998). *The expression of the emotions in man and animals*, 3rd edn, ed. P. Ekman. New York: Oxford University Press.

Dasborough, M.T. (2006). Cognitive asymmetry in employee emotional reactions to leadership behaviors. *The Leadership Quarterly*, **17**, 163–78.

Davidson, D. (1980). *Essays on actions and events*. Oxford: Clarendon Press.

Davidson, R.J. (1992). Prolegomenon to the structure of emotion: gleanings from neuropsychology. *Cognition and Emotion*, **6**, 245–68.

Davidson, R.J. (1998). Affective style and affective disorders: perspectives from affective neuroscience. *Cognition and Emotion*, **12**, 307–30.

Davidson, R.J. (2000). Affective style, psychopathology and resiliance: brain mechanisms and plasticity. *American Psychologist*, **55**, 1196–214.

Davidson, R.J. (2003a). Seven sins in the study of emotion: correctives from affective neuroscience. *Brain and Cognition*, **52**, 129–32.

Davidson, R.J. (2003b). Affective neuroscience and psychophysiology: toward a synthesis. *Psychophysiology*, **40**, 655–65.

References

Davidson, R.J. (2004a). Well-being and affective style: neural substrates and biobehavioral correlates. *Philosophical Transactions of the Royal Society B: Biological Sciences*, **359**, 1395–411.

Davidson, R.J. (2004b). What does the prefrontal cortex 'do' in affect: perspectives in frontal EEG asymmetry research. *Biological Psychology*, **67**, 219–34.

Davidson, R.J. and Fox, N.A. (1982). Asymmetrical brain activity discriminates between positive and negative affective stimuli in human infants. *Science*, **218**, 1235–7.

Davidson, R.J. and Irwin, W. (1999). The functional neuroanatomy of emotion and affective style. *Trends in Cognitive Science*, **3**, 11–21.

Davidson, R.J. and Sutton, S.K. (1995). Affective neuroscience: the emergence of a discipline. *Current Opinion in Neurobiology*, **5**, 217–24.

Davidson, R.J., Ekman, P., Saron, C.D., Senulis, J.A., *et al.* (1990a). Approach–withdrawal and cerebral asymmetry: emotional expression and brain physiology: I. *Journal of Personality and Social Psychology*, **58**, 330–341.

Davidson, R.J., Chapman, J.P., Chapman, L.J., and Henriques, J.B. (1990b). Asymmetrical brain electrical activity discriminates between psychometrically-matched verbal and spatial cognitive tasks. *Psychophysiology*, **27**, 528–43.

Davidson, R.J., Putnam, K.M., and Larson, C.L. (2000). Dysfunction in the neural circuitry of emotion regulation—a possible prelude to violence. *Science*, **289**, 591–4.

Davidson, R.J., Pizzagalli, D., Nitschke, J.B., and Putnam, K.M. (2002). Depression: perspectives from affective neuroscience. *Annual Review of Psychology*, **53**, 545–74.

Davidson, R.J., Scherer, K.R., and Goldsmith, H.H. (eds) (2003a). *Handbook of affective sciences*. New York: Oxford University Press.

Davidson, R.J., Pizzagalli, D., Nitschke, J.H., and Kalin, N.H. (2003b). Parsing the subcomponents of emotion and disorders of emotion: perspectives from affective neuroscience. In: R.J. Davidson, K.R. Scherer, and H.H. Goldsmith (eds), *Handbook of affective sciences*, pp. 8–24. New York, Oxford University Press.

Davies, S. (1994). *Musical meaning and expression*, Ithaca, NY: Cornell University Press.

Davitz, J. (1969). *Language of emotion*. New York: Academic Press.

Dawkins, R. and Krebs, J.R. (1978). Animal signals: information or manipulation. In: J.R. Krebs and N.B. Davies (eds), *Behavioural ecology: an evolutionary approach*, pp. 282–309. Oxford: Blackwell.

Dawson, M.E. and Nuechterlein, K.H. (1984). Psychophysiological dysfunctions in the developmental course of schizophrenic disorders. *Schizophrenia Bulletin*, **10**, 204–32.

Dawson, M.E. and Schell, A.M. (1982). Electrodermal responses to attended and non-attended significant stimuli during dichotic listening. *Journal of Experimental Psychology: Human Perception and Performance*, **8**, 315–24.

Dawson, M.E., Schell, A.M., and Filion, D.L. (2000). The electrodermal system. In: J.T. Cacioppo, L.G. Tassinary, and G.G. Berntson (eds), *Handbook of psychophysiology*, 2nd edn, pp. 200–223. New York: Cambridge University Press.

Dawson, M., Schell, D., and Filion, D.L. (2007). The electrodermal system. In: J.T. Cacioppo, L.G. Tassinary, and G.G. Berntson (eds), *Handbook of psychophysiology*, 3rd edn, pp. 159–81. Cambridge: Cambridge University Press.

Decety, J. and Hodges, S.D. (2006). A social cognitive neuroscience model of human empathy. In: P.A.M. van Lange (ed.), *Bridging social psychology: benefits of transdisciplinary approaches*, pp. 103–9. Mahwah, NJ: Lawrence Erlbaum Associates.

Decety, J. and Lamm, C. (2006). Human empathy through the lens of social neuroscience. *The Scientific World Journal*, **6**, 1146–63.

Decety, J. and Jackson, P.L. (2006). A social neuroscience perspective of empathy. *Current Directions in Psychological Science*, **15**, 54–8.

Deci, E.L. (1975). *Intrinsic motivation*. New York: Plenum.

Deci, E.L. and Ryan, R.M. (1985). *Intrinsic motivation and self-determination in human behavior*. New York: Plenum Press.

De Houwer, J., Thomas, S., and Baeyens, F. (2001). Associative learning of likes and dislikes: a review of 25 years of research on human evaluative conditioning. *Psychological Bulletin*, **127**, 853–69.

Dekker, J. and Everaerd, W. (1988). Attentional effects on sexual arousal. *Psychophysiology*, **25**, 45–54.

DeLancey, C. (2002). *Passionate engines: what emotions reveal about mind and artificial intelligence*. Oxford: Oxford University Press.

Dellarosa Cummins, D. and Cummins, R. (1999). Biological preparedness and evolutionary explanation. *Cognition*, **73**, B37–B53.

Delplanque, S., Grandjean, D., Chrea, C., Aymard, L., Cayeux, I., Le Calvé, B., *et al.* (2008). Emotional processing of odors: evidence for a non-linear relation between pleasantness and familiarity evaluations. *Chemical Senses*, **33**, 469–79.

Delplanque, S., Grandjean, D., Chrea, C., Coppin, G., Aymard, L., Cayeux, I., *et al.* (in press). Sequential unfolding of novelty and pleasantness appraisals of odors: evidence from facial electromyography and autonomic reactions. *Emotion*

Dembo, T. (1931). Der Ärger als dynamisches Problem. In: K. Lewin (ed.), Untersuchungen zur Handlungs- und Affekt-Psychologie, X, *Psychologische Forschung*, **15**, 1–144. (Engl. transl. in De Rivera, J. (ed.) (1976). *Field theory as human-science: contributions of Lewin's Berlin group*. New York: Gardner.)

De Meijer, M. (1989). The contribution of general features of body movement to the attribution of emotions. *Journal of Nonverbal Behavior*, **13**, 247–68.

Denham, S. (1998). *Emotional development in young children*. New York: Guilford Press.

Denham, S.A. and Burton, R. (2003). *Social and emotional prevention and intervention programming for preschoolers*. New York: Kluwer Academic/Plenum.

Dennett, D. (1991). *Consciousness explained*. Boston, MA: Little Brown.

Dennett, D.C. (2006). *Breaking the spell: religion as a natural phenomenon*. London: Allen Lane.

Deonna, J. and Teroni, F. (2008). *Qu'est-ce qu'une émotion?* Paris: Librairie. Philosophique.

Depue, R.A. and Collins, P.F. (1999). Neurobiology of the structure of personality: dopamine, facilitation of incentive motivation, and extraversion. *Behavioral and Brain Sciences*, **22**, 491–517.

Depue, R.A. and Iacono, W.G. (1989). Neurobehavioral aspects of affective disorders. *Annual Review of Psychology*, **40**, 457–92.

de Rivera, J. and Grinkis, C. (1986). Emotions as social relationships. *Motivation and Emotion*, **10**, 351–69.

de Rivera, J. and Páez, D. (2007). Emotional climate, human security, and cultures of peace. *Journal of Social Issues*, **63**, 233–53.

de Rivera, J., Kurrein, R., and Olsen, N. (2007). The emotional climate of nations and their culture of peace. *Journal of Social Issues*, **63**, 255–72.

DeSteno, D., Petty R.E., Wegener, D.T., and Rucker, D.D. (2000). Beyond valence in the perception of likelihood: the role of emotion specificity. *Journal of Personality and Social Psychology*, **78**, 397–416.

DeSteno, D., Petty, R.E., Rucker, D.D., Wegener, D.T., and Braverman, J. (2004). Discrete emotions and persuasion: the role of emotion-induced expectancies. *Journal of Personality and Social Psychology*, **86**, 43–56.

Dewaele, J.-M. and Pavlenko, A. (2002). Emotion vocabulary in interlanguage. *Language and Learning*, **52**, 263–322.

Dewey, J. (1959). *Art as experience*. New York: Capricorn Books.

Dewsbury, D.A. (1999) The proximate and the ultimate: past, present and future. *Behavioural Process*, **46**, 189–99.

Dhabhar, F.S. and McEwen, B.S. (1999). Enhancing versus suppressive effects of stress hormones on skin immune function. *Proceedings of the National Academy of Sciences USA*, **96**, 1059–64.

Dhabhar, F.S. and McEwen, B.S. (2001). Bidirectional effects of stress and glucocorticoid hormones on immune function: possible explanations of paradoxical observations. In: R. Ader, D.L. Felton, and N. Cohen (eds), *Psychoneuroimmunology*, pp. 301–38. San Diego, CA: Academic Press.

Diamond, L.M. (2003). What does sexual orientation orient? A biobehavioral model distinguishing romantic love and sexual desire. *Psychological Review*, **110**, 173–92.

Dickinson, A. and Dearing, M.F. (1979) Appetitive-aversive interactions and inhibitory processes. In: A.B. Dickinson (ed.), *Mechanisms of learning and motivation*, pp. 203–31. Hillsdale, NJ: Lawrence Erlbaum Associates.

Diener, E. and Lucas, R.E. (1999). Personality and subjective well-being. In: D. Kahneman, E. Diener, and N. Schwarz (eds), *Well-being: the foundations of hedonic psychology*, pp. 213–29. New York: Russell Sage.

Diener, E. and Seligman, M.E. (2002). Very happy people. *Psychological Science*, **13**, 81–4.

Diener, E., Suh, E.M. Lucas, R.E., and Smith, H.L. (1999). Subjective well-being: three decades of progress. *Psychological Bulletin*, **125**, 276–302.

Digman, J.M. (1990). Personality structure: emergence of the five-factor model. *Annual Review of Psychology*, **41**, 417–40.

van Dijk, W.W. (1999). *Dashed hopes and shattered dreams: on the psychology of disappointment*. Doctoral thesis, University of Amsterdam, The Netherlands.

van Dijk, W.W. and van der Pligt, J. (1997). The impact of probability and magnitude of outcome on disappointment and elation. *Organizational Behavior and Human Decision Processes*, **69**, 277–84.

van Dijk, W.W. and van Harreveld, F. (2008). Disappointment and regret. In: N.M. Ashkanasy and C.L. Cooper (eds), *Research companion to emotions in organizations*, pp. 90–102. London: Edward Elgar Publishers.

van Dijk, W.W., Ouwerkerk, J.W., Goslinga, S., and Nieweg, M. (2005). Deservingness and Schadenfreude. *Cognition and Emotion*, **19**, 933–9.

Dimberg, U. and Ohman, A. (1996). Behold the wrath: psychophysiological responses to facial stimuli. *Motivation and Emotion*, **20**, 149–82.

Dinarello, C.A. (2005). Blocking IL-1 in systemic inflammation. *Journal of Experimental Medicine*, **201**, 1355–9.

Dishion, T.J., Bullock, B.M., and Granic, I. (2002). Pragmatism in modeling peer influence: dynamics, outcomes, and change processes. *Development and Psychopathology*, **14**, 969–81.

Ditto, P.H., Pizarro, D.A., Epstein, E.B., Jacobson, J.A., and MacDonald, T.K. (2006). Visceral influences on risk-taking behavior. *Journal of Behavioral Decision Making*, **19**, 99–113.

Dixon, A.F. (1998). *Primate sexuality. comparative studies of the prosimians, monkeys, apes, and human beings*. Oxford: Oxford University Press.

Dixon, T. (2003). *From passions to emotions*. Cambridge: Cambridge University Press.

D'Mello, S.K., Craig, S.D., Sullins, J., and Graesser, A.C. (2006). Predicting affective states expressed through an emote-aloud procedure from autotutor's mixed-initiative dialogue. *International Journal of Artificial Intelligence in Education*, **16**, 3–28.

Dodge, K.A., Lansford, J.E., Burks, V.S., Bates, J.E., Pettit, G.S., Fontaine, R., and Price, J.M. (2003). Peer rejection and social information processing factors in the development of aggressive behavior problems in children. *Child Development*, **74**, 374–93.

Dohrenwend, B.P., Turner, J.B., Turse, N.A., Adams, B.G., Koenen, K.C., and Marshall, R. (2006). The psychological risks of Vietnam for U.S. veterans: a revisit with new data. *Science*, **313**, 979–82.

Dolan, R.J. (2002). Emotion, cognition, and behavior. *Science*, **298**, 1191–4.

Dolan, R.J. and Vuilleumier, P. (2003). Amygdala automaticity in emotional processing. *Annals of the New York Academy of Sciences*, **985**, 348–55.

Dolcos, F., LaBar, K.S., and Cabeza, R. (2004). Interaction between the amygdala and the medial temporal lobe memory system predicts better memory for emotional events. *Neuron*, **42**, 855–63.

Dolcos, F., LaBar, K.S., and Cabeza, R. (2005). Remembering one year later: role of the amygdala and the medial temporal lobe memory system in retrieving emotional memories. *Proceedings of the National Academy of Sciences USA*, **102**, 2626–31.

Dollard, J., Doob, L.W., Miller, N.E., Mowrer, O.H., and Sears, R.R. (1939). *Frustration and aggression*. New Haven, CT: Yale University Press.

Donaldson, Z.R. and Young, L.J. (2008). Oxytocin, vasopressin, and the neurogenetics of sociality. *Science*, **322**, 900–904.

Doty, R.L. (2003). Mammalian pheromones: fact or fantasy? In: R.L. Doty (ed.), *Handbook of olfaction and gustation*, 2nd edn, pp. 345–83. New York: Marcel Dekker.

Douglas-Cowie, E., Cowie, R., and Campbell, N. (eds) (2003). *Speech Communication*, **40**(1–2) (special issue on speech and emotion).

Douglas-Hamilton, I., Bhalla, S., Wittemyer, G., and Vollrath, F. (2006). Behavioural reactions of elephants towards a dying and deceased matriarch. *Applied Animal Behavioral Science*, **100**, 87–102.

Dovidio, J.F. (1984). Helping behavior and altruism: an empirical and conceptual overview. In: L. Berkowitz (ed.), *Advances in experimental social psychology*, Vol. 17, pp. 361–427. New York: Academic Press.

Dovidio, J.F., Allen, J.L., and Schroeder, D.A. (1990). Specificity of empathy-induced helping: evidence for altruistic

References

motivation. *Journal of Personality and Social Psychology*, **59**, 249–60.

Dovidio, J.F., Piliavin, J.A., Schroeder, D.A., and Penner, L.A. (2006). *The social psychology of prosocial behavior*. Mahwah, NJ: Lawrence Erlbaum Associates.

Draghi-Lorenz, R., Reddy, V., and Costall, A. (2001). Rethinking the development of 'nonbasic' emotions: a critical review of existing theories. *Developmental Review*, **21**, 263–304.

Draine, S.C. and Greenwald, A.G. (1998). Replicable unconscious semantic priming. *Journal of Experimental Psychology: General*, **127**, 286–303.

Dretske, F. (1981). *Knowledge and the flow of information*. Cambridge, MA: MIT Press.

Dretske, F. (1988). *Explaining behavior: reasons in a world of causes*. Cambridge, MA: MIT Press.

Duchenne, G.B. (1862/1990). *The mechanism of human facial expression* (transl. R.A. Cuthbertson). New York: Cambridge University Press. (Original published in French, 1862.)

Duffy, E. (1941). An explanation of 'emotional' phenomena without the use of the concept 'emotion'. *Journal of General Psychology*, **25**, 283–93.

Duncker, K. (1941). On pleasure, emotion and striving. *Philosophy and Phenomenological Research*, **1**, 391–430.

Dunn, A.J. and Berridge, C.W. (1990). Physiological and behavioral responses to corticotropin-releasing factor administration: is CRF a mediator of anxiety or stress responses? *Brain Research Reviews*, **15**, 71–100.

Dunn, B.D., Dalgleish, T., and Lawrence, A. (2006). The somatic marker hypothesis: a critical evaluation. *Neuroscience and Biobehavioral Reviews*, **30**, 239–71.

Dunn, J. (2003). Emotional development in early childhood: a social relationship perspective. In: R.J. Davidson, K.R. Scherer, and H.H. Goldsmith (eds), *Handbook of affective sciences*, pp. 332–46. New York: Oxford University Press.

Dunn, R.P. and Strick, P.L. (1996). The corticospinal system: a structural framework for the central control of movement. In: L.B. Rowell and J.T. Sheperd (eds), *Handbook of physiology. exercise: integration and regulation of multiple systems*, pp. 217–54. New York: Oxford University Press.

Durbin, C., Klein, D.N., Hayden, E.P., Buckley, M.E., and Moerk, K.C. (2005). Temperamental emotionality in preschoolers and parental mood disorders. *Journal of Abnormal Psychology*, **114**, 28–37.

Durkheim, E. (1995). *The elementary forms of religious life* (translated with an Introduction by K.E. Fields). New York: The Free Press.

Duval, S. and Wicklund, R.A. (1972). *A theory of objective self-awareness*. New York: Academic Press.

Dworkin, B.R., Elbert, T., Rau, H., Birbaumer, N., Pauli, P., Droste, C., *et al.* (1994). Central effects of baroreceptor activation in humans: attenuation of skeletal reflexes and pain perception. *Proceedings of the National Academy of Sciences USA*, **91**, 6329–33.

Dzokoto, V. and Okazaki, S. (2006). Happiness in the eye and the heart: somatic referencing in West African emotion lexica. *Journal of Black Psychology*, **32**, 117–40.

Eagly, A.H., Beall, A.E., and Sternberg, R.J. (eds) (2004). *The psychology of gender*, 2nd edn. New York: Guilford Press.

Easterlin, R.A. (1974). Does economic growth improve the human lot? Some empirical evidence. In: P.A. David and M. W. Reder (eds), *Nations and households in economic growth*, pp. 89–125. New York: Academic Press.

Easterlin, R.A. (1995). Will raising the incomes of all increase the happiness of all? *Journal of Economic Behavior and Organization*, **27**, 35–47.

Edelman, G.M. (2006). *Second nature: brain science and human knowledge*. New Haven, CT: Yale University Press.

Edmans, A., Garcia, D., and Norli, O. (2007). Sports sentiment and stock returns. *Journal of Finance*, **62**, 1967–98.

Efran, J.S. and Spangler, T.J. (1979). Why grown-ups cry. *Motivation and Emotion*, **3**, 63–72.

Eibl-Eibesfeldt, I. (1989). *Human ethology*. Hawthorne, NY: Aldine de Gruyter.

Eid, M. (2001). Advanced statistical methods for the study of appraisal and emotional reaction. In: K.R. Scherer, A. Schorr, and T. Johnstone (eds), *Appraisal processes in emotion: theory, methods, research*, pp. 319–30. New York: Oxford University Press.

Eigsti, I., Zayas, V., Mischel, W., Shoda, Y., Ayduk, O., Dadlani, M.B., Davidson, M.C., Aber, J., and Casey, B.J. (2006). Predicting cognitive control from preschool to late adolescence and young adulthood. *Psychological Science*, **17**, 478–84.

Eisenberg, N. (2000). Emotion, regulation, and moral development. *Annual Review of Psychology*, **51**, 665–97.

Eisenberg, N. and Fabes, R. (1990). Empathy: conceptualization, measurement and relation to prosocial behavior. *Motivation and Emotion*, **14**, 131–49.

Eisenberg, N. and Fabes, R.A. (1992). Emotion, regulation, and the development of social competence. In: M.S. Clark (ed.), *Emotion and social behavior: Vol 14. Review of personality and social psychology*, pp. 119–50. Newbury Park, CA: Sage.

Eisenberg, N. and Spinrad, T.L. (2004). Emotion-related regulation. Sharpening the definition. *Child Development*, **75**, 334–9.

Eisenberg, N., Fabes, R.A., Bustamante, D., Mathy, R.M., Miller, P.A., and Lindholm, E. (1988). Differentiation of vicariously induced emotional reactions in children. *Developmental Psychology*, **24**, 237–46.

Eisenberg, N., Fabes, R.A., Miller, P.A., Fultz, J., Shell, R., Mathy, R.M., and Reno, R.R. (1989). Relation of sympathy and distress to prosocial behavior: a multimethod study. *Journal of Personality and Social Psychology*, **57**, 55–66.

Eisenberg, N., Fabes, R.A., Murphy, B., Karbon, M., Maszk, P., Smith, M., *et al.* (1994a). The relations of emotionality and regulation to dispositional and situational empathy-related responding. *Journal of Personality and Social Psychology*, **66**, 776–97.

Eisenberg, N., Fabes, R.A., Nyman, M., Bernzweig, J., and Pinuelas, A. (1994b). The relations of emotionality and regulation to children's anger-related reactions. *Child Development*, **65**, 109–28.

Eisenberg, N., Fabes, R.A., Murphy, B., Karbon, M., Smith, M., and Maszk, P. (1996). The relations of children's dispositional empathy-related responding to their emotionality, regulation, and social functioning. *Developmental Psychology*, **32**, 195–209.

Eisenberg, N., Cumberland, A., and Spinrad, T.L. (1998). Parental socialization of emotion. *Psychological Inquiry*, **9**, 241–73.

Eisenberg, N., Fabes, R.A., Guthrie, I.K., and Reiser, M. (2000). Dispositional emotionality and regulation: their role in predicting quality of social functioning. *Journal of Personality and Social Psychology*, **78**, 136–57.

Eisenberg, N., Losoya, S., and Spinrad, T. (2003). Affect and prosocial responding. In R.J. Davidson, K.R. Scherer, and H.H. Goldsmith (eds), *Handbook of affective sciences*, pp. 787–803. New York: Oxford University Press.

Eisenberg, N., Spinrad, T.L, and Sadovsky, A. (2006a). Empathy-related responding in children. In: M. Killen and J.G. Smetana (eds), *Handbook of moral development*, pp. 515–49). Mahwah, NJ: Lawrence Erlbaum Associates.

Eisenberg, N., Fabes, R.A., and Spinrad, T.L. (2006b). Prosocial behavior. In: N. Eisenberg (ed.) *Handbook of child psychology: Vol. 3. Social, emotional, and personality development*, 6th edn, pp. 646–718 (series editors W. Damon and R.M. Lerner). New York: Wiley.

Ekman, P. (1972). Universal and cultural differences in facial expression of emotion. In: J.R. Cole (ed.), *Nebraska Symposium on Motivation, 1971*, pp. 207–83. Lincoln, NE: Nebraska University Press.

Ekman, P. (1989). The argument and evidence about universals in facial expressions of emotion. In: H. Wagner and A. Manstead (eds), *Handbook of psychophysiology: the biological psychology of emotions and social processes*, pp. 143–64. London: John Wiley.

Ekman, P. (1992a). An argument for basic emotions. *Cognition and Emotion*, **6**, 169–200.

Ekman, P. (1992b). Are there basic emotions? *Psychological Review*, **99**, 550–553.

Ekman, P. (1993). Facial expression and emotion. *American Psychologist*, **48**, 384–92.

Ekman, P. (1999). Basic emotions. In: T. Dalgleish and T. Power (eds), *The handbook of cognition and emotion*, pp. 45–60. Chichester: John Wiley.

Ekman, P. (2003). *Emotions revealed*. New York, Times Books.

Ekman, P. and Davidson, R.J. (1994). How is evidence of universals in antecedents of emotions explained? In: *The nature of emotion: fundamental questions*, pp. 144–77. New York: Oxford University Press.

Ekman, P. and Friesen, W.V. (1967). Head and body cues in the perception of emotion: a reformulation. *Perceptual and Motor Skills*, **24**, 711–24.

Ekman, P. and Friesen, W. (1969). The repertoire of nonverbal behavior: categories, origins, usage, and coding. *Semiotica*, **1**, 49–98.

Ekman, P. and Friesen, W.V. (1975). *Unmasking the face; a guide to recognizing emotions from facial clues*. Englewood Cliffs, NJ: Prentice-Hall.

Ekman, P. and Friesen, W.V. (1978). *Facial action coding system: investigator's guide*. Palo Alto, CA: Consulting Psychologists Press.

Ekman, P. and Friesen, W. (1982). *Rationale and reliability for EMFACS*. San Francisco, CA.

Ekman, P. and Friesen, W.V. (1986). A new pan-cultural facial expression of emotion. *Motivation and Emotion*, **10**, 159–68.

Ekman, P. and Rosenberg, E.L. (eds) (2005). *What the face reveals: basic and applied studies of spontaneous expression using the Facial Action Coding System (FACS)*. New York, Oxford University Press.

Ekman, P., Friesen, W.V., O'Sullivan, M., and Scherer, K.R. (1980). Relative importance of face, body and speech in judgments of personality and affect. *Journal of Personality and Social Psychology*, **38**, 270–277.

Ekman, P., Levenson, R.W., and Friesen, W. (1983). Autonomic nervous system activity distinguishes among emotions. *Science*, **221**, 1208–10.

Ekman, P., Davidson, R.J., and Friesen, W.V. (1990). The Duchenne smile: emotional expression and brain physiology: II. *Journal of Personality and Social Psychology*, **58**, 342–53.

Ekman, P., Friesen, W.V., and Hager, J.C. (eds) (2002). *Facial action coding system*: Salt Lake City, UT: Research Nexus, Network Research Information.

Eley, T.C., Bolton, D., O'Connor, T.G., Perrin, S., Smith, P., and Plomin, R. (2003). A twin study of anxiety-related behaviours in pre-school children. *Journal of Child Psychology and Psychiatry*, **44**, 945–60.

Elfenbein, H.A. and Ambady, N. (2002). On the universality and cultural specificity of emotion recognition: a meta-analysis. *Psychological Bulletin*, **128**, 203–35.

Elfenbein, H.A., Beaupré, M.G., Levesque, M., and Hess, U. (2007). Toward a dialect theory: cultural differences in the expression and recognition of posed facial expressions *Emotion*, **7**, 131–46.

Elison, J. and Harter, S. (2007). Humiliation: causes, correlates, and consequences. In: J.L. Tracy, R.W. Robins, and J.P. Tangney (eds), *The self-conscious emotions: theory and research*, pp. 310–329. New York: Guilford Press.

Elliot, A.J. and Devine, P.G. (1994). On the motivational nature of cognitive dissonance: dissonance as psychological discomfort. *Journal of Personality and Social Psychology*, **67**, 382–94.

Elliot, A.J. and Dweck, C.S. (2005). Competence and motivation. Competence as the core of achievement motivation. In: A.J. Elliot and C.S. Dweck (eds), *Handbook of competence and motivation*, pp. 3–12. New York: Guilford.

Elliot, A.J. and Dweck, C.S. (eds) (2005). *Handbook of competence and motivation*. New York: Guilford Press.

Elliott, C. (2003). *Better than well: American medicine meets the American dream*. New York: Norton.

Ellsberg, D. (1961). Risk, ambiguity, and the Savage axioms. *Quarterly Journal of Economics*, **75**, 643–69.

Ellsworth, P.C. (1991). Some implications of cognitive appraisal theories of emotion. In: K. Strongman (ed.), *International review of studies on emotion*, pp. 143–61. New York: Wiley.

Ellsworth, P.C. (1994a). Sense, culture, and sensibility. In: S. Kitayama and H.R. Markus (eds), *Emotion and culture: empirical studies of mutual influence*, pp. 23–50. Washington, DC: American Psychological Association.

Ellsworth, P. (1994b). Levels of thought and levels of emotion. In: P. Ekman and R.J. Davidson (eds), *The nature of emotion: fundamental questions*, pp. 192–6. New York: Oxford University Press.

Ellsworth, P.C. (1994c). William James and emotion: is a century of fame worth a century of misunderstanding? *Psychological Review*, **101**, 222–9.

Ellsworth, P.C. and Scherer, K.R. (2003). Appraisal processes in emotion. In: R.J. Davidson, K.R. Scherer, and H.H. Goldsmith (eds), *Handbook of affective sciences*, pp. 572–95. Oxford: Oxford University Press.

Ellsworth, P.C. and Smith, C.A. (1988). From appraisal to emotion: differences among unpleasant feelings. *Motivation and Emotion*, **12**, 271–302.

437

References

Elster, J. (1999). *Alchemies of the mind: rationality and the emotions*. Cambridge: Cambridge University Press.

Emmons, R.A. and McCullough, M.E. (2003). Counting blessings versus burdens: an experimental investigation of gratitude and subjective well-being in daily life. *Journal of Personality and Social Psychology*, **84**, 377–89.

Emmons, R.A. and McCullough, M.E. (eds) (2004). *The psychology of gratitude*. New York: Oxford University Press.

Erickson, E. (1968). *Identity: youth and crisis*. New York: Norton.

Ernst, M., Pine, D.S., and Hardin, M. (2006). Triadic model of the neurobiology of motivated behavior in adolescence. *Psychological Medicine*, **36**, 299–312.

Estes, W.K. (1944). An experimental study of punishment. *Psychological Monographs*, **57**(3), no. 263.

Etkin, A., Egner, T., Peraza, D.M., Kandel, E.R., and Hirsch, J. (2006). Resolving emotional conflict: a role for the rostral anterior cingulate cortex in modulating activity in the amygdala. *Neuron*, **51**, 871–82.

Everitt, B.J., Cardinal, R.N., Parkinson, J.A. and Robbins, T.W. (2003). Appetitive behavior: impact of amygdala-dependent mechanisms of emotional learning. *Ann Ny Acad Sci*, **985**, 233–250.

Everson-Rose, S.A. and Lewis, T.T. (2005). Psychosocial factors and cardiovascular diseases. *Annual Review of Public Health*, **26**, 469–500.

Eysenck, H.J. (1981). *A model for personality*. New York: Springer.

Eysenck, H.J. and Eysenck, M.W. (1985). *Personality and individual differences: a natural science approach*. New York: Plenum Press.

Eysenck, M.W. (2004). Trait anxiety, repressors and cognitive bias. In: J. Yiend (ed.), *Cognition, emotion and psychopathology: theoretical, empirical and clinical directions*, pp. 49–67. Cambridge: Cambridge University Press.

Eysenck, S.B.G., Eysenck, H.J., and Barrett, P. (1985). A revised version of the Psychoticism Scale. *Personality and Individual Differences*, **6**, 21–9.

Fabrigar, L.R. and Petty, R.E. (1999). The role of the affective and cognitive bases of attitudes in susceptibility to affectively and cognitively based persuasion. *Personality and Social Psychology Bulletin*, **25**, 363–81.

Fabrigar, L.R., Visser, P.S., and Browne, M.W. (1997). Conceptual and methodological issues in testing the circumplex structure of data in personality and social psychology. *Personality and Social Psychology Bulletin*, **1**, 184–203.

Fallgatter, A., Jatzke, S., Bartsch, A., Hamelbeck, B., and Lesch, K. (1999). Serotonin transporter promoter polymorphism influences topography of inhibitory motor control. *International Journal of Neuropsychopharmacology*, **2**, 115–20.

Fanselow, M.S. and Poulos, A.M. (2005). The neuroscience of mammalian associative learning. *Annual Review of Psychology*, **56**, 207–34.

Fawzy, F.I. and Fawzy, N.W. (1998). Psychoeducational interventions. In: J. Holland (ed.), *Psycho-oncology*, pp. 676–93. New York: Oxford University Press.

Fazio, R.H. (1990). Multiple processes by which attitudes guide behavior: the mode model as an integrative framework. In: M.P. Zanna (ed.), *Advances in experimental social psychology*, Vol. 23, pp. 75–109. New York: Academic Press.

Fazio, R.H. and Olson, M.A. (2003). Implicit measures in social cognition research: their meaning and use. *Annual Review of Psychology*, **54**, 297–327.

Feagin, S.L. (1996). *Reading with feeling: the aesthetics of appreciation*. Ithaca, NY: Cornell University Press.

Fechner, G.T. (1876). *Vorschule der Ästhetik (Foundations of aesthetics)*. Leipzig: Breitkopf and Härtel.

Fehr, E. and Camerer, C.E. (2007). Social neuroeconomics: the neural circuitry of social preferences. *Trends in Cognitive Science*, **11**, 419–27.

Fehr, E. and Fischbacher, U. (2002). Why social preferences matter—the impact of non-selfish motives on competition, cooperation and incentives. *Economic Journal*, **112**, C1–C33.

Fehr, E., and Fischbacher, U. (2004). Third-party punishment and social norms. *Evolution and Human Behavior*, **25**, 63–87.

Fehr, E. and Schmidt, K. (2002). Theories of fairness and reciprocity—evidence and economic application. In: M. Dewatripont, L.P. Hansen, and S.J. Turnovsky (eds), *Advances in economics and econometrics—8th World Congress*, Econometric Society Monographs, pp. 208–57. Cambridge: Cambridge University Press.

Fehr, E., Kirchsteiger, G. and Riedl, A. (1993). Does fairness prevent market clearing? An experimental investigation. *Quarterly Journal of Economics*, **108**, 437–59.

Fehr, E., Fischbacher, U. and Gächter, S. (2002). Strong reciprocity, human cooperation, and the enforcement of social norms. *Human Nature*, **13**, 1–25.

Fellous, J.-M. and Arbib, M. (eds) (2005). *Who needs emotions? The brain meets the robot*. New York: Oxford University Press.

Ferguson, T.J. and Stegge, H. (1998). Measuring guilt in children: a rose by any other name still has thorns. In: J. Bybee (ed.) *Guilt and children*, pp. 19–74. San Diego, CA: Academic Press.

Fernandez-Dols, J.M., Carrera, P., Hurtado de Mendoza, A., and Oceja, L. (2007). Emotional climate as emotion accessibility: how countries prime emotions. *Journal of Social Issues*, **63**, 339–52.

Fernandez-Fernandez, R., Martini, A.C., Navarro, V.M., Castellano, J.M., Dieguez, C., Aguilar, E., *et al.* (2006). Novel signals for the integration of energy balance and reproduction. *Molecular and Cellular Endocrinology*, **254–255**, 127–32.

Ferrari, P.F., Gallese, V., Rizzolatti, G., and Fogassi, L. (2003). Mirror neurons responding to the observation of ingestive and communicative mouth actions in the monkey ventral premotor cortex. *European Journal of Neuroscience*, **17**, 1703–14.

Ferris, C.F., Stolberg, T., Kulkarni, P., Murugavel, M., Blanchard, R., Blanchard, D.C., Febo, M., Brevard, M., and Simon, N.G. (2008). Imaging the neural circuitry and chemical control of aggressive motivation. *BMC Neuroscience*, **9**, 111 (doi:10.1186/1471-2202-9-111).

Ferster, C.B. and Skinner, B.F. (1957). *Schedules of reinforcement*. New York: Appleton-Century-Crofts.

Festinger, L. (1957). *A theory of cognitive dissonance*. Evanston, IL: Row, Peterson.

Fiedler, K. (2008) Language: a toolbox for sharing and influencing social reality. *Perspectives on Psychological Science*, **3**, 38–47.

Field, A.P. (2005). Learning to like (or dislike): associative learning of preferences. In: A.J. Wills (ed.), *New directions in human associative learning*, pp. 221–52. Mahwah, NJ: Lawrence Erlbaum Associates.

Field, A.P. (2006a). Is conditioning a useful framework for understanding the development and treatment of phobias? *Clinical Psychology Review*, **26**, 857–75.

Field, A.P. (2006b). The behavioral inhibition system and the verbal information pathway to children's fears. *Journal of Abnormal Psychology*, 115, 742–52.

Field, A.P. and Nightingale, Z.C. (2009). What if Little Albert had escaped? *Clinical Child Psychology and Psychiatry*, 14, 343–51.

Fields, H.L. (1992). Is there a facilitating component to central pain modulation ? *American Pain Society Journal*, 1, 71–8.

Fine, C. and Blair, R.J.R. (2000). The cognitive and emotional effects of amygdala damage. *Neuroreport*, 6, 435–50.

Finkel, N.J. (1995). *Commonsense justice: juror' notions of the law.* Cambridge, MA: Harvard University Press.

Finkel, N.J. and Parrott, W.G. (2006). *Emotions and culpability: how the law is at odds with psychology, jurors, and itself.* Washington, DC: American Psychological Association.

von Fintel K and Matthewson L (2008). Universals in semantics. *The Linguistic Review*, 25, 139–201.

Fischer, A.H. and Manstead, A.S.R. (2000). The relation between gender and emotion in different cultures. In: A.H. Fischer (ed.), *Gender and emotion: social psychological perspectives*, pp. 71–98. New York: Cambridge University Press.

Fischer, K.W. and Rose, S.P. (1994). Dynamic development of coordination of components in brain and behavior: a framework for theory and research. In: G. Dawson and K.W. Fischer (eds), *Human behavior and the developing brain*, pp. 3–66. New York: Guilford Press.

Fisher, C.D. (2002). Antecedents and consequences of real-time affective reactions at work. *Motivation and Emotion*, 26, 3–30.

Fisher, H.E. (2004). *Why we love: the nature and chemistry of romantic love.* New York: Henry Holt and Company.

Fiske, S.T. (1992). Thinking is for doing: portraits of social cognition from daguerreotype to laser photo. *Journal of Personality and Social Psychology*, 63, 877–89.

Fiske, S.T. and Taylor, S.E. (2008). *Social cognition: from brains to culture*, Chs 13, 14. New York: Wiley.

Fitzgerald, D.A., Angstadt, M., Jelsone, L.M., Nathan, P.J., and Phan, K.L. (2006). Beyond threat: amygdala reactivity across multiple expressions of facial affect. *Neuroimage*, 30, 1441–8.

Flaubert, G. (1964). *Sentimental education.* Harmondsworth: Penguin. (Original work published 1869.)

Foa, E.B. and Kozak, M.J. (1986). Emotional processing of fear: exposure to corrective information. *Psychological Bulletin*, 99, 20–35.

Foa, E.B., Liebowitz, M.R., Kozak, M.J., Davies, S.O., Campeas, R., Franklin, M.E., et al. (2005a). Treatment of obsessive compulsive disorder by exposure and ritual prevention, clomipramine, and their combination: a randomized, placebo-controlled trial. *American Journal of Psychiatry*, 162, 151–61.

Foa, E.B., Hembree, E.A., Cahill, S.P., Rauch, S.A.M., Riggs, D. S., Feeny, N.C. et al. (2005b). Randomized trial of prolonged exposure for posttraumatic stress disorder with and without cognitive restructuring: Outcome at academic and community clinics. *Journal of Consulting and Clinical Psychology*, 73, 953–64.

Fodor, J.A. (1987). *Psychosemantics: the problem of meaning in the philosophy of mind.* Cambridge, MA: MIT Press.

Fodor, J.A. (2001). *The mind doesn't work that way.* Cambridge, MA: MIT Press.

Fogel, A., Nwokah, E., Dedo, J.Y., Messinger, K., Dickson, K.L., Matusov, E., and Holt, S.A. (1992). Social process theory of emotion: a dynamic systems approach. *Social Development*, 1, 122–42.

Folkman, S. and Lazarus, R.S. (1980). Analysis of coping in a middle-aged community sample. *Journal of Health and Social Behavior*, 21, 219–39.

Folkman, S. and Lazarus, R.S. (1985). If it changes it must be a process: study of emotion and coping during three stages of a college examination. *Journal of Personality and Social Psychology*, 48, 150–170.

Folkman, S. and Lazarus, R.S. (1988). *The ways of coping.* Palo Alto, CA: Consulting Psychologists Press.

Fontaine, J.R.J., Luyten, P., De Boeck, P., Corveleyn, J., Fernandez, M., Herrera, D., et al. (2006). Untying the Gordian Knot of guilt and shame: the structure of guilt and shame reactions based on situation and person variation in Belgium, Hungary, and Peru. *Journal of Cross-Cultural Psychology*, 37, 273–92.

Fontaine, J.R.J., Scherer, K.R., Roesch, E.B., and Ellsworth, P.C. (2007). The world of emotions is not two dimensional. *Psychological Science*, 18, 1050–1057.

Ford, T., Goodman, R., and Meltzer, H. (1999). The British Child and Adolescent Mental Health Survey: the prevalence of DSM-IV disorders. *Journal of the American Academy of Child and Adolescent Psychiatry*, 42, 1203–11.

Forgas, J.P. (1995). Mood and judgment: the affect infusion model (AIM). *Psychological Bulletin*, 117, 39–66.

Forgas. J.P. (ed.) (1999). *Feeling and thinking: the role of affect in social cognition.* Cambridge: Cambridge University Press.

Forgas, J.P. (2002). Feeling and doing: affective influences on interpersonal behavior. *Psychological Inquiry*, 13, 1–28.

Forgas, J.P. (2003). Affective influences on attitudes and judgments. In: R.J. Davidson, K.R. Scherer, and H.H. Goldsmith (eds) *Handbook of affective science*, pp. 596–618. New York: Oxford University Press.

Forgas, J.P. and Vargas, P.T. (2004). The effects of mood on social judgment and reasoning. In: M. Lewis and J.M. Haviland (eds), *Handbook of emotions*, 2nd edn, pp. 350–367. New York: Guilford Press.

Foucault, M. (1965). *Madness and civilisation: a history of insanity in the Age of Reason.* Translation by R. Howard of an abridged version of *Folie et déraison. Histoire de la folie à l'âge classique* (Paris: Librairie Plon, 1961). London: Tavistock.

Foucault, M. (2006). *History of madness.* English translation of *Histoire de la folie à l'âge classique*, (Paris: Gallimard, 1972). London: Routledge.

Fouts, H., Lamb, M., and Hewlett, B. (2004). Infant crying in hunter–gatherer cultures. *Behavioral and Brain Sciences*, 27, 462–3.

Fowles, D.C. (1988). Psychophysiology and psychopathology: a motivational approach. *Psychophysiology*, 25, 373–91.

Fox, B.H. (1998). Psychosocial factors in cancer incidence and prognosis. In: J. Holland (ed.), *Psycho-oncology*, pp. 110–124. New York: Oxford University Press.

Frank, M.J. and Claus, E.D. (2006). Anatomy of a decision: striatal-orbitofrontal interactions in reinforcement learning, decision making, and reversal. *Psychological Review*, 113, 300–326.

Frank. R.H. (1988). *Passions within reason: the strategic role of the emotions.* New York: Norton.

References

Frankfurt, H.G. (1988). *The importance of what we care about.* Cambridge: Cambridge University Press.

Frederick, S. and Loewenstein, G. (1999). Hedonic adaptation. In: D. Kahneman, E. Diener, and N. Schwartz (eds), *Well-being: the foundations of hedonic psychology*, pp. 302–29. New York: Russell Sage Foundation.

Fredrickson, B.L. (1998). What good are positive emotions? *Review of General Psychology*, **2**, 300–319.

Fredrickson, B.L. (2001). The role of positive emotions in positive psychology: the broaden-and-build theory of positive emotions. *American Psychologist*, **56**, 218–26.

Fredrickson, B.L. and Branigan, C.A. (2005). Positive emotions broaden the scope of attention and thought-action repertoires. *Cognition and Emotion*, **19**, 313–32.

Fredrikson, M., Annas, P., Fischer, H., and Wik, G. (1996). Gender and age differences in the prevalence of specific fears and phobias. *Behaviour Research and Therapy*, **34**, 33–9.

Freeman, D., Garety, P.A., Kuipers, E., Fowler, D., and Bebbington, P.E. (2002). A cognitive model of persecutory delusions. *British Journal of Clinical Psychology*, **41**, 331–47.

Freeman, E.R., Bloom, D.A., and McGuire, E.J. (2001). A brief history of testosterone. *Journal of Urology*, **165**, 371–3.

Freese, J.L. and Amaral, D.G. (2005). The organization of projections from the amygdala to visual cortical areas TE and VI in the macaque monkey. *Journal of Comparative Neurology*, **486**, 295–317.

French, J.R.P. and Raven, B. (1959). The bases of social power. In: D. Cartwright (ed.), *Studies in social power*, pp. 150–167). Ann Arbor, MI: University of Michigan.

Freud, A. (1936). Ego and the mechanisms of defence. In: *The writings of Anna Freud*, Vol. 2. New York: International University Press.

Freud, S. (1914/1957). *On narcissism: an introduction*, Standard Edition Vol. 14, pp. 73–102. London: Hogarth Press.

Freud, S. (1915/1957). *Instincts and their vicissitudes*, Standard Edition Vol. 14. London: Hogarth Press.

Freud, S. (1917/1984). *Mourning and melancholia*, Pelican Freud Library Vol. 11. Harmondsworth: Penguin.

Freud, S. (1923). *The ego and the id*, Standard Edition Vol. 19. London: Hogarth Press.

Freud, S. (1928). *The future of an illusion*, Standard Edition Vol. 21. London: Hogarth.

Freud, S. (1933). *New introductory lectures on psycho-analysis*, Standard Edition Vol. 22. London: Hogarth Press.

Frick, P.J. and Morris, A.S. (2004). Temperament and developmental pathways to severe conduct problems. *Journal of Clinical Child and Adolescent Psychology*, **33**, 54–68.

Fridhandler, B.M. (1986). Conceptual note on state, trait, and the state-trait distinction. *Journal of Personality and Social Psychology*, **50**, 169–74.

Fridlund, A.J. (1992). Darwin's anti-Darwinism in the *Expression of the Emotions in Man and Animals*. In: K.T. Strongman (ed.), *International review of studies of emotion*, Vol. 2, pp. 117–37. Chichester: John Wiley.

Friedman, N.P. and Miyake, A. (2004). The relations among inhibition and interference control functions: a latent-variable analysis. *Journal of Experimental Psychology: General*, **133**, 101–35.

Fries, P. (2005). A mechanism for cognitive dynamics: neuronal communication through neuronal coherence. *Trends in Cognitive Science*, **9**, 474–80.

Frijda, N.H. (1986). *The emotions.* Cambridge: Cambridge University Press.

Frijda, N.H. (1993). Moods, emotion episodes, and emotions. In: M. Lewis and J.M. Haviland (eds), *Handbook of emotions*, 1st edn, pp. 381–403. New York: Guilford Press.

Frijda, N.H. (1994). Varieties of affect: emotions and episodes, moods and sentiments. In: P. Ekman and R.J. Davidson (eds), *The nature of emotion*, pp. 59–67. New York: Oxford University Press.

Frijda, N.H. (2007). *The laws of emotion.* Mahwah, NJ: Lawrence Erlbaum Associates.

Frijda, N.H. (2007a). Appraisal. In: *The laws of emotion*, pp. 93–121. Mahwah, NJ: Lawrence Erlbaum Associates.

Frijda, N.H. (2007b). Klaus Scherer's article on 'What are emotions?': comments. *Social Science Information*, **46**, 381–443.

Frijda, N.H. (ed.) (2007c). *Social Science Information*, **46**(3) (Special Issue on emotions).

Frijda, N.H. and Mesquita, B. (1994). The social roles and functions of emotions. In: S. Kitayama and H.R. Markus (eds), *Emotion and culture: empirical studies of mutual influence*, pp. 51–88. Washington, DC: American Psychological Association.

Frijda, N.H. and Sundararajan, L. (2007). Emotion refinement: a theory inspired by Chinese poetics. *Perspectives on Psychological Science*, **2**, 227–41.

Frijda, N.H. and Zeelenberg, M. (2001). Appraisal: what is the dependent? In: K.R. Scherer, A. Schorr, and T. Johnstone (eds), *Appraisal processes in emotion: theory, methods, research*, pp. 141–55. New York: Oxford University Press.

Frijda, N.H., Kuipers, P., and ter Schure, E. (1989). Relations among emotion, appraisal, and emotional action readiness. *Journal of Personality and Social Psychology*, **57**, 212–28.

Frijda, N.H., Mesquita, B., Sonnemans, J., and van Goozen, S. (1991). The duration of affective phenomena, or emotions, sentiments and passions. In: K.T. Strongman (ed.), *International review of emotion*, Vol. 1. Chichester: Wiley.

Frijda, N.H., Markam, S., Sato, K., and Wiers, R. (1995). Emotions and emotion words. In: J.A. Russell, J.M. Fernandez-Dols, A.S.R. Manstead, and J.C. Wellenkamp (eds.), *Everyday conceptions of emotion: an introduction to the psychology, anthropology, and linguistics of emotion*, pp. 121–43. Dordrecht: Kluwer Academic.

Frith, U. (2006). *Autism: explaining the enigma.* Oxford: Blackwell.

Fromm, E. (1950). *Psychoanalysis and religion.* New Haven, CT: Yale University Press.

Fum, D., Missier, F.D., and Stocco, A. (2007). The cognitive modeling of human behavior: why a model is (sometimes) better than 10,000 words, *Cognitive Systems Research*, **8**, 135–42.

Funayama, E.S., Grillon, C.G., Davis, M., and Phelps, E.A. (2001). A double dissociation in the affective modulation of startle in humans: effects of unilateral temporal lobectomy. *Journal of Cognitive Neuroscience*, **13**, 721–9.

Furukawa, T.A., Watanabe, N., and Churchill, R. (2006). Psychotherapy plus antidepressant for panic disorder with or without agoraphobia: systematic review. *British Journal of Psychiatry*, **188**, 305–12.

Gabrielsson, A. and Juslin, P.N. (2003). Emotional expression in music. In: R.J. Davidson, K.R. Scherer, and H.H. Goldsmith (eds), *Handbook of affective sciences*, pp. 503–34. New York: Oxford University Press.

Gabrielsson, A. and Lindström, E. (2001). The influence of musical structure on emotional expression. In: P.N. Juslin and J.A. Sloboda (eds), *Music and emotion: theory and research*, pp. 223–48. Oxford: Oxford University Press.

Gächter, S. and Falk, A. (2002). Reputation and reciprocity: consequences for the labour relation. *Scandinavian Journal of Economics*, 104, 1–26.

Gadanho, S.C. (2003). *Learning* behavior-selection by emotions and cognition in a multi-goal robot task. *Journal of Machine Learning Research*, 4, 385–412.

Gainotti, G. (1972). Emotional behavior and hemispheric side of the lesion. *Cortex*, 8, 41–55.

Galambos, N.L. and Costigan, C.L. (2003). Emotional and personality development in adolescence. In: R.M. Lerner, M.A. Easterbrooks, and J. Mistry (eds) *Handbook of psychology, developmental psychology*, Vol. 6, pp. 351–72. Hoboken, NJ: John Wiley and Sons, Inc.

Gallup, G.G. (1982). Self-awareness and the emergence of mind in primates. *American Journal of Primatology*, 2, 237–48.

Garcia, J. and Koelling, R.A. (1966). Relation of cue to consequence in avoidance learning. *Psychonomic Science*, 4, 123–4.

Gati, I. and Ben-Shakar, G. (1990). Novelty and significance in orientation and habituation: a feature-matching approach. *Journal of Experimental Psychology: General*, 119, 251–63.

Geers, A.L. and Lassiter, G.D. (1999). Affective expectations and information gain: Evidence for assimilation and contrast effects in affective experience. *Journal of Experimental Social Psychology*, 35, 394–413.

de Gelder, B. and Bertelson, P. (2003). Multisensory integration, perception and ecological validity. *Trends in Cognitive Sciences*, 7, 460–467.

de Gelder, B. and Vroomen, J. (2000a). The perception of emotions by ear and by eye. *Cognition and Emotion*, 14, 289–311.

de Gelder, B. and Vroomen, J. (2000b). Bimodal emotion perception: integration across separate modalities, cross-modal perceptual grouping or perception of multimodal events? *Cognition and Emotion*, 14, 321–4.

Gendolla, G.H.E. (2000). On the impact of mood on behavior: an integrative theory and a review. *Review of General Psychology*, 4, 378–408.

Gendolla, G.H.E. (2004). The intensity of motivation when the self is involved: an application of Brehm's theory of motivation to effort-related cardiovascular response. In: R. A. Wright, J. Greenberg, and S.S. Brehm (eds), *Motivational analyses of social behavior*, pp. 205–24. Mahwah, NJ: Lawrence Erlbaum Associates.

Gendolla, G.H.E. and Wright, R.A. (2005). Motivation in social settings: studies of effort-related cardiovascular arousal. In: J.P. Forgas, K. Williams, and W. von Hippel (eds), *Social motivation*, pp. 71–90. New York: Cambridge University Press.

Georgiadis, J.R. and Holstege, G. (2005). Human brain activation during sexual stimulation of the penis. *Journal of Comparative Neurology*, 493, 33–8.

Gerrig, R.J. (1993). *Experiencing narrative worlds : on the psychological activities of reading*. New Haven, CT: Yale University Press.

Gershon, M.D. and Tack, J. (2007). The serotonin signaling system: from basic understanding to drug development for functional GI disorders. *Gastroenterology*, 132, 397–414.

Ghaemi, S.N., Boiman, E.E., and Goodwin, F.K. (2000). Diagnosing bipolar disorder and the effect of antidepressants: a naturalistic study. *Journal of Clinical Psychiatry*, 61, 804–8, quiz 809.

Ghazanfar, A.A., Turesson, H.K., Maier, J.X., van Dinther, R., Patterson, R.D., and Logothetis, N.K. (2007). Vocal tract resonances as indexical cues in rhesus monkeys. *Current Biology*, 17, 425–30.

Gianaros, P.J., Derbyshire, S.W.G., May, J.C., Siegle, G.J., Gamalo, M.A., and Jennings, J.R. (2005). Anterior cingulate activity correlates with blood pressure during stress. *Psychophysiology*, 42, 627–35.

Gibbard, A. (1990). *Wise choices, apt feelings: a theory of normative judgment*. Cambridge, MA: Harvard University Press.

Gibbon, J. (1977). Scalar expectancy theory and Weber's law in animal timing. *Psychological Review*, 84, 279–325.

Gigerenzer, G. (2007). *Gut feelings: the intelligence of the unconscious*. New York: Viking Press.

Gigerenzer, G. and Selten, R. (eds) (2001). *Bounded rationality: the adaptive toolbox*. Cambridge, MA: MIT Press.

Gigerenzer, G., Todd, P.M., and the ABC Research Group (1999). *Simple heuristics that make us smart*. New York; Oxford University Press.

Gilbert, D.T. and Wilson, T.D. (2000). Miswanting: some problems in the forecasting of future affective states. In: J. Forgas (ed.), *Thinking and feeling: the role of affect in social cognition*, 178–200 Cambridge: Cambridge University Press.

Gilbert, D.T., Lieberman, M.D., Morewedge, C.K., and Wilson, T.D. (2004). The peculiar longevity of things not so bad. *Psychological Science*, 15, 14–19.

Gilbert, P. (2005). Compassion and cruelty: a biopsychosocial approach. In: P. Gilbert (ed.), *Compassion. Conceptualisations, research and use in psychotherapy*, pp. 9–74. London: Routledge.

Gilbertson, M.W., Shenton, M.E., Ciszewski, A., Kasai, K., Lasko, N.B., Orr, S.P., et al. (2002). Smaller hippocampal volume predicts pathologic vulnerability to psychological trauma. *Nature Neuroscience*, 5, 1242–7.

Giles, J. (2004). *The nature of sexual desire*. Westport, CT: Praeger.

Gilovich, T. and Medvec, V.H. (1995). The experience of regret: what, when, and why. *Psychological Review*, 102, 379–95.

Ginet, C. (1990). *On action*. Cambridge: Cambridge University Press.

Gintis, H. (2000). Strong reciprocity and human sociality. *Journal of Theoretical Biology*, 206, 169–179.

Giordano, L.A., Bickel, W.K., Loewenstein, G., Jacobs, E.A., Marsch L., and Badger, G.J. (2002). Mild opioid deprivation increases the degree that opioid-dependent outpatients discount delayed heroin and money. *Psychopharmacology*, 163, 174–82.

Glaeser, E., Laibson, D., Scheinkman, J., and Soutter, C. (2000). Measuring trust. *Quarterly Journal of Economics*, 115, 811–46.

Glucksberg, S. (2001). *Understanding figurative language: from metaphor to idioms*. New York: Oxford University Press.

References

Goldberg, L.R. (2006). The International Personality Item Pool and the future of public-domain personality measures. *Journal of Research in Personality*, **40**, 84–96.

Goldie, P. (2000). *The emotions: a philosophical exploration*. Oxford: Clarendon.

Goldie, P. (2004). *On personality*. London: Routledge.

Goldman, A. (1977). Plain sex. *Philosophy and Public Affairs*, **6**, 267–87.

Goldman, A.I. (2006). *Simulating minds: the philosophy, psychology, and neuroscience of mindreading*. New York: Oxford University Press.

Goldman, A.I. and Sripada, C.S. (2005). Simulationist models of face-based emotion recognition. *Cognition*, **94**, 193–213.

Goldsmith, H.H., Davidson, R.J., and Pollak, S. (2008). Developmental neuroscience perspectives on emotion regulation. *Child Development Perspectives*, 2, 132–40.

Gollwitzer, P.M. (1996). The volitional benefits of planning. In: P.M. Gollwitzer and J.A. Bargh (eds), *The psychology of action: linking cognition and motivation to behavior*, pp. 287–312. New York: Guilford Press.

Goodman, S.H. and Gotlib, I.H. (1999). Risk for psychopathology in the children of depressed mothers: a developmental model for understanding mechanisms of transmission. *Psychological Review*, **106**, 458–90.

Goodwin, G.M. and Sachs, G. (2004). *Bipolar disorder*. Oxford: Healthpress.

van Goozen, S.H.M., Matthys, W., Cohen-Kettenis, P.T., Buitelaar, J.K., and van Engeland, H. (2000). Hypothalamic-pituitary-adrenal axis and autonomic nervous system activity in disruptive children and matched controls. *Journal of the American Academy of Child and Adolescent Psychiatry*, **39**, 1438–45.

van Goozen, S.H.M., Fairchild, G., Snoek, H., and Harold, G.T. (2007). The evidence for a neurobiological model of childhood antisocial behavior. *Psychological Bulletin*, **133**, 149–82.

Gordon, R. (1987). *The structure of emotions*. Cambridge: Cambridge University Press.

Gorfein, D.S. and MacLeod, C.M. (2007). *Inhibition in cognition*. Washington, DC: American Psychological Association.

Gortmaker, S.L., Kagan, J., Caspi, A., and Silva, P.A. (1997). Daylength during pregnancy and shyness in children. *Developmental Psychobiology*, **41**, 107–14.

Gosling, S.D. (2001). From mice to men: what can we learn about personality from animal research? *Psychological Bulletin*, **127**, 45–86.

Gotlib, I.H. and Hammen, C.L. (eds) (2002). *Handbook of depression*. New York: Guilford Press.

Gotlib, I.H., Joormann, J., Minor, K.L., and Cooney, R.E. (2006). Cognitive and biological functioning in children at risk for depression. In: T. Canli (ed.), *Biology of personality and individual differences*, pp. 353–81. New York: Guilford Press.

Gotlib, I.H., Joorman, J., Minor, K.L., and Hallmayer, J. (2008). HPA-Axis reactivity may underlie the associations among the 5-HTTLPR polymorphism, stress and risk for depression. *Biological Psychiatry*, **63**, 847–51.

Gottman, J.M. (1994). *What predicts divorce? The relationship between marital processes and marital outcomes*. Hillsdale, NJ: Lawrence Erlbaum Associates.

Gould, S.J. (1991). *Bully for brontosaurus. reflections in natural history*. New York: Norton.

Gramming, P. and Sundberg, J. (1988). Spectrum factors relevant to phonetogram measurement. *Journal of the Acoustical Society of America*, **83**, 2352–60.

Grandey, A.A. (2003). When 'the show must go on': surface acting and deep acting as determinants of emotional exhaustion and peer-rated service delivery. *Academy of Management Journal*, **46**, 86–96.

Grandey, A.A., Tam, A.P., and Brauburger, A.L. (2002). Affective states and traits in the workplace: diary and survey data from young workers. *Motivation and Emotion*, **26**, 31–55.

Grandjean, D. and Scherer, K.R. (2008). Unpacking the cognitive architecture of emotion processes. *Emotion*, **8**, 341–51.

Grandjean, D., Sander, D., Pourtois, G., Schwartz, S., Seghier, M.L., Scherer, K.R., *et al.* (2005). The voices of wrath: brain responses to angry prosody in meaningless speech. *Nature Neuroscience*, **8**, 145–6.

Grandjean, D., Sander, D., and Scherer, K.R. (2008). Conscious emotional experience emerges as a function of multilevel, appraisal-driven response synchronization. *Consciousness and Cognition*, **17**, 484–95.

Gratch, J. and Marsella, S. (2004). A domain-independent framework for modeling emotion. *Cognitive Systems Research*, **5**, 269–306.

Gratch, J. and Marsella, S. (2005). Lessons from emotion psychology for the design of lifelike characters. *Applied Artificial Intelligence*, **19**, 215–33.

Gray, J.A. (1982). *The neuropsychology of anxiety: an enquiry into the functions of the septo-hippocampal system*. New York: Oxford University Press.

Gray, J.A. (1987). *Fear and stress*, Cambridge: Cambridge University Press.

Gray, J.A. (1994). Three fundamental emotion systems. In: P. Ekman and R.J. Davidson (eds), *The nature of emotion: fundamental questions*, pp. 243–7. New York: Oxford University Press.

Gray, J.A. and McNaughton, N. (2000). *The neuropsychology of anxiety: an enquiry into the functions of the septo-hippocampal system*, 2nd edn. Oxford: Oxford University Press.

Graziano, W.G. and Eisenberg, N. (1997). Agreeableness: a dimension of personality. In: R. Hogan, R. Johnson, and S. Briggs (eds), *Handbook of personality psychology*, pp. 795–824. San Diego, CA: Academic Press.

Grebner, S., Elfering, A., Semmer, N.K., Kaiser-Probst, C., and Schlapbach, M.-L. (2004). Stressful situations at work and in private life among young workers: an event sampling approach. *Social Indicators Research*, **67**, 11–49.

Greenberg, D.L., Rice, H.J., Cooper, J.J., Cabeza, R., Rubin, D.C., and LaBar, K.S. (2005). Co-activation of the amygdala, hippocampus and inferior frontal gyrus during autobiographical memory retrieval. *Neuropsychologia*, **43**, 659–74.

Greene, J.D., Sommerville, R.B., Nystrom, L.E., Darley, J.M., and Cohen, J.D. (2001). An fMRI investigation of emotional engagement in moral judgment. *Science*, **293**, 2105–8.

Greenspan, P. (1980). A case of mixed feelings: ambivalence and the logic of emotion. In: A.O. Rorty (ed.), *Explaining emotions*, pp. 223–250. Berkeley, CA: University of California Press.

Greenspan, P. (1988). *Emotions and reasons: an enquiry into emotional justification*. New York: Routledge.

Greenwald, A.G. (1980). The totalitarian ego: fabrication and revision of personal history. *American Psychologist*, **35**, 603–18.

Gregg, T.R. and Siegel, A. (2001). Brain structures and neurotransmitters regulating aggression in cats: implications for human aggression. *Progress in Neuropsychopharmacology and Biological Psychiatry*, **25**, 91–140.

Grey, W.D. (ed.) (2007). *Integrated models of cognitive systems.* New York: Oxford University Press.

Griffiths, P.E. (1997). *What emotions really are: the problem of psychological categories.* Chicago: University of Chicago Press.

Griffiths, P.E. (2003). Basic emotions, complex emotions, Machiavellian emotions. In: A. Hatzimoysis (ed.), *Philosophy and the emotions*, pp. 39–67. Cambridge: Cambridge University Press.

Grobras, M.H. and Paus, T. (2006). Brain networks involved in viewing angry hands or faces. *Cerebral Cortex*, **16**, 1087–96.

Gross, D.M. (2006). *The secret history of emotion: from Aristotle's Rhetoric to modern brain science.* Chicago: University of Chicago Press.

Gross, J.J. (1998). Antecedent- and response-focused emotion regulation: divergent consequences for experience, expression, and physiology. *Journal of Personality and Social Psychology*, **74**, 224–37.

Gross, J.J. (2002). Emotion regulation: affect, cognition, and social consequences. *Psychophysiology*, **39**, 281–91.

Gross, J.J. (ed.) (2007). *Handbook of emotion regulation.* New York: Guilford Press.

Gross, J.J. and John, O.P. (2003). Individual differences in two emotion regulation processes: implications for affect, relationships, and well-being. *Journal of Personality and Social Psychology*, **85**, 348–62.

Gross, J.J. and Keltner, D. (eds) (1999). Functional accounts of emotion. *Journal of Cognition and Emotion*, **13**(5) (special issue).

Gross, J.J. and Thompson, R.A. (2007). Emotion regulation: conceptual foundations. In: J.J. Gross (ed.), *Handbook of emotion regulation*, pp. 3–24. New York: Guilford Press.

Grossberg, S. (1971). On the dynamics of operant conditioning. *Journal of Theoretical Biology*, **33**, 225–55.

Groves, D.A. and Brown, V.J. (2005). Vagal nerve stimulation: a review of its applications and potential mechanisms that mediate its clinical effects. *Neuroscience and Biobehavioral Reviews*, **29**, 493–500.

Guerrero, L.K. and Floyd, K. (2006). *Nonverbal communication in close relationships.* Mahwah, NJ: Lawrence Erlbaum Associates.

Gunnar, M., Marvinney, D., Isensee, J., and Fisch, R.O. (1989). Coping with uncertainty: new models of the relations between hormonal, behavioral, and cognitive processes. In: D.S. Palermo (ed.), *Coping with uncertainty: behavioral and developmental perspectives*, pp. 101–29. Hillsdale, NJ: Lawrence Erlbaum Associates.

Gustafson, G.E., Wood, R.M., and Green, J.A. (2000). Can we hear the causes of infants' crying? In: R.G. Barr, B. Hopkins, and J.A. Green (eds), *Cry as a sign, a symptom, and a signal. Clinical, emotional and developmental aspects of infant and toddler crying*, pp. 8–22. London: MacKeith Press.

Güth, W., Schmittberger, R. and Schwarze, B. (1982). An experimental analysis of ultimatum bargaining. *Journal of Economic Behavior and Organization*, **3**, 367–88.

Guttenplan, S. (1994). An essay on mind. In: S. Guttenplan (ed.), *A companion to the philosophy of mind*, pp. 1–107. Oxford: Blackwell.

Guttman, L. (1957). A new approach to factor analysis: the radex. In: P.F. Lazarsfeld (ed.), *Mathematical thinking in the social sciences*, pp. 258–348. New York: Columbia University Press.

Habib, K.E., Weld, K.P., Rice, K.C., Pushkas, J., Champoux, M., Listwak, S., *et al.* (2000). Oral administration of a corticotropin-releasing hormone receptor antagonist significantly attenuates behavioral, neuroendocrine, and autonomic responses to stress in primates. *Proceedings of the National Academy of Sciences USA*, **97**, 6079–84.

Haidt, J. (2001). The emotional dog and its rational tail: a social intuitionist approach to moral judgment. *Psychological Review*, **108**, 814–34.

Haidt, J. (2002). Dialogue between my head and my heart: affective influences on moral judgment. *Psychological Inquiry*, **13**, 54–6.

Haidt, J. (2003). The moral emotions. In: R.J. Davidson, K.R. Scherer, and H.H. Goldsmith (eds), *Handbook of affective sciences*, pp. 852–70. New York: Oxford University Press.

Haidt, J., McCauley, C.R., and Rozin, P. (1994). A scale to measure disgust sensitivity. *Personality and Individual Differences*, **16**, 701–13.

Halberstadt, A., Denham, S.A., and Dunsmore, J. (2001). Affective social competence. *Social Development*, **10**, 79–119.

Hall, C.S. and Lindzey, G. (1970). *Theories of personality*, 2nd edn. New York: Wiley.

Hall, J.A. (2006). Gender differences in nonverbal communication: similarities, differences, stereotypes, and origins. In: V. L. Manusov and M.L. Patterson (eds), *The handbook of nonverbal communication*, pp. 201–18. Thousand Oaks, CA: Sage.

Hall, J.A. and Bernieri, F.J. (eds) (2001). *Interpersonal sensitivity: theory and measurement.* Mahwah, NJ: Lawrence Erlbaum Associates.

Hall, J.A., Coats, E.J., and Smith LeBeau, L. (2005a). Nonverbal behavior and the vertical dimension of social relations: a meta-analysis. *Psychological Bulletin*, **131**, 898–924.

Hall, J.A., Bernieri, F.J., and Carney, D.R. (2005b). Nonverbal behavior and interpersonal sensitivity. In: J.A. Harrigan, R. Rosenthal, and K.R. Scherer (eds), *The new handbook of methods in nonverbal behavior research*, pp. 237–81. Oxford: Oxford University Press.

Hamann, S. (2003). Nosing in on the emotional brain. *Nature Neuroscience*, **6**, 106–8.

Hamann, S., Herman, R.A., Nolan, C.L., and Wallen, K. (2004). Men and women differ in amygdala response to visual sexual stimuli. *Nature Neuroscience*, **7**, 411–16.

Hamilton, W.D. (1964). Genetical evolution of social behaviour I and II. *Journal of Theoretical Biology*, **7**, 1–52.

Hammerstein, P. (2003). *Genetic and cultural evolution of cooperation.* Cambridge, MA: MIT Press.

Hammond, K.R. and Stewart, T.R. (eds) (2001). *The essential Brunswik: beginnings, explications, applications.* New York: Oxford University Press.

Hantouche, E.G., Akiskal, H.S., Lancrenon, S., Allilaire, J.F., Sechter, D., Azorin, J.M., Bourgeois, M., *et al.* (1998). Systematic clinical methodology for validating bipolar-II disorder: data in mid-stream from a French national multi-site study (EPIDEP). *Journal of Affective Disorders*, **50**, 163–73.

References

Harackiewicz, J.M., Manderlink, G., and Sansone, C. (1984). Rewarding pinball wizardry: effects of evaluation and cue value on intrinsic interest. *Journal of Personality and Social Psychology*, **47**, 287–300.

Harber, K.D. and Cohen, D.J. (2005). The emotional broadcaster theory of social sharing. *Journal of Language and Social Psychology*, **24**, 382–400.

Harding, G. (1986). Constructing addiction as a moral failing. *Sociology of Health and Illness*, **8**, 75–86.

Hare, R.D. (2003). *Hare Psychopathy Checklist–Revised (PCL-R)*, 2nd edn. Toronto: Multi Health Systems.

Hare, R.M. (1952). *The language of morals*. Oxford: Clarendon Press.

Hareli, S. and Weiner, B. (2002). Social emotions and personality inferences: a scaffold for a new direction in the study of achievement motivation. *Educational Psychologist*, **37**, 183–93.

Hariri, A.R. and Holmes, A. (2006). Genetics of emotional regulation: the role of the serotonin transporter in neural function. *Trends in Cognitive Sciences*, **10**, 182–91.

Hariri, A.R., Mattay, V.S., Tessitore, A., Kolachana, B., Fera, F., Goldman, D., Egan, M.F., and Weinberger, D.R. (2002). Serotonin transporter genetic variation and the response of the human amygdala. *Science*, **297**, 400–403.

Hariri, A.R., Drabant, E.M., and Weinberger, D.R. (2006). Imaging genetics: perspectives from studies of genetically driven variation in serotonin function and corticolimbic affective processing. *Biological Psychiatry*, **59**, 888–97.

Harré, P.L. (ed.) (1986). *The social construction of emotions*. Oxford: Basil Blackwell.

Harrigan, J.A. (2005). Proxemics, kinesics, and gaze. In: J.A. Harrigan, R. Rosenthal, and K.R. Scherer (eds), *The new handbook of methods in nonverbal behavior research*, pp. 137–98. New York: Oxford University Press.

Harrigan, J.A., Rosenthal, R., and Scherer, K.R. (eds) (2006). *The new handbook of methods in nonverbal behavior research*. Oxford: Oxford University Press.

Harris, P.L. (2000). *The work of the imagination*. Oxford: Blackwell.

Harris, P.L. (2006). Social cognition. In: W. Damon, R. Lerner, D. Kuhn, and R, Siegler (eds), *Handbook of child psychology, volume 2: cognition, perception and language*, 6th edition, pp. 811–58. New York: John Wiley.

Harris P.L. (2008). Children's understanding of emotion. In: M. Lewis, J. Haviland-Jones, and L. Feldman Barrett (eds), *Handbook of emotions*, 3rd edn, pp. 320–331. New York: Guilford Press.

Harris, P.L., Johnson, C.N., Hutton, D., Andrews, G., and Cooke, T. (1989). Young children's theory of mind and emotion. *Cognition and Emotion*, **3**, 379–400.

Harris, P.L., de Rosnay, M., and Pons, F. (2005). Language and children's understanding of mental states. *Current Directions in Psychological Science*, **14**, 69–73.

Harris, W.V. (2001). *Restraining rage: the ideology of anger control in classical antiquity*. Cambridge, MA: Harvard University Press.

Harrison, N.A., Singer, T., and Rothstein, P. (2006). Pupillary contagion: central mechanisms engaged in sadness processing. *Social Cognitive and Affective Neuroscience*, **1**, 5–17.

Hart, B.L. (1988). Biological basis of the behavior of sick animals. *Neuroscience and Biobehavioral Reviews*, **12**, 123–37.

Harvey, A.G. (2005). Unwanted intrusive thoughts in insomnia. In: D.A. Clark (ed.), *Intrusive thoughts in clinical disorders: theory, research, and treatment*, pp. 86–118. New York: Guilford Press.

Harvey, J.H. (2002). *Perspectives on loss and trauma*. Thousand Oaks, CA: Sage.

Harvey, J.H. and Miller, E. (1998). Toward a psychology of loss. *Psychological Science*, **9**, 429–34.

Hassin, R.R., Aarts, H., and Ferguson, M. (2005). Automatic goal inferences. *Journal of Experimental Social Psychology*, **41**, 129–40.

Hastie, R. and Rasinski, K.A. (1988) The concept of accuracy in social judgment. In: D. Bar-Tal and A.W. Kruglanski (eds), *The social psychology of knowledge*, 193–208. New York, Cambridge University Press.

Hatfield, E. and Rapson, R.L. (1993). *Love, sex, and intimacy: their psychology, biology, and history*. New York: HarperCollins.

Hatfield, E. and Rapson, R.L. (2005). *Love and sex: cross-cultural perspectives*. Lanham, MD: University Press of America.

Hatfield, E., Cacioppo, J.T., and Rapson, R.L. (1992). Primitive emotional contagion. In: M.S. Clark (ed.), *Emotion and social behavior: review of personality and social psychology*, Vol. 4, pp. 151–77. Newbury Park, CA: Sage.

Hatfield, E., Cacioppo, J.T., and Rapson, R.L. (1994). *Emotional contagion: studies in emotion and social interaction*. Cambridge: Cambridge University Press.

Hatfield, E., Rapson, R.L., and Martel, L.D. (2007). Passionate love and sexual desire. In: S. Kitayama and D. Cohen (eds), *Handbook of cultural psychology*, pp. 760–779. New York: Guilford Press.

Haxby, J.V., Hoffman, E.A., and Gobbini, M. I. (2000). The distributed human neural system for face perception. *Trends in Cognitive Science*, **4**, 223–33.

Hay, D.F. (2007). The gradual emergence of sex differences in aggression: alternative hypotheses. *Psychological Medicine*, **37**, 1527–38.

Hayashi, N., Ostrom, E., Walker, J., and Yamagishi, T. (1999). Reciprocity, trust, and the sense of control—a cross-societal study. *Rationality and Society*, **11**, 27–46.

Healy, D. (1997). *The antidepressant era*. Cambridge, MA: Harvard University Press.

Healey, J. and Picard, R.W. (2005). Detecting stress during real-world driving tasks using physiological sensors. *IEEE Transactions on Intelligent Transportation Systems*, **6**, 156–66.

Heckhansen, H. (1991). *Motivation and action*. Berlin: Springer-verlag.

Hegel, G.W.F. (1975). *Aesthetics: lectures on fine art*, Vol. 1, transl. T.M. Knox. Oxford: Clarendon.

Heider, F. (1958). *The psychology of interpersonal relations*. New York: Wiley.

Heinz, A., Braus, D.F., Smolka, M.N., Wrase, J., Puls, I., Hermann, D., *et al.* (2005). Amygdala-prefrontal coupling depends on a genetic variation of the serotonin transporter. *Nature Neuroscience*, **8**, 20–21.

Heinz, A., Smolka, M.N., Braus, D.F., Wrase, J., Beck, A., Flor, H., Mann, K., *et al.* (2007). Serotonin transporter genotype (5-HTTLPR): effects of neutral and undefined conditions on amygdala activation. *Biological Psychiatry*, **61**, 1011–14.

Helson, H. (1948). Adaptation level as a basis for a quantitative theory of frames of reference. *Psychological Review*, **55**, 297–313.

Helson, H. (1964). *Adaptation-level theory: an experimental and systematic approach to behavior*. New York: Harper and Row.

Henrich, J. and Gil-White, F.J. (2001). The evolution of prestige: freely conferred status as a mechanism for enhancing the benefits of cultural transmission. *Evolution and Human Behavior*, 22, 165–96.

Henry, J.P. (1982). The relation of social to biological processes in disease. *Social Science and Medicine*, 16, 369–80.

Hergenhan, B.R. and Olson, M.H. (2005). *An introduction to theories of learning*, 7th edn. Upper Saddle River, NJ: Pearson.

Herman, J.P., Figueiredo, H., Mueller, N.K., Ulrich-Lai, Y., Ostrander, M.M., Choi, D.C., et al. (2003). Central mechanisms of stress integration: hierarchical circuitry controlling hypothalamo-pituitary-adrenocortical responsiveness. *Frontiers in Neuroendocrinology*, 24, 151–80.

Hermans, D., Baeyens, F., and Eelen, P. (2003). On the acquisition and activation of evaluative information in memory: the study of evaluative learning. In: J. Musch and K.C. Klauer (eds), *The psychology of evaluation*, pp. 139–68. Mahwah, NJ: Lawrence Erlbaum Associates.

Hermans, D., Craske, M.G., Mineka, S., and Lovibond, P.F. (2006). Extinction in human fear conditioning. *Biological Psychiatry*, 60, 361–8.

Herrmann, M.J., Huter, T., Muller, F., Muhlberger, A., Pauli, P., Reif, A., et al. (2007). Additive effects of serotonin transporter and tryptophan hydroxylase-2 gene variation on emotional processing. *Cerebral Cortex*, 17, 1160–1163.

Hertenstein, M.J. (2002). Touch: its communicative functions in infancy. *Human Development*, 45, 70–94.

Hertwig, R. and Todd, P.M. (2003). More is not always better: the benefits of cognitive limits. In: D. Hardman and L. Macchi (eds), *Reasoning and decision making: a handbook*, pp. 275–305. Chichester; Wiley.

Herz, R.S., Schankler, C., and Beland, S. (2004). Olfaction, emotion, and associative learning: effects on motivated behavior. *Motivation and Emotion*, 284, 363–83.

Hess, U., Kappas, A., and Scherer, K.R. (1998). Multichannel communication of emotion: synthetic signal production. In: K.R. Scherer (ed.), *Facets of emotion: recent research*, pp. 161–82. Hillsdale, NJ: Lawrence Erlbaum Associates.

Hess, U., Blairy, S., and Philippot, P. (1999). Facial mimicry In: P. Philippot, R. Feldman, and E. Coats (eds), *The social context of nonverbal behavior*, pp. 213–41. Cambridge: Cambridge University Press.

Hess, U., Adams, R.B. Jr, and Kleck, R.E. (2007). When two do the same it might not mean the same: the perception of emotional expressions shown by men and women. In: U. Hess and P. Philippot (eds), *Group dynamics and emotional expression*, pp. 33–50. New York: Cambridge University Press.

Hess, U., Thibault, P., Levesque, M., and Matsumoto, D. The mislabeling of contempt is not an English language phenomenon. Unpublished manuscript.

Hess, W.R. (1957). *The functional organization of the diencephalon*. New York: Grune and Stratton.

Het, S., Ramlow, G., and Wolf, O.T. (2005). A meta-analytic review of the effects of acute cortisol administration on human memory. *Psychoneuroendocrinology*, 30, 771–84.

Heuer, F. and Reisberg, D. (1990). Vivid memories of emotional events: the accuracy of remembered minutiae. *Memory and Cognition*, 18, 496–506.

Higgins, E.T. (1987). Self-discrepancy: a theory relating self and affect. *Psychological Review*, 94, 319–40.

Higgins, E.T. (1997). Beyond pleasure and pain. *American Psychologist*, 52, 1280–1300.

Higgins, E.T. and Pittman, T. (2008). Motives of the human animal: comprehending, managing, and sharing inner states. *Annual Review of Psychology*, 59, 361–85.

Hill, J. and Maughan, B. (2001). *Conduct disorders in childhood and adolescence*. Cambridge: Cambridge University Press.

Hiroto, D.S. and Seligman, M.E.P. (1975). Generality of learned helplessness in man. *Journal of Personality and Social Psychology*, 31, 311–27.

Hirsch, C.R. and Mathews, A. (2000). Impaired positive inferential bias in social phobia. *Journal of Abnormal Psychology*, 109, 705–12.

Hirshleifer, D. and Shumway, T. (2003). Good day sunshine: stock returns and the weather. *Journal of Finance*, 58, 1009–32.

Hjort, M. and Laver, S. (eds) (1997). *Emotion and the arts*. New York: Oxford University Press.

Hobson, P. (2002). *The cradle of thought: exploring the origins of thinking*. London: Macmillan.

Hochschild, A. (1983). *The managed heart*. Los Angeles, CA: University of California Press.

Hockey, G.R.J. (1997). Compensatory control in the regulation of human performance under stress and high workload: a cognitive-energetical framework. *Biological Psychology*, 45, 73–93.

Hoebel, B.G., Rada, P.V., Mark, G.P., and Pothos, E.N. (1999). Neural systems for reinforcement and inhibition of behavior: relevance to eating, addiction, and depression. In: D. Kahneman, E. Diener, and N. Schwarz (eds), *Well-being: the foundations of hedonic psychology*, pp. 558–71. New York: Sage.

Hoffman, M.L. (2000). *Empathy and moral development: implications for caring and justice*. New York: Cambridge University Press.

Hofstede, G. (1980). *Culture's consequences: international differences in work-related values*. Beverly Hills, CA: Sage.

Hogan, P.C. (2003). *The mind and its stories*. Cambridge: Cambridge University Press.

Holland, P.C. and Gallagher, M. (2004). Amygdala-frontal interactions and reward expectancy. *Current Opinion in Neurobiology*, 14, 148–55.

Hollon, S., DeRubeis, R., Shelton, R., Amsterdam, J., Salomon, R., O'Reardon, J., et al. (2005). Prevention of relapse following cognitive therapy vs medications in moderate to severe depression. *Archives of General Psychiatry*, 62, 417–22.

van Hooff, J.A.R.A.M. (1967). The facial displays of the catarrhine monkeys and apes. In: D. Morris (ed.), *Primate ethology*, pp. 7–68. Chicago: Aldine.

van Hooff, J.A.R.A.M. (1972). A comparative approach to the phylogeny of laughter and smiling. In: R.A. Hinde (ed.), *Non-verbal communication*, pp. 209–41. Cambridge: Cambridge University Press.

Hopf, H.C., Muller-Forell, W., and Hopf, N.J. (1992). Localization of emotional and volitional facial paresis. *Neurology*, 42, 1918–23.

Horan, W.P., Kring, A.M., and Blanchard, J.J. (2006). Anhedonia in schizophrenia: a review of assessment strategies. *Schizophrenia Bulletin*, 32, 259–73.

Hornak, J., Bramham, J., Rolls, E.T., Morris, R.G., O'Doherty, J., Bullock, P.R., et al. (2003). Changes in emotion after

445

References

circumscribed surgical lesions of the orbitofrontal and cingulate cortices. *Brain*, **126**, 1691–712.

Hornak, J., O'Doherty, J., Bramham, J., Rolls, E.T., Morris, R.G., Bullock, P.R., *et al.* (2004). Reward-related reversal learning after surgical excisions in orbitofrontal and dorsolateral prefrontal cortex in humans. *Journal of Cognitive Neuroscience*, **16**, 463–78.

Horowitz, M.J., Markman, H.C., Stinson, C.H., Fridhandler, B., and Ghannam, J.H. (1990). A classification theory of defense. In: J.L. Singer (ed.), *Repression and dissociation: implications for personality theory, psychopathology, and health. The John D. and Catherine T. MacArthur Foundation series on mental health and development*, pp. 61–84. Chicago, IL: University of Chicago Press.

Horstmann, G. (2006). Latency and duration of the action interuption and surprise. *Cognition and Emotion*, **20**, 242–73.

Horwitz, A.V. (2002). *Creating mental illness*. Chicago, IL: University of Chicago Press.

Horwitz, A.V. and Wakefield, J.C. (2007). *The loss of sadness. How psychiatry transformed normal sorrow into depressive disorder*. New York: Oxford University Press.

Hovland, C.I., Lumsdaine, A.A., and Sheffield, F.D. (1949). *Studies in social psychology during World War II*, Vol. 3. Princeton, NJ: Princeton University Press.

Hu, P., Stylos-Allan, M., and Walker, M.P. (2006). Sleep facilitates consolidation of emotional declarative memory. *Psychological Science*, **17**, 891–8.

Hudlicka, E. and Cañamero, L. (eds) (2004). *Architectures for modeling emotion: cross-disciplinary foundations. Papers from the 2004 AAAI Spring Symposium*. Technical Report SS-04-02. Menlo Park, CA: AAAI Press.

Hudson, R. and Distel, H. (2002). The individuality of odor perception. In: C. Rouby, B. Schaal, D. Dubois, R. Gervais, and A. Holley (eds), *Olfaction, taste, and cognition*, pp. 408–20. Cambridge: Cambridge University Press.

Hull, C.L. (1943). *Principles of behaviour*. New York: Appleton-Century-Crofts.

Hume, D. (1739/1740). *A treatise of human nature*, II.ii.i. (Reprinted 1969, Harmondsworth: Penguin.)

Hume, D. (1751/1975). *Enquiries concerning the principles of morals*, ed. L.A. Selby-Bigge (3rd edn with P.H. Nidditch). Oxford: Clarendon.

Hume, D. (1888/1978). *A treatise of human nature*, 2nd edn, ed. L.A. Selby-Bigge (revised and with notes by P.H. Nidditch). Oxford: Clarendon Press. (Original publication 1739.)

Hume, D. (1970). An enquiry concerning the principles of morals. In: L. A. Selby-Bigge (ed.), *Enquiries concerning the human understanding and concerning the principles of morals*. Oxford: Clarendon.

Humphrey, S.P. and Williamson, R.T. (2001). A review of saliva: normal composition, flow, and function. *Journal of Prosthetic Dentistry*, **85**, 162–9.

Huskinson, T.L.H. and Haddock, G. (2004). Individual differences in attitude structure: variance in chronic reliance on affective and cognitive information. *Journal of Experimental Social Psychology*, **40**, 82–90.

Huy, Q.N. (2005). An emotion based view of strategic renewal. *Advances in Strategic Management*, **22**, 3–37.

Iacoboni, M. (2005). Understanding others: imitation, language, and empathy. In: S. Hurley and N. Chater (eds), *Perspectives on imitation: from neuroscience to social science.*

Volume 1: Mechanisms of imitation and imitation in animals, pp. 77–101. Cambridge, MA: MIT Press.

Hyman, S., Chisholm, D., Kessler, R., Patel, V., and Whiteford, H. (2006). Mental disorders. In: D.T. Jamison, *et al.* (eds), *Disease control priorities in developing countries*, 2nd edn, pp. 605–25. New York: Oxford University Press.

Iacoboni, M. and Dapretto, M. (2006). The mirror neuron system and the consequences of its dysfunction. *Nature Reviews Neuroscience*, **7**, 942–51.

IASP—International Association for the Study of Pain (Subcommittee on Taxonomy) (1979). Pain terms: a list with definitions and notes as usage. *Pain*, **6**, 249–52.

Iida, A. and Campbell, N. (2003). Speech database design for a concatenative text-to-speech synthesis system for individuals with communication disorders. *International Journal of Speech Technology*, **6**, 379–92.

Ikemoto, S. and Panksepp, J. (1999) The role of nucleus accumbens dopamine in motivated behavior: a unifying interpretation with special reference to reward-seeking. *Brain Research Reviews*, **31**, 6–14.

Immelmann, K. and Beer, C. (1989). *A dictionary of ethology*. Cambridge, MA: Harvard University Press.

Ingram, R.E., Miranda, J., and Segal, Z. (1988). *Cognitive vulnerability to depression*. New York: Guilford Press.

Inwood, B. (1985). *Ethics and human action in early Stoicism*, Ch. 5. Oxford: Oxford University Press.

Irwin, M.R. and Miller, A.H. (2007). Depressive disorders and immunity: 20 years of progress and discovery. *Brain, Behavior, and Immunity*, **21**, 374–83.

Irwin, W., Davidson, R.J., Lowe, M.J., Mock, B.J., Sorenson, J.A., and Turski, P.A. (1996). Human amygdala activation detected with echo-planar functional magnetic resonance imaging. *NeuroReport*, **7**, 1765–9.

Isbister, K. and Höök, K. (eds) (2007). *International Journal of Human-Computer Studies*, **65**(4) (special issue on evaluating affective interactions).

Isen, A.M. (2000). Positive affect and decision making. In: M. Lewis and J.M. Haviland (eds), *Handbook of emotions*, 2nd edn, pp. 417–35. New York: Guilford Press.

Isen, A.M. and Levin, P.F. (1972). The effect of feeling good on helping: cookies and kindness. *Journal of Personality and Social Psychology*, **15**, 294–301.

Isen, A.M., Niedenthal, P., and Cantor, N. (1992). The influence of positive affect on social categorization. *Motivation and Emotion*, **16**, 65–78.

Iwase, M., Ouchi, Y., Okada, H., Yokoyama, C., Nobezawa, S., Yoshikawa, E., *et al.* (2002). Neural substrates of human facial expression of pleasant emotion induced by comic films: a PET study. *Neuroimage*, **17**, 758–68.

Izard, C.E. (1971). *The face of emotion*. New York: Appleton-Century-Crofts.

Izard, C.E. (1977). *Human emotions*. New York: Plenum Press.

Izard, C.E. (1990a). The substrates and function of emotion feelings: William James and current emotion theory. *Personality and Social Psychology Bulletin*, **16**, 626–35.

Izard, C.E. (1990b). Facial expressions and the regulation of emotions. *Journal of Personality and Social Psychology*, **58**, 487–98.

Izard, C.E. (1992). Basic emotions, relations among emotions, and emotion-cognition relations. *Psychological Review*, **99**, 561–5.

Izard, C.E. (2002). Translating emotion theory and research into preventive interventions. *Psychological Bulletin*, **128**, 796–824.

Izard, C.E. (2007). Basic emotions, natural kinds, emotion schemas, and a new paradigm. *Perspectives on Psychological Science*, **2**, 260–280.

Izard, C.E. and Ackerman, B.P. (2000). Motivational, organizational, and regulatory functions of discrete emotions. In: M. Lewis and J.M. Haviland-Jones (eds), *Handbook of emotions*, 2nd edn, pp. 253–322. New York: Guilford Press.

Izard, C.E., Hembree, E.A., and Huebner, R.R. (1987). Infants' emotion expressions to acute pain: developmental change and stability of individual differences. *Developmental Psychology*, **23**, 105–13.

Izard, C.E., Fantauzzo, C.A., Castle, J.M., Haynes, O.M., Rayias, M.F., and Putnam, P.H. (1995). The ontogeny and significance of infants' facial expressions in the first 9 months of life. *Developmental Psychology*, **31**, 997–1013.

Jackson, D.C., Malmstadt, J.R., Larson, C.L., and Davidson, R.J. (2000). Suppression and enhancement of emotional responses to unpleasant pictures. *Psychophysiology*, **37**, 515–22.

Jackson, D.C., Mueller, C.J., Dolski, I.V., Dalton, K.M., Nitschke, J.B., Urry, H.L., *et al.* (2003). Now you feel it, now you don't: frontal brain electrical asymmetry and individual differences in emotion regulation. *Psychological Science*, **14**, 612–17.

Jackson, F. (1982). Epiphenomenal qualia. *Philosophical Quarterly*, **32**, 127–36.

Jackson, P.L., Meltzoff, A.N. and Decety, J. (2005). How do we perceive the pain of others: a window into the neural processes involved in empathy. *NeuroImage*, **24**, 771–9.

Jackson, P.L., Brunet, E., Meltzoff, A.N., and Decety, J. (2006). Empathy examined through the neural mechanisms involved in imagining how I feel versus how you feel pain. *Neuropsychologia*, **44**, 752–61.

Jackson, S.W. (1986). *Melancholia and depression: from Hippocratic times to modern times*. New Haven, CT: Yale University Press.

Jacobs, N., Kemis, G., Peeters, F., Derom, C., Vlietnick, R., and van Os, J. (2006). Stress-related negative affectivity and genetically altered serotonin transporter function. *Archives of General Psychiatry*, **63**, 989–96.

Jacobsen, R. (2006). Desire, sexual. In: A. Soble (ed.), *Sex from Plato to Paglia: a philosophical encyclopedia*, pp. 222–9. Westport, CT: Greenwood Press.

James, W. (1884). What is an emotion? *Mind*, **9**, 188–205.

James, W. (1890/1983). *The principles of psychology*. New York: Macmillan. (Reprinted 1983, Cambridge, MA: Harvard University Press.)

James, W. (1894). The physical basis of emotion. *Psychological Review*, **1**, 516–29.

James, W. (1961/1902). *The varieties of religious experience*. New York: Macmillan.

Jamison, K.R. (1993). *Touched with fire: manic-depressive illness and the artistic temperament*. New York: Free Press.

Jankowiak, W. (ed.) (1995). *Romantic passion*. New York: Columbia University Press.

Jellinek, E.M. (1960). *The disease concept of alcoholism*. New Haven, CT: College and University Press.

Jenkins, R., Lewis, P., Bebbington, P., Brugha, T., Farrell, M., Gill, B., *et al.* (1997). The National Psychiatric Morbidity Surveys of Great Britain: initial findings from the Household Survey. *Psychological Medicine*, **27**, 775–89.

Jensen, P.S., Hoagwood, K., and Zitner, L. (2006). What's in a name? Problems versus prospects in current diagnostic approaches. In: D. Cicchetti and D.J. Cohen (eds), *Developmental psychopathology, Vol. 1, Theory and Method*, 2nd edn, pp. 24–40. New York: Wiley.

Jespersen, O. (1922). *Language: its nature, development and origin*. London: Allen and Unwin.

Jiang, Y. and He, S. (2006). Cortical responses to invisible faces: dissociating subsystems for facial-information processing. *Current Biology*, **16**, 2023–9.

Johnson, E.J., Hershey, J., Meszaros, J., and Kunreuther, H. (1993). Framing, probability distortions, and insurance decisions. *Journal of Risk and Uncertainty*, **7**, 35–51.

Johnson, M.H. (2005). Subcortical face processing. *Nature Reviews Neuroscience*, **6**, 766–74.

Johnson, S.L. (2005). Mania and dysregulation in goal pursuit: a review. *Clinical Psychology Review*, **25**, 241–62.

Johnson-Laird, P.N. and Oatley, K. (1989). The language of emotions: an analysis of a semantic field. *Cognition and Emotion*, **3**, 81–123.

Johnstone, T. and Scherer, K.R. (2000). Vocal communciation of emotion. In: M. Lewis and J. Haviland-Jones (eds), *Handbook of emotions*, 2nd edn, pp. 220–235. New York: Guilford Press.

Johnstone, T, van Reekum, C.M., Hird, K., Kirsner, K., and Scherer, K.R. (2005). Affective speech elicited with a computer game. *Emotion*, **5**, 513–18.

Johnstone, T., van Reekum, C.M., Urry, H.L., Kalin, N.H., and Davidson R.J. (2007). Failure to regulate: Counter-productive recruitment of top-down prefrontal-subcortical circuitry in major depression. *Journal of Neuroscience*, **27**, 8877–84.

Joireman, J., Strathman, A., and Balliet, D. (2006). Considering future consequences: an integrative model. In: L.J. Sanna and E.C. Chang (eds), *Judgments over time: the interplay of thoughts, feelings, and behaviors*, pp. 82–99. New York: Oxford University Press.

Jones, E. and Wessely, S. (2005). *Shell shock to PTSD: military psychiatry from 1900 to the Gulf War*. Hove: Psychology Press.

Jones, E.E., Kanouse, D.E., Kelley, H.H., Nisbett, R.E,, Valins, S. and Weiner, B. (1972). *Attribution: perceiving the causes of behavior*. Morristown, NJ: General Learning.

Jones, H.E. (1935). The galvanic skin response as related to overt emotional expression. *American Journal of Psychology*, **47**, 241–51.

Jones, S.H. and Bentall, R.P. (2006). *The psychology of bipolar disorder*. Oxford: Oxford University Press.

Jones, S., Mansell, W., and Waller, L. (2006). Appraisal of hypomania-relevant experiences: development of a questionnaire to assess positive self-dispositional appraisals in bipolar and behavioural high risk samples. *Journal of Affective Disorders*, **93**, 19–28.

Joormann, J., Talbot, L., and Gotlib, I.H. (2007). Biased processing of emotional information in girls at risk for depression. *Journal of Abnormal Psychology*, **116**, 135–43.

Joukamaa, M., Kokkonen, P., Veijola, J., Laksy, K., Karvonen, J.T., Jokelainen, J., *et al.* (2003). Social situation of expectant mothers and alexithymia 31 years later in their offspring: a prospective study. *Psychosomatic Medicine*, **65**, 307–12.

References

Judd, L.L., Schettler, P.J., Akiskal, H.S., Maser, J., Coryell, W., Solomon, D., *et al.* (2003). Long-term symptomatic status of bipolar I vs. bipolar II disorders. *International Journal of Neuropsychopharmacology*, **6**, 127–37.

Jung-Beeman, M., Bowden, E., Haberman, J., Frymiare, J.L., Arambel-Liu, S., Greenblatt, R., *et al.* (2004). Neural activity when people solve verbal problems with insight. *PLoS Biology*, **2**, 500–510.

Jürgens, U. (1979) Vocalization as an emotional indicator—neuroethological study in the squirrel monkey. *Behaviour*, **69**, 89–117.

Juslin, P.N. (2000). Cue utilization in communication of emotion in music performance: relating performance to perception. *Journal of Experimental Psychology: Human Perception and Performance*, **26**, 1797–813.

Juslin, P.N. and Laukka, P. (2003). Communication of emotions in vocal expression and music performance: different channels, same code? *Psychological Bulletin*, **129**, 770–814.

Juslin, P.N. and Scherer, K.R. (2005). Vocal expression of affect. In: J.A. Harrigan, R. Rosenthal, and K.R. Scherer (eds), *The new handbook of methods in nonverbal behavior research*, pp. 65–135. New York: Oxford University Press.

Juslin, P.N. and Sloboda, J.A. (eds) (2010). *Handbook of music and emotion: Theory, research, applications.* New York: Oxford University Press.

Kaas, J. (1990). Somatosensory system. In: G. Paxinos (ed.), *The human nervous system*, 1st edn, pp. 813–44. New York: Academic Press.

Kagan, J. (2003). Behavioral inhibition as a temperamental category. In: R.J. Davidson, K.R. Scherer, and H.H. Goldsmith (eds), *Handbook of affective sciences*, pp. 320–331. Oxford: Oxford University Press.

Kagan, J. (2006). *An argument for mind.* New Haven, CT: Yale University Press.

Kagan, J. (2007). *What is emotion?*. New Haven, CT: Yale University Press.

Kagan, J. and Fox, N.A. (2006). Biology, culture, and temperamental biases. In: N. Eisenberg (ed.), *Handbook of child psychology, volume 3: social, emotional, and personality development*, 6th edn, pp. 167–225 (series editors W. Damon and R. Lerner). New York: John Wiley.

Kagan, J. and Snidman, N. (2004). *The long shadow of temperament.* Cambridge, MA: Harvard University Press.

Kahan, D.M. and Nussbaum, M.C. (1996). Two conceptions of emotion in criminal law. *Columbia Law Review*, **96**, 269–374.

Kahneman, D. (1999). Objective happiness. In: D. Kahneman, E. Diener, and N. Schwarz (eds), *Well-being: the foundations of hedonic psychology*, pp. 3–25. New York: Russell Sage Foundation.

Kahneman, D. (2000). Experienced utility and objective happiness: a moment-based approach. In: D. Kahneman and A. Tversky (eds), *Choices, values, and frames*, pp. 673–92. New York: Cambridge University Press.

Kahneman, D. (2003). A perspective on judgment and choice: mapping bounded rationality. *American Psychologist*, **58**, 697–720.

Kahneman, D. and Frederick, S. (2002). Representativeness revisited: attribute substitution in intuitive judgment. In: T. Gilovich, D. Griffin, and D. Kahneman (eds), *Heuristics and biases: the psychology of intuitive judgment*, pp. 49–81. New York. Cambridge University Press.

Kahneman, D. and Frederick, S. (2005). A model of heuristic judgment. In: K.J. Holyoak and R.G. Morrison (eds), *The Cambridge handbook of thinking and reasoning*, pp. 267–93. Cambridge: Cambridge University Press.

Kahneman, D. and Tversky, A. (1979). Prospect theory: an analysis of decision under risk. *Econometrica*, **47**, 263–91.

Kahneman, D. and Tversky, A. (1982). The simulation heuristic. In: D. Kahneman, P. Slovic, and A. Tversky (eds), *Judgment under uncertainty: heuristics and biases*, pp. 201–8. Cambridge: Cambridge University Press.

Kahneman, D., Slovic, P., and Tversky, A. (1982). *Judgment under uncertainty: heuristics and biases.* Cambridge: Cambridge University Press.

Kahneman, D., Diener, E., and Schwarz, N. (1999). *Well-being: the foundations of hedonic psychology.* New York: Russell Sage.

Kahneman, D., Krueger, A., Schkade, D., Schwarz, N., and Stone, A. (2006). Would you be happier if you were richer? A focusing illusion. *Science*, **312**, 1908–10.

Kaiser, S. and Scherer, K.R. (1998). Models of 'normal' emotions applied to facial and vocal expressions in clinical disorders. In: W.F. Flack, Jr and J.D. Laird (eds), *Emotions in psychopathology*, pp. 81–98. New York: Oxford University Press.

Kalat, J.W. (2007). *Biological psychology.* Belmont, CA: Thomson.

Kalin, N.H., Larson, C., Shelton, S.E., and Davidson, R.J. (1998). Asymmetric frontal brain activity, cortisol, and behavior associated with fearful temperament in rhesus monkeys. *Behavioral Neuroscience*, **112**, 286–92.

el Kaliouby, R. and Robinson, P. (2005). In: *Real-time vision for human-computer interaction*, pp. 181–200. Berlin: Springer-Verlag.

el Kaliouby, R., Picard, R.W. and Baron-Cohen, S. (2006). Affective computing and autism. *Annals of the New York Academy of Sciences*, **1093**, 228–48.

Kalisch. R., Korenfeld, E., Stephen, K.E., Weiskopf, N., Seymour, B., and Dolan, R.J. (2006). Context-dependent human extinction memory is mediated by a ventromedial prefrontal hippocampal network. *Journal of Neuroscience*, **26**, 9503–11.

Kalivas, P. and Volkow, N.D. (2005). The neural basis of addiction: a pathology of motivation and choice. *American Journal of Psychiatry*, **162**, 1403–13.

Kaltsas, G.A. and Chrousos, G. (2007). The neuroendocrinology of stress. In: J.T. Cacioppo, L.G. Tassinary, and G.G. Berntson (eds), *Handbook of psychophysiology*, 3rd edn, pp. 303–18. Cambridge: Cambridge University Press.

Kamarck, T.W., Muldoon, M.F., Shiffman, S., Sutton-Tyrrell, K., Gwaltney, C., and Janicki, D.L. (2004). Experiences of demand and control in daily life as correlates of subclinical carotid atherosclerosis in a healthy older sample. *Health Psychology*, **23**, 24–32.

Kamin, L.J. (1968). 'Attention-like' processes in classical conditioning. In: M.R. Jones (ed.), *Miami Symposium on the Prediction of Behavior, 1967: Aversive stimulation*, pp. 9–31. Coral Gables, FL: University of Miami Press.

Kant, I. (1785/1959). *Foundations of the metaphysics of morals*, transl. L. White Beck. New York: MacMillan Library of Liberal Arts.

Kant, I. (1986). *Kritik der praktischen Vernunft.* Stuttgart: Reclam.

Kant, I. (2000). *Critique of the power of judgment*, transl. P. Guyer and E. Matthews. Cambridge: Cambridge University Press.

Kaplan, H.S. (1995). *The sexual desire disorders: dysfunctional regulation of sexual motivation*. New York: Brunner/Mazel.

Kaplan, J. and Iacoboni, M. (2006). Getting a grip on other minds: mirror neurons, intention understanding and cognitive empathy. *Social Neuroscience*, **1**, 175–83.

Kaplan, S. and Kaplan, R. (1982). *Cognition and environment: functioning in an uncertain world*. New York: Praeger.

Karama, S., Lecours, A.R., Leroux, J.M., Bourgouin, P., Beaudoin, G., Joubert, S., *et al.* (2002). Areas of brain activation in males and females during viewing of erotic film excerpts. *Human Brain Mapping*, **16**, 1–13.

Karlson, P. and Lüscher, M (1959). 'Pheromones': a new term for a class of biologically active substances. *Nature*, **183**, 55–6.

Kaster, R.A. (2005). *Emotion, restraint, and community in ancient Rome*. Oxford: Oxford University Press.

Katon, W.J. (2006). Panic disorder. *New England Journal of Medicine*, **354**, 2360–2367.

Katz, D. and Stotland, E. (1959). A preliminary statement to a theory of attitude structure and change. In: S. Koch (ed.), *Psychology: a study of a science*, Vol. 3, pp. 423–75. New York: McGraw-Hill.

Katz, L.D. (2006). Pleasure. *Stanford Encyclopedia of Philosophy* <http://plato.stanford.edu/entries/pleasure/>.

Keane, T.M., Marshall, A.D., and Taft, C.T. (2006). Posttraumatic stress disorder: etiology, epidemiology, and treatment outcome. *Annual Review of Clinical Psychology*, **2**, 161–97.

Keeler, W. (1983). Shame and stage fright in Java. *Ethos*, **11**, 152–65.

Keenan, A. and Newton, T.J. (1985). Stressful events, stressors and psychological strains in young professional engineers. *Journal of Occupational Behaviour*, **6**, 151–6.

Keil, A., Moratti, S., Sabatinelli, D., Bradley, M.M., and Lang, P.J. (2005). Additive effects of emotional content and spatial selective attention on electrocortical facilitation. *Cerebral Cortex*, **15**, 1187–97.

Kellerman, H. (1990). Emotion and the organization of primary process. In: R. Plutchik and H. Kellerman (eds), *Emotion, psychopathology, and psychotherapy*, pp. 89–113. San Diego, CA: Academic Press.

Kelley, K.W. (1985). Immunological consequences of changing environmental stimuli. In: G.P. Moberg (ed.), *Animal stress*, pp. 193–233. Bethesda, MD: American Physiological Society.

Kelley, K.W., Weigent, D.A., and Kooijman, R. (2007). Protein hormones and immunity. *Brain, Behavior, and Immunity*, **21**, 384–92.

Kelly, J.R. and Barsade, S.G. (2001). Mood and emotions in small groups and work teams. *Organizational Behavior and Human Decision Processes*, **86**, 99–130.

Kelso, J.A.S. (1995). *Dynamic patterns: the self-organization of brain and behavior*. Cambridge, MA: MIT Press.

Keltner, D. and Buswell, B.N. (1996). Evidence for the distinctness of embarrassment, shame, and guilt: a study of recalled antecedents and facial expressions of emotion. *Cognition and Emotion*, **10**, 155–71.

Keltner, D. and Buswell, B.N. (1997). Embarrassment: its distinct form and appeasement functions. *Psychological Bulletin*, **122**, 250–270.

Keltner, D. and Gross, J. (1999). Functional theories of emotions. *Cognition and Emotion*, **13**, 467–80.

Keltner, D. and Haidt, J. (1999). Social functions of emotions at four levels of analysis. *Cognition and Emotion*, **13**, 505–21.

Keltner, D. and Haidt, J. (2001). Social functions of emotions. In: T. Mayne and G.A. Bonanno (eds), *Emotions: current issues and future directions*, pp. 192–213. New York: Guilford Press.

Keltner, D. and Haidt, J. (2003). Approaching awe, a moral, spiritual, and aesthetic emotion. *Cognition and Emotion*, **17**, 297–314.

Keltner, D. and Kring, A.M. (1998) Emotion, social function, and psychopathology. *Review of General Psychology*, **2**, 320–342.

Keltner, D., Ekman, P., Gonzaga, G.C., and Beer, J. (2003). Facial expression of emotion. In: R.J. Davidson, K.R. Scherer, and H. H. Goldsmith (eds), *Handbook of affective sciences*, pp. 415–32. New York: Oxford University Press.

Keltner, D., Haidt, J., and Shiota, M.N. (2006a). Social functionalism and the evolution of emotions. In: M. Schaller, J. Simpson, and D. Kenrick (eds), *Evolution and social psychology: frontiers of social psychology*, pp. 115–42. Madison, CT, Psychosocial Press.

Keltner, D., Oatley, K., and Jenkins, J.M. (2006b). *Understanding emotions*. Oxford: Blackwell Publishing.

Kemper, T.D. (1978). *A social interactional theory of emotions*. New York: Wiley.

Kendler, K.S., Thornton, L.M., and Gardner, C.O. (2001). Genetic risk, number of previous depressive episodes, and stressful life events in predicting onset of major depression. *American Journal of Psychiatry*, **158**, 582–6.

Kendler, K.S., Halberstadt, L.J., Butera, F., Myers, J., Bouchard, T.J., and Ekman, P. (2008). The similarity of facial expressions in response to emotion-inducing films in reared apart twins. *Psychological Medicine*, **38**, 1475–83.

Kendon, A. (2004). *Gesture: visible action as utterance*. Cambridge: Cambridge University Press.

Kenny, A. (1963). *Action, emotion and will*. London: Routledge and Kegan Paul.

Kensinger, E.A. and Corkin, S. (2004). Two routes to emotional memory: distinct neural processes for valence and arousal. *Proceedings of the National Academy of Sciences USA*, **101**, 3310–3315.

Kent, S., Bluthe, R.M., Dantzer, R., Hardwick, A.J., Kelley, K.W., Rothwell, N.J., and Vannice, J.L. (1992a). Different receptor mechanisms mediate the pyrogenic and behavioral effects of interleukin 1. *Proceedings of the National Academy of Sciences USA*, **89**, 9117–20.

Kent, S., Bluthe, R.M., Kelley, K.W., and Dantzer, R. (1992b). Sickness behavior as a new target for drug development. *Trends in Pharmacological Science*, **13**, 24–8.

Kessler, R.C., Sonnega, A., Bromet, E., Hughes, M., and Nelson, C.B. (1995). Posttraumatic stress disorder in the National Comorbidity Survey. *Archives of General Psychiatry*, **52**, 1048–60.

Kessler, R., Stang, P., Wittchen, H., Ustun, T., Roy-Byrne, P., and Walters, E. (1998). Lifetime panic-depression comorbidity in the National Comorbidity Survey. *Archives of General Psychiatry*, **55**, 801–8.

Kessler, R.C., Berglund, P., Demler, O., Jin, R., Merikangas, K.R., and Walters, E.E. (2005). Lifetime prevalence and

References

age-of-onset distributions of DSM-IV disorders in the National Comorbidity Survey Replication. *Archives of General Psychiatry*, **62**, 593–602.

Kessler, R.C., Chiu, W.T., Jin, R., Ruscio, A.M., Shear, M., and Walters, E.E. (2006). The epidemiology of panic attacks, panic disorder, and agoraphobia in the National Comorbidity Survey Replication. *Archives of General Psychiatry*, **63**, 415–24.

Kiecolt-Glaser, J.K. and Newton, T.L. (2001). Marriage and health: his and hers. *Psychological Bulletin*, **127**, 472–503.

Kiecolt-Glaser, J.K., McGuire, L., Robles, T.F., and Glaser, R. (2002). Emotions, morbidity, and mortality: new perspectives from psychoneuroimmunology. *Annual Review of Psychology*, **53**, 83–107.

Kihlstrom, J.F., Mulvaney, S., Tobias, B.A., and Tobis, I.P. (2000). The emotional unconscious. In: E. Eich, J.F. Kihlstrom, G.H. Bower, J.P. Forgas, and P.M. Niedenthal (eds), *Cognition and emotion*, pp. 30–86. New York: Oxford University Press.

Killias, M., Somonin, M., and De Puy, J. (2005). *Violence experienced by women in Switzerland over their lifespan*. Bern: Staempfli Publishers.

Kin, N.W. and Sanders, V.M. (2006). It takes nerve to tell T and B cells what to do. *Journal of Leukocyte Biology*, **79**, 1093–104.

Kipper, S. and Todt, D. (2003). The role of rhythm and pitch in the evaluation of human laughter. *Journal of Nonverbal Behavior*, **27**, 255–72.

Kipps, C.M., Duggins, A.J., McCusker, E.A., and Calder, A.J. (2007). Disgust and happiness recognition correlate with anteroventral insula and amygdala volume respectively in preclinical Huntington's disease. *Journal of Cognitive Neuroscience*, **19**, 1206–17.

Kirkpatrick, L.A. and Ellis, B.J. (2001). An evolutionary-psychological approach to self-esteem: multiple domains and multiple functions. In: G.J.O. Fletcher and M.S. Clark (eds), *Blackwell handbook of social psychology: interpersonal processes*, pp. 411–36. Oxford: Blackwell.

Kirmayer, L.J., Groleau, D., Looper, K.J., and Dao, M.D. (2004). Explaining medically unexplained symptoms. *Canadian Journal of Psychiatry*, **49**, 663–72.

Kirsch, I. (1999). *How expectancies shape experience*. Washington, DC: American Psychological Association.

Kissler, J., Assadollahi, R., and Herbert, C. (2006). Emotional and semantic networks in visual word processing: insights from ERP studies. *Progress in Brain Research*, **156**, 47–84.

Kitayama, S., Markus, H.R., Matsumoto, H., and Norasakkunkit, V. (1997). Individual and collective processes in the construction of the self: self-enhancement in the United States and self-criticism in Japan. *Journal of Personality and Social Psychology*, **72**, 1245–67.

Kitayama, S., Mesquita, B., and Karasawa, M. (2006a). Cultural affordances and emotional experience: socially engaging and disengaging emotions in Japan and the United States. *Journal of Personality and Social Psychology*, **91**, 890–903.

Kitayama, S., Mesquita, B., and Karasawa, M. (2006b). The emotional basis of independent and interdependent selves: socially disengaging and engaging emotions in the US and Japan. *Journal of Personality and Social Psychology*, **91**, 890–903.

Kitayama, S., Duffy, S., and Uchida, Y.K. (2007). Self as cultural mode of being. In: S. Kitayama and D. Cohen (eds),

The handbook of cultural psychology, pp. 136–74. New York: Guilford Press.

Kivy, P. (1989). *Sound sentiment: an essay on the musical emotions, the arts and their philosophies*. Philadelphia, PA: Temple University Press.

Klauer, K.C. and Musch, J. (2003). Affective priming: findings and theories. In: J. Musch and K.C. Klauer (eds), *The psychology of evaluation*, pp. 7–50. Mahwah, NJ: Lawrence Erlbaum Associates.

Klein, D.F. (1981). Anxiety reconceptualized. In: D.F. Klein and J.G. Rabkin (eds), *Anxiety: new research and changing concepts*, pp. 235–63. New York: Raven Press.

Klein, D.F. (1993). False suffocation alarms, spontaneous panics, and related conditions: an integrative hypothesis. *Archives of General Psychiatry*, **50**, 306–17.

Klein, D., Shankman, S., and McFarland, B. (2006). Classification of mood disorders. In: D. Stein, D. Kupfer, and A. Schatzberg (eds), *Textbook of mood disorders*, pp. 171–232. Arlington, VA: American Psychiatric Publishing.

Klein, J., Moon, Y., and Picard, R.W. (2002). This computer responds to user frustration: theory, design, results, and implications. *Interacting with Computers*, **14**, 119–40.

Kleinsmith, L.J. and Kaplan, S. (1964). Interaction of arousal and recall interval in nonsense syllable paired-associate learning. *Journal of Experimental Psychology*, **67**, 124–6.

Klinger, E. (1975). Consequences of commitment to and disengagement from incentives. *Psychological Review*, **82**, 1–25.

de Kloet, E.R. (2003). Hormones, brain and stress. *Endocrine Regulations*, **37**, 51–68.

Klopf, A.H. (1988). A neural model of classical conditioning. *Psychobiology*, **16**, 85–125.

Kluver, H. and Bucy, P.C. (1937). 'Psychic blindness' and other symptoms following bilateral temporal lobectomy in rhesus monkeys. *American Journal of Physiology*, **119**, 352–3.

Knapp, M.L. and Hall, J.A. (2010). *Nonverbal communication in human interaction*, 7th edn. Belmont, CA: Wadsworth.

Knight, F.H. (1921). *Risk, uncertainty, and profit*. New York: Houghton Mifflin.

Knoch, D., Pascual-Leone, A., Meyer, K., Treyer, V., and Fehr, E. (2006). Diminishing reciprocal fairness by disrupting the right prefrontal cortex. *Science*, **314**, 829–32.

Kobak, R.R. and Sceery, A. (1988). Attachment in late adolescence: working models, affect regulation, and representations of self and others. *Child Development*, **59**, 135–46.

Kochanska, G. (1997). Multiple pathways to conscience for children with different temperaments: from toddlerhood to age 5. *Developmental Psychology*, **33**, 228–40.

Kogut, T. and Ritov, I. (2005). The 'identified victim' effect: an identified group, or just a single individual? *Journal of Behavioral Decision Making*, **18**, 157–67.

Koh, K.B. (1998). Emotion and immunity. *Journal of Psychosomatic Research*, **45**, 107–15.

Köhler, W. (1935). *The place of value in a world of facts*. New York: New American Library.

Konorski, J. (1967). *Integrative activity of the brain: an interdisciplinary approach*. Chicago, IL: University of Chicago Press.

Konstan, D. (2006). *The emotions of the ancient Greeks: studies in Aristotle and classical literature*. Toronto: University of Toronto Press.

Konstan, D. and Rutter, N.K. (2003). *Envy, spite and jealousy: the rivalrous emotions in ancient Greece*. Edinburgh: Edinburgh University Press.

Kopnisky, K.L., Stoff, D.M., and Rausch, D.M. (2004). Workshop report: the effects of psychological variables on the progression of HIV-1 disease. *Brain, Behavior, and Immunity*, **18**, 246–61.

Kopnisky, K., Bao, J., and Lin, Y. (2007). Neurobiology of HIV, psychiatric and substance abuse comorbidity research: workshop report. *Brain, Behavior, and Immunity*, **21**, 428–41.

Korb, S., Grandjean, D., and Scherer, K.R. (2008). Motor commands of facial expressions: the Bereitschaftspotential preceding voluntary smiles. *Brain Topography*, **20**, 232–8.

Korsgaard, Ch. (1996). The sources of normativity. Cambridge: Cambridge University Press.

Korsten, N.J., Fragopanagos, N., Hartley, M., Taylor, N., and Taylor, N. (2006) Attention as a controller. *Neural Networks*, **19**, 1408–21.

Korsten, N., Fragopanagos, N., and Taylor, J.G. (2007). Neural substructures for appraisal in emotion: self-esteem and depression. *Lecture Notes in Computer Science (Proceedings of ICANN 2007)*, **2007**(4669), 850–858.

Korte, S.M., Koolhaas, J.M., Wingfield, J.C., and McEwen, B.S. (2005). The Darwinian concept of stress: benefits of allostasis and costs of allostatic load and the trade-offs in health and disease (review). *Neuroscience and Biobehavioral Reviews*, **29**, 3–38.

Kosfeld, M., Heinrichs, M., Zak, P.J., Fischbacher, U., and Fehr, E. (2005). Oxytocin increases trust in humans. *Nature*, **435**, 673–6.

Kosslyn, S.M. and Koenig, O. (1995). *Wet mind, the new cognitive neuroscience*. New York: Free Press.

Kövecses, Z. (2000). *Metaphor and emotion*. Cambridge: Cambridge University Press.

Kövecses Z. (2005). *Metaphor in culture: universality and variation*. New York: Cambridge University Press.

Kramer, P. (1997). *Listening to Prozac*. New York: Penguin Books.

Krantz, D.S., Sheps, D.S., Carney, R.M., and Natelson, B.H. (2000). Effects of mental stress in patients with coronary artery disease: evidence and clinical implications. *Journal of the American Medical Association*, **283**, 1800–1802.

Krauss, R.M. and Fussell, S.R. (1996). Social psychological models of interpersonal communication. In: E.T. Higgins and A.W. Kruglanski (eds), *Social psychology: handbook of basic principles*, pp. 655–701. New York: Guilford Press.

Kringelbach, M.L. and Rolls, E.T. (2004). The functional neuroanatomy of the human orbitofrontal cortex: evidence from neuroimaging and neuropsychology. *Progress in Neurobiology*, **72**, 341–72.

Krishnakumar, A. and Buehler, C. (2000). Interparental conflict and parenting behaviors. A meta-analytic review. *Family Relations*, **49**, 25–44.

Kristjánsson, K. (2006). *Justifying emotions: pride and jealousy*. London: Routledge.

Kroenke, K. and Swindle, R. (2000). Cognitive-behavioural therapy for somatization and symptom syndromes: a critical review of controlled trials. *Psycotherapy and Psychosomatics*, **69**, 205–15.

Krueger, R.F. and Tackett, J.L. (2006). *Personality and psychopathology*. New York: Guilford Press.

Kubovy, M. (1999). On the pleasures of the mind. In: D. Kahneman, E. Diener, and N. Schwarz (eds), *Well-being: the foundations of hedonic psychology*, pp. 134–54. New York: Russell Sage.

Kubzansky, L.D. (2005). Personality, emotion, and health. In: W.W. Eaton (ed.), *Medical and psychiatric comorbidity over the course of life*, pp. 197–211. Arlington, VA: American Psychiatric Publishing.

Kubzansky, L.D. and Kawachi, I. (2000). Going to the heart of the matter: do negative emotions cause coronary heart disease? *Journal of Psychosomatic Research*, **48**, 323–37.

Kulka, R.A., Schlenger, W.E., Fairbank, J.A., Hough, R.L., Jordan, B.K., Marmar, C.R., *et al.* (1990). *Trauma and the Vietnam War generation: report of findings from the National Vietnam Veterans Readjustment Study*. New York: Brunner/Mazel.

Kuppens, P., Van Mechelen, I., Smits, D.J.M., and De Boeck, P. (2003). The appraisal basis of anger: specificity, necessity and sufficiency of components. *Emotion*, **3**, 254–69.

Kutchins, H. and Kirk, S.A. (1997). *Making us crazy. DSM—the psychiatric bible and the creation of mental disorders*. New York: Free Press.

Kwan, V.S.M., Bond, M.H., and Singelis, T.M. (1997). Pancultural explanations for life satisfaction: adding relationship harmony to self-esteem. *Journal of Personality and Social Psychology*, **73**, 1038–51.

Laan, E. and Everaerd, W. (1995). Determinants of female sexual arousal: psychophysiological theory and data. *Annual Review of Sex Research*, **6**, 32–76.

LaBar, K.S. and Cabeza, R. (2006). Cognitive neuroscience of emotional memory. *Nature Reviews Neuroscience*, **7**, 54–64.

LaBar, K.S. and Phelps, E.A. (1998). Arousal-mediated memory consolidation: role of the medial temporal lobe in humans. *Psychological Science*, **9**, 527–40.

LaBar, K.S. and Phelps, E.A. (2005). Reinstatement of conditioned fear in humans is context-dependent and impaired in amnesia. *Behavioral Neuroscience*, **119**, 677–86.

LaBar, K.S., Gitelman, D.R., Parrish, T.B., Kim, Y.-H., Nobre, A., and Mesulam, M.-M. (2001). Hunger selectively modulates corticolimbic activation to food stimuli in humans. *Behavioral Neuroscience*, **115**, 493–500.

Labouvie-Vief, G. (2005). The psychology of emotions and ageing. In: M.L. Johnson (ed.), *The Cambridge handbook of age and aging*, pp. 229–37. Cambridge: Cambridge University Press.

Labouvie-Vief, G. and Márquez González, M. (2004). Dynamic integration: affect optimization and differentiation in development. In: D.Y. Dai and R.J. Sternberg (eds), *Motivation, emotion, and cognition: integrative perspectives on intellectual functioning and development*, pp. 237–72. Mahwah, NJ: Lawrence Erlbaum Associates.

Lachter, J., Forster, K.I., and Ruthruff, E. (2004). Forty-five years after Broadbent (1958): still no identification without attention. *Psychological Review*, **111**, 880–913.

Lackner, J.R. and Dizio, P.A. (2000). Aspects of body self-calibration. *Trends in Cognitive Science*, **4**, 279–88.

Ladefoged, P. (1967). *Three areas of experimental phonetics*. London: Oxford University Press.

Ladygina-Kohts, N.N. (2002). *Infant chimpanzee and human child: a classic 1935 comparative study of ape emotions and intelligence*, ed. F.B.M. de Waal. Oxford: Oxford University Press.

References

Lagattuta, K.H. and Wellman, H.M. (2001). Thinking about the past: early knowledge about links between prior experience, thinking, and emotion. *Child Development*, **72**, 82–102.

Laidlaw, K. (2004). Depression in older adults. In: M.J. Power (ed.), *Mood disorders: a handbook of science and practice*, pp. 337–52. Chichester: Wiley.

Lakin, J.L. and Chartrand, T.L. (2003). Using nonconscious behavioral mimicry to create affiliation and rapport. *Psychological Science*, **14**, 334–9.

Lakoff, G. (1993). The contemporary theory of metaphor. In: A. Ortony (ed.), *Metaphor and thought*, pp. 202–51. Cambridge: Cambridge University Press.

Lakoff, G. and Johnson, M. (1980). *Metaphors we live by*. Chicago: University of Chicago Press.

Lamarque, P. (1995). Tragedy and moral value. *Australasian Journal of Philosophy*, **73**, 239–49.

Lamm, C., Batson, C.D., and Decety, J. (2007). The neural basis of human empathy—effects of perspective-taking and cognitive appraisal. *Journal of Cognitive Neuroscience*, **19**, 42–58.

Lanctôt, N. and Hess, U. (2007). The timing of appraisals. *Emotion*, **7**, 207–12.

Landman, J. (1993). *Regret: the persistence of the possible*. New York: Oxford University Press.

Lane, R. and Schwartz, G.E. (1987). Levels of emotional awareness: a cognitive-developmental theory and its application. *American Journal of Psychiatry*, **144**, 133–43.

Lang, A. (2000). The limited capacity model of mediated message processing. *Journal of Communication*, **50**, 46–70.

Lang, P.J. (1980). Behavioral treatment and bio-behavioral assessment: computer applications. In: J.B. Sidowski, J.H. Johnson, and T.A. Williams (eds), *Technology in mental health care delivery systems*, pp. 119–37. Norwood, NJ: Ablex Publishing.

Lang, P.J. (1985). The cognitive psychophysiology of emotion: fear and anxiety. In: A.H. Hussain and J.D. Maser (eds), *Anxiety and the anxiety disorders*, pp. 131–70. Hillsdale, NJ: Lawrence Erlbaum Associates.

Lang, P.J. (1994). The varieties of emotional experience: a meditation on James–Lange theory. *Psychological Review*, **101**, 211–21.

Lang, P.J. (1995). The emotion probe. Studies of motivation and attention. *American Psychologist*, **50**, 372–85.

Lang, P.J. and Davis, M. (2006). Emotion, motivation, and the brain: reflex foundations in animal and human research. *Progress in Brain Research*, **156**, 3–29.

Lang, P.J., Bradley, M.M., and Cuthbert, B.N. (1990). Emotion, attention, and the startle reflex. *Psychological Review*, **97**, 377–39.

Lang, P.J., Bradley, M.M., and Cuthbert, B.N. (1997a). Motivated attention: affect, activation, and action. In: P.J. Lang, R.F. Simons, and M.T. Balaban (eds), *Attention and orienting: sensory and motivational processes*, pp. 97–135. Mahwah, NJ: Lawrence Erlbaum Associates.

Lang, P.J., Simons, R.F., and Balaban, M.T. (eds) (1997b). *Attention and orienting: sensory and motivational processes*. Mahwah, NJ: Lawrence Erlbaum Associates.

Langer, S.K. (1967). *Mind: an essay on human feeling* (abridged and edited by G. Van Den Heuvel). Baltimore, MD: Johns Hopkins Press.

Langford, D.J., Crager, S.E., Shehzad, Z., Smith, S.B., Sotocinal, S.G., Levenstadt, J.S., Chanda, M.L., Levitin, D.J., and Mogil, J.S. (2006). Social modulation of pain as evidence for empathy in mice. *Science*, **312**, 1967–70.

Langley, J.N. (1916). Sketch of the progress of discovery in the eighteenth century as regards the autonomic nervous system. *Journal of Physiology*, **50**, 225–58.

La Rochefoucauld (1665/1959). *Maxims* (transl. L. Tancock). Harmondsworth: Penguin Books. (Original work published 1665.)

Larsen, J.K., Brand, N., Bermond, B., and Hijman, R. (2003). Cognitive and emotional characteristics of alexithymia–a review of neurobiological studies. *Journal of Psychosomatic Research*, **54**, 533–41.

Larsen, J.T., McGraw, A.P., and Cacioppo, J.T. (2001). Can people feel happy and sad at the same time? *Journal of Personality and Social Psychology*, **81**, 684–96.

Larsen, P.R., Kronenberg, H.M., Melmed, S., and Polonsky, K.S (2003). *Williams textbook of endocrinology*, 10th edn. Philadelphia, PA: Saunders.

Larsen, R.J. and Diener, E. (1992). Problems and promises with the circumplex model of emotion. *Review of Personality and Social Psychology*, **13**, 25–59.

Larson, C.L., Schaefer, H.S., Siegle, G.J., Jackson, C.A.B., Anderle, M.J., and Davidson, R.J. (2006). Fear is fast in phobics: amygdala activation in response to fear-relevant stimuli. *Biological Psychiatry*, **60**, 410–417.

Larson, R. and Almeida, D. (1999). Emotional transmission in the daily lives of families: a new paradigm for studying family process. *Journal of Marriage and the Family*, **61**, 5–20.

Larson, R. and Asmussen, L. (1991). Anger, worry, and hurt in early adolescence: an enlarging world of negative emotions. In: M.E. Colten and S. Gore (eds), *Adolescent stress: causes and consequences*, pp. 21–41. Hawthorne, NY: Aldine de Gruyter.

Latané, B. and Darley, J.M. (1970). *The unresponsive bystander: why doesn't he help?* New York: Appleton-Century-Crofts.

Laukka, P., Juslin, P., and Bresin, R. (2005). A dimensional approach to vocal expression of emotion. *Cognition and Emotion*, **19**, 633–53.

Lazarus, R.S. (1966). *Psychological stress and the coping process*. New York: McGraw Hill.

Lazarus, R.S. (1968). Emotions and adaptation: conceptual and empirical relations. In: W.J. Arnold (ed.), *Nebraska Symposium on Motivation*, pp. 175–270. Lincoln, NE: University of Nebraska Press.

Lazarus, R.S. (1991). *Emotion and adaptation*. New York: Oxford University Press.

Lazarus, R.S. (2001). Relational meaning and discrete emotions. In: K.R. Scherer, A. Schorr, and T. Johnstone (eds), *Appraisal processes in emotion: theory, methods, research*, pp. 37–67. New York: Oxford University Press.

Lazarus, R.S. and Cohen-Charash, Y. (2001). Discrete emotions in organizations. In: R.L. Payne and C.L. Cooper (eds), *Emotions at work: theory, research and applications for management*, pp. 45–81. New York: Wiley.

Lazarus, R.S. and Folkman, S. (1984). *Stress, appraisal, and coping*. New York: Springer.

Lazarus, R.S. and Launier, R. (1978). Stress-related transactions between person and environment. In: L.A. Pervin and M. Lewis (eds), *Perspectives in interactional psychology*, pp. 287–327. New York: Plenum.

Leary, M.R. (2000). Affect, cognition, and the social emotions. In: J.P. Forgas (ed.), *Feeling and thinking*, pp. 331–56. Cambridge: Cambridge University Press.

Leary, M.R. and Baumeister, R.F. (2000). The nature and function of self-esteem: sociometer theory. In: M. Zanna (ed.), *Advances in experimental social psychology*, Vol. 32, pp. 1–62. San Diego, CA: Academic Press.

Leavens, D.A., Aureli, F., and Hopkins, W.D. (2004). Behavioral evidence for the cutaneous expression of emotion in a chimpanzee (*Pan troglodytes*). *Behaviour*, 141, 979–97.

LeDoux, J.E. (1991). Emotion and the limbic system concept. *Concepts in Neuroscience*, 2, 169–99.

LeDoux, J.E. (1996). *The emotional brain*. New York: Simon and Schuster.

LeDoux, J.E. (1998a). *The emotional brain: the mysterious underpinnings of emotional life*. New York: Simon and Schuster.

LeDoux, J.E. (1998b). Fear and the brain: where have we been, and where are we going? *Biological Psychiatry*, 44, 1229–38.

LeDoux, J.E. (2000). Emotion circuits in the brain. *Annual Review of Neuroscience*, 23, 155–84.

LeDoux, J.E. (2002). *Synaptic self: how our brains become who we are*. New York: Viking.

LeDoux, J. (2007). The amygdala. *Current Biology*, 17, R868–R874.

LeDoux, J.E. (2008a). Amygdala. *Scholarpedia*, 3, 2698.

LeDoux, J.E. (2008b). Emotional coloration of consciousness: how feelings come about. In: L.W. Weiskrantz and M. Davies (eds), *Frontiers of consciousness: the Chichele Lectures*, pp. 69–130. Oxford: Oxford University Press.

LeDoux, J.E. and Gorman, J.M. (2001). A call to action: overcoming anxiety through active coping. *American Journal of Psychiatry*, 158, 1953–5.

Ledyard, J. (1995). Public goods: a survey of experimental research. In: J. Kagel and A. Roth (eds), *Handbook of experimental economics*, pp. 111–94. Princeton, NJ: Princeton University Press.

Leiris, M. (1958). *La possession et ses aspects théâtraux chez les Ethiopiens de Gondar*. Paris: Plon.

Leith, K.P. and Baumeister, R.F. (1998). Empathy, shame, guilt, and narratives of interpersonal conflicts: guilt-prone people are better at perspective taking. *Journal of Personality*, 66, 2–37.

Leknes, S. and Tracey, I. (2008). A common neurobiology for pain and pleasure. *Nature Reviews Neuroscience*, 9, 314–20.

Lemon, R.N., Kirkwood, P.A., Maier, M.A., Nakajima, K., and Nathan, P. (2004). Direct and indirect pathways for corticospinal control of upper limb motoneurons in the primate. *Progress in Brain Research*, 143, 263–79.

Lengbeyer, L. (2007). Situated cognition: the perspect model. In: D. Spurrett, D. Ross, H. Kincaid, and L. Stephens (eds), *Distributed cognition and the will: individual volition and social context*, pp. 227–54. Cambridge, MA: MIT Press.

Le Page, M. (2005). Orgasms: a real 'turn-off' for women. *New Scientist*, 186, 14.

Lerner, J.S. and Keltner, D. (2001). Fear, anger, and risk. *Journal of Personality and Social Psychology*, 81, 146–59.

Lerner, J.S., Goldberg, J.H., and Tetlock, P.E. (1998). Sober second thought: the effects of accountability, anger and authoritarianism on attributions of responsibility. *Personality and Social Psychology Bulletin*, 24, 563–74.

Lerner, J.S., Small, D.A., and Loewenstein, G. (2004). Heart strings and purse strings: carry-over effects of emotions on economic transactions. *Psychological Science*, 15, 337–41.

Lesch, K.P., Bengel, D., Heils, A., Sabol, S.Z., Greenberg, B. D., Petri, S., *et al.* (1996). Association of anxiety-related traits with a polymorphism in the serotonin transporter gene regulatory region. *Science*, 274, 1527–31.

Leserman, J., Jackson, E.D, Petitto, J.M., Golden, R.N., Silva, S.G., Perkins, D.O., *et al.* (1999). Progression to AIDS: the effects of stress, depressive symptoms, and social support. *Psychosomatic Medicine*, 61, 397–406.

Leshner, A.I. (1980). The interaction of experience and neuroendocrine factors in determining behavioral adaptations to aggression. *Progress in Brain Research*, 53, 427–38.

Levenson, R.W. (1999) The intrapersonal functions of emotion. *Cognition and Emotion*, 13, 481–504.

Levenson, R.W. (2003). Autonomic specificity and emotion. In: R.J. Davidson, K.R. Scherer, and H.H. Goldsmith (eds), *Handbook of affective sciences*. New York, Oxford University Press.

Levenson, R.W. (2005). *FACS/EMFACS emotion predictions*. Berkeley, CA (computer program available from R. W. Levenson, University of California, Berkeley).

Levenson, R.W., Ekman, P., Heider, K., and Friesen, W.V. (1992). Emotion and autonomic nervous system activity in the Minangkabau of West Sumatra. *Journal of Personality and Social Psychology*, 62, 972–88.

Leventhal, G.S. (1980). What should be done with equity theory? New approaches to the study of fairness in social relationships. In: K.S. Gergen, M.S. Greenberg, and R.H. Willis (eds), *Social exchange: advances in theory and research*, pp. 27–55. New York: Plenum.

Leventhal, H. (1984). A perceptual-motor theory of emotion. *Advances in Experimental Social Psychology*, 17, 117–82.

Leventhal, H. and Scherer, K.R. (1987). The relationship of emotion to cognition: a functional approach to a semantic controversy. *Cognition and Emotion*, 1, 3–28.

Leventhal, H., Weinman, J., Leventhal, E.A., and Phillips, L. A. (2008). Health psychology: the search for pathways between behavior and health. *Annual Review of Psychology*, 59, 477–505.

Levi, I. (1967). *Gambling with truth*. New York: Alfred A. Knopf.

Levine, D.S. (2007). Neural network modeling of emotion. *Physics of Life Reviews*, 4, 37–63.

Levinson, J. (1996). Musical expressiveness. In: *The pleasures of aesthetics: philosophical essays*, pp. 90–125. Ithaca, NY: Cornell University Press.

Levinson, J. (1997). Emotion in response to art: a survey of the terrain. In: M. Hjort and S. Laver (eds), *Emotion and the arts*, pp. 20–34. Oxford: Oxford University Press.

Levy, R.I. (1984a). Emotion, knowing, and culture. In: R.A. Shweder and R.A. Levine (eds), *Culture theory: essays on mind, self, and emotion*, pp. 214–37. Cambridge: Cambridge University Press.

Levy, R.I. (1984b). The emotions in comparative perspective. In: K.R. Scherer and P. Ekman (eds), *Approaches to emotion*, pp. 397–410. Hillsdale, NJ: Lawrence Erlbaum Associates.

References

Lewin, K. (ed.) (1925a). Untersuchungen zur Handlungs- und Affekt-Psychologie. *Psychologische Forschung*, 7.

Lewin, K. (1925b). I. Vorbemerkungen über die psychischen Kräfte und Energien und über die Struktur der Seele. In: K. Lewin (ed.), Untersuchungen zur Handlungs- und Affekt-Psychologie. *Psychologische Forschung*, 7, 294–329. (Engl. transl. of Part 1. Comments concerning psychological forces and energies and the structure of the psyche. In: D. Rapaport (ed.) (1951). *Organization and pathology of thought. Selected sources*, pp. 76–94. New York: Columbia University Press. Engl. transl. of Part 2. On the structure of the mind. In: K. Lewin (ed.) (1935). *A dynamic theory of personality*, pp. 43–65. New York: McGraw-Hill.)

Lewin, K. (1925c). II. Vorsatz, Wille und Bedürfnis. In: K. Lewin (ed.) (1925). Untersuchungen zur Handlungs- und Affekt-Psychologie. *Psychologische Forschung*, 7, 330–385. (Engl. transl. Intention, will and need. In: D. Rapaport (ed.) (1951). *Organization and pathology of thought. Selected sources*. New York: Columbia University Press.)

Lewin, K. (1926). Untersuchungen zur Handlungs- und Affekt-Psychologie. II.: Vorsatz, Wille und Bedürfnis. *Psychologische Forschung*, 7, 330–385.

Lewin, K. (1935). *A dynamic theory of personality*. New York: McGraw-Hill.

Lewin, K., Dembo, T., Festinger, L., and Sears, P.S. (1944). Level of aspiration. In: J.M. Hunt (ed.), *Personality and the behavior disorders*, pp. 333–78. New York: Ronald Press.

Lewis, M. (1993). Self-conscious emotions: embarrassment, pride, shame, and guilt. In: M. Lewis and J.M. Haviland (eds), *Handbook of emotions*, 1st edn, pp. 353–64. New York: Guilford Press.

Lewis, M. (2000a). Self-conscious emotions: embarrassment, pride, shame, and guilt. In: M. Lewis and J.M. Haviland-Jones (eds), *Handbook of emotions*, 2nd edn, pp. 623–36. New York: Guilford Press.

Lewis, M. (2000b). The emergence of human emotions. In: M. Lewis and J. Haviland-Jones (eds), *Handbook of emotions*, 2nd edn, pp. 265–80). New York: Guilford Press.

Lewis, M. (2008). The emergence of human emotions. In: M. Lewis, J. Haviland-Jones, and L. Feldman Barrett (eds), *Handbook of emotions*, 3rd edn, pp. 304–19. New York: Guilford Press.

Lewis, M. and Brooks, J. (1978). Self-knowledge and emotional development. In: M. Lewis and L. Rosenblum (eds), *The development of affect*, pp. 205–26. New York: Plenum.

Leyhausen, P. (1967). Biologie von Ausdruck und Eindruck. Teil 1. (The biology of expression and impression. Part 1). *Psychologische Forschung*, 31, 113–76.

Libby, P. (2002). Inflammation in atherosclerosis. *Nature*, 420, 868–74.

Lim, M.M., Wang, Z., Olazabal, D.E., Ren, X., Terwilliger, E.F., and Young, L.J. (2004). Enhanced partner preference in a promiscuous species by manipulating the expression of a single gene. *Nature*, 429, 754–7.

Lind, E.A., Kanfer, R., and Early, P. (1990). Voice, control, and procedural justice: instrumental and non-instrumental concerns in fairness judgments. *Journal of Personality and Social Psychology*, 59, 952–9.

Lipp, O.V., Oughton, N., and LeLievre, J. (2003). Evaluative learning in human Pavlovian conditioning: extinct, but still there? *Learning and Motivation*, 34, 219–39.

Lipps, T. (1965). Empathy and aesthetic pleasure. In: K. Aschenbrenner and A. Isenberg (eds), *Aesthetic theories: studies in the philosophy of art*, pp. 403–12. Englewood Cliffs, NJ: Prentice Hall.

Locher, P., Martindale, C., and Dorfman, L. (eds) (2006). *New directions in aesthetics, creativity, and the arts*. Amityville, NY: Baywood.

Locke, E.A. and Latham, G.P. (1990). *A theory of goal setting and performance*. Englewood Cliffs, NJ: Prentice Hall.

Loewenstein, G. (1987). Anticipation and the valuation of delayed consumption. *Economic Journal*, 97, 666–84.

Loewenstein, G. (1996). Out of control: visceral influences on behavior. *Organizational Behavior and Human Decision Processes*, 65, 272–92.

Loewenstein, G. and Lerner, J.S. (2003). The role of affect in decision making. In: R.J. Davidson, K.R. Scherer, and H.H. Goldsmith, (eds), *Handbook of affective sciences*, pp. 619–42. New York: Oxford University Press.

Loewenstein, G. and Schkade, D. (1999). Wouldn't it be nice? Predicting future feelings. In: D. Kahneman and E. Diener (eds), *Well-being: the foundation of hedonic psychology*, pp. 85–105. New York: Russell Sage Foundation.

Loewenstein, G.F., Thompson, L., and Bazerman, M.H. (1989). Social utility and decision making in interpersonal contexts. *Journal of Personality and Social Psychology*, 57, 426–41.

Loewenstein, G., Weber, E.U., Hsee, C.K., and Welch, N. (2001). Risk as feelings. *Psychological Bulletin*, 127, 267–86.

Longino, H. (2006). The social dimensions of scientific knowledge. In: E.N. Zalta (ed.), *Stanford encyclopedia of philosophy*, Fall 2006 edn <http://plato.stanford.edu/archives/fall2006/entries/scientific-knowledge-social/>.

Loomes, G. and Sugden, R. (1982). Regret theory: an alternative theory of rational choice under uncertainty. *Economic Journal*, 92, 805–24.

Loquendo (2007). *Emotional TTS voices*. Available online at: <http://www.loquendo.com/en/technology/emotional_tts.htm> (last accessed 9 December 2008).

Lord, R.G., Klimoski, R.J., and Kanfer, R. (eds) (2002). *Emotions in the workplace*. San Francisco, CA: Jossey Bass.

Lorenz, E.N. (1963). Deterministic nonperiodic flow. *Journal of Atmospheric Science*, 20, 130–141.

Lorenz, K. (1943). Die angeborenen Formen möglicher Erfahrung (The innate forms of potential experience). *Zeitschrift für Tierpsychologie*, 5, 233–519.

Lorenz, K. (1981). *The foundations of ethology*. New York: Springer.

Lorini, E. and Castelfranchi, C. (2007). The cognitive structure of surprise: looking for basic principles. *Topoi: an International Review of Philosophy*, 26, 133–49.

Lovibond, P.F. and Shanks, D.R. (2002). The role of awareness in Pavlovian conditioning: empirical evidence and theoretical implications. *Journal of Experimental Psychology: Animal Behavior Processes*, 28, 3–26.

Lowman, C., Hunt, W.A., Litten, R.Z., and Drummond, D. (2000) Research perspectives on alcohol craving: an overview. *Addiction*, 95, S45–S54.

Lucas, R.E. and Baird, B.M. (2004). Extraversion and emotional reactivity. *Journal of Personality and Social Psychology*, 86, 473–85.

Luce, M.F. (1998). Choosing to avoid: coping with negatively emotion-laden consumer decisions. *Journal of Consumer Research*, **24**, 409–33.

Luo, Q., Holroyd, T., Jones, M., Hendler, T., and Blair J. (2007). Neural dynamics for facial threat processing as revealed by gamma band synchronization using MEG. *Neuroimage*, **34**, 839–47.

Luthar, S.S., Cicchetti, D., and Becker, B. (2000). The construct of resilience: a critical evaluation and guidelines for future work. *Child Development*, **71**, 543–62.

Lykken, D.T. (1995). *The antisocial personalities*. Hillsdale, NJ: Lawrence Erlbaum Associates.

Lykken, D. and Tellegen, A. (1996). Happiness is a stochastic phenomenon. *Psychological Science*, **7**, 186–89.

Lyons, W. (1980). *Emotion*. Cambridge: Cambridge University Press.

Lyubomirsky, S., King, L., and Diener, E. (2005a). The benefits of frequent positive affect: does happiness lead to success? *Psychological Bulletin*, **131**, 803–55.

Lyubomirsky, S., Sheldon, K.M., and Schkade, D. (2005b). Pursuing happiness: the architecture of sustainable change. *Review of General Psychology*, **9**, 11–31.

McArthur, R. and Borsini, F. (2006). Animal models of depression in drug discovery: a historical perspective. *Pharmacology Biochemistry and Behavior*, **84**, 436–52.

McCarthy, E.D. (1994). The social construction of emotions: new directions from cultural theory. In: W.M. Wentworth and J. Ryan (eds), *Social perspective on emotion*, Vol. 2, pp. 267–80. Greenwich, CT: JAI Press.

McClelland, D.C. (1987). *Human motivation*. Cambridge: Cambridge University Press.

McClelland, D.C., Atkinson, J.W., Clark, R.A., and Lowell, E.L. (1953). *The achievement motive*. New York: Appleton-Century-Crofts.

McClure, S.M., Laibson, D.I., Loewenstein, G., and Cohen, J.D. (2004). Separate neural systems value immediate and delayed monetary rewards. *Science*, **306**, 503–7.

McCrae, R.R. and Costa, P.T. (1997). Personality trait structure as a human universal. *American Psychologist*, **52**, 509–16.

McCrae, R.R. and Costa, P.T. (2005). *Personality in adulthood*, 2nd edn. New York: Guilford Press.

McCrae, R.R., Costa, P.T., Martin, T.A., Oryol, V.E., Rukavishnikov, A.A., Senin, I.G., Hřebíčková, M., and Urbánek, T. (2004). Consensual validation of personality traits across cultures. *Journal of Research in Personality*, **38**, 179–201.

McCullough, M.E., Emmons, R.A., and Tsang, J. (2002). The grateful disposition: a conceptual and empirical topography. *Journal of Personality and Social Psychology*, **82**, 112–27.

McEwen, B.S. (1998). Protective and damaging effects of stress mediators. *New England Journal of Medicine*, **338**, 171–9.

McEwen, B. (2004). *Roles of vasopressin and oxytocin in memory processing*. Advances in Pharmacology, Vol. 50, Amsterdam: Elsevier.

McEwen, B.S. and Seeman, T. (2003). Stress and affect: applicability to the concepts of allostasis and allostatic load. In: R.J. Davidson, K.R. Scherer, and H.H. Goldsmith (eds), *Handbook of affective sciences*, pp. 1117–38. New York: Oxford University Press.

McEwen, B.S. and Wingfield, J.C. (2003). The concept of allostasis in biology and biomedicine. *Hormones and Behavior*, **43**, 2–15.

McFarland, D. (1987). *The Oxford companion to animal behaviour*. Oxford: Oxford University Press.

McGaugh, J.L. (1995). Emotional activation, neuromodulatory systems, and memory. In: D. L. Schacter (ed.), *Memory distortion: how minds, brains, and societies reconstruct the past*, pp. 255–73. Cambridge, MA: Harvard University Press.

McGaugh, J.L. (2004). The amygdala modulates the consolidation of memories of emotionally arousing experiences. *Annual Review of Neuroscience*, **27**, 1–28.

McGaugh, J.L. and Cahill, L. (2003). Emotion and memory: central and peripheral contributions. In: R.J. Davidson, K.R. Scherer and H.H. Goldsmith (eds), *Handbook of affective sciences*, pp. 93–116. New York: Oxford University Press.

McGuffin, P., Rijsdijk, F., Andrew, M., Sham, P., Katz, R., and Cardno, A. (2003). The heritability of bipolar affective disorder and the genetic relationship to unipolar depression. *Archives of General Psychiatry*, **60**, 497–502.

McIntosh, D.N. (1996). Facial feedback hypotheses: evidence, implications, and directions. *Motivation and Emotion*, **20**, 121–47.

McIntosh, D.N., Druckman, D., and Zajonc, R.B. (1994). Socially induced affect. In: D. Druckman and R.A. Bjork (eds), *Learning, remembering, believing: enhancing human performance*, pp. 251–76. Washington, DC: National Academy Press.

McKenna, M.C., Zevon, M.A., Corn, B., and Rounds, J. (1999). Psychosocial factors and the development of breast cancer: a meta-analysis. *Health Psychology*, **18**, 520–531.

Mackie, D.M. and Smith, E.R. (2002). Intergroup emotions: prejudice reconceptualized as differentiated reactions to out-groups. In: J.P. Forgas and K.D. Williams (eds), *The social self: cognitive, interpersonal and intergroup perspectives*, pp. 309–26. Philadelphia, PA: Psychology Press.

Mackie, D.M., Silver, L., and Smith, E.R. (2004). Intergroup emotions: emotion as an intergroup phenomenon. In: L.Z. Tiedens and C.W. Leach (eds), *The social life of emotions*, pp. 227–45. Cambridge: Cambridge University Press.

Mackie, D.M., Maitner, A.T., and Smith, E.R. (2009). Intergroup emotions theory. In: T.D. Nelson (ed.), *Handbook of prejudice, stereotyping, and discrimination*. New York: Psychology Press.

McLaughlin, B. (1995). Philosophy of mind. In: R. Audi (ed.), *Cambridge dictionary of philosophy*, pp. 597–606. Cambridge: Cambridge University Press.

McLellan, A.T., Lewis, D.C., O'Brien, C.P., and Kleber, H.D. (2000). Drug dependence, a chronic medical illness: implications for treatment, insurance, and outcomes evaluation. *Journal of the American Medical Association*, **284**, 1689–95.

MacLeod, C., Mathews, A., and Tata, P. (1986). Attentional bias in emotional disorders. *Journal of Abnormal Psychology*, **95**, 15–20.

MacLeod, C., Campbell, L., Rutherford, E., and Wilson, E. (2004). The causal status of anxiety-linked attentional and interpretive bias. In: J. Yiend (ed.), *Cognition, emotion and psychopathology: theoretical, empirical and clinical directions*, pp. 172–89. Cambridge: Cambridge University Press.

McNally, R.J. (1981). Phobias and preparedness: instructional reversal of electrodermal conditioning to fear-relevant stimuli. *Psychological Reports*, **48**, 175–80.

References

McNally, R.J. (1994). *Panic disorder: a critical analysis*. New York: Guilford Press.

McNally, R.J. (2001). On the scientific status of cognitive appraisal models of anxiety disorder. *Behaviour Research and Therapy*, **39**, 513–21.

McNally, R.J. (2002). Anxiety sensitivity and panic disorder. *Biological Psychiatry*, **52**, 938–46.

McNally, R.J. (2003a). Progress and controversy in the study of posttraumatic stress disorder. *Annual Review of Psychology*, **54**, 229–52.

McNally, R.J. (2003b). *Remembering trauma*. Cambridge, MA: Belknap Press/Harvard University Press.

McNally, R.J. (2006). Cognitive abnormalities in posttraumatic stress disorder. *Trends in Cognitive Sciences*, **10**, 271–7.

McNally, R.J. (2007). PTSD and Vietnam veterans. *Science*, **315**, 185–6.

McNally, R.J. and Reese, H.E. (2009). Information-processing approaches to understanding anxiety disorders. In: M.M. Antony and M.B. Stein (eds), *Oxford handbook of anxiety and anxiety disorders*, pp. 136–52. Oxford: Oxford University Press.

McNally, R.K., Bryant, R.A., and Ehlers, A. (2003). Does early psychological intervention promote recovery from posttraumatic stress? *Psychological Science in the Public Interest*, **4**, 45–79.

McNaughton, N. and Corr, P.J. (2004). A two-dimensional neuropsychology of defense: fear/anxiety and defensive distance. *Neuroscience and Biobehavioral Reviews*, **28**, 285–305.

McNeill, D. (2005). *Gesture and thought*. Chicago: University of Chicago Press.

McVittie, C. (2006). Critical health psychology, pluralism and dilemmas: the importance of being critical. *Journal of Health Psychology*, **11**, 373–7.

Magai, C. (2001). Emotions over the life course. In: J.E. Birren and K.W. Schaie (eds), *Handbook of the psychology of aging*, 5th edn, pp. 399–426. San Diego, CA: Academic Press.

Maher, M., Mora, P., and Leventhal, H. (2006). Depression as a predictor of perceived social support and demand: a componential approach using a prospective sample of older adults. *Emotion*, **6**, 450–458.

Mai, F. (2004). Somatization disorder: a practical review. *Canadian Journal of Psychiatry*, **49**, 652–62.

Maia, T.V. and McClelland, J.L. (2004). A reexamination of the evidence for the somatic marker hypothesis: what participants really know in the Iowa Gambling Task. *Proceedings of the National Academy of Sciences USA*, **101**, 16075–80.

Maia, T.V. and McClelland, J.L. (2005). The somatic marker hypothesis: still many questions but no answers: response to Bechara *et al*. *Trends in Cogitive Sciences*, **9**, 162–4.

Maier, N. (1956). Frustration theory: restatement and extension. *Psychological Review*, **63**, 370–388.

Maier, S.F., Seligman, M.E.P., and Solomon, R.L. (1969). Pavlovian fear conditioning and learned helplessness: effects of escape and avoidance behavior of (a) the CS-UCS contingency and (b) the independence of voluntary responding. In: B.A. Campbell and R.M. Church (eds), *Punishment and aversive behavior*, pp. 299–342. New York: Appleton-Century-Crofts.

Makagon, M.M., Funayama, E.S., and Owren, M.J. (2008). An acoustic analysis of laughter produced by congenitally deaf and normally hearing college students. *Journal of the Acoustical Society of America*, **124**, 472–83.

Malarkey, W.B. and Mills, P.J. (2007). Endocrinology: the active partner in PNI research. *Brain, Behavior, and Immunity*, **21**, 161–8.

Mallon, R. and Stich, S. (2000). The odd couple: the compatibility of social construction and evolutionary psychology. *Philosophy of Science*, **67**, 133–54.

Malpaux, B., Thiery, J.C., and Chemineau, P. (1999). Melatonin and the seasonal control of reproduction. *Reproduction Nutrition Development*, **39**, 355–66.

Mandler, G. (1990). A constructivist theory of emotion. In: N.S. Stein, B.L. Leventhal and T. Trabasso (eds), *Psychological and biological approaches to emotion*, pp. 21–44. Hillsdale, NJ: Lawrence Erlbaum Associates.

Manser, M.B., Bell, M.B., and Fletcher, L.B. (2001). The information that receivers extract from alarm calls in suricates. *Proceedings of the Royal Society B: Biological Sciences*, **268**, 2485–91.

Manuck, S.B., Kaplan, J.R., and Clarkson, T.B. (1983). Behaviorally induced heart rate reactivity and atherosclerosis in cynomolgus monkeys. *Psychosomatic Medicine*, **45**, 95–108.

Manusov, V. (ed.) (2005). *The sourcebook of nonverbal measures*. Mahwah, NJ: Lawrence Erlbaum Associates.

Manusov, V.L. and Patterson, M.L. (eds) (2006). *The handbook of nonverbal communication*. Thousand Oaks, CA: Sage.

Maquet, P., Peters, J., Aerts, J., Delfiore, G., Degueldre, C., Luxen, A., *et al.* (1996). Functional neuroanatomy of human rapid-eye-movement sleep and dreaming. *Nature*, **383**, 163–6.

Maren, S. (2005). Synaptic mechanisms of associative memory in the amygdala. *Neuron*, **47**, 783–6.

Marin, R.S. (1996). Apathy: concept, syndrome, neural mechanisms, and treatment. *Seminars in Clinical Neuropsychiatry*, **1**, 304–14.

Markon, K.E., Krueger, R.F., and Watson, D. (2005). Delineating the structure of normal and abnormal personality: an integrative hierarchical approach. *Journal of Personality and Social Psychology*, **88**, 139–57.

Markowitz, H.M. (1952). The utility of wealth. *Journal of Political Economy*, **60**, 151–8.

Markus, H.R. (1977). Self-schemata and processing information about the self. *Journal of Personality and Social Psychology*, **35**, 63–78.

Markus, H.R. and Kitayama, S. (1991). Culture and the self: implications for cognition, emotion, and motivation. *Psychological Review*, **98**, 224–53.

Markus, H.R. and Kitayama, S. (1994). The cultural construction of self and emotion: implications for social behavior. In: S. Kitayama and H.R. Markus (eds), *Emotion and culture: empirical studies of mutual influence*, pp. 89–130. Washington, DC: American Psychological Association.

Marsella, S., Gratch, J., and Rickel, J. (2004). In: H. Prendinger and M. Ishizuka (eds), *Life-like characters tools, affective functions and applications*, p. 46. New York: Springer.

Marsh, A.A., Adams, R.B., Jr, and Kleck, R.E. (2005). Why do fear and anger look the way they do? Form and social function in facial expressions. *Personality and Social Psychology Bulletin*, **31**, 73–86.

Martin, L.L. and Clore, G.L. (eds) (2001). *Theories of mood and cognition: a user's guidebook*. Mahwah, NJ: Lawrence Erlbaum Associates.

Martin, L.L. and Tesser, A. (1996). Some ruminative thoughts. In: R.S. Weyer (ed.), *Ruminative thoughts. Advances in social* cognition, Vol. 9, pp. 1–47. Hillsdale, NJ: Lawrence Erlbaum Associates.

Martin, L.L., Ward, D.W., Achee, J.W., and Wyer, R.S. (1993). Mood as input: people have to interpret the motivational implications of their moods. *Journal of Personality and Social Psychology*, **64**, 317–26.

Martin, L.L., Abend, T.A., Sedikides, C., and Green, J. (1997). How would I feel if...? Mood as input to a role fulfillment evaluation process. *Journal of Personality and Social Psychology*, **73**, 242–53.

Martin, R.A. (1998). Approaches to the sense of humor: a historical review. In: W. Ruch (ed.) The sense of humor, pp. 15–62. New York: Mouton de Gruyter.

Martin, R.A. (2007). *The psychology of humor: an integrative approach*. Burlington, MA: Elsevier Academic Press.

Marwell, G. and Ames, R.E. (1979). Experiments on the provision of public-goods. Resources, interest, group-size, and the free-rider problem. *American Journal of Sociology*, **84**, 1335–60.

Mascolo, M.J., Fischer, K.W., and Li, J. (2003). Dynamic development of component systems of emotions: pride, shame, and guilt in China and the United States. In: R.J. Davidson, K.R. Scherer, and H.H. Goldsmith (eds), *Handbook of affective sciences*, pp. 375–408. New York: Oxford University Press.

Maslow, A.H. (1964). *Religions, values, and peak-experiences*. Columbus OH, Ohio State University Press.

Massaro, D.W. (1998). *Perceiving talking faces*. Cambridge, MA: MIT Press.

Masterson, F.A. and Crawford, M. (1982). The defense motivation system: a theory of avoidance behavior. *Behavioral and Brain Sciences*, **5**, 661–96.

Masuko, T., Miyanaga, K., and Kobayashi, T. see <http://www.isca-speech.org/archive/interspeech_2004/i04_1437.html>.

Mathews, A. and MacLeod, C. (2002). Induced processing biases have casual effects on anxiety. *Cognition and Emotion*, **16**, 331–54.

Matravers, D. (2005). The challenge of irrationalism, and how not to meet it. In: M. Kieran (ed.), *Contemporary debates in aesthetics and the philosophy of art*, pp. 254–64. Oxford: Blackwell.

Matsumoto, D. (2001). Culture and emotion. In: D. Matsumoto (ed.), *The handbook of culture and psychology*. New York, Oxford University Press.

Matsumoto, D. (2009). Culture and emotional expression. In: C.-Y. Chiu, Y.-Y. Hong, S. Shavitt, and R.S. Wyer (eds), *Problems and solutions in cross-cultural theory, research, and application*. New York, Psychology Press. 271–287.

Matsumoto, D. and Ekman, P. (1989). American–Japanese cultural differences in intensity ratings of facial expressions of emotion. *Motivation and Emotion*, **13**, 143–57.

Matsumoto, D. and Ekman, P. (2004). The relationship among expressions, labels, and descriptions of contempt. *Journal of Personality and Social Psychology*, **87**, 529–40.

Matsumoto, D. and Willingham, B. (2009). Spontaneous facial expressions of emotion of blind individuals. *Journal of Personality and Social Psychology*, **96**(1), 1–10.

Matsumoto, D. and Wilson, J. (2008). Culture, emotion, and motivation. In: R.M. Sorrentino and S. Yamaguchi (eds), *Handbook of motivation and cognition across cultures*, pp. 541–64. New York, Elsevier.

Matsumoto, D., Haan, N., Gary, Y., Theodorou, P., and Cooke-Carney, C. (1986). Preschoolers' moral actions and emotions in prisoner's dilemma. *Developmental Psychology*, **22**, 663–70.

Matsumoto, D., Kudoh, T., Scherer, K.R., and Wallbott, H.G. (1988). Antecedents of and reactions to emotions in the United States and Japan. *Journal of Cross-Cultural Psychology*, **19**, 267–86.

Matsumoto, D., Ekman, P., and Fridlund, A. (1991). Analyzing nonverbal behavior. In: P.W. Dowrick (ed.), *Practical guide to using video in the behavioral sciences*, pp. 153–65. New York: John Wiley and Sons.

Matsumoto, D., Yoo, S.H., Alexandre, J., Altarriba, J., Anguas-Wong, A.M., Arriola, M., Ataca, B., Bauer, L.M., and Bond, M.H. (2006). Universal effects of contexts on display rules for emotional behaviors. *Submitted for publication*.

Matsumoto, D., Keltner, D., Shiota, M.N., O'Sullivan, M., and Frank, M.G. (2008). Facial expressions of emotion. In: M. Lewis, J.M. Haviland-Jones, and L. Feldman Barrett (eds), *Handbook of emotions*, 3rd edn, pp. 211–34. New York, Guilford Press.

Matthews, G., Zeidner, M., and Roberts, R.D. (2002). *Emotional intelligence: science and myth*. Cambridge, MA: MIT Press.

Matthews, G., Deary, I.J., and Whiteman, M.C. (2003). *Personality traits*, 2nd edn. Cambridge: Cambridge University Press.

Maunsell, J.H. (2004). Neuronal representations of cognitive state: reward or attention? *Trends in Cognitive Sciences*, **8**, 261–5.

Mauro, R., Sato, K., and Tucker, J. (1992). The role of appraisal in human emouons: a cross-cultural study. *Journal of Personality and Social Psychology*, **62**, 301–17.

Mauss, I.B., Levenson, R.W., McCarter, L., Wilhelm, F.H., and Gross, J.J. (2005). The tie that binds? Coherence among emotion experience, behavior, and physiology. *Emotion*, **5**, 175–90.

Maxwell, J.S. and Davidson, R.J. (2007). Emotion as motion: asymmetries in approach and avoidant actions. *Psychological Science*, **18**, 1113–19.

Mayberg, H.S., Lozano, A.M., Voon, V., McNeely, H.E., Seinosicz, D., Hamani, C., Schwalb, J.M., and Kennedy, S.H. (2005). Deep brain stimulation for treatment-resistant depression. *Neuron*, **45**, 651–60.

Mayer, E.A., Naliboff, B.D., and Craig, A.D. (2006). Neuroimaging of the brain–gut axis: from basic understanding to treatment of functional GI disorders. *Gastroenterology*, **131**, 1925–42.

Mayer, J.D. and Salovey, P. (1997). What is emotional intelligence? In: P. Salovey and D. Sluyter (eds), *Emotional development and emotional intelligence: implications for educators*, pp. 3–31. New York: Basic Books.

Mayer, J.D., Roberts, R.D., and Barsade, S.G. (2008a). Human abilities: emotional intelligence. *Annual Review of Psychology*, **59**, 507–36.

Mayer, J.D., Salovey, P., Caruso, D.R., and Sitarenios, G. (2003). Measuring emotional intelligence with the MSCEIT V2.0. *Emotion*, **3**, 97–105.

Mayer, J.D., Salovey, P., and Caruso, D.R. (2008b). Emotional intelligence: new ability or eclectic traits? *American Psychologist*, **63**, 503–17.

Mayou, R., Kirmayer, L.J., Simon, G., Kroenke, K., and Sharpe, M. (2005). Somatoform disorders: time for a new approach in DSM-IV. *American Journal of Psychiatry*, **162**, 847–55.

References

Mayr, E. (1982). *The growth of biological thought: diversity, evolution, and inheritance.* Cambridge, MA: The Belknap Press of Harvard University Press.

Mayr, E. (2004). *What makes biology unique?: considerations on the autonomy of a scientific discipline.* New York: Cambridge University Press.

Mehrabian, A. (1972). *Nonverbal communication.* Chicago, IL: Aldine.

Meier, S. (2007). A survey on economic theories and field evidence on pro-social behavior. In: B.S. Frey and A. Stutzer (eds), *Economics and psychology. A promising new cross-disciplinary field,* pp. 51–88. Cambridge, MA: MIT Press.

Mele, A.R. (1992). *Springs of action.* Oxford: Oxford University Press.

Mellers, B.A., Schwartz, A., Ho, K., and Ritov, I. (1997). Decision affect theory: emotional reactions to the outcomes of risky options. *Psychological Science,* 8, 423–9.

Melzack, R. and Wall, P.D. (1965). Pain mechanisms: a new theory. *Science,* 150, 971–9.

Menon, U. and Shweder. R.A. (1994). Kali's tongue: cultural psychology and the power of shame in Orissa, India. In: S. Kitayama and H.R. Markus (eds), *Emotion and culture: empirical studies of mutual influence,* pp. 241–84. Washington, DC: American Psychological Association.

Merker, B. (2007). Consciousness without a cerebral cortex: a challenge for neuroscience and medicine. *Behavioral and Brain Sciences,* 30, 63–81.

Mesquita, B. (2001). Emotions in collectivist and individualist contexts. *Journal of Personality and Social Psychology,* 80, 68–74.

Mesquita, B. (2003). Emotions as dynamic cultural phenomena. In: R.J. Davidson, K.R. Scherer, and H. Goldsmith (eds), *Handbook of affective sciences,* pp. 871–90. New York: Oxford University Press.

Mesquita, B. and Ellsworth, P.C. (2003). The role of culture in appraisal. In: K.R. Scherer, A. Schorr, and T. Johnstone (eds). *Appraisal processes in emotion: theory, methods, research,* pp. 233–48. New York: Oxford University Press.

Mesquita, B. and Frijda, N.H. (1992). Cultural variations in emotions: a review. *Psychological Bulletin,* 112, 179–204.

Mesquita, B. and Karasawa, M. (2002). Different emotional lives. *Cognition and Emotion,* 16, 127–41.

Mesquita, B. and Karasawa, M. (2004). Self-conscious emotions as dynamic cultural processes. *Psychological Inquiry,* 15, 161–6.

Mesquita, B. and Leu, J. (2007). The cultural psychology of emotion. In: S. Kitayama and D. Cohen (eds), *The handbook of cultural psychology,* pp. 734–59. New York: Guilford Press.

Mesquita, B., Frijda, N.H., and Scherer, K.R. (1997). Culture and emotion. In: J.E. Berry, P.B. Dasen, and T.S. Saraswathi (eds), *Handbook of cross-cultural psychology: Vol. 2. Basic processes and developmental psychology,* pp. 255–97. Boston, MA: Allyn and Bacon.

Mesquita, B., Karasawa, M., Haire, A., Izumi, S., Hayashi, A., and Idzelis, M. (2007). *What do I feel? The role of cultural models in emotion representations.* Unpublished manuscript, Wake Forest University, Winston-Salem, NC.

Metcalfe, J. and Jacobs, W.J. (1998). Emotional memory: effects of stress on 'cool' and 'hot' memory systems. *Psychology of Learning and Motivation,* 38, 187–221.

Metcalfe, J. and Mischel, W. (1999). A hot/cool system analysis of delay of gratification: dynamics of willpower. *Psychological Review,* 106, 3–26.

Meyer, L.B. (1956). *Emotion and meaning in music.* Chicago, IL: Chicago University Press.

Meyer, V. (1966). Modification of expectations in cases with obsessional rituals. *Behaviour Research and Therapy,* 4, 273–80.

Meyer, W.-U., Reisenzein, R., and Schützwohl, A. (1997). Towards a process analysis of emotions: the case of surprise. *Motivation and Emotion,* 21, 251–74.

Meyer-Lindenberg, A. and Weinberger, D.R. (2006) Intermediate phenotypes and genetic mechanisms of psychiatric disorders. *Nature Reviews Neuroscience,* 7, 818–27.

Meyer-Lindenberg, A., Buckholtz, J.W., Kolachana, B.R., Hariri, A, Pezawas, L., Blasi, G., *et al.* (2006) Neural mechanisms of genetic risk for impulsivity and violence in humans. *Proceedings of the National Academy of Sciences USA,* 103, 6269–74.

Miall, D.S. and Kuiken, D. (2002). A feeling for fiction: becoming what we behold. *Poetics,* 30, 221–41.

Mikula, G., Scherer, K.R., and Athenstaedt, U. (1998). The role of injustice in the elicitation of differential emotional reactions. *Personality and Social Psychology Bulletin,* 24, 769–83.

Mikulincer, M. and Shaver, P.R. (2003). The attachment behavioral system in adulthood: activation, psychodynamics, and interpersonal processes. In: M.P. Zanna (ed.), *Advances in experimental social psychology,* Vol. 35, pp. 53–152. San Diego, CA: Academic Press.

Mikulincer, M. and Shaver, P. R. (2005). Attachment theory and emotions in close relationships: exploring the attachment-related dynamics of emotional reactions to relational events. *Personal Relationships,* 12, 149–68.

Mikulincer, M., Florian, V., and Weller, A. (1993). Attachment styles, coping strategies, and posttraumatic psychological distress: the impact of the Gulf War in Israel. *Journal of Personality and Social Psychology,* 64, 817–26.

Milinski, M., Semmann, D., Bakker, T.C.M., and Krambeck, H.J. (2001). Cooperation through indirect reciprocity: image scoring or standing strategy? *Proceedings of the Royal Society B: Biological Sciences,* 268, 2495–501.

Millar, M.G. and Tesser, A. (1986). Effects of affective and cognitive focus on the attitude-behavior relation. *Journal of Personality and Social Psychology,* 51, 270–276.

Miller, E.K. and Cohen, J.D. (2001). An integrative theory of prefrontal cortex function. *Annual Review of Neuroscience,* 24, 167–202.

Miller, N.E. (1948). Studies of fear as an acquirable drive: I. Fear as motivation and fear-reduction as reinforcement in the learning of new responses. *Journal of Experimental Psychology,* 38, 89–101.

Miller, P. and Eisenberg, N. (1988). The relation of empathy to aggression and externalizing/antisocial behavior. *Psychological Bulletin,* 103, 324–44.

Miller, S.B. (2004). *Disgust. The gatekeeper emotion.* Hillsdale, NJ: The Analytic Press.

Miller, W.I. (1997). *The anatomy of disgust.* Cambridge, MA: Harvard University Press.

Mills, D.L., Coffey-Corina, S.A., and Neville, H.J. (1997). Language comprehension and cerebral specialization from 13–20 months. *Developmental Neuropsychology,* 13, 397–445.

Mineka, S., Davidson, M., Cook, M., and Keir, R. (1984). Observational conditioning of snake fear in rhesus monkeys. *Journal of Abnormal Psychology,* 93, 355–72.

Mischel, W. (1974). Processes in delay of gratification. In: L. Berkowitz (ed.), *Advances in experimental social psychology*, Vol. 7, pp. 249–92. New York: Academic Press.

Mischel, W. and Ayduk, O. (2004). Willpower in a cognitive-affective processing system: the dynamics of delay of gratification. In: R.F. Baumeister and K.D. Vohs (eds), *Handbook of self-regulation: research, theory, and applications*, pp. 99–129. New York: Guilford Press.

Mischel, W., Shoda, Y., and Rodriguez, M.L. (1989). Delay of gratification in children. *Science*, **244**, 933–8.

Mitchell, J.P., Banaji, M.R., and Macrae, C.N. (2005). The link between social cognition and self-referential thought in the medial prefrontal cortex. *Journal of Cognitive Neuroscience*, **17**, 1306–15.

Masuko, T., Miyanaga, K., and Kobayashi, T. (2004). A style control technique for HMM-based speech synthesis. In: *Proceedings of the 8th International Conference of Spoken Language Processing, Jeju, Korea (Proc. INTERSPEECH 2004-ICSLP)*, pp. 1437–40 <http://www.isca-speech.org/archive/interspeech_2004/i04_1437.html>.

Moenter, S.M., Defazio, A.R., Pitts, G.R., and Nunemaker, C.S. (2003). Mechanisms underlying episodic gonadotropin-releasing hormone secretion. *Frontiers in Neuroendocrinology*, **24**, 79–93.

Moffitt, T.E. (2005). The new look of behavioral genetics in developmental psychopathology: gene–environment interplay in antisocial behaviors. *Psychological Bulletin*, **131**, 533–54.

Moors, A. (2009). Theories of emotion causation: a review. *Cognition and Emotion* **23**, 625–62.

Moors, A. and De Houwer, J. (2005). Automatic processing of dominance and submissiveness. *Experimental Psychology*, **52**, 296–302.

Moors, A. and De Houwer, J. (2006). Automaticity: a theoretical and conceptual analysis. *Psychological Bulletin*, **132**, 297–326.

Moors, A., De Houwer, J., Hermans, D., and Eelen, P. (2005). Unintentional processing of motivational valence. *Quarterly Journal of Experimental Psychology: A*, **58**, 1043–63.

Moos, R.H. and Moos, B.S. (2006). Rates and predictors of relapse after natural and treated remission from alcohol use disorders. *Addiction*, **101**, 212–22.

Morecraft, R.J., Stilwell-Morecraft, K.S., and Rossing, W.R. (2004). The motor cortex and facial expression: new insights from neuroscience. *Neurologist*, **10**, 235–49.

Morgan, S. (2003). Dark desires. *Ethical Theory and Moral Practice*, **6**, 377–410.

Morling, B., Kitayama, S., and Miyamoto, Y. (2002). Cultural practices emphasize influence in the U.S. and adjustment in Japan. *Personality and Social Psychology Bulletin*, **28**, 311–23.

Morris, J.S., DeGelder, B., Weiskrantz, L., and Dolan, R.J. (2001). Differential extrageniculostriate and amygdala responses to presentation of emotional faces in a cortically blind field. *Brain*, **124**, 1241–52.

Morris, W.N. (1989). *Mood: the frame of mind*. New York: Springer.

Morris, W., Hirsch, M.W., Smale, S., and Devaney, R. (2003). *Differential equations, dynamical systems, and an introduction to chaos*. San Diego, CA: Academic Press.

Mountcastle, V.B. (1958). Somatic functions of the nervous system. *Annual Review of Physiology*, **20**, 471–508.

Mowrer, O.H. (1956). Two-factor learning theory reconsidered, with special reference to secondary reinforcement and the role of habit. *Psychological Review*, **63**, 114–28.

Müller, J. (ed) (1997). *Autonomous Agents '97* (online proceedings available at <http://sigart.acm.org/proceedings/agents97/>).

Mulligan, K. (1995). Musil's *Analyse des Gefühls*. In: B. Böschenstein and M.-L. Roth (eds), *Hommage à Robert Musil*, pp. 87–110. Berne: Lang.

Munafo, M.R., Clark, T.G., and Flint, J. (2005). Promise and ptfalls in the meta-analysis of genetic association studies: a response to Sen and Shinka. *Molecular Psychiatry*, **10**, 895–7.

Murphy, D. (2006). *Psychiatry in the scientific image*. Cambridge, MA: MIT Press.

Murphy, F.C., Nimmo-Smith, I., and Lawrence, A.D. (2003). Functional neuroanatomy of emotions: a meta-analysis. *Cognitive Affective and Behavioral Neuroscience*, **3**, 207–33.

Murphy, S.T. and Zajonc, R.B. (1993). Affect, cognition, and awareness: affective priming with optimal and suboptimal stimulus exposures. *Journal of Personality and Social Psychology*, **64**, 723–39.

Murray, H.A. (1938). *Explorations in personality*. New York: Oxford University Press.

Murray, L. and Trevarthen, C. (1985). Emotional regulation on interactions between two-month-olds and their mothers. In: T.M. Field and N.A. Fox (eds), *Social perception in infants*, pp. 177–97. Norwood, NJ: Ablex.

Musil, R. (1995). *The man without qualities*, Vols 1 and 2 (transl. by S. Wilkins and B. Pike), pp. 1239–47, 1258–65, 1304–11. London: Macmillan/Picador.

Nabi, R.L. (2007). Emotion and persuasion: a social cognitive perspective. In: D.R. Roskos-Ewoldsen and J. Monahan (eds), *Communication and social cognition: theories and methods*, pp. 377–98. Mahwah, NJ: Lawrence Erlbaum Associates.

Narayanan, R.T., Seidenbecher, T., Sangha, S., Stork, O., and Pape, H.C. (2007). Theta resynchronization during reconsolidation of remote contextual fear memory. *Neuroreport*, **18**, 1107–11.

Nass, C., Jonsson, I.-M., Harris, H., Reaves, B., Endo, J., Brave, S., and Takayama, L. (2004). Improving automotive safety by pairing driver emotion and car voice emotion, pp. 1973–6. In: *CHI ACM*, Portland, Oregon.

National Institute of Drug Abuse (2006). *Principles of drug abuse treatment for criminal justice populations*. NIH Publication 06–5316. Bethesda, MD: National Institutes of Health.

Neisser, U. (1982). Snapshots or benchmarks. In: U. Neisser (ed.), *Memory observed: remembering in natural contexts*, pp. 43–48. San Francisco, CA: W. H. Freeman.

Nelson, C.A. (1987). The recognition of facial expression in the first two years of life: mechanisms of development. *Developmental Psychology*, **58**, 889–909.

Nelson, R.J. (2005). *An introduction to behavioral neuroendocrinology*, 3rd edn. Sunderland, MA: Sinauer.

Nesse, R.M. (1990). Evolutionary explanations of emotions. *Human Nature*, **1**, 261–89.

Nesse, R.M. (1999). Proximate and evolutionary studies of anxiety, stress, and depression: synergy at the interface. *Neuroscience and Biobehavioral Reviews*, **23**, 895–903.

Nesse, R.M. (2000). Is depression an adaptation? *Archives of General Psychiatry*, **57**, 14–20.

Nesse, R.M. (2001). *Evolution and the capacity for commitment*. New York: Russell Sage Foundation.

Nesse, R.M. (2004). Natural selection and the elusiveness of happiness. *Philosophical Transactions of the Royal Society B: Biological Sciences*, **359**, 1333–47.

References

Nesse, R.M. (2005). Natural selection and the regulation of defenses: a signal detection analysis of the smoke detector principle. *Evolution and Human Behavior*, **26**, 88–105.

Nesse, R.M. (2007). Runaway social selection for displays of partner value and altruism. *Journal of Biological Theory*, **2**, 1–13.

Nesse, R.M. and Jackson, E.D. (2006). Evolution: psychiatric nosology's missing biological foundation. *Clinical Neuropsychiatry*, **3**, 121–31.

Neu, J. (2000). *A tear is an intellectual thing: the meanings of emotion*. Oxford: Oxford University Press.

Neumann, R. (2000). The causal influences of attributions on emotions: a procedural priming approach. *Psychological Science*, **11**, 179–82.

Newman, J.P. and Lorenz, A.R. (2003). Response modulation and emotion processing: implications for psychopathy and other dysregulatory psychopathology. In: R.J. Davidson, K.R. Scherer, and H.H. Goldsmith (eds), *Handbook of affective sciences*, pp. 904–29. New York: Oxford University Press.

Nichols, S. (2004). *Sentimental rules*. Oxford: Oxford University Press.

Niedenthal, P.M., Barsalou, L.W., Winkielman, P., Krauth-Gruber, S., and Ric, F. (2005a). Embodiment in attitudes, social perception, and emotion. *Personality and Social Psychology Review*, **9**, 184–211.

Niedenthal, P., Feldman-Barrett, L., and Winkielman, P. (eds) (2005b). *The unconscious in emotion*. New York: Guilford.

Nietzsche, F. (1889/2003). *Twilight of the idols*, transl. R.J. Hollingdale. London: Penguin Classics.

Niiya, Y., Ellsworth, P.C., and Yamaguchi, S. (2006). Amae in Japan and the United States: an exploration of a 'culturally unique' emotion. *Emotion*, **6**, 279–95.

Nilsonne, Å. (1987). Acoustic analysis of speech variables during depression and after improvement. *Acta Psychiatrica Scandinavica*, **76**, 235–45.

Nisbett, R.E. and Schachter, S. (1966). Cognitive manipulation of pain. *Journal of Experimental Social Psychology*, **2**, 227–36.

Nitschke, J.B., Sarinopoulos, I., Mackiewicz, K.L., Schaefer, H.S., and Davidson, R.J. (2006). Functional neuroanatomy of aversion and its anticipation. *Neuroimage*, **29**, 106–16.

Niv, Y., Joel, D., and Dayan, P. (2006). A normative perspective on motivation. *Trends in Cognitive Science*, **10**, 375–81.

Nixon, C.L. and Watson, A.C. (2001). Family experiences and eraly emotion understanding. *Merrill-Palm Quarterly*, **47**, 300–322.

Nolen-Hoeksema, S. (1991). Responses to depression and their effects on the duration of depressive episodes. *Journal of Abnormal Psychology*, **100**, 569–82.

Nolen-Hoeksema, S. (1993). Sex differences in control of depression. In: D.M. Wegner and J.W. Pennebaker (eds), *Handbook of mental control*, pp. 306–24. Englewood Cliffs, NJ: Prentice-Hall.

Nordgren, L.,van der Pligt, J., and van Harreveld, F.(2006). Visceral drives in retrospect: explanations about the inaccessible past. *Psychological Science*, **17**, 635–40.

Norgren, R. (1985). Taste and the autonomic nervous system. *Chemical Senses*, **10**, 143–61.

Norman, D. (2004). *Emotional design. Why we love (or hate) everyday things*. New York: Basic Books.

Nowak, M.A. and Sigmund, K. (1998). Evolution of indirect reciprocity by image scoring. *Nature*, **393**, 573–7.

Nowicki, S., Jr and Duke, M.P. (1994). Individual differences in the nonverbal communication of affect: the Diagnostic Analysis of Nonverbal Accuracy Scale. *Journal of Nonverbal Behavior*, **18**, 9–35.

Nussbaum, M. (1990). *Love's knowledge*. Oxford: Oxford University Press.

Nussbaum, M. (1994). *The therapy of desire: theory and practice in Hellenistic ethics*. Princeton, NJ: Princeton University Press.

Nussbaum, M.C. (2001). *Upheavals of thought: the intelligence of emotions*. Cambridge: Cambridge University Press.

Oakes, T.R., Pizzagalli, D.A., Hendrick, A.M., Horras, K.A., Larson, C.L., Abercrombie, H.C., *et al.* (2004). Functional coupling of simultaneous electrical and metabolic activity in the human brain. *Human Brain Mapping*, **21**, 257–70.

Oakley, J. (1992). *Morality and the emotions*. London: Routledge and Kegan Paul.

Oatley, K. (1991). Living together. Review of C Lutz's *Unnatural emotions: everyday sentiments on a Micronesian atoll and their challenge to Western theory*. *Cognition and Emotion*, **5**, 65–79.

Oatley, K. (1992). *Best laid schemes: the psychology of emotions, studies in emotion and social interaction*. Cambridge: Cambridge University Press.

Oatley, K. (2000). The sentiments and beliefs of distributed cognition. In: N.H. Frijda, A.S.R. Manstead, and S. Bem (eds), *Emotions and beliefs: how feelings influence thoughts*, pp. 78–107. New York: Cambridge University Press.

Oatley, K. (2003). Creative expression and communication of emotions in the visual and narrative arts. In: R.J. Davidson, K.R. Scherer, and H.H. Goldsmith (eds), *Handbook of affective sciences*, pp. 481–502. New York: Oxford University Press.

Oatley, K. (2004a). *Emotions: a brief history*. Oxford: Blackwell Publishing.

Oatley, K. (2004b). From the emotions of conversation to the passions of fiction. In: N.H. Frijda, A.S.R. Manstead, and A. Fischer (eds), *Feelings and emotions: the Amsterdam Symposium*, pp. 98–115. New York: Cambridge University Press.

Oatley, K. and Duncan, E. (1994). The experience of emotions in everyday life. *Cognition and Emotion*, **8**, 369–81.

Oatley, K. and Johnson-Laird, P.N. (1987). Towards a cognitive theory of emotions. *Cognition and Emotion*, **1**, 29–50.

Oatley, K. and Johnson-Laird, P.N. (1996). The communicative theory of emotions: empirical tests, mental models, and implications for social interaction. In: L.L. Martin and A. Tesser (eds), *Striving and feeling: interactions among goals, affect, and self-regulation*, pp. 363–93. Mahwah, NJ: Lawrence Erlbaum Associates.

Obrist, P.A. (1981). *Cardiovascular psychophysiology*. New York: Plenum Press.

Ochsner, K.N. (2000) Are affective events richly recollected or simply familiar? The experience and process of recognizing feelings past. *Journal of Experimental Psychology: General*, **129**, 242–61.

Ochsner, K.N. and Gross, J.J. (2005). The cognitive control of emotion. *Trends in Cognitive Science*, **9**, 242–9.

Ochsner, K.N., Bunge, S.A., Gross, J.J., and Gabrieli, J.D. (2002). Rethinking feelings: an fMRI study of the cognitive regulation of emotion. *Journal of Cognitive Neuroscience*, **14**, 1215–29.

Ochsner, K.N., Ray, R.D., Cooper, J.C., Robertson, E.R., Chopra, S., Gabrieli, J.D., and Gross, J.J. (2004). For better or for worse: neural systems supporting the cognitive down- and up-regulation of negative emotion. *Neuroimage*, **23**, 483–99.

Öhman, A. (2008). Fear and anxiety: overlaps and dissociations. In: M. Lewis, J.M. Haviland-Jones, and L. Feldman Barrett (eds), *Handbook of emotions*, 3rd edn., pp. 709–29. New York: Guilford Press.

Öhman, A. and Mineka, S. (2001). Fears, phobias, and preparedness: toward an evolved module of fear and fear learning. *Psychological Review*, **108**, 483–522.

Öhman, A. and Wiens, S. (2003). On the automaticity of autonomic responses in emotion: an evolutionary perspective. In: R.J. Davidson, K.R. Scherer, and H.H. Hill (eds), *Handbook of affective sciences*, pp. 256–75. New York: Oxford University Press.

Öhman, A., Hamm, A., and Hugdahl, K. (2000a). Cognition and the autonomic nervous system: orienting, anticipation, and conditioning. In: J.T. Cacioppo, L.G. Tassinary and G.G. Berntson (eds), *Handbook of psychophysiology*, 2nd edn, pp. 553–75. New York: Cambridge University Press.

Öhman, A., Flykt, A., and Lundqvist, D. (2000b). Unconscious emotion: evolutionary perspectives, psychophysiological data and neuropsychological mechanisms. In: R.D. Lane, L. Nadel, and G. Ahern (eds), *Cognitive neuroscience of emotion*, pp. 296–327. New York: Oxford University Press.

Öhman, A., Flykt, A., and Esteves, F. (2001). Emotion drives attention: detecting the snake in the grass. *Journal of Experimental Psychology: General*, **130**, 466–78.

Oishi, S. and Diener, E. (2001). Goals, culture, and subjective well-being. *Personality and Social Psychology Bulletin*, **27**, 1674–82.

Olatunji, B.O. and Sawchuk, C.N. (2005). Disgust: characteristic features, social manifestations, and clinical implications. *Journal of Social and Clinical Psychology*, **24**, 932–62.

Olds, J. and Milner, P. (1954). Positive reinforcement produced by electrical stimulation of septal area and other regions of the brain. *Journal of Comparative and Physiological Psychology*, **47**, 419–27.

Oliver, R.L. (1996). *Satisfaction: a behavioral perspective on the consumer*. New York: McGraw-Hill.

Olivier, B., Mos, J., van Oorschot, R., and Hen, R. (1995). Serotonin receptors and animal models of aggressive behavior. *Pharmacopsychiatry*, **28**(Suppl 2), 80–90.

Olofsson, J.K., Nordin, S., Sequeira, H., and Polich, J. (2008). Affective picture processing: an integrative review of ERP findings. *Biological Psychology*, **77**, 247–65.

Olson, J.M., Roese, N.J., and Zanna, M.P. (1996). Expectancies. In: E.T. Higgins and A.W. Kruglanski (eds), *Social psychology: handbook of basic principles*, pp. 211–38. New York: Guilford Press.

Olson, K.R. and Weber, D.A. (2004). Relations between big five traits and fundamental motives. *Psychological Reports*, **95**, 795–802.

Olsson, A. and Phelps, E.A. (2004). Learned fear of 'unseen' faces after Pavlovian, observational, and instructed fear. *Psychological Science*, **15**, 822–8.

Olsson, A. and Phelps, E.A. (2007). Social learning of fear. *Nature Neuroscience*, **10**, 1095–102.

Omoto, A.M. and Snyder, M. (1995). Sustained helping without obligation: motivation, longevity of service, and per-ceived attitude change among AIDS volunteers. *Journal of Personality and Social Psychology*, **68**, 671–87.

O'Neil, R. and Parke, R.D. (2000). Family–peer relationships: the role of emotion regulation, cognitive understanding, and attentional processes as mediating processes. In: K. Kerns, J. Contreras, and A.M. Neal-Barnett (eds), *Family and peers: linking two social worlds*, pp. 195–225. New York: Greenwood Praeger.

Orr, S.P., McNally, R.J., Rosen, G.M., and Shalev, A.Y. (2004). Psychophysiologic reactivity: Implications for conceptualizing PTSD. In: G.M. Rosen (ed.), *Posttraumatic stress disorder: issues and controversies*, pp. 101–26. Chichester: Wiley.

Ortony, A. (1987). Is guilt an emotion? *Cognition and Emotion*, **1**, 283–98.

Ortony, A. (1993). *Metaphor and thought*. New York: Cambridge University Press.

Ortony, A. (2003). On making believable emotional agents believable. In: R. Trappl, P. Petta, and S. Payr (eds), *Emotions in humans and artifacts*, pp.189–212. Cambridge, MA: MIT Press.

Ortony, A., Clore, G.L., and Collins, A. (1988). *The cognitive structure of emotions*. New York: Cambridge University Press.

Ortony, A., Norman, D.A., and Revelle, W. (2005). Effective functioning: a three level model of affect, motivation, cognition, and behavior. In: J. Fellous and M. Arbib (eds), *Who needs emotions? The brain meets the machine*, pp. 173–202. New York: Oxford Univeristy Press.

Osgood, C.E., Suci, G.J., and Tannenbaum, P.H. (1957). *The measurement of meaning*. Urbana, IL: University of Illinois Press.

Osgood, C.E., May, W.H., and Miron, M.S. (1975). *Cross-cultural universals in affective meaning*. Urbana, IL: University of Illinois Press.

O'Shaughnessy, B. (1980). *The will*, 2 vols. Cambridge: Cambridge University Press.

Searle, J.R. (1983). *Intentionality, an essay in the philosophy of mind*. Cambridge: Cambridge University Press.

Öst, L.-G., Fellenius, J., and Sterner, U. (1991). Applied tension, exposure in vivo, and tension-only in the treatment of blood phobia. *Behaviour Research and Therapy*, **29**, 561–74.

Oster, H. (2004). *BabyFACS: Facial Action Coding System for infants and young children*. New York: New York University.

Ott, E. (2002). *Chaos in dynamical systems*, 2nd edn. New York: Cambridge University Press.

Otto, R. (1917). *Das Heilige. Über das Irrationale in der Idee des Göttlichen und sein Verhältnis zum Rationalen*. Gotha: L. Klotz. (The idea of the Holy : an inquiry into the non-rational factor in the idea of the divine and its relation to the rational, 2nd edn, transl. by J.W. Harvey. London: Oxford University Press, 1950.)

Owren, M.J. and Bachorowski, J.-A. (2001). The evolution of emotional expression: a 'selfish gene' account of smiling and laughter in early hominids and humans. In: T.J. Mayne and G.A. Bonanno (eds), *Emotions: current issues and future directions*, pp. 152–91. New York: Guilford Press.

Owren, M.J. and Bachorowski, J.-A. (2003). Reconsidering the evolution of nonlinguistic communication: the case of laughter. *Journal of Nonverbal Behavior*, **27**, 183–200.

Owren, M.J. and Rendall, D. (1997). An affect-conditioning model of nonhuman primate vocal signaling. In: D.H.

References

Owings, M.D. Beecher, and N.S. Thompson (eds), *Perspectives in Ethology*, pp. 299–346. New York: Plenum Press.

Owren, M.J. and Rendall, D. (2001). Sound on the rebound: bringing form and function back to the forefront in understanding nonhuman primate vocal signaling. *Evolutionary Anthropology*, **10**, 58–71.

Páez, D., Basabe, N., Ubillos, S., and González-Castro, J.L. (2007). Social sharing, participation in demonstrations, emotional climate, and coping with collective violence after the March 11th Madrid bombings. *Journal of Social Issues*, **63**, 323–37.

Panksepp, J. (1992). A critical role for 'affective neuroscience' in resolving what is basic about basic emotions. *Psychological Review*, **99**, 554–60.

Panksepp, J. (1998). *Affective neuroscience: the foundations of human and animal emotions*. New York: Oxford University Press.

Panksepp, J. (2005). Affective consciousness: core emotional feelings in animals and humans. *Consciousness and Cognition*, **14**, 30–80.

Panther, K. and Radden, G. (eds) (1999). *Metonymy in language and thought*. Amsterdam: John Benjamins.

Pantic, M. and Rothkrantz, L.J.M. (2003). Towards an affect-sensitive multimodal human-computer interaction. *Proceedings of the IEEE*, **91**, 1370–1390.

Parke, F.I. and Waters, K. (1996). *Computer facial animation*. Wellesley, MA: A. K. Peters.

Parkinson, B. and Totterdell, P. (1999). Classifying affect-regulation strategies. *Cognition and Emotion*, **13**, 277.

Parkinson, B., Fischer, A.H., and Manstead, A.S.R. (2005). *Emotion in social relations: cultural, group, and interpersonal processes*. New York: Psychology Press.

Parr, L.A. (2001). Cognitive and physiological markers of emotional awareness in chimpanzees, *Pan troglodytes. Animal Cognition*, **4**, 223–9.

Parr, L.A. and Hopkins, W.D. (2001). Brain temperature asymmetries and emotional perception in chimpanzees, *Pan troglodytes. Physiology and Behavior*, **71**, 363–71.

Parrott, W.G. (1991). The emotional experiences of envy and jealousy. In: P. Salovey (ed.), *The psychology of jealousy and envy*, pp. 3–30. New York: Guilford Press.

Parrott, W.G., and Rodriguez Mosquera, P.M. (2008). On the pleasures and displeasures of being envied. In R.H. Smith (ed.), *Envy: Theory and research*, pp. 117–32. New York: Oxford University Press.

Parsons, L.M. and Osherson, D. (2001). New evidence for distinct right and left brain systems for deductive versus probabilistic reasoning. *Cerebral Cortex*, **11**, 954–65.

Paster, G.K., Rowe, K., and Floyd-Wilson, M. (eds) (2004). *Reading the passions: essays on the cultural history of emotion*. Philadelphia, PA: University of Pennsylvania Press.

Patrick, C.J. (ed.) (2006). *Handbook of psychopathy*. New York: Guilford Press.

Paus, T. (2001). Primate anterior cingulate cortex: where motor control, drive and cognition interface. *Nature Reviews Neuroscience*, **2**, 417–24.

Pavlenko, A. (2005). *Emotions and multilingualism*. Cambridge: Cambridge University Press.

Pavlov, V.A. and Tracey, K.J. (2005). The cholinergic anti-inflammatory pathway. *Brain, Behavior, and Immunity*, **19**, 493–9.

Payne, J.W., Bettman, J.R., and Johnson, E.J. (1993). *The adaptive decision maker*. Cambridge: Cambridge University Press.

Payne, K., Thompson, M., and Kramer, L. (2003). Elephant calling patterns as indicators of group size and composition: the basis for an acoustic monitoring system. *African Journal of Ecology*, **41**, 99–107.

Payne, R.L. and Cooper, C.L. (eds) (2001). *Emotions at work: theory, research and applications for management*. New York: Wiley.

Pearce, J.M. and Bouton, M.E. (2001). Theories of associative learning in animals. *Annual Review of Psychology*, **52**, 111–39.

Pearlin, L.I. and Schooler, C. (1978). The structure of coping. *Journal of Health and Social Behavior*, **22**, 337–56.

Pedersen, S., Vitaro, F., Barker, E.D., and Borge, A.I.H. (2007). The timing of middle-childhood peer rejection and friendship: Linking early behavior to early-adolescent adjustment. *Child Development*, **78**, 1037–51.

Pediatric OCD Treatment Study Team (2004). Cognitive-behavioral therapy, sertraline, and their combination for children and adolescents with obsessive-compulsive disorder: a randomized controlled trial. *Journal of the American Medical Association*, **292**, 1969–76.

Peele, S. (1987). A moral vision of addiction: how people's values determine whether they become and remain addicts. *Journal of Drug Issues*, **17**, 187–215.

Peleg, G., Katzir, G., Peleg, O., Kamara, M., Brodsky, L., Hel-Or, H., Keren, D., and Nevo, E. (2006). Heriditary family signature of facial expression. *Proceedings of the National Academy of Sciences USA*, **103**, 15921–6.

Peng, K. and Nisbett, R.E. (1999). Culture, dialectics, and reasoning about contradiction. *American Psychologist*, **54**, 741–54.

Pennebaker, J.W. (1997). *Opening up: the healing power of expressing emotions*. New York: Guilford Press.

Penner, L.A. (2002). The causes of sustained volunteerism: an interactionist perspective. *Journal of Social Issues*, **58**, 447–67.

Penner, L.A., Dovidio, J.F., Piliavin, J.A., and Schroeder, D.A. (2005). Prosocial behavior: multi-level perspectives. *Annual Review of Psychology*, **56**, 365–92.

Perlis, M.L. and Nielsen, T.A. (1993). Mood regulation, dreaming and nightmares: evaluation of a desensitization function for REM sleep. *Dreaming*, **3**, 243–57.

Pernkopf, E., Platzer, W., and Monsen, H. (1989). *Atlas of topographic and applied human anatomy. Vol. 1. Head and neck*, 3rd edn. Baltimore, MD: Urban and Schwarzenberg.

Perrez, M., Watzek, D., Michel, G., Schoebi, D., Wilhelm, P., and Hänggi, Y. (2005). Facets of emotion regulation in families with adolescents: a new research approach. In: H. Kriesi, P. Farago, M. Kohli, and M. Zarin-Nejadan (eds), *Contemporary Switzerland. Revisiting the special case*, pp. 61–80. New York: Palgrave Macmillan.

Perris, C. (1966). A study of bipolar (manic-depressive) and unipolar recurrent depressive psychoses *Acta Psychiatrica Scandinavia Supplement*, **194**, 9–14.

Perris, C. (1974). A study of cycloid psychoses. *Acta Psychiatrica Scandinavica*, **253**, 1–77.

Perris, C. (1992). The distinction between unipolar and bipolar mood disorders. A 25-years perspective. *Encephale*, **18**, 9–13.

Persaud, N., McLeod, P., and Cowey, A. (2007). Post-decision wagering objectively measures awareness. *Nature Neuroscience*, **10**, 257–61.

Perunovic, W.Q.E., Heller, D., and Rafaeli, E. (2007). Within-person changes in the structure of emotion: the role of cultural identification and language. *Psychological Science*, **18**, 607–13.

Pessoa, L. (2005). To what extent are emotional visual stimuli processed without attention and awareness? *Current Opinion in Neurobiology*, **15**, 188–96.

Pessoa, L. (2008). On the relationship between emotion and cognition. *Nature Reviews Neuroscience*, **9**, 148–58.

Pessoa, L., Kastner, S., and Ungerleider, L.G. (2002). Attentional control of the processing of neutral and emotional stimuli. *Brain Research. Cognitive Brain Research*, **15**, 31–45.

Peterson, C. (2000). The future of optimism. *American Psychologist*, **55**, 44–55.

Peterson, C. and Seligman, M.E.P. (1984). Causal explanations as a risk factor for depression: theory and evidence. *Psychological Review*, **91**, 347–74.

Petrides, K.V. and Furnham, A. (2001). Trait emotional intelligence: psychometric investigation with reference to established trait taxonomies. *European Journal of Personality*, **15**, 425–48.

Petrides, K.V. and Furnham, A. (2003). Trait emotional intelligence: behavioural validation in two studies of emotion recognition and reactivity to mood induction. *European Journal of Personality*, **17**, 39–57.

Petty, R.E. and Cacioppo, J.T. (1986). The elaboration likelihood model of persuasion. In: L. Berkowitz (ed.), *Advances in experimental social psychology*, Vol. 19, pp. 123–205. New York: Academic Press.

Petty, R.E. and Wegener, D.T. (1998). Attitude change: multiple roles for persuasion variables. In: D. Gilbert, S. Fiske, and G. Lindzey (eds), *The handbook of social psychology*, (4th edn, pp. 323–90). New York: McGraw-Hill.

Petty, R.E., Schumann, D.W., Richman, S.A., and Strathman, A.J. (1993). Positive mood and persuasion: Different roles for affect under high and low elaboration conditions. *Journal of Personality and Social Psychology*, **64**, 5–20.

Petty, R.E., Briñol, P., and Tormala, Z.L. (2002). Thought confidence as a determinant of persuasion: the self-validation hypothesis. *Journal of Personality and Social Psychology*, **82**, 722–41.

Petty, R.E., Fabrigar, L.R., and Wegener, D.T. (2003). Emotional factors in attitudes and persuasion. In: R.J. Davidson, K.R. Scherer, and H.H. Goldsmith (eds), *Handbook of affective sciences*, pp. 752–72. Oxford: Oxford University Press.

Pezawas, L., Meyer-Lindenberg, A., Drabant, E.M., Verchinski, B.A., Munoz, K.E., Kolachana, B.S., et al. (2005). 5-HTTLPR polymorphism impacts human cingulate-amygdala interactions: a genetic susceptibility mechanism for depression. *Nature Neuroscience*, **8**, 828–34.

Pfeifer, M., Goldsmith, H.H., Davidson, R.J., and Rickman, M. (2002). Continuity and change in inhibited and uninhibited children. *Child Development*, **73**, 1474–85.

Pfeifer, R. (1994). The Fungus Eater approach to emotion: a view from artificial intelligence. *Cognitive Studies*, **1**, 42–57.

Pham, M.T., Cohen, J.B., Pracejus, J.W., and Hughes, G.D. (2001). Affect monitoring and the primacy of feelings in judgment. *Journal of Consumer Research*, **28**, 167–88.

Phan, K.L., Wager, T., Taylor, S.F., and Liberzon, I. (2002). Functional neuroanatomy of emotion: a meta-analysis of emotion activation studies in PET and fMRI. *NeuroImage*, **16**, 331–48.

Phan, K.L., Taylor, S.F., Welsh, R.C., Decker, L.R., Noll, D.C., Nichols, T.E., Britton, J.C., and Liberzon, I. (2003). Activation of the medial prefrontal cortex and extended amygdala by individual ratings of emotional arousal: a fMRI study. *Biological Psychiatry*, **53**, 211–15.

Phelps, E.A. (2006). Emotion and cognition: insights from studies of the human amygdala. *Annual Review of Psychology*, **57**, 27–53.

Phelps, E.A. and LeDoux, J.E. (2005). Neural systems underlying emotion behavior: from animal models to human function. *Neuron*, **48**, 175–87.

Phelps, E.A., LaBar, K.S., and Spencer, D.D. (1997). Memory for emotional words following unilateral temporal lobectomy. *Brain and Cognition*, **35**, 85–109.

Phelps, E.A., O'Connor, K.J., Gatenby, J.C., Grillon, C., Gore, J.C., and Davis, M. (2001). Activation of the left amygdala to a cognitive representation of fear. *Nature Neuroscience*, **4**, 437–41.

Phelps, E.A., Delgado, M.R., Nearing, K.I., and LeDoux, J.E. (2004). Extinction learning in humans: role of the amygdala and vmPFC. *Neuron*, **43**, 897–905.

Phelps, E.A., Ling, S., and Carrasco, M. (2006). Emotion facilitates perception and potentiates the perceptual benefits of attention. *Psychological Science*, **17**, 292–9.

Piaget, J. (1952). *The origins of intelligence in children*. New York: International Universities Press.

Picard, R.W. (1997). *Affective computing*. Cambridge, MA: MIT Press.

Picard, R.W., Vyzas, E., and Healey, J. (2001). Toward machine emotional intelligence: analysis of affective physiological state. *IEEE Transactions on Pattern Analysis and Machine Intelligence*, **23**, 1175–91.

Pickering, A.D. and Gray, J.A. (1999). The neuroscience of personality. In: L. A. Pervin and O. P. John (eds), *Handbook of personality: theory and research*, pp. 277–99. New York: Guilford Press.

Pickering, A.D. and Gray, J.A. (2001). Dopamine, appetitive reinforcement, and the neuropsychology of human learning: an individual differences approach. In: A. Eliasz and A. Angleitner (eds), *Advances in research on temperament*, pp. 113–49. Lengerich, Germany: PABST Science Publishers.

Pighin, F., Hecker, J., Lischinski, D., Szeliski, R., and Salesin, D. (1998). Synthesizing realistic facial expressions from photographs. *International Conference on Computer Graphics and Interactive Techniques. Proceedings of the 25th annual conference on computer graphics and interactive techniques*, pp. 75–84. New York: Association for Computing Machinery.

Pilcher, J.J. and Huffcutt, A.I. (1996). Effects of sleep deprivation on performance: a meta-analysis. *Sleep*, **19**, 318–26.

Piliavin, J.A., Dovidio, J.F., Gaertner, S.L., and Clark, R.D. III (1981). *Emergency intervention*. New York: Academic.

Piliavin, J.A., Grube, J.A., and Callero, P.L. (2002). Role as a resource for action in public service. *Journal of Social Issues*, **58**, 469–85.

Pitcher, G. (1970). Pain perception. *Philosophical Review*, **79**, 368–93.

Pitkänen, A., Savander, V., and LeDoux, J.E. (1997). Organization of intra-amygdaloid circuitries in the rat: an emerging framework for understanding functions of the amygdala. *Trends in Neurosciences*, **20**, 517–23.

Pittman, T.S. (1998). Motivation. In: D.T. Gilbert, S.T. Fiske, and G. Lindzey (eds), *Handbook of social psychology*, 4th edn, Vol. 1, pp. 549–90. New York: McGraw Hill.

References

Pizzagalli, D.A., Jahn, A.L., and O'Shea, J.P. (2005). Toward an objective characterization of an anhedonic phenotype: a signal-detection approach. *Biological Psychiatry*, **57**, 319–27.

Plassmann, H., O'Doherty, J., Shiv, B., and Rangel, A. (2008). Marketing actions can modulate neural representations of experienced pleasantness. *Proceedings of the National Academy of Sciences USA*, **105**, 1050–1054.

Plato (1993). *Republic*, transl. R. Waterfield. Oxford: Oxford University Press.

Plessner, H. (1941). *Lachen und Weinen: eine Untersuchung nach den Grenzen des Menschlichen Verhaltens*. Arnhem: Van Loghum Slaterus.

Plotnik, J., de Waal, F.B.M., and Reiss, D. (2006). Self-recognition in an Asian elephant. *Proceedings of the National Academy of Sciences USA*, **103**, 17053–7.

Plutchik, R. (1980). *Emotion: a psychoevolutionary synthesis*. New York: Harper Row.

Plutchik, R. (1984). Emotion: a general psychoevolutionary theory. In: K.R. Scherer and P. Ekman (eds), *Approaches to emotion*, pp. 197–219. Hillsdale, NJ: Lawrence Erlbaum Associates.

Plutchik, R. (2003). *Emotions and life: perspectives from psychology, biology, and evolution*. Washington, DC: American Psychological Association.

Pons, F. and Harris, P.L. (2005). Longitudinal change and longitudinal stability of individual differences in children's emotion understanding. *Cognition and Emotion*, **19**, 1158–74.

Portmann, J. (1999). *When bad things happen to other people*. London: Routledge.

Power, M.J. (ed.) (2004). *Mood disorders: a handbook of science and practice*. Chichester: John Wiley.

Premack, D. (1959). Toward empirical behavioral laws: Vol. I. Positive reinforcement. *Psychological Review*, **66**, 219–33.

Prendinger, H. and Ishizuka, M. (eds) (2004). *Life-like characters: tools, affective functions, and applications*. Berlin: Springer-Verlag.

Prendinger, H., Mori, J., and Ishizuka, M. (2005). Using human physiology to evaluate subtle expressivity of a virtual quizmaster in a mathematical game. *Internationa Journal of Human–Computer Studies*, **62**, 231–45.

Preston, S.D. and de Waal, F.B.M. (2002). Empathy: its ultimate and proximate bases. *Behavioral and Brain Sciences*, **25**, 1–72.

Preuschoft, S. and van Hooff, J.A.R.A.M. (1995). Homologizing primate facial displays: a critical review of methods. *Folia primatologica*, **65**, 121–37.

Pribram, K.H. (1991). *Brain and perception: holonomy and structure in figural processing*. Hillsdale, NJ: Lawrence Erlbaum Associates.

Price, D.D. (2000). Psychological and neural mechanisms of the affective dimension of pain. *Science*, **288**, 1769–72.

Price, H.H. (1969) *Belief*. London: George Allen and Unwin.

Price, M.E., Cosmides, L., and Tooby, J. (2002). Punitive sentiment as an anti-free rider psychological device. *Evolution and Human Behavior*, **23**, 203–31.

Prigogene, I. and Stengers, I. (1984). *Order out of chaos*. New York: Bantam.

Primoratz, I. (1999). *Ethics and sex*. London: Routledge.

Prinz, J. (2004). *Gut reactions: a perceptual theory of emotion*. Oxford: Oxford University Press.

Prinz, J. (2005). Are emotions feelings? *Journal of Consciousness Studies*, **12**(8–10), 9–16.

van Prooijen, J.W., van den Bos, K., and Wilke, H.A.M. (2004). The role of standing in the psychology of procedural justice: toward theoretical integration. In: W. Stroebe and M. Hewstone (eds), *European review of social psychology*, pp. 33–58. Hove: Psychology Press.

Provine, R.R. (2000). *Laughter: a scientific investigation*. New York: Viking.

Pruyser, P.W. (1976). *The minister as diagnostician: personal problems in pastoral perspective*. Philadelphia, PA: Westminster Press.

Pugh, S.D. (2001). Service with a smile: emotional contagion in the service encounter. *Academy of Management Journal*, **44**, 1018–27.

de Quervain, D.J.F., Fischbacher, U., Treyer, V., et al. (2004). The neural basis of altruistic punishment. *Science*, **305**, 1254–8.

Quirk, G.J., Russo, G.K., Barron, J.L., and Lebron, K. (2000). The role of ventromedial prefrontal cortex in the recovery of extinguished fear. *Journal of Neuroscience*, **20**, 6225–31.

Quirk, G.J., Garcia, R., and Gonzalez-Lima, F. (2006). Prefrontal mechanisms in extinction of conditioned fear. *Biological Psychiatry*, **60**, 337–43.

Rafaeli, A. and Sutton, R.I. (1987). The expression of emotion as part of the work role. *Academy of Management Review*, **12**, 23–37.

Rafaeli, A. and Sutton, R.I. (1989). The expression of emotion in organizational life. In L.L. Cummings and B.M. Staw (eds), *Research in organizational behavior*, Vol. 11, pp. 1–42. Greenwich, CT: JAI Press.

Rafaeli, A. and Sutton, R.I. (1990). Busy stores and demanding customers: how do they affect the display of positive emotion? *Academy of Management Journal*, **33**, 623–37.

Rafaeli, A. and Sutton, R.I. (1991). Emotional contrast strategies as means of social influence: lessons from criminal interrogators and bill collectors. *Academy of Management Journal*, **34**, 749–75.

Rafaeli, E., Rogers, G.M., and Revelle, W. (2007). Affective synchrony: individual differences in mixed emotions. *Personality and Social Psychology Bulletin*, **33**, 915–32.

Raine, A. (2002a). Annotation: the role of prefrontal deficits, low autonomic arousal, and early health factors in the development of antisocial and aggressive behavior in children. *Journal of Child Psychology and Psychiatry*, **43**, 417–34.

Raine, A. (2002b). Biosocial studies of antisocial and violent behavior in children and adults: a review. *Journal of Abnormal Child Psychology*, **30**, 311–26.

Raine, A., Venables, P.H., and Mednick, S. A. (1997). Low resting heart rate at age 3 years predisposes to aggression at age 11 years: evidence from the Mauritius Child Health Project. *Journal of the American Academy of Child and Adolescent Psychiatry*, **36**, 1457–64.

Raison, C.L., Capuron, L., and Miller, A.H. (2006). Cytokines sing the blues: inflammation and the pathogenesis of depression. *Trends in Immunology*, **27**, 24–31.

Ramon y Cajal, S. (1899–1904). *Textura del sistema nervioso del hombre y de los vertebrados*. Madrid: Imprenta N Moya.

Ramsden, S.R. and Hubbard, J.A. (2002). Family expressiveness and parental emotion coaching: their role in children's emotion regulation and aggression. *Journal of Abnormal Child Psychology*, **30**, 657–67.

Ranulf, S. (1938). *Moral indignation and middle class psychology. A sociological study.* Copenhagen: Levin and Munksgaard.

Rao, H., Gillihan, S.J., Wang, J., Korczykowski, M., Sankoorikal, G.M., Kaercher, K.A., *et al.* (2007). Genetic variation in serotonin transporter alters resting brain function in healthy individuals. *Biological Psychiatry*, **62**, 600–606.

Rawls, J. (1971). *A theory of justice.* Cambridge, MA: Harvard University Press.

Raz, N. (2000). Aging of the brain and its impact on cognitive performance: integration of structural and functional findings. In: F.I.M. Craik and T.A. Salthouse (eds), *The handbook of aging and cognition*, 2nd edn, pp. 1–90. Hillsdale, NJ: Lawrence Erbaum Associates.

Reber, A.S. (1985). *Dictionary of psychology.* London: Penguin Books.

Reddy, W.M. (2001). *The navigation of feeling: a framework for the history of emotions.* Cambridge: Cambridge University Press.

van Reekum, C.M. and Scherer, K.R. (1997). Levels of processing for emotion-antecedent appraisal. In: G. Matthews (ed.), *Cognitive science perspectives on personality and emotion*, pp. 259–300. Amsterdam: Elsevier Science.

van Reekum, C., Banse, R., Johnstone, T., Etter, A., Wehrle, T., and Scherer, K.R. (2004). Psychophysiological responses to appraisal responses in a computer game. *Cognition and Emotion*, **18**, 663–88.

van Reekum, R., Stuss, D.T., and Ostrander, L. (2005). Apathy: why care? *Journal of Neuropsychiatry and Clinical Neurosciences*, **17**, 7–19.

Reeves, B. and Nass, C. (1996). *The media equation.* New York: Cambridge University Press.

Regan, P.C. and Berscheid, E. (1999). *Lust: what we know about human sexual desire.* Thousand Oaks, CA: Sage.

Reich, J.W., Zautra, A.J., and Davis, M. (2003). Dimensions of affect relationships: models and their integrative implications. *Review of General Psychology*, **7**, 66–83.

Reilly, J. (2006). How faces come to serve grammar: the development of non-manual morphology in ASL. In: B. Schick, M. Marschark, and P. Spencer (eds), *Advances in the development of sign language by deaf children*, pp. 262–90. Oxford: Oxford University Press.

Reilly, J. and Seibert, L. (2003). Language and emotion. In: R.J. Davidson, K.R. Scherer, and H.H. Goldsmith (eds), *Handbook of affective sciences*, pp. 535–58. New York: Oxford University Press.

Reilly, J.S., Larsen, J., Stiles, J., and Trauner, D. (1995). Affective facial expression in infants with focal brain damage. *Neuropsychologia*, **33**, 83–99.

Reisenzein, R. (1983). The Schachter theory of emotion: two decades later. *Psychological Bulletin*, **94**, 239–64.

Reisenzein, R. (1994). Pleasure-activation theory and the intensity of emotions. *Journal of Personality and Social Psychology*, **67**, 525–39.

Reisenzein, R. (2000a). The subjective experience of surprise. In: H. Bless and J.P. Forgas (eds), *The message within: the role of subjective experience in social cognition and behavior*, pp. 262–79. Philadelphia, PA: Psychology Press.

Reisenzein, R. (2000b). Exploring the strength of association between the components of emotion syndromes: the case of surprise. *Cognition and Emotion*, **14**, 1–38.

Reisenzein, R. (2001). Appraisal processes conceptualized from a schema-theoretic perspective: contributions to a process analysis of emotions. In: In: K.R. Scherer, A. Schorr, and T. Johnstone (eds), *Appraisal processes in emotion: theory, methods, research*, pp. 187–204. New York: Oxford University Press.

Reisenzein, R. (2003a). Stumpf's kognitiv-evaluative Theorie der Emotionen. In: L. Sprung and W. Schönpflug (eds), *Zur Geschichte der Psychologie in Berlin*, pp. 227–74. Frankfurt am Main: Lang.

Reisenzein, R. (2003b). Die Emotionstheorie von Meinong. In: R. Reisenzein, W.-U. Meyer, and A. Schützwohl (eds), *Einführung in die Emotionspsychologie, Band III: Kognitive Emotionstheorien*, Ch. 1. Bern: Huber.

Reisenzein, R., Meyer, W.-U., and Schutzwohl, A. (1995). James and the physical basis of emotion: a comment on Ellsworth. *Psychological Review*, **102**, 757–61.

Reiss, D. and Marino, L. (2001). Mirror self-recognition in the bottlenose dolphin: a case of cognitive convergence. *Proceedings of the National Academy of Sciences USA*, **98**, 5937–42.

Reiss, S. and McNally, R.J. (1985). Expectancy model of fear. In: S. Reiss and R.R. Bootzin (eds), *Theoretical issues in behavior therapy*, pp. 107–21. San Diego, CA: Academic Press.

Renninger, K.A., Hidi, S., and Krapp, A. (1992). *The role of interest in learning and development.* Hillsdale, NJ: Lawrence Erlbaum Associates.

Rescorla, R.A. (1968). Probability of shock in the presence and absence of CS in fear conditioning. *Journal of Comparative and Physiological Psychology*, **66**, 1–5.

Rescorla, R.A. (2000). Extinction can be enhanced by a concurrent excitor. *Journal of Experimental Psychology: Animal Behavior Processes*, **26**, 251–60.

Rescorla, R.A. and Wagner, A.R. (1972). A theory of Pavlovian conditioning: variations in the effectiveness of reinforcement and nonreinforcement. In: A.H. Black and W.F. Prokasy (eds), *Classical conditioning II: current theory and research*, pp. 64–99. New York: Appleton-Century-Crofts.

Reuter, M., Schmitz, A., Corr, P., and Hennig, J. (2006). Molecular genetics support Gray's personality theory: the interaction of COMT and DRD2 polymorphisms predicts the behavioral approach system. *International Journal of Neuropsychopharmacology*, **9**, 155–66.

Reuter-Lorenz, P. and Davidson, R.J. (1981). Differential contributions of the two cerebral hemispheres to the perception of happy and sad faces. *Neuropsychologia*, **19**, 609–13.

Revelle, W. (1995). Personality processes. *Annual Review of Psychology*, **46**, 295–328.

Rhodes, G. and Zebrowitz, L.A. (eds) (2002). *Facial attractivnesss: evolutionary, cognitive, and social perspectives.* Westport, CT: Ablex.

Richards, I.A. (1936). *The philosophy of rhetoric.* London: Oxford University Press.

Richardson, M.P., Strange, B.A. and Dolan, R.J. (2004). Encoding of emotional memories depends on amygdala and hippocampus and their interactions. *Nature Neuroscience*, **7**, 278–85.

Richter, M. and Gendolla, G.H.E. (2007). Incentive value and cardiovascular reactivity in active coping. *International Journal of Psychophysiology*, **63**, 294–301.

References

Richters, J.E. and Hinshaw, S.P. (1999). The abduction of disorder in psychiatry. *Journal of Abnormal Psychology*, **108**, 438–45.

Rick, S. and Loewenstein, G. (2008). The role of emotion in economic behavior. In: M. Lewis, J.M. Haviland-Jones, and L. Feldman Barrett (eds), *Handbook of emotions*, 3rd edn, Ch. 9. New York: Guilford Press.

Ridley, A. (2003). Tragedy. In: J. Levinson (ed.), *The Oxford handbook of aesthetics*, pp. 408–20. Oxford: Oxford University Press.

Rief, W. and Sharpe, M. (2004). Somatoform disorders—new approaches to classification, conceptualization, and treatment. *Journal of Psychosomatic Research*, **56**, 387–90.

Rimé, B. (2005). *Le partage social des émotions* (The social sharing of emotion). Paris: Presses Universitaires de France.

Rimé, B. (2007). Interpersonal emotion regulation. In: J.J. Gross (ed.), *Handbook of emotion regulation*, pp. 466–85. New York: Guilford Press.

Rimé, B. (2009). Emotion elicits the social sharing of emotion: Theory and empirical review. *Emotion Review*, **7**, 60–85.

Rimé, B., Finkenauer, C., Luminet, O., Zech, E., and Philippot, P. (1998). Social sharing of emotion: new evidence and new questions. In: W. Stroebe and M. Hewstone (eds), *European Review of Social Psychology*, Vol. 9, pp. 145–89. Chichester: Wiley.

Rinn, W.E. (1984). The neuropsychology of facial expression: a review of the neurological and psychological mechanisms for producing facial expressions. *Psychological Bulletin*, **95**, 52–77.

Riskind, J.H., Williams, N.L., Gessner, T.L., Chrosniak, L.D., and Cortina, J.M. (2000). The looming maladaptive style: anxiety, danger, and schematic processing. *Journal of Personality and Social Psychology*, **79**, 837–52.

Rizzolatti, G. and Craighero, L. (2004). The mirror-neuron system. *Annual Review of Neuroscience*, **27**, 169–92.

Rizzolatti, G., Fadiga, L., Gallese, V., and Fogassi, L. (1996). Premotor cortex and the recognition of motor actions. *Cognitive Brain Research*, **3**, 131–41.

Roberts, B.W. and DelVecchio, W.F. (2000). The rank-order consistency of personality from childhood to old age: a quantitative review of longitudinal studies. *Psychological Bulletin*, **126**, 3–25.

Robinson, D. (2005). *Deeper than reason: emotion and its role in literature, music, and art*. New York: Oxford University Press.

Robinson, M.D. and Clore, G.L. (2002). Belief and feeling: evidence for an accessibility model of emotional self-report. *Psychological Bulletin*, **128**, 934–60.

Robinson, T.E. and Berridge, K.C. (1993). The neural basis of drug craving: an incentive-sensitization theory of addiction. *Brain Research Reviews*, **18**, 247–91.

Roese, N. and Olson, J.M. (1995). *What might have been: the psychology of counterfactual thinking*. Hillsdale, NJ: Lawrence Erlbaum Associates.

Roese, N.J. and Summerville, A. (2005). What we regret most . . . and why. *Personality and Social Psychology Bulletin*, **31**, 1273–85.

Rogers, G.M. and Revelle, W. (1998). Personality, mood, and the evaluation of affective and neutral word pairs. *Journal of Personality and Social Psychology*, **74**, 1592–605.

Rogers, R.W. (1983). Cognitive and physiological processes in fear appeals and attitude change: a revised theory of protection motivation. In: J.T. Cacioppo and R.E. Petty (eds), *Social psychophysiology: a sourcebook*, pp. 153–76. New York: Guilford Press.

Rohleder, N., Wolf, J.M., Maldonado, E.F., and Kirschbaum, C. (2006). The psychosocial stress-induced increase in salivary alpha-amylase is independent of saliva flow rate. *Psychophysiology*, **43**, 645–52.

Roland, C. and Foxx, R.M. (2003). Self-respect: a neglected concept. *Philosophical Psychology*, **16**, 247–87.

Rolls, E.T. (2000). Précis of 'The brain and emotion'. *Behavioral and Brain Sciences*, **23**, 177–234.

Rolls, E.T. (2004). The functions of the orbitofrontal cortex. *Brain and Cognition*, **55**, 11–29.

Rolls, E.T. (2005). *Emotion explained*. New York: Oxford University Press.

Rolls, E.T. (2006). Brain mechanisms underlying flavour and appetite. *Philosophical Transactions of the Royal Society B: Biological Sciences* **361**, 1123–36.

Rolls, E.T. (2008). *Memory, attention, and decision-making: a computational neuroscience approach*. Oxford: Oxford University Press.

Rolls, E.T. (2009). The anterior and midcingulate cortices and reward. In: B.A. Vogt (ed.), *Cingulate neurobiology and disease*. Oxford: Oxford University Press (in press).

Rolls, E.T., Browing, A.S., Inoue, K., and Hernadi, I. (2005). Novel visual stimuli activate a population of neurons in the primate orbitofrontal cortex. *Neurobiology of Learning and Memory*, **84**, 111–23.

Room, R. (1983). Sociological aspects of the disease concept of alcoholism. In: R.G. Smart, F.B. Glaser, Y. Israel, H. Kalant, R.E. Popham, and W. Schmidt (eds), *Research advances in alcoholism and drug problems*, Vol. 7, pp. 47–91. New York: Plenum Press.

Rorty, A. (ed.) (1980). *Explaining emotions*. Los Angeles, CA: University of California Press.

Rosaldo, M.Z. (1980). *Knowledge and passion: Ilongot notions of self and social life*. Cambridge: Cambridge University Press.

Roseman, I.J. (1984). Cognitive determinants of emotion: a structural theory. In: P. Shaver (ed.), *Review of personality and social psychology*, Vol. 5, pp. 11–36. Beverly Hills, CA: Sage.

Roseman, I.J. (1991). Appraisal determinants of discrete emotions. *Cognition and Emotion*, **5**, 161–200.

Roseman, I.J. (2001). A model of appraisal in the emotion system: integrating theory, research, and applications. In: K.R. Scherer, A. Schorr, and T. Johnstone (eds), *Appraisal processes in emotion: theory, methods, research*, pp. 68–91. New York: Oxford University Press.

Roseman, I.J., Antoniou, A.A., and Jose, P.E. (1996). Appraisal determinants of emotions: constructing a more accurate and comprehensive theory. *Cognition and Emotion*, **10**, 241–77.

Roseman, I.J. and Kaiser, S.(2001). Applications of appraisal theory to understanding, diagnosing, and treating emotion pathology. In: K.R. Scherer, A. Schorr, and T. Johnstone (eds), *Appraisal theories of emotions: theories, methods, research*, pp. 249–70. New York: Oxford University Press.

Roseman, I.J. and Smith, C.A. (2001). Appraisal theory: overview, assumptions, varieties, controversies. In: K.R. Scherer, A. Schorr, and T. Johnstone (eds.). *Appraisal processes in emotion: theory, methods, research*, pp. 3–19. New York: Oxford University Press.

Roseman, I.J., Wiest, C., and Swartz, T.S. (1994). Phenomenology, behaviors, and goals differentiate discrete emotions. *Journal of Personality and Social Psychology*, **67**, 206–21.

Rosenberg, E.L. and Ekman, P. (1994). Coherence between expressive and experiential systems in emotion. *Cognition and Emotion*, **8**, 201–29.

Rosenblatt, P.C., Walsh, R.P., and Jackson, D.A. (1976). *Grief and mourning in cross-cultural perspective*. New Haven, CT: HRAF Press.

Rosengren, A., Hawken, S., Ounpuu, S., Sliwa, K., Zubaid, M., Almahmeed, W.A., *et al.* (2004). Association of psychosocial risk factors with risk of acute myocardial infarction in 11,119 cases and 13,648 controls from 52 countries (the INTERHEART study): case-control study. *Lancet*, **364**, 953–62.

Rosenkranz, M.A., Jackson, D.C., Dalton, K.M., Dolski, I., Ryff, C.D., Singer, B.H., Muller, D., Kalin, N.H., and Davidson, R.J. (2003). Affective style and *in vivo* immune response: neurobehavioral mechanisms. *Proceedings of the National Academy of Sciences USA*, **100**, 11148–52.

Rosenkranz, M.A., Busse, W.W., Johnstone, T., Swenson, C.A., Crisafi, G.M., Jackson, M.M., Bosch, J.A., Sheridan, J.F., and Davidson, R.J. (2005). Neural circuitry underlying the interaction between emotion and asthma symptom exacerbation. *Proceedings of the National Academy of Sciences USA*, **102**, 13319–24.

Rosenthal, R., Hall, J.A., DiMatteo, M.R., Rogers, P.L., and Archer, D. (1979). *Sensitivity to nonverbal communication: the PONS test*. Baltimore, MD: The Johns Hopkins University Press.

Rosenwein, B.H. (2006). *Emotional communities in the early Middle Ages*. Ithaca, NY: Cornell University Press.

de Rosis, F., Novielli, N., Carofiglio, V., Cavalluzzi, A., and Carolis, B.D. (2006) User modeling and adaptation in health promotion dialogs with an animated character. *International Journal of Biomedical Informatics*, **39**, 514–31.

Roth, A. and Fonagy, P. (2004). *What works for whom: a critical review of psychotherapy research*, 2nd edn. New York, Guilford Press.

Roth, W.T., Wilhelm, F.H., and Pettit, D. (2005). Are current theories of panic falsifiable? *Psychological Bulletin*, **131**, 171–92.

Rothbart, M.K. (1999). Temperament in childhood. In: J.A. Kohnstamm, J.E. Bates, and M.K. Rothbart (eds), *Temperament in childhood*, pp. 59–76. New York: Wiley.

Rothbart, M.K. and Bates, J.E. (1998). Temperament. In: N. Eisenberg (ed.), *Handbook of child psychology. Vol. 3: Social, emotional, and personality development*, pp. 105–76. New York: Wiley.

Rothbart, M.K., Ahadi, S.A., and Hershey, K.L. (1994). Temperament and social behavior in childhood. *Merrill-Palmer Quarterly*, **40**, 21–39.

Rothbaum, B.O. and Mellman, T.A. (2001). Dreams and exposure therapy in PTSD. *Journal of Traumatic Stress*, **14**, 481–90.

Rottenstreich, Y. and Hsee, C.K. (2001). Money, kisses, and electric shocks: on the affective psychology of risk. *Psychological Science*, **12**, 185–90.

Rotter, J.B. (1966). Generalized expectancies for internal versus external control of reinforcement. *Psychological Monographs*, **80** (1, Whole No. 609).

Rozanski, A., Blumenthal, J.A., Davidson, K.W., Saab, P., and Kubzansky, L.D. (2005). The epidemiology, pathophysiology, and management of psychosocial risk factors in cardiac practice: the emerging field of behavioral cardiology. *Journal of the American College of Cardiology*, **45**, 637–51.

Rozin, P. (1999). Preadaptation and the puzzles and properties of pleasure. In: D. Kahneman, E. Diener, and N. Schwarz (eds), *Well-being: the foundations of hedonic psychology*, pp. 109–33. New York: Russell Sage.

Rozin, P. and Fallon, A.E. (1987). A perspective on disgust. *Psychological Review*, **94**, 23–41.

Rozin, P. and Royzman, E.B. (2001). Negativity bias, negativity dominance, and contagion. *Personality and Social Psychology Review*, **5**, 296–320.

Rozin, P., Lowery, L., Imada, S., and Haidt, J. (1999). The CAD triad hypothesis: a mapping between three moral emotions (contempt, anger, disgust) and three moral codes (community, autonomy, divinity). *Journal of Personality and Social Psychology*, **76**, 574–86.

Rozin, P., Taylor, C., Ross, L., Bennett, G., and Hejmadi, A. (2005). General and specific abilities to recognise negative emotions, especially disgust, as portrayed in the face and the body. *Cognition and Emotion*, **19**, 397–412.

Rozin, P., Haidt, J., and McCauley, C.R. (2000). Disgust. In: M. Lewis, J.M. Haviland-Jones, and L. Feldman Barrett (eds), *Handbook of emotions*, 3rd edn, pp. 757–76. New York: Guilford Press.

Ruch, W. (1993). Exhilaration and humor. In: M. Lewis and J.M. Haviland (eds), *Handbook of emotions*, 1st edn, pp. 605–16. New York: Guilford Press.

Ruch, W. (1997). State and trait cheerfulness and the induction of exhilaration: a FACS study. *European Psychologist*, **2**, 328–41.

Ruch, W. and Ekman, P. (2001). The expressive pattern of laughter. In: A. Kazniak (ed.), *Emotion, qualia, and consciousness*, pp. 426–43. Tokyo: World Scientific.

Rudrauf, D., David, O., Lachaux, J.P., Kovach, C.K., Martinerie, J., Renault, B., *et al.* (2008). Rapid interactions between the ventral visual stream and emotion-related structures rely on a two-pathway architecture. *Journal of Neuroscience*, **28**, 2793–803.

Ruelle, D. (1991). *Chance and chaos*. Princeton, NJ: Princeton University Press.

Ruiz, J.I. (2007). Emotional climate in organizations: applications in Latin American prisons. *Journal of Social Issues*, **63**, 289–306.

Ruse, M. (1995). Reductionism. In: T. Honderich (ed.), *Oxford companion to philosophy*, pp. 750–751. Oxford: Oxford University Press.

Rush, A., Trivedi, M., Wisnieski, S., Niernberg, A., Stewart, J., Warden, D., *et al.* (2006). Acute and longer-term outcomes in depressed outpatients requiring one or several treatment steps: a STAR*D report. *Amercian Journal of Psychiatry*, **163**, 1905–17.

Rushworth, M.F., Walton, M.E., Kennerley, S.W., and Bannerman, D.M. (2004). Action sets and decisions in the medial frontal cortex. *Trends in Cognitive Sciences*, **8**, 410–417.

Russell, J.A. (1980). A circumplex model of affect. *Journal of Personality and Social Psychology*, **39**, 1161–78.

Russell, J.A. (1991). Culture and the categorization of emotions. *Psychological Bulletin*, **110**, 426–50.

Russell, J.A. (1999). On the bipolarity of positive and negative affect. *Psychological Bulletin*, **125**, 3–30.

References

Russell, J. (2003). Core affect and the psychological construction of emotion. *Psychological Review*, **100**, 145–72.

Russell, J.A. and Barrett, L.F. (1999). Core affect, prototypical emotional episodes, and other things called emotion: dissecting the elephant. *Journal of Personality and Social Psychology*, **76**, 805–19.

Russell, J.A. and Carroll, J.M. (1999). On the bipolarity of positive and negative affect. *Psychological Bulletin*, **125**, 3–30.

Russell, J.A. and Fernández-Dols, J.M. (eds) (1997). *The psychology of facial expression*. Cambridge: Cambridge University Press.

Russell, J.A. and Mehrabian, A. (1977). Evidence for a three-factor theory of emotions. *Journal of Research in Personality*, **11**, 273–94.

Russell, J.A., Lewicka, M., and Niit, T. (1989). A cross-cultural study of a circumplex model of affect. *Journal of Personality and Social Psychology*, **57**, 848–56.

Rutter, M. and Silberg, J. (2002). Gene-environment interplay in relation to emotional and behavioral disturbance. *Annual Review of Psychology*, **53**, 463–90.

Saarni, C. (1990). Emotional competence. In: R. Thompson (ed), *Nebraska Symposium: socioemotional development*, pp. 115–61. Lincoln, NB: University of Nebraska Press.

Saarni, C. (1999). *The development of emotional competence*. New York: Guilford Press.

Saarni, C., Campos, J., Camras, L., and Witherington, D. (2006). Emotional development: action, communication and understanding. In: N. Eisenberg (ed.), *Handbook of child psychology: social, emotional, and personality development*, 6th edn, pp. 226–99 (series editors W. Damon and R. Lerner). New York: John Wiley.

Sabatinelli, D., Bradley, M.M., Fitzsimmons, J.R., and Lang, P.J. (2005). Parallel amygdala and inferotemporal activation reflect emotional intensity and fear relevance. *Neuroimage*, **24**, 1265–70.

Salkovskis, P.M. (1985). Obsessional compulsive problems: a cognitive-behavioral analysis. *Behaviour Research and Therapy*, **23**, 571–83.

Salovey, P. and Grewal, D. (2005). The science of emotional intelligence. *Current Directions in Psychological Science*, **14**, 281–5.

Salovey, P. and Mayer, J.D. (1990). Emotional intelligence. *Imagination, Cognition, and Personality*, **9**, 185–211.

Salovey, P. and Rodin, J. (1984). Some antecedents and consequences of social-comparison jealousy. *Journal of Personality and Social Psychology*, **47**, 780–792.

Sander, D. (2008). Basic tastes and basic emotions: basic problems, and perspectives for a nonbasic solution (commentary). *Behavioral and Brain Sciences*, **31**, 88.

Sander, D. and Koenig, O. (2002). No inferiority complex in the study of emotion complexity: a cognitive neuroscience computational architecture of emotion. *Cognitive Science Quarterly*, **2**, 249–272.

Sander, D., Grafman, J., and Zalla, T. (2003). The human amygdala: an evolved system for relevance detection. *Reviews in the Neurosciences*, **14**, 303–16.

Sander, D., Grandjean, D., and Scherer, K.R. (2005). A systems approach to appraisal mechanisms in emotion. *Neural Networks*, **18**, 317–52.

Sanfey, A.G., Rilling, J.K., Aronson, J.A., Nystrom, L.E., and Cohen, J.D. (2003). The neural basis of economic decision-making in the ultimatum game. *Science*, **300**, 1755–8.

Sansone, C. and Thoman, D.B. (2005). Interest as the missing motivator in self-regulation. *European Psychologist*, **10**, 175–86.

Saper, C.B., Cano, G., and Scammell, T.E. (2005). Homeostatic, circadian, and emotional regulation of sleep. *Journal of Comprehensive Neurology*, **493**, 92–8.

Saucier, G. and Goldberg, L.R. (2001). Lexical studies of indigenous personality factors: premises, products, and prospects. *Journal of Personality*, **69**, 847–79.

Schachter, S. and Singer, J. (1962). Cognitive, social and physiological determinants of emotional state. *Psychological Review*, **69**, 379–99.

Schaefer, A., Braver, T.S., Reynolds, J.R., Burgess, G.C., Yarkoni, T., and Gray, J.R. (2006). Individual differences in amygdala activity predict response speed during working memory. *Journal of Neuroscience*, **26**, 10120–10128.

Schaal, B., Soussignan, R., and Marlier, L. (2002). Olfactory cognition at the start of life: the perinatal shaping of selective odor responsiveness. In: C. Rouby, B. Schaal, D. Dubois, R. Gervais, and A. Holley (eds), *Olfaction, taste, and cognition*, pp. 421–40. Cambridge: Cambridge University Press.

Scheff, T.J. (1988). Shame and conformity. the deference-emotion system. *American Review of Sociology*, **53**, 395–406.

Scheff, T.J. (1990). *Microsociology: discourse, emotion and social structure*. Chicago, IL: Chicago University Press.

Scheiner, E., Hammerschmidt, K., Jürgens, U., and Zwirner, P. (2004). The influence of hearing impairment on preverbal emotional vocalizations of infants. *Folia Phoniatrica Logopaedia*, **56**, 27–40.

Scheler, M. (1961). *Ressentiment*. New York: Free Press of Glencoe. (Original work published 1912.)

Scheler, M. (1973). *Formalism in ethics and non-formal ethics of value. A new attempt toward the foundation of an ethical personalism*, pp. 328–44. Evanston, IL: Northwestern University Press.

Schell, A.M., Dawson, M.E., Rissling, A., Ventura, J., Subotnik, K.L., Gitlin, M.J., *et al.* (2005). Electrodermal predictors of functional outcome and negative symptoms in schizophrenia. *Psychophysiology*, **42**, 483–92.

Scherer, K.R. (1978). Personality inference from voice quality: the loud voice of extroversion. *European Journal of Social Psychology*, **8**, 467–87.

Scherer, K.R. (1982). Emotion as a process: function, origin, and regulation. *Social Science Information*, **21**, 555–70.

Scherer, K.R. (1984a). On the nature and function of emotion: a component process approach. In: K.R. Scherer and P. Ekman (eds), *Approaches to emotion*, pp. 293–318. Hillsdale, NJ: Lawrence Erlbaum Associates.

Scherer, K.R. (1984b). Emotion as a multicomponent process: a model and some cross-cultural data. In: P. Shaver (ed), *Review of personality and social psychology*, Vol. 5, pp. 37–63. Beverley-Hills, CA: Sage.

Scherer, K.R. (1985). Vocal affect signalling: a comparative approach. In: J. Rosenblatt, C. Beer, M.-C. Busnel, and P.J. B. Slater (eds), *Advances in the study of behavior*, Vol. 15, pp. 189–244. New York: Academic Press.

Scherer, K.R. (1986a). Vocal affect expression: a review and model for future research. *Psychological Bulletin*, **99**, 143–65.

Scherer, K.R. (1986b). Emotion experiences across European cultures: a summary statement. In: K.R. Scherer, H.G. Wallbott, and A.B. Summerfield (eds), *Experiencing emotion:*

a cross-cultural study, pp. 173–89. New York: Cambridge University Press.

Scherer, K.R. (1992). Vocal affect expression as symptom, symbol, and appeal. In: H. Papousek, U. Jürgens, and M. Papousek (eds), *Nonverbal vocal communication: comparative and developmental approaches*, pp. 43–60. Cambridge: Cambridge University Press.

Scherer, K.R. (1994a). Affect bursts. In: S. van Goozen, N.E. van de Poll, and J.A. Sergeant (eds), *Emotions: essays on emotion theory*, pp. 161–96. Hillsdale, NJ: Lawrence Erlbaum Associates.

Scherer, K.R. (1994b) Emotions serve to decouple stimulus and response. In: P. Ekman and R.J. Davidson (eds), *The nature of emotion: fundamental questions*, pp. 127–39. New York: Oxford University Press.

Scherer, K.R. (1994c). Toward a concept of 'modal emotions'. In: P. Ekman and R.J. Davidson (eds), *The nature of emotion: fundamental questions*, pp. 25–31. New York: Oxford University Press.

Scherer, K.R. (1997). The role of culture in emotion-antecedent appraisal. *Journal of Personality and Social Psychology*, **73**, 902–22.

Scherer, K.R. (1999a). Appraisal theories. In: T. Dalgleish and M. Power (eds), *Handbook of cognition and emotion*, pp. 637–63. Chichester: Wiley.

Scherer, K.R. (1999b). On the sequential nature of appraisal processes: indirect evidence from a recognition task. *Cognition and Emotion*, **13**, 763–93.

Scherer, K.R. (2001a). Appraisal considered as a process of multilevel sequential checking. In: K.R. Scherer, A. Schorr, and T. Johnstone (eds), *Appraisal processes in emotion: theory, methods, research*, pp. 92–120. New York: Oxford University Press.

Scherer, K.R. (2001b). Feelings integrate the central representation of appraisal-driven response organization in emotion. In: A.S.R. Manstead, N.H. Frijda, and A.H. Fischer (eds), *Feelings and emotions: the Amsterdam Symposium*, pp. 136–57. Cambridge: Cambridge University Press.

Scherer, K.R. (2001c). The nature and study of appraisal: a review of the issues. In: K.R. Scherer, A. Schorr, and T. Johnstone (eds), *Appraisal processes in emotion: theory, methods, research*, pp. 369–92. New York: Oxford University Press.

Scherer, K.R. (2003). Vocal communication of emotion: a review of research paradigms. *Speech Communication*, **40**, 227–56.

Scherer, K.R. (2004). Feelings integrate the central representation of appraisal-driven response organization in emotion. In: A.S.R. Manstead, N.H. Frijda, and A.H. Fischer (eds), *Feelings and emotions: the Amsterdam Symposium*, pp. 136–57. Cambridge: Cambridge University Press.

Scherer, K.R. (2005). What are emotions? And how can they be measured? *Social Science Information*, **44**, 693–727.

Scherer, K.R. (2007). Component models of emotion can inform the quest for emotional competence. In: G. Matthews, M. Zeidner, and R.D. Roberts (eds), *The science of emotional intelligence: knowns and unknowns*, pp. 101–26. New York: Oxford University Press.

Scherer, K.R. and Ceschi, G. (1997). Lost luggage emotion: a field study of emotion-antecedent appraisal. *Motivation and Emotion*, **21**, 211–35.

Scherer, K.R. and Ekman, P. (eds) (1984). *Approaches to emotion*. Hillsdale, NJ: Lawrence Erlbaum Associates.

Scherer, K.R. and Ekman, P. (2005). Methodological issues in studying nonverbal behavior. In: J.A. Harrigan, R. Rosenthal, and K.R. Scherer (eds), *The new handbook of methods in nonverbal behavior research*, pp. 471–512. New York: Oxford University Press.

Scherer, K.R. and Ellgring, H. (2007a). Are facial expressions of emotion produced by categorical affect programs or dynamically driven by appraisal? *Emotion*, **7**, 113–30.

Scherer, K.R. and Ellgring, R.H. (2007b). Multimodal expression of emotion: affect programs or componential appraisal patterns? *Emotion*, **7**, 158–71.

Scherer, K.R. and Grandjean, D. (2008). Inferences from facial expressions of emotion have many facets. *Cognition and Emotion*, **22**, 789–801.

Scherer K.R. and Peper, M. (2001). Psychological theories of emotion and neuropsychological research. In: F. Boller and J. Grafman (eds), *Handbook of neuropsychology*, Vol. 5, pp. 17–48. Amsterdam: Elsevier.

Scherer, K.R. and Tannenbaum, P.H. (1986). Emotional experiences in everyday life: a survey approach. *Motivation and Emotion*, **10**, 295–314.

Scherer, K.R. and Wallbott, H.G. (1985). Analysis of nonverbal behavior. In: T.A. van Dijk (ed.), *Handbook of discourse analysis*, pp.199–230. London: Academic Press.

Scherer, K.R. and Wallbott, H. (1994). Evidence for universality and cultural variation of differential emotion response-patterning. *Journal of Personality and Social Psychology*, **66**, 310–328.

Scherer, K.R., and Zentner, M.R. (2001). Emotional effects of music: production rules. In: P.N. Juslin and J.A. Sloboda (eds), *Music and emotion: theory and research*, pp. 361–92. Oxford: Oxford University Press.

Scherer, K.R., Wallbott, H.G., Matsumoto, D., and Kudoh, T. (1988). Emotional experience in cultural context: a comparison between Europe, Japan, and the United States. In: K.R. Scherer (ed.), *Facets of emotion: recent research*, pp. 5–30. Hillsdale, NJ: Lawrence Erlbaum Associates.

Scherer, K.R., Schorr, A., and Johnstone, T. (2001a). *Appraisal processes in emotion: theory, methods, research*. New York: Oxford University Press.

Scherer, K.R., Banse, R., and Wallbott, H. (2001b). Emotion inferences from vocal expression correlate across languages and cultures. *Journal of Cross-Cultural Psychology*, **32**, 76–92.

Scherer, K.R., Johnstone, T., and Klasmeyer, G. (2003). Vocal expression of emotion. In: R.J. Davidson, K.R. Scherer, and H.H. Goldsmith (eds), *Handbook of affective sciences*, pp. 433–56. New York: Oxford University Press.

Scherer, K.R., Wranik, T., Sangsue, J., Tran, V., and Scherer, U. (2004). Emotions in everyday life: probability of occurrence, risk factors, appraisal and reaction pattern. *Social Science Information*, **43**, 499–570.

Scherer, K.R., Dan, E.S., and Flykt, A. (2006). What determines a feeling's position in affective space? A case for appraisal. *Cognition and Emotion*, **20**, 92–113.

Schinka, J.A., Busch, R.M., and Robichaux-Keene, N. (2004). A meta-analysis of the association between the serotonin transporter gene polymorphism (5-HTTLPR) and trait anxiety. *Molecular Psychiatry*, **9**, 197–202.

Schino, G., Perretta, G., Taglioni, A., Monaco, V., and Troisi, A. (1996). Primate displacement activities as an ethopharmacological model of anxiety. *Anxiety*, **2**, 186–91.

References

Schino, G., Geminiani, S., Rosati, L., and Aureli, F. (2004). Behavioral and emotional response of Japanese macaque (*Macaca fuscata*) mothers after their offspring receive an aggression. *Journal of Comparative Psychology*, **118**, 340–346.

Schlenker, B.R. (1980). *Impression management: the self-concept, social identity, and interpersonal relations*. Monterey, CA: Brooks/Cole.

Schlosberg, H. (1952). The description of facial expressions in terms of two dimensions. *Journal of Experimental Psychology*, **44**, 229–37.

Schlosberg, H. (1954). Three dimensions of emotion. *Psychological Review*, **61**, 81–8.

Schmidt, K.L. and Cohn, J.F. (2001). Human facial expressions as adaptations: evolutionary questions in facial expression research. *Yearbook of Physical Anthropology*, **44**, 3–24.

Schmidt, N.B., Lerew, D.R., and Jackson, R.J. (1999). Prospective evaluation of anxiety sensitivity in the pathogenesis of panic: replication and extension. *Journal of Abnormal Psychology*, **108**, 532–7.

Schmidt, N.B., Zvolensky, M.J., and Maner, J.L. (2006). Anxiety sensitivity: prospective prediction of panic attacks and Axis I pathology. *Journal of Psychiatric Research*, **40**, 691–9.

Schneider, K. and Josephs, I. (1991). *Journal of Nonverbal Behavior*, **15**, 185–98.

Schneirla, T.C. (1959). An evolutionary and developmental theory of biphasic processes underlying approach and withdrawal. In: M.R. Jones (ed.), *Current theory and research in motivation*, pp. 1–49. Lincoln, NB: University of Nebraska Press.

Schoebi, D., Plancherel, B., Tschumakov, M., and Perrez, M. (2006). La punition corporelle des enfants en Suisse et en Russie. *La Revue International de l'Éducation Familiale*, **19**, 53–75.

Schoeck, H. (1969). *Envy: a theory of social behaviour* (transl. M. Glenny and B. Ross). Indianapolis, IN: Liberty Press. (Original work published 1966.)

Schopenhauer, A. (1966). *The world as will and representation*, transl. E.F.J. Payne. New York: Dover.

Schorr, A. (2001). Appraisal: the evolution of an idea. In: K.R. Scherer, A. Schorr, and T. Johnstone (eds), *Appraisal processes in emotion*, pp. 20–36. New York: Oxford University Press.

Schröder, M. (2003). Experimental study of affect bursts. *Speech Communication*, **40**, 99–116.

Schröder, M. (2006). Expressing degree of activation in synthetic speech. *IEEE Transactions on Audio, Speech and Language Processing*, **14**, 1128–36.

Schröder, M. (2008). Approaches to emotional expressivity in synthetic speech. In: K. Izdebski (ed.), *Emotions in the human voice, Volume 3: Culture and perception*, pp. 307–21. San Diego, CA: Plural.

Schroeder, T. (2004). *Three faces of desire*. New York: Oxford University Press.

Schupp, H.T., Flaisch, T., Stockburger, J., and Junghofer, M. (2006). Emotion and attention: event-related brain potential studies. *Progress in Brain Research*, **156**, 31–51.

Schut, H. and Stroebe, M. (2005). Interventions to enhance adaptation to bereavement. *Journal of Palliative Medicine*, **8**, S140–S147.

Schutte, N.S., Malouff, J.M., Hall, L.E., Haggerty, D.J., Cooper, J.T., *et al.* (1998). Development and validation of a measure of emotional intelligence. *Personality and Individual Differences*, **25**, 167–77.

Schutz, P.A. and Pekrun, R. (eds) (2007). *Emotion in education*. Amsterdam: Elsevier/Academic Press.

Schwarz, N. (2001) Feeling as information: implications for affective influences in information processing. In: L.L. Martin and G.L. Clore (eds), *Theories of mood and cognition: a user's guidebook*, pp. 159–76. Mahwah, NJ: Lawrence Erlbaum Associates.

Schwarz, N. and Clore, G.L. (1983). Mood, misattribution, and judgments of well-being: Informative and directive functions of affective states. *Journal of Personality and Social Psychology*, **45**, 513–23.

Schwarz, N. and Clore, G.L. (1988). How do I feel about it? Informative functions of affective states. In: K. Fiedler and J. Forgas (eds), *Affect, cognition, and social behavior*, pp. 44–62. Gottingen: Hogrefe.

Schwarz, N. and Clore, G.L. (2007). Feelings and phenomenal experience. In: E.T. Higgins and A.W. Kruglanski (eds), *Social psychology: handbook of basic principles*, 2nd edn, pp. 385–407. New York: Guilford Press.

Schwarz, N. and Strack, F. (1999). Reports of subjective well-being: judgmental processes and their methodological implications. In: D. Kahneman, E. Diener, and N. Schwarz (eds), *Well-being: the foundations of hedonic psychology*, pp. 61–84. New York: Russell Sage Foundation.

Schwitzgebel, E. (2002). How well do we know our own conscious experience? The case of visual imagery. *Journal of Consciousness Studies*, **9**, 35–53.

Schwitzgebel, E. (2006). Belief. In: E.N. Zalta (ed.), *Stanford encyclopedia of philosophy*, Fall 2006 edn <http://plato.stanford.edu/archives/fall2006/entries/belief/>.

Scott, J.P. and Fuller, J. (1965). *Genetics of the social behavior of the dog*. Chicago, IL: University of Chicago Press.

Scruton, R. (1986). *Sexual desire: a moral philosophy of the erotic*. New York: Free Press.

Searle, J.R. (1983). *Intentionality*. Cambridge: Cambridge University Press.

Segal, Z.V., Kennedy, S., Gemar, M., Hood, K., Pedersen, R., and Buis, T. (2006). Cognitive reactivity to sad mood provocation and the prediction of depressive relapse. *Archives of General Psychiatry*, **63**, 750–55.

Segerstrom, S.C. (2005). Optimism and immunity: do positive thoughts always lead to positive effects? *Brain, Behavior, and Immunity*, **19**, 195–200.

Seligman, M.E.P. (1971). Phobias and preparedness. *Behavior Therapy*, **2**, 307–20.

Seligman, M.E.P. (1975). *Helplessness: on depression, development, and death*. San Francisco, CA: Freeman.

Selten, J.-P. and Cantor-Graae, E. (2005). Social defeat: risk factor for psychosis? *British Journal of Psychiatry*, **187**, 101–2.

Selye, H. (1964). *From dream to discovery*. New York: McGraw-Hill.

Selye, H. (1987). *Stress without distress*. London: Transworld.

Semmer, N.K. (2003). Individual differences, work stress and health. In: M.J. Schabracq, J.A. Winnubst, and C.L. Cooper (eds), *Handbook of work and health psychology*, 2nd edn, pp. 83–120. Chichester: Wiley.

Semmer, N.K., McGrath, J.E., and Beehr, T.A. (2005). Conceptual issues in research on stress and health. In: C.L. Cooper (ed.), *Handbook of stress and health*, 2nd edn, pp. 1–43. New York: CRC Press.

Sen, S., Burmeister, M., and Ghosh, D. (2004). Meta-analysis of the association between a serotonin transporter promoter polymorphism (5-HTTLPR) and anxiety-related personality traits. *American Journal of Medical Genetics Part B: Neuropsychiatric Genetics*, **127**, 85–9.

Sergerie, K., Chochol, C., and Armony, J.L. (2008). The role of the amygdala in emotional processing: a quantitative meta-analysis of functional neuroimaging studies. *Neuroscience and Biobehavioral Reviews*, **32**, 811–30.

Seymour, B. and Dolan, R. (2008). Emotion, decision making, and the amygdala. *Neuron*, **58**, 662–71.

Shaffer, J.A. (1978). Sexual desire. *Journal of Philosophy*, **75**, 175–89.

Shamay-Tsoory, S.G., Tibi-Elhanany, Y., and Aharon-Peretz, J. (2007). The green-eyed monster and malicious joy: the neuroanatomical bases of envy and gloating (Schadenfreude). *Brain*, **130**, 1663–78.

Shand, A.F. (1914). *The foundations of character: being a study of the tendencies of the emotions and sentiments*. London: Macmillan.

Shankman, S.A., Klein, D.N., Tenke, C.E., andBruder, G.E. (2007). Reward sensitivity in depression: a biobehavioral study. *Journal of Abnormal Psychology*, **116**, 95–104.

Shanks, D.R. (2004). Judging covariation and causation. In: D. J. Koehler and N. Harvey (eds), *Handbook of judgment and decision making*, pp. 220–239. Oxford: Blackwell.

Sharot, T. and Phelps, E.A. (2004). How arousal modulates memory: disentangling the effects of attention and retention. *Cognitive, Affective, and Behavioral Neuroscience*, **4**, 294–306.

Sharot, T., Delgado, M.R., and Phelps, E.A. (2004). How emotion enhances the feeling of remembering. *Nature Neuroscience*, **7**, 1376–80.

Shaver, P.R., Schwartz, J.C., Kirson, D., and O'Connor, C. (1987). Emotion knowledge: further exploration of a prototype approach. *Journal of Personality and Social Psychology*, **52**, 1061–86.

Shepard, R.N. (1978). The circumplex and related topological manifolds in the study of perception. In: S. Shye (ed.), *Theory construction and data analysis in the behavioral sciences*, pp. 29–80. Washington, DC: Jossey Bass.

Sheps, D.S., McMahon, R.P., Becker, L., Carney, R.M., Freedland, K.E., Cohen, J.D., *et al.* (2002). Mental stress-induced ischemia and all-cause mortality in patients with coronary artery disease: results from the psychophysiological investigations of Myocardial Ischemia study. *Circulation*, **105**, 1780–1784.

Shields, R.W., Jr (1993). Functional anatomy of the autonomic nervous system. *Journal of Clinical Neurophysiology*, **10**, 2–13.

Shields, S. (1984). Reports of bodily change in anxiety, sadness and anger. *Motivation and Emotion*, **81**, 1–21.

Shin, L.M., Orr, S.P., Carson, M.A., Rauch, S.L., Macklin, M. L., Lasko, N.B., *et al.* (2004). Regional cerebral blood flow in the amygdala and medial prefrontal cortex during traumatic imagery in male and female Vietnam veterans with PTSD. *Archives of General Psychiatry*, **61**, 168–76.

Shiv, B. and Fedorikhin, A. (1999). Heart and mind in conflict: the interplay of affect and cognition in consumer decision making. *Journal of Consumer Research*, **26**, 278–92.

Shiv, B., Loewenstein, G., Bechara, A., Damasio, H., and Damasio, A.R. (2005). Investment behavior and the negative side of emotion. *Psychological Science*, **16**, 435–9.

Shoemaker, S. (1982). The inverted spectrum. *Journal of Philosophy*, **79**, 357–81.

Shrauger, J.S. and Schoeneman, T.J. (1979). Symbolic interactionist view of self-concept: through the glass darkly. *Psychological Bulletin*, **86**, 549–73.

Shweder, R.A. (1993). The cultural psychology of the emotions. In: M. Lewis and J. M. Haviland (eds), *Handbook of emotions*, 1st edn, pp. 417–31. New York: Guilford Press.

Siddle, D. (ed.) (1983). *Orienting and habituation: perspectives in human research*. Chichester: Wiley.

Siddle, D.A.T. and Lipp, O.V. (1997). Orienting, habituation and information processing: the effects of omission, the role of expectancy and the problem of dishabituation. In: P.J. Lang, R.F. Simons, and M.T. Balaban (eds), *Attention and orienting: sensory motivational processes*, 1st edn, pp. 23–40. Mahwah, NJ: Lawrence Erlbaum Associates.

Siegel, A., Bhatt, S., Bhatt, R., and Zalcman, S.S. (2007). The neurobiological bases for development of pharmacological treatments of aggressive disorders. *Current Neuropharmacology*, **5**, 135–47.

Siegle, G.J. and Hasselmo, M.E. (2002). Using connectionist models to guide assessment of psychological disorder. *Psychological Assessment*, **14**, 263–78.

Siegman, A.W. and Feldstein, S. (eds) (1985). *Multichannel integrations of nonverbal behavior*. Hillsdale, NJ: Lawrence Erlbaum Associates.

Sifneos, P.E. (1973). Prevalence of alexithymic characteristics in psychosomatic patients. *Psychotherapy and Psychosomatics*, **22**, 255–62.

Sifneos, P.E. (1996). Alexithymia: past and present. *American Journal of Psychiatry*, **153**, 137–42.

Silk, J.S., Steinberg, L., and Morris, A.S. (2003). Adolescents' emotion regulation in daily life: links to depressive symptoms and problem behavior. *Child Development*, **74**, 1869–80.

Silverman, W.K. and Dick-Niederhauser, A. (2004). Separation anxiety disorder. In: T.L. Morris and J.S. March (eds), *Anxiety disorders in children and adolescents*, 2nd edn, pp. 164–88. New York: Guilford Press.

Silvia, P.J. (2005). Emotional responses to art: from collation and arousal to cognition and emotion. *Review of General Psychology*, **9**, 342–57.

Silvia, P.J. (2006a). Artistic training and interest in visual art: applying the appraisal model of aesthetic emotions. *Empirical Studies of the Arts*, **24**, 139–61.

Silvia, P.J. (2006b). *Exploring the psychology of interest*. New York: Oxford University Press.

Simon, H. (1978). Rational decision making in organizations. *The American Economic Review*, **69**, 493–513.

Simpson, J.A. (1990). The influence of attachment styles on romantic relationships. *Journal of Personality and Social Psychology*, **59**, 971–80.

Simpson, J.A., Collins, W.A., Tran, S., and Haydon, K.C. (2007). Attachment and the experience and expression of emotions in adult romantic relationships: a developmental perspective. *Journal of Personality and Social Psychology*, **92**, 355–67.

Singer, B. and Toates, F.M. (1987). Sexual motivation. *Journal of Sex Research*, **23**, 481–501.

Singer, T., Seymour, B., O'Doherty, J., Kaube, H., Dolan, R.J., and Frith, C.D. (2004). Empathy for pain involves the affective but not sensory components of pain. *Science*, **303**, 1157–62.

References

Singer, T., Seymour, B., O'Doherty, J.P., Stephan, K.E., Dolan, R.J., and Frith, C.D. (2006). Empathic neural responses are modulated by the perceived fairness of others. *Nature*, **439**, 466–9.

Skinner, B.F. (1938). *The behavior of organisms: an experimental analysis.* Englewood Cliffs, NJ: Prentice-Hall.

Skinner, B.F. (1965/1953). *Science and human behavior.* New York: Macmillan/The Free Press.

Sloboda, J. and Juslin, P.N. (2001). Psychological perspectives on music and emotion. In: P.N. Juslin and J.A. Sloboda (eds), *Music and emotion: theory and research*, pp. 71–104. Oxford: Oxford University Press.

Slovic, P. and Peters, E. (2006). Risk perception and affect. *Current Directions in Psychological Science*, **15**, 322–5.

Slovic, P., Finucane, M., Peters, E., and MacGregor, D.G. (2001). *The affect heuristic. Intuitive judgment: heuristics and biases.* New York: Cambridge University Press.

Slovic, P., Finucane, M.L., Peters, E., and MacGregor, D.G. (2002). In: T. Gilovich, D. Griffin, and D. Kahneman (eds), *Heuristics and biases: the psychology of intuitive judgment*, pp. 397–420. New York: Cambridge University Press.

Small, D.A. and Loewenstein, G. (2003). Helping 'a' victim or helping 'THE' victim: altruism and identifiability. *Journal of Risk and Uncertainty*, **26**, 5–16.

Smith, A. (1976/1759). *The theory of moral sentiments* (ed. D.D. Raphael and A.L. Macfie). Oxford: Clarendon Press.

Smith, A. (1982/1759). *The theory of the moral sentiments* (ed. D.D. Raphael and A.L. Macfie). Indianapolis, IA: Liberty Fund.

Smith, B. (ed.) (1988). *Foundations of Gestalt theory.* Munich: Philosophia Verlag.

Smith, B. (1994). *Austrian philosophy. The legacy of Franz Brentano*, Chs 5, 8, 9. Chicago: Open Court.

Smith, C.A. (1991). The self, appraisal, and coping. In: C.R. Snyder and D.R. Forsyth (eds), *Handbook of social and clinical psychology: the health perspective*, pp. 116–37. New York: Pergamon Press.

Smith, C.A. and Ellsworth, P.C. (1985). Patterns of cognitive appraisal in emotion. *Journal of Personality and Social Psychology*, **48**, 813–38.

Smith, C.A. and Ellsworth, P.C. (1987). Patterns of appraisal and emotion related to taking an exam. *Journal of Personality and Social Psychology*, **52**, 475–88.

Smith, C.A. and Kirby, L.D. (2001). Toward delivering on the promise of appraisal theory. In: K.R. Scherer, A. Schorr, and T. Johnstone (eds), *Appraisal processes in emotion: theory, methods, research*, pp. 121–38. New York: Oxford University Press.

Smith, C.A. and Lazarus, R.S. (1990). Emotion and adaptation. In: L.A. Pervin (ed.), *Handbook of personality: theory and research*, pp. 609–37. New York: Guilford Press.

Smith, C.A. and Lazarus, R.S. (1993). Appraisal components, core relational themes, and the emotions. *Cognition and Emotion*, **7**, 233–69.

Smith, C.A. and Scott, H.H. (1997). A componential approach to the meaning of facial expressions. In: J.A. Russell and J.-M. Fernández-Dol (eds), *The psychology of facial expression*, pp. 229–54. Cambridge: Cambridge University Press.

Smith, C.A., Haynes, K.N., Lazarus, R.S., and Pope, L.K. (1993). In search of the 'hot' cognitions: attributions, ap-praisals, and their relation to emotion. *Journal of Personality and Social Psychology*, **65**, 916–29.

Smith, E.R. (1993). Social identity and social emotions: toward new conceptualizations of prejudice. In: D.M. Mackie and D.L. Hamilton (eds), *Affect, cognition, and stereotyping: interactive processes in group perception*, pp. 297–31. San Diego, CA: Academic Press.

Smith, E.R. and Mackie, D.M. (2008). Intergroup emotions. In: M. Lewis, J.M. Haviland-Jones, and L. Feldman Barrett (eds), *Handbook of emotions*, 3rd edn, pp. 428–39. New York: Guilford Publications.

Smith, G.T., Fischer, S., Cyders, M.A., Annus, A.M., Spillane, N.S., and McCarthy, D.M. (2007). On the validity and utility of discriminating among impulsivity-like traits. *Assessment*, **14**, 155–70.

Smith, J.M. (1964). Group selection and kin selection. *Nature*, **201**, 1145–7.

Smith, M.C., Bentin, S., and Spalek, T.M. (2001). Attention constraints of semantic activation during visual word recognition. *Journal of Experimental Psychology: Learning, Memory, and Cognition*, **27**, 1289–98.

Smith, M.L., Cottrell, G.W., Gosselin, F., and Schyns, P.G. (2005). Transmitting and decoding facial expressions. *Psychological Science*, **16**, 184–9.

Smith, N.K., Cacioppo, J.T., Larsen, J.T., and Chartrand, T.L. (2003). May I have your attention, please: electrocortical responses to positive and negative stimuli. *Neuropsychologia*, **41**, 171–83.

Smith, R.H. (2003). Envy and its transmutations. In: L.Z. Tiedens and C.W. Leach (eds), *The social life of emotions*, pp. 43–63. Cambridge: Cambridge University Press.

Smith, R.H. and Kim, S.H. (2007). Comprehending envy. *Psychological Bulletin*, **133**, 46–64.

Smith, R.H., Parrott, W.G., Ozer, D., and Moniz, A. (1994). Subjective injustice and inferiority as predictors of hostile and depressive feelings in envy. *Personality and Social Psychology Bulletin*, **20**, 705–11.

Snibbe, A.C. and Markus, H.R. (2005). You can't always get what you want: educational attainment, agency, and choice. *Journal of Personality and Social Psychology*, **88**, 703–20.

Snider, J.G. and Osgood, C.S. (eds) (1969). *Semantic differential technique: a sourcebook.* Chicago, IL: Aldine.

Snyder, C.R. (ed.) (2000). *Handbook of hope: theory, measures, and applications.* San Diego, CA: Academic Press.

Sober, E. and Wilson, D.S. (1998). *Unto others: the evolution and psychology of unselfish behavior.* Cambridge, MA: Harvard University Press.

Sokolov, E.N., Spinks, J.A., Näätänen, R., and Lyytinen, H. (2002). *The orienting response in information processing.* Mahwah, NJ: Lawrence Erlbaum Associates.

Solomon, R.C. (1976). *The passions: the myth and nature of human emotion.* Garden City, NY: Doubleday.

Solomon, R. (1978). Emotions and anthropology: the logic of emotional world views. *Inquiry*, **21**, 181–99.

Solomon, R. (1990). In defense of sentimentality. *Philosophy and Literature*, **14**, 304–23.

Soltis, J. (2004). The signal functions of early infant crying. *Behavioral and Brain Sciences*, **27**, 443–90.

Soltysik, S. and Jelen, P. (2005). In rats, sighs correlate with relief. *Physiology and Behavior*, **85**, 598–602.

Sorabji, R. (2000). *Emotion and peace of mind*. Oxford: Oxford University Press.

Sorce, J.F., Emde, R.N., Campos, J.J., and Klinnert, M.D. (1985). Maternal emotional signaling: its effect on the visual cliff behavior of one-year-olds. *Developmental Psychology*, **21**, 195–200.

de Sousa, R. (1987). *The rationality of emotion*. Cambridge, MA: MIT Press.

de Sousa, R. (2001). Moral emotions. *Ethical Theory and Moral Practice*, **4**, 109–26.

de Sousa, R. (2003). Emotion. In: E.N. Zalta (ed.), *Stanford encyclopedia of philosophy*, Spring 2003 edn <http://plato.stanford.edu/archives/spr2003/entries/emotion/>.

de Sousa, R. (2007). *Why think? Evolution and the rational mind*. New York: Oxford University Press.

Soussignan, R. (2002). Duchenne smile, emotional experience and autonomic reactivity: a test of the facial feedback hypothesis. *Emotion*, **2**, 52–74.

Spackman, M.P., Belcher, J.C., Calapp, J.W., and Taylor, A. (2002). An analysis of subjective and objective instruction forms on mock-juries' murder/manslaughter distinctions. *Law and Human Behavior*, **26**, 605–23.

Spear, L.P. (2000). Neurobehavioral changes in adolescence. *Current Directions in Psychological Science*, **9**, 111–14.

Spector, P.E. (1997). The role of frustration in antisocial behavior at work. In: R.A. Jiacalone and J. Greenberg (eds), *Anti-social behavior in organizations*, pp. 1–17. Thousand Oaks, CA: Sage.

Spielberger, C.D. (1985). Anxiety, cognition and affect: a state-trait perspective. In: A.H. Hussain and J.D. Maser (eds), *Anxiety and the anxiety disorders*, pp. 171–82. Hillsdale, NJ: Lawrence Erlbaum Associates.

Spielberger, C.D., Sydeman, S.J., Owen, A.E., and Marsh, B.J. (1999). Measuring anxiety and anger with the state-trait anxiety inventory (STAI) and the state-trait anger expression inventory (STAXI). In: M.E. Maruish (ed.), *The use of psychological testing for treatment planning and outcomes assessment*, 2nd edn, pp. 993–1021. Mahwah, NJ: Lawrence Erlbaum Associates.

Spitzberg, B.H. and Cupach, W.R. (eds). (2007). *The dark side of interpersonal communication*, 2nd edn. Mahwah, NJ: Lawrence Erlbaum Associates.

Spitzer, R.L. and Endicott, I. (1978). Medical and mental disorder: proposed definition and criteria. In: R.L. Spitzer and D.F. Klein (eds), *Critical issues in psychiatric diagnosis*, pp. 15–40. New York: Raven Press.

Spitzer, R.L. and Williams, I.B.W. (1988). Basic principles in the development of DSM-III. In: I.E. Mezzich and M. von Cranach (eds), *International classification in psychiatry: unity and diversity*, pp. 81–8. Cambridge: Cambridge University Press.

Stanovich, K. (2004). *The robot's rebellion: finding meaning in the age of Darwin*. Chicago: Chicago University Press.

Stearns, P.N. (1989). *Jealousy: the evolution of an emotion in American history*. New York: New York University Press.

Steblay, N.M. (1992). A meta-analytic review of the weapon focus effect. *Law and Human Behavior*, **16**, 413–24.

Steckler, T., Kalin, N.H., and Reul, J.M.H.M. (2005). *Handbook of stress and the brain*, Vols 1 and 2. Amsterdam: Elsevier.

Stein, E. (1989/1916). *On the problem of empathy* (transl. W. Stein). Washington, DC: ICS Publications.

Stein, N.L. and Trabasso, T. (1992). The organisation of emotional experience: creating links among emotion, thinking, language, and intentional action. *Cognition and Emotion*, **6**, 225–44.

Steinberg, L. (2004). *Risk taking in adolescence: what changes, and why?* In: R.E. Dahl and L.P. Spear (eds), *Adolescent brain development, vulnerabilities and opportunities*, pp. 51–8. New York: New York Academy of Sciences.

Stelmack, R.M. and Stalikas, A. (1991). Galen and the humour theory of temperament. *Personality and Individual Differences*, **12**, 255–63.

Stenberg, C. and Campos, J. (1990). The development of anger expression in infancy. In: N. Stein, B. Leventhal, and T. Trabasso (eds), *Psychological and biological approaches to emotion*, pp. 247–82. Hillsdale, NJ: Lawrence Erlbaum Associates.

Sternberg, R.J. (1998). *Cupid's arrow: the course of love through time*. Cambridge: Cambridge University Press.

Stephens, G.L. and Graham, G. (2000). *When self-consciousness breaks*. Cambridge, MA: MIT Press.

Steptoe, A. (ed.) (2007). *Depression and physical illness*. Cambridge: Cambridge University Press.

Stern, D.N. (1985). *The interpersonal world of the infant*. New York: Basic Books.

Stern, I. and Marks, I.M. (1973). Brief and prolonged flooding. *Archives of General Psychiatry*, **28**, 270–276.

Stevens, J.R. and Hauser, M.D. (2004). Why be nice? Psychological constraints on the evolution of cooperation. *Trends in Cognitive Sciences*, **8**, 60–65.

Stewart, I.N. and Peregoy, P.L. (1983). Catastrophe theory modeling in psychology. *Psychological Bulletin*, **94**, 336–62.

Stickgold, R., Hobson, J.A., Fosse, R., and Fosse, M. (2001). Sleep, learning, and dreams: off-line memory reprocessing. *Science*, **294**, 1052–7.

Stocker, M. and Hegeman, E. (1996). *Valuing emotions*. Cambridge: Cambridge University Press.

Stone, A.A., Turkkan, J.S., Bachrach, C.A., Jobe, J.B., Kurtzman, H.S., and Cain, V.S. (2000). *The science of self-report*. Mahwah, NJ: Lawrence Erlbaum Associates.

Stone, A.A., Schwartz, J.E., Schwarz, N., Schkade, D., Krueger, A., and Kahneman, D. (2006). A population approach to the study of emotion: diurnal rhythms of a working day examined with the day reconstruction method. *Emotion*, **6**, 139–49.

Storbeck, J., Robinson, M.D., and McCourt, M.E. (2006). Semantic processing precedes affect retrieval: the neurological case for cognitive primacy in visual processing. *Review of General Psychology*, **10**, 41–55.

Storm, C. and Storm, T. (1987). A taxonomic study of the vocabulary of emotions. *Journal of Personality and Social Psychology*, **53**, 805–16.

Storr, A. (1988). *Churchill's black dog, Kafka's mice, and other phenomena of the human mind*. New York: Grove Weidenfeld.

Strawson, G. (1994). *Mental reality*. Cambridge, MA: MIT Press.

Strawson, P. (1974). Freedom and resentment. In: *Freedom and resentment and other essays*. London: Methuen.

Strayer, J. (1987). Affective and cognitive perspectives on empathy. In: N. Eisenberg and J. Strayer (eds), *Empathy and its development*, pp. 218–44. New York: Cambridge University Press.

References

Strigo, I.A., Duncan, G.H., Boivin, M., and Bushnell, M.C. (2003). Differentiation of visceral and cutaneous pain in the human brain. *Journal of Neurophysiology*, **89**, 3294–303.

Stroebe, M.S., Hansson, R.O., Stroebe, W., and Schut, H. (eds) (2001). *Handbook of bereavement research*. Washington, DC: American Psychology Association.

Stroebe, M., Schut, H., and Stroebe, W. (2007). Health outcomes of bereavement. *The Lancet*, **370**, 1960–1973.

Strongman, K.T. (1987). *The psychology of emotion*. Chichester: John Wiley.

Stuart, S. and Noyes, R. (1999). Attachment and interpersonal communication in somatization. *Psychosomatics*, **40**, 34–43.

Stumpf, C. (1928). *Gefühl und Gefühlsempfindung*. Leipzig: Barth.

Sullivan, M.W., Bennett, D.S., and Lewis, M. (2003). Darwin's view self-evaluative emotions as context-specific emotions. *Annals of the New York Academy of Sciences*, **1000**, 304–8.

Sundararajan, L. (2008). *Kong* (emptiness): a Chinese Buddhist emotion. In: W. Lemmens and W. Van Herck (eds), *Religious emotions/some philosophical explorations*, pp. 183–97. Cambridge: Cambridge Scholars Publishing.

Sundberg, J. (1987). *The science of the singing voice*. DeKalb, IL: Northern Illinois University Press.

Sundberg, J. and Nordenberg, M. (2006) Effects of vocal loudness variation on spectrum balanceas reflected by the alpha measure of long-term-average spectra of speech. *Journal of the Acoustical Society of America*, **120**, 453–7.

Sundberg, J., Ternström, S., Perkins, W., and Gramming, P. (1988). Long-time-average spectrum analysis of phonatory effects of noise and filtered auditory feedback. *Journal of Phonetics*, **16**, 203–19.

Suri, R. and Schultz, W. (1998). Learning of sequential movements by neural network model with dopamine-like reinforcement signal. *Experimental Brain Research*, **121**, 350–354.

Susskind, J.M., Littlewort, G., Bartlett, M.S., Movellan, J., and Anderson, A.K. (2007). Human and computer recognition of facial expressions of emotion. *Neuropsychologia*, **45**, 152–62.

Susskind, J.M., Lee, D.H. Cusi, A, Feiman, R., Grabski, W., and Anderson A.K. (2008). Expressing fear enhances sensory acquisition. *Nature Neuroscience*, **11**, 843–50.

Sutton, J., Smith, P.K., and Swettenham, J., (1999). Bullying and 'theory of mind': a critique of the 'social skills deficit' view of antisocial behaviour. *Social Development*, **8**, 117–27.

Sutton, R.I. and Rafaeli, A. (1988). Untangling the relationship between displayed emotions and organizational sales: the case of convenience stores. *Academy of Management Journal*, **31**, 461–87.

Sutton, R.S. and Barto, A.G. (1981). Toward a modern theory of adaptive networks: expectation and prediction. *Psychological Review*, **88**, 135–70.

Swaab, D.F. (2007). Sexual differentiation of the brain and behavior. *Best Practice and Research Clinical Endocrinology and Metabolism*, **21**, 431–44.

Swanson, L.W. and Petrovich, G.D. (1998). What is the amygdala? *Trends in Neurosciences*, **21**, 323–31.

Szentagothai, J. (1984). Downward causation? *Annual Review of Neuroscience*, **7**, 1–11.

Tabibnia, G. and Zaidel, E. (2005). Alexithymia, interhemispheric transfer, and right hemispheric specialization: a critical review. *Psychotherapy and Psychosomatics*, **74**, 81–92.

Tajfel, H. (1978). *Differentiation between social groups: studies in the social psychology of intergroup relations*. London: Academic Press.

Tajfel, H., Flament, C., Billig, M., and Bundy, R.P. (1971). Social categorization and intergroup behavior. *European Journal of Social Psychology*, **1**, 149–78.

Talarico, J.M., LaBar, K.S., and Rubin, D.C. (2004). Emotional intensity predicts autobiographical memory experience. *Memory and Cognition*, **32**, 1118–32.

Tamir, M., Robinson, M.D., Clore, G.L., Martin, L.L., and Whitaker, D.J. (2004). Are we puppets on a string?: The contextual meaning of unconscious expressive cues. *Personality and Social Psychology Bulletin*, **30**, 237–49.

Tan, E. and Frijda, N.H. (1999). Sentiment in film viewing. In: C. Plantinga and G.M. Smith (eds), *Passionate views. Film, cognition, and emotion*, pp. 48–64. Baltimore, MD: The Johns Hopkins University Press.

Tangney, J.P. (1991). Moral affect: the good, the bad, and the ugly. *Journal of Personality and Social Personality*, **61**, 598–607.

Tangney, J.P. (1998). How does guilt differ from shame? In: J. Bybee (ed.), *Guilt and Children*, pp. 1–17. San Diego, CA: Academic Press.

Tangney, J.P. and Dearing, R.L. (2002). *Shame and guilt*. New York: Guilford Press.

Tangney, J.P. and Fischer, K.W. (eds) (1995). *Self-conscious emotions: the psychology of shame, guilt, embarrassment, and pride*. New York: Guilford Press.

Tangney, J.P., Miller, R.S., Flicker, L., and Barlow, D.H. (1996). Are shame, guilt, and embarrassment distinct emotions? *Journal of Personality and Social Psychology*, **70**, 1256–69.

Tangney, J.P., Stuewig, J., and Mashek, D.J. (2007). Moral emotions and moral behavior. *Annual Review of Psychology*, **58**, 345–72.

Tappolet, C. (2000). *Emotions et valeurs*. Paris: Presses Universitaires de France.

Taylor, C. (1966). *Action and purpose*. Englewood Cliffs, NJ: Prentice-Hall.

Taylor, G. (1985). *Pride, shame and guilt. emotions of self-assessment*. Oxford: Clarendon.

Taylor, G.J. (2004). Alexithymia: 25 years of theory and research. In: I. Nyklicek, L. Temoshok, and A. Vingerhoets (eds), *Emotional expression and health*, pp. 137–53. Andover: Brunner-Routledge.

Taylor, J.G. and Fragopanagos, N. (2004). Modelling human attention and emotions. In: Proceedings of the International Joint Conference on Neural Networks 2004, Special Session on Attention and Emotion, pp. 501–6. Berlin: Springer.

Taylor, S.E. and Brown, J.D. (1988). Illusion and well-being: a social psychological perspective on mental health. *Psychological Bulletin*, **103**, 193–210.

Teasdale, J.D. (1999). Multi-level theories of cognition-emotion relations. In: T. Dalgleish and M.J. Power (eds), *Handbook of cognition and emotion*, pp. 665–81. New York: John Wiley and Sons.

Tellegen, A., Watson, D., and Clark, L.A. (1999). On the dimensional and hierarchical structure of affect. *Psychological Science*, **10**, 297–303.

Terry, W.S. (2003). *Learning and memory*, 2nd edn. Boston, MA: Allyn and Bacon.

Tett, R.P., Fox, K.E., and Wang, A. (2005). Development and validation of a self-report measure of emotional intelligence as a multidimensional trait domain. *Personality and Social Psychology Bulletin*, **31**, 859–88.

Thagard, P. and Aubie, B. (2008). Emotional consciousness: a neural model of how cognitive appraisal and somatic perception interact to produce qualitative experience. *Consciousness and Cognition*, **17**, 811–34.

Thalberg, I.. (1977). *Perception, emotion and action*. New Haven, CT: Yale University Press.

Thayer, R.E. (1987). Problem perception, optimism, and related states as a function of time of day (diurnal rhythm) and moderate exercise: two arousal systems in interaction. *Motivation and Emotion*, **11**, 19–36.

Thayer, R.E. (1989). *The biopsychology of mood and arousal*. New York: Oxford University Press.

Thayer, R.E., Newman, J.R., and McClain, T.M. (1993). The self-regulation of mood: strategies for changing a bad mood, raising energy, and reducing tension. *Journal of Personality and Social Psychology*, **67**, 910–925.

Thelen, E. (1995). Motor development: a new synthesis. *American Psychologist*, **50**, 79–95.

Theobald, B.-J., Matthews, I., Mangini, M., Spies, J.R., Brick, T., Cohn, J.F., et al. (2009) (forthcoming). Mapping and manipulating facial expression. Language and Speech, 52(2 & 3).

Thibaut, J.W. and Walker, W.L. (1975). *Procedural justice: a psychological analysis*. Hillsdale, NJ: Lawrence Erlbaum Associates.

Thoits, P.A. and Hewitt, L.N. (2001). Volunteer work and well-being. *Journal of Health and Social Behavior*, **42**, 115–31.

Thompson, A. and Bolger, N. (1999). Emotional transmission in couples under stress. *Journal of Marriage and the Family*, **61**, 38–48.

Thompson, R.A. (1991). Emotional regulation and emotional development. *Educational Psychology Review*, **3**, 269–307.

Thorndike, E.L. (1911). *Animal intelligence*. New York: Macmillan.

Thorndike, E.L. (1931). *Human learning*. New York: Century.

Thrash, T.M. and Elliot, A.J. (2004). Inspiration: core characteristics, component processes, antecedents, and function. *Journal of Personality and Social Psychology*, **87**, 957.

Tice, D.M. (1992). Self-presentation and self-concept change: the looking glass self as magnifying glass. *Journal of Personality and Social Psychology*, **63**, 435–51.

Tiedens, L.Z. and Linton, S. (2001). Judgment under emotional certainty and uncertainty: the effects of specific emotions on information processing. *Journal of Personality and Social Psychology*, **81**, 973–88.

Tiedens, L., Ellsworth, P.C., and Mesquita, B. (2000). Sentimental stereotypes: emotional expectations for high and low status group members. *Personality and Social Psychology Bulletin*, **26**, 560–574.

Tiger, L. (1979). *Optimism: the biology of hope*. New York: Simon and Schuster.

Tinbergen, N. (1963). On the aims and methods of ethology. *Zeitschrift für Tierpsychologie*, **20**, 410–463.

Titchener, E.B. (1909). *A text-book of psychology*. New York: Macmillan.

Titze, I. (1994). *Principles of voice production*. Englewood Cliffs, NJ: Prentice Hall.

Tolin, D.F. and Foa, E.B. (2006). Sex differences in trauma and posttraumatic stress disorder: a quantitative review of 25 years of research. *Psychological Bulletin*, **132**, 959–92.

Tolman, E.C. and Honzik, C.H. (1930). Introduction and removal of reward, and maze performance in rats. *University of California Publications in Psychology*, **4**, 257–75.

Tom, S.M., Fox, C.R., Trepel, C., and Poldrack, R.A. (2007). The neural basis of loss aversion in decision-making under risk. *Science*, **315**, 515–18.

Tomarken, A.J., Davidson, R.J., Wheeler, R.E., and Kinney, L. (1992a). Psychometric properties of resting anterior EEG asymmetry: temporal stability and internal consistency. *Psychophysiology*, **29**, 576–92.

Tomarken, A.J., Davidson, R.J., Wheeler, R.E., and Doss, R.C. (1992b). Individual differences in anterior brain asymmetry and fundamental dimensions of emotion. *Journal of Personality and Social Psychology*, **62**, 676–87.

Tomasello, M. (2001). Perceiving intentions and learning words in the second year of life. In: M. Tomasello and E. Bates (eds), *Language development: the essential readings*, pp. 111–28. Oxford: Blackwell.

Tomkins, S.S. (1962). *Affect, imagery, consciousness: Vol. 1. The positive affects*. New York: Springer.

Tomkins, S.S. (1963). *Affect, imagery, consciousness: Vol. II. The negative affects*. New York: Springer.

Tooby, J. and Cosmides, L. (1990). The past explains the present: emotional adaptations and the structure of ancestral environments. *Ethology and Sociobiology*, **11**, 375–424.

Tooby, J. and Cosmides, L. (2000). Evolutionary psychology and the emotions. In: M. Lewis and J. Haviland-Jones (eds), *Handbook of emotions*, 2nd edn, pp. 91–115. New York: Guilford Press.

Tracy, J.L. and Robins, R.W. (2004). Show your pride: evidence for a discrete emotion expression. *Psychological Science*, **15**, 194–7.

Tracy, J.L. and Robins, R.W. (2007). The nature of pride. In: J.L. Tracy, R.W. Robins, and J.P. Tangney (eds), *The self-conscious emotions: theory and research*, pp. 263–82. New York: Guilford Press.

Tracy, J.L., Robins, R.W., and Tangney, J.P. (eds) (2007). *The self-conscious emotions: theory and research*. New York: Guilford Press.

Trappl, R., Petta, P., and Payr, S. (eds) (2003). *Emotions in humans and artifacts*. Cambridge, MA: MIT Press.

Tremblay, R.E. and Nagin, D.S. (2005). The developmental origins of physical aggression in humans. In Tremblay, R.E., Hartup, W.W., and Archer, J. (eds), *Developmental origins of aggression*, pp. 83–106. New York: Guilford Press.

Tremblay, R.E., Hartup, W.W., and Archer, J. (2005). *Developmental origins of aggression*. New York: Guilford Press.

Trevarthen, C. and Hubley, P. (1978). Secondary intersubjectivity: confidence, confiding and acts of meaning in the first year. In: A. Lock (ed.), *Action, gesture and symbol: the emergence of language*, pp. 183–229. New York: Academic Press.

Triandis, H.C. (1995). *Individualism and collectivism*. Boulder, CO: Westview Press.

Trivers, R.L. (1971). The evolution of reciprocal altruism. *Quarterly Review of Biology*, **46**, 35–57.

Tronick, E.Z., Als, H., Adamson, L., Wise, S., and Brazelton, T.B. (1978). The infant's response to entrapment between contradictory messages in face-to-face interaction. *Journal of the American Academy of Child Psychiatry*, **17**, 1–13.

Tsai, J.L. (2007). Ideal affect: cultural causes and behavioral consequences. *Perspectives on Psychological Science*, **2**, 242–59.

References

Tsai, J.L., Miao, F.F., Seppala, E., Fung, H.H., and Yeung, D.Y. (2007). Influence and adjustment goals: Sources of cultural differences in ideal affect. *Journal of Personality and Social Psychology*, **92**, 1102–17.

Tschan, F., Rochat, S., and Zapf, D. (2005). It's not only clients. Studying emotion work with clients and co-workers with an event-sampling approach. *Journal of Occupational and Organizational Psychology*, **78**, 195–220.

Tsiamyrtzis, P., Dowdall, J., Shastri, D., Pavlidis, I., Frank, M.G., and Ekman, P. (2006). Imaging facial physiology for the detection of deceit. *International Journal of Computer Vision*, **71**, 197–214.

Tversky, A. and Kahneman, D. (1974). Judgment under uncertainty: heuristics and biases. *Science*, **185**, 1124–31.

Tversky, A. and Kahneman, D. (1983). Extensional versus intuitive reasoning: the conjunction fallacy in probability judgment. *Psychological Review*, **90**, 293–315.

Tye, M. (1995). *Ten problems of consciousness*. Cambridge, MA: MIT Press.

Tye, M. (2003). Qualia. In: E.N. Zalta (ed.), *Stanford encyclopedia of philosophy*, Summer 2003 edn <http://plato.stanford.edu/archives/sum2003/entries/qualia/>.

Tyler, T.R. and Blader, S.L. (2000). *Cooperation in groups: procedural justice, social identity, and behavioral engagement*. Philadelphia, PA: Psychology Press.

Uchino, B.N., Smith, T.W., Holt-Lunstad, J.L., Campo, R., and Reblin, M. (2007). Stress and illness. In: J. Cacioppo, L. Tassinary, and G. Berntson (eds), *Handbook of psychophysiology*, 3rd, edn, pp. 608–32. New York: Cambridge University Press.

UPI (2006). Spy software used in call centers. <http.//www.physorg.com/news80412604.html> accessed Nov 19, 2008. United Press International.

Urry, H.L., Nitschke, J.B., Dolski, I., Jackson, D.C., Dalton, K.M., Mueller, C.J., et al. (2004). Making a life worth living: neural correlates of well-being. *Psychological Science*, **15**, 367–72.

Urry, H.L., van Reekum, C.M., Johnstone, T., Kalin, N.H., Thurow, M.E., Schaefer, H.S., et al. (2006). Amygdala and ventromedial prefrontal cortex are inversely coupled during regulation of negative affect and predict the diurnal pattern of cortisol secretion among older adults. *Journal of Neuroscience*, **26**, 4415–25.

Uttl, B., Ohta, N., and Siegenthaler, A.L. (eds) (2006). *Memory and emotion: interdisciplinary perspectives*. Malden, MA: Blackwell Publishing.

Vallacher, R.R. and Nowak, A. (1997). The emergence of dynamical social psychology. *Psychological Inquiry*, **8**, 73–99.

Vallacher, R.R., Read, S.J., and Nowak, A. (eds) (2002). The dynamical perspective in personality and social psychology. (Special issue). *Personality and Social Psychology Review*, **6**(4).

Van Boven, L., Loewenstein, G., and Dunning, D. (2005). The illusion of courage in social predictions: underestimating the impact of fear of embarrassment on other people. *Organizational Behavior and Human Decision Processes*, **96**, 130–141.

Van Coillie, H. and Van Mechelen, I. (2006). A taxonomy of anger-related behaviors in young adults. *Motivation and Emotion*, **30**, 57–74.

Van den Stock, J., Righart, R., and de Gelder, B. (2007). Body expressions influence recognition of emotions in the face and voice. *Emotion*, **7**, 487–94.

Van Diest, I., Thayer, J.F., Vandeputte, B., Van de Woestijne, K.P., and Van den Bergh, O. (2006). Anxiety and respiratory variability. *Physiology and Behavior*, **82**, 189–95.

Van Dijk, E. and Zeelenberg, M. (2005). On the psychology of 'if only': regret and the comparison between factual and counterfactual outcomes. *Organizational Behavior and Human Decision Processes*, **97**, 152–60.

Vickers, K. and McNally, R.J. (2004). Panic disorder and suicide attempt in the National Comorbidity Survey. *Journal of Abnormal Psychology*, **113**, 582–91.

Vileikyte, L., Leventhal, H., Gonzalez, J.D., Peyrot, M., Rubin, R.R., Ulbrecht, J.S., et al. (2005). Diabetic peripheral neuropathy and depression: the association revisited. *Diabetes Care*, **28**, 2378–83.

Vilhjálmsson, H., Cantelmo, N., Cassell, J., Chafai, N., Kipp, M., Kopp, S., et al. (2007). The behavior markup language: recent developments and challenges. In: C. Pelachaud et al. (eds), *Intelligent Virtual Agents. 7th International Working Conference, IVA 2007, Paris, France, September 17–19, 2007* (Lecture Notes in Artificial Intelligence Vol. 4722), pp. 99–111. Berlin: Springer-Verlag.

Vingerhoets, A.J.J.M. and Cornelius, R.R. (eds) (2001). *Adult crying. A biopsychosocial approach*. Hove: Brunner-Routledge.

Virkkunen, M. and Linnoila, M. (1987). Serotonin in early-onset alcoholism. *Recent Developments in Alcoholism*, **13**, 173–89.

Vogt, B.A. (ed.) (2009). *Cingulate neurobiology and disease*. Oxford: Oxford University Press.

Vohs, K.D., Baumeister, R.F., and Loewenstein, G. (eds) (2007). *Do emotions help or hurt decision making?* New York: Russell Sage Foundation.

Vorst, H.C.M. and Bermond, B. (2001). Validity and reliability of the Bermond–Vorst Alexithymia Questionnaire. *Personality and Individual Differences*, **30**, 413–34.

Vrana, S.R., Spence, E.L., and Lang, P.J. (1988). The startle probe response: a new measure of emotion? *Journal of Abnormal Psychology*, **97**, 487–91.

Vrana S.R., Cuthbert, B.N., and Lang, P.J. (1989). Processing fearful and neutral sentences: memory and heart rate change. *Cognition and Emotion*, **3**, 179–95.

Vuilleumier, P. (2005). How brains beware: neural mechanisms of emotional attention. *Trends in Cognitive Sciences*, **9**, 585–94.

Vuilleumier, P. (2009). The role of the amygdala in perception and attention. In: P.J. Whalen and E.A. Phelps (eds), *The human amygdala*. New York: Guilford Press.

Vuilleumier, P., Armony, J., Driver, J., and Dolan, R.J. (2003). Distinct spatial frequency sensitivities for processing faces and emotional expressions. *Nature Neuroscience*, **6**, 624–31.

Vuilleumier, P., Richardson, M.P., Armony, J.L., Driver, J., and Dolan, R.J. (2004). Distant influences of amygdala lesion on visual cortical activation during emotional face processing. *Nature Neuroscience*, **7**, 1271–8.

Vygotsky, L. (1934/1986). *Thought and language*. Cambridge, MA : MIT Press.

de Waal, F.B.M. (1996). *Good natured: the origins of right and wrong in humans and other animals*. Cambridge, MA: Harvard University Press.

de Waal, F.B.M. (1999). Anthropomorphism and anthropodenial: consistency in our thinking about humans and other animals. *Philosophical Topics*, **27**, 255–80.

de Waal, F.B.M. (2000). Primates–a natural heritage of conflict resolution. *Science*, **289**, 586–90.

de Waal, F.B.M. (2003). Darwin's legacy and the study of primate visual communication. In: P. Ekman, J. Campos, R.J. Davidson, and F.B.M. de Waal (eds), *Emotions inside out: 130 years after Darwin's The Expression of Emotion in Man and Animals*. New York: New York Academy of Sciences.

de Waal, F. (2006). *Primates and philosophers: how morality evolved* (ed. S. Macedo and J. Ober). Princeton, NJ: Princeton University Press.

de Waal, F.B.M. and Aureli, F. (1996). Consolation, reconciliation, and a possible cognitive difference between macaque and chimpanzee. In: A.E. Russon, K.A. Bard, and S.T. Parker (eds), *Reaching into thought: the minds of the great apes*, pp. 80–110. Cambridge: Cambridge University Press.

de Waal, F.B.M. and Luttrell, L.M. (1985). The formal hierarchy of rhesus monkeys: an investigation of the bared-teeth display. *American Journal of Primatology*, **9**, 73–85.

de Waal, F.B.M. and van Roosmalen, A. (1979). Reconciliation and consolation among chimpanzees. *Behavioral Ecology and Sociobiology*, **5**, 55–66.

Wachsmuth, I. and Knoblich, G. (eds). (2008). *Modeling communication with robots and virtual humans* (Lecture Notes in Artificial Intelligence Vol. 4930). Berlin: Springer-Verlag.

Wadhwa, M., Shiv, B., and Nowlis, S.M. (2008). A bite to whet the reward appetite: the influence of sampling on reward-seeking behaviors. *Journal of Marketing Research*, **45**, 403–13.

Wager, T.D., Phan, K.L., Liberzon, I., and Taylor, S.F. (2003). Valence, gender, and lateralization of functional brain anatomy in emotion: a meta-analysis of findings from neuroimaging. *Neuroimage*, **19**, 513–31.

Wakefield, J.C. (1992a). Disorder as a harmful dysfunction: a conceptual critique of *DSM-III-R*'s definition of mental disorder. *Psychological Review*, **99**, 232–47.

Wakefield, J.C. (1992b). The concept of mental disorder: on the boundary between biological facts and social values. *American Psychologist*, **47**, 373–88.

Wakefield, J.C. (1999a). Evolutionary versus prototype analyses of the concept of disorder. *Journal of Abnormal Psychology*, **108**, 374–99.

Wakefield, J.C. (1999b). Mental disorder as a black box essentialist concept. *Journal of Abnormal Psychology*, **108**, 465–72.

Wakefield, J.C. (2003). Dysfunction as a factual component of disorder. *Behaviour Research and Therapy*, **41**, 969–90.

Wakefield, J.C. and Horwitz, A.V. (2007). *The loss of sadness: how psychiatry transformed normal sorrow into depressive disorder*. New York: Oxford University Press.

Wall, P.D. (1978). The gate control theory of pain mechanisms: a re-examination and re-statement. *Brain*, **101**, 1–18.

Wallace, J. (1994). *Responsibility and the moral sentiments*. Cambridge, MA: Harvard University Press.

Wallbott, H.G. (1998). Bodily expression of emotion. *European Journal of Social Psychology*, **28**, 879–96.

Wallis, J.D. and Miller, E.K. (2003). Neuronal activity in primate dorsolateral and orbital prefrontal cortex during performance of a reward preference task. *European Journal of Neuroscience*, **18**, 2069–81.

Walton, K. (1990). *Mimesis as make-believe: on the foundations of the representational arts*. Cambridge, MA: Harvard University Press.

Watanuki, S. and Kim, Y.K. (2005). Physiological responses induced by pleasant stimuli. *Journal of Physiological Anthropology and Applied Human Science*, **24**, 135–8.

Watkins, L.R. and Maier, S.F. (2005). Immune regulation of central nervous system functions: from sickness responses to pathological pain. *Journal of Internal Medicine*, **257**, 139–55.

Watson, D. and Clark, L.A. (1997). Extraversion and its positive emotional core. In: R. Hogan, J. Johnson, and S. Briggs (eds), *Handbook of personality psychology*, pp. 767–93. San Diego, CA: Academic Press.

Watson, D. and Tellegen, A. (1985). Toward a consensual structure of mood. *Psychological Bulletin*, **98**, 219–35.

Watson, D., Clark, L.A., and Tellegen, A. (1988). Development and validation of brief measures of positive and negative affect: the PANAS scales. *Journal of Personality and Social Psychology*, **54**, 1063–70.

Watson, D., Wiese, D., Vaidya, J., and Tellegen, A. (1999). The two general activation systems of affect: structural findings, evolutionary considerations, and psychobiological evidence. *Journal of Personality and Social Psychology*, **76**, 820–838.

Watson, J.B. (1919). *Psychology from the standpoint of a behaviorist*. Philadelphia: Lippincott.

Watson, J.B. and Rayner, R. (1920). Conditioned emotional reactions. *Journal of Experimental Psychology*, **3**, 1–14.

Watson, J.S. (1979). Perception of contingency as a determinant of social responsiveness. In: E. Thoman (ed.), *The origins of social responsiveness*, pp. 33–64. Hillsdale, NJ: Lawrence Erlbaum Associates.

Watts, F.N. (1992). Applications of current cognitive theories of the emotions to the conceptualization of emotional disorders. *British Journal of Clinical Psychology*, **31**, 153–67.

Watts, F. (2007). Emotion regulation and religion. In: J.J. Gross (ed.), *Handbook of emotion regulation*, pp. 504–22. New York: Guilford Press.

Webster, J.C., Oakley, R.H., Jewell, C.M., and Cidlowski, J.A. (2001). Proinflammatory cytokines regulate human glucocorticoid receptor gene expression and lead to the accumulation of the dominant negative B isoform: a mechanism for the generation of glucocorticoid resistance. *Proceedings of the National Academy of Sciences USA*, **98**, 6865–70.

Wedekind, C. and Milinski, M. (2000). Cooperation through image scoring in humans. *Science*, **288**, 850–852.

Wedgwood, R. (2002). The aim of belief. *Philosophical Perspectives*, **16**, 267–97.

Wegener, D.T. and Petty, R.E. (1997). The flexible correction model: the role of naïve theories of bias in bias correction. In: M.P. Zanna (ed.), *Advances in experimental social psychology*, Vol. 29, pp. 141–208. New York: Academic Press.

Wegener, D.T., Petty, R.E., and Smith, S.M. (1995). Positive mood can increase or decrease message scrutiny: the hedonic contingency view of mood and message processing. *Journal of Personality and Social Psychology*, **69**, 5–15.

Wegner, D. (2002). *The illusion of conscious will*. Cambridge, MA: MIT Press.

Weigand, D. (ed.) (2004). *Emotion in dialogic interaction: advances in the complex*. Amsterdam: John Benjamins.

Weigert, A.J. (1991). *Mixed emotions: certain steps toward understanding ambivalence*. Albany, NY: State University of New York Press.

References

Weiner, B. (1982). The emotional consequences of causal attributions. In: M.S. Clark and S.T. Fiske (eds), *Affect and cognition*, pp. 185–209. Hillsdale, NJ: Lawrence Erlbaum Associates.

Weiner, B. (1986). *An attributional theory of motivation and emotion*. New York: Springer-Verlag.

Weiner, B. (1995). *Judgments of responsibility: a foundation for a theory of social conduct*. New York: Guilford.

Weiner, B. (2006). *Social motivation, justice, and the moral emotions*. Mahwah, NJ: Lawrence Erlbaum Associates.

Weiss, H.M. and Cropanzano, R. (1996). Affective events theory: a theoretical discussion of the structure, consequences of affective experiences at work. *Research in Organizational Behavior*, **18**, 1–74.

Weiss, H., Suckow, K., and Cropanzano, R. (1999). Effects of justice conditions on discrete emotions. *Journal of Applied Psychology*, **84**, 786–94.

Wellman, H.M., Cross, D., and Watson, J. (2001). Meta-analysis of theory-of-mind development: the truth about false belief. *Child Development*, **72**, 655–84.

Wells, K., Sturm, R., Sherbourne, C., and Meredith, L. (1996). *Caring for depression*. Cambridge, MA: Harvard University Press.

Whalen, P.J., Shin, L.M., McInerney, S.C., Fischer, H., Wright, C.I., and Rauch, S.L. (2001). A functional MRI study of human amygdala responses to facial expressions of fear versus anger. *Emotion*, **1**, 70–83.

Whalen, P.J., Kagan, J., Cook, R.G., Davis, F.C., Kim, H., Polis, S., McLaren, D.G., Somerville, L.H., McLean, A.A., Maxwell, J.S., Johnstone, T. (2004). Human amygdala responsivity to masked fearful eye whites. *Science*, **306**, 2061.

Wheeler, R.E., Davidson, R.J., and Tomarken, A.J. (1993). Frontal brain asymmetry and emotional reactivity: a biological substrate of affective style. *Psychophysiology*, **30**, 82–9.

Whitehouse, H. (2004). Rites of terror: emotion, metaphor, and memory in Melanesian initiation cults. In: J. Corrigan (ed.), *Religion and emotion. approaches and interpretations*, pp. 133–48. Oxford: Oxford University Press.

Whiteside, S.P. and Lynam, D.R. (2001). The five factor model and impulsivity: using a structural model of personality to understand impulsivity. *Personality and Individual Differences*, **30**, 669–89.

Whorf, B.L. (1956). *Language, thought, and reality*. New York: John Wiley.

Wicker, B., Keysers, C., Plailly, J., Royet, J.P., Gallese, V., and Rizzolatti, G. (2003). Both of us disgusted in my insula: the common neural basis of seeing and feeling disgust. *Neuron*, **40**, 655–64.

Wicklund, R.A. and Gollwitzer, P.M. (1982). *Symbolic self-completion*. Hillsdale, NJ: Lawrence Erlbaum Associates.

Wierzbicka, A. (1999). *Emotions across languages and cultures: diversity and universals*. Cambridge: Cambridge University Press.

Wiggins, D. (1987). A sensible subjectivism? In: *Needs, values, truth: essays in the philosophy of value*, pp. 185–214. Oxford: Basil Blackwell.

Wild, B., Rodden, F.A., Rapp, A., Erb, M., Grodd, W., and Ruch, W. (2006). Humor and smiling: cortical regions selective for cognitive, affective, and volitional components. *Neurology*, **66**, 887–93.

Wilde, O. (1890/1988). *A picture of Dorian Gray*. New York: Norton.

Williams, B. (1985). *Ethics and the limits of philosophy*. London: Fontana Paperbacks.

Williams, B. (1993). *Shame and necessity*. Berkeley, CA: University of California Press.

Williams, J.M.G., Watts, F.N., MacLeod, C., and Mathews, A. (eds) (1997). *Cognitive psychology and emotional disorders*, 2nd edn. Chichester: Wiley.

Williams, L.M., Liddell, B.J., Kemp, A.H., Bryant, R.A., Meares, R.A., Peduto, A.S., Gordon, E. (2006). Amygdala-prefrontal dissociation of subliminal and supraliminal fear. *Human Brain Mapping*, **27**, 652–61.

Williams, P. and Aaker, J.L. (2002). Can mixed emotions peacefully coexist? *Journal of Consumer Research*, **28**, 636–49.

Wilson, E., MacLeod, C., Mathews, A., and Rutherford, E. (2006). The causal role of interpretive bias in anxiety reactivity. *Journal of Abnormal Psychology*, **115**, 103–11.

Wilson, E.O. (1975). *Sociobiology: the new synthesis*. Cambridge, MA: Harvard University Press.

Wilson, J. (2000). Volunteering. *Annual Review of Sociology*, **26**, 215–40.

Wilson, J. and Musick, M.A. (2003). Doing well by doing good: volunteering and occupational achievement among American women. *Sociological Quarterly*, **44**, 433–51.

Wilson, J.R.S. (1972). *Emotion and object*. Cambridge: Cambridge University Press.

Wilson, M. and Daly, M. (2004). Do pretty women inspire men to discount the future? *Proceedings of the Royal Society B: Biological Sciences*, **271**(Suppl. 4), S177–S179.

Wilson, T.D. and Gilbert, D.T. (2003). Affective forecasting. In: M.P. Zanna (ed.), *Advances in experimental social psychology*, pp. 345–411. San Diego, CA: Academic Press.

Wilson, T.D. and Gilbert, D.T. (2005). Affective forecasting: knowing what to want. *Current Directions in Psychological Science*, **14**, 131–4.

Wilson, T.D. and Gilbert, D.T. (2008). Explaining away: a model of affective adaptation. *Perspectives on Psychological Science*, **5**, 370–86.

Wilson, T.D. and Klaaren, K.J. (1992). 'Expectation whirls me round': the role of affective expectations on affective experiences. In: M.S. Clark (ed.), *Review of personality and social psychology: emotion and social behavior*, Vol. 14, pp. 1–31. Newbury Park, CA: Sage.

Wilson, T.D. and Schooler, J.W. (1991). Thinking too much: introspection can reduce the quality of preferences and decisions. *Journal of Personality and Social Psychology*, **60**, 181–92.

Wilson, T.D., Lisle, D.J., Schooler, J.W., Hodges, S.D., Klaaren, K.J., and LaFleur, S.J. (1993). Introspecting about reasons can reduce post-choice satisfaction. *Personality and Social Psychology Bulletin*, **19**, 331–9.

Wilson, T.D., Wheatley, T.P., Meyers, J.M., Gilbert, D.T., and Axsom, D. (2000). Focalism: a source of durability bias in affective forecasting. *Journal of Personality and Social Psychology*, **78**, 821–36.

Wilson, T.D., Centerbar, D.B., Kermer, D.A., and Gilbert, D.T. (2005). The pleasures of uncertainty: prolonging positive moods in ways people do not anticipate. *Journal of Personality and Social Psychology*, **88**, 5–21.

Wilt, J. and Revelle, W. (2009). Extraversion and emotional reactivity. In: M. Leary and R.H. Hoyle (eds), *Handbook of individual differences in social behavior*. New York: Guilford Press.

Winkielman, P. and Berridge, K.C. (2004). Unconscious emotion. *Current Directions in Psychological Science*, **13**, 120–123.

Winkielman, P., Berridge, K.C., and Willbarger, J.L. (2005a). Emotion, behavior, and conscious experience: once more without feeling. In: L.F.Barrett, P.M. Niedenthal, and P. Winkielman (eds), *Emotion and consciousness*, pp. 335–63. New York: Guilford Press.

Winkielman, P., Berridge, K.C., and Wilbarger, J.L. (2005b). Unconscious affective reactions to masked happy versus angry faces influence consumption behavior and judgments of value. *Personality and Social Psychology Bulletin*, 1, 121–35.

Winston, J.S., Gottfried, J.A., Kilner, J.M., and Dolan, R.J. (2005). Integrated neural representations of odor intensity and affective valence in human amygdala. *Journal of Neuroscience*, 25, 8903–7.

Witasek, S. (1904). *Grundzüge der allgemeinen Ästhetik*. Leipzig: Barth.

Witkiewitz, K. and Marlatt, G.A. (2004). Relapse prevention for alcohol and drug problems: that was Zen, this is Tao. *American Psychologist*, 59, 224–35.

Wolfe, J.M. and Horowitz, T.S. (2004). What attributes guide the deployment of visual attention and how do they do it? *Nature Reviews Neuroscience*, 5, 495–501.

Wollheim, R. (1999). On the so called moral emotions. In: *On the emotions*, pp. 148–224. New Haven, CT: Yale University Press.

Wood, J.V., Michela, J.L., and Giordano, C. (2000). Downward comparison in everyday life: reconciling self-enhancement models with the mood-cognition priming model. *Journal of Personality and Social Psychology*, 79, 563–79.

Woodworth, R.S. (1918). *Dynamic psychology*. New York: Columbia University Press.

Woodworth, R.S. (1938). *Experimental psychology*. New York: Holt.

Wordsworth, W. (1802). Preface to *Lyrical Ballads* of 1802. In: S. Gill (ed.), *William Wordsworth*. Oxford: Oxford University Press (1984 edition).

World Health Organization (1992). *The ICD-10 classification of mental and behavioural disorders. Clinical descriptions and diagnostic guidelines*. Geneva: World Health Organization (2002). *World report on violence and health*, ed. E.G. Krug, L.L. Dahlman, J.A. Mercy, A.B. Zwi, and R. Lozano. Geneva: WHO.

Wranik, T. and Scherer, K.S. (2008). Why do I get angry? A componential appraisal approach. To appear in M. Potegal, G. Stemmler, and C. Spielberger (eds), *A handbook of anger: constituent and concomitant biological, psychological, and social processes*. Cambridge: Cambridge University Press.

Wright, P. and Liu, Y. (2006). Neutral faces activate the amygdala during identity matching. *Neuroimage*, 29, 628–36.

Wright, R.A. (1996). Brehm's theory of motivation as a model of effort and cardiovascular response. In: P.M. Gollwitzer and J.A. Bargh (eds), *The psychology of action*, pp. 424–53. New York: Guilford Press.

Wright, R.A. and Kirby, L.D. (2001). Effort determination of cardiovascular response: an integrative analysis with applications in social psychology. In: M.P. Zanna (ed.), *Advances in experimental social psychology*, Vol. 33, pp. 255–307. New York: Academic Press.

Wundt, W. (1896). *Grundriss der Psychologie*. Leipzig: Engelmann.

Wundt, W. (1924). *An introduction to psychology* (transl. R. Pintner). London: Allen ans Unwin. (Original work published 1912.)

Wyer, R.S. Jr and Albarracín, D. (2005). Belief formation, organization, and change: cognitive and motivational influences. In: D. Albarracín, B.T. Johnson, and M.P. Zanna (eds), *The handbook of attitudes*, pp. 273–322. Mahwah, NJ: Lawrence Erlbaum Associates.

Wysocki, C.J. and Preti, G. (2004). Facts, fallacies, fears and frustrations with human pheromones. *Anatomical Record*, 281A, 1201–11.

Xiao, J., Baker, S., Matthews, I., and Kanade, T. (2004). Real-time combined 2D + 3D active appearance models. *Proceedings of the IEEE Conference on Computer Vision and Pattern Recognition*, Vol. 2, pp. 535–42.

Yates, B.J. and Stocker, S.D. (1998). Integration of somatic and visceral inputs by the brainstem: functional considerations. *Experimental Brain Research*, 119, 269–75.

Yehuda, R. and McFarlane, A.C. (1995). Conflict between current knowledge about posttraumatic stress disorder and its original conceptual basis. *American Journal of Psychiatry*, 152, 1705–13.

Yerkes, R.M. (1925). *Almost human*. New York: Century.

Yerkes, R.M. and Dodson, J.D. (1908). The relation of strength of stimulus to rapidity of habit-formation. *Journal of Comparative Neurology and Psychology*, 18, 459–82.

Yiend, J. and Mackintosh, B. (2004). The experimental modification of processing biases. In: J. Yiend (ed.), *Cognition, emotion and psychopathology: theoretical, empirical and clinical directions*, pp. 190–210. Cambridge: Cambridge University Press.

Yik, M.S.M., Russell, J.A., and Feldman-Barrett, L. (1999). Structure of self-reported current affect: integration and beyond. *Journal of Personality and Social Psychology*, 77, 600–619.

Young, A.W., Rowland, D., Calder, A.J., Etcoff, N.L., Seth, A., and Perrett, D.I. (1997). Facial expression megamix: tests of dimensional and category accounts of emotion recognition. *Cognition*, 63, 271–313.

Young, M.P., Scannel, J.W., Burns, G.A.P.C., and Blakemore, C. (1994). Analysis of connectivity: neural systems in the cerebral cortex. *Reviews in the Neurosciences*, 5, 227–49.

Young, P.T. (1959). The role of affective processes in learning and behavior. *Psychological Review*, 66, 104–25.

Yue, X., Vessel, E.A., and Biederman, I. (2007). The neural basis of scene preferences. *Neuroreport*, 18, 525–9.

Yzerbyt, V.Y., Dumont, M., Gordijn, E., and Wigboldus, D. (2002). Intergroup emotions and self-categorization: the impact of perspective-taking on reactions to victims of harmful behavior. In: D.M. Mackie and E.R. Smith (eds), *From prejudice to intergroup emotions*, pp. 67–88. New York: Psychology Press.

Zagzebski, L. (1996). *Virtues of the mind: an inquiry into the nature of virtue and the ethical foundations of knowledge*. Cambridge: Cambridge University Press.

Zahn-Waxler, C., Radke-Yarrow, M., Wagner, E., and Chapman, M. (1992). Development of concern for others. *Developmental Psychology*, 28, 126–36.

Zajonc, R.B. (1998). Emotions. In: D.T. Gilbert, S.T. Fiske, and G. Lindzey (eds), *Handbook of social psychology*, Vol. 1, 4th edn, pp. 591–634. New York: McGraw Hill.

Zajonc, R.B. (2000). Feeling and thinking: closing the debate over the independence of affect. In: J.P. Forgas (ed.), *Feeling and thinking: the role of affect in social cognition*, pp. 31–58. New York: Cambridge University Press.

References

Zajonc, R.B. (2001). Mere exposure: a gateway to the subliminal. *Current Directions in Psychological Science*, **10**, 224–8.

Zajonc, R.B. and Markus, H. (1982). Affective and cognitive factors in preference. *Journal of Consumer Research*, **9**, 123–31.

Zalcman, S.S. and Siegel, A. (2006). The neurobiology of aggression and rage: role of cytokines. *Brain, Behavior, and Immunity*, **20**, 507–14.

Zammuner, V.L., Petitbon, E. (2006). The recognition of emotional qualities expressed in music. In, M. Baroni, A.R. Adessi, R. Caterina, M. Costa (eds), *Proceedings of the 9th International Conference on Music Perception and Cognition* (ICMPC9), pp. 402–07, Bologna/Italy, August 22–26 2006 <http://www.marlocosta.it/icmpc2006/pdfs190.pdf>.

Zanna, M.P. and Rempel, J.K. (1988). Attitudes: a new look at an old concept. In: D. Bar-Tal and A.W. Kruglanski (eds), *The social psychology of knowledge*, pp. 315–34. Cambridge: Cambridge University Press.

Zapf, D. and Holz, M. (2006). On the positive and negative effects of emotion work in organizations. *European Journal of Work and Organizational Psychology*, **15**, 1–28.

Zech, E., Rimé, B., and Nils, F. (2004). Social sharing of emotion, emotional recovery, and interpersonal aspects. In: P. Philippot and R. Feldman (eds), *The regulation of emotion*, pp. 157–85. Mahwah, NJ: Lawrence Erlbaum Associates.

Zeelenberg, M. and Pieters, R. (2007). A theory of regret regulation 1.0. *Journal of Consumer Psychology*, **17**, 3–18.

Zeelenberg, M., van Dijk, W.W., Manstead, A.S.R., and van der Pligt, J. (2000). On bad decisions and disconfirmed expectancies: regret, disappointment and decision-making. *Cognition and Emotion*, **14**, 521–41.

Zeelenberg, M., Van den Bos, K., Van Dijk, E., and Pieters, R. (2002). The inaction effect in the psychology of regret. *Journal of Personality and Social Psychology*, **82**, 314–27.

Zeeman, E.C. (1977). *Catastrophe theory: selected papers 1972–1977*. Reading, MA: Benjamin.

Zeidner, M. and Endler, N.S. (1996). *Handbook of coping: theory, research, applications*. New York: John Wiley and Sons.

Zeifman, D.M. (2001). An ethological analysis of human infant crying: answering Tinbergen's four questions. *Developmental Psychobiology*, **39**, 265–85.

Zermatten, A., Van der Linden, M., d'Acremont, M., Jermann, F., and Bechara, A. (2005). Impulsivity and decision making. *Journal of Nervous and Mental Disease*, **193**, 647–50.

Ziegler, T.E., Savage, A., Scheffler, G., and Snowdon, C.T. (1987). The endocrinology of puberty and reproductive functioning in female cotton-top tamarins (*Saguinus oedipus*) under varying social conditions. *Biology of Reproduction*, **37**, 618–27.

Zillmann, D. (1983). Transfer of excitation in emotional behavior. In: J.T. Cacioppo and R.E. Petty (eds), *Social psychophysiology: a sourcebook*, pp. 215–40. New York: Guilford Press.

Zillmann, D. (1988). Mood management: using entertainment to full advantage. In: L. Donohew and H.E. Sypher (eds), *Communication, social cognition, and affect*, pp. 147–71. Hillsdale, NJ: Lawrence Erlbaum Associates.

Zinck, A. and Newen, A. (2008). Classifying emotions: a developmental account. *Synthese*, **161**, 1–25.

Zipes, D.P., Libby, P., Bonow, R.O., and Braunwald, E. (2005). *Braunwald's heart disease: a textbook of cardiovascular medicine*, 7th edn. Philadelphia, PA: Elsevier Saunders.

Zohar, D., Tzischinsky, O., Epsten, R., and Lavie, P. (2005). The effects of sleep loss on medical residents' emotional reactions to work events: a cognitive-energy model. *Sleep*, **28**, 47–54.

Zuckerman, M. (1979). *Sensation seeking: beyond the optimum level of arousal*. Hillsdale, NJ: Lawrence Erlbaum Associates.

Name Index

Aaker, J.L. 257
Abbott, D.H. 320
Abe, J.A. 117
Abel, M. 371
Abrahamsson, M. 408
Abramson, L.Y. 62
Abu-Lughod, L. 107, 397
Ackerknecht, E.H. 65
Ackerman, B.P. 117, 150
Àdàm, G. 223
Adams, R.B. 167, 331
Adelman, P.K. 154
Ader, R. 67, 214, 304, 322
Adolphs, R. 30, 167, 251, 332, 333, 376
Aggleton, J. 28, 30, 32
Ågmo, A. 365, 367
Ainsworth, M.D.S. 53
AISB '05 68
Aksan, N. 261
Albarracin, D. 76
Alberti, L.B. 8
Alcock, J. 159
Alden, L.E. 369
Aldwin, C.M. 102
Alexander, R.D. 24
Allen, S.R. 340
Allport, G.W. 342
Almeida, D. 180
Amaral, D.G. 56, 236, 380
Ambady, N. 154, 200, 398
American Psychiatric Association 10, 40, 114, 123, 208, 247, 273, 287, 298, 307, 310, 311, 322, 323
American Psychological Association 308
Ames, R.E. 25
Amodio, D.M. 39
Amsel, A. 188
Anagnostaras, S.G. 236
Anderson, A.K. 55, 56, 167
Anderson, C.A. 22, 23
Anderson, C.M. 26
Andrade, E.B. 249
Andreoni, J. 24, 26
Andrew, M. 260
Andrew, R.J. 167
Angel, L. 256
Angyal, A. 121
Arambel-Liu, S. 253
Arbib, M. 68, 342
Archer, J. 42, 77
Argyle, M. 240, 268, 413

Aristotle 7, 45, 59, 119, 144, 146, 203, 206, 207, 226, 238, 252, 329, 383, 401
Armon-Jones, C. 98
Armony, J.L. 95, 97
Armor, D.A. 120, 121
Armstrong, D. 298
Arnold, M.B. 1, 45, 46, 144, 147, 339, 372
Aron, A. 244
Aron, E.N. 244
Aronson, J.A. 313
Arrow, K.J. 79, 392
Arsenio, W.F. 262
Asendorpf, J.B. 368, 369
Ashkanasy, N.M. 416
Asmussen, L. 5
Atkinson, A.P. 197
Atkinson, J.W. 266, 346
Aubie, B. 388
Aue, T. 48, 362
Aureli, F. 34, 35
Austin, J.T. 267
Ausubel, D.P. 199, 367
Averill, J.R. 33, 98, 99, 146, 157, 226, 236
Axelrod, R. 24
Aydede, M. 298
Ayduk, O. 113, 114

Bach, D.R. 31
Bachorowski, J.-A. 234, 235
Badger, G.J. 132
Baeyens, F. 52
Bagby, R.M. 23
Bagozzi, R.P. 216
Bailey, J.M. 366
Bailly, G. 407
Baird, B.M. 305
Baker, S. 179
Bakermans-Kranenburg, M.J. 309
Baldwin, J.M. 224
Balleine, B.W. 276, 278
Bamberg, M. 240, 241
Bandes, S.A. 236
Bandura, A. 164, 293
Banks, W.A. 213
Banse, R. 406
Bänziger, T. 81
Bar, M. 57
Barbalet, J.M. 380
Barclay, L.J. 415
Bard, P. 83, 229, 276

Jensen, P.S. 123
Jesperson, O. 241
Jiang, Y. 332
Jin, R. 348
John, O.P. 339
Johnson, E.J. 80, 112
Johnson, M. 253
Johnson, S.L. 114, 245, 332
Johnson-Laird, P.N. 42, 47, 147, 240, 340, 372
Johnstone, T. 16, 49, 405, 406
Jones, E.E. 62, 311
Jones, H.E. 169, 222
Jones, S.H. 248
Joormann, J. 348
Jorris, W.N. 129, 259
Josephs, I. 12, 13
Joukamaa, M. 23
Judd, L.L. 247
Jung-Beeman, M. 253
Jürgens, U. 37
Juslin, P.N. 7, 8, 9, 81, 269, 271, 405, 406, 411

Kaas, J. 380
Kagan, J. 43, 222, 284, 365, 369, 389, 390
Kahan, D.M. 236
Kahneman, D. 3, 79, 105, 111, 131, 200, 206, 240, 265, 274, 312, 313, 348, 372, 413, 414
Kaiser, S. 45, 305
Kalat, J.W. 346
Kalin, N.H. 17
el Kaliouby, R. 12
Kalisch, R. 236
Kalivas, P. 4
Kaltsas, G.A. 303
Kamarck, T.W. 384
Kamin, L.J. 51
Kanade, T. 176, 179
Kanfer, R. 416
Kant, I. 6, 265, 284
Kaplan, K.S. 255, 367
Kaplan, R. 225
Kaplan, S. 225, 250
Karama, S. 366
Karasawa, M. 107, 314
Karlson, P. 306
Kaster, R.A. 206
Katon, W.J. 299
Katz, D. 59
Katz, L.D. 309
Katz, R. 260
Kawachi, I. 205
Keane, T.M. 312
Keats, J. 8
Keeler, W. 187
Keenan, A. 414, 415
Keil, A. 56
Kellerman, H. 304
Kelley, J.R. 414
Kelley, K.W. 212, 214, 321

Kelso, J.A.S. 126, 127, 129
Keltner, D. 5, 33, 112, 138, 146, 159, 163, 164, 175, 188, 189, 275, 351, 357, 372, 395
Kemper, T.D. 379
Kendler, K.S. 115
Kendon, A. 196
Kennedy, R. 105
Kennedy, S. 260
Kenny, A. 144
Kensinger, E.A. 252
Kent, S. 213
Kermer, D.A. 16
Kessler, R.C. 259, 299, 311, 348
Keynes, J.M. 131
Kiecolt-Glaser, J.K. 205, 384, 385
Kihlstrom, J.F. 359, 360, 395
Killias, M. 180
Kim, S.H. 156
Kim, Y.K. 212
Kin, N.W. 212
Kinney, K.S. 303
Kipper, S. 234
Kipps, C.M. 141
Kirby, L.D. 45, 46, 48, 135
Kirk, S.A. 123
Kirkpatrick, L.A. 376
Kirmayer, L.J. 323
Kirsch, I. 164
Kirschbaum, C. 352
Kissler, J. 240
Kitayama, S. 91, 215, 216, 314, 399
Kivy, P. 8
Klaaren, K.J. 164
Klasmeyer, G. 406
Klauer, K.C. 315
Kleck, F.E. 167
Klein, D.F. 260, 298, 299
Klein, D.J. 382
Klein, J. 13
Kleinsmith, L.J. 250
Klimoski, R.J. 416
Klinger, E. 163
de Kloet, E.R. 321
Klopf, A.H. 97
Kluver, H. 236, 277
Knapp, M.L. 283
Knickmeyer, R.C. 64
Knight, F.H. 395
Knoblich, G. 139, 140
Knoch, D. 180
Kobak, R.R. 53
Kochanska, G. 261
Koelling, R.A. 51
Koenig, O. 94
Kogut, T. 132
Koh, K.B. 212
Köhler, W. 196
Konorski, J. 335
Konstan, D. 156, 206